Stan Lee PRESENTS

ESSENTIAL

Fantastic Four

VOL. 1

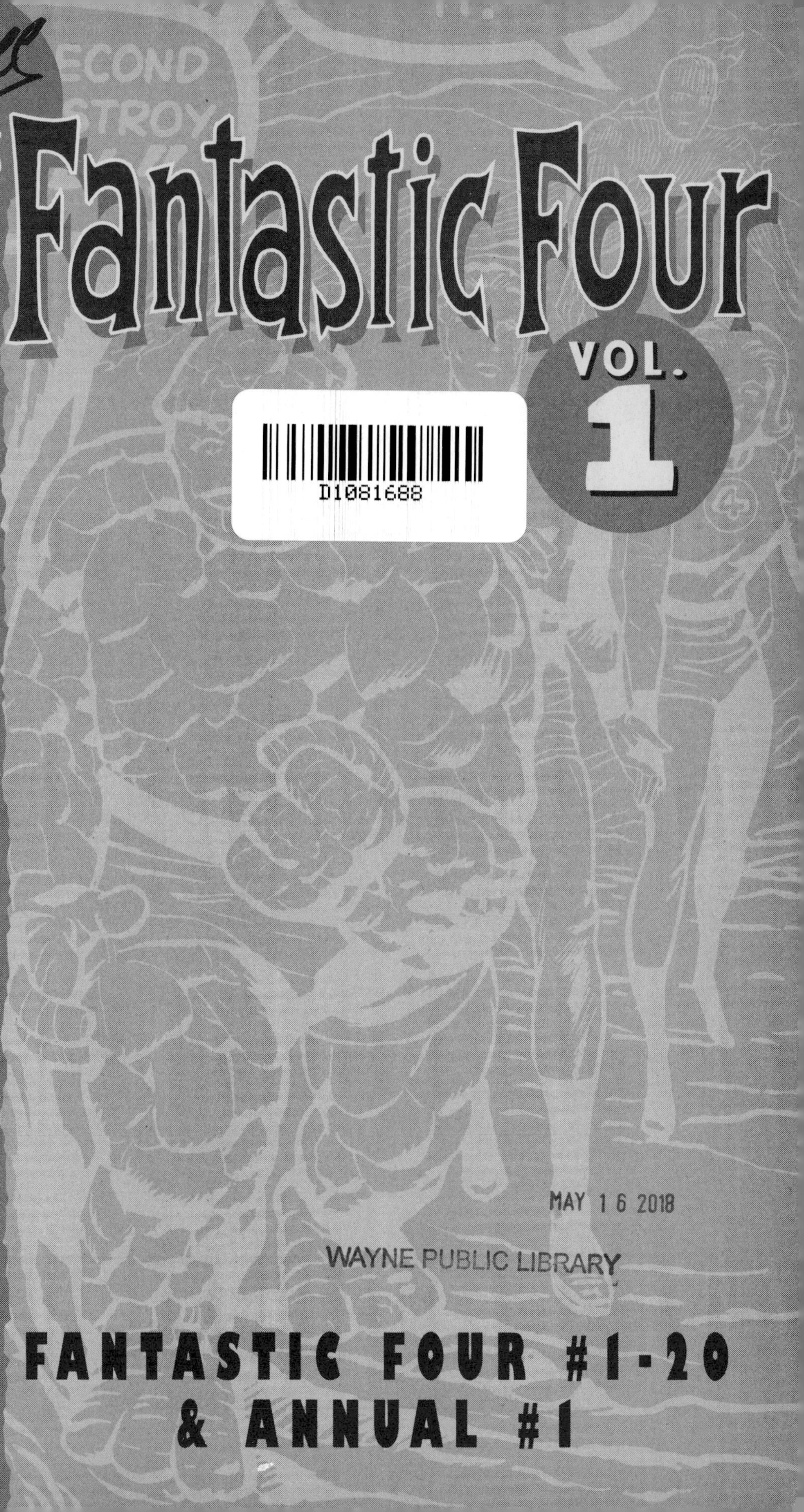

FANTASTIC FOUR #1-20
& ANNUAL #1

The Fantastic Four #1

WRITER: STAN LEE
PENCILER: JACK KIRBY
INKER: UNKNOWN
LETTERER: ART SIMEK

The Fantastic Four #2

WRITER: STAN LEE
PENCILER: JACK KIRBY
INKER: UNKNOWN
LETTERER: JOHN DUFFY

The Fantastic Four #3

WRITER: STAN LEE
PENCILER: JACK KIRBY
INKER: SOL BRODSKY
LETTERER: ART SIMEK

The Fantastic Four #4

WRITER: STAN LEE
PENCILER: JACK KIRBY
INKER: SOL BRODSKY
LETTERER: ART SIMEK

The Fantastic Four #5

WRITER: STAN LEE
PENCILER: JACK KIRBY
INKER: JOE SINNOTT
LETTERER: ART SIMEK

The Fantastic Four #6

WRITER: STAN LEE
PENCILER: JACK KIRBY
INKER: DICK AYERS
LETTERER: UNKNOWN

The Fantastic Four #7

WRITER: STAN LEE
PENCILER: JACK KIRBY
INKER: DICK AYERS
LETTERER: UNKNOWN

The Fantastic Four #8

WRITER: STAN LEE
PENCILER: JACK KIRBY
INKER: DICK AYERS
LETTERER: ART SIMEK

The Fantastic Four #9

WRITER: STAN LEE
PENCILER: JACK KIRBY
INKER: DICK AYERS
LETTERER: ART SIMEK

The Fantastic Four #10

WRITER: STAN LEE
PENCILER: JACK KIRBY
INKER: DICK AYERS
LETTERER: ART SIMEK

The Fantastic Four #11

WRITER: STAN LEE
PENCILER: JACK KIRBY
INKER: DICK AYERS
LETTERER: ART SIMEK

The Fantastic Four #12

WRITER: STAN LEE
PENCILER: JACK KIRBY
INKER: DICK AYERS
LETTERER: ART SIMEK

The Fantastic Four #13

WRITER: STAN LEE
PENCILER: JACK KIRBY
INKER: STEVE DITKO
LETTERER: ART SIMEK

The Fantastic Four #14

WRITER: STAN LEE
PENCILER: JACK KIRBY
INKER: DICK AYERS
LETTERER: ART SIMEK

The Fantastic Four #15

WRITER: STAN LEE
PENCILER: JACK KIRBY
INKER: DICK AYERS
LETTERER: ART SIMEK

The Fantastic Four #16

WRITER: STAN LEE
PENCILER: JACK KIRBY
INKER: DICK AYERS
LETTERER: ART SIMEK

The Fantastic Four #17

WRITER: STAN LEE
PENCILER: JACK KIRBY
INKER: DICK AYERS
LETTERER: ART SIMEK

The Fantastic Four #18

WRITER: STAN LEE
PENCILER: JACK KIRBY
INKER: DICK AYERS
LETTERER: ART SIMEK

The Fantastic Four #19

WRITER: STAN LEE
PENCILER: JACK KIRBY
INKER: DICK AYERS
LETTERER: SAM ROSEN

The Fantastic Four #20

WRITER: STAN LEE
PENCILER: JACK KIRBY
INKER: DICK AYERS
LETTERER: ART SIMEK

The Fantastic Four Annual #1

WRITER: STAN LEE
PENCILER: JACK KIRBY
INKERS: DICK AYERS, STEVE DITKO & SOL BRODSKY
LETTERERS: ART SIMEK & RAY HOLLOWAY

REPRINT CREDITS

MARVEL ESSENTIAL DESIGN:
JOHN "JG" ROSHELL OF COMICRAFT
COVER ART:
JACK KIRBY
COLLECTION EDITOR:
MARK D. BEAZLEY
ASSISTANT EDITOR:
JENNIFER GRÜNWALD
SENIOR EDITOR, SPECIAL PROJECTS:
JEFF YOUNGQUIST
ART RECONSTRUCTION:
POND SCUM, KEITH WILLIAMS & PHIL LORD

DIRECTOR OF SALES:
DAVID GABRIEL
BOOK DESIGNER & PRODUCTION:
TERNARD SOLOMON
CREATIVE DIRECTOR:
TOM MARVELLI
EDITOR IN CHIEF:
JOE QUESADA
PUBLISHER:
DAN BUCKLEY
SPECIAL THANKS TO TOM BREVOORT & RALPH MACCHIO

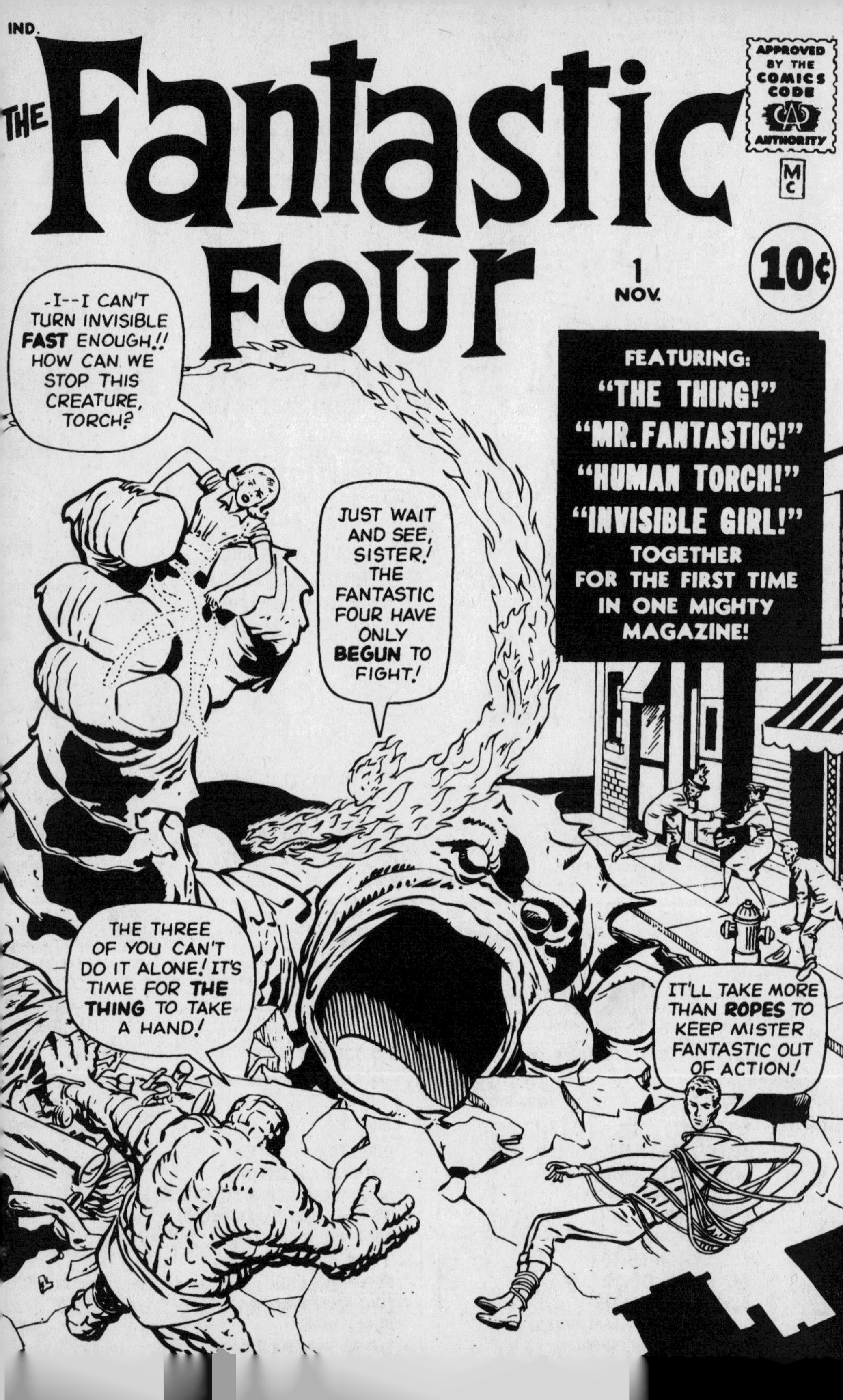
IND.
THE Fantastic FOUR
APPROVED BY THE COMICS CODE AUTHORITY
MC
1 NOV.
10¢
-I--I CAN'T TURN INVISIBLE FAST ENOUGH!! HOW CAN WE STOP THIS CREATURE, TORCH?
FEATURING: "THE THING!" "MR. FANTASTIC!" "HUMAN TORCH!" "INVISIBLE GIRL!" TOGETHER FOR THE FIRST TIME IN ONE MIGHTY MAGAZINE!
JUST WAIT AND SEE, SISTER! THE FANTASTIC FOUR HAVE ONLY BEGUN TO FIGHT!
THE THREE OF YOU CAN'T DO IT ALONE! IT'S TIME FOR THE THING TO TAKE A HAND!
IT'LL TAKE MORE THAN ROPES TO KEEP MISTER FANTASTIC OUT OF ACTION!

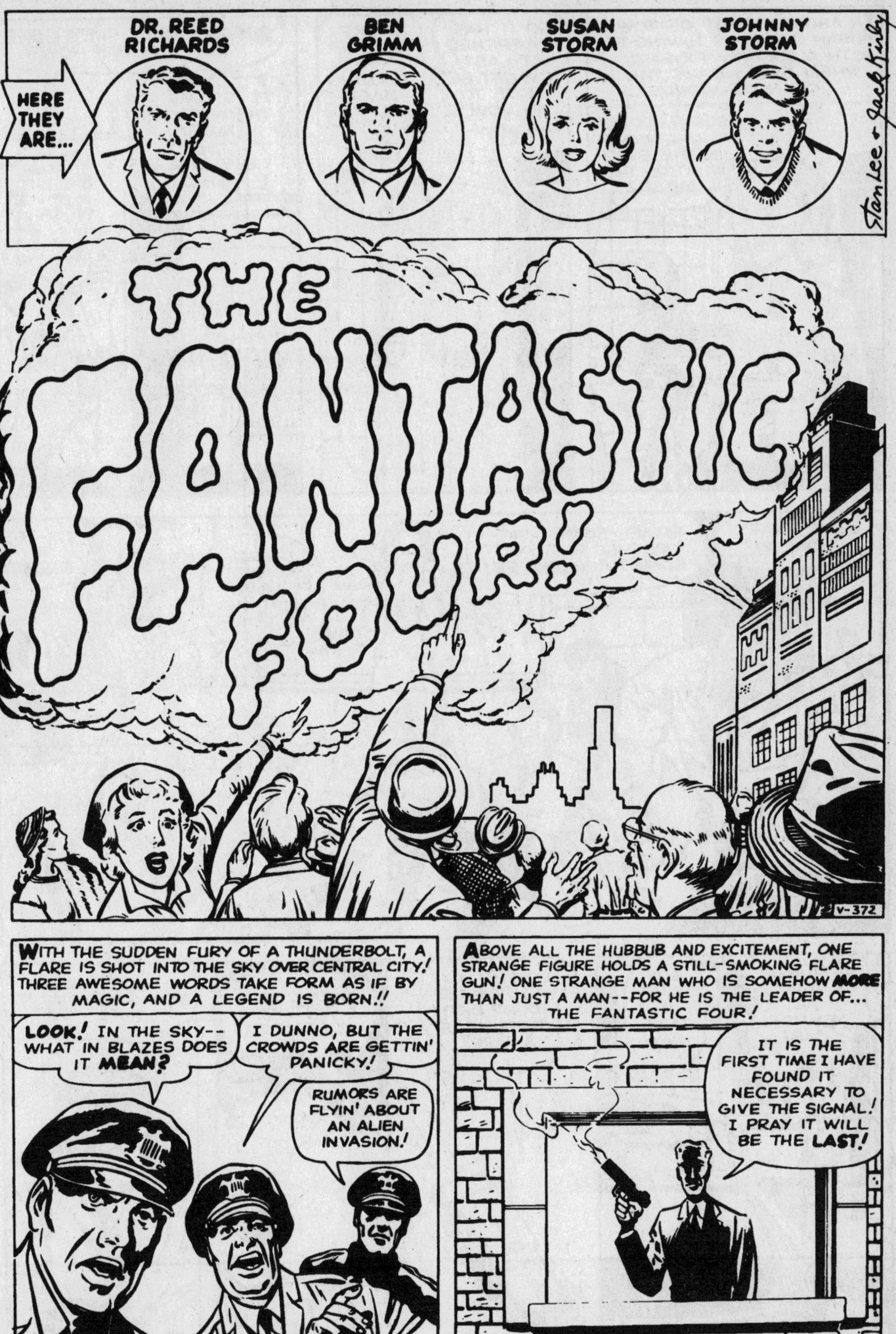

DR. REED RICHARDS
BEN GRIMM
SUSAN STORM
JOHNNY STORM
HERE THEY ARE...
Stan Lee + Jack Kirby
THE FANTASTIC FOUR!
V-372
WITH THE SUDDEN FURY OF A THUNDERBOLT, A FLARE IS SHOT INTO THE SKY OVER CENTRAL CITY! THREE AWESOME WORDS TAKE FORM AS IF BY MAGIC, AND A LEGEND IS BORN!!
LOOK! IN THE SKY-- WHAT IN BLAZES DOES IT MEAN?
I DUNNO, BUT THE CROWDS ARE GETTIN' PANICKY!
RUMORS ARE FLYIN' ABOUT AN ALIEN INVASION!
ABOVE ALL THE HUBBUB AND EXCITEMENT, ONE STRANGE FIGURE HOLDS A STILL-SMOKING FLARE GUN! ONE STRANGE MAN WHO IS SOMEHOW MORE THAN JUST A MAN--FOR HE IS THE LEADER OF... THE FANTASTIC FOUR!
IT IS THE FIRST TIME I HAVE FOUND IT NECESSARY TO GIVE THE SIGNAL! I PRAY IT WILL BE THE LAST!
1

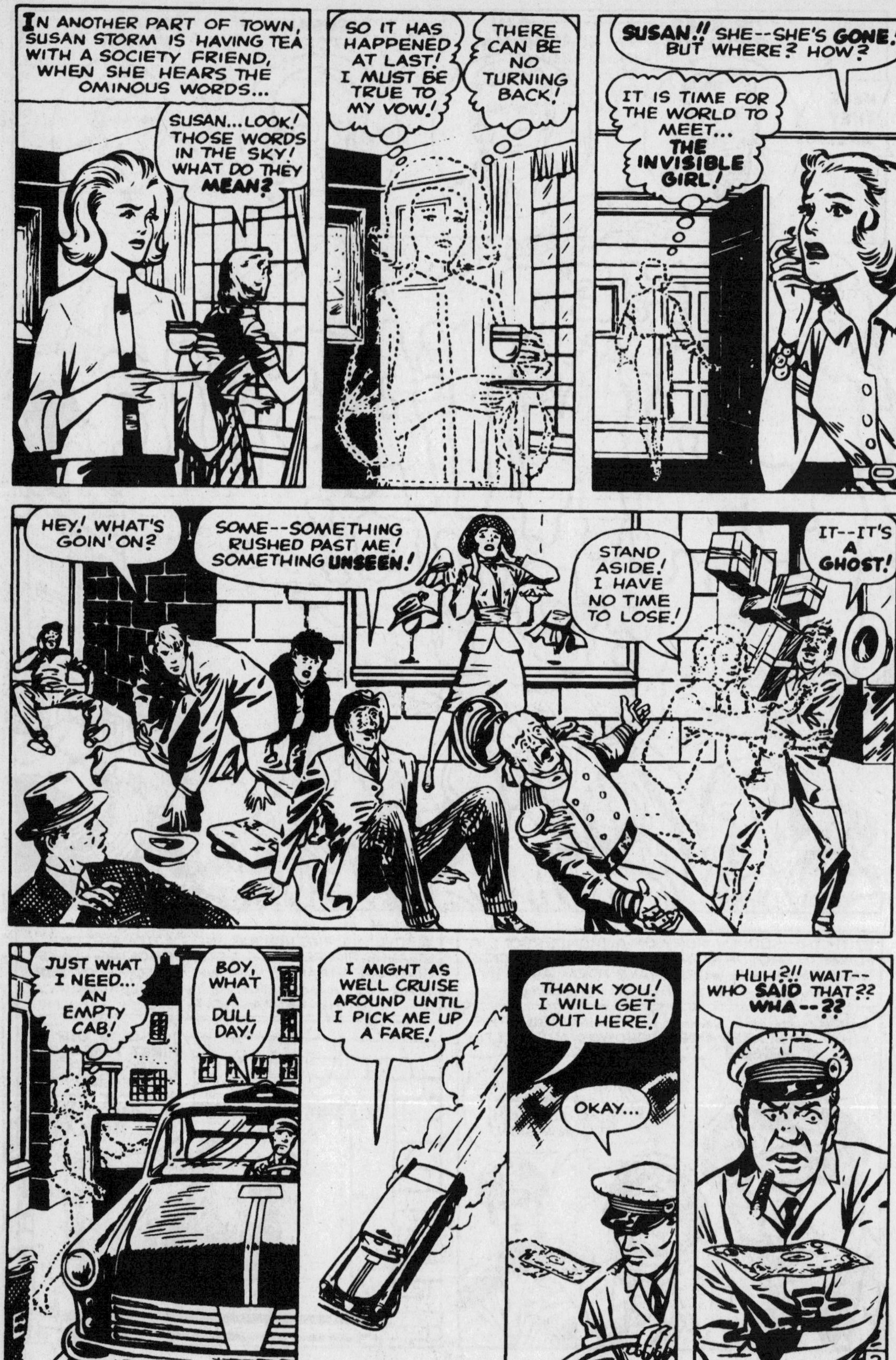
IN ANOTHER PART OF TOWN, SUSAN STORM IS HAVING TEA WITH A SOCIETY FRIEND, WHEN SHE HEARS THE OMINOUS WORDS...
SUSAN...LOOK! THOSE WORDS IN THE SKY! WHAT DO THEY MEAN?
SO IT HAS HAPPENED AT LAST! I MUST BE TRUE TO MY VOW!
THERE CAN BE NO TURNING BACK!
SUSAN!! SHE--SHE'S GONE! BUT WHERE? HOW?
IT IS TIME FOR THE WORLD TO MEET... THE INVISIBLE GIRL!
HEY! WHAT'S GOIN' ON?
SOME--SOMETHING RUSHED PAST ME! SOMETHING UNSEEN!
STAND ASIDE! I HAVE NO TIME TO LOSE!
IT--IT'S A GHOST!
JUST WHAT I NEED... AN EMPTY CAB!
BOY, WHAT A DULL DAY!
I MIGHT AS WELL CRUISE AROUND UNTIL I PICK ME UP A FARE!
THANK YOU! I WILL GET OUT HERE!
OKAY...
HUH?!! WAIT-- WHO SAID THAT?? WHA--??
2

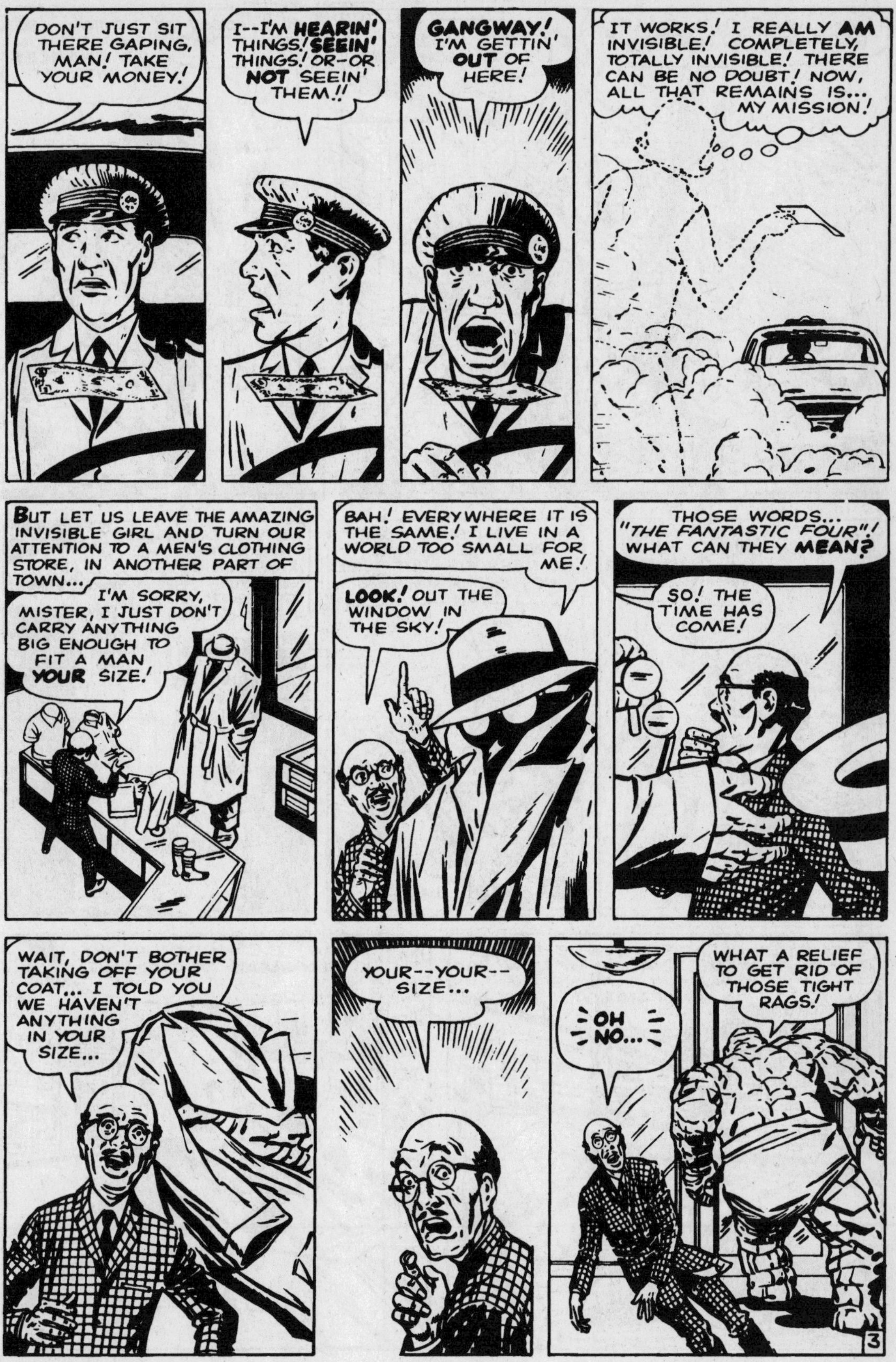
DON'T JUST SIT THERE GAPING, MAN! TAKE YOUR MONEY!
I--I'M HEARIN' THINGS! SEEIN' THINGS! OR--OR NOT SEEIN' THEM!!
GANGWAY! I'M GETTIN' OUT OF HERE!
IT WORKS! I REALLY AM INVISIBLE! COMPLETELY, TOTALLY INVISIBLE! THERE CAN BE NO DOUBT! NOW, ALL THAT REMAINS IS... MY MISSION!
BUT LET US LEAVE THE AMAZING INVISIBLE GIRL AND TURN OUR ATTENTION TO A MEN'S CLOTHING STORE, IN ANOTHER PART OF TOWN...
I'M SORRY, MISTER, I JUST DON'T CARRY ANYTHING BIG ENOUGH TO FIT A MAN YOUR SIZE!
BAH! EVERYWHERE IT IS THE SAME! I LIVE IN A WORLD TOO SMALL FOR ME!
LOOK! OUT THE WINDOW IN THE SKY!
THOSE WORDS... "THE FANTASTIC FOUR"! WHAT CAN THEY MEAN?
SO! THE TIME HAS COME!
WAIT, DON'T BOTHER TAKING OFF YOUR COAT... I TOLD YOU WE HAVEN'T ANYTHING IN YOUR SIZE...
YOUR--YOUR--SIZE...
WHAT A RELIEF TO GET RID OF THOSE TIGHT RAGS!
OH NO...
3

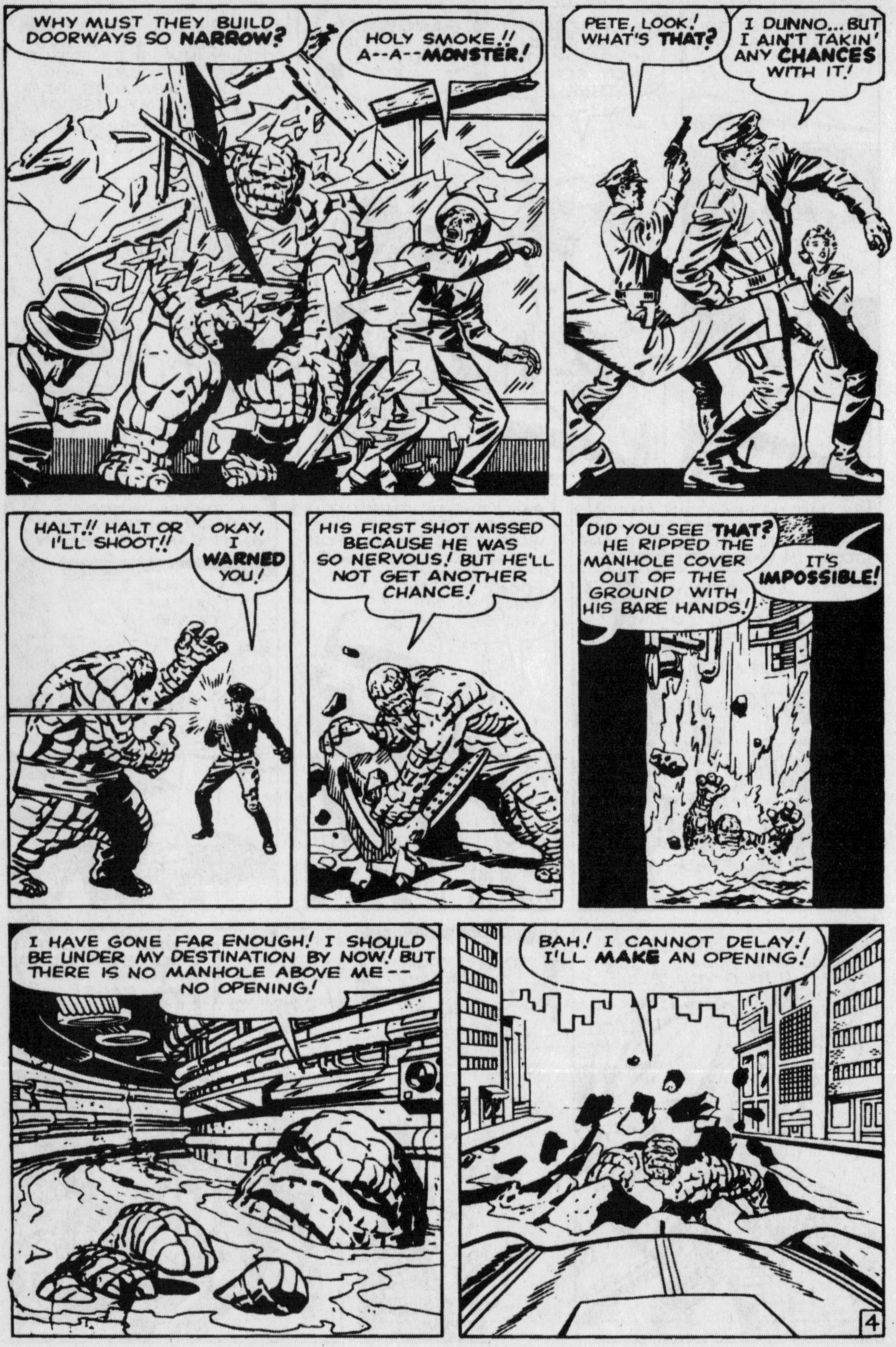
WHY MUST THEY BUILD DOORWAYS SO **NARROW?**
HOLY SMOKE.!! A--A--**MONSTER!**
PETE, LOOK! WHAT'S **THAT?**
I DUNNO... BUT I AIN'T TAKIN' ANY **CHANCES** WITH IT!
HALT!! HALT OR I'LL SHOOT!!
OKAY, I **WARNED** YOU!
HIS FIRST SHOT MISSED BECAUSE HE WAS SO NERVOUS! BUT HE'LL NOT GET ANOTHER CHANCE!
DID YOU SEE **THAT?** HE RIPPED THE MANHOLE COVER OUT OF THE GROUND WITH HIS BARE HANDS!
IT'S **IMPOSSIBLE!**
I HAVE GONE FAR ENOUGH! I SHOULD BE UNDER MY DESTINATION BY NOW! BUT THERE IS NO MANHOLE ABOVE ME -- NO OPENING!
BAH! I CANNOT DELAY! I'LL **MAKE** AN OPENING!
4

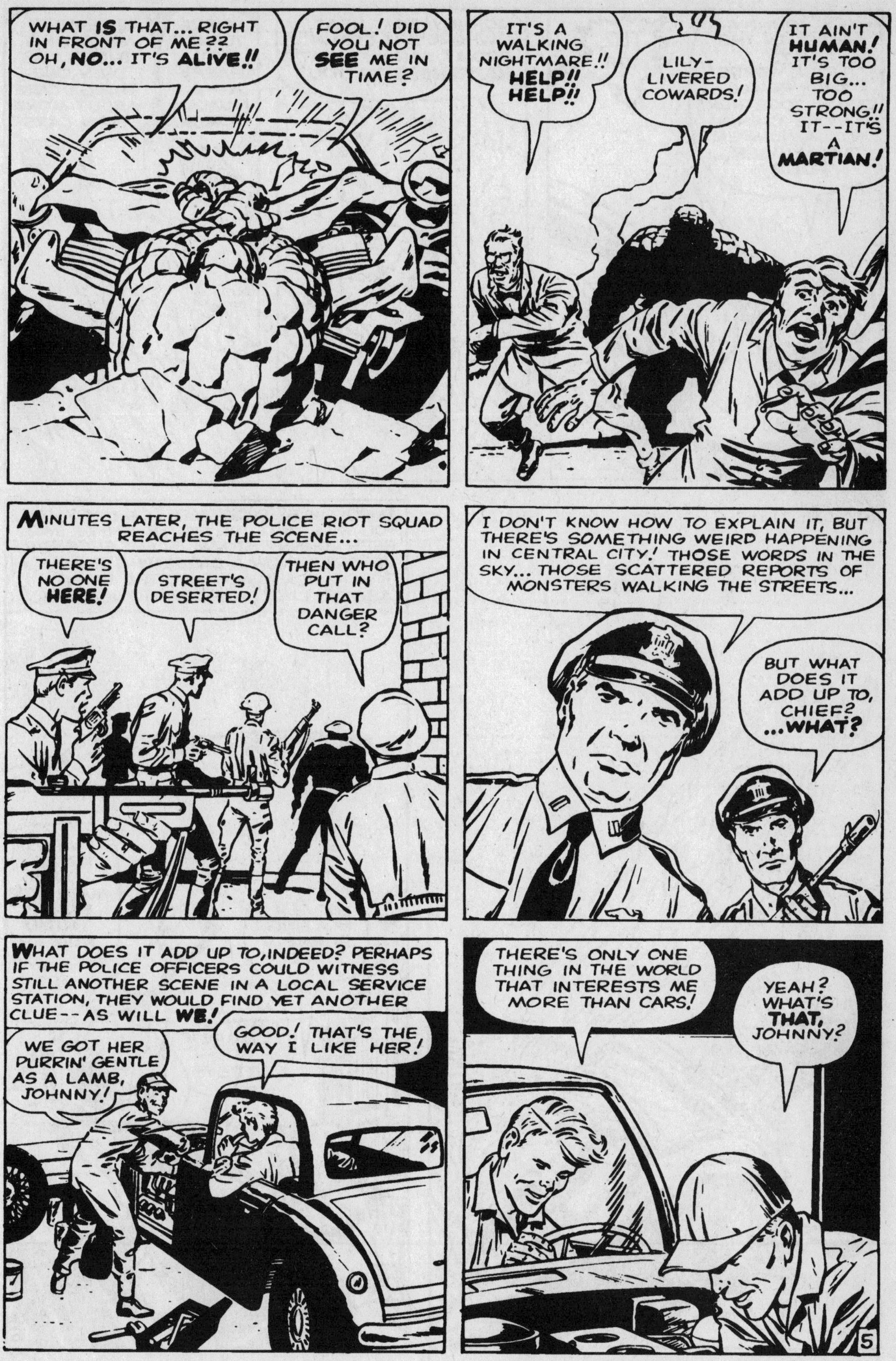
WHAT **IS** THAT... RIGHT IN FRONT OF ME?? OH, **NO**... IT'S **ALIVE!!**
FOOL! DID YOU NOT **SEE** ME IN TIME?
IT'S A WALKING NIGHTMARE!! **HELP!! HELP!!**
LILY-LIVERED COWARDS!
IT AIN'T **HUMAN!** IT'S TOO BIG... TOO STRONG!! IT--IT'S A **MARTIAN!**
MINUTES LATER, THE POLICE RIOT SQUAD REACHES THE SCENE...
THERE'S NO ONE **HERE!**
STREET'S DESERTED!
THEN WHO PUT IN THAT DANGER CALL?
I DON'T KNOW HOW TO EXPLAIN IT, BUT THERE'S SOMETHING WEIRD HAPPENING IN CENTRAL CITY! THOSE WORDS IN THE SKY... THOSE SCATTERED REPORTS OF MONSTERS WALKING THE STREETS...
BUT WHAT DOES IT ADD UP TO, CHIEF? **...WHAT?**
WHAT DOES IT ADD UP TO, INDEED? PERHAPS IF THE POLICE OFFICERS COULD WITNESS STILL ANOTHER SCENE IN A LOCAL SERVICE STATION, THEY WOULD FIND YET ANOTHER CLUE--AS WILL **WE!**
WE GOT HER PURRIN' GENTLE AS A LAMB, JOHNNY!
GOOD! THAT'S THE WAY I LIKE HER!
THERE'S ONLY ONE THING IN THE WORLD THAT INTERESTS ME MORE THAN CARS!
YEAH? WHAT'S **THAT,** JOHNNY?
5

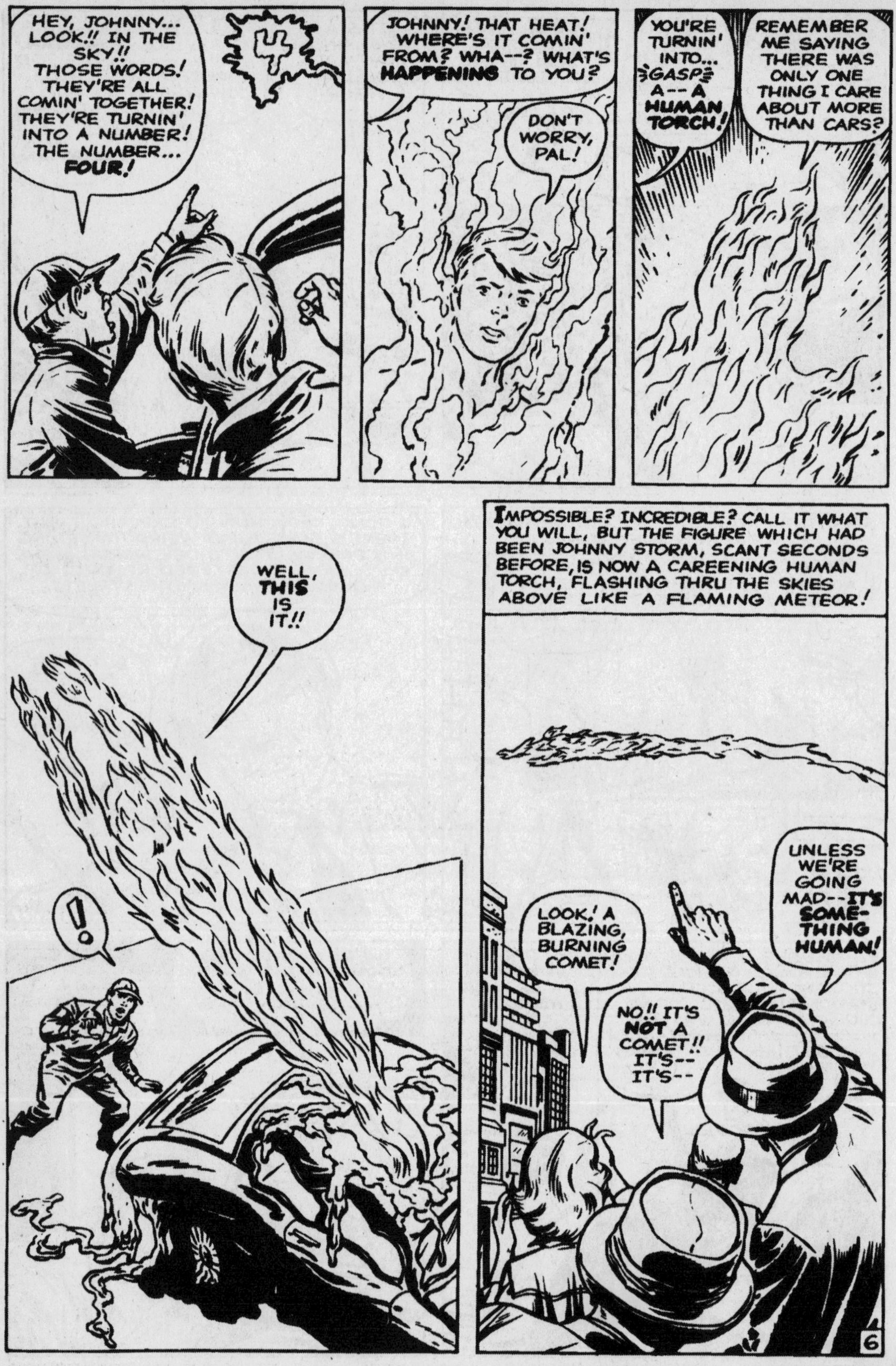
HEY, JOHNNY... LOOK!! IN THE SKY!! THOSE WORDS! THEY'RE ALL COMIN' TOGETHER! THEY'RE TURNIN' INTO A NUMBER! THE NUMBER... FOUR!
4
JOHNNY! THAT HEAT! WHERE'S IT COMIN' FROM? WHA--? WHAT'S HAPPENING TO YOU?
DON'T WORRY, PAL!
YOU'RE TURNIN' INTO... GASP A--A HUMAN TORCH!
REMEMBER ME SAYING THERE WAS ONLY ONE THING I CARE ABOUT MORE THAN CARS?
WELL, THIS IS IT!!
!
IMPOSSIBLE? INCREDIBLE? CALL IT WHAT YOU WILL, BUT THE FIGURE WHICH HAD BEEN JOHNNY STORM, SCANT SECONDS BEFORE, IS NOW A CAREENING HUMAN TORCH, FLASHING THRU THE SKIES ABOVE LIKE A FLAMING METEOR!
LOOK! A BLAZING, BURNING COMET!
UNLESS WE'RE GOING MAD--IT'S SOMETHING HUMAN!
NO!! IT'S NOT A COMET!! IT'S-- IT'S--
6

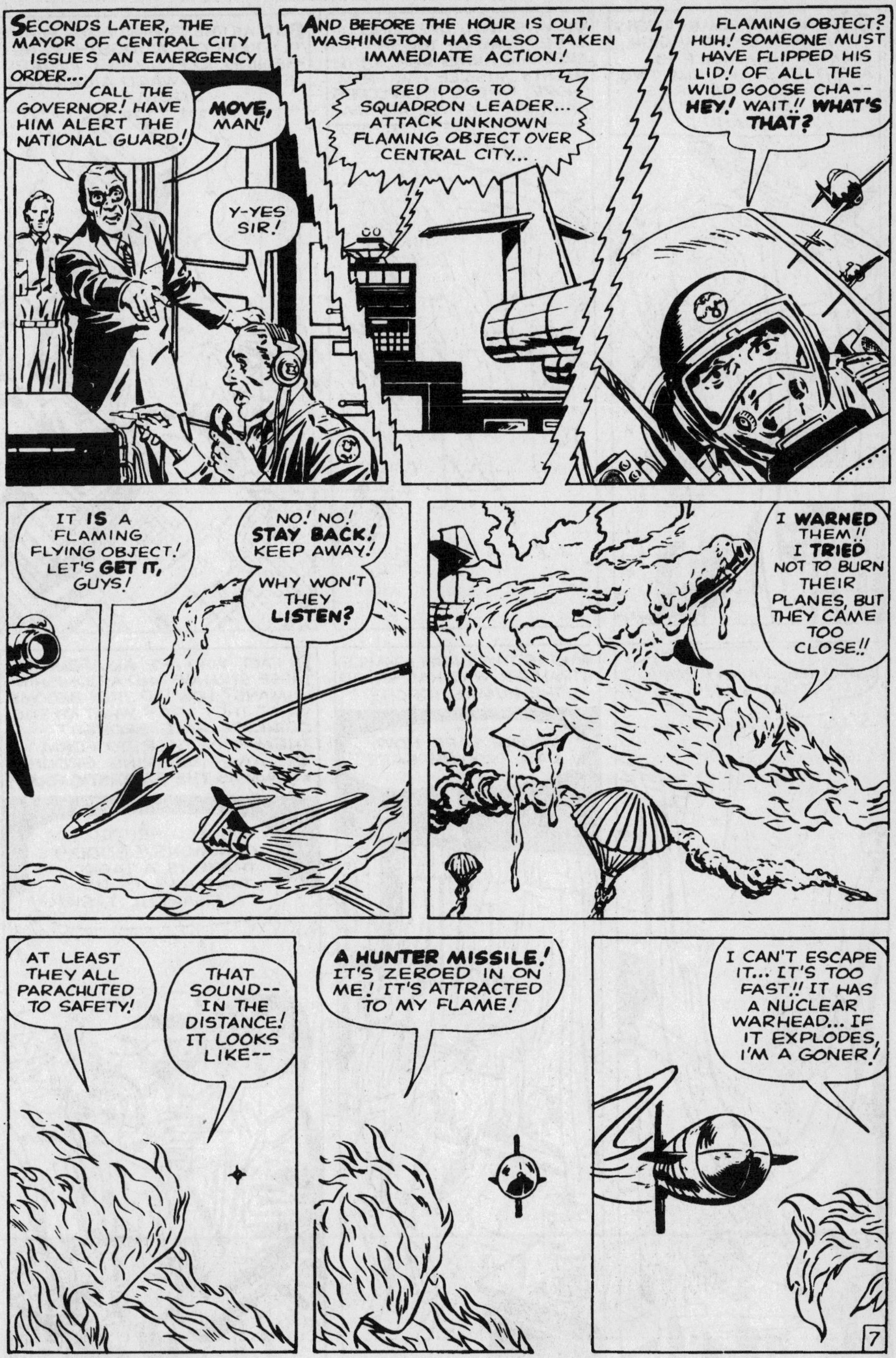
SECONDS LATER, THE MAYOR OF CENTRAL CITY ISSUES AN EMERGENCY ORDER...
CALL THE GOVERNOR! HAVE HIM ALERT THE NATIONAL GUARD!
MOVE, MAN!
Y-YES SIR!
AND BEFORE THE HOUR IS OUT, WASHINGTON HAS ALSO TAKEN IMMEDIATE ACTION!
RED DOG TO SQUADRON LEADER... ATTACK UNKNOWN FLAMING OBJECT OVER CENTRAL CITY...
FLAMING OBJECT? HUH! SOMEONE MUST HAVE FLIPPED HIS LID! OF ALL THE WILD GOOSE CHA-- HEY! WAIT!! WHAT'S THAT?
IT IS A FLAMING FLYING OBJECT! LET'S GET IT, GUYS!
NO! NO! STAY BACK! KEEP AWAY!
WHY WON'T THEY LISTEN?
I WARNED THEM!! I TRIED NOT TO BURN THEIR PLANES, BUT THEY CAME TOO CLOSE!!
AT LEAST THEY ALL PARACHUTED TO SAFETY!
THAT SOUND-- IN THE DISTANCE! IT LOOKS LIKE--
A HUNTER MISSILE! IT'S ZEROED IN ON ME! IT'S ATTRACTED TO MY FLAME!
I CAN'T ESCAPE IT... IT'S TOO FAST!! IT HAS A NUCLEAR WARHEAD... IF IT EXPLODES, I'M A GONER!
7

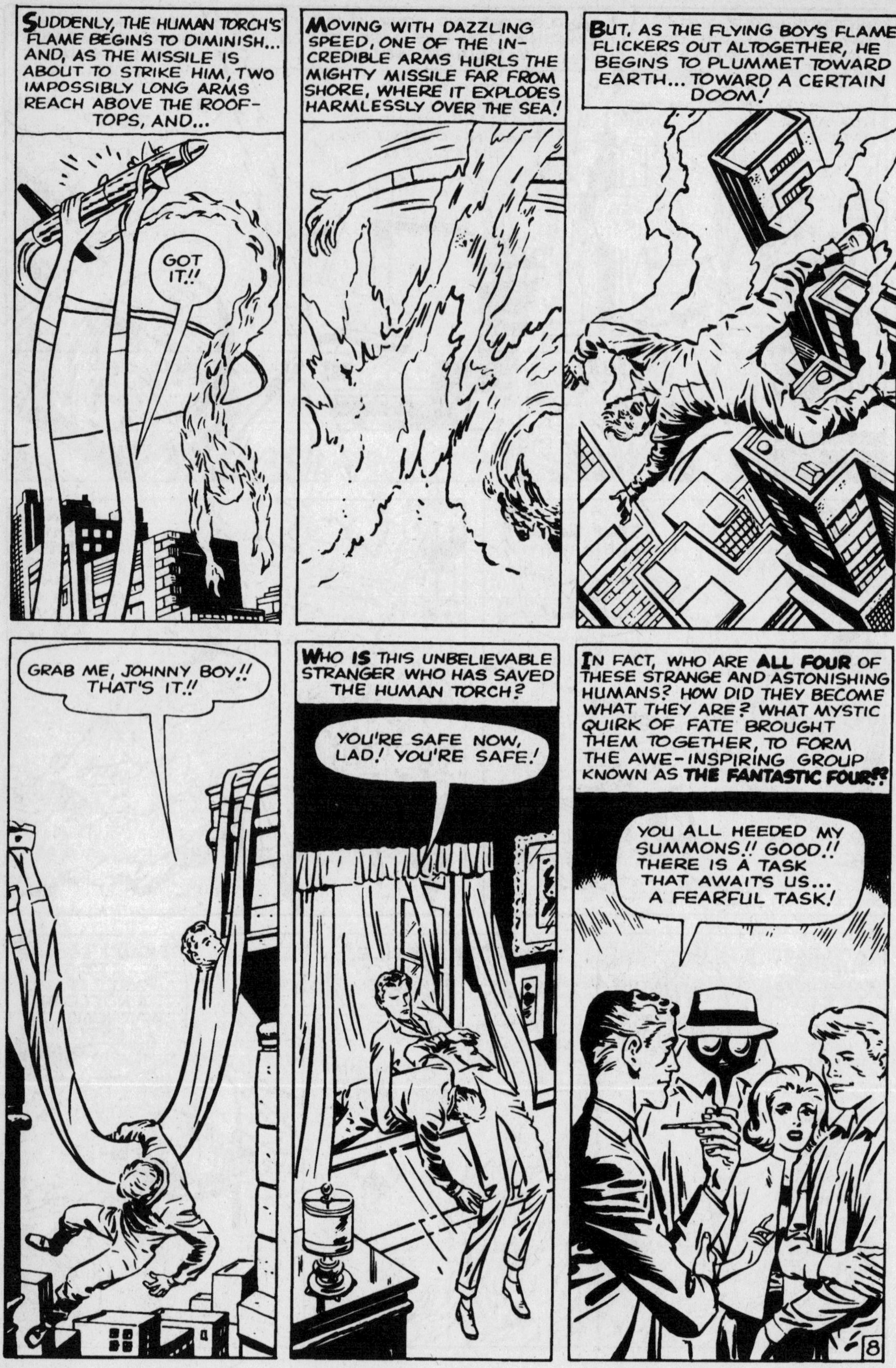
SUDDENLY, THE HUMAN TORCH'S FLAME BEGINS TO DIMINISH... AND, AS THE MISSILE IS ABOUT TO STRIKE HIM, TWO IMPOSSIBLY LONG ARMS REACH ABOVE THE ROOF-TOPS, AND...
GOT IT!!
MOVING WITH DAZZLING SPEED, ONE OF THE INCREDIBLE ARMS HURLS THE MIGHTY MISSILE FAR FROM SHORE, WHERE IT EXPLODES HARMLESSLY OVER THE SEA!
BUT, AS THE FLYING BOY'S FLAME FLICKERS OUT ALTOGETHER, HE BEGINS TO PLUMMET TOWARD EARTH... TOWARD A CERTAIN DOOM!
GRAB ME, JOHNNY BOY!! THAT'S IT!!
WHO IS THIS UNBELIEVABLE STRANGER WHO HAS SAVED THE HUMAN TORCH?
YOU'RE SAFE NOW, LAD! YOU'RE SAFE!
IN FACT, WHO ARE ALL FOUR OF THESE STRANGE AND ASTONISHING HUMANS? HOW DID THEY BECOME WHAT THEY ARE? WHAT MYSTIC QUIRK OF FATE BROUGHT THEM TOGETHER, TO FORM THE AWE-INSPIRING GROUP KNOWN AS THE FANTASTIC FOUR??
YOU ALL HEEDED MY SUMMONS!! GOOD!! THERE IS A TASK THAT AWAITS US... A FEARFUL TASK!
8

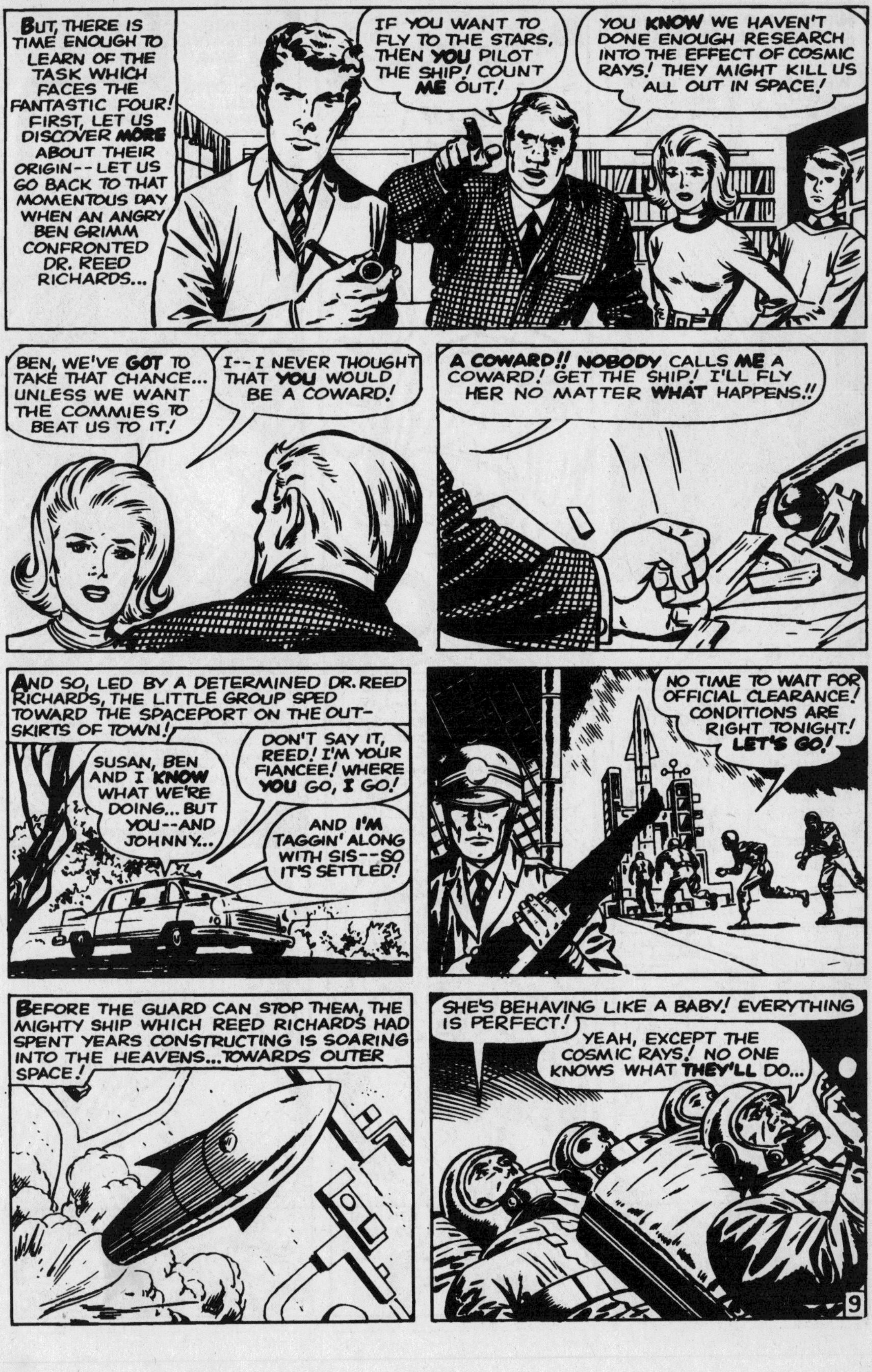
BUT, THERE IS TIME ENOUGH TO LEARN OF THE TASK WHICH FACES THE FANTASTIC FOUR! FIRST, LET US DISCOVER MORE ABOUT THEIR ORIGIN--LET US GO BACK TO THAT MOMENTOUS DAY WHEN AN ANGRY BEN GRIMM CONFRONTED DR. REED RICHARDS...
IF YOU WANT TO FLY TO THE STARS, THEN YOU PILOT THE SHIP! COUNT ME OUT!
YOU KNOW WE HAVEN'T DONE ENOUGH RESEARCH INTO THE EFFECT OF COSMIC RAYS! THEY MIGHT KILL US ALL OUT IN SPACE!
BEN, WE'VE GOT TO TAKE THAT CHANCE... UNLESS WE WANT THE COMMIES TO BEAT US TO IT!
I--I NEVER THOUGHT THAT YOU WOULD BE A COWARD!
A COWARD!! NOBODY CALLS ME A COWARD! GET THE SHIP! I'LL FLY HER NO MATTER WHAT HAPPENS!!
AND SO, LED BY A DETERMINED DR. REED RICHARDS, THE LITTLE GROUP SPED TOWARD THE SPACEPORT ON THE OUT-SKIRTS OF TOWN!
SUSAN, BEN AND I KNOW WHAT WE'RE DOING... BUT YOU--AND JOHNNY...
DON'T SAY IT, REED! I'M YOUR FIANCEE! WHERE YOU GO, I GO!
AND I'M TAGGIN' ALONG WITH SIS--SO IT'S SETTLED!
NO TIME TO WAIT FOR OFFICIAL CLEARANCE! CONDITIONS ARE RIGHT TONIGHT! LET'S GO!
BEFORE THE GUARD CAN STOP THEM, THE MIGHTY SHIP WHICH REED RICHARDS HAD SPENT YEARS CONSTRUCTING IS SOARING INTO THE HEAVENS...TOWARDS OUTER SPACE!
SHE'S BEHAVING LIKE A BABY! EVERYTHING IS PERFECT!
YEAH, EXCEPT THE COSMIC RAYS! NO ONE KNOWS WHAT THEY'LL DO...
9

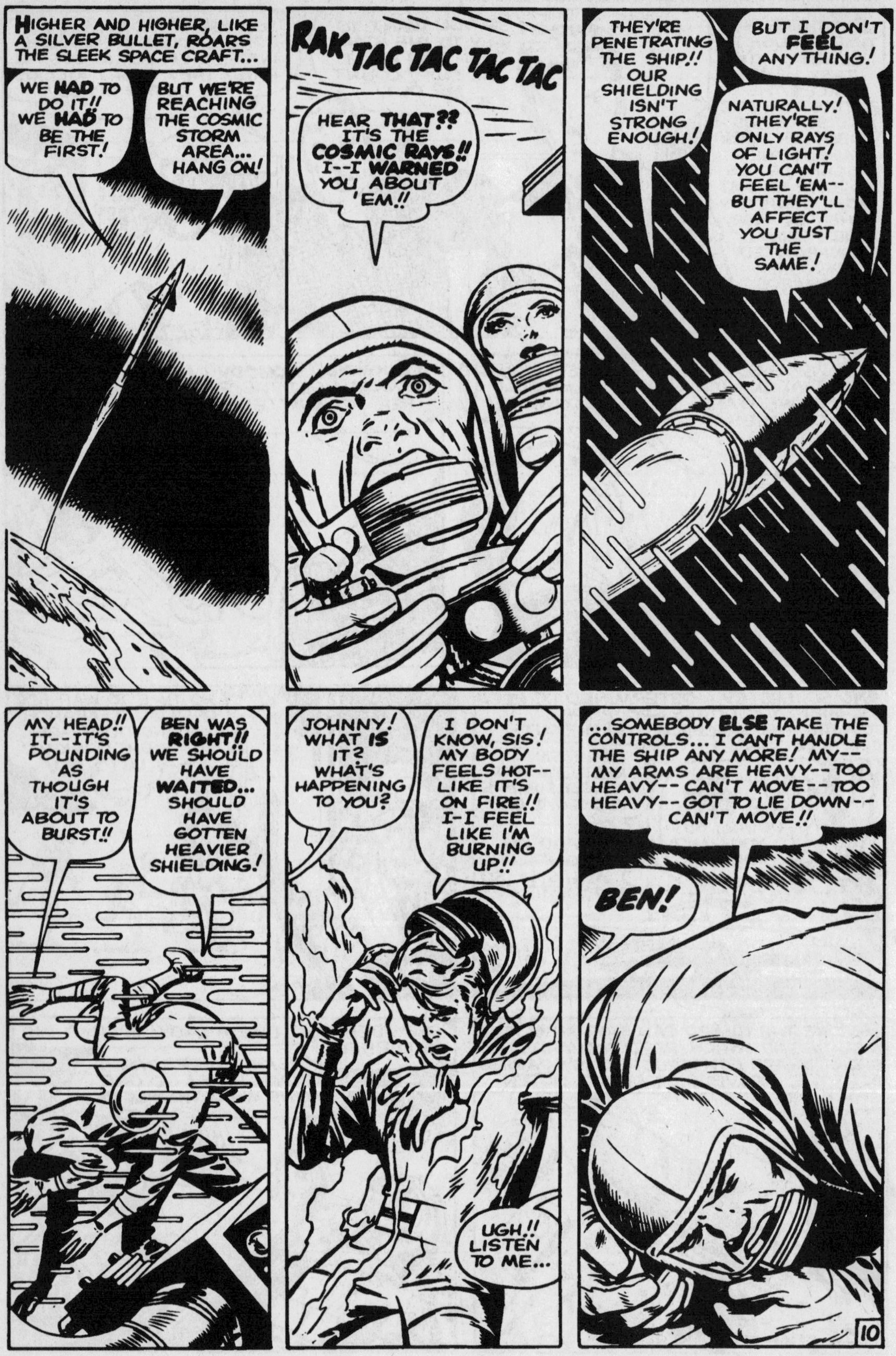
HIGHER AND HIGHER, LIKE A SILVER BULLET, ROARS THE SLEEK SPACE CRAFT...
WE HAD TO DO IT!! WE HAD TO BE THE FIRST!
BUT WE'RE REACHING THE COSMIC STORM AREA... HANG ON!
RAK TAC TAC TAC TAC
HEAR THAT?? IT'S THE COSMIC RAYS!! I--I WARNED YOU ABOUT 'EM!!
THEY'RE PENETRATING THE SHIP!! OUR SHIELDING ISN'T STRONG ENOUGH!
BUT I DON'T FEEL ANYTHING!
NATURALLY! THEY'RE ONLY RAYS OF LIGHT! YOU CAN'T FEEL 'EM-- BUT THEY'LL AFFECT YOU JUST THE SAME!
MY HEAD!! IT--IT'S POUNDING AS THOUGH IT'S ABOUT TO BURST!!
BEN WAS RIGHT!! WE SHOULD HAVE WAITED... SHOULD HAVE GOTTEN HEAVIER SHIELDING!
JOHNNY! WHAT IS IT? WHAT'S HAPPENING TO YOU?
I DON'T KNOW, SIS! MY BODY FEELS HOT-- LIKE IT'S ON FIRE!! I-I FEEL LIKE I'M BURNING UP!!
UGH!! LISTEN TO ME...
...SOMEBODY ELSE TAKE THE CONTROLS... I CAN'T HANDLE THE SHIP ANY MORE! MY-- MY ARMS ARE HEAVY--TOO HEAVY-- CAN'T MOVE--TOO HEAVY--GOT TO LIE DOWN-- CAN'T MOVE!!
BEN!
10

AT THAT MOMENT, THE POWERFUL SHIP'S AUTOMATIC PILOT TOOK OVER, AND MANAGED TO RETURN THE SLEEK ROCKET SAFELY TO EARTH, IN A ROUGH, BUT NON-FATAL LANDING!

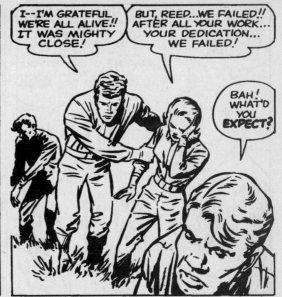

I--I'M GRATEFUL WE'RE ALL ALIVE!! IT WAS MIGHTY CLOSE!

BUT, REED...WE FAILED!! AFTER ALL YOUR WORK... YOUR DEDICATION... WE FAILED!

BAH! WHAT'D YOU EXPECT?

BUT WE'RE STILL NOT COMPLETELY SAFE! WE STILL HAVE TO SEE WHETHER THE COSMIC RAYS AFFECTED US IN ANY WAY!

OH, REED... I FEEL SO STRANGE!

SUSAN! LOOK AT SUSAN!!

WHAT'S WRONG?

YOU'RE =GASP= FADING AWAY!!

OH, NO!! NO!!

IT'S IMPOSSIBLE!!

SOMEHOW THE COSMIC RAYS HAVE ALTERED YOUR ATOMIC STRUCTURE...MAKING YOU GROW INVISIBLE!

SIS! I CAN'T SEE YOU AT ALL ANY MORE!

HOW... HOW LONG WILL IT LAST?

THERE'S NO WAY OF KNOWING!!

WHA--WHAT IF SHE NEVER GETS VISIBLE AGAIN??

LOOK!! I SEE HER!

I'M MYSELF AGAIN! IT HAPPENED SO SUDDENLY...ALL BY ITSELF!

11

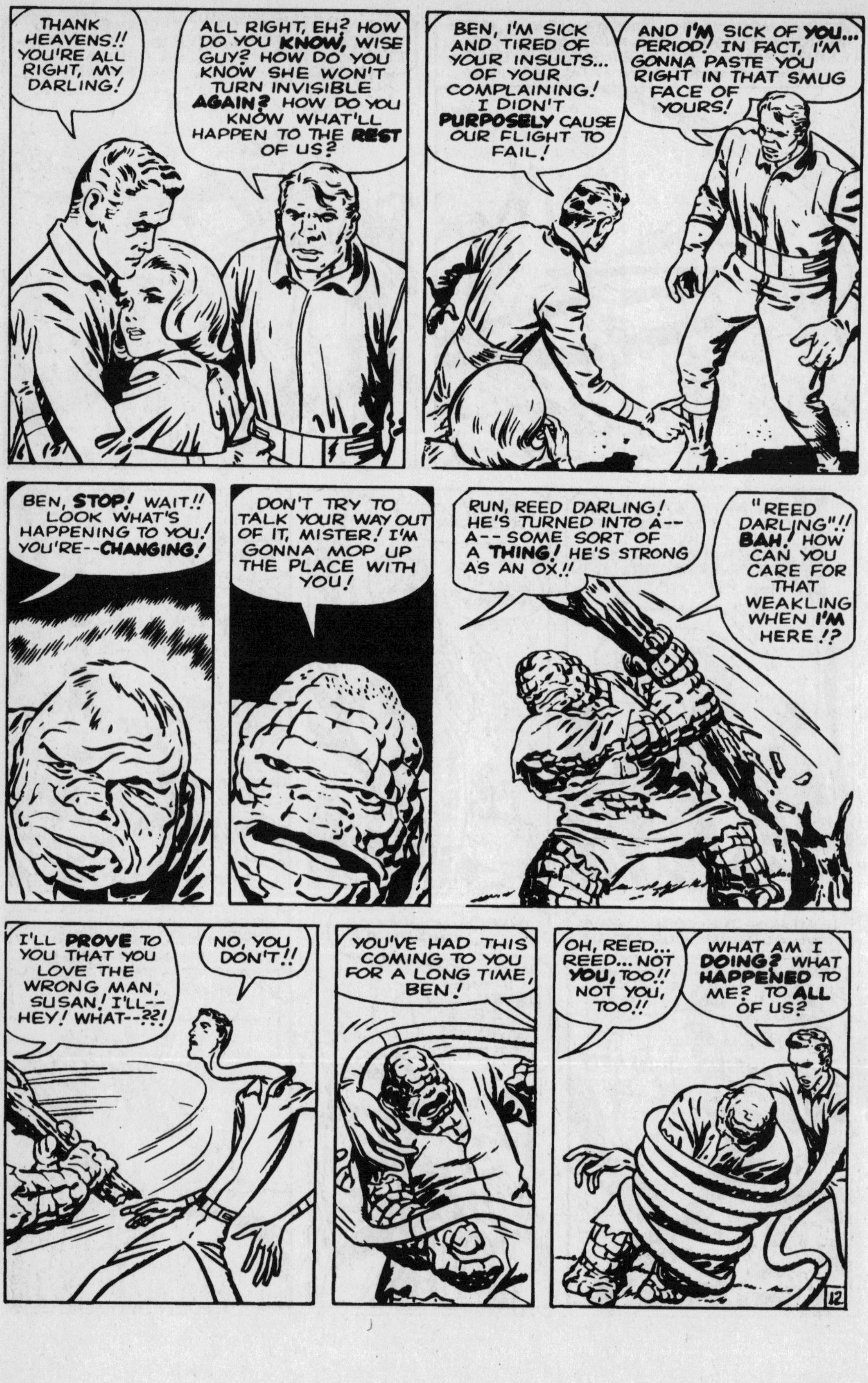
THANK HEAVENS!! YOU'RE ALL RIGHT, MY DARLING!
ALL RIGHT, EH? HOW DO YOU KNOW, WISE GUY? HOW DO YOU KNOW SHE WON'T TURN INVISIBLE AGAIN? HOW DO YOU KNOW WHAT'LL HAPPEN TO THE REST OF US?
BEN, I'M SICK AND TIRED OF YOUR INSULTS... OF YOUR COMPLAINING! I DIDN'T PURPOSELY CAUSE OUR FLIGHT TO FAIL!
AND I'M SICK OF YOU... PERIOD! IN FACT, I'M GONNA PASTE YOU RIGHT IN THAT SMUG FACE OF YOURS!
BEN, STOP! WAIT!! LOOK WHAT'S HAPPENING TO YOU! YOU'RE--CHANGING!
DON'T TRY TO TALK YOUR WAY OUT OF IT, MISTER! I'M GONNA MOP UP THE PLACE WITH YOU!
RUN, REED DARLING! HE'S TURNED INTO A-- A--SOME SORT OF A THING! HE'S STRONG AS AN OX!!
"REED DARLING"!! BAH! HOW CAN YOU CARE FOR THAT WEAKLING WHEN I'M HERE!?
I'LL PROVE TO YOU THAT YOU LOVE THE WRONG MAN, SUSAN! I'LL-- HEY! WHAT--??!
NO, YOU DON'T!!
YOU'VE HAD THIS COMING TO YOU FOR A LONG TIME, BEN!
OH, REED... REED... NOT YOU, TOO!! NOT YOU, TOO!!
WHAT AM I DOING? WHAT HAPPENED TO ME? TO ALL OF US?
12

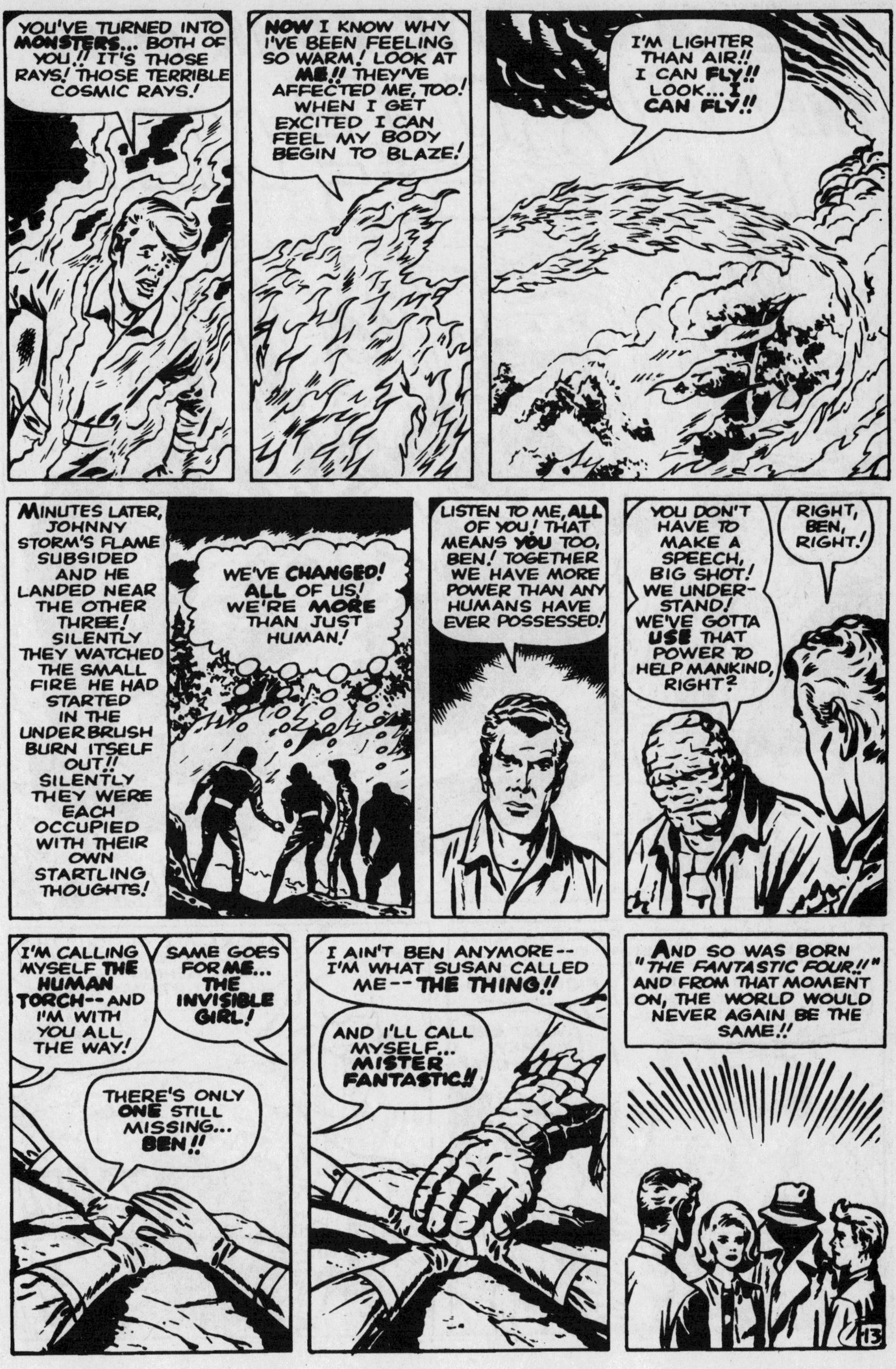
YOU'VE TURNED INTO MONSTERS... BOTH OF YOU!! IT'S THOSE RAYS! THOSE TERRIBLE COSMIC RAYS!
NOW I KNOW WHY I'VE BEEN FEELING SO WARM! LOOK AT ME!! THEY'VE AFFECTED ME, TOO! WHEN I GET EXCITED I CAN FEEL MY BODY BEGIN TO BLAZE!
I'M LIGHTER THAN AIR!! I CAN FLY!! LOOK... I CAN FLY!!
MINUTES LATER, JOHNNY STORM'S FLAME SUBSIDED AND HE LANDED NEAR THE OTHER THREE! SILENTLY THEY WATCHED THE SMALL FIRE HE HAD STARTED IN THE UNDERBRUSH BURN ITSELF OUT!! SILENTLY THEY WERE EACH OCCUPIED WITH THEIR OWN STARTLING THOUGHTS!
WE'VE CHANGED! ALL OF US! WE'RE MORE THAN JUST HUMAN!
LISTEN TO ME, ALL OF YOU! THAT MEANS YOU TOO, BEN! TOGETHER WE HAVE MORE POWER THAN ANY HUMANS HAVE EVER POSSESSED!
YOU DON'T HAVE TO MAKE A SPEECH, BIG SHOT! WE UNDERSTAND! WE'VE GOTTA USE THAT POWER TO HELP MANKIND, RIGHT?
RIGHT, BEN, RIGHT!
I'M CALLING MYSELF THE HUMAN TORCH-- AND I'M WITH YOU ALL THE WAY!
SAME GOES FOR ME... THE INVISIBLE GIRL!
THERE'S ONLY ONE STILL MISSING... BEN!!
I AIN'T BEN ANYMORE-- I'M WHAT SUSAN CALLED ME-- THE THING!!
AND I'LL CALL MYSELF... MISTER FANTASTIC!!
AND SO WAS BORN "THE FANTASTIC FOUR!!" AND FROM THAT MOMENT ON, THE WORLD WOULD NEVER AGAIN BE THE SAME!!
13

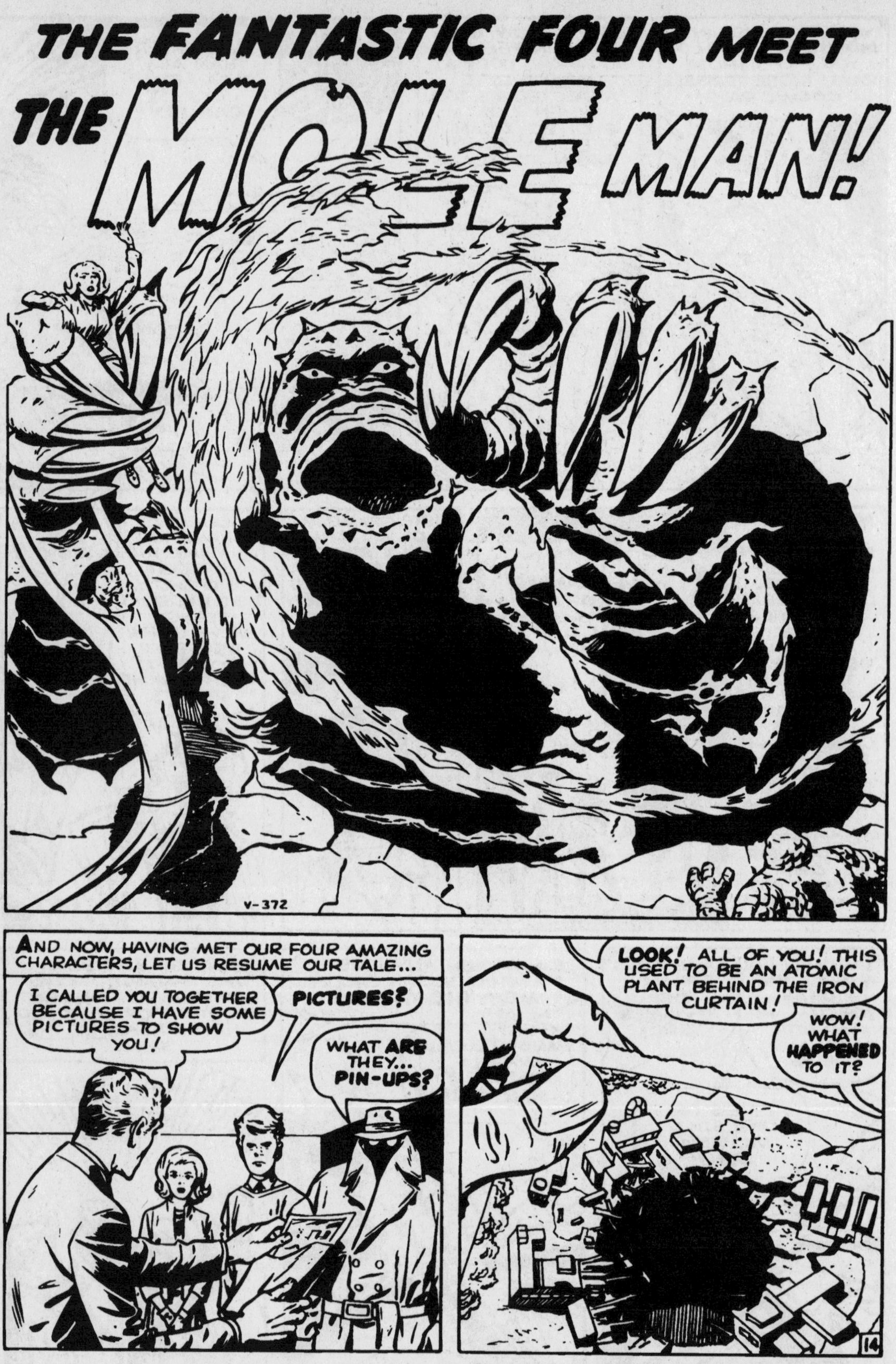
THE FANTASTIC FOUR MEET
THE MOLE MAN!
V-372
AND NOW, HAVING MET OUR FOUR AMAZING CHARACTERS, LET US RESUME OUR TALE...
I CALLED YOU TOGETHER BECAUSE I HAVE SOME PICTURES TO SHOW YOU!
PICTURES?
WHAT ARE THEY... PIN-UPS?
LOOK! ALL OF YOU! THIS USED TO BE AN ATOMIC PLANT BEHIND THE IRON CURTAIN!
WOW! WHAT HAPPENED TO IT?
14

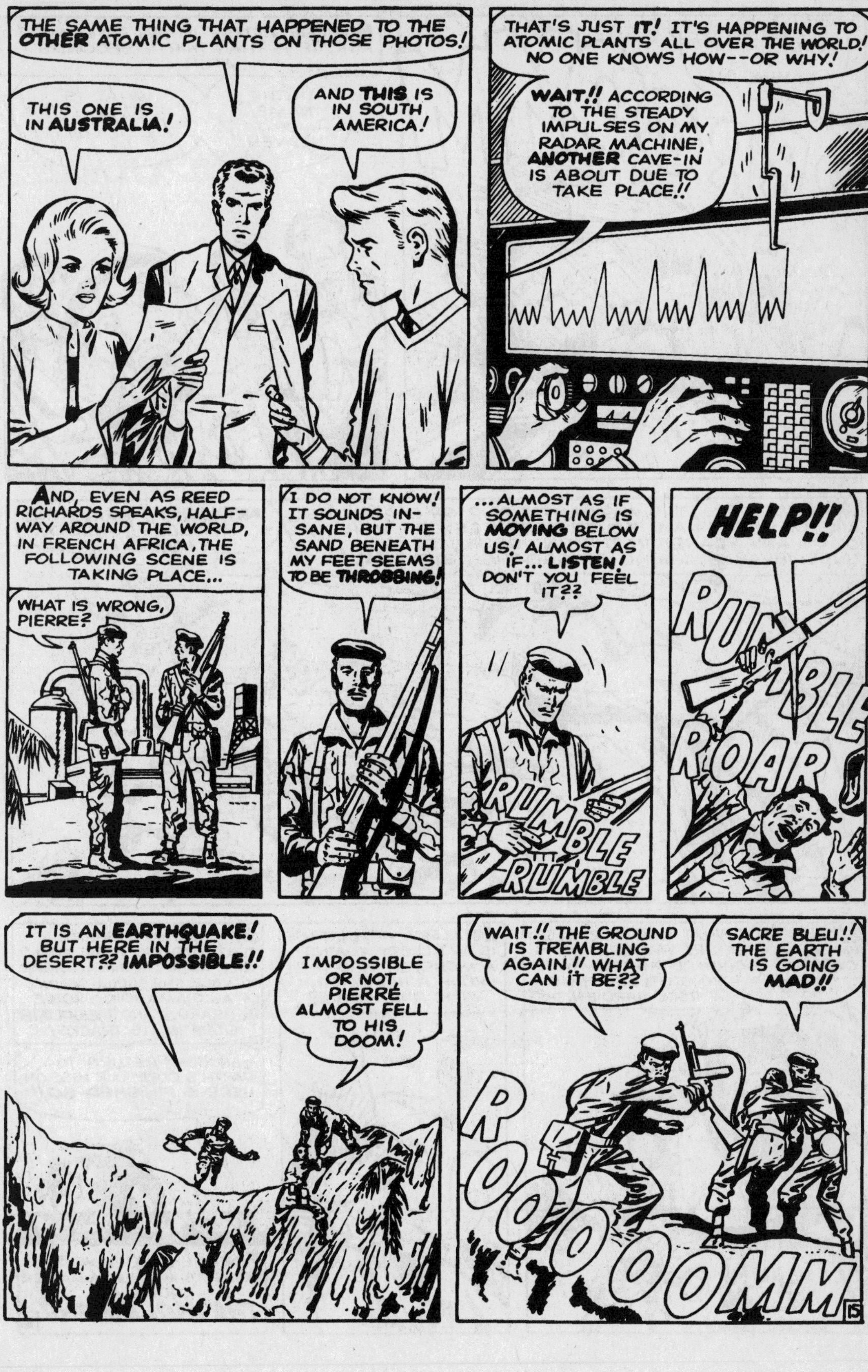
THE SAME THING THAT HAPPENED TO THE OTHER ATOMIC PLANTS ON THOSE PHOTOS!
THIS ONE IS IN AUSTRALIA!
AND THIS IS IN SOUTH AMERICA!
THAT'S JUST IT! IT'S HAPPENING TO ATOMIC PLANTS ALL OVER THE WORLD! NO ONE KNOWS HOW--OR WHY!
WAIT!! ACCORDING TO THE STEADY IMPULSES ON MY RADAR MACHINE, ANOTHER CAVE-IN IS ABOUT DUE TO TAKE PLACE!!
AND, EVEN AS REED RICHARDS SPEAKS, HALF-WAY AROUND THE WORLD, IN FRENCH AFRICA, THE FOLLOWING SCENE IS TAKING PLACE...
WHAT IS WRONG, PIERRE?
I DO NOT KNOW! IT SOUNDS IN-SANE, BUT THE SAND BENEATH MY FEET SEEMS TO BE THROBBING!
...ALMOST AS IF SOMETHING IS MOVING BELOW US! ALMOST AS IF... LISTEN! DON'T YOU FEEL IT??
RUMBLE RUMBLE
HELP!!
RUMBLE
ROAR
IT IS AN EARTHQUAKE! BUT HERE IN THE DESERT?? IMPOSSIBLE!!
IMPOSSIBLE OR NOT, PIERRE ALMOST FELL TO HIS DOOM!
WAIT!! THE GROUND IS TREMBLING AGAIN!! WHAT CAN IT BE??
SACRE BLEU!! THE EARTH IS GOING MAD!!
ROOOOOOMM

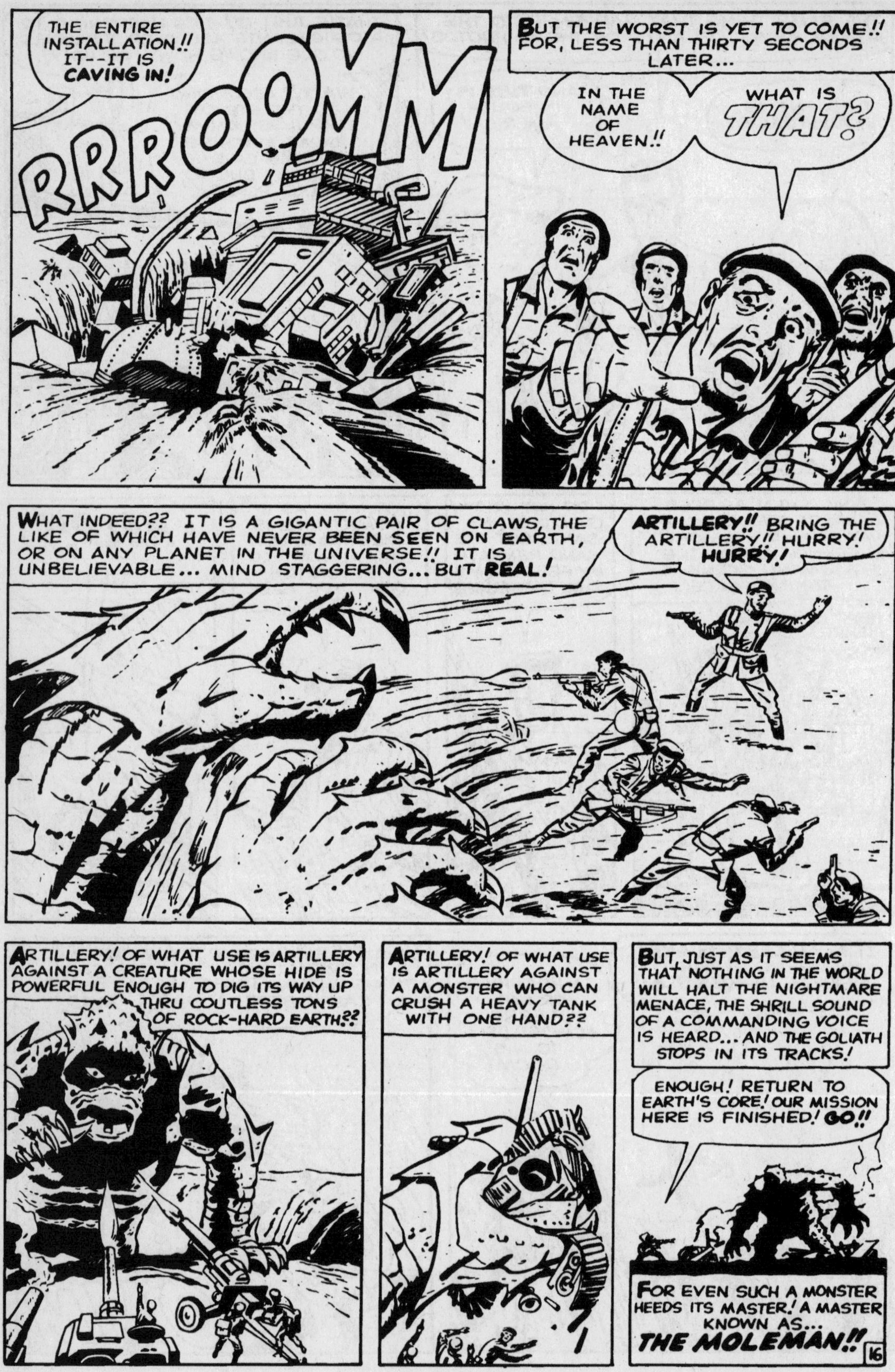
THE ENTIRE INSTALLATION!! IT--IT IS CAVING IN!
RRROOMM
BUT THE WORST IS YET TO COME!! FOR, LESS THAN THIRTY SECONDS LATER...
IN THE NAME OF HEAVEN!!
WHAT IS THAT?
WHAT INDEED?? IT IS A GIGANTIC PAIR OF CLAWS, THE LIKE OF WHICH HAVE NEVER BEEN SEEN ON EARTH, OR ON ANY PLANET IN THE UNIVERSE!! IT IS UNBELIEVABLE... MIND STAGGERING... BUT REAL!
ARTILLERY!! BRING THE ARTILLERY!! HURRY! HURRY!
ARTILLERY! OF WHAT USE IS ARTILLERY AGAINST A CREATURE WHOSE HIDE IS POWERFUL ENOUGH TO DIG ITS WAY UP THRU COUTLESS TONS OF ROCK-HARD EARTH??
ARTILLERY! OF WHAT USE IS ARTILLERY AGAINST A MONSTER WHO CAN CRUSH A HEAVY TANK WITH ONE HAND??
BUT, JUST AS IT SEEMS THAT NOTHING IN THE WORLD WILL HALT THE NIGHTMARE MENACE, THE SHRILL SOUND OF A COMMANDING VOICE IS HEARD... AND THE GOLIATH STOPS IN ITS TRACKS!
ENOUGH! RETURN TO EARTH'S CORE! OUR MISSION HERE IS FINISHED! GO!!
FOR EVEN SUCH A MONSTER HEEDS ITS MASTER! A MASTER KNOWN AS... THE MOLEMAN!!
16

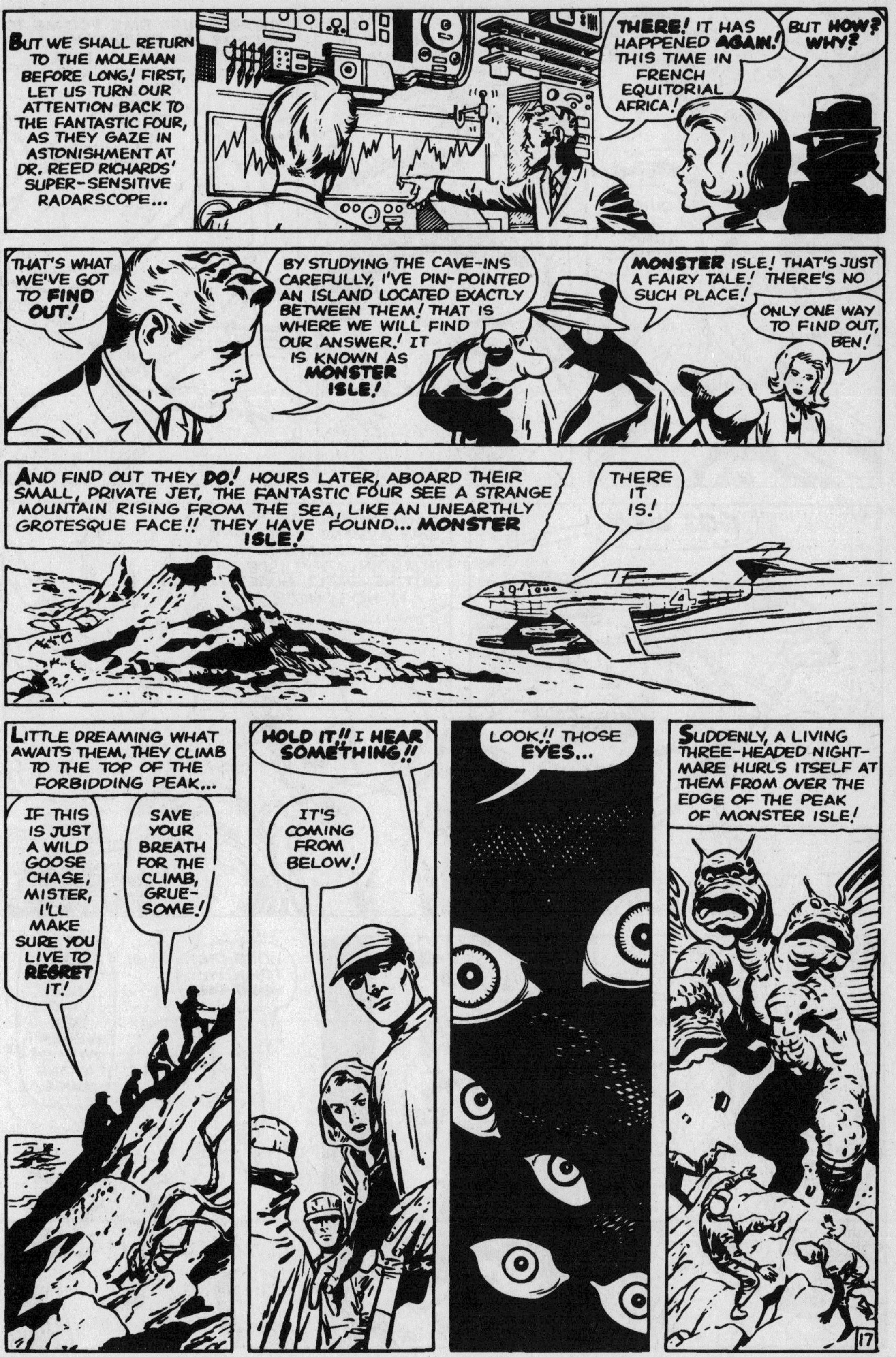
BUT WE SHALL RETURN TO THE MOLEMAN BEFORE LONG! FIRST, LET US TURN OUR ATTENTION BACK TO THE FANTASTIC FOUR, AS THEY GAZE IN ASTONISHMENT AT DR. REED RICHARDS' SUPER-SENSITIVE RADARSCOPE...
THERE! IT HAS HAPPENED AGAIN! THIS TIME IN FRENCH EQUITORIAL AFRICA!
BUT HOW? WHY?
THAT'S WHAT WE'VE GOT TO FIND OUT!
BY STUDYING THE CAVE-INS CAREFULLY, I'VE PIN-POINTED AN ISLAND LOCATED EXACTLY BETWEEN THEM! THAT IS WHERE WE WILL FIND OUR ANSWER! IT IS KNOWN AS MONSTER ISLE!
MONSTER ISLE! THAT'S JUST A FAIRY TALE! THERE'S NO SUCH PLACE!
ONLY ONE WAY TO FIND OUT, BEN!
AND FIND OUT THEY DO! HOURS LATER, ABOARD THEIR SMALL, PRIVATE JET, THE FANTASTIC FOUR SEE A STRANGE MOUNTAIN RISING FROM THE SEA, LIKE AN UNEARTHLY GROTESQUE FACE!! THEY HAVE FOUND... MONSTER ISLE!
THERE IT IS!
LITTLE DREAMING WHAT AWAITS THEM, THEY CLIMB TO THE TOP OF THE FORBIDDING PEAK...
IF THIS IS JUST A WILD GOOSE CHASE, MISTER, I'LL MAKE SURE YOU LIVE TO REGRET IT!
SAVE YOUR BREATH FOR THE CLIMB, GRUE-SOME!
HOLD IT!! I HEAR SOMETHING!!
IT'S COMING FROM BELOW!
LOOK!! THOSE EYES...
SUDDENLY, A LIVING THREE-HEADED NIGHT-MARE HURLS ITSELF AT THEM FROM OVER THE EDGE OF THE PEAK OF MONSTER ISLE!
17

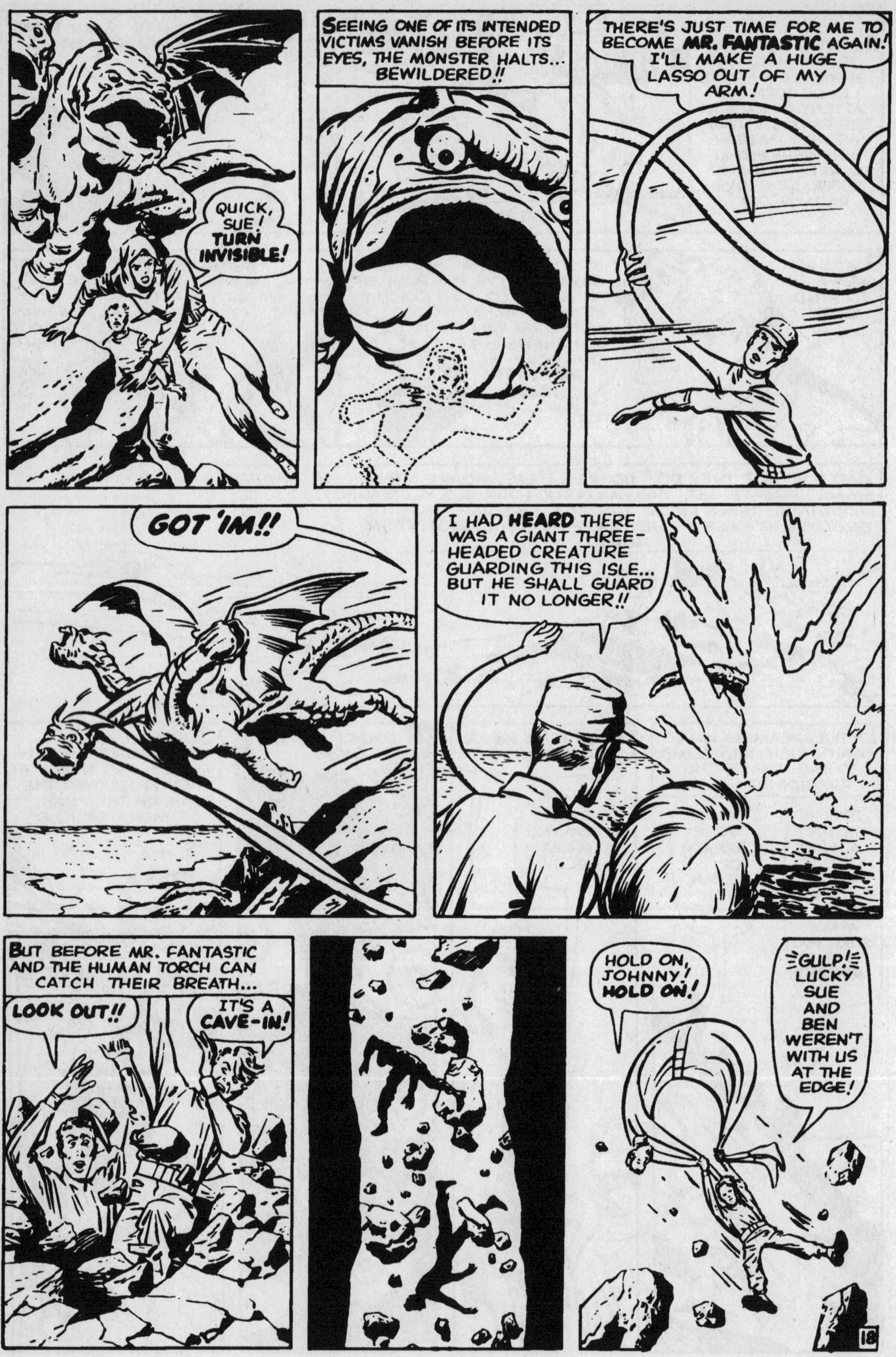
QUICK, SUE! TURN INVISIBLE!
SEEING ONE OF ITS INTENDED VICTIMS VANISH BEFORE ITS EYES, THE MONSTER HALTS... BEWILDERED!!
THERE'S JUST TIME FOR ME TO BECOME MR. FANTASTIC AGAIN! I'LL MAKE A HUGE LASSO OUT OF MY ARM!
GOT 'IM!!
I HAD HEARD THERE WAS A GIANT THREE-HEADED CREATURE GUARDING THIS ISLE... BUT HE SHALL GUARD IT NO LONGER!!
BUT BEFORE MR. FANTASTIC AND THE HUMAN TORCH CAN CATCH THEIR BREATH...
LOOK OUT!!
IT'S A CAVE-IN!
HOLD ON, JOHNNY! HOLD ON!
GULP! LUCKY SUE AND BEN WEREN'T WITH US AT THE EDGE!
18

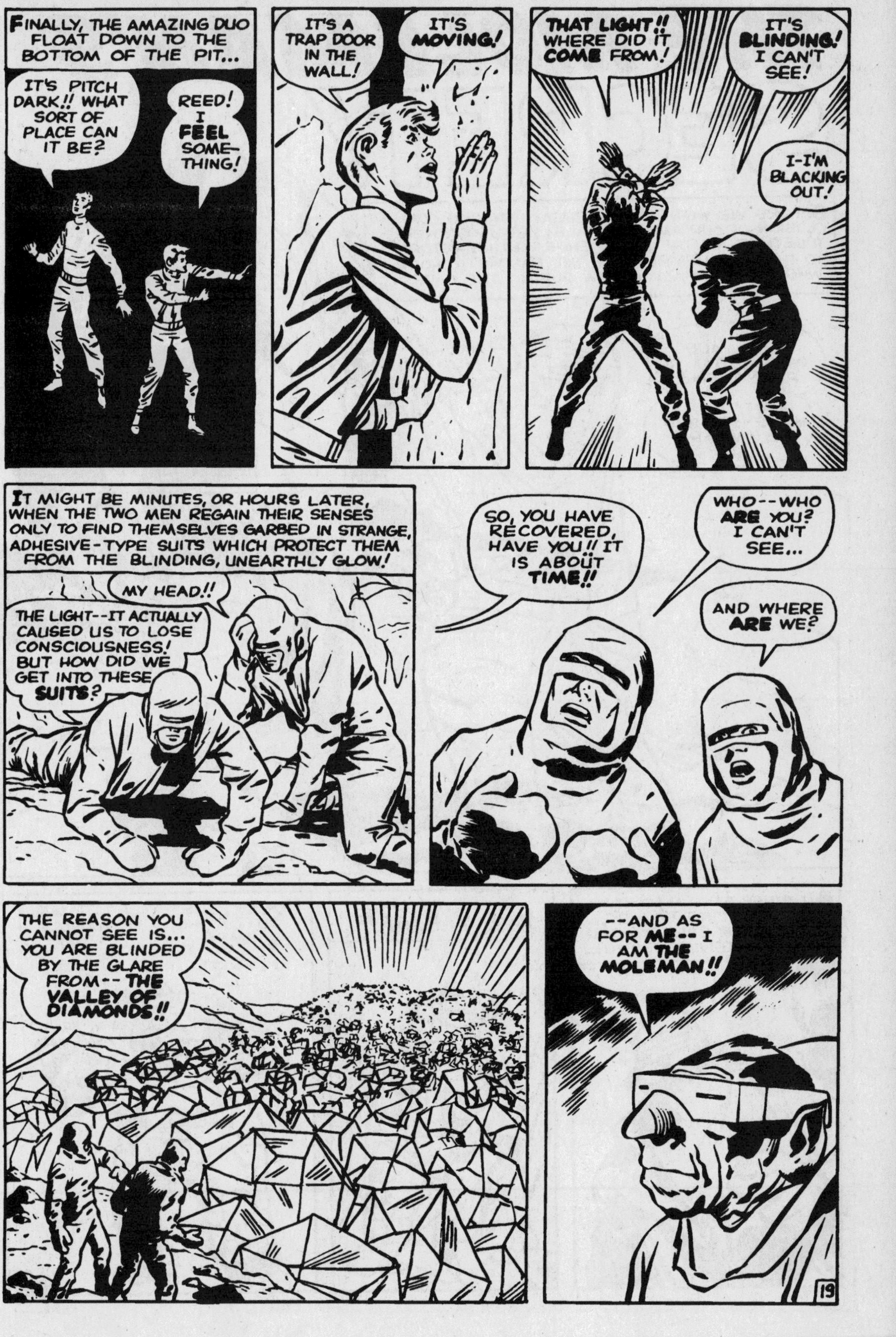
FINALLY, THE AMAZING DUO FLOAT DOWN TO THE BOTTOM OF THE PIT...
IT'S PITCH DARK!! WHAT SORT OF PLACE CAN IT BE?
REED! I FEEL SOME-THING!
IT'S A TRAP DOOR IN THE WALL!
IT'S MOVING!
THAT LIGHT!! WHERE DID IT COME FROM!
IT'S BLINDING! I CAN'T SEE!
I-I'M BLACKING OUT!
IT MIGHT BE MINUTES, OR HOURS LATER, WHEN THE TWO MEN REGAIN THEIR SENSES ONLY TO FIND THEMSELVES GARBED IN STRANGE, ADHESIVE-TYPE SUITS WHICH PROTECT THEM FROM THE BLINDING, UNEARTHLY GLOW!
MY HEAD!!
THE LIGHT--IT ACTUALLY CAUSED US TO LOSE CONSCIOUSNESS! BUT HOW DID WE GET INTO THESE SUITS?
SO, YOU HAVE RECOVERED, HAVE YOU!! IT IS ABOUT TIME!!
WHO--WHO ARE YOU? I CAN'T SEE...
AND WHERE ARE WE?
THE REASON YOU CANNOT SEE IS... YOU ARE BLINDED BY THE GLARE FROM--THE VALLEY OF DIAMONDS!!
--AND AS FOR ME--I AM THE MOLEMAN!!

THE MOLEMAN'S SECRET!

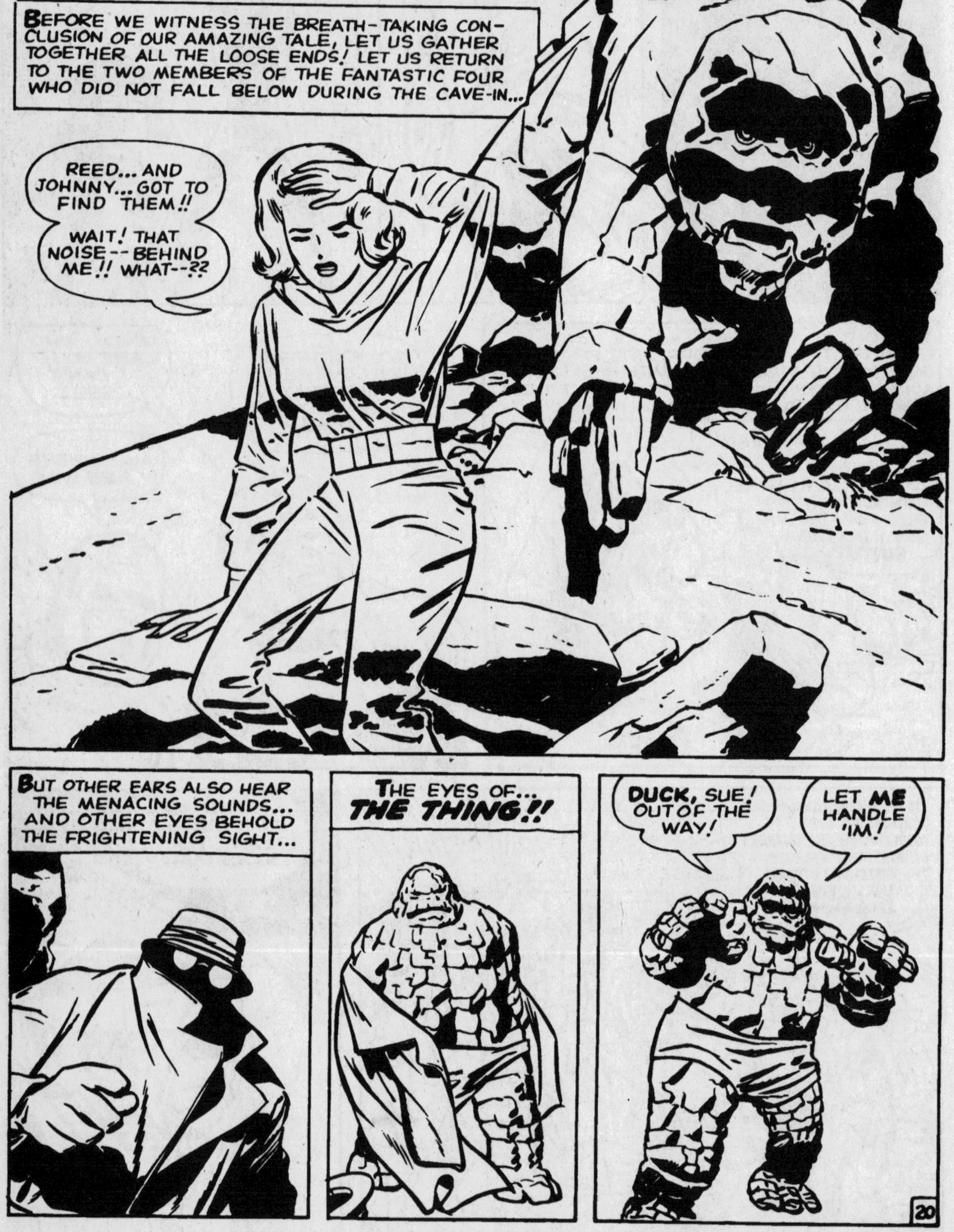

BEFORE WE WITNESS THE BREATH-TAKING CONCLUSION OF OUR AMAZING TALE, LET US GATHER TOGETHER ALL THE LOOSE ENDS! LET US RETURN TO THE TWO MEMBERS OF THE FANTASTIC FOUR WHO DID NOT FALL BELOW DURING THE CAVE-IN...
REED... AND JOHNNY... GOT TO FIND THEM!!
WAIT! THAT NOISE--BEHIND ME!! WHAT--??
BUT OTHER EARS ALSO HEAR THE MENACING SOUNDS... AND OTHER EYES BEHOLD THE FRIGHTENING SIGHT...
THE EYES OF... THE THING!!
DUCK, SUE! OUT OF THE WAY!
LET ME HANDLE 'IM!

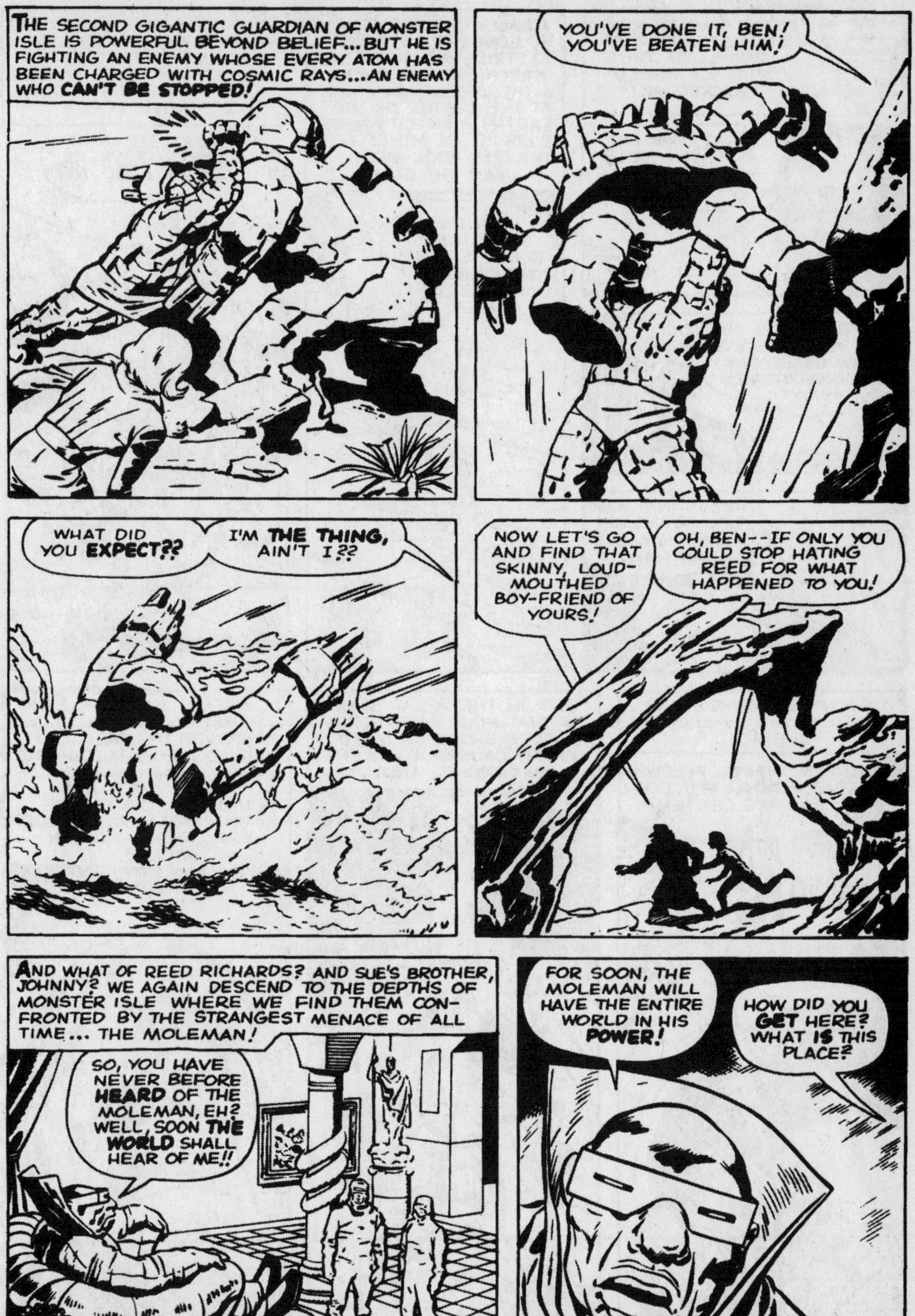
THE SECOND GIGANTIC GUARDIAN OF MONSTER ISLE IS POWERFUL BEYOND BELIEF... BUT HE IS FIGHTING AN ENEMY WHOSE EVERY ATOM HAS BEEN CHARGED WITH COSMIC RAYS... AN ENEMY WHO **CAN'T BE STOPPED!**
YOU'VE DONE IT, BEN! YOU'VE BEATEN HIM!
WHAT DID YOU **EXPECT??**
I'M **THE THING,** AIN'T I??
NOW LET'S GO AND FIND THAT SKINNY, LOUD-MOUTHED BOY-FRIEND OF YOURS!
OH, BEN--IF ONLY YOU COULD STOP HATING REED FOR WHAT HAPPENED TO YOU!
AND WHAT OF REED RICHARDS? AND SUE'S BROTHER, JOHNNY? WE AGAIN DESCEND TO THE DEPTHS OF MONSTER ISLE WHERE WE FIND THEM CONFRONTED BY THE STRANGEST MENACE OF ALL TIME... THE MOLEMAN!
SO, YOU HAVE NEVER BEFORE **HEARD** OF THE MOLEMAN, EH? WELL, SOON **THE WORLD** SHALL HEAR OF ME!!
FOR SOON, THE MOLEMAN WILL HAVE THE ENTIRE WORLD IN HIS **POWER!**
HOW DID YOU **GET** HERE? WHAT **IS** THIS PLACE?

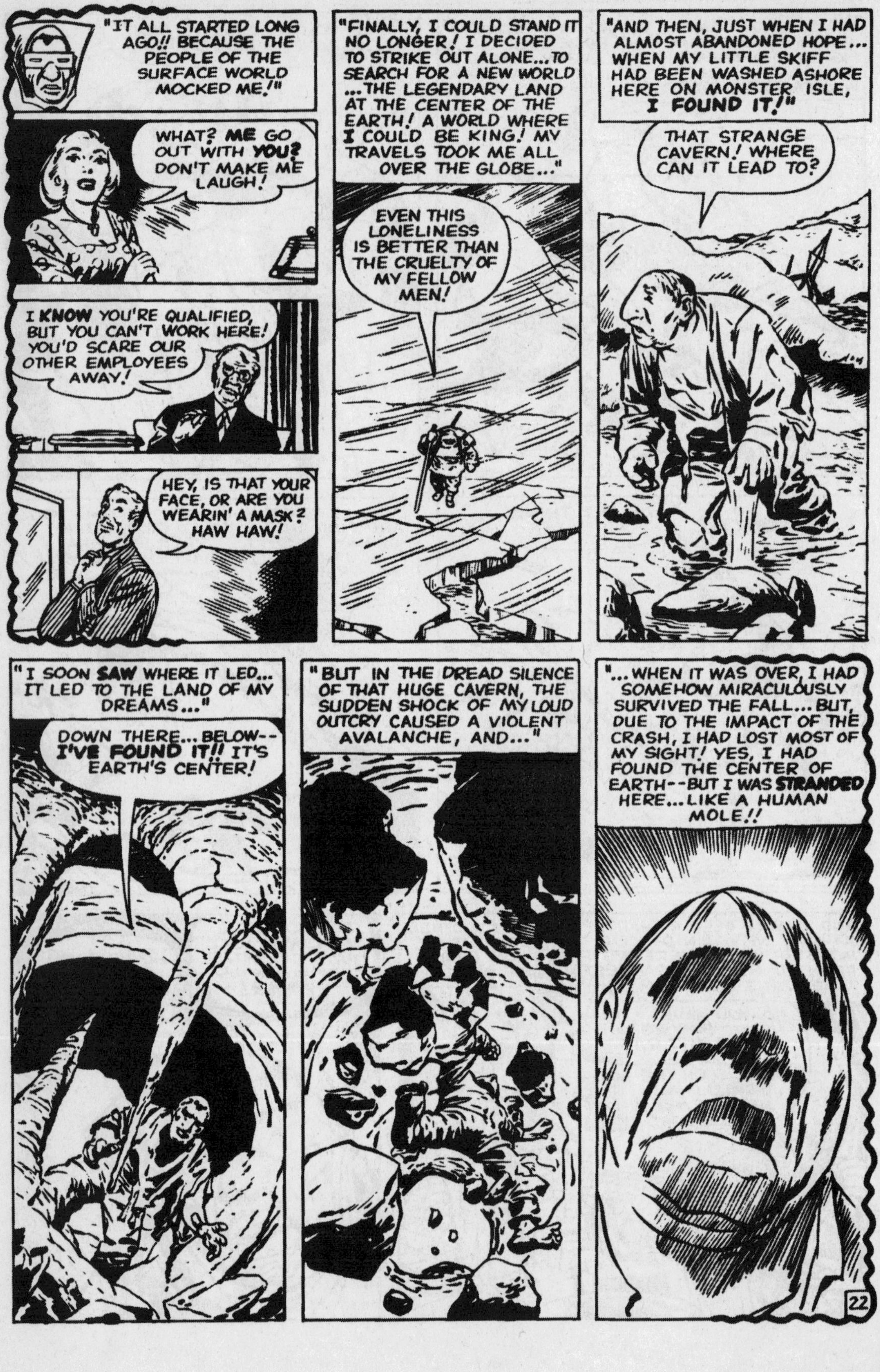

"IT ALL STARTED LONG AGO!! BECAUSE THE PEOPLE OF THE SURFACE WORLD MOCKED ME!"
WHAT? ME GO OUT WITH YOU? DON'T MAKE ME LAUGH!
I KNOW YOU'RE QUALIFIED, BUT YOU CAN'T WORK HERE! YOU'D SCARE OUR OTHER EMPLOYEES AWAY!
HEY, IS THAT YOUR FACE, OR ARE YOU WEARIN' A MASK? HAW HAW!
"FINALLY, I COULD STAND IT NO LONGER! I DECIDED TO STRIKE OUT ALONE...TO SEARCH FOR A NEW WORLD ...THE LEGENDARY LAND AT THE CENTER OF THE EARTH! A WORLD WHERE I COULD BE KING! MY TRAVELS TOOK ME ALL OVER THE GLOBE..."
EVEN THIS LONELINESS IS BETTER THAN THE CRUELTY OF MY FELLOW MEN!
"AND THEN, JUST WHEN I HAD ALMOST ABANDONED HOPE... WHEN MY LITTLE SKIFF HAD BEEN WASHED ASHORE HERE ON MONSTER ISLE, I FOUND IT!"
THAT STRANGE CAVERN! WHERE CAN IT LEAD TO?
"I SOON SAW WHERE IT LED... IT LED TO THE LAND OF MY DREAMS..."
DOWN THERE... BELOW-- I'VE FOUND IT!! IT'S EARTH'S CENTER!
"BUT IN THE DREAD SILENCE OF THAT HUGE CAVERN, THE SUDDEN SHOCK OF MY LOUD OUTCRY CAUSED A VIOLENT AVALANCHE, AND..."
"...WHEN IT WAS OVER, I HAD SOMEHOW MIRACULOUSLY SURVIVED THE FALL... BUT, DUE TO THE IMPACT OF THE CRASH, I HAD LOST MOST OF MY SIGHT! YES, I HAD FOUND THE CENTER OF EARTH--BUT I WAS STRANDED HERE...LIKE A HUMAN MOLE!!
22

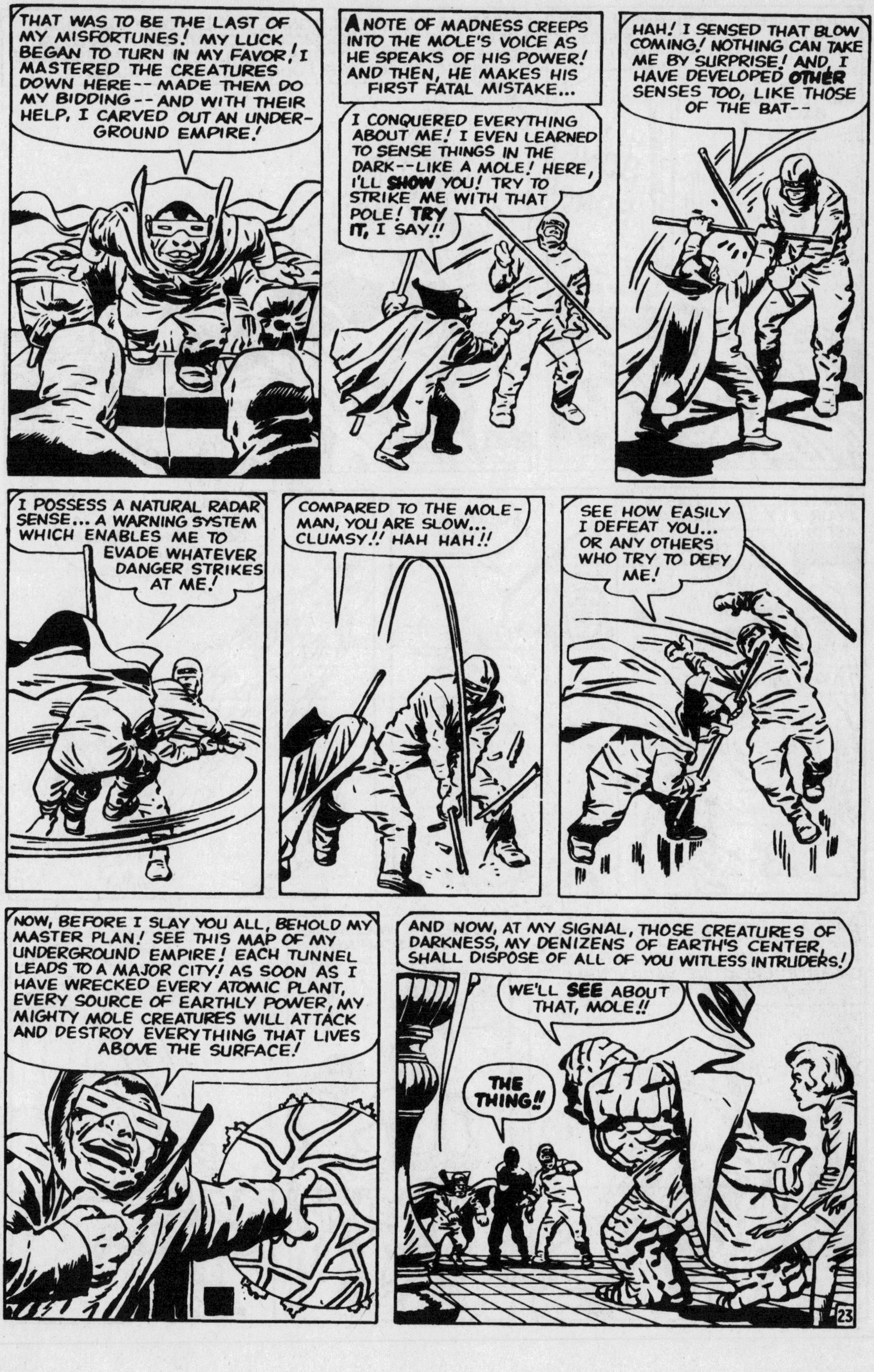
THAT WAS TO BE THE LAST OF MY MISFORTUNES! MY LUCK BEGAN TO TURN IN MY FAVOR! I MASTERED THE CREATURES DOWN HERE-- MADE THEM DO MY BIDDING--AND WITH THEIR HELP, I CARVED OUT AN UNDERGROUND EMPIRE!
A NOTE OF MADNESS CREEPS INTO THE MOLE'S VOICE AS HE SPEAKS OF HIS POWER! AND THEN, HE MAKES HIS FIRST FATAL MISTAKE...
I CONQUERED EVERYTHING ABOUT ME! I EVEN LEARNED TO SENSE THINGS IN THE DARK--LIKE A MOLE! HERE, I'LL SHOW YOU! TRY TO STRIKE ME WITH THAT POLE! TRY IT, I SAY!!
HAH! I SENSED THAT BLOW COMING! NOTHING CAN TAKE ME BY SURPRISE! AND, I HAVE DEVELOPED OTHER SENSES TOO, LIKE THOSE OF THE BAT--
I POSSESS A NATURAL RADAR SENSE... A WARNING SYSTEM WHICH ENABLES ME TO EVADE WHATEVER DANGER STRIKES AT ME!
COMPARED TO THE MOLE-MAN, YOU ARE SLOW... CLUMSY!! HAH HAH!!
SEE HOW EASILY I DEFEAT YOU... OR ANY OTHERS WHO TRY TO DEFY ME!
NOW, BEFORE I SLAY YOU ALL, BEHOLD MY MASTER PLAN! SEE THIS MAP OF MY UNDERGROUND EMPIRE! EACH TUNNEL LEADS TO A MAJOR CITY! AS SOON AS I HAVE WRECKED EVERY ATOMIC PLANT, EVERY SOURCE OF EARTHLY POWER, MY MIGHTY MOLE CREATURES WILL ATTACK AND DESTROY EVERYTHING THAT LIVES ABOVE THE SURFACE!
AND NOW, AT MY SIGNAL, THOSE CREATURES OF DARKNESS, MY DENIZENS OF EARTH'S CENTER, SHALL DISPOSE OF ALL OF YOU WITLESS INTRUDERS!
WE'LL SEE ABOUT THAT, MOLE!!
THE THING!!
23

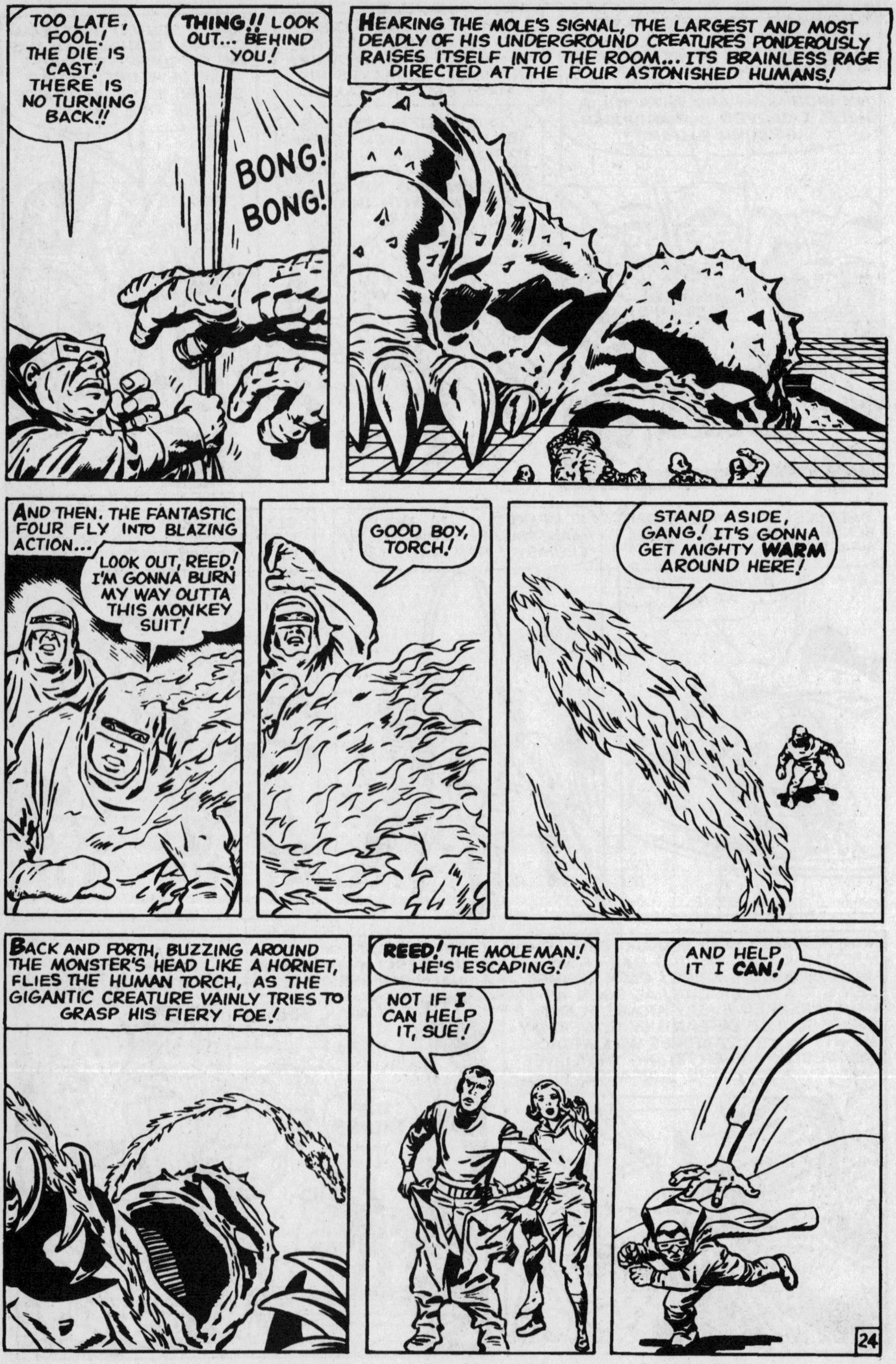
TOO LATE, FOOL! THE DIE IS CAST! THERE IS NO TURNING BACK!!
THING!! LOOK OUT... BEHIND YOU!
BONG! BONG!
HEARING THE MOLE'S SIGNAL, THE LARGEST AND MOST DEADLY OF HIS UNDERGROUND CREATURES PONDEROUSLY RAISES ITSELF INTO THE ROOM... ITS BRAINLESS RAGE DIRECTED AT THE FOUR ASTONISHED HUMANS!
AND THEN. THE FANTASTIC FOUR FLY INTO BLAZING ACTION...
LOOK OUT, REED! I'M GONNA BURN MY WAY OUTTA THIS MONKEY SUIT!
GOOD BOY, TORCH!
STAND ASIDE, GANG! IT'S GONNA GET MIGHTY WARM AROUND HERE!
BACK AND FORTH, BUZZING AROUND THE MONSTER'S HEAD LIKE A HORNET, FLIES THE HUMAN TORCH, AS THE GIGANTIC CREATURE VAINLY TRIES TO GRASP HIS FIERY FOE!
REED! THE MOLE MAN! HE'S ESCAPING!
NOT IF I CAN HELP IT, SUE!
AND HELP IT I CAN!

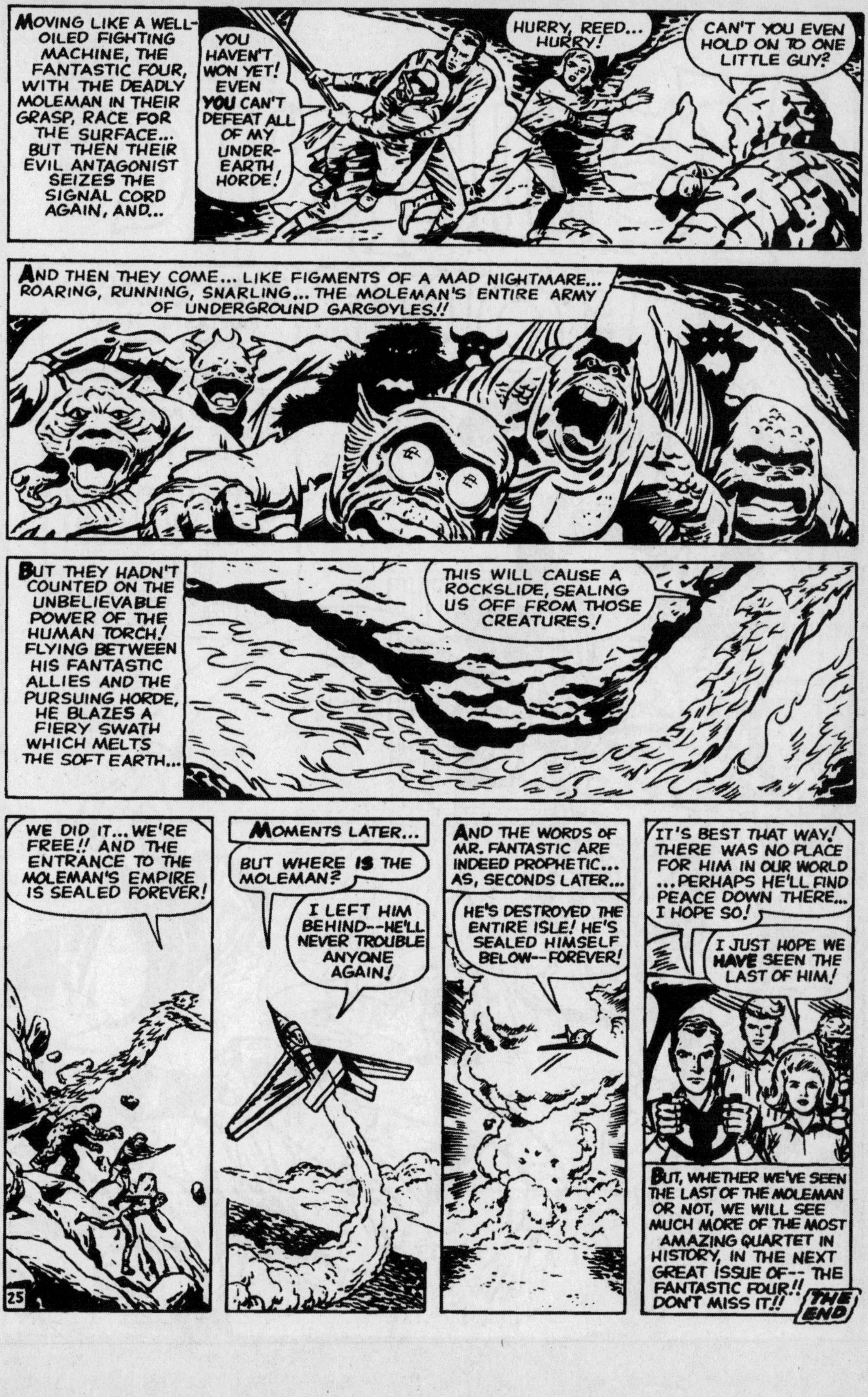
MOVING LIKE A WELL-OILED FIGHTING MACHINE, THE FANTASTIC FOUR, WITH THE DEADLY MOLEMAN IN THEIR GRASP, RACE FOR THE SURFACE... BUT THEN THEIR EVIL ANTAGONIST SEIZES THE SIGNAL CORD AGAIN, AND...
YOU HAVEN'T WON YET! EVEN YOU CAN'T DEFEAT ALL OF MY UNDER-EARTH HORDE!
HURRY, REED... HURRY!
CAN'T YOU EVEN HOLD ON TO ONE LITTLE GUY?
AND THEN THEY COME... LIKE FIGMENTS OF A MAD NIGHTMARE... ROARING, RUNNING, SNARLING... THE MOLEMAN'S ENTIRE ARMY OF UNDERGROUND GARGOYLES!!
BUT THEY HADN'T COUNTED ON THE UNBELIEVABLE POWER OF THE HUMAN TORCH! FLYING BETWEEN HIS FANTASTIC ALLIES AND THE PURSUING HORDE, HE BLAZES A FIERY SWATH WHICH MELTS THE SOFT EARTH...
THIS WILL CAUSE A ROCKSLIDE, SEALING US OFF FROM THOSE CREATURES!
WE DID IT... WE'RE FREE!! AND THE ENTRANCE TO THE MOLEMAN'S EMPIRE IS SEALED FOREVER!
25
MOMENTS LATER...
BUT WHERE IS THE MOLEMAN?
I LEFT HIM BEHIND--HE'LL NEVER TROUBLE ANYONE AGAIN!
AND THE WORDS OF MR. FANTASTIC ARE INDEED PROPHETIC... AS, SECONDS LATER...
HE'S DESTROYED THE ENTIRE ISLE! HE'S SEALED HIMSELF BELOW--FOREVER!
IT'S BEST THAT WAY! THERE WAS NO PLACE FOR HIM IN OUR WORLD ...PERHAPS HE'LL FIND PEACE DOWN THERE... I HOPE SO!
I JUST HOPE WE HAVE SEEN THE LAST OF HIM!
BUT, WHETHER WE'VE SEEN THE LAST OF THE MOLEMAN OR NOT, WE WILL SEE MUCH MORE OF THE MOST AMAZING QUARTET IN HISTORY, IN THE NEXT GREAT ISSUE OF-- THE FANTASTIC FOUR!! DON'T MISS IT!!
THE END

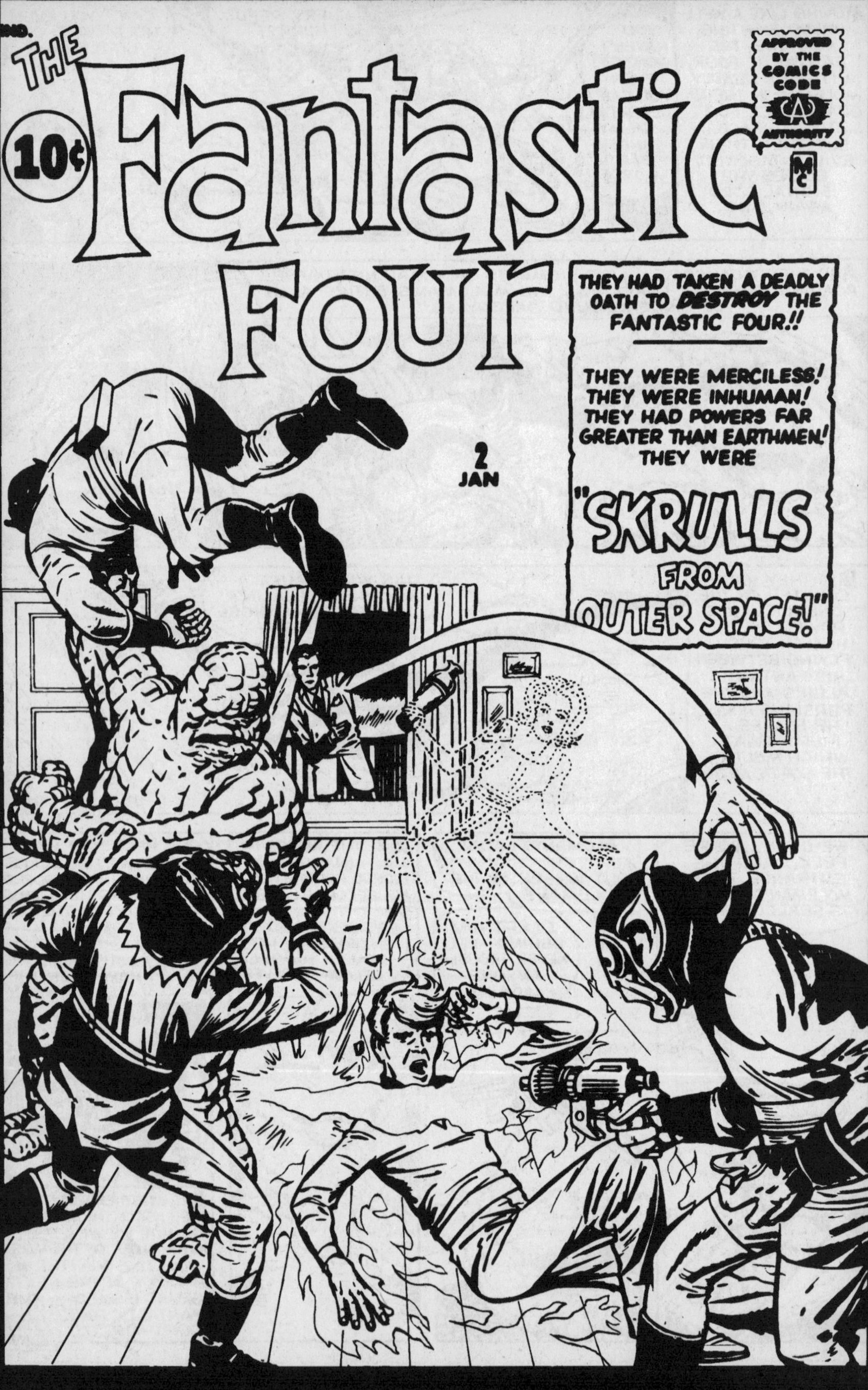
THE
Fantastic
FOUR
10¢
APPROVED BY THE COMICS CODE AUTHORITY
MC
2
JAN
THEY HAD TAKEN A DEADLY OATH TO DESTROY THE FANTASTIC FOUR!!
THEY WERE MERCILESS! THEY WERE INHUMAN! THEY HAD POWERS FAR GREATER THAN EARTHMEN! THEY WERE
"SKRULLS FROM OUTER SPACE!"

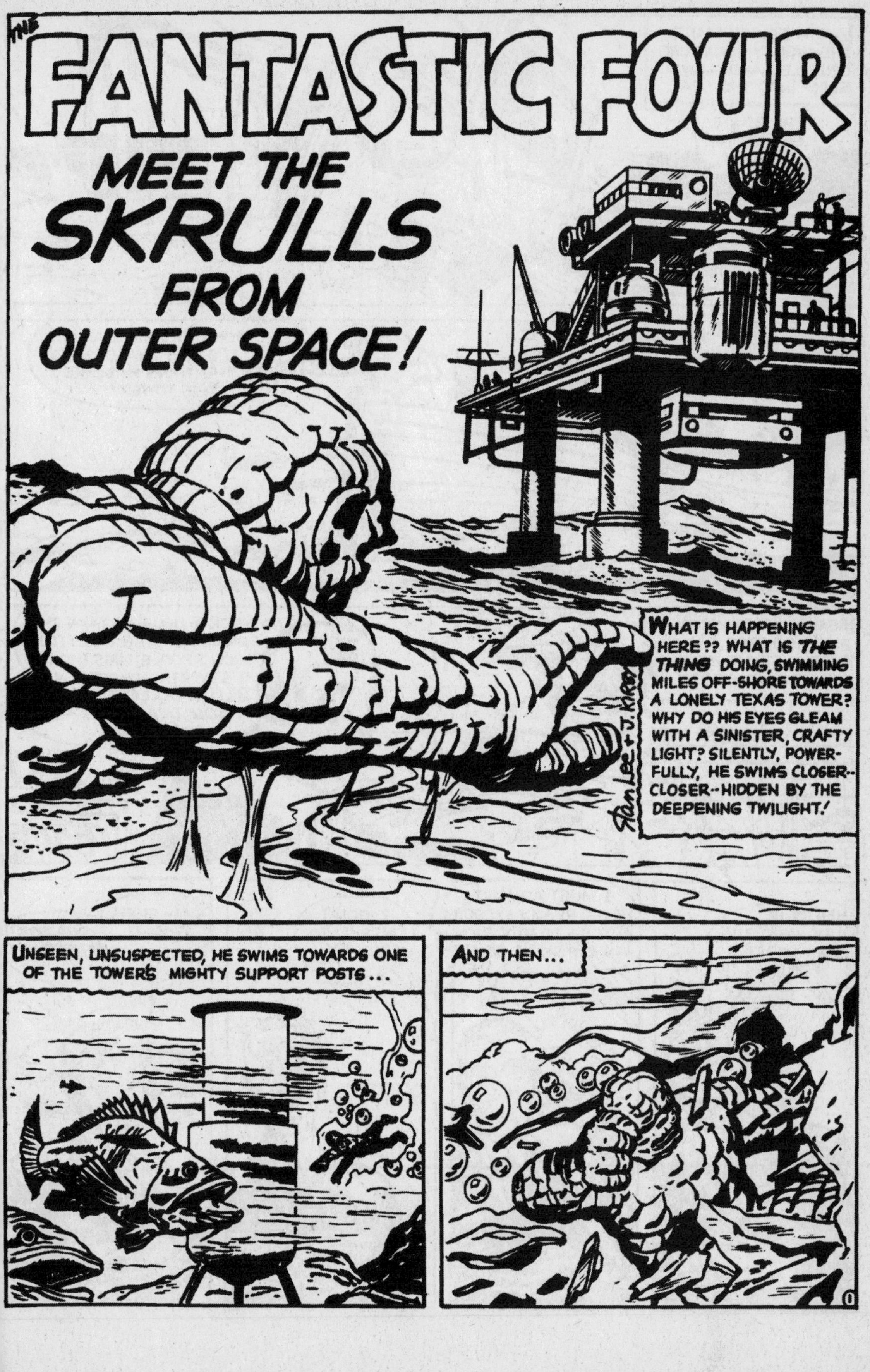
THE
FANTASTIC FOUR
MEET THE SKRULLS FROM OUTER SPACE!
WHAT IS HAPPENING HERE?? WHAT IS THE THING DOING, SWIMMING MILES OFF-SHORE TOWARDS A LONELY TEXAS TOWER? WHY DO HIS EYES GLEAM WITH A SINISTER, CRAFTY LIGHT? SILENTLY, POWERFULLY, HE SWIMS CLOSER-- CLOSER--HIDDEN BY THE DEEPENING TWILIGHT!
Stan Lee + J. Kirby
UNSEEN, UNSUSPECTED, HE SWIMS TOWARDS ONE OF THE TOWER'S MIGHTY SUPPORT POSTS...
AND THEN...
1

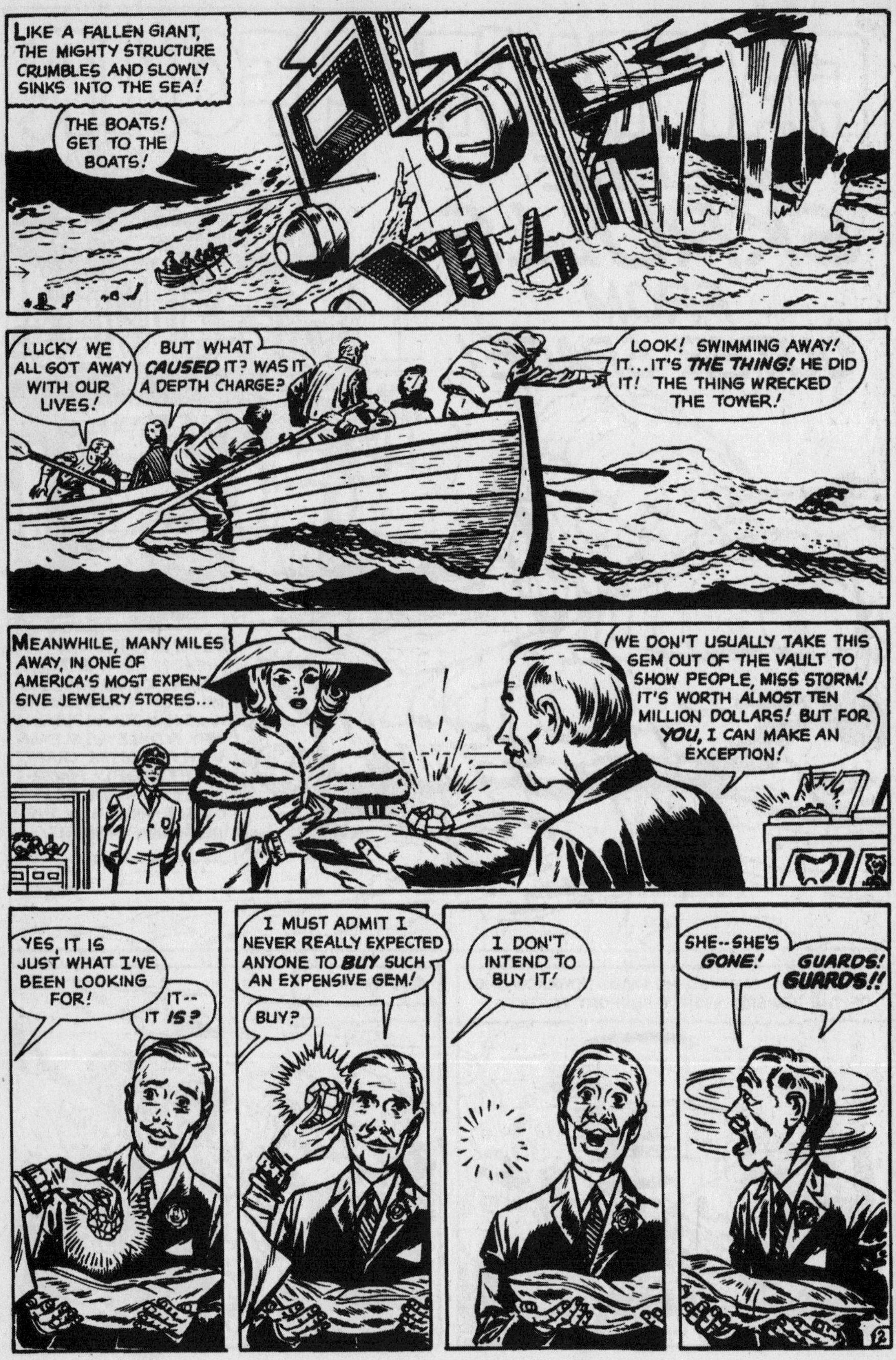
LIKE A FALLEN GIANT, THE MIGHTY STRUCTURE CRUMBLES AND SLOWLY SINKS INTO THE SEA!
THE BOATS! GET TO THE BOATS!
LUCKY WE ALL GOT AWAY WITH OUR LIVES!
BUT WHAT CAUSED IT? WAS IT A DEPTH CHARGE?
LOOK! SWIMMING AWAY! IT...IT'S THE THING! HE DID IT! THE THING WRECKED THE TOWER!
MEANWHILE, MANY MILES AWAY, IN ONE OF AMERICA'S MOST EXPENSIVE JEWELRY STORES...
WE DON'T USUALLY TAKE THIS GEM OUT OF THE VAULT TO SHOW PEOPLE, MISS STORM! IT'S WORTH ALMOST TEN MILLION DOLLARS! BUT FOR YOU, I CAN MAKE AN EXCEPTION!
YES, IT IS JUST WHAT I'VE BEEN LOOKING FOR!
IT-- IT IS?
I MUST ADMIT I NEVER REALLY EXPECTED ANYONE TO BUY SUCH AN EXPENSIVE GEM!
BUY?
I DON'T INTEND TO BUY IT!
SHE--SHE'S GONE!
GUARDS! GUARDS!!
2

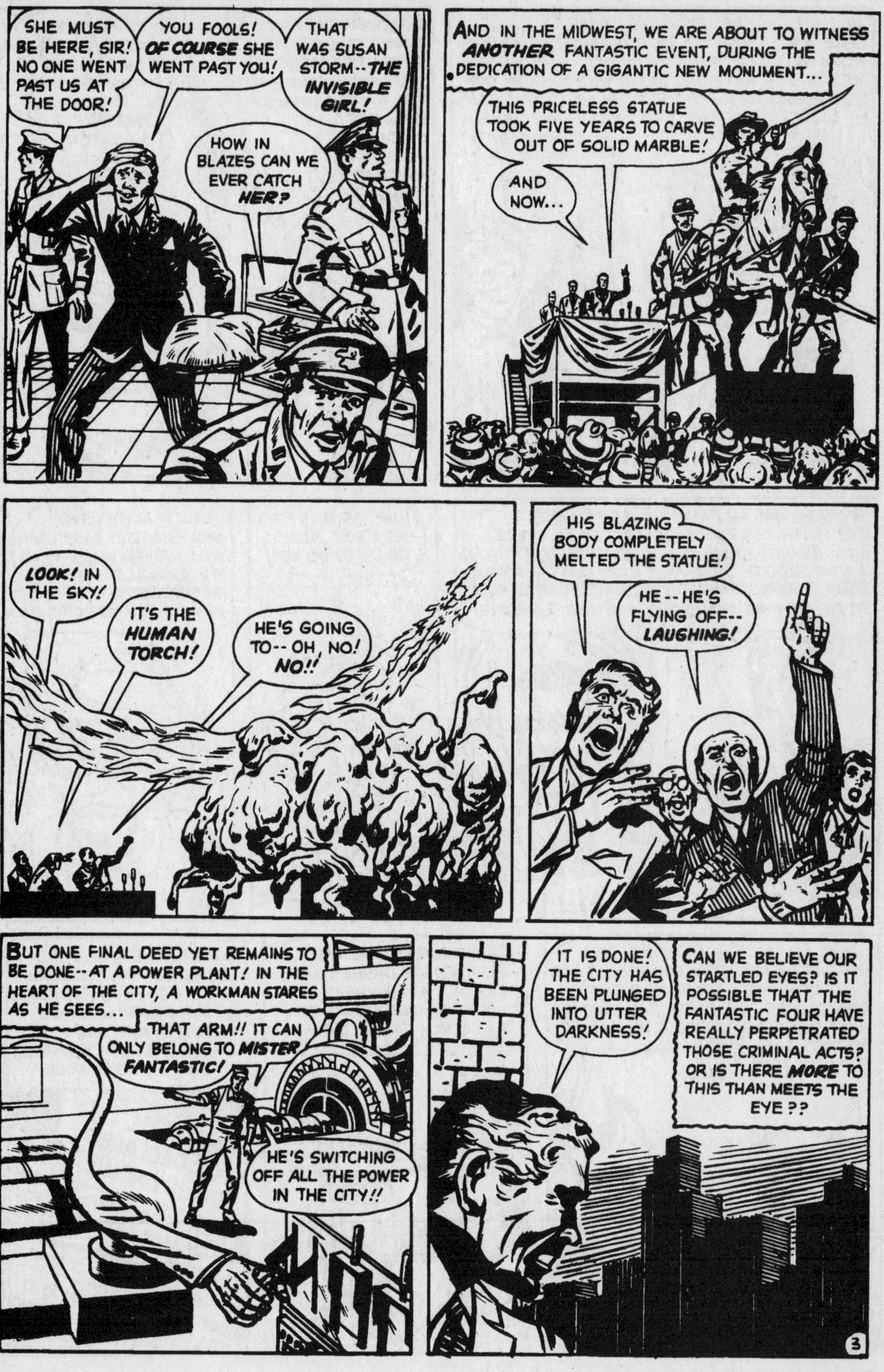

SHE MUST BE HERE, SIR! NO ONE WENT PAST US AT THE DOOR!
YOU FOOLS! OF COURSE SHE WENT PAST YOU!
THAT WAS SUSAN STORM--THE INVISIBLE GIRL!
HOW IN BLAZES CAN WE EVER CATCH HER?
AND IN THE MIDWEST, WE ARE ABOUT TO WITNESS ANOTHER FANTASTIC EVENT, DURING THE DEDICATION OF A GIGANTIC NEW MONUMENT...
THIS PRICELESS STATUE TOOK FIVE YEARS TO CARVE OUT OF SOLID MARBLE!
AND NOW...
LOOK! IN THE SKY!
IT'S THE HUMAN TORCH!
HE'S GOING TO-- OH, NO! NO!!
HIS BLAZING BODY COMPLETELY MELTED THE STATUE!
HE--HE'S FLYING OFF-- LAUGHING!
BUT ONE FINAL DEED YET REMAINS TO BE DONE--AT A POWER PLANT! IN THE HEART OF THE CITY, A WORKMAN STARES AS HE SEES...
THAT ARM!! IT CAN ONLY BELONG TO MISTER FANTASTIC!
HE'S SWITCHING OFF ALL THE POWER IN THE CITY!!
IT IS DONE! THE CITY HAS BEEN PLUNGED INTO UTTER DARKNESS!
CAN WE BELIEVE OUR STARTLED EYES? IS IT POSSIBLE THAT THE FANTASTIC FOUR HAVE REALLY PERPETRATED THOSE CRIMINAL ACTS? OR IS THERE MORE TO THIS THAN MEETS THE EYE??
3

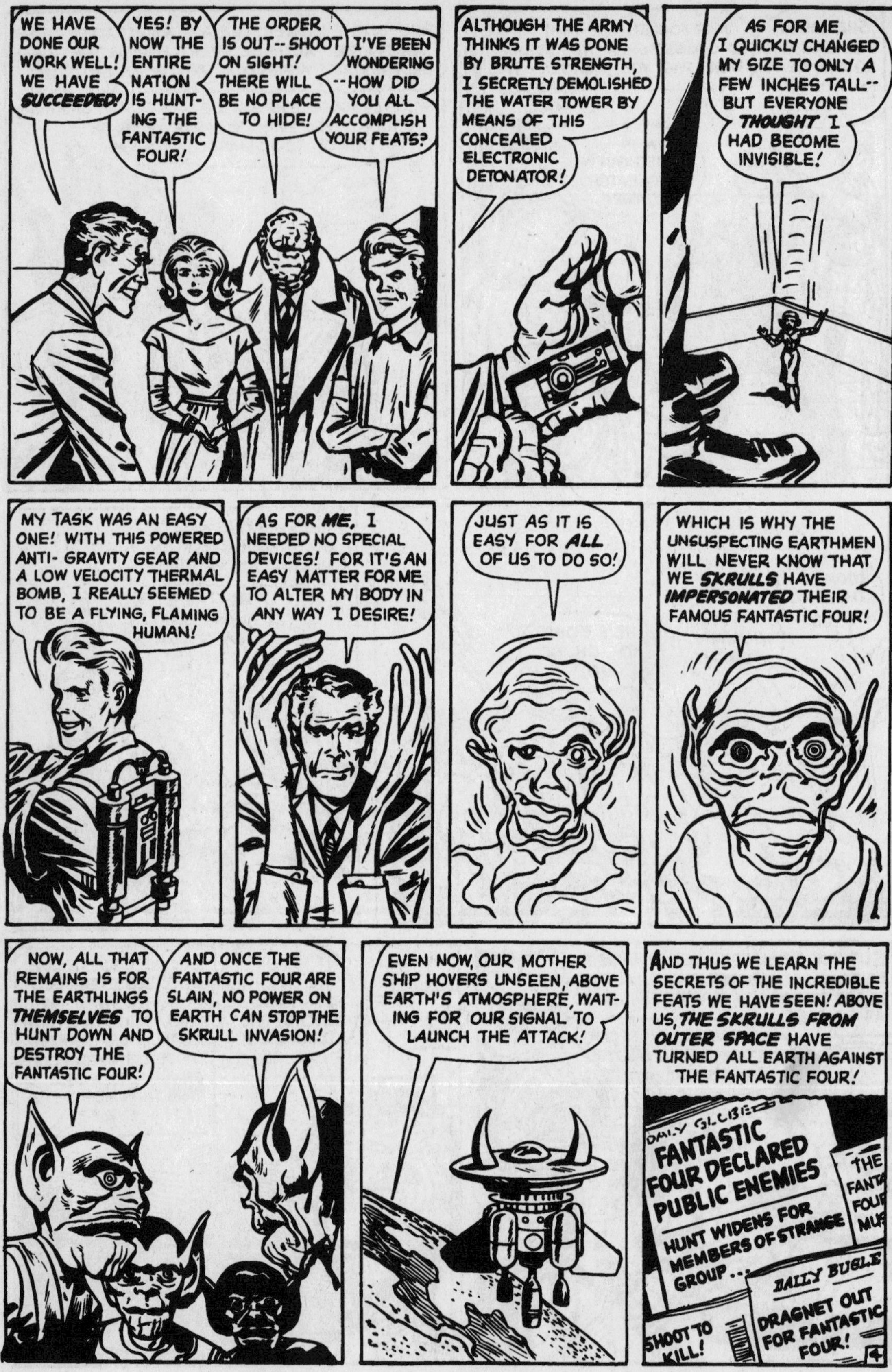
WE HAVE DONE OUR WORK WELL! WE HAVE SUCCEEDED!
YES! BY NOW THE ENTIRE NATION IS HUNTING THE FANTASTIC FOUR!
THE ORDER IS OUT-- SHOOT ON SIGHT! THERE WILL BE NO PLACE TO HIDE!
I'VE BEEN WONDERING --HOW DID YOU ALL ACCOMPLISH YOUR FEATS?
ALTHOUGH THE ARMY THINKS IT WAS DONE BY BRUTE STRENGTH, I SECRETLY DEMOLISHED THE WATER TOWER BY MEANS OF THIS CONCEALED ELECTRONIC DETONATOR!
AS FOR ME, I QUICKLY CHANGED MY SIZE TO ONLY A FEW INCHES TALL-- BUT EVERYONE THOUGHT I HAD BECOME INVISIBLE!
MY TASK WAS AN EASY ONE! WITH THIS POWERED ANTI- GRAVITY GEAR AND A LOW VELOCITY THERMAL BOMB, I REALLY SEEMED TO BE A FLYING, FLAMING HUMAN!
AS FOR ME, I NEEDED NO SPECIAL DEVICES! FOR IT'S AN EASY MATTER FOR ME TO ALTER MY BODY IN ANY WAY I DESIRE!
JUST AS IT IS EASY FOR ALL OF US TO DO SO!
WHICH IS WHY THE UNSUSPECTING EARTHMEN WILL NEVER KNOW THAT WE SKRULLS HAVE IMPERSONATED THEIR FAMOUS FANTASTIC FOUR!
NOW, ALL THAT REMAINS IS FOR THE EARTHLINGS THEMSELVES TO HUNT DOWN AND DESTROY THE FANTASTIC FOUR!
AND ONCE THE FANTASTIC FOUR ARE SLAIN, NO POWER ON EARTH CAN STOP THE SKRULL INVASION!
EVEN NOW, OUR MOTHER SHIP HOVERS UNSEEN, ABOVE EARTH'S ATMOSPHERE, WAITING FOR OUR SIGNAL TO LAUNCH THE ATTACK!
AND THUS WE LEARN THE SECRETS OF THE INCREDIBLE FEATS WE HAVE SEEN! ABOVE US, THE SKRULLS FROM OUTER SPACE HAVE TURNED ALL EARTH AGAINST THE FANTASTIC FOUR!
DAILY GLOBE
FANTASTIC FOUR DECLARED PUBLIC ENEMIES
HUNT WIDENS FOR MEMBERS OF STRANGE GROUP...
DAILY BUGLE
DRAGNET OUT FOR FANTASTIC FOUR!
SHOOT TO KILL!
4

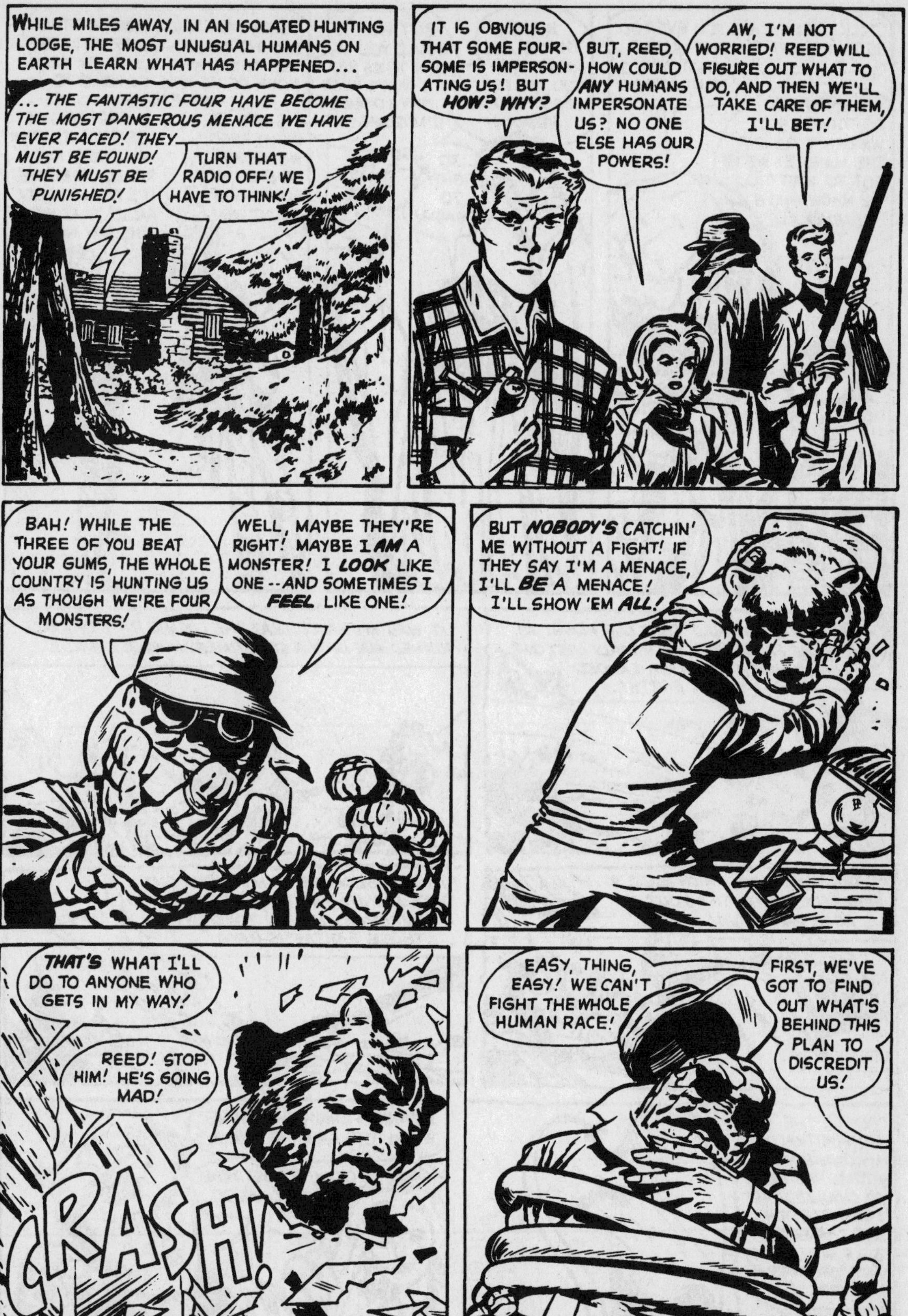
WHILE MILES AWAY, IN AN ISOLATED HUNTING LODGE, THE MOST UNUSUAL HUMANS ON EARTH LEARN WHAT HAS HAPPENED...
... THE FANTASTIC FOUR HAVE BECOME THE MOST DANGEROUS MENACE WE HAVE EVER FACED! THEY MUST BE FOUND! THEY MUST BE PUNISHED!
TURN THAT RADIO OFF! WE HAVE TO THINK!
IT IS OBVIOUS THAT SOME FOURSOME IS IMPERSONATING US! BUT HOW? WHY?
BUT, REED, HOW COULD ANY HUMANS IMPERSONATE US? NO ONE ELSE HAS OUR POWERS!
AW, I'M NOT WORRIED! REED WILL FIGURE OUT WHAT TO DO, AND THEN WE'LL TAKE CARE OF THEM, I'LL BET!
BAH! WHILE THE THREE OF YOU BEAT YOUR GUMS, THE WHOLE COUNTRY IS HUNTING US AS THOUGH WE'RE FOUR MONSTERS!
WELL, MAYBE THEY'RE RIGHT! MAYBE I AM A MONSTER! I LOOK LIKE ONE -- AND SOMETIMES I FEEL LIKE ONE!
BUT NOBODY'S CATCHIN' ME WITHOUT A FIGHT! IF THEY SAY I'M A MENACE, I'LL BE A MENACE! I'LL SHOW 'EM ALL!
THAT'S WHAT I'LL DO TO ANYONE WHO GETS IN MY WAY!
REED! STOP HIM! HE'S GOING MAD!
CRASH!
EASY, THING, EASY! WE CAN'T FIGHT THE WHOLE HUMAN RACE!
FIRST, WE'VE GOT TO FIND OUT WHAT'S BEHIND THIS PLAN TO DISCREDIT US!

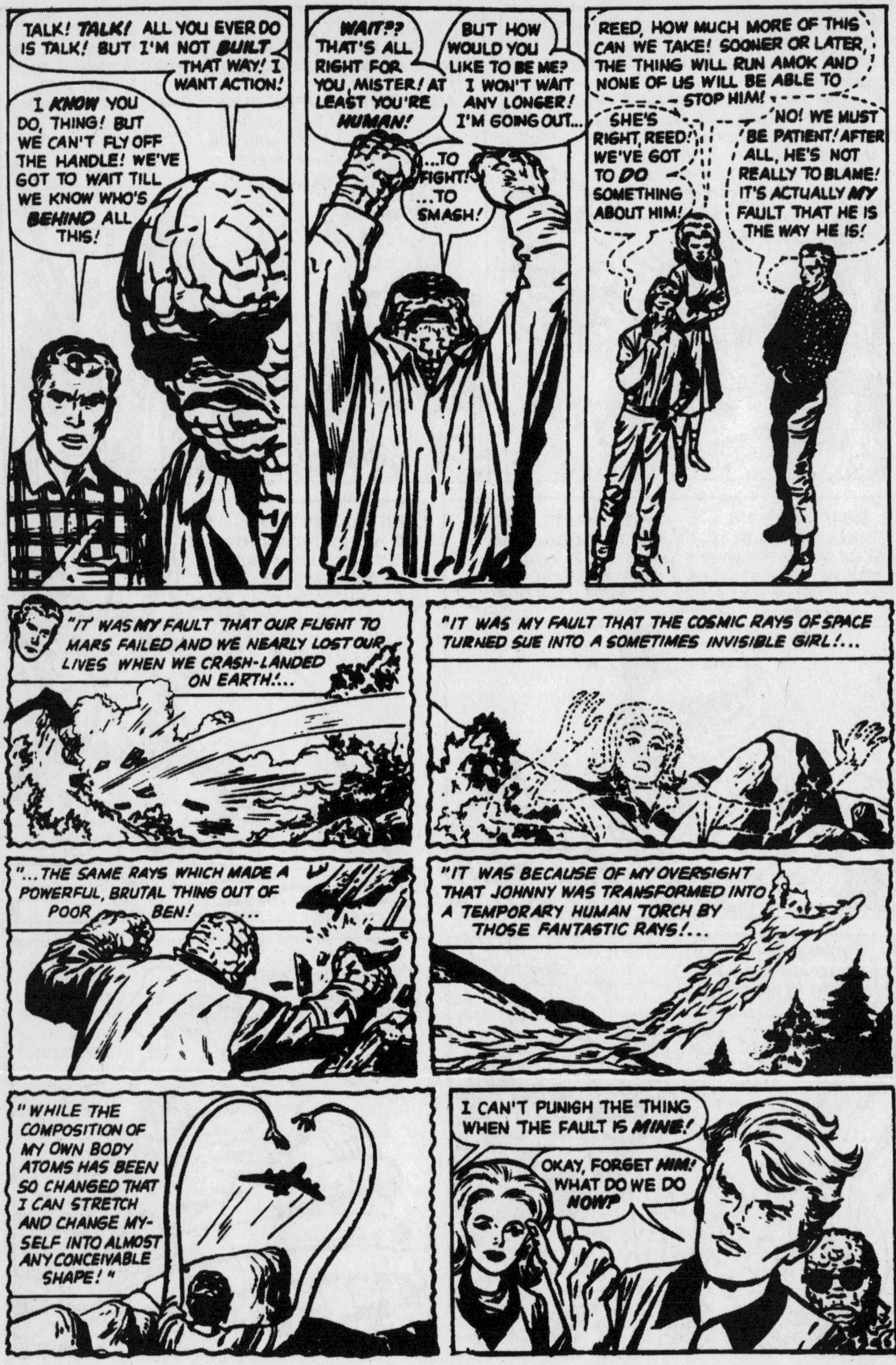
TALK! TALK! ALL YOU EVER DO IS TALK! BUT I'M NOT BUILT THAT WAY! I WANT ACTION!
I KNOW YOU DO, THING! BUT WE CAN'T FLY OFF THE HANDLE! WE'VE GOT TO WAIT TILL WE KNOW WHO'S BEHIND ALL THIS!
WAIT?? THAT'S ALL RIGHT FOR YOU, MISTER! AT LEAST YOU'RE HUMAN!
BUT HOW WOULD YOU LIKE TO BE ME? I WON'T WAIT ANY LONGER! I'M GOING OUT...
...TO FIGHT! ...TO SMASH!
REED, HOW MUCH MORE OF THIS CAN WE TAKE! SOONER OR LATER, THE THING WILL RUN AMOK AND NONE OF US WILL BE ABLE TO STOP HIM!
SHE'S RIGHT, REED! WE'VE GOT TO DO SOMETHING ABOUT HIM!
NO! WE MUST BE PATIENT! AFTER ALL, HE'S NOT REALLY TO BLAME! IT'S ACTUALLY MY FAULT THAT HE IS THE WAY HE IS!
"IT WAS MY FAULT THAT OUR FLIGHT TO MARS FAILED AND WE NEARLY LOST OUR LIVES WHEN WE CRASH-LANDED ON EARTH!...
"IT WAS MY FAULT THAT THE COSMIC RAYS OF SPACE TURNED SUE INTO A SOMETIMES INVISIBLE GIRL!...
"...THE SAME RAYS WHICH MADE A POWERFUL, BRUTAL THING OUT OF POOR BEN!...
"IT WAS BECAUSE OF MY OVERSIGHT THAT JOHNNY WAS TRANSFORMED INTO A TEMPORARY HUMAN TORCH BY THOSE FANTASTIC RAYS!...
"WHILE THE COMPOSITION OF MY OWN BODY ATOMS HAS BEEN SO CHANGED THAT I CAN STRETCH AND CHANGE MY-SELF INTO ALMOST ANY CONCEIVABLE SHAPE!"
I CAN'T PUNISH THE THING WHEN THE FAULT IS MINE!
OKAY, FORGET HIM! WHAT DO WE DO NOW?

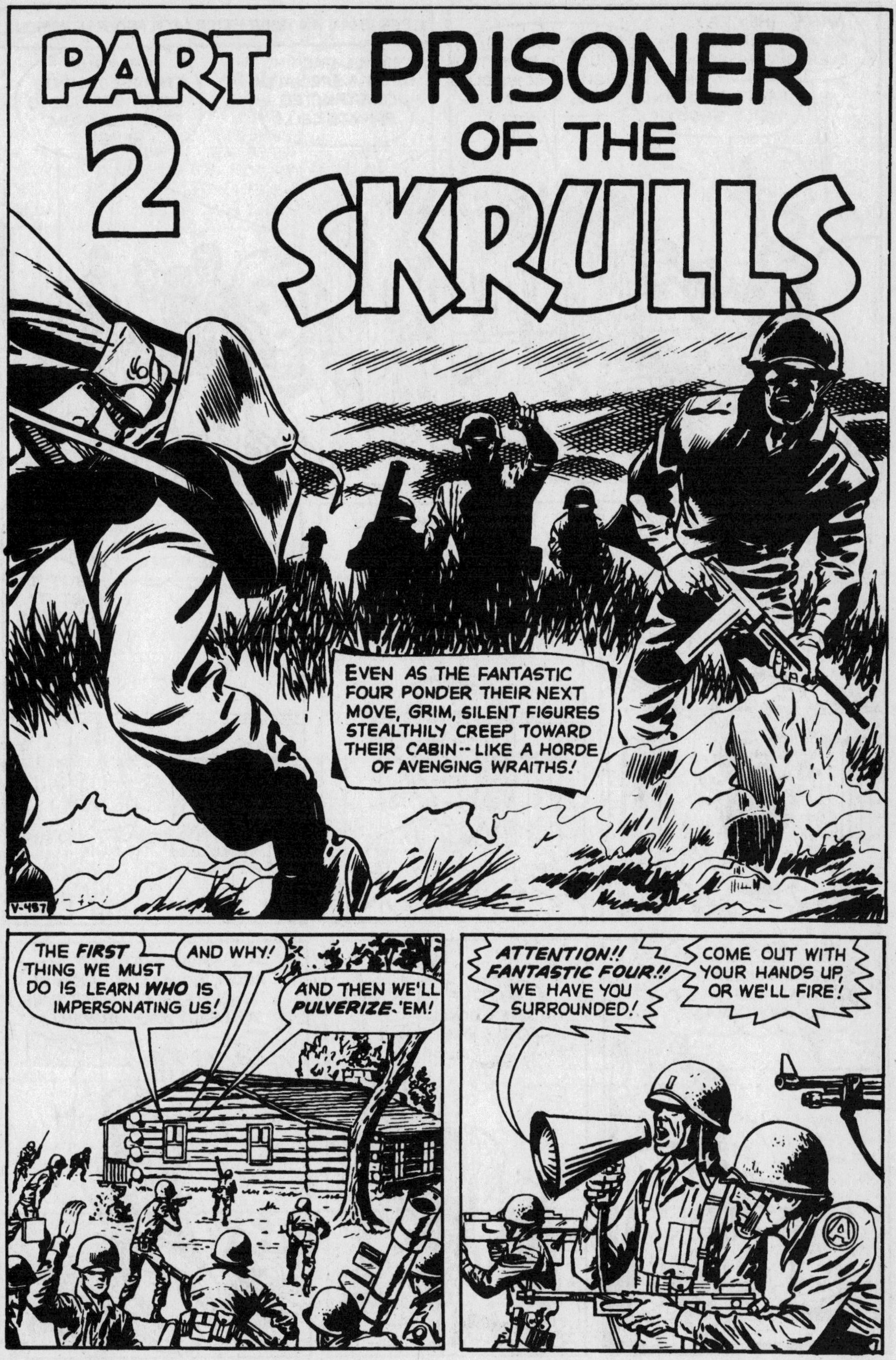
PART 2
PRISONER OF THE SKRULLS
EVEN AS THE FANTASTIC FOUR PONDER THEIR NEXT MOVE, GRIM, SILENT FIGURES STEALTHILY CREEP TOWARD THEIR CABIN -- LIKE A HORDE OF AVENGING WRAITHS!
V-487
THE FIRST THING WE MUST DO IS LEARN WHO IS IMPERSONATING US!
AND WHY!
AND THEN WE'LL PULVERIZE 'EM!
ATTENTION!! FANTASTIC FOUR!! WE HAVE YOU SURROUNDED!
COME OUT WITH YOUR HANDS UP, OR WE'LL FIRE!

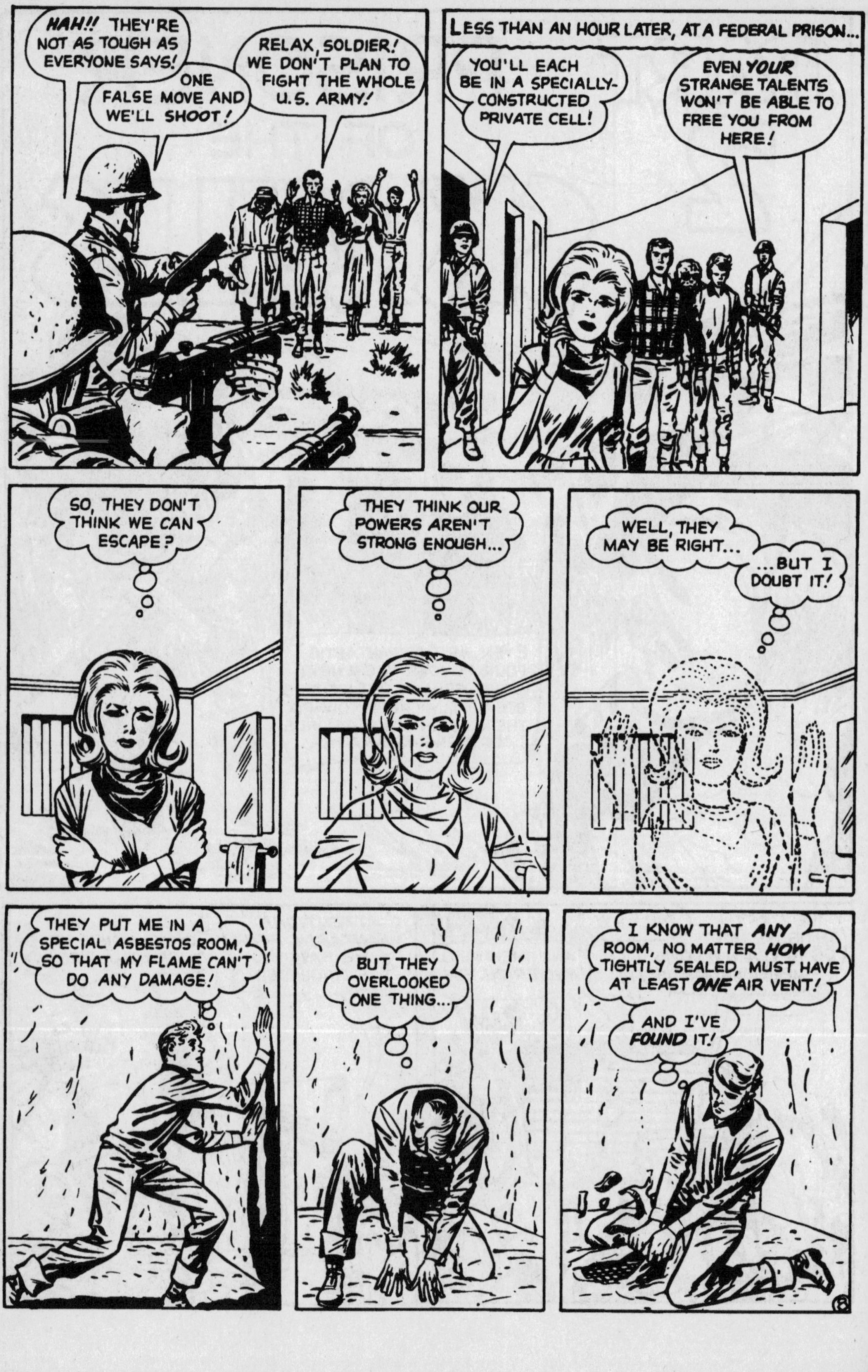
HAH!! THEY'RE NOT AS TOUGH AS EVERYONE SAYS!
ONE FALSE MOVE AND WE'LL SHOOT!
RELAX, SOLDIER! WE DON'T PLAN TO FIGHT THE WHOLE U.S. ARMY!
LESS THAN AN HOUR LATER, AT A FEDERAL PRISON...
YOU'LL EACH BE IN A SPECIALLY-CONSTRUCTED PRIVATE CELL!
EVEN YOUR STRANGE TALENTS WON'T BE ABLE TO FREE YOU FROM HERE!
SO, THEY DON'T THINK WE CAN ESCAPE?
THEY THINK OUR POWERS AREN'T STRONG ENOUGH...
WELL, THEY MAY BE RIGHT...
...BUT I DOUBT IT!
THEY PUT ME IN A SPECIAL ASBESTOS ROOM, SO THAT MY FLAME CAN'T DO ANY DAMAGE!
BUT THEY OVERLOOKED ONE THING...
I KNOW THAT ANY ROOM, NO MATTER HOW TIGHTLY SEALED, MUST HAVE AT LEAST ONE AIR VENT!
AND I'VE FOUND IT!
8

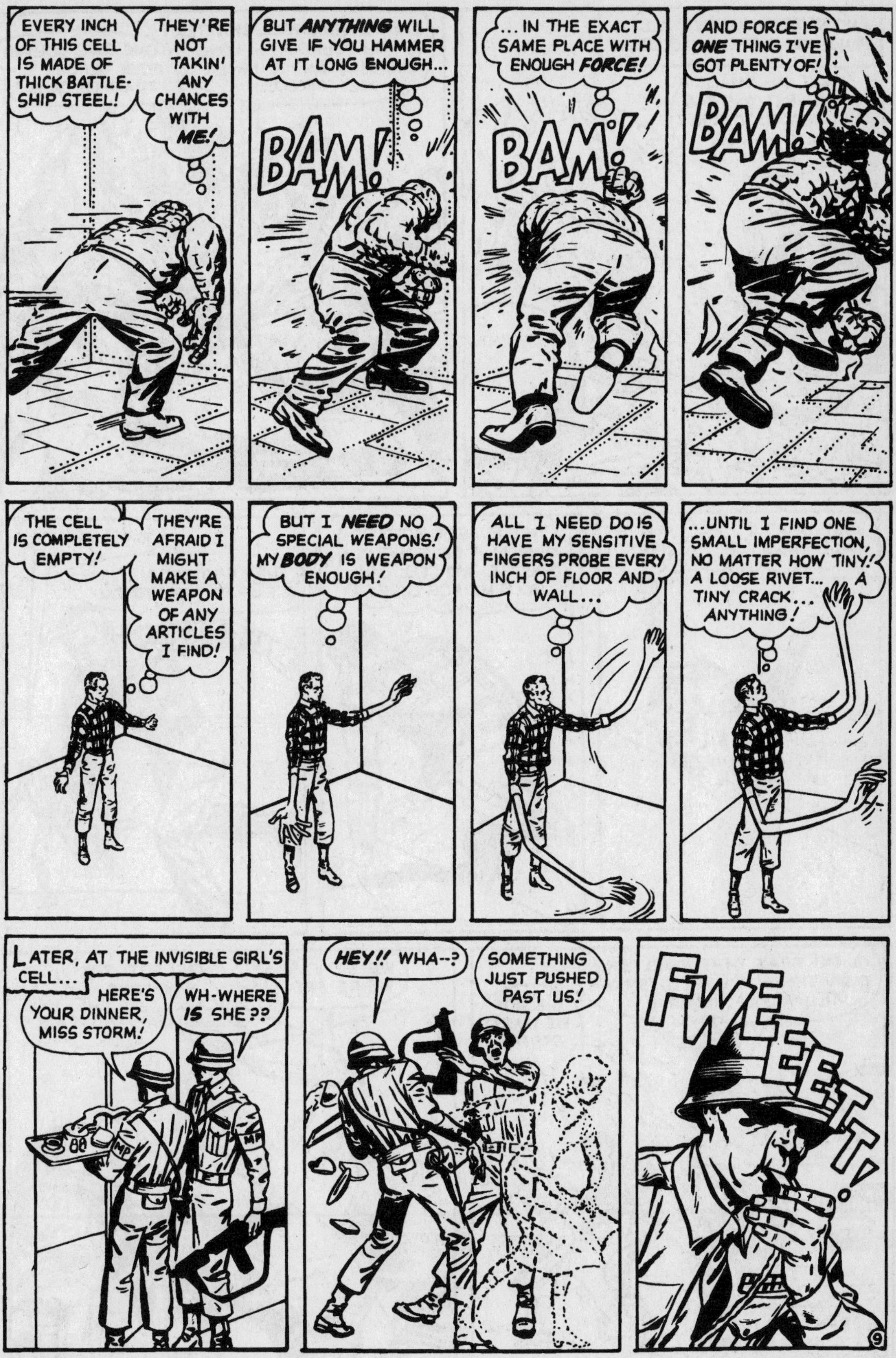
EVERY INCH OF THIS CELL IS MADE OF THICK BATTLE-SHIP STEEL!
THEY'RE NOT TAKIN' ANY CHANCES WITH ME!
BUT ANYTHING WILL GIVE IF YOU HAMMER AT IT LONG ENOUGH...
BAM!
...IN THE EXACT SAME PLACE WITH ENOUGH FORCE!
BAM!
AND FORCE IS ONE THING I'VE GOT PLENTY OF!
BAM!
THE CELL IS COMPLETELY EMPTY!
THEY'RE AFRAID I MIGHT MAKE A WEAPON OF ANY ARTICLES I FIND!
BUT I NEED NO SPECIAL WEAPONS! MY BODY IS WEAPON ENOUGH!
ALL I NEED DO IS HAVE MY SENSITIVE FINGERS PROBE EVERY INCH OF FLOOR AND WALL...
...UNTIL I FIND ONE SMALL IMPERFECTION, NO MATTER HOW TINY! A LOOSE RIVET... A TINY CRACK... ANYTHING!
LATER, AT THE INVISIBLE GIRL'S CELL...
HERE'S YOUR DINNER, MISS STORM!
WH-WHERE IS SHE??
HEY!! WHA--?
SOMETHING JUST PUSHED PAST US!
FWEEEET!
9

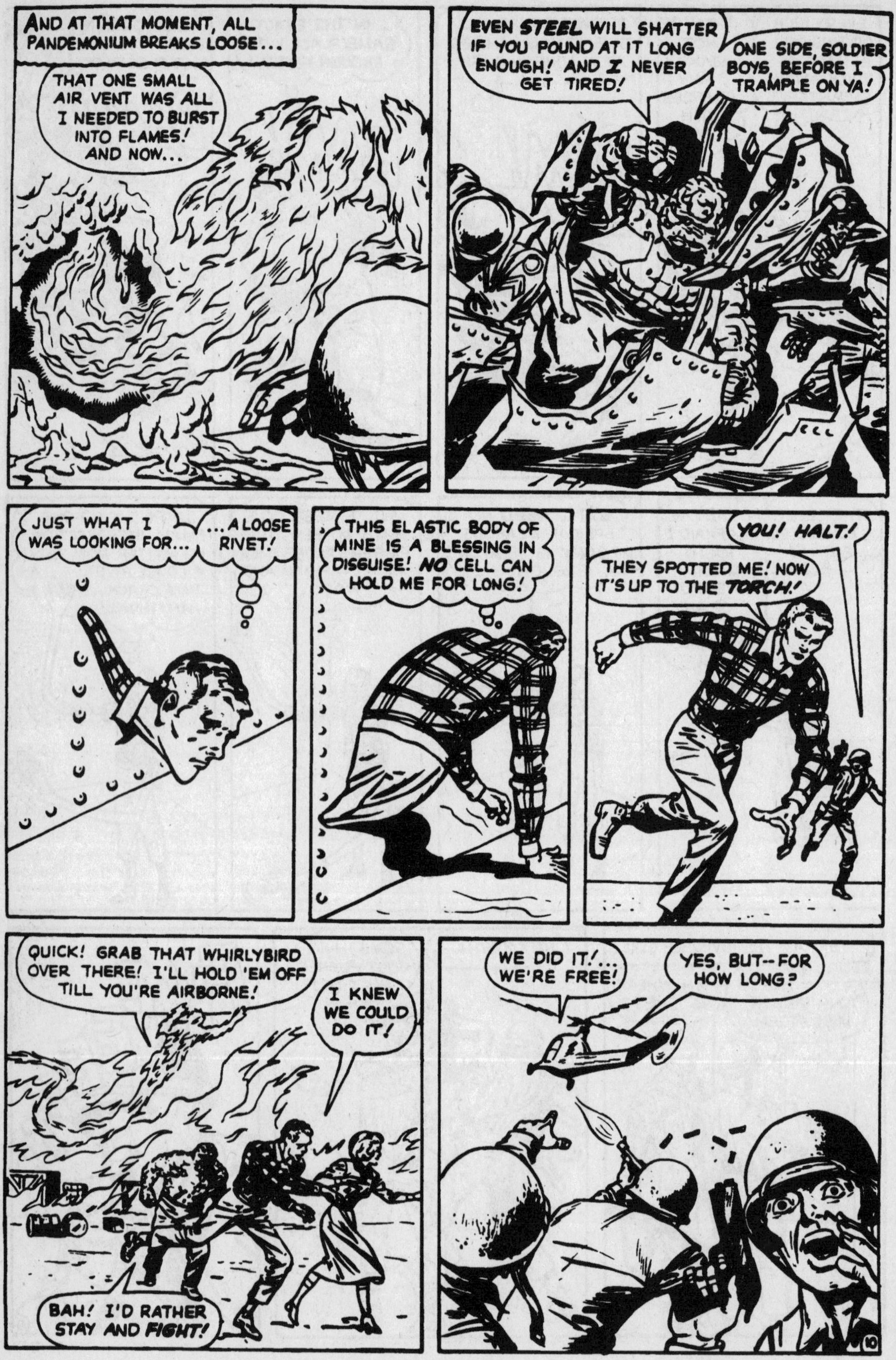
AND AT THAT MOMENT, ALL PANDEMONIUM BREAKS LOOSE...
THAT ONE SMALL AIR VENT WAS ALL I NEEDED TO BURST INTO FLAMES! AND NOW...
EVEN STEEL WILL SHATTER IF YOU POUND AT IT LONG ENOUGH! AND I NEVER GET TIRED!
ONE SIDE, SOLDIER BOYS, BEFORE I TRAMPLE ON YA!
JUST WHAT I WAS LOOKING FOR...
...A LOOSE RIVET!
THIS ELASTIC BODY OF MINE IS A BLESSING IN DISGUISE! NO CELL CAN HOLD ME FOR LONG!
YOU! HALT!
THEY SPOTTED ME! NOW IT'S UP TO THE TORCH!
QUICK! GRAB THAT WHIRLYBIRD OVER THERE! I'LL HOLD 'EM OFF TILL YOU'RE AIRBORNE!
I KNEW WE COULD DO IT!
BAH! I'D RATHER STAY AND FIGHT!
WE DID IT!... WE'RE FREE!
YES, BUT--FOR HOW LONG?
10

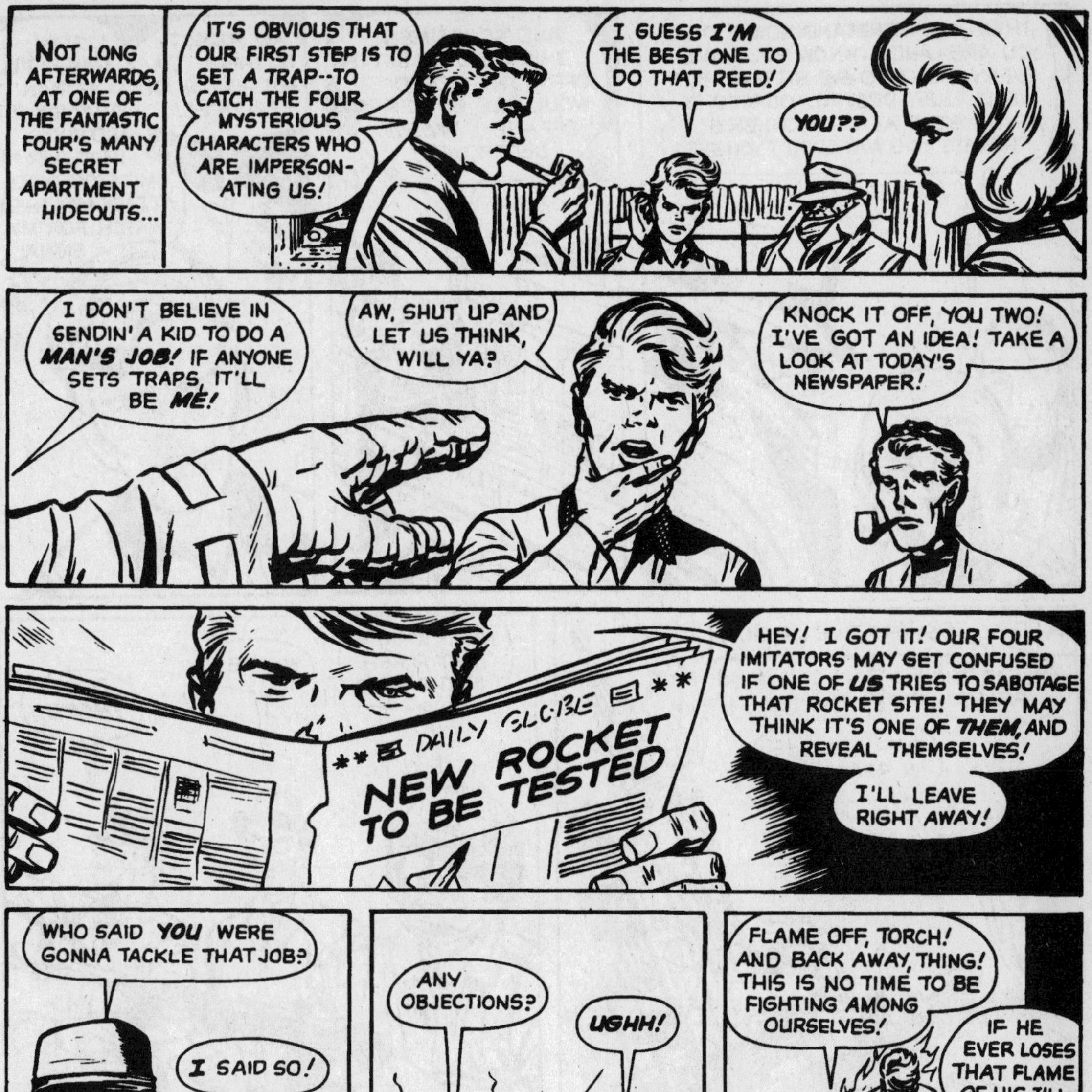
NOT LONG AFTERWARDS, AT ONE OF THE FANTASTIC FOUR'S MANY SECRET APARTMENT HIDEOUTS...
IT'S OBVIOUS THAT OUR FIRST STEP IS TO SET A TRAP--TO CATCH THE FOUR MYSTERIOUS CHARACTERS WHO ARE IMPERSON-ATING US!
I GUESS I'M THE BEST ONE TO DO THAT, REED!
YOU??
I DON'T BELIEVE IN SENDIN' A KID TO DO A MAN'S JOB! IF ANYONE SETS TRAPS, IT'LL BE ME!
AW, SHUT UP AND LET US THINK, WILL YA?
KNOCK IT OFF, YOU TWO! I'VE GOT AN IDEA! TAKE A LOOK AT TODAY'S NEWSPAPER!
DAILY GLOBE
NEW ROCKET TO BE TESTED
HEY! I GOT IT! OUR FOUR IMITATORS MAY GET CONFUSED IF ONE OF US TRIES TO SABOTAGE THAT ROCKET SITE! THEY MAY THINK IT'S ONE OF THEM, AND REVEAL THEMSELVES!
I'LL LEAVE RIGHT AWAY!
WHO SAID YOU WERE GONNA TACKLE THAT JOB?
I SAID SO!
ANY OBJECTIONS?
UGHH!
FLAME OFF, TORCH! AND BACK AWAY, THING! THIS IS NO TIME TO BE FIGHTING AMONG OURSELVES!
IF HE EVER LOSES THAT FLAME OF HIS, I'LL--
11

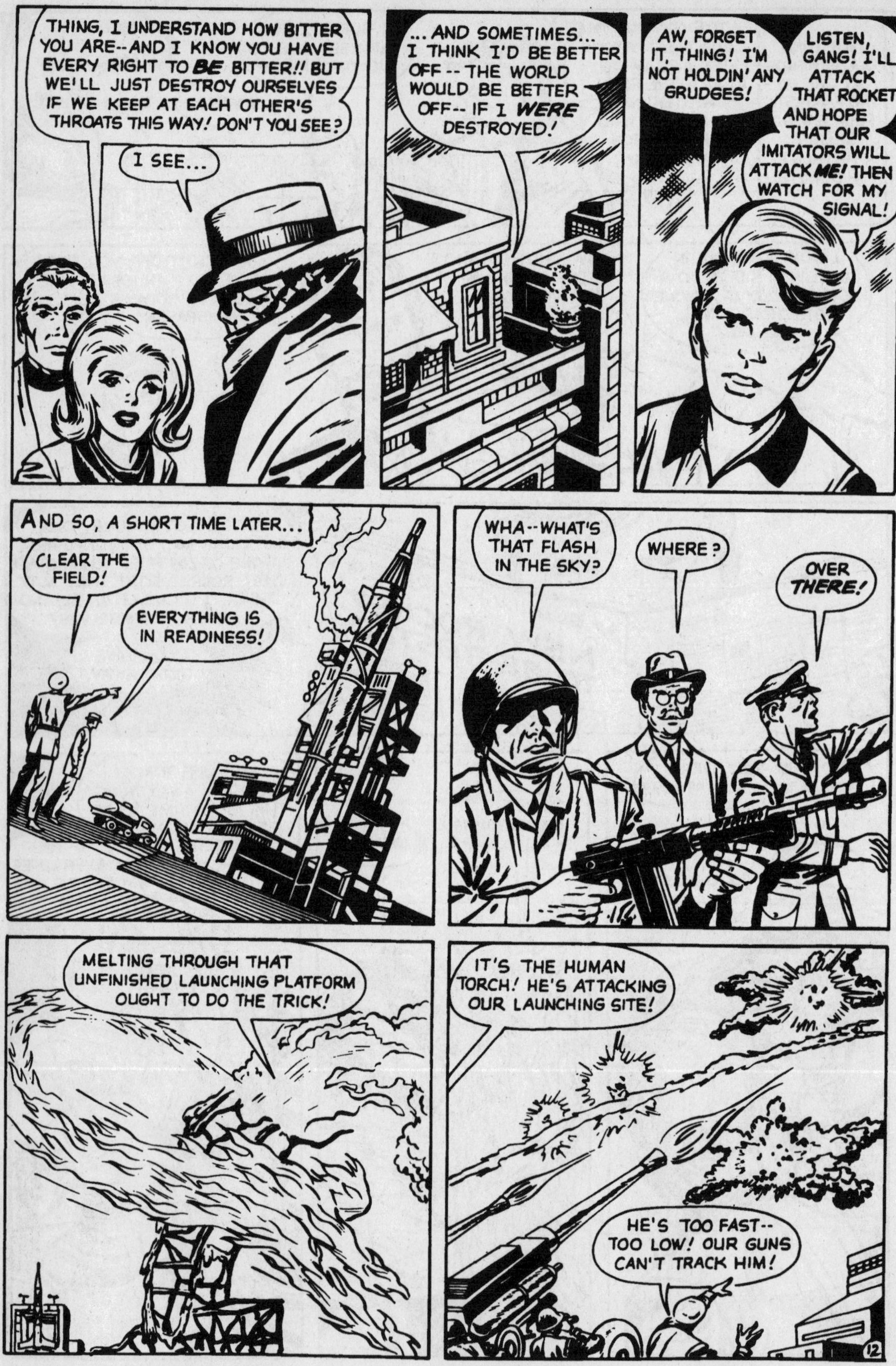
THING, I UNDERSTAND HOW BITTER YOU ARE--AND I KNOW YOU HAVE EVERY RIGHT TO BE BITTER!! BUT WE'LL JUST DESTROY OURSELVES IF WE KEEP AT EACH OTHER'S THROATS THIS WAY! DON'T YOU SEE?
I SEE...
...AND SOMETIMES... I THINK I'D BE BETTER OFF -- THE WORLD WOULD BE BETTER OFF-- IF I WERE DESTROYED!
AW, FORGET IT, THING! I'M NOT HOLDIN' ANY GRUDGES!
LISTEN, GANG! I'LL ATTACK THAT ROCKET AND HOPE THAT OUR IMITATORS WILL ATTACK ME! THEN WATCH FOR MY SIGNAL!
AND SO, A SHORT TIME LATER...
CLEAR THE FIELD!
EVERYTHING IS IN READINESS!
WHA--WHAT'S THAT FLASH IN THE SKY?
WHERE?
OVER THERE!
MELTING THROUGH THAT UNFINISHED LAUNCHING PLATFORM OUGHT TO DO THE TRICK!
IT'S THE HUMAN TORCH! HE'S ATTACKING OUR LAUNCHING SITE!
HE'S TOO FAST-- TOO LOW! OUR GUNS CAN'T TRACK HIM!
12

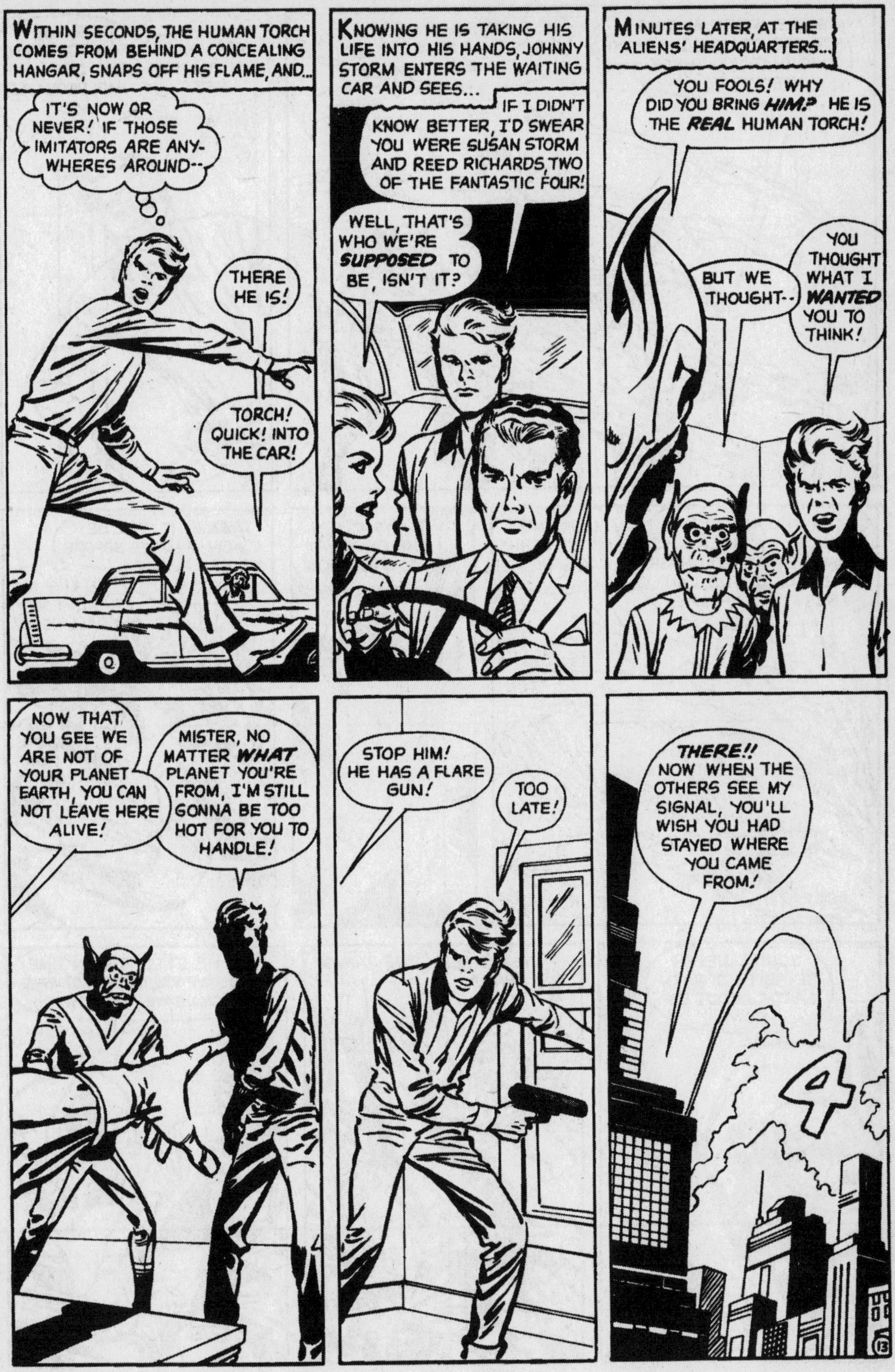
WITHIN SECONDS, THE HUMAN TORCH COMES FROM BEHIND A CONCEALING HANGAR, SNAPS OFF HIS FLAME, AND...
IT'S NOW OR NEVER! IF THOSE IMITATORS ARE ANY-WHERES AROUND--
THERE HE IS!
TORCH! QUICK! INTO THE CAR!
KNOWING HE IS TAKING HIS LIFE INTO HIS HANDS, JOHNNY STORM ENTERS THE WAITING CAR AND SEES...
IF I DIDN'T KNOW BETTER, I'D SWEAR YOU WERE SUSAN STORM AND REED RICHARDS, TWO OF THE FANTASTIC FOUR!
WELL, THAT'S WHO WE'RE SUPPOSED TO BE, ISN'T IT?
MINUTES LATER, AT THE ALIENS' HEADQUARTERS...
YOU FOOLS! WHY DID YOU BRING HIM? HE IS THE REAL HUMAN TORCH!
BUT WE THOUGHT--
YOU THOUGHT WHAT I WANTED YOU TO THINK!
NOW THAT YOU SEE WE ARE NOT OF YOUR PLANET EARTH, YOU CAN NOT LEAVE HERE ALIVE!
MISTER, NO MATTER WHAT PLANET YOU'RE FROM, I'M STILL GONNA BE TOO HOT FOR YOU TO HANDLE!
STOP HIM! HE HAS A FLARE GUN!
TOO LATE!
THERE!! NOW WHEN THE OTHERS SEE MY SIGNAL, YOU'LL WISH YOU HAD STAYED WHERE YOU CAME FROM!
4
13

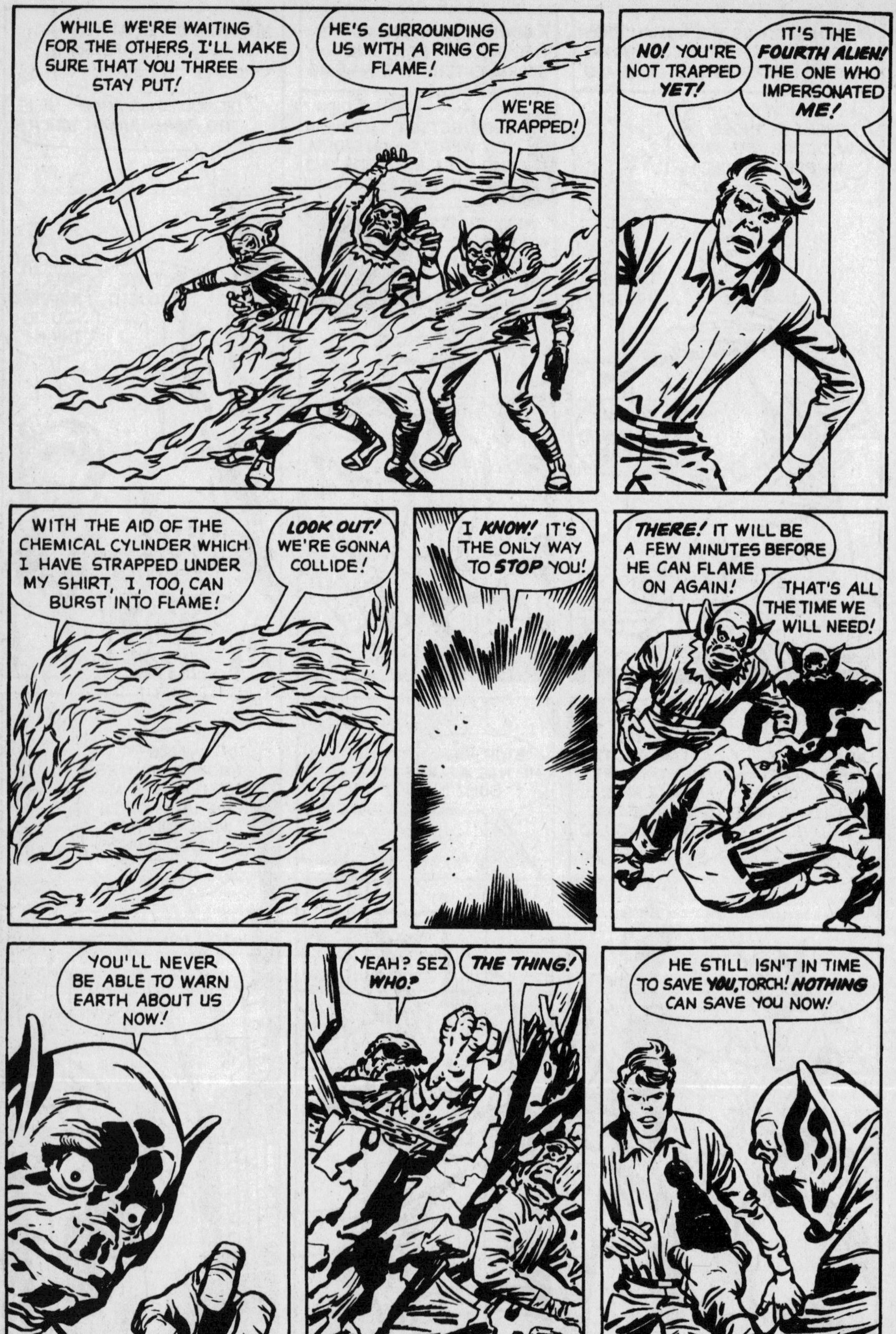
WHILE WE'RE WAITING FOR THE OTHERS, I'LL MAKE SURE THAT YOU THREE STAY PUT!
HE'S SURROUNDING US WITH A RING OF FLAME!
WE'RE TRAPPED!
NO! YOU'RE NOT TRAPPED YET!
IT'S THE FOURTH ALIEN! THE ONE WHO IMPERSONATED ME!
WITH THE AID OF THE CHEMICAL CYLINDER WHICH I HAVE STRAPPED UNDER MY SHIRT, I, TOO, CAN BURST INTO FLAME!
LOOK OUT! WE'RE GONNA COLLIDE!
I KNOW! IT'S THE ONLY WAY TO STOP YOU!
THERE! IT WILL BE A FEW MINUTES BEFORE HE CAN FLAME ON AGAIN!
THAT'S ALL THE TIME WE WILL NEED!
YOU'LL NEVER BE ABLE TO WARN EARTH ABOUT US NOW!
YEAH? SEZ WHO?
THE THING!
HE STILL ISN'T IN TIME TO SAVE YOU, TORCH! NOTHING CAN SAVE YOU NOW!
14

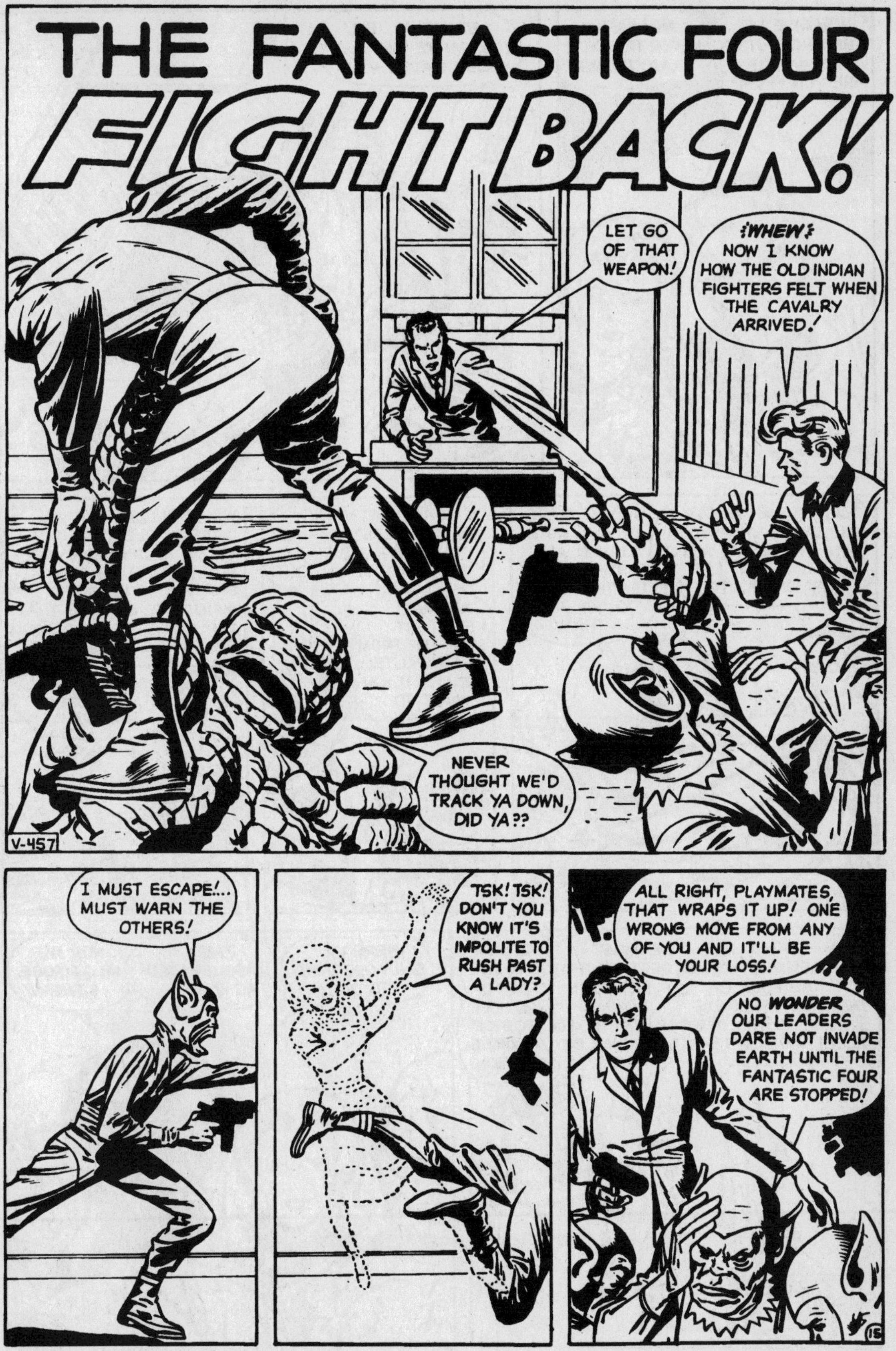
THE FANTASTIC FOUR
FIGHT BACK!
LET GO OF THAT WEAPON!
¡WHEW! NOW I KNOW HOW THE OLD INDIAN FIGHTERS FELT WHEN THE CAVALRY ARRIVED!
NEVER THOUGHT WE'D TRACK YA DOWN, DID YA??
V-457
I MUST ESCAPE!... MUST WARN THE OTHERS!
TSK! TSK! DON'T YOU KNOW IT'S IMPOLITE TO RUSH PAST A LADY?
ALL RIGHT, PLAYMATES, THAT WRAPS IT UP! ONE WRONG MOVE FROM ANY OF YOU AND IT'LL BE YOUR LOSS!
NO WONDER OUR LEADERS DARE NOT INVADE EARTH UNTIL THE FANTASTIC FOUR ARE STOPPED!
15

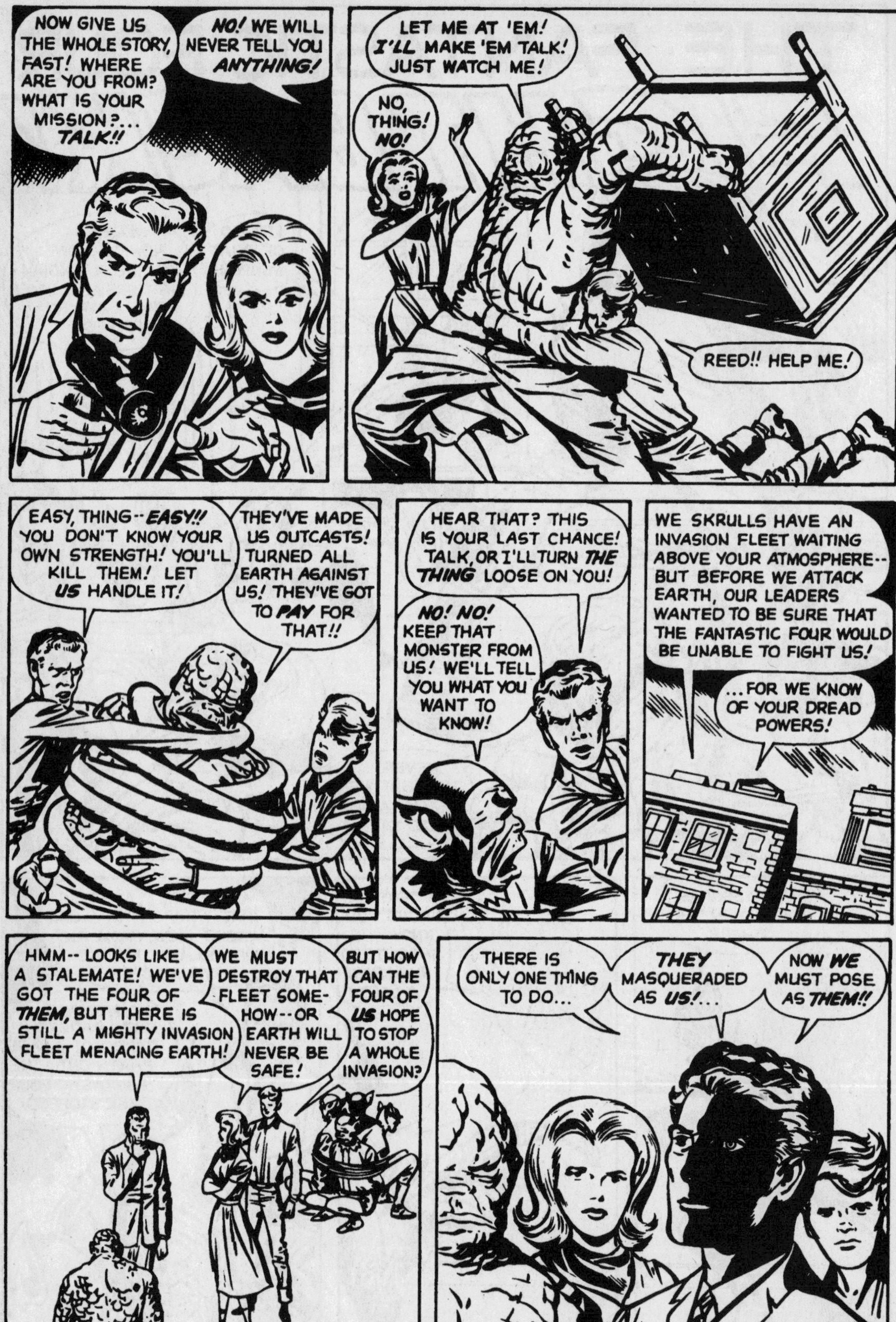
NOW GIVE US THE WHOLE STORY, FAST! WHERE ARE YOU FROM? WHAT IS YOUR MISSION?... TALK!!
NO! WE WILL NEVER TELL YOU ANYTHING!
LET ME AT 'EM! I'LL MAKE 'EM TALK! JUST WATCH ME!
NO, THING! NO!
REED!! HELP ME!
EASY, THING--EASY!! YOU DON'T KNOW YOUR OWN STRENGTH! YOU'LL KILL THEM! LET US HANDLE IT!
THEY'VE MADE US OUTCASTS! TURNED ALL EARTH AGAINST US! THEY'VE GOT TO PAY FOR THAT!!
HEAR THAT? THIS IS YOUR LAST CHANCE! TALK, OR I'LL TURN THE THING LOOSE ON YOU!
NO! NO! KEEP THAT MONSTER FROM US! WE'LL TELL YOU WHAT YOU WANT TO KNOW!
WE SKRULLS HAVE AN INVASION FLEET WAITING ABOVE YOUR ATMOSPHERE-- BUT BEFORE WE ATTACK EARTH, OUR LEADERS WANTED TO BE SURE THAT THE FANTASTIC FOUR WOULD BE UNABLE TO FIGHT US!
...FOR WE KNOW OF YOUR DREAD POWERS!
HMM-- LOOKS LIKE A STALEMATE! WE'VE GOT THE FOUR OF THEM, BUT THERE IS STILL A MIGHTY INVASION FLEET MENACING EARTH!
WE MUST DESTROY THAT FLEET SOME-HOW--OR EARTH WILL NEVER BE SAFE!
BUT HOW CAN THE FOUR OF US HOPE TO STOP A WHOLE INVASION?
THERE IS ONLY ONE THING TO DO...
THEY MASQUERADED AS US!...
NOW WE MUST POSE AS THEM!!
16

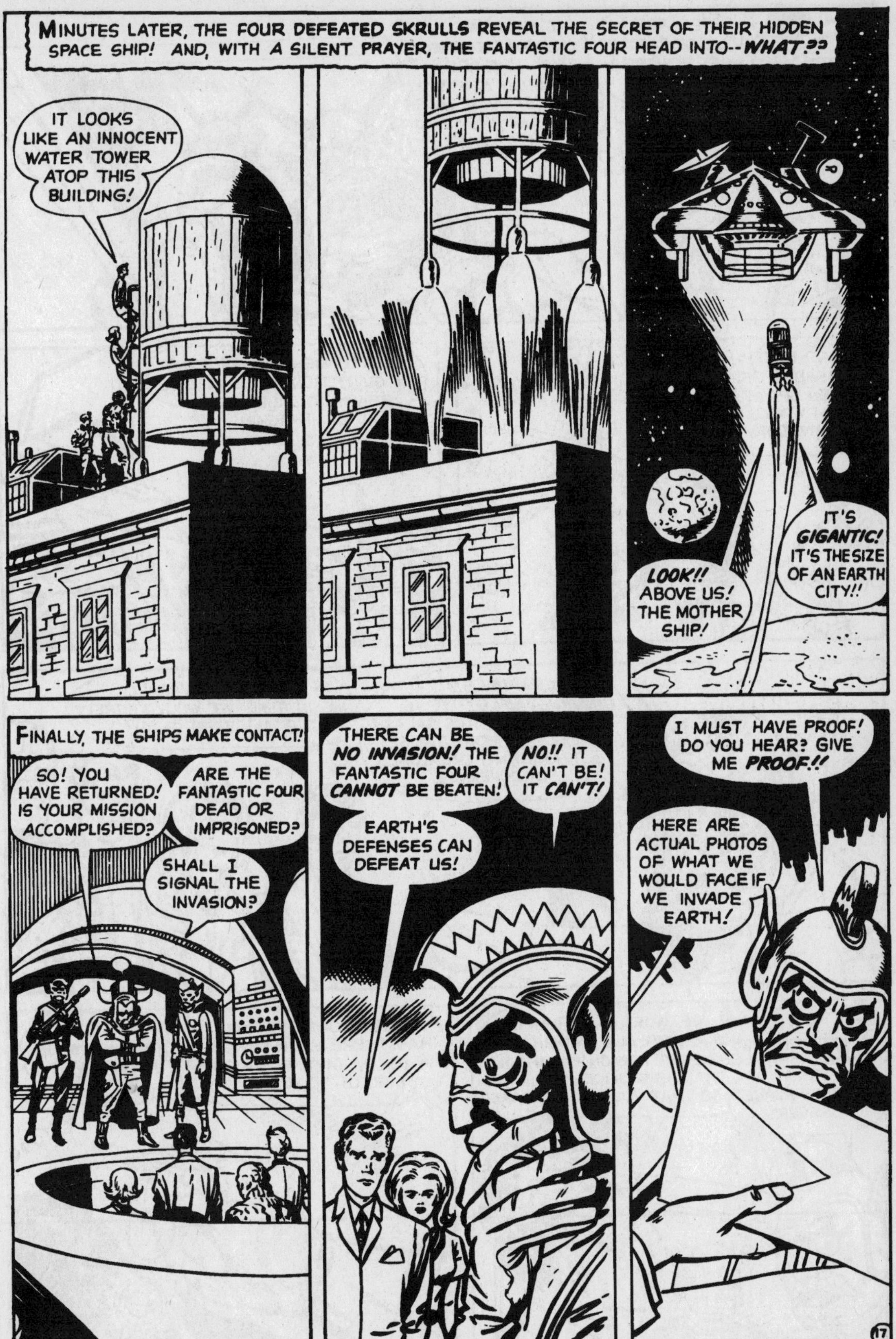
MINUTES LATER, THE FOUR DEFEATED SKRULLS REVEAL THE SECRET OF THEIR HIDDEN SPACE SHIP! AND, WITH A SILENT PRAYER, THE FANTASTIC FOUR HEAD INTO--WHAT??
IT LOOKS LIKE AN INNOCENT WATER TOWER ATOP THIS BUILDING!
LOOK!! ABOVE US! THE MOTHER SHIP!
IT'S GIGANTIC! IT'S THE SIZE OF AN EARTH CITY!!
FINALLY, THE SHIPS MAKE CONTACT!
SO! YOU HAVE RETURNED! IS YOUR MISSION ACCOMPLISHED?
ARE THE FANTASTIC FOUR DEAD OR IMPRISONED?
SHALL I SIGNAL THE INVASION?
THERE CAN BE NO INVASION! THE FANTASTIC FOUR CANNOT BE BEATEN!
EARTH'S DEFENSES CAN DEFEAT US!
NO!! IT CAN'T BE! IT CAN'T!
I MUST HAVE PROOF! DO YOU HEAR? GIVE ME PROOF!!
HERE ARE ACTUAL PHOTOS OF WHAT WE WOULD FACE IF WE INVADE EARTH!
17

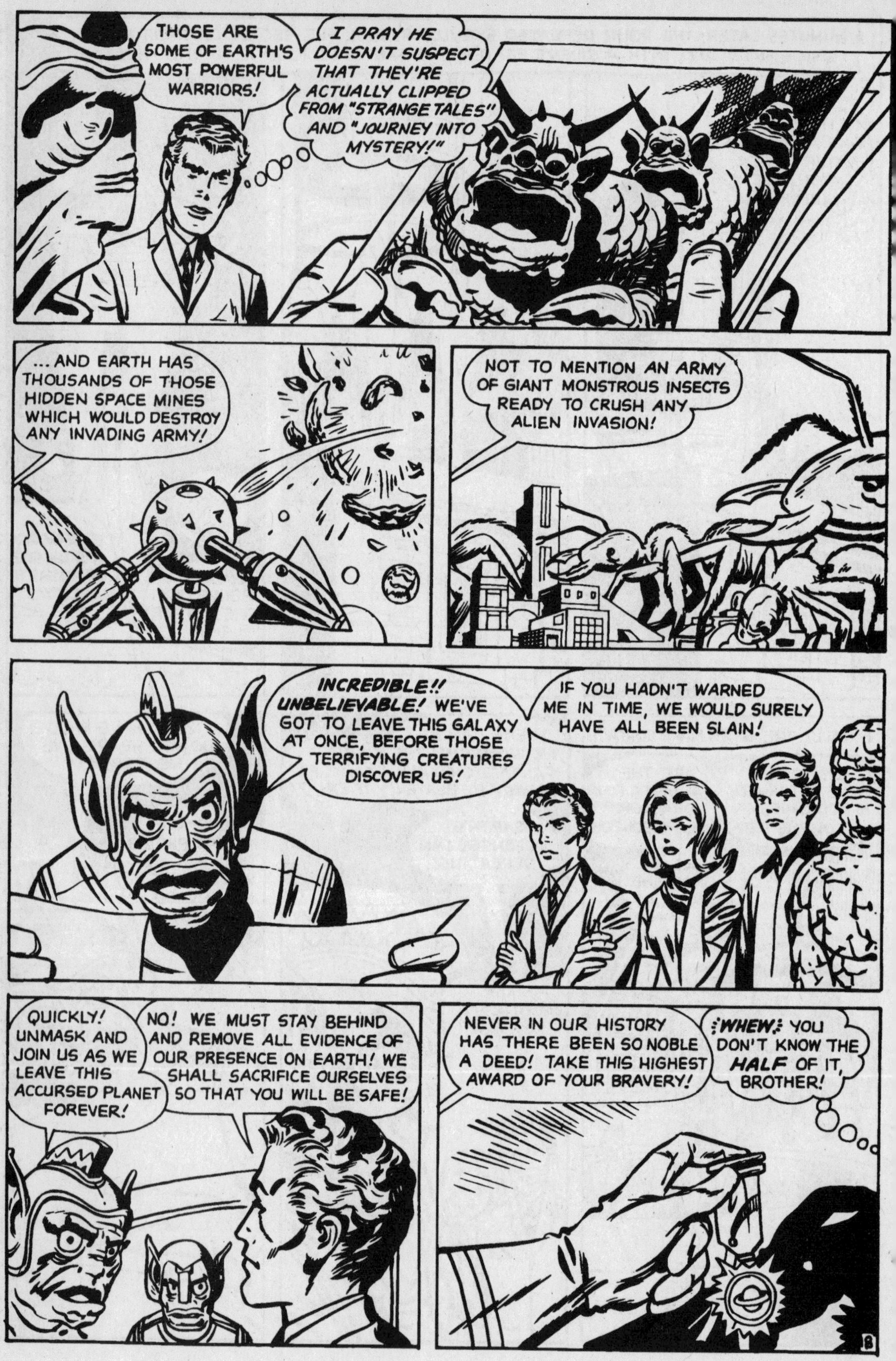
THOSE ARE SOME OF EARTH'S MOST POWERFUL WARRIORS!
I PRAY HE DOESN'T SUSPECT THAT THEY'RE ACTUALLY CLIPPED FROM "STRANGE TALES" AND "JOURNEY INTO MYSTERY!"
... AND EARTH HAS THOUSANDS OF THOSE HIDDEN SPACE MINES WHICH WOULD DESTROY ANY INVADING ARMY!
NOT TO MENTION AN ARMY OF GIANT MONSTROUS INSECTS READY TO CRUSH ANY ALIEN INVASION!
INCREDIBLE!! UNBELIEVABLE! WE'VE GOT TO LEAVE THIS GALAXY AT ONCE, BEFORE THOSE TERRIFYING CREATURES DISCOVER US!
IF YOU HADN'T WARNED ME IN TIME, WE WOULD SURELY HAVE ALL BEEN SLAIN!
QUICKLY! UNMASK AND JOIN US AS WE LEAVE THIS ACCURSED PLANET FOREVER!
NO! WE MUST STAY BEHIND AND REMOVE ALL EVIDENCE OF OUR PRESENCE ON EARTH! WE SHALL SACRIFICE OURSELVES SO THAT YOU WILL BE SAFE!
NEVER IN OUR HISTORY HAS THERE BEEN SO NOBLE A DEED! TAKE THIS HIGHEST AWARD OF YOUR BRAVERY!
WHEW! YOU DON'T KNOW THE HALF OF IT, BROTHER!
8

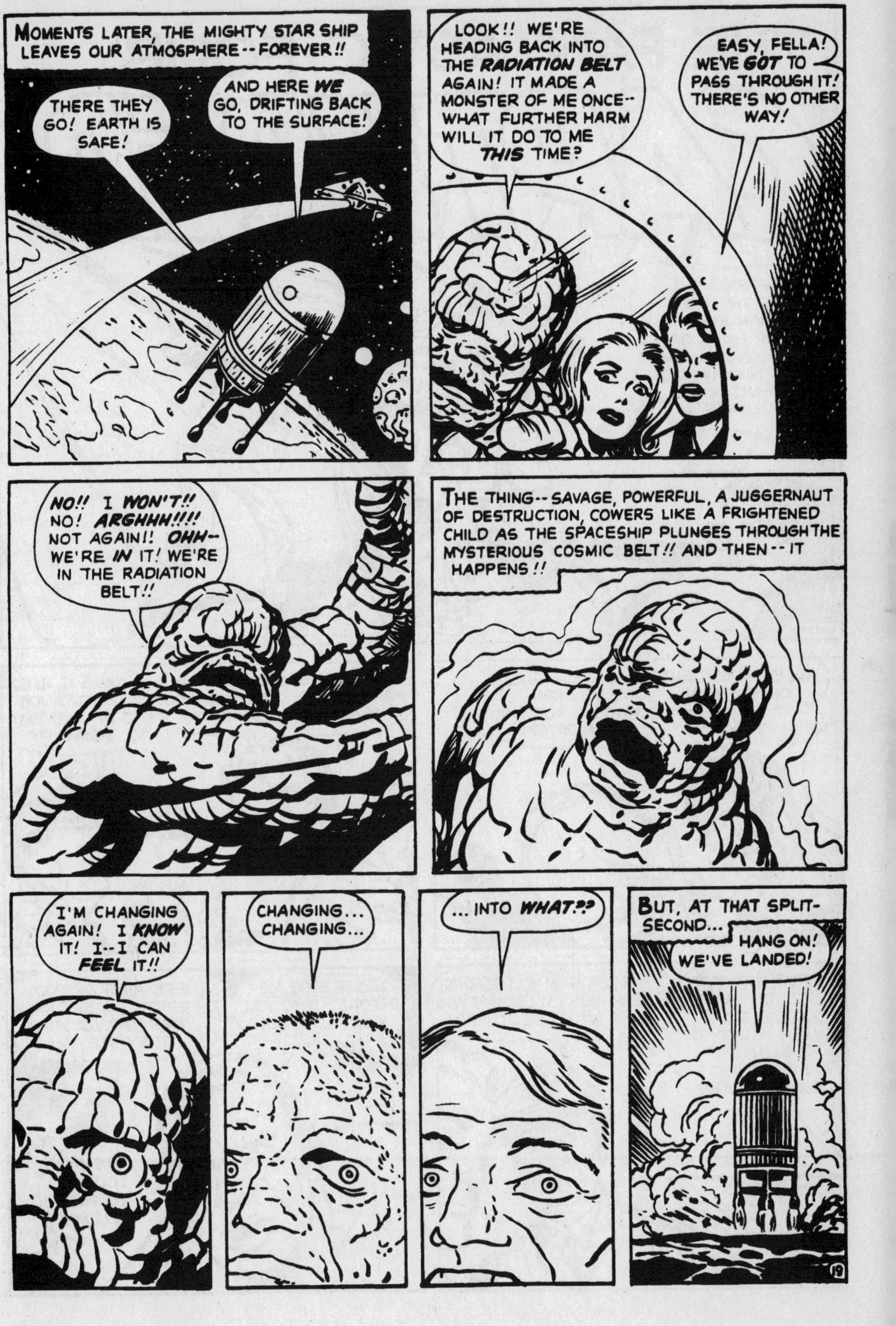
MOMENTS LATER, THE MIGHTY STAR SHIP LEAVES OUR ATMOSPHERE--FOREVER!!
THERE THEY GO! EARTH IS SAFE!
AND HERE WE GO, DRIFTING BACK TO THE SURFACE!
LOOK!! WE'RE HEADING BACK INTO THE RADIATION BELT AGAIN! IT MADE A MONSTER OF ME ONCE--WHAT FURTHER HARM WILL IT DO TO ME THIS TIME?
EASY, FELLA! WE'VE GOT TO PASS THROUGH IT! THERE'S NO OTHER WAY!
NO!! I WON'T!! NO! ARGHHH!!!! NOT AGAIN!! OHH--WE'RE IN IT! WE'RE IN THE RADIATION BELT!!
THE THING--SAVAGE, POWERFUL, A JUGGERNAUT OF DESTRUCTION, COWERS LIKE A FRIGHTENED CHILD AS THE SPACESHIP PLUNGES THROUGH THE MYSTERIOUS COSMIC BELT!! AND THEN--IT HAPPENS!!
I'M CHANGING AGAIN! I KNOW IT! I--I CAN FEEL IT!!
CHANGING... CHANGING...
...INTO WHAT??
BUT, AT THAT SPLIT-SECOND...
HANG ON! WE'VE LANDED!
19

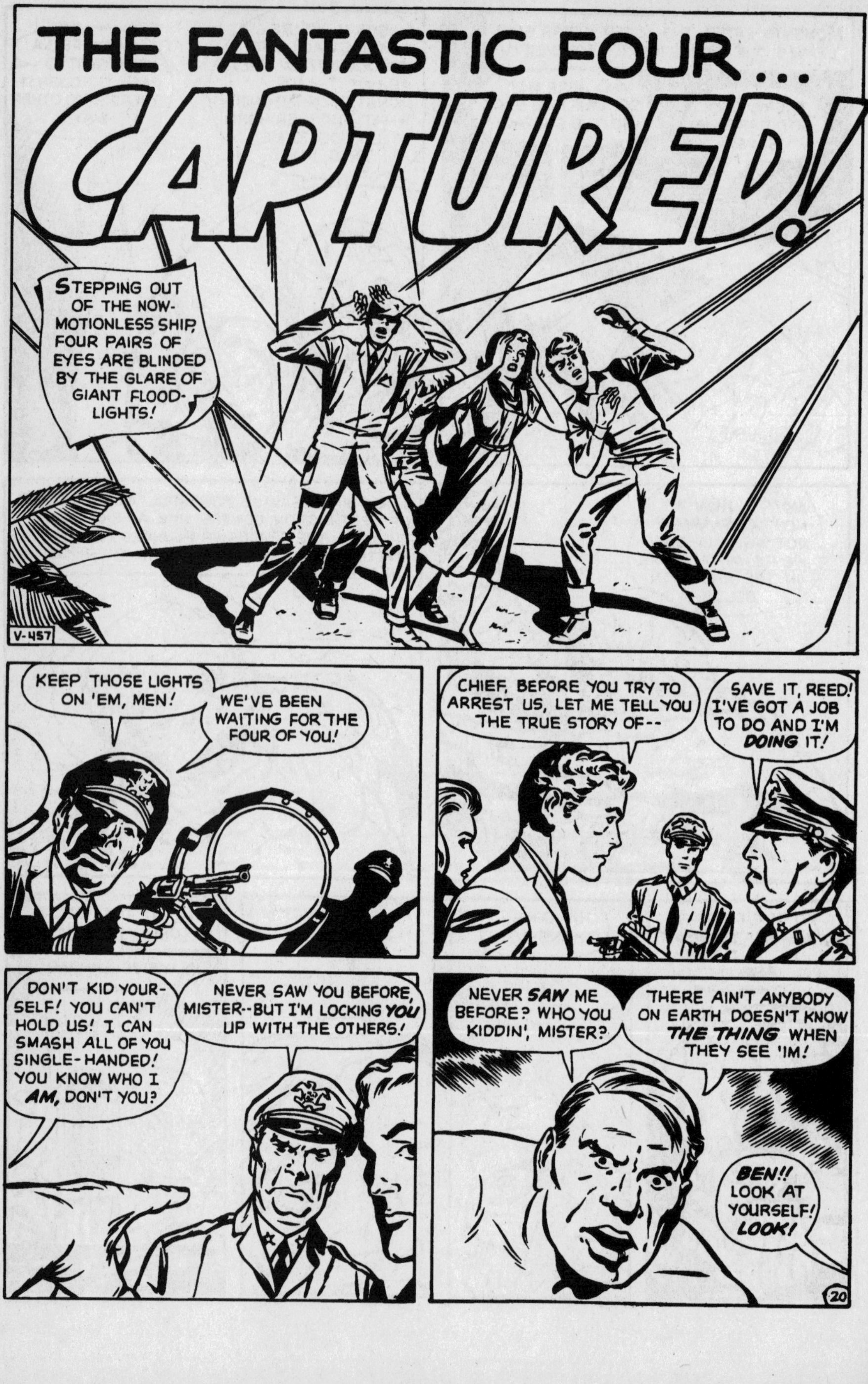
THE FANTASTIC FOUR...
CAPTURED!
STEPPING OUT OF THE NOW-MOTIONLESS SHIP, FOUR PAIRS OF EYES ARE BLINDED BY THE GLARE OF GIANT FLOOD-LIGHTS!
V-457
KEEP THOSE LIGHTS ON 'EM, MEN!
WE'VE BEEN WAITING FOR THE FOUR OF YOU!
CHIEF, BEFORE YOU TRY TO ARREST US, LET ME TELL YOU THE TRUE STORY OF--
SAVE IT, REED! I'VE GOT A JOB TO DO AND I'M DOING IT!
DON'T KID YOURSELF! YOU CAN'T HOLD US! I CAN SMASH ALL OF YOU SINGLE-HANDED! YOU KNOW WHO I AM, DON'T YOU?
NEVER SAW YOU BEFORE, MISTER--BUT I'M LOCKING YOU UP WITH THE OTHERS!
NEVER SAW ME BEFORE? WHO YOU KIDDIN', MISTER?
THERE AIN'T ANYBODY ON EARTH DOESN'T KNOW THE THING WHEN THEY SEE 'IM!
BEN!! LOOK AT YOURSELF! LOOK!
20

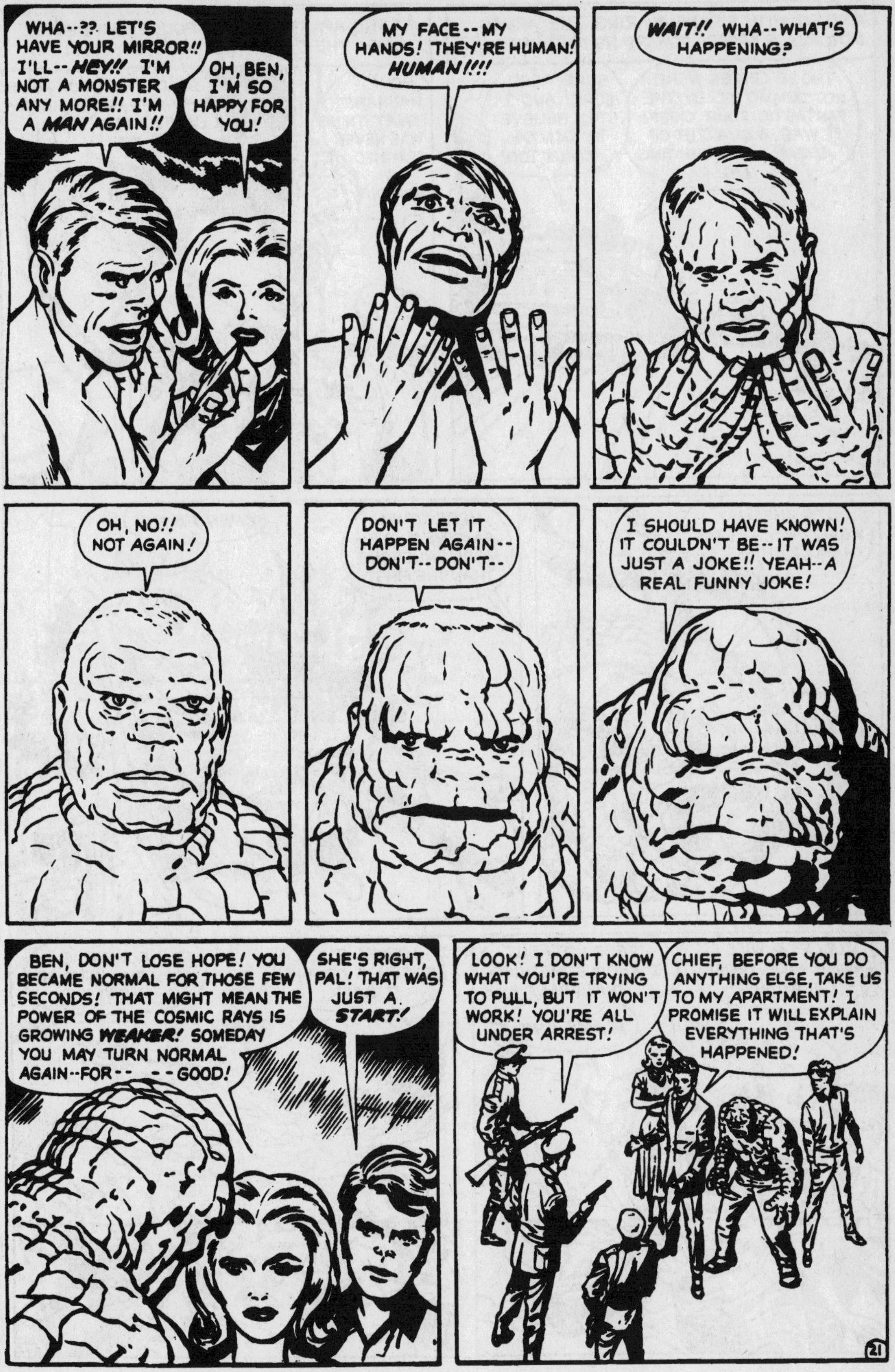
WHA--?? LET'S HAVE YOUR MIRROR!! I'LL--HEY!! I'M NOT A MONSTER ANY MORE!! I'M A MAN AGAIN!!
OH, BEN, I'M SO HAPPY FOR YOU!
MY FACE--MY HANDS! THEY'RE HUMAN! HUMAN!!!!
WAIT!! WHA--WHAT'S HAPPENING?
OH, NO!! NOT AGAIN!
DON'T LET IT HAPPEN AGAIN-- DON'T--DON'T--
I SHOULD HAVE KNOWN! IT COULDN'T BE--IT WAS JUST A JOKE!! YEAH--A REAL FUNNY JOKE!
BEN, DON'T LOSE HOPE! YOU BECAME NORMAL FOR THOSE FEW SECONDS! THAT MIGHT MEAN THE POWER OF THE COSMIC RAYS IS GROWING WEAKER! SOMEDAY YOU MAY TURN NORMAL AGAIN--FOR-- --GOOD!
SHE'S RIGHT, PAL! THAT WAS JUST A START!
LOOK! I DON'T KNOW WHAT YOU'RE TRYING TO PULL, BUT IT WON'T WORK! YOU'RE ALL UNDER ARREST!
CHIEF, BEFORE YOU DO ANYTHING ELSE, TAKE US TO MY APARTMENT! I PROMISE IT WILL EXPLAIN EVERYTHING THAT'S HAPPENED!
21

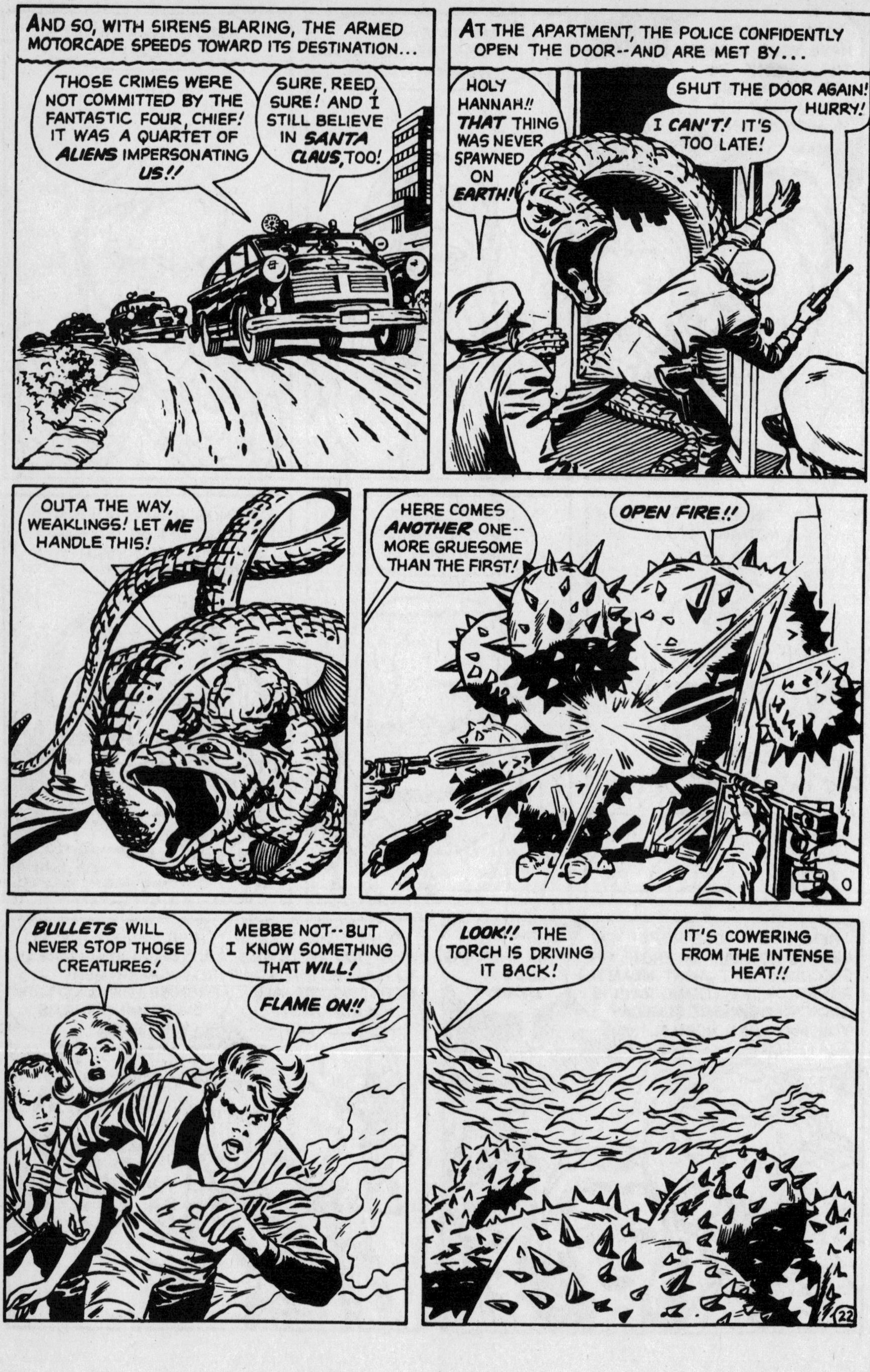

AND SO, WITH SIRENS BLARING, THE ARMED MOTORCADE SPEEDS TOWARD ITS DESTINATION...
THOSE CRIMES WERE NOT COMMITTED BY THE FANTASTIC FOUR, CHIEF! IT WAS A QUARTET OF ALIENS IMPERSONATING US!!
SURE, REED, SURE! AND I STILL BELIEVE IN SANTA CLAUS, TOO!
AT THE APARTMENT, THE POLICE CONFIDENTLY OPEN THE DOOR--AND ARE MET BY...
HOLY HANNAH!! THAT THING WAS NEVER SPAWNED ON EARTH!
SHUT THE DOOR AGAIN! HURRY!
I CAN'T! IT'S TOO LATE!
OUTA THE WAY, WEAKLINGS! LET ME HANDLE THIS!
HERE COMES ANOTHER ONE-- MORE GRUESOME THAN THE FIRST!
OPEN FIRE!!
BULLETS WILL NEVER STOP THOSE CREATURES!
MEBBE NOT--BUT I KNOW SOMETHING THAT WILL!
FLAME ON!!
LOOK!! THE TORCH IS DRIVING IT BACK!
IT'S COWERING FROM THE INTENSE HEAT!!
22

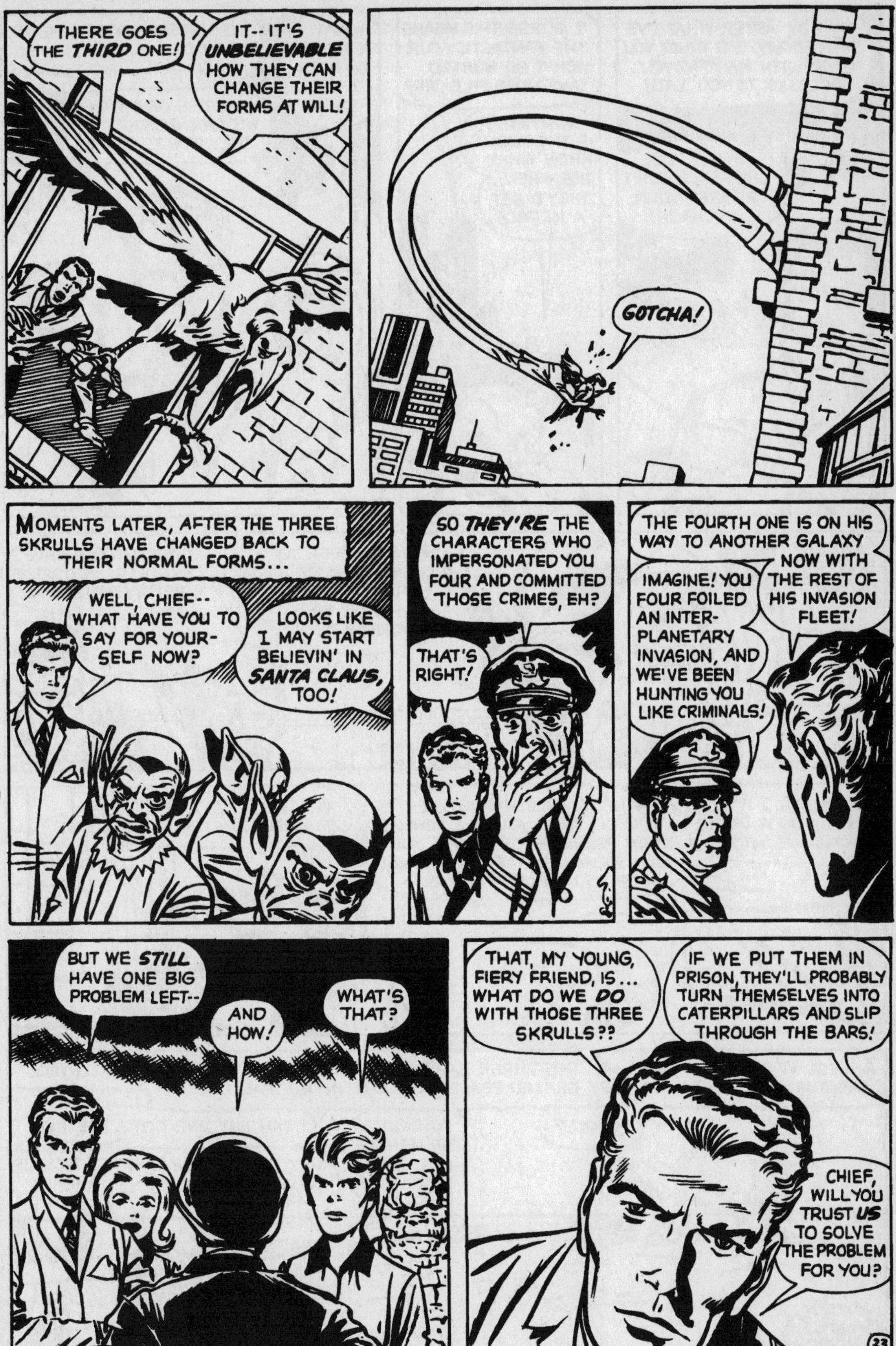
THERE GOES THE THIRD ONE!
IT-- IT'S UNBELIEVABLE HOW THEY CAN CHANGE THEIR FORMS AT WILL!
GOTCHA!
MOMENTS LATER, AFTER THE THREE SKRULLS HAVE CHANGED BACK TO THEIR NORMAL FORMS...
WELL, CHIEF-- WHAT HAVE YOU TO SAY FOR YOURSELF NOW?
LOOKS LIKE I MAY START BELIEVIN' IN SANTA CLAUS, TOO!
SO THEY'RE THE CHARACTERS WHO IMPERSONATED YOU FOUR AND COMMITTED THOSE CRIMES, EH?
THAT'S RIGHT!
THE FOURTH ONE IS ON HIS WAY TO ANOTHER GALAXY NOW WITH THE REST OF HIS INVASION FLEET!
IMAGINE! YOU FOUR FOILED AN INTER-PLANETARY INVASION, AND WE'VE BEEN HUNTING YOU LIKE CRIMINALS!
BUT WE STILL HAVE ONE BIG PROBLEM LEFT--
AND HOW!
WHAT'S THAT?
THAT, MY YOUNG, FIERY FRIEND, IS... WHAT DO WE DO WITH THOSE THREE SKRULLS??
IF WE PUT THEM IN PRISON, THEY'LL PROBABLY TURN THEMSELVES INTO CATERPILLARS AND SLIP THROUGH THE BARS!
CHIEF, WILL YOU TRUST US TO SOLVE THE PROBLEM FOR YOU?
23

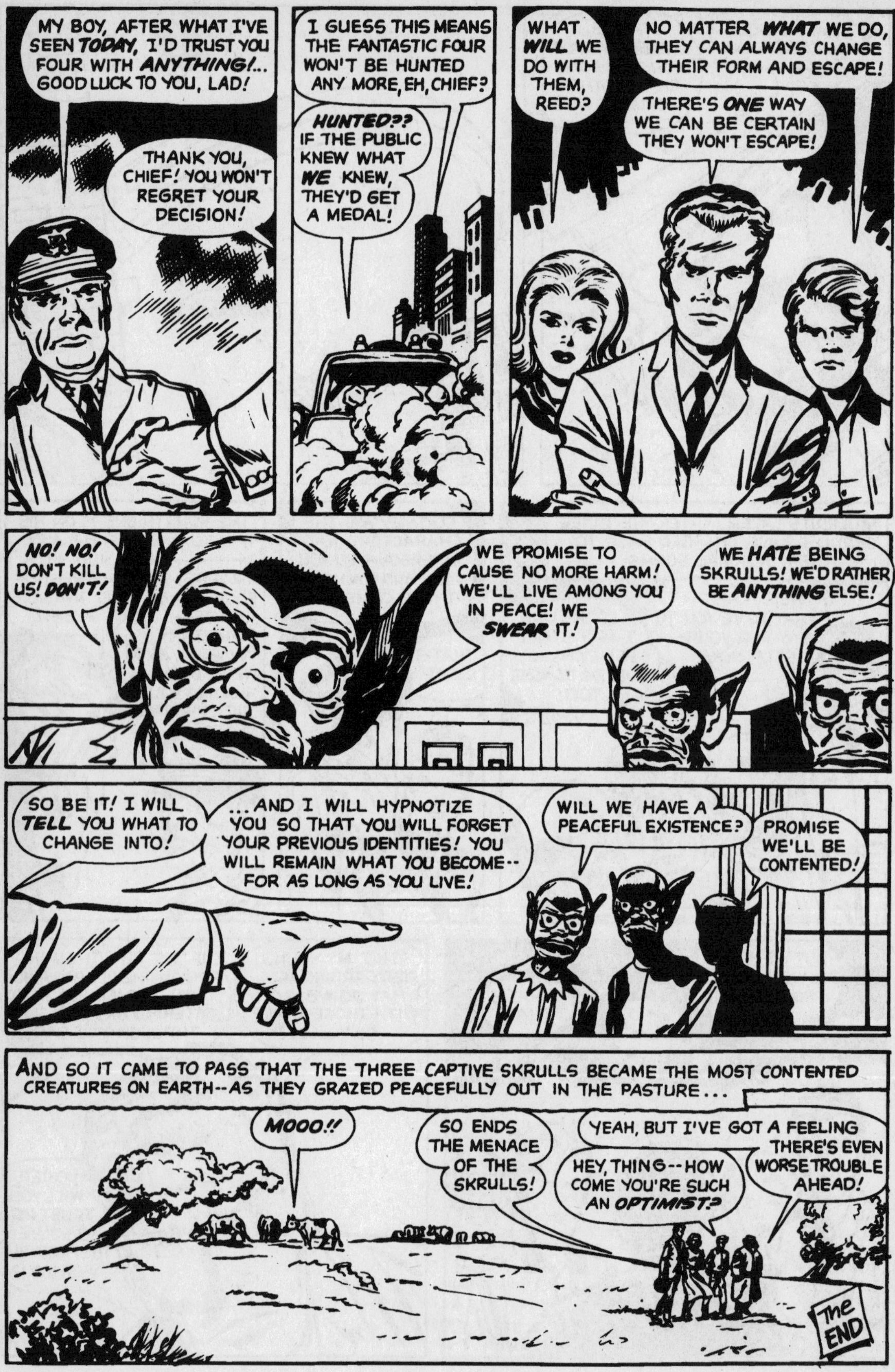

MY BOY, AFTER WHAT I'VE SEEN TODAY, I'D TRUST YOU FOUR WITH ANYTHING!... GOOD LUCK TO YOU, LAD!
THANK YOU, CHIEF! YOU WON'T REGRET YOUR DECISION!
I GUESS THIS MEANS THE FANTASTIC FOUR WON'T BE HUNTED ANY MORE, EH, CHIEF?
HUNTED?? IF THE PUBLIC KNEW WHAT WE KNEW, THEY'D GET A MEDAL!
WHAT WILL WE DO WITH THEM, REED?
NO MATTER WHAT WE DO, THEY CAN ALWAYS CHANGE THEIR FORM AND ESCAPE!
THERE'S ONE WAY WE CAN BE CERTAIN THEY WON'T ESCAPE!
NO! NO! DON'T KILL US! DON'T!
WE PROMISE TO CAUSE NO MORE HARM! WE'LL LIVE AMONG YOU IN PEACE! WE SWEAR IT!
WE HATE BEING SKRULLS! WE'D RATHER BE ANYTHING ELSE!
SO BE IT! I WILL TELL YOU WHAT TO CHANGE INTO!
...AND I WILL HYPNOTIZE YOU SO THAT YOU WILL FORGET YOUR PREVIOUS IDENTITIES! YOU WILL REMAIN WHAT YOU BECOME-- FOR AS LONG AS YOU LIVE!
WILL WE HAVE A PEACEFUL EXISTENCE?
PROMISE WE'LL BE CONTENTED!
AND SO IT CAME TO PASS THAT THE THREE CAPTIVE SKRULLS BECAME THE MOST CONTENTED CREATURES ON EARTH--AS THEY GRAZED PEACEFULLY OUT IN THE PASTURE...
MOOO!!
SO ENDS THE MENACE OF THE SKRULLS!
HEY, THING--HOW COME YOU'RE SUCH AN OPTIMIST?
YEAH, BUT I'VE GOT A FEELING THERE'S EVEN WORSE TROUBLE AHEAD!
THE END

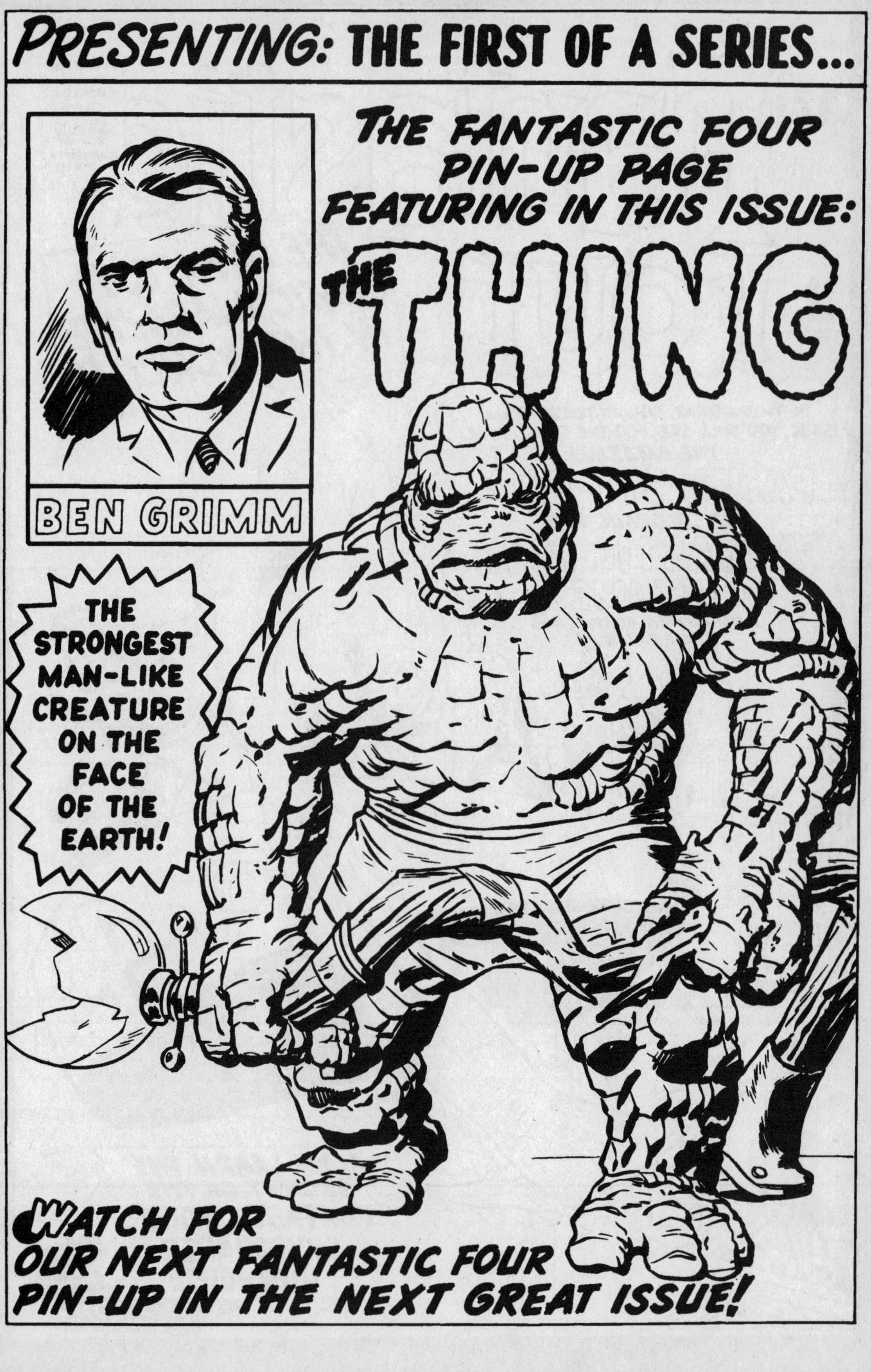
PRESENTING: THE FIRST OF A SERIES...
THE FANTASTIC FOUR PIN-UP PAGE FEATURING IN THIS ISSUE:
THE THING
BEN GRIMM
THE STRONGEST MAN-LIKE CREATURE ON THE FACE OF THE EARTH!
WATCH FOR OUR NEXT FANTASTIC FOUR PIN-UP IN THE NEXT GREAT ISSUE!

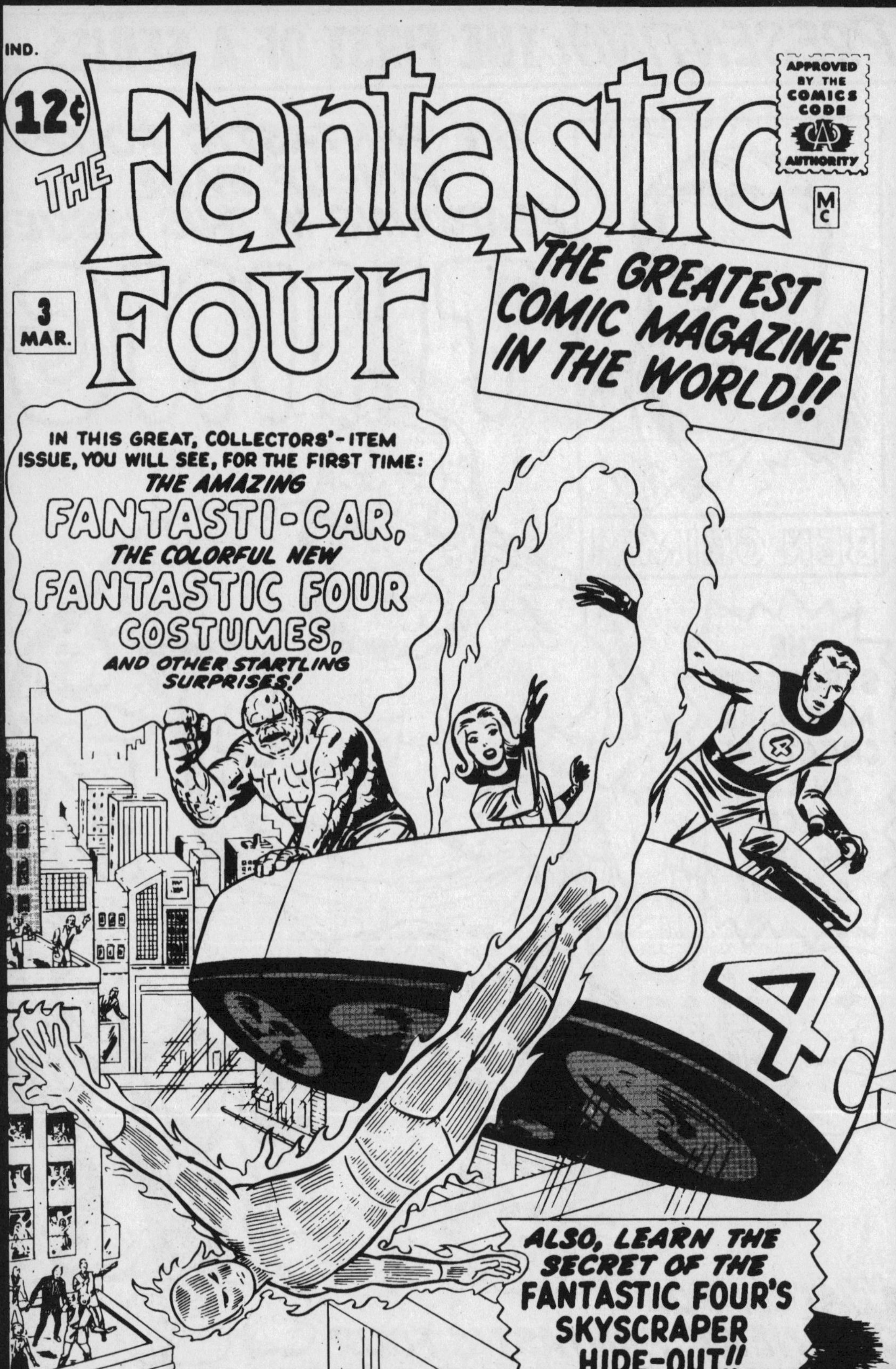

IND.
12¢
THE Fantastic Four
3 MAR.
APPROVED BY THE COMICS CODE AUTHORITY
MC
THE GREATEST COMIC MAGAZINE IN THE WORLD!!
IN THIS GREAT, COLLECTORS'-ITEM ISSUE, YOU WILL SEE, FOR THE FIRST TIME: THE AMAZING FANTASTI-CAR, THE COLORFUL NEW FANTASTIC FOUR COSTUMES, AND OTHER STARTLING SURPRISES!
ALSO, LEARN THE SECRET OF THE FANTASTIC FOUR'S SKYSCRAPER HIDE-OUT!!

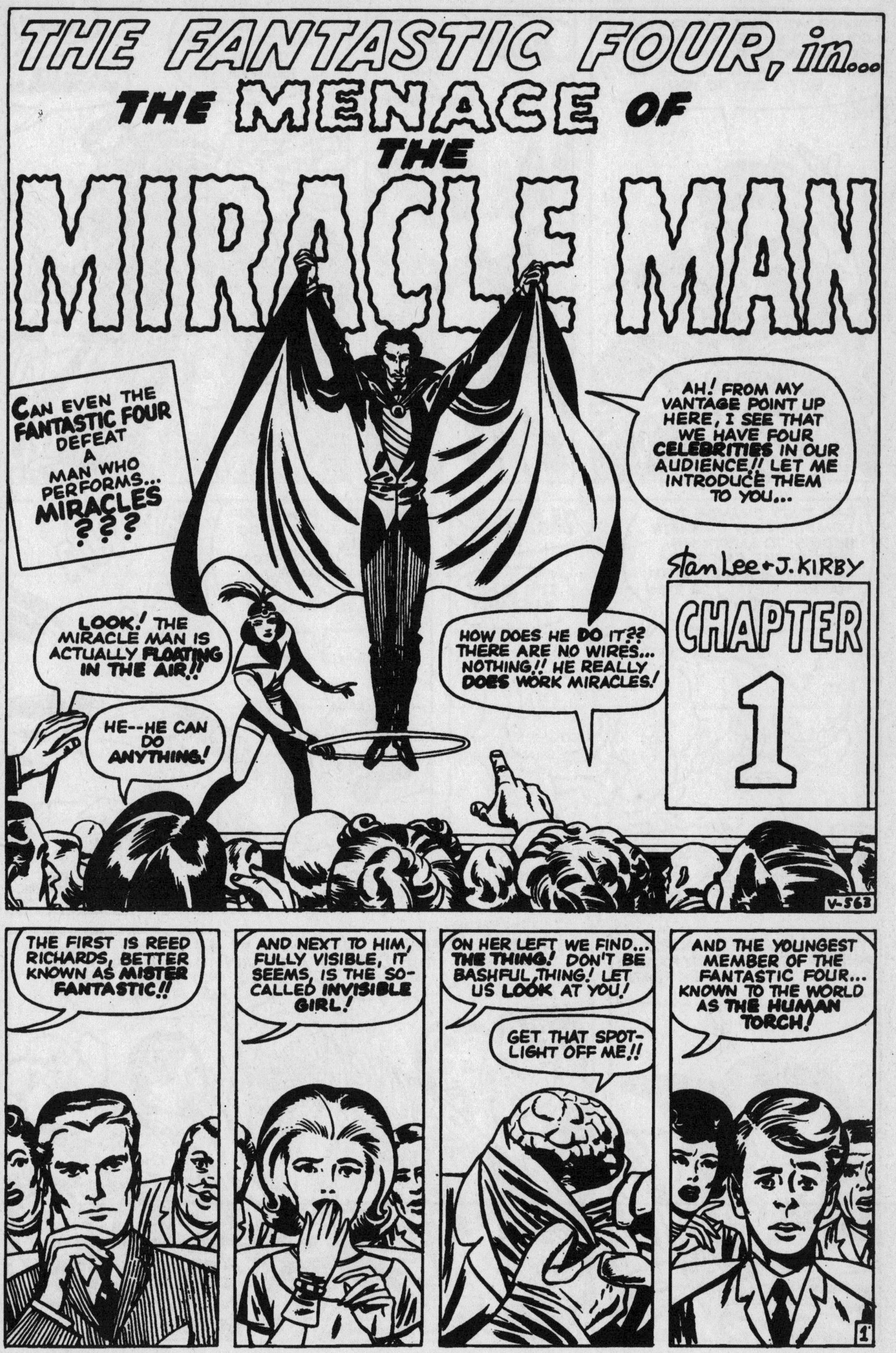
THE FANTASTIC FOUR, in...
THE MENACE OF THE MIRACLE MAN
CAN EVEN THE FANTASTIC FOUR DEFEAT A MAN WHO PERFORMS... MIRACLES ???
AH! FROM MY VANTAGE POINT UP HERE, I SEE THAT WE HAVE FOUR CELEBRITIES IN OUR AUDIENCE!! LET ME INTRODUCE THEM TO YOU...
Stan Lee + J. KIRBY
CHAPTER 1
LOOK! THE MIRACLE MAN IS ACTUALLY FLOATING IN THE AIR!!
HE--HE CAN DO ANYTHING!
HOW DOES HE DO IT?? THERE ARE NO WIRES... NOTHING!! HE REALLY DOES WORK MIRACLES!
V-563
THE FIRST IS REED RICHARDS, BETTER KNOWN AS MISTER FANTASTIC!!
AND NEXT TO HIM, FULLY VISIBLE, IT SEEMS, IS THE SO-CALLED INVISIBLE GIRL!
ON HER LEFT WE FIND... THE THING! DON'T BE BASHFUL, THING! LET US LOOK AT YOU!
GET THAT SPOT-LIGHT OFF ME!!
AND THE YOUNGEST MEMBER OF THE FANTASTIC FOUR... KNOWN TO THE WORLD AS THE HUMAN TORCH!
1

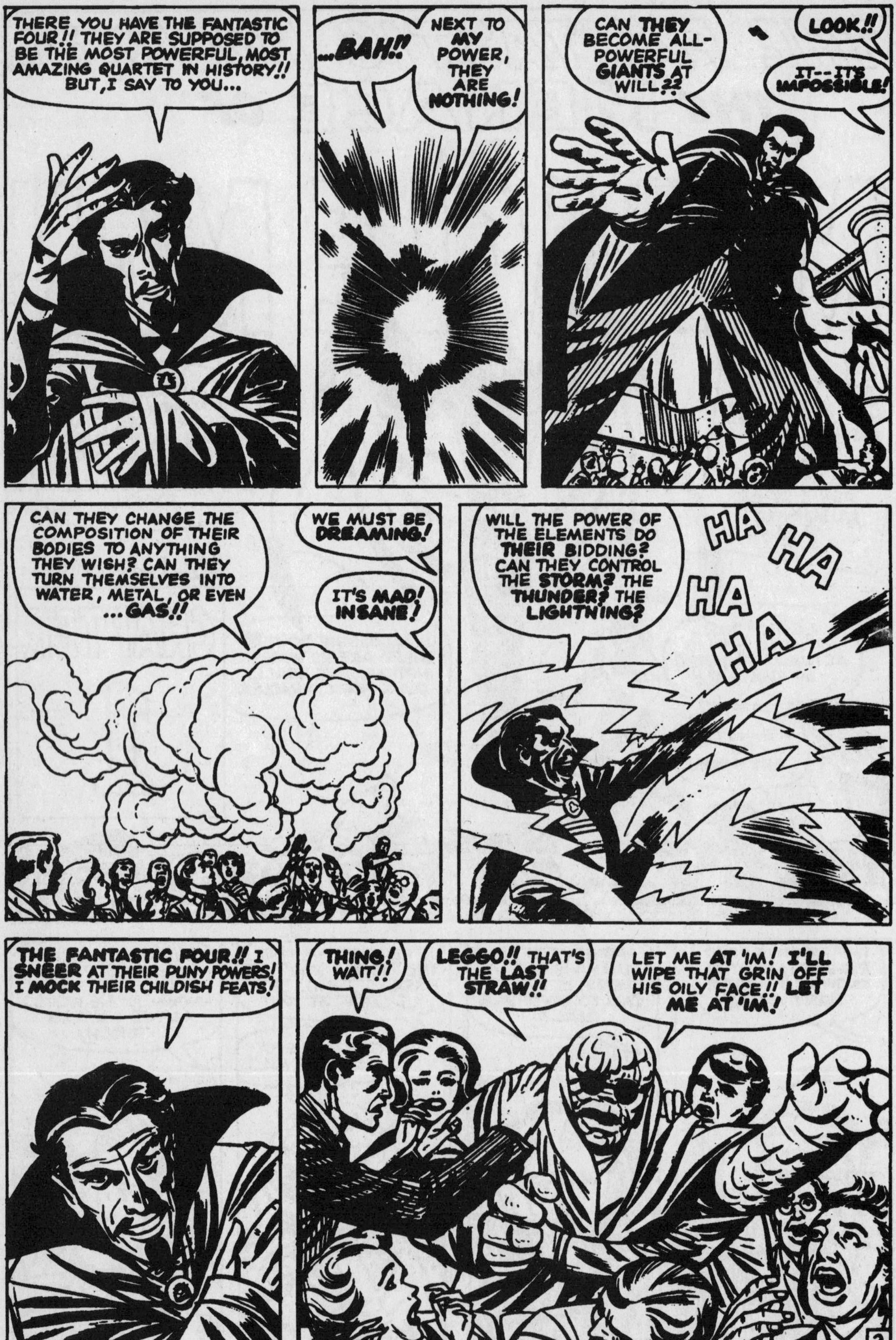
THERE YOU HAVE THE FANTASTIC FOUR!! THEY ARE SUPPOSED TO BE THE MOST POWERFUL, MOST AMAZING QUARTET IN HISTORY!! BUT, I SAY TO YOU...
...BAH!!
NEXT TO MY POWER, THEY ARE NOTHING!
CAN THEY BECOME ALL-POWERFUL GIANTS AT WILL??
LOOK!!
IT--IT'S IMPOSSIBLE!
CAN THEY CHANGE THE COMPOSITION OF THEIR BODIES TO ANYTHING THEY WISH? CAN THEY TURN THEMSELVES INTO WATER, METAL, OR EVEN ...GAS!!
WE MUST BE DREAMING!
IT'S MAD! INSANE!
WILL THE POWER OF THE ELEMENTS DO THEIR BIDDING? CAN THEY CONTROL THE STORM? THE THUNDER? THE LIGHTNING?
HA HA HA HA
THE FANTASTIC FOUR!! I SNEER AT THEIR PUNY POWERS! I MOCK THEIR CHILDISH FEATS!
THING! WAIT!!
LEGGO!! THAT'S THE LAST STRAW!!
LET ME AT 'IM! I'LL WIPE THAT GRIN OFF HIS OILY FACE!! LET ME AT 'IM!
2

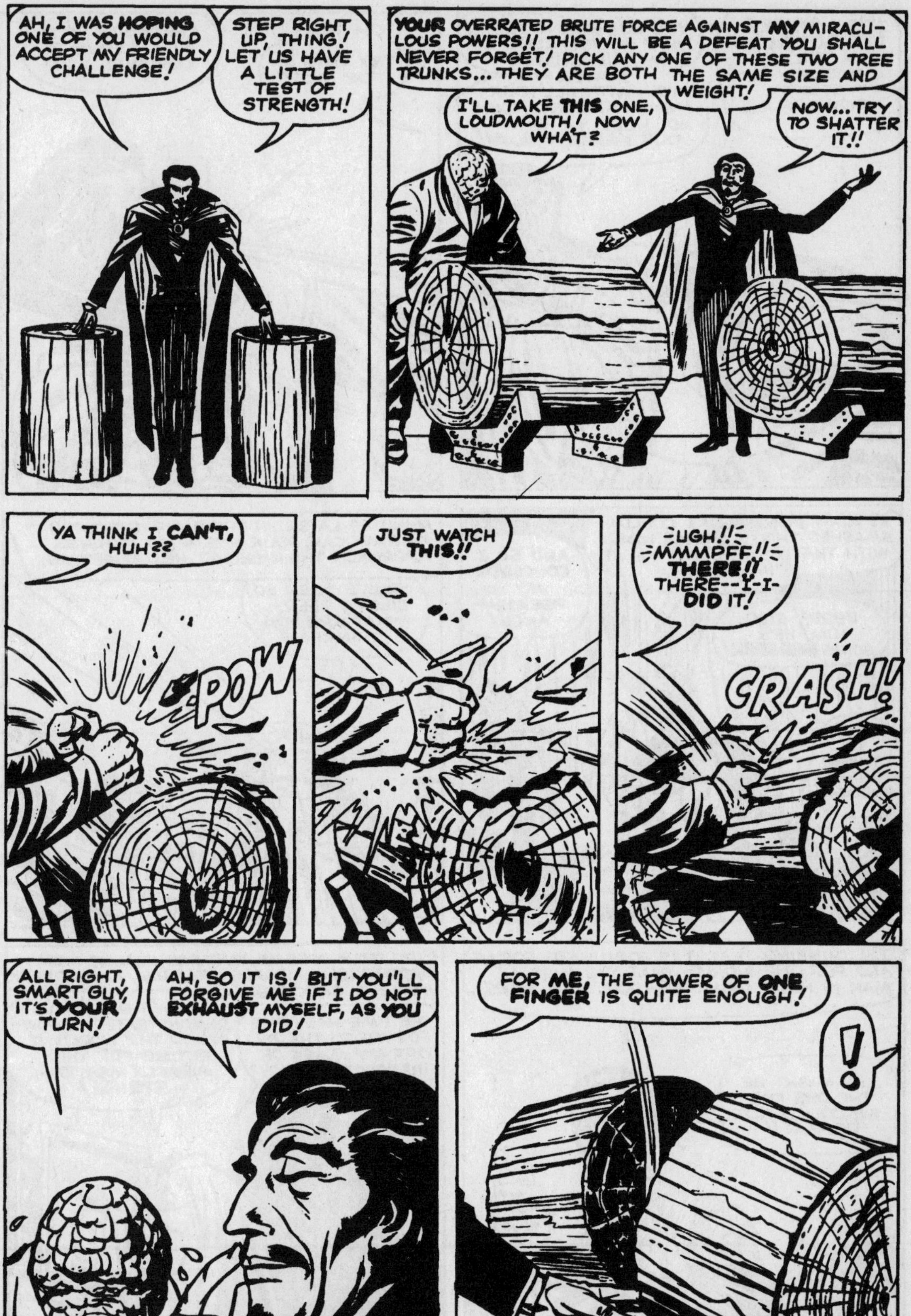

AH, I WAS HOPING ONE OF YOU WOULD ACCEPT MY FRIENDLY CHALLENGE!
STEP RIGHT UP, THING! LET US HAVE A LITTLE TEST OF STRENGTH!
YOUR OVERRATED BRUTE FORCE AGAINST MY MIRACULOUS POWERS!! THIS WILL BE A DEFEAT YOU SHALL NEVER FORGET! PICK ANY ONE OF THESE TWO TREE TRUNKS... THEY ARE BOTH THE SAME SIZE AND WEIGHT!
I'LL TAKE THIS ONE, LOUDMOUTH! NOW WHAT?
NOW... TRY TO SHATTER IT!!
YA THINK I CAN'T, HUH??
POW
JUST WATCH THIS!!
UGH!! MMMPFF!! THERE!! THERE--I-I-DID IT!
CRASH!
ALL RIGHT, SMART GUY, IT'S YOUR TURN!
AH, SO IT IS! BUT YOU'LL FORGIVE ME IF I DO NOT EXHAUST MYSELF, AS YOU DID!
FOR ME, THE POWER OF ONE FINGER IS QUITE ENOUGH!
!
3

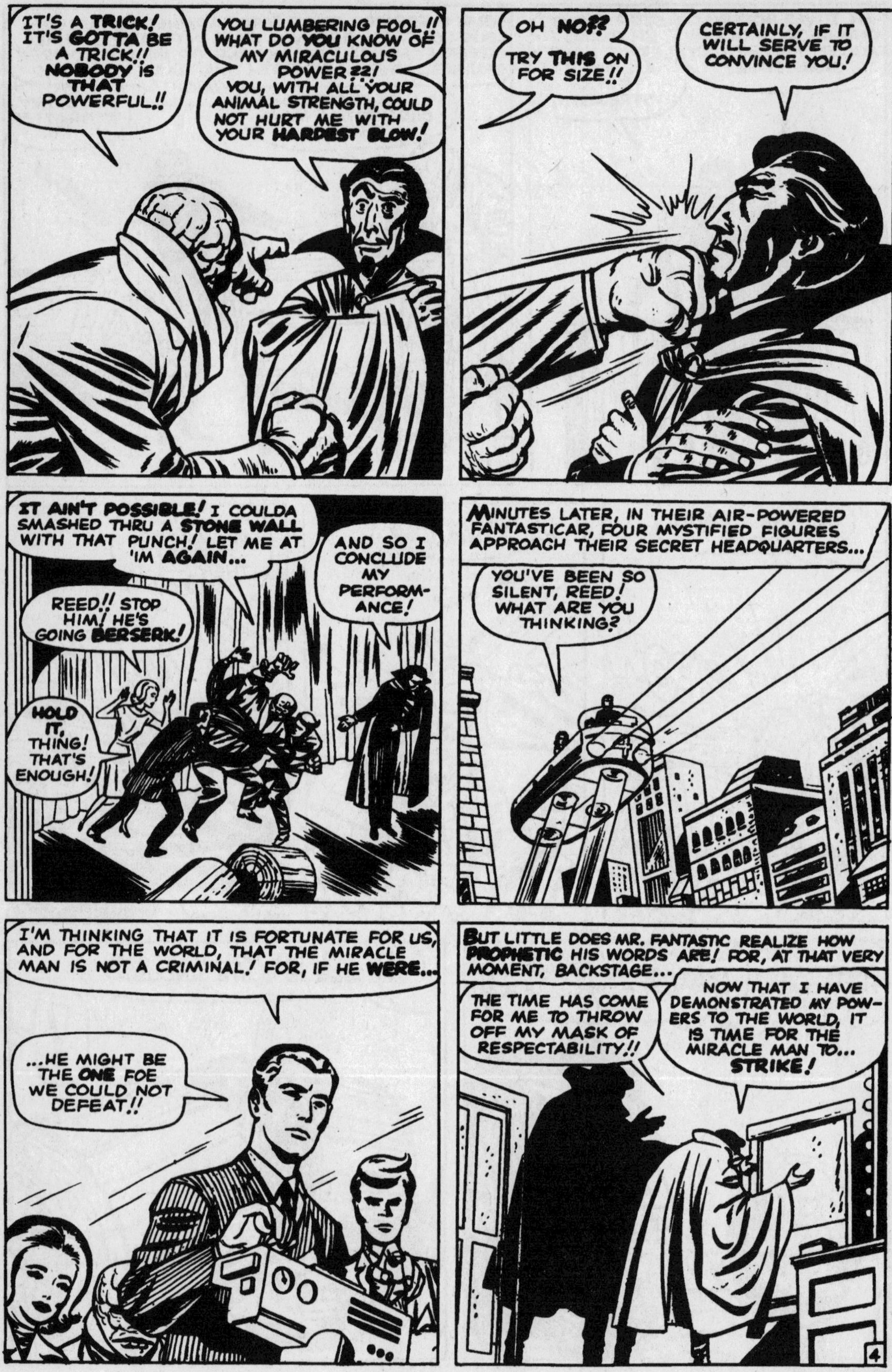

IT'S A TRICK! IT'S GOTTA BE A TRICK!! NOBODY IS THAT POWERFUL!!
YOU LUMBERING FOOL!! WHAT DO YOU KNOW OF MY MIRACULOUS POWER??! YOU, WITH ALL YOUR ANIMAL STRENGTH, COULD NOT HURT ME WITH YOUR HARDEST BLOW!
OH NO?? TRY THIS ON FOR SIZE!!
CERTAINLY, IF IT WILL SERVE TO CONVINCE YOU!
IT AIN'T POSSIBLE! I COULDA SMASHED THRU A STONE WALL WITH THAT PUNCH! LET ME AT 'IM AGAIN...
AND SO I CONCLUDE MY PERFORMANCE!
REED!! STOP HIM! HE'S GOING BERSERK!
HOLD IT, THING! THAT'S ENOUGH!
MINUTES LATER, IN THEIR AIR-POWERED FANTASTICAR, FOUR MYSTIFIED FIGURES APPROACH THEIR SECRET HEADQUARTERS...
YOU'VE BEEN SO SILENT, REED! WHAT ARE YOU THINKING?
I'M THINKING THAT IT IS FORTUNATE FOR US, AND FOR THE WORLD, THAT THE MIRACLE MAN IS NOT A CRIMINAL! FOR, IF HE WERE...
...HE MIGHT BE THE ONE FOE WE COULD NOT DEFEAT!!
BUT LITTLE DOES MR. FANTASTIC REALIZE HOW PROPHETIC HIS WORDS ARE! FOR, AT THAT VERY MOMENT, BACKSTAGE...
THE TIME HAS COME FOR ME TO THROW OFF MY MASK OF RESPECTABILITY!!
NOW THAT I HAVE DEMONSTRATED MY POWERS TO THE WORLD, IT IS TIME FOR THE MIRACLE MAN TO... STRIKE!
4

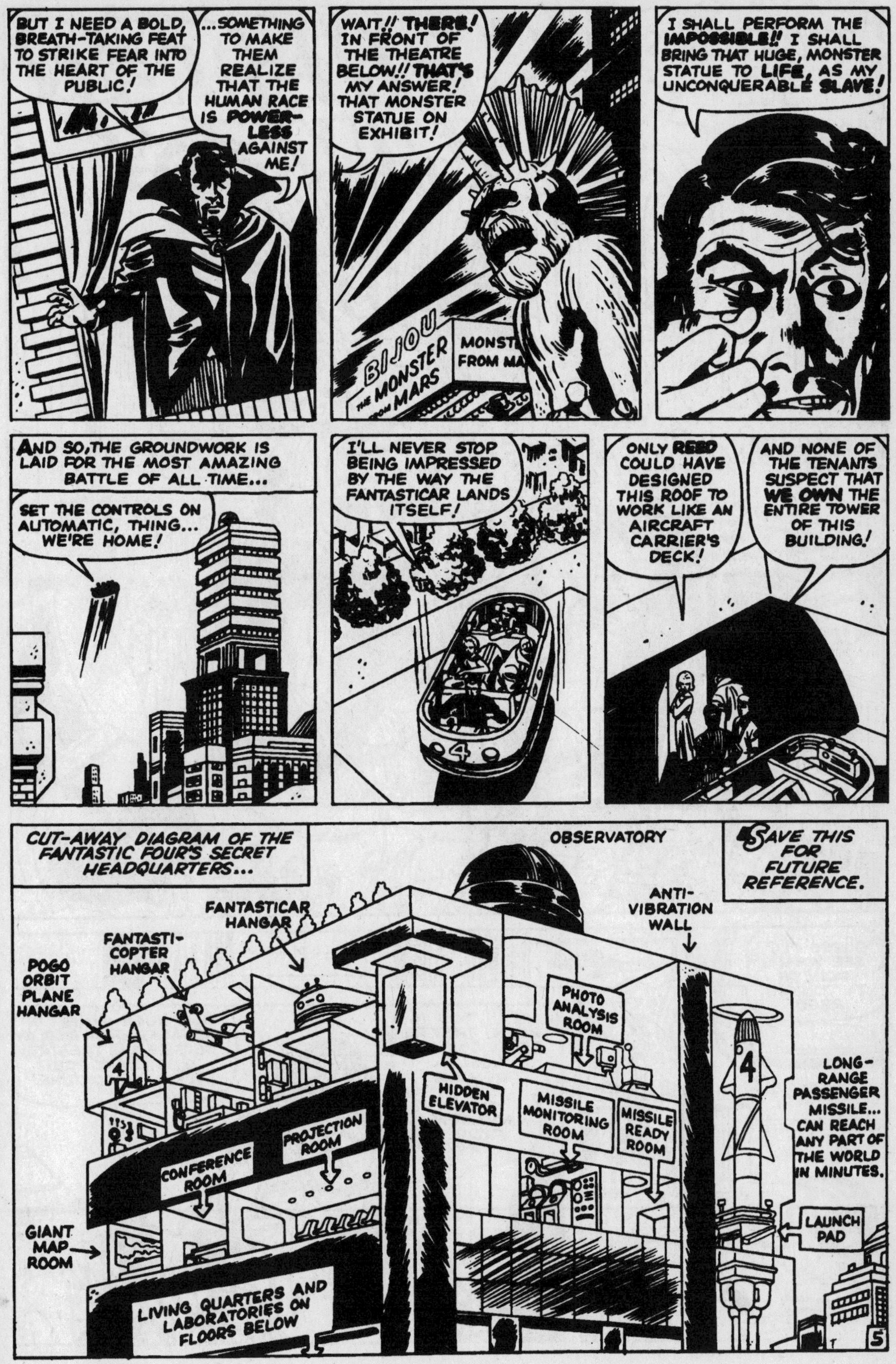
BUT I NEED A BOLD, BREATH-TAKING FEAT TO STRIKE FEAR INTO THE HEART OF THE PUBLIC!
...SOMETHING TO MAKE THEM REALIZE THAT THE HUMAN RACE IS POWER-LESS AGAINST ME!
WAIT!! THERE! IN FRONT OF THE THEATRE BELOW!! THAT'S MY ANSWER! THAT MONSTER STATUE ON EXHIBIT!
BIJOU
THE MONSTER FROM MARS
I SHALL PERFORM THE IMPOSSIBLE!! I SHALL BRING THAT HUGE, MONSTER STATUE TO LIFE, AS MY UNCONQUERABLE SLAVE!
AND SO, THE GROUNDWORK IS LAID FOR THE MOST AMAZING BATTLE OF ALL TIME...
SET THE CONTROLS ON AUTOMATIC, THING... WE'RE HOME!
I'LL NEVER STOP BEING IMPRESSED BY THE WAY THE FANTASTICAR LANDS ITSELF!
ONLY REED COULD HAVE DESIGNED THIS ROOF TO WORK LIKE AN AIRCRAFT CARRIER'S DECK!
AND NONE OF THE TENANTS SUSPECT THAT WE OWN THE ENTIRE TOWER OF THIS BUILDING!
CUT-AWAY DIAGRAM OF THE FANTASTIC FOUR'S SECRET HEADQUARTERS...
OBSERVATORY
SAVE THIS FOR FUTURE REFERENCE.
FANTASTICAR HANGAR
FANTASTI-COPTER HANGAR
POGO ORBIT PLANE HANGAR
ANTI-VIBRATION WALL
PHOTO ANALYSIS ROOM
HIDDEN ELEVATOR
MISSILE MONITORING ROOM
MISSILE READY ROOM
LONG-RANGE PASSENGER MISSILE... CAN REACH ANY PART OF THE WORLD IN MINUTES.
PROJECTION ROOM
CONFERENCE ROOM
GIANT MAP ROOM
LAUNCH PAD
LIVING QUARTERS AND LABORATORIES ON FLOORS BELOW
5

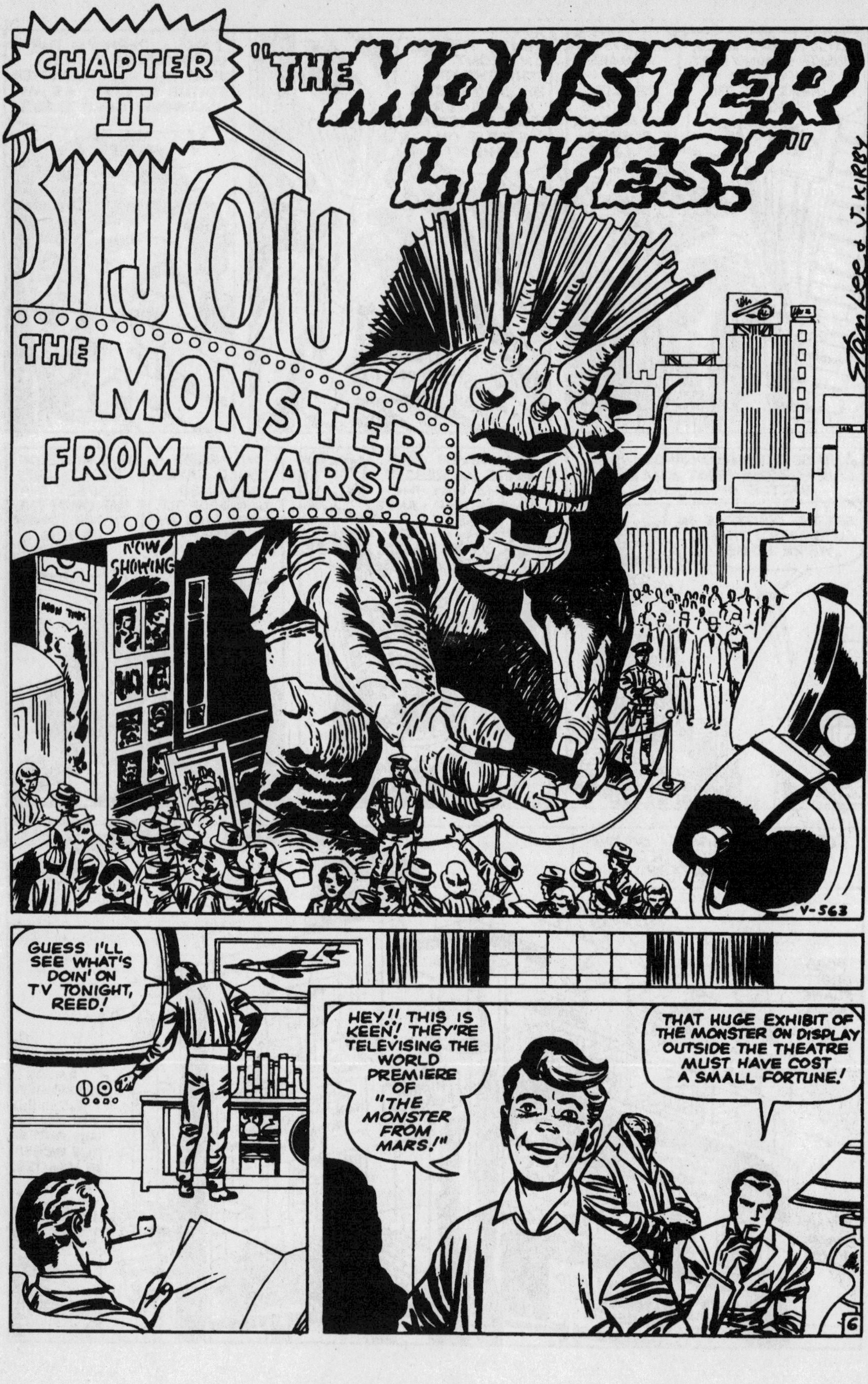
CHAPTER II
"THE MONSTER LIVES!"
Stan Lee & J. Kirby
BIJOU
THE MONSTER FROM MARS!
NOW SHOWING
V-563
GUESS I'LL SEE WHAT'S DOIN' ON TV TONIGHT, REED!
HEY!! THIS IS KEEN! THEY'RE TELEVISING THE WORLD PREMIERE OF "THE MONSTER FROM MARS!"
THAT HUGE EXHIBIT OF THE MONSTER ON DISPLAY OUTSIDE THE THEATRE MUST HAVE COST A SMALL FORTUNE!
6

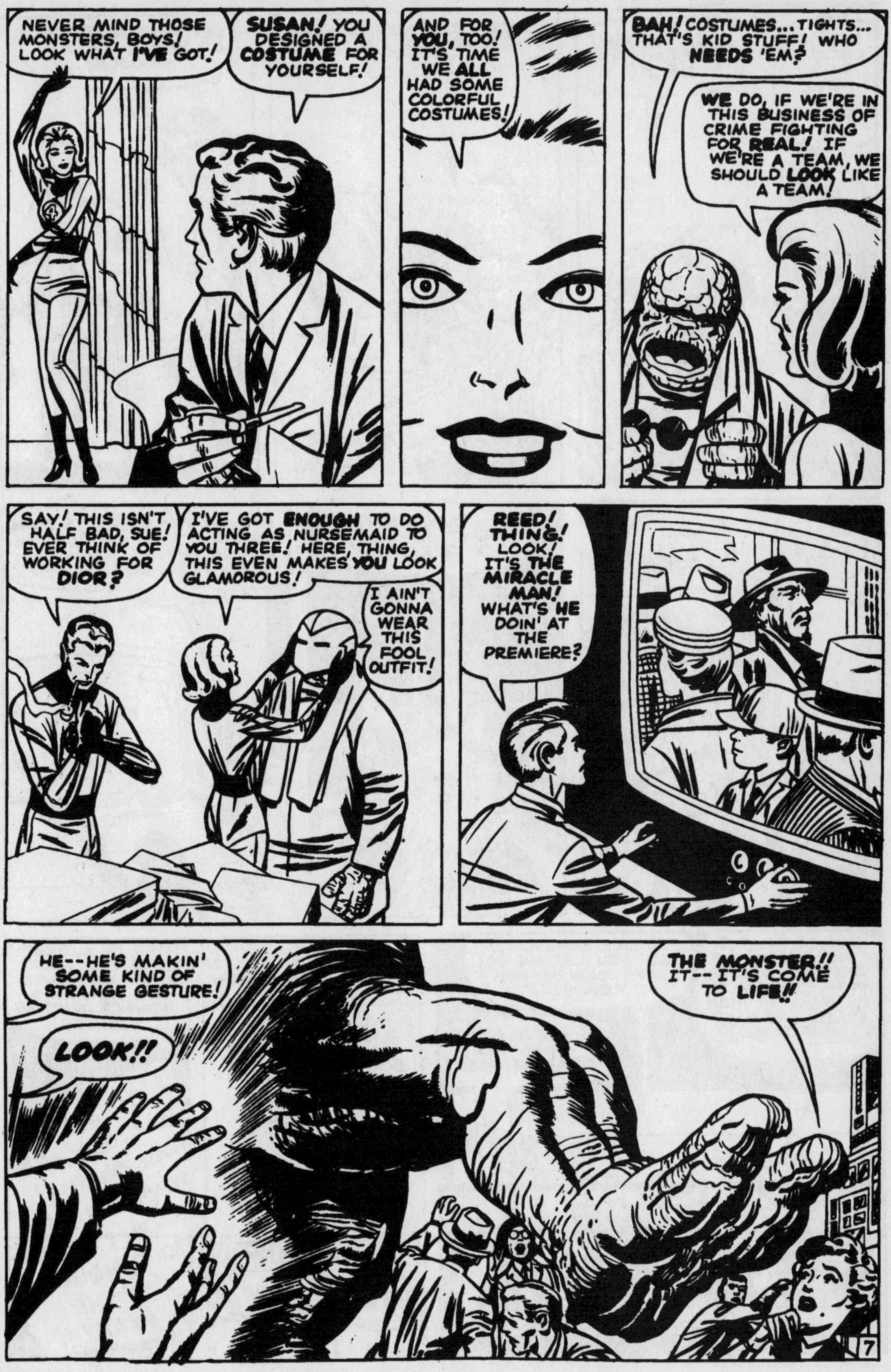

NEVER MIND THOSE MONSTERS, BOYS! LOOK WHAT I'VE GOT!
SUSAN! YOU DESIGNED A COSTUME FOR YOURSELF!
AND FOR YOU, TOO! IT'S TIME WE ALL HAD SOME COLORFUL COSTUMES!
BAH! COSTUMES... TIGHTS... THAT'S KID STUFF! WHO NEEDS 'EM?
WE DO, IF WE'RE IN THIS BUSINESS OF CRIME FIGHTING FOR REAL! IF WE'RE A TEAM, WE SHOULD LOOK LIKE A TEAM!
SAY! THIS ISN'T HALF BAD, SUE! EVER THINK OF WORKING FOR DIOR?
I'VE GOT ENOUGH TO DO ACTING AS NURSEMAID TO YOU THREE! HERE, THING, THIS EVEN MAKES YOU LOOK GLAMOROUS!
I AIN'T GONNA WEAR THIS FOOL OUTFIT!
REED! THING! LOOK! IT'S THE MIRACLE MAN! WHAT'S HE DOIN' AT THE PREMIERE?
HE--HE'S MAKIN' SOME KIND OF STRANGE GESTURE!
LOOK!!
THE MONSTER!! IT--IT'S COME TO LIFE!!
7

GET THE CROWDS BACK! WE'LL TRY TO STOP IT!

KEEP FIRING!! I'LL RADIO FOR HELP!!

JUMP, JOE! HE'S SQUEEZIN' THE CAR LIKE IT'S A PAPER BOX!

SET THAT BAZOOKA UP HERE!! ON THE DOUBLE!

OKAY!! LET 'IM HAVE IT!!

NO... WAIT!! LOOK!!

HE--HE VANISHED!! RIGHT IN FRONT OF OUR EYES!

POP!

IT WAS THE MIRACLE MAN! HE DID IT! HE CAUSED THE WHOLE THING! I DON'T KNOW HOW, BUT HE DID IT!

CLICK!

THIS IS WHAT I DREADED!! THE ONE MAN WHOSE POWERS SEEM TO BE GREATER THAN OURS... HE MUST BE STOPPED!!

POWER--SHMOWER!! JUST YOU LET ME GET MY HANDS ON HIM AGAIN...!!

WE--WE'VE GOT TO WARN THE COMMISSIONER!

BUT, AS SUE IS ABOUT TO LEARN, THE COMMISSIONER HAS ALREADY BEEN WARNED...

PHONE CALL FOR YOU, SIR, FROM THE FANTASTIC FOUR!

GOOD! I WANT TO READ THEM THIS NOTE I RECEIVED!

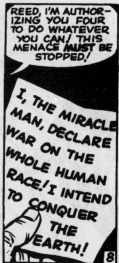

REED, I'M AUTHORIZING YOU FOUR TO DO WHATEVER YOU CAN! THIS MENACE MUST BE STOPPED!

I, THE MIRACLE MAN, DECLARE WAR ON THE WHOLE HUMAN RACE! I INTEND TO CONQUER THE EARTH!

8

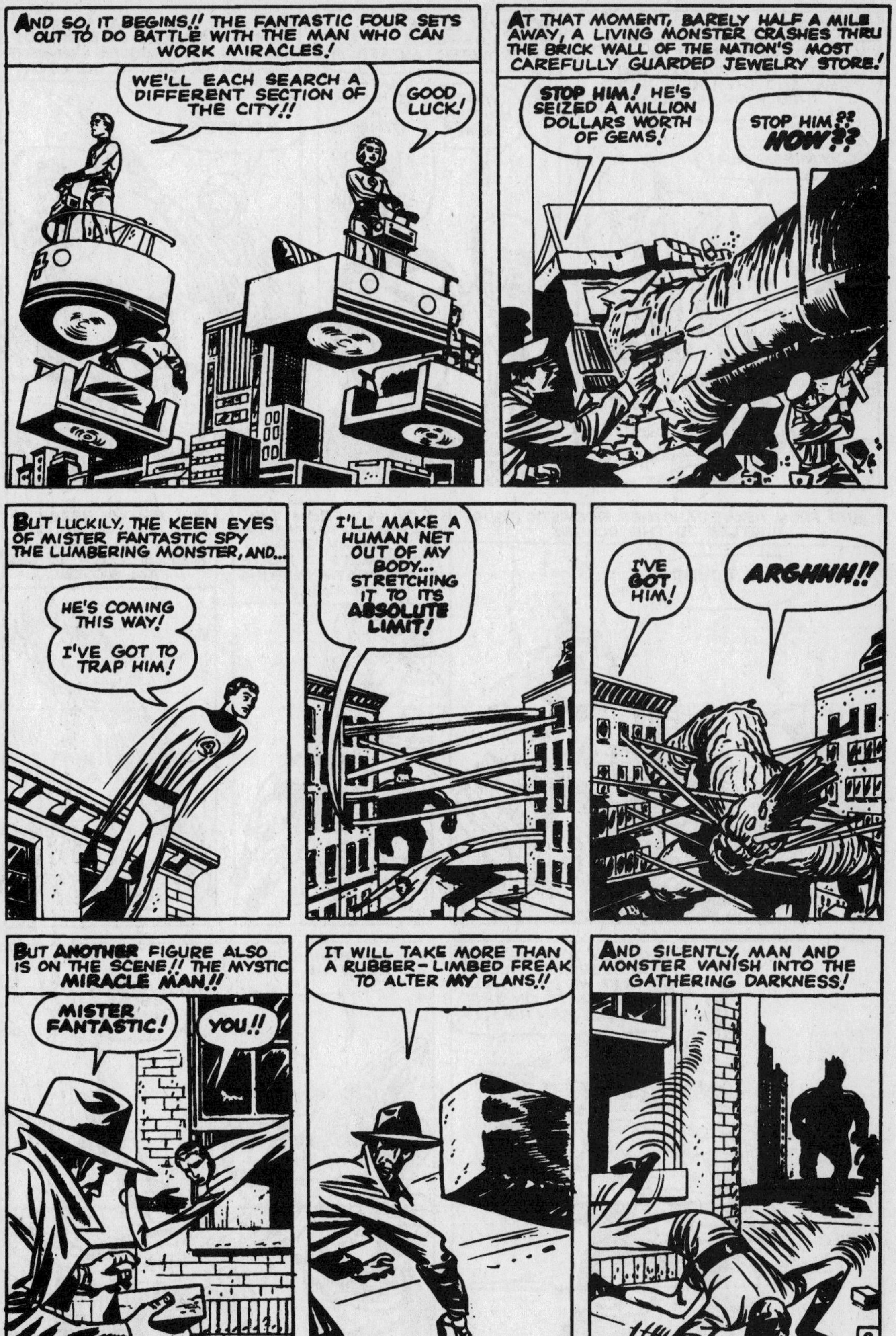
AND SO, IT BEGINS!! THE FANTASTIC FOUR SETS OUT TO DO BATTLE WITH THE MAN WHO CAN WORK MIRACLES!
WE'LL EACH SEARCH A DIFFERENT SECTION OF THE CITY!!
GOOD LUCK!
AT THAT MOMENT, BARELY HALF A MILE AWAY, A LIVING MONSTER CRASHES THRU THE BRICK WALL OF THE NATION'S MOST CAREFULLY GUARDED JEWELRY STORE!
STOP HIM! HE'S SEIZED A MILLION DOLLARS WORTH OF GEMS!
STOP HIM?? HOW??
BUT LUCKILY, THE KEEN EYES OF MISTER FANTASTIC SPY THE LUMBERING MONSTER, AND...
HE'S COMING THIS WAY!
I'VE GOT TO TRAP HIM!
I'LL MAKE A HUMAN NET OUT OF MY BODY... STRETCHING IT TO ITS ABSOLUTE LIMIT!
I'VE GOT HIM!
ARGHHH!!
BUT ANOTHER FIGURE ALSO IS ON THE SCENE!! THE MYSTIC MIRACLE MAN!!
MISTER FANTASTIC!
YOU!!
IT WILL TAKE MORE THAN A RUBBER-LIMBED FREAK TO ALTER MY PLANS!!
AND SILENTLY, MAN AND MONSTER VANISH INTO THE GATHERING DARKNESS!
9

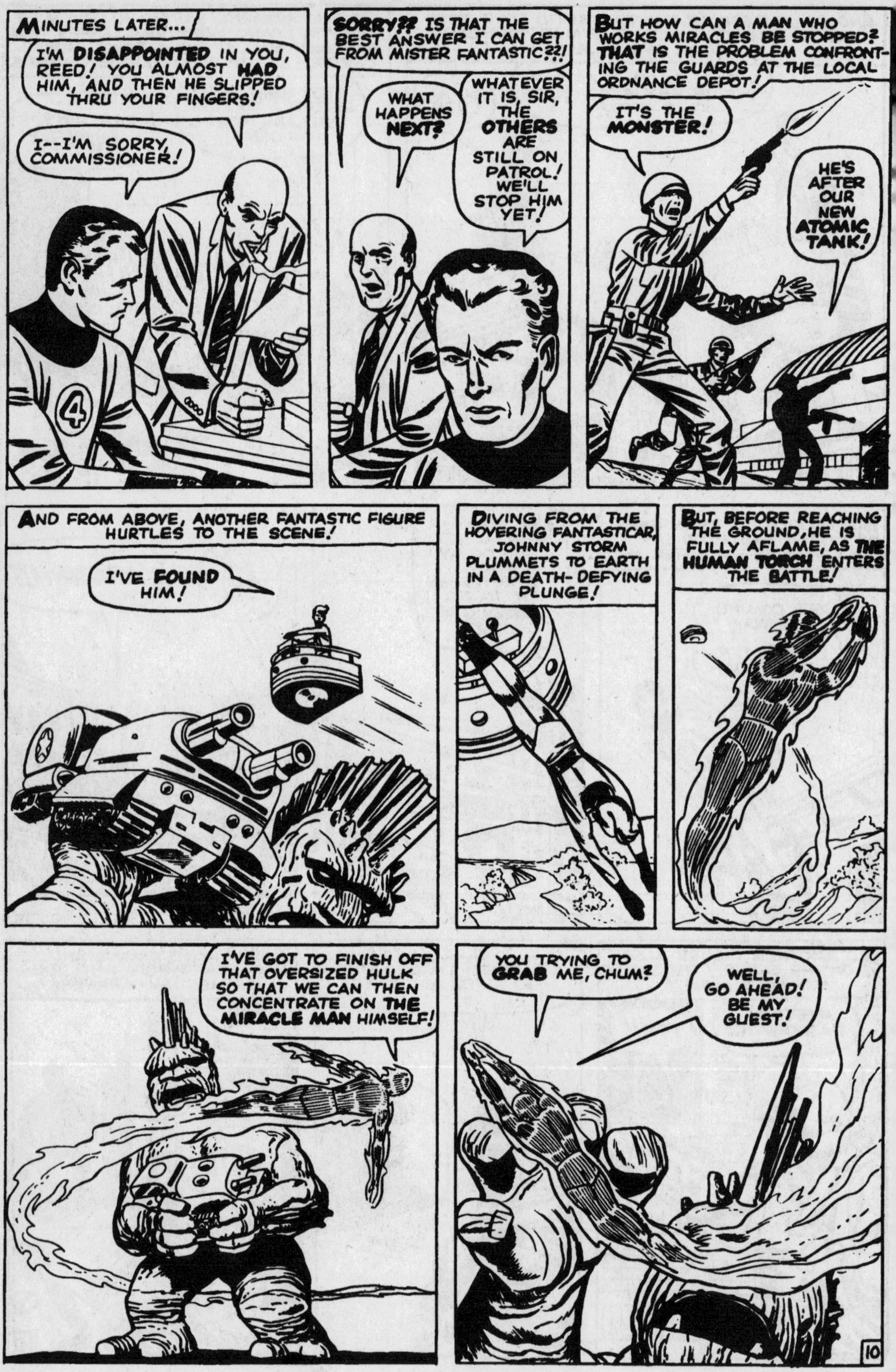

MINUTES LATER...
I'M DISAPPOINTED IN YOU, REED! YOU ALMOST HAD HIM, AND THEN HE SLIPPED THRU YOUR FINGERS!
I--I'M SORRY, COMMISSIONER!
SORRY?? IS THAT THE BEST ANSWER I CAN GET FROM MISTER FANTASTIC??!
WHAT HAPPENS NEXT?
WHATEVER IT IS, SIR, THE OTHERS ARE STILL ON PATROL! WE'LL STOP HIM YET!
BUT HOW CAN A MAN WHO WORKS MIRACLES BE STOPPED? THAT IS THE PROBLEM CONFRONTING THE GUARDS AT THE LOCAL ORDNANCE DEPOT!
IT'S THE MONSTER!
HE'S AFTER OUR NEW ATOMIC TANK!
AND FROM ABOVE, ANOTHER FANTASTIC FIGURE HURTLES TO THE SCENE!
I'VE FOUND HIM!
DIVING FROM THE HOVERING FANTASTICAR, JOHNNY STORM PLUMMETS TO EARTH IN A DEATH-DEFYING PLUNGE!
BUT, BEFORE REACHING THE GROUND, HE IS FULLY AFLAME, AS THE HUMAN TORCH ENTERS THE BATTLE!
I'VE GOT TO FINISH OFF THAT OVERSIZED HULK SO THAT WE CAN THEN CONCENTRATE ON THE MIRACLE MAN HIMSELF!
YOU TRYING TO GRAB ME, CHUM?
WELL, GO AHEAD! BE MY GUEST!
10

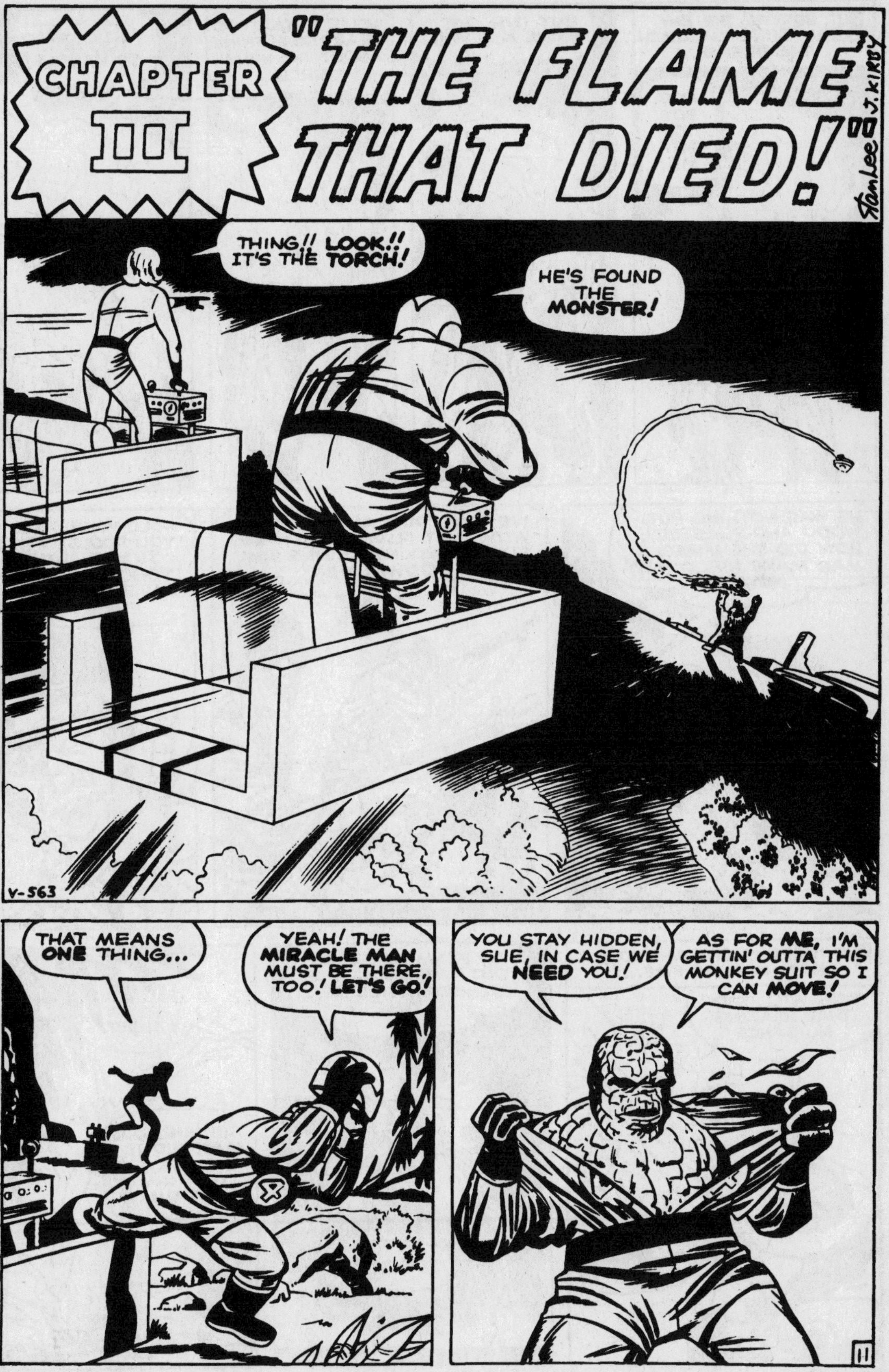

CHAPTER III
"THE FLAME THAT DIED!"
Stan Lee
J. KIRBY
THING!! LOOK!! IT'S THE TORCH!
HE'S FOUND THE MONSTER!
V-563
THAT MEANS ONE THING...
YEAH! THE MIRACLE MAN MUST BE THERE, TOO! LET'S GO!
YOU STAY HIDDEN, SUE, IN CASE WE NEED YOU!
AS FOR ME, I'M GETTIN' OUTTA THIS MONKEY SUIT SO I CAN MOVE!
11

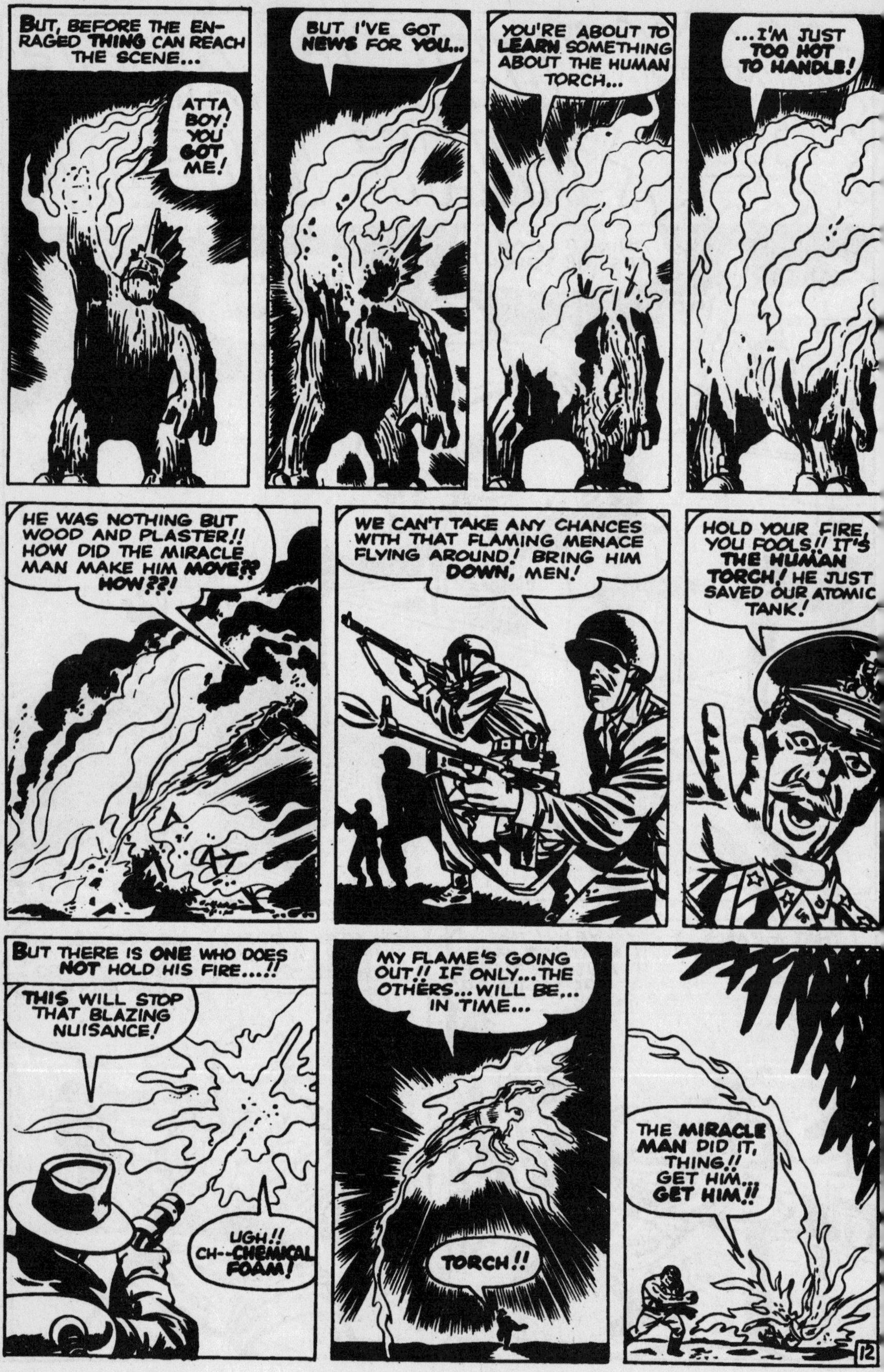
BUT, BEFORE THE ENRAGED THING CAN REACH THE SCENE...
ATTA BOY! YOU GOT ME!
BUT I'VE GOT NEWS FOR YOU...
YOU'RE ABOUT TO LEARN SOMETHING ABOUT THE HUMAN TORCH...
...I'M JUST TOO HOT TO HANDLE!
HE WAS NOTHING BUT WOOD AND PLASTER!! HOW DID THE MIRACLE MAN MAKE HIM MOVE?? HOW??!
WE CAN'T TAKE ANY CHANCES WITH THAT FLAMING MENACE FLYING AROUND! BRING HIM DOWN, MEN!
HOLD YOUR FIRE, YOU FOOLS!! IT'S THE HUMAN TORCH! HE JUST SAVED OUR ATOMIC TANK!
BUT THERE IS ONE WHO DOES NOT HOLD HIS FIRE....!!
THIS WILL STOP THAT BLAZING NUISANCE!
UGH!! CH--CHEMICAL FOAM!
MY FLAME'S GOING OUT!! IF ONLY...THE OTHERS...WILL BE... IN TIME...
TORCH!!
THE MIRACLE MAN DID IT, THING!! GET HIM... GET HIM!!
12

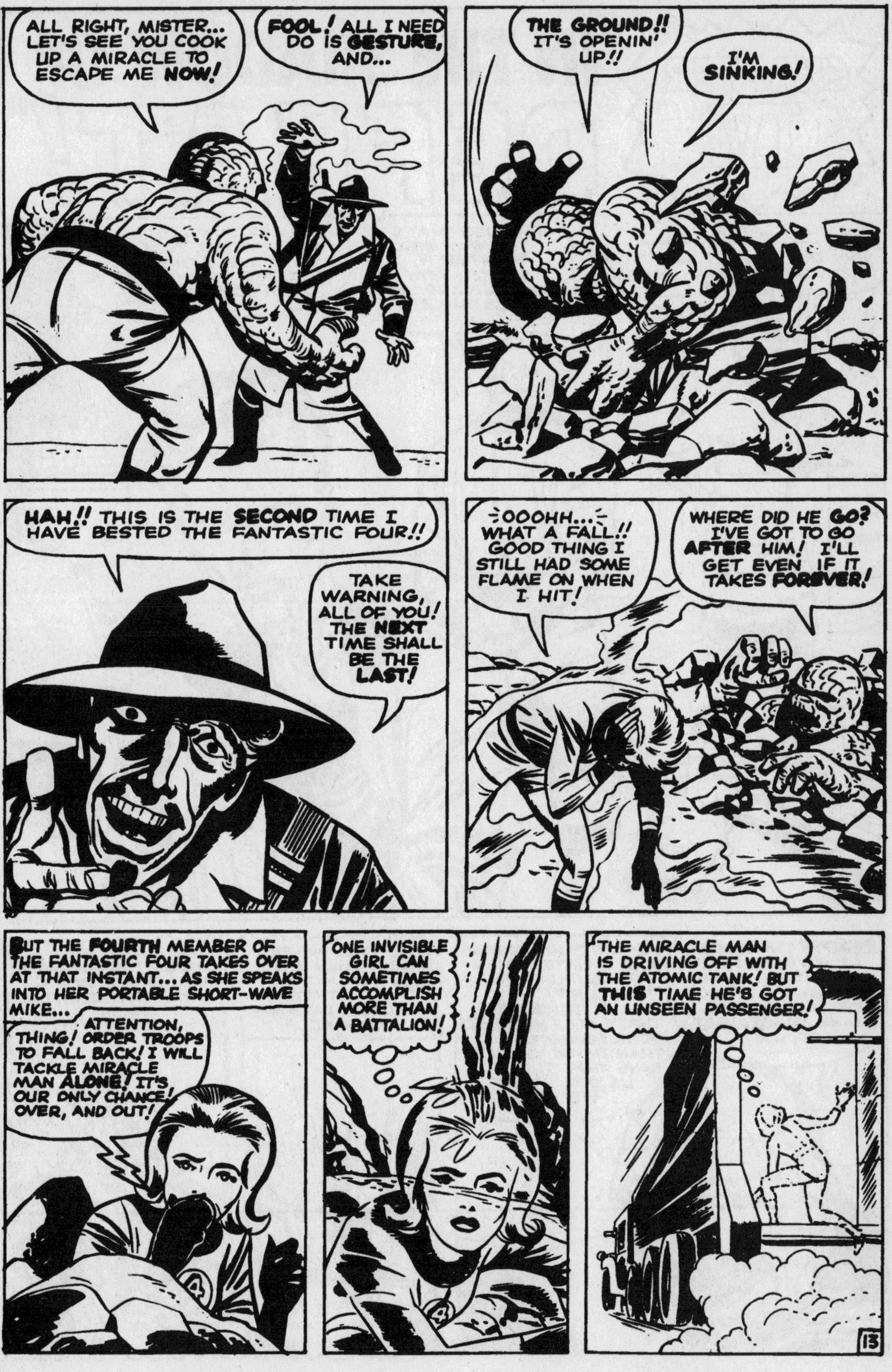

ALL RIGHT, MISTER... LET'S SEE YOU COOK UP A MIRACLE TO ESCAPE ME NOW!
FOOL! ALL I NEED DO IS GESTURE, AND...
THE GROUND!! IT'S OPENIN' UP!!
I'M SINKING!
HAH!! THIS IS THE SECOND TIME I HAVE BESTED THE FANTASTIC FOUR!!
TAKE WARNING, ALL OF YOU! THE NEXT TIME SHALL BE THE LAST!
OOOHH... WHAT A FALL!! GOOD THING I STILL HAD SOME FLAME ON WHEN I HIT!
WHERE DID HE GO? I'VE GOT TO GO AFTER HIM! I'LL GET EVEN IF IT TAKES FOREVER!
BUT THE FOURTH MEMBER OF THE FANTASTIC FOUR TAKES OVER AT THAT INSTANT... AS SHE SPEAKS INTO HER PORTABLE SHORT-WAVE MIKE...
ATTENTION, THING! ORDER TROOPS TO FALL BACK! I WILL TACKLE MIRACLE MAN ALONE! IT'S OUR ONLY CHANCE! OVER, AND OUT!
ONE INVISIBLE GIRL CAN SOMETIMES ACCOMPLISH MORE THAN A BATTALION!
THE MIRACLE MAN IS DRIVING OFF WITH THE ATOMIC TANK! BUT THIS TIME HE'S GOT AN UNSEEN PASSENGER!
13

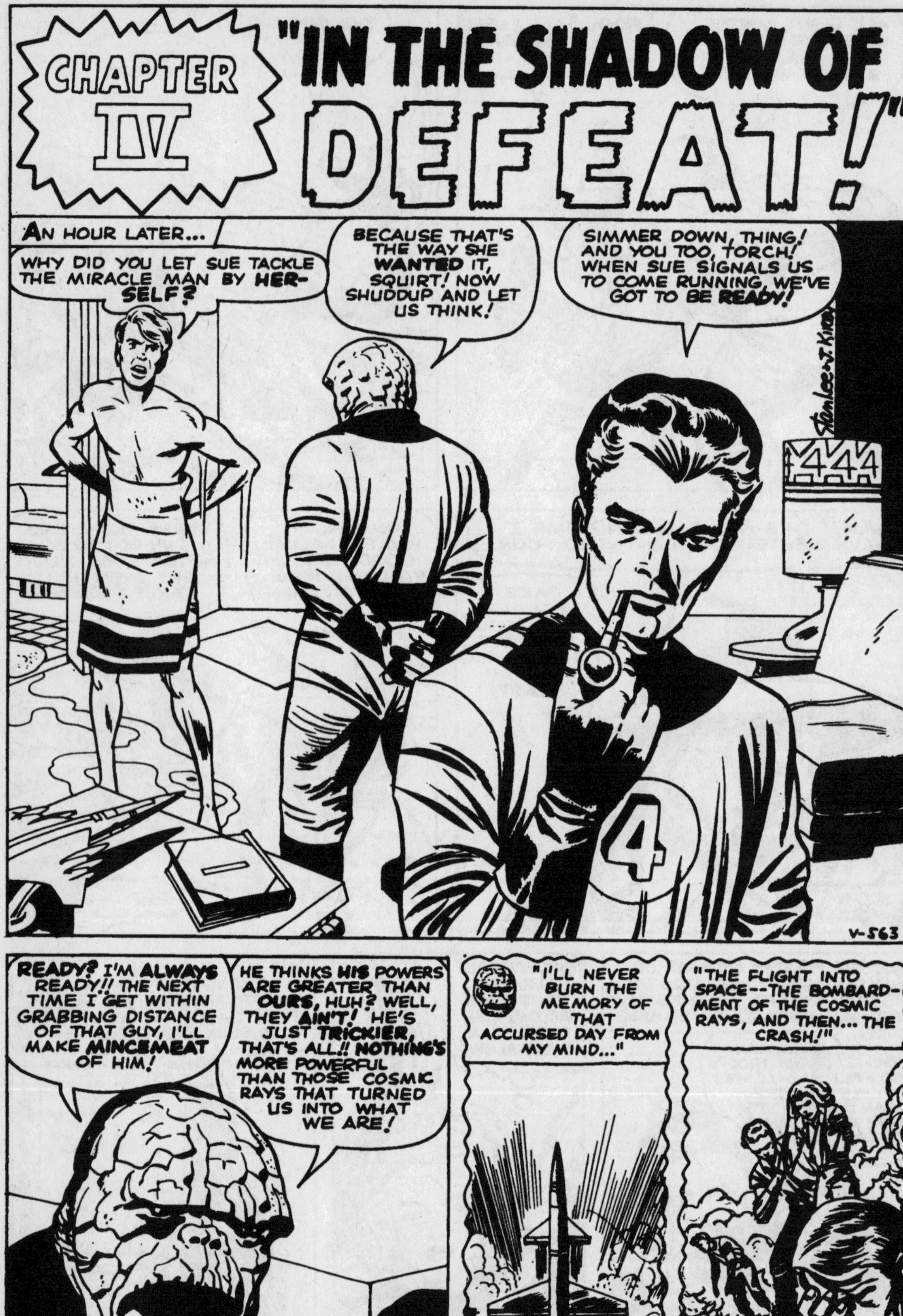
CHAPTER IV
"IN THE SHADOW OF DEFEAT!"
AN HOUR LATER...
WHY DID YOU LET SUE TACKLE THE MIRACLE MAN BY HER-SELF?
BECAUSE THAT'S THE WAY SHE WANTED IT, SQUIRT! NOW SHUDDUP AND LET US THINK!
SIMMER DOWN, THING! AND YOU TOO, TORCH! WHEN SUE SIGNALS US TO COME RUNNING, WE'VE GOT TO BE READY!
444
4
V-563
READY? I'M ALWAYS READY!! THE NEXT TIME I GET WITHIN GRABBING DISTANCE OF THAT GUY, I'LL MAKE MINCEMEAT OF HIM!
HE THINKS HIS POWERS ARE GREATER THAN OURS, HUH? WELL, THEY AIN'T! HE'S JUST TRICKIER, THAT'S ALL!! NOTHING'S MORE POWERFUL THAN THOSE COSMIC RAYS THAT TURNED US INTO WHAT WE ARE!
"I'LL NEVER BURN THE MEMORY OF THAT ACCURSED DAY FROM MY MIND..."
"THE FLIGHT INTO SPACE--THE BOMBARDMENT OF THE COSMIC RAYS, AND THEN... THE CRASH!"
14

"I'LL NEVER FORGET SEEING SUSAN GROW INVISIBLE RIGHT BEFORE MY EYES!"
"OR THE LOOK ON ALL YOUR FACES AS I TALKED TO YOU, WHILE I WAS STILL BEN GRIMM..."
"...BEFORE I BEGAN TO... CHANGE..."
"...INTO THE THING!"
"AND HOW ABOUT YOU, REED? HOW DID YOU FEEL WHEN, DURING OUR BATTLE, YOU REALIZED YOU HAD CHANGED, TOO?"
"...YOUR LIMBS HAD TURNED TO ELASTIC! YOU COULD MOLD THEM INTO ANY SHAPE!"
"BUT THE MOST UNCANNY THING OF ALL WAS SEEING JOHNNY'S BODY TURN TO LIVING FLAME!"
"BEING LIGHTER THAN AIR, AS HE BLAZED LIKE A HUMAN TORCH, HE WAS ACTUALLY ABLE TO FLY! GRAVITY MEANT NOTHING TO HIM!"
"THAT'S WHEN WE DECIDED THAT OUR DESTINIES WERE ALL ENTWINED, AND SO WE DECIDED TO REMAIN TOGETHER, AS THE FANTASTIC FOUR!"
FATE HAS BEEN GOOD TO US, BEN! WE'VE BEEN ABLE TO USE OUR POWERS TO HELP MANKIND... TO FIGHT EVIL AND INJUSTICE!
SURE! IT'S BEEN GREAT FOR YOU! BUT WHAT ABOUT ME! I'M JUST A WALKIN' FRIGHT! AN UGLY, GRUESOME THING!
15

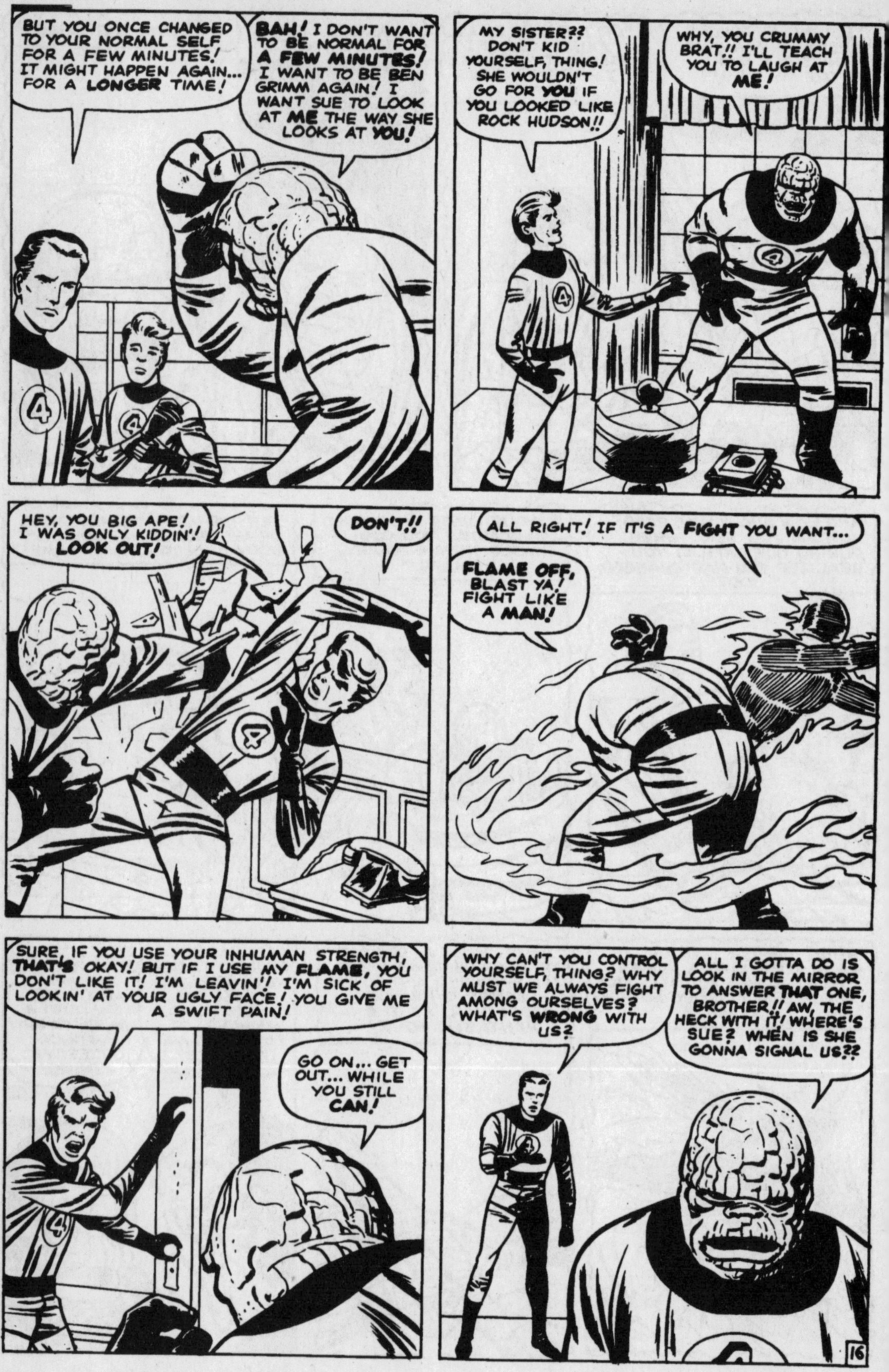
BUT YOU ONCE CHANGED TO YOUR NORMAL SELF FOR A FEW MINUTES! IT MIGHT HAPPEN AGAIN... FOR A LONGER TIME!
BAH! I DON'T WANT TO BE NORMAL FOR A FEW MINUTES! I WANT TO BE BEN GRIMM AGAIN! I WANT SUE TO LOOK AT ME THE WAY SHE LOOKS AT YOU!
MY SISTER?? DON'T KID YOURSELF, THING! SHE WOULDN'T GO FOR YOU IF YOU LOOKED LIKE ROCK HUDSON!!
WHY, YOU CRUMMY BRAT!! I'LL TEACH YOU TO LAUGH AT ME!
HEY, YOU BIG APE! I WAS ONLY KIDDIN'! LOOK OUT!
DON'T!!
ALL RIGHT! IF IT'S A FIGHT YOU WANT...
FLAME OFF, BLAST YA! FIGHT LIKE A MAN!
SURE, IF YOU USE YOUR INHUMAN STRENGTH, THAT'S OKAY! BUT IF I USE MY FLAME, YOU DON'T LIKE IT! I'M LEAVIN'! I'M SICK OF LOOKIN' AT YOUR UGLY FACE! YOU GIVE ME A SWIFT PAIN!
GO ON... GET OUT... WHILE YOU STILL CAN!
WHY CAN'T YOU CONTROL YOURSELF, THING? WHY MUST WE ALWAYS FIGHT AMONG OURSELVES? WHAT'S WRONG WITH US?
ALL I GOTTA DO IS LOOK IN THE MIRROR TO ANSWER THAT ONE, BROTHER!! AW, THE HECK WITH IT! WHERE'S SUE? WHEN IS SHE GONNA SIGNAL US??
16

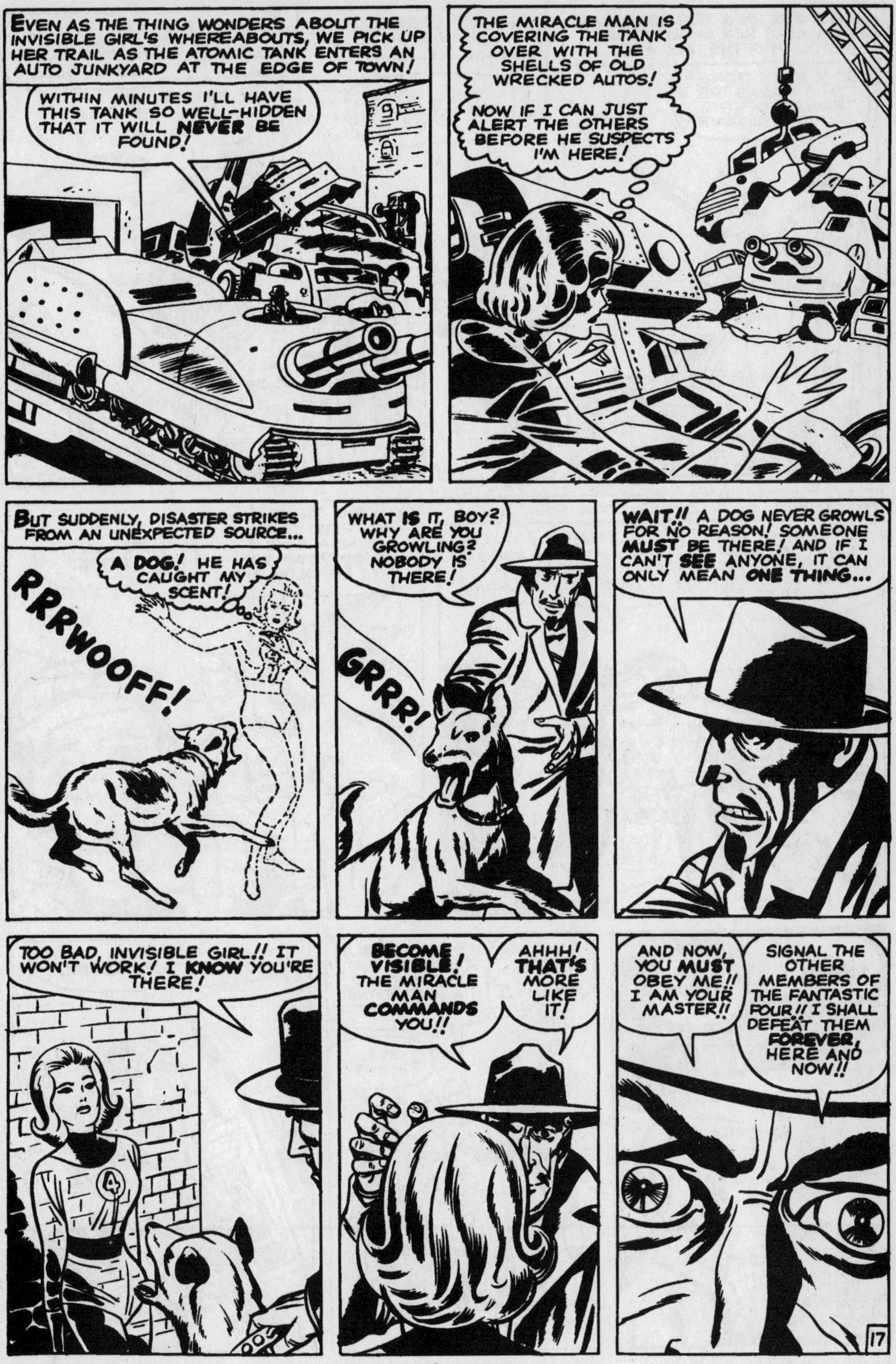

EVEN AS THE THING WONDERS ABOUT THE INVISIBLE GIRL'S WHEREABOUTS, WE PICK UP HER TRAIL AS THE ATOMIC TANK ENTERS AN AUTO JUNKYARD AT THE EDGE OF TOWN!
WITHIN MINUTES I'LL HAVE THIS TANK SO WELL-HIDDEN THAT IT WILL NEVER BE FOUND!
THE MIRACLE MAN IS COVERING THE TANK OVER WITH THE SHELLS OF OLD WRECKED AUTOS!
NOW IF I CAN JUST ALERT THE OTHERS BEFORE HE SUSPECTS I'M HERE!
BUT SUDDENLY, DISASTER STRIKES FROM AN UNEXPECTED SOURCE...
A DOG! HE HAS CAUGHT MY SCENT!
RRRWOOFF!
WHAT IS IT, BOY? WHY ARE YOU GROWLING? NOBODY IS THERE!
GRRR!
WAIT!! A DOG NEVER GROWLS FOR NO REASON! SOMEONE MUST BE THERE! AND IF I CAN'T SEE ANYONE, IT CAN ONLY MEAN ONE THING...
TOO BAD, INVISIBLE GIRL!! IT WON'T WORK! I KNOW YOU'RE THERE!
BECOME VISIBLE! THE MIRACLE MAN COMMANDS YOU!!
AHHH! THAT'S MORE LIKE IT!
AND NOW, YOU MUST OBEY ME!! I AM YOUR MASTER!!
SIGNAL THE OTHER MEMBERS OF THE FANTASTIC FOUR!! I SHALL DEFEAT THEM FOREVER, HERE AND NOW!!
17

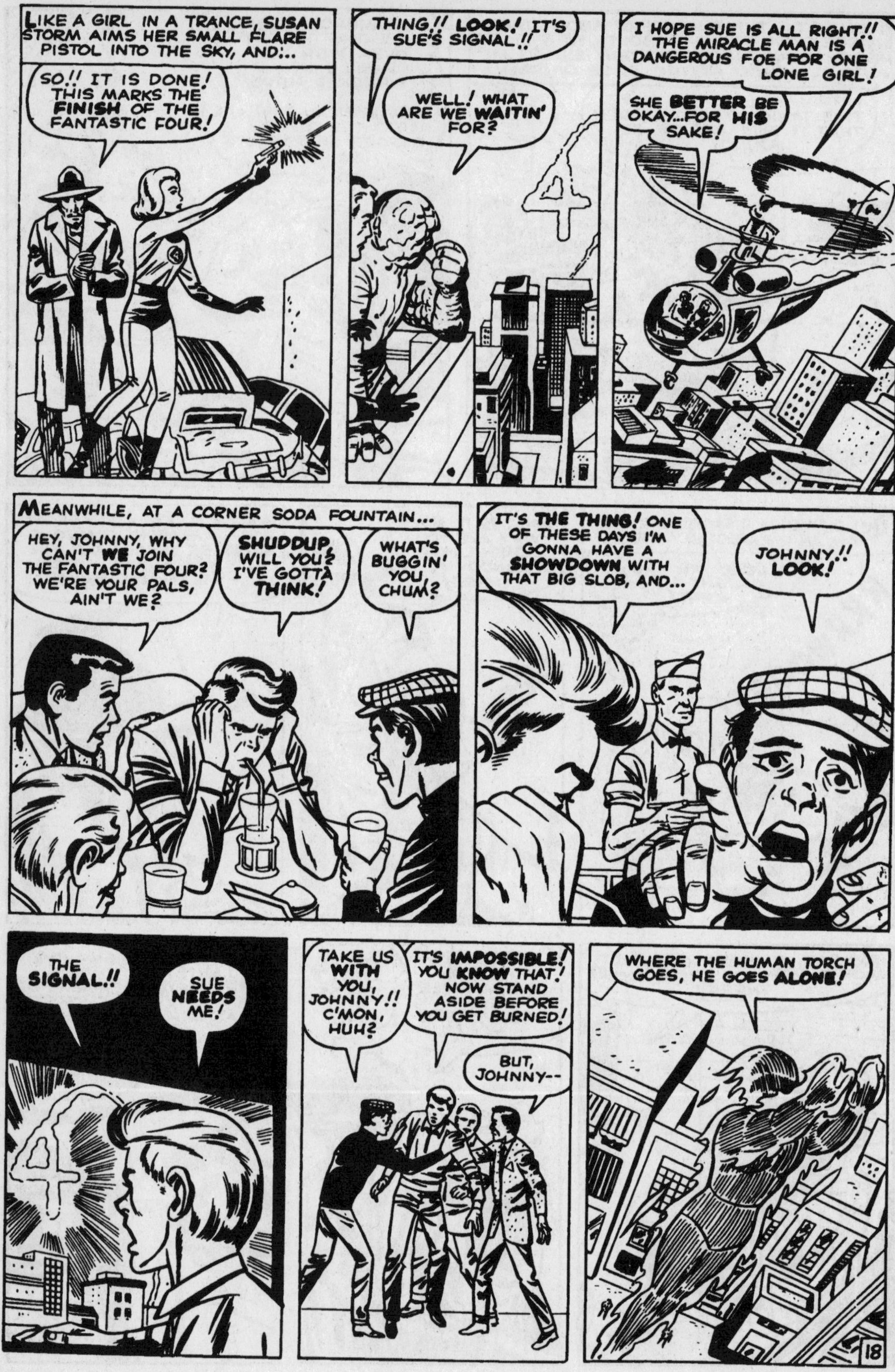
LIKE A GIRL IN A TRANCE, SUSAN STORM AIMS HER SMALL FLARE PISTOL INTO THE SKY, AND:...
SO!! IT IS DONE! THIS MARKS THE FINISH OF THE FANTASTIC FOUR!
THING!! LOOK! IT'S SUE'S SIGNAL!!
WELL! WHAT ARE WE WAITIN' FOR?
I HOPE SUE IS ALL RIGHT!! THE MIRACLE MAN IS A DANGEROUS FOE FOR ONE LONE GIRL!
SHE BETTER BE OKAY...FOR HIS SAKE!
MEANWHILE, AT A CORNER SODA FOUNTAIN...
HEY, JOHNNY, WHY CAN'T WE JOIN THE FANTASTIC FOUR? WE'RE YOUR PALS, AIN'T WE?
SHUDDUP, WILL YOU? I'VE GOTTA THINK!
WHAT'S BUGGIN' YOU, CHUM?
IT'S THE THING! ONE OF THESE DAYS I'M GONNA HAVE A SHOWDOWN WITH THAT BIG SLOB, AND...
JOHNNY!! LOOK!
THE SIGNAL!!
SUE NEEDS ME!
TAKE US WITH YOU, JOHNNY!! C'MON, HUH?
IT'S IMPOSSIBLE! YOU KNOW THAT! NOW STAND ASIDE BEFORE YOU GET BURNED!
BUT, JOHNNY--
WHERE THE HUMAN TORCH GOES, HE GOES ALONE!
18

CHAPTER V "THE FINAL CHALLENGE!"

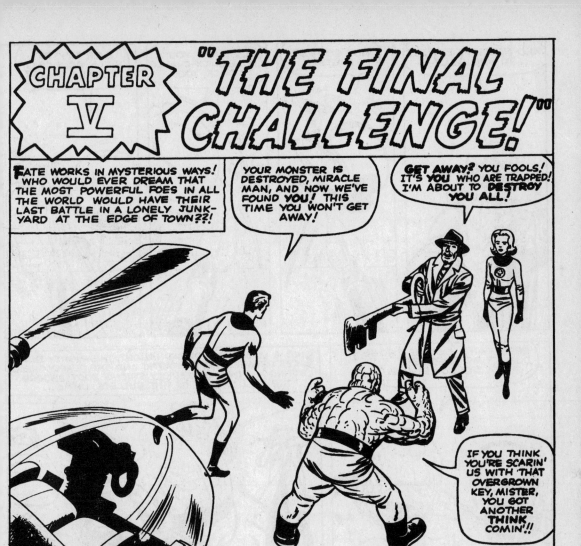

FATE WORKS IN MYSTERIOUS WAYS! WHO WOULD EVER DREAM THAT THE MOST POWERFUL FOES IN ALL THE WORLD WOULD HAVE THEIR LAST BATTLE IN A LONELY JUNK-YARD AT THE EDGE OF TOWN??!

YOUR MONSTER IS DESTROYED, MIRACLE MAN, AND NOW WE'VE FOUND YOU! THIS TIME YOU WON'T GET AWAY!

GET AWAY? YOU FOOLS! IT'S YOU WHO ARE TRAPPED! I'M ABOUT TO DESTROY YOU ALL!

IF YOU THINK YOU'RE SCARIN' US WITH 'THAT OVERGROWN KEY, MISTER, YOU GOT ANOTHER THINK COMIN'!!

Stan Lee + J. Kirby

V-

C'MON, REED, WHAT ARE WE WAITIN' FOR? LET'S PULVERIZE HIM!

HOLD IT, THING! THERE'S MORE TO THAT KEY THAN MEETS THE EYE!

YOU ARE VERY PERCEPTIVE, MISTER FANTASTIC!! TOO BAD YOU ARE ABOUT TO DIE!

THIS IS MORE THAN JUST AN OVERSIZED KEY...

...BEFORE YOUR VERY EYES, I CAN MAKE IT CHANGE INTO...

A MACHINE GUN!!!

19

AND NOW, FAREWELL! ...TO YOU **ALL!**

NOT SO FAST, MISTER...

I'LL SHOW YOU A LITTLE QUICK-CHANGE TRICK, TOO!

EVER TRY TO HIT A BOUNCING RUBBER BALL??

REED CAN'T DODGE THOSE DUM-DUMS **FOREVER!** I GOTTA **DO** SOMETHING!!

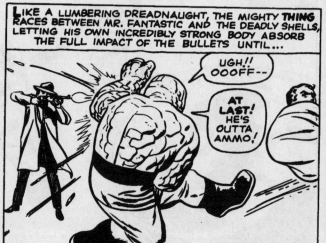

LIKE A LUMBERING DREADNAUGHT, THE MIGHTY **THING** RACES BETWEEN MR. FANTASTIC AND THE DEADLY SHELLS, LETTING HIS OWN INCREDIBLY STRONG BODY ABSORB THE FULL IMPACT OF THE BULLETS UNTIL...

UGH!! OOOFF--

AT LAST! HE'S OUTTA AMMO!

THING! YOU SAVED ME!

BIG DEAL!! YOU BETTER MOVE, BROTHER, BEFORE LAUGHING BOY GETS AWAY WITH SUE AGAIN!

BUT BEFORE THE EXHAUSTED MR. FANTASTIC OR THE BATTERED THING CAN ACT, THE MIRACLE MAN REACHES THE ATOMIC TANK, AND...

HE'S ESCAPING!

20

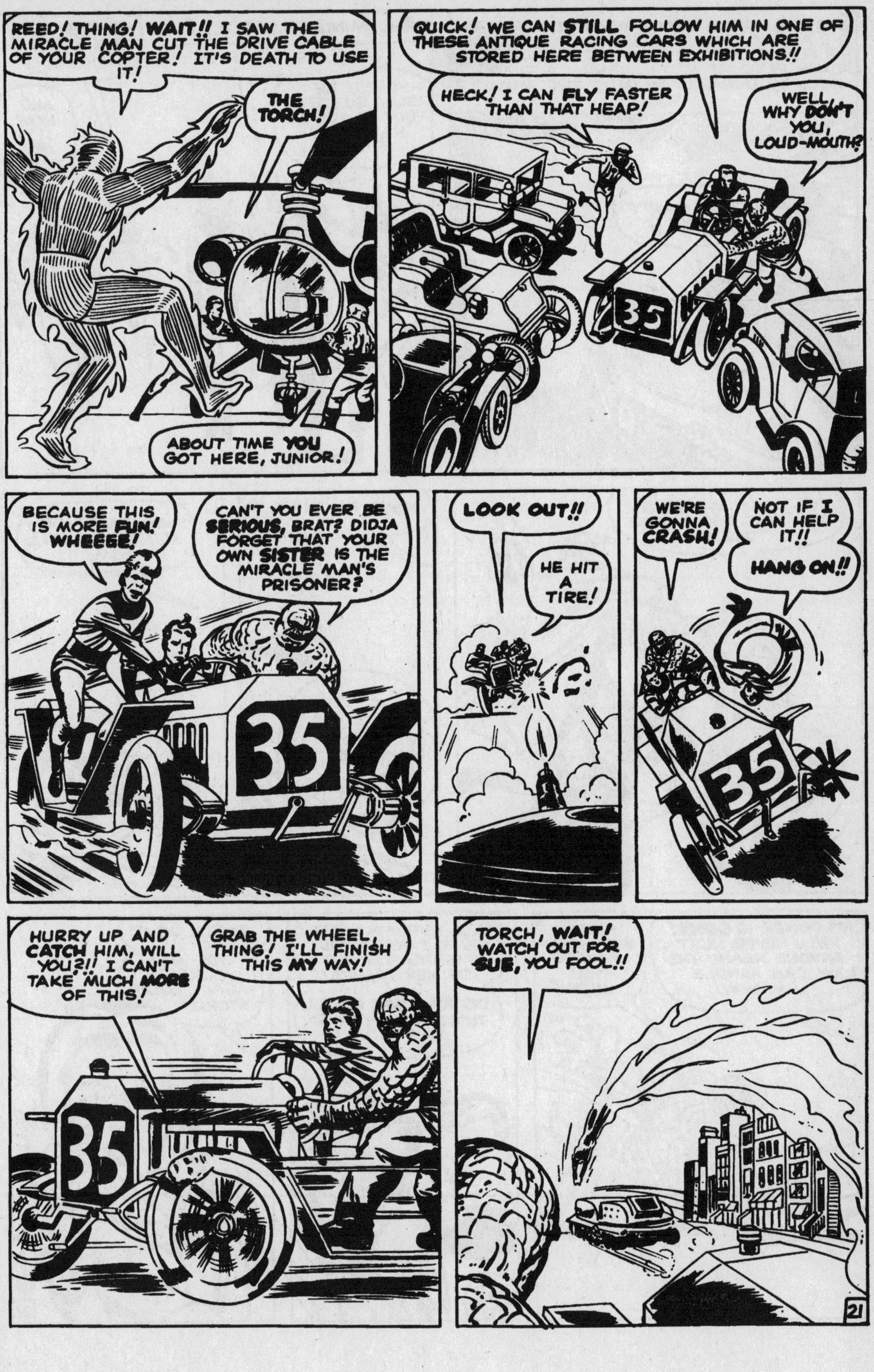
REED! THING! WAIT!! I SAW THE MIRACLE MAN CUT THE DRIVE CABLE OF YOUR COPTER! IT'S DEATH TO USE IT!
THE TORCH!
ABOUT TIME YOU GOT HERE, JUNIOR!
QUICK! WE CAN STILL FOLLOW HIM IN ONE OF THESE ANTIQUE RACING CARS WHICH ARE STORED HERE BETWEEN EXHIBITIONS!!
HECK! I CAN FLY FASTER THAN THAT HEAP!
WELL, WHY DON'T YOU, LOUD-MOUTH?
35
BECAUSE THIS IS MORE FUN! WHEEEE!
CAN'T YOU EVER BE SERIOUS, BRAT? DIDJA FORGET THAT YOUR OWN SISTER IS THE MIRACLE MAN'S PRISONER?
35
LOOK OUT!!
HE HIT A TIRE!
WE'RE GONNA CRASH!
NOT IF I CAN HELP IT!! HANG ON!!
35
HURRY UP AND CATCH HIM, WILL YOU?!! I CAN'T TAKE MUCH MORE OF THIS!
GRAB THE WHEEL, THING! I'LL FINISH THIS MY WAY!
35
TORCH, WAIT! WATCH OUT FOR SUE, YOU FOOL!!

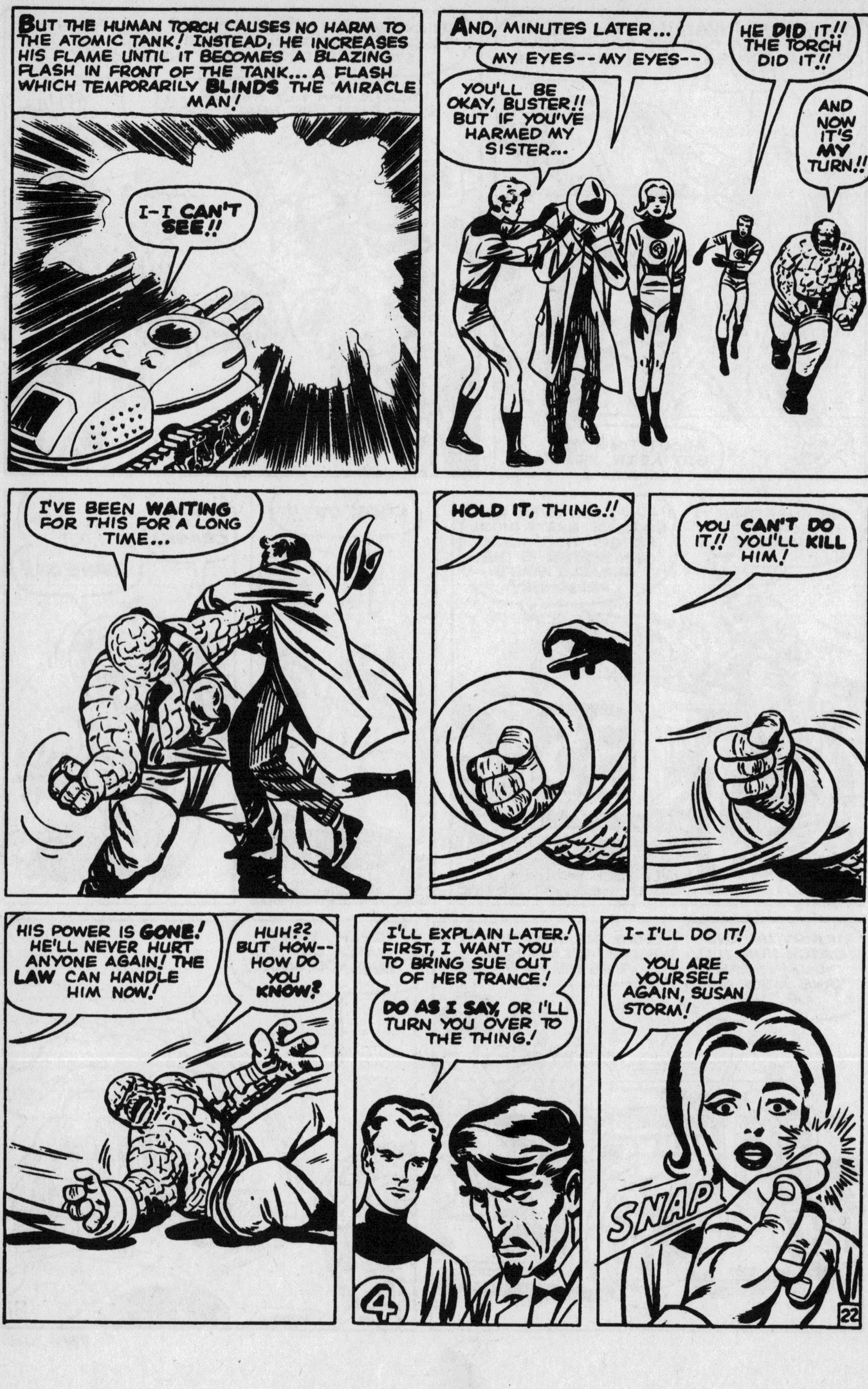
BUT THE HUMAN TORCH CAUSES NO HARM TO THE ATOMIC TANK! INSTEAD, HE INCREASES HIS FLAME UNTIL IT BECOMES A BLAZING FLASH IN FRONT OF THE TANK... A FLASH WHICH TEMPORARILY BLINDS THE MIRACLE MAN!
I-I CAN'T SEE!!
AND, MINUTES LATER...
MY EYES-- MY EYES--
YOU'LL BE OKAY, BUSTER!! BUT IF YOU'VE HARMED MY SISTER...
HE DID IT!! THE TORCH DID IT!!
AND NOW IT'S MY TURN!!
I'VE BEEN WAITING FOR THIS FOR A LONG TIME...
HOLD IT, THING!!
YOU CAN'T DO IT!! YOU'LL KILL HIM!
HIS POWER IS GONE! HE'LL NEVER HURT ANYONE AGAIN! THE LAW CAN HANDLE HIM NOW!
HUH?? BUT HOW-- HOW DO YOU KNOW?
I'LL EXPLAIN LATER! FIRST, I WANT YOU TO BRING SUE OUT OF HER TRANCE!
DO AS I SAY, OR I'LL TURN YOU OVER TO THE THING!
I-I'LL DO IT!
YOU ARE YOURSELF AGAIN, SUSAN STORM!
SNAP
22

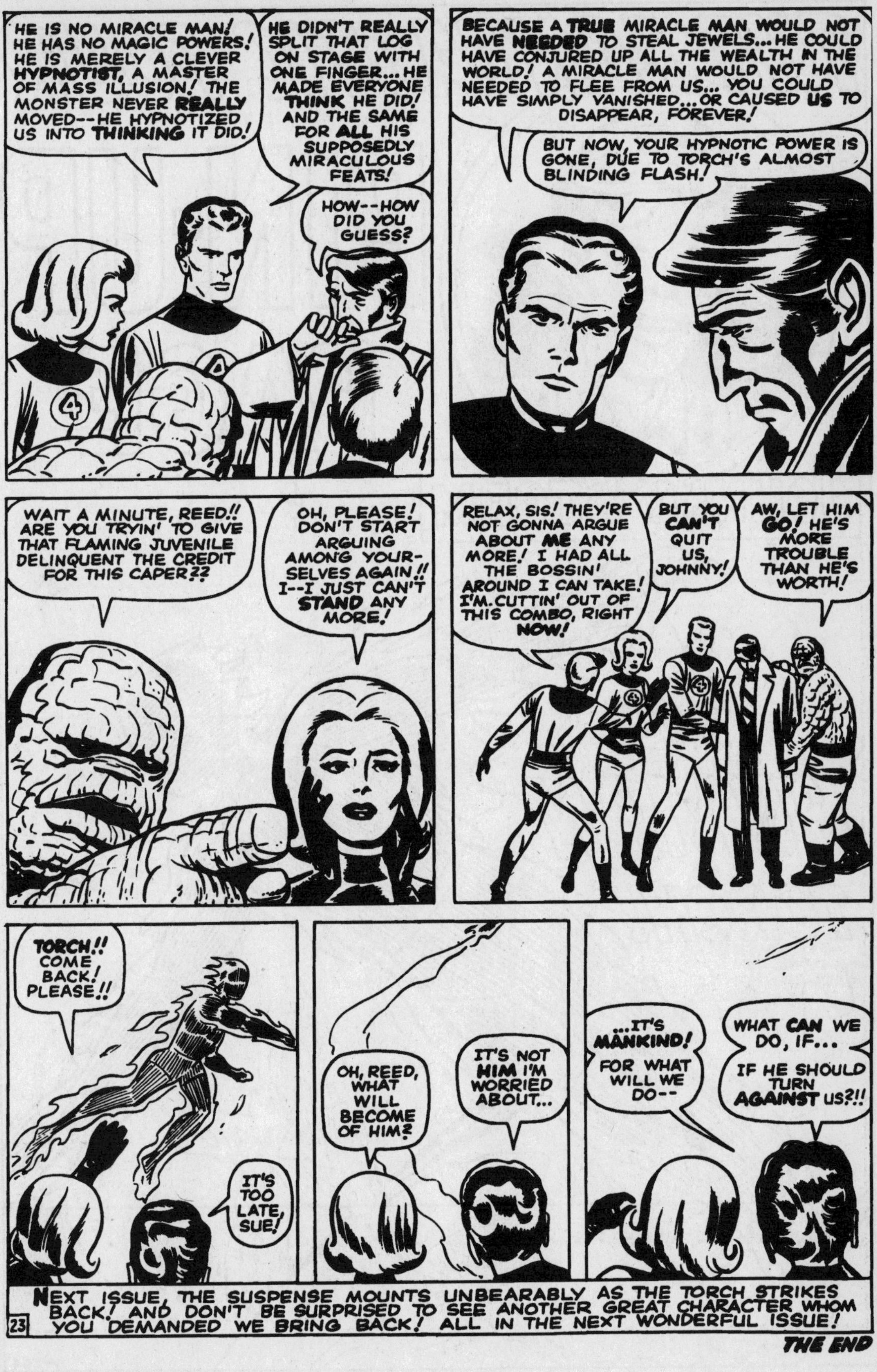
HE IS NO MIRACLE MAN! HE HAS NO MAGIC POWERS! HE IS MERELY A CLEVER HYPNOTIST, A MASTER OF MASS ILLUSION! THE MONSTER NEVER REALLY MOVED--HE HYPNOTIZED US INTO THINKING IT DID!
HE DIDN'T REALLY SPLIT THAT LOG ON STAGE WITH ONE FINGER...HE MADE EVERYONE THINK HE DID! AND THE SAME FOR ALL HIS SUPPOSEDLY MIRACULOUS FEATS!
HOW--HOW DID YOU GUESS?
BECAUSE A TRUE MIRACLE MAN WOULD NOT HAVE NEEDED TO STEAL JEWELS...HE COULD HAVE CONJURED UP ALL THE WEALTH IN THE WORLD! A MIRACLE MAN WOULD NOT HAVE NEEDED TO FLEE FROM US... YOU COULD HAVE SIMPLY VANISHED...OR CAUSED US TO DISAPPEAR, FOREVER!
BUT NOW, YOUR HYPNOTIC POWER IS GONE, DUE TO TORCH'S ALMOST BLINDING FLASH!
WAIT A MINUTE, REED!! ARE YOU TRYIN' TO GIVE THAT FLAMING JUVENILE DELINQUENT THE CREDIT FOR THIS CAPER??
OH, PLEASE! DON'T START ARGUING AMONG YOURSELVES AGAIN!! I--I JUST CAN'T STAND ANY MORE!
RELAX, SIS! THEY'RE NOT GONNA ARGUE ABOUT ME ANY MORE! I HAD ALL THE BOSSIN' AROUND I CAN TAKE! I'M. CUTTIN' OUT OF THIS COMBO, RIGHT NOW!
BUT YOU CAN'T QUIT US, JOHNNY!
AW, LET HIM GO! HE'S MORE TROUBLE THAN HE'S WORTH!
TORCH!! COME BACK! PLEASE!!
IT'S TOO LATE, SUE!
OH, REED, WHAT WILL BECOME OF HIM?
IT'S NOT HIM I'M WORRIED ABOUT...
...IT'S MANKIND! FOR WHAT WILL WE DO--
WHAT CAN WE DO, IF... IF HE SHOULD TURN AGAINST US?!!
NEXT ISSUE, THE SUSPENSE MOUNTS UNBEARABLY AS THE TORCH STRIKES BACK! AND DON'T BE SURPRISED TO SEE ANOTHER GREAT CHARACTER WHOM YOU DEMANDED WE BRING BACK! ALL IN THE NEXT WONDERFUL ISSUE!
23

THE END

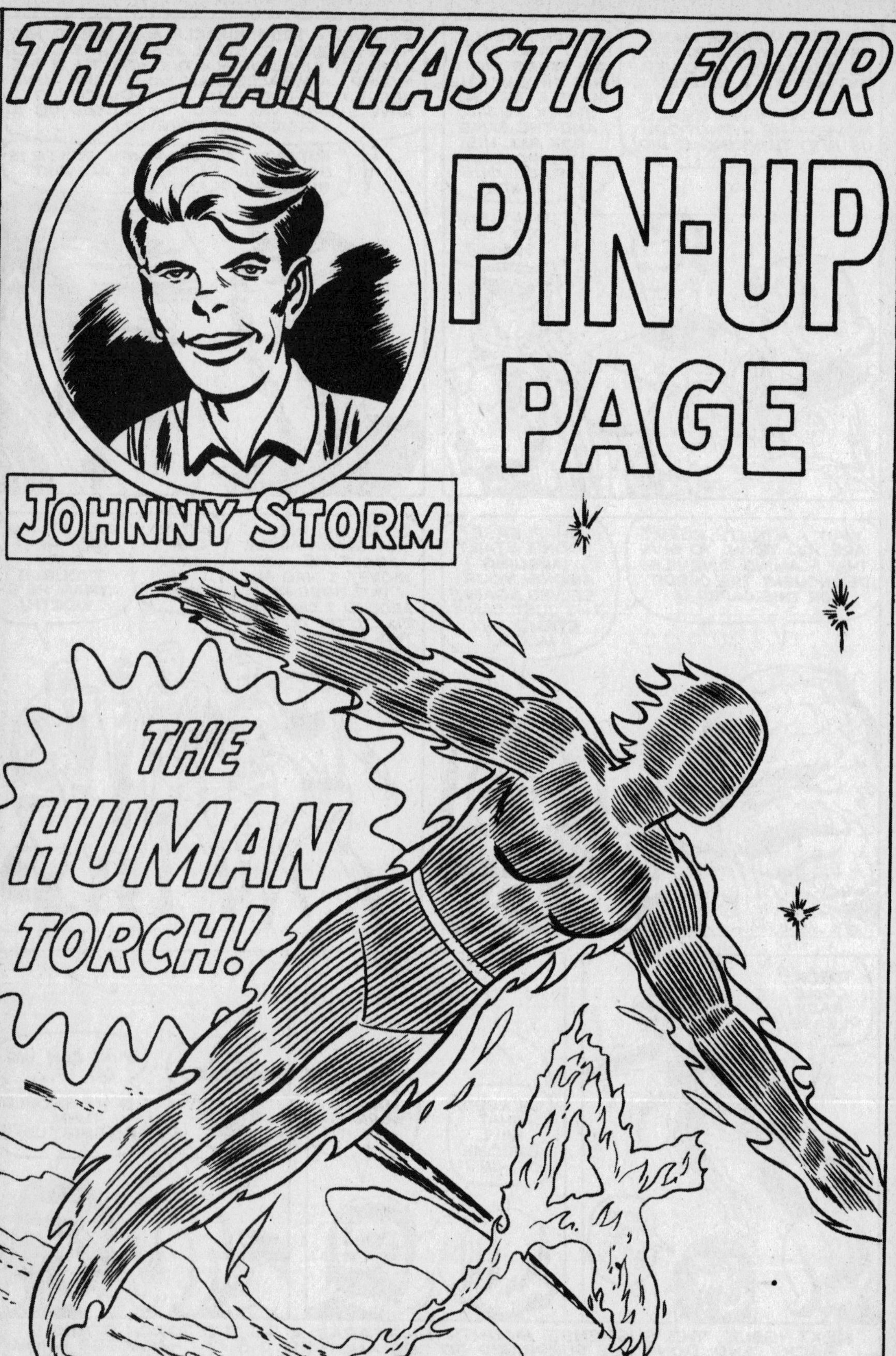
THE FANTASTIC FOUR
PIN-UP PAGE
JOHNNY STORM
THE HUMAN TORCH!
V-564

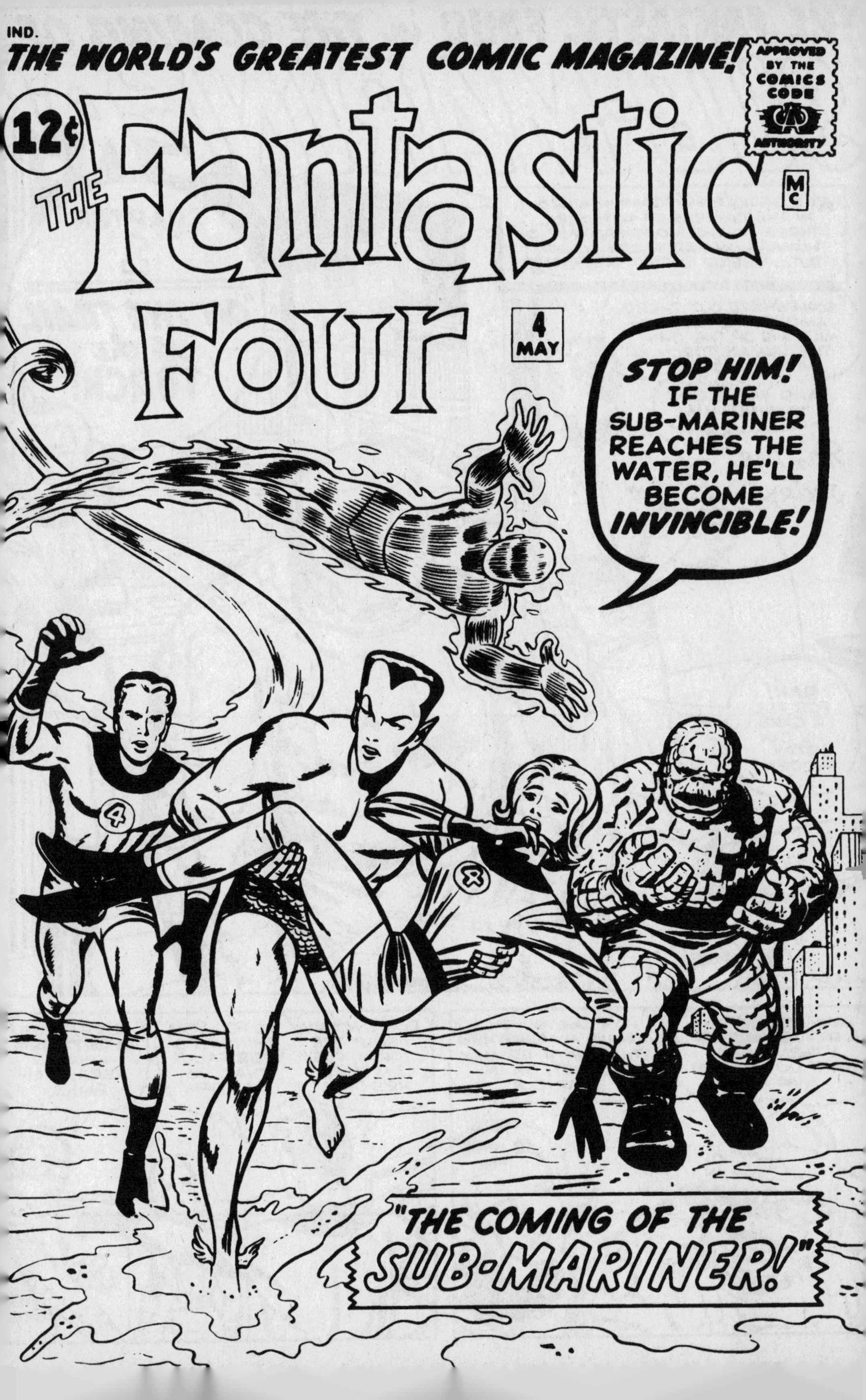
IND.
THE WORLD'S GREATEST COMIC MAGAZINE!
APPROVED BY THE COMICS CODE AUTHORITY
12¢
THE Fantastic Four
MC
4 MAY
STOP HIM! IF THE SUB-MARINER REACHES THE WATER, HE'LL BECOME INVINCIBLE!
"THE COMING OF THE SUB-MARINER!"

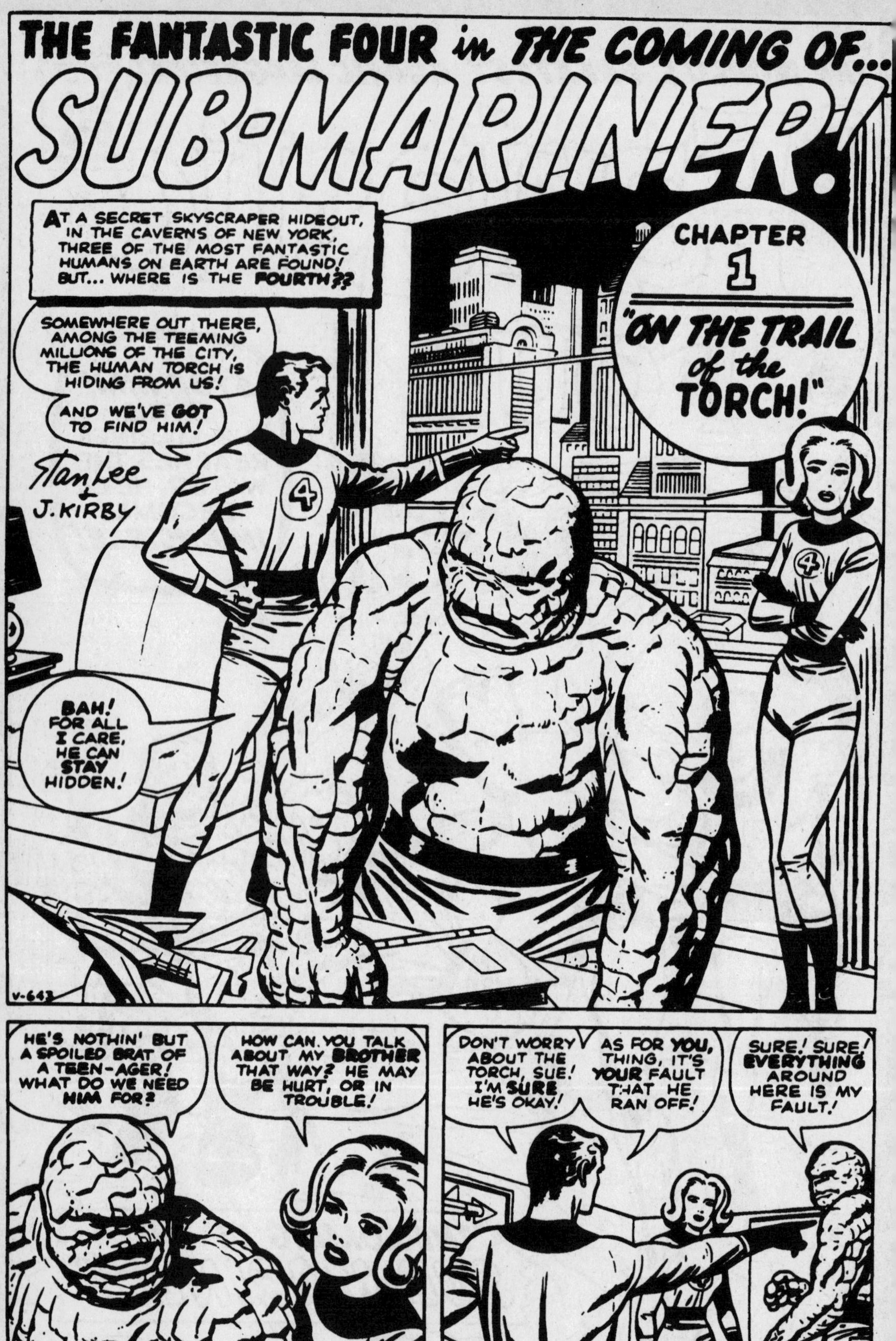
THE FANTASTIC FOUR in THE COMING OF...
SUB-MARINER!
AT A SECRET SKYSCRAPER HIDEOUT, IN THE CAVERNS OF NEW YORK, THREE OF THE MOST FANTASTIC HUMANS ON EARTH ARE FOUND! BUT... WHERE IS THE FOURTH??
CHAPTER 1
"ON THE TRAIL of the TORCH!"
SOMEWHERE OUT THERE, AMONG THE TEEMING MILLIONS OF THE CITY, THE HUMAN TORCH IS HIDING FROM US!
AND WE'VE GOT TO FIND HIM!
Stan Lee & J. KIRBY
BAH! FOR ALL I CARE, HE CAN STAY HIDDEN!
V-643
HE'S NOTHIN' BUT A SPOILED BRAT OF A TEEN-AGER! WHAT DO WE NEED HIM FOR?
HOW CAN YOU TALK ABOUT MY BROTHER THAT WAY? HE MAY BE HURT, OR IN TROUBLE!
DON'T WORRY ABOUT THE TORCH, SUE! I'M SURE HE'S OKAY!
AS FOR YOU, THING, IT'S YOUR FAULT THAT HE RAN OFF!
SURE! SURE! EVERYTHING AROUND HERE IS MY FAULT!
1

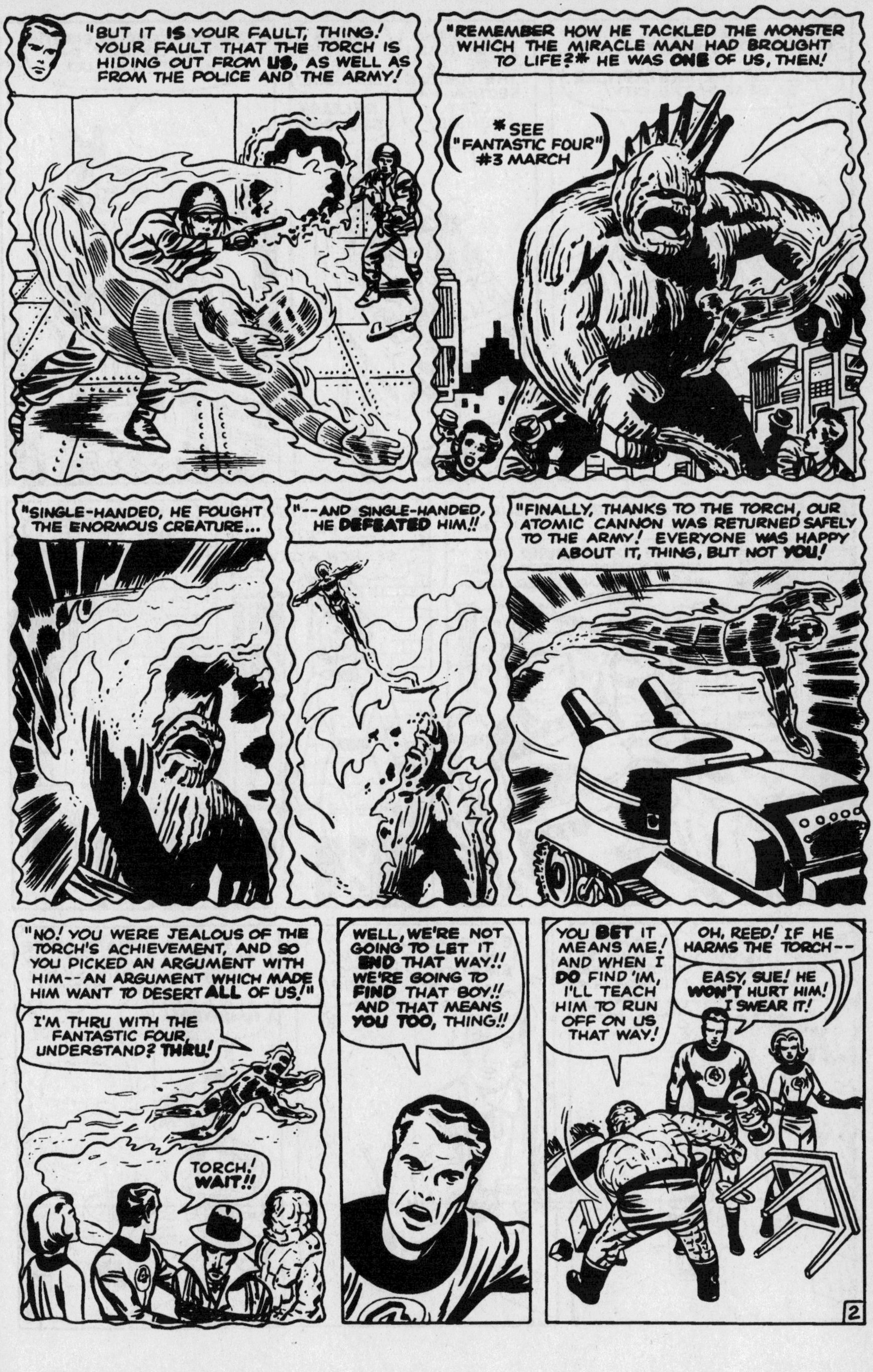

"BUT IT IS YOUR FAULT, THING! YOUR FAULT THAT THE TORCH IS HIDING OUT FROM US, AS WELL AS FROM THE POLICE AND THE ARMY!
"REMEMBER HOW HE TACKLED THE MONSTER WHICH THE MIRACLE MAN HAD BROUGHT TO LIFE?* HE WAS ONE OF US, THEN!
(*SEE "FANTASTIC FOUR" #3 MARCH)
"SINGLE-HANDED, HE FOUGHT THE ENORMOUS CREATURE...
"--AND SINGLE-HANDED, HE DEFEATED HIM!!
"FINALLY, THANKS TO THE TORCH, OUR ATOMIC CANNON WAS RETURNED SAFELY TO THE ARMY! EVERYONE WAS HAPPY ABOUT IT, THING, BUT NOT YOU!
"NO! YOU WERE JEALOUS OF THE TORCH'S ACHIEVEMENT, AND SO YOU PICKED AN ARGUMENT WITH HIM--AN ARGUMENT WHICH MADE HIM WANT TO DESERT ALL OF US!"
I'M THRU WITH THE FANTASTIC FOUR, UNDERSTAND? THRU!
TORCH! WAIT!!
WELL, WE'RE NOT GOING TO LET IT END THAT WAY!! WE'RE GOING TO FIND THAT BOY!! AND THAT MEANS YOU TOO, THING!!
YOU BET IT MEANS ME! AND WHEN I DO FIND 'IM, I'LL TEACH HIM TO RUN OFF ON US THAT WAY!
OH, REED! IF HE HARMS THE TORCH--
EASY, SUE! HE WON'T HURT HIM! I SWEAR IT!
2

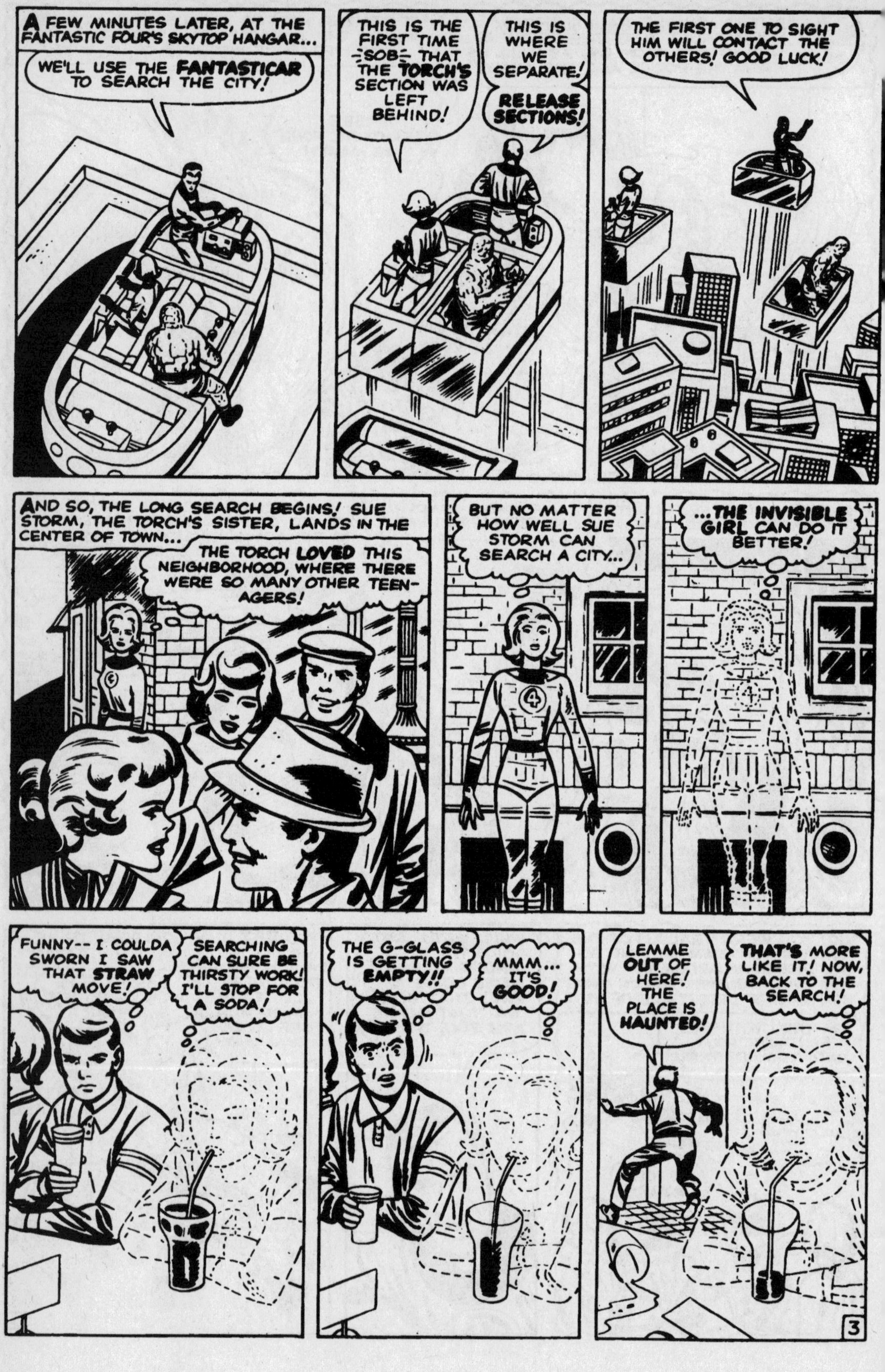

A FEW MINUTES LATER, AT THE FANTASTIC FOUR'S SKYTOP HANGAR...
WE'LL USE THE FANTASTICAR TO SEARCH THE CITY!
THIS IS THE FIRST TIME -SOB- THAT THE TORCH'S SECTION WAS LEFT BEHIND!
THIS IS WHERE WE SEPARATE! RELEASE SECTIONS!
THE FIRST ONE TO SIGHT HIM WILL CONTACT THE OTHERS! GOOD LUCK!
AND SO, THE LONG SEARCH BEGINS! SUE STORM, THE TORCH'S SISTER, LANDS IN THE CENTER OF TOWN...
THE TORCH LOVED THIS NEIGHBORHOOD, WHERE THERE WERE SO MANY OTHER TEEN-AGERS!
BUT NO MATTER HOW WELL SUE STORM CAN SEARCH A CITY...
...THE INVISIBLE GIRL CAN DO IT BETTER!
FUNNY-- I COULDA SWORN I SAW THAT STRAW MOVE!
SEARCHING CAN SURE BE THIRSTY WORK! I'LL STOP FOR A SODA!
THE G-GLASS IS GETTING EMPTY!!
MMM... IT'S GOOD!
LEMME OUT OF HERE! THE PLACE IS HAUNTED!
THAT'S MORE LIKE IT! NOW, BACK TO THE SEARCH!
3

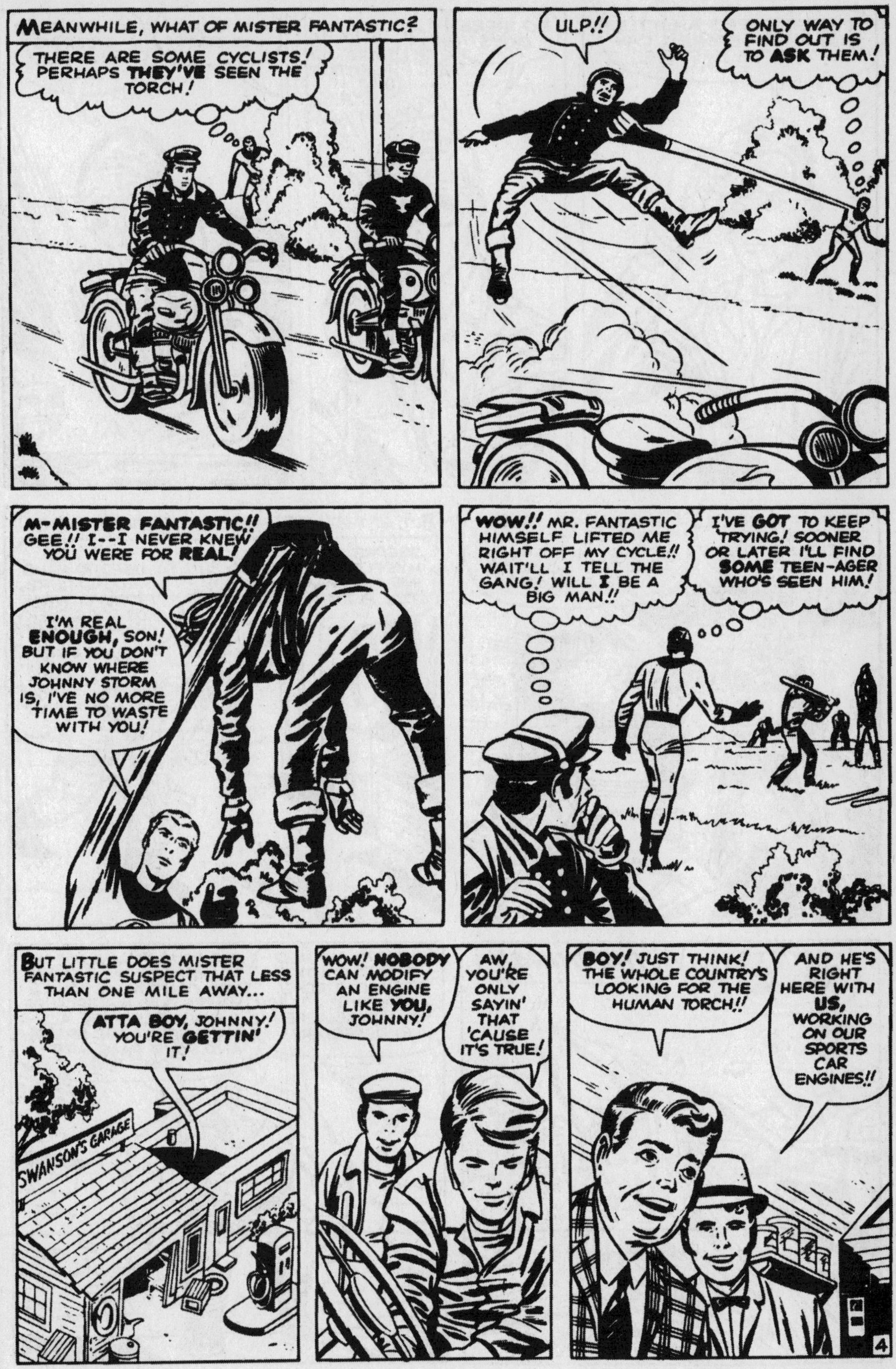
MEANWHILE, WHAT OF MISTER FANTASTIC?
THERE ARE SOME CYCLISTS! PERHAPS THEY'VE SEEN THE TORCH!
ULP!!
ONLY WAY TO FIND OUT IS TO ASK THEM!
M-MISTER FANTASTIC!! GEE!! I--I NEVER KNEW YOU WERE FOR REAL!
I'M REAL ENOUGH, SON! BUT IF YOU DON'T KNOW WHERE JOHNNY STORM IS, I'VE NO MORE TIME TO WASTE WITH YOU!
WOW!! MR. FANTASTIC HIMSELF LIFTED ME RIGHT OFF MY CYCLE!! WAIT'LL I TELL THE GANG! WILL I BE A BIG MAN!!
I'VE GOT TO KEEP TRYING! SOONER OR LATER I'LL FIND SOME TEEN-AGER WHO'S SEEN HIM!
BUT LITTLE DOES MISTER FANTASTIC SUSPECT THAT LESS THAN ONE MILE AWAY...
ATTA BOY, JOHNNY! YOU'RE GETTIN' IT!
SWANSON'S GARAGE
WOW! NOBODY CAN MODIFY AN ENGINE LIKE YOU, JOHNNY!
AW, YOU'RE ONLY SAYIN' THAT 'CAUSE IT'S TRUE!
BOY! JUST THINK! THE WHOLE COUNTRY'S LOOKING FOR THE HUMAN TORCH!!
AND HE'S RIGHT HERE WITH US, WORKING ON OUR SPORTS CAR ENGINES!!
4

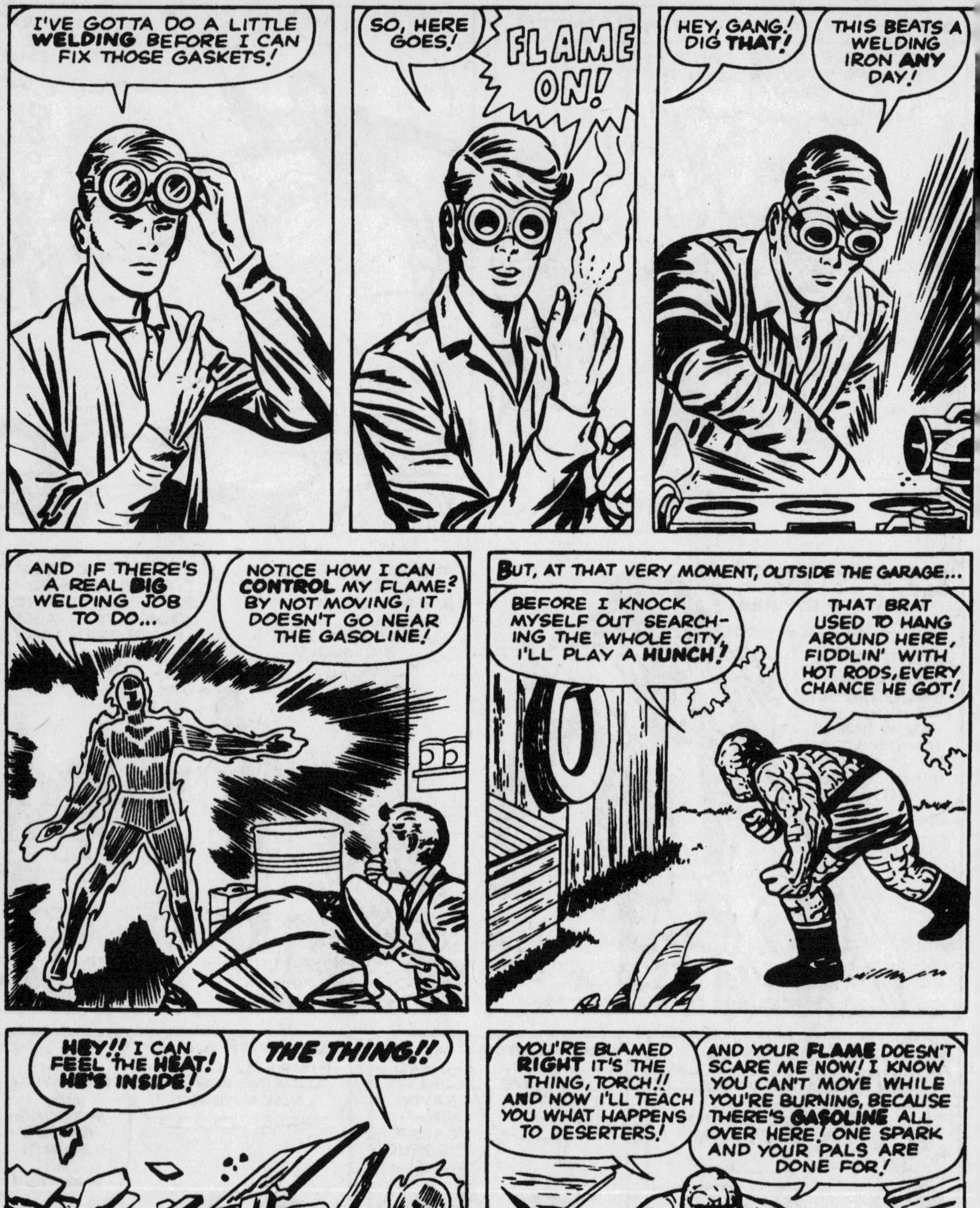
I'VE GOTTA DO A LITTLE WELDING BEFORE I CAN FIX THOSE GASKETS!
SO, HERE GOES!
FLAME ON!
HEY, GANG! DIG THAT!
THIS BEATS A WELDING IRON ANY DAY!
AND IF THERE'S A REAL BIG WELDING JOB TO DO...
NOTICE HOW I CAN CONTROL MY FLAME? BY NOT MOVING, IT DOESN'T GO NEAR THE GASOLINE!
BUT, AT THAT VERY MOMENT, OUTSIDE THE GARAGE...
BEFORE I KNOCK MYSELF OUT SEARCHING THE WHOLE CITY, I'LL PLAY A HUNCH!
THAT BRAT USED TO HANG AROUND HERE, FIDDLIN' WITH HOT RODS, EVERY CHANCE HE GOT!
HEY!! I CAN FEEL THE HEAT! HE'S INSIDE!
THE THING!!
YOU'RE BLAMED RIGHT IT'S THE THING, TORCH!! AND NOW I'LL TEACH YOU WHAT HAPPENS TO DESERTERS!
AND YOUR FLAME DOESN'T SCARE ME NOW! I KNOW YOU CAN'T MOVE WHILE YOU'RE BURNING, BECAUSE THERE'S GASOLINE ALL OVER HERE! ONE SPARK AND YOUR PALS ARE DONE FOR!
5

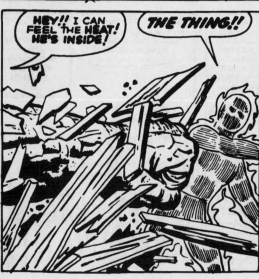

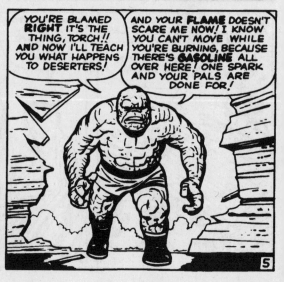

CHAPTER 2 ENTER THE SUB-MARINER!

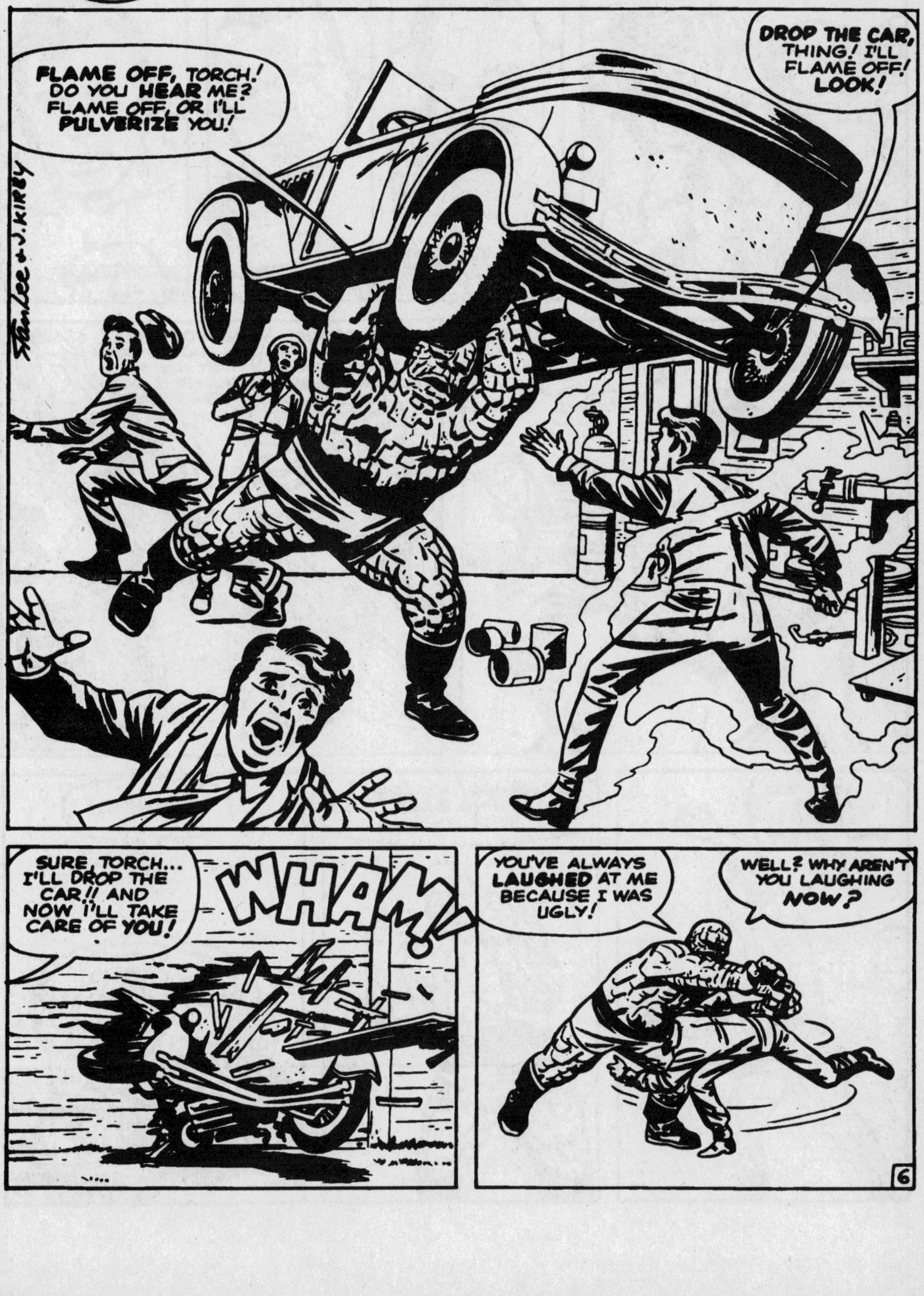
FLAME OFF, TORCH! DO YOU HEAR ME? FLAME OFF, OR I'LL PULVERIZE YOU!
DROP THE CAR, THING! I'LL FLAME OFF! LOOK!
Stan Lee + J. Kirby
SURE, TORCH... I'LL DROP THE CAR!! AND NOW I'LL TAKE CARE OF YOU!
WHAM!
YOU'VE ALWAYS LAUGHED AT ME BECAUSE I WAS UGLY!
WELL? WHY AREN'T YOU LAUGHING NOW?

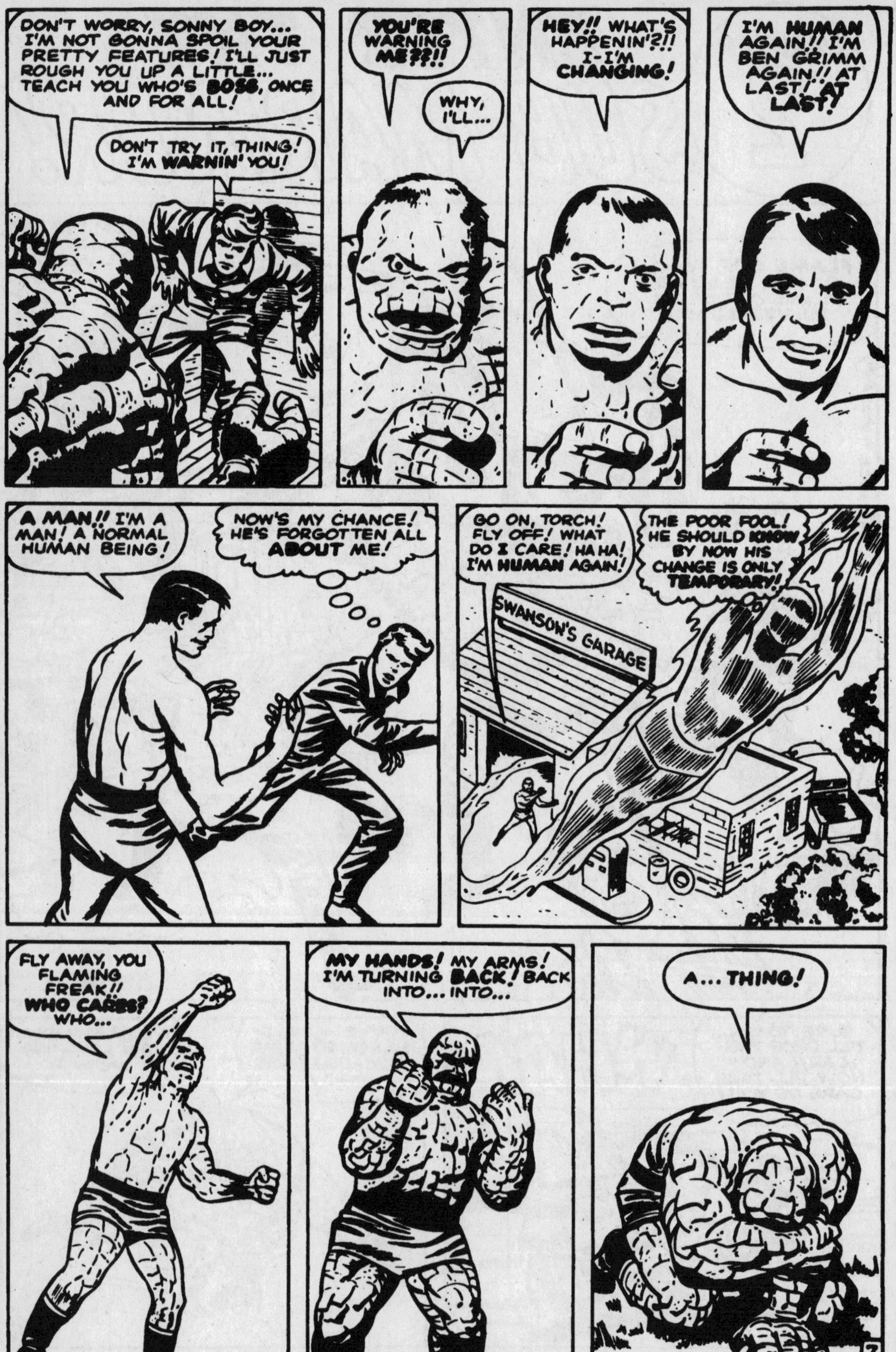
DON'T WORRY, SONNY BOY... I'M NOT GONNA SPOIL YOUR PRETTY FEATURES! I'LL JUST ROUGH YOU UP A LITTLE... TEACH YOU WHO'S BOSS, ONCE AND FOR ALL!
DON'T TRY IT, THING! I'M WARNIN' YOU!
YOU'RE WARNING ME??!!
WHY, I'LL...
HEY!! WHAT'S HAPPENIN'?!! I-I'M CHANGING!
I'M HUMAN AGAIN!! I'M BEN GRIMM AGAIN!! AT LAST! AT LAST!
A MAN!! I'M A MAN! A NORMAL HUMAN BEING!
NOW'S MY CHANCE! HE'S FORGOTTEN ALL ABOUT ME!
GO ON, TORCH! FLY OFF! WHAT DO I CARE! HA HA! I'M HUMAN AGAIN!
THE POOR FOOL! HE SHOULD KNOW BY NOW HIS CHANGE IS ONLY TEMPORARY!
SWANSON'S GARAGE
FLY AWAY, YOU FLAMING FREAK!! WHO CARES? WHO...
MY HANDS! MY ARMS! I'M TURNING BACK! BACK INTO... INTO...
A... THING!

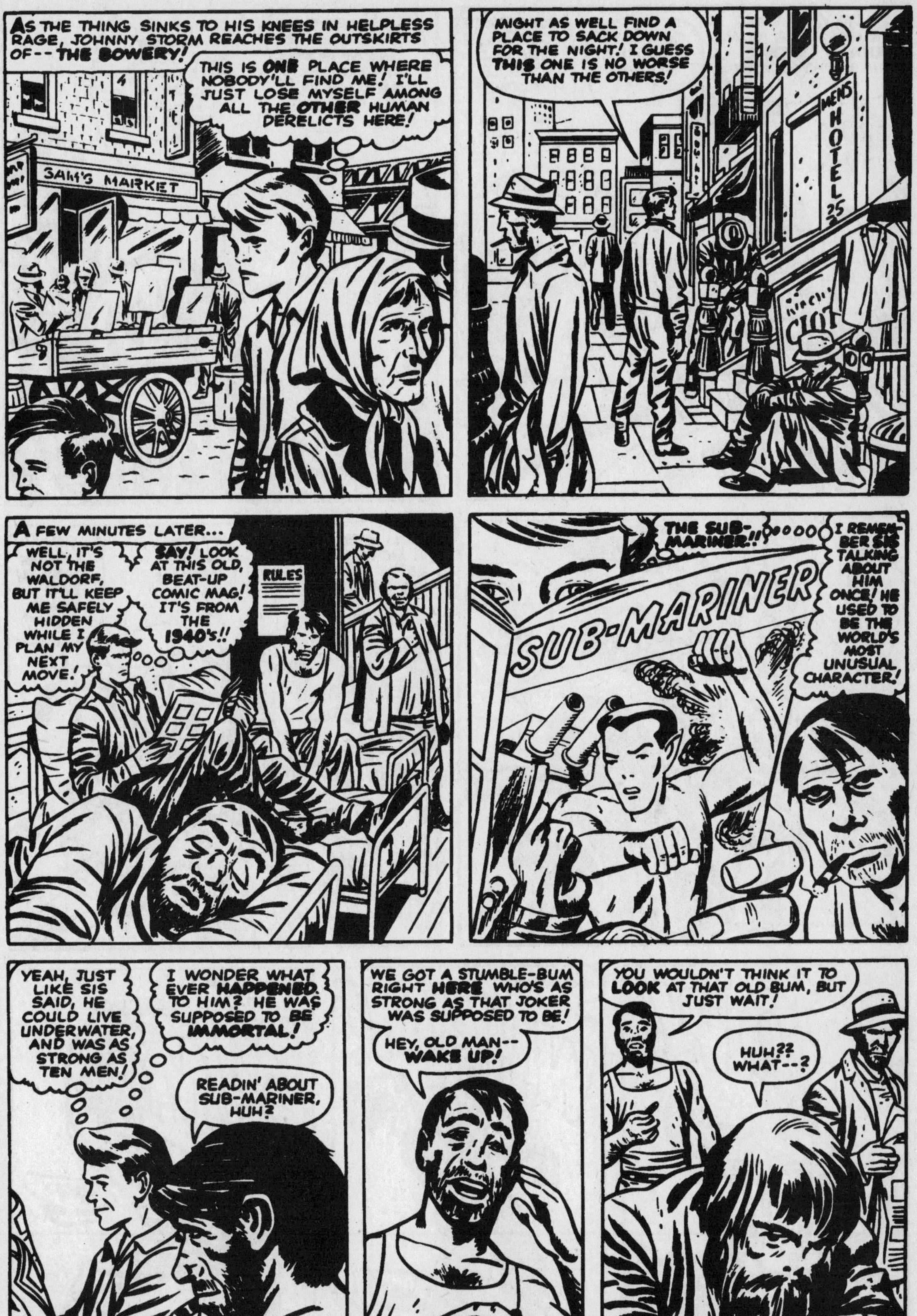

AS THE THING SINKS TO HIS KNEES IN HELPLESS RAGE, JOHNNY STORM REACHES THE OUTSKIRTS OF-- THE BOWERY!
THIS IS ONE PLACE WHERE NOBODY'LL FIND ME! I'LL JUST LOSE MYSELF AMONG ALL THE OTHER HUMAN DERELICTS HERE!
SAM'S MARKET
MIGHT AS WELL FIND A PLACE TO SACK DOWN FOR THE NIGHT! I GUESS THIS ONE IS NO WORSE THAN THE OTHERS!
MEN'S HOTEL 25
A FEW MINUTES LATER...
WELL, IT'S NOT THE WALDORF, BUT IT'LL KEEP ME SAFELY HIDDEN WHILE I PLAN MY NEXT MOVE!
SAY! LOOK AT THIS OLD, BEAT-UP COMIC MAG! IT'S FROM THE 1940's!!
RULES
THE SUB-MARINER!!
I REMEMBER SIS TALKING ABOUT HIM ONCE! HE USED TO BE THE WORLD'S MOST UNUSUAL CHARACTER!
SUB-MARINER
YEAH, JUST LIKE SIS SAID, HE COULD LIVE UNDERWATER, AND WAS AS STRONG AS TEN MEN!
I WONDER WHAT EVER HAPPENED TO HIM? HE WAS SUPPOSED TO BE IMMORTAL!
READIN' ABOUT SUB-MARINER, HUH?
WE GOT A STUMBLE-BUM RIGHT HERE WHO'S AS STRONG AS THAT JOKER WAS SUPPOSED TO BE!
HEY, OLD MAN-- WAKE UP!
YOU WOULDN'T THINK IT TO LOOK AT THAT OLD BUM, BUT JUST WAIT!
HUH?? WHAT--?
8

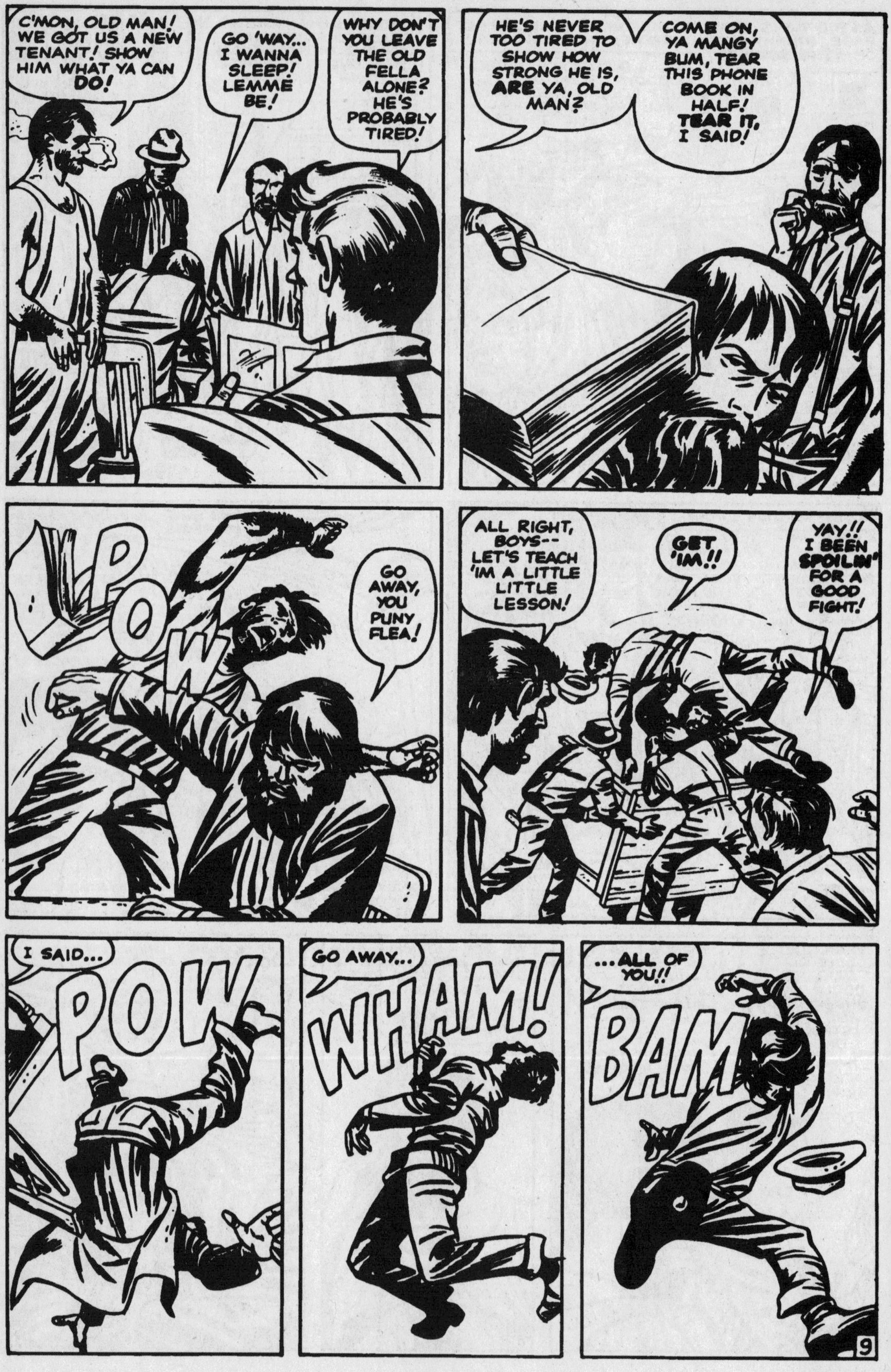
C'MON, OLD MAN! WE GOT US A NEW TENANT! SHOW HIM WHAT YA CAN DO!
GO 'WAY... I WANNA SLEEP! LEMME BE!
WHY DON'T YOU LEAVE THE OLD FELLA ALONE? HE'S PROBABLY TIRED!
HE'S NEVER TOO TIRED TO SHOW HOW STRONG HE IS, ARE YA, OLD MAN?
COME ON, YA MANGY BUM, TEAR THIS PHONE BOOK IN HALF! TEAR IT, I SAID!
POW
GO AWAY, YOU PUNY FLEA!
ALL RIGHT, BOYS-- LET'S TEACH 'IM A LITTLE LITTLE LESSON!
GET 'IM!!
YAY!! I BEEN SPOILIN' FOR A GOOD FIGHT!
I SAID...
POW
GO AWAY...
WHAM!
...ALL OF YOU!!
BAM
9

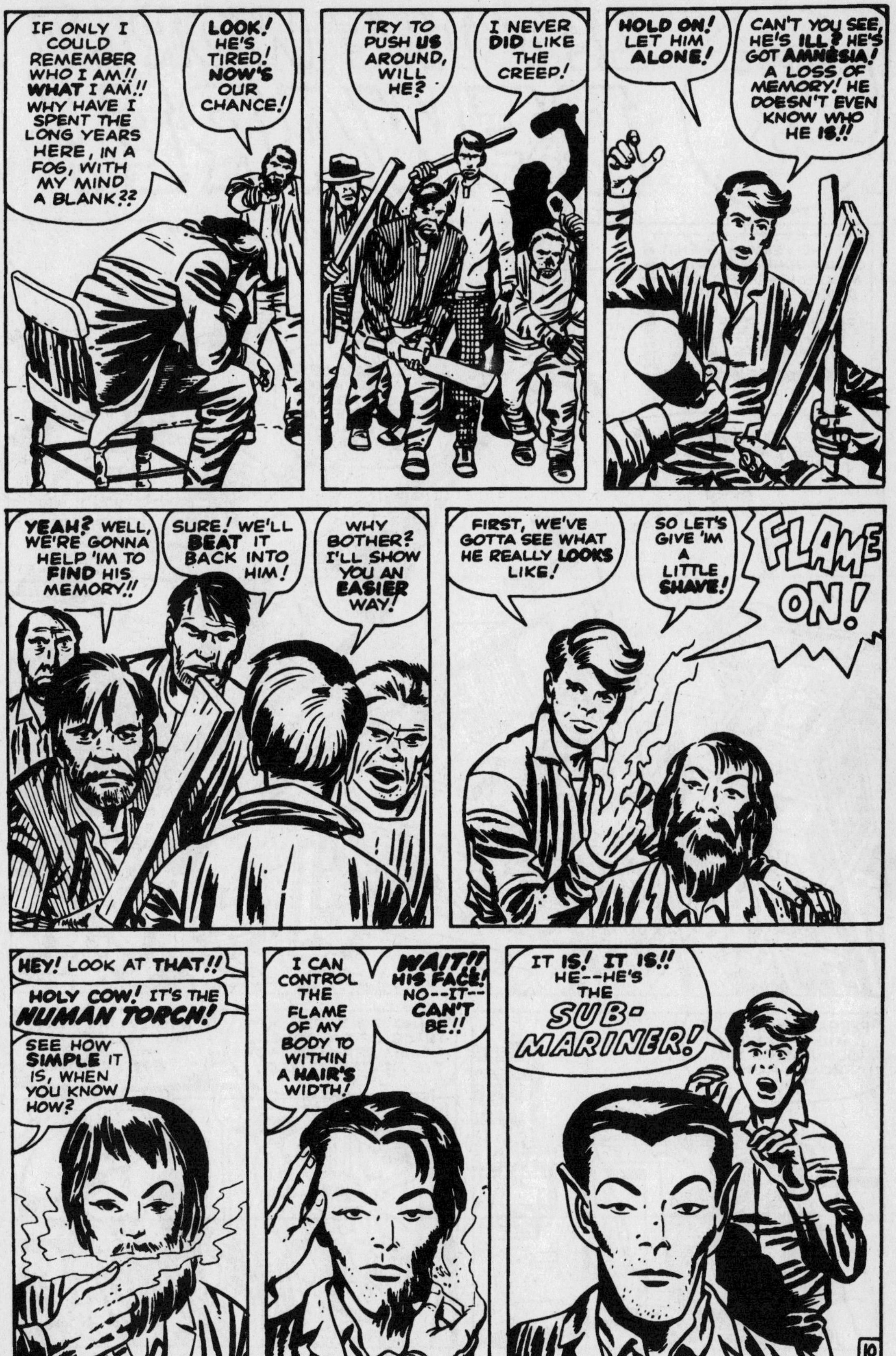
IF ONLY I COULD REMEMBER WHO I AM!! WHAT I AM!! WHY HAVE I SPENT THE LONG YEARS HERE, IN A FOG, WITH MY MIND A BLANK??
LOOK! HE'S TIRED! NOW'S OUR CHANCE!
TRY TO PUSH US AROUND, WILL HE?
I NEVER DID LIKE THE CREEP!
HOLD ON! LET HIM ALONE!
CAN'T YOU SEE, HE'S ILL? HE'S GOT AMNESIA! A LOSS OF MEMORY! HE DOESN'T EVEN KNOW WHO HE IS!!
YEAH? WELL, WE'RE GONNA HELP 'IM TO FIND HIS MEMORY!!
SURE! WE'LL BEAT IT BACK INTO HIM!
WHY BOTHER? I'LL SHOW YOU AN EASIER WAY!
FIRST, WE'VE GOTTA SEE WHAT HE REALLY LOOKS LIKE!
SO LET'S GIVE 'IM A LITTLE SHAVE!
FLAME ON!
HEY! LOOK AT THAT!!
HOLY COW! IT'S THE HUMAN TORCH!
SEE HOW SIMPLE IT IS, WHEN YOU KNOW HOW?
I CAN CONTROL THE FLAME OF MY BODY TO WITHIN A HAIR'S WIDTH!
WAIT!! HIS FACE! NO--IT--CAN'T BE!!
IT IS! IT IS!! HE--HE'S THE SUB-MARINER!
10

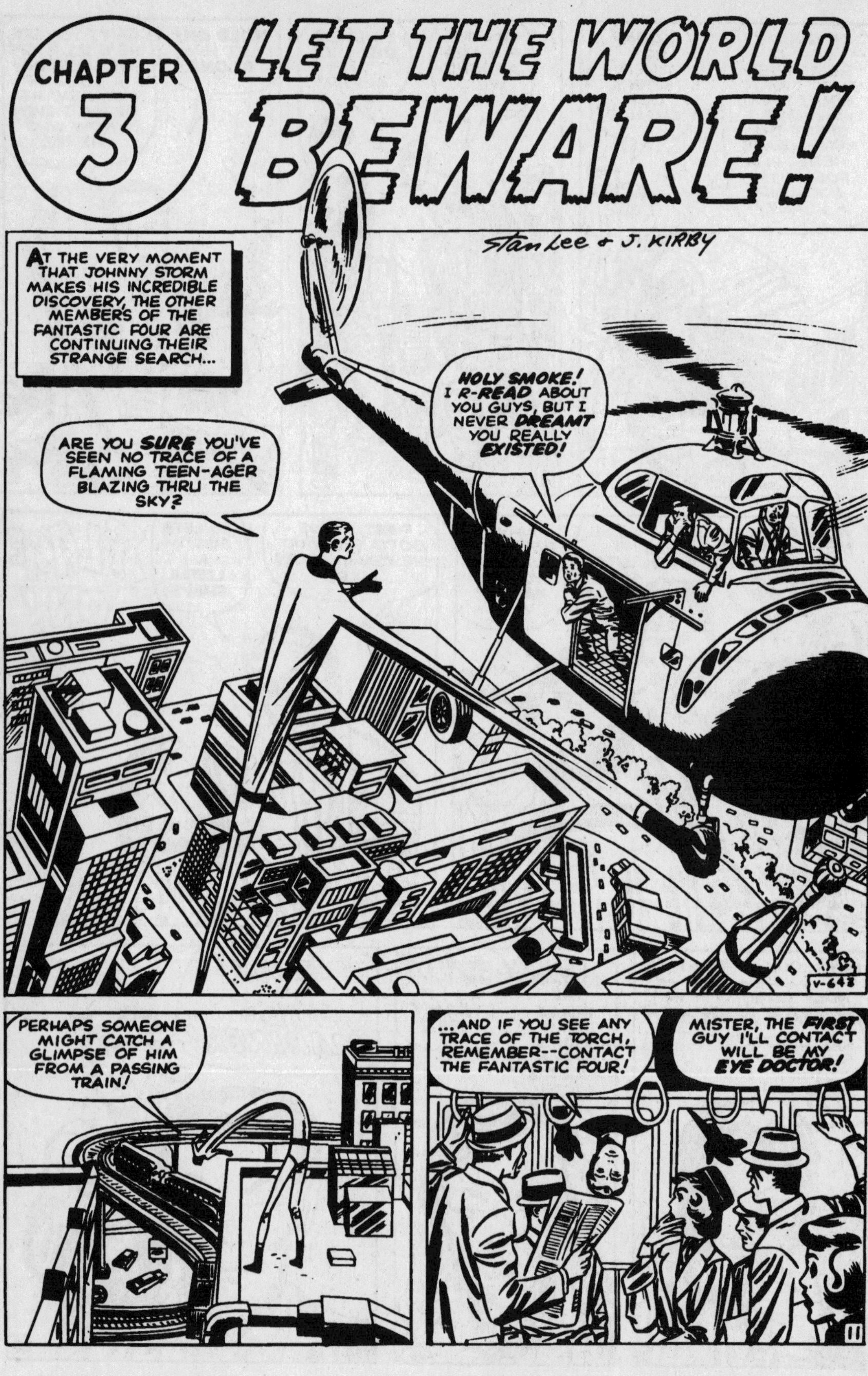
CHAPTER 3
LET THE WORLD BEWARE!
STAN LEE & J. KIRBY
AT THE VERY MOMENT THAT JOHNNY STORM MAKES HIS INCREDIBLE DISCOVERY, THE OTHER MEMBER'S OF THE FANTASTIC FOUR ARE CONTINUING THEIR STRANGE SEARCH...
ARE YOU SURE YOU'VE SEEN NO TRACE OF A FLAMING TEEN-AGER BLAZING THRU THE SKY?
HOLY SMOKE! I R-READ ABOUT YOU GUYS, BUT I NEVER DREAMT YOU REALLY EXISTED!
V-643
PERHAPS SOMEONE MIGHT CATCH A GLIMPSE OF HIM FROM A PASSING TRAIN!
...AND IF YOU SEE ANY TRACE OF THE TORCH, REMEMBER--CONTACT THE FANTASTIC FOUR!
MISTER, THE FIRST GUY I'LL CONTACT WILL BE MY EYE DOCTOR!
11

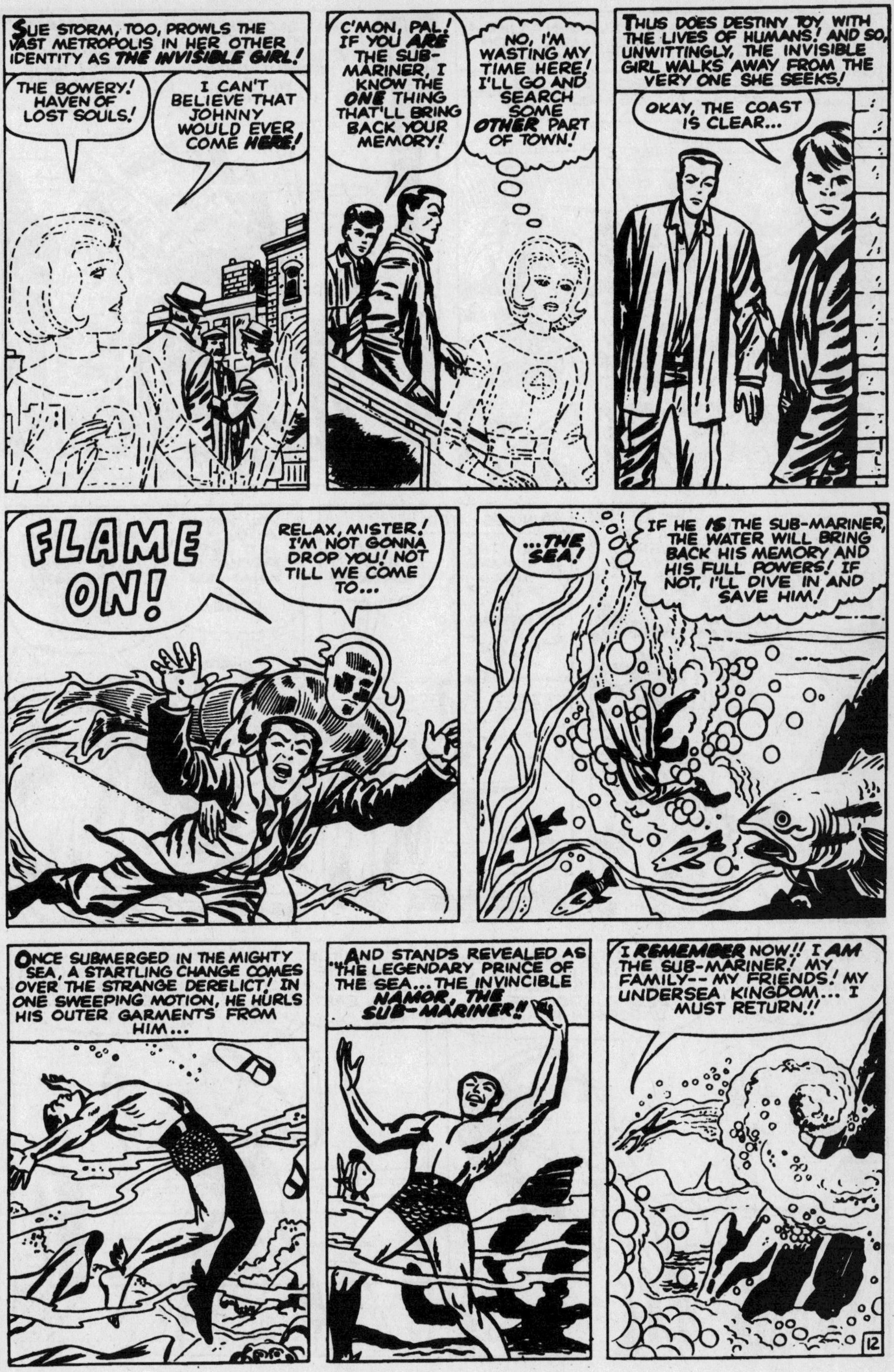
SUE STORM, TOO, PROWLS THE VAST METROPOLIS IN HER OTHER IDENTITY AS THE INVISIBLE GIRL!
THE BOWERY! HAVEN OF LOST SOULS!
I CAN'T BELIEVE THAT JOHNNY WOULD EVER COME HERE!
C'MON, PAL! IF YOU ARE THE SUB-MARINER, I KNOW THE ONE THING THAT'LL BRING BACK YOUR MEMORY!
NO, I'M WASTING MY TIME HERE! I'LL GO AND SEARCH SOME OTHER PART OF TOWN!
THUS DOES DESTINY TOY WITH THE LIVES OF HUMANS! AND SO, UNWITTINGLY, THE INVISIBLE GIRL WALKS AWAY FROM THE VERY ONE SHE SEEKS!
OKAY, THE COAST IS CLEAR...
FLAME ON!
RELAX, MISTER! I'M NOT GONNA DROP YOU! NOT TILL WE COME TO...
...THE SEA!
IF HE IS THE SUB-MARINER, THE WATER WILL BRING BACK HIS MEMORY AND HIS FULL POWERS! IF NOT, I'LL DIVE IN AND SAVE HIM!
ONCE SUBMERGED IN THE MIGHTY SEA, A STARTLING CHANGE COMES OVER THE STRANGE DERELICT! IN ONE SWEEPING MOTION, HE HURLS HIS OUTER GARMENTS FROM HIM...
...AND STANDS REVEALED AS THE LEGENDARY PRINCE OF THE SEA... THE INVINCIBLE NAMOR, THE SUB-MARINER!!
I REMEMBER NOW!! I AM THE SUB-MARINER! MY FAMILY-- MY FRIENDS! MY UNDERSEA KINGDOM... I MUST RETURN!!
12

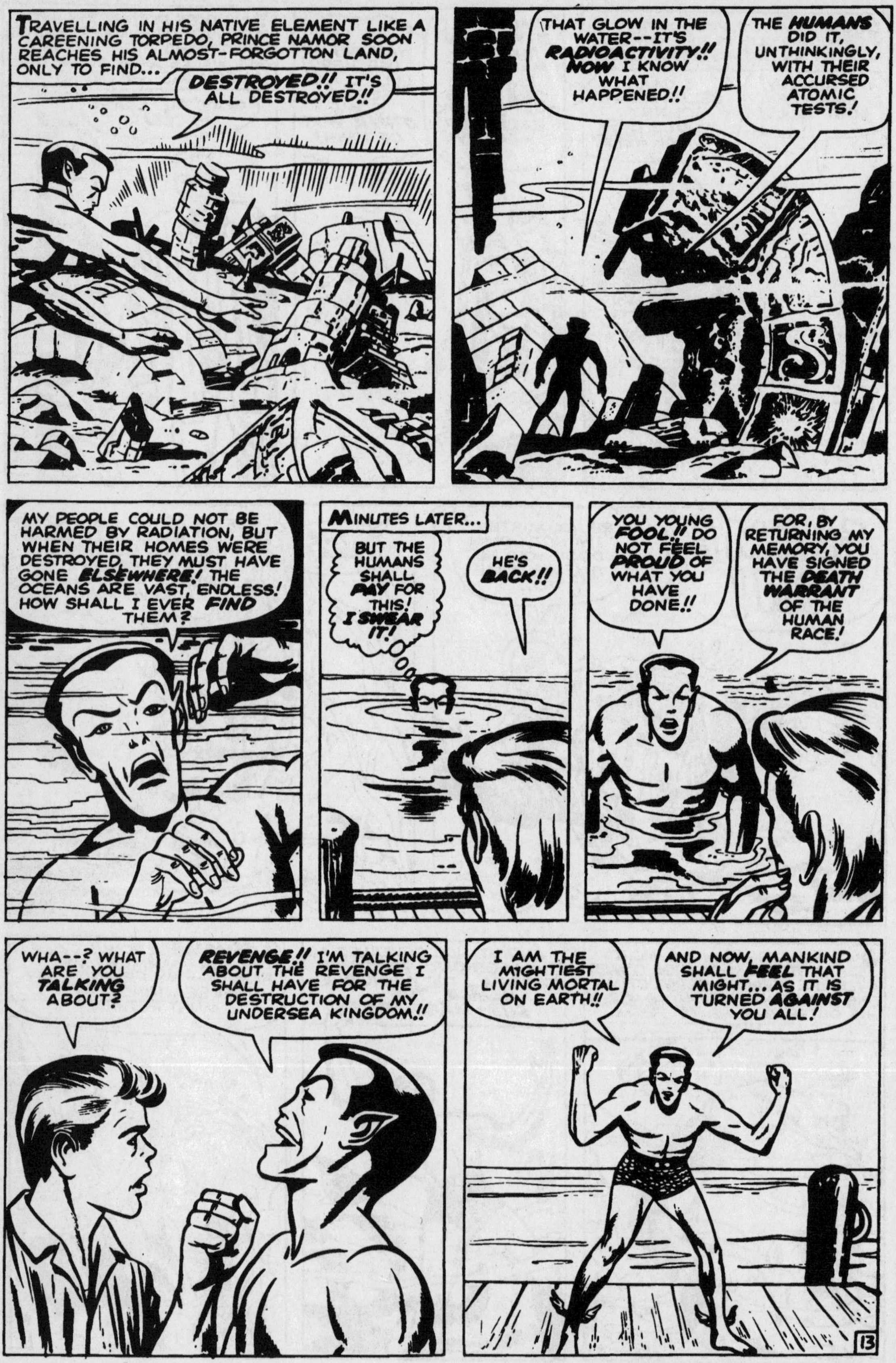
TRAVELLING IN HIS NATIVE ELEMENT LIKE A CAREENING TORPEDO, PRINCE NAMOR SOON REACHES HIS ALMOST-FORGOTTON LAND, ONLY TO FIND...
DESTROYED!! IT'S ALL DESTROYED!!
THAT GLOW IN THE WATER--IT'S RADIOACTIVITY!! NOW I KNOW WHAT HAPPENED!!
THE HUMANS DID IT, UNTHINKINGLY, WITH THEIR ACCURSED ATOMIC TESTS!
MY PEOPLE COULD NOT BE HARMED BY RADIATION, BUT WHEN THEIR HOMES WERE DESTROYED, THEY MUST HAVE GONE ELSEWHERE! THE OCEANS ARE VAST, ENDLESS! HOW SHALL I EVER FIND THEM?
MINUTES LATER...
BUT THE HUMANS SHALL PAY FOR THIS! I SWEAR IT!
HE'S BACK!!
YOU YOUNG FOOL!! DO NOT FEEL PROUD OF WHAT YOU HAVE DONE!!
FOR, BY RETURNING MY MEMORY, YOU HAVE SIGNED THE DEATH WARRANT OF THE HUMAN RACE!
WHA--? WHAT ARE YOU TALKING ABOUT?
REVENGE!! I'M TALKING ABOUT THE REVENGE I SHALL HAVE FOR THE DESTRUCTION OF MY UNDERSEA KINGDOM!!
I AM THE MIGHTIEST LIVING MORTAL ON EARTH!!
AND NOW, MANKIND SHALL FEEL THAT MIGHT... AS IT IS TURNED AGAINST YOU ALL!
13

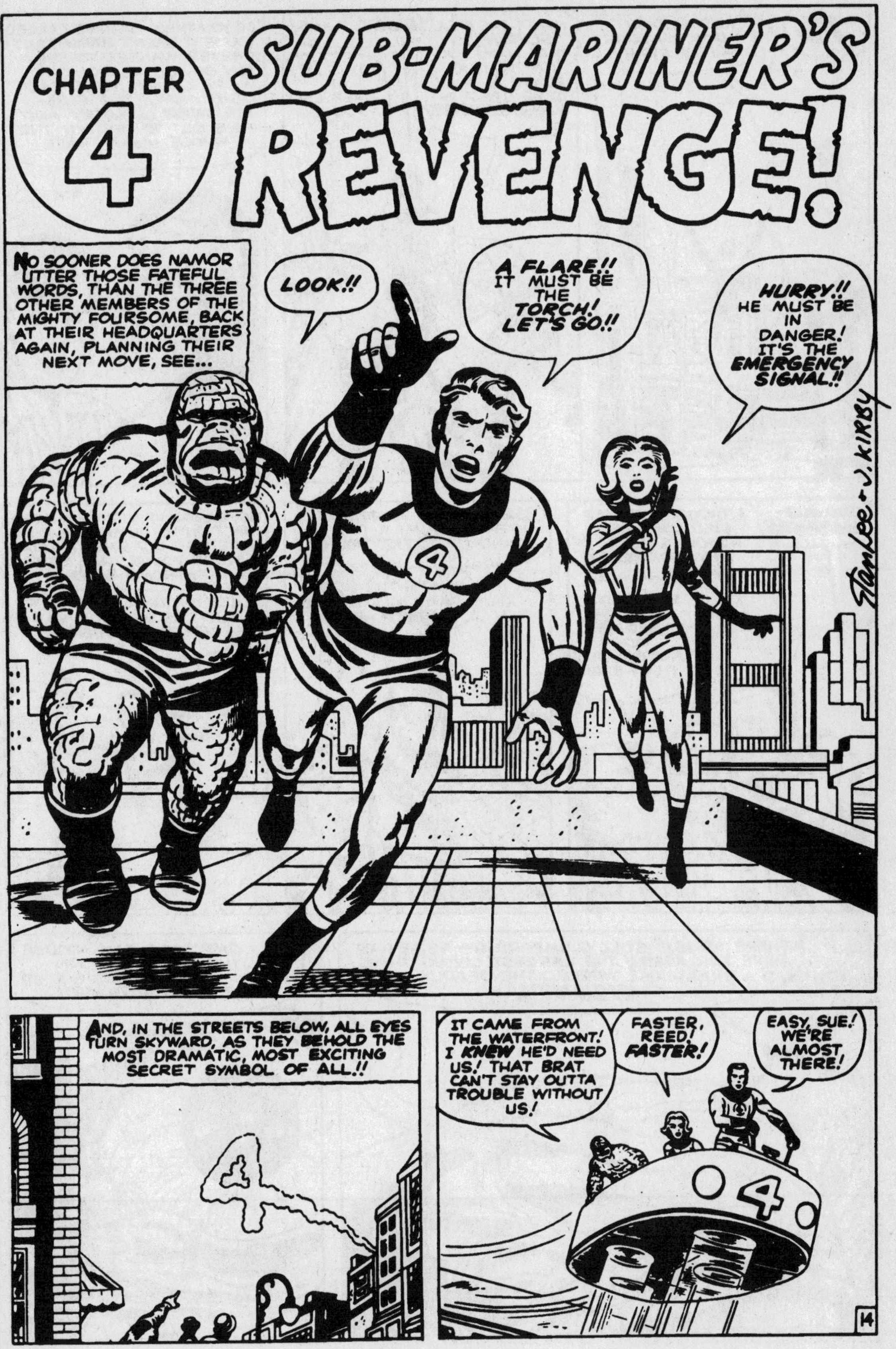
CHAPTER 4
SUB-MARINER'S REVENGE!
NO SOONER DOES NAMOR UTTER THOSE FATEFUL WORDS, THAN THE THREE OTHER MEMBERS OF THE MIGHTY FOURSOME, BACK AT THEIR HEADQUARTERS AGAIN, PLANNING THEIR NEXT MOVE, SEE...
LOOK!!
A FLARE!! IT MUST BE THE TORCH! LET'S GO!!
HURRY!! HE MUST BE IN DANGER! IT'S THE EMERGENCY SIGNAL!!
STAN LEE • J. KIRBY
AND, IN THE STREETS BELOW, ALL EYES TURN SKYWARD, AS THEY BEHOLD THE MOST DRAMATIC, MOST EXCITING SECRET SYMBOL OF ALL!!
4
IT CAME FROM THE WATERFRONT! I KNEW HE'D NEED US! THAT BRAT CAN'T STAY OUTTA TROUBLE WITHOUT US!
FASTER, REED! FASTER!
EASY, SUE! WE'RE ALMOST THERE!
4
14

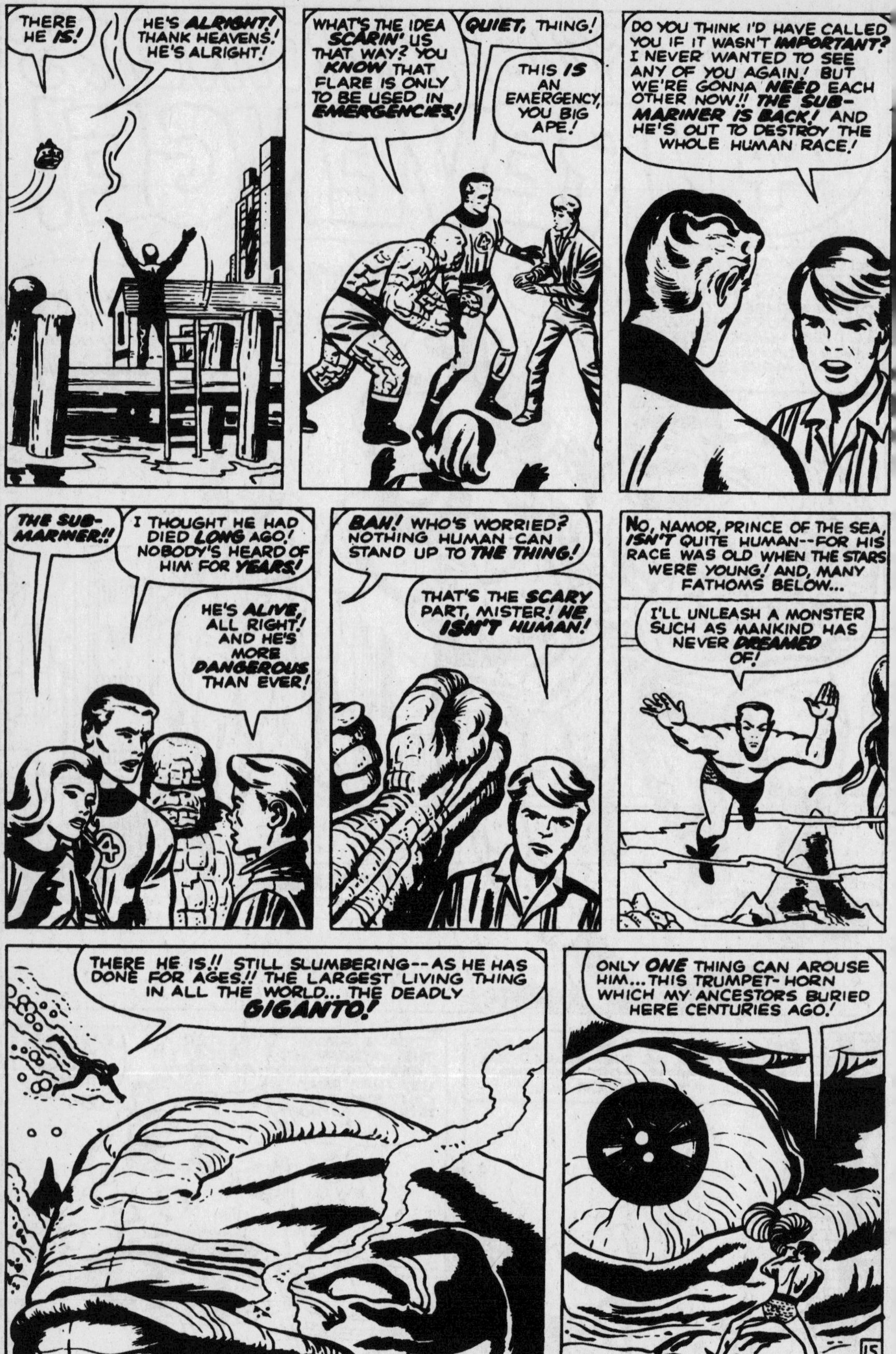

THERE HE IS!
HE'S ALRIGHT! THANK HEAVENS! HE'S ALRIGHT!
WHAT'S THE IDEA SCARIN' US THAT WAY? YOU KNOW THAT FLARE IS ONLY TO BE USED IN EMERGENCIES!
QUIET, THING!
THIS IS AN EMERGENCY, YOU BIG APE!
DO YOU THINK I'D HAVE CALLED YOU IF IT WASN'T IMPORTANT? I NEVER WANTED TO SEE ANY OF YOU AGAIN! BUT WE'RE GONNA NEED EACH OTHER NOW!! THE SUB-MARINER IS BACK! AND HE'S OUT TO DESTROY THE WHOLE HUMAN RACE!
THE SUB-MARINER!!
I THOUGHT HE HAD DIED LONG AGO! NOBODY'S HEARD OF HIM FOR YEARS!
HE'S ALIVE, ALL RIGHT! AND HE'S MORE DANGEROUS THAN EVER!
BAH! WHO'S WORRIED? NOTHING HUMAN CAN STAND UP TO THE THING!
THAT'S THE SCARY PART, MISTER! HE ISN'T HUMAN!
NO, NAMOR, PRINCE OF THE SEA, ISN'T QUITE HUMAN--FOR HIS RACE WAS OLD WHEN THE STARS WERE YOUNG! AND, MANY FATHOMS BELOW...
I'LL UNLEASH A MONSTER SUCH AS MANKIND HAS NEVER DREAMED OF!
THERE HE IS!! STILL SLUMBERING--AS HE HAS DONE FOR AGES!! THE LARGEST LIVING THING IN ALL THE WORLD... THE DEADLY GIGANTO!
ONLY ONE THING CAN AROUSE HIM... THIS TRUMPET-HORN WHICH MY ANCESTORS BURIED HERE CENTURIES AGO!
15

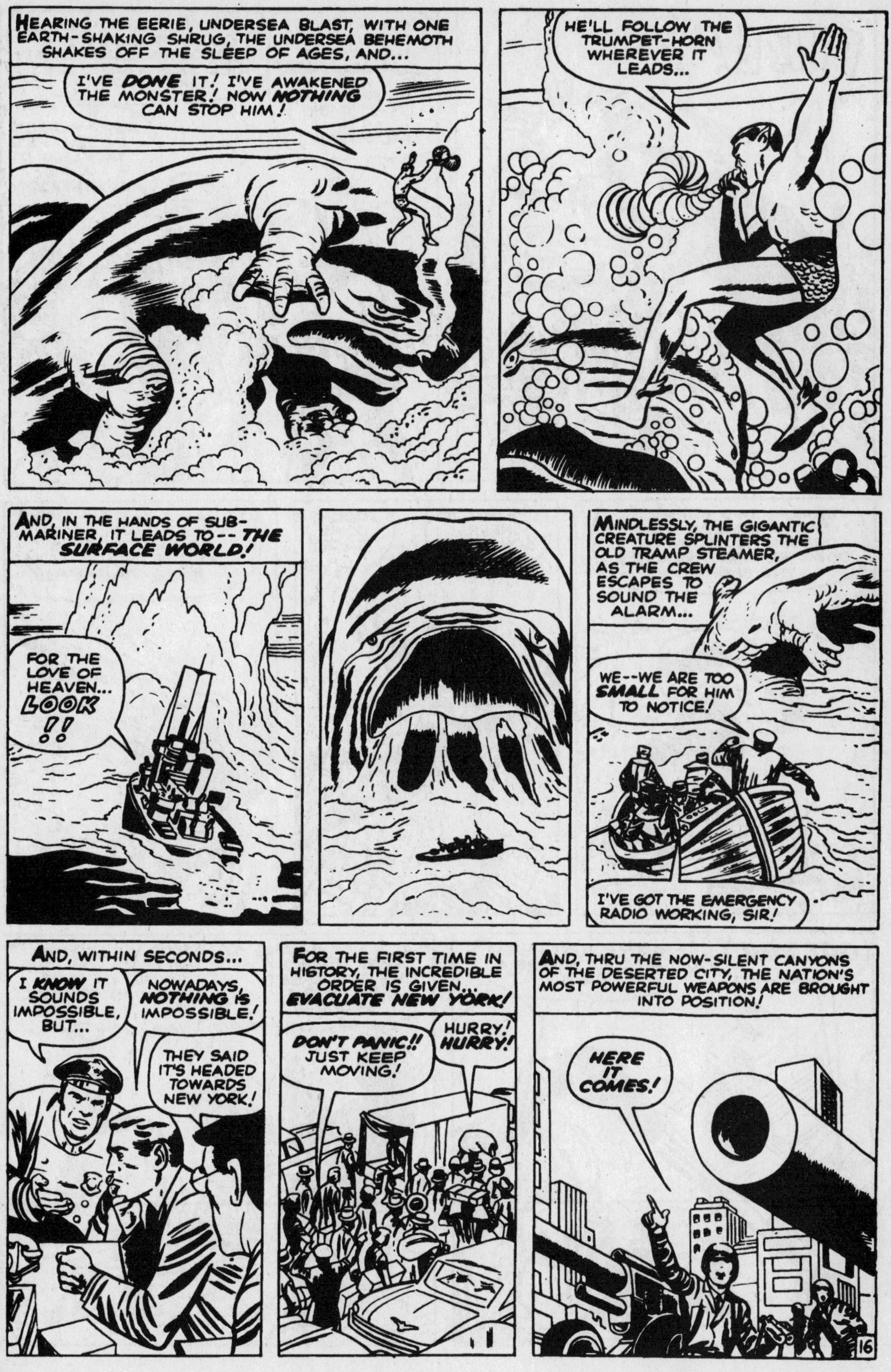
HEARING THE EERIE, UNDERSEA BLAST, WITH ONE EARTH-SHAKING SHRUG, THE UNDERSEA BEHEMOTH SHAKES OFF THE SLEEP OF AGES, AND...
I'VE DONE IT! I'VE AWAKENED THE MONSTER! NOW NOTHING CAN STOP HIM!
HE'LL FOLLOW THE TRUMPET-HORN WHEREVER IT LEADS...
AND, IN THE HANDS OF SUB-MARINER, IT LEADS TO-- THE SURFACE WORLD!
FOR THE LOVE OF HEAVEN... LOOK !!
MINDLESSLY, THE GIGANTIC CREATURE SPLINTERS THE OLD TRAMP STEAMER, AS THE CREW ESCAPES TO SOUND THE ALARM...
WE--WE ARE TOO SMALL FOR HIM TO NOTICE!
I'VE GOT THE EMERGENCY RADIO WORKING, SIR!
AND, WITHIN SECONDS...
I KNOW IT SOUNDS IMPOSSIBLE, BUT...
NOWADAYS, NOTHING IS IMPOSSIBLE!
THEY SAID IT'S HEADED TOWARDS NEW YORK!
FOR THE FIRST TIME IN HISTORY, THE INCREDIBLE ORDER IS GIVEN... EVACUATE NEW YORK!
DON'T PANIC!! JUST KEEP MOVING!
HURRY! HURRY!
AND, THRU THE NOW-SILENT CANYONS OF THE DESERTED CITY, THE NATION'S MOST POWERFUL WEAPONS ARE BROUGHT INTO POSITION!
HERE IT COMES!
16

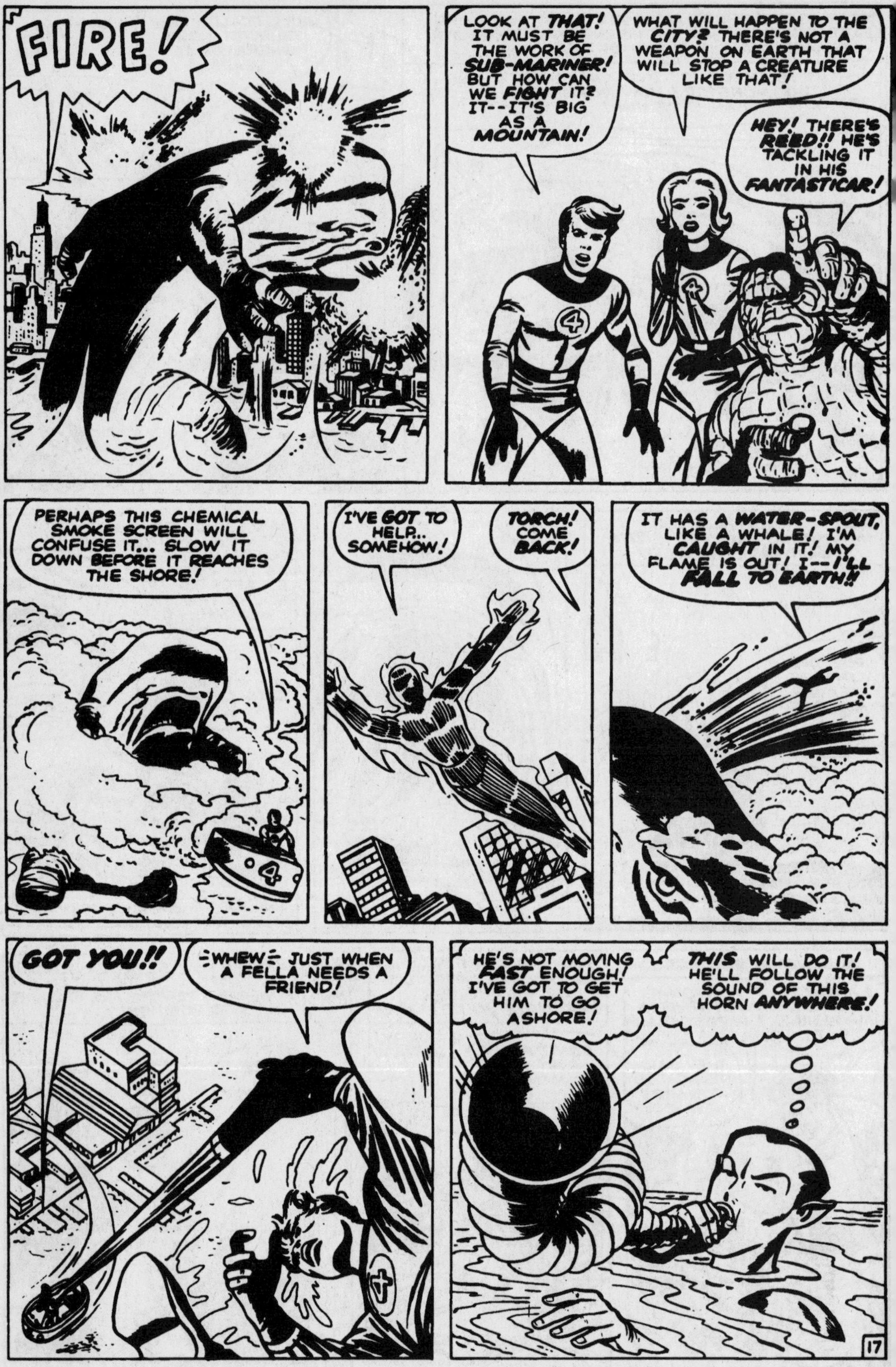
FIRE!
LOOK AT THAT! IT MUST BE THE WORK OF SUB-MARINER! BUT HOW CAN WE FIGHT IT? IT--IT'S BIG AS A MOUNTAIN!
WHAT WILL HAPPEN TO THE CITY? THERE'S NOT A WEAPON ON EARTH THAT WILL STOP A CREATURE LIKE THAT!
HEY! THERE'S REED!! HE'S TACKLING IT IN HIS FANTASTICAR!
PERHAPS THIS CHEMICAL SMOKE SCREEN WILL CONFUSE IT... SLOW IT DOWN BEFORE IT REACHES THE SHORE!
I'VE GOT TO HELP.. SOMEHOW!
TORCH! COME BACK!
IT HAS A WATER-SPOUT, LIKE A WHALE! I'M CAUGHT IN IT! MY FLAME IS OUT! I--I'LL FALL TO EARTH!!
GOT YOU!!
WHEW JUST WHEN A FELLA NEEDS A FRIEND!
HE'S NOT MOVING FAST ENOUGH! I'VE GOT TO GET HIM TO GO ASHORE!
THIS WILL DO IT! HE'LL FOLLOW THE SOUND OF THIS HORN ANYWHERE!

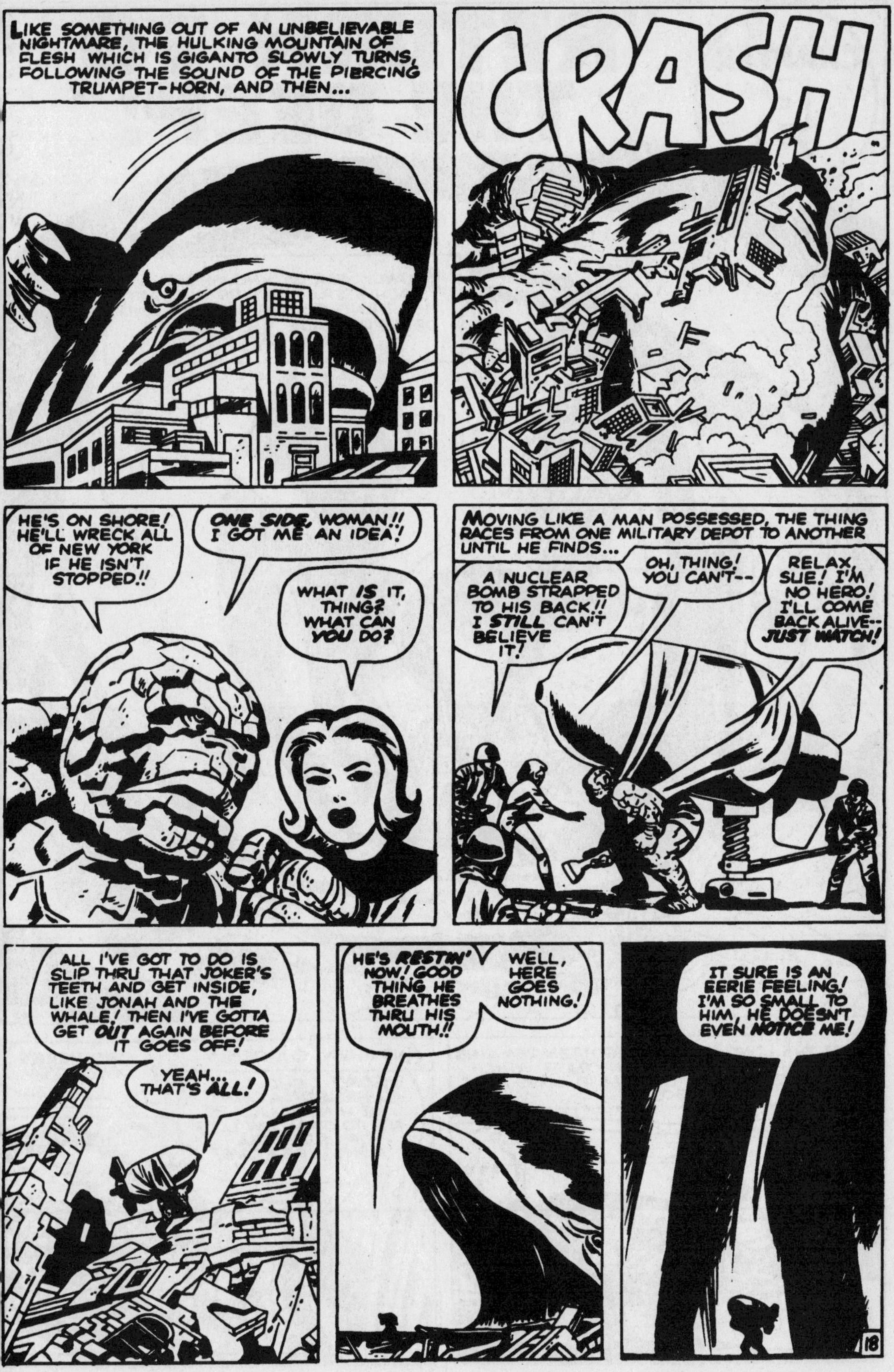
LIKE SOMETHING OUT OF AN UNBELIEVABLE NIGHTMARE, THE HULKING MOUNTAIN OF FLESH WHICH IS GIGANTO SLOWLY TURNS, FOLLOWING THE SOUND OF THE PIERCING TRUMPET-HORN, AND THEN...
CRASH
HE'S ON SHORE! HE'LL WRECK ALL OF NEW YORK IF HE ISN'T STOPPED!!
ONE SIDE, WOMAN!! I GOT ME AN IDEA!
WHAT IS IT, THING? WHAT CAN YOU DO?
MOVING LIKE A MAN POSSESSED, THE THING RACES FROM ONE MILITARY DEPOT TO ANOTHER UNTIL HE FINDS...
A NUCLEAR BOMB STRAPPED TO HIS BACK!! I STILL CAN'T BELIEVE IT!
OH, THING! YOU CAN'T--
RELAX, SUE! I'M NO HERO! I'LL COME BACK ALIVE-- JUST WATCH!
ALL I'VE GOT TO DO IS SLIP THRU THAT JOKER'S TEETH AND GET INSIDE, LIKE JONAH AND THE WHALE! THEN I'VE GOTTA GET OUT AGAIN BEFORE IT GOES OFF!
YEAH... THAT'S ALL!
HE'S RESTIN' NOW! GOOD THING HE BREATHES THRU HIS MOUTH!!
WELL, HERE GOES NOTHING!
IT SURE IS AN EERIE FEELING! I'M SO SMALL TO HIM, HE DOESN'T EVEN NOTICE ME!
18

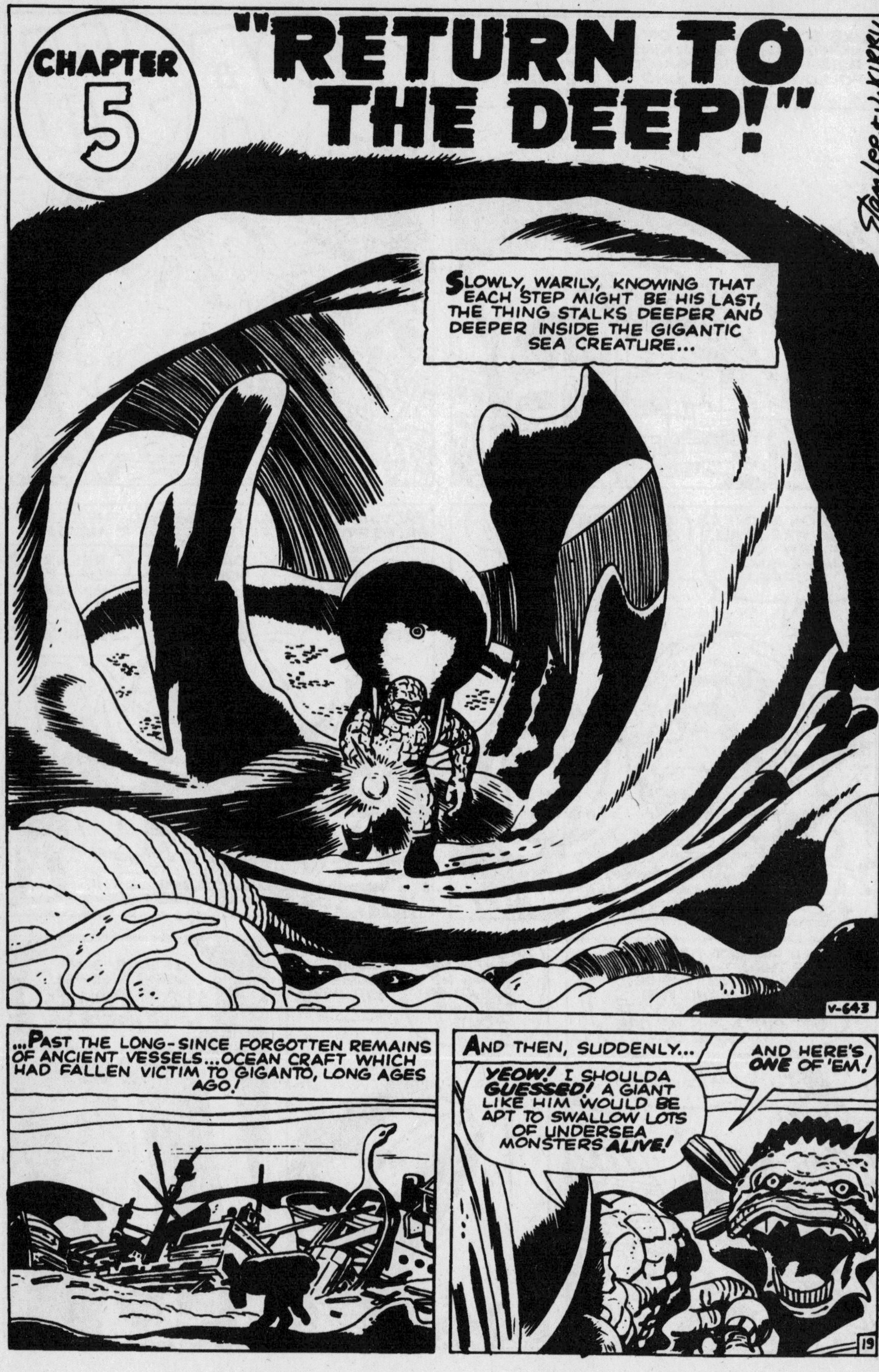
CHAPTER 5
"RETURN TO THE DEEP!"
SLOWLY, WARILY, KNOWING THAT EACH STEP MIGHT BE HIS LAST, THE THING STALKS DEEPER AND DEEPER INSIDE THE GIGANTIC SEA CREATURE...
V-643
...PAST THE LONG-SINCE FORGOTTEN REMAINS OF ANCIENT VESSELS...OCEAN CRAFT WHICH HAD FALLEN VICTIM TO GIGANTO, LONG AGES AGO!
AND THEN, SUDDENLY...
YEOW! I SHOULDA GUESSED! A GIANT LIKE HIM WOULD BE APT TO SWALLOW LOTS OF UNDERSEA MONSTERS ALIVE!
AND HERE'S ONE OF 'EM!
19

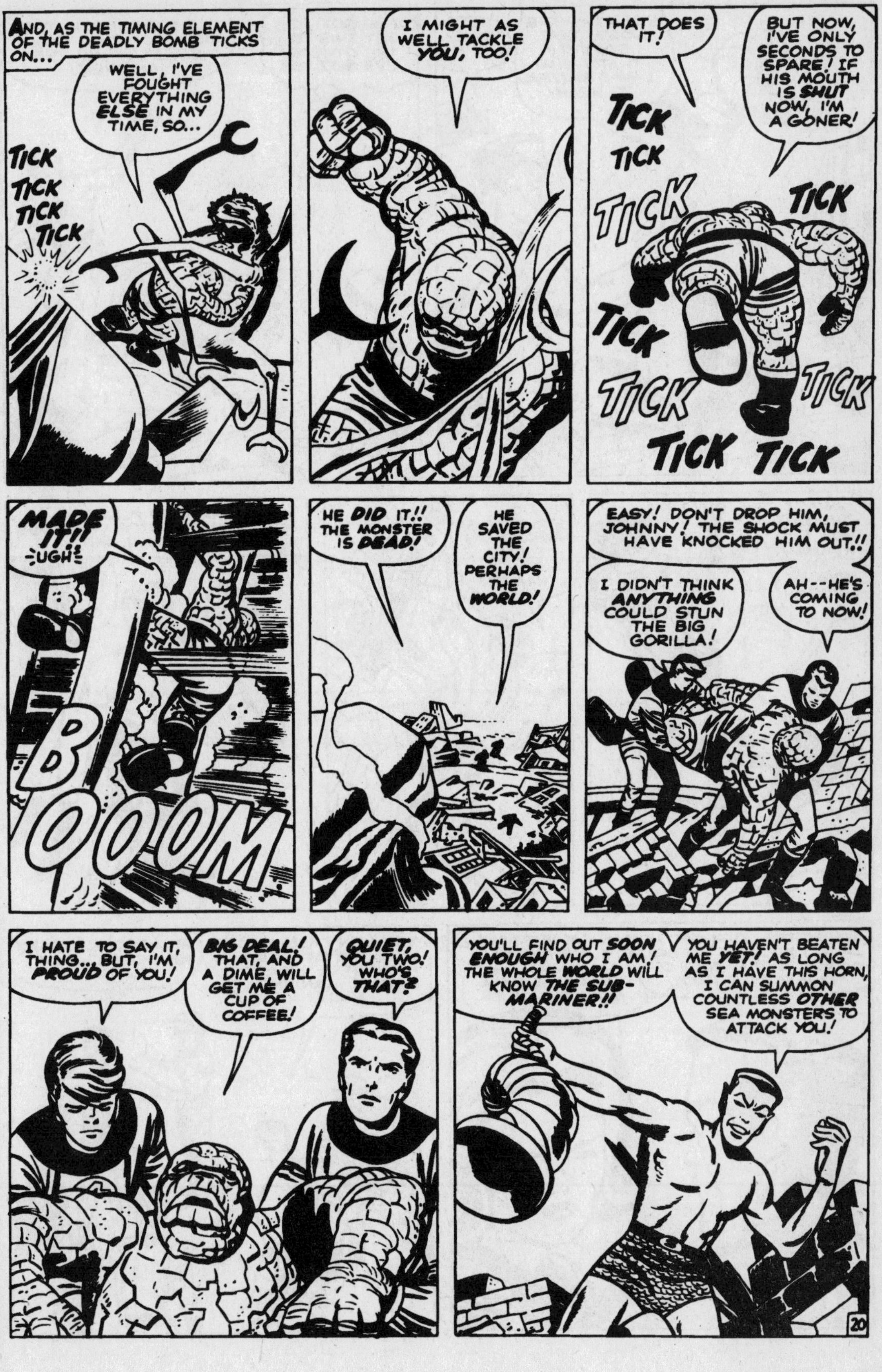
AND, AS THE TIMING ELEMENT OF THE DEADLY BOMB TICKS ON...
WELL, I'VE FOUGHT EVERYTHING ELSE IN MY TIME, SO...
TICK
TICK
TICK
TICK
I MIGHT AS WELL TACKLE YOU, TOO!
THAT DOES IT!
BUT NOW, I'VE ONLY SECONDS TO SPARE! IF HIS MOUTH IS SHUT NOW, I'M A GONER!
TICK
TICK
TICK
TICK
TICK
TICK
TICK
TICK
TICK
MADE IT!! UGH
BOOOM
HE DID IT!! THE MONSTER IS DEAD!
HE SAVED THE CITY! PERHAPS THE WORLD!
EASY! DON'T DROP HIM, JOHNNY! THE SHOCK MUST HAVE KNOCKED HIM OUT!!
I DIDN'T THINK ANYTHING COULD STUN THE BIG GORILLA!
AH--HE'S COMING TO NOW!
I HATE TO SAY IT, THING... BUT, I'M PROUD OF YOU!
BIG DEAL! THAT, AND A DIME, WILL GET ME A CUP OF COFFEE!
QUIET, YOU TWO! WHO'S THAT?
YOU'LL FIND OUT SOON ENOUGH WHO I AM! THE WHOLE WORLD WILL KNOW THE SUB-MARINER!!
YOU HAVEN'T BEATEN ME YET! AS LONG AS I HAVE THIS HORN, I CAN SUMMON COUNTLESS OTHER SEA MONSTERS TO ATTACK YOU!
20

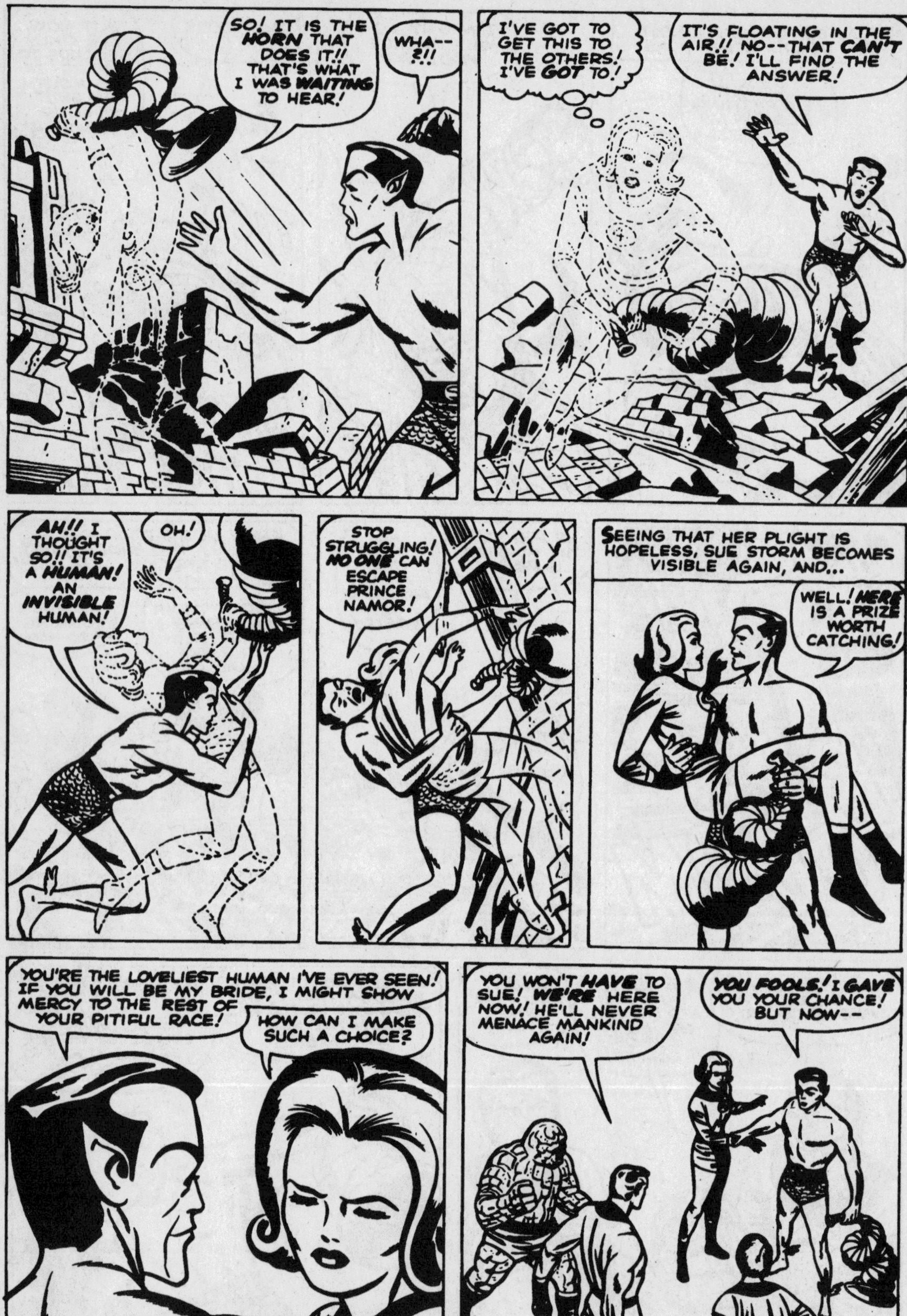
SO! IT IS THE HORN THAT DOES IT!! THAT'S WHAT I WAS WAITING TO HEAR!
WHA-- ?!!
I'VE GOT TO GET THIS TO THE OTHERS! I'VE GOT TO!
IT'S FLOATING IN THE AIR!! NO--THAT CAN'T BE! I'LL FIND THE ANSWER!
AH!! I THOUGHT SO!! IT'S A HUMAN! AN INVISIBLE HUMAN!
OH!
STOP STRUGGLING! NO ONE CAN ESCAPE PRINCE NAMOR!
SEEING THAT HER PLIGHT IS HOPELESS, SUE STORM BECOMES VISIBLE AGAIN, AND...
WELL! HERE IS A PRIZE WORTH CATCHING!
YOU'RE THE LOVELIEST HUMAN I'VE EVER SEEN! IF YOU WILL BE MY BRIDE, I MIGHT SHOW MERCY TO THE REST OF YOUR PITIFUL RACE!
HOW CAN I MAKE SUCH A CHOICE?
YOU WON'T HAVE TO SUE! WE'RE HERE NOW! HE'LL NEVER MENACE MANKIND AGAIN!
YOU FOOLS! I GAVE YOU YOUR CHANCE! BUT NOW--
21

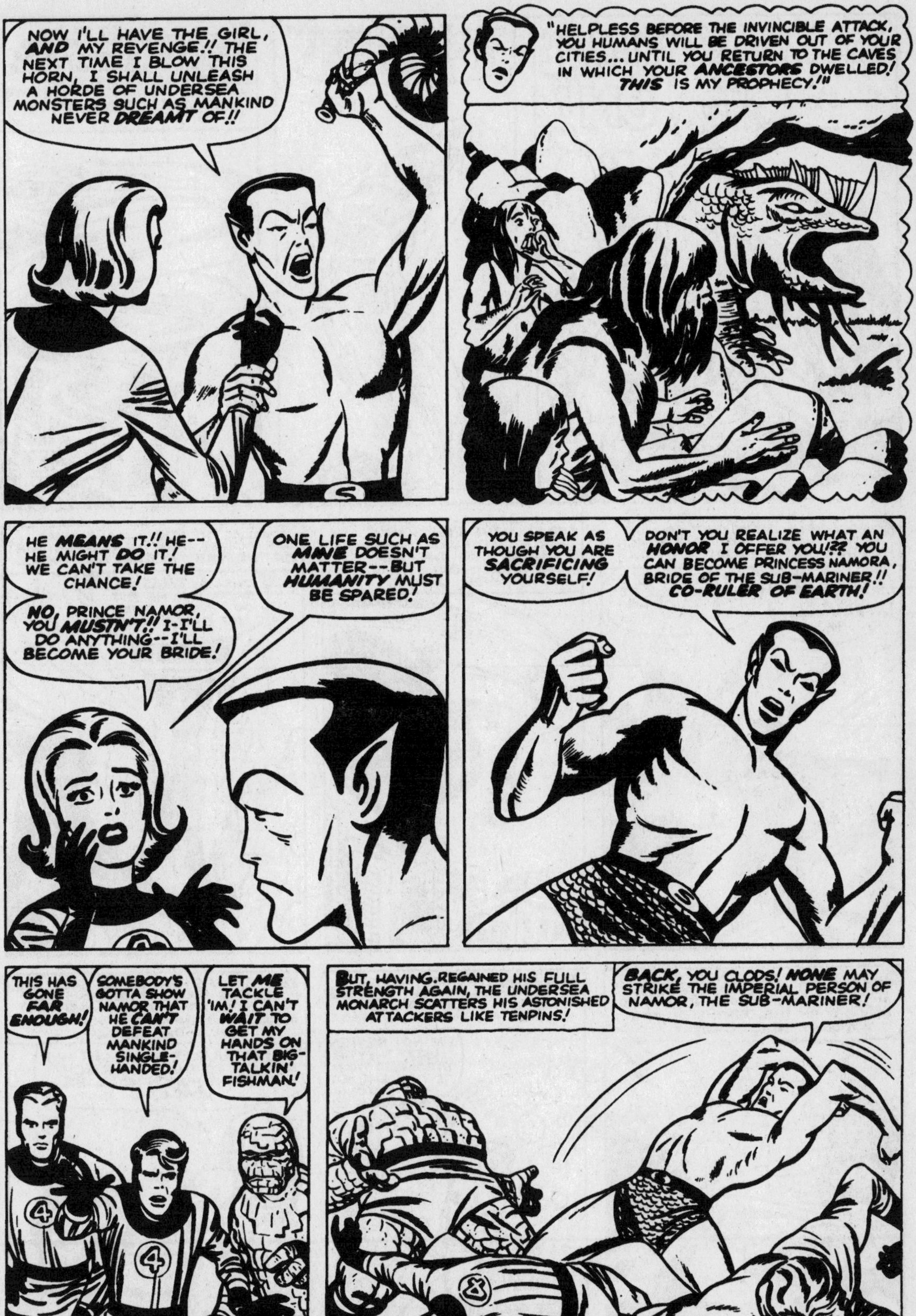
NOW I'LL HAVE THE GIRL, AND MY REVENGE!! THE NEXT TIME I BLOW THIS HORN, I SHALL UNLEASH A HORDE OF UNDERSEA MONSTERS SUCH AS MANKIND NEVER DREAMT OF!!
"HELPLESS BEFORE THE INVINCIBLE ATTACK, YOU HUMANS WILL BE DRIVEN OUT OF YOUR CITIES... UNTIL YOU RETURN TO THE CAVES IN WHICH YOUR ANCESTORS DWELLED! THIS IS MY PROPHECY!"
HE MEANS IT!! HE--HE MIGHT DO IT! WE CAN'T TAKE THE CHANCE!
NO, PRINCE NAMOR, YOU MUSTN'T!! I-I'LL DO ANYTHING--I'LL BECOME YOUR BRIDE!
ONE LIFE SUCH AS MINE DOESN'T MATTER--BUT HUMANITY MUST BE SPARED!
YOU SPEAK AS THOUGH YOU ARE SACRIFICING YOURSELF!
DON'T YOU REALIZE WHAT AN HONOR I OFFER YOU!?? YOU CAN BECOME PRINCESS NAMORA, BRIDE OF THE SUB-MARINER!! CO-RULER OF EARTH!
THIS HAS GONE FAR ENOUGH!
SOMEBODY'S GOTTA SHOW NAMOR THAT HE CAN'T DEFEAT MANKIND SINGLE-HANDED!
LET ME TACKLE 'IM! I CAN'T WAIT TO GET MY HANDS ON THAT BIG-TALKIN' FISHMAN!
BUT, HAVING REGAINED HIS FULL STRENGTH AGAIN, THE UNDERSEA MONARCH SCATTERS HIS ASTONISHED ATTACKERS LIKE TENPINS!
BACK, YOU CLODS! NONE MAY STRIKE THE IMPERIAL PERSON OF NAMOR, THE SUB-MARINER!
22

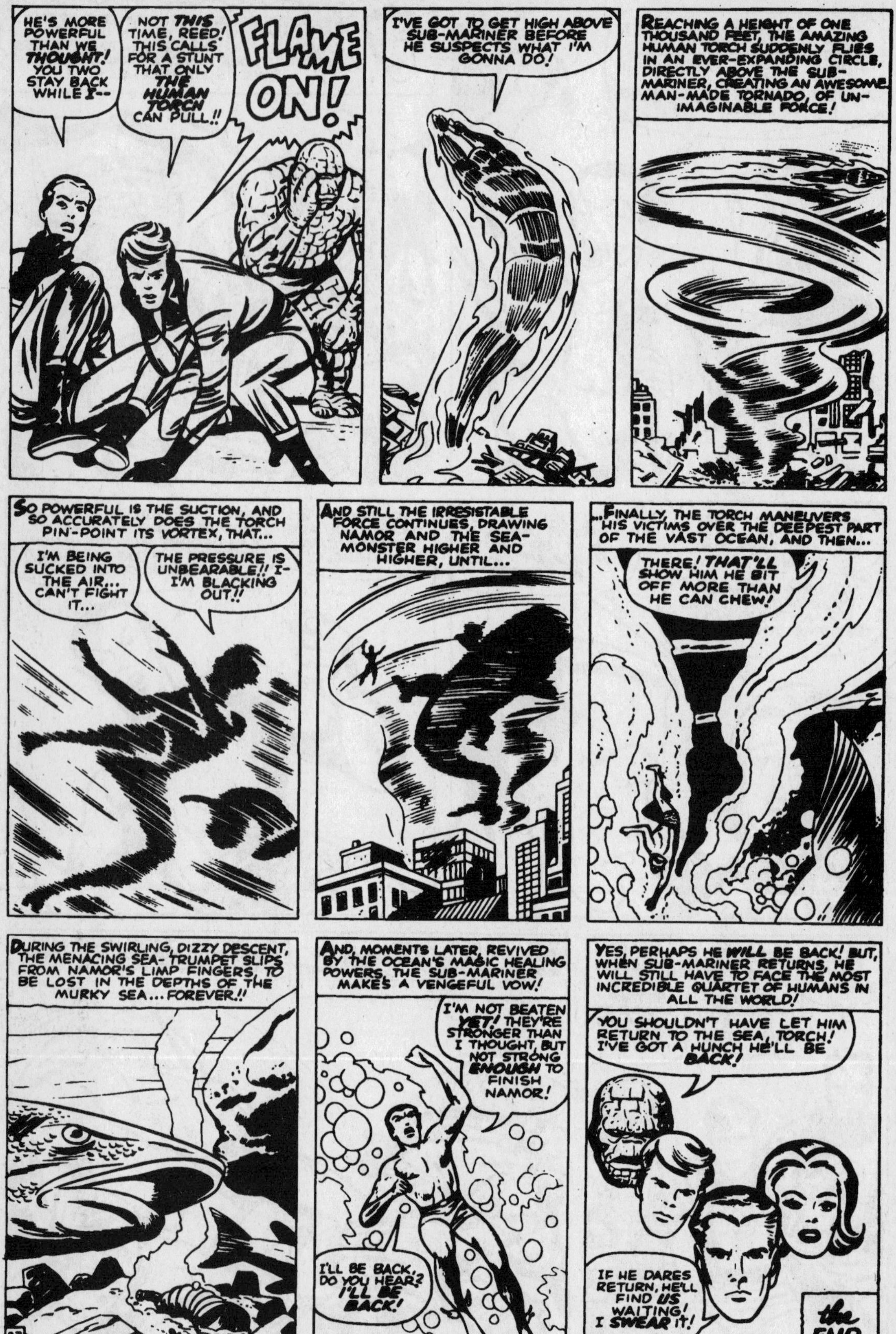

HE'S MORE POWERFUL THAN WE THOUGHT! YOU TWO STAY BACK WHILE I--
NOT THIS TIME, REED! THIS CALLS FOR A STUNT THAT ONLY THE HUMAN TORCH CAN PULL!!
FLAME ON!
I'VE GOT TO GET HIGH ABOVE SUB-MARINER BEFORE HE SUSPECTS WHAT I'M GONNA DO!
REACHING A HEIGHT OF ONE THOUSAND FEET, THE AMAZING HUMAN TORCH SUDDENLY FLIES IN AN EVER-EXPANDING CIRCLE, DIRECTLY ABOVE THE SUB-MARINER, CREATING AN AWESOME MAN-MADE TORNADO, OF UN-IMAGINABLE FORCE!
SO POWERFUL IS THE SUCTION, AND SO ACCURATELY DOES THE TORCH PIN-POINT ITS VORTEX, THAT...
I'M BEING SUCKED INTO THE AIR... CAN'T FIGHT IT...
THE PRESSURE IS UNBEARABLE!! I-I'M BLACKING OUT!!
AND STILL THE IRRESISTABLE FORCE CONTINUES, DRAWING NAMOR AND THE SEA-MONSTER HIGHER AND HIGHER, UNTIL...
...FINALLY, THE TORCH MANEUVERS HIS VICTIMS OVER THE DEEPEST PART OF THE VAST OCEAN, AND THEN...
THERE! THAT'LL SHOW HIM HE BIT OFF MORE THAN HE CAN CHEW!
DURING THE SWIRLING, DIZZY DESCENT, THE MENACING SEA-TRUMPET SLIPS FROM NAMOR'S LIMP FINGERS, TO BE LOST IN THE DEPTHS OF THE MURKY SEA... FOREVER!!
23
AND, MOMENTS LATER, REVIVED BY THE OCEAN'S MAGIC HEALING POWERS, THE SUB-MARINER MAKES A VENGEFUL VOW!
I'M NOT BEATEN YET! THEY'RE STRONGER THAN I THOUGHT, BUT NOT STRONG ENOUGH TO FINISH NAMOR!
I'LL BE BACK, DO YOU HEAR? I'LL BE BACK!
YES, PERHAPS HE WILL BE BACK! BUT, WHEN SUB-MARINER RETURNS, HE WILL STILL HAVE TO FACE THE MOST INCREDIBLE QUARTET OF HUMANS IN ALL THE WORLD!
YOU SHOULDN'T HAVE LET HIM RETURN TO THE SEA, TORCH! I'VE GOT A HUNCH HE'LL BE BACK!
IF HE DARES RETURN, HE'LL FIND US WAITING! I SWEAR IT!
THE END

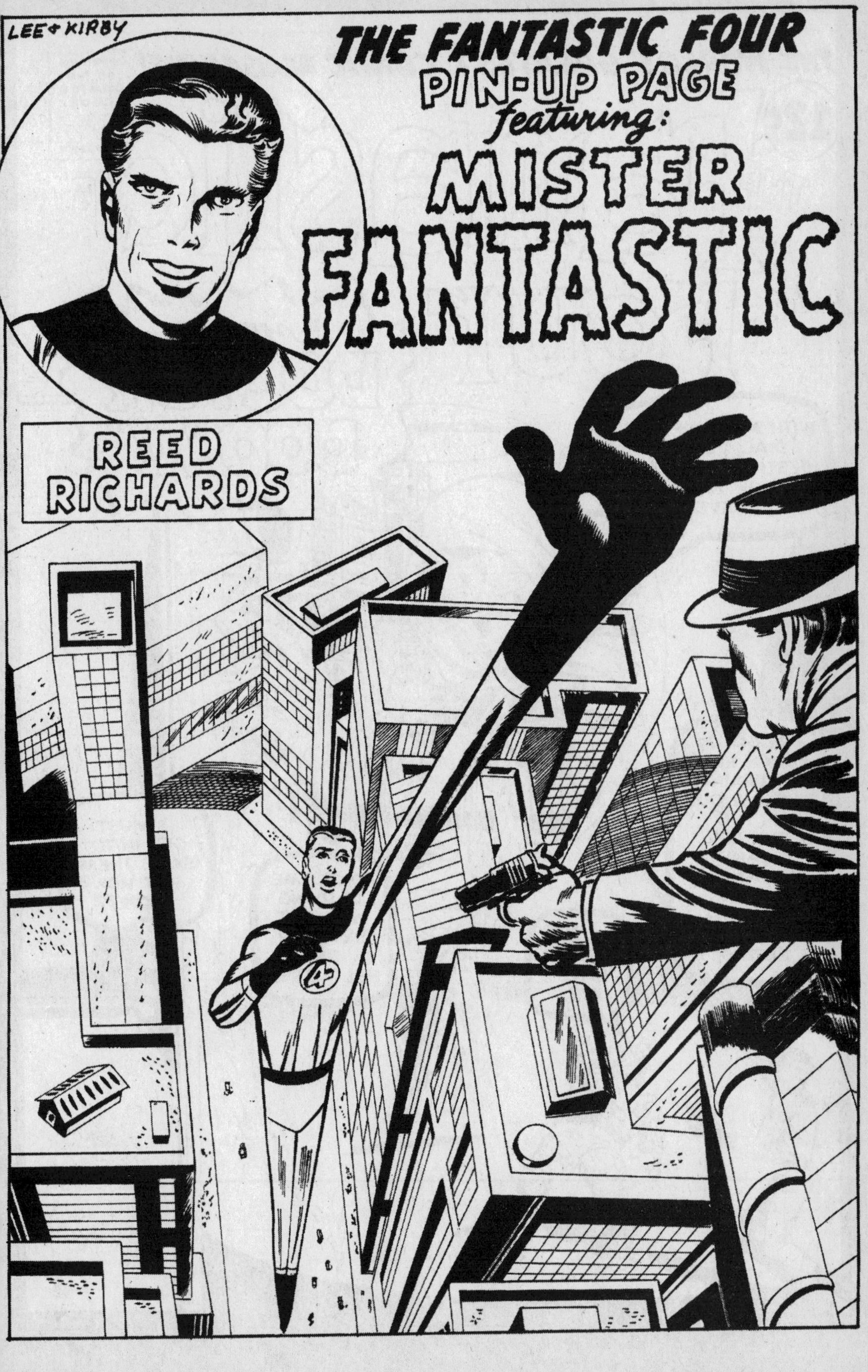
LEE & KIRBY
THE FANTASTIC FOUR
PIN-UP PAGE
featuring:
MISTER
FANTASTIC
REED
RICHARDS

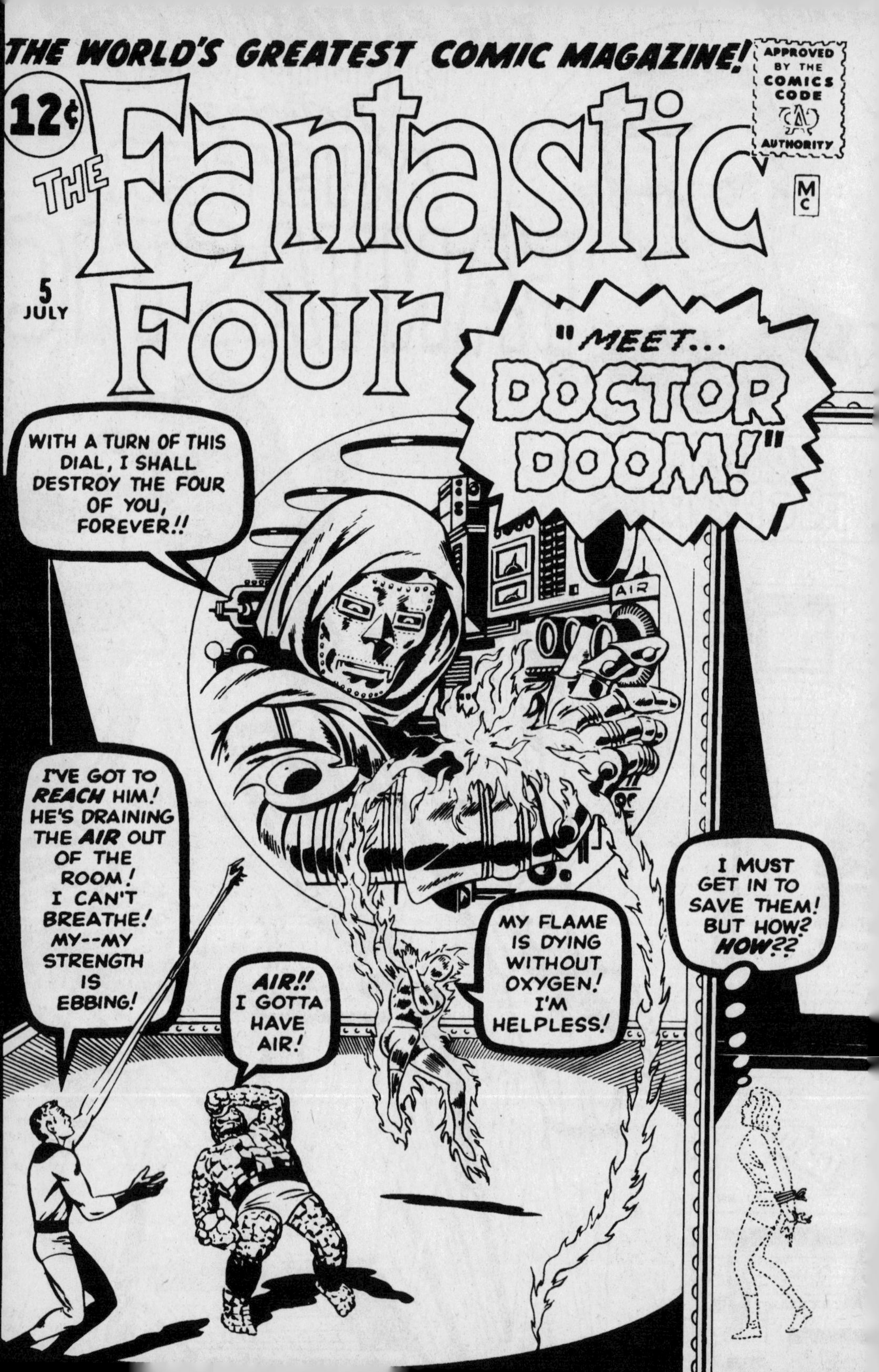
THE WORLD'S GREATEST COMIC MAGAZINE!
APPROVED BY THE COMICS CODE AUTHORITY
12¢
THE Fantastic Four
MC
5 JULY
"MEET... DOCTOR DOOM!"
WITH A TURN OF THIS DIAL, I SHALL DESTROY THE FOUR OF YOU, FOREVER!!
AIR
I'VE GOT TO REACH HIM! HE'S DRAINING THE AIR OUT OF THE ROOM! I CAN'T BREATHE! MY--MY STRENGTH IS EBBING!
AIR!! I GOTTA HAVE AIR!
MY FLAME IS DYING WITHOUT OXYGEN! I'M HELPLESS!
I MUST GET IN TO SAVE THEM! BUT HOW? HOW??

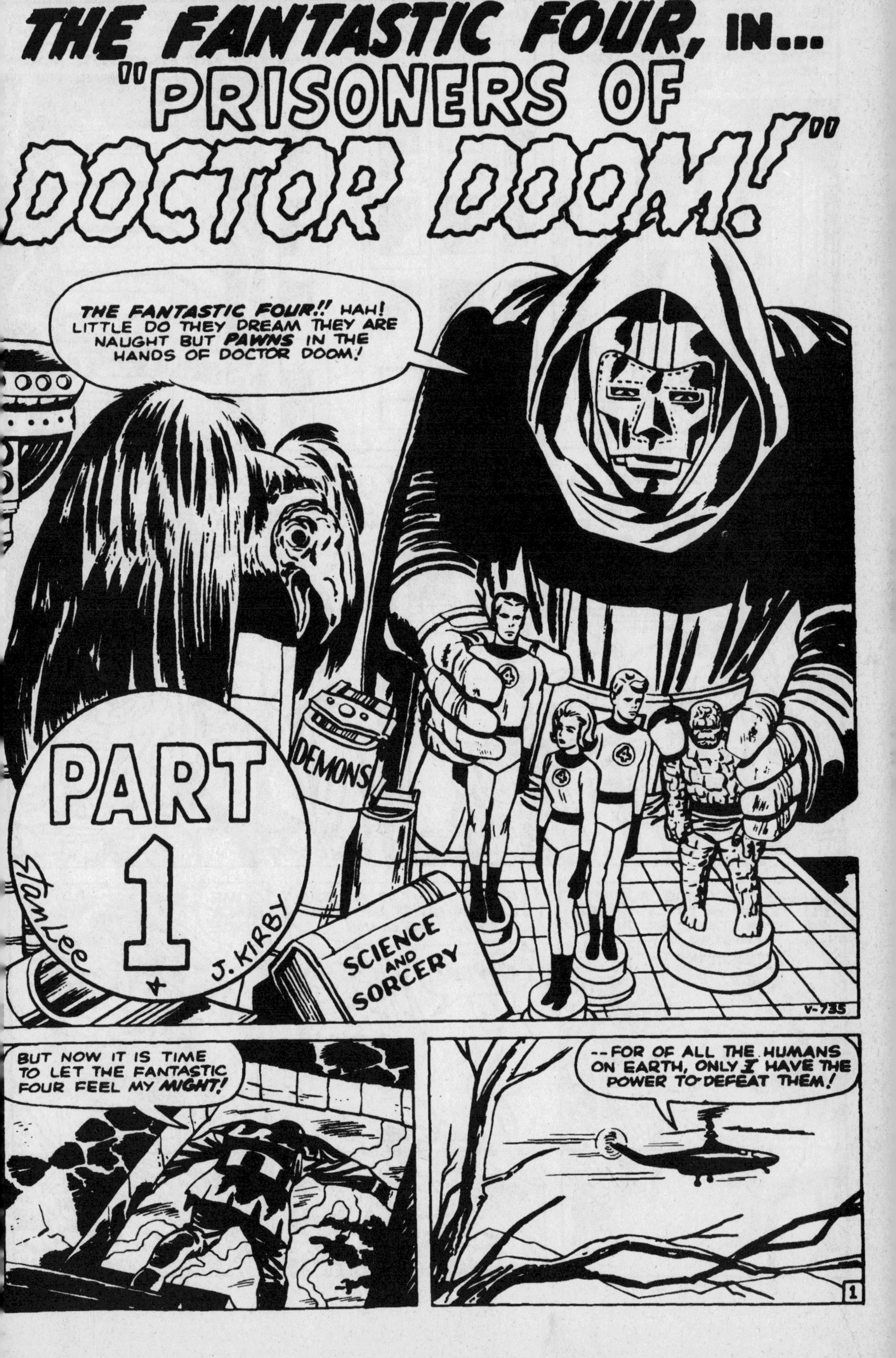
THE FANTASTIC FOUR, IN...
"PRISONERS OF DOCTOR DOOM!"
THE FANTASTIC FOUR!! HAH! LITTLE DO THEY DREAM THEY ARE NAUGHT BUT PAWNS IN THE HANDS OF DOCTOR DOOM!
DEMONS
PART 1
STAN LEE + J. KIRBY
SCIENCE AND SORCERY
V-735
BUT NOW IT IS TIME TO LET THE FANTASTIC FOUR FEEL MY MIGHT!
--FOR OF ALL THE HUMANS ON EARTH, ONLY I HAVE THE POWER TO DEFEAT THEM!
1

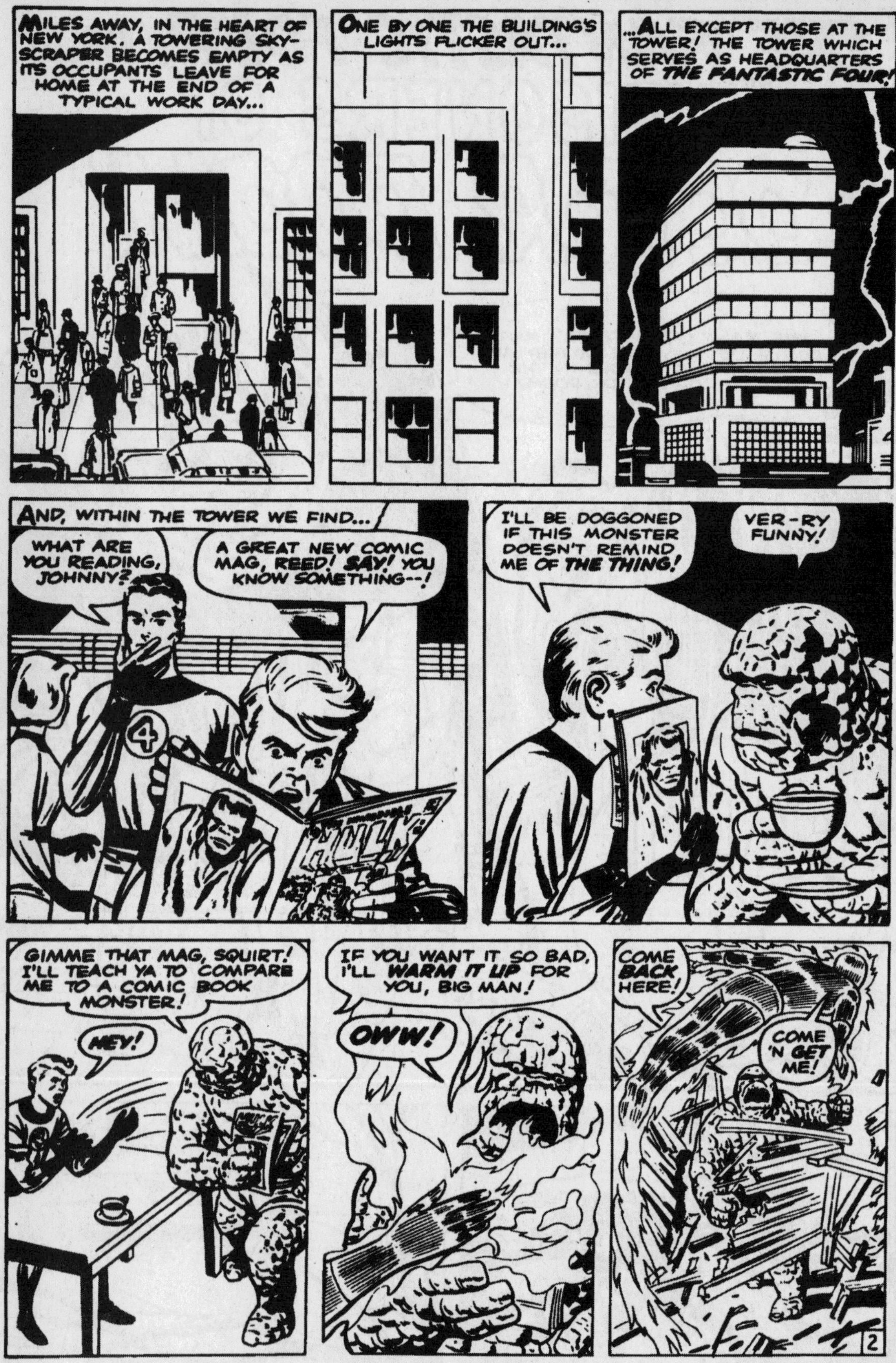
MILES AWAY, IN THE HEART OF NEW YORK, A TOWERING SKY-SCRAPER BECOMES EMPTY AS ITS OCCUPANTS LEAVE FOR HOME AT THE END OF A TYPICAL WORK DAY...
ONE BY ONE THE BUILDING'S LIGHTS FLICKER OUT...
...ALL EXCEPT THOSE AT THE TOWER! THE TOWER WHICH SERVES AS HEADQUARTERS OF THE FANTASTIC FOUR!
AND, WITHIN THE TOWER WE FIND...
WHAT ARE YOU READING, JOHNNY?
A GREAT NEW COMIC MAG, REED! SAY! YOU KNOW SOMETHING--!
I'LL BE DOGGONED IF THIS MONSTER DOESN'T REMIND ME OF THE THING!
VER-RY FUNNY!
GIMME THAT MAG, SQUIRT! I'LL TEACH YA TO COMPARE ME TO A COMIC BOOK MONSTER!
HEY!
IF YOU WANT IT SO BAD, I'LL WARM IT UP FOR YOU, BIG MAN!
OWW!
COME BACK HERE!
COME 'N GET ME!
2

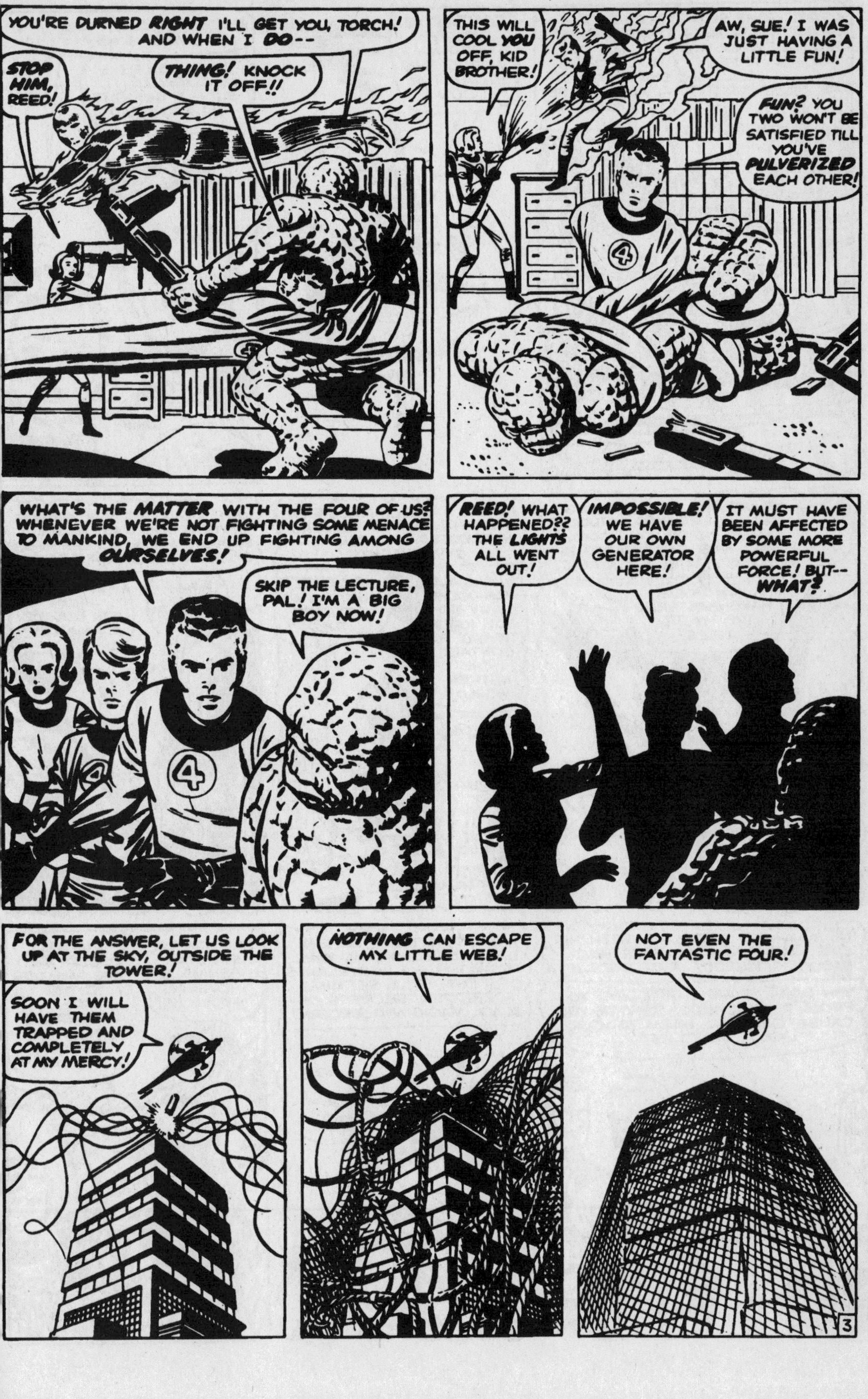
YOU'RE DURNED RIGHT I'LL GET YOU, TORCH! AND WHEN I DO--
STOP HIM, REED!
THING! KNOCK IT OFF!!
THIS WILL COOL YOU OFF, KID BROTHER!
AW, SUE! I WAS JUST HAVING A LITTLE FUN!
FUN? YOU TWO WON'T BE SATISFIED TILL YOU'VE PULVERIZED EACH OTHER!
WHAT'S THE MATTER WITH THE FOUR OF US? WHENEVER WE'RE NOT FIGHTING SOME MENACE TO MANKIND, WE END UP FIGHTING AMONG OURSELVES!
SKIP THE LECTURE, PAL! I'M A BIG BOY NOW!
REED! WHAT HAPPENED?? THE LIGHTS ALL WENT OUT!
IMPOSSIBLE! WE HAVE OUR OWN GENERATOR HERE!
IT MUST HAVE BEEN AFFECTED BY SOME MORE POWERFUL FORCE! BUT-- WHAT?
FOR THE ANSWER, LET US LOOK UP AT THE SKY, OUTSIDE THE TOWER!
SOON I WILL HAVE THEM TRAPPED AND COMPLETELY AT MY MERCY!
NOTHING CAN ESCAPE MY LITTLE WEB!
NOT EVEN THE FANTASTIC FOUR!
3

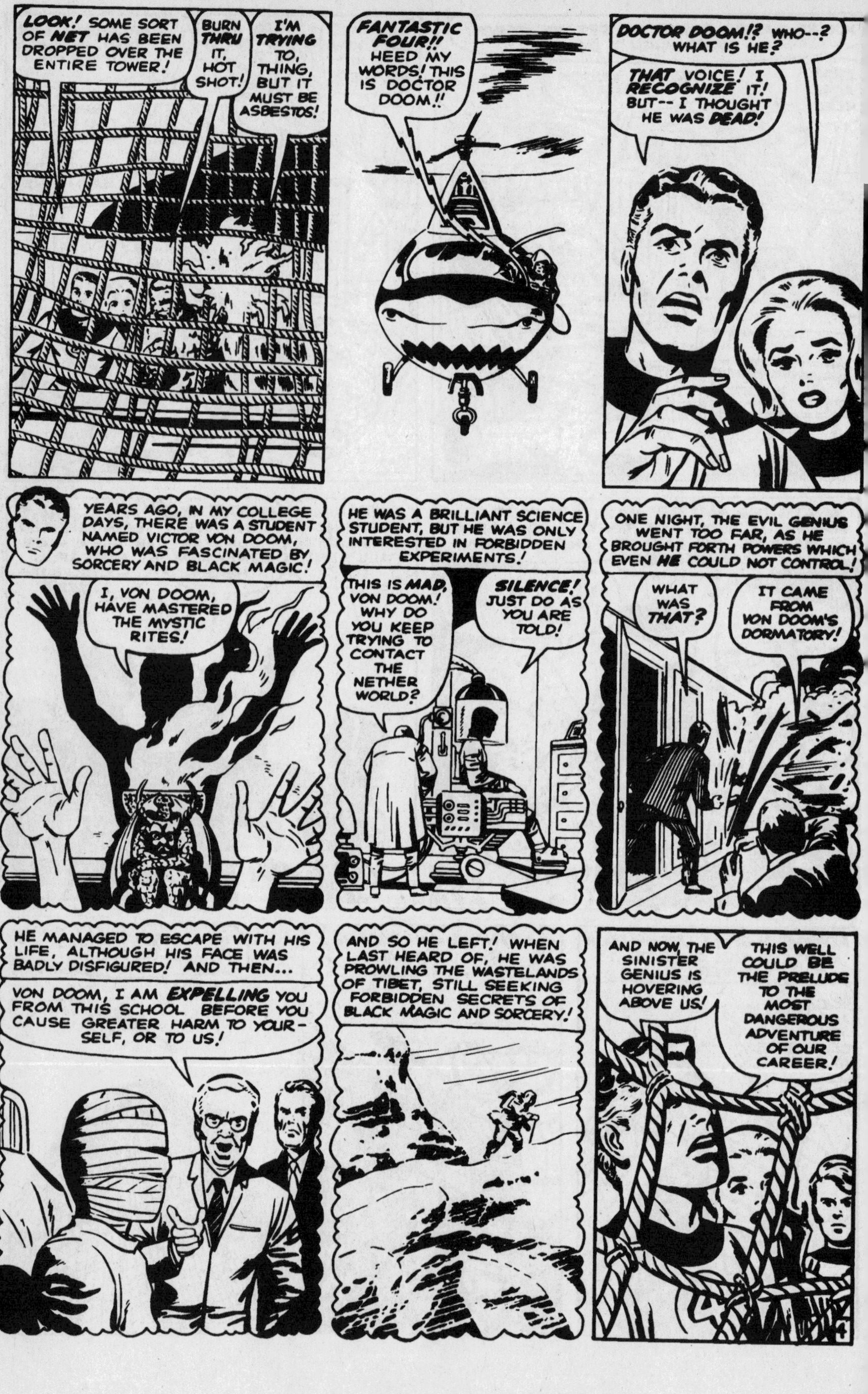

LOOK! SOME SORT OF NET HAS BEEN DROPPED OVER THE ENTIRE TOWER!
BURN THRU IT, HOT SHOT!
I'M TRYING TO, THING, BUT IT MUST BE ASBESTOS!
FANTASTIC FOUR!! HEED MY WORDS! THIS IS DOCTOR DOOM!!
DOCTOR DOOM!? WHO--? WHAT IS HE?
THAT VOICE! I RECOGNIZE IT! BUT-- I THOUGHT HE WAS DEAD!
YEARS AGO, IN MY COLLEGE DAYS, THERE WAS A STUDENT NAMED VICTOR VON DOOM, WHO WAS FASCINATED BY SORCERY AND BLACK MAGIC!
I, VON DOOM, HAVE MASTERED THE MYSTIC RITES!
HE WAS A BRILLIANT SCIENCE STUDENT, BUT HE WAS ONLY INTERESTED IN FORBIDDEN EXPERIMENTS!
THIS IS MAD, VON DOOM! WHY DO YOU KEEP TRYING TO CONTACT THE NETHER WORLD?
SILENCE! JUST DO AS YOU ARE TOLD!
ONE NIGHT, THE EVIL GENIUS WENT TOO FAR, AS HE BROUGHT FORTH POWERS WHICH EVEN HE COULD NOT CONTROL!
WHAT WAS THAT?
IT CAME FROM VON DOOM'S DORMATORY!
HE MANAGED TO ESCAPE WITH HIS LIFE, ALTHOUGH HIS FACE WAS BADLY DISFIGURED! AND THEN...
VON DOOM, I AM EXPELLING YOU FROM THIS SCHOOL BEFORE YOU CAUSE GREATER HARM TO YOUR-SELF, OR TO US!
AND SO HE LEFT! WHEN LAST HEARD OF, HE WAS PROWLING THE WASTELANDS OF TIBET, STILL SEEKING FORBIDDEN SECRETS OF BLACK MAGIC AND SORCERY!
AND NOW, THE SINISTER GENIUS IS HOVERING ABOVE US!
THIS WELL COULD BE THE PRELUDE TO THE MOST DANGEROUS ADVENTURE OF OUR CAREER!

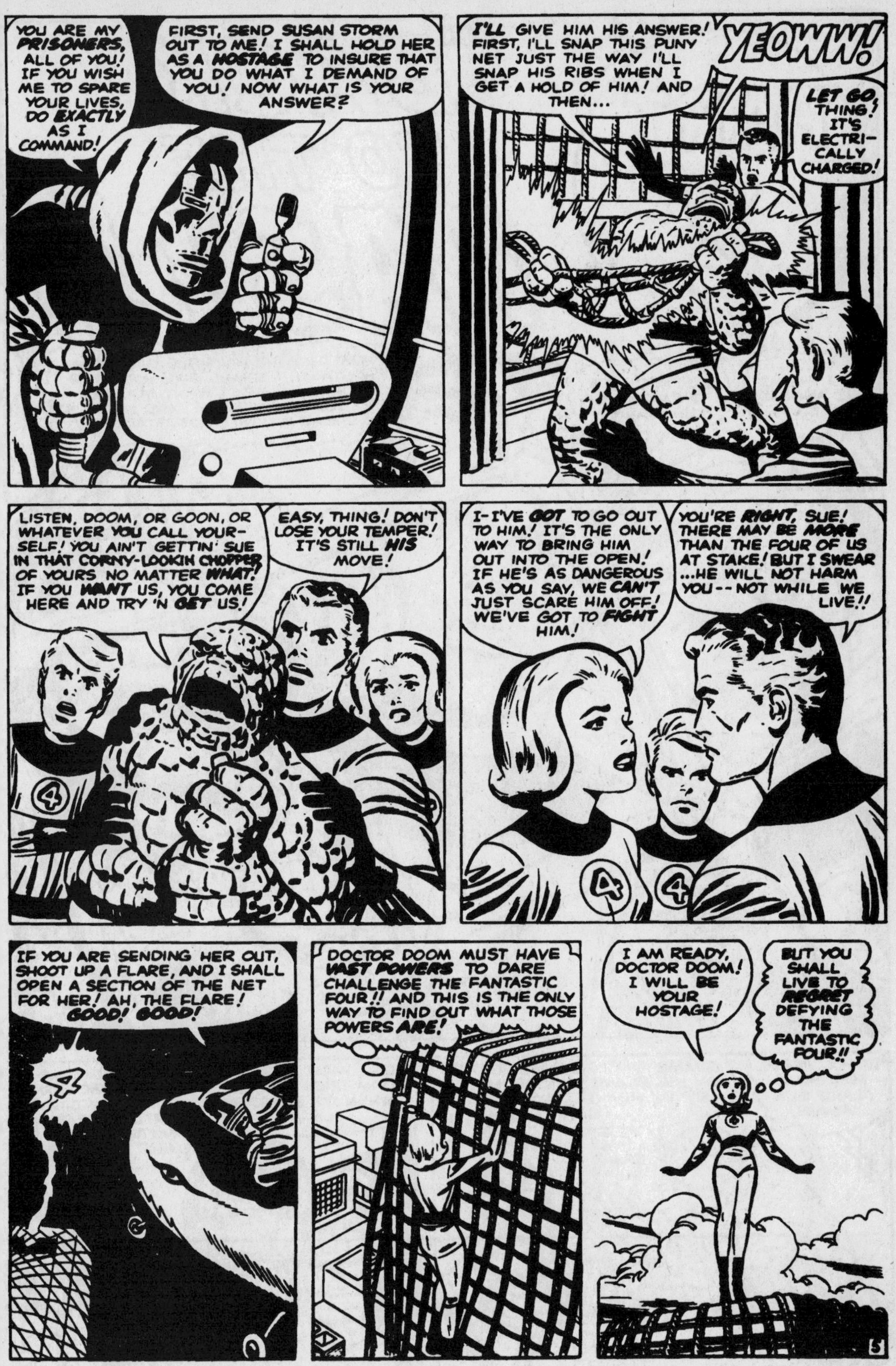
YOU ARE MY PRISONERS, ALL OF YOU! IF YOU WISH ME TO SPARE YOUR LIVES, DO EXACTLY AS I COMMAND!
FIRST, SEND SUSAN STORM OUT TO ME! I SHALL HOLD HER AS A HOSTAGE TO INSURE THAT YOU DO WHAT I DEMAND OF YOU! NOW WHAT IS YOUR ANSWER?
I'LL GIVE HIM HIS ANSWER! FIRST, I'LL SNAP THIS PUNY NET JUST THE WAY I'LL SNAP HIS RIBS WHEN I GET A HOLD OF HIM! AND THEN...
YEOWW!
LET GO, THING! IT'S ELECTRICALLY CHARGED!
LISTEN, DOOM, OR GOON, OR WHATEVER YOU CALL YOURSELF! YOU AIN'T GETTIN' SUE IN THAT CORNY-LOOKIN CHOPPER OF YOURS NO MATTER WHAT! IF YOU WANT US, YOU COME HERE AND TRY 'N GET US!
EASY, THING! DON'T LOSE YOUR TEMPER! IT'S STILL HIS MOVE!
I-I'VE GOT TO GO OUT TO HIM! IT'S THE ONLY WAY TO BRING HIM OUT INTO THE OPEN! IF HE'S AS DANGEROUS AS YOU SAY, WE CAN'T JUST SCARE HIM OFF! WE'VE GOT TO FIGHT HIM!
YOU'RE RIGHT, SUE! THERE MAY BE MORE THAN THE FOUR OF US AT STAKE! BUT I SWEAR ...HE WILL NOT HARM YOU -- NOT WHILE WE LIVE!!
IF YOU ARE SENDING HER OUT, SHOOT UP A FLARE, AND I SHALL OPEN A SECTION OF THE NET FOR HER! AH, THE FLARE! GOOD! GOOD!
4
DOCTOR DOOM MUST HAVE VAST POWERS TO DARE CHALLENGE THE FANTASTIC FOUR!! AND THIS IS THE ONLY WAY TO FIND OUT WHAT THOSE POWERS ARE!
I AM READY, DOCTOR DOOM! I WILL BE YOUR HOSTAGE!
BUT YOU SHALL LIVE TO REGRET DEFYING THE FANTASTIC FOUR!!
5

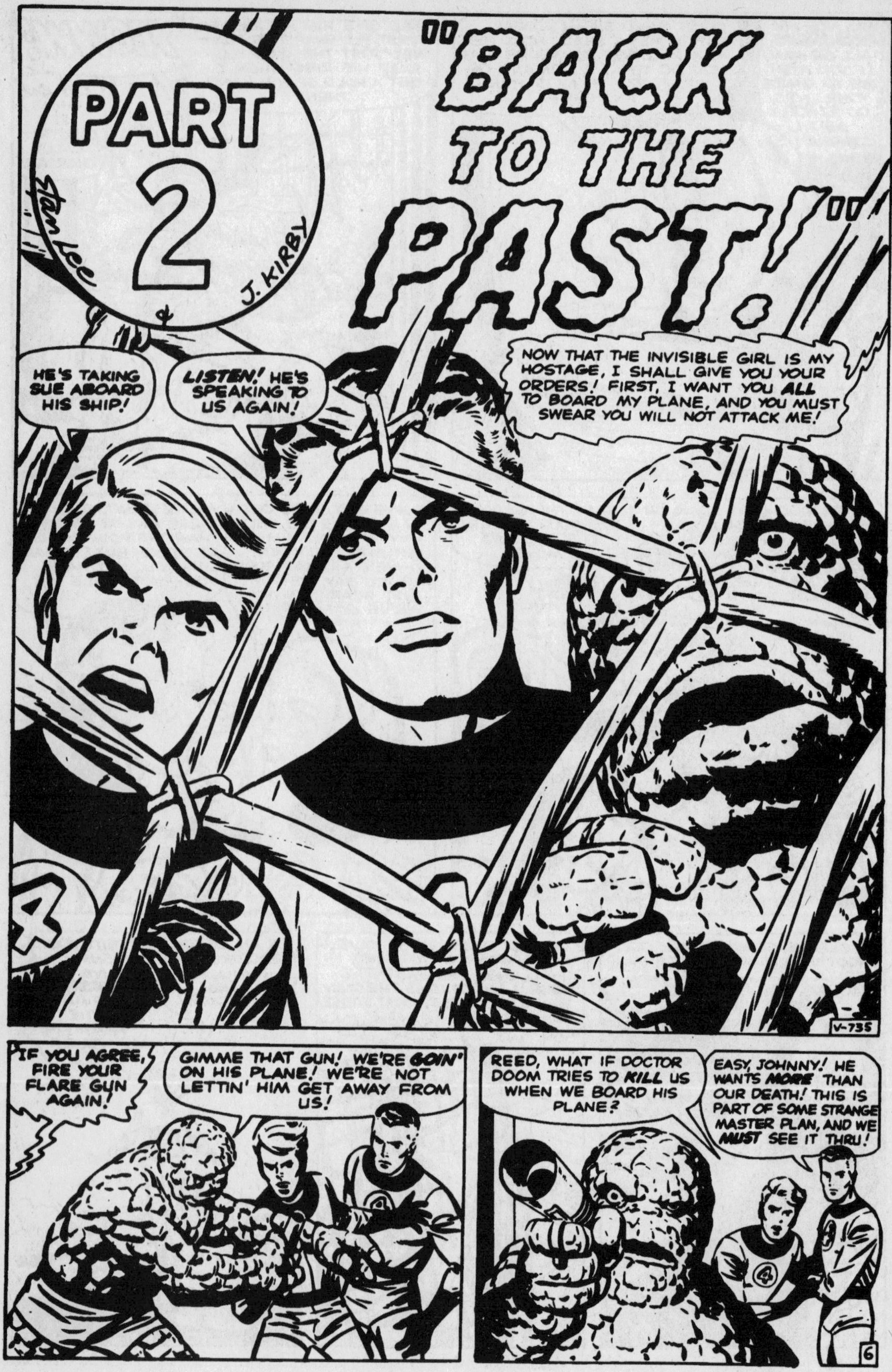
PART 2
"BACK TO THE PAST!"
Stan Lee & J. KIRBY
HE'S TAKING SUE ABOARD HIS SHIP!
LISTEN! HE'S SPEAKING TO US AGAIN!
NOW THAT THE INVISIBLE GIRL IS MY HOSTAGE, I SHALL GIVE YOU YOUR ORDERS! FIRST, I WANT YOU ALL TO BOARD MY PLANE, AND YOU MUST SWEAR YOU WILL NOT ATTACK ME!
V-735
IF YOU AGREE, FIRE YOUR FLARE GUN AGAIN!
GIMME THAT GUN! WE'RE GOIN' ON HIS PLANE! WE'RE NOT LETTIN' HIM GET AWAY FROM US!
REED, WHAT IF DOCTOR DOOM TRIES TO KILL US WHEN WE BOARD HIS PLANE?
EASY, JOHNNY! HE WANTS MORE THAN OUR DEATH! THIS IS PART OF SOME STRANGE MASTER PLAN, AND WE MUST SEE IT THRU!
6

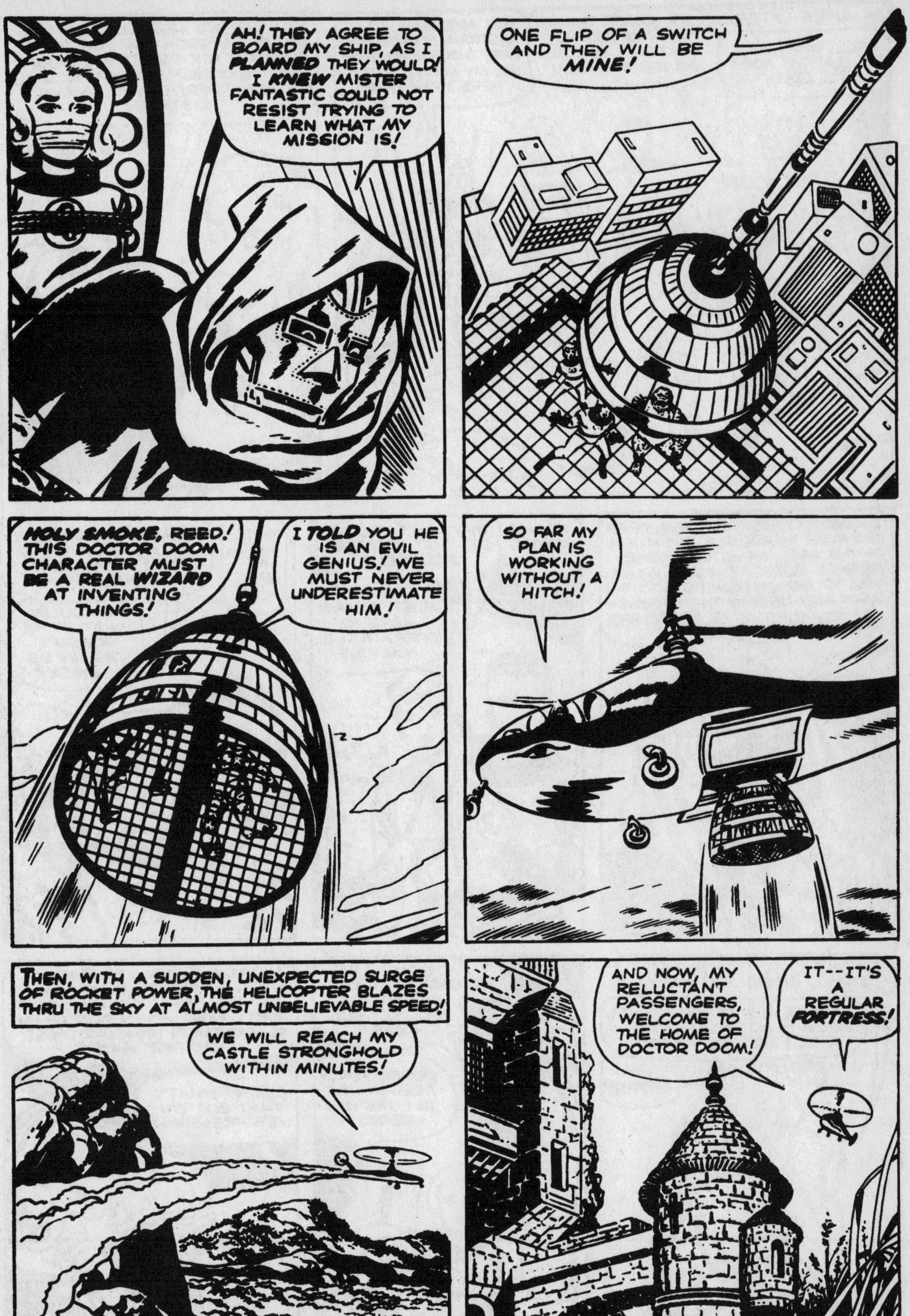
AH! THEY AGREE TO BOARD MY SHIP, AS I PLANNED THEY WOULD! I KNEW MISTER FANTASTIC COULD NOT RESIST TRYING TO LEARN WHAT MY MISSION IS!
ONE FLIP OF A SWITCH AND THEY WILL BE MINE!
HOLY SMOKE, REED! THIS DOCTOR DOOM CHARACTER MUST BE A REAL WIZARD AT INVENTING THINGS!
I TOLD YOU HE IS AN EVIL GENIUS! WE MUST NEVER UNDERESTIMATE HIM!
SO FAR MY PLAN IS WORKING WITHOUT A HITCH!
THEN, WITH A SUDDEN, UNEXPECTED SURGE OF ROCKET POWER, THE HELICOPTER BLAZES THRU THE SKY AT ALMOST UNBELIEVABLE SPEED!
WE WILL REACH MY CASTLE STRONGHOLD WITHIN MINUTES!
AND NOW, MY RELUCTANT PASSENGERS, WELCOME TO THE HOME OF DOCTOR DOOM!
IT--IT'S A REGULAR FORTRESS!
7

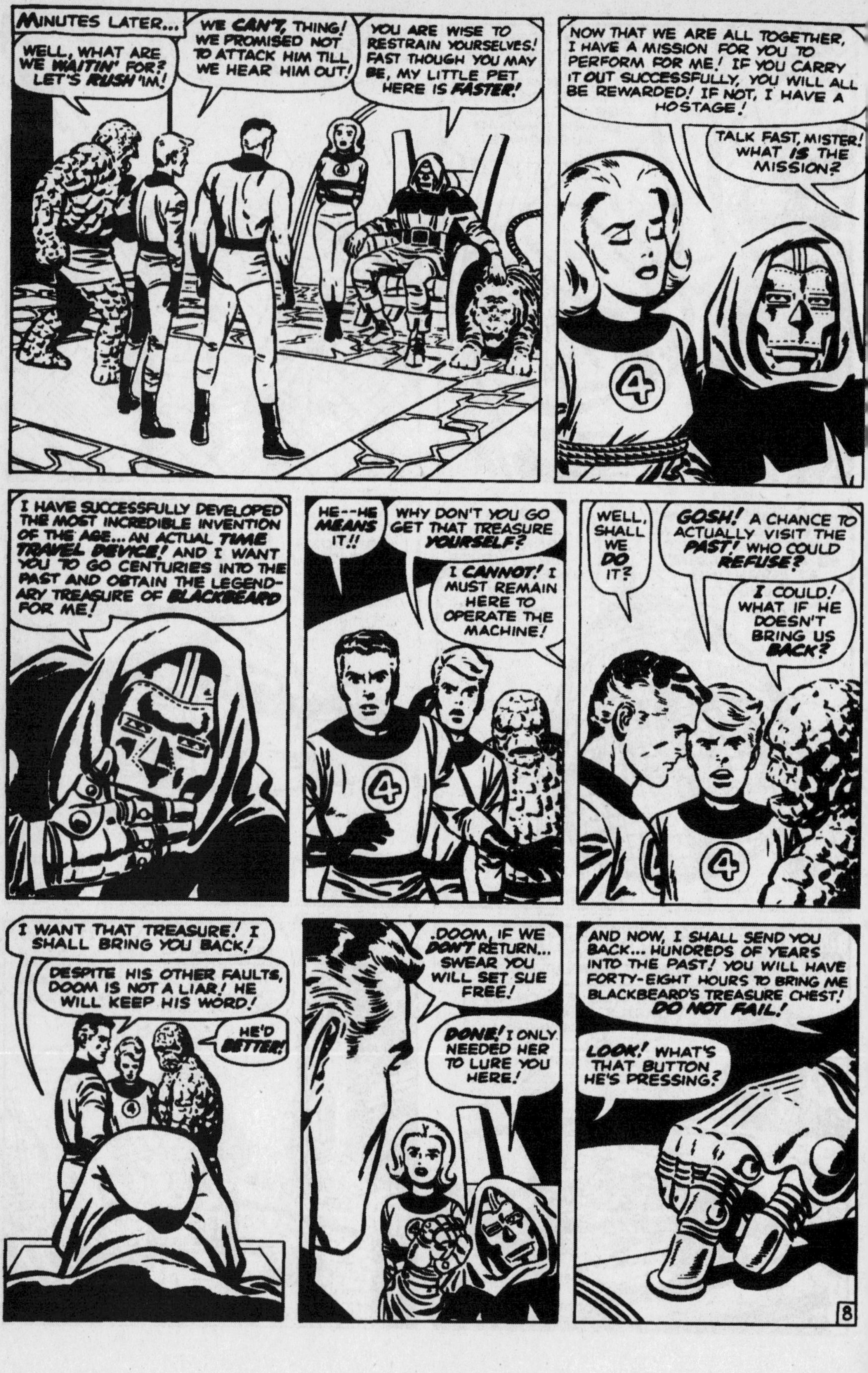
MINUTES LATER...
WELL, WHAT ARE WE WAITIN' FOR? LET'S RUSH 'IM!
WE CAN'T, THING! WE PROMISED NOT TO ATTACK HIM TILL WE HEAR HIM OUT!
YOU ARE WISE TO RESTRAIN YOURSELVES! FAST THOUGH YOU MAY BE, MY LITTLE PET HERE IS FASTER!
NOW THAT WE ARE ALL TOGETHER, I HAVE A MISSION FOR YOU TO PERFORM FOR ME! IF YOU CARRY IT OUT SUCCESSFULLY, YOU WILL ALL BE REWARDED! IF NOT, I HAVE A HOSTAGE!
TALK FAST, MISTER! WHAT IS THE MISSION?
I HAVE SUCCESSFULLY DEVELOPED THE MOST INCREDIBLE INVENTION OF THE AGE... AN ACTUAL TIME TRAVEL DEVICE! AND I WANT YOU TO GO CENTURIES INTO THE PAST AND OBTAIN THE LEGENDARY TREASURE OF BLACKBEARD FOR ME!
HE--HE MEANS IT!!
WHY DON'T YOU GO GET THAT TREASURE YOURSELF?
I CANNOT! I MUST REMAIN HERE TO OPERATE THE MACHINE!
WELL, SHALL WE DO IT?
GOSH! A CHANCE TO ACTUALLY VISIT THE PAST! WHO COULD REFUSE?
I COULD! WHAT IF HE DOESN'T BRING US BACK?
I WANT THAT TREASURE! I SHALL BRING YOU BACK!
DESPITE HIS OTHER FAULTS, DOOM IS NOT A LIAR! HE WILL KEEP HIS WORD!
HE'D BETTER!
DOOM, IF WE DON'T RETURN... SWEAR YOU WILL SET SUE FREE!
DONE! I ONLY NEEDED HER TO LURE YOU HERE!
AND NOW, I SHALL SEND YOU BACK... HUNDREDS OF YEARS INTO THE PAST! YOU WILL HAVE FORTY-EIGHT HOURS TO BRING ME BLACKBEARD'S TREASURE CHEST! DO NOT FAIL!
LOOK! WHAT'S THAT BUTTON HE'S PRESSING?

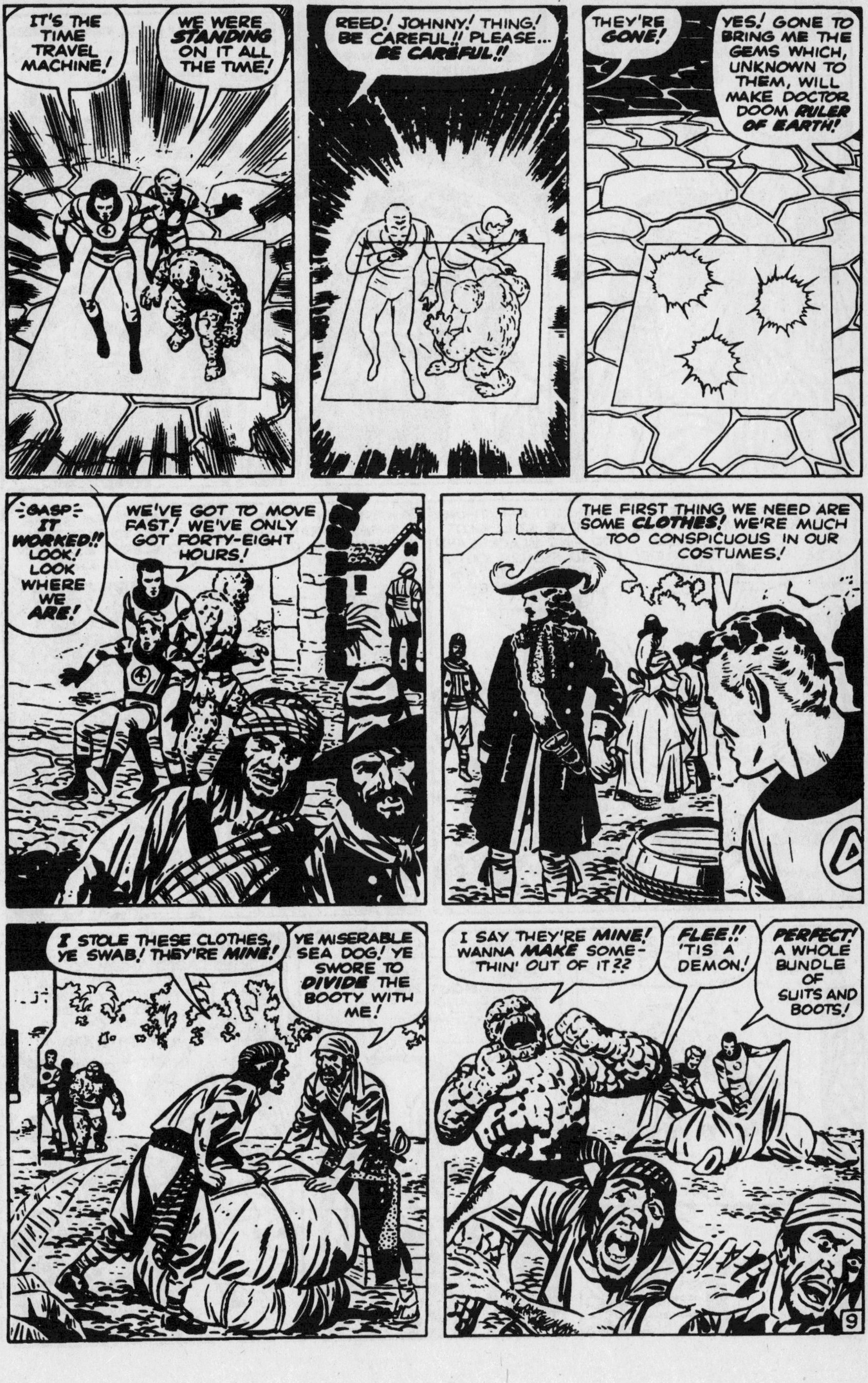
IT'S THE TIME TRAVEL MACHINE!
WE WERE STANDING ON IT ALL THE TIME!
REED! JOHNNY! THING! BE CAREFUL!! PLEASE... BE CAREFUL!!
THEY'RE GONE!
YES! GONE TO BRING ME THE GEMS WHICH, UNKNOWN TO THEM, WILL MAKE DOCTOR DOOM RULER OF EARTH!
-GASP- IT WORKED!! LOOK! LOOK WHERE WE ARE!
WE'VE GOT TO MOVE FAST! WE'VE ONLY GOT FORTY-EIGHT HOURS!
THE FIRST THING WE NEED ARE SOME CLOTHES! WE'RE MUCH TOO CONSPICUOUS IN OUR COSTUMES!
I STOLE THESE CLOTHES, YE SWAB! THEY'RE MINE!
YE MISERABLE SEA DOG! YE SWORE TO DIVIDE THE BOOTY WITH ME!
I SAY THEY'RE MINE! WANNA MAKE SOME-THIN' OUT OF IT??
FLEE!! 'TIS A DEMON!
PERFECT! A WHOLE BUNDLE OF SUITS AND BOOTS!
9

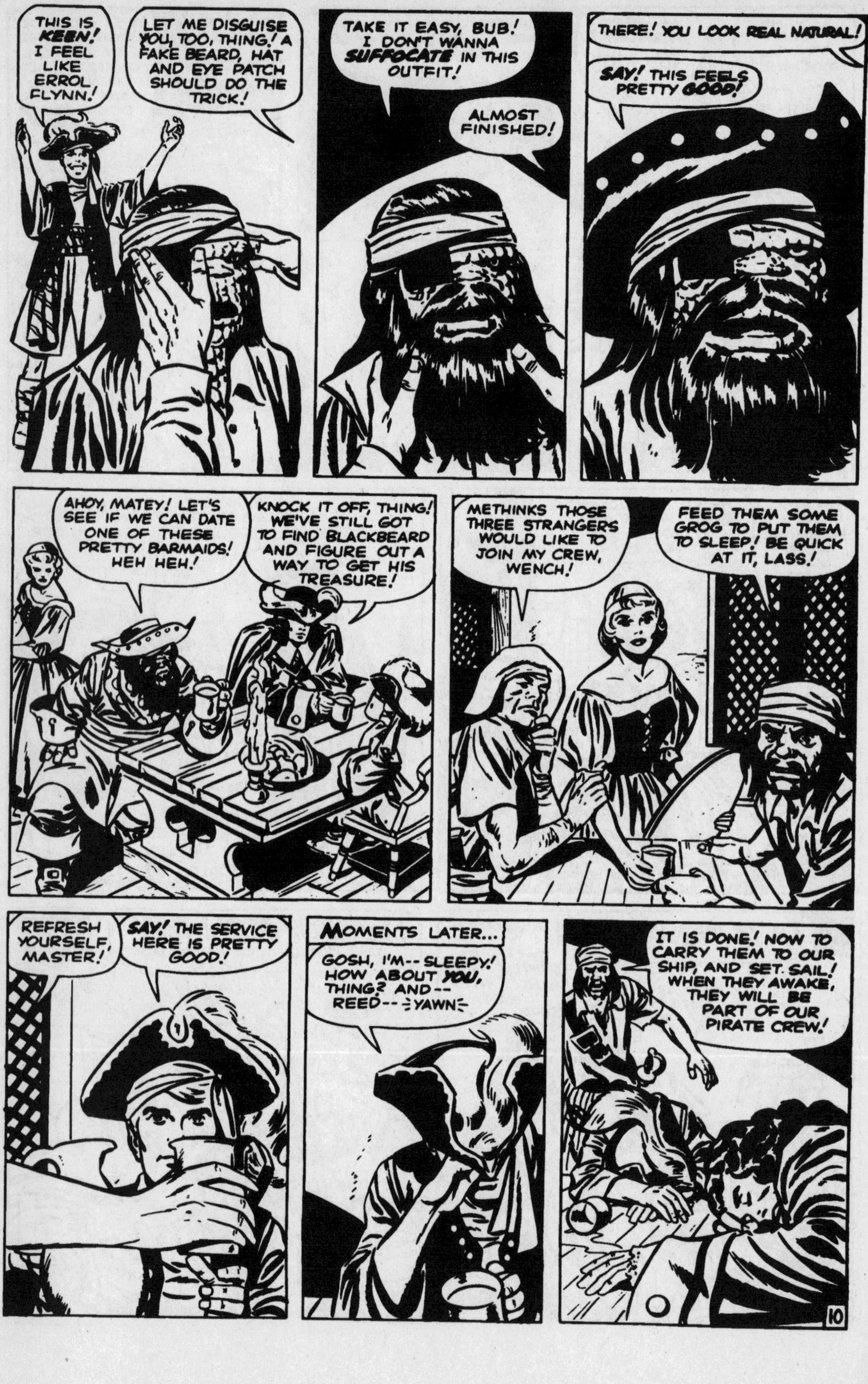

THIS IS KEEN! I FEEL LIKE ERROL FLYNN!
LET ME DISGUISE YOU, TOO, THING! A FAKE BEARD, HAT AND EYE PATCH SHOULD DO THE TRICK!
TAKE IT EASY, BUB! I DON'T WANNA SUFFOCATE IN THIS OUTFIT!
ALMOST FINISHED!
THERE! YOU LOOK REAL NATURAL!
SAY! THIS FEELS PRETTY GOOD!
AHOY, MATEY! LET'S SEE IF WE CAN DATE ONE OF THESE PRETTY BARMAIDS! HEH HEH!
KNOCK IT OFF, THING! WE'VE STILL GOT TO FIND BLACKBEARD AND FIGURE OUT A WAY TO GET HIS TREASURE!
METHINKS THOSE THREE STRANGERS WOULD LIKE TO JOIN MY CREW, WENCH!
FEED THEM SOME GROG TO PUT THEM TO SLEEP! BE QUICK AT IT, LASS!
REFRESH YOURSELF, MASTER!
SAY! THE SERVICE HERE IS PRETTY GOOD!
MOMENTS LATER...
GOSH, I'M-- SLEEPY! HOW ABOUT YOU, THING? AND-- REED-- YAWN
IT IS DONE! NOW TO CARRY THEM TO OUR SHIP, AND SET SAIL! WHEN THEY AWAKE, THEY WILL BE PART OF OUR PIRATE CREW!
10

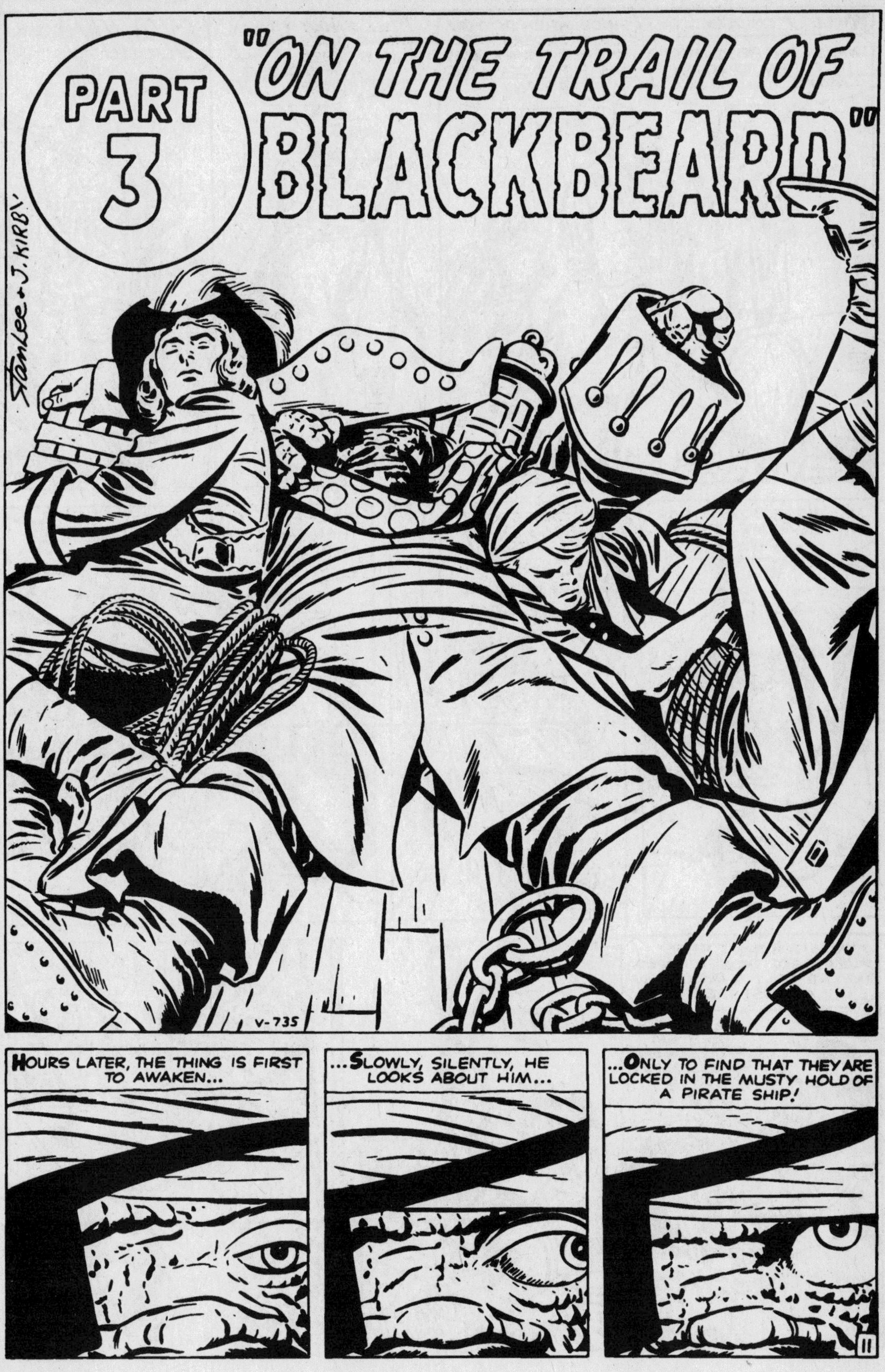
PART 3
"ON THE TRAIL OF BLACKBEARD"
Stan Lee + J. Kirby
V-735
HOURS LATER, THE THING IS FIRST TO AWAKEN...
...SLOWLY, SILENTLY, HE LOOKS ABOUT HIM...
...ONLY TO FIND THAT THEY ARE LOCKED IN THE MUSTY HOLD OF A PIRATE SHIP!
11

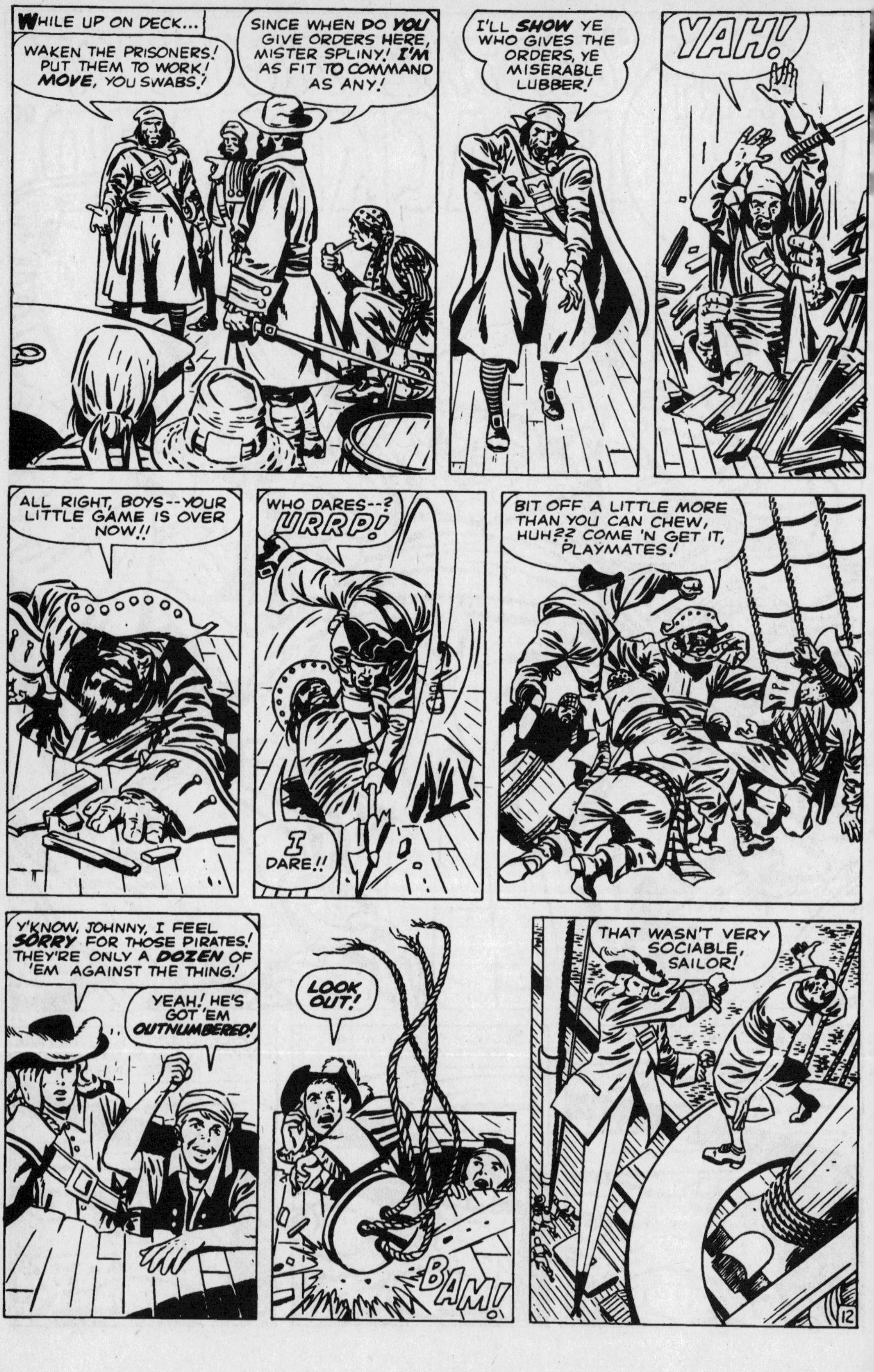
WHILE UP ON DECK...
WAKEN THE PRISONERS! PUT THEM TO WORK! MOVE, YOU SWABS!
SINCE WHEN DO YOU GIVE ORDERS HERE, MISTER SPLINY! I'M AS FIT TO COMMAND AS ANY!
I'LL SHOW YE WHO GIVES THE ORDERS, YE MISERABLE LUBBER!
YAH!
ALL RIGHT, BOYS--YOUR LITTLE GAME IS OVER NOW!!
WHO DARES--? URRP!
I DARE!!
BIT OFF A LITTLE MORE THAN YOU CAN CHEW, HUH?? COME 'N GET IT, PLAYMATES!
Y'KNOW, JOHNNY, I FEEL SORRY FOR THOSE PIRATES! THEY'RE ONLY A DOZEN OF 'EM AGAINST THE THING!
YEAH! HE'S GOT 'EM OUTNUMBERED!
LOOK OUT!
BAM!
THAT WASN'T VERY SOCIABLE, SAILOR!
12

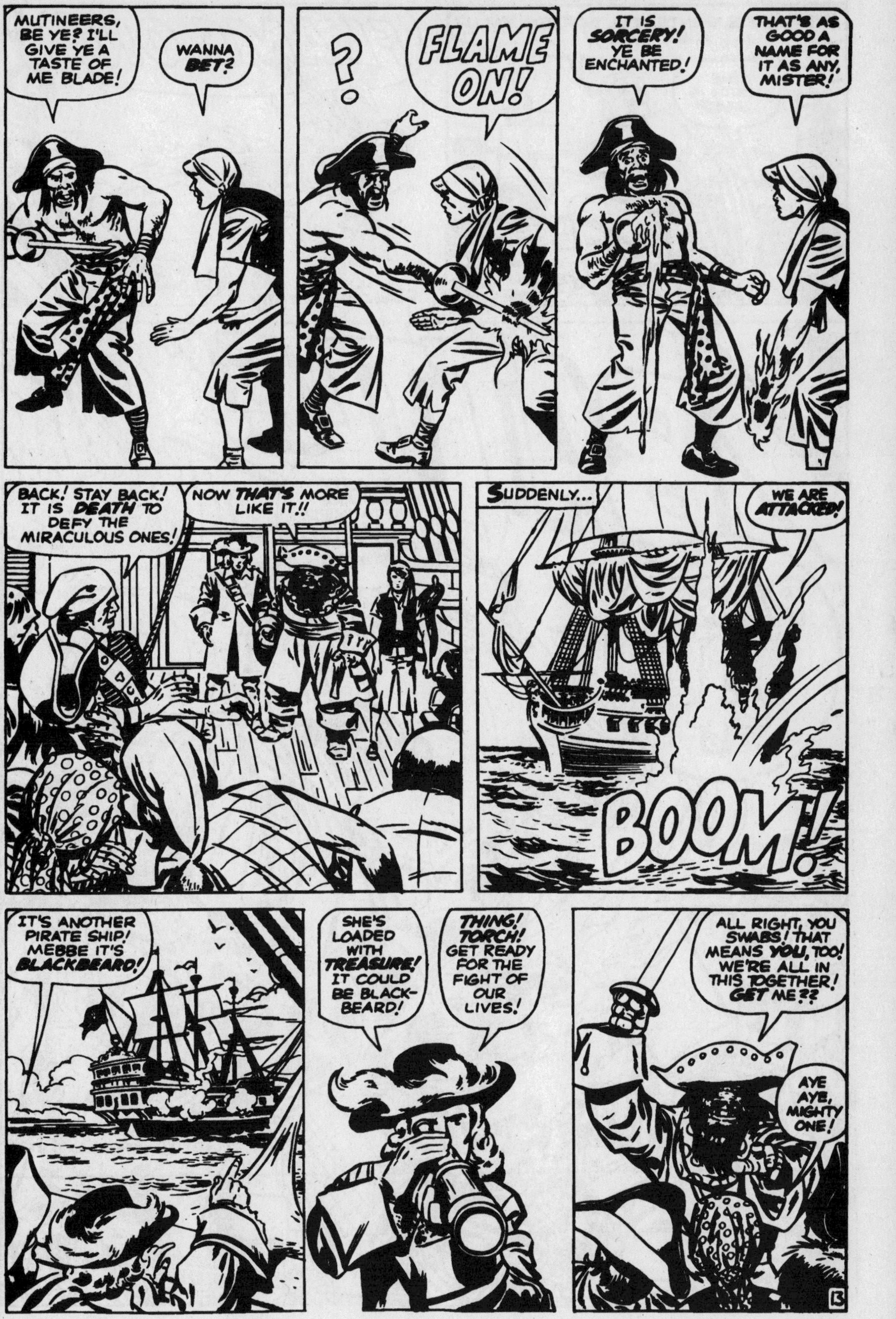
MUTINEERS, BE YE? I'LL GIVE YE A TASTE OF ME BLADE!
WANNA BET?
?
FLAME ON!
IT IS SORCERY! YE BE ENCHANTED!
THAT'S AS GOOD A NAME FOR IT AS ANY, MISTER!
BACK! STAY BACK! IT IS DEATH TO DEFY THE MIRACULOUS ONES!
NOW THAT'S MORE LIKE IT!!
SUDDENLY...
WE ARE ATTACKED!
BOOM!
IT'S ANOTHER PIRATE SHIP! MEBBE IT'S BLACKBEARD!
SHE'S LOADED WITH TREASURE! IT COULD BE BLACK-BEARD!
THING! TORCH! GET READY FOR THE FIGHT OF OUR LIVES!
ALL RIGHT, YOU SWABS! THAT MEANS YOU, TOO! WE'RE ALL IN THIS TOGETHER! GET ME??
AYE AYE, MIGHTY ONE!
13

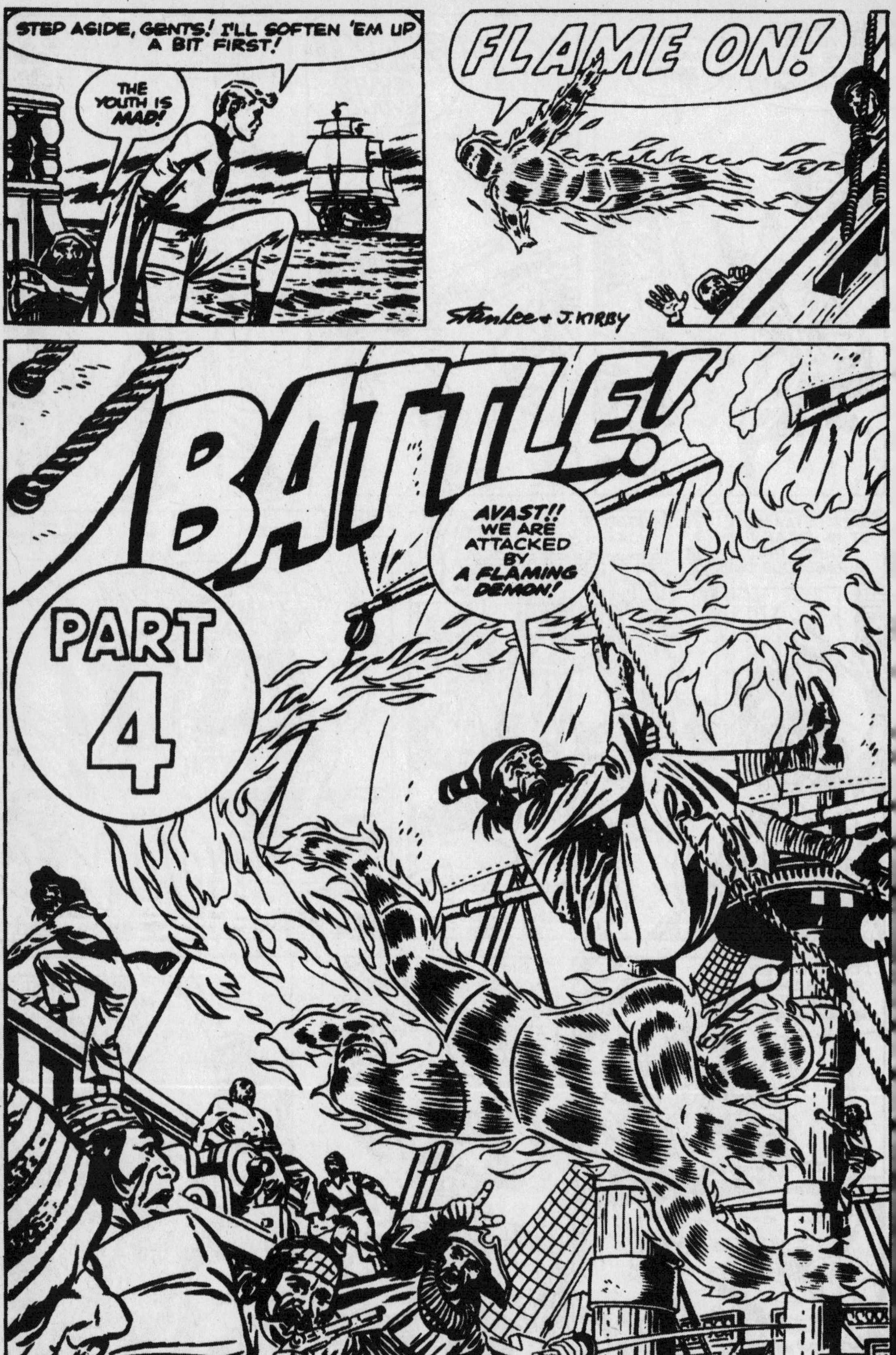

STEP ASIDE, GENTS! I'LL SOFTEN 'EM UP A BIT FIRST!
THE YOUTH IS MAD!
FLAME ON!
Stan Lee + J. KIRBY
BATTLE!
PART 4
AVAST!! WE ARE ATTACKED BY A FLAMING DEMON!
V-735
14

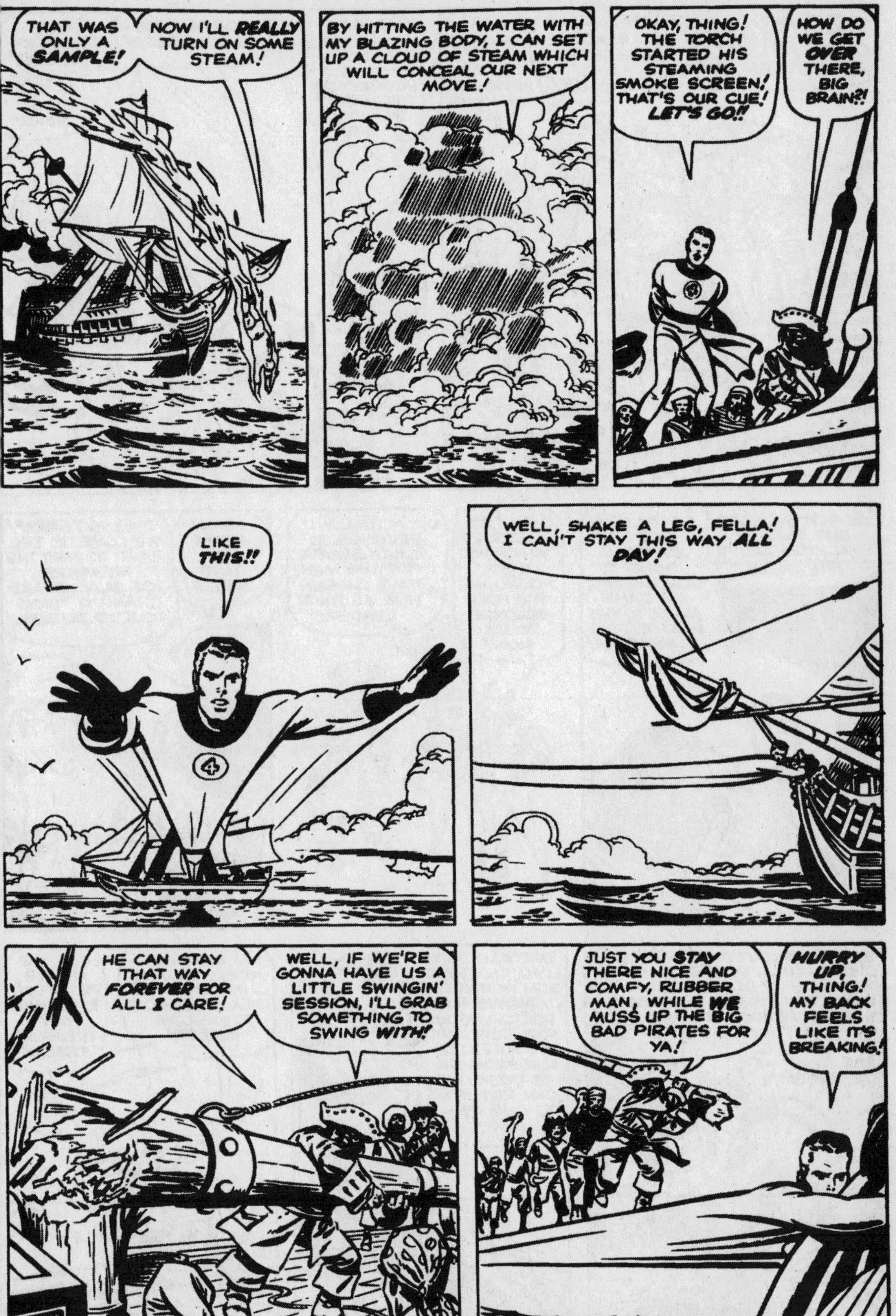

THAT WAS ONLY A SAMPLE!
NOW I'LL REALLY TURN ON SOME STEAM!
BY HITTING THE WATER WITH MY BLAZING BODY, I CAN SET UP A CLOUD OF STEAM WHICH WILL CONCEAL OUR NEXT MOVE!
OKAY, THING! THE TORCH STARTED HIS STEAMING SMOKE SCREEN! THAT'S OUR CUE! LET'S GO!!
HOW DO WE GET OVER THERE, BIG BRAIN?!
LIKE THIS!!
WELL, SHAKE A LEG, FELLA! I CAN'T STAY THIS WAY ALL DAY!
HE CAN STAY THAT WAY FOREVER FOR ALL I CARE!
WELL, IF WE'RE GONNA HAVE US A LITTLE SWINGIN' SESSION, I'LL GRAB SOMETHING TO SWING WITH!
JUST YOU STAY THERE NICE AND COMFY, RUBBER MAN, WHILE WE MUSS UP THE BIG BAD PIRATES FOR YA!
HURRY UP, THING! MY BACK FEELS LIKE IT'S BREAKING!
15

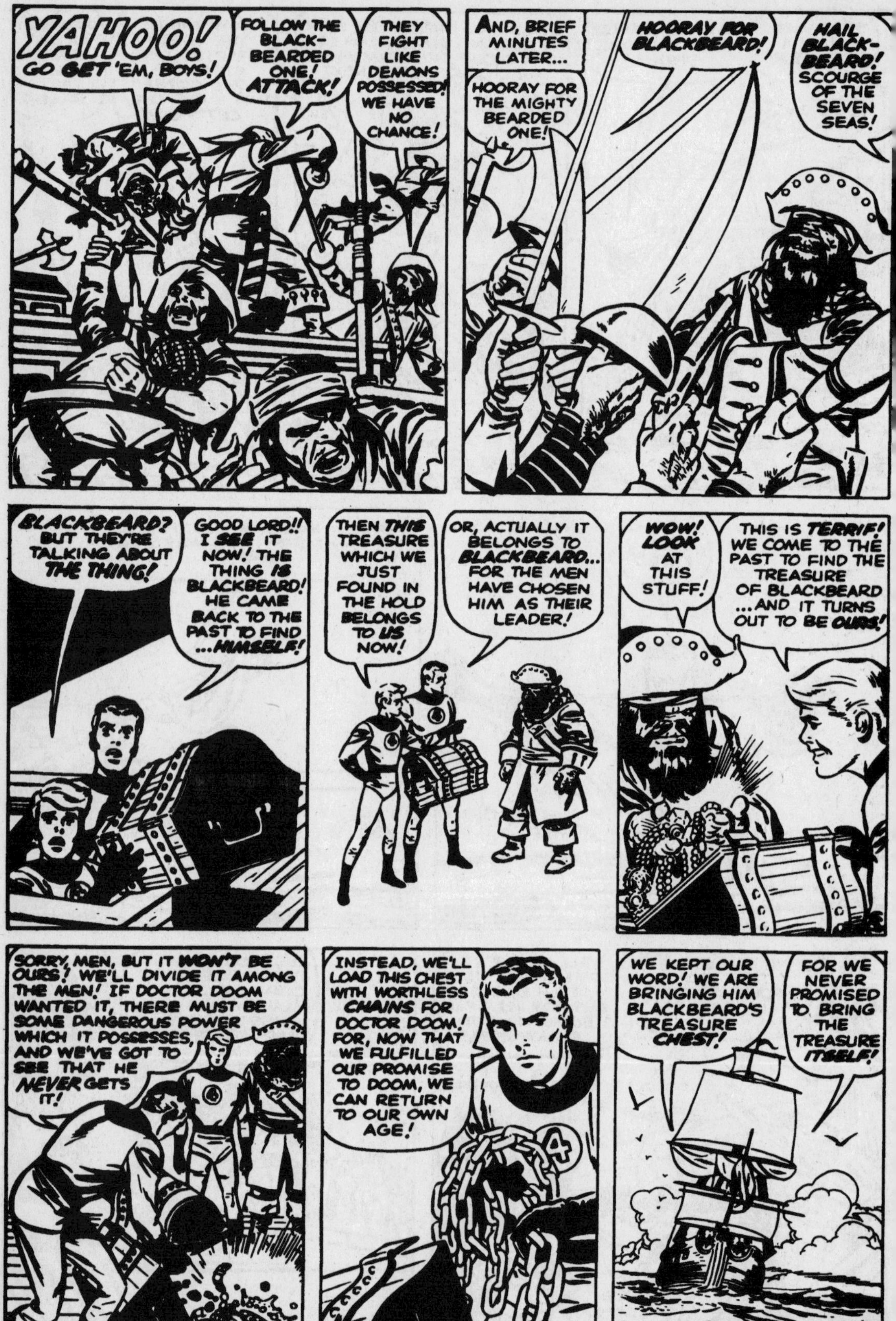

YAHOO! GO GET 'EM, BOYS!
FOLLOW THE BLACK-BEARDED ONE! ATTACK!
THEY FIGHT LIKE DEMONS POSSESSED! WE HAVE NO CHANCE!
AND, BRIEF MINUTES LATER...
HOORAY FOR THE MIGHTY BEARDED ONE!
HOORAY FOR BLACKBEARD!
HAIL BLACK-BEARD! SCOURGE OF THE SEVEN SEAS!
BLACKBEARD? BUT THEY'RE TALKING ABOUT THE THING!
GOOD LORD!! I SEE IT NOW! THE THING IS BLACKBEARD! HE CAME BACK TO THE PAST TO FIND ...HIMSELF!
THEN THIS TREASURE WHICH WE JUST FOUND IN THE HOLD BELONGS TO US NOW!
OR, ACTUALLY IT BELONGS TO BLACKBEARD... FOR THE MEN HAVE CHOSEN HIM AS THEIR LEADER!
WOW! LOOK AT THIS STUFF!
THIS IS TERRIF! WE COME TO THE PAST TO FIND THE TREASURE OF BLACKBEARD ...AND IT TURNS OUT TO BE OURS!
SORRY, MEN, BUT IT WON'T BE OURS! WE'LL DIVIDE IT AMONG THE MEN! IF DOCTOR DOOM WANTED IT, THERE MUST BE SOME DANGEROUS POWER WHICH IT POSSESSES, AND WE'VE GOT TO SEE THAT HE NEVER GETS IT!
INSTEAD, WE'LL LOAD THIS CHEST WITH WORTHLESS CHAINS FOR DOCTOR DOOM! FOR, NOW THAT WE FULFILLED OUR PROMISE TO DOOM, WE CAN RETURN TO OUR OWN AGE!
WE KEPT OUR WORD! WE ARE BRINGING HIM BLACKBEARD'S TREASURE CHEST!
FOR WE NEVER PROMISED TO BRING THE TREASURE ITSELF!
16

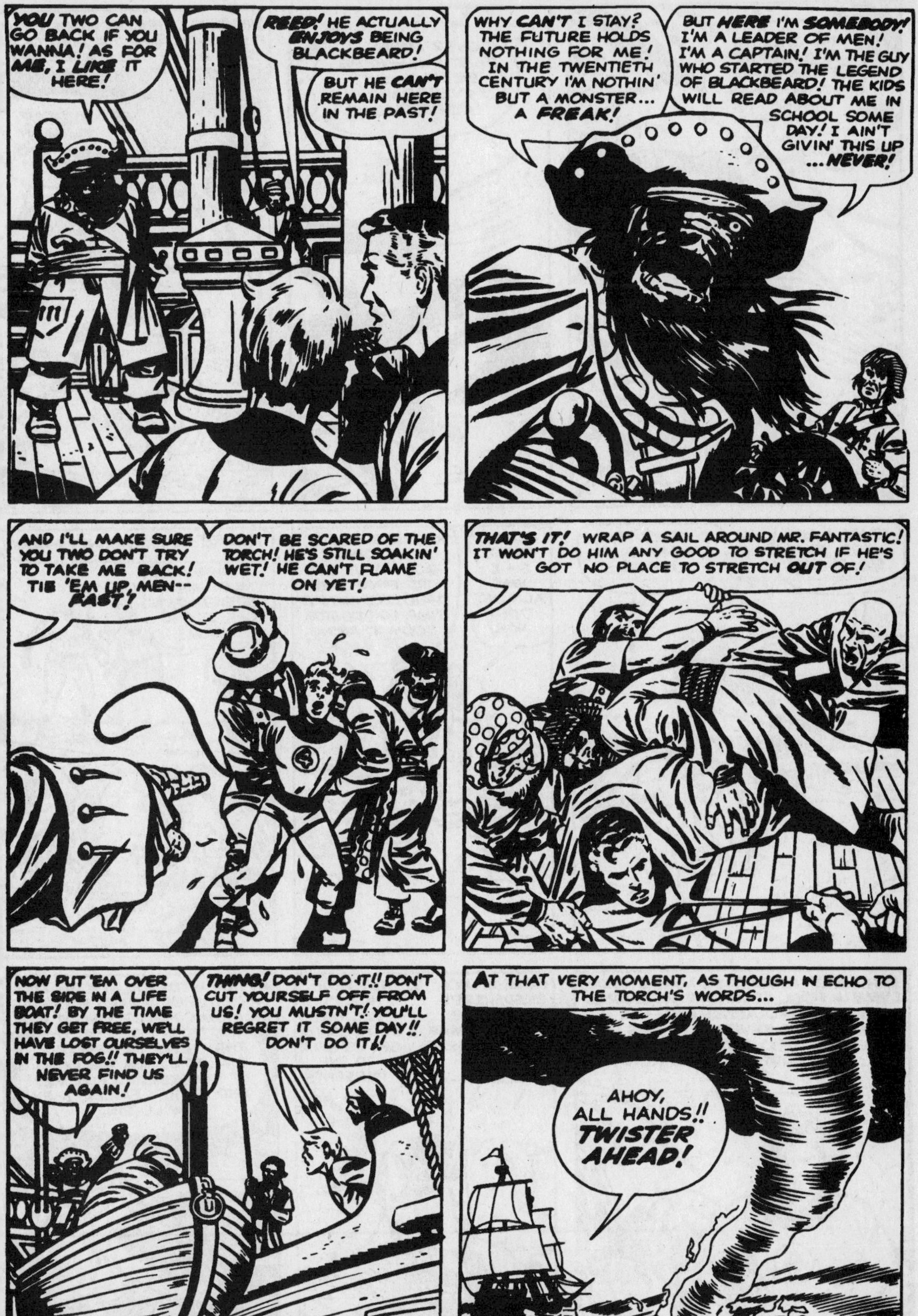
YOU TWO CAN GO BACK IF YOU WANNA! AS FOR ME, I LIKE IT HERE!
REED! HE ACTUALLY ENJOYS BEING BLACKBEARD!
BUT HE CAN'T REMAIN HERE IN THE PAST!
WHY CAN'T I STAY? THE FUTURE HOLDS NOTHING FOR ME! IN THE TWENTIETH CENTURY I'M NOTHIN' BUT A MONSTER... A FREAK!
BUT HERE I'M SOMEBODY! I'M A LEADER OF MEN! I'M A CAPTAIN! I'M THE GUY WHO STARTED THE LEGEND OF BLACKBEARD! THE KIDS WILL READ ABOUT ME IN SCHOOL SOME DAY! I AIN'T GIVIN' THIS UP ...NEVER!
AND I'LL MAKE SURE YOU TWO DON'T TRY TO TAKE ME BACK! TIE 'EM UP, MEN-- FAST!
DON'T BE SCARED OF THE TORCH! HE'S STILL SOAKIN' WET! HE CAN'T FLAME ON YET!
THAT'S IT! WRAP A SAIL AROUND MR. FANTASTIC! IT WON'T DO HIM ANY GOOD TO STRETCH IF HE'S GOT NO PLACE TO STRETCH OUT OF!
NOW PUT 'EM OVER THE SIDE IN A LIFE BOAT! BY THE TIME THEY GET FREE, WE'LL HAVE LOST OURSELVES IN THE FOG!! THEY'LL NEVER FIND US AGAIN!
THING! DON'T DO IT!! DON'T CUT YOURSELF OFF FROM US! YOU MUSTN'T! YOU'LL REGRET IT SOME DAY!! DON'T DO IT!!
AT THAT VERY MOMENT, AS THOUGH IN ECHO TO THE TORCH'S WORDS...
AHOY, ALL HANDS!! TWISTER AHEAD!
17

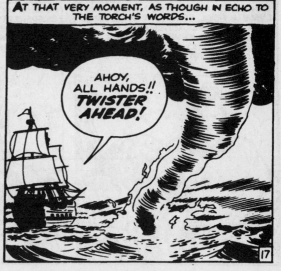

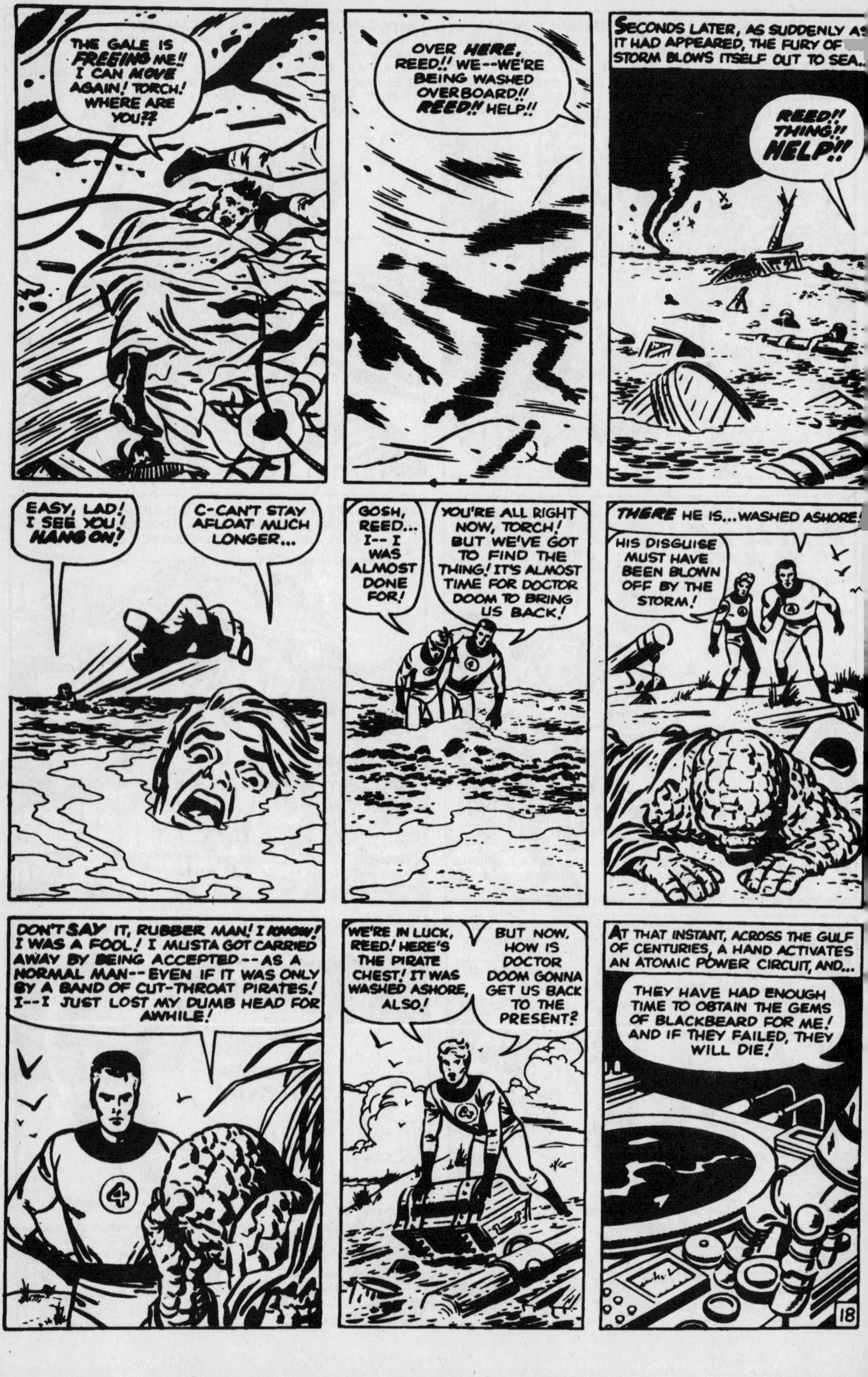
THE GALE IS FREEING ME!! I CAN MOVE AGAIN! TORCH! WHERE ARE YOU??
OVER HERE, REED!! WE--WE'RE BEING WASHED OVERBOARD!! REED!! HELP!!
SECONDS LATER, AS SUDDENLY AS IT HAD APPEARED, THE FURY OF STORM BLOWS ITSELF OUT TO SEA...
REED!! THING!! HELP!!
EASY, LAD! I SEE YOU! HANG ON!
C-CAN'T STAY AFLOAT MUCH LONGER...
GOSH, REED... I-- I WAS ALMOST DONE FOR!
YOU'RE ALL RIGHT NOW, TORCH! BUT WE'VE GOT TO FIND THE THING! IT'S ALMOST TIME FOR DOCTOR DOOM TO BRING US BACK!
THERE HE IS...WASHED ASHORE!
HIS DISGUISE MUST HAVE BEEN BLOWN OFF BY THE STORM!
DON'T SAY IT, RUBBER MAN! I KNOW! I WAS A FOOL! I MUSTA GOT CARRIED AWAY BY BEING ACCEPTED--AS A NORMAL MAN--EVEN IF IT WAS ONLY BY A BAND OF CUT-THROAT PIRATES! I--I JUST LOST MY DUMB HEAD FOR AWHILE!
WE'RE IN LUCK, REED! HERE'S THE PIRATE CHEST! IT WAS WASHED ASHORE, ALSO!
BUT NOW, HOW IS DOCTOR DOOM GONNA GET US BACK TO THE PRESENT?
AT THAT INSTANT, ACROSS THE GULF OF CENTURIES, A HAND ACTIVATES AN ATOMIC POWER CIRCUIT, AND...
THEY HAVE HAD ENOUGH TIME TO OBTAIN THE GEMS OF BLACKBEARD FOR ME! AND IF THEY FAILED, THEY WILL DIE!
18

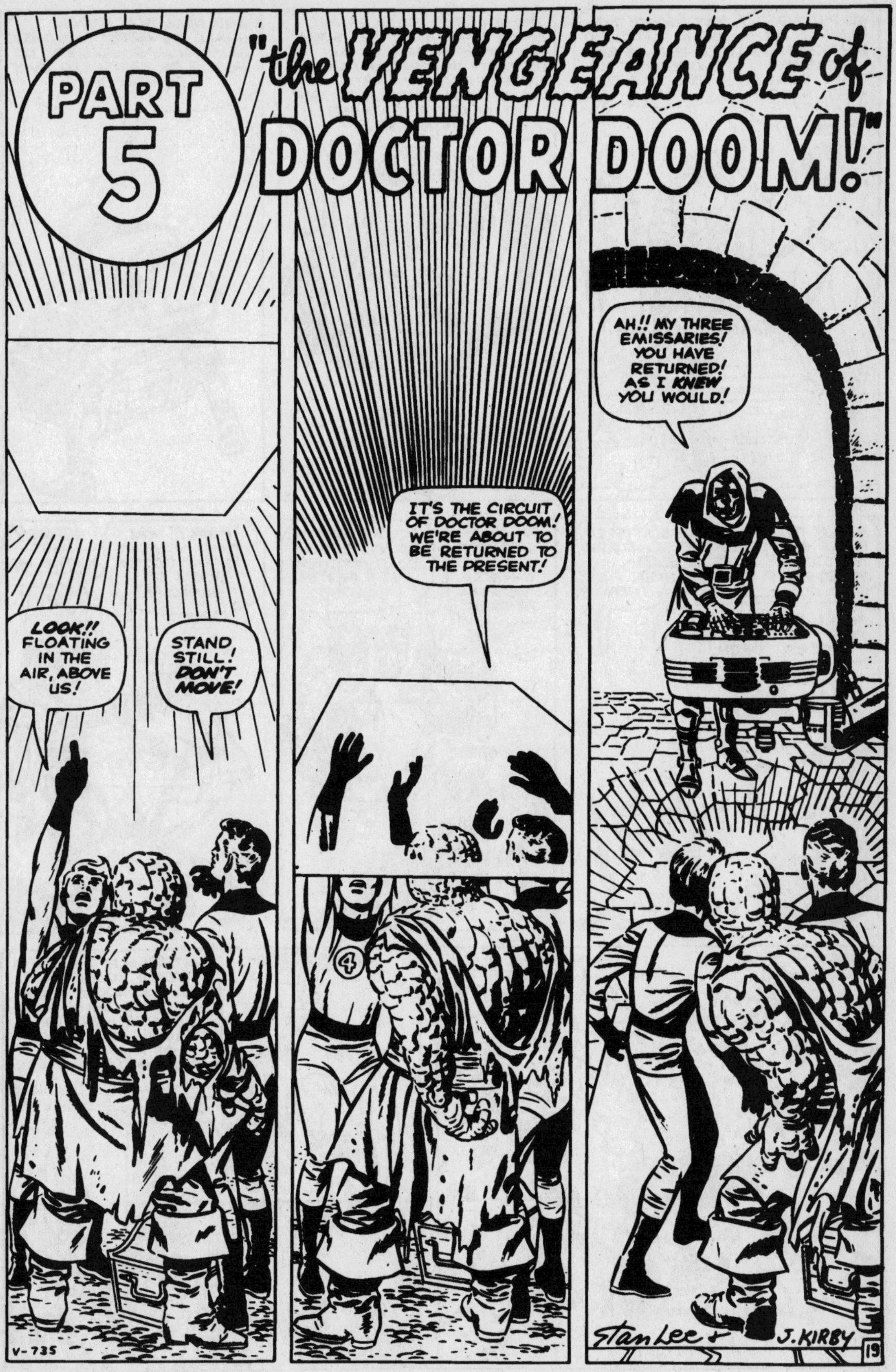
PART 5
"the VENGEANCE of DOCTOR DOOM!"
LOOK!! FLOATING IN THE AIR, ABOVE US!
STAND STILL! DON'T MOVE!
IT'S THE CIRCUIT OF DOCTOR DOOM! WE'RE ABOUT TO BE RETURNED TO THE PRESENT!
AH!! MY THREE EMISSARIES! YOU HAVE RETURNED! AS I KNEW YOU WOULD!
Stan Lee + J. KIRBY
V-735
19

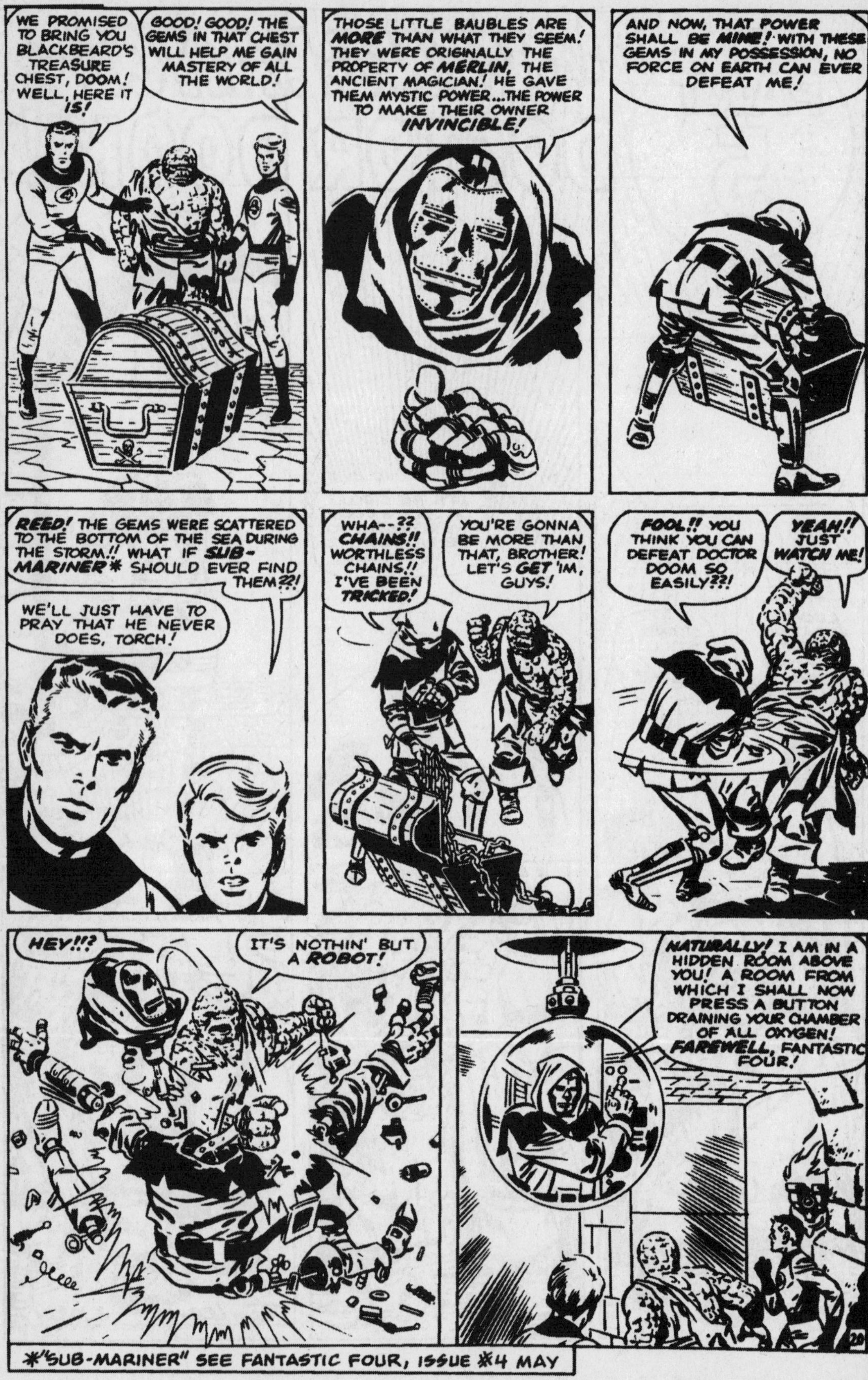
WE PROMISED TO BRING YOU BLACKBEARD'S TREASURE CHEST, DOOM! WELL, HERE IT IS!
GOOD! GOOD! THE GEMS IN THAT CHEST WILL HELP ME GAIN MASTERY OF ALL THE WORLD!
THOSE LITTLE BAUBLES ARE MORE THAN WHAT THEY SEEM! THEY WERE ORIGINALLY THE PROPERTY OF MERLIN, THE ANCIENT MAGICIAN! HE GAVE THEM MYSTIC POWER...THE POWER TO MAKE THEIR OWNER INVINCIBLE!
AND NOW, THAT POWER SHALL BE MINE! WITH THESE GEMS IN MY POSSESSION, NO FORCE ON EARTH CAN EVER DEFEAT ME!
REED! THE GEMS WERE SCATTERED TO THE BOTTOM OF THE SEA DURING THE STORM!! WHAT IF SUB-MARINER* SHOULD EVER FIND THEM??!
WE'LL JUST HAVE TO PRAY THAT HE NEVER DOES, TORCH!
WHA--?? CHAINS!! WORTHLESS CHAINS!! I'VE BEEN TRICKED!
YOU'RE GONNA BE MORE THAN THAT, BROTHER! LET'S GET 'IM, GUYS!
FOOL!! YOU THINK YOU CAN DEFEAT DOCTOR DOOM SO EASILY??!
YEAH!! JUST WATCH ME!
HEY!!?
IT'S NOTHIN' BUT A ROBOT!
NATURALLY! I AM IN A HIDDEN ROOM ABOVE YOU! A ROOM FROM WHICH I SHALL NOW PRESS A BUTTON DRAINING YOUR CHAMBER OF ALL OXYGEN! FAREWELL, FANTASTIC FOUR!
*"SUB-MARINER" SEE FANTASTIC FOUR, ISSUE *4 MAY

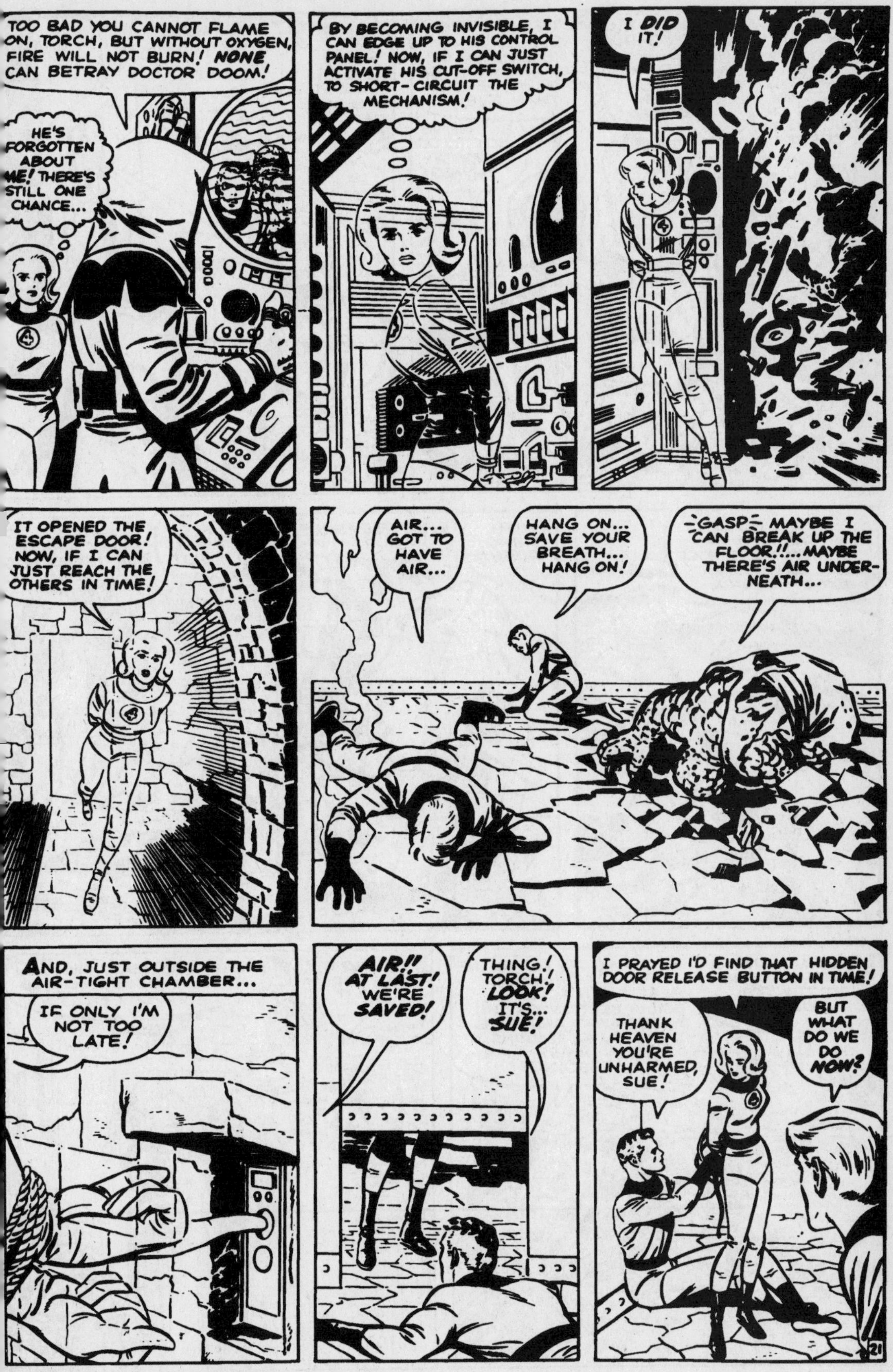
TOO BAD YOU CANNOT FLAME ON, TORCH, BUT WITHOUT OXYGEN, FIRE WILL NOT BURN! NONE CAN BETRAY DOCTOR DOOM!
HE'S FORGOTTEN ABOUT ME! THERE'S STILL ONE CHANCE...
BY BECOMING INVISIBLE, I CAN EDGE UP TO HIS CONTROL PANEL! NOW, IF I CAN JUST ACTIVATE HIS CUT-OFF SWITCH, TO SHORT-CIRCUIT THE MECHANISM!
I DID IT!
IT OPENED THE ESCAPE DOOR! NOW, IF I CAN JUST REACH THE OTHERS IN TIME!
AIR... GOT TO HAVE AIR...
HANG ON... SAVE YOUR BREATH... HANG ON!
-GASP- MAYBE I CAN BREAK UP THE FLOOR!!... MAYBE THERE'S AIR UNDERNEATH...
AND, JUST OUTSIDE THE AIR-TIGHT CHAMBER...
IF ONLY I'M NOT TOO LATE!
AIR!! AT LAST! WE'RE SAVED!
THING! TORCH! LOOK! IT'S... SUE!
I PRAYED I'D FIND THAT HIDDEN DOOR RELEASE BUTTON IN TIME!
THANK HEAVEN YOU'RE UNHARMED, SUE!
BUT WHAT DO WE DO NOW?
21

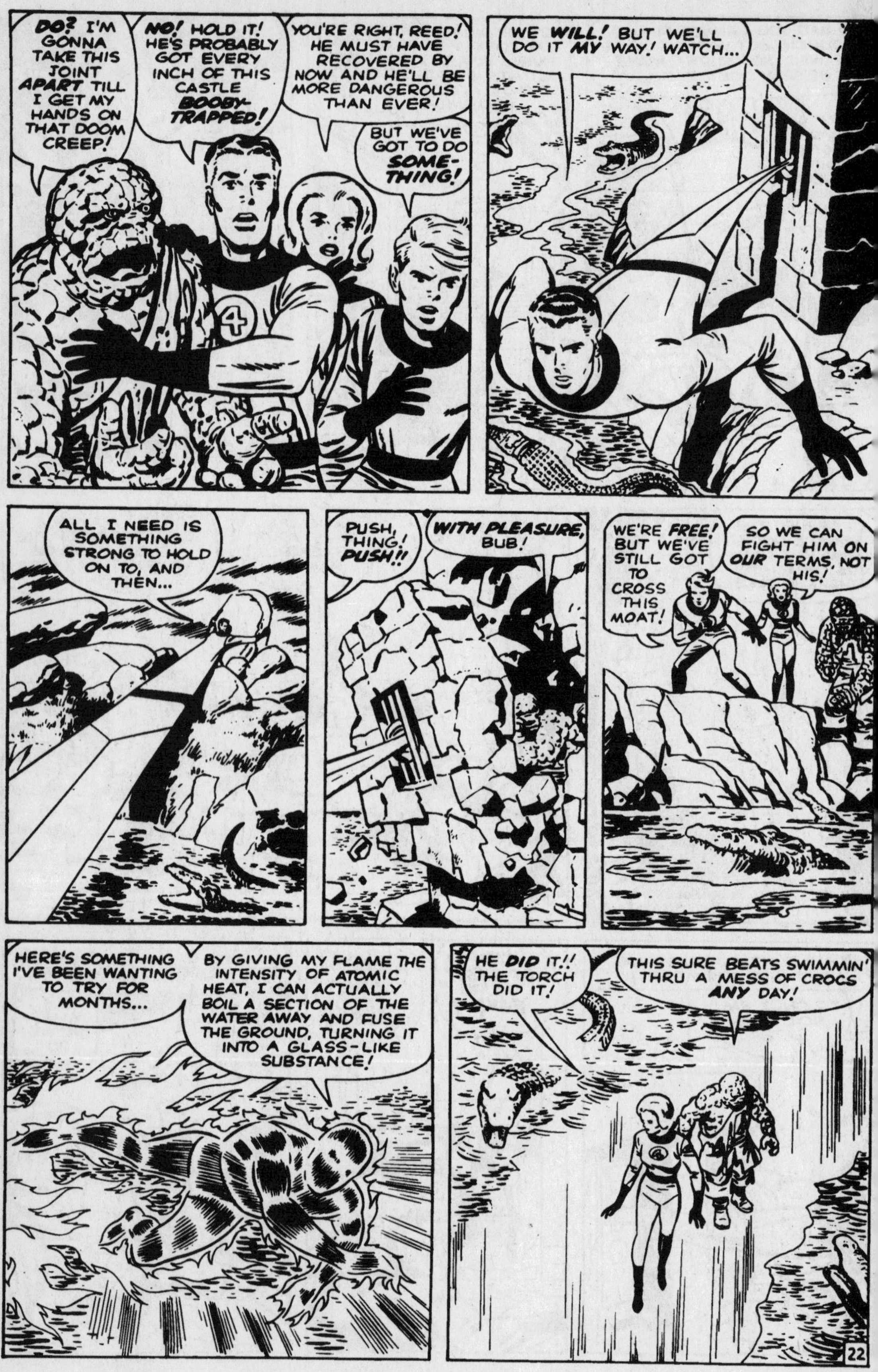

DO? I'M GONNA TAKE THIS JOINT APART TILL I GET MY HANDS ON THAT DOOM CREEP!
NO! HOLD IT! HE'S PROBABLY GOT EVERY INCH OF THIS CASTLE BOOBY-TRAPPED!
YOU'RE RIGHT, REED! HE MUST HAVE RECOVERED BY NOW AND HE'LL BE MORE DANGEROUS THAN EVER!
BUT WE'VE GOT TO DO SOMETHING!
WE WILL! BUT WE'LL DO IT MY WAY! WATCH...
ALL I NEED IS SOMETHING STRONG TO HOLD ON TO, AND THEN...
PUSH, THING! PUSH!!
WITH PLEASURE, BUB!
WE'RE FREE! BUT WE'VE STILL GOT TO CROSS THIS MOAT!
SO WE CAN FIGHT HIM ON OUR TERMS, NOT HIS!
HERE'S SOMETHING I'VE BEEN WANTING TO TRY FOR MONTHS...
BY GIVING MY FLAME THE INTENSITY OF ATOMIC HEAT, I CAN ACTUALLY BOIL A SECTION OF THE WATER AWAY AND FUSE THE GROUND, TURNING IT INTO A GLASS-LIKE SUBSTANCE!
HE DID IT!! THE TORCH DID IT!
THIS SURE BEATS SWIMMIN' THRU A MESS OF CROCS ANY DAY!
22

NOW, I'LL JUST CREATE A CIRCLE OF FLAME AROUND THE CASTLE, AND SMOKE DOCTOR DOOM OUT!!

BAH! LET HIM USE HIS FLAME! I HOPE HE BURNS MY FORTRESS TO THE GROUND, SO THAT NONE WILL EVER LEARN MY MANY SECRETS!

AS FOR ME, THE GREATEST SCIENTIFIC BRAIN OF ALL TIME IS NOT WITHOUT HIS OWN EMERGENCY ESCAPE DEVICES...SUCH AS MY ROCKET-POWERED FLYING HARNESS!

I HAVE BEEN CHEATED OUT OF THE MAGIC GEMS OF MERLIN, BUT I SHALL STILL ESCAPE...TO FIND NEW HIDDEN SITE WHERE I CAN PLAN FOR MY CONQUEST OF EARTH!

TORCH! LOOK!

I'VE GOT TO GO AFTER HIM! MANKIND WILL NEVER BE SAFE IF DOCTOR DOOM ESCAPES!

EVEN YOUR MIRACULOUS FLAME CANNOT MATCH THE THRUST OF MY ROCKETS, TORCH!

HE'S RIGHT! I--I'M GROWING WEAK!

TOO MUCH STRAIN... CAN'T GO ON--FLAME DYING--

GOT TO KEEP ENOUGH FLAME TO BREAK MY FALL...GOT TO...

TORCH!! THAT WAS A GREAT TRY!

BAH! THEY DON'T PAY OFF FOR ALSO-RANS!

GOSH, FIRST SUB-MARINER, AND NOW DOCTOR DOOM LOOSE ON EARTH! WHAT HAPPENS NEXT?!

WE'LL DEVOTE OUR LIVES TO TRACKING THEM DOWN! WE CAN DO NO MORE!

AND NEXT TIME I'LL HANDLE THINGS MY WAY!

the END

SURPRISE FOLLOWS SURPRISE IN THE NEXT FABULOUS ISSUE OF THE FANTASTIC FOUR!!

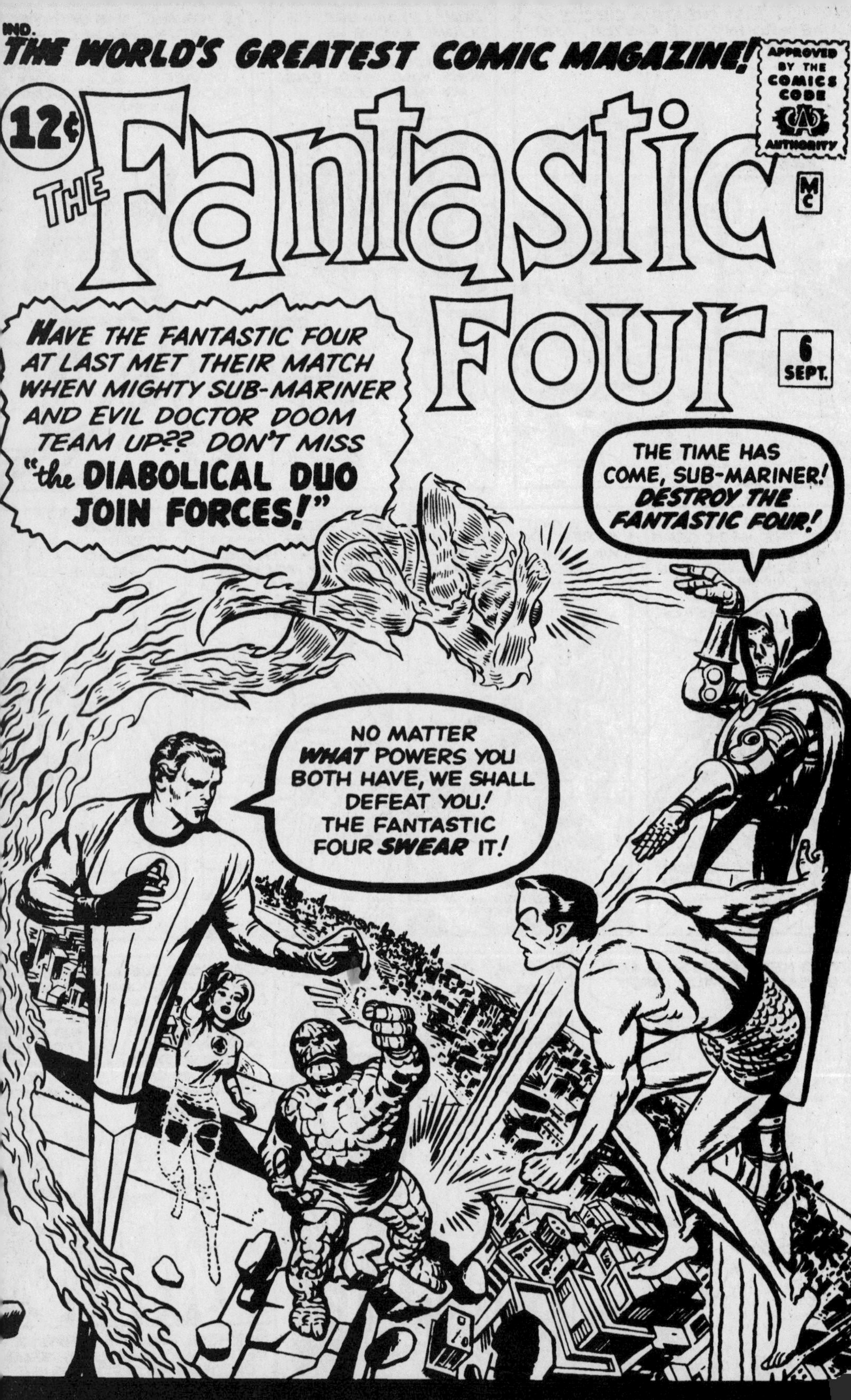

IND.
THE WORLD'S GREATEST COMIC MAGAZINE!
APPROVED BY THE COMICS CODE AUTHORITY
12¢
THE Fantastic Four
MC
6 SEPT.
HAVE THE FANTASTIC FOUR AT LAST MET THEIR MATCH WHEN MIGHTY SUB-MARINER AND EVIL DOCTOR DOOM TEAM UP?? DON'T MISS "the DIABOLICAL DUO JOIN FORCES!"
THE TIME HAS COME, SUB-MARINER! DESTROY THE FANTASTIC FOUR!
NO MATTER WHAT POWERS YOU BOTH HAVE, WE SHALL DEFEAT YOU! THE FANTASTIC FOUR SWEAR IT!

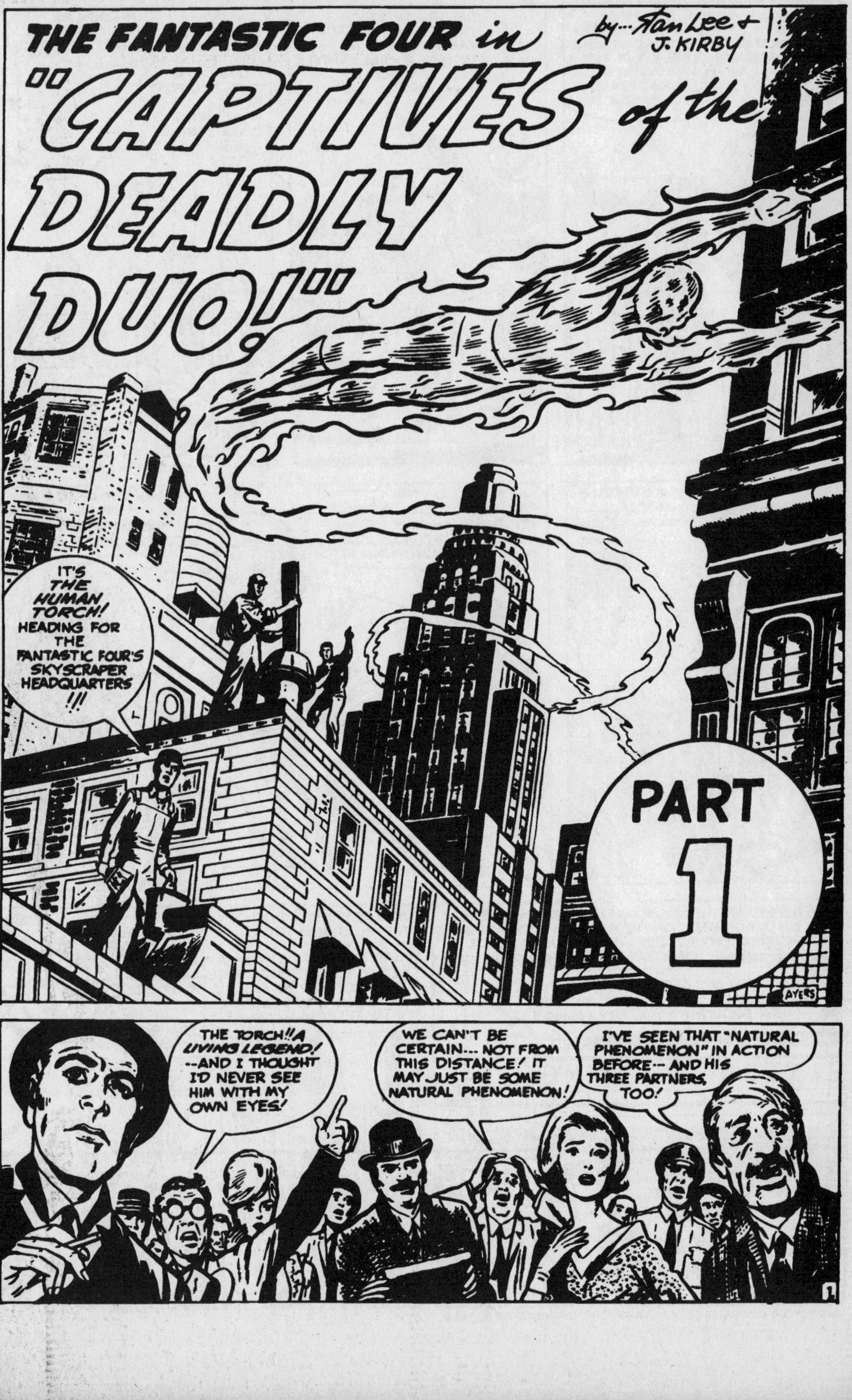
THE FANTASTIC FOUR in
"CAPTIVES of the DEADLY DUO!"
by... Stan Lee & J. KIRBY
IT'S THE HUMAN TORCH! HEADING FOR THE FANTASTIC FOUR'S SKYSCRAPER HEADQUARTERS!!!
PART 1
AYERS
THE TORCH!! A LIVING LEGEND! --AND I THOUGHT I'D NEVER SEE HIM WITH MY OWN EYES!
WE CAN'T BE CERTAIN... NOT FROM THIS DISTANCE! IT MAY JUST BE SOME NATURAL PHENOMENON!
I'VE SEEN THAT "NATURAL PHENOMENON" IN ACTION BEFORE-- AND HIS THREE PARTNERS, TOO!
1

IT'S KINDA HARD TO MAKE UP YOUR MIND! YOU SEE THESE STRANGE THINGS---HEAR ALL THOSE INCREDIBLE STORIES...

IT'S MASS HYSTERIA, PETE! I COULD NO MORE BELIEVE IN THE FANTASTIC FOUR THAN I COULD IN FLYING SAUCERS!

THE HUMAN TORCH...THE THING...MISTER FANTASTIC...THE INVISIBLE GIRL...THEY'RE ALL CREATURES OF THE IMAGI---- HEY! WHA---?

HARRY--- SOMETHING PUSHED US OFF OUR FEET--- SOMETHING THAT BRUSHED BY US... SOMETHING --- WE CAN'T SEE!

PARDON ME, GENTLEMEN... I MUST GET BY...

A VOICE.. ...OUT OF THE THIN AIR!... A GIRL'S VOICE!

LOOK!... MATERIALIZING BEFORE OUR VERY EYES...

---THE INVISIBLE GIRL!

SHE'S ONE OF THE FANTASTIC FOUR! IMAGINE HER BEING AMONG US ALL THIS TIME.... WITHOUT OUR KNOWING IT!

IT'S ENOUGH TO GIVE ONE THE SHIVERS!

FIRST THE HUMAN TORCH---AND NOW HER! SOMETHING'S UP FOR SURE!

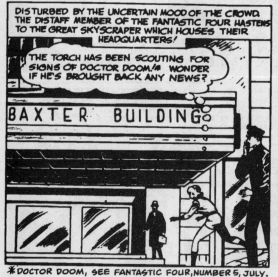

DISTURBED BY THE UNCERTAIN MOOD OF THE CROWD, THE DISTAFF MEMBER OF THE FANTASTIC FOUR HASTENS TO THE GREAT SKYSCRAPER WHICH HOUSES THEIR HEADQUARTERS!

THE TORCH HAS BEEN SCOUTING FOR SIGNS OF DOCTOR DOOM.* I WONDER IF HE'S BROUGHT BACK ANY NEWS?

BAXTER BUILDING

IN A REMOTE CORNER OF THE BUSTLING LOBBY...

THIS EXPRESS ELEVATOR SEEMS TO BE WORKING-- BUT NOT FOR ME! I'LL NEVER GET TO DELIVER MY TELEGRAM!

ARE YOU DELIVERING ANY MESSAGES TO THE FANTASTIC FOUR, SON?

ER--- NO, MA'AM... (GULP)

*DOCTOR DOOM, SEE FANTASTIC FOUR, NUMBER 5, JULY.

2

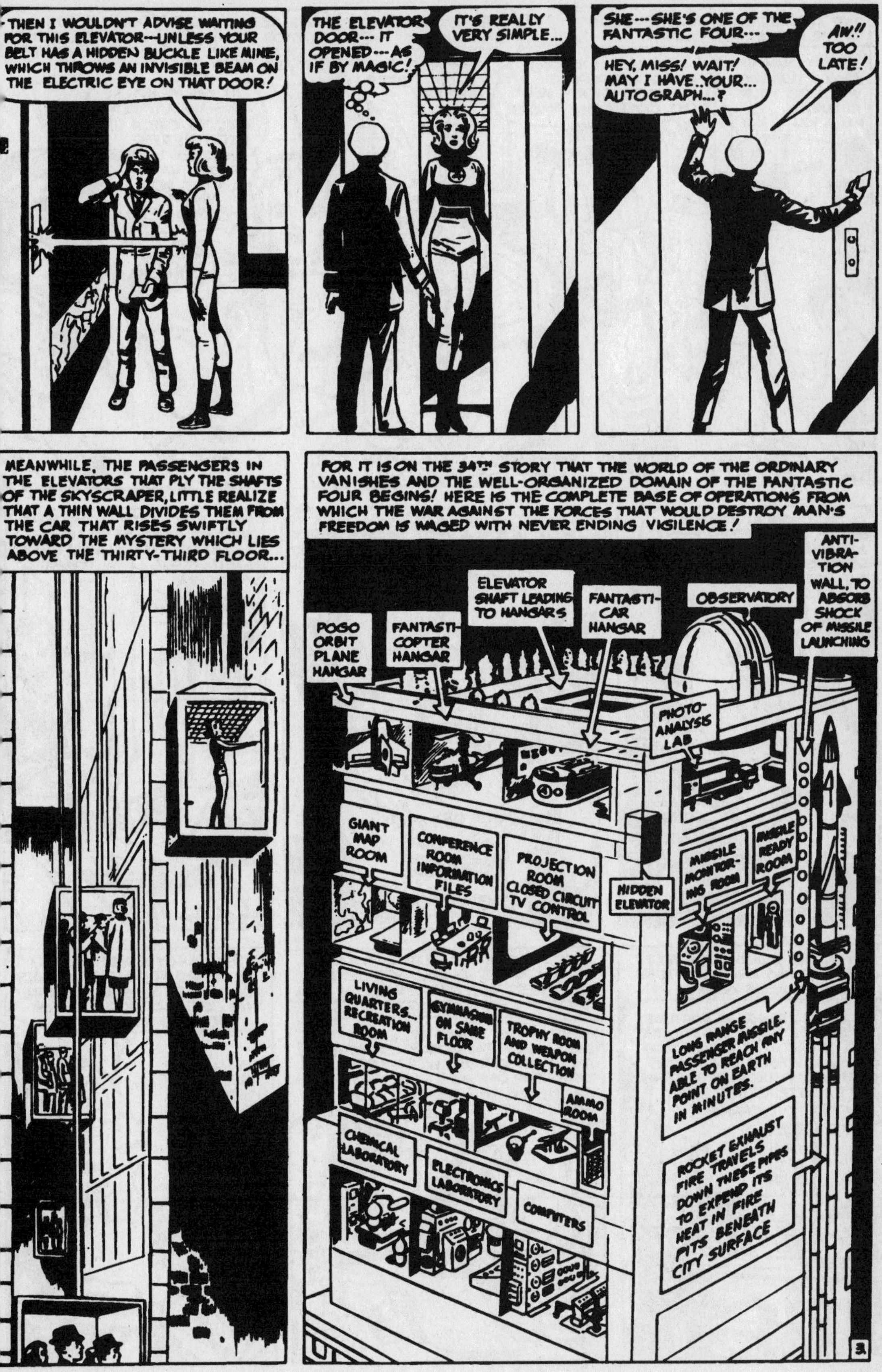
THEN I WOULDN'T ADVISE WAITING FOR THIS ELEVATOR---UNLESS YOUR BELT HAS A HIDDEN BUCKLE LIKE MINE, WHICH THROWS AN INVISIBLE BEAM ON THE ELECTRIC EYE ON THAT DOOR!
THE ELEVATOR DOOR--- IT OPENED---AS IF BY MAGIC!
IT'S REALLY VERY SIMPLE...
SHE---SHE'S ONE OF THE FANTASTIC FOUR---
HEY, MISS! WAIT! MAY I HAVE..YOUR... AUTOGRAPH...?
AW!! TOO LATE!
MEANWHILE, THE PASSENGERS IN THE ELEVATORS THAT PLY THE SHAFTS OF THE SKYSCRAPER, LITTLE REALIZE THAT A THIN WALL DIVIDES THEM FROM THE CAR THAT RISES SWIFTLY TOWARD THE MYSTERY WHICH LIES ABOVE THE THIRTY-THIRD FLOOR...
FOR IT IS ON THE 34TH STORY THAT THE WORLD OF THE ORDINARY VANISHES AND THE WELL-ORGANIZED DOMAIN OF THE FANTASTIC FOUR BEGINS! HERE IS THE COMPLETE BASE OF OPERATIONS FROM WHICH THE WAR AGAINST THE FORCES THAT WOULD DESTROY MAN'S FREEDOM IS WAGED WITH NEVER ENDING VIGILENCE!
POGO ORBIT PLANE HANGAR
FANTASTI-COPTER HANGAR
ELEVATOR SHAFT LEADING TO HANGARS
FANTASTI-CAR HANGAR
OBSERVATORY
ANTI-VIBRATION WALL, TO ABSORB SHOCK OF MISSILE LAUNCHING
PHOTO-ANALYSIS LAB
GIANT MAP ROOM
CONFERENCE ROOM INFORMATION FILES
PROJECTION ROOM CLOSED CIRCUIT TV CONTROL
HIDDEN ELEVATOR
MISSILE MONITORING ROOM
MISSILE READY ROOM
LIVING QUARTERS... RECREATION ROOM
GYMNASIUM ON SAME FLOOR
TROPHY ROOM AND WEAPON COLLECTION
AMMO ROOM
LONG RANGE PASSENGER MISSILE. ABLE TO REACH ANY POINT ON EARTH IN MINUTES.
CHEMICAL LABORATORY
ELECTRONICS LABORATORY
COMPUTERS
ROCKET EXHAUST FIRE TRAVELS DOWN THESE PIPES TO EXPEND ITS HEAT IN FIRE PITS BENEATH CITY SURFACE
3

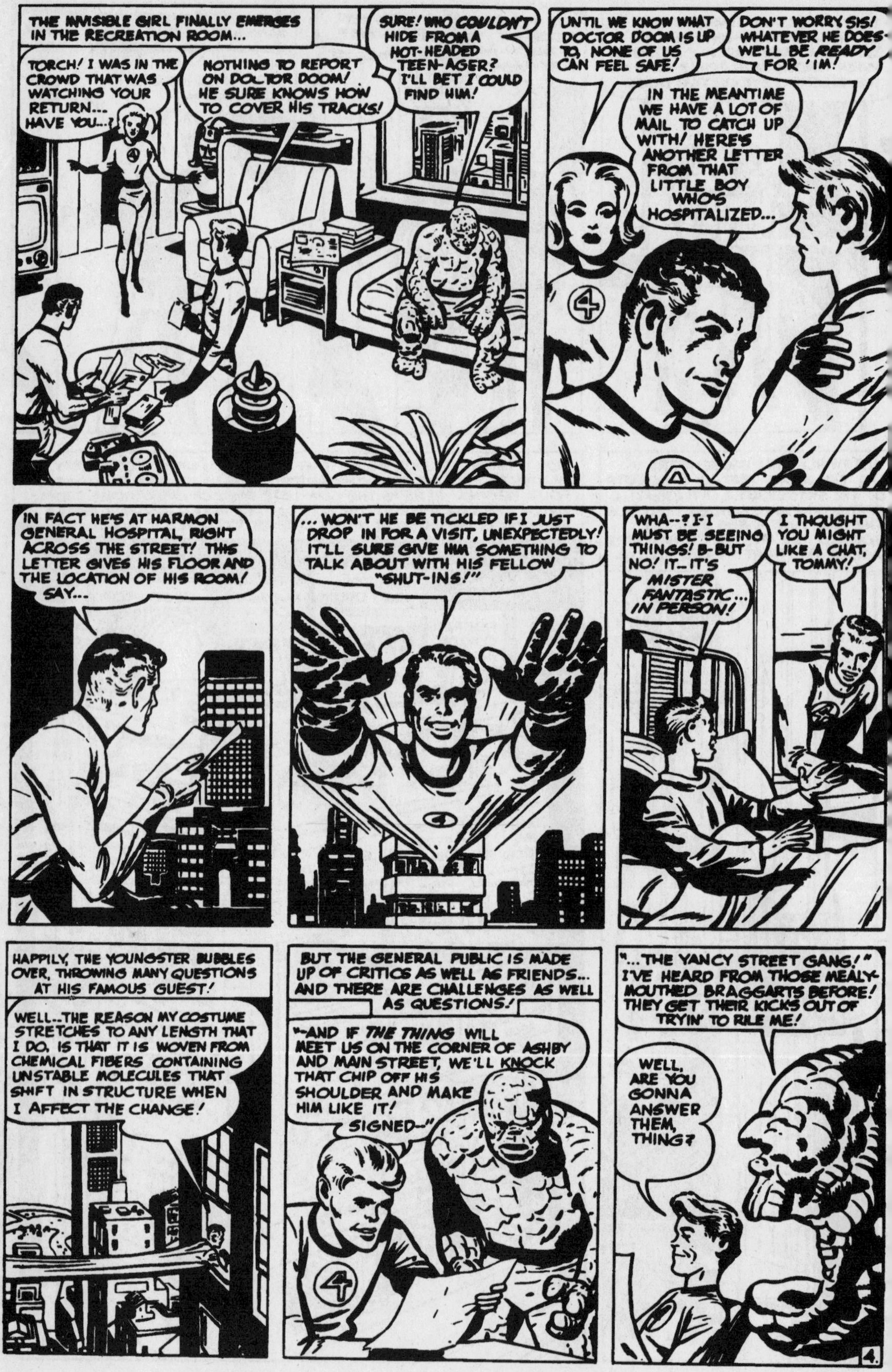
THE INVISIBLE GIRL FINALLY EMERGES IN THE RECREATION ROOM...
TORCH! I WAS IN THE CROWD THAT WAS WATCHING YOUR RETURN... HAVE YOU...?
NOTHING TO REPORT ON DOCTOR DOOM! HE SURE KNOWS HOW TO COVER HIS TRACKS!
SURE! WHO COULDN'T HIDE FROM A HOT-HEADED TEEN-AGER? I'LL BET I COULD FIND HIM!
UNTIL WE KNOW WHAT DOCTOR DOOM IS UP TO, NONE OF US CAN FEEL SAFE!
DON'T WORRY SIS! WHATEVER HE DOES-- WE'LL BE READY FOR 'IM!
IN THE MEANTIME WE HAVE A LOT OF MAIL TO CATCH UP WITH! HERE'S ANOTHER LETTER FROM THAT LITTLE BOY WHO'S HOSPITALIZED...
IN FACT HE'S AT HARMON GENERAL HOSPITAL, RIGHT ACROSS THE STREET! THIS LETTER GIVES HIS FLOOR AND THE LOCATION OF HIS ROOM! SAY...
...WON'T HE BE TICKLED IF I JUST DROP IN FOR A VISIT, UNEXPECTEDLY! IT'LL SURE GIVE HIM SOMETHING TO TALK ABOUT WITH HIS FELLOW "SHUT-INS!"
WHA--? I-I MUST BE SEEING THINGS! B-BUT NO! IT--IT'S MISTER FANTASTIC... IN PERSON!
I THOUGHT YOU MIGHT LIKE A CHAT, TOMMY!
HAPPILY, THE YOUNGSTER BUBBLES OVER, THROWING MANY QUESTIONS AT HIS FAMOUS GUEST!
WELL--THE REASON MY COSTUME STRETCHES TO ANY LENGTH THAT I DO, IS THAT IT IS WOVEN FROM CHEMICAL FIBERS CONTAINING UNSTABLE MOLECULES THAT SHIFT IN STRUCTURE WHEN I AFFECT THE CHANGE!
BUT THE GENERAL PUBLIC IS MADE UP OF CRITICS AS WELL AS FRIENDS... AND THERE ARE CHALLENGES AS WELL AS QUESTIONS!
"--AND IF THE THING WILL MEET US ON THE CORNER OF ASHBY AND MAIN STREET, WE'LL KNOCK THAT CHIP OFF HIS SHOULDER AND MAKE HIM LIKE IT! SIGNED--"
"...THE YANCY STREET GANG!" I'VE HEARD FROM THOSE MEALY-MOUTHED BRAGGARTS BEFORE! THEY GET THEIR KICKS OUT OF TRYIN' TO RILE ME!
WELL, ARE YOU GONNA ANSWER THEM, THING?
4.

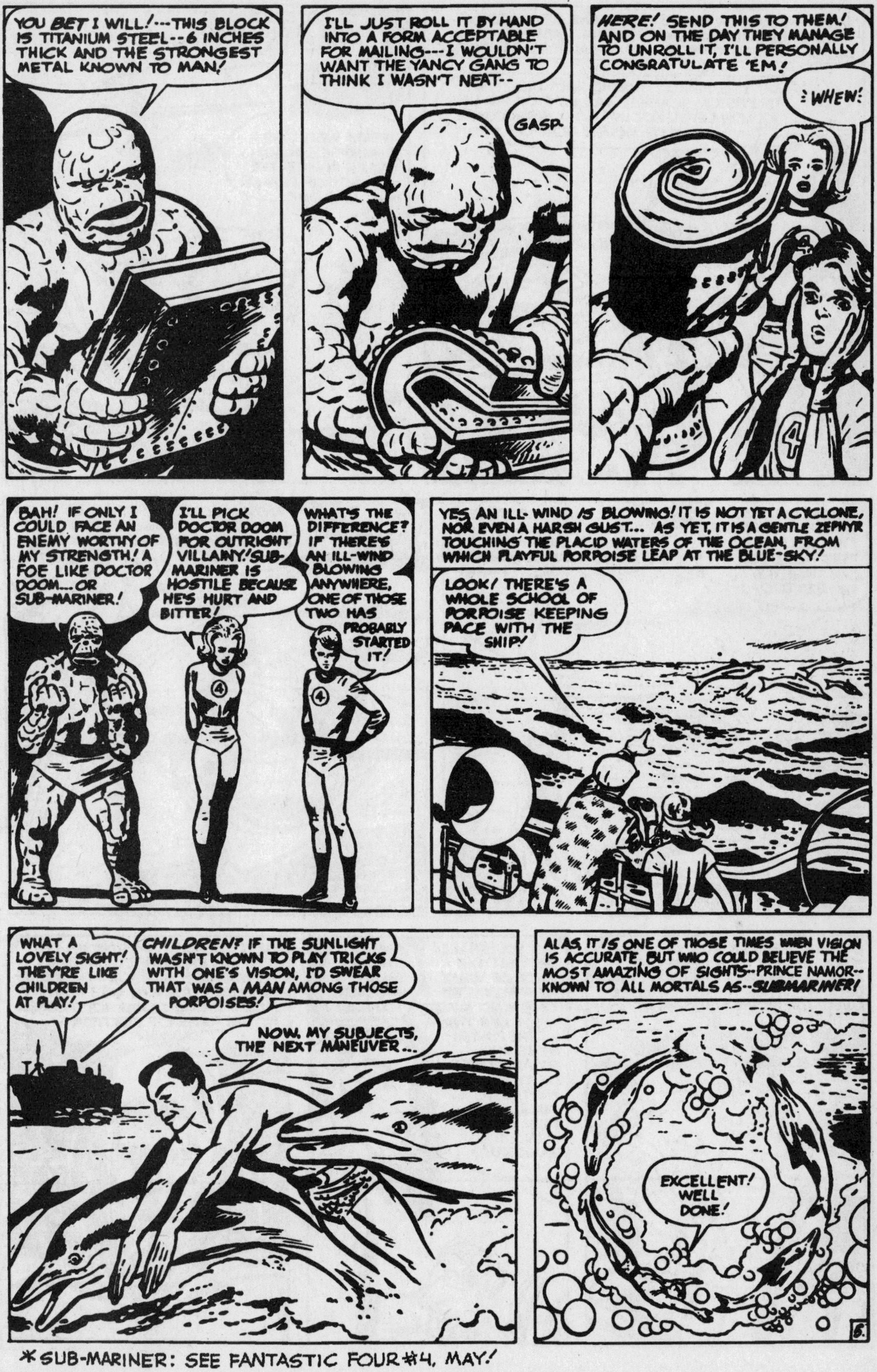
YOU BET I WILL!---THIS BLOCK IS TITANIUM STEEL--6 INCHES THICK AND THE STRONGEST METAL KNOWN TO MAN!
I'LL JUST ROLL IT BY HAND INTO A FORM ACCEPTABLE FOR MAILING---I WOULDN'T WANT THE YANCY GANG TO THINK I WASN'T NEAT--
GASP
HERE! SEND THIS TO THEM! AND ON THE DAY THEY MANAGE TO UNROLL IT, I'LL PERSONALLY CONGRATULATE 'EM!
WHEW!
BAH! IF ONLY I COULD FACE AN ENEMY WORTHY OF MY STRENGTH! A FOE LIKE DOCTOR DOOM... OR SUB-MARINER!
I'LL PICK DOCTOR DOOM FOR OUTRIGHT VILLAINY! SUB-MARINER IS HOSTILE BECAUSE HE'S HURT AND BITTER!
WHAT'S THE DIFFERENCE? IF THERE'S AN ILL-WIND BLOWING ANYWHERE, ONE OF THOSE TWO HAS PROBABLY STARTED IT!
YES AN ILL-WIND IS BLOWING! IT IS NOT YET A CYCLONE, NOR EVEN A HARSH GUST... AS YET, IT IS A GENTLE ZEPHYR TOUCHING THE PLACID WATERS OF THE OCEAN, FROM WHICH PLAYFUL PORPOISE LEAP AT THE BLUE-SKY!
LOOK! THERE'S A WHOLE SCHOOL OF PORPOISE KEEPING PACE WITH THE SHIP!
WHAT A LOVELY SIGHT! THEY'RE LIKE CHILDREN AT PLAY!
CHILDREN? IF THE SUNLIGHT WASN'T KNOWN TO PLAY TRICKS WITH ONE'S VISION, I'D SWEAR THAT WAS A MAN AMONG THOSE PORPOISES!
NOW, MY SUBJECTS, THE NEXT MANEUVER...
ALAS, IT IS ONE OF THOSE TIMES WHEN VISION IS ACCURATE, BUT WHO COULD BELIEVE THE MOST AMAZING OF SIGHTS--PRINCE NAMOR--KNOWN TO ALL MORTALS AS--SUBMARINER!
EXCELLENT! WELL DONE!
6.

* SUB-MARINER: SEE FANTASTIC FOUR #4, MAY!

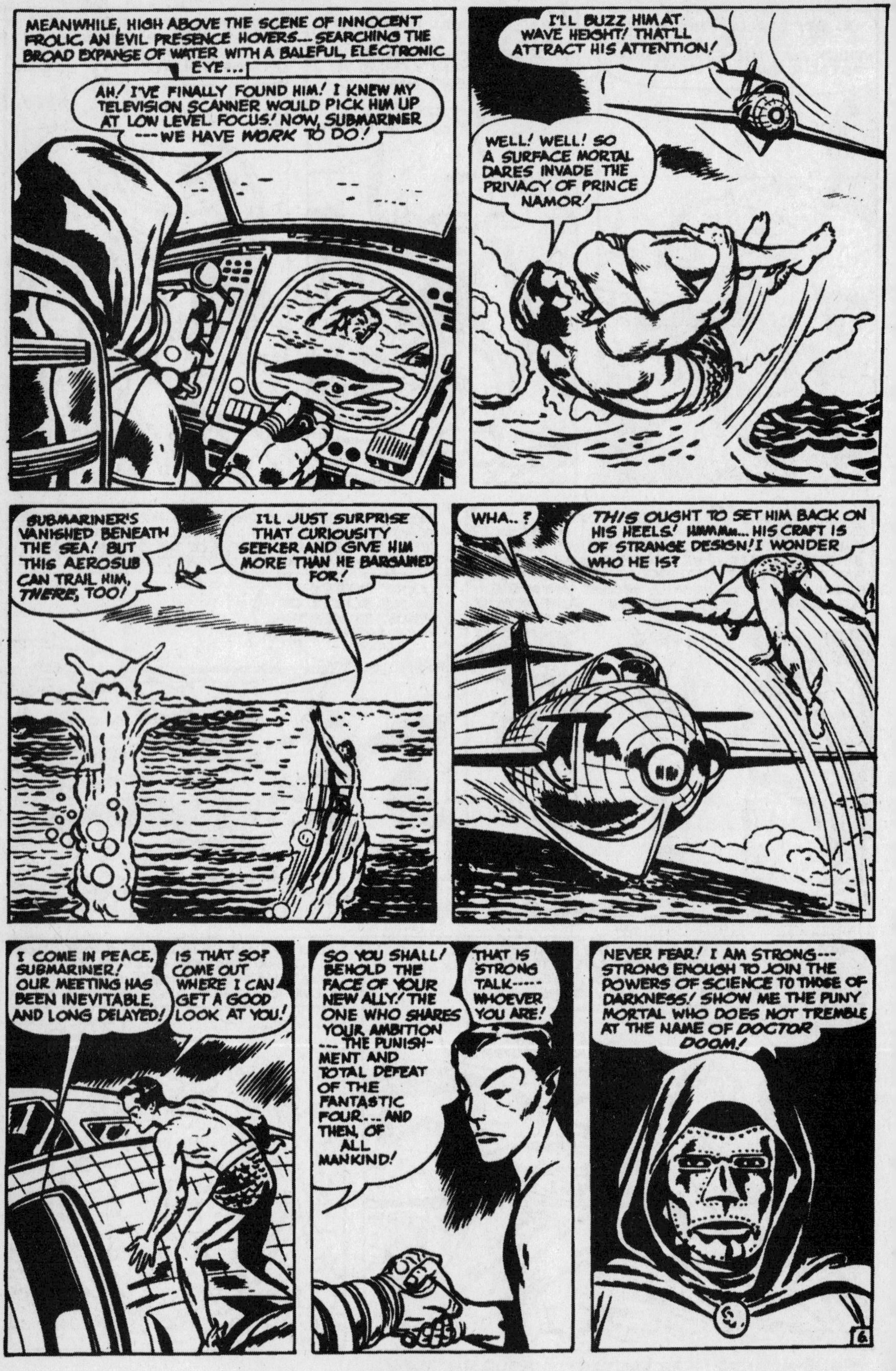
MEANWHILE, HIGH ABOVE THE SCENE OF INNOCENT FROLIC, AN EVIL PRESENCE HOVERS... SEARCHING THE BROAD EXPANSE OF WATER WITH A BALEFUL, ELECTRONIC EYE...
AH! I'VE FINALLY FOUND HIM! I KNEW MY TELEVISION SCANNER WOULD PICK HIM UP AT LOW LEVEL FOCUS! NOW, SUBMARINER ---WE HAVE WORK TO DO!
I'LL BUZZ HIM AT WAVE HEIGHT! THAT'LL ATTRACT HIS ATTENTION!
WELL! WELL! SO A SURFACE MORTAL DARES INVADE THE PRIVACY OF PRINCE NAMOR!
SUBMARINER'S VANISHED BENEATH THE SEA! BUT THIS AEROSUB CAN TRAIL HIM, THERE, TOO!
I'LL JUST SURPRISE THAT CURIOUSITY SEEKER AND GIVE HIM MORE THAN HE BARGAINED FOR!
WHA..?
THIS OUGHT TO SET HIM BACK ON HIS HEELS! HMMM... HIS CRAFT IS OF STRANGE DESIGN! I WONDER WHO HE IS?
I COME IN PEACE, SUBMARINER! OUR MEETING HAS BEEN INEVITABLE, AND LONG DELAYED!
IS THAT SO? COME OUT WHERE I CAN GET A GOOD LOOK AT YOU!
SO YOU SHALL! BEHOLD THE FACE OF YOUR NEW ALLY! THE ONE WHO SHARES YOUR AMBITION --- THE PUNISHMENT AND TOTAL DEFEAT OF THE FANTASTIC FOUR... AND THEN, OF ALL MANKIND!
THAT IS STRONG TALK----- WHOEVER YOU ARE!
NEVER FEAR! I AM STRONG--- STRONG ENOUGH TO JOIN THE POWERS OF SCIENCE TO THOSE OF DARKNESS! SHOW ME THE PUNY MORTAL WHO DOES NOT TREMBLE AT THE NAME OF DOCTOR DOOM!
6

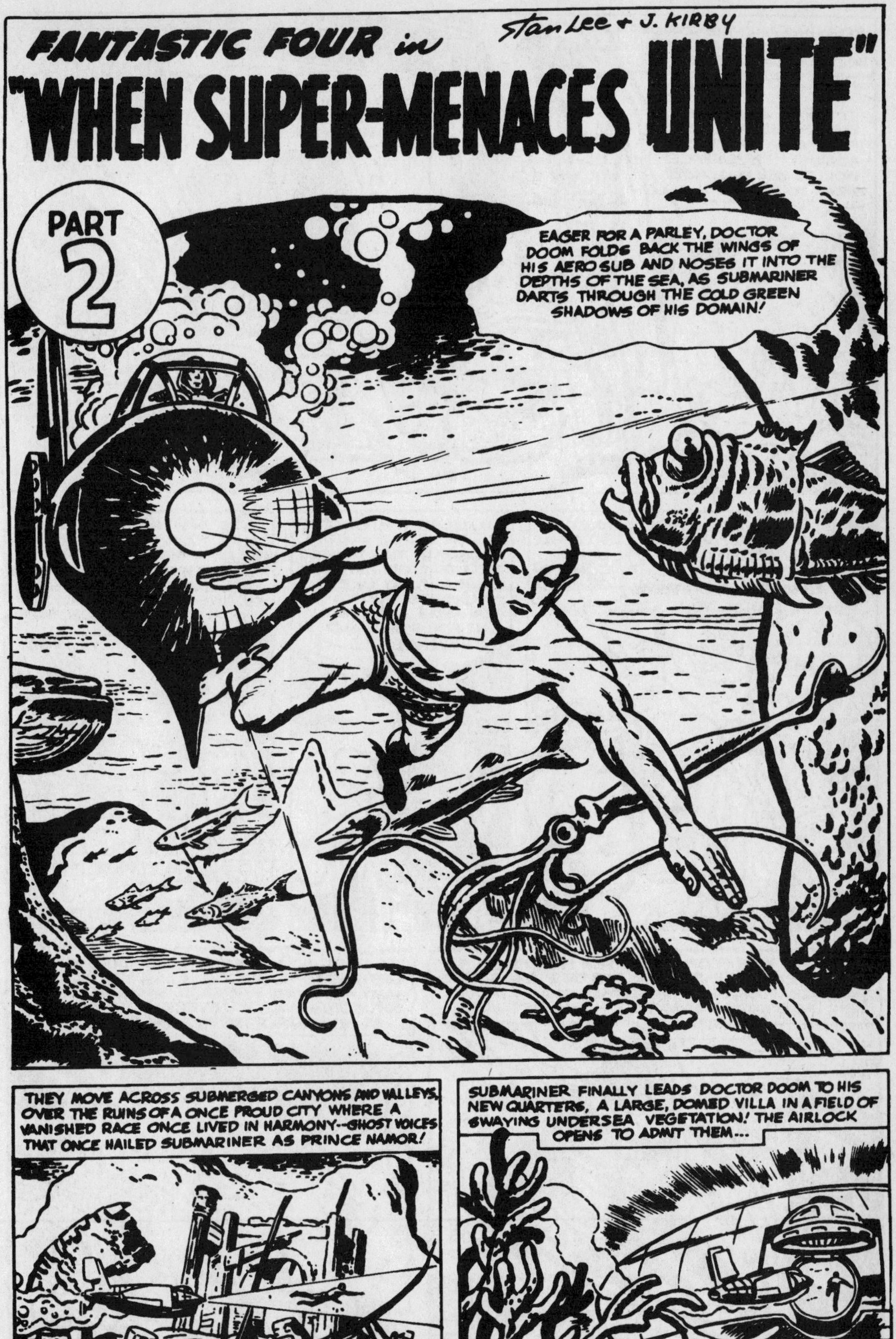
FANTASTIC FOUR in
Stan Lee + J. Kirby
"WHEN SUPER-MENACES UNITE"
PART 2
EAGER FOR A PARLEY, DOCTOR DOOM FOLDS BACK THE WINGS OF HIS AERO SUB AND NOSES IT INTO THE DEPTHS OF THE SEA, AS SUBMARINER DARTS THROUGH THE COLD GREEN SHADOWS OF HIS DOMAIN!
THEY MOVE ACROSS SUBMERGED CANYONS AND VALLEYS, OVER THE RUINS OF A ONCE PROUD CITY WHERE A VANISHED RACE ONCE LIVED IN HARMONY--GHOST VOICES THAT ONCE HAILED SUBMARINER AS PRINCE NAMOR!
SUBMARINER FINALLY LEADS DOCTOR DOOM TO HIS NEW QUARTERS, A LARGE, DOMED VILLA IN A FIELD OF SWAYING UNDERSEA VEGETATION! THE AIRLOCK OPENS TO ADMIT THEM...
7

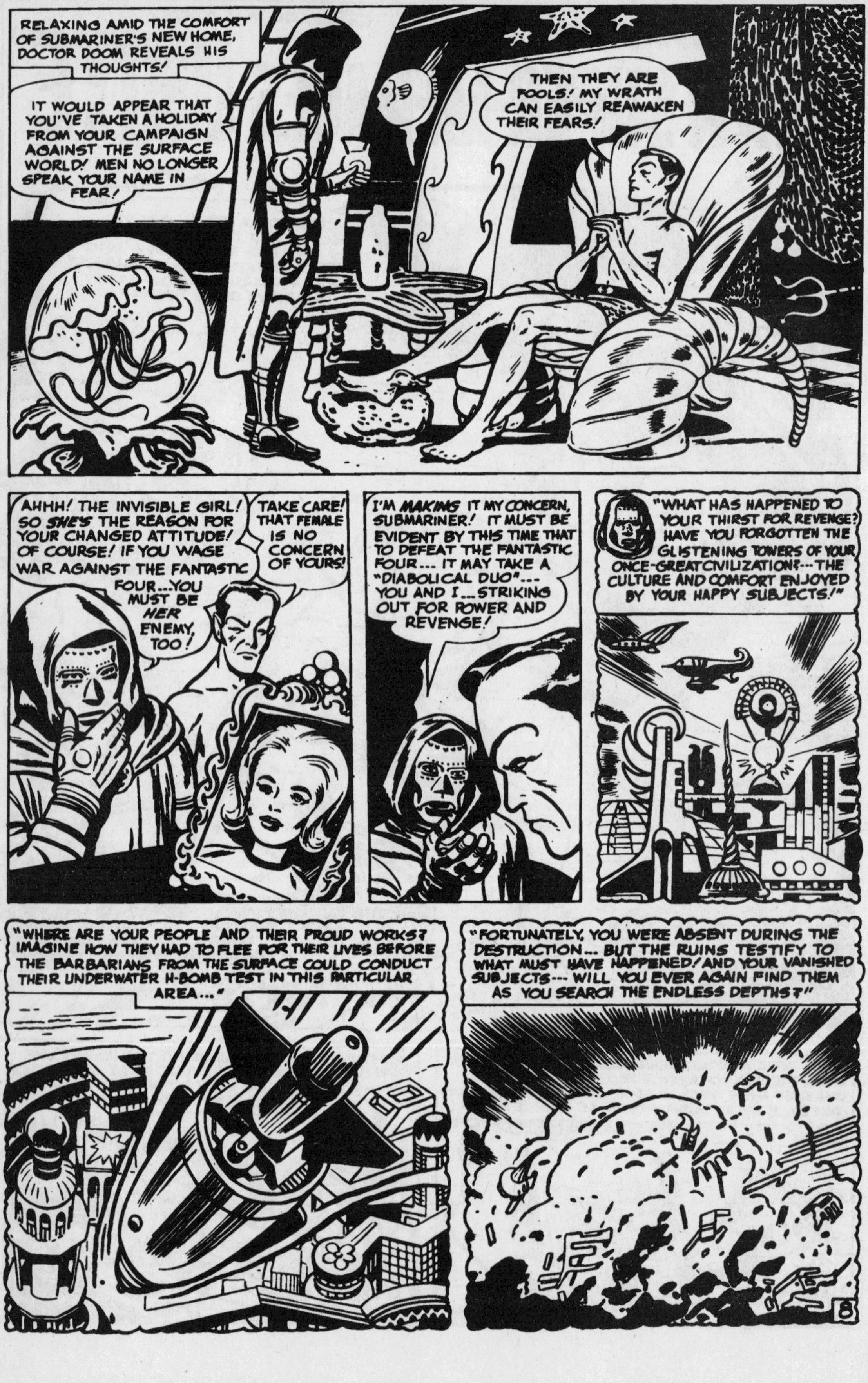
RELAXING AMID THE COMFORT OF SUBMARINER'S NEW HOME, DOCTOR DOOM REVEALS HIS THOUGHTS!
IT WOULD APPEAR THAT YOU'VE TAKEN A HOLIDAY FROM YOUR CAMPAIGN AGAINST THE SURFACE WORLD! MEN NO LONGER SPEAK YOUR NAME IN FEAR!
THEN THEY ARE FOOLS! MY WRATH CAN EASILY REAWAKEN THEIR FEARS!
AHHH! THE INVISIBLE GIRL! SO SHE'S THE REASON FOR YOUR CHANGED ATTITUDE! OF COURSE! IF YOU WAGE WAR AGAINST THE FANTASTIC FOUR...YOU MUST BE HER ENEMY, TOO!
TAKE CARE! THAT FEMALE IS NO CONCERN OF YOURS!
I'M MAKING IT MY CONCERN, SUBMARINER! IT MUST BE EVIDENT BY THIS TIME THAT TO DEFEAT THE FANTASTIC FOUR... IT MAY TAKE A "DIABOLICAL DUO"... YOU AND I... STRIKING OUT FOR POWER AND REVENGE!
"WHAT HAS HAPPENED TO YOUR THIRST FOR REVENGE? HAVE YOU FORGOTTEN THE GLISTENING TOWERS OF YOUR ONCE-GREAT CIVILIZATION?---THE CULTURE AND COMFORT ENJOYED BY YOUR HAPPY SUBJECTS!"
"WHERE ARE YOUR PEOPLE AND THEIR PROUD WORKS? IMAGINE HOW THEY HAD TO FLEE FOR THEIR LIVES BEFORE THE BARBARIANS FROM THE SURFACE COULD CONDUCT THEIR UNDERWATER H-BOMB TEST IN THIS PARTICULAR AREA..."
"FORTUNATELY, YOU WERE ABSENT DURING THE DESTRUCTION... BUT THE RUINS TESTIFY TO WHAT MUST HAVE HAPPENED! AND YOUR VANISHED SUBJECTS--- WILL YOU EVER AGAIN FIND THEM AS YOU SEARCH THE ENDLESS DEPTHS?"
8

IMAGINE-- YOUR GREAT AND PROUD PEOPLE--- STRUGGLING FOR THOUSANDS OF YEARS DEFEATING ALL THE TERRORS OF THE DEEP TO BUILD A CIVILIZATION SUPERB AND BEAUTIFUL... YES, BEAUTIFUL AND GLOWING WITH LIFE--- UNTIL THAT LAST TERRIFYING MOMENT... WHEN THAT MONSTER OF A BOMB LODGED IN THE MIDST OF THAT BEAUTY...

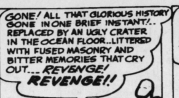

GONE! ALL THAT GLORIOUS HISTORY GONE IN ONE BRIEF INSTANT!.. REPLACED BY AN UGLY CRATER IN THE OCEAN FLOOR...LITTERED WITH FUSED MASONRY AND BITTER MEMORIES THAT CRY OUT.... REVENGE! *REVENGE!!*

REVENGE UPON THE SURFACE WORLD WHICH DID THIS IN ITS IGNORANCE! REVENGE UPON HUMANITY'S DEFENDERS! DEATH TO THE FANTASTIC FOUR!

I...I. I CANNOT HARM THE *GIRL!* BUT I WILL AID YOU IN DEFEATING THE *OTHERS!*

VERY WELL THEN! I AGREE! BUT BEFORE I TELL YOU OF MY PLAN, LET ME DEMONSTRATE THE POWER OF MY MAGNETIC BRAINCHILDREN!

I CALL THIS CYLINDER A "GRABBER"! AT A TOUCH OF THIS CONTROL KNOB, I CAN LAUNCH IT IN ANY DIRECTION! *OBSERVE!*

TRAVELING ON ITS MAGNETIC BEAM, THE GRABBER SWIFTLY, TIRELESSLY COVERS VAST DISTANCES OF THE UNDERSEA KINGDOM...

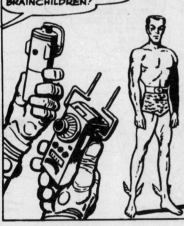

AS IF IT HAD A WILL OF ITS OWN, THE GRABBER ZEROES IN ON THE HEAD OF A HUGE PAGAN IDOL, MIRED FOR CENTURIES IN THE OOZE OF THE SEA BOTTOM...

THE HUGE MASS BEGINS TO STIR, TREMBLING IN THE PULL OF A TITANIC, UNSEEN FORCE! SLOWLY IT IS LIFTED FROM THE STRONG GRIP OF ITS AGE OLD PRISON...

THEN, WITH ONE SUDDEN, FRIGHTFUL YANK, THE MAMMOTH IDOL'S HEAD BREAKS FREE AND DRIFTS LIKE A FEATHER ON THE MAGNETIC CURRENT TRAVELLED BY THE GRABBER!

9.

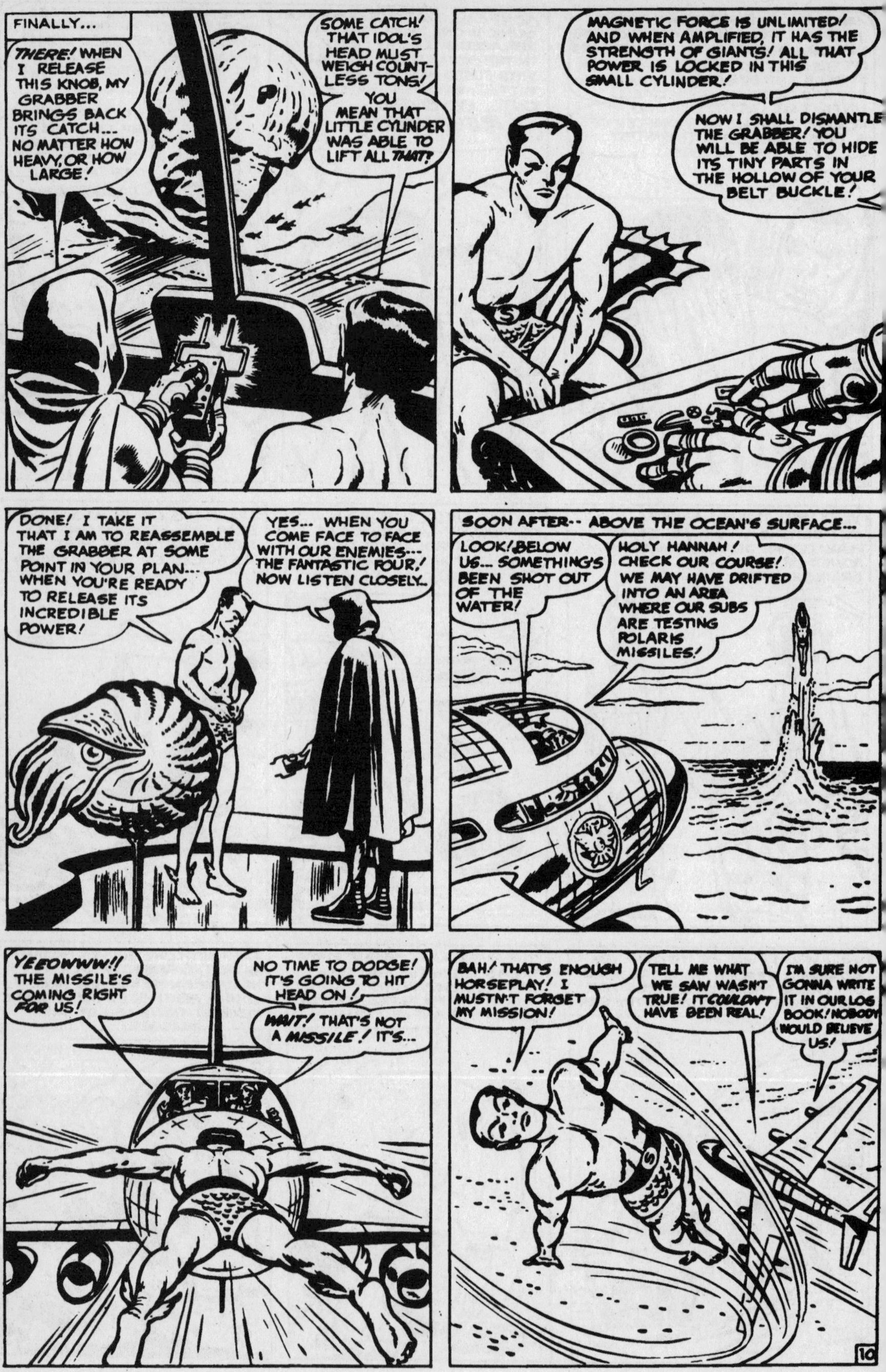
FINALLY...
THERE! WHEN I RELEASE THIS KNOB, MY GRABBER BRINGS BACK ITS CATCH... NO MATTER HOW HEAVY, OR HOW LARGE!
SOME CATCH! THAT IDOL'S HEAD MUST WEIGH COUNTLESS TONS!
YOU MEAN THAT LITTLE CYLINDER WAS ABLE TO LIFT ALL THAT?
MAGNETIC FORCE IS UNLIMITED! AND WHEN AMPLIFIED, IT HAS THE STRENGTH OF GIANTS! ALL THAT POWER IS LOCKED IN THIS SMALL CYLINDER!
NOW I SHALL DISMANTLE THE GRABBER! YOU WILL BE ABLE TO HIDE ITS TINY PARTS IN THE HOLLOW OF YOUR BELT BUCKLE!
DONE! I TAKE IT THAT I AM TO REASSEMBLE THE GRABBER AT SOME POINT IN YOUR PLAN... WHEN YOU'RE READY TO RELEASE ITS INCREDIBLE POWER!
YES... WHEN YOU COME FACE TO FACE WITH OUR ENEMIES--- THE FANTASTIC FOUR! NOW LISTEN CLOSELY...
SOON AFTER-- ABOVE THE OCEAN'S SURFACE...
LOOK! BELOW US... SOMETHING'S BEEN SHOT OUT OF THE WATER!
HOLY HANNAH! CHECK OUR COURSE! WE MAY HAVE DRIFTED INTO AN AREA WHERE OUR SUBS ARE TESTING POLARIS MISSILES!
YEEOWWW!! THE MISSILE'S COMING RIGHT FOR US!
NO TIME TO DODGE! IT'S GOING TO HIT HEAD ON!
WAIT! THAT'S NOT A MISSILE! IT'S...
BAH! THAT'S ENOUGH HORSEPLAY! I MUSTN'T FORGET MY MISSION!
TELL ME WHAT WE SAW WASN'T TRUE! IT COULDN'T HAVE BEEN REAL!
I'M SURE NOT GONNA WRITE IT IN OUR LOG BOOK! NOBODY WOULD BELIEVE US!
10

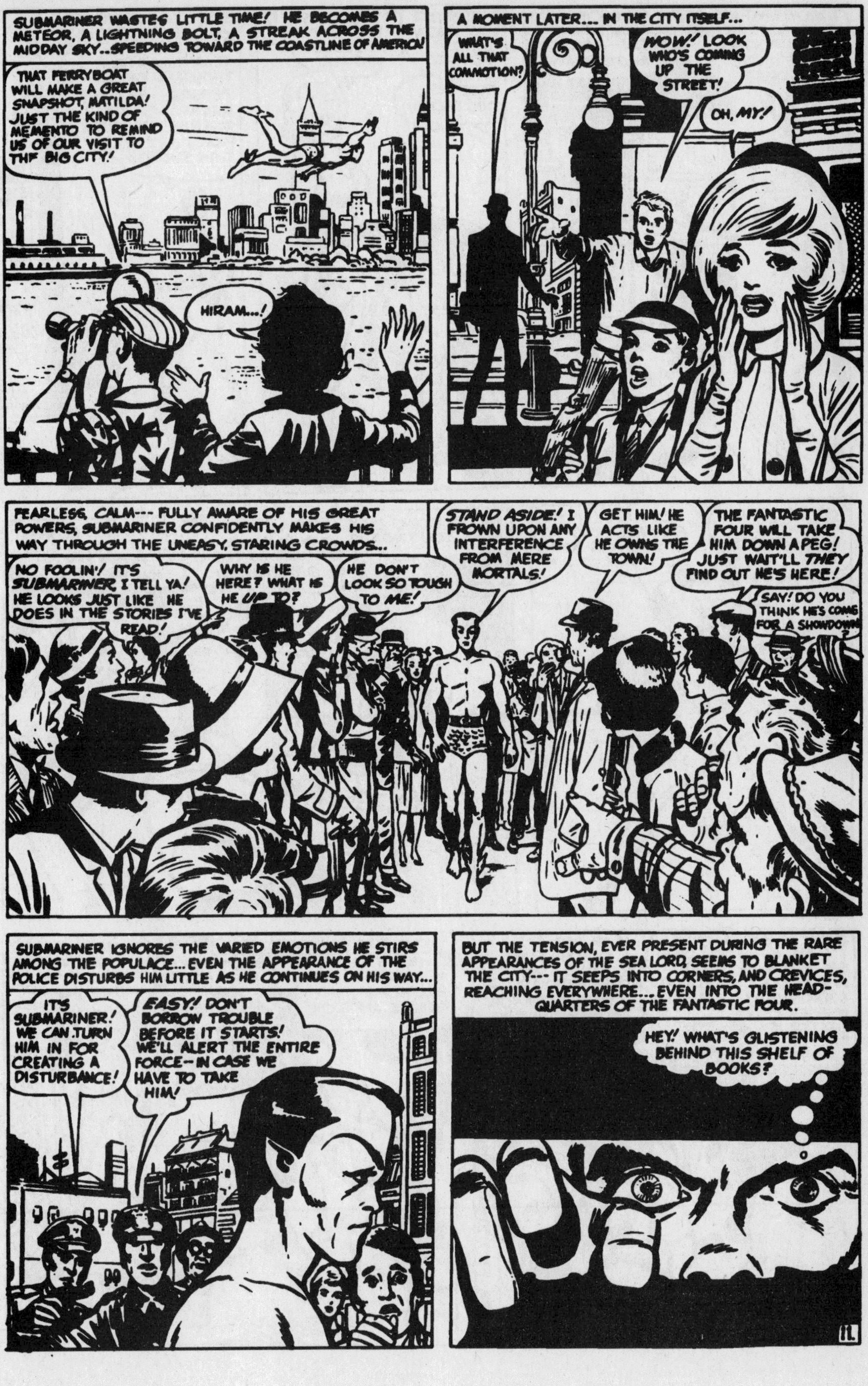

SUBMARINER WASTES LITTLE TIME! HE BECOMES A METEOR, A LIGHTNING BOLT, A STREAK ACROSS THE MIDDAY SKY..SPEEDING TOWARD THE COASTLINE OF AMERICA!
THAT FERRYBOAT WILL MAKE A GREAT SNAPSHOT, MATILDA! JUST THE KIND OF MEMENTO TO REMIND US OF OUR VISIT TO THE BIG CITY!
HIRAM...!
A MOMENT LATER... IN THE CITY ITSELF...
WHAT'S ALL THAT COMMOTION?
WOW! LOOK WHO'S COMING UP THE STREET!
OH, MY!
FEARLESS, CALM--- FULLY AWARE OF HIS GREAT POWERS, SUBMARINER CONFIDENTLY MAKES HIS WAY THROUGH THE UNEASY, STARING CROWDS..
NO FOOLIN'! IT'S SUBMARINER, I TELL YA! HE LOOKS JUST LIKE HE DOES IN THE STORIES I'VE READ!
WHY IS HE HERE? WHAT IS HE UP TO?
HE DON'T LOOK SO TOUGH TO ME!
STAND ASIDE! I FROWN UPON ANY INTERFERENCE FROM MERE MORTALS!
GET HIM! HE ACTS LIKE HE OWNS THE TOWN!
THE FANTASTIC FOUR WILL TAKE HIM DOWN A PEG! JUST WAIT'LL THEY FIND OUT HE'S HERE!
SAY! DO YOU THINK HE'S COME FOR A SHOWDOWN?
SUBMARINER IGNORES THE VARIED EMOTIONS HE STIRS AMONG THE POPULACE... EVEN THE APPEARANCE OF THE POLICE DISTURBS HIM LITTLE AS HE CONTINUES ON HIS WAY...
IT'S SUBMARINER! WE CAN TURN HIM IN FOR CREATING A DISTURBANCE!
EASY! DON'T BORROW TROUBLE BEFORE IT STARTS! WE'LL ALERT THE ENTIRE FORCE-- IN CASE WE HAVE TO TAKE HIM!
BUT THE TENSION, EVER PRESENT DURING THE RARE APPEARANCES OF THE SEA LORD, SEEMS TO BLANKET THE CITY--- IT SEEPS INTO CORNERS, AND CREVICES, REACHING EVERYWHERE... EVEN INTO THE HEAD-QUARTERS OF THE FANTASTIC FOUR.
HEY! WHAT'S GLISTENING BEHIND THIS SHELF OF BOOKS?
11.

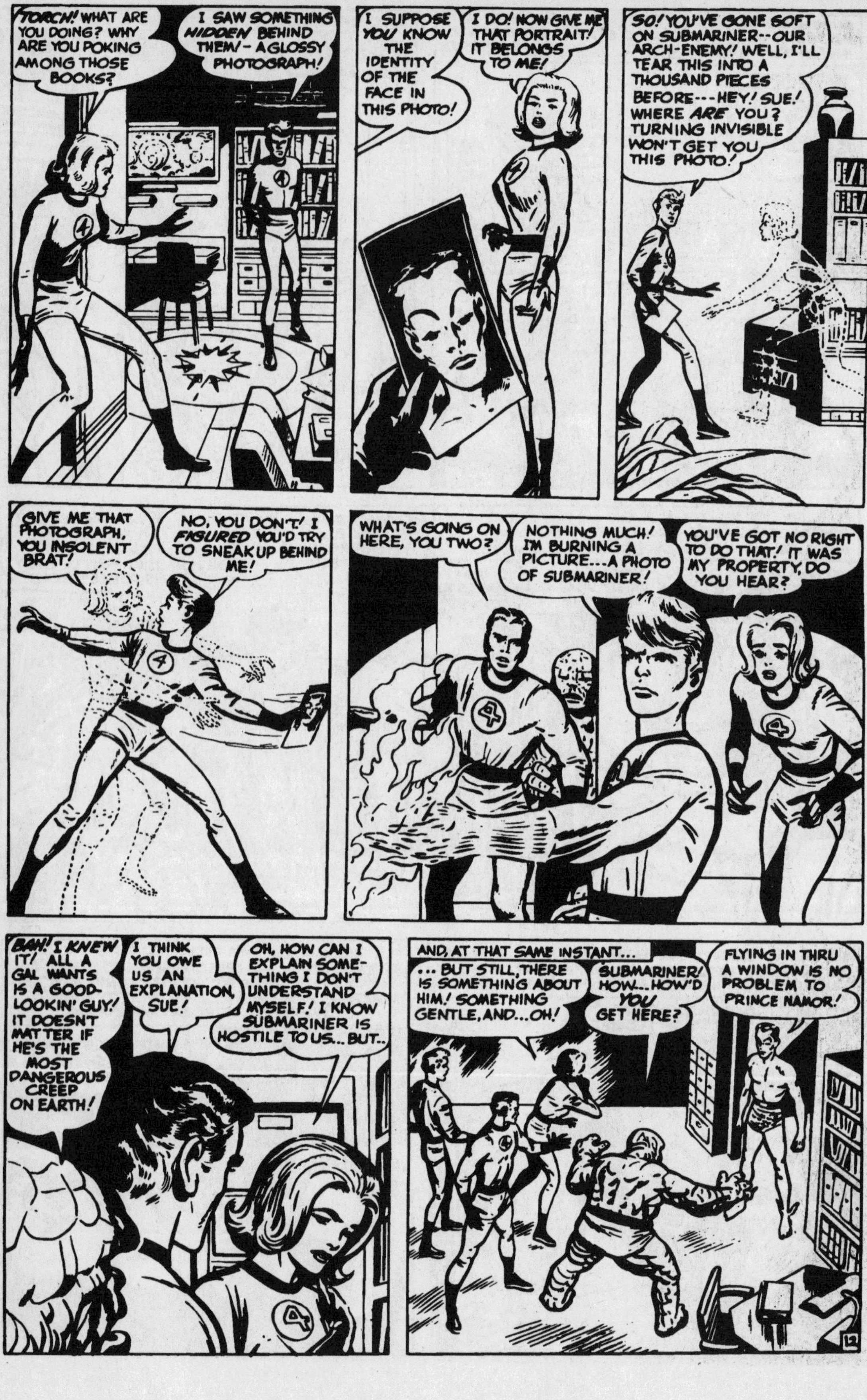
TORCH! WHAT ARE YOU DOING? WHY ARE YOU POKING AMONG THOSE BOOKS?
I SAW SOMETHING HIDDEN BEHIND THEM! - A GLOSSY PHOTOGRAPH!
I SUPPOSE YOU KNOW THE IDENTITY OF THE FACE IN THIS PHOTO!
I DO! NOW GIVE ME THAT PORTRAIT! IT BELONGS TO ME!
SO! YOU'VE GONE SOFT ON SUBMARINER--OUR ARCH-ENEMY! WELL, I'LL TEAR THIS INTO A THOUSAND PIECES BEFORE---HEY! SUE! WHERE ARE YOU? TURNING INVISIBLE WON'T GET YOU THIS PHOTO!
GIVE ME THAT PHOTOGRAPH, YOU INSOLENT BRAT!
NO, YOU DON'T! I FIGURED YOU'D TRY TO SNEAK UP BEHIND ME!
WHAT'S GOING ON HERE, YOU TWO?
NOTHING MUCH! I'M BURNING A PICTURE... A PHOTO OF SUBMARINER!
YOU'VE GOT NO RIGHT TO DO THAT! IT WAS MY PROPERTY, DO YOU HEAR?
BAH! I KNEW IT! ALL A GAL WANTS IS A GOOD-LOOKIN' GUY! IT DOESN'T MATTER IF HE'S THE MOST DANGEROUS CREEP ON EARTH!
I THINK YOU OWE US AN EXPLANATION, SUE!
OH, HOW CAN I EXPLAIN SOMETHING I DON'T UNDERSTAND MYSELF! I KNOW SUBMARINER IS HOSTILE TO US... BUT...
AND, AT THAT SAME INSTANT...
... BUT STILL, THERE IS SOMETHING ABOUT HIM! SOMETHING GENTLE, AND...OH!
SUBMARINER! HOW...HOW'D YOU GET HERE?
FLYING IN THRU A WINDOW IS NO PROBLEM TO PRINCE NAMOR!
12

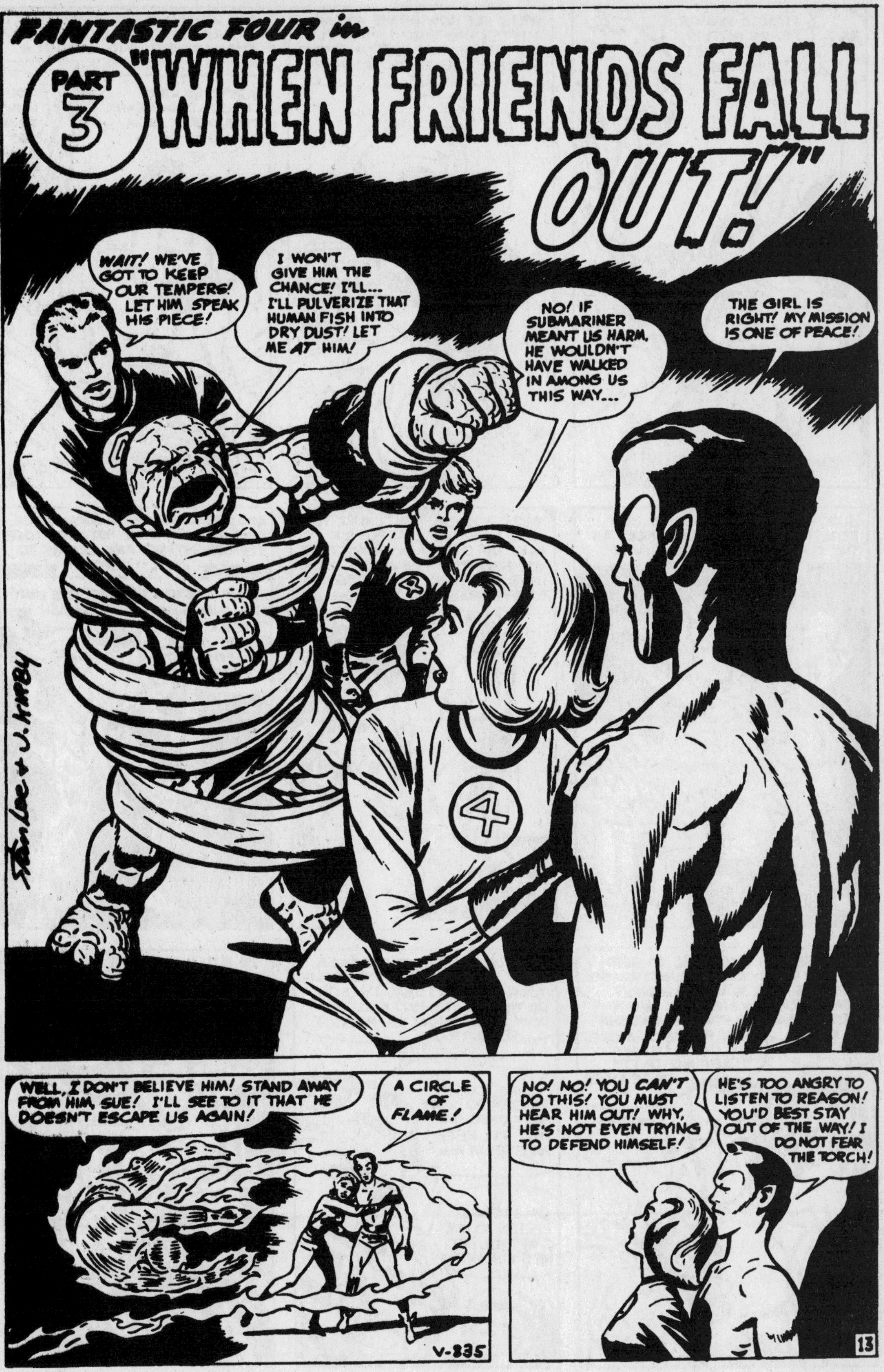

FANTASTIC FOUR in
PART 3
"WHEN FRIENDS FALL OUT!"
WAIT! WE'VE GOT TO KEEP OUR TEMPERS! LET HIM SPEAK HIS PIECE!
I WON'T GIVE HIM THE CHANCE! I'LL... I'LL PULVERIZE THAT HUMAN FISH INTO DRY DUST! LET ME AT HIM!
NO! IF SUBMARINER MEANT US HARM, HE WOULDN'T HAVE WALKED IN AMONG US THIS WAY...
THE GIRL IS RIGHT! MY MISSION IS ONE OF PEACE!
Stan Lee + J. Kirby
WELL, I DON'T BELIEVE HIM! STAND AWAY FROM HIM, SUE! I'LL SEE TO IT THAT HE DOESN'T ESCAPE US AGAIN!
A CIRCLE OF FLAME!
V-835
NO! NO! YOU CAN'T DO THIS! YOU MUST HEAR HIM OUT! WHY, HE'S NOT EVEN TRYING TO DEFEND HIMSELF!
HE'S TOO ANGRY TO LISTEN TO REASON! YOU'D BEST STAY OUT OF THE WAY! I DO NOT FEAR THE TORCH!
13

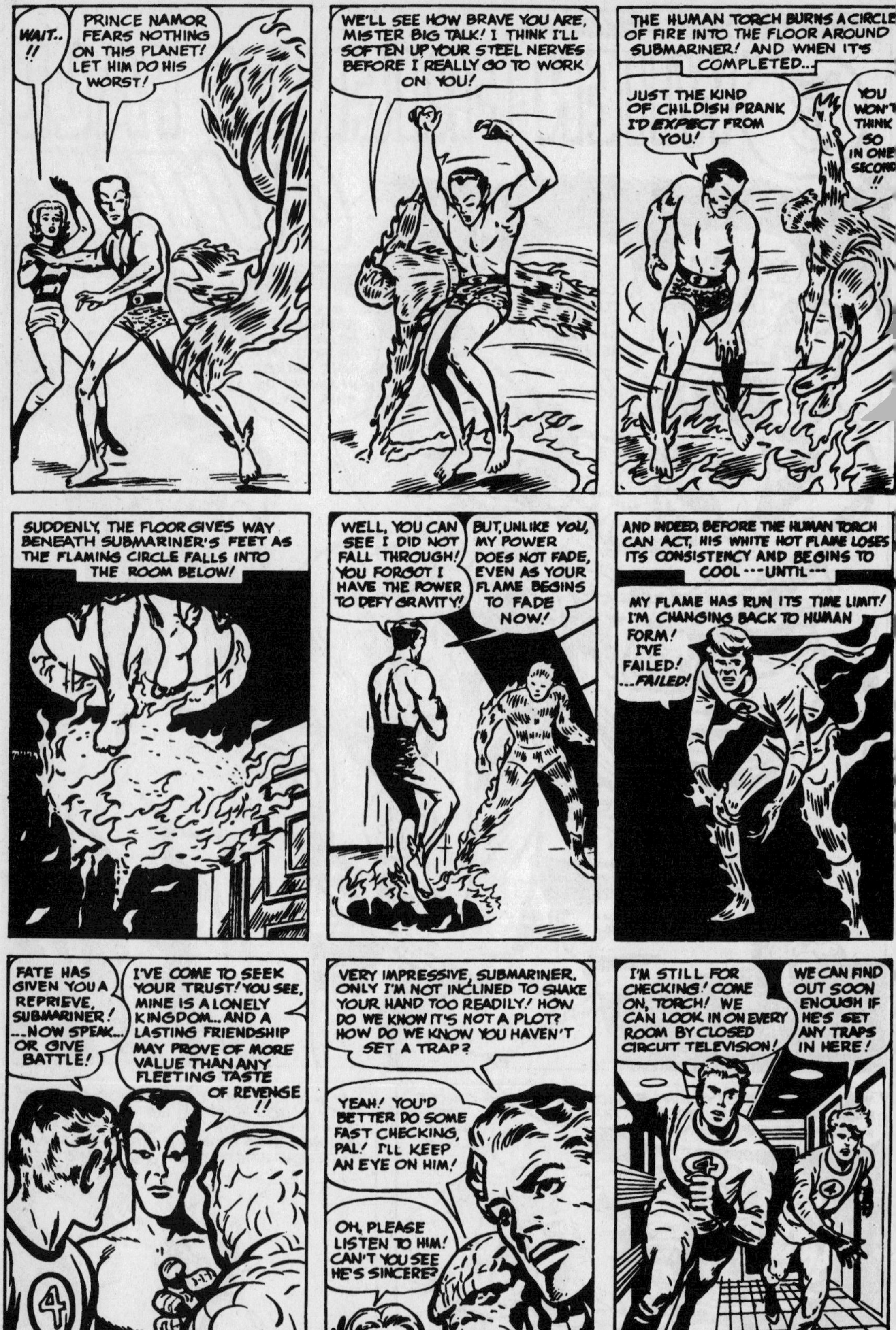
WAIT.. !!
PRINCE NAMOR FEARS NOTHING ON THIS PLANET! LET HIM DO HIS WORST!
WE'LL SEE HOW BRAVE YOU ARE, MISTER BIG TALK! I THINK I'LL SOFTEN UP YOUR STEEL NERVES BEFORE I REALLY GO TO WORK ON YOU!
THE HUMAN TORCH BURNS A CIRCLE OF FIRE INTO THE FLOOR AROUND SUBMARINER! AND WHEN IT'S COMPLETED...
JUST THE KIND OF CHILDISH PRANK I'D EXPECT FROM YOU!
YOU WON'T THINK SO IN ONE SECOND !!
SUDDENLY, THE FLOOR GIVES WAY BENEATH SUBMARINER'S FEET AS THE FLAMING CIRCLE FALLS INTO THE ROOM BELOW!
WELL, YOU CAN SEE I DID NOT FALL THROUGH! YOU FORGOT I HAVE THE POWER TO DEFY GRAVITY!
BUT, UNLIKE YOU, MY POWER DOES NOT FADE, EVEN AS YOUR FLAME BEGINS TO FADE NOW!
AND INDEED, BEFORE THE HUMAN TORCH CAN ACT, HIS WHITE HOT FLAME LOSES ITS CONSISTENCY AND BEGINS TO COOL---UNTIL---
MY FLAME HAS RUN ITS TIME LIMIT! I'M CHANGING BACK TO HUMAN FORM! I'VE FAILED! ...FAILED!
FATE HAS GIVEN YOU A REPRIEVE, SUBMARINER! ...NOW SPEAK... OR GIVE BATTLE!
I'VE COME TO SEEK YOUR TRUST! YOU SEE, MINE IS A LONELY KINGDOM... AND A LASTING FRIENDSHIP MAY PROVE OF MORE VALUE THAN ANY FLEETING TASTE OF REVENGE !!
VERY IMPRESSIVE, SUBMARINER. ONLY I'M NOT INCLINED TO SHAKE YOUR HAND TOO READILY! HOW DO WE KNOW IT'S NOT A PLOT? HOW DO WE KNOW YOU HAVEN'T SET A TRAP?
YEAH! YOU'D BETTER DO SOME FAST CHECKING, PAL! I'LL KEEP AN EYE ON HIM!
OH, PLEASE LISTEN TO HIM! CAN'T YOU SEE HE'S SINCERE?
I'M STILL FOR CHECKING! COME ON, TORCH! WE CAN LOOK IN ON EVERY ROOM BY CLOSED CIRCUIT TELEVISION!
WE CAN FIND OUT SOON ENOUGH IF HE'S SET ANY TRAPS IN HERE!
14

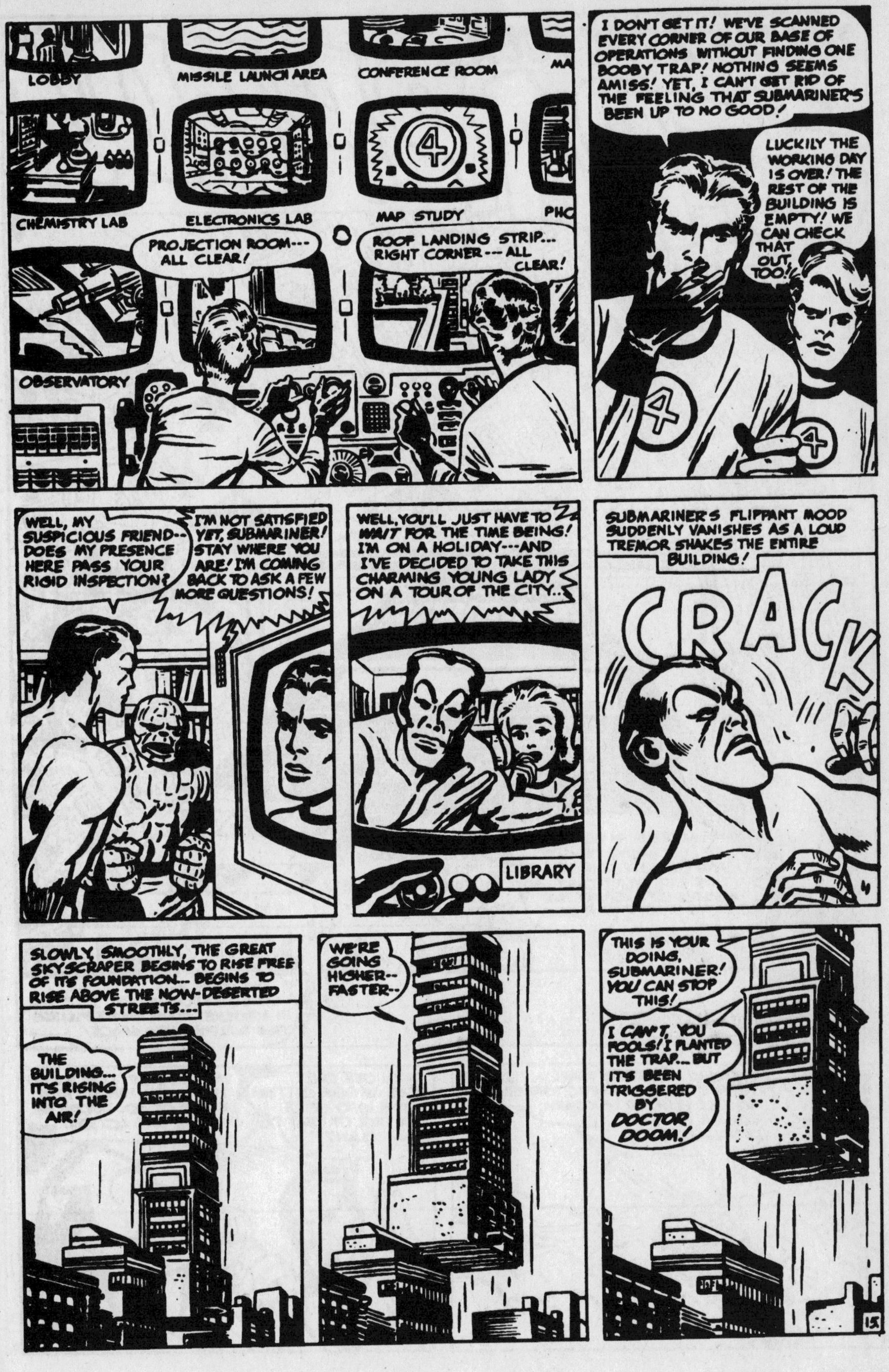
LOBBY
MISSILE LAUNCH AREA
CONFERENCE ROOM
CHEMISTRY LAB
ELECTRONICS LAB
MAP STUDY
PROJECTION ROOM--- ALL CLEAR!
ROOF LANDING STRIP... RIGHT CORNER --- ALL CLEAR!
OBSERVATORY
I DON'T GET IT! WE'VE SCANNED EVERY CORNER OF OUR BASE OF OPERATIONS WITHOUT FINDING ONE BOOBY TRAP! NOTHING SEEMS AMISS! YET, I CAN'T GET RID OF THE FEELING THAT SUBMARINER'S BEEN UP TO NO GOOD!
LUCKILY THE WORKING DAY IS OVER! THE REST OF THE BUILDING IS EMPTY! WE CAN CHECK THAT OUT, TOO!
WELL, MY SUSPICIOUS FRIEND-- DOES MY PRESENCE HERE PASS YOUR RIGID INSPECTION?
I'M NOT SATISFIED YET, SUBMARINER! STAY WHERE YOU ARE! I'M COMING BACK TO ASK A FEW MORE QUESTIONS!
WELL, YOU'LL JUST HAVE TO WAIT FOR THE TIME BEING! I'M ON A HOLIDAY---AND I'VE DECIDED TO TAKE THIS CHARMING YOUNG LADY ON A TOUR OF THE CITY..
LIBRARY
SUBMARINER'S FLIPPANT MOOD SUDDENLY VANISHES AS A LOUD TREMOR SHAKES THE ENTIRE BUILDING!
CRACK
SLOWLY, SMOOTHLY, THE GREAT SKYSCRAPER BEGINS TO RISE FREE OF ITS FOUNDATION... BEGINS TO RISE ABOVE THE NOW-DESERTED STREETS...
THE BUILDING... IT'S RISING INTO THE AIR!
WE'RE GOING HIGHER-- FASTER--
THIS IS YOUR DOING, SUBMARINER! YOU CAN STOP THIS!
I CAN'T, YOU FOOLS! I PLANTED THE TRAP... BUT IT'S BEEN TRIGGERED BY DOCTOR DOOM!
15

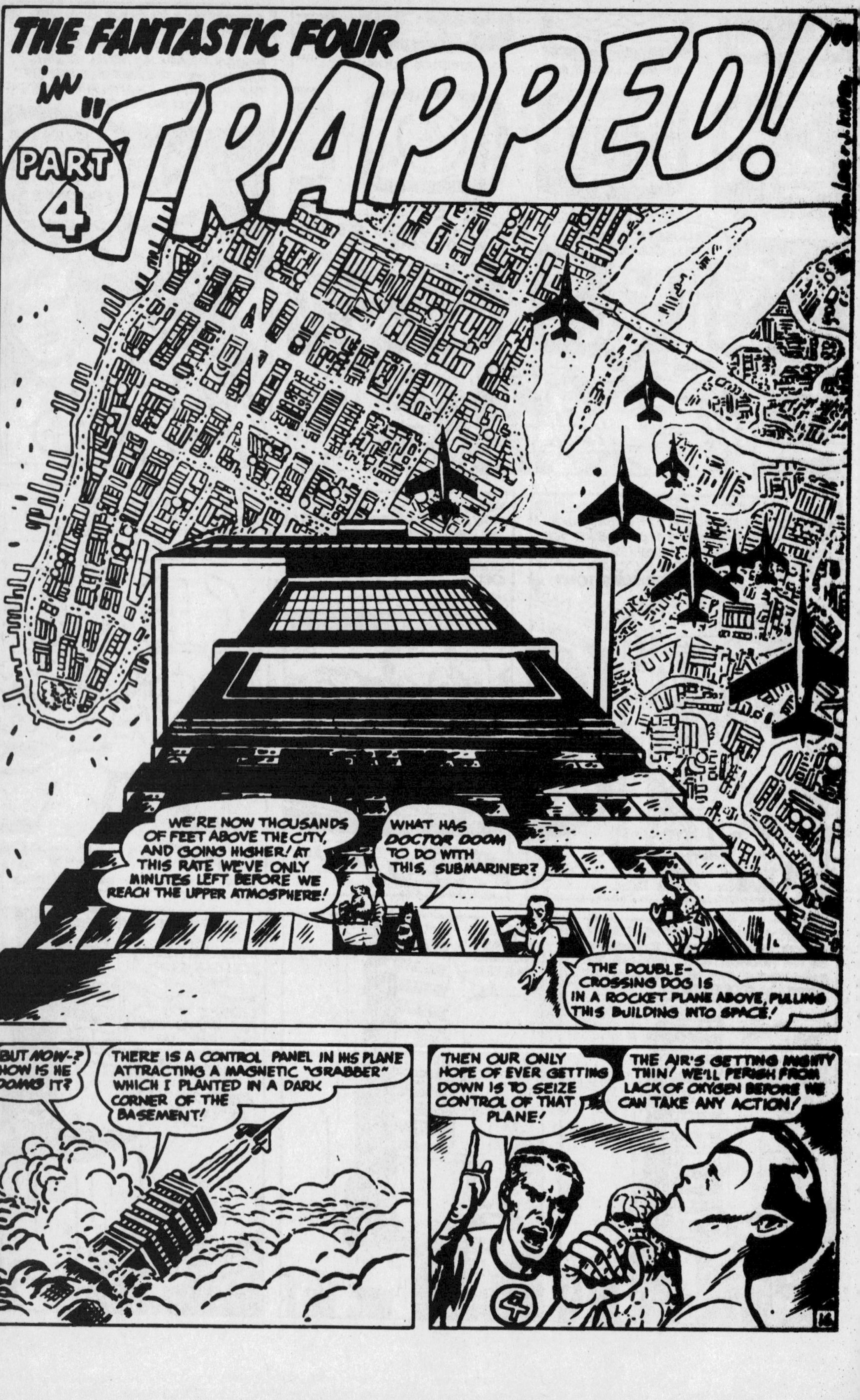
THE FANTASTIC FOUR
in "TRAPPED!"
PART 4
WE'RE NOW THOUSANDS OF FEET ABOVE THE CITY, AND GOING HIGHER! AT THIS RATE WE'VE ONLY MINUTES LEFT BEFORE WE REACH THE UPPER ATMOSPHERE!
WHAT HAS DOCTOR DOOM TO DO WITH THIS, SUBMARINER?
THE DOUBLE-CROSSING DOG IS IN A ROCKET PLANE ABOVE, PULLING THIS BUILDING INTO SPACE!
BUT NOW-? HOW IS HE DOING IT?
THERE IS A CONTROL PANEL IN HIS PLANE ATTRACTING A MAGNETIC "GRABBER" WHICH I PLANTED IN A DARK CORNER OF THE BASEMENT!
THEN OUR ONLY HOPE OF EVER GETTING DOWN IS TO SEIZE CONTROL OF THAT PLANE!
THE AIR'S GETTING MIGHTY THIN! WE'LL PERISH FROM LACK OF OXYGEN BEFORE WE CAN TAKE ANY ACTION!
16

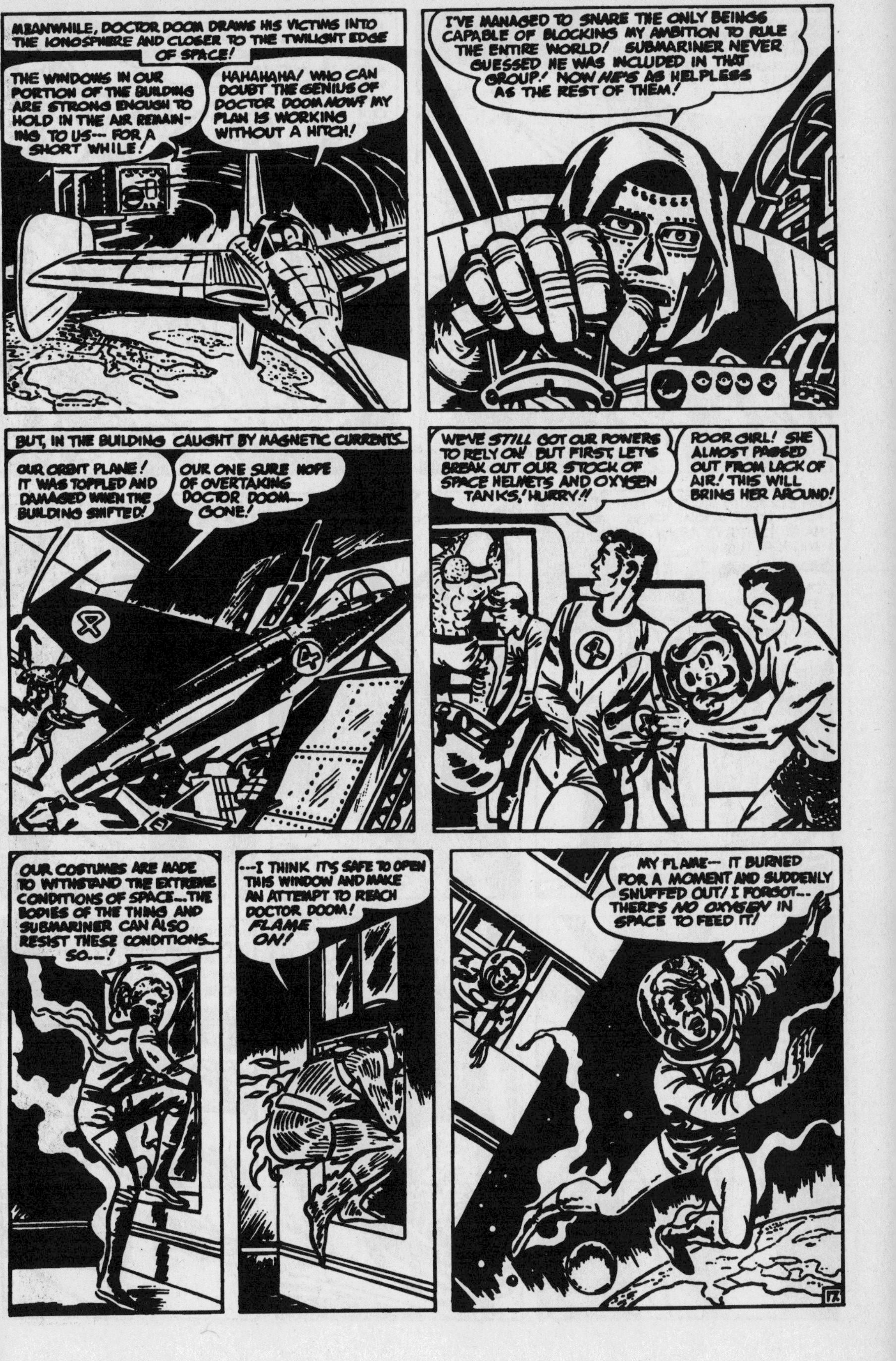
MEANWHILE, DOCTOR DOOM DRAWS HIS VICTIMS INTO THE IONOSPHERE AND CLOSER TO THE TWILIGHT EDGE OF SPACE!
THE WINDOWS IN OUR PORTION OF THE BUILDING ARE STRONG ENOUGH TO HOLD IN THE AIR REMAINING TO US--- FOR A SHORT WHILE!
HAHAHAHA! WHO CAN DOUBT THE GENIUS OF DOCTOR DOOM NOW? MY PLAN IS WORKING WITHOUT A HITCH!
I'VE MANAGED TO SNARE THE ONLY BEINGS CAPABLE OF BLOCKING MY AMBITION TO RULE THE ENTIRE WORLD! SUBMARINER NEVER GUESSED HE WAS INCLUDED IN THAT GROUP! NOW HE'S AS HELPLESS AS THE REST OF THEM!
BUT, IN THE BUILDING CAUGHT BY MAGNETIC CURRENTS...
OUR ORBIT PLANE! IT WAS TOPPLED AND DAMAGED WHEN THE BUILDING SHIFTED!
OUR ONE SURE HOPE OF OVERTAKING DOCTOR DOOM... GONE!
WE'VE STILL GOT OUR POWERS TO RELY ON! BUT FIRST, LET'S BREAK OUT OUR STOCK OF SPACE HELMETS AND OXYGEN TANKS, HURRY!!
POOR GIRL! SHE ALMOST PASSED OUT FROM LACK OF AIR! THIS WILL BRING HER AROUND!
OUR COSTUMES ARE MADE TO WITHSTAND THE EXTREME CONDITIONS OF SPACE...THE BODIES OF THE THING AND SUBMARINER CAN ALSO RESIST THESE CONDITIONS... SO...!
--I THINK IT'S SAFE TO OPEN THIS WINDOW AND MAKE AN ATTEMPT TO REACH DOCTOR DOOM! FLAME ON!
MY FLAME--- IT BURNED FOR A MOMENT AND SUDDENLY SNUFFED OUT! I FORGOT... THERE'S NO OXYGEN IN SPACE TO FEED IT!
17

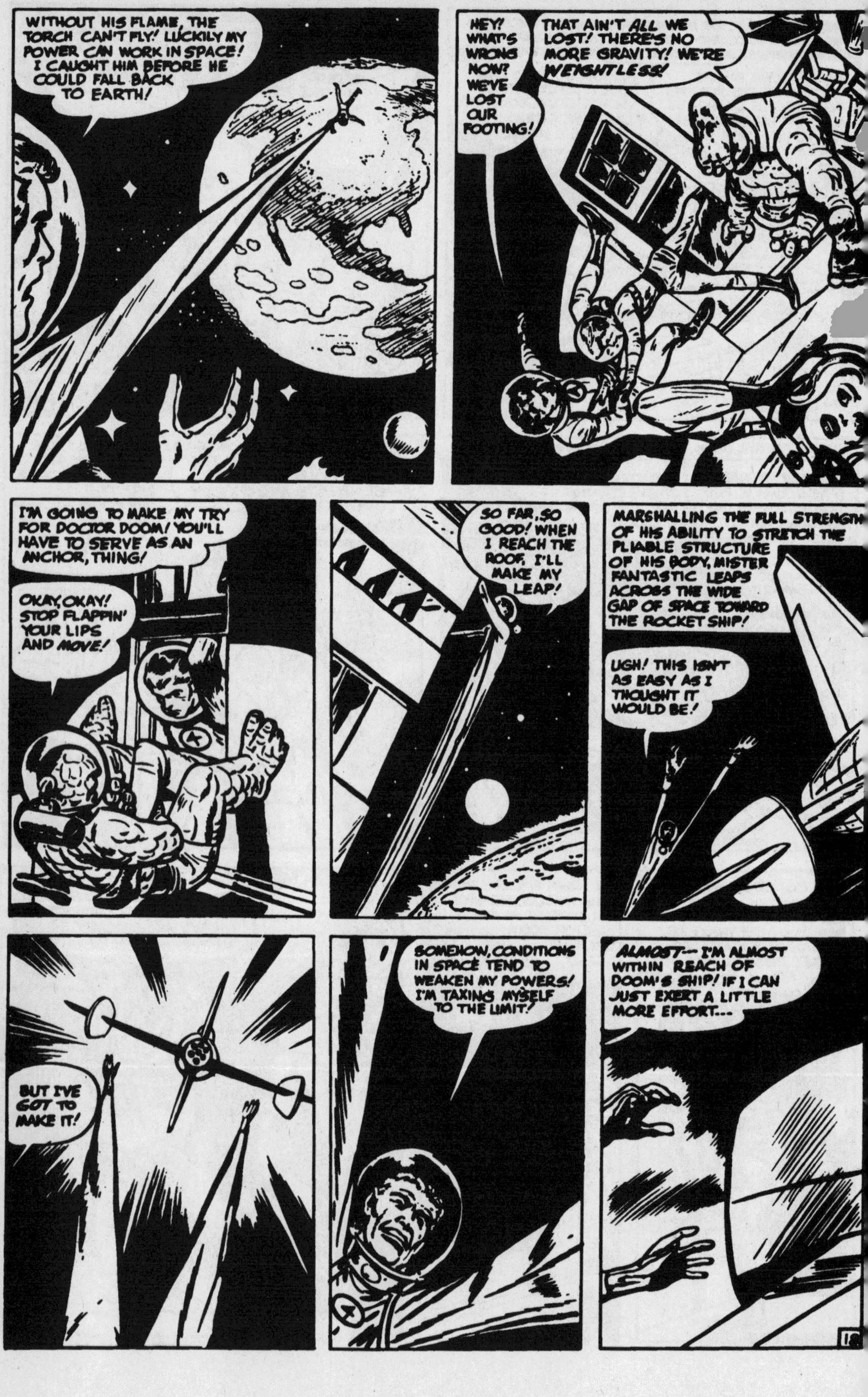
WITHOUT HIS FLAME, THE TORCH CAN'T FLY! LUCKILY MY POWER CAN WORK IN SPACE! I CAUGHT HIM BEFORE HE COULD FALL BACK TO EARTH!
HEY! WHAT'S WRONG NOW? WE'VE LOST OUR FOOTING!
THAT AIN'T ALL WE LOST! THERE'S NO MORE GRAVITY! WE'RE WEIGHTLESS!
I'M GOING TO MAKE MY TRY FOR DOCTOR DOOM! YOU'LL HAVE TO SERVE AS AN ANCHOR, THING!
OKAY, OKAY! STOP FLAPPIN' YOUR LIPS AND MOVE!
SO FAR, SO GOOD! WHEN I REACH THE ROOF, I'LL MAKE MY LEAP!
MARSHALLING THE FULL STRENGTH OF HIS ABILITY TO STRETCH THE PLIABLE STRUCTURE OF HIS BODY, MISTER FANTASTIC LEAPS ACROSS THE WIDE GAP OF SPACE TOWARD THE ROCKET SHIP!
UGH! THIS ISN'T AS EASY AS I THOUGHT IT WOULD BE!
BUT I'VE GOT TO MAKE IT!
SOMEHOW, CONDITIONS IN SPACE TEND TO WEAKEN MY POWERS! I'M TAXING MYSELF TO THE LIMIT!
ALMOST-- I'M ALMOST WITHIN REACH OF DOOM'S SHIP! IF I CAN JUST EXERT A LITTLE MORE EFFORT...

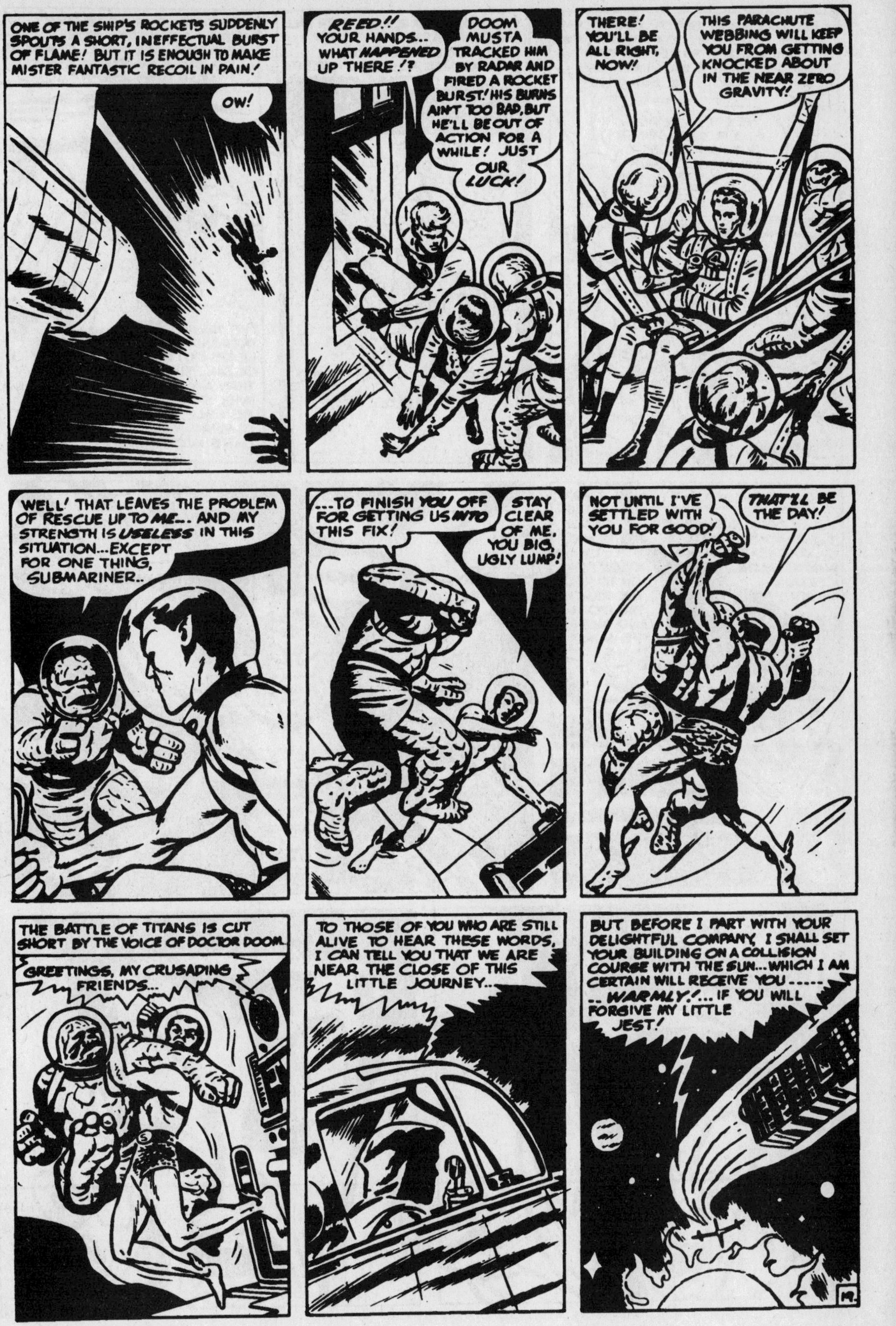
ONE OF THE SHIP'S ROCKETS SUDDENLY SPOUTS A SHORT, INEFFECTUAL BURST OF FLAME! BUT IT IS ENOUGH TO MAKE MISTER FANTASTIC RECOIL IN PAIN!
OW!
REED!! YOUR HANDS.. WHAT HAPPENED UP THERE!?
DOOM MUSTA TRACKED HIM BY RADAR AND FIRED A ROCKET BURST! HIS BURNS AIN'T TOO BAD, BUT HE'LL BE OUT OF ACTION FOR A WHILE! JUST OUR LUCK!
THERE! YOU'LL BE ALL RIGHT, NOW!
THIS PARACHUTE WEBBING WILL KEEP YOU FROM GETTING KNOCKED ABOUT IN THE NEAR ZERO GRAVITY!
WELL! THAT LEAVES THE PROBLEM OF RESCUE UP TO ME... AND MY STRENGTH IS USELESS IN THIS SITUATION...EXCEPT FOR ONE THING, SUBMARINER..
...TO FINISH YOU OFF FOR GETTING US INTO THIS FIX!
STAY CLEAR OF ME, YOU BIG, UGLY LUMP!
NOT UNTIL I'VE SETTLED WITH YOU FOR GOOD!
THAT'LL BE THE DAY!
THE BATTLE OF TITANS IS CUT SHORT BY THE VOICE OF DOCTOR DOOM.
GREETINGS, MY CRUSADING FRIENDS...
TO THOSE OF YOU WHO ARE STILL ALIVE TO HEAR THESE WORDS, I CAN TELL YOU THAT WE ARE NEAR THE CLOSE OF THIS LITTLE JOURNEY..
BUT BEFORE I PART WITH YOUR DELIGHTFUL COMPANY, I SHALL SET YOUR BUILDING ON A COLLISION COURSE WITH THE SUN...WHICH I AM CERTAIN WILL RECEIVE YOU .... WARMLY!... IF YOU WILL FORGIVE MY LITTLE JEST!
19.

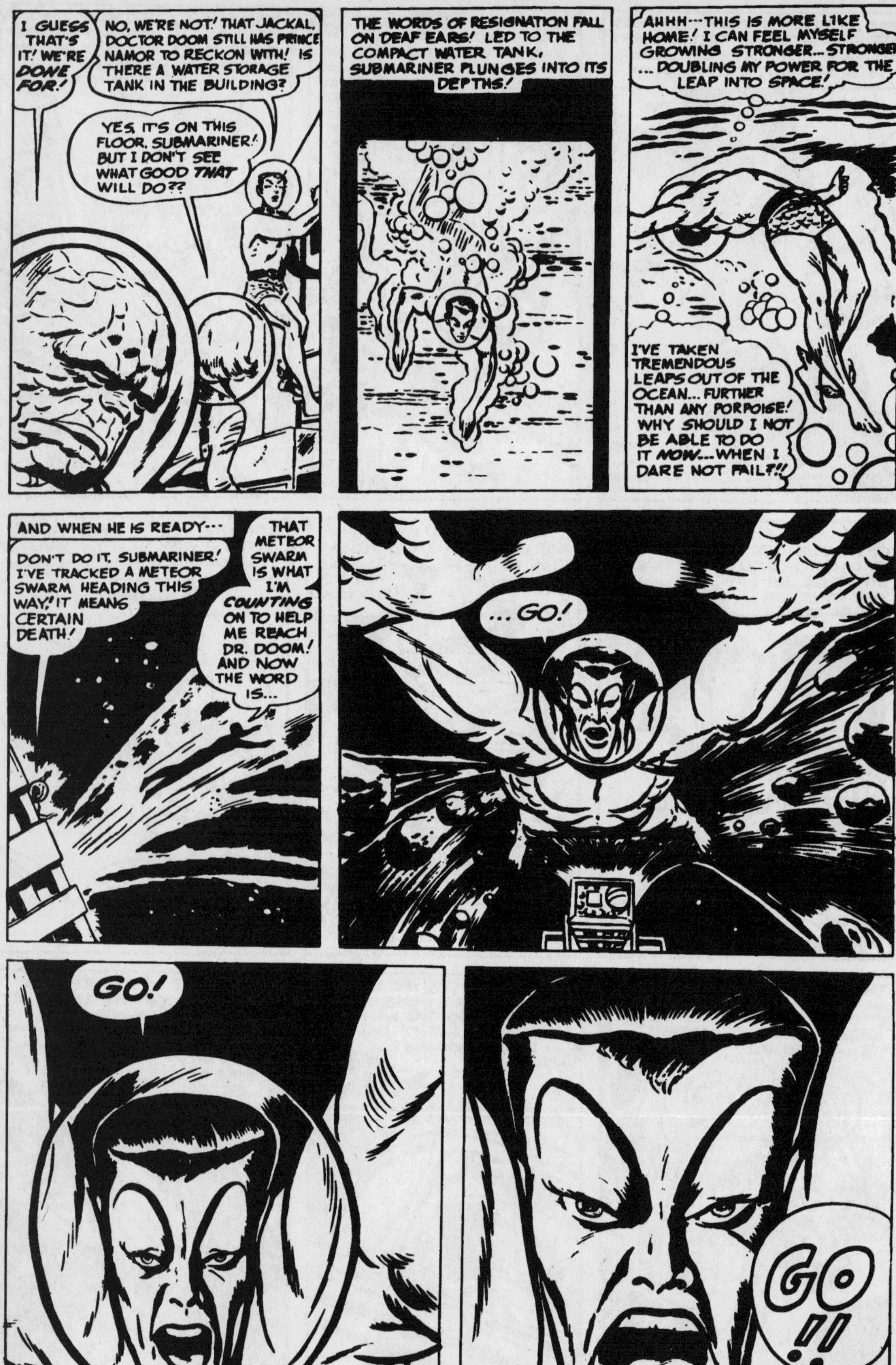

I GUESS THAT'S IT! WE'RE DONE FOR!
NO, WE'RE NOT! THAT JACKAL, DOCTOR DOOM STILL HAS PRINCE NAMOR TO RECKON WITH! IS THERE A WATER STORAGE TANK IN THE BUILDING?
YES, IT'S ON THIS FLOOR, SUBMARINER! BUT I DON'T SEE WHAT GOOD THAT WILL DO??
THE WORDS OF RESIGNATION FALL ON DEAF EARS! LED TO THE COMPACT WATER TANK, SUBMARINER PLUNGES INTO ITS DEPTHS!
AHHH---THIS IS MORE LIKE HOME! I CAN FEEL MYSELF GROWING STRONGER... STRONGER ... DOUBLING MY POWER FOR THE LEAP INTO SPACE!
I'VE TAKEN TREMENDOUS LEAPS OUT OF THE OCEAN... FURTHER THAN ANY PORPOISE! WHY SHOULD I NOT BE ABLE TO DO IT NOW... WHEN I DARE NOT FAIL?!!
AND WHEN HE IS READY---
DON'T DO IT, SUBMARINER! I'VE TRACKED A METEOR SWARM HEADING THIS WAY! IT MEANS CERTAIN DEATH!
THAT METEOR SWARM IS WHAT I'M COUNTING ON TO HELP ME REACH DR. DOOM! AND NOW THE WORD IS...
...GO!
GO!
GO!!
20

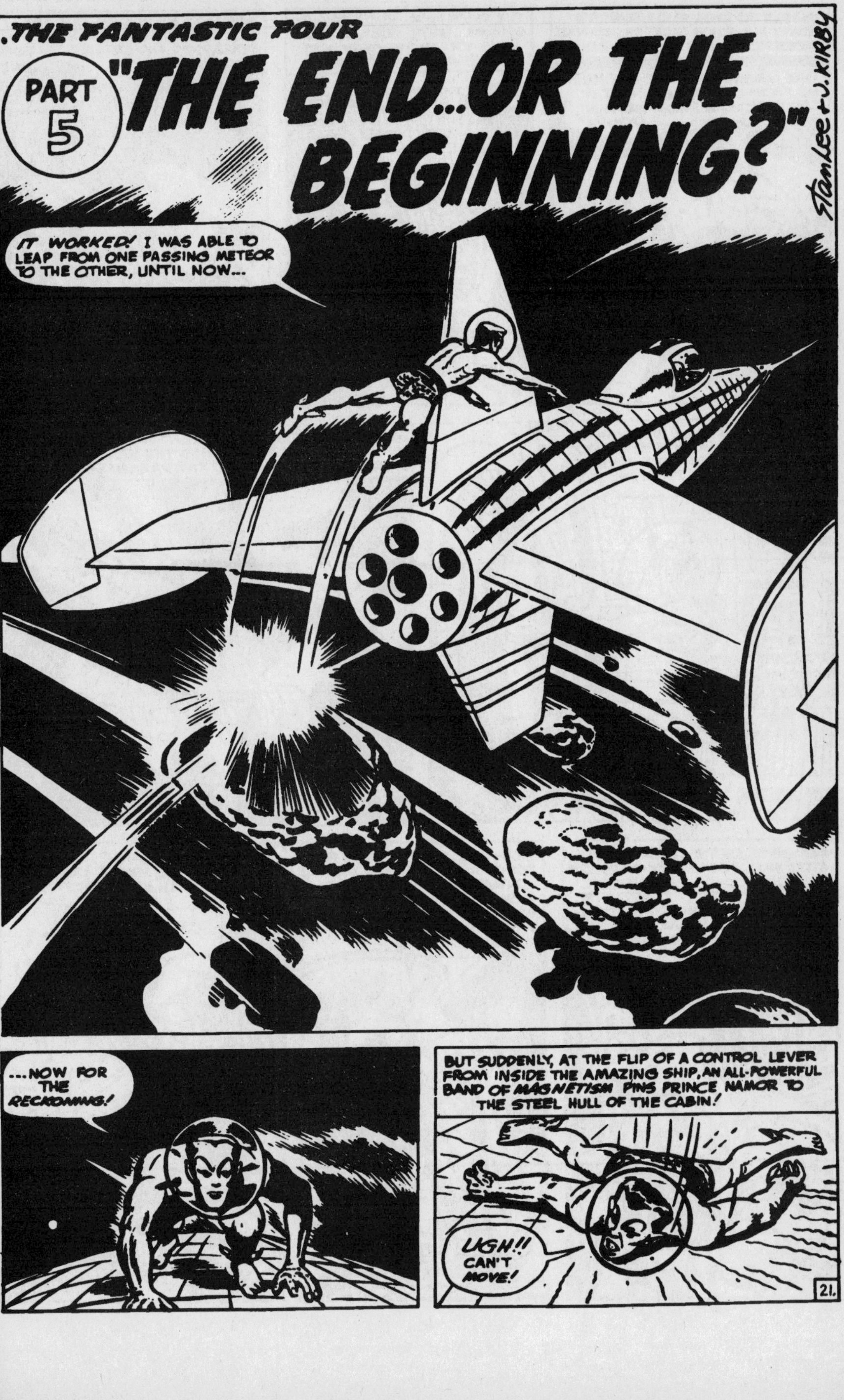

.THE FANTASTIC FOUR
PART 5
"THE END...OR THE BEGINNING?"
Stan Lee + J. Kirby
IT WORKED! I WAS ABLE TO LEAP FROM ONE PASSING METEOR TO THE OTHER, UNTIL NOW...
...NOW FOR THE RECKONING!
BUT SUDDENLY, AT THE FLIP OF A CONTROL LEVER FROM INSIDE THE AMAZING SHIP, AN ALL-POWERFUL BAND OF MAGNETISM PINS PRINCE NAMOR TO THE STEEL HULL OF THE CABIN!
UGH!! CAN'T MOVE!
21.

UNABLE TO RISE, SUBMARINER'S POWERFUL FISTS EXERT TREMENDOUS PRESSURE ON THE FUSELAGE BENEATH HIM!

THIS MAGNETIC FORCE MAY KEEP ME FROM GETTING *UP*... BUT IT CAN'T STOP ME FROM *GOING DOWN!*

THE THICK METAL BUCKLES AND GROANS... UNTIL SUBMARINER'S ARMS CRASH THROUGH INTO THE SHIP'S INTERIOR!

WHEN THE AIR RUSHES OUT, THE HULL BENEATH SUBMARINER COLLAPSES, AND CARRIES HIM DOWN WITH IT!

NOW IF I CAN ONLY BREAK INTO THE PILOT'S CABIN BEFORE DOCTOR DOOM MAKES HIS NEXT MOVE! I'M SURE HE KNOWS I'M IN THE SHIP!

SUDDENLY, A THOUSAND GREAT HAMMER-BLOWS OF ELECTRICITY SMASH INTO THE SEA MONARCH, HURLING HIM BACK INTO THE DARKNESS.

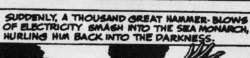

CRACK

MEANWHILE, ON THE OTHER SIDE OF THE STEEL WALL, DOCTOR DOOM LISTENS FOR SOUNDS OF MOVEMENT...

I DON'T HEAR A THING! THAT'S THE END OF SUBMARINER! HIS ATTEMPT TO STOP ME WAS THE LAST!

VOLTS

NOW, ALL I HAVE TO DO IS PUSH DOWN THIS LEVER AND BREAK CONTACT WITH THE BUILDING! SLOWLY BUT SURELY IT WILL SPIRAL INTO THE SUN... TAKING WITH IT THE REST OF MY ENEMIES!

OWWW!! I-I CAN'T *TOUCH* ANYTHING! THE WHOLE CABIN IS CHARGED WITH *ELECTRICITY!*

22

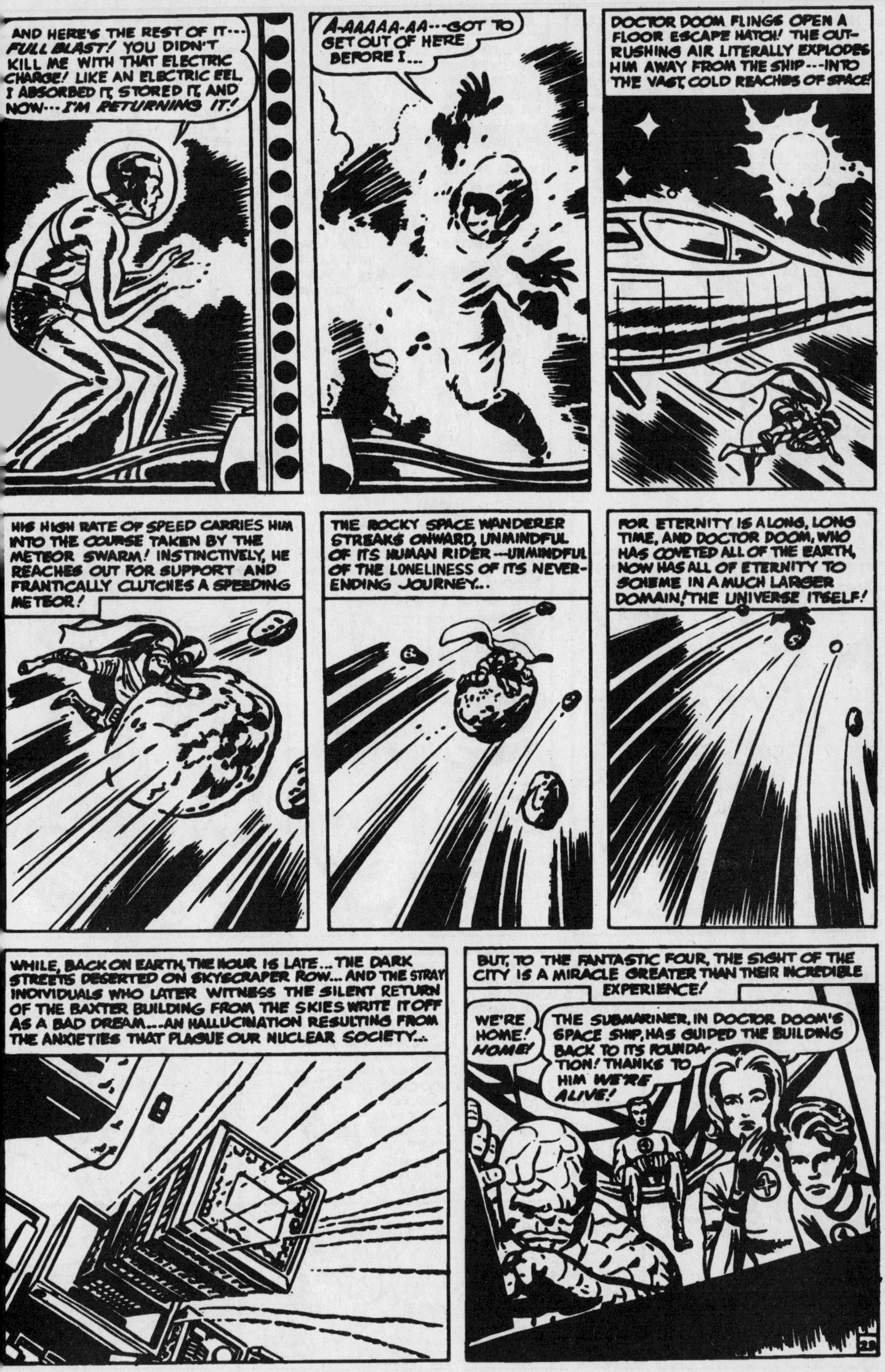
AND HERE'S THE REST OF IT--- FULL BLAST! YOU DIDN'T KILL ME WITH THAT ELECTRIC CHARGE! LIKE AN ELECTRIC EEL, I ABSORBED IT, STORED IT, AND NOW--- I'M RETURNING IT!
A-AAAAA-AA---GOT TO GET OUT OF HERE BEFORE I...
DOCTOR DOOM FLINGS OPEN A FLOOR ESCAPE HATCH! THE OUT-RUSHING AIR LITERALLY EXPLODES HIM AWAY FROM THE SHIP---INTO THE VAST, COLD REACHES OF SPACE!
HIS HIGH RATE OF SPEED CARRIES HIM INTO THE COURSE TAKEN BY THE METEOR SWARM! INSTINCTIVELY, HE REACHES OUT FOR SUPPORT AND FRANTICALLY CLUTCHES A SPEEDING METEOR!
THE ROCKY SPACE WANDERER STREAKS ONWARD, UNMINDFUL OF ITS HUMAN RIDER---UNMINDFUL OF THE LONELINESS OF ITS NEVER-ENDING JOURNEY...
FOR ETERNITY IS A LONG, LONG TIME, AND DOCTOR DOOM, WHO HAS COVETED ALL OF THE EARTH, NOW HAS ALL OF ETERNITY TO SCHEME IN A MUCH LARGER DOMAIN! THE UNIVERSE ITSELF!
WHILE, BACK ON EARTH, THE HOUR IS LATE... THE DARK STREETS DESERTED ON SKYSCRAPER ROW... AND THE STRAY INDIVIDUALS WHO LATER WITNESS THE SILENT RETURN OF THE BAXTER BUILDING FROM THE SKIES WRITE IT OFF AS A BAD DREAM...AN HALLUCINATION RESULTING FROM THE ANXIETIES THAT PLAGUE OUR NUCLEAR SOCIETY...
BUT, TO THE FANTASTIC FOUR, THE SIGHT OF THE CITY IS A MIRACLE GREATER THAN THEIR INCREDIBLE EXPERIENCE!
WE'RE HOME! HOME!
THE SUBMARINER, IN DOCTOR DOOM'S SPACE SHIP, HAS GUIDED THE BUILDING BACK TO ITS FOUNDATION! THANKS TO HIM WE'RE ALIVE!
23

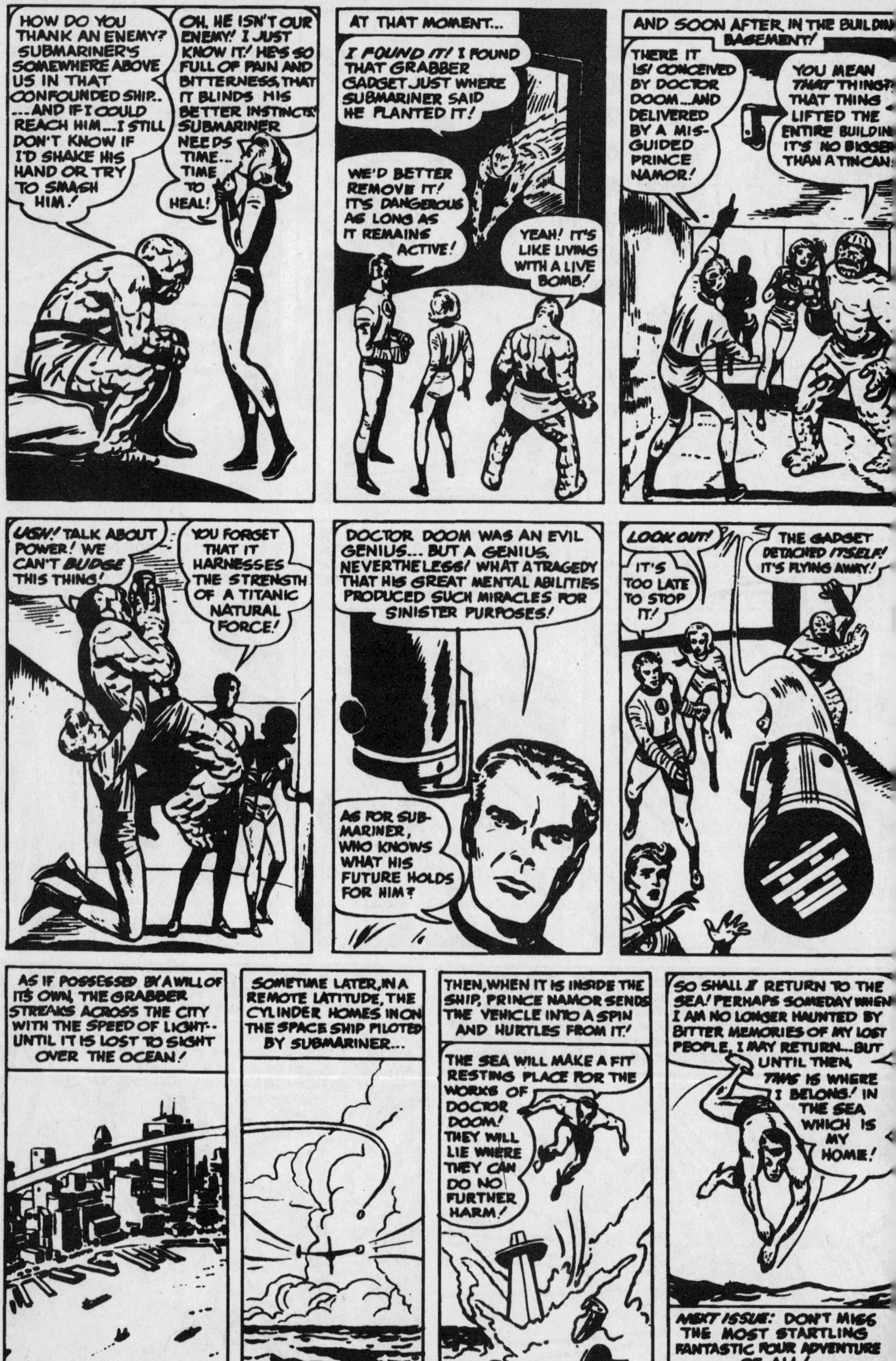
HOW DO YOU THANK AN ENEMY? SUBMARINER'S SOMEWHERE ABOVE US IN THAT CONFOUNDED SHIP.. ...AND IF I COULD REACH HIM...I STILL DON'T KNOW IF I'D SHAKE HIS HAND OR TRY TO SMASH HIM!
OH, HE ISN'T OUR ENEMY! I JUST KNOW IT! HE'S SO FULL OF PAIN AND BITTERNESS, THAT IT BLINDS HIS BETTER INSTINCTS! SUBMARINER NEEDS TIME... TIME TO HEAL!
AT THAT MOMENT...
I FOUND IT! I FOUND THAT GRABBER GADGET JUST WHERE SUBMARINER SAID HE PLANTED IT!
WE'D BETTER REMOVE IT! IT'S DANGEROUS AS LONG AS IT REMAINS ACTIVE!
YEAH! IT'S LIKE LIVING WITH A LIVE BOMB!
AND SOON AFTER, IN THE BUILDIN BASEMENT!
THERE IT IS! CONCEIVED BY DOCTOR DOOM...AND DELIVERED BY A MIS-GUIDED PRINCE NAMOR!
YOU MEAN THAT THING? THAT THING LIFTED THE ENTIRE BUILDIN IT'S NO BIGGER THAN A TIN CAN
UGH! TALK ABOUT POWER! WE CAN'T BUDGE THIS THING!
YOU FORGET THAT IT HARNESSES THE STRENGTH OF A TITANIC NATURAL FORCE!
DOCTOR DOOM WAS AN EVIL GENIUS... BUT A GENIUS, NEVERTHELESS! WHAT A TRAGEDY THAT HIS GREAT MENTAL ABILITIES PRODUCED SUCH MIRACLES FOR SINISTER PURPOSES!
AS FOR SUB-MARINER, WHO KNOWS WHAT HIS FUTURE HOLDS FOR HIM?
LOOK OUT!
IT'S TOO LATE TO STOP IT!
THE GADGET DETACHED ITSELF! IT'S FLYING AWAY!
AS IF POSSESSED BY A WILL OF ITS OWN, THE GRABBER STREAKS ACROSS THE CITY WITH THE SPEED OF LIGHT-- UNTIL IT IS LOST TO SIGHT OVER THE OCEAN!
24
SOMETIME LATER, IN A REMOTE LATITUDE, THE CYLINDER HOMES IN ON THE SPACE SHIP PILOTED BY SUBMARINER...
THEN, WHEN IT IS INSIDE THE SHIP, PRINCE NAMOR SENDS THE VEHICLE INTO A SPIN AND HURTLES FROM IT!
THE SEA WILL MAKE A FIT RESTING PLACE FOR THE WORKS OF DOCTOR DOOM! THEY WILL LIE WHERE THEY CAN DO NO FURTHER HARM!
SO SHALL I RETURN TO THE SEA! PERHAPS SOMEDAY WHEN I AM NO LONGER HAUNTED BY BITTER MEMORIES OF MY LOST PEOPLE, I MAY RETURN...BUT UNTIL THEN, THIS IS WHERE I BELONG! IN THE SEA WHICH IS MY HOME!
NEXT ISSUE: DON'T MISS THE MOST STARTLING FANTASTIC FOUR ADVENTURE OF ALL! WATCH FOR IT!!
-THE END-

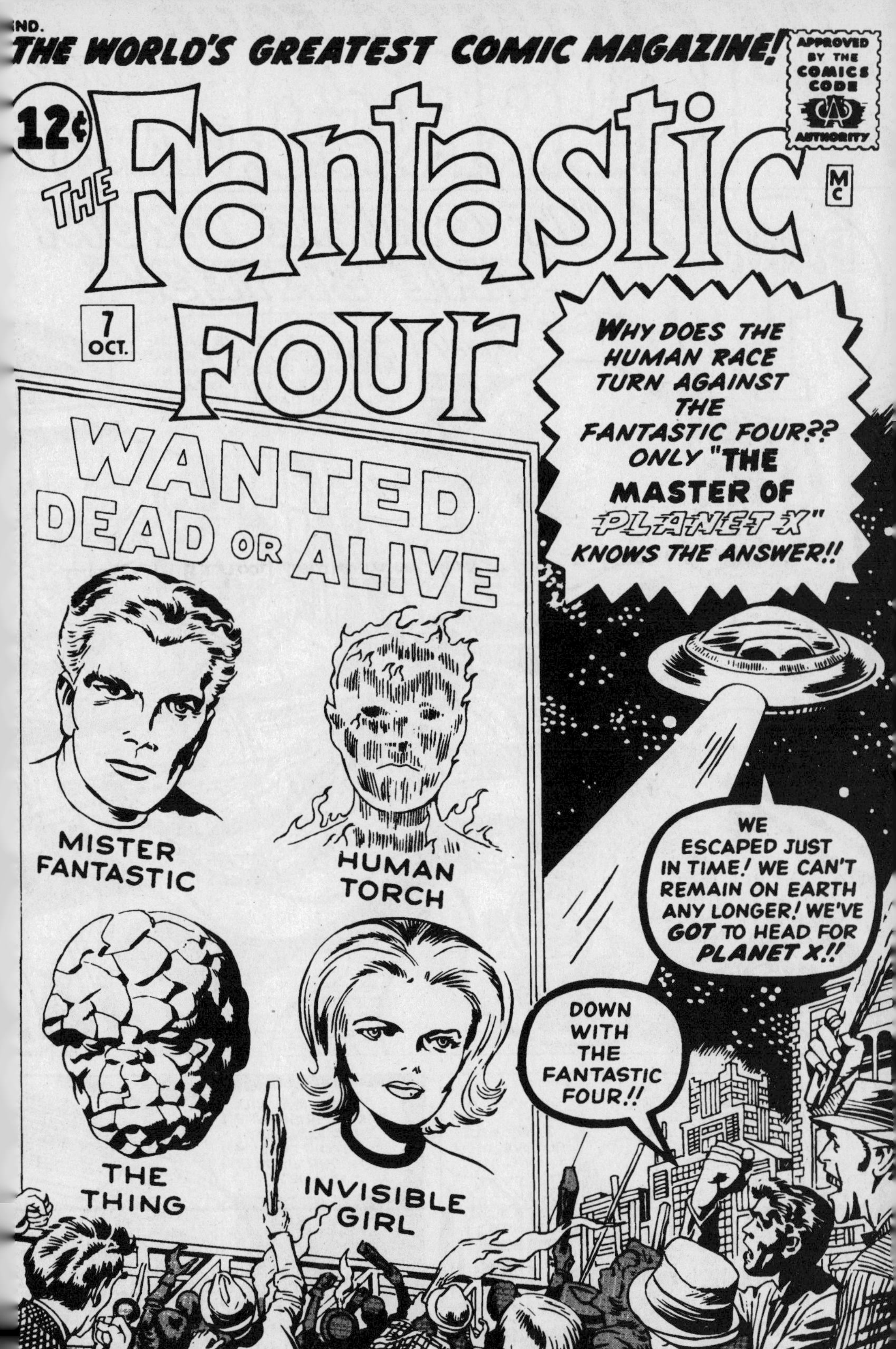
IND.
THE WORLD'S GREATEST COMIC MAGAZINE!
APPROVED BY THE COMICS CODE AUTHORITY
12¢
THE Fantastic Four
MC
7 OCT.
WHY DOES THE HUMAN RACE TURN AGAINST THE FANTASTIC FOUR?? ONLY "THE MASTER OF PLANET X" KNOWS THE ANSWER!!
WANTED DEAD OR ALIVE
MISTER FANTASTIC
HUMAN TORCH
THE THING
INVISIBLE GIRL
WE ESCAPED JUST IN TIME! WE CAN'T REMAIN ON EARTH ANY LONGER! WE'VE GOT TO HEAD FOR PLANET X!!
DOWN WITH THE FANTASTIC FOUR!!

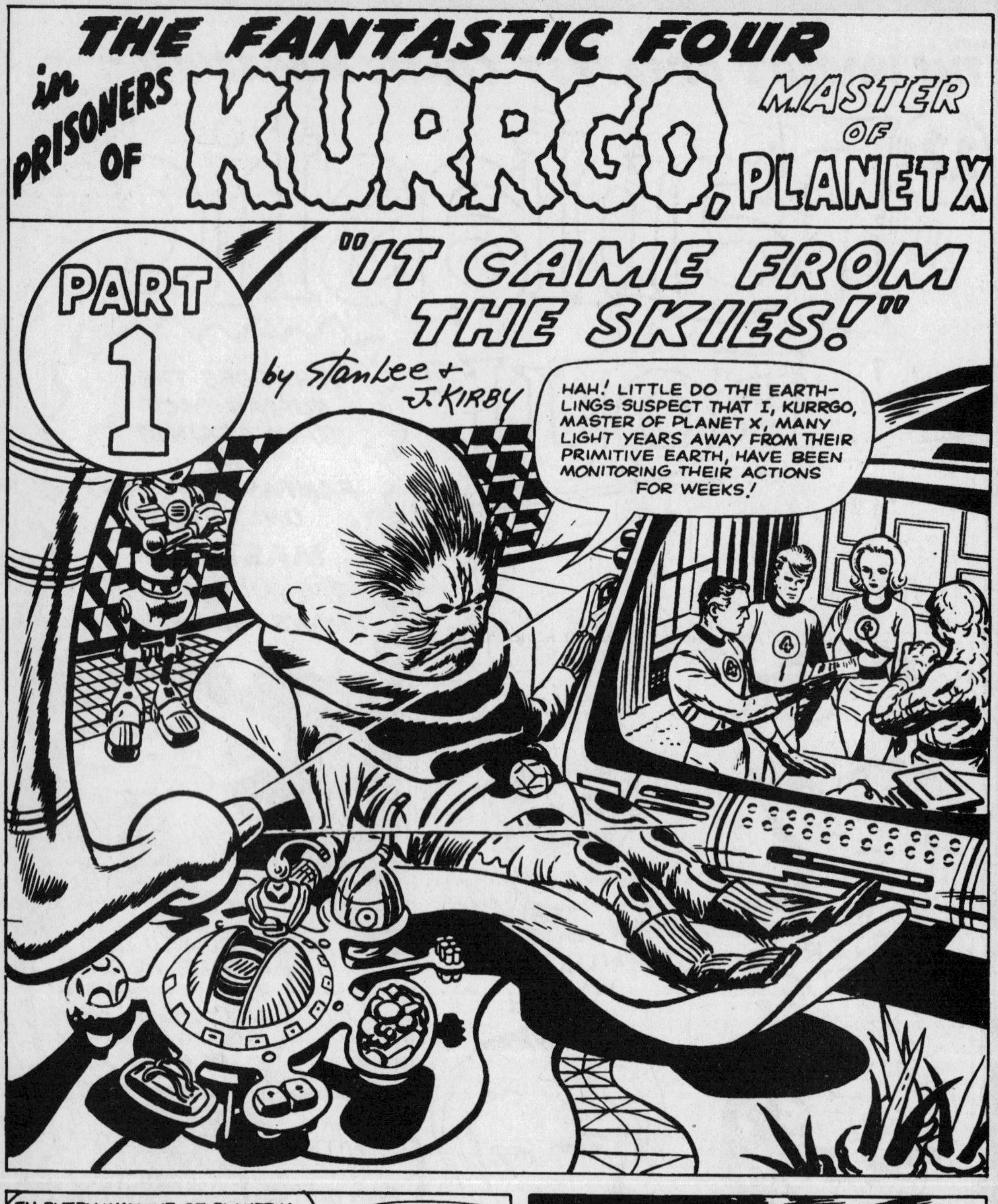

THE FANTASTIC FOUR
in PRISONERS OF KURRGO, MASTER OF PLANET X
PART 1
"IT CAME FROM THE SKIES!"
by Stan Lee & J. Kirby
HAH! LITTLE DO THE EARTHLINGS SUSPECT THAT I, KURRGO, MASTER OF PLANET X, MANY LIGHT YEARS AWAY FROM THEIR PRIMITIVE EARTH, HAVE BEEN MONITORING THEIR ACTIONS FOR WEEKS!
IN EVERY WAY WE OF PLANET X ARE THE EARTHLINGS' SUPERIORS! WE ARE A FAR OLDER RACE, A FAR WISER ONE! OUR SCIENCE IS A THOUSAND YEARS MORE ADVANCED THAN THEIRS!
SO, WHAT A PITY IT IS THAT THEY WILL SURVIVE, WHILE WE...
...WHILE WE WILL SOON PERISH WHEN THAT RUNAWAY ASTEROID COLLIDES WITH OUR LUCKLESS PLANET!
1

OH, KURRGO, MY LORD! IF ONLY WE HAD ENOUGH SPACE SHIPS TO ENABLE US TO **FLEE** OUR PLANET BEFORE THE HOLOCAUST!

FOOL! YOU **KNOW** WE HAVE ONLY **TWO** SPACE SHIPS ON PLANET X! FOR WE HAVE NEVER CARED FOR SPACE TRAVEL!

BUT **ONE** OF THOSE SHIPS IS EVEN **NOW** BLAZING TOWARDS **EARTH**... TOWARDS THE ONLY FOUR CREATURES IN ALL THE UNIVERSE WHO MIGHT FIND A WAY TO SAVE US!

"PILOTED BY MY OWN PERSONAL ROBOT, THE SHIP MUST LAND ON EARTH AND CAPTURE THE **FANTASTIC FOUR!** THEN, THEY ARE TO BE BROUGHT TO PLANET X, AS MY PRISONERS!"

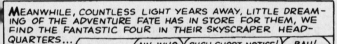

MEANWHILE, COUNTLESS LIGHT YEARS AWAY, LITTLE DREAMING OF THE ADVENTURE FATE HAS IN STORE FOR THEM, WE FIND THE FANTASTIC FOUR IN THEIR SKYSCRAPER HEADQUARTERS...

WE HAVEN'T MUCH TIME! WE'RE DUE TO APPEAR IN WASHINGTON LATER, TO ATTEND A GOVERNMENT DINNER IN OUR HONOR!

AW, WHO **NEEDS** IT, REED? I'M NOT EVEN HUNGRY!

SUCH SHORT NOTICE! I HAVEN'T GOT A THING TO WEAR!

BAH! IT'S JUST A WASTE OF TIME! I AIN'T GOIN'!

"THE THING'S **RIGHT**, REED! HECK, WE'RE NO SPEECH-MAKERS! IMAGINE WHAT WOULD HAPPEN IF I HAVE TO TRY TO SAY SOMETHING CLEVER--!"

THAT REMINDS ME OF A JOKE I HEARD ABOUT TWO BEATNIKS...

...OR, EH, AH, MAYBE YOU'VE ALREADY **HEARD** IT...?

"I'D PROBABLY GET ALL TENSE AND NERVOUS, AND THE THE NEXT THING WE KNOW, IT WOULD BE JUST MY LUCK TO BURST INTO **FLAME!**"

THAT'S FOOLISH AND YOU **KNOW** IT, TORCH! NOW, DOES ANYONE **ELSE** HAVE A BEEF?

YOU **BET!**

"CAN YA IMAGINE HOW **I'D** LOOK IN FRONT OF ALL THOSE CONGRESSMEN AT A BIG STATE DINNER? THEY'D THINK I WAS NUTTY IF I KEPT ALL BUNDLED UP, BUT I'D SCARE 'EM TO DEATH IF I TOOK MY HAT AND COAT OFF!"

13

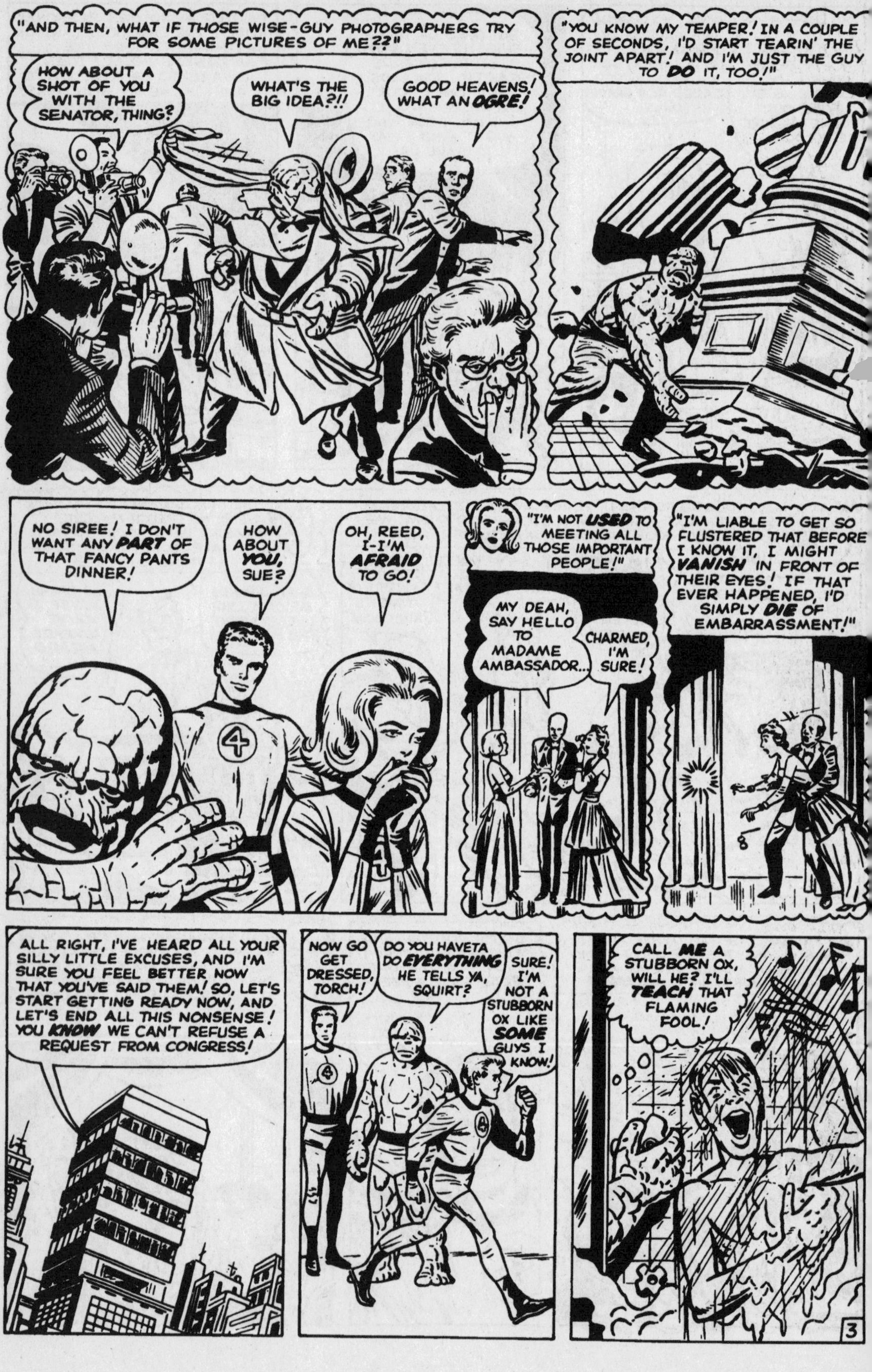
"AND THEN, WHAT IF THOSE WISE-GUY PHOTOGRAPHERS TRY FOR SOME PICTURES OF ME??"
HOW ABOUT A SHOT OF YOU WITH THE SENATOR, THING?
WHAT'S THE BIG IDEA?!!
GOOD HEAVENS! WHAT AN OGRE!
"YOU KNOW MY TEMPER! IN A COUPLE OF SECONDS, I'D START TEARIN' THE JOINT APART! AND I'M JUST THE GUY TO DO IT, TOO!"
NO SIREE! I DON'T WANT ANY PART OF THAT FANCY PANTS DINNER!
HOW ABOUT YOU, SUE?
OH, REED, I-I'M AFRAID TO GO!
"I'M NOT USED TO MEETING ALL THOSE IMPORTANT PEOPLE!"
MY DEAH, SAY HELLO TO MADAME AMBASSADOR...
CHARMED, I'M SURE!
"I'M LIABLE TO GET SO FLUSTERED THAT BEFORE I KNOW IT, I MIGHT VANISH IN FRONT OF THEIR EYES! IF THAT EVER HAPPENED, I'D SIMPLY DIE OF EMBARRASSMENT!"
ALL RIGHT, I'VE HEARD ALL YOUR SILLY LITTLE EXCUSES, AND I'M SURE YOU FEEL BETTER NOW THAT YOU'VE SAID THEM! SO, LET'S START GETTING READY NOW, AND LET'S END ALL THIS NONSENSE! YOU KNOW WE CAN'T REFUSE A REQUEST FROM CONGRESS!
NOW GO GET DRESSED, TORCH!
DO YOU HAVETA DO EVERYTHING HE TELLS YA, SQUIRT?
SURE! I'M NOT A STUBBORN OX LIKE SOME GUYS I KNOW!
CALL ME A STUBBORN OX, WILL HE? I'LL TEACH THAT FLAMING FOOL!
3

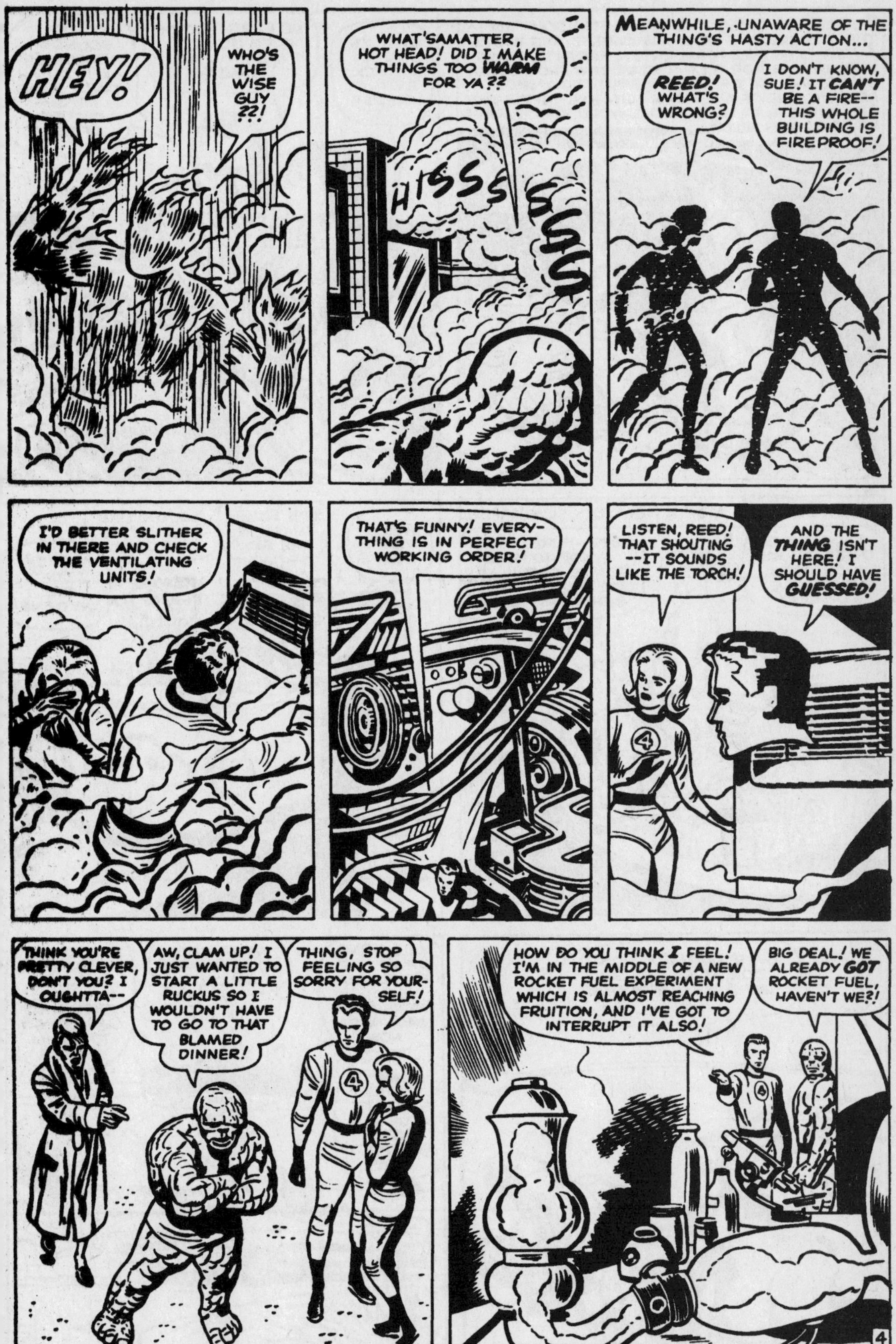
HEY!
WHO'S THE WISE GUY ??!
WHAT'SAMATTER, HOT HEAD! DID I MAKE THINGS TOO WARM FOR YA??
HISSSSSSSS
MEANWHILE, UNAWARE OF THE THING'S HASTY ACTION...
REED! WHAT'S WRONG?
I DON'T KNOW, SUE! IT CAN'T BE A FIRE-- THIS WHOLE BUILDING IS FIREPROOF!
I'D BETTER SLITHER IN THERE AND CHECK THE VENTILATING UNITS!
THAT'S FUNNY! EVERYTHING IS IN PERFECT WORKING ORDER!
LISTEN, REED! THAT SHOUTING --IT SOUNDS LIKE THE TORCH!
AND THE THING ISN'T HERE! I SHOULD HAVE GUESSED!
THINK YOU'RE PRETTY CLEVER, DON'T YOU? I OUGHTTA--
AW, CLAM UP! I JUST WANTED TO START A LITTLE RUCKUS SO I WOULDN'T HAVE TO GO TO THAT BLAMED DINNER!
THING, STOP FEELING SO SORRY FOR YOURSELF!
HOW DO YOU THINK I FEEL! I'M IN THE MIDDLE OF A NEW ROCKET FUEL EXPERIMENT WHICH IS ALMOST REACHING FRUITION, AND I'VE GOT TO INTERRUPT IT ALSO!
BIG DEAL! WE ALREADY GOT ROCKET FUEL, HAVEN'T WE?!
4

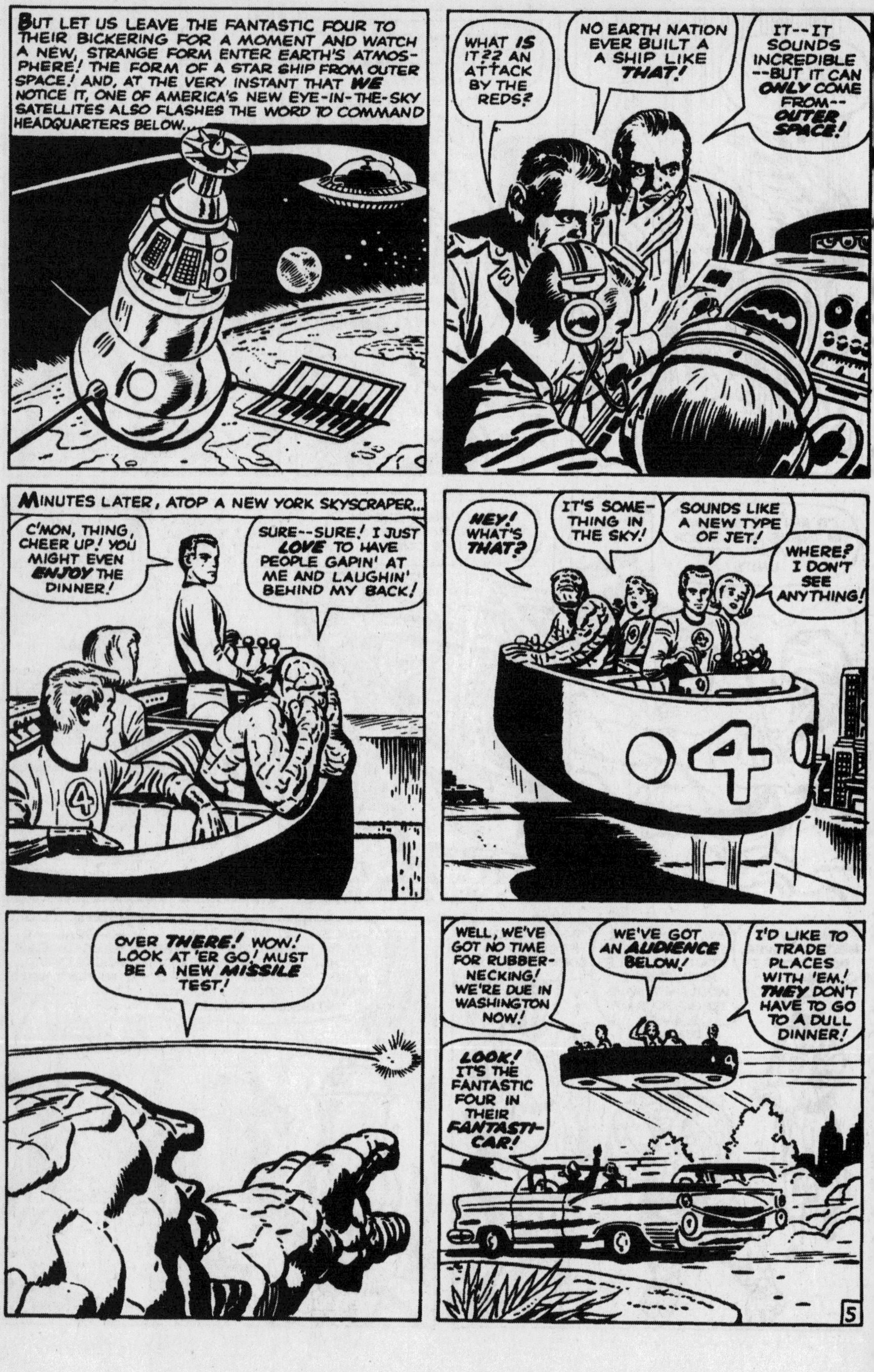
BUT LET US LEAVE THE FANTASTIC FOUR TO THEIR BICKERING FOR A MOMENT AND WATCH A NEW, STRANGE FORM ENTER EARTH'S ATMOSPHERE! THE FORM OF A STAR SHIP FROM OUTER SPACE! AND, AT THE VERY INSTANT THAT WE NOTICE IT, ONE OF AMERICA'S NEW EYE-IN-THE-SKY SATELLITES ALSO FLASHES THE WORD TO COMMAND HEADQUARTERS BELOW...
WHAT IS IT?? AN ATTACK BY THE REDS?
NO EARTH NATION EVER BUILT A SHIP LIKE THAT!
IT--IT SOUNDS INCREDIBLE --BUT IT CAN ONLY COME FROM-- OUTER SPACE!
MINUTES LATER, ATOP A NEW YORK SKYSCRAPER...
C'MON, THING, CHEER UP! YOU MIGHT EVEN ENJOY THE DINNER!
SURE--SURE! I JUST LOVE TO HAVE PEOPLE GAPIN' AT ME AND LAUGHIN' BEHIND MY BACK!
HEY! WHAT'S THAT?
IT'S SOMETHING IN THE SKY!
SOUNDS LIKE A NEW TYPE OF JET!
WHERE? I DON'T SEE ANYTHING!
4
OVER THERE! WOW! LOOK AT 'ER GO! MUST BE A NEW MISSILE TEST!
WELL, WE'VE GOT NO TIME FOR RUBBERNECKING! WE'RE DUE IN WASHINGTON NOW!
WE'VE GOT AN AUDIENCE BELOW!
I'D LIKE TO TRADE PLACES WITH 'EM! THEY DON'T HAVE TO GO TO A DULL DINNER!
LOOK! IT'S THE FANTASTIC FOUR IN THEIR FANTASTI-CAR!
5

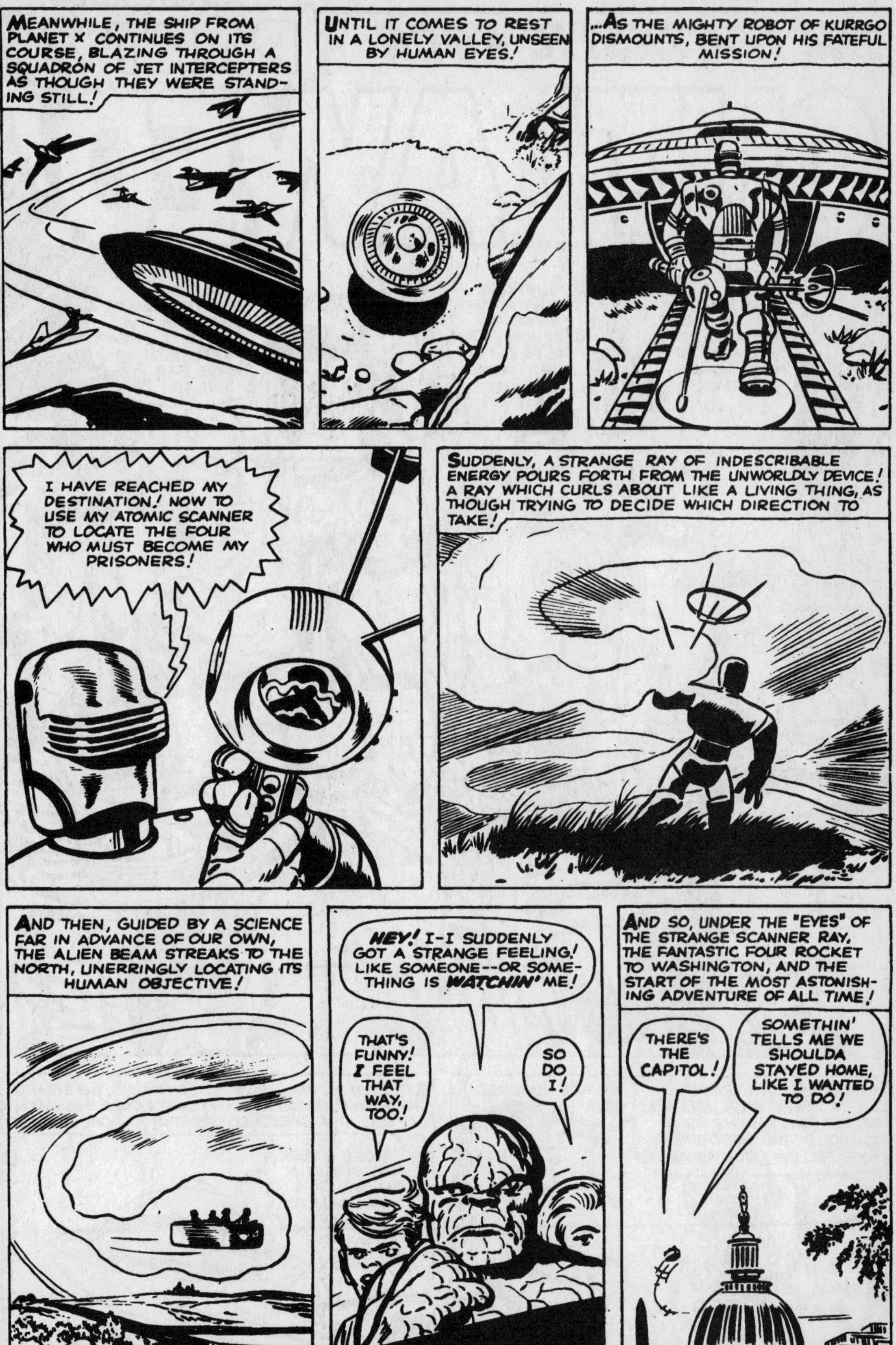
MEANWHILE, THE SHIP FROM PLANET X CONTINUES ON ITS COURSE, BLAZING THROUGH A SQUADRON OF JET INTERCEPTERS AS THOUGH THEY WERE STANDING STILL!
UNTIL IT COMES TO REST IN A LONELY VALLEY, UNSEEN BY HUMAN EYES!
...AS THE MIGHTY ROBOT OF KURRGO DISMOUNTS, BENT UPON HIS FATEFUL MISSION!
I HAVE REACHED MY DESTINATION! NOW TO USE MY ATOMIC SCANNER TO LOCATE THE FOUR WHO MUST BECOME MY PRISONERS!
SUDDENLY, A STRANGE RAY OF INDESCRIBABLE ENERGY POURS FORTH FROM THE UNWORLDLY DEVICE! A RAY WHICH CURLS ABOUT LIKE A LIVING THING, AS THOUGH TRYING TO DECIDE WHICH DIRECTION TO TAKE!
AND THEN, GUIDED BY A SCIENCE FAR IN ADVANCE OF OUR OWN, THE ALIEN BEAM STREAKS TO THE NORTH, UNERRINGLY LOCATING ITS HUMAN OBJECTIVE!
HEY! I-I SUDDENLY GOT A STRANGE FEELING! LIKE SOMEONE--OR SOMETHING IS WATCHIN' ME!
THAT'S FUNNY! I FEEL THAT WAY, TOO!
SO DO I!
AND SO, UNDER THE "EYES" OF THE STRANGE SCANNER RAY, THE FANTASTIC FOUR ROCKET TO WASHINGTON, AND THE START OF THE MOST ASTONISHING ADVENTURE OF ALL TIME!
THERE'S THE CAPITOL!
SOMETHIN' TELLS ME WE SHOULDA STAYED HOME, LIKE I WANTED TO DO!
6

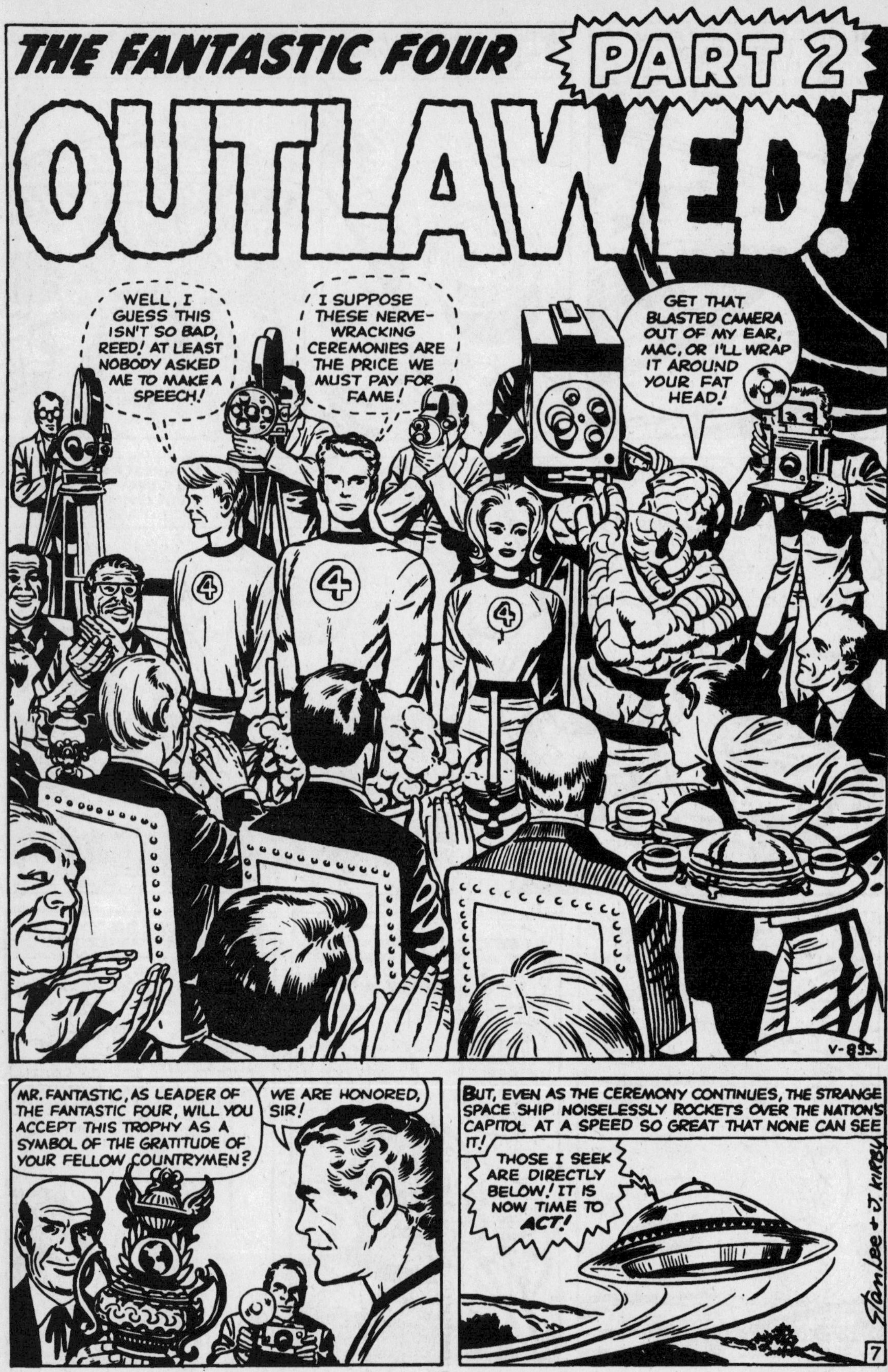
THE FANTASTIC FOUR
PART 2
OUTLAWED!
WELL, I GUESS THIS ISN'T SO BAD, REED! AT LEAST NOBODY ASKED ME TO MAKE A SPEECH!
I SUPPOSE THESE NERVE-WRACKING CEREMONIES ARE THE PRICE WE MUST PAY FOR FAME!
GET THAT BLASTED CAMERA OUT OF MY EAR, MAC, OR I'LL WRAP IT AROUND YOUR FAT HEAD!
V-833
MR. FANTASTIC, AS LEADER OF THE FANTASTIC FOUR, WILL YOU ACCEPT THIS TROPHY AS A SYMBOL OF THE GRATITUDE OF YOUR FELLOW COUNTRYMEN?
WE ARE HONORED, SIR!
BUT, EVEN AS THE CEREMONY CONTINUES, THE STRANGE SPACE SHIP NOISELESSLY ROCKETS OVER THE NATION'S CAPITOL AT A SPEED SO GREAT THAT NONE CAN SEE IT!
THOSE I SEEK ARE DIRECTLY BELOW! IT IS NOW TIME TO ACT!
Stan Lee + J. Kirby
7

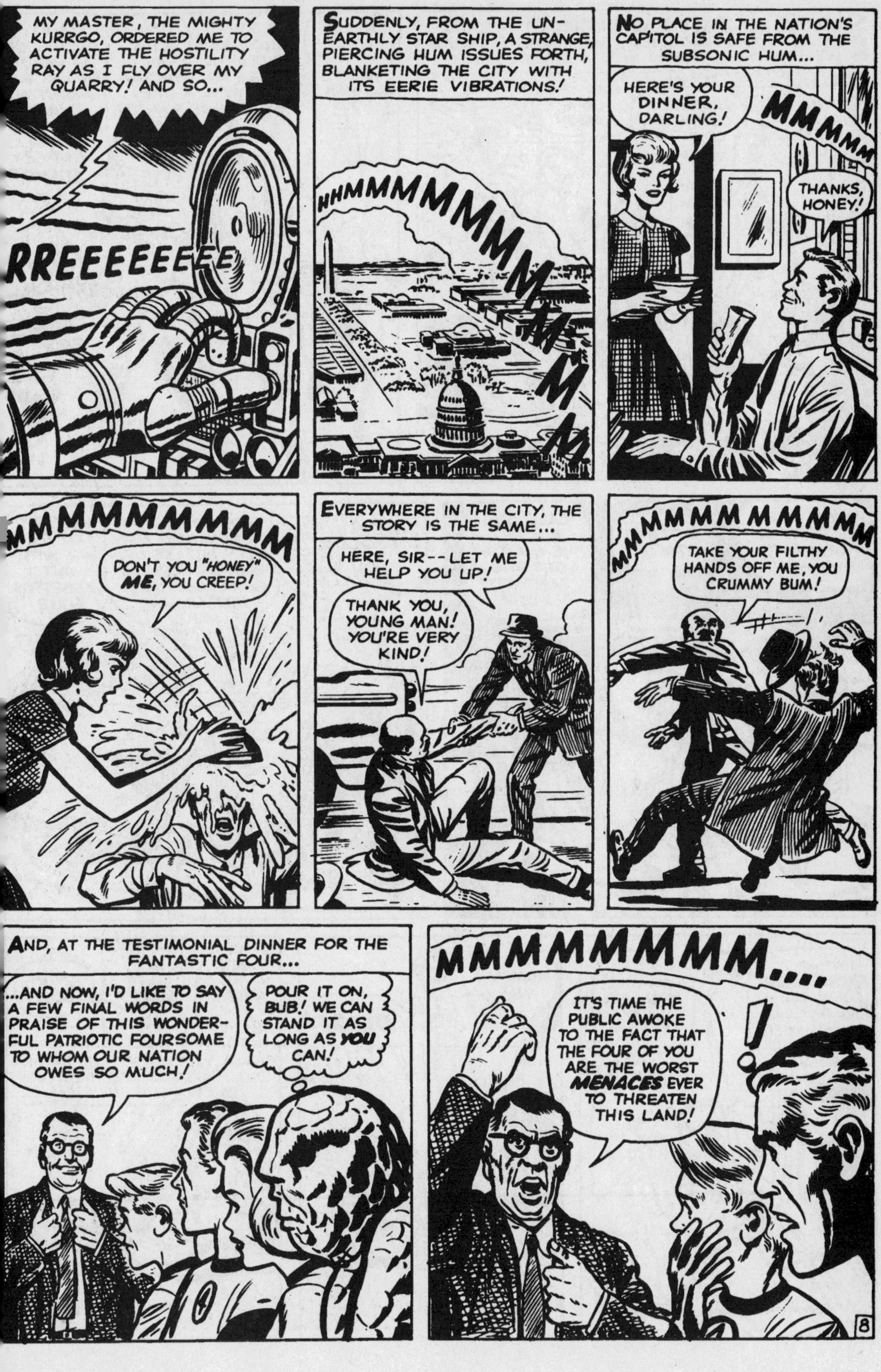

MY MASTER, THE MIGHTY KURRGO, ORDERED ME TO ACTIVATE THE HOSTILITY RAY AS I FLY OVER MY QUARRY! AND SO...
RREEEEEEEE
SUDDENLY, FROM THE UNEARTHLY STAR SHIP, A STRANGE, PIERCING HUM ISSUES FORTH, BLANKETING THE CITY WITH ITS EERIE VIBRATIONS!
HHMMMMMMMMMMM
NO PLACE IN THE NATION'S CAPITOL IS SAFE FROM THE SUBSONIC HUM...
HERE'S YOUR DINNER, DARLING!
MMMMM
THANKS, HONEY!
MMMMMMMMMM
DON'T YOU "HONEY" ME, YOU CREEP!
EVERYWHERE IN THE CITY, THE STORY IS THE SAME...
HERE, SIR--LET ME HELP YOU UP!
THANK YOU, YOUNG MAN! YOU'RE VERY KIND!
MMMMMMMMMMMMM
TAKE YOUR FILTHY HANDS OFF ME, YOU CRUMMY BUM!
AND, AT THE TESTIMONIAL DINNER FOR THE FANTASTIC FOUR...
...AND NOW, I'D LIKE TO SAY A FEW FINAL WORDS IN PRAISE OF THIS WONDERFUL PATRIOTIC FOURSOME TO WHOM OUR NATION OWES SO MUCH!
POUR IT ON, BUB! WE CAN STAND IT AS LONG AS YOU CAN!
MMMMMMMMM....
IT'S TIME THE PUBLIC AWOKE TO THE FACT THAT THE FOUR OF YOU ARE THE WORST MENACES EVER TO THREATEN THIS LAND!
!
8

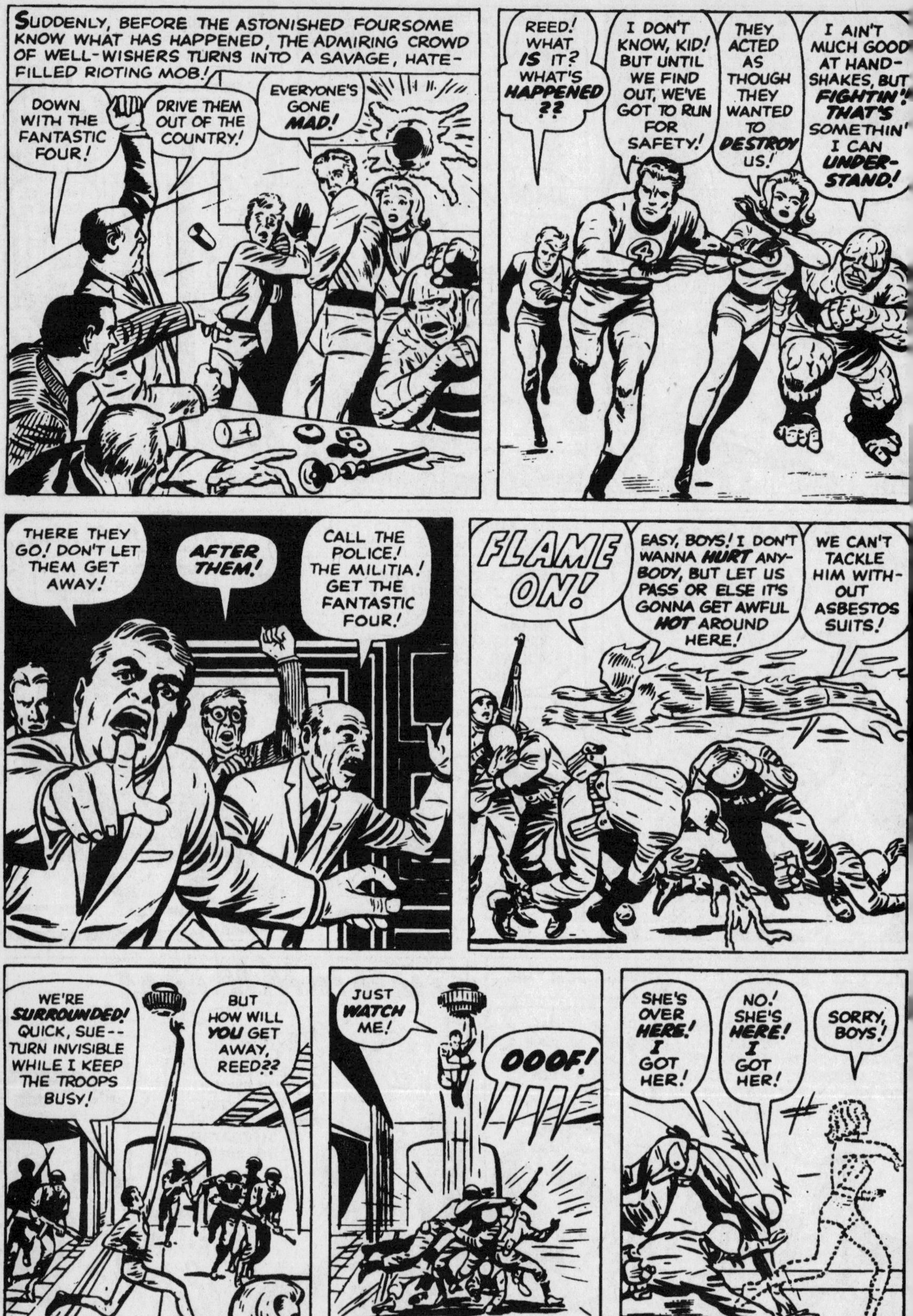

SUDDENLY, BEFORE THE ASTONISHED FOURSOME KNOW WHAT HAS HAPPENED, THE ADMIRING CROWD OF WELL-WISHERS TURNS INTO A SAVAGE, HATE-FILLED RIOTING MOB!
DOWN WITH THE FANTASTIC FOUR!
DRIVE THEM OUT OF THE COUNTRY!
EVERYONE'S GONE MAD!
REED! WHAT IS IT? WHAT'S HAPPENED??
I DON'T KNOW, KID! BUT UNTIL WE FIND OUT, WE'VE GOT TO RUN FOR SAFETY!
THEY ACTED AS THOUGH THEY WANTED TO DESTROY US!
I AIN'T MUCH GOOD AT HAND-SHAKES, BUT FIGHTIN'! THAT'S SOMETHIN' I CAN UNDER-STAND!
THERE THEY GO! DON'T LET THEM GET AWAY!
AFTER THEM!
CALL THE POLICE! THE MILITIA! GET THE FANTASTIC FOUR!
FLAME ON!
EASY, BOYS! I DON'T WANNA HURT ANY-BODY, BUT LET US PASS OR ELSE IT'S GONNA GET AWFUL HOT AROUND HERE!
WE CAN'T TACKLE HIM WITH-OUT ASBESTOS SUITS!
WE'RE SURROUNDED! QUICK, SUE-- TURN INVISIBLE WHILE I KEEP THE TROOPS BUSY!
BUT HOW WILL YOU GET AWAY, REED??
JUST WATCH ME!
OOOF!
SHE'S OVER HERE! I GOT HER!
NO! SHE'S HERE! I GOT HER!
SORRY, BOYS!
9

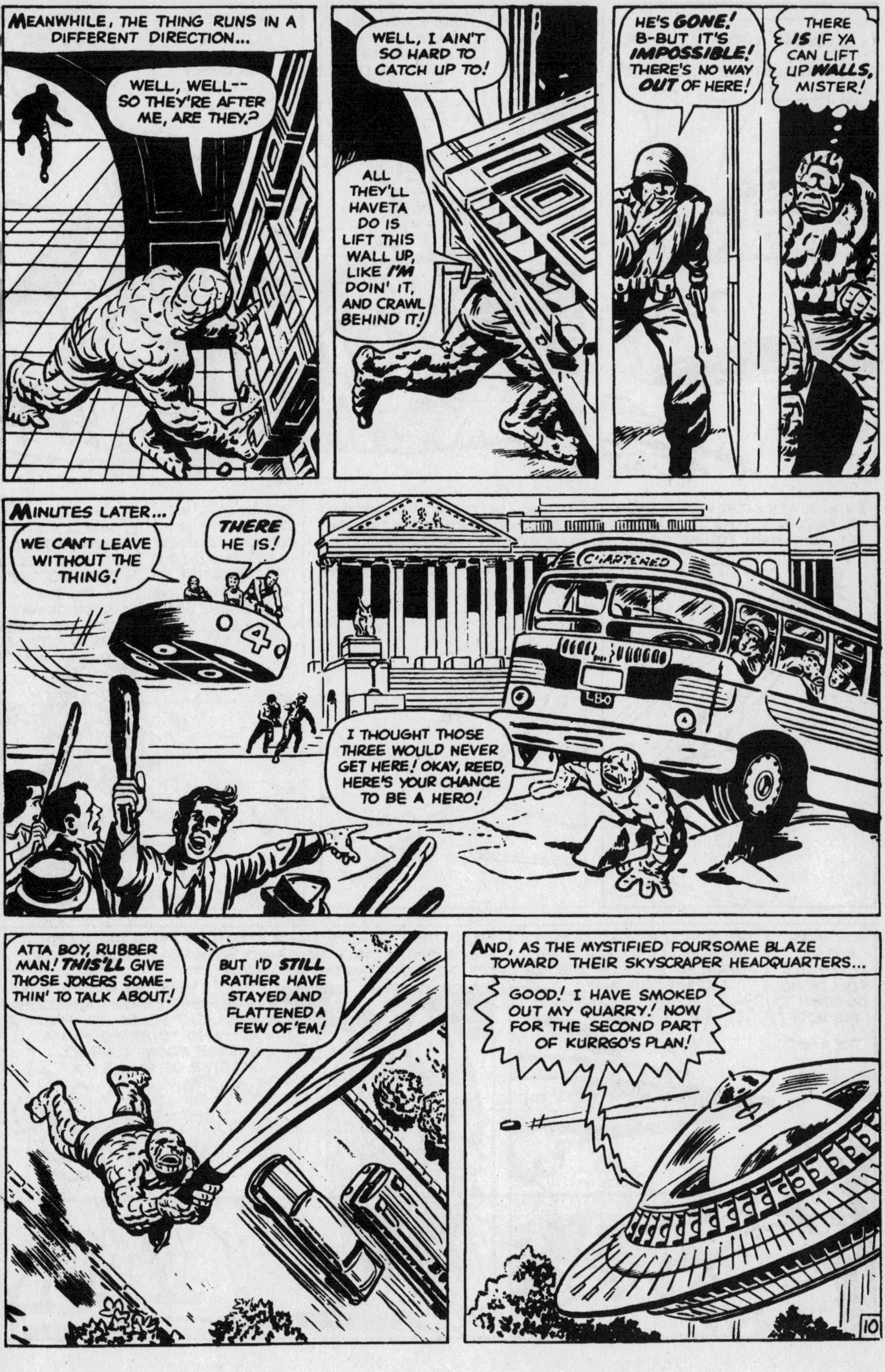
MEANWHILE, THE THING RUNS IN A DIFFERENT DIRECTION...
WELL, WELL-- SO THEY'RE AFTER ME, ARE THEY?
WELL, I AIN'T SO HARD TO CATCH UP TO!
ALL THEY'LL HAVETA DO IS LIFT THIS WALL UP, LIKE I'M DOIN' IT, AND CRAWL BEHIND IT!
HE'S GONE! B-BUT IT'S IMPOSSIBLE! THERE'S NO WAY OUT OF HERE!
THERE IS IF YA CAN LIFT UP WALLS, MISTER!
MINUTES LATER...
WE CAN'T LEAVE WITHOUT THE THING!
THERE HE IS!
CHARTERED
I THOUGHT THOSE THREE WOULD NEVER GET HERE! OKAY, REED, HERE'S YOUR CHANCE TO BE A HERO!
ATTA BOY, RUBBER MAN! THIS'LL GIVE THOSE JOKERS SOME-THIN' TO TALK ABOUT!
BUT I'D STILL RATHER HAVE STAYED AND FLATTENED A FEW OF 'EM!
AND, AS THE MYSTIFIED FOURSOME BLAZE TOWARD THEIR SKYSCRAPER HEADQUARTERS...
GOOD! I HAVE SMOKED OUT MY QUARRY! NOW FOR THE SECOND PART OF KURRGO'S PLAN!
10

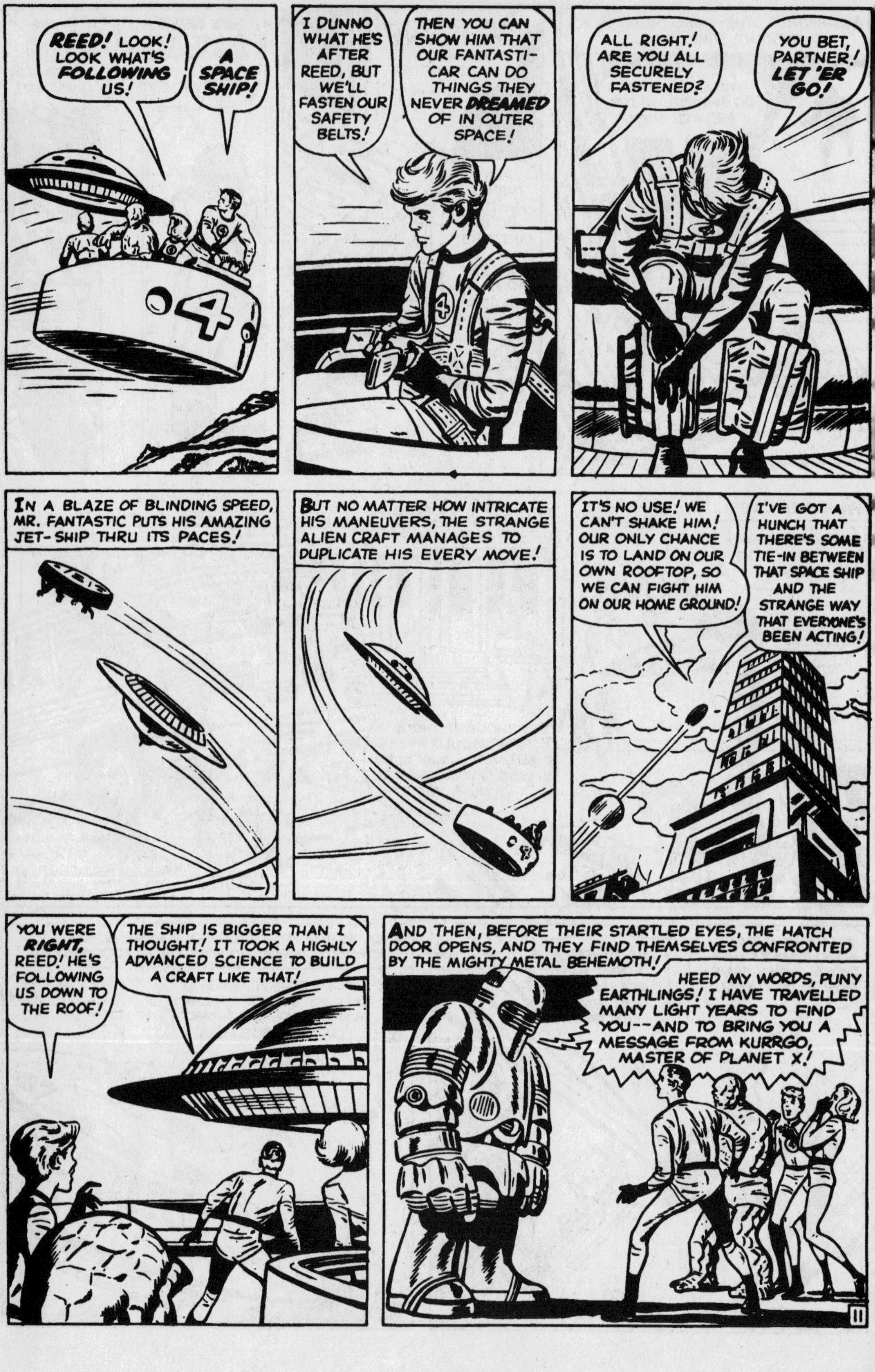
REED! LOOK! LOOK WHAT'S FOLLOWING US!
A SPACE SHIP!
I DUNNO WHAT HE'S AFTER REED, BUT WE'LL FASTEN OUR SAFETY BELTS!
THEN YOU CAN SHOW HIM THAT OUR FANTASTI-CAR CAN DO THINGS THEY NEVER DREAMED OF IN OUTER SPACE!
ALL RIGHT! ARE YOU ALL SECURELY FASTENED?
YOU BET, PARTNER! LET 'ER GO!
IN A BLAZE OF BLINDING SPEED, MR. FANTASTIC PUTS HIS AMAZING JET-SHIP THRU ITS PACES!
BUT NO MATTER HOW INTRICATE HIS MANEUVERS, THE STRANGE ALIEN CRAFT MANAGES TO DUPLICATE HIS EVERY MOVE!
IT'S NO USE! WE CAN'T SHAKE HIM! OUR ONLY CHANCE IS TO LAND ON OUR OWN ROOFTOP, SO WE CAN FIGHT HIM ON OUR HOME GROUND!
I'VE GOT A HUNCH THAT THERE'S SOME TIE-IN BETWEEN THAT SPACE SHIP AND THE STRANGE WAY THAT EVERYONE'S BEEN ACTING!
YOU WERE RIGHT, REED! HE'S FOLLOWING US DOWN TO THE ROOF!
THE SHIP IS BIGGER THAN I THOUGHT! IT TOOK A HIGHLY ADVANCED SCIENCE TO BUILD A CRAFT LIKE THAT!
AND THEN, BEFORE THEIR STARTLED EYES, THE HATCH DOOR OPENS, AND THEY FIND THEMSELVES CONFRONTED BY THE MIGHTY METAL BEHEMOTH!
HEED MY WORDS, PUNY EARTHLINGS! I HAVE TRAVELLED MANY LIGHT YEARS TO FIND YOU--AND TO BRING YOU A MESSAGE FROM KURRGO, MASTER OF PLANET X!
11

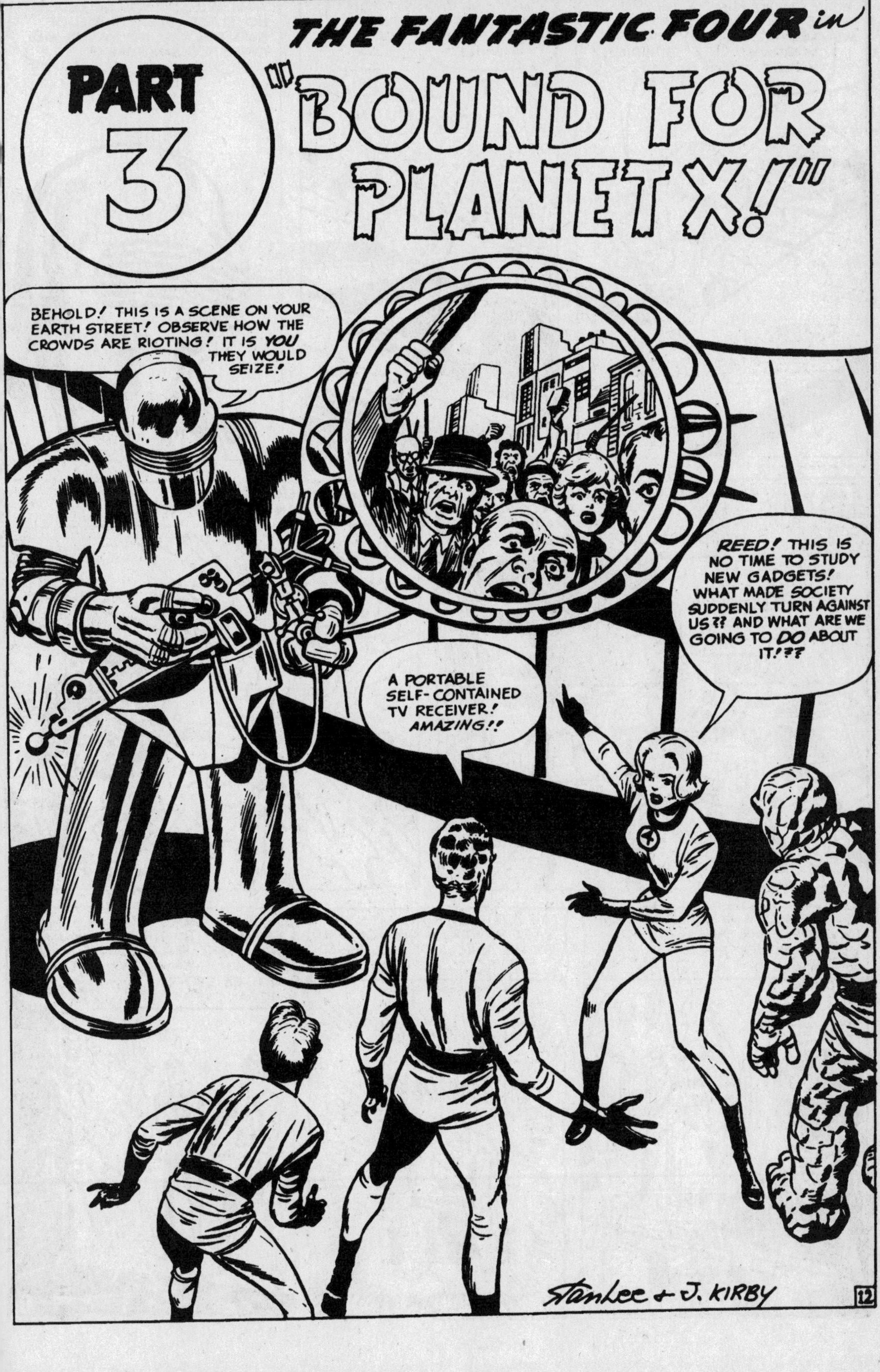
THE FANTASTIC FOUR in
PART 3
"BOUND FOR PLANET X!"
BEHOLD! THIS IS A SCENE ON YOUR EARTH STREET! OBSERVE HOW THE CROWDS ARE RIOTING! IT IS YOU THEY WOULD SEIZE!
REED! THIS IS NO TIME TO STUDY NEW GADGETS! WHAT MADE SOCIETY SUDDENLY TURN AGAINST US?? AND WHAT ARE WE GOING TO DO ABOUT IT!??
A PORTABLE SELF-CONTAINED TV RECEIVER! AMAZING!!
Stan Lee + J. KIRBY
12

HOLY SMOKE, SIS! THERE ISN'T MUCH WE *CAN* DO!! LOOK DOWN THERE!

THEY'RE TRYING TO STORM THE BUILDING!

ONLY ONE THING TO DO! WE'VE GOT TO GET OUT OF THE COUNTRY FOR A WHILE!

THAT WILL DO YOU NO GOOD! NO PLACE ON EARTH WILL BE SAFE FOR YOU! NO NATION WILL OFFER YOU SANCTUARY!

"NO MATTER *WHERE* YOU GO, NO MATTER WHAT CONTINENT YOU FLEE TO, YOU WILL BE HUNTED BY YOUR FELLOW HUMANS AS THOUGH YOU ARE FOUR MONSTERS!"

"MEN WITH CHEMICAL FOAM WILL RENDER THE HUMAN TORCH HELPLESS..."

"EVENTUALLY, A WAY WILL BE FOUND TO CONFINE MR. FANTASTIC SO THAT HIS POWER TO CHANGE HIS SHAPE WILL AVAIL HIM NOTHING---"

"AS FOR THE THING, EVEN HIS VAST POWER CAN BE CONTAINED BY THE FORCES OF HARNESSED ELECTRICAL ENERGY."

"WHILE A RADIOACTIVE ARM-BAND FASTENED TO THE INVISIBLE GIRL WILL MAKE HER PRESENCE ALWAYS KNOWN, EVEN THOUGH SHE CAN NOT BE SEEN BY HUMAN EYES!"

TICK!TAC-TAC-TAC-TAC-TAC

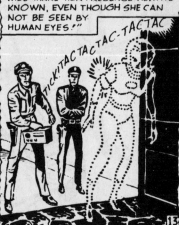

13

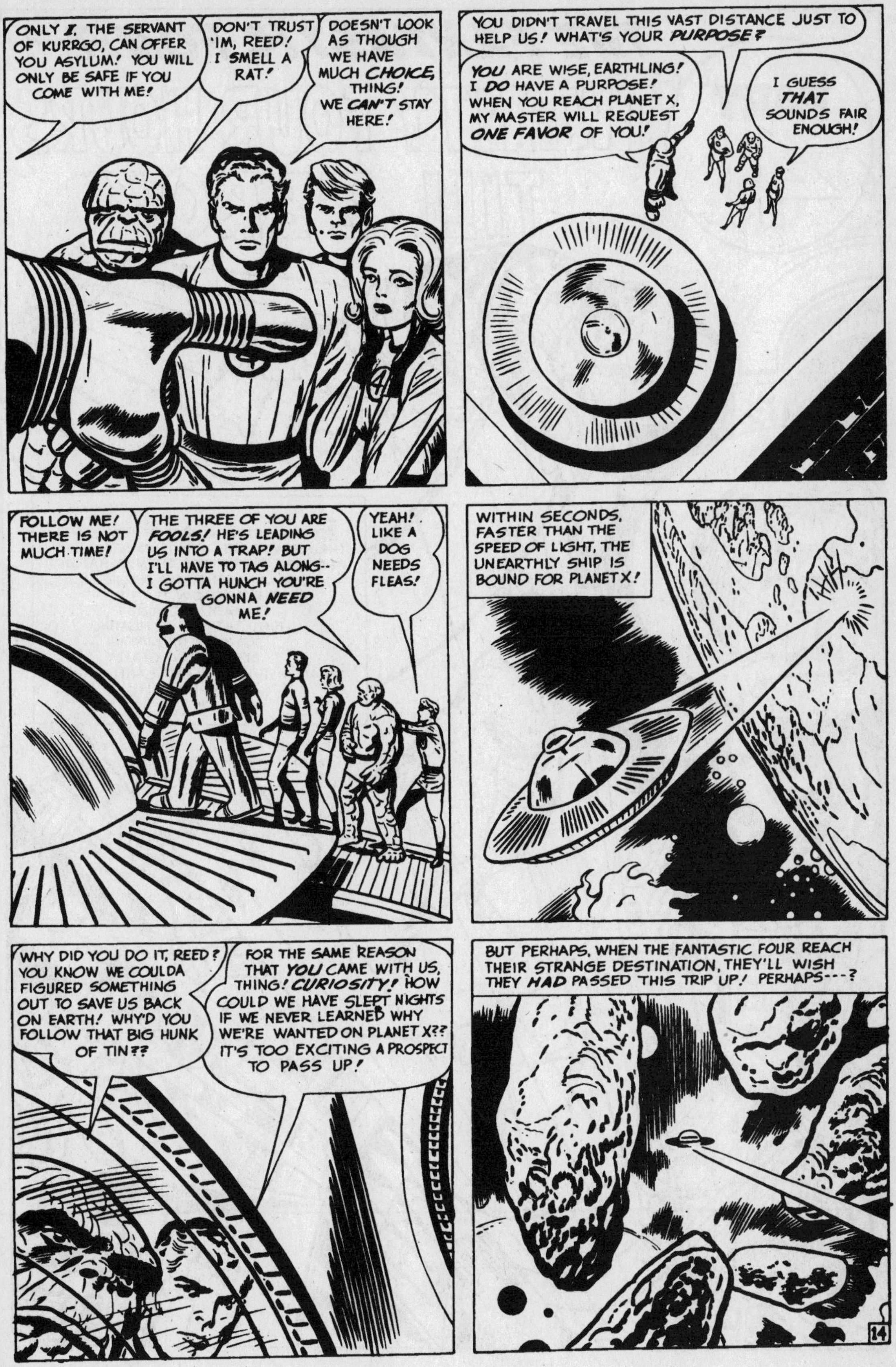
ONLY I, THE SERVANT OF KURRGO, CAN OFFER YOU ASYLUM! YOU WILL ONLY BE SAFE IF YOU COME WITH ME!
DON'T TRUST 'IM, REED! I SMELL A RAT!
DOESN'T LOOK AS THOUGH WE HAVE MUCH CHOICE, THING! WE CAN'T STAY HERE!
YOU DIDN'T TRAVEL THIS VAST DISTANCE JUST TO HELP US! WHAT'S YOUR PURPOSE?
YOU ARE WISE, EARTHLING! I DO HAVE A PURPOSE! WHEN YOU REACH PLANET X, MY MASTER WILL REQUEST ONE FAVOR OF YOU!
I GUESS THAT SOUNDS FAIR ENOUGH!
FOLLOW ME! THERE IS NOT MUCH TIME!
THE THREE OF YOU ARE FOOLS! HE'S LEADING US INTO A TRAP! BUT I'LL HAVE TO TAG ALONG-- I GOTTA HUNCH YOU'RE GONNA NEED ME!
YEAH! LIKE A DOG NEEDS FLEAS!
WITHIN SECONDS, FASTER THAN THE SPEED OF LIGHT, THE UNEARTHLY SHIP IS BOUND FOR PLANET X!
WHY DID YOU DO IT, REED? YOU KNOW WE COULDA FIGURED SOMETHING OUT TO SAVE US BACK ON EARTH! WHY'D YOU FOLLOW THAT BIG HUNK OF TIN??
FOR THE SAME REASON THAT YOU CAME WITH US, THING! CURIOSITY! HOW COULD WE HAVE SLEPT NIGHTS IF WE NEVER LEARNED WHY WE'RE WANTED ON PLANET X?? IT'S TOO EXCITING A PROSPECT TO PASS UP!
BUT PERHAPS, WHEN THE FANTASTIC FOUR REACH THEIR STRANGE DESTINATION, THEY'LL WISH THEY HAD PASSED THIS TRIP UP! PERHAPS---?
14

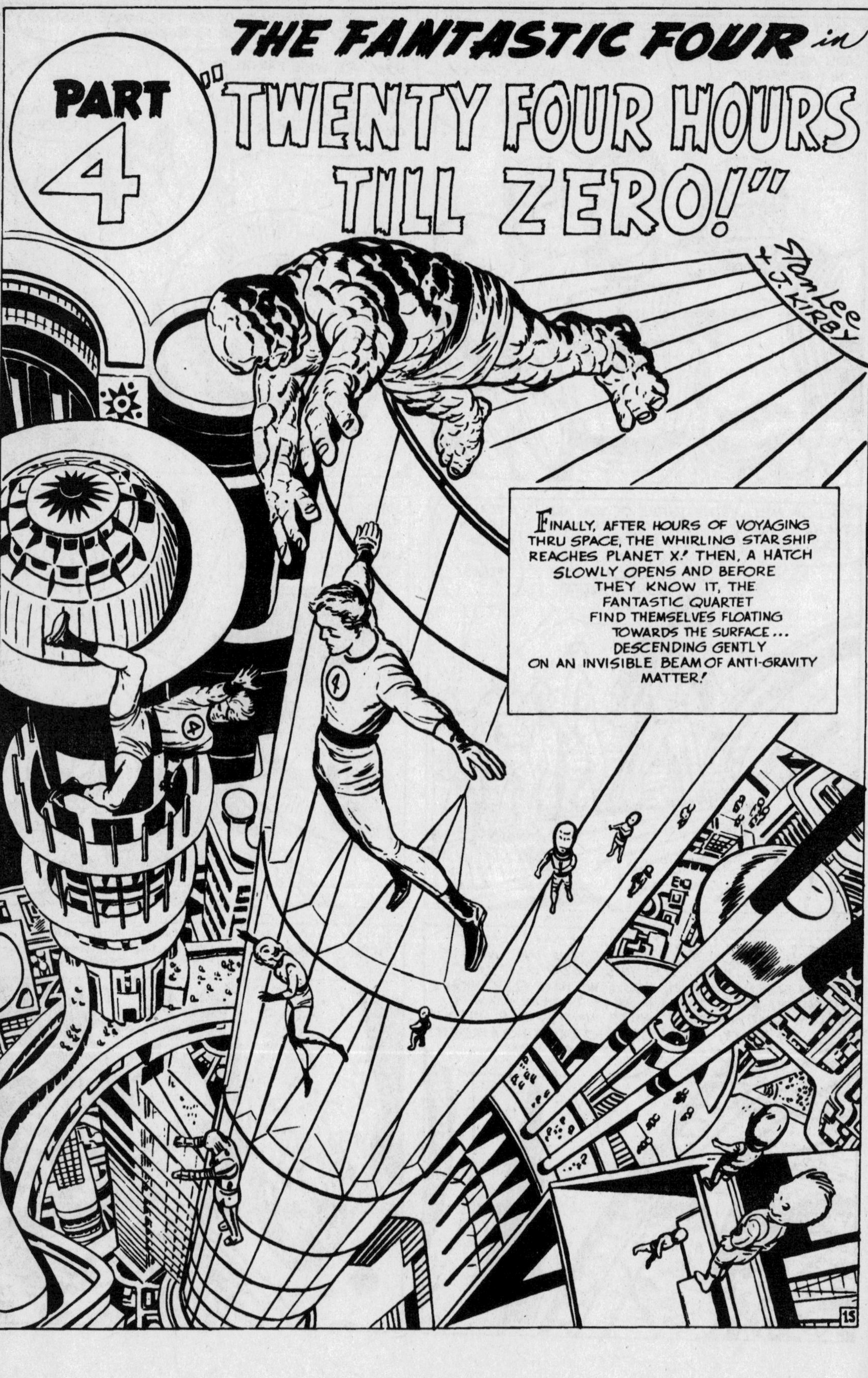
THE FANTASTIC FOUR in
PART 4
"TWENTY FOUR HOURS TILL ZERO!"
Stan Lee + J. Kirby
FINALLY, AFTER HOURS OF VOYAGING THRU SPACE, THE WHIRLING STARSHIP REACHES PLANET X! THEN, A HATCH SLOWLY OPENS AND BEFORE THEY KNOW IT, THE FANTASTIC QUARTET FIND THEMSELVES FLOATING TOWARDS THE SURFACE... DESCENDING GENTLY ON AN INVISIBLE BEAM OF ANTI-GRAVITY MATTER!
15

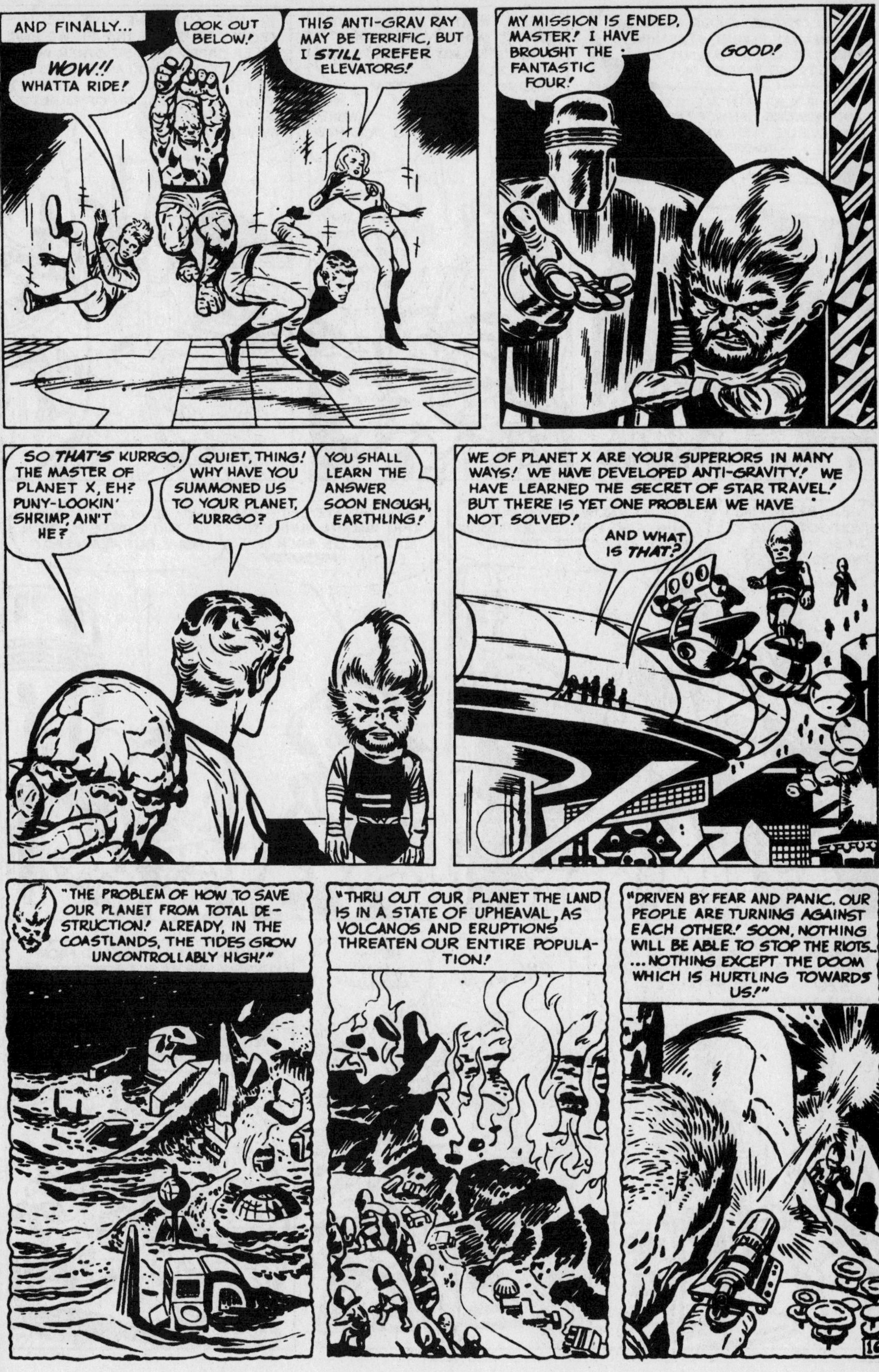

AND FINALLY...
WOW!! WHATTA RIDE!
LOOK OUT BELOW!
THIS ANTI-GRAV RAY MAY BE TERRIFIC, BUT I STILL PREFER ELEVATORS!
MY MISSION IS ENDED, MASTER! I HAVE BROUGHT THE FANTASTIC FOUR!
GOOD!
SO THAT'S KURRGO, THE MASTER OF PLANET X, EH? PUNY-LOOKIN' SHRIMP, AIN'T HE?
QUIET, THING! WHY HAVE YOU SUMMONED US TO YOUR PLANET, KURRGO?
YOU SHALL LEARN THE ANSWER SOON ENOUGH, EARTHLING!
WE OF PLANET X ARE YOUR SUPERIORS IN MANY WAYS! WE HAVE DEVELOPED ANTI-GRAVITY! WE HAVE LEARNED THE SECRET OF STAR TRAVEL! BUT THERE IS YET ONE PROBLEM WE HAVE NOT SOLVED!
AND WHAT IS THAT?
"THE PROBLEM OF HOW TO SAVE OUR PLANET FROM TOTAL DE-STRUCTION! ALREADY, IN THE COASTLANDS, THE TIDES GROW UNCONTROLLABLY HIGH!"
"THRU OUT OUR PLANET THE LAND IS IN A STATE OF UPHEAVAL, AS VOLCANOS AND ERUPTIONS THREATEN OUR ENTIRE POPULA-TION!
"DRIVEN BY FEAR AND PANIC, OUR PEOPLE ARE TURNING AGAINST EACH OTHER! SOON, NOTHING WILL BE ABLE TO STOP THE RIOTS... ...NOTHING EXCEPT THE DOOM WHICH IS HURTLING TOWARDS US!"
16

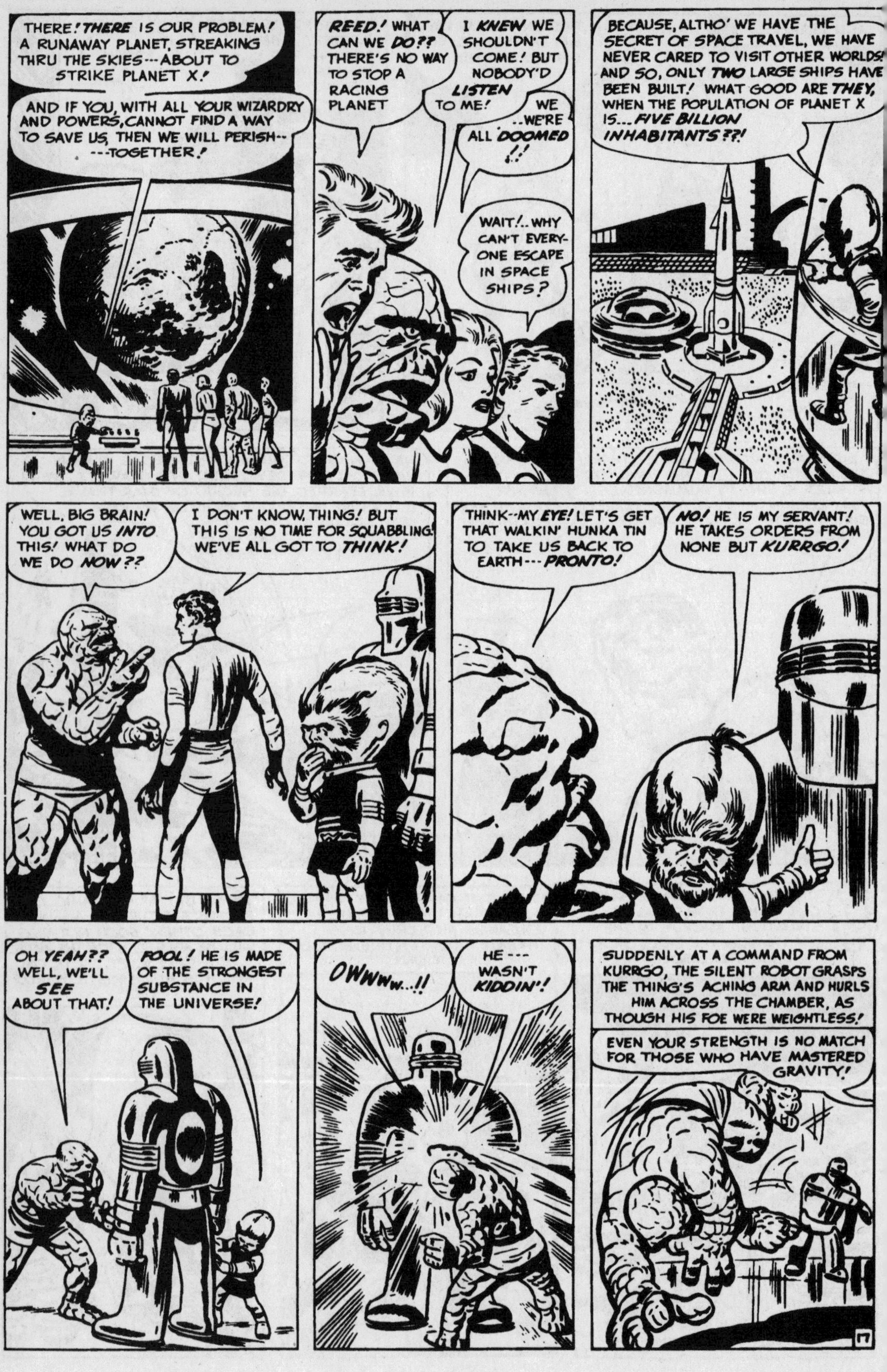
THERE! THERE IS OUR PROBLEM! A RUNAWAY PLANET, STREAKING THRU THE SKIES---ABOUT TO STRIKE PLANET X!
AND IF YOU, WITH ALL YOUR WIZARDRY AND POWERS, CANNOT FIND A WAY TO SAVE US, THEN WE WILL PERISH-- ---TOGETHER!
REED! WHAT CAN WE DO?? THERE'S NO WAY TO STOP A RACING PLANET
I KNEW WE SHOULDN'T COME! BUT NOBODY'D LISTEN TO ME!
WE ..WE'RE ALL DOOMED !!
WAIT!.. WHY CAN'T EVERYONE ESCAPE IN SPACE SHIPS?
BECAUSE, ALTHO' WE HAVE THE SECRET OF SPACE TRAVEL, WE HAVE NEVER CARED TO VISIT OTHER WORLDS! AND SO, ONLY TWO LARGE SHIPS HAVE BEEN BUILT! WHAT GOOD ARE THEY, WHEN THE POPULATION OF PLANET X IS... FIVE BILLION INHABITANTS??!
WELL, BIG BRAIN! YOU GOT US INTO THIS! WHAT DO WE DO NOW??
I DON'T KNOW, THING! BUT THIS IS NO TIME FOR SQUABBLING! WE'VE ALL GOT TO THINK!
THINK--MY EYE! LET'S GET THAT WALKIN' HUNKA TIN TO TAKE US BACK TO EARTH---PRONTO!
NO! HE IS MY SERVANT! HE TAKES ORDERS FROM NONE BUT KURRGO!
OH YEAH?? WELL, WE'LL SEE ABOUT THAT!
FOOL! HE IS MADE OF THE STRONGEST SUBSTANCE IN THE UNIVERSE!
OWWww...!!
HE--- WASN'T KIDDIN'!
SUDDENLY AT A COMMAND FROM KURRGO, THE SILENT ROBOT GRASPS THE THING'S ACHING ARM AND HURLS HIM ACROSS THE CHAMBER, AS THOUGH HIS FOE WERE WEIGHTLESS!
EVEN YOUR STRENGTH IS NO MATCH FOR THOSE WHO HAVE MASTERED GRAVITY!
17

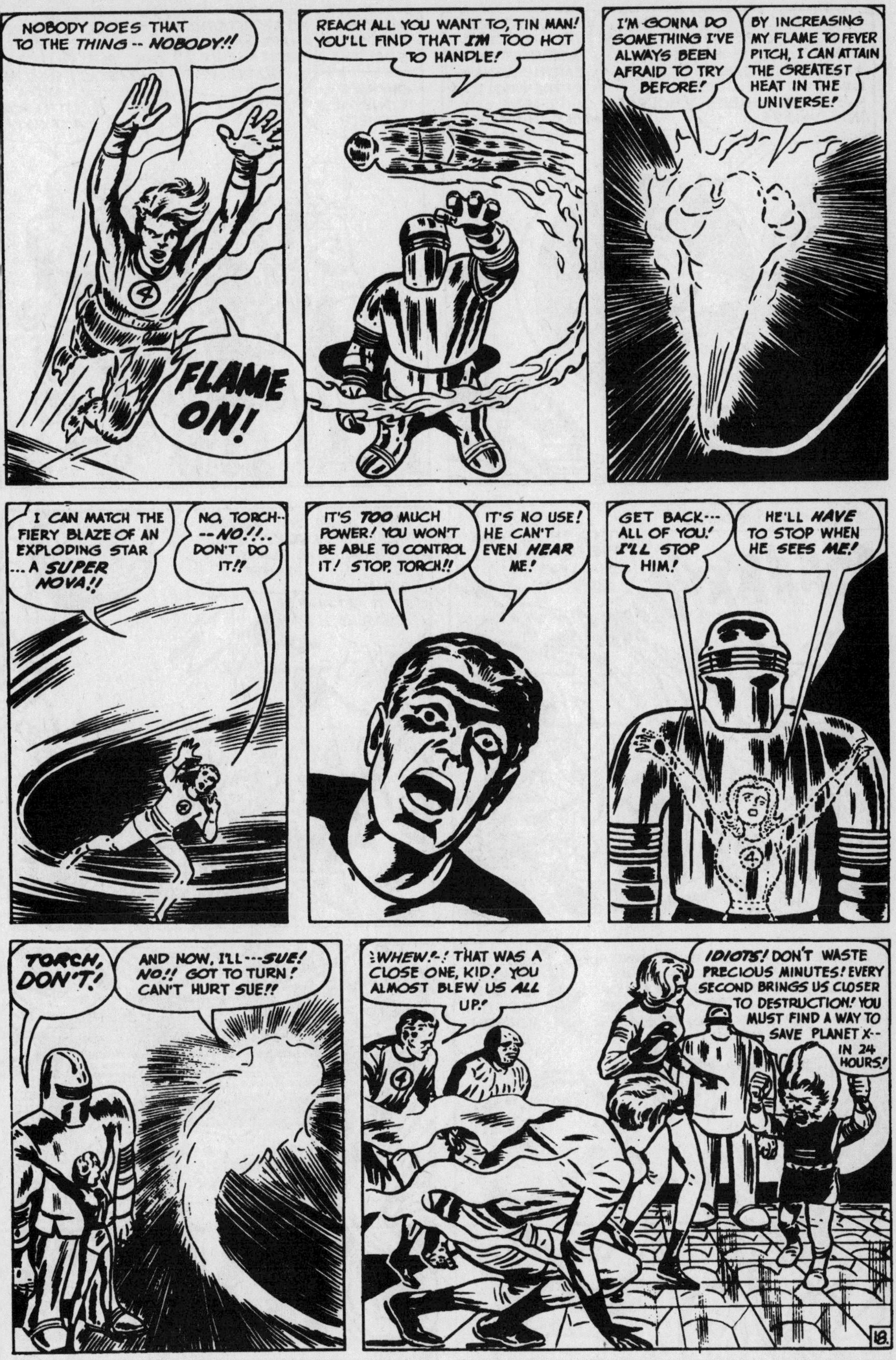
NOBODY DOES THAT TO THE THING -- NOBODY!!
FLAME ON!
REACH ALL YOU WANT TO, TIN MAN! YOU'LL FIND THAT I'M TOO HOT TO HANDLE!
I'M GONNA DO SOMETHING I'VE ALWAYS BEEN AFRAID TO TRY BEFORE!
BY INCREASING MY FLAME TO FEVER PITCH, I CAN ATTAIN THE GREATEST HEAT IN THE UNIVERSE!
I CAN MATCH THE FIERY BLAZE OF AN EXPLODING STAR ...A SUPER NOVA!!
NO, TORCH-- --NO!!.. DON'T DO IT!!
IT'S TOO MUCH POWER! YOU WON'T BE ABLE TO CONTROL IT! STOP, TORCH!!
IT'S NO USE! HE CAN'T EVEN HEAR ME!
GET BACK--- ALL OF YOU! I'LL STOP HIM!
HE'LL HAVE TO STOP WHEN HE SEES ME!
TORCH, DON'T!
AND NOW, I'LL---SUE! NO!! GOT TO TURN! CAN'T HURT SUE!!
WHEW!-! THAT WAS A CLOSE ONE, KID! YOU ALMOST BLEW US ALL UP!
IDIOTS! DON'T WASTE PRECIOUS MINUTES! EVERY SECOND BRINGS US CLOSER TO DESTRUCTION! YOU MUST FIND A WAY TO SAVE PLANET X-- IN 24 HOURS!
18.

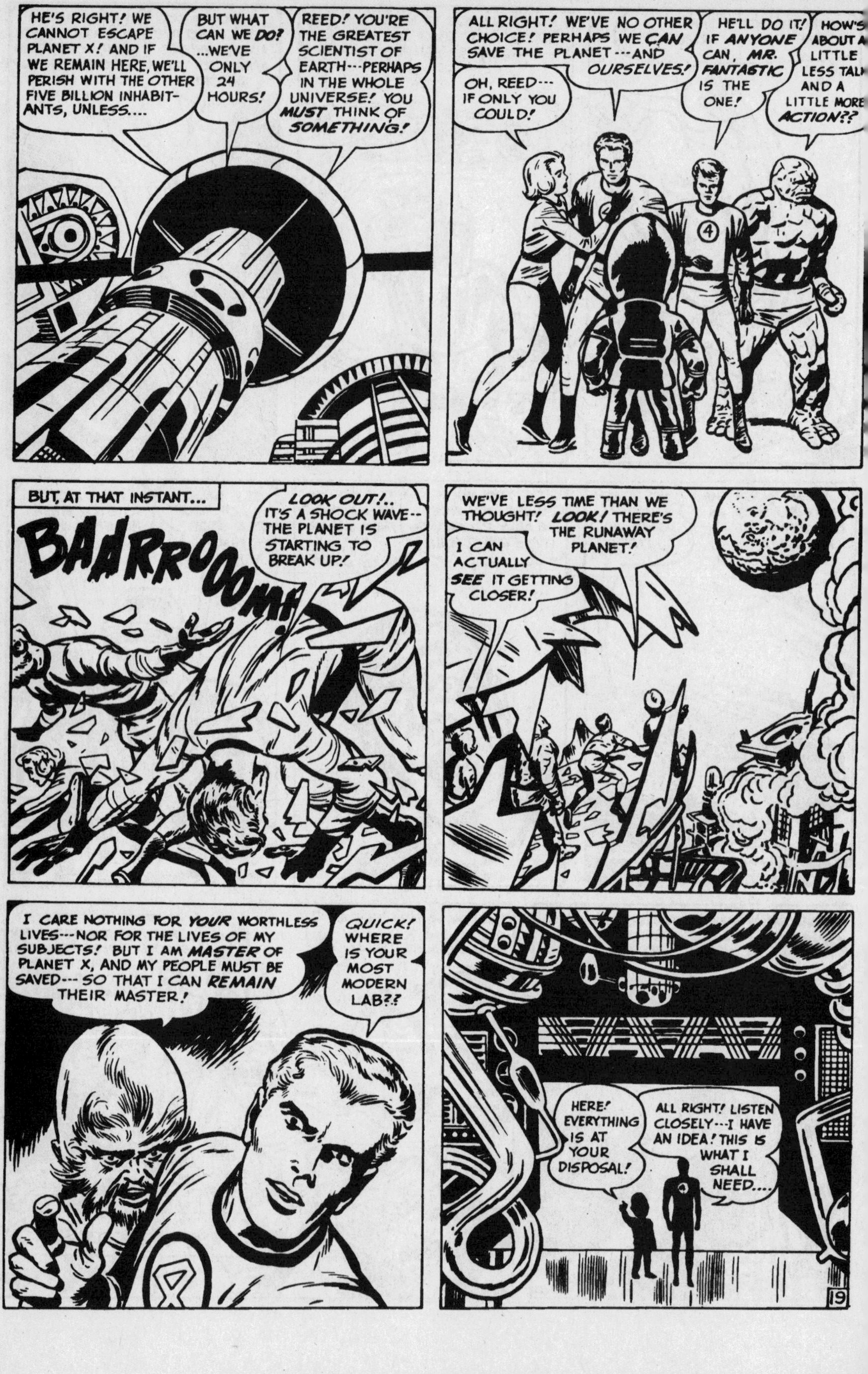
HE'S RIGHT! WE CANNOT ESCAPE PLANET X! AND IF WE REMAIN HERE, WE'LL PERISH WITH THE OTHER FIVE BILLION INHABIT-ANTS, UNLESS....
BUT WHAT CAN WE DO? ...WE'VE ONLY 24 HOURS!
REED! YOU'RE THE GREATEST SCIENTIST OF EARTH---PERHAPS IN THE WHOLE UNIVERSE! YOU MUST THINK OF SOMETHING!
ALL RIGHT! WE'VE NO OTHER CHOICE! PERHAPS WE CAN SAVE THE PLANET---AND OURSELVES!
OH, REED--- IF ONLY YOU COULD!
HE'LL DO IT! IF ANYONE CAN, MR. FANTASTIC IS THE ONE!
HOW'S ABOUT A LITTLE LESS TALK AND A LITTLE MORE ACTION??
BUT, AT THAT INSTANT...
BAARROOOMM
LOOK OUT!.. IT'S A SHOCK WAVE-- THE PLANET IS STARTING TO BREAK UP!
WE'VE LESS TIME THAN WE THOUGHT! LOOK! THERE'S THE RUNAWAY PLANET!
I CAN ACTUALLY SEE IT GETTING CLOSER!
I CARE NOTHING FOR YOUR WORTHLESS LIVES---NOR FOR THE LIVES OF MY SUBJECTS! BUT I AM MASTER OF PLANET X, AND MY PEOPLE MUST BE SAVED--- SO THAT I CAN REMAIN THEIR MASTER!
QUICK! WHERE IS YOUR MOST MODERN LAB??
HERE! EVERYTHING IS AT YOUR DISPOSAL!
ALL RIGHT! LISTEN CLOSELY---I HAVE AN IDEA! THIS IS WHAT I SHALL NEED....
19

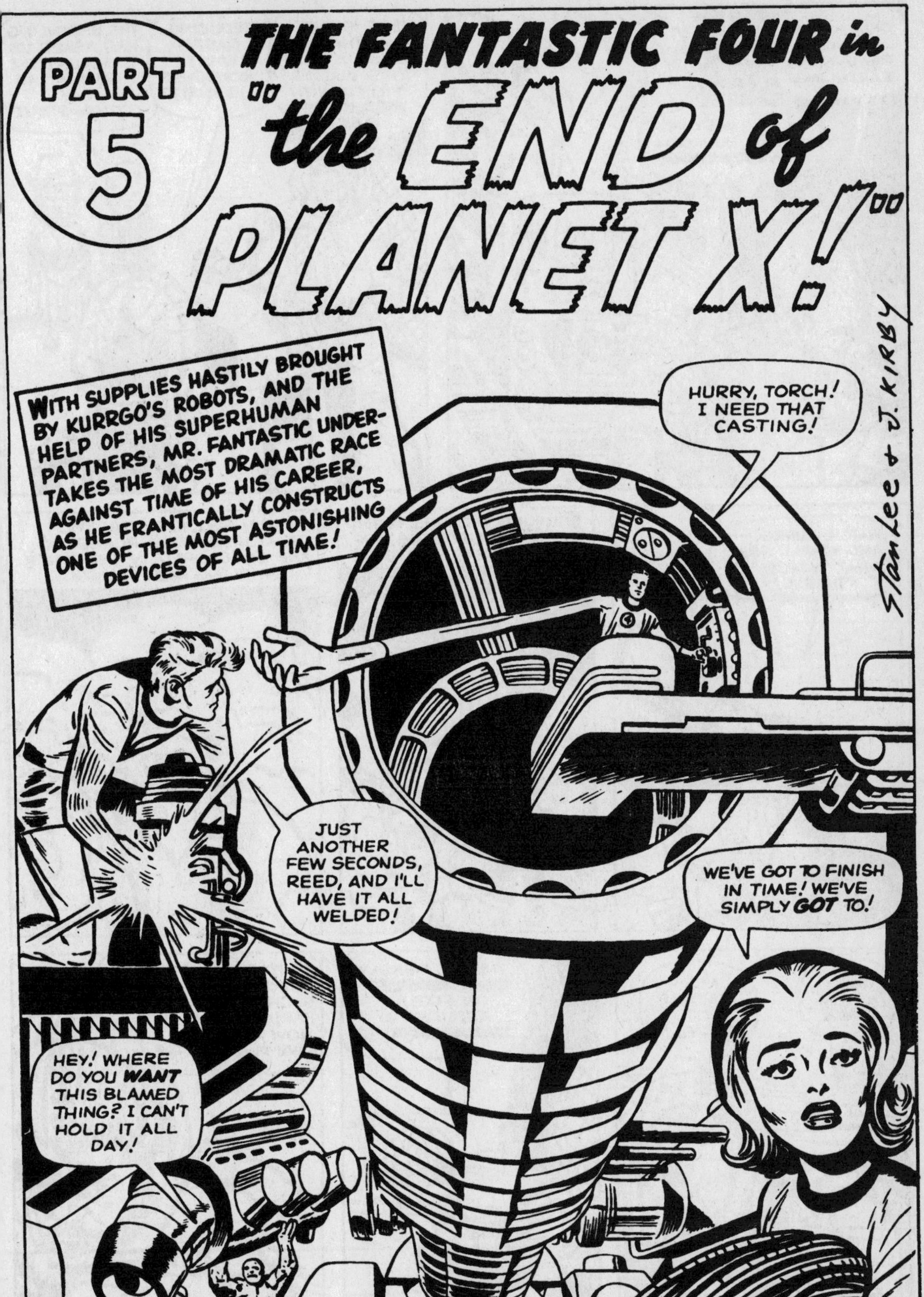
PART 5
THE FANTASTIC FOUR in
"the END of PLANET X!"
Stan Lee + J. KIRBY
WITH SUPPLIES HASTILY BROUGHT BY KURRGO'S ROBOTS, AND THE HELP OF HIS SUPERHUMAN PARTNERS, MR. FANTASTIC UNDER-TAKES THE MOST DRAMATIC RACE AGAINST TIME OF HIS CAREER, AS HE FRANTICALLY CONSTRUCTS ONE OF THE MOST ASTONISHING DEVICES OF ALL TIME!
HURRY, TORCH! I NEED THAT CASTING!
JUST ANOTHER FEW SECONDS, REED, AND I'LL HAVE IT ALL WELDED!
WE'VE GOT TO FINISH IN TIME! WE'VE SIMPLY GOT TO!
HEY! WHERE DO YOU WANT THIS BLAMED THING? I CAN'T HOLD IT ALL DAY!
AYERS
V-895
20

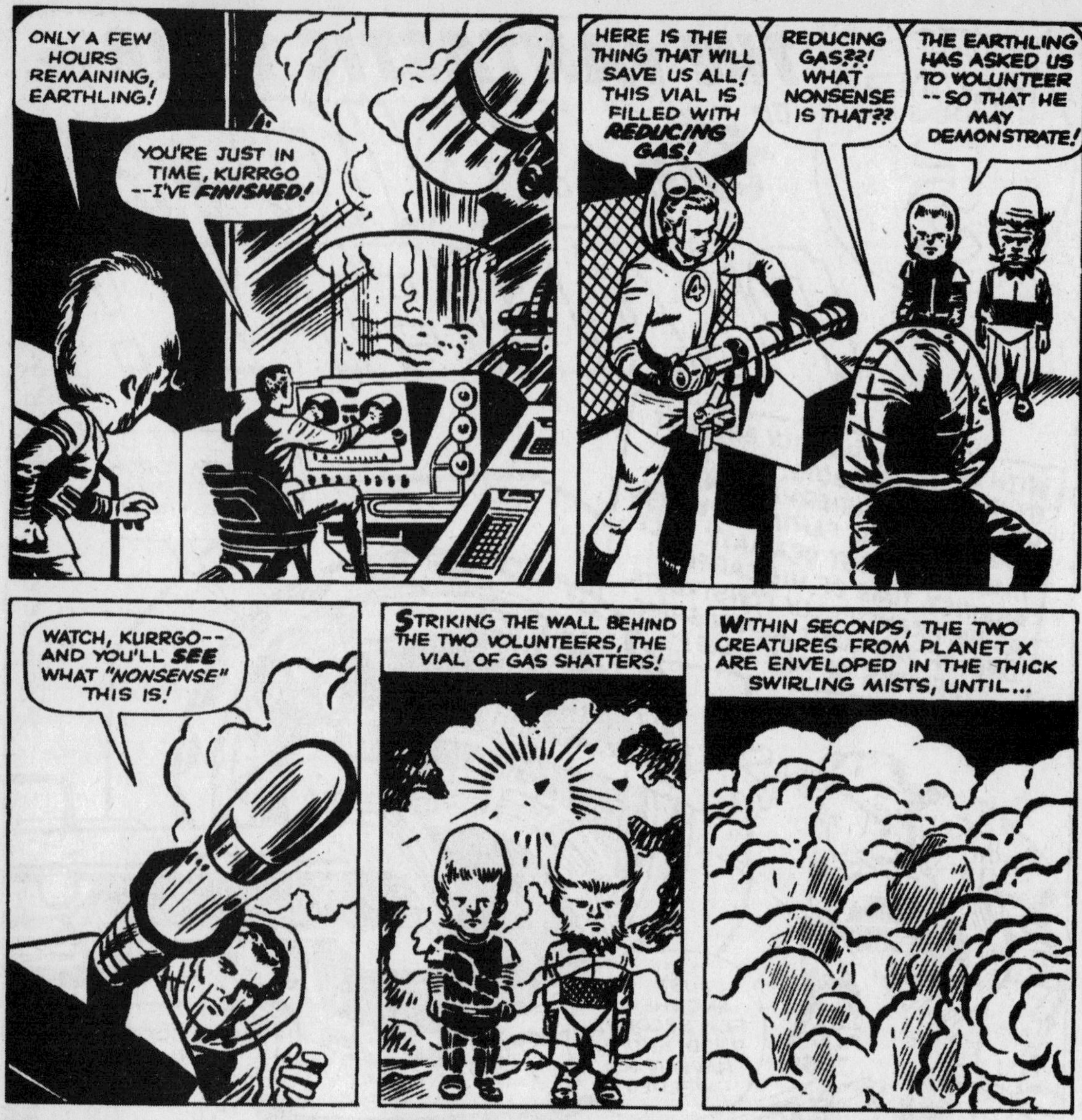
ONLY A FEW HOURS REMAINING, EARTHLING!
YOU'RE JUST IN TIME, KURRGO --I'VE FINISHED!
HERE IS THE THING THAT WILL SAVE US ALL! THIS VIAL IS FILLED WITH REDUCING GAS!
REDUCING GAS??! WHAT NONSENSE IS THAT??
THE EARTHLING HAS ASKED US TO VOLUNTEER --SO THAT HE MAY DEMONSTRATE!
WATCH, KURRGO-- AND YOU'LL SEE WHAT "NONSENSE" THIS IS!
STRIKING THE WALL BEHIND THE TWO VOLUNTEERS, THE VIAL OF GAS SHATTERS!
WITHIN SECONDS, THE TWO CREATURES FROM PLANET X ARE ENVELOPED IN THE THICK SWIRLING MISTS, UNTIL...
THEY- THEY'RE GONE!
NO, KURRGO! NOT GONE!
THEY'VE MERELY BEEN REDUCED IN SIZE! REDUCED A THOUSANDFOLD!
IT- IT IS INCREDIBLE! BUT OF WHAT USE ARE SUCH ELABORATE PARLOR TRICKS?? HOW WILL THIS SAVE PLANET X???
21

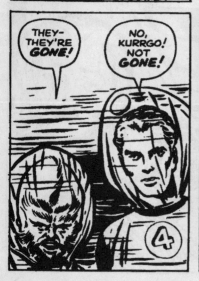

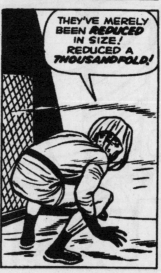

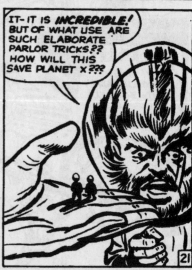

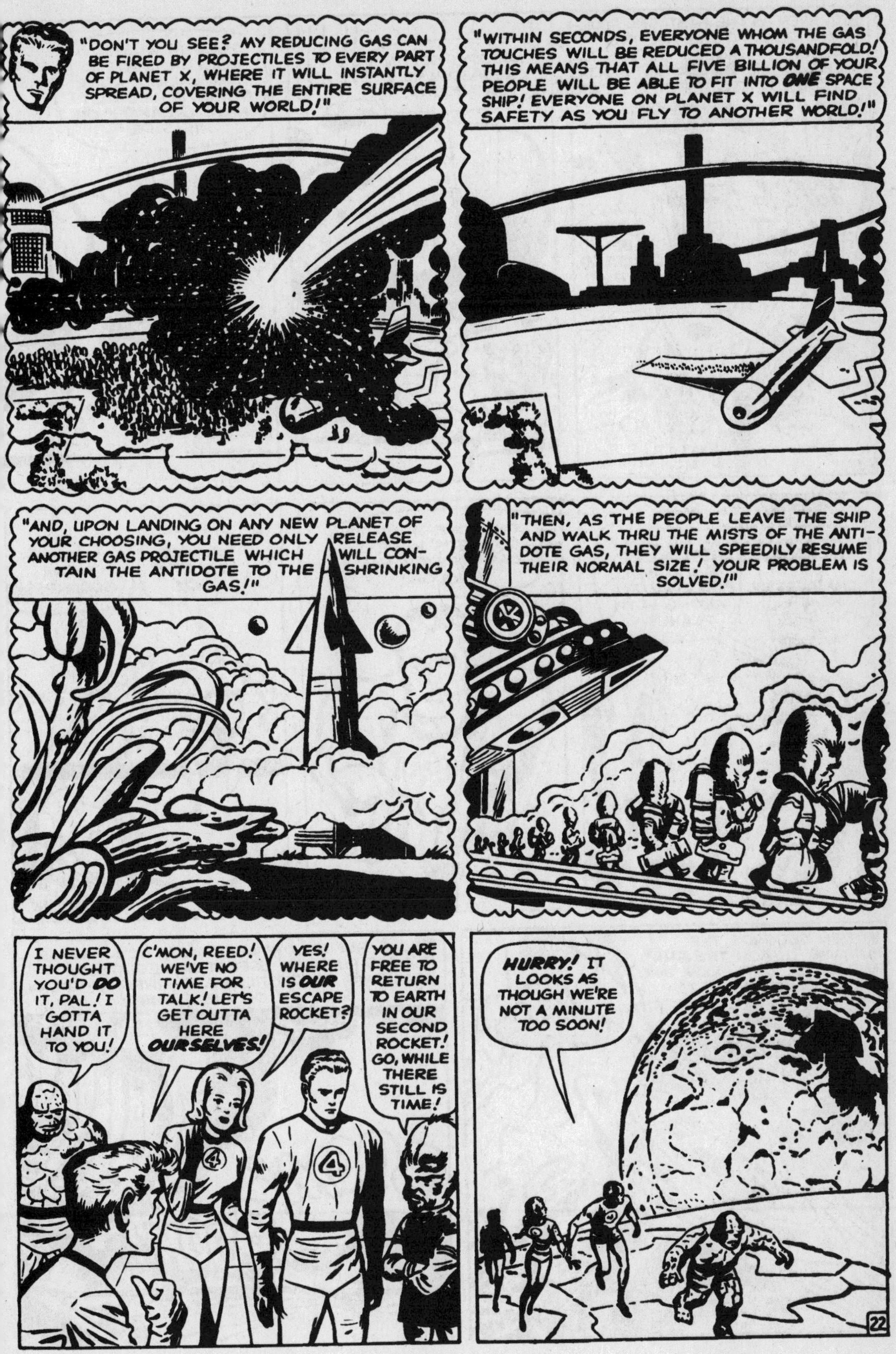
"DON'T YOU SEE? MY REDUCING GAS CAN BE FIRED BY PROJECTILES TO EVERY PART OF PLANET X, WHERE IT WILL INSTANTLY SPREAD, COVERING THE ENTIRE SURFACE OF YOUR WORLD!"
"WITHIN SECONDS, EVERYONE WHOM THE GAS TOUCHES WILL BE REDUCED A THOUSANDFOLD! THIS MEANS THAT ALL FIVE BILLION OF YOUR PEOPLE WILL BE ABLE TO FIT INTO ONE SPACE SHIP! EVERYONE ON PLANET X WILL FIND SAFETY AS YOU FLY TO ANOTHER WORLD!"
"AND, UPON LANDING ON ANY NEW PLANET OF YOUR CHOOSING, YOU NEED ONLY RELEASE ANOTHER GAS PROJECTILE WHICH WILL CONTAIN THE ANTIDOTE TO THE SHRINKING GAS!"
"THEN, AS THE PEOPLE LEAVE THE SHIP AND WALK THRU THE MISTS OF THE ANTIDOTE GAS, THEY WILL SPEEDILY RESUME THEIR NORMAL SIZE! YOUR PROBLEM IS SOLVED!"
I NEVER THOUGHT YOU'D DO IT, PAL! I GOTTA HAND IT TO YOU!
C'MON, REED! WE'VE NO TIME FOR TALK! LET'S GET OUTTA HERE OURSELVES!
YES! WHERE IS OUR ESCAPE ROCKET?
YOU ARE FREE TO RETURN TO EARTH IN OUR SECOND ROCKET! GO, WHILE THERE STILL IS TIME!
HURRY! IT LOOKS AS THOUGH WE'RE NOT A MINUTE TOO SOON!
22

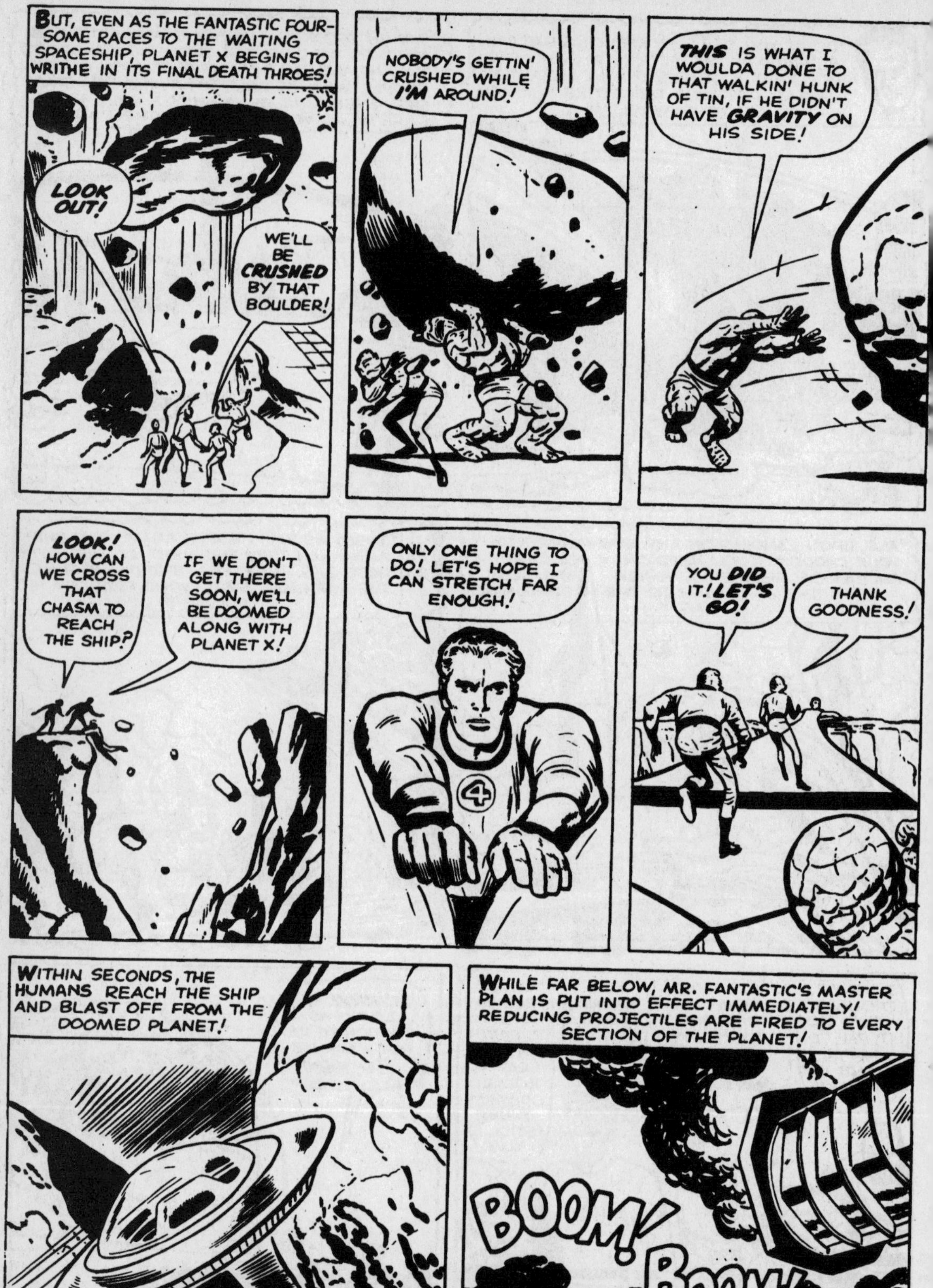

BUT, EVEN AS THE FANTASTIC FOURSOME RACES TO THE WAITING SPACESHIP, PLANET X BEGINS TO WRITHE IN ITS FINAL DEATH THROES!
LOOK OUT!
WE'LL BE CRUSHED BY THAT BOULDER!
NOBODY'S GETTIN' CRUSHED WHILE I'M AROUND!
THIS IS WHAT I WOULDA DONE TO THAT WALKIN' HUNK OF TIN, IF HE DIDN'T HAVE GRAVITY ON HIS SIDE!
LOOK! HOW CAN WE CROSS THAT CHASM TO REACH THE SHIP?
IF WE DON'T GET THERE SOON, WE'LL BE DOOMED ALONG WITH PLANET X!
ONLY ONE THING TO DO! LET'S HOPE I CAN STRETCH FAR ENOUGH!
YOU DID IT! LET'S GO!
THANK GOODNESS!
WITHIN SECONDS, THE HUMANS REACH THE SHIP AND BLAST OFF FROM THE DOOMED PLANET!
WHILE FAR BELOW, MR. FANTASTIC'S MASTER PLAN IS PUT INTO EFFECT IMMEDIATELY! REDUCING PROJECTILES ARE FIRED TO EVERY SECTION OF THE PLANET!
BOOM! BOOM!

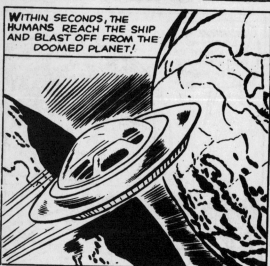

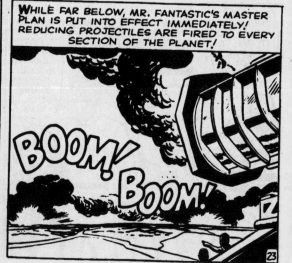

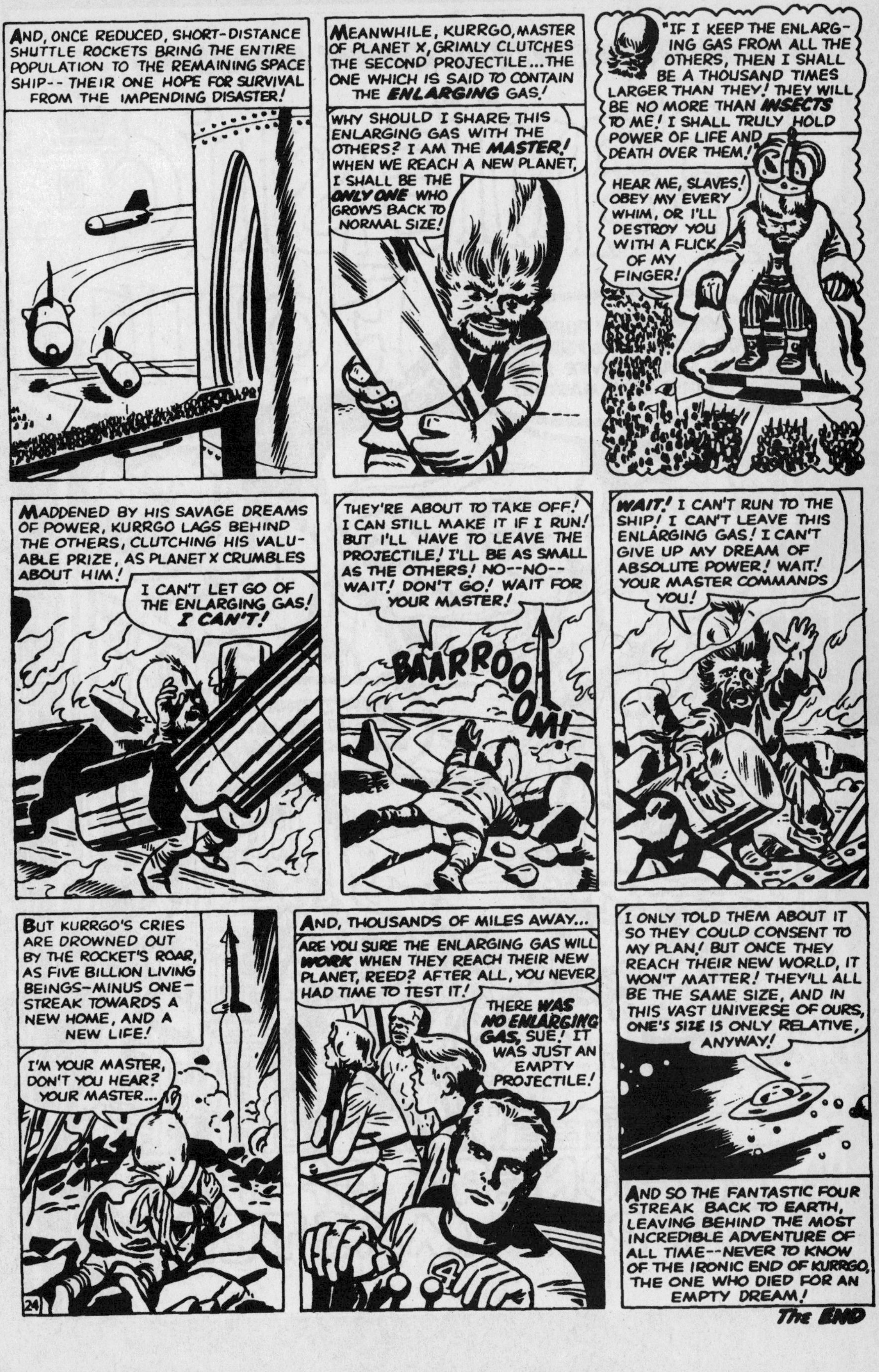
AND, ONCE REDUCED, SHORT-DISTANCE SHUTTLE ROCKETS BRING THE ENTIRE POPULATION TO THE REMAINING SPACE SHIP-- THEIR ONE HOPE FOR SURVIVAL FROM THE IMPENDING DISASTER!
MEANWHILE, KURRGO, MASTER OF PLANET X, GRIMLY CLUTCHES THE SECOND PROJECTILE... THE ONE WHICH IS SAID TO CONTAIN THE ENLARGING GAS!
WHY SHOULD I SHARE THIS ENLARGING GAS WITH THE OTHERS? I AM THE MASTER! WHEN WE REACH A NEW PLANET, I SHALL BE THE ONLY ONE WHO GROWS BACK TO NORMAL SIZE!
"IF I KEEP THE ENLARGING GAS FROM ALL THE OTHERS, THEN I SHALL BE A THOUSAND TIMES LARGER THAN THEY! THEY WILL BE NO MORE THAN INSECTS TO ME! I SHALL TRULY HOLD POWER OF LIFE AND DEATH OVER THEM!"
HEAR ME, SLAVES! OBEY MY EVERY WHIM, OR I'LL DESTROY YOU WITH A FLICK OF MY FINGER!
MADDENED BY HIS SAVAGE DREAMS OF POWER, KURRGO LAGS BEHIND THE OTHERS, CLUTCHING HIS VALUABLE PRIZE, AS PLANET X CRUMBLES ABOUT HIM!
I CAN'T LET GO OF THE ENLARGING GAS! I CAN'T!
THEY'RE ABOUT TO TAKE OFF! I CAN STILL MAKE IT IF I RUN! BUT I'LL HAVE TO LEAVE THE PROJECTILE! I'LL BE AS SMALL AS THE OTHERS! NO--NO-- WAIT! DON'T GO! WAIT FOR YOUR MASTER!
BAARROOOOM!
WAIT! I CAN'T RUN TO THE SHIP! I CAN'T LEAVE THIS ENLARGING GAS! I CAN'T GIVE UP MY DREAM OF ABSOLUTE POWER! WAIT! YOUR MASTER COMMANDS YOU!
BUT KURRGO'S CRIES ARE DROWNED OUT BY THE ROCKET'S ROAR, AS FIVE BILLION LIVING BEINGS-MINUS ONE- STREAK TOWARDS A NEW HOME, AND A NEW LIFE!
I'M YOUR MASTER, DON'T YOU HEAR? YOUR MASTER...
AND, THOUSANDS OF MILES AWAY...
ARE YOU SURE THE ENLARGING GAS WILL WORK WHEN THEY REACH THEIR NEW PLANET, REED? AFTER ALL, YOU NEVER HAD TIME TO TEST IT!
THERE WAS NO ENLARGING GAS, SUE! IT WAS JUST AN EMPTY PROJECTILE!
I ONLY TOLD THEM ABOUT IT SO THEY COULD CONSENT TO MY PLAN! BUT ONCE THEY REACH THEIR NEW WORLD, IT WON'T MATTER! THEY'LL ALL BE THE SAME SIZE, AND IN THIS VAST UNIVERSE OF OURS, ONE'S SIZE IS ONLY RELATIVE, ANYWAY!
AND SO THE FANTASTIC FOUR STREAK BACK TO EARTH, LEAVING BEHIND THE MOST INCREDIBLE ADVENTURE OF ALL TIME--NEVER TO KNOW OF THE IRONIC END OF KURRGO, THE ONE WHO DIED FOR AN EMPTY DREAM!
24
The END

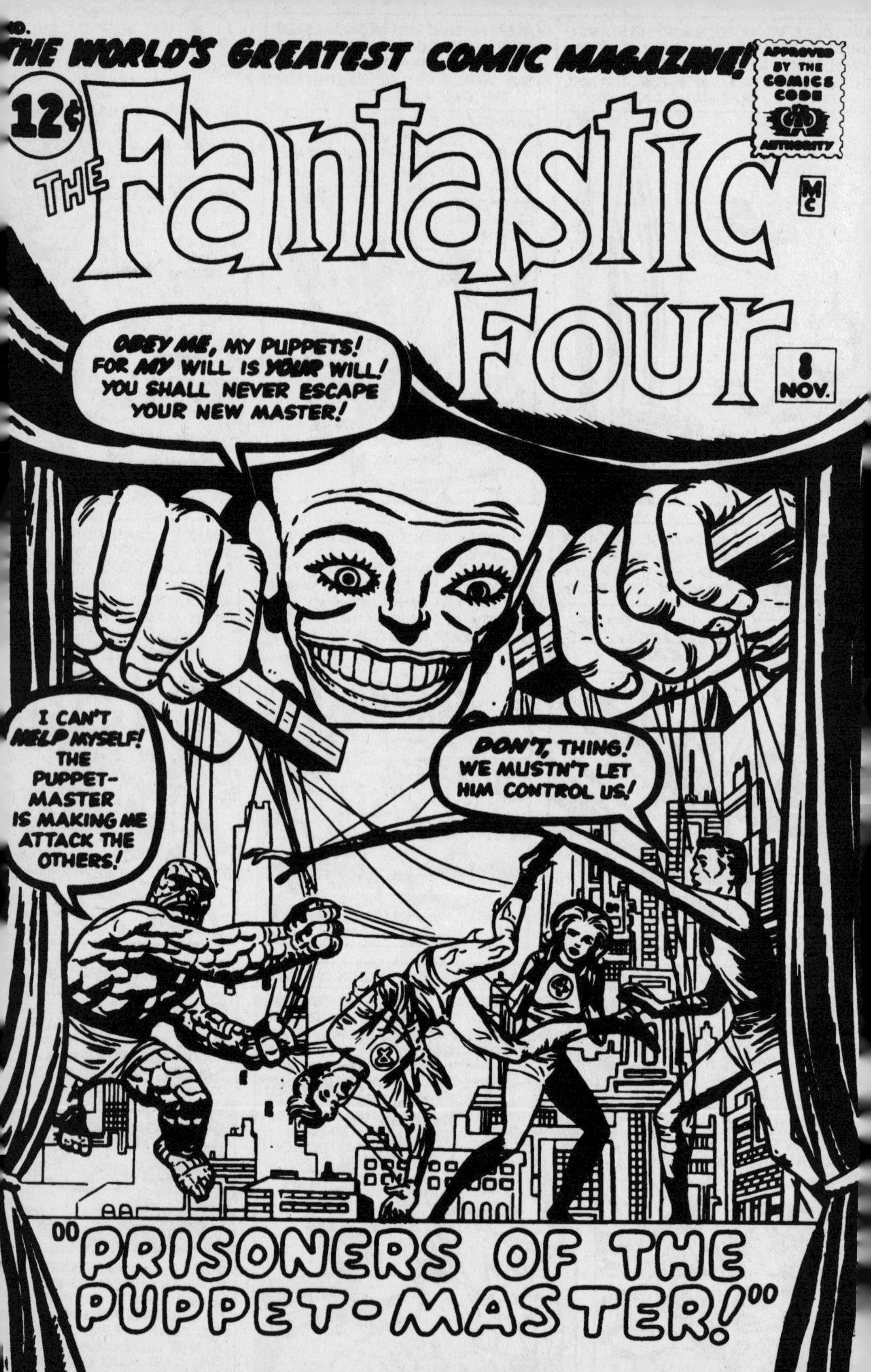
NO.
THE WORLD'S GREATEST COMIC MAGAZINE!
APPROVED BY THE COMICS CODE AUTHORITY
12¢
THE Fantastic Four
MC
8 NOV.
OBEY ME, MY PUPPETS! FOR MY WILL IS YOUR WILL! YOU SHALL NEVER ESCAPE YOUR NEW MASTER!
I CAN'T HELP MYSELF! THE PUPPET-MASTER IS MAKING ME ATTACK THE OTHERS!
DON'T, THING! WE MUSTN'T LET HIM CONTROL US!
"PRISONERS OF THE PUPPET-MASTER!"

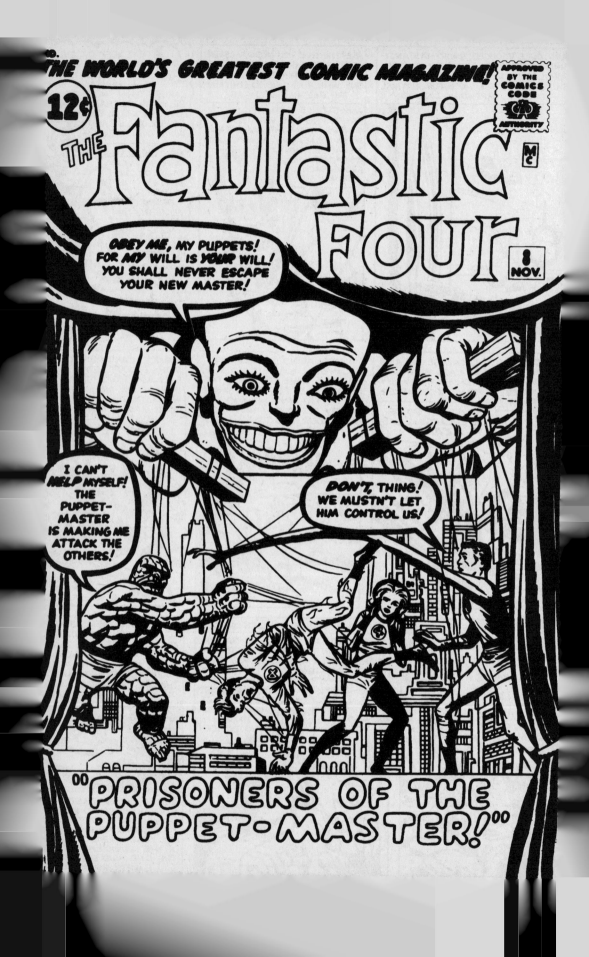

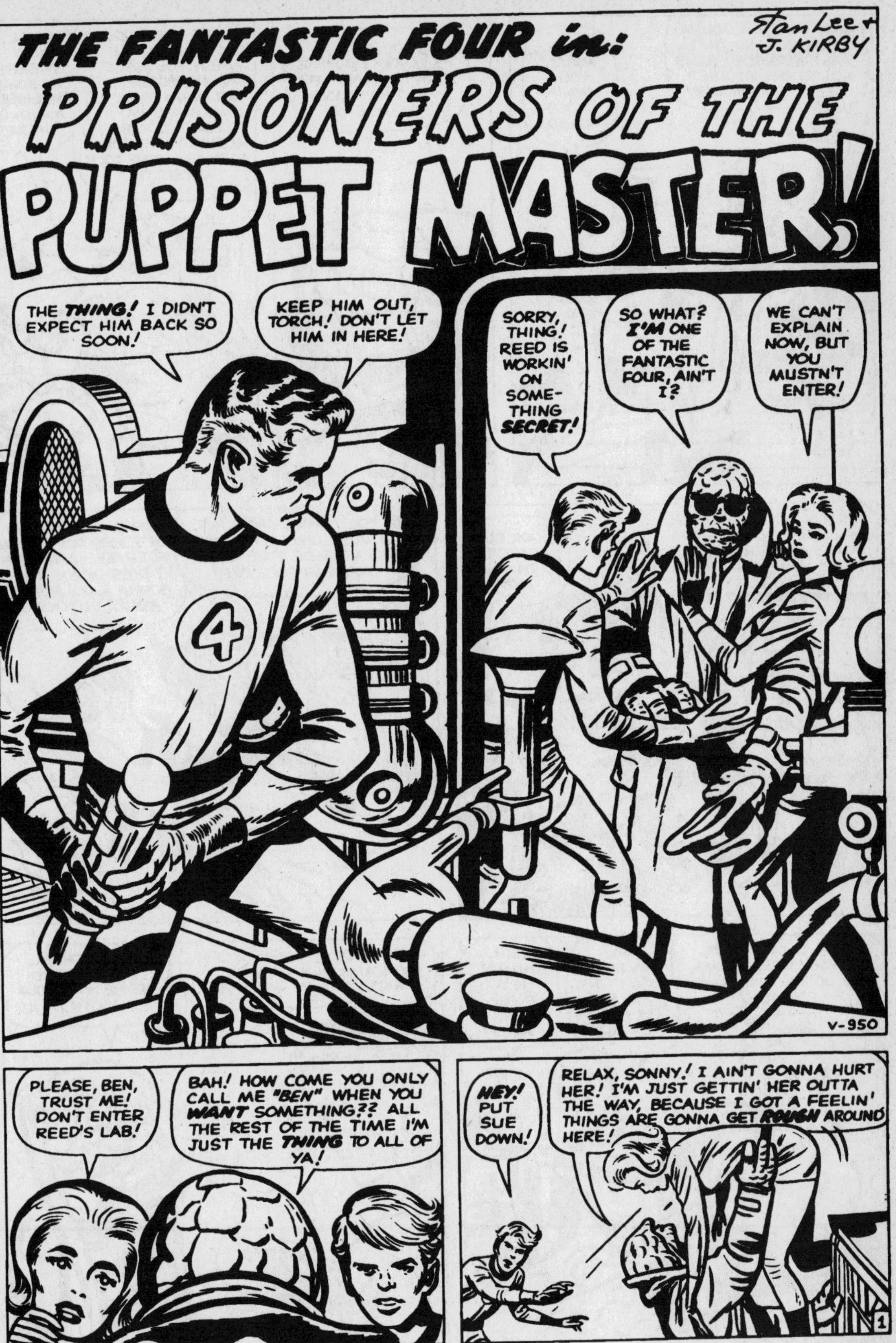
Stan Lee + J. KIRBY
THE FANTASTIC FOUR in: PRISONERS OF THE PUPPET MASTER!
THE THING! I DIDN'T EXPECT HIM BACK SO SOON!
KEEP HIM OUT, TORCH! DON'T LET HIM IN HERE!
SORRY, THING! REED IS WORKIN' ON SOME-THING SECRET!
SO WHAT? I'M ONE OF THE FANTASTIC FOUR, AIN'T I?
WE CAN'T EXPLAIN NOW, BUT YOU MUSTN'T ENTER!
V-950
PLEASE, BEN, TRUST ME! DON'T ENTER REED'S LAB!
BAH! HOW COME YOU ONLY CALL ME "BEN" WHEN YOU WANT SOMETHING?? ALL THE REST OF THE TIME I'M JUST THE THING TO ALL OF YA!
HEY! PUT SUE DOWN!
RELAX, SONNY! I AIN'T GONNA HURT HER! I'M JUST GETTIN' HER OUTTA THE WAY, BECAUSE I GOT A FEELIN' THINGS ARE GONNA GET ROUGH AROUND HERE!
1

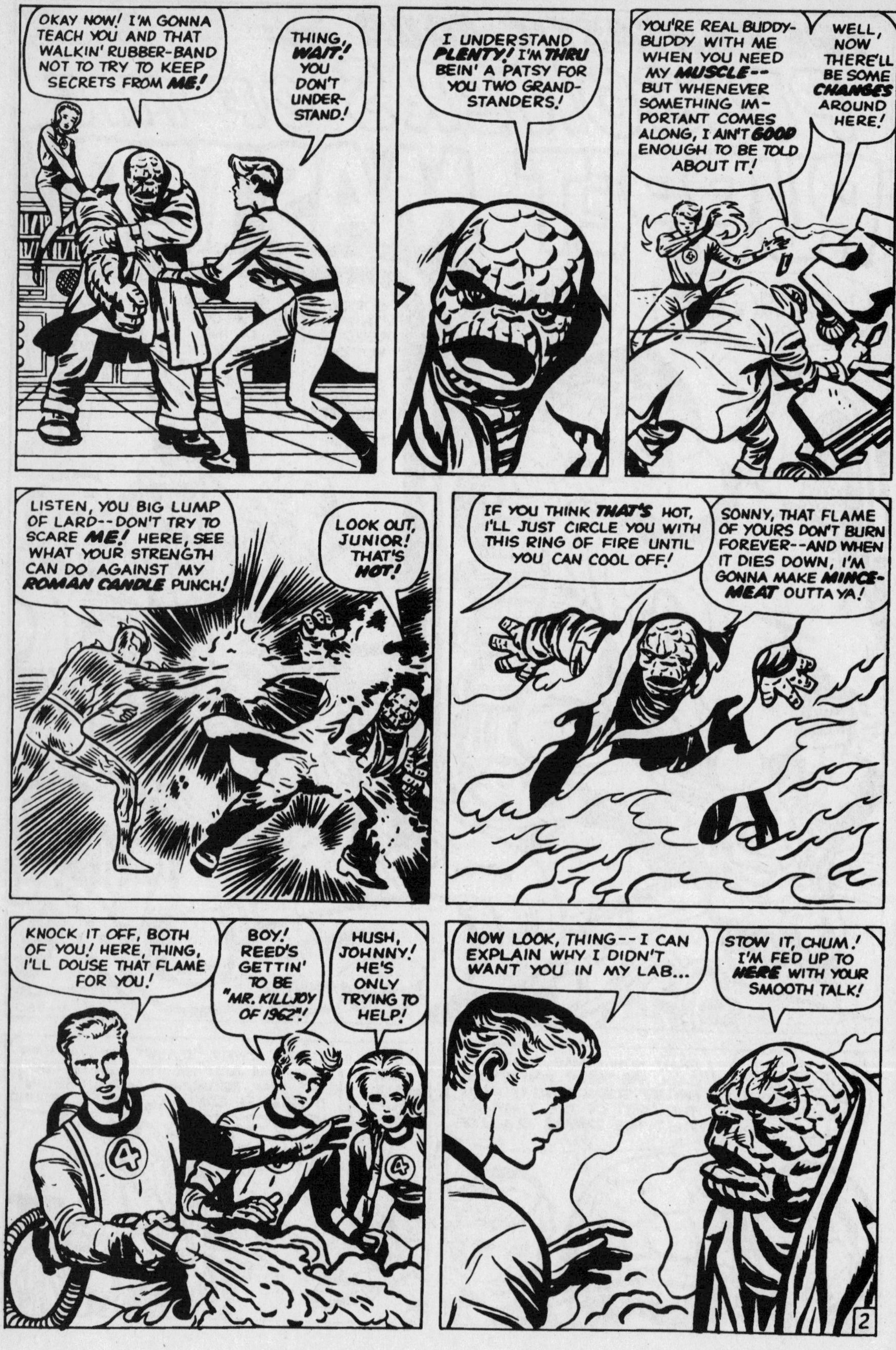
OKAY NOW! I'M GONNA TEACH YOU AND THAT WALKIN' RUBBER-BAND NOT TO TRY TO KEEP SECRETS FROM ME!
THING, WAIT! YOU DON'T UNDER-STAND!
I UNDERSTAND PLENTY! I'M THRU BEIN' A PATSY FOR YOU TWO GRAND-STANDERS!
YOU'RE REAL BUDDY-BUDDY WITH ME WHEN YOU NEED MY MUSCLE-- BUT WHENEVER SOMETHING IM-PORTANT COMES ALONG, I AIN'T GOOD ENOUGH TO BE TOLD ABOUT IT!
WELL, NOW THERE'LL BE SOME CHANGES AROUND HERE!
LISTEN, YOU BIG LUMP OF LARD--DON'T TRY TO SCARE ME! HERE, SEE WHAT YOUR STRENGTH CAN DO AGAINST MY ROMAN CANDLE PUNCH!
LOOK OUT, JUNIOR! THAT'S HOT!
IF YOU THINK THAT'S HOT, I'LL JUST CIRCLE YOU WITH THIS RING OF FIRE UNTIL YOU CAN COOL OFF!
SONNY, THAT FLAME OF YOURS DON'T BURN FOREVER--AND WHEN IT DIES DOWN, I'M GONNA MAKE MINCE-MEAT OUTTA YA!
KNOCK IT OFF, BOTH OF YOU! HERE, THING, I'LL DOUSE THAT FLAME FOR YOU!
BOY! REED'S GETTIN' TO BE "MR. KILLJOY OF 1962"!
HUSH, JOHNNY! HE'S ONLY TRYING TO HELP!
NOW LOOK, THING--I CAN EXPLAIN WHY I DIDN'T WANT YOU IN MY LAB...
STOW IT, CHUM! I'M FED UP TO HERE WITH YOUR SMOOTH TALK!

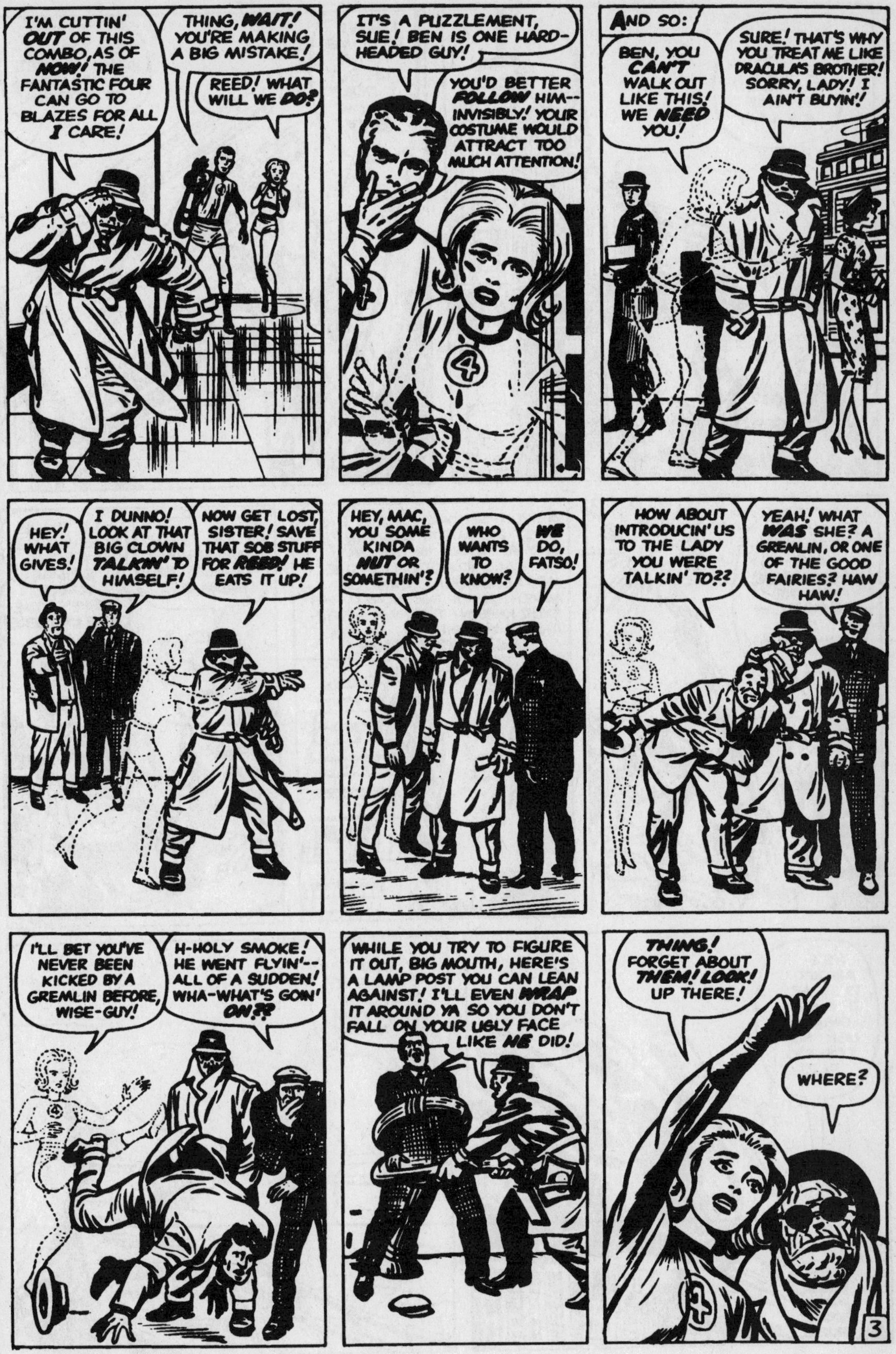
I'M CUTTIN' OUT OF THIS COMBO, AS OF NOW! THE FANTASTIC FOUR CAN GO TO BLAZES FOR ALL I CARE!
THING, WAIT! YOU'RE MAKING A BIG MISTAKE!
REED! WHAT WILL WE DO?
IT'S A PUZZLEMENT, SUE! BEN IS ONE HARD-HEADED GUY!
YOU'D BETTER FOLLOW HIM-- INVISIBLY! YOUR COSTUME WOULD ATTRACT TOO MUCH ATTENTION!
AND SO:
BEN, YOU CAN'T WALK OUT LIKE THIS! WE NEED YOU!
SURE! THAT'S WHY YOU TREAT ME LIKE DRACULA'S BROTHER! SORRY, LADY! I AIN'T BUYIN'!
HEY! WHAT GIVES!
I DUNNO! LOOK AT THAT BIG CLOWN TALKIN' TO HIMSELF!
NOW GET LOST, SISTER! SAVE THAT SOB STUFF FOR REED! HE EATS IT UP!
HEY, MAC, YOU SOME KINDA NUT OR SOMETHIN'?
WHO WANTS TO KNOW?
WE DO, FATSO!
HOW ABOUT INTRODUCIN' US TO THE LADY YOU WERE TALKIN' TO??
YEAH! WHAT WAS SHE? A GREMLIN, OR ONE OF THE GOOD FAIRIES? HAW HAW!
I'LL BET YOU'VE NEVER BEEN KICKED BY A GREMLIN BEFORE, WISE-GUY!
H-HOLY SMOKE! HE WENT FLYIN'-- ALL OF A SUDDEN! WHA-WHAT'S GOIN' ON??
WHILE YOU TRY TO FIGURE IT OUT, BIG MOUTH, HERE'S A LAMP POST YOU CAN LEAN AGAINST! I'LL EVEN WRAP IT AROUND YA SO YOU DON'T FALL ON YOUR UGLY FACE LIKE HE DID!
THING! FORGET ABOUT THEM! LOOK! UP THERE!
WHERE?
3

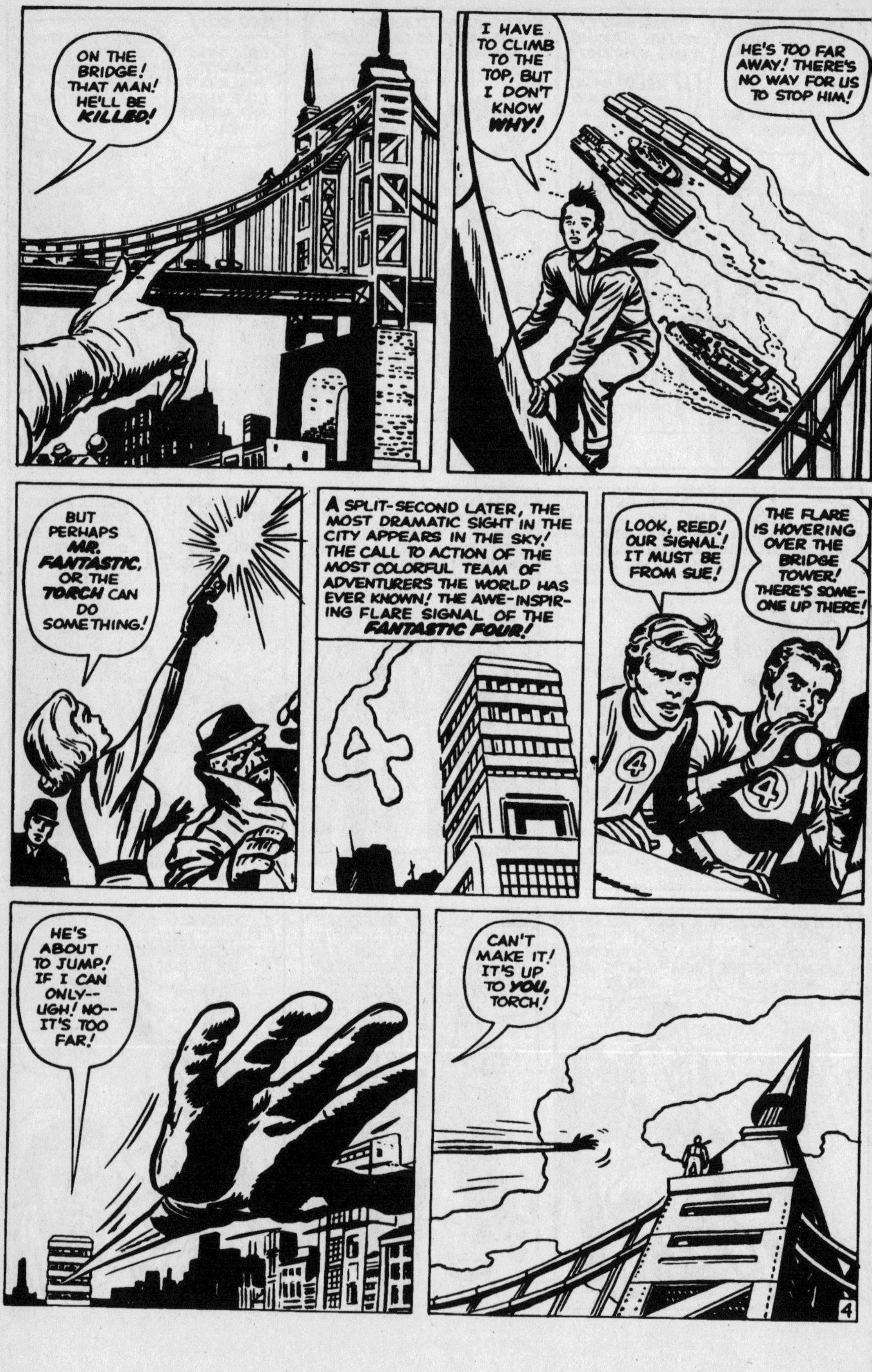

ON THE BRIDGE! THAT MAN! HE'LL BE KILLED!
I HAVE TO CLIMB TO THE TOP, BUT I DON'T KNOW WHY!
HE'S TOO FAR AWAY! THERE'S NO WAY FOR US TO STOP HIM!
BUT PERHAPS MR. FANTASTIC, OR THE TORCH CAN DO SOMETHING!
A SPLIT-SECOND LATER, THE MOST DRAMATIC SIGHT IN THE CITY APPEARS IN THE SKY! THE CALL TO ACTION OF THE MOST COLORFUL TEAM OF ADVENTURERS THE WORLD HAS EVER KNOWN! THE AWE-INSPIRING FLARE SIGNAL OF THE FANTASTIC FOUR!
LOOK, REED! OUR SIGNAL! IT MUST BE FROM SUE!
THE FLARE IS HOVERING OVER THE BRIDGE TOWER! THERE'S SOMEONE UP THERE!
HE'S ABOUT TO JUMP! IF I CAN ONLY-- UGH! NO-- IT'S TOO FAR!
CAN'T MAKE IT! IT'S UP TO YOU, TORCH!
4

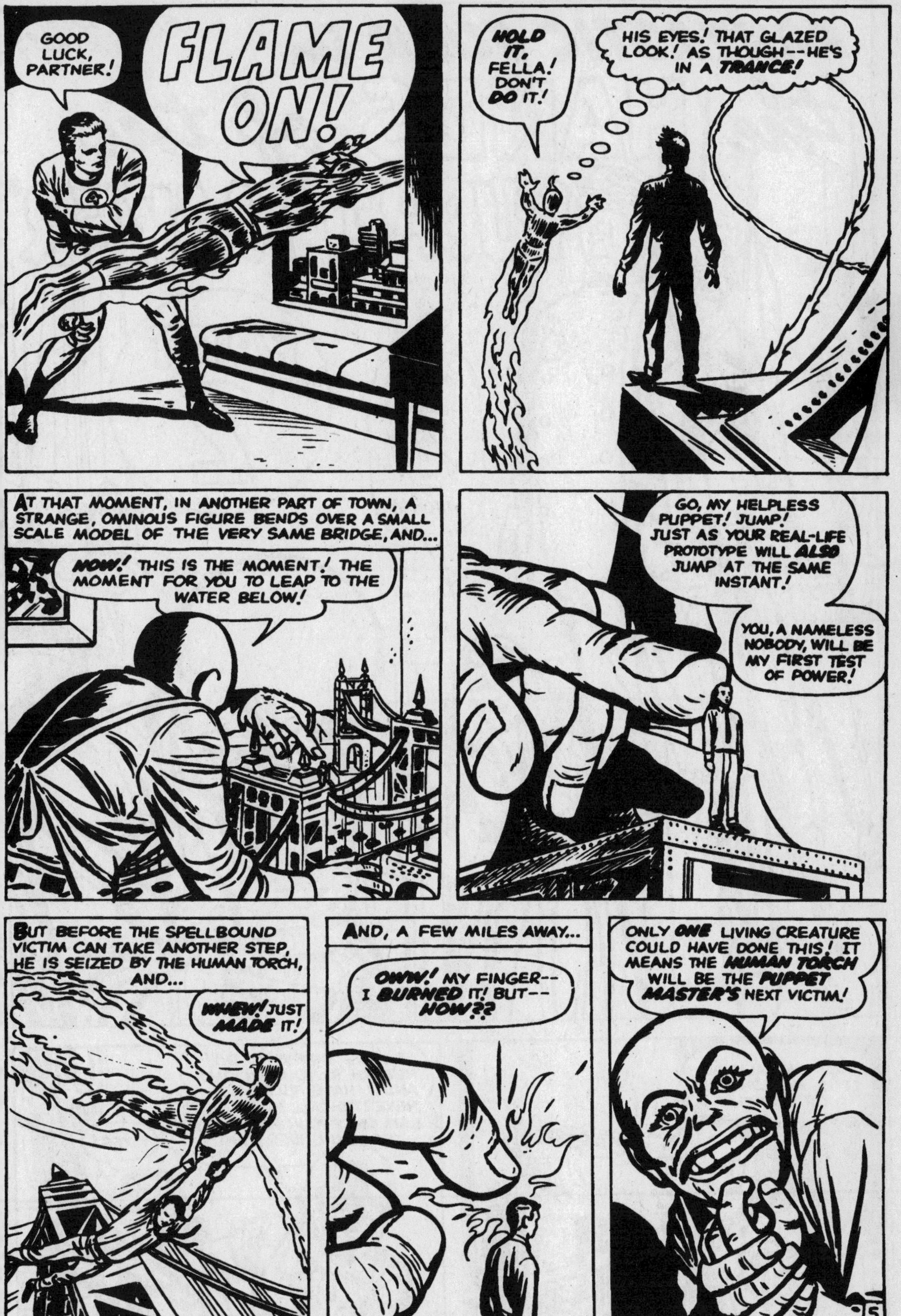

GOOD LUCK, PARTNER!
FLAME ON!
HOLD IT, FELLA! DON'T DO IT!
HIS EYES! THAT GLAZED LOOK! AS THOUGH--HE'S IN A TRANCE!
AT THAT MOMENT, IN ANOTHER PART OF TOWN, A STRANGE, OMINOUS FIGURE BENDS OVER A SMALL SCALE MODEL OF THE VERY SAME BRIDGE, AND...
NOW! THIS IS THE MOMENT! THE MOMENT FOR YOU TO LEAP TO THE WATER BELOW!
GO, MY HELPLESS PUPPET! JUMP! JUST AS YOUR REAL-LIFE PROTOTYPE WILL ALSO JUMP AT THE SAME INSTANT!
YOU, A NAMELESS NOBODY, WILL BE MY FIRST TEST OF POWER!
BUT BEFORE THE SPELLBOUND VICTIM CAN TAKE ANOTHER STEP, HE IS SEIZED BY THE HUMAN TORCH, AND...
WHEW! JUST MADE IT!
AND, A FEW MILES AWAY...
OWW! MY FINGER-- I BURNED IT! BUT-- HOW??
ONLY ONE LIVING CREATURE COULD HAVE DONE THIS! IT MEANS THE HUMAN TORCH WILL BE THE PUPPET MASTER'S NEXT VICTIM!
5

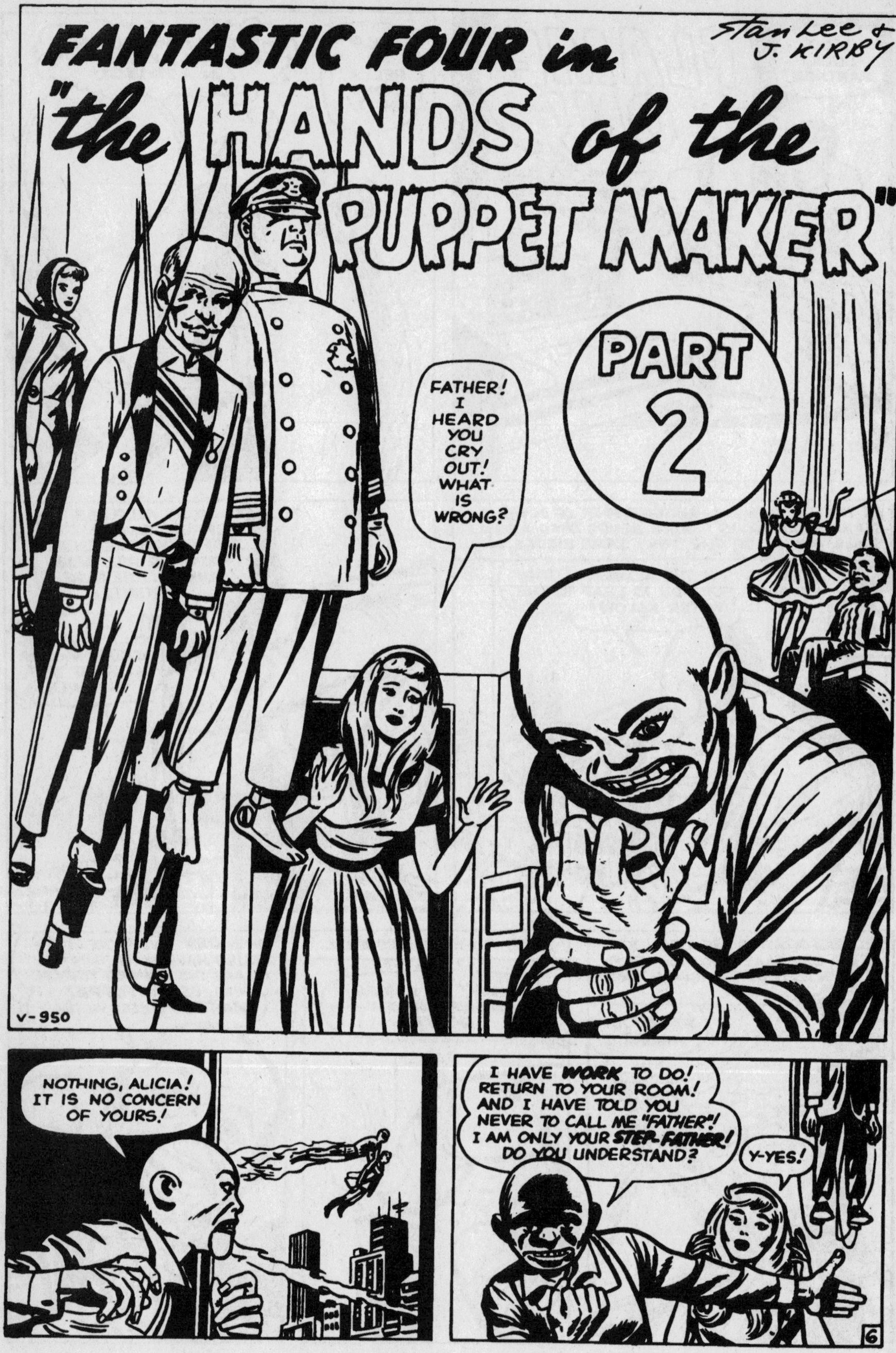
FANTASTIC FOUR in
"the HANDS of the PUPPET MAKER"
Stan Lee & J. KIRBY
PART 2
FATHER! I HEARD YOU CRY OUT! WHAT IS WRONG?
V-950
NOTHING, ALICIA! IT IS NO CONCERN OF YOURS!
I HAVE WORK TO DO! RETURN TO YOUR ROOM! AND I HAVE TOLD YOU NEVER TO CALL ME "FATHER"! I AM ONLY YOUR STEP-FATHER! DO YOU UNDERSTAND?
Y-YES!
6

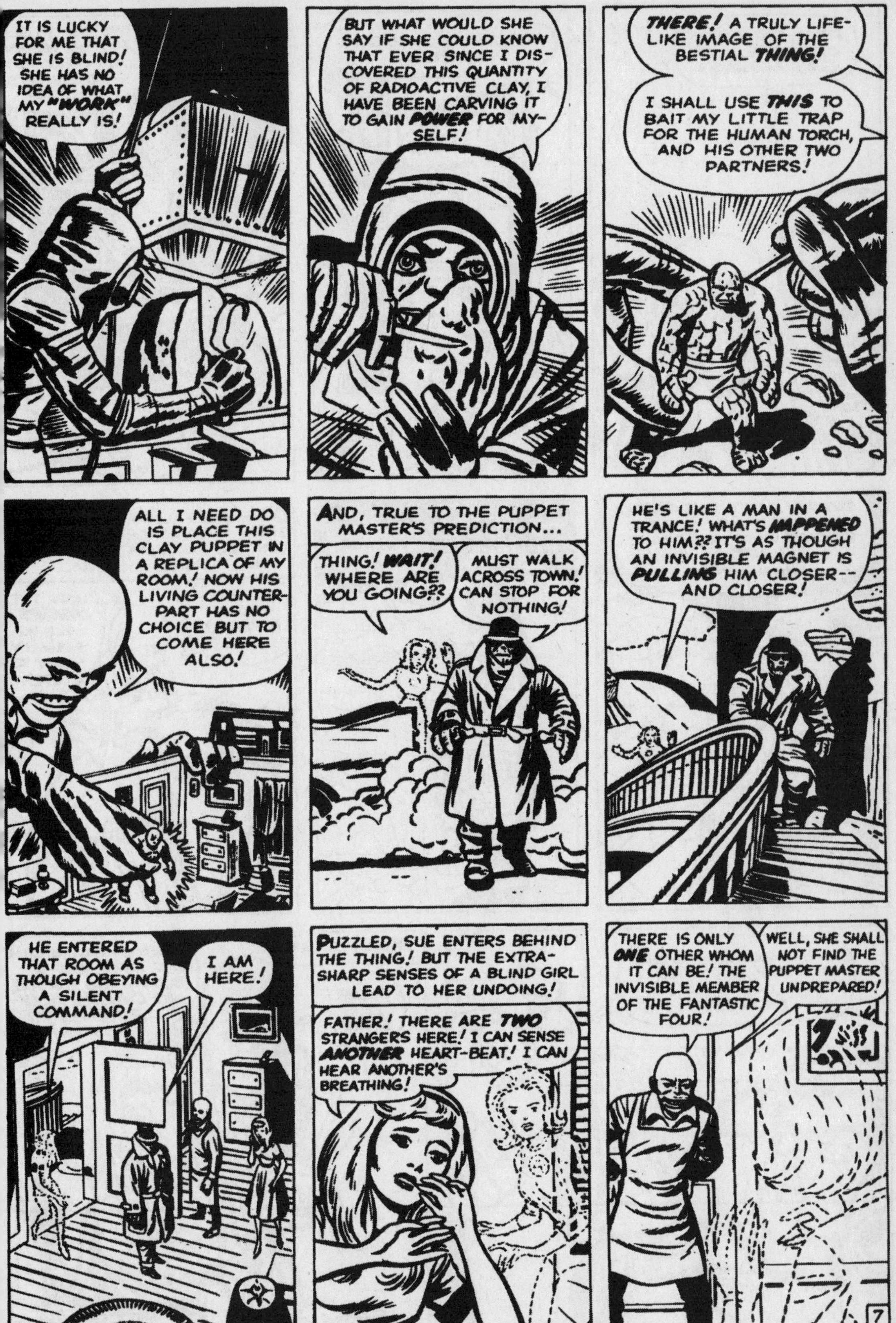
IT IS LUCKY FOR ME THAT SHE IS BLIND! SHE HAS NO IDEA OF WHAT MY "WORK" REALLY IS!
BUT WHAT WOULD SHE SAY IF SHE COULD KNOW THAT EVER SINCE I DISCOVERED THIS QUANTITY OF RADIOACTIVE CLAY, I HAVE BEEN CARVING IT TO GAIN POWER FOR MYSELF!
THERE! A TRULY LIFE-LIKE IMAGE OF THE BESTIAL THING!
I SHALL USE THIS TO BAIT MY LITTLE TRAP FOR THE HUMAN TORCH, AND HIS OTHER TWO PARTNERS!
ALL I NEED DO IS PLACE THIS CLAY PUPPET IN A REPLICA OF MY ROOM! NOW HIS LIVING COUNTERPART HAS NO CHOICE BUT TO COME HERE ALSO!
AND, TRUE TO THE PUPPET MASTER'S PREDICTION...
THING! WAIT! WHERE ARE YOU GOING??
MUST WALK ACROSS TOWN! CAN STOP FOR NOTHING!
HE'S LIKE A MAN IN A TRANCE! WHAT'S HAPPENED TO HIM?? IT'S AS THOUGH AN INVISIBLE MAGNET IS PULLING HIM CLOSER-- AND CLOSER!
HE ENTERED THAT ROOM AS THOUGH OBEYING A SILENT COMMAND!
I AM HERE!
PUZZLED, SUE ENTERS BEHIND THE THING! BUT THE EXTRA-SHARP SENSES OF A BLIND GIRL LEAD TO HER UNDOING!
FATHER! THERE ARE TWO STRANGERS HERE! I CAN SENSE ANOTHER HEART-BEAT! I CAN HEAR ANOTHER'S BREATHING!
THERE IS ONLY ONE OTHER WHOM IT CAN BE! THE INVISIBLE MEMBER OF THE FANTASTIC FOUR!
WELL, SHE SHALL NOT FIND THE PUPPET MASTER UNPREPARED!
7

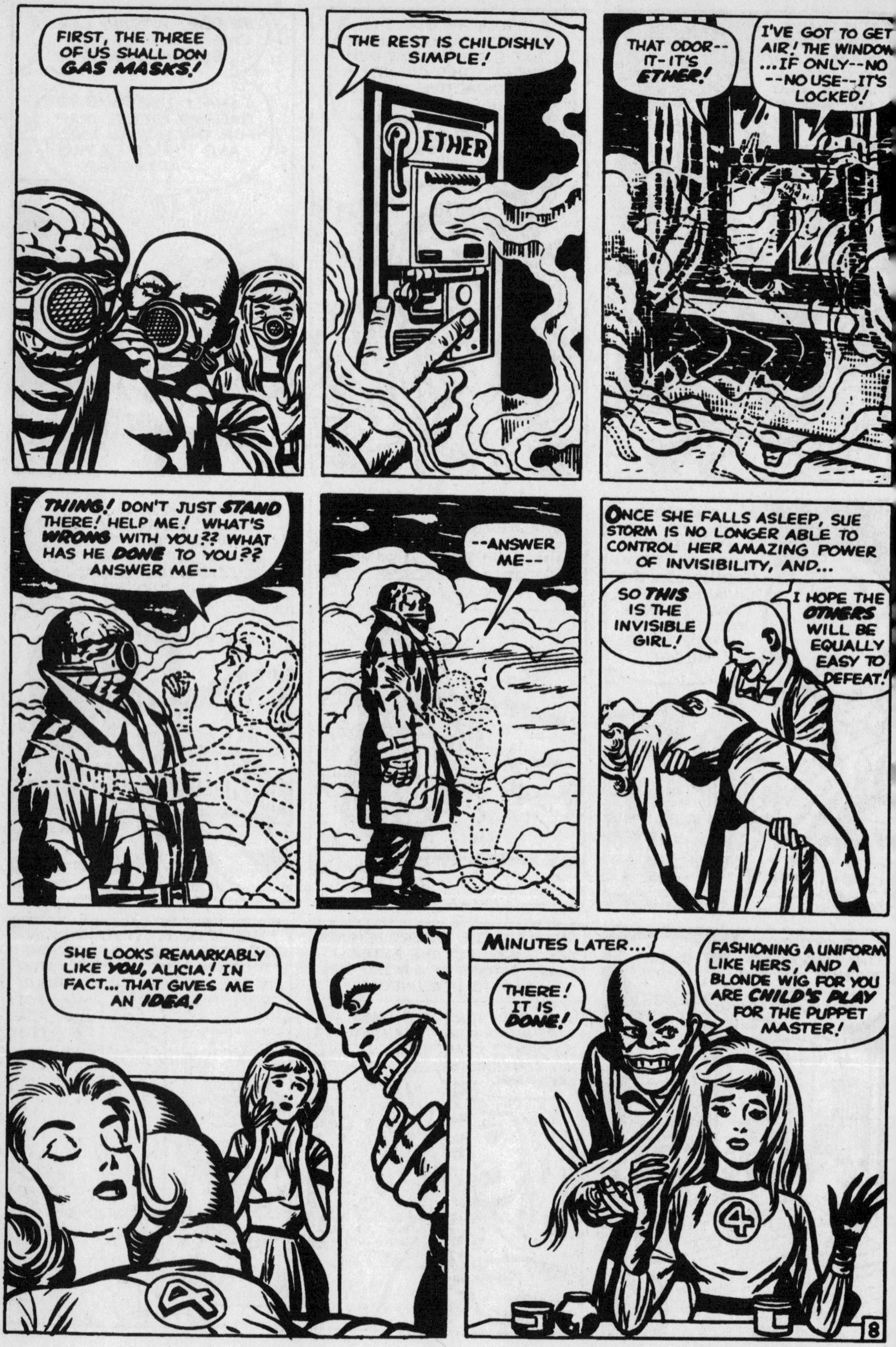
FIRST, THE THREE OF US SHALL DON GAS MASKS!
THE REST IS CHILDISHLY SIMPLE!
ETHER
THAT ODOR-- IT-IT'S ETHER!
I'VE GOT TO GET AIR! THE WINDOW ...IF ONLY--NO --NO USE--IT'S LOCKED!
THING! DON'T JUST STAND THERE! HELP ME! WHAT'S WRONG WITH YOU?? WHAT HAS HE DONE TO YOU?? ANSWER ME--
--ANSWER ME--
ONCE SHE FALLS ASLEEP, SUE STORM IS NO LONGER ABLE TO CONTROL HER AMAZING POWER OF INVISIBILITY, AND...
SO THIS IS THE INVISIBLE GIRL!
I HOPE THE OTHERS WILL BE EQUALLY EASY TO DEFEAT!
SHE LOOKS REMARKABLY LIKE YOU, ALICIA! IN FACT... THAT GIVES ME AN IDEA!
MINUTES LATER...
THERE! IT IS DONE!
FASHIONING A UNIFORM LIKE HERS, AND A BLONDE WIG FOR YOU ARE CHILD'S PLAY FOR THE PUPPET MASTER!
8

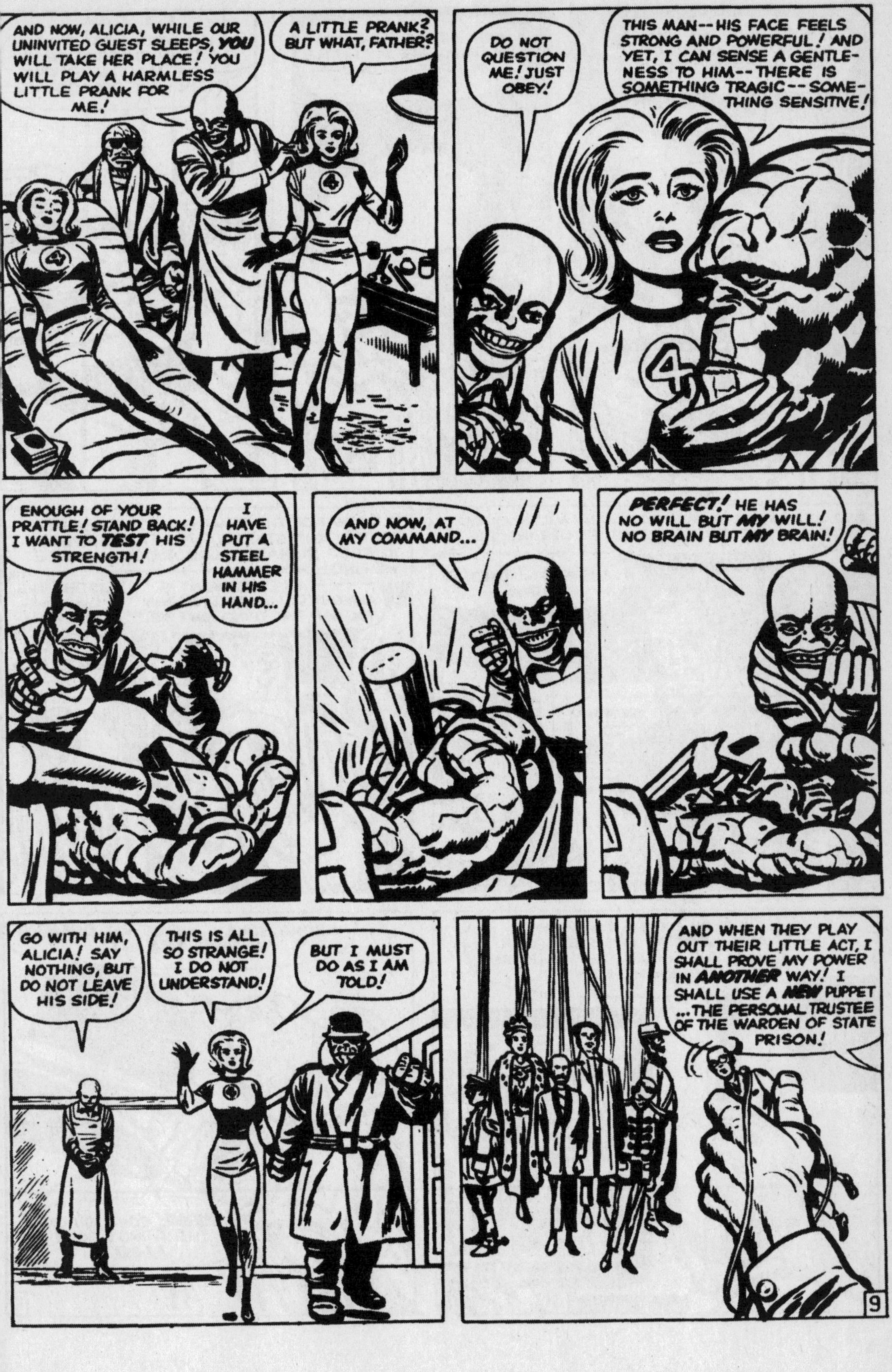
AND NOW, ALICIA, WHILE OUR UNINVITED GUEST SLEEPS, YOU WILL TAKE HER PLACE! YOU WILL PLAY A HARMLESS LITTLE PRANK FOR ME!
A LITTLE PRANK? BUT WHAT, FATHER?
DO NOT QUESTION ME! JUST OBEY!
THIS MAN--HIS FACE FEELS STRONG AND POWERFUL! AND YET, I CAN SENSE A GENTLENESS TO HIM--THERE IS SOMETHING TRAGIC--SOMETHING SENSITIVE!
ENOUGH OF YOUR PRATTLE! STAND BACK! I WANT TO TEST HIS STRENGTH!
I HAVE PUT A STEEL HAMMER IN HIS HAND...
AND NOW, AT MY COMMAND...
PERFECT! HE HAS NO WILL BUT MY WILL! NO BRAIN BUT MY BRAIN!
GO WITH HIM, ALICIA! SAY NOTHING, BUT DO NOT LEAVE HIS SIDE!
THIS IS ALL SO STRANGE! I DO NOT UNDERSTAND!
BUT I MUST DO AS I AM TOLD!
AND WHEN THEY PLAY OUT THEIR LITTLE ACT, I SHALL PROVE MY POWER IN ANOTHER WAY! I SHALL USE A NEW PUPPET ...THE PERSONAL TRUSTEE OF THE WARDEN OF STATE PRISON!
9

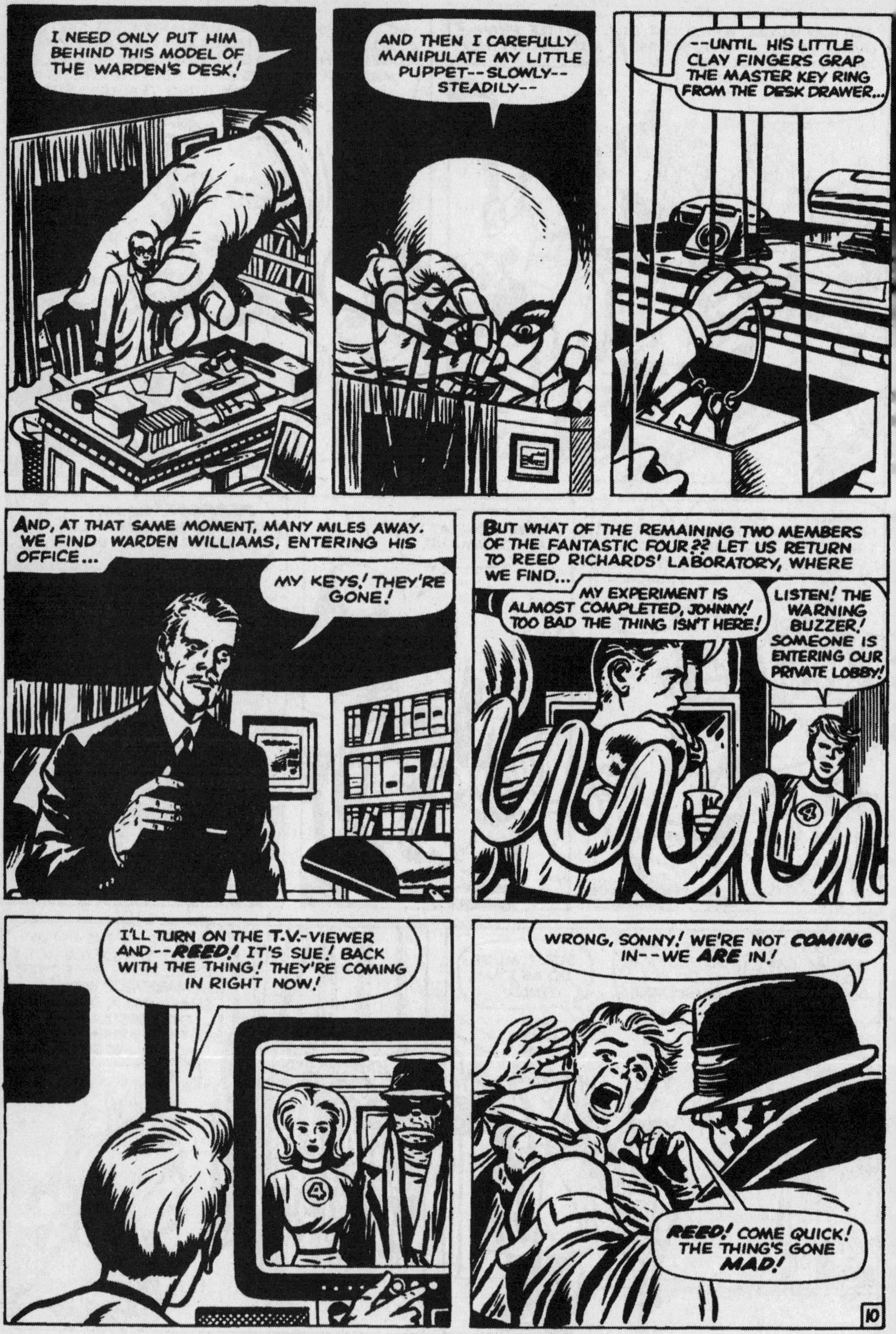
I NEED ONLY PUT HIM BEHIND THIS MODEL OF THE WARDEN'S DESK!
AND THEN I CAREFULLY MANIPULATE MY LITTLE PUPPET--SLOWLY--STEADILY--
--UNTIL HIS LITTLE CLAY FINGERS GRAP THE MASTER KEY RING FROM THE DESK DRAWER...
AND, AT THAT SAME MOMENT, MANY MILES AWAY. WE FIND WARDEN WILLIAMS, ENTERING HIS OFFICE...
MY KEYS! THEY'RE GONE!
BUT WHAT OF THE REMAINING TWO MEMBERS OF THE FANTASTIC FOUR?? LET US RETURN TO REED RICHARDS' LABORATORY, WHERE WE FIND...
MY EXPERIMENT IS ALMOST COMPLETED, JOHNNY! TOO BAD THE THING ISN'T HERE!
LISTEN! THE WARNING BUZZER! SOMEONE IS ENTERING OUR PRIVATE LOBBY!
I'LL TURN ON THE T.V.-VIEWER AND--REED! IT'S SUE! BACK WITH THE THING! THEY'RE COMING IN RIGHT NOW!
WRONG, SONNY! WE'RE NOT COMING IN--WE ARE IN!
REED! COME QUICK! THE THING'S GONE MAD!
10

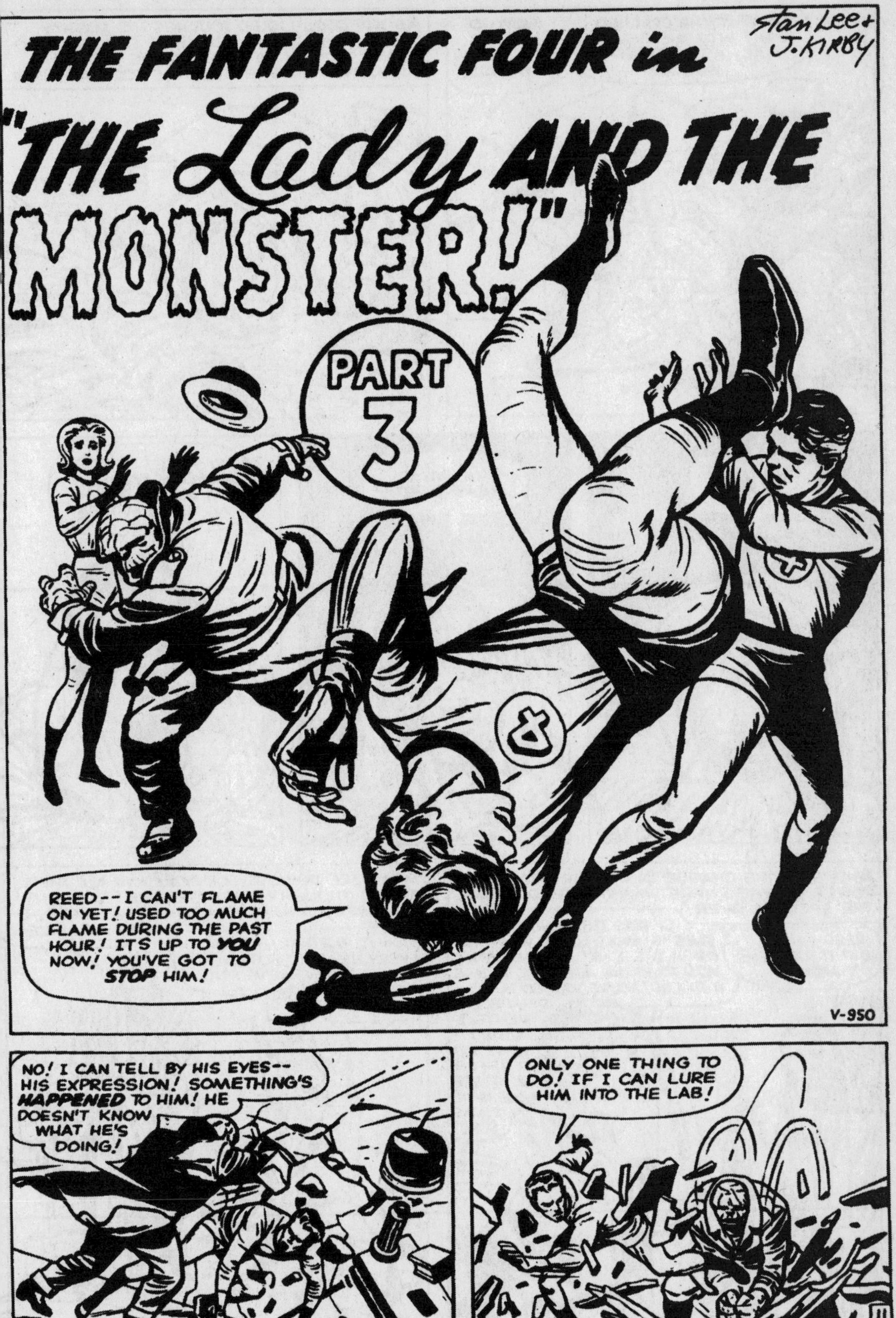
Stan Lee + J. Kirby
THE FANTASTIC FOUR in
"THE Lady AND THE MONSTER!"
PART 3
REED--I CAN'T FLAME ON YET! USED TOO MUCH FLAME DURING THE PAST HOUR! IT'S UP TO YOU NOW! YOU'VE GOT TO STOP HIM!
V-950
NO! I CAN TELL BY HIS EYES--HIS EXPRESSION! SOMETHING'S HAPPENED TO HIM! HE DOESN'T KNOW WHAT HE'S DOING!
ONLY ONE THING TO DO! IF I CAN LURE HIM INTO THE LAB!
11

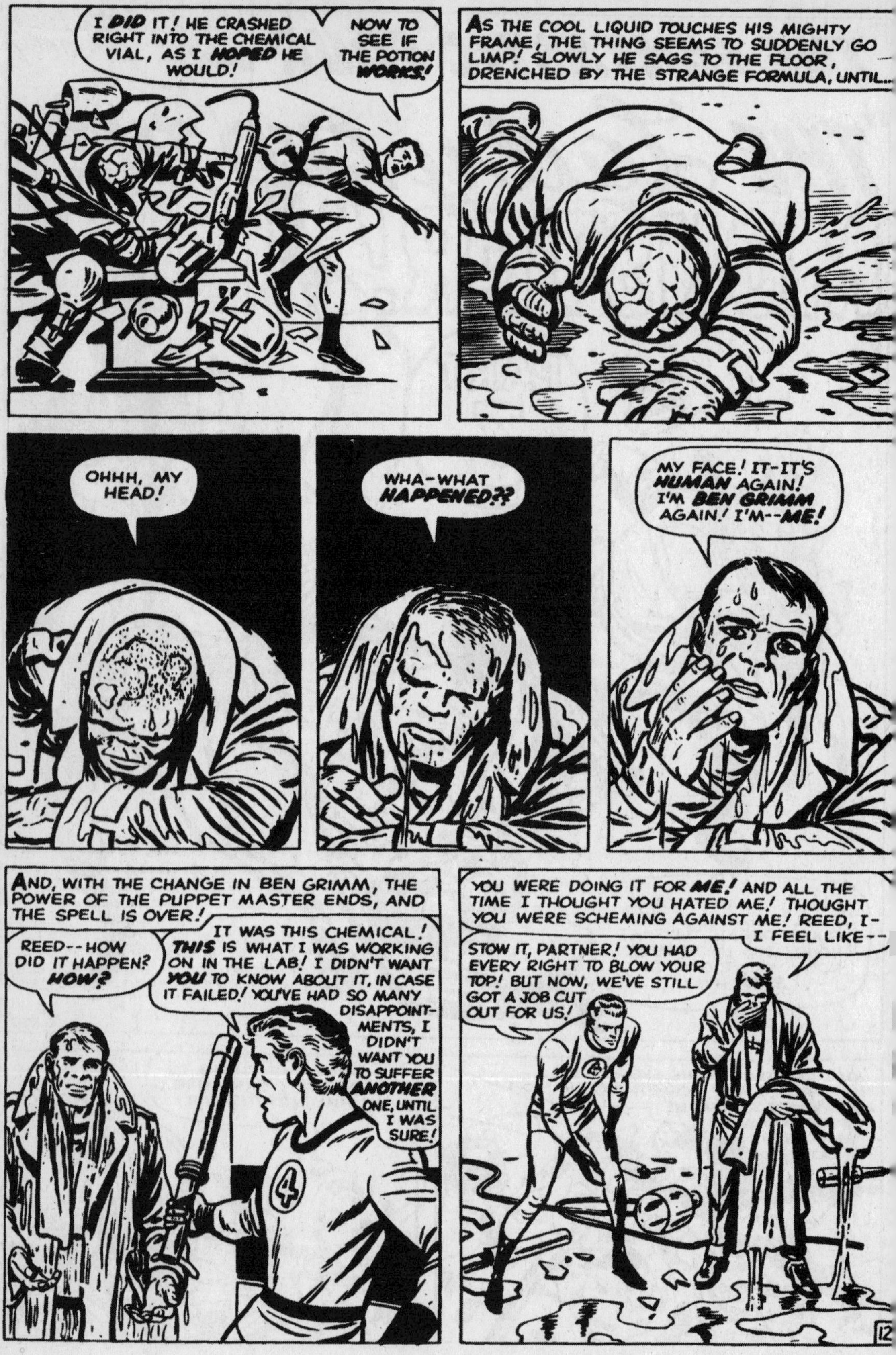
I DID IT! HE CRASHED RIGHT INTO THE CHEMICAL VIAL, AS I HOPED HE WOULD!
NOW TO SEE IF THE POTION WORKS!
AS THE COOL LIQUID TOUCHES HIS MIGHTY FRAME, THE THING SEEMS TO SUDDENLY GO LIMP! SLOWLY HE SAGS TO THE FLOOR, DRENCHED BY THE STRANGE FORMULA, UNTIL...
OHHH, MY HEAD!
WHA-WHAT HAPPENED??
MY FACE! IT-IT'S HUMAN AGAIN! I'M BEN GRIMM AGAIN! I'M--ME!
AND, WITH THE CHANGE IN BEN GRIMM, THE POWER OF THE PUPPET MASTER ENDS, AND THE SPELL IS OVER!
REED--HOW DID IT HAPPEN? HOW?
IT WAS THIS CHEMICAL! THIS IS WHAT I WAS WORKING ON IN THE LAB! I DIDN'T WANT YOU TO KNOW ABOUT IT, IN CASE IT FAILED! YOU'VE HAD SO MANY DISAPPOINT-MENTS, I DIDN'T WANT YOU TO SUFFER ANOTHER ONE, UNTIL I WAS SURE!
YOU WERE DOING IT FOR ME! AND ALL THE TIME I THOUGHT YOU HATED ME! THOUGHT YOU WERE SCHEMING AGAINST ME! REED, I-I FEEL LIKE--
STOW IT, PARTNER! YOU HAD EVERY RIGHT TO BLOW YOUR TOP! BUT NOW, WE'VE STILL GOT A JOB CUT OUT FOR US!
12

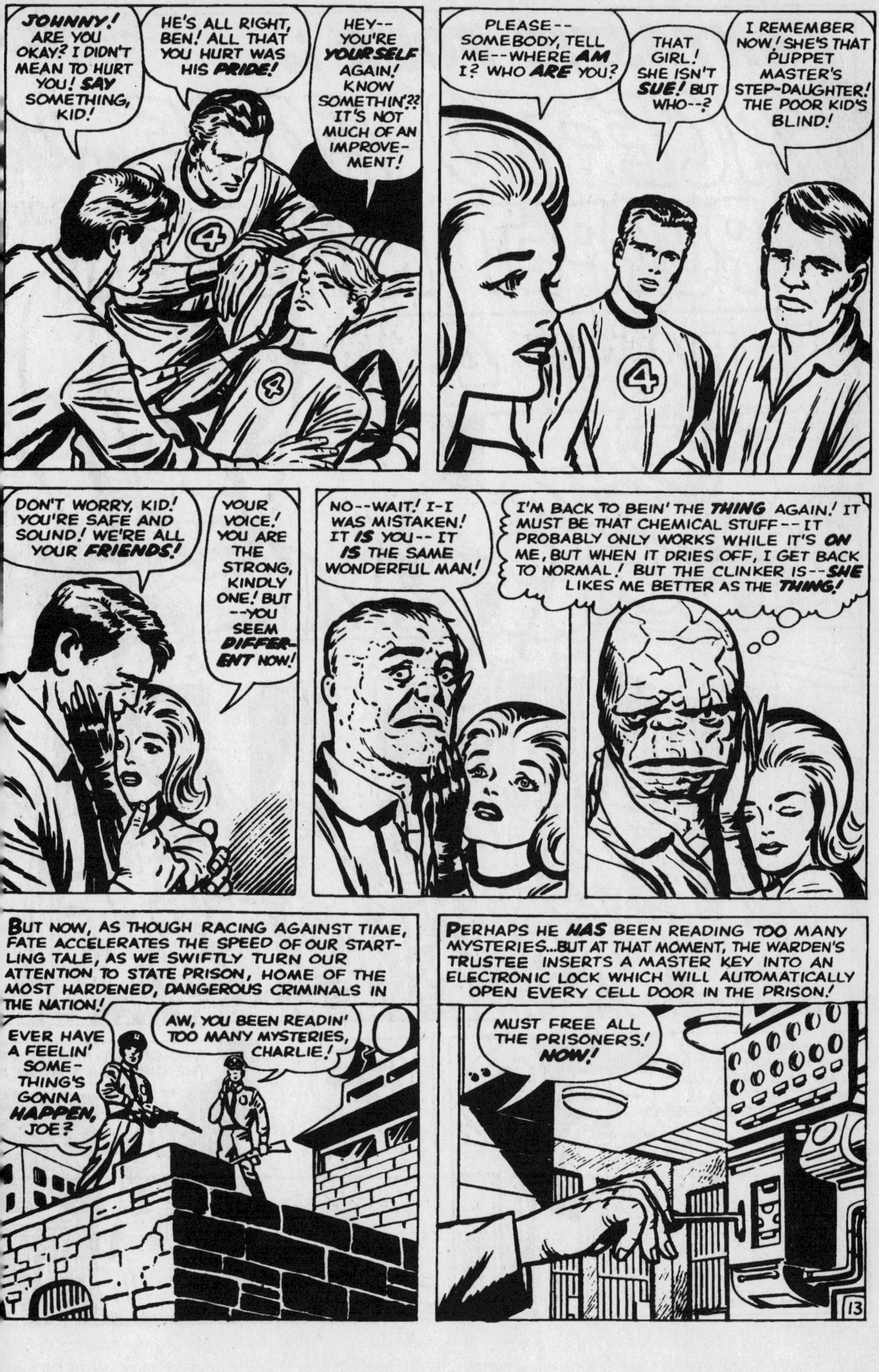
JOHNNY! ARE YOU OKAY? I DIDN'T MEAN TO HURT YOU! SAY SOMETHING, KID!
HE'S ALL RIGHT, BEN! ALL THAT YOU HURT WAS HIS PRIDE!
HEY-- YOU'RE YOURSELF AGAIN! KNOW SOMETHIN'?? IT'S NOT MUCH OF AN IMPROVEMENT!
PLEASE-- SOMEBODY, TELL ME--WHERE AM I? WHO ARE YOU?
THAT GIRL! SHE ISN'T SUE! BUT WHO--?
I REMEMBER NOW! SHE'S THAT PUPPET MASTER'S STEP-DAUGHTER! THE POOR KID'S BLIND!
DON'T WORRY, KID! YOU'RE SAFE AND SOUND! WE'RE ALL YOUR FRIENDS!
YOUR VOICE! YOU ARE THE STRONG, KINDLY ONE! BUT --YOU SEEM DIFFERENT NOW!
NO--WAIT! I-I WAS MISTAKEN! IT IS YOU-- IT IS THE SAME WONDERFUL MAN!
I'M BACK TO BEIN' THE THING AGAIN! IT MUST BE THAT CHEMICAL STUFF--IT PROBABLY ONLY WORKS WHILE IT'S ON ME, BUT WHEN IT DRIES OFF, I GET BACK TO NORMAL! BUT THE CLINKER IS--SHE LIKES ME BETTER AS THE THING!
BUT NOW, AS THOUGH RACING AGAINST TIME, FATE ACCELERATES THE SPEED OF OUR STARTLING TALE, AS WE SWIFTLY TURN OUR ATTENTION TO STATE PRISON, HOME OF THE MOST HARDENED, DANGEROUS CRIMINALS IN THE NATION!
EVER HAVE A FEELIN' SOMETHING'S GONNA HAPPEN, JOE?
AW, YOU BEEN READIN' TOO MANY MYSTERIES, CHARLIE!
PERHAPS HE HAS BEEN READING TOO MANY MYSTERIES...BUT AT THAT MOMENT, THE WARDEN'S TRUSTEE INSERTS A MASTER KEY INTO AN ELECTRONIC LOCK WHICH WILL AUTOMATICALLY OPEN EVERY CELL DOOR IN THE PRISON!
MUST FREE ALL THE PRISONERS! NOW!
13

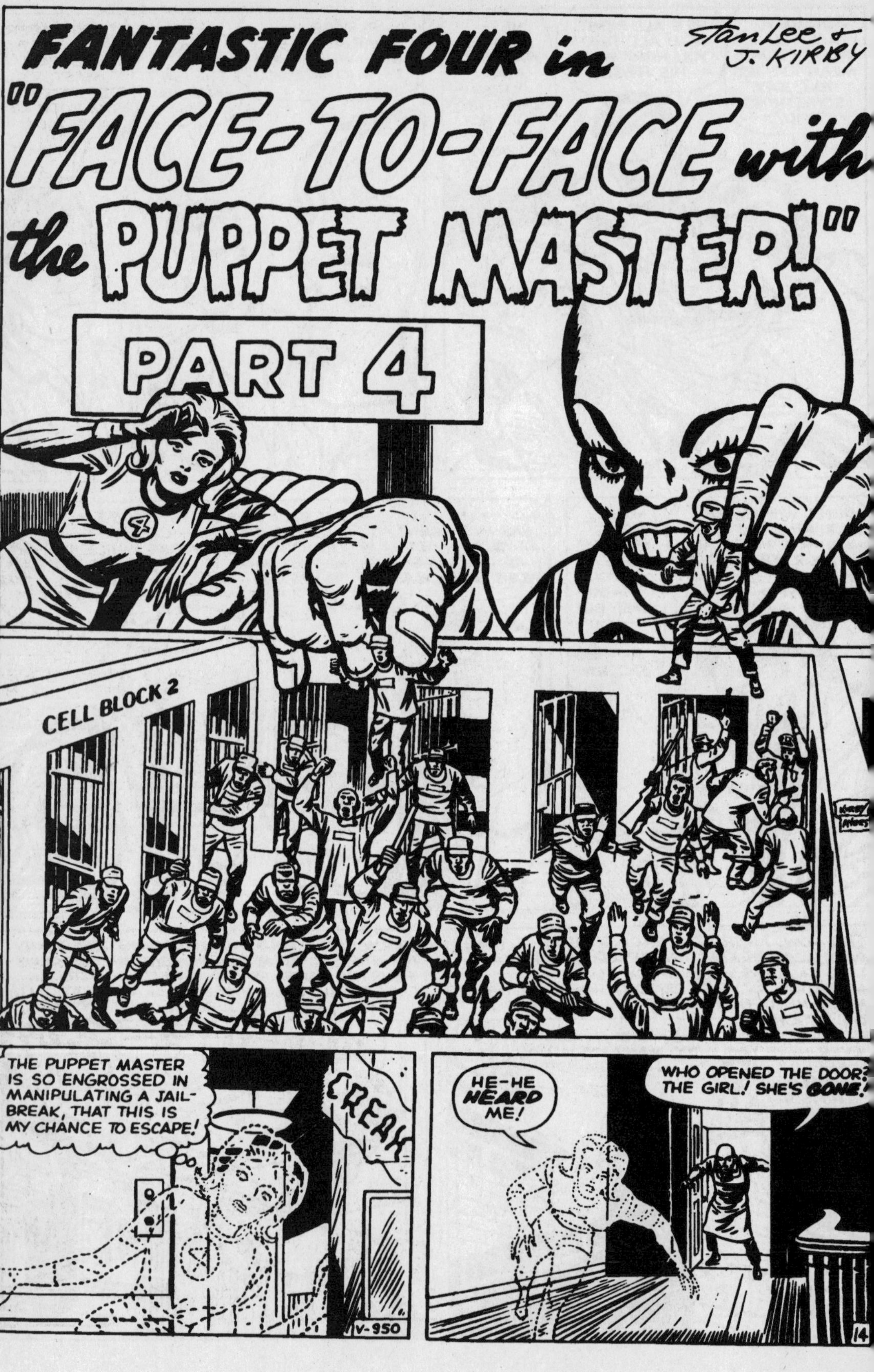
FANTASTIC FOUR in
"FACE-TO-FACE with the PUPPET MASTER!"
Stan Lee & J. KIRBY
PART 4
CELL BLOCK 2
THE PUPPET MASTER IS SO ENGROSSED IN MANIPULATING A JAIL-BREAK, THAT THIS IS MY CHANCE TO ESCAPE!
CREAK
HE-HE HEARD ME!
WHO OPENED THE DOOR? THE GIRL! SHE'S GONE!
V-950
14

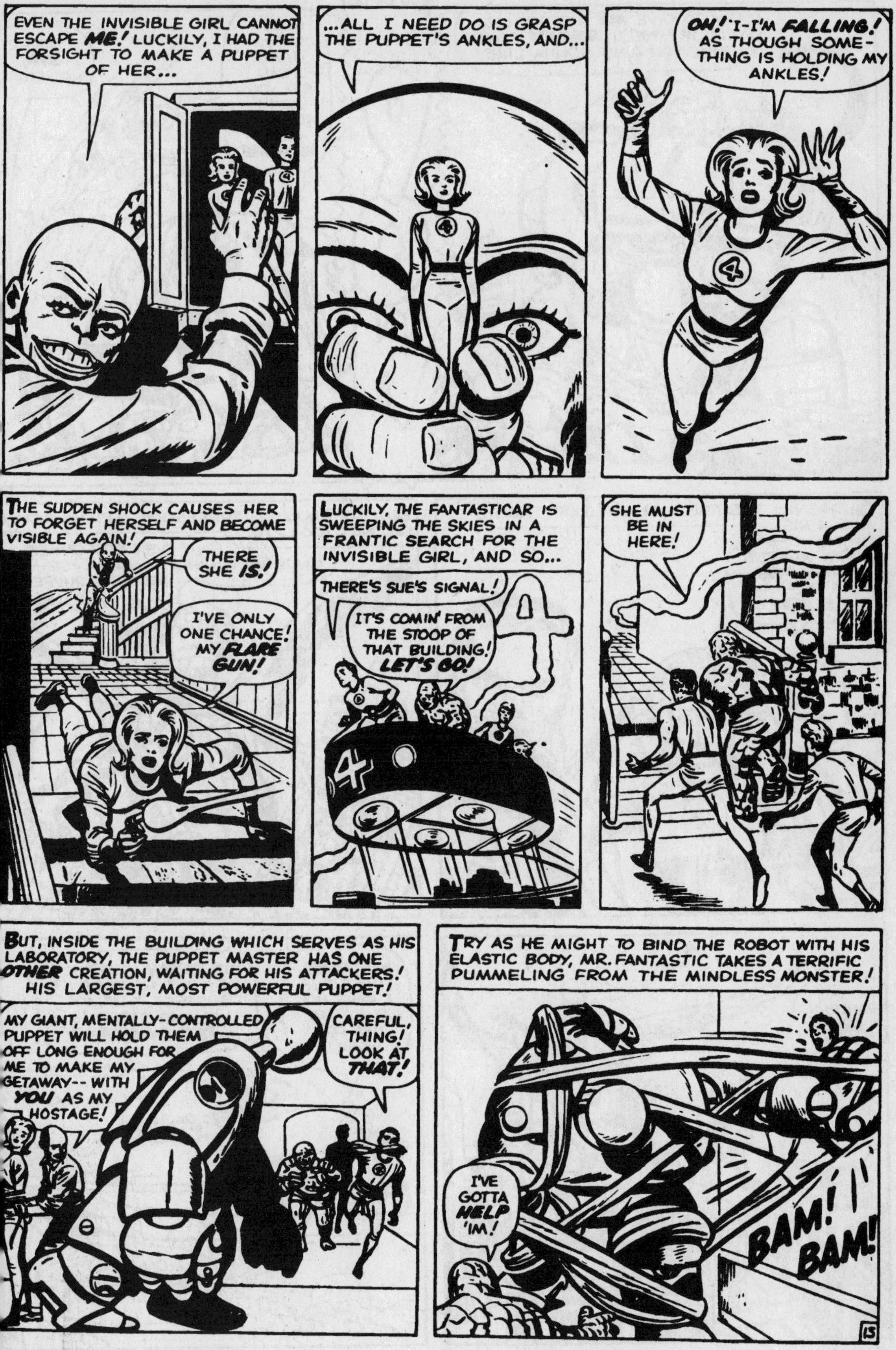
EVEN THE INVISIBLE GIRL CANNOT ESCAPE ME! LUCKILY, I HAD THE FORSIGHT TO MAKE A PUPPET OF HER...
...ALL I NEED DO IS GRASP THE PUPPET'S ANKLES, AND...
OH! I-I'M FALLING! AS THOUGH SOME-THING IS HOLDING MY ANKLES!
THE SUDDEN SHOCK CAUSES HER TO FORGET HERSELF AND BECOME VISIBLE AGAIN!
THERE SHE IS!
I'VE ONLY ONE CHANCE! MY FLARE GUN!
LUCKILY, THE FANTASTICAR IS SWEEPING THE SKIES IN A FRANTIC SEARCH FOR THE INVISIBLE GIRL, AND SO...
THERE'S SUE'S SIGNAL!
IT'S COMIN' FROM THE STOOP OF THAT BUILDING! LET'S GO!
SHE MUST BE IN HERE!
BUT, INSIDE THE BUILDING WHICH SERVES AS HIS LABORATORY, THE PUPPET MASTER HAS ONE OTHER CREATION, WAITING FOR HIS ATTACKERS! HIS LARGEST, MOST POWERFUL PUPPET!
MY GIANT, MENTALLY-CONTROLLED PUPPET WILL HOLD THEM OFF LONG ENOUGH FOR ME TO MAKE MY GETAWAY-- WITH YOU AS MY HOSTAGE!
CAREFUL, THING! LOOK AT THAT!
TRY AS HE MIGHT TO BIND THE ROBOT WITH HIS ELASTIC BODY, MR. FANTASTIC TAKES A TERRIFIC PUMMELING FROM THE MINDLESS MONSTER!
I'VE GOTTA HELP 'IM!
BAM! BAM!
15

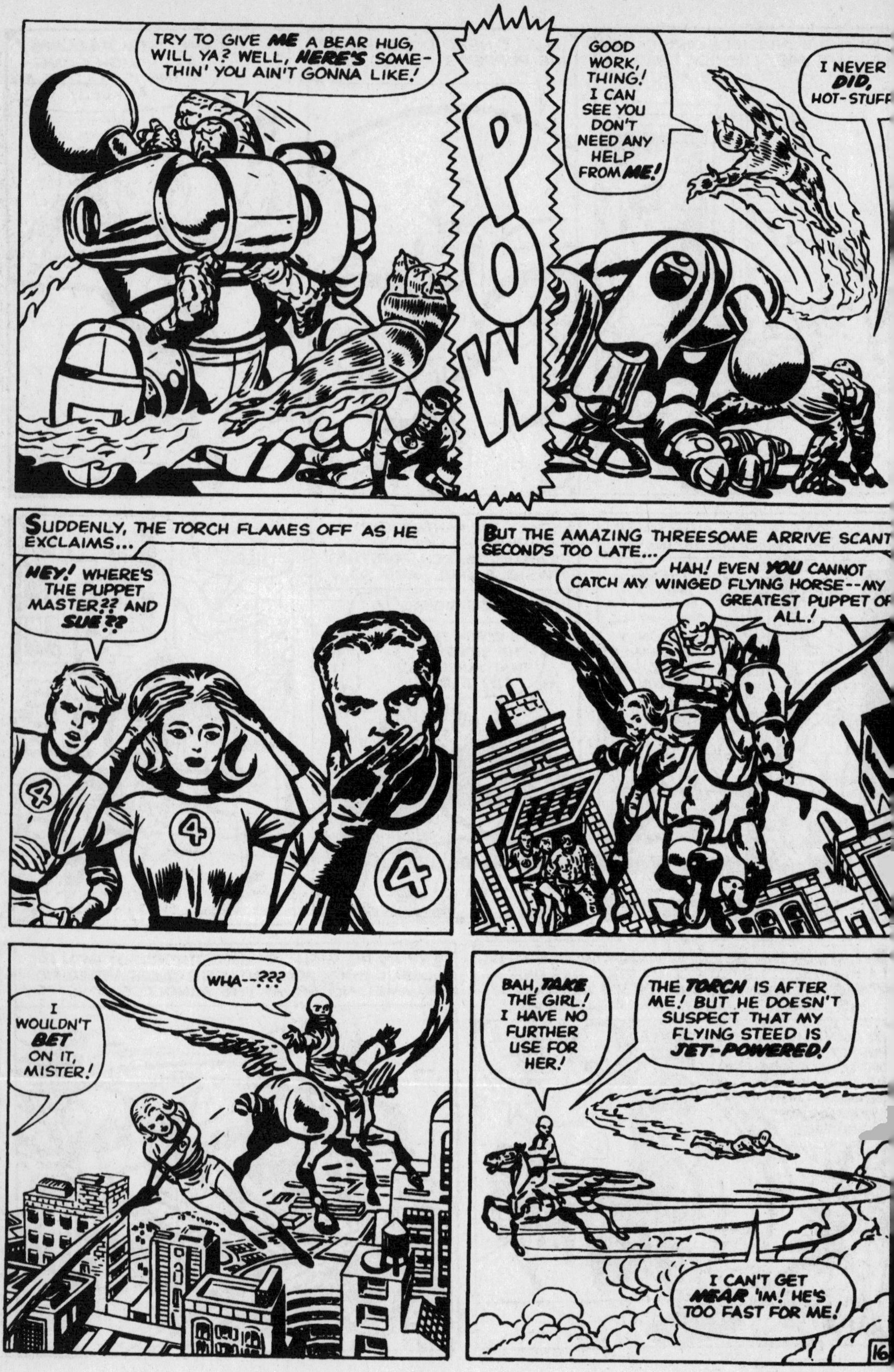
TRY TO GIVE ME A BEAR HUG, WILL YA? WELL, HERE'S SOME-THIN' YOU AIN'T GONNA LIKE!
POW
GOOD WORK, THING! I CAN SEE YOU DON'T NEED ANY HELP FROM ME!
I NEVER DID, HOT-STUFF
SUDDENLY, THE TORCH FLAMES OFF AS HE EXCLAIMS...
HEY! WHERE'S THE PUPPET MASTER?? AND SUE??
BUT THE AMAZING THREESOME ARRIVE SCANT SECONDS TOO LATE...
HAH! EVEN YOU CANNOT CATCH MY WINGED FLYING HORSE--MY GREATEST PUPPET OF ALL!
I WOULDN'T BET ON IT, MISTER!
WHA--???
BAH, TAKE THE GIRL! I HAVE NO FURTHER USE FOR HER!
THE TORCH IS AFTER ME! BUT HE DOESN'T SUSPECT THAT MY FLYING STEED IS JET-POWERED!
I CAN'T GET NEAR 'IM! HE'S TOO FAST FOR ME!
16

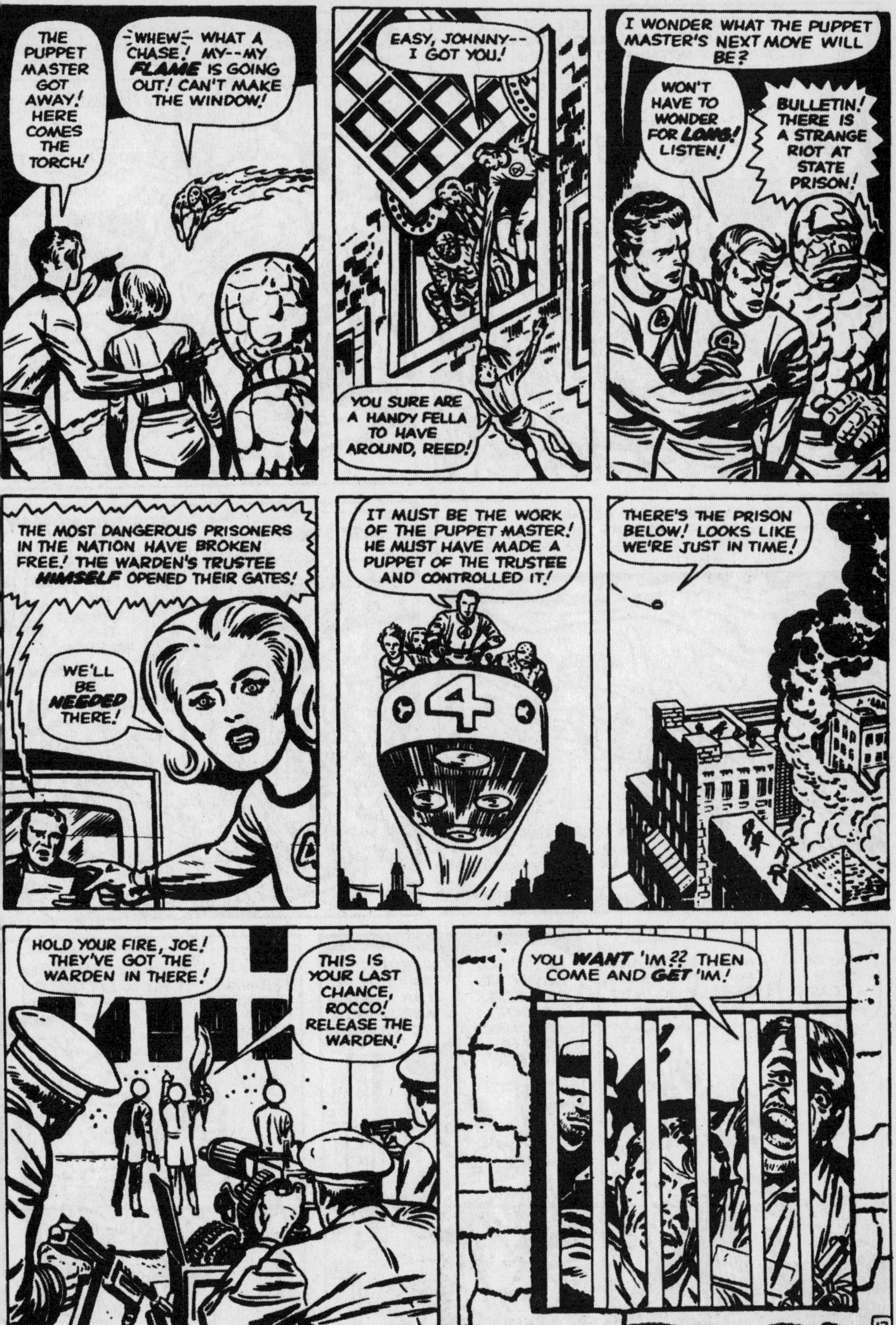
THE PUPPET MASTER GOT AWAY! HERE COMES THE TORCH!
WHEW— WHAT A CHASE! MY--MY FLAME IS GOING OUT! CAN'T MAKE THE WINDOW!
EASY, JOHNNY-- I GOT YOU!
YOU SURE ARE A HANDY FELLA TO HAVE AROUND, REED!
I WONDER WHAT THE PUPPET MASTER'S NEXT MOVE WILL BE?
WON'T HAVE TO WONDER FOR LONG! LISTEN!
BULLETIN! THERE IS A STRANGE RIOT AT STATE PRISON!
THE MOST DANGEROUS PRISONERS IN THE NATION HAVE BROKEN FREE! THE WARDEN'S TRUSTEE HIMSELF OPENED THEIR GATES!
WE'LL BE NEEDED THERE!
IT MUST BE THE WORK OF THE PUPPET MASTER! HE MUST HAVE MADE A PUPPET OF THE TRUSTEE AND CONTROLLED IT!
THERE'S THE PRISON BELOW! LOOKS LIKE WE'RE JUST IN TIME!
HOLD YOUR FIRE, JOE! THEY'VE GOT THE WARDEN IN THERE!
THIS IS YOUR LAST CHANCE, ROCCO! RELEASE THE WARDEN!
YOU WANT 'IM?? THEN COME AND GET 'IM!
17

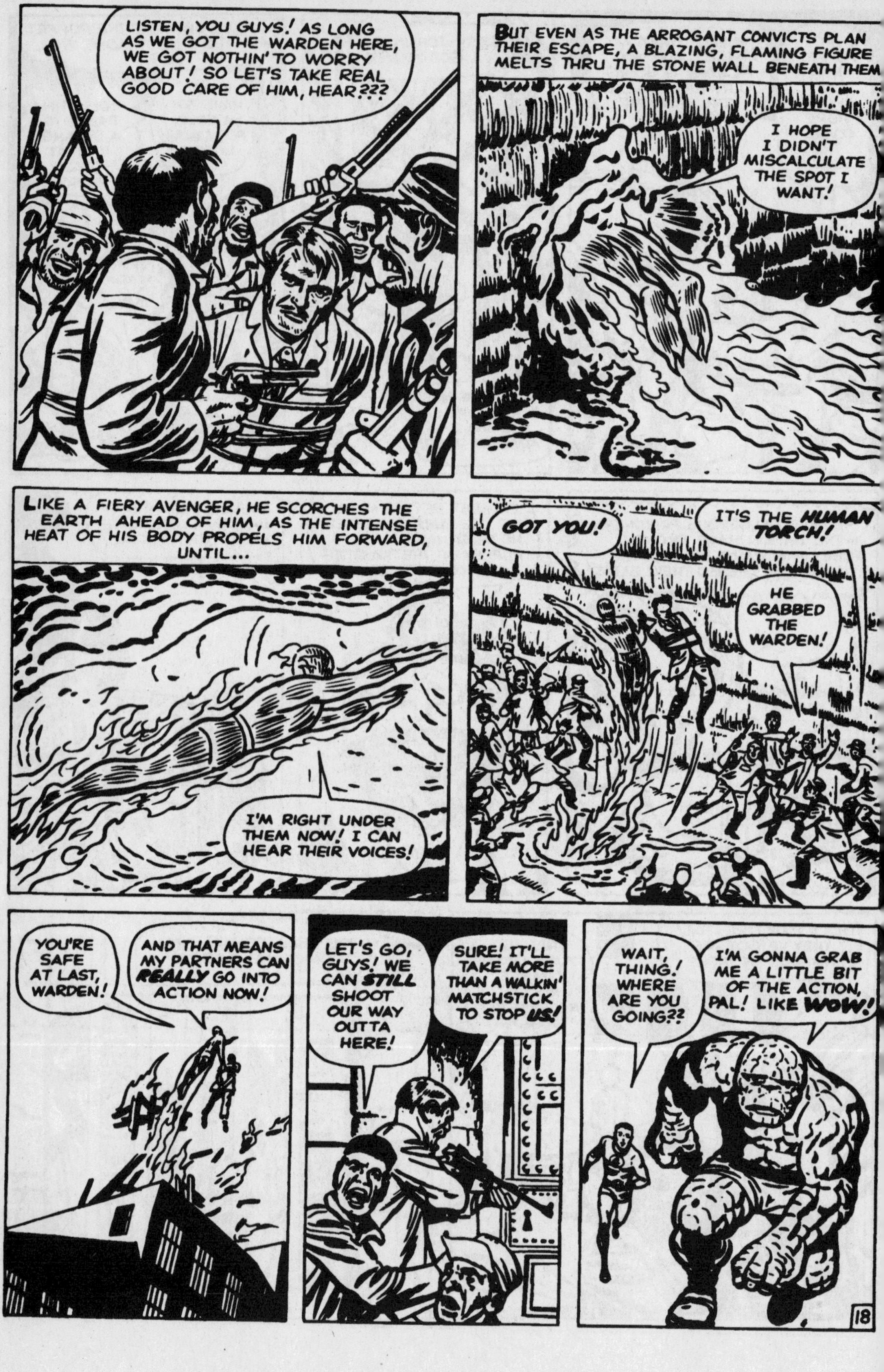
LISTEN, YOU GUYS! AS LONG AS WE GOT THE WARDEN HERE, WE GOT NOTHIN' TO WORRY ABOUT! SO LET'S TAKE REAL GOOD CARE OF HIM, HEAR???
BUT EVEN AS THE ARROGANT CONVICTS PLAN THEIR ESCAPE, A BLAZING, FLAMING FIGURE MELTS THRU THE STONE WALL BENEATH THEM
I HOPE I DIDN'T MISCALCULATE THE SPOT I WANT!
LIKE A FIERY AVENGER, HE SCORCHES THE EARTH AHEAD OF HIM, AS THE INTENSE HEAT OF HIS BODY PROPELS HIM FORWARD, UNTIL...
I'M RIGHT UNDER THEM NOW! I CAN HEAR THEIR VOICES!
GOT YOU!
IT'S THE HUMAN TORCH!
HE GRABBED THE WARDEN!
YOU'RE SAFE AT LAST, WARDEN!
AND THAT MEANS MY PARTNERS CAN REALLY GO INTO ACTION NOW!
LET'S GO, GUYS! WE CAN STILL SHOOT OUR WAY OUTTA HERE!
SURE! IT'LL TAKE MORE THAN A WALKIN' MATCHSTICK TO STOP US!
WAIT, THING! WHERE ARE YOU GOING??
I'M GONNA GRAB ME A LITTLE BIT OF THE ACTION, PAL! LIKE WOW!
18

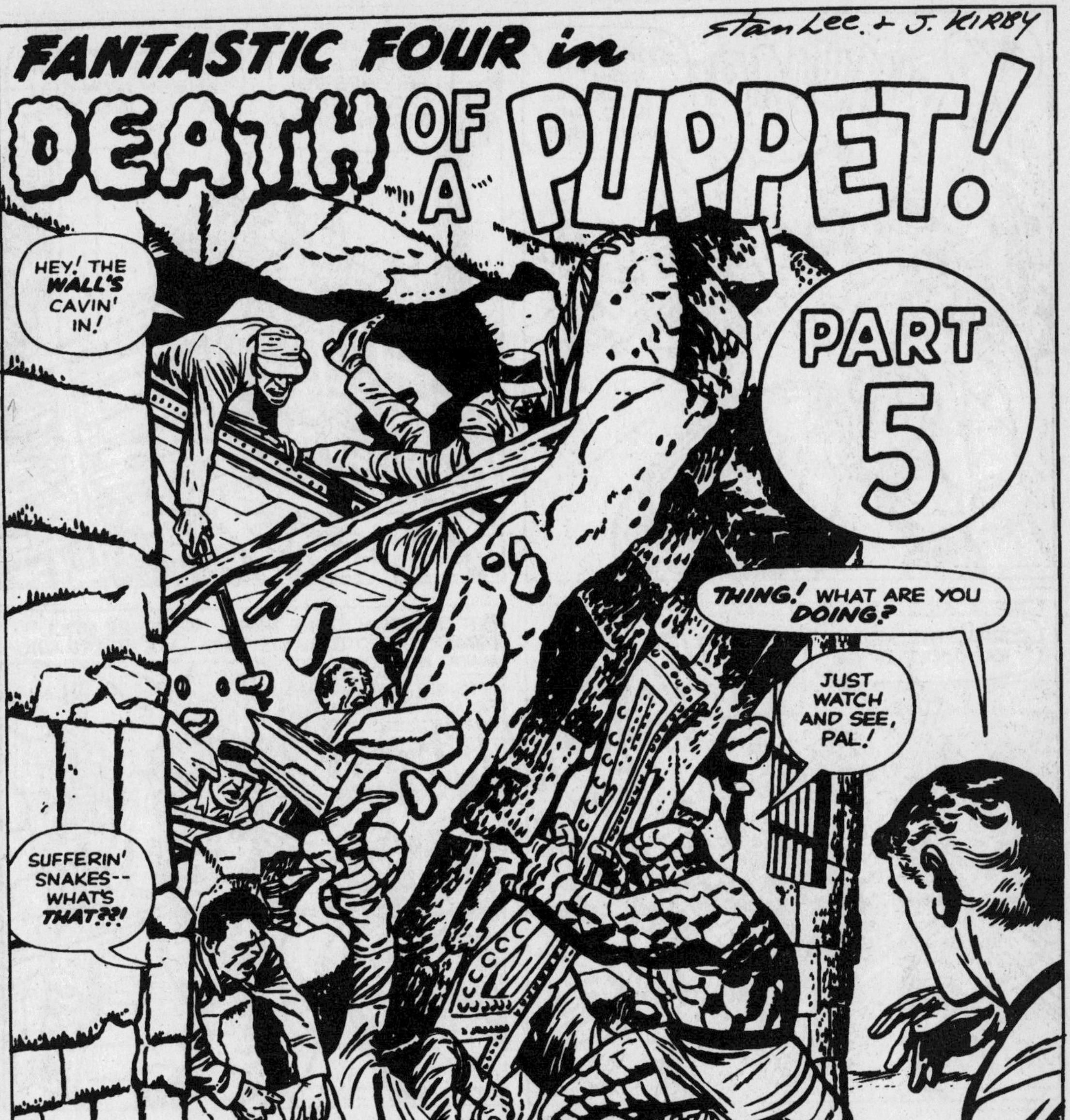
Stan Lee + J. Kirby
FANTASTIC FOUR in
DEATH OF A PUPPET!
HEY! THE WALL'S CAVIN' IN!
PART 5
THING! WHAT ARE YOU DOING?
JUST WATCH AND SEE, PAL!
SUFFERIN' SNAKES-- WHAT'S THAT??!
V-950

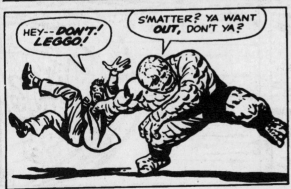

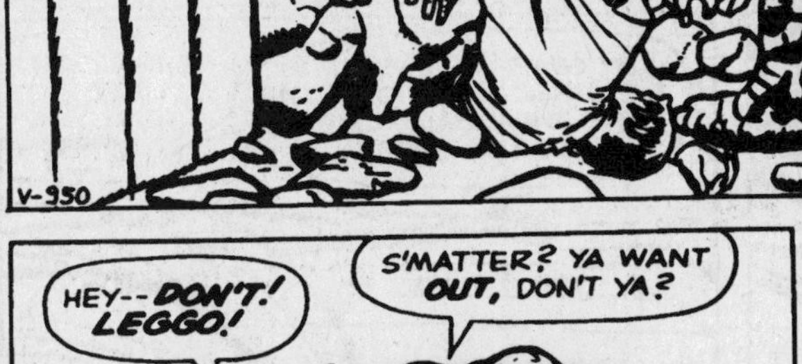
HEY-- DON'T! LEGGO!
S'MATTER? YA WANT OUT, DON'T YA?

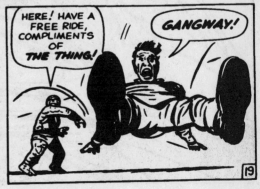

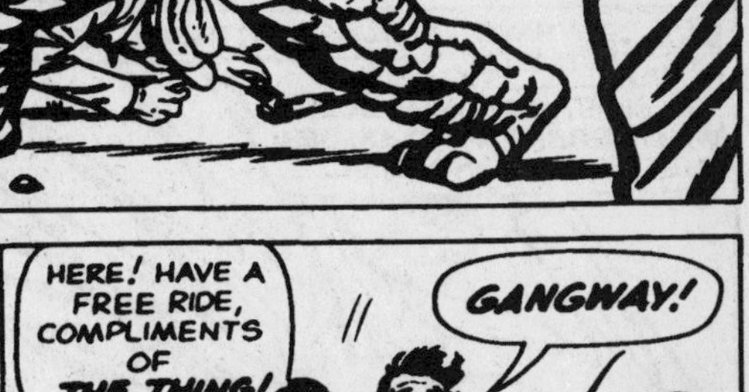
HERE! HAVE A FREE RIDE, COMPLIMENTS OF THE THING!
GANGWAY!

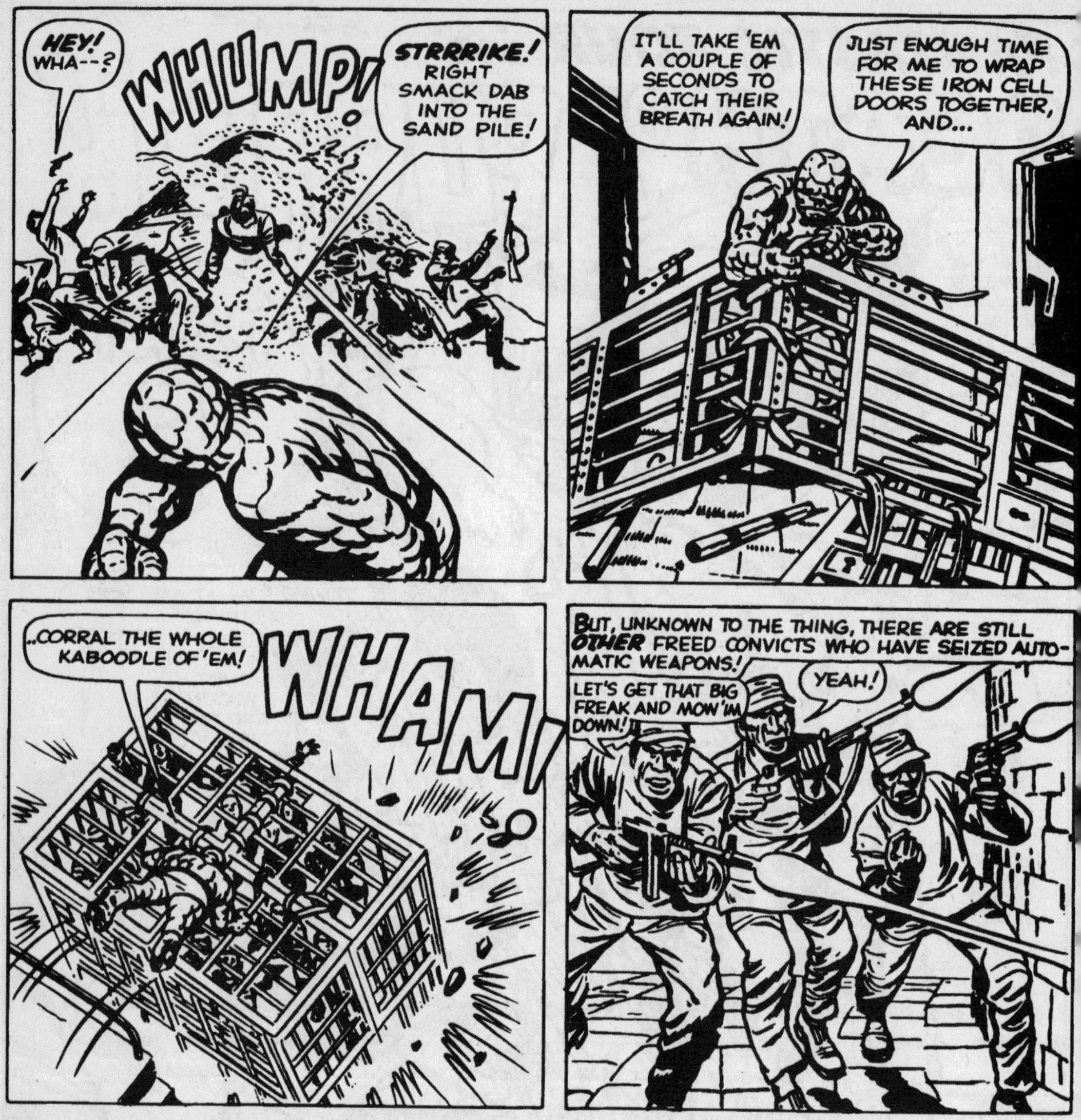
HEY! WHA--?
WHUMP!
STRRRIKE! RIGHT SMACK DAB INTO THE SAND PILE!
IT'LL TAKE 'EM A COUPLE OF SECONDS TO CATCH THEIR BREATH AGAIN!
JUST ENOUGH TIME FOR ME TO WRAP THESE IRON CELL DOORS TOGETHER, AND...
..CORRAL THE WHOLE KABOODLE OF 'EM!
WHAM!
BUT, UNKNOWN TO THE THING, THERE ARE STILL OTHER FREED CONVICTS WHO HAVE SEIZED AUTOMATIC WEAPONS!
LET'S GET THAT BIG FREAK AND MOW 'IM DOWN!
YEAH!
BUT THEY HAVE RECKONED WITHOUT THE AMAZING MR. FANTASTIC!
THE ELASTICITY OF MY BODY WILL ENABLE ME TO ABSORB THE SHELLS, AND THEN...
...BY SNAPPING MYSELF IN THE OTHER DIRECTION, I CAN FIRE THEM BACK LIKE A SLING-SHOT!
TWANG!
20

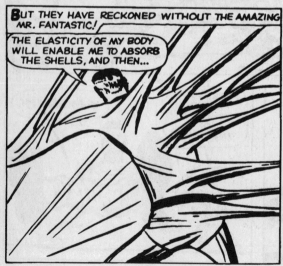

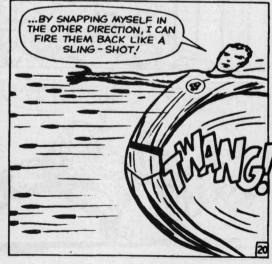

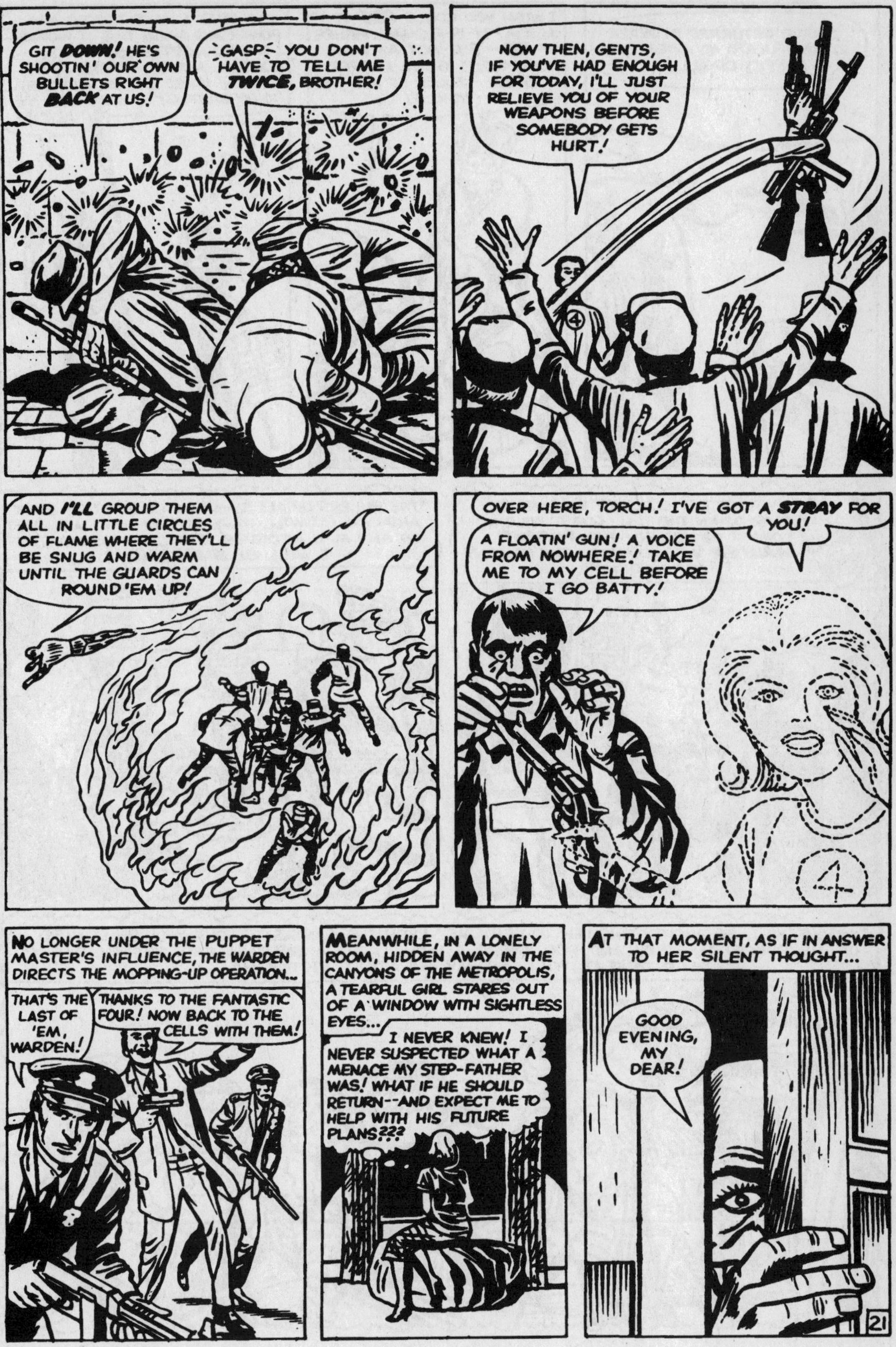

GIT DOWN! HE'S SHOOTIN' OUR OWN BULLETS RIGHT BACK AT US!
-GASP- YOU DON'T HAVE TO TELL ME TWICE, BROTHER!
NOW THEN, GENTS, IF YOU'VE HAD ENOUGH FOR TODAY, I'LL JUST RELIEVE YOU OF YOUR WEAPONS BEFORE SOMEBODY GETS HURT!
AND I'LL GROUP THEM ALL IN LITTLE CIRCLES OF FLAME WHERE THEY'LL BE SNUG AND WARM UNTIL THE GUARDS CAN ROUND 'EM UP!
OVER HERE, TORCH! I'VE GOT A STRAY FOR YOU!
A FLOATIN' GUN! A VOICE FROM NOWHERE! TAKE ME TO MY CELL BEFORE I GO BATTY!
NO LONGER UNDER THE PUPPET MASTER'S INFLUENCE, THE WARDEN DIRECTS THE MOPPING-UP OPERATION...
THAT'S THE LAST OF 'EM, WARDEN!
THANKS TO THE FANTASTIC FOUR! NOW BACK TO THE CELLS WITH THEM!
MEANWHILE, IN A LONELY ROOM, HIDDEN AWAY IN THE CANYONS OF THE METROPOLIS, A TEARFUL GIRL STARES OUT OF A WINDOW WITH SIGHTLESS EYES...
I NEVER KNEW! I NEVER SUSPECTED WHAT A MENACE MY STEP-FATHER WAS! WHAT IF HE SHOULD RETURN--AND EXPECT ME TO HELP WITH HIS FUTURE PLANS???
AT THAT MOMENT, AS IF IN ANSWER TO HER SILENT THOUGHT...
GOOD EVENING, MY DEAR!
21

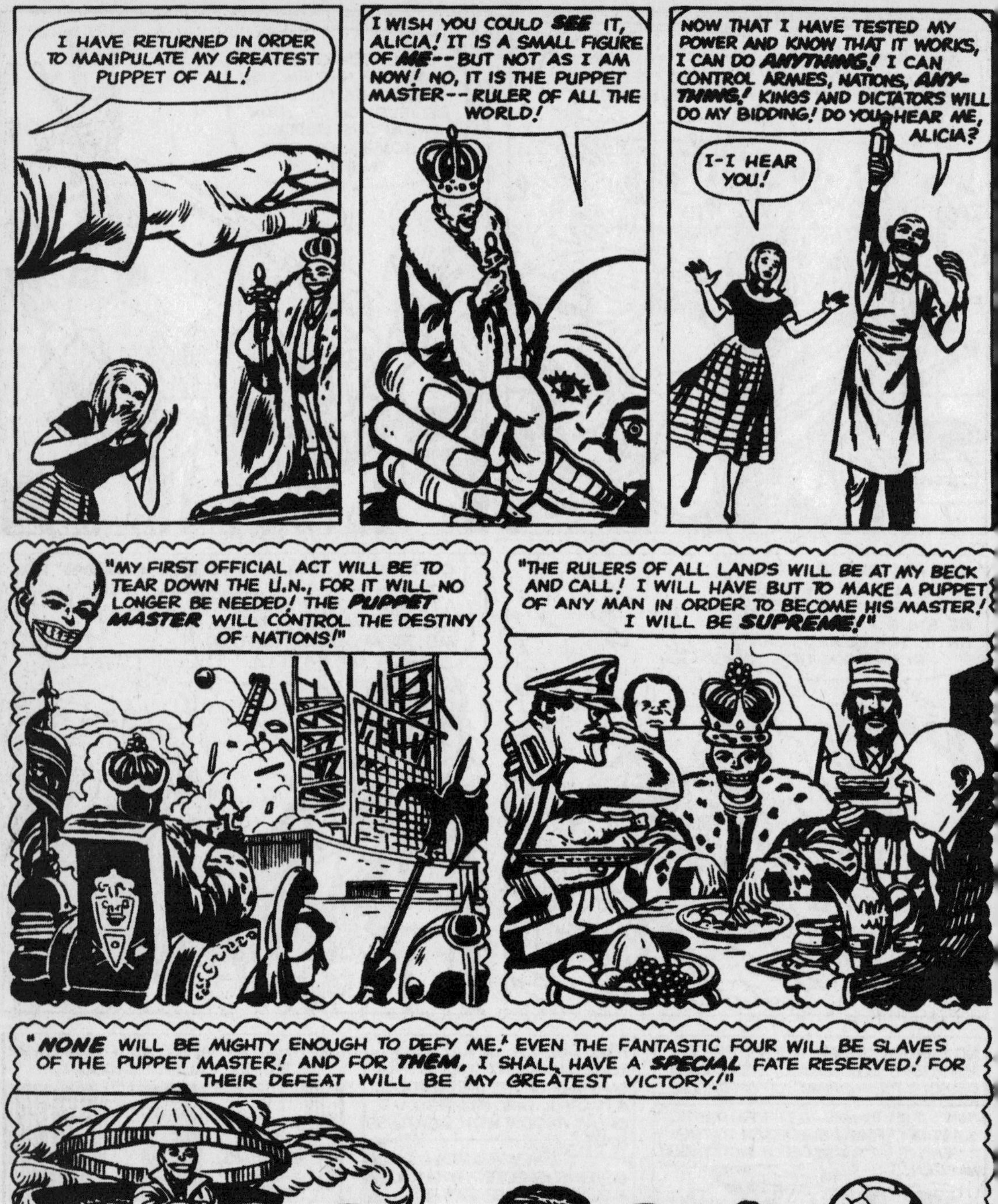

I HAVE RETURNED IN ORDER TO MANIPULATE MY GREATEST PUPPET OF ALL!
I WISH YOU COULD SEE IT, ALICIA! IT IS A SMALL FIGURE OF ME-- BUT NOT AS I AM NOW! NO, IT IS THE PUPPET MASTER-- RULER OF ALL THE WORLD!
NOW THAT I HAVE TESTED MY POWER AND KNOW THAT IT WORKS, I CAN DO ANYTHING! I CAN CONTROL ARMIES, NATIONS, ANYTHING! KINGS AND DICTATORS WILL DO MY BIDDING! DO YOU HEAR ME, ALICIA?
I-I HEAR YOU!
"MY FIRST OFFICIAL ACT WILL BE TO TEAR DOWN THE U.N., FOR IT WILL NO LONGER BE NEEDED! THE PUPPET MASTER WILL CONTROL THE DESTINY OF NATIONS!"
"THE RULERS OF ALL LANDS WILL BE AT MY BECK AND CALL! I WILL HAVE BUT TO MAKE A PUPPET OF ANY MAN IN ORDER TO BECOME HIS MASTER! I WILL BE SUPREME!"
"NONE WILL BE MIGHTY ENOUGH TO DEFY ME! EVEN THE FANTASTIC FOUR WILL BE SLAVES OF THE PUPPET MASTER! AND FOR THEM, I SHALL HAVE A SPECIAL FATE RESERVED! FOR THEIR DEFEAT WILL BE MY GREATEST VICTORY!"
PUPPET MASTER REX
4

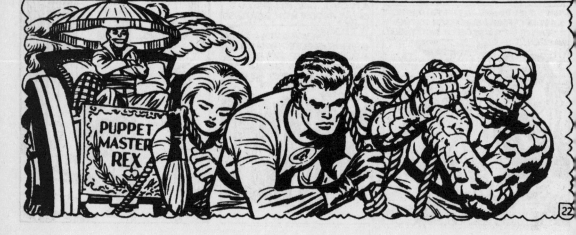

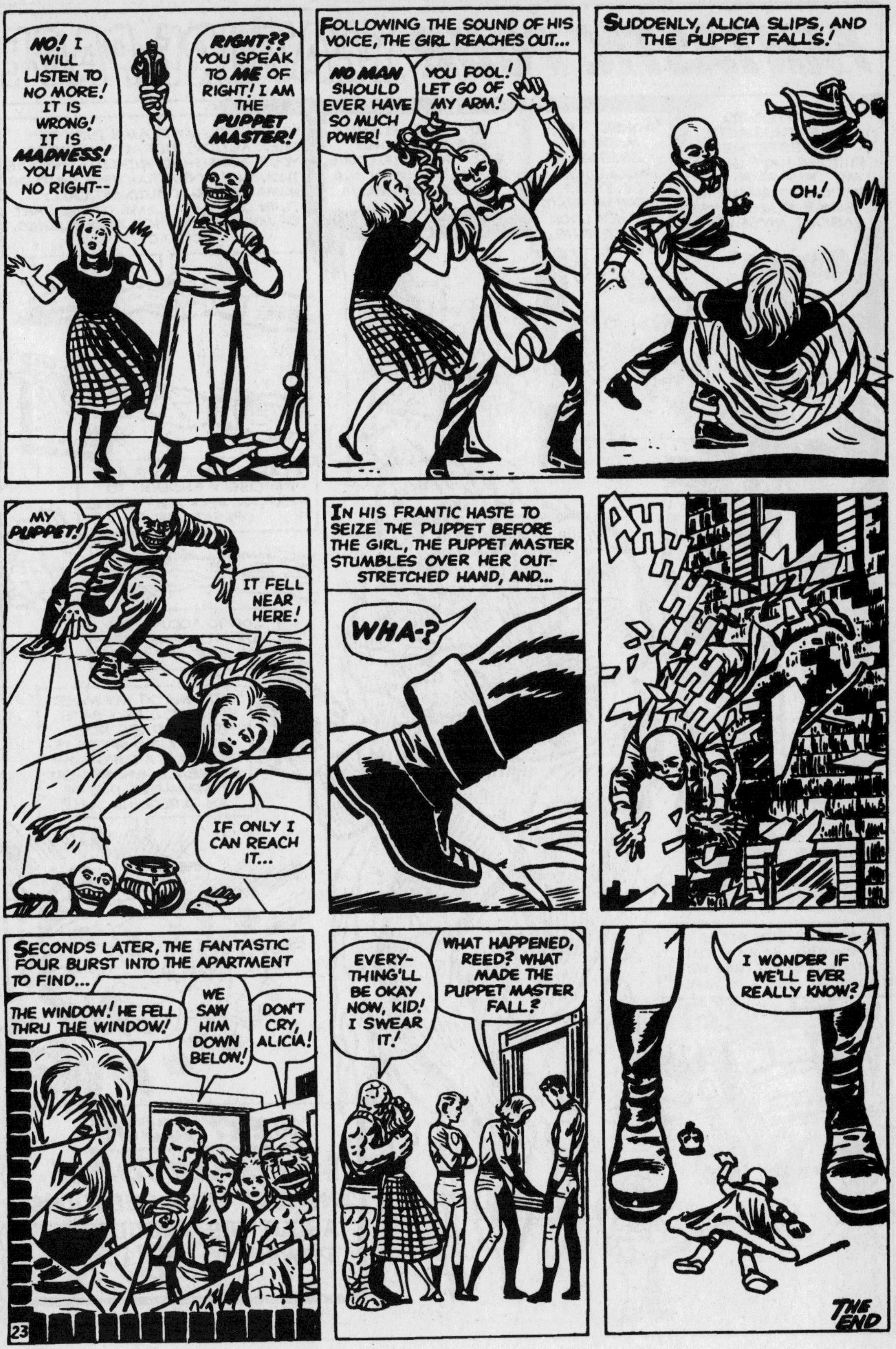
NO! I WILL LISTEN TO NO MORE! IT IS WRONG! IT IS MADNESS! YOU HAVE NO RIGHT--
RIGHT?? YOU SPEAK TO ME OF RIGHT! I AM THE PUPPET MASTER!
FOLLOWING THE SOUND OF HIS VOICE, THE GIRL REACHES OUT...
NO MAN SHOULD EVER HAVE SO MUCH POWER!
YOU FOOL! LET GO OF MY ARM!
SUDDENLY, ALICIA SLIPS, AND THE PUPPET FALLS!
OH!
MY PUPPET!
IT FELL NEAR HERE!
IF ONLY I CAN REACH IT...
IN HIS FRANTIC HASTE TO SEIZE THE PUPPET BEFORE THE GIRL, THE PUPPET MASTER STUMBLES OVER HER OUT-STRETCHED HAND, AND...
WHA-?
AHHHHHHH
SECONDS LATER, THE FANTASTIC FOUR BURST INTO THE APARTMENT TO FIND...
THE WINDOW! HE FELL THRU THE WINDOW!
WE SAW HIM DOWN BELOW!
DON'T CRY, ALICIA!
EVERY-THING'LL BE OKAY NOW, KID! I SWEAR IT!
WHAT HAPPENED, REED? WHAT MADE THE PUPPET MASTER FALL?
I WONDER IF WE'LL EVER REALLY KNOW?
THE END
23

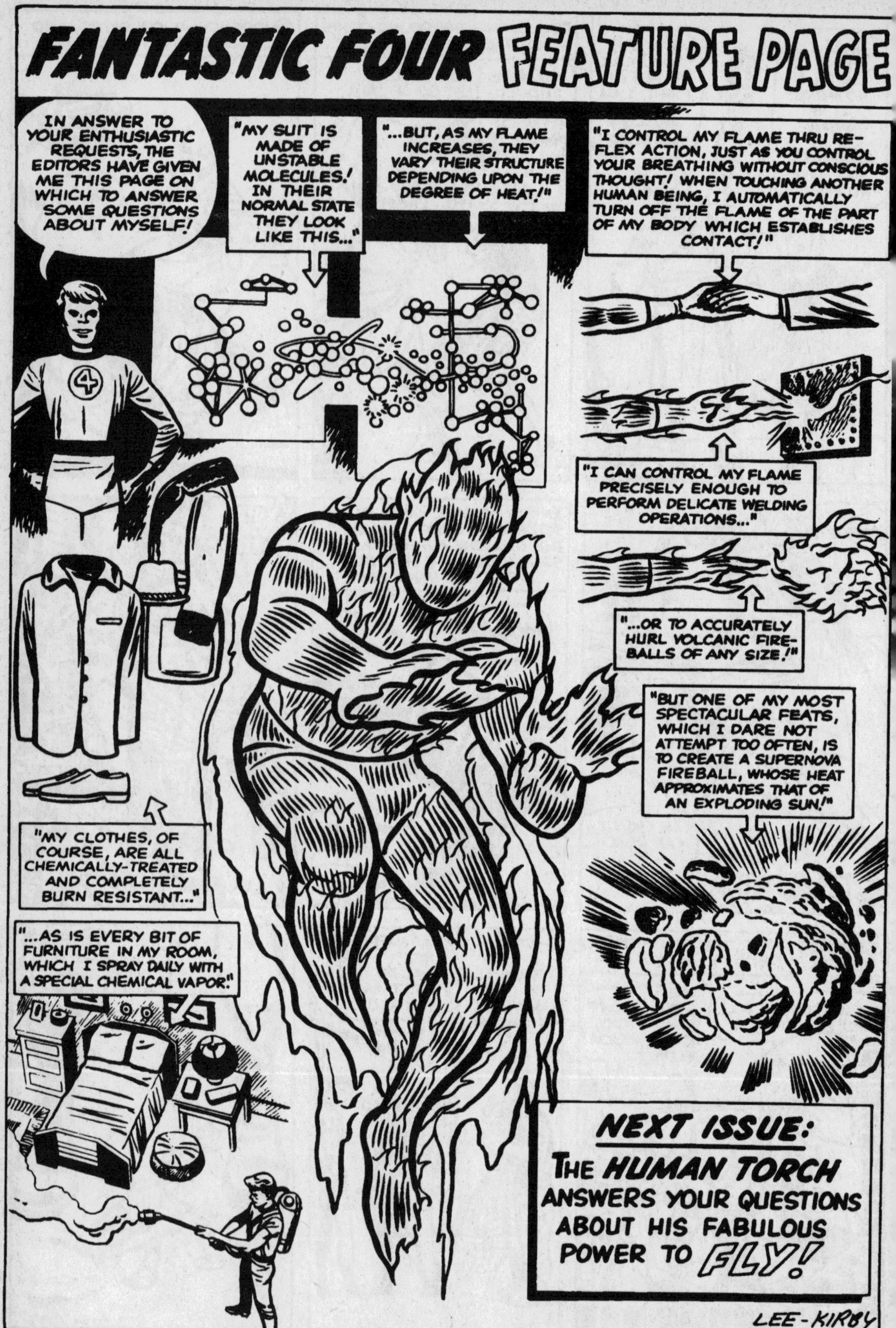
FANTASTIC FOUR FEATURE PAGE
IN ANSWER TO YOUR ENTHUSIASTIC REQUESTS, THE EDITORS HAVE GIVEN ME THIS PAGE ON WHICH TO ANSWER SOME QUESTIONS ABOUT MYSELF!
"MY SUIT IS MADE OF UNSTABLE MOLECULES! IN THEIR NORMAL STATE THEY LOOK LIKE THIS..."
"...BUT, AS MY FLAME INCREASES, THEY VARY THEIR STRUCTURE DEPENDING UPON THE DEGREE OF HEAT!"
"I CONTROL MY FLAME THRU REFLEX ACTION, JUST AS YOU CONTROL YOUR BREATHING WITHOUT CONSCIOUS THOUGHT! WHEN TOUCHING ANOTHER HUMAN BEING, I AUTOMATICALLY TURN OFF THE FLAME OF THE PART OF MY BODY WHICH ESTABLISHES CONTACT!"
"I CAN CONTROL MY FLAME PRECISELY ENOUGH TO PERFORM DELICATE WELDING OPERATIONS..."
"...OR TO ACCURATELY HURL VOLCANIC FIREBALLS OF ANY SIZE!"
"BUT ONE OF MY MOST SPECTACULAR FEATS, WHICH I DARE NOT ATTEMPT TOO OFTEN, IS TO CREATE A SUPERNOVA FIREBALL, WHOSE HEAT APPROXIMATES THAT OF AN EXPLODING SUN!"
"MY CLOTHES, OF COURSE, ARE ALL CHEMICALLY-TREATED AND COMPLETELY BURN RESISTANT..."
"...AS IS EVERY BIT OF FURNITURE IN MY ROOM, WHICH I SPRAY DAILY WITH A SPECIAL CHEMICAL VAPOR!"
NEXT ISSUE:
THE HUMAN TORCH ANSWERS YOUR QUESTIONS ABOUT HIS FABULOUS POWER TO FLY!
LEE-KIRBY

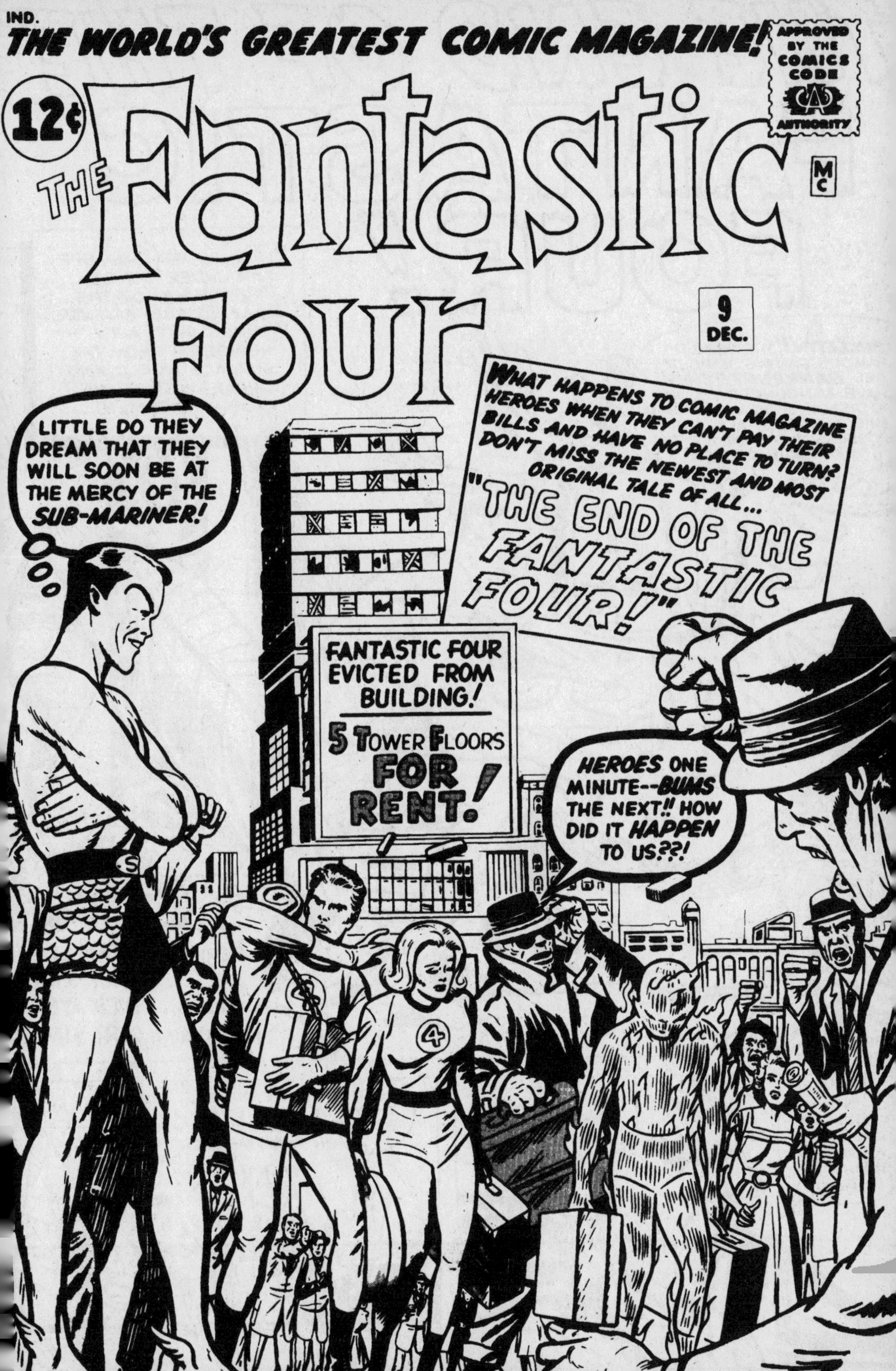
IND.
THE WORLD'S GREATEST COMIC MAGAZINE!
APPROVED BY THE COMICS CODE AUTHORITY
12¢
THE Fantastic Four
MC
9 DEC.
WHAT HAPPENS TO COMIC MAGAZINE HEROES WHEN THEY CAN'T PAY THEIR BILLS AND HAVE NO PLACE TO TURN? DON'T MISS THE NEWEST AND MOST ORIGINAL TALE OF ALL... "THE END OF THE FANTASTIC FOUR!"
LITTLE DO THEY DREAM THAT THEY WILL SOON BE AT THE MERCY OF THE SUB-MARINER!
FANTASTIC FOUR EVICTED FROM BUILDING!
5 TOWER FLOORS FOR RENT!
HEROES ONE MINUTE--BUMS THE NEXT!! HOW DID IT HAPPEN TO US??!

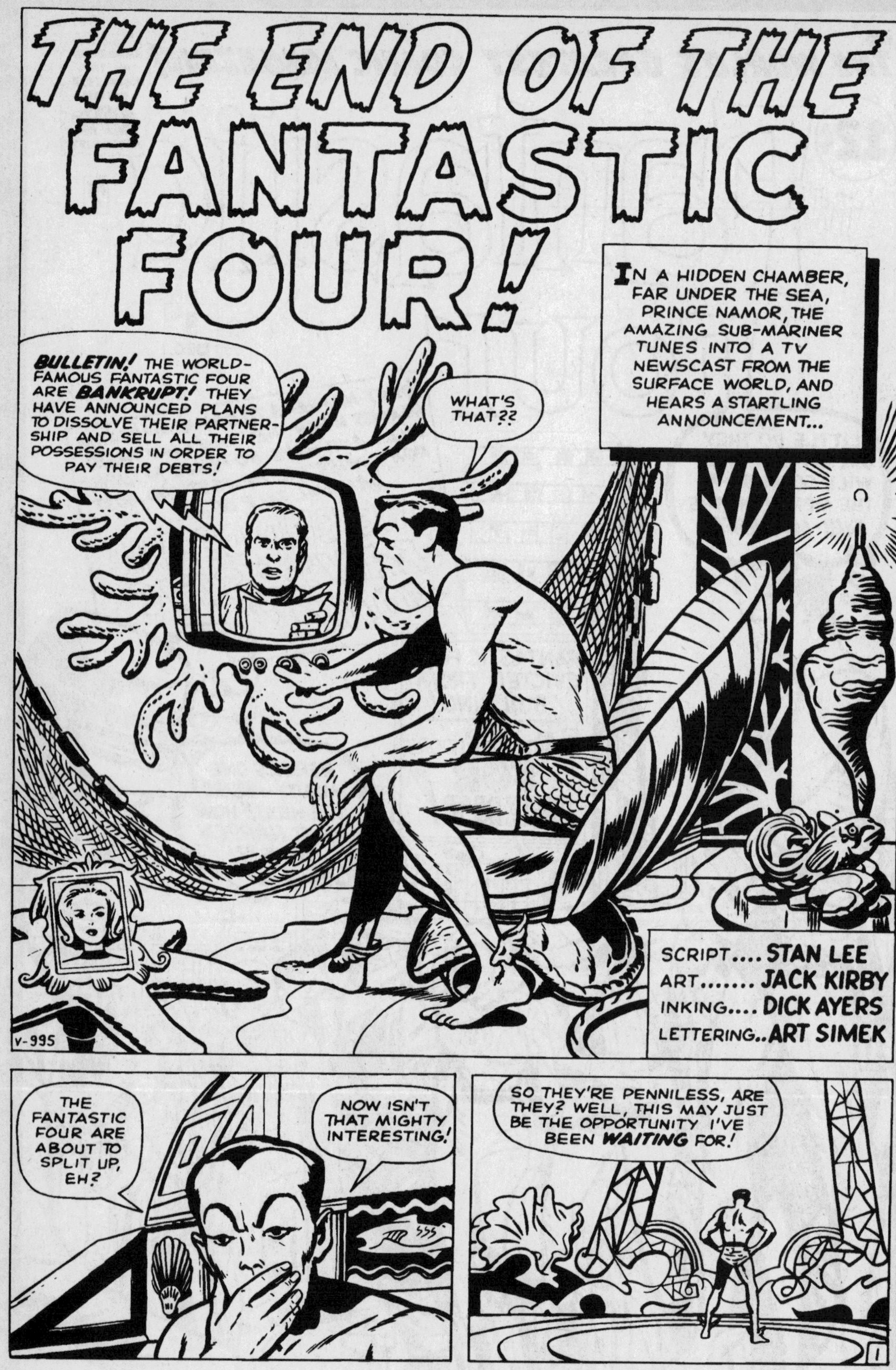
THE END OF THE FANTASTIC FOUR!
IN A HIDDEN CHAMBER, FAR UNDER THE SEA, PRINCE NAMOR, THE AMAZING SUB-MARINER TUNES INTO A TV NEWSCAST FROM THE SURFACE WORLD, AND HEARS A STARTLING ANNOUNCEMENT...
BULLETIN! THE WORLD-FAMOUS FANTASTIC FOUR ARE BANKRUPT! THEY HAVE ANNOUNCED PLANS TO DISSOLVE THEIR PARTNERSHIP AND SELL ALL THEIR POSSESSIONS IN ORDER TO PAY THEIR DEBTS!
WHAT'S THAT??
SCRIPT.... STAN LEE
ART........ JACK KIRBY
INKING.... DICK AYERS
LETTERING..ART SIMEK
V-995
THE FANTASTIC FOUR ARE ABOUT TO SPLIT UP, EH?
NOW ISN'T THAT MIGHTY INTERESTING!
SO THEY'RE PENNILESS, ARE THEY? WELL, THIS MAY JUST BE THE OPPORTUNITY I'VE BEEN WAITING FOR!
1

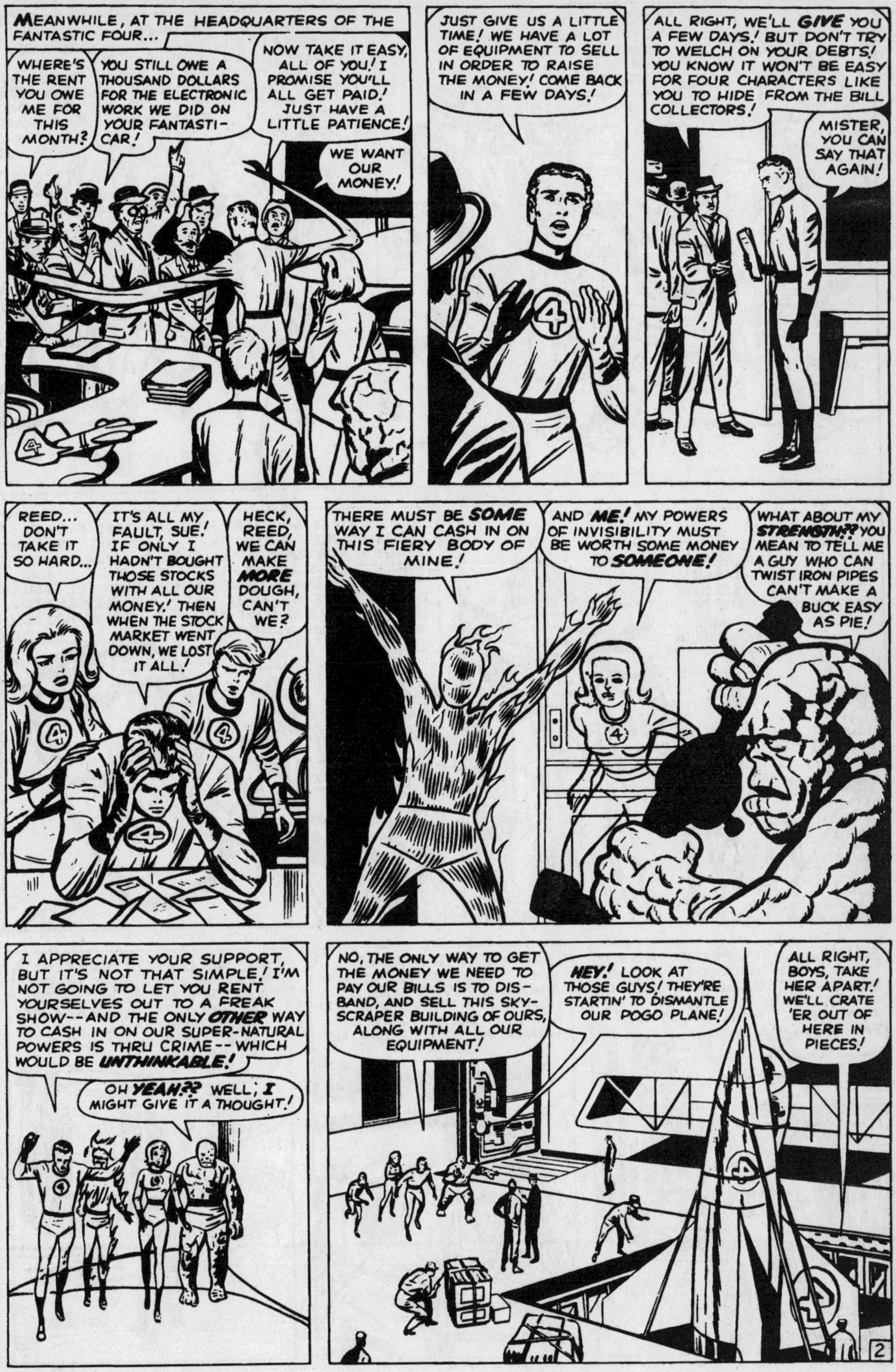
MEANWHILE, AT THE HEADQUARTERS OF THE FANTASTIC FOUR...
WHERE'S THE RENT YOU OWE ME FOR THIS MONTH?
YOU STILL OWE A THOUSAND DOLLARS FOR THE ELECTRONIC WORK WE DID ON YOUR FANTASTI-CAR!
NOW TAKE IT EASY, ALL OF YOU! I PROMISE YOU'LL ALL GET PAID! JUST HAVE A LITTLE PATIENCE!
WE WANT OUR MONEY!
JUST GIVE US A LITTLE TIME! WE HAVE A LOT OF EQUIPMENT TO SELL IN ORDER TO RAISE THE MONEY! COME BACK IN A FEW DAYS!
ALL RIGHT, WE'LL GIVE YOU A FEW DAYS! BUT DON'T TRY TO WELCH ON YOUR DEBTS! YOU KNOW IT WON'T BE EASY FOR FOUR CHARACTERS LIKE YOU TO HIDE FROM THE BILL COLLECTORS!
MISTER, YOU CAN SAY THAT AGAIN!
REED... DON'T TAKE IT SO HARD...
IT'S ALL MY FAULT, SUE! IF ONLY I HADN'T BOUGHT THOSE STOCKS WITH ALL OUR MONEY! THEN WHEN THE STOCK MARKET WENT DOWN, WE LOST IT ALL!
HECK, REED, WE CAN MAKE MORE DOUGH, CAN'T WE?
THERE MUST BE SOME WAY I CAN CASH IN ON THIS FIERY BODY OF MINE!
AND ME! MY POWERS OF INVISIBILITY MUST BE WORTH SOME MONEY TO SOMEONE!
WHAT ABOUT MY STRENGTH?? YOU MEAN TO TELL ME A GUY WHO CAN TWIST IRON PIPES CAN'T MAKE A BUCK EASY AS PIE!
I APPRECIATE YOUR SUPPORT, BUT IT'S NOT THAT SIMPLE! I'M NOT GOING TO LET YOU RENT YOURSELVES OUT TO A FREAK SHOW--AND THE ONLY OTHER WAY TO CASH IN ON OUR SUPER-NATURAL POWERS IS THRU CRIME--WHICH WOULD BE UNTHINKABLE!
OH YEAH?? WELL, I MIGHT GIVE IT A THOUGHT!
NO, THE ONLY WAY TO GET THE MONEY WE NEED TO PAY OUR BILLS IS TO DIS-BAND, AND SELL THIS SKY-SCRAPER BUILDING OF OURS, ALONG WITH ALL OUR EQUIPMENT!
HEY! LOOK AT THOSE GUYS! THEY'RE STARTIN' TO DISMANTLE OUR POGO PLANE!
ALL RIGHT, BOYS, TAKE HER APART! WE'LL CRATE 'ER OUT OF HERE IN PIECES!
2

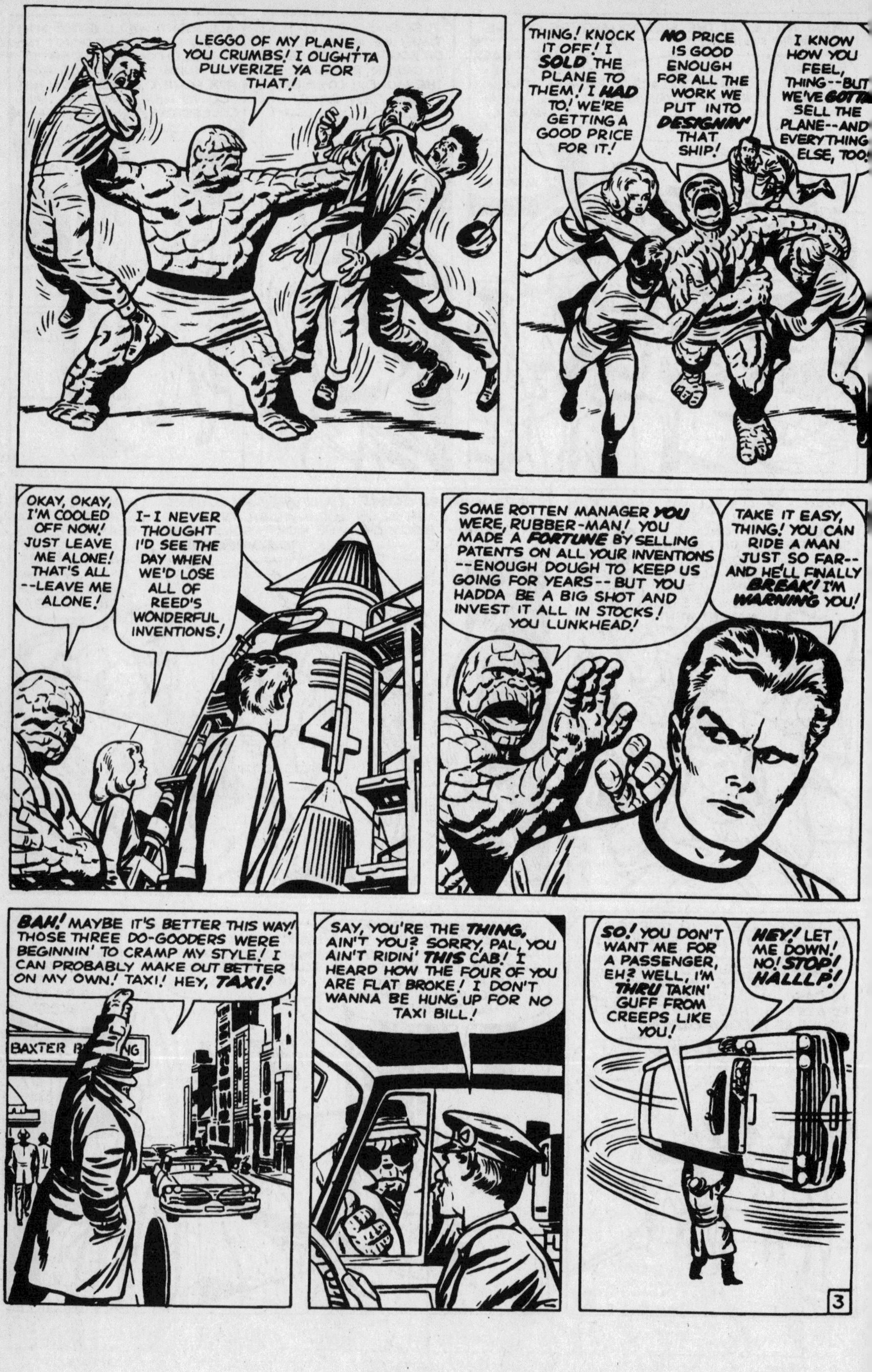
LEGGO OF MY PLANE, YOU CRUMBS! I OUGHTTA PULVERIZE YA FOR THAT!
THING! KNOCK IT OFF! I SOLD THE PLANE TO THEM! I HAD TO! WE'RE GETTING A GOOD PRICE FOR IT!
NO PRICE IS GOOD ENOUGH FOR ALL THE WORK WE PUT INTO DESIGNIN' THAT SHIP!
I KNOW HOW YOU FEEL, THING--BUT WE'VE GOTTA SELL THE PLANE--AND EVERYTHING ELSE, TOO!
OKAY, OKAY, I'M COOLED OFF NOW! JUST LEAVE ME ALONE! THAT'S ALL --LEAVE ME ALONE!
I-I NEVER THOUGHT I'D SEE THE DAY WHEN WE'D LOSE ALL OF REED'S WONDERFUL INVENTIONS!
SOME ROTTEN MANAGER YOU WERE, RUBBER-MAN! YOU MADE A FORTUNE BY SELLING PATENTS ON ALL YOUR INVENTIONS --ENOUGH DOUGH TO KEEP US GOING FOR YEARS--BUT YOU HADDA BE A BIG SHOT AND INVEST IT ALL IN STOCKS! YOU LUNKHEAD!
TAKE IT EASY, THING! YOU CAN RIDE A MAN JUST SO FAR--AND HE'LL FINALLY BREAK! I'M WARNING YOU!
BAH! MAYBE IT'S BETTER THIS WAY! THOSE THREE DO-GOODERS WERE BEGINNIN' TO CRAMP MY STYLE! I CAN PROBABLY MAKE OUT BETTER ON MY OWN! TAXI! HEY, TAXI!
SAY, YOU'RE THE THING, AIN'T YOU? SORRY, PAL, YOU AIN'T RIDIN' THIS CAB! I HEARD HOW THE FOUR OF YOU ARE FLAT BROKE! I DON'T WANNA BE HUNG UP FOR NO TAXI BILL!
SO! YOU DON'T WANT ME FOR A PASSENGER, EH? WELL, I'M THRU TAKIN' GUFF FROM CREEPS LIKE YOU!
HEY! LET ME DOWN! NO! STOP! HALLLP!
3

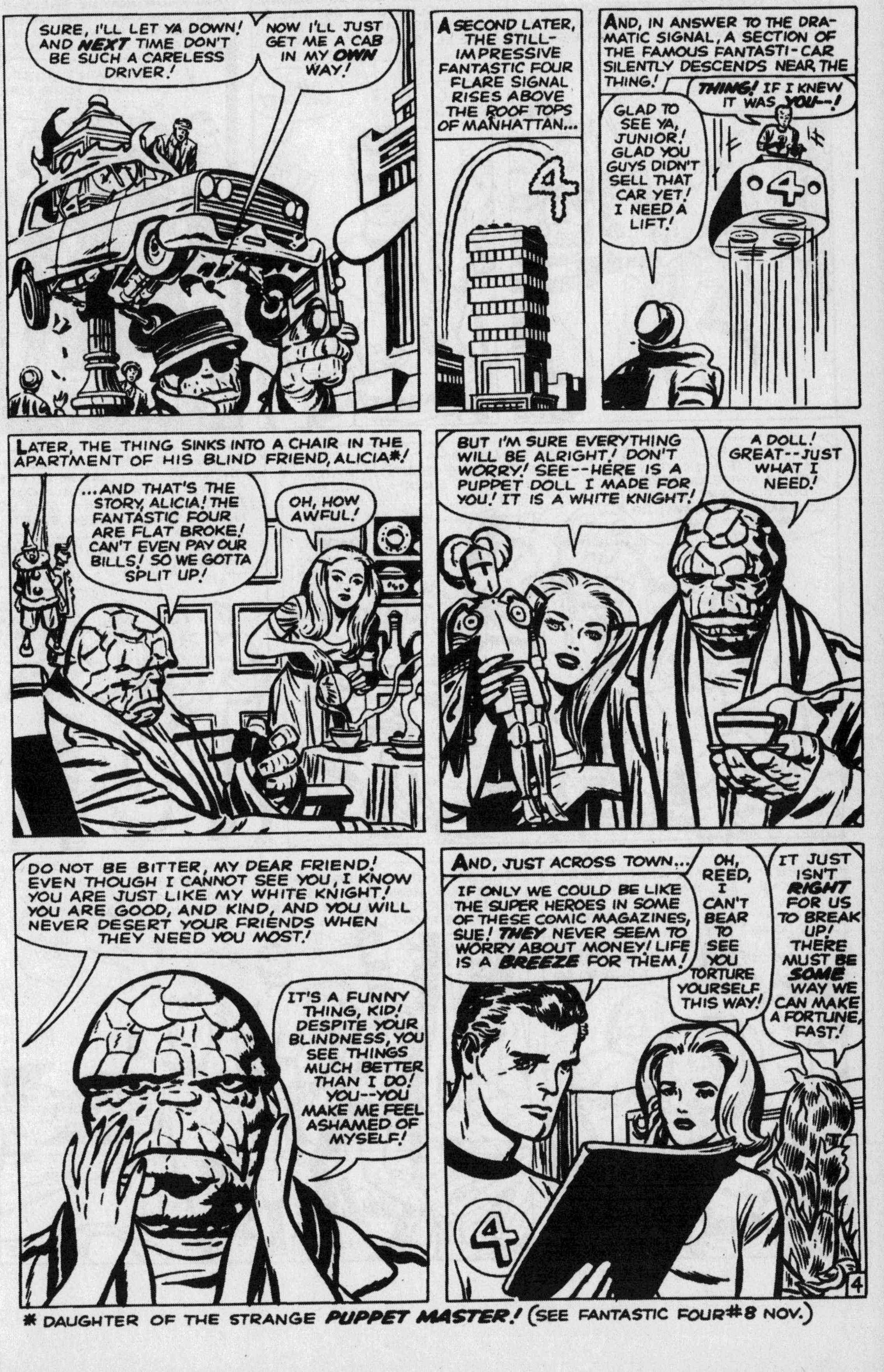
SURE, I'LL LET YA DOWN! AND NEXT TIME DON'T BE SUCH A CARELESS DRIVER!
NOW I'LL JUST GET ME A CAB IN MY OWN WAY!
A SECOND LATER, THE STILL-IMPRESSIVE FANTASTIC FOUR FLARE SIGNAL RISES ABOVE THE ROOF TOPS OF MANHATTAN...
4
AND, IN ANSWER TO THE DRAMATIC SIGNAL, A SECTION OF THE FAMOUS FANTASTI-CAR SILENTLY DESCENDS NEAR THE THING!
THING! IF I KNEW IT WAS YOU--!
GLAD TO SEE YA, JUNIOR! GLAD YOU GUYS DIDN'T SELL THAT CAR YET! I NEED A LIFT!
4
LATER, THE THING SINKS INTO A CHAIR IN THE APARTMENT OF HIS BLIND FRIEND, ALICIA*!
...AND THAT'S THE STORY, ALICIA! THE FANTASTIC FOUR ARE FLAT BROKE! CAN'T EVEN PAY OUR BILLS! SO WE GOTTA SPLIT UP!
OH, HOW AWFUL!
BUT I'M SURE EVERYTHING WILL BE ALRIGHT! DON'T WORRY! SEE--HERE IS A PUPPET DOLL I MADE FOR YOU! IT IS A WHITE KNIGHT!
A DOLL! GREAT--JUST WHAT I NEED!
DO NOT BE BITTER, MY DEAR FRIEND! EVEN THOUGH I CANNOT SEE YOU, I KNOW YOU ARE JUST LIKE MY WHITE KNIGHT! YOU ARE GOOD, AND KIND, AND YOU WILL NEVER DESERT YOUR FRIENDS WHEN THEY NEED YOU MOST!
IT'S A FUNNY THING, KID! DESPITE YOUR BLINDNESS, YOU SEE THINGS MUCH BETTER THAN I DO! YOU--YOU MAKE ME FEEL ASHAMED OF MYSELF!
AND, JUST ACROSS TOWN...
IF ONLY WE COULD BE LIKE THE SUPER HEROES IN SOME OF THESE COMIC MAGAZINES, SUE! THEY NEVER SEEM TO WORRY ABOUT MONEY! LIFE IS A BREEZE FOR THEM!
OH, REED, I CAN'T BEAR TO SEE YOU TORTURE YOURSELF THIS WAY!
IT JUST ISN'T RIGHT FOR US TO BREAK UP! THERE MUST BE SOME WAY WE CAN MAKE A FORTUNE, FAST!
4
4

* DAUGHTER OF THE STRANGE **PUPPET MASTER!** (SEE FANTASTIC FOUR #8 NOV.)

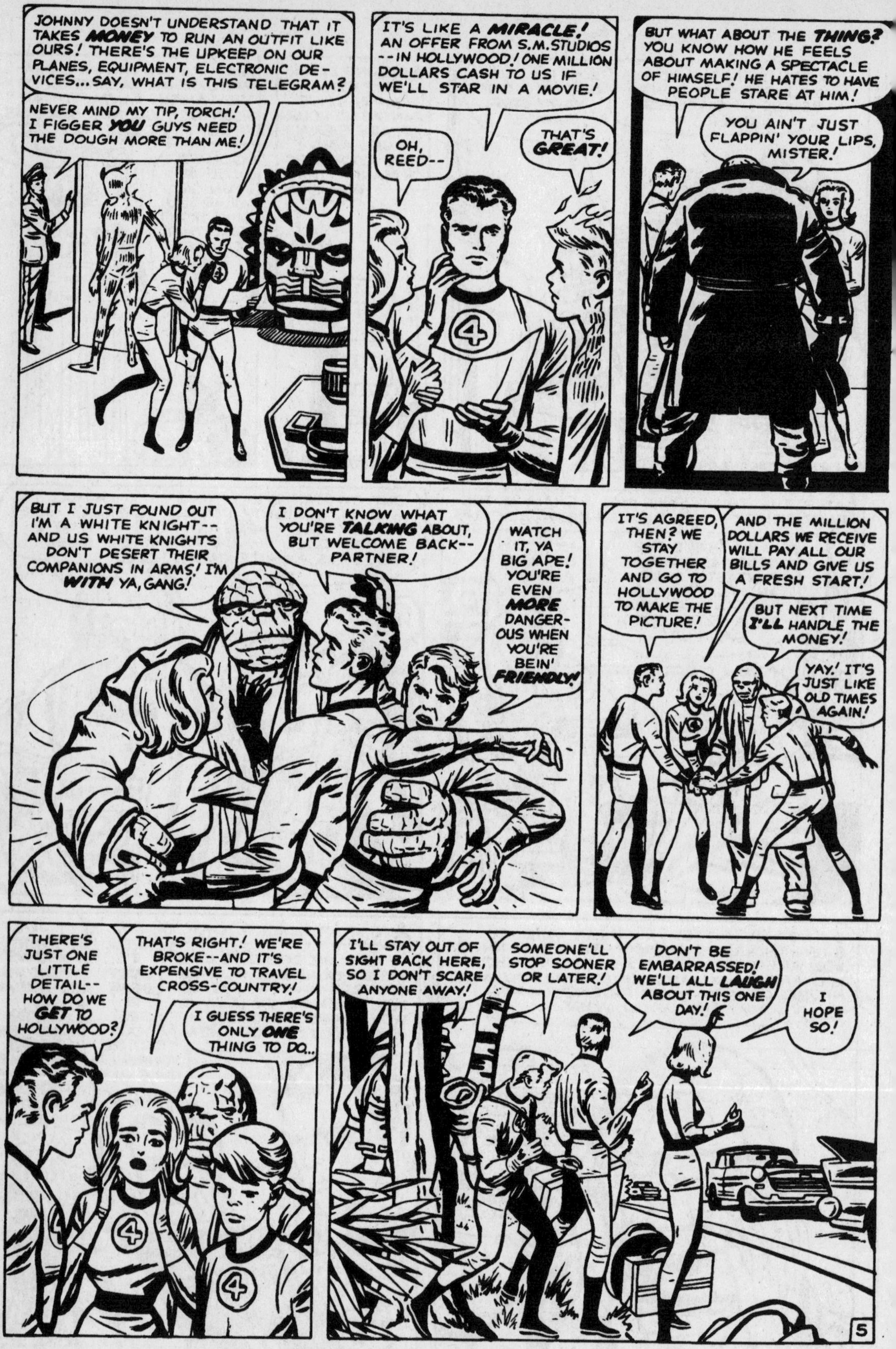

JOHNNY DOESN'T UNDERSTAND THAT IT TAKES MONEY TO RUN AN OUTFIT LIKE OURS! THERE'S THE UPKEEP ON OUR PLANES, EQUIPMENT, ELECTRONIC DEVICES... SAY, WHAT IS THIS TELEGRAM?
NEVER MIND MY TIP, TORCH! I FIGGER YOU GUYS NEED THE DOUGH MORE THAN ME!
IT'S LIKE A MIRACLE! AN OFFER FROM S.M. STUDIOS --IN HOLLYWOOD! ONE MILLION DOLLARS CASH TO US IF WE'LL STAR IN A MOVIE!
OH, REED--
THAT'S GREAT!
BUT WHAT ABOUT THE THING? YOU KNOW HOW HE FEELS ABOUT MAKING A SPECTACLE OF HIMSELF! HE HATES TO HAVE PEOPLE STARE AT HIM!
YOU AIN'T JUST FLAPPIN' YOUR LIPS, MISTER!
BUT I JUST FOUND OUT I'M A WHITE KNIGHT--AND US WHITE KNIGHTS DON'T DESERT THEIR COMPANIONS IN ARMS! I'M WITH YA, GANG!
I DON'T KNOW WHAT YOU'RE TALKING ABOUT, BUT WELCOME BACK--PARTNER!
WATCH IT, YA BIG APE! YOU'RE EVEN MORE DANGEROUS WHEN YOU'RE BEIN' FRIENDLY!
IT'S AGREED, THEN? WE STAY TOGETHER AND GO TO HOLLYWOOD TO MAKE THE PICTURE!
AND THE MILLION DOLLARS WE RECEIVE WILL PAY ALL OUR BILLS AND GIVE US A FRESH START!
BUT NEXT TIME I'LL HANDLE THE MONEY!
YAY! IT'S JUST LIKE OLD TIMES AGAIN!
THERE'S JUST ONE LITTLE DETAIL--HOW DO WE GET TO HOLLYWOOD?
THAT'S RIGHT! WE'RE BROKE--AND IT'S EXPENSIVE TO TRAVEL CROSS-COUNTRY!
I GUESS THERE'S ONLY ONE THING TO DO...
I'LL STAY OUT OF SIGHT BACK HERE, SO I DON'T SCARE ANYONE AWAY!
SOMEONE'LL STOP SOONER OR LATER!
DON'T BE EMBARRASSED! WE'LL ALL LAUGH ABOUT THIS ONE DAY!
I HOPE SO!
5

PART 2 SUB-MARINER GIVES THE ORDERS!

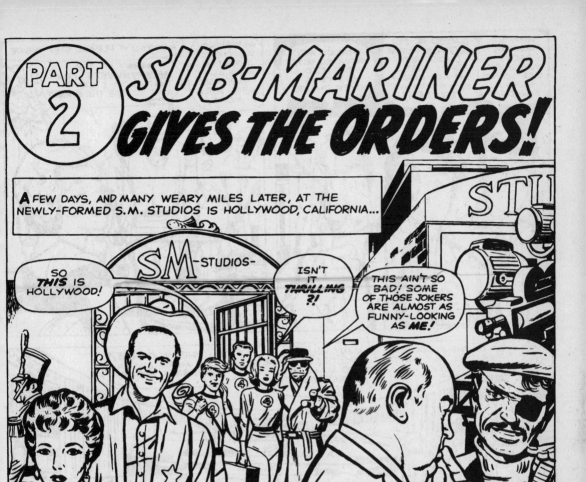

A FEW DAYS, AND MANY WEARY MILES LATER, AT THE NEWLY-FORMED S.M. STUDIOS IS HOLLYWOOD, CALIFORNIA...

SO *THIS* IS HOLLYWOOD!

ISN'T IT *THRILLING* ?!

THIS AIN'T SO BAD! SOME OF THOSE JOKERS ARE ALMOST AS FUNNY-LOOKING AS *ME!*

V-995

GOSH! WITH ALL THE CELEBRITIES AROUND HERE, NOBODY'S EVEN NOTICING *US!*

LET'S BE GLAD THEY *AREN'T!* NEXT THING FOR US TO DO IS FIND OUT WHERE WE'RE SUPPOSED TO REPORT TO!

SAY, CURLY, WHERE'S THE HEAD OFFICE OF THIS JOINT?

R-RIGHT B-BEHIND YOU!!!

6

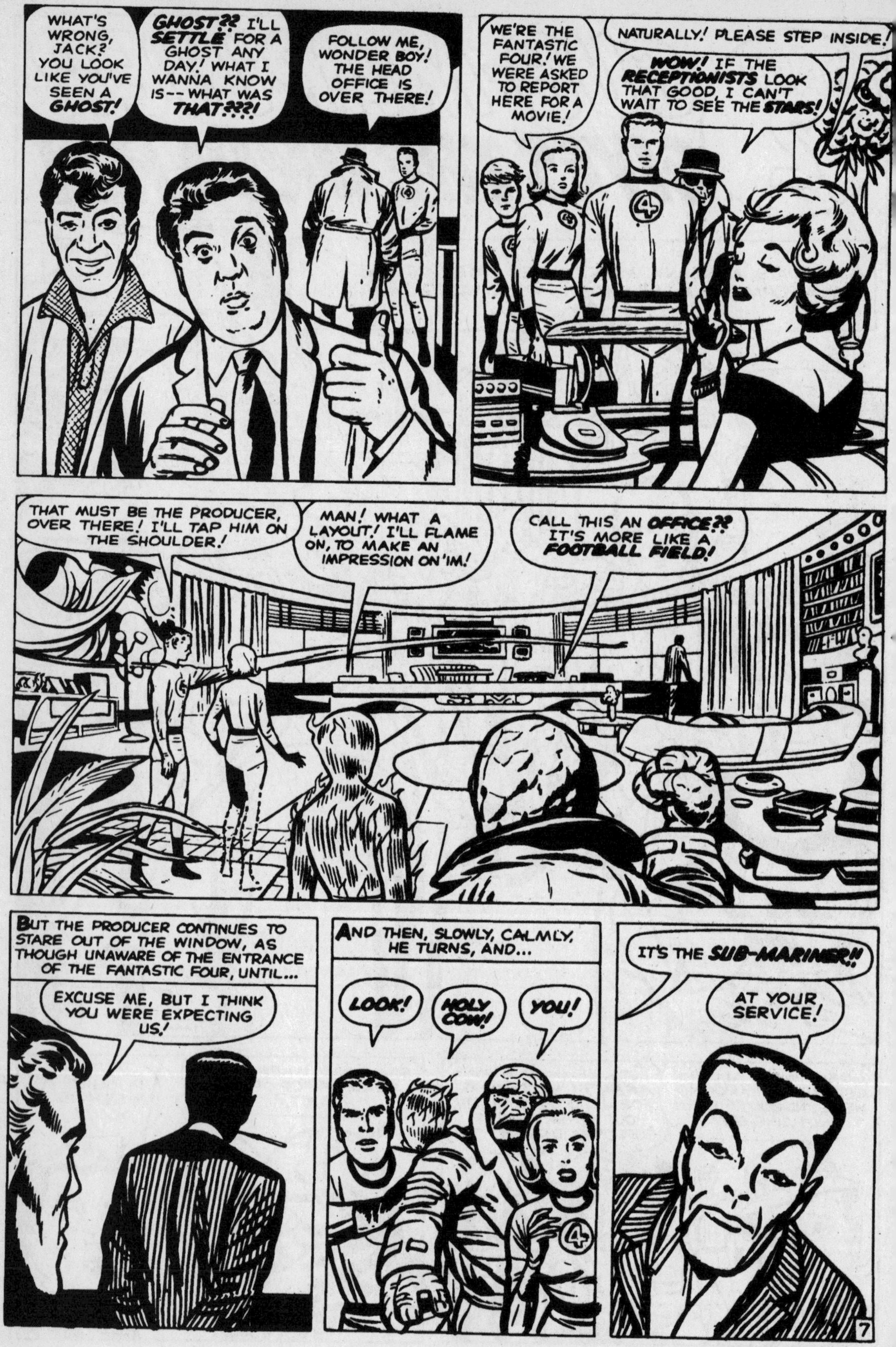
WHAT'S WRONG, JACK? YOU LOOK LIKE YOU'VE SEEN A GHOST!
GHOST?? I'LL SETTLE FOR A GHOST ANY DAY! WHAT I WANNA KNOW IS-- WHAT WAS THAT???!
FOLLOW ME, WONDER BOY! THE HEAD OFFICE IS OVER THERE!
WE'RE THE FANTASTIC FOUR! WE WERE ASKED TO REPORT HERE FOR A MOVIE!
NATURALLY! PLEASE STEP INSIDE!
WOW! IF THE RECEPTIONISTS LOOK THAT GOOD, I CAN'T WAIT TO SEE THE STARS!
THAT MUST BE THE PRODUCER, OVER THERE! I'LL TAP HIM ON THE SHOULDER!
MAN! WHAT A LAYOUT! I'LL FLAME ON, TO MAKE AN IMPRESSION ON 'IM!
CALL THIS AN OFFICE?? IT'S MORE LIKE A FOOTBALL FIELD!
BUT THE PRODUCER CONTINUES TO STARE OUT OF THE WINDOW, AS THOUGH UNAWARE OF THE ENTRANCE OF THE FANTASTIC FOUR, UNTIL...
EXCUSE ME, BUT I THINK YOU WERE EXPECTING US!
AND THEN, SLOWLY, CALMLY, HE TURNS, AND...
LOOK!
HOLY COW!
YOU!
IT'S THE SUB-MARINER!!
AT YOUR SERVICE!
7

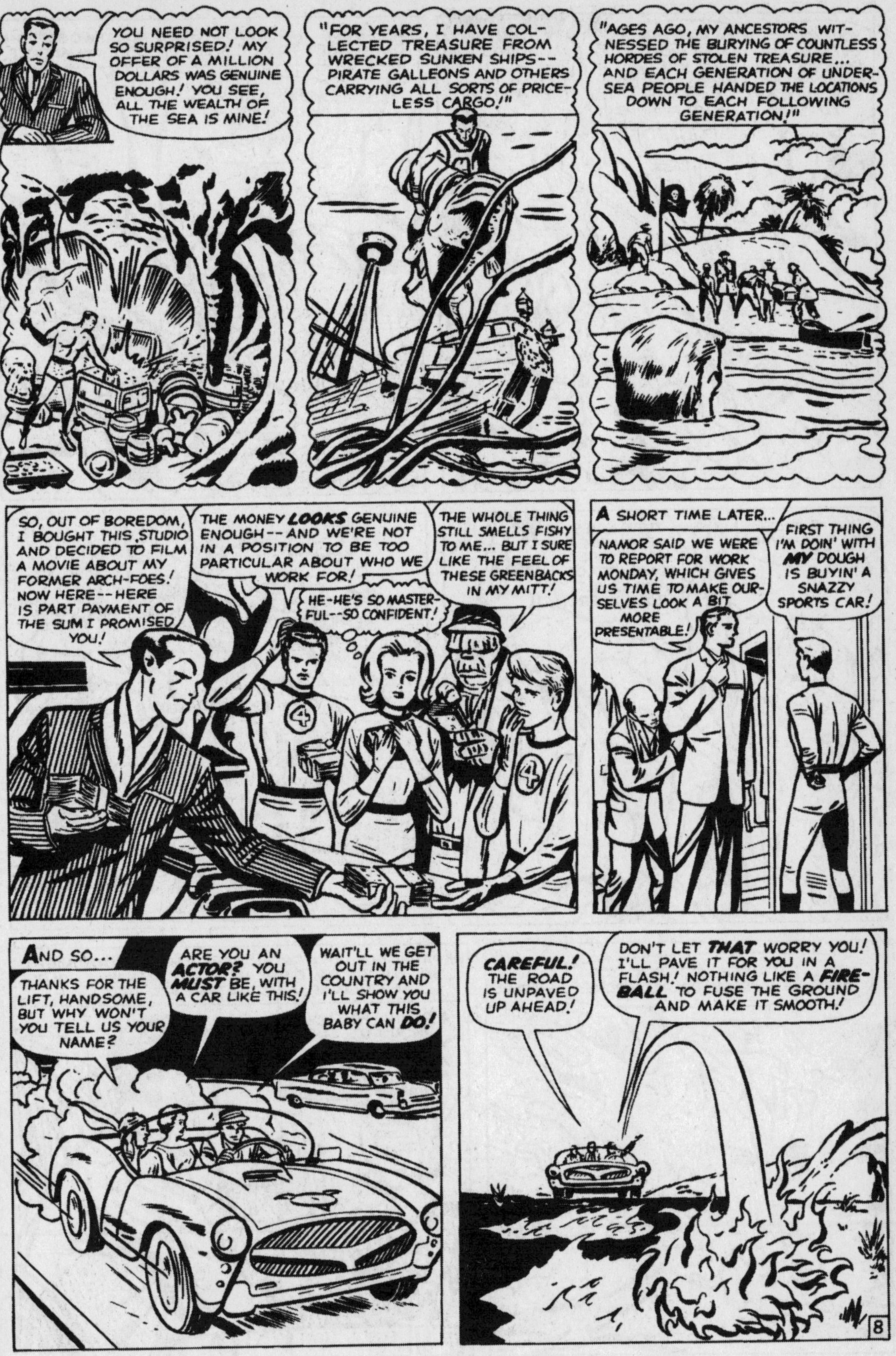
YOU NEED NOT LOOK SO SURPRISED! MY OFFER OF A MILLION DOLLARS WAS GENUINE ENOUGH! YOU SEE, ALL THE WEALTH OF THE SEA IS MINE!
"FOR YEARS, I HAVE COLLECTED TREASURE FROM WRECKED SUNKEN SHIPS-- PIRATE GALLEONS AND OTHERS CARRYING ALL SORTS OF PRICELESS CARGO!"
"AGES AGO, MY ANCESTORS WITNESSED THE BURYING OF COUNTLESS HORDES OF STOLEN TREASURE... AND EACH GENERATION OF UNDERSEA PEOPLE HANDED THE LOCATIONS DOWN TO EACH FOLLOWING GENERATION!"
SO, OUT OF BOREDOM, I BOUGHT THIS STUDIO AND DECIDED TO FILM A MOVIE ABOUT MY FORMER ARCH-FOES! NOW HERE--HERE IS PART PAYMENT OF THE SUM I PROMISED YOU!
THE MONEY LOOKS GENUINE ENOUGH--AND WE'RE NOT IN A POSITION TO BE TOO PARTICULAR ABOUT WHO WE WORK FOR!
HE-HE'S SO MASTERFUL--SO CONFIDENT!
THE WHOLE THING STILL SMELLS FISHY TO ME... BUT I SURE LIKE THE FEEL OF THESE GREENBACKS IN MY MITT!
A SHORT TIME LATER...
NAMOR SAID WE WERE TO REPORT FOR WORK MONDAY, WHICH GIVES US TIME TO MAKE OURSELVES LOOK A BIT MORE PRESENTABLE!
FIRST THING I'M DOIN' WITH MY DOUGH IS BUYIN' A SNAZZY SPORTS CAR!
AND SO...
THANKS FOR THE LIFT, HANDSOME, BUT WHY WON'T YOU TELL US YOUR NAME?
ARE YOU AN ACTOR? YOU MUST BE, WITH A CAR LIKE THIS!
WAIT'LL WE GET OUT IN THE COUNTRY AND I'LL SHOW YOU WHAT THIS BABY CAN DO!
CAREFUL! THE ROAD IS UNPAVED UP AHEAD!
DON'T LET THAT WORRY YOU! I'LL PAVE IT FOR YOU IN A FLASH! NOTHING LIKE A FIREBALL TO FUSE THE GROUND AND MAKE IT SMOOTH!
8

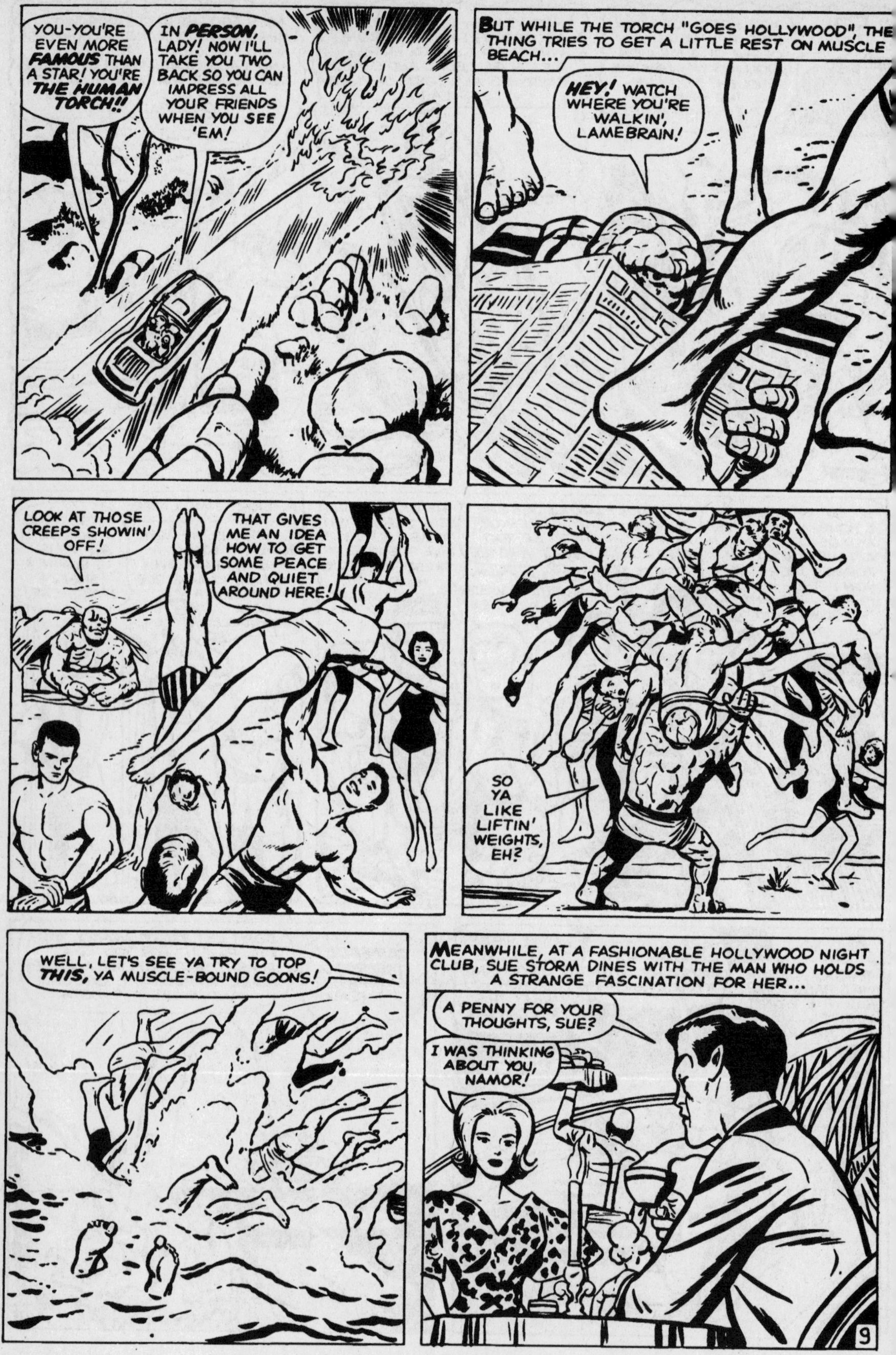
YOU-YOU'RE EVEN MORE FAMOUS THAN A STAR! YOU'RE THE HUMAN TORCH!!
IN PERSON, LADY! NOW I'LL TAKE YOU TWO BACK SO YOU CAN IMPRESS ALL YOUR FRIENDS WHEN YOU SEE 'EM!
BUT WHILE THE TORCH "GOES HOLLYWOOD", THE THING TRIES TO GET A LITTLE REST ON MUSCLE BEACH...
HEY! WATCH WHERE YOU'RE WALKIN', LAMEBRAIN!
LOOK AT THOSE CREEPS SHOWIN' OFF!
THAT GIVES ME AN IDEA HOW TO GET SOME PEACE AND QUIET AROUND HERE!
SO YA LIKE LIFTIN' WEIGHTS, EH?
WELL, LET'S SEE YA TRY TO TOP THIS, YA MUSCLE-BOUND GOONS!
MEANWHILE, AT A FASHIONABLE HOLLYWOOD NIGHT CLUB, SUE STORM DINES WITH THE MAN WHO HOLDS A STRANGE FASCINATION FOR HER...
A PENNY FOR YOUR THOUGHTS, SUE?
I WAS THINKING ABOUT YOU, NAMOR!
9

YOU'VE BEEN SO KIND TO US-- SO GENEROUS! I WAS WONDERING *WHY*?

I'LL GIVE YOU YOUR ANSWER AFTER THE PICTURE IS FINISHED, SUE! WE START THE FILMING SOON!

AND, NOT LONG AFTERWARD, A SLEEK SCHOONER SAILS TO A RARELY VISITED SECTION OF THE FOGGY MEDITERRANEAN.

LAND HO! IT IS *HIDDEN ISLE*, JUST WHERE PRINCE NAMOR SAID IT WOULD BE!

HIDDEN ISLE HAS BEEN UNKNOWN FOR CENTURIES! I DISCOVERED IT RECENTLY ON MY TRAVELS! IT IS *THERE* WE SHALL FILM THE FIRST SCENES OF MY PICTURE --THE SCENES STARRING MR. FANTASTIC!

WHAT ABOUT MY *SCRIPT*?

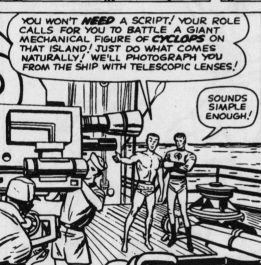

YOU WON'T *NEED* A SCRIPT! YOUR ROLE CALLS FOR YOU TO BATTLE A GIANT MECHANICAL FIGURE OF *CYCLOPS* ON THAT ISLAND! JUST DO WHAT COMES NATURALLY! WE'LL PHOTOGRAPH YOU FROM THE SHIP WITH TELESCOPIC LENSES!

SOUNDS SIMPLE ENOUGH!

NO NEED TO LAUNCH A BOAT FOR ME -- I'LL REACH THE ISLE IN MY *OWN* WAY!

MINUTES LATER...

NO SIGN OF THE MECHANICAL CYCLOPS YET! WONDER WHAT IT LOOKS LIKE? MUST BE A BIG, SHAGGY MONSTER, LIKE THE ONE USED IN THE OLD-TIME MOVIE KING KONG!

THE FOOL *FELL* FOR IT! WAIT TILL HE LEARNS THAT THE CYCLOPS *ISN'T* MECHANICAL! IT'S THE *REAL* CYCLOPS, WHO WON'T ALLOW ANY HUMAN TO LEAVE HIS ISLE-- ALIVE! NOW TO RETURN HOME! WE'RE *FINISHED* HERE!

AFTER ALL THESE CENTURIES-- A HUMAN INTRUDER!

CYCLOPS!! YOU'RE-- YOU'RE *ALIVE*!

10

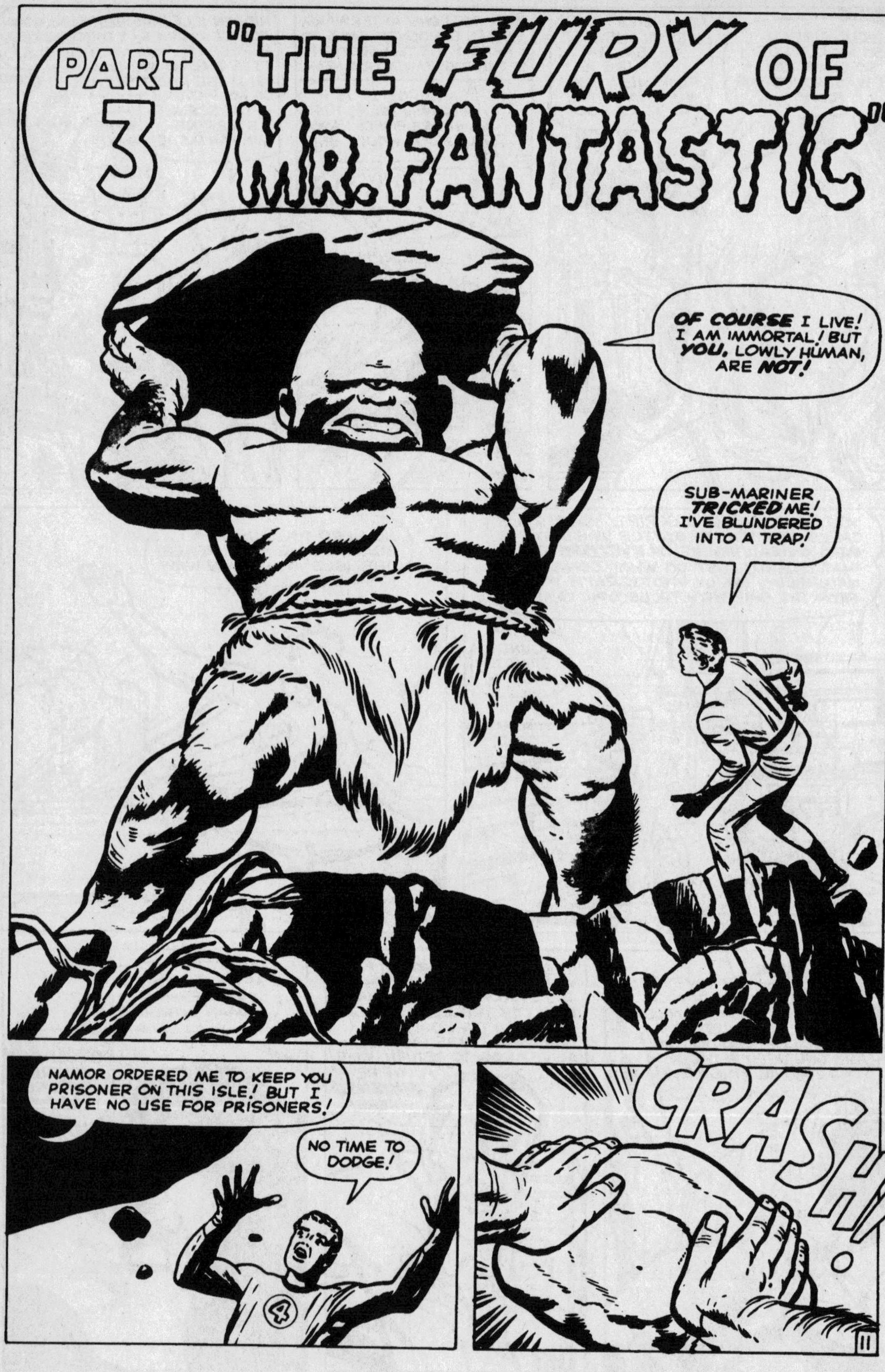
PART 3
"THE FURY OF MR. FANTASTIC"
OF COURSE I LIVE! I AM IMMORTAL! BUT YOU, LOWLY HUMAN, ARE NOT!
SUB-MARINER TRICKED ME! I'VE BLUNDERED INTO A TRAP!
NAMOR ORDERED ME TO KEEP YOU PRISONER ON THIS ISLE! BUT I HAVE NO USE FOR PRISONERS!
NO TIME TO DODGE!
CRASH!
11

SECONDS LATER, AFTER THE DUST HAS CLEARED...

ONE THING NAMOR *FORGOT* TO TELL YOU-- THE REASON THEY CALL ME *MR. FANTASTIC!*

RUN, PUNY HUMAN! RUN TILL YOU DROP! THERE IS NO ESCAPE FROM HIDDEN ISLE! SOONER OR LATER I SHALL CRUSH YOU!

.WELL, DON'T JUST *STAND* THERE! IF YOU'RE GONNA THROW THAT THING, THEN *THROW* IT!

THOSE WILL BE THE LAST WORDS YOU'LL EVER UTTER!

I *HOPED* YOU'D DO THAT! AND NOW...

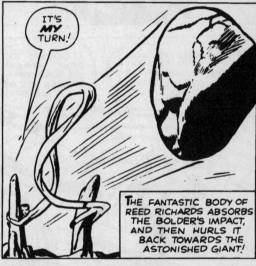

IT'S *MY* TURN!

THE FANTASTIC BODY OF REED RICHARDS ABSORBS THE BOLDER'S IMPACT, AND THEN HURLS IT BACK TOWARDS THE ASTONISHED GIANT!

YOU ARE *MORE* THAN HUMAN! BUT STILL NO MATCH FOR *CYCLOPS!*

MY STRENGTH IS TOO GREAT! *NOTHING* YOU CAN DO WILL STOP ME!

THE DINOSAURS WERE STRONG, TOO-- BUT LOOK WHAT HAPPENED TO *THEM!*

12

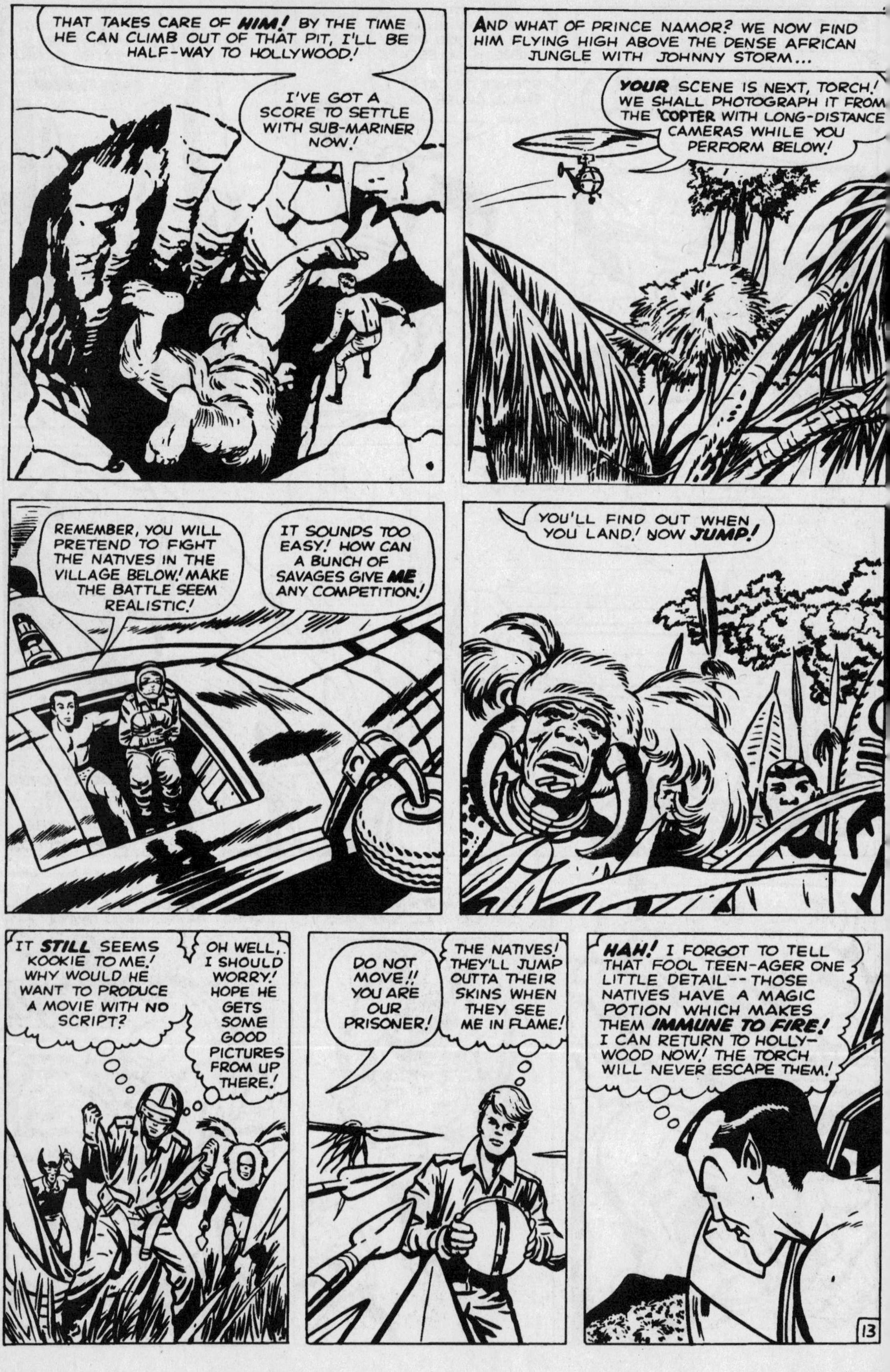

THAT TAKES CARE OF HIM! BY THE TIME HE CAN CLIMB OUT OF THAT PIT, I'LL BE HALF-WAY TO HOLLYWOOD!
I'VE GOT A SCORE TO SETTLE WITH SUB-MARINER NOW!
AND WHAT OF PRINCE NAMOR? WE NOW FIND HIM FLYING HIGH ABOVE THE DENSE AFRICAN JUNGLE WITH JOHNNY STORM...
YOUR SCENE IS NEXT, TORCH! WE SHALL PHOTOGRAPH IT FROM THE 'COPTER WITH LONG-DISTANCE CAMERAS WHILE YOU PERFORM BELOW!
REMEMBER, YOU WILL PRETEND TO FIGHT THE NATIVES IN THE VILLAGE BELOW! MAKE THE BATTLE SEEM REALISTIC!
IT SOUNDS TOO EASY! HOW CAN A BUNCH OF SAVAGES GIVE ME ANY COMPETITION!
YOU'LL FIND OUT WHEN YOU LAND! NOW JUMP!
IT STILL SEEMS KOOKIE TO ME! WHY WOULD HE WANT TO PRODUCE A MOVIE WITH NO SCRIPT?
OH WELL, I SHOULD WORRY! HOPE HE GETS SOME GOOD PICTURES FROM UP THERE!
DO NOT MOVE!! YOU ARE OUR PRISONER!
THE NATIVES! THEY'LL JUMP OUTTA THEIR SKINS WHEN THEY SEE ME IN FLAME!
HAH! I FORGOT TO TELL THAT FOOL TEEN-AGER ONE LITTLE DETAIL-- THOSE NATIVES HAVE A MAGIC POTION WHICH MAKES THEM IMMUNE TO FIRE! I CAN RETURN TO HOLLY-WOOD NOW! THE TORCH WILL NEVER ESCAPE THEM!
13

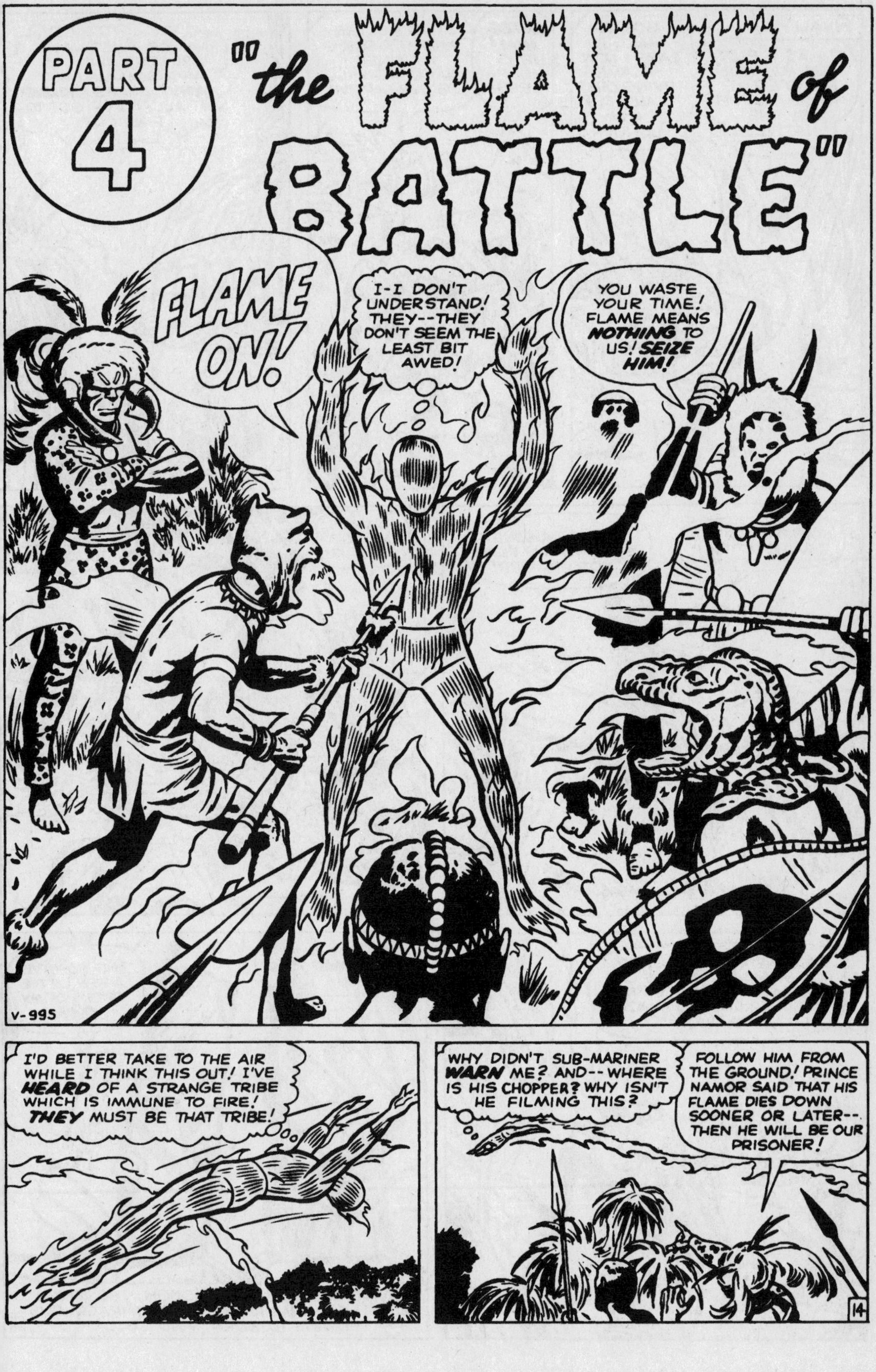
PART 4
"the FLAME of BATTLE"
FLAME ON!
I-I DON'T UNDERSTAND! THEY--THEY DON'T SEEM THE LEAST BIT AWED!
YOU WASTE YOUR TIME! FLAME MEANS NOTHING TO US! SEIZE HIM!
V-995
I'D BETTER TAKE TO THE AIR WHILE I THINK THIS OUT! I'VE HEARD OF A STRANGE TRIBE WHICH IS IMMUNE TO FIRE! THEY MUST BE THAT TRIBE!
WHY DIDN'T SUB-MARINER WARN ME? AND--WHERE IS HIS CHOPPER? WHY ISN'T HE FILMING THIS?
FOLLOW HIM FROM THE GROUND! PRINCE NAMOR SAID THAT HIS FLAME DIES DOWN SOONER OR LATER--. THEN HE WILL BE OUR PRISONER!
14

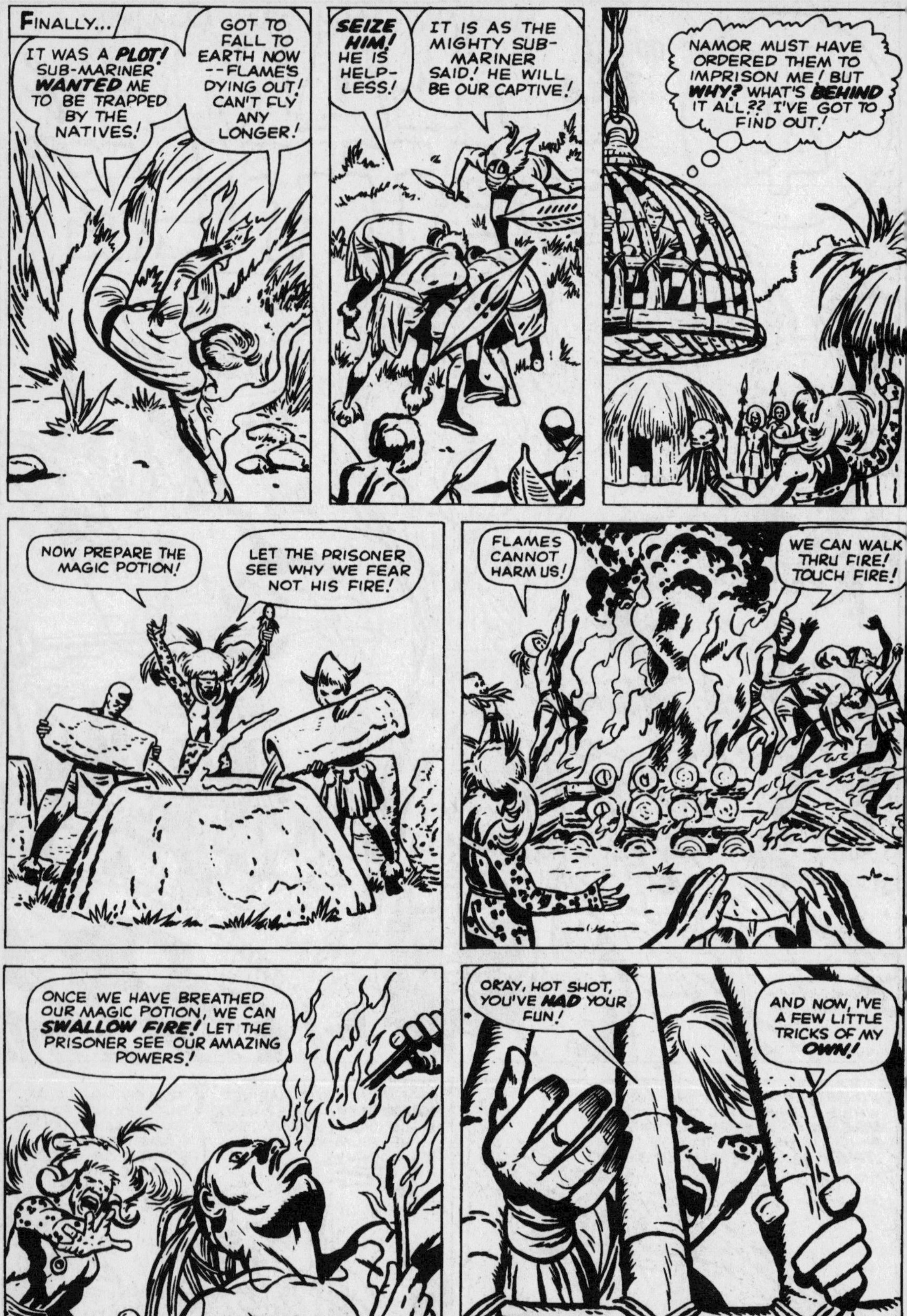
FINALLY...
IT WAS A PLOT! SUB-MARINER WANTED ME TO BE TRAPPED BY THE NATIVES!
GOT TO FALL TO EARTH NOW --FLAME'S DYING OUT! CAN'T FLY ANY LONGER!
SEIZE HIM! HE IS HELP-LESS!
IT IS AS THE MIGHTY SUB-MARINER SAID! HE WILL BE OUR CAPTIVE!
NAMOR MUST HAVE ORDERED THEM TO IMPRISON ME! BUT WHY? WHAT'S BEHIND IT ALL?? I'VE GOT TO FIND OUT!
NOW PREPARE THE MAGIC POTION!
LET THE PRISONER SEE WHY WE FEAR NOT HIS FIRE!
FLAMES CANNOT HARM US!
WE CAN WALK THRU FIRE! TOUCH FIRE!
ONCE WE HAVE BREATHED OUR MAGIC POTION, WE CAN SWALLOW FIRE! LET THE PRISONER SEE OUR AMAZING POWERS!
OKAY, HOT SHOT, YOU'VE HAD YOUR FUN!
AND NOW, I'VE A FEW LITTLE TRICKS OF MY OWN!
HAVING RESTED LONG ENOUGH, THE TORCH'S BODY AGAIN HAS REGAINED ITS MIRACULOUS POWER TO BURN, AND SO...
15

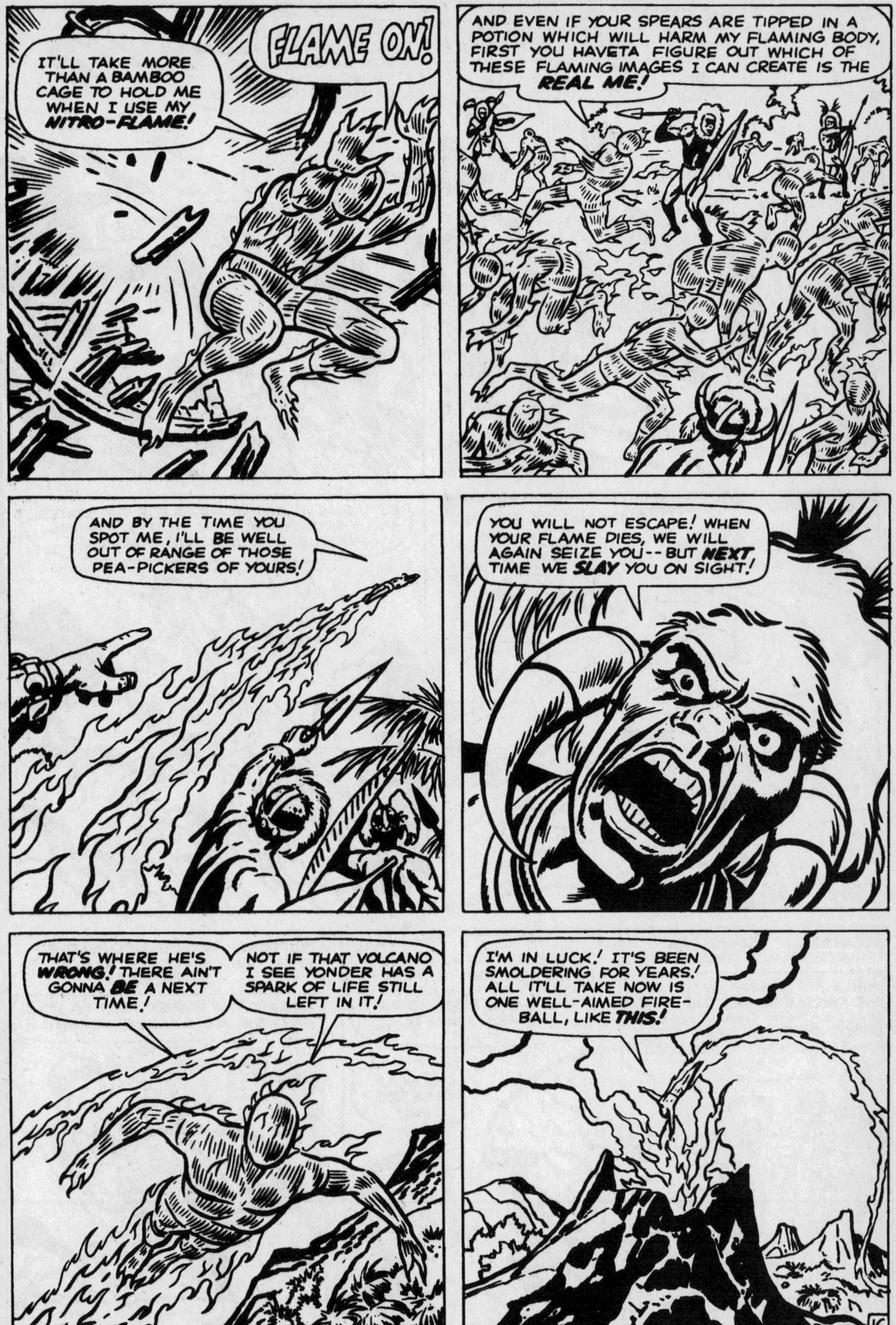

IT'LL TAKE MORE THAN A BAMBOO CAGE TO HOLD ME WHEN I USE MY NITRO-FLAME!
FLAME ON!
AND EVEN IF YOUR SPEARS ARE TIPPED IN A POTION WHICH WILL HARM MY FLAMING BODY, FIRST YOU HAVETA FIGURE OUT WHICH OF THESE FLAMING IMAGES I CAN CREATE IS THE REAL ME!
AND BY THE TIME YOU SPOT ME, I'LL BE WELL OUT OF RANGE OF THOSE PEA-PICKERS OF YOURS!
YOU WILL NOT ESCAPE! WHEN YOUR FLAME DIES, WE WILL AGAIN SEIZE YOU-- BUT NEXT TIME WE SLAY YOU ON SIGHT!
THAT'S WHERE HE'S WRONG! THERE AIN'T GONNA BE A NEXT TIME!
NOT IF THAT VOLCANO I SEE YONDER HAS A SPARK OF LIFE STILL LEFT IN IT!
I'M IN LUCK! IT'S BEEN SMOLDERING FOR YEARS! ALL IT'LL TAKE NOW IS ONE WELL-AIMED FIRE-BALL, LIKE THIS!
16

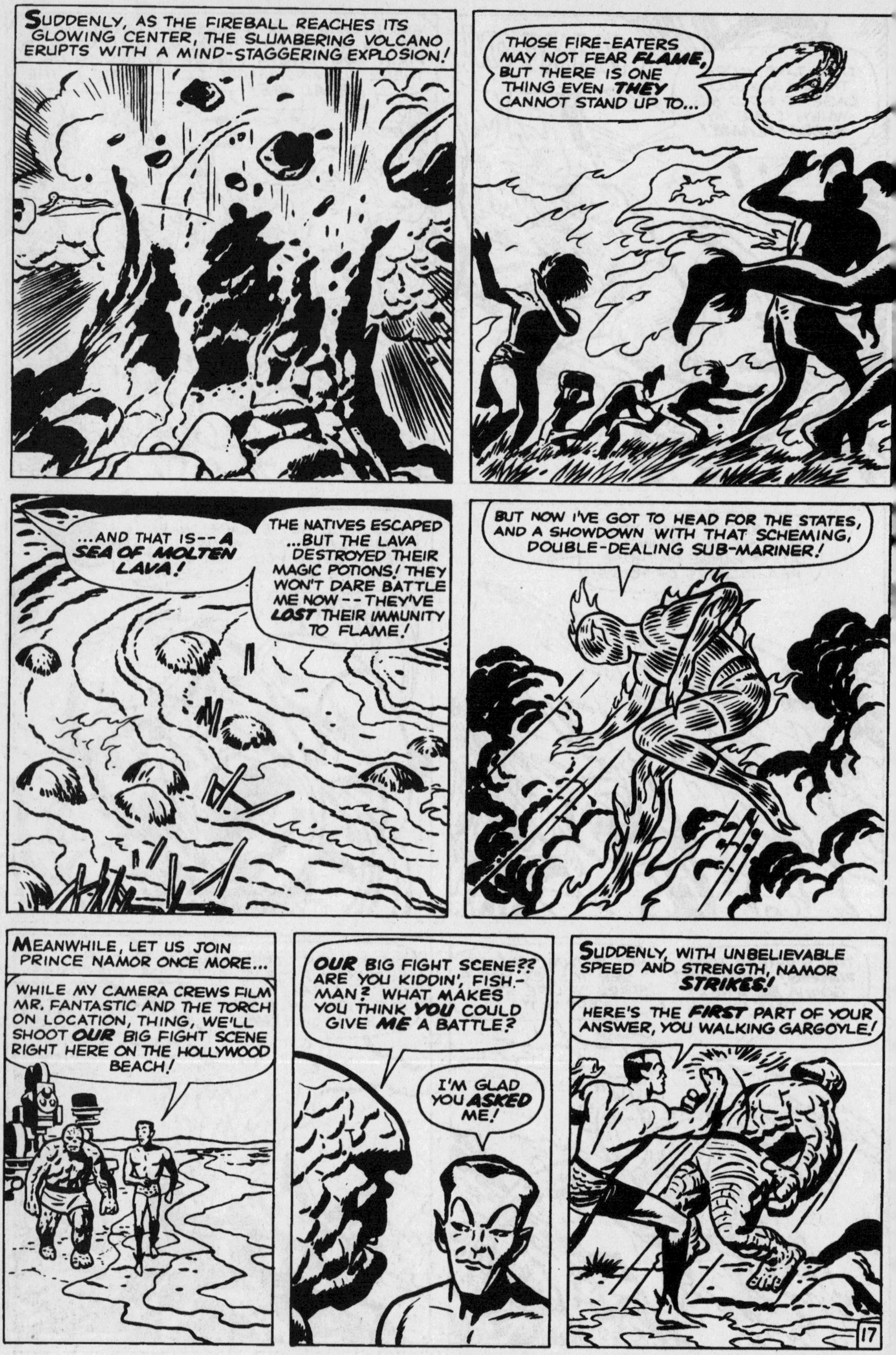
SUDDENLY, AS THE FIREBALL REACHES ITS GLOWING CENTER, THE SLUMBERING VOLCANO ERUPTS WITH A MIND-STAGGERING EXPLOSION!
THOSE FIRE-EATERS MAY NOT FEAR FLAME, BUT THERE IS ONE THING EVEN THEY CANNOT STAND UP TO...
...AND THAT IS--A SEA OF MOLTEN LAVA!
THE NATIVES ESCAPED ...BUT THE LAVA DESTROYED THEIR MAGIC POTIONS! THEY WON'T DARE BATTLE ME NOW--THEY'VE LOST THEIR IMMUNITY TO FLAME!
BUT NOW I'VE GOT TO HEAD FOR THE STATES, AND A SHOWDOWN WITH THAT SCHEMING, DOUBLE-DEALING SUB-MARINER!
MEANWHILE, LET US JOIN PRINCE NAMOR ONCE MORE...
WHILE MY CAMERA CREWS FILM MR. FANTASTIC AND THE TORCH ON LOCATION, THING, WE'LL SHOOT OUR BIG FIGHT SCENE RIGHT HERE ON THE HOLLYWOOD BEACH!
OUR BIG FIGHT SCENE?? ARE YOU KIDDIN', FISH-MAN? WHAT MAKES YOU THINK YOU COULD GIVE ME A BATTLE?
I'M GLAD YOU ASKED ME!
SUDDENLY, WITH UNBELIEVABLE SPEED AND STRENGTH, NAMOR STRIKES!
HERE'S THE FIRST PART OF YOUR ANSWER, YOU WALKING GARGOYLE!
17

I'VE BEEN WAITING FOR A CHANCE TO ROUGH YOU UP FOR A LONG TIME, GRUESOME!

YEAH? WELL, IT LOOKS LIKE YA DIDN'T WAIT LONG ENOUGH, LOUD-MOUTH!

WHUMP!

NOTHING PLEASES ME MORE THAN TO HAVE A FOE GET OVER-CONFIDENT!

HUH?

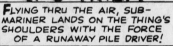

FLYING THRU THE AIR, SUB-MARINER LANDS ON THE THING'S SHOULDERS WITH THE FORCE OF A RUNAWAY PILE DRIVER!

TIME AND AGAIN THE MIGHTY MONARCH OF THE SEA HURLS HIMSELF HIGH ABOVE HIS VICTIM, AND THEN...

...OVER AND OVER HE HAMMERS THE STUNNED THING DEEPER AND DEEPER INTO THE SOGGY SAND BELOW!

OKAY, WET-HEAD, YOU HAD YOUR FUN! JUST LET ME SHOVE THIS MUD OFF ME, AND I'LL MAKE MINCE-MEAT OUTTA YA!

YOU'RE NOT BEATEN YET??!

FOR A MOMENT, THE FIGHT IS A STAND-OFF, AS THE WEARY THING LUMBERS GROGGILY ONTO SHORE--ONE QUESTION REPEATING OVER AND OVER AGAIN IN HIS ACHING HEAD...

WHY DOESN'T NAMOR GET TIRED?? WHERE DOES HIS STRENGTH COME FROM??

AND THEN, IN A BLINDING FLASH, THE ANSWER COMES TO HIM...

THE WATER! I SHOULDA GUESSED! THAT'S WHY HE WANTED TO FIGHT ON THE BEACH!

THIS IS IT, MISTER!

18

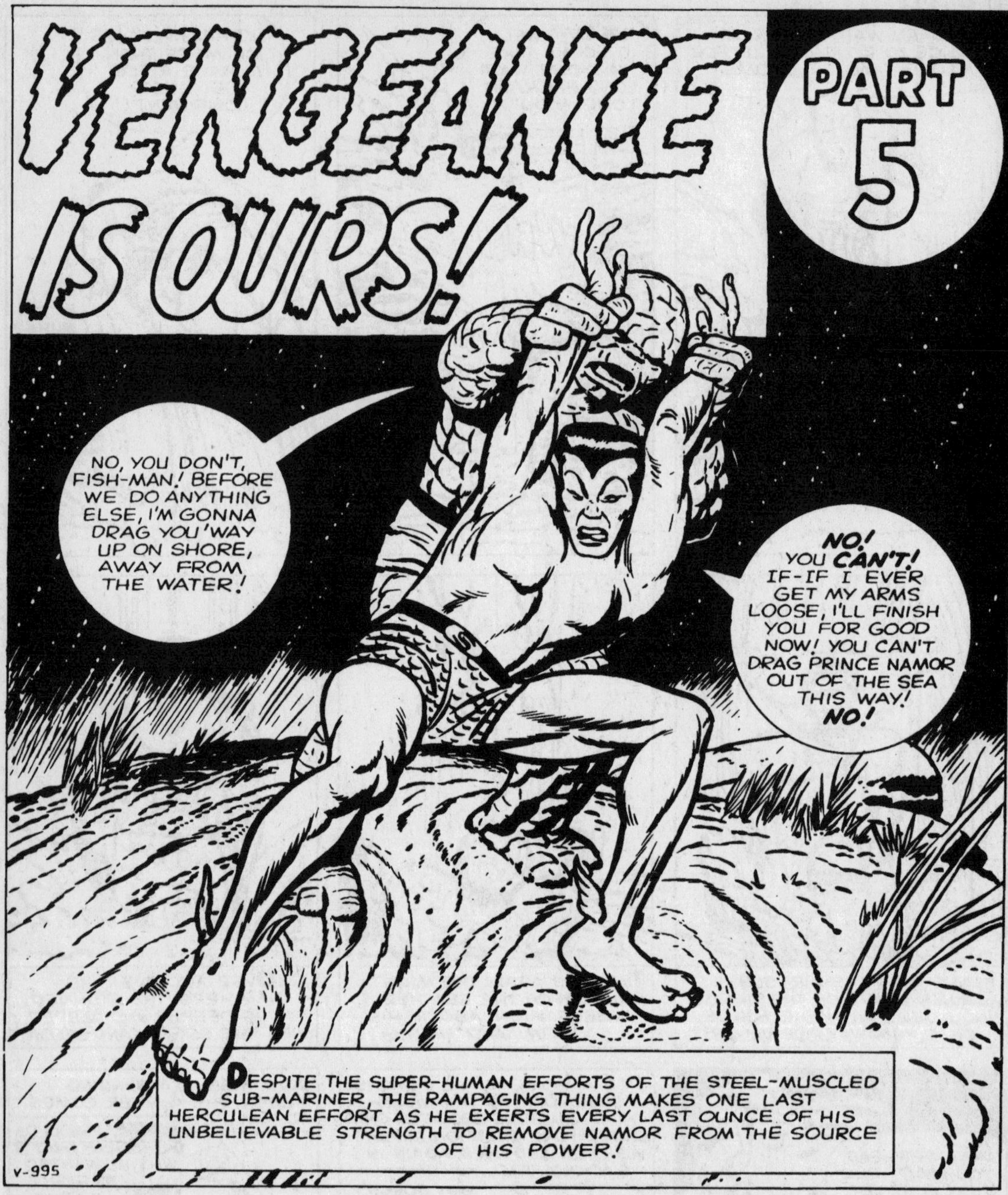
VENGEANCE IS OURS!
PART 5
NO, YOU DON'T, FISH-MAN! BEFORE WE DO ANYTHING ELSE, I'M GONNA DRAG YOU 'WAY UP ON SHORE, AWAY FROM THE WATER!
NO! YOU CAN'T! IF-IF I EVER GET MY ARMS LOOSE, I'LL FINISH YOU FOR GOOD NOW! YOU CAN'T DRAG PRINCE NAMOR OUT OF THE SEA THIS WAY! NO!
DESPITE THE SUPER-HUMAN EFFORTS OF THE STEEL-MUSCLED SUB-MARINER, THE RAMPAGING THING MAKES ONE LAST HERCULEAN EFFORT AS HE EXERTS EVERY LAST OUNCE OF HIS UNBELIEVABLE STRENGTH TO REMOVE NAMOR FROM THE SOURCE OF HIS POWER!
V-995

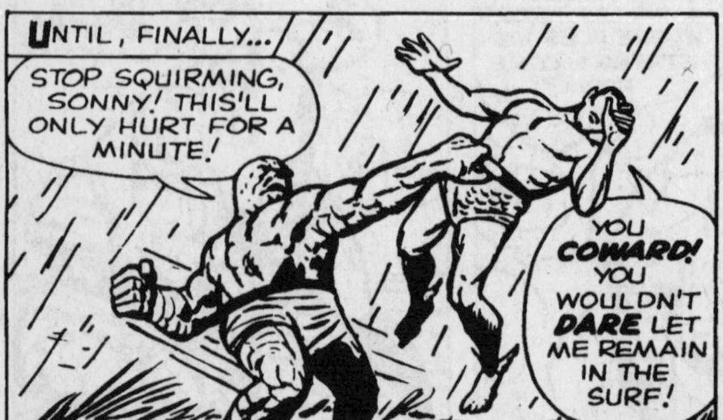
UNTIL, FINALLY...
STOP SQUIRMING, SONNY! THIS'LL ONLY HURT FOR A MINUTE!
YOU COWARD! YOU WOULDN'T DARE LET ME REMAIN IN THE SURF!

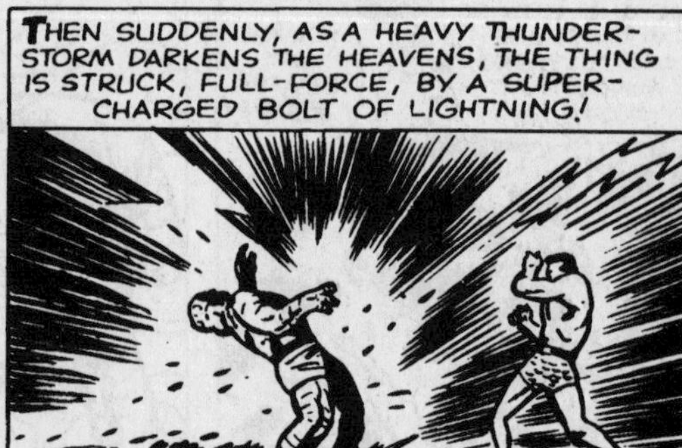
THEN SUDDENLY, AS A HEAVY THUNDER-STORM DARKENS THE HEAVENS, THE THING IS STRUCK, FULL-FORCE, BY A SUPER-CHARGED BOLT OF LIGHTNING!
19

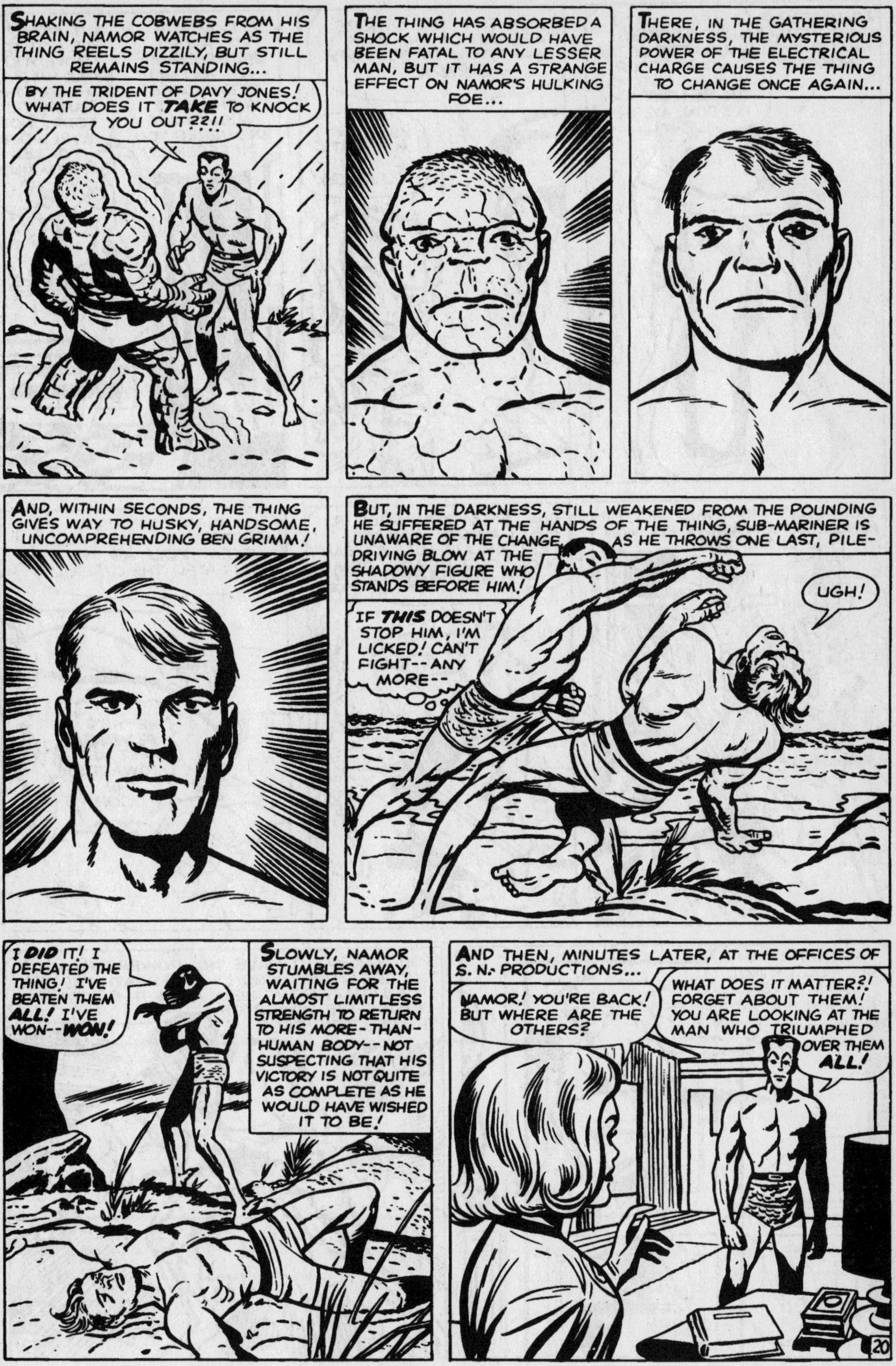
SHAKING THE COBWEBS FROM HIS BRAIN, NAMOR WATCHES AS THE THING REELS DIZZILY, BUT STILL REMAINS STANDING...
BY THE TRIDENT OF DAVY JONES! WHAT DOES IT TAKE TO KNOCK YOU OUT??!!
THE THING HAS ABSORBED A SHOCK WHICH WOULD HAVE BEEN FATAL TO ANY LESSER MAN, BUT IT HAS A STRANGE EFFECT ON NAMOR'S HULKING FOE...
THERE, IN THE GATHERING DARKNESS, THE MYSTERIOUS POWER OF THE ELECTRICAL CHARGE CAUSES THE THING TO CHANGE ONCE AGAIN...
AND, WITHIN SECONDS, THE THING GIVES WAY TO HUSKY, HANDSOME, UNCOMPREHENDING BEN GRIMM!
BUT, IN THE DARKNESS, STILL WEAKENED FROM THE POUNDING HE SUFFERED AT THE HANDS OF THE THING, SUB-MARINER IS UNAWARE OF THE CHANGE, AS HE THROWS ONE LAST, PILE-DRIVING BLOW AT THE SHADOWY FIGURE WHO STANDS BEFORE HIM!
IF THIS DOESN'T STOP HIM, I'M LICKED! CAN'T FIGHT--ANY MORE--
UGH!
I DID IT! I DEFEATED THE THING! I'VE BEATEN THEM ALL! I'VE WON--WON!
SLOWLY, NAMOR STUMBLES AWAY, WAITING FOR THE ALMOST LIMITLESS STRENGTH TO RETURN TO HIS MORE-THAN-HUMAN BODY--NOT SUSPECTING THAT HIS VICTORY IS NOT QUITE AS COMPLETE AS HE WOULD HAVE WISHED IT TO BE!
AND THEN, MINUTES LATER, AT THE OFFICES OF S. N. PRODUCTIONS...
NAMOR! YOU'RE BACK! BUT WHERE ARE THE OTHERS?
WHAT DOES IT MATTER?! FORGET ABOUT THEM! YOU ARE LOOKING AT THE MAN WHO TRIUMPHED OVER THEM ALL!
20

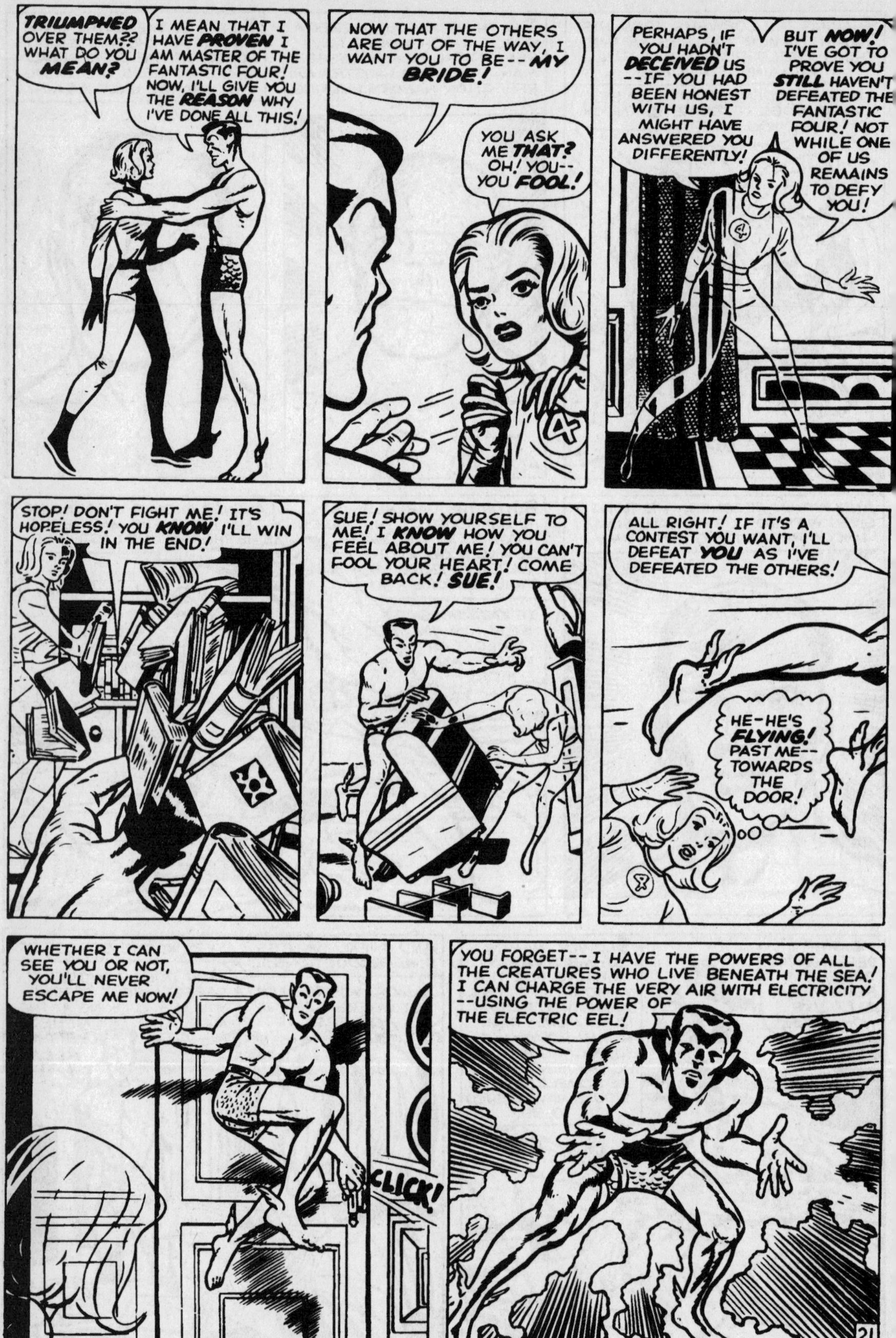
TRIUMPHED OVER THEM?? WHAT DO YOU MEAN?
I MEAN THAT I HAVE PROVEN I AM MASTER OF THE FANTASTIC FOUR! NOW, I'LL GIVE YOU THE REASON WHY I'VE DONE ALL THIS!
NOW THAT THE OTHERS ARE OUT OF THE WAY, I WANT YOU TO BE--MY BRIDE!
YOU ASK ME THAT? OH! YOU--YOU FOOL!
PERHAPS, IF YOU HADN'T DECEIVED US --IF YOU HAD BEEN HONEST WITH US, I MIGHT HAVE ANSWERED YOU DIFFERENTLY!
BUT NOW! I'VE GOT TO PROVE YOU STILL HAVEN'T DEFEATED THE FANTASTIC FOUR! NOT WHILE ONE OF US REMAINS TO DEFY YOU!
STOP! DON'T FIGHT ME! IT'S HOPELESS! YOU KNOW I'LL WIN IN THE END!
SUE! SHOW YOURSELF TO ME! I KNOW HOW YOU FEEL ABOUT ME! YOU CAN'T FOOL YOUR HEART! COME BACK! SUE!
ALL RIGHT! IF IT'S A CONTEST YOU WANT, I'LL DEFEAT YOU AS I'VE DEFEATED THE OTHERS!
HE-HE'S FLYING! PAST ME--TOWARDS THE DOOR!
WHETHER I CAN SEE YOU OR NOT, YOU'LL NEVER ESCAPE ME NOW!
CLICK!
YOU FORGET--I HAVE THE POWERS OF ALL THE CREATURES WHO LIVE BENEATH THE SEA! I CAN CHARGE THE VERY AIR WITH ELECTRICITY --USING THE POWER OF THE ELECTRIC EEL!
21

I MYSELF AM NOT WITHOUT RESOURCES, NAMOR!
THIS CARPET, THROWN OVER YOU, WILL PROVIDE INSULATION FOR ME--PROTECTING ME FROM THE ELECTRIC CURRENT!
YOU ARE WORTHY OF ME, FEMALE! IN EVERY WAY! BUT HERE IS A POWER YOU CANNOT COMBAT! THE RADAR SENSE OF THE CAVE FISH FROM THE LOWEST DEPTHS OF THE SEA!
THEY HAVE NO EYES, BUT CAN SENSE THE PRESENCE OF OTHERS BY USING THEIR RADAR-TYPE INSTINCTS! AS I SHALL DO WITH YOU!
EDITOR'S NOTE: TO EXPLAIN MORE FULLY HOW NAMOR USES HIS "RADAR VISION", THIS IS THE WAY SUE ACTUALLY IS... INVISIBLE TO THE NORMAL EYE!
BUT, TO NAMOR, USING HIS "RADAR VISION", THIS IS THE WAY THE INVISIBLE GIRL APPEARS TO HIM --LIKE AN IMAGE ON A RADAR SCREEN!
NOW THAT I KNOW WHERE YOU ARE, YOU CAN ELUDE ME NO LONGER!
TAKE YOUR HANDS OFF ME, YOU--YOU BARBARIAN!
YOUR STRUGGLES ARE USELESS! I LIKE A WOMAN WITH SPIRIT! ONLY SUCH A FEMALE CAN BE A FITTING MATE FOR NAMOR, THE MONARCH OF THE SEA!
NO! I'M NOT BEATEN YET! I'LL--WHAT'S THAT??!
CRASH!
ALL RIGHT, NAMOR THIS IS IT! RELEASE THAT GIRL!
KEEP OUTTA THIS, REED! YOU PROMISED I COULD HAVE 'IM FIRST!
OH NO! THAT'S MY SISTER HE'S THREATENING! HE'S MINE!
22

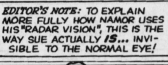

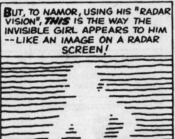

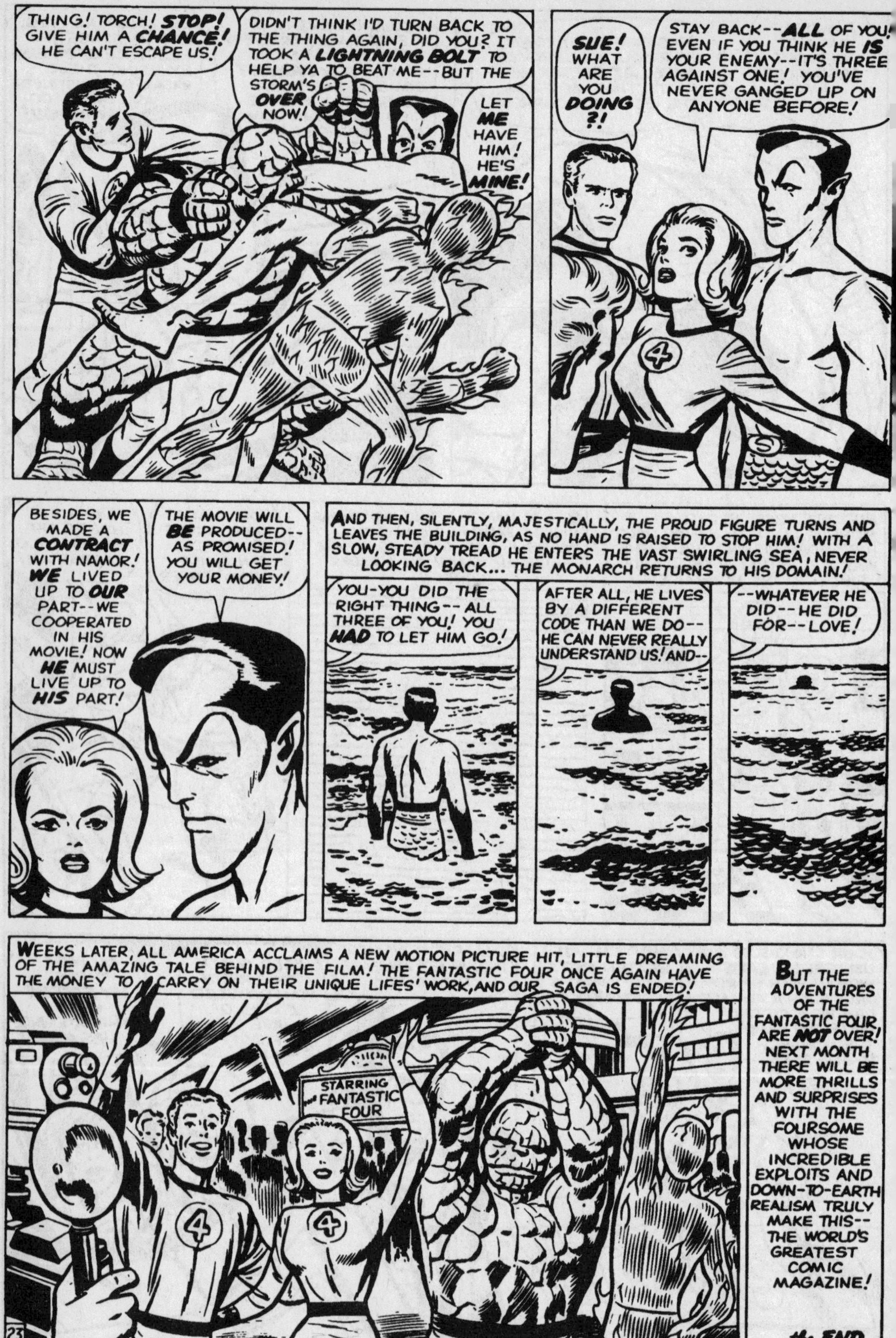
THING! TORCH! STOP! GIVE HIM A CHANCE! HE CAN'T ESCAPE US!
DIDN'T THINK I'D TURN BACK TO THE THING AGAIN, DID YOU? IT TOOK A LIGHTNING BOLT TO HELP YA TO BEAT ME--BUT THE STORM'S OVER NOW!
LET ME HAVE HIM! HE'S MINE!
STAY BACK--ALL OF YOU! EVEN IF YOU THINK HE IS YOUR ENEMY--IT'S THREE AGAINST ONE! YOU'VE NEVER GANGED UP ON ANYONE BEFORE!
SUE! WHAT ARE YOU DOING ?!
BESIDES, WE MADE A CONTRACT WITH NAMOR! WE LIVED UP TO OUR PART--WE COOPERATED IN HIS MOVIE! NOW HE MUST LIVE UP TO HIS PART!
THE MOVIE WILL BE PRODUCED--AS PROMISED! YOU WILL GET YOUR MONEY!
AND THEN, SILENTLY, MAJESTICALLY, THE PROUD FIGURE TURNS AND LEAVES THE BUILDING, AS NO HAND IS RAISED TO STOP HIM! WITH A SLOW, STEADY TREAD HE ENTERS THE VAST SWIRLING SEA, NEVER LOOKING BACK... THE MONARCH RETURNS TO HIS DOMAIN!
YOU-YOU DID THE RIGHT THING--ALL THREE OF YOU! YOU HAD TO LET HIM GO!
AFTER ALL, HE LIVES BY A DIFFERENT CODE THAN WE DO--HE CAN NEVER REALLY UNDERSTAND US! AND--
--WHATEVER HE DID--HE DID FOR--LOVE!
WEEKS LATER, ALL AMERICA ACCLAIMS A NEW MOTION PICTURE HIT, LITTLE DREAMING OF THE AMAZING TALE BEHIND THE FILM! THE FANTASTIC FOUR ONCE AGAIN HAVE THE MONEY TO CARRY ON THEIR UNIQUE LIFES' WORK, AND OUR SAGA IS ENDED!
STARRING FANTASTIC FOUR
23
BUT THE ADVENTURES OF THE FANTASTIC FOUR ARE NOT OVER! NEXT MONTH THERE WILL BE MORE THRILLS AND SURPRISES WITH THE FOURSOME WHOSE INCREDIBLE EXPLOITS AND DOWN-TO-EARTH REALISM TRULY MAKE THIS--THE WORLD'S GREATEST COMIC MAGAZINE!
the END

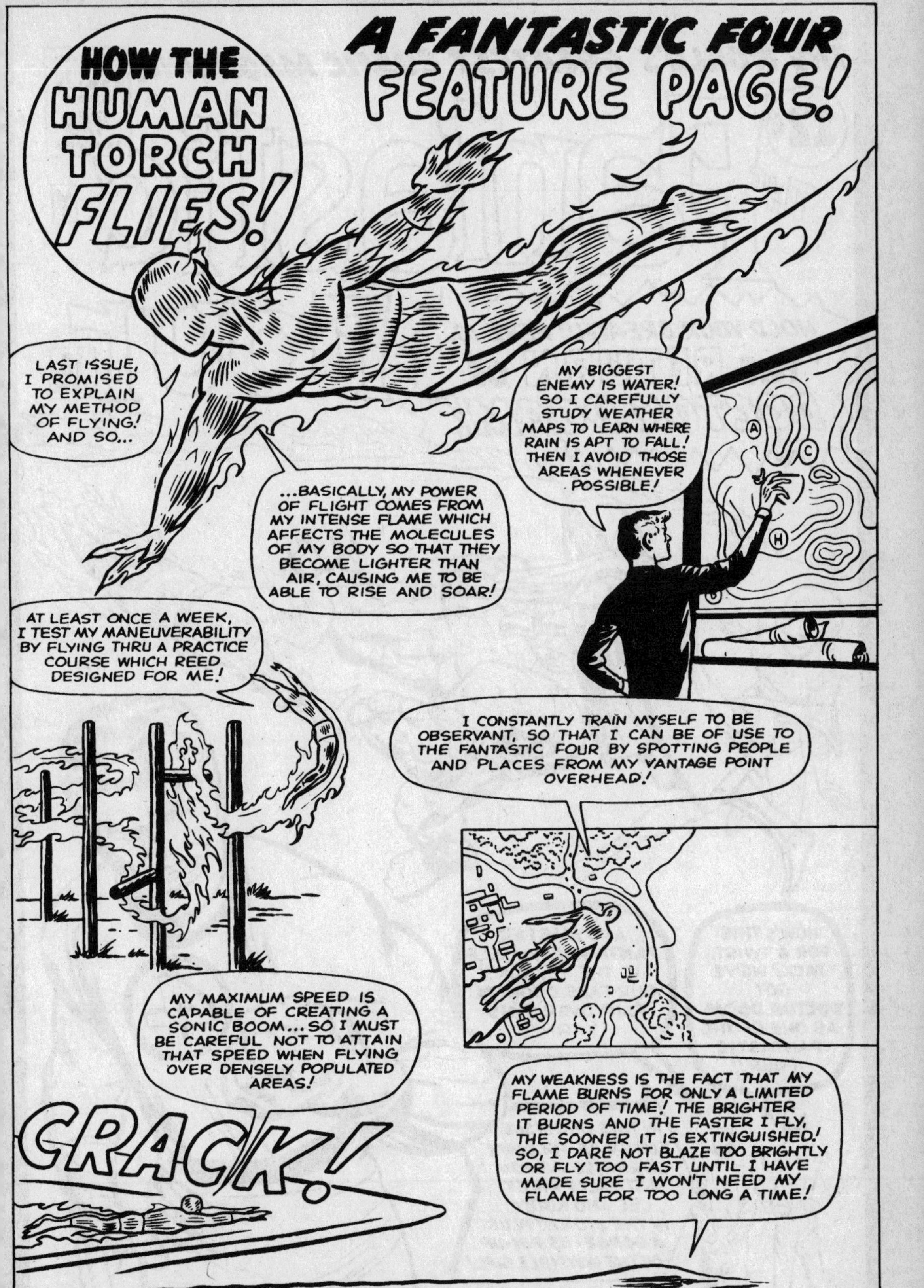
HOW THE HUMAN TORCH FLIES!
A FANTASTIC FOUR FEATURE PAGE!
LAST ISSUE, I PROMISED TO EXPLAIN MY METHOD OF FLYING! AND SO...
...BASICALLY, MY POWER OF FLIGHT COMES FROM MY INTENSE FLAME WHICH AFFECTS THE MOLECULES OF MY BODY SO THAT THEY BECOME LIGHTER THAN AIR, CAUSING ME TO BE ABLE TO RISE AND SOAR!
MY BIGGEST ENEMY IS WATER! SO I CAREFULLY STUDY WEATHER MAPS TO LEARN WHERE RAIN IS APT TO FALL! THEN I AVOID THOSE AREAS WHENEVER POSSIBLE!
AT LEAST ONCE A WEEK, I TEST MY MANEUVERABILITY BY FLYING THRU A PRACTICE COURSE WHICH REED DESIGNED FOR ME!
I CONSTANTLY TRAIN MYSELF TO BE OBSERVANT, SO THAT I CAN BE OF USE TO THE FANTASTIC FOUR BY SPOTTING PEOPLE AND PLACES FROM MY VANTAGE POINT OVERHEAD!
MY MAXIMUM SPEED IS CAPABLE OF CREATING A SONIC BOOM... SO I MUST BE CAREFUL NOT TO ATTAIN THAT SPEED WHEN FLYING OVER DENSELY POPULATED AREAS!
CRACK!
MY WEAKNESS IS THE FACT THAT MY FLAME BURNS FOR ONLY A LIMITED PERIOD OF TIME! THE BRIGHTER IT BURNS AND THE FASTER I FLY, THE SOONER IT IS EXTINGUISHED! SO, I DARE NOT BLAZE TOO BRIGHTLY OR FLY TOO FAST UNTIL I HAVE MADE SURE I WON'T NEED MY FLAME FOR TOO LONG A TIME!
Stan Lee + J. KIRBY

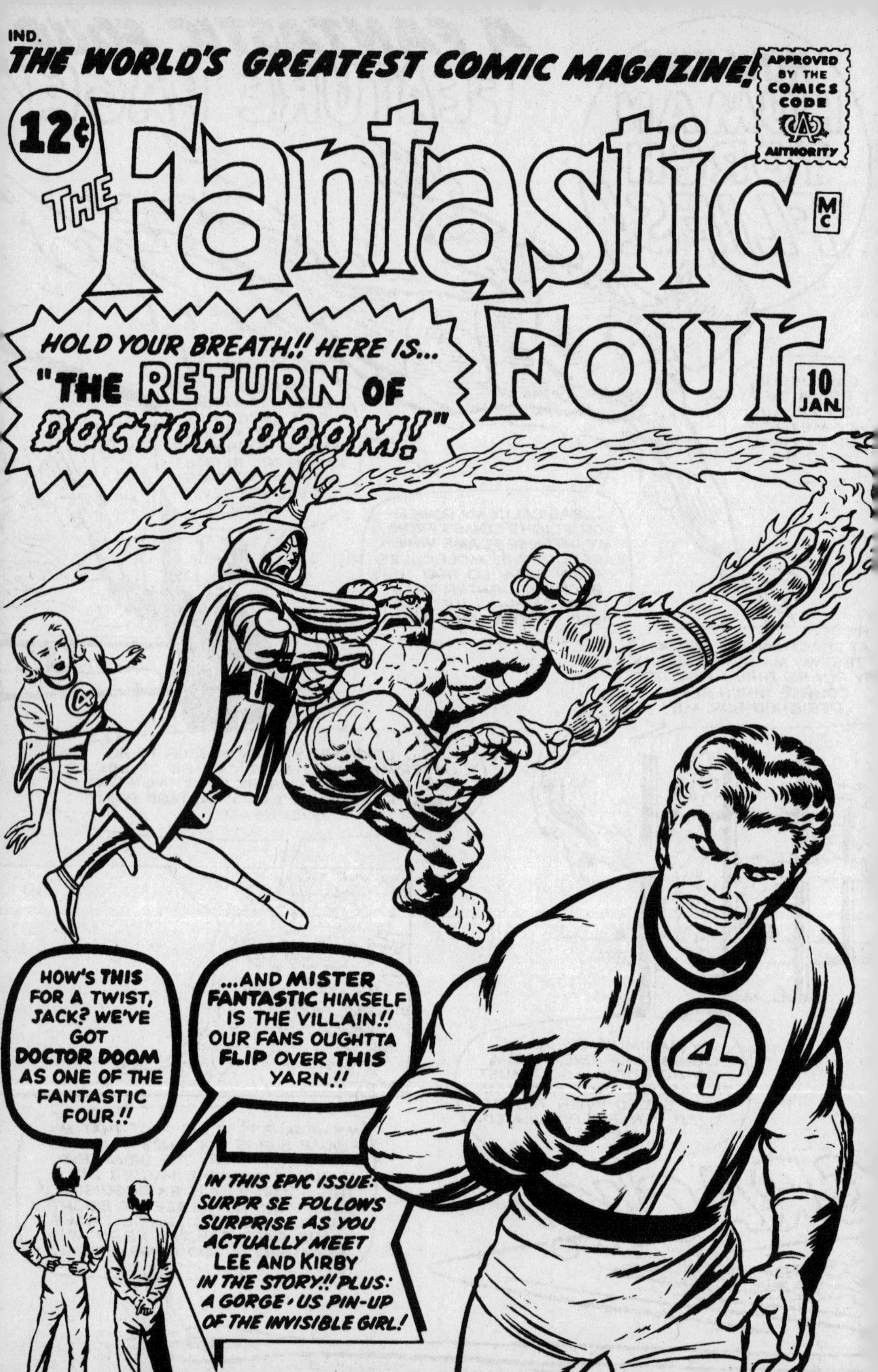
IND.
THE WORLD'S GREATEST COMIC MAGAZINE!
APPROVED BY THE COMICS CODE AUTHORITY
12¢
THE Fantastic Four
MC
10 JAN.
HOLD YOUR BREATH!! HERE IS... "THE RETURN OF DOCTOR DOOM!"
HOW'S THIS FOR A TWIST, JACK? WE'VE GOT DOCTOR DOOM AS ONE OF THE FANTASTIC FOUR!!
...AND MISTER FANTASTIC HIMSELF IS THE VILLAIN!! OUR FANS OUGHTTA FLIP OVER THIS YARN!!
IN THIS EPIC ISSUE: SURPR SE FOLLOWS SURPRISE AS YOU ACTUALLY MEET LEE AND KIRBY IN THE STORY!! PLUS: A GORGE US PIN-UP OF THE INVISIBLE GIRL!

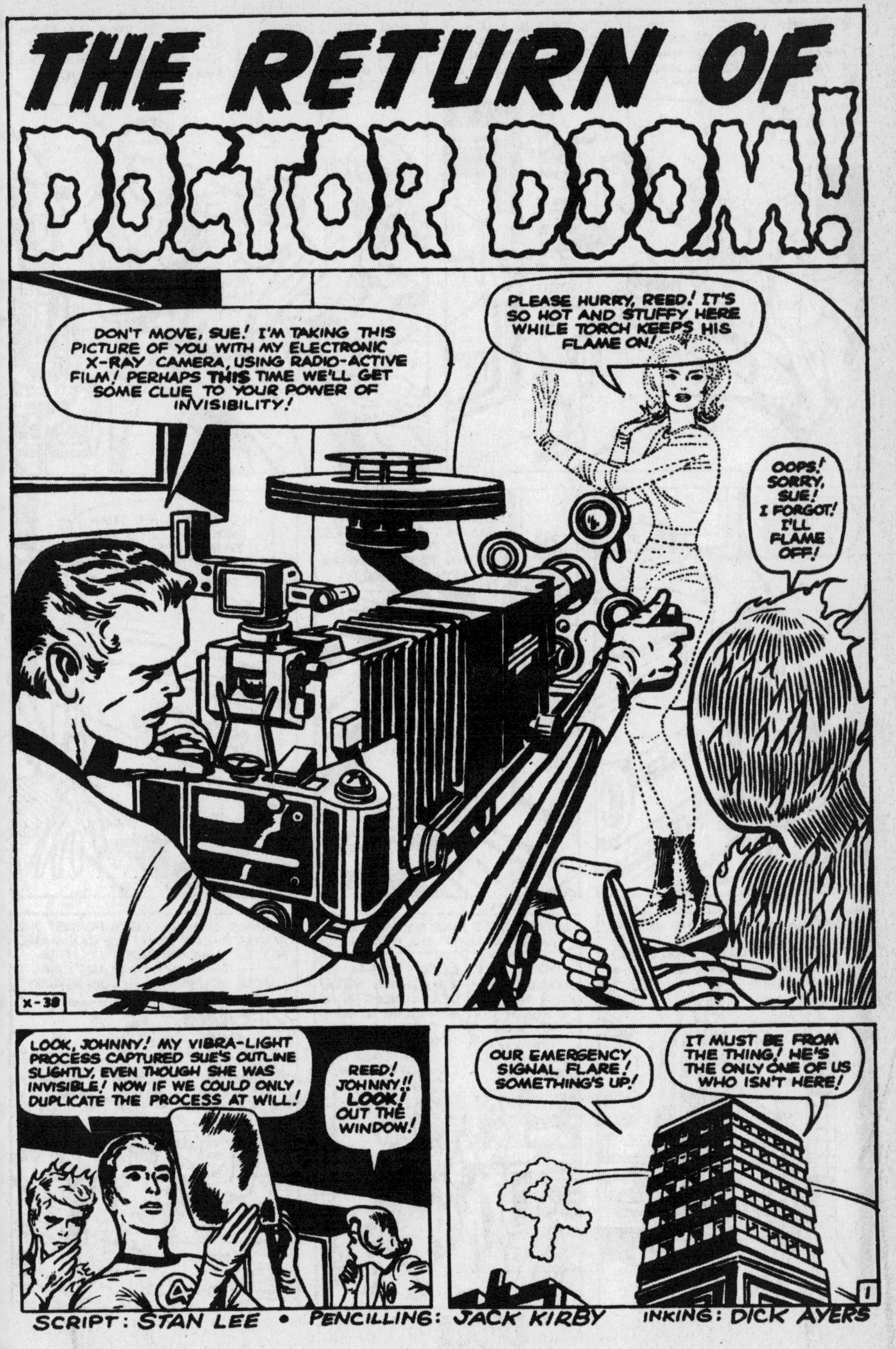
THE RETURN OF DOCTOR DOOM!
DON'T MOVE, SUE! I'M TAKING THIS PICTURE OF YOU WITH MY ELECTRONIC X-RAY CAMERA, USING RADIO-ACTIVE FILM! PERHAPS THIS TIME WE'LL GET SOME CLUE TO YOUR POWER OF INVISIBILITY!
PLEASE HURRY, REED! IT'S SO HOT AND STUFFY HERE WHILE TORCH KEEPS HIS FLAME ON!
OOPS! SORRY, SUE! I FORGOT! I'LL FLAME OFF!
X-38
LOOK, JOHNNY! MY VIBRA-LIGHT PROCESS CAPTURED SUE'S OUTLINE SLIGHTLY, EVEN THOUGH SHE WAS INVISIBLE! NOW IF WE COULD ONLY DUPLICATE THE PROCESS AT WILL!
REED! JOHNNY!! LOOK! OUT THE WINDOW!
OUR EMERGENCY SIGNAL FLARE! SOMETHING'S UP!
IT MUST BE FROM THE THING! HE'S THE ONLY ONE OF US WHO ISN'T HERE!
1

SCRIPT: STAN LEE • PENCILLING: JACK KIRBY INKING: DICK AYERS

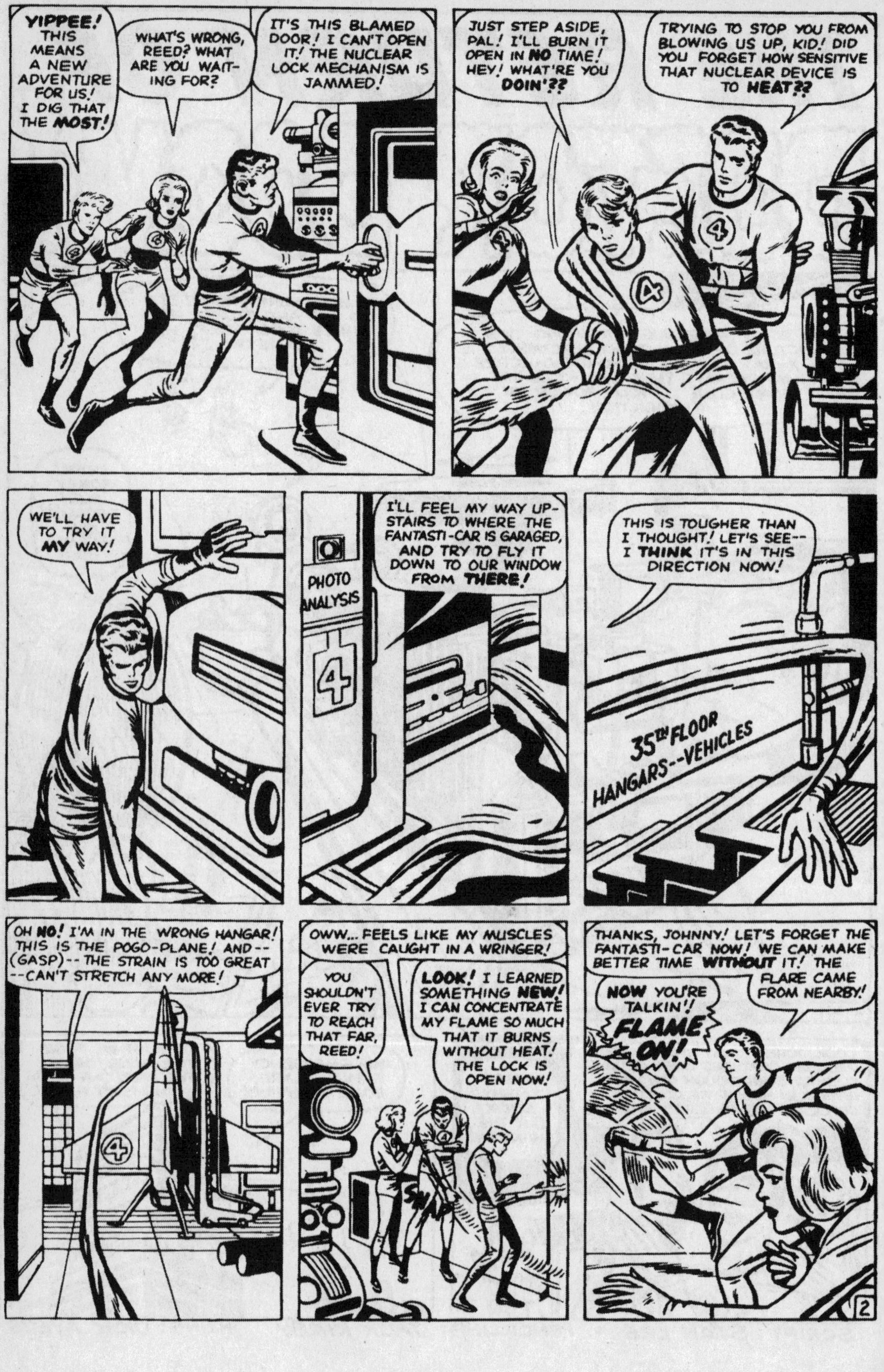
YIPPEE! THIS MEANS A NEW ADVENTURE FOR US! I DIG THAT THE MOST!
WHAT'S WRONG, REED? WHAT ARE YOU WAITING FOR?
IT'S THIS BLAMED DOOR! I CAN'T OPEN IT! THE NUCLEAR LOCK MECHANISM IS JAMMED!
JUST STEP ASIDE, PAL! I'LL BURN IT OPEN IN NO TIME! HEY! WHAT'RE YOU DOIN'??
TRYING TO STOP YOU FROM BLOWING US UP, KID! DID YOU FORGET HOW SENSITIVE THAT NUCLEAR DEVICE IS TO HEAT??
WE'LL HAVE TO TRY IT MY WAY!
PHOTO ANALYSIS
I'LL FEEL MY WAY UPSTAIRS TO WHERE THE FANTASTI-CAR IS GARAGED, AND TRY TO FLY IT DOWN TO OUR WINDOW FROM THERE!
THIS IS TOUGHER THAN I THOUGHT! LET'S SEE-- I THINK IT'S IN THIS DIRECTION NOW!
35TH FLOOR HANGARS--VEHICLES
OH NO! I'M IN THE WRONG HANGAR! THIS IS THE POGO-PLANE! AND--(GASP)-- THE STRAIN IS TOO GREAT --CAN'T STRETCH ANY MORE!
OWW... FEELS LIKE MY MUSCLES WERE CAUGHT IN A WRINGER!
YOU SHOULDN'T EVER TRY TO REACH THAT FAR, REED!
LOOK! I LEARNED SOMETHING NEW! I CAN CONCENTRATE MY FLAME SO MUCH THAT IT BURNS WITHOUT HEAT! THE LOCK IS OPEN NOW!
THANKS, JOHNNY! LET'S FORGET THE FANTASTI-CAR NOW! WE CAN MAKE BETTER TIME WITHOUT IT! THE FLARE CAME FROM NEARBY!
NOW YOU'RE TALKIN'! FLAME ON!
2

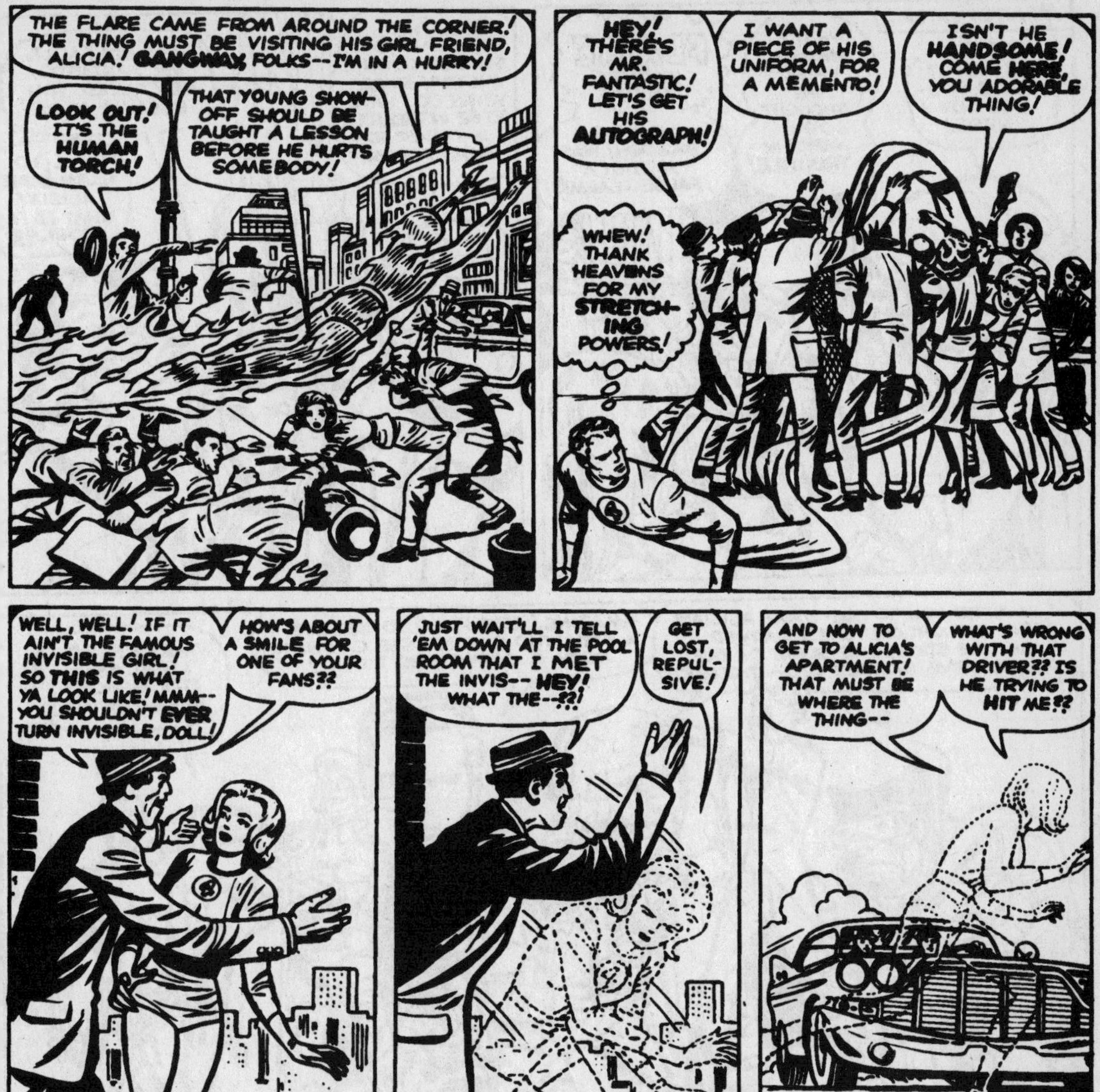
THE FLARE CAME FROM AROUND THE CORNER! THE THING MUST BE VISITING HIS GIRL FRIEND, ALICIA! GANGWAY, FOLKS--I'M IN A HURRY!
LOOK OUT! IT'S THE HUMAN TORCH!
THAT YOUNG SHOW-OFF SHOULD BE TAUGHT A LESSON BEFORE HE HURTS SOMEBODY!
HEY! THERE'S MR. FANTASTIC! LET'S GET HIS AUTOGRAPH!
I WANT A PIECE OF HIS UNIFORM, FOR A MEMENTO!
ISN'T HE HANDSOME! COME HERE, YOU ADORABLE THING!
WHEW! THANK HEAVENS FOR MY STRETCHING POWERS!
WELL, WELL! IF IT AIN'T THE FAMOUS INVISIBLE GIRL! SO THIS IS WHAT YA LOOK LIKE! MMM-- YOU SHOULDN'T EVER TURN INVISIBLE, DOLL!
HOW'S ABOUT A SMILE FOR ONE OF YOUR FANS??
JUST WAIT'LL I TELL 'EM DOWN AT THE POOL ROOM THAT I MET THE INVIS-- HEY! WHAT THE--?!
GET LOST, REPULSIVE!
AND NOW TO GET TO ALICIA'S APARTMENT! THAT MUST BE WHERE THE THING--
WHAT'S WRONG WITH THAT DRIVER?? IS HE TRYING TO HIT ME??
OH! I FORGOT! I'M INVISIBLE! HE DOESN'T SEE ME!
I'VE GOT TO TURN VISIBLE --NOW!
HOLY SMOKE! WHERE'D THAT GAL COME FROM??
WHEW! HE JUST MISSED ME!
SCREEEEEEEEEEEEEE!
HONEST, OFFICER--IT WASN'T MY FAULT!
I KNOW-- I KNOW! I SAW HER, TOO!

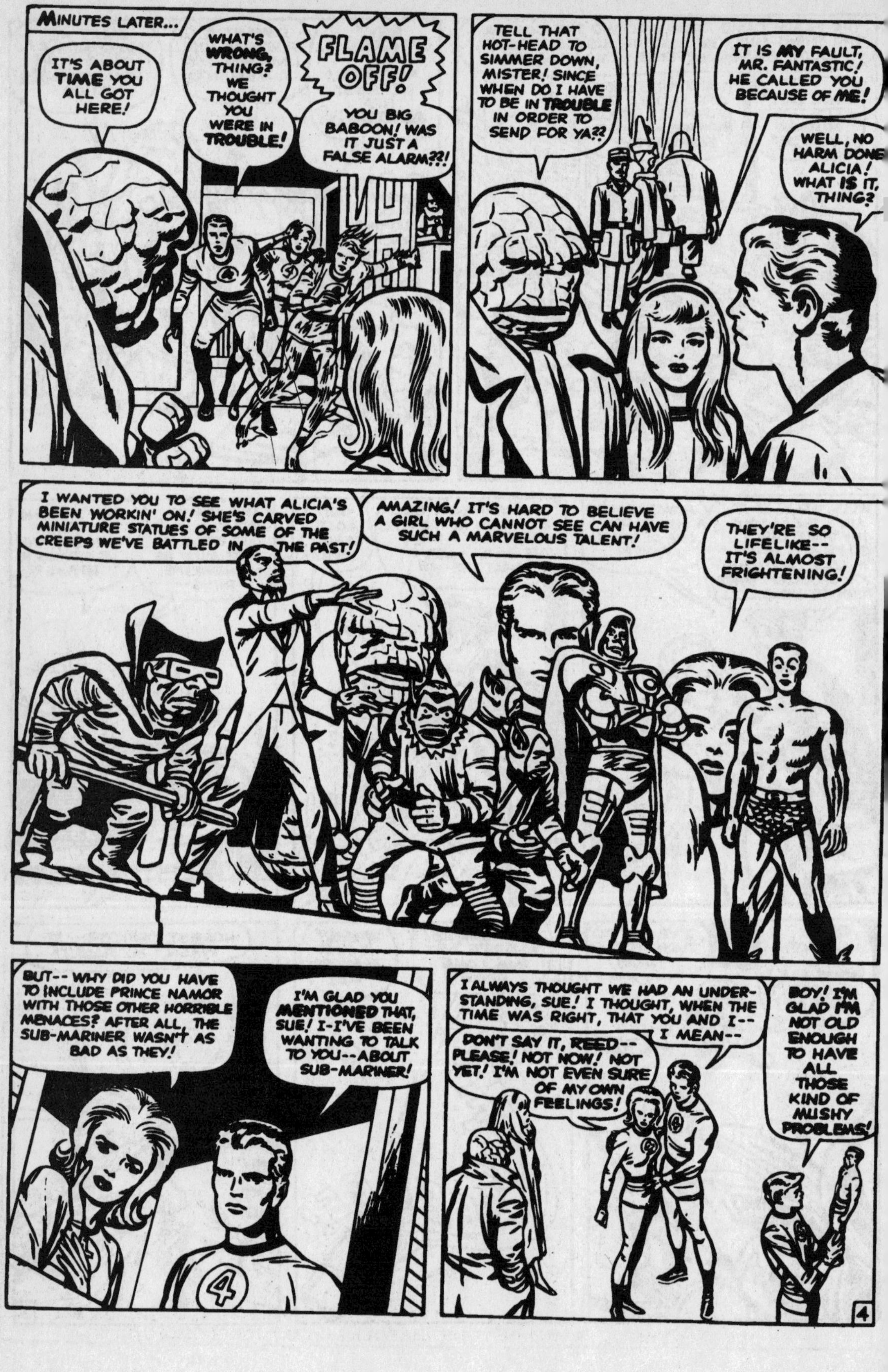
MINUTES LATER...
IT'S ABOUT TIME YOU ALL GOT HERE!
WHAT'S WRONG, THING? WE THOUGHT YOU WERE IN TROUBLE!
FLAME OFF!
YOU BIG BABOON! WAS IT JUST A FALSE ALARM??!
TELL THAT HOT-HEAD TO SIMMER DOWN, MISTER! SINCE WHEN DO I HAVE TO BE IN TROUBLE IN ORDER TO SEND FOR YA??
IT IS MY FAULT, MR. FANTASTIC! HE CALLED YOU BECAUSE OF ME!
WELL, NO HARM DONE ALICIA! WHAT IS IT, THING?
I WANTED YOU TO SEE WHAT ALICIA'S BEEN WORKIN' ON! SHE'S CARVED MINIATURE STATUES OF SOME OF THE CREEPS WE'VE BATTLED IN THE PAST!
AMAZING! IT'S HARD TO BELIEVE A GIRL WHO CANNOT SEE CAN HAVE SUCH A MARVELOUS TALENT!
THEY'RE SO LIFELIKE-- IT'S ALMOST FRIGHTENING!
BUT-- WHY DID YOU HAVE TO INCLUDE PRINCE NAMOR WITH THOSE OTHER HORRIBLE MENACES? AFTER ALL, THE SUB-MARINER WASN'T AS BAD AS THEY!
I'M GLAD YOU MENTIONED THAT, SUE! I-I'VE BEEN WANTING TO TALK TO YOU--ABOUT SUB-MARINER!
I ALWAYS THOUGHT WE HAD AN UNDERSTANDING, SUE! I THOUGHT, WHEN THE TIME WAS RIGHT, THAT YOU AND I-- I MEAN--
DON'T SAY IT, REED-- PLEASE! NOT NOW! NOT YET! I'M NOT EVEN SURE OF MY OWN FEELINGS!
BOY! I'M GLAD I'M NOT OLD ENOUGH TO HAVE ALL THOSE KIND OF MUSHY PROBLEMS!
4

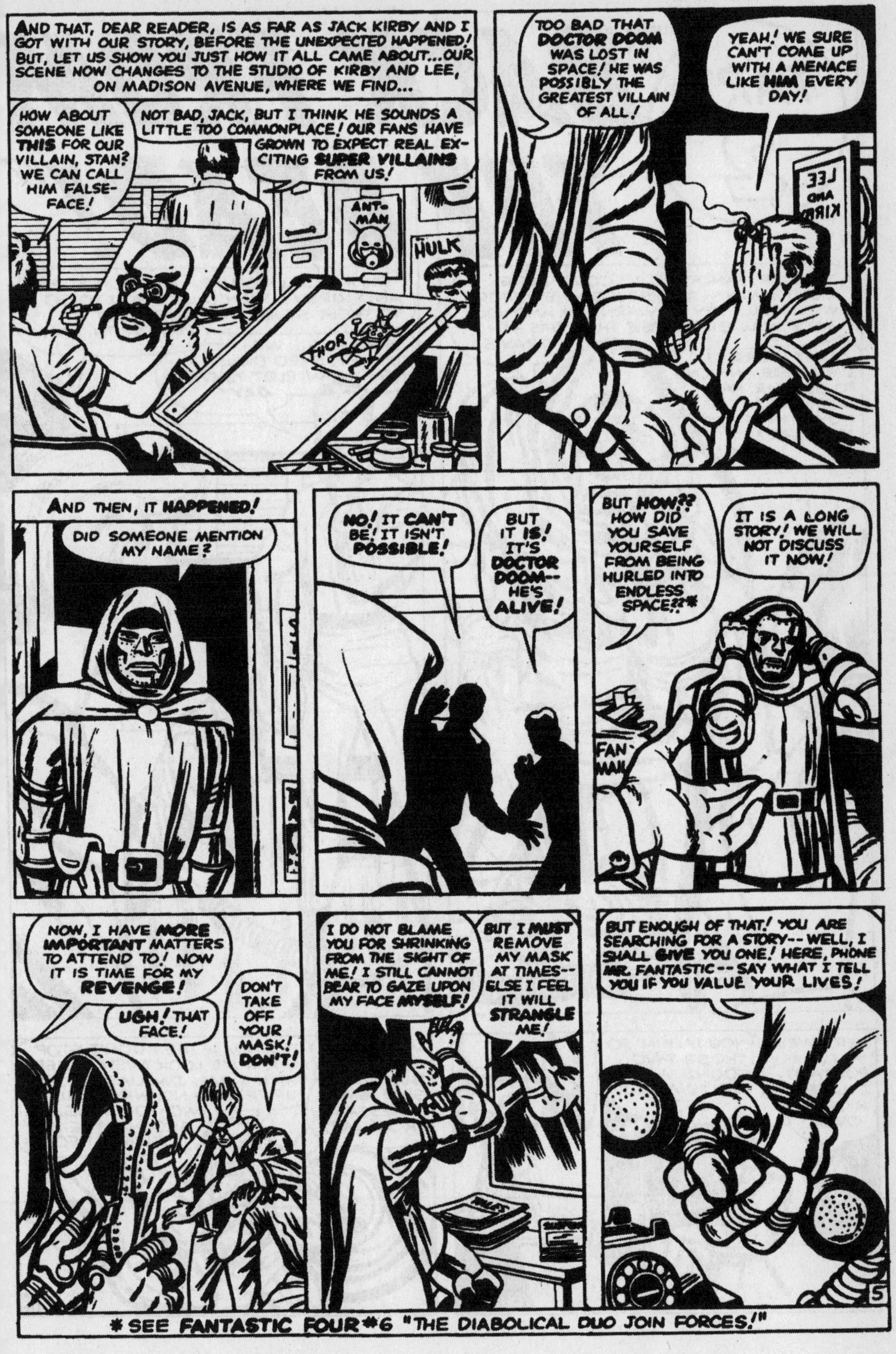
AND THAT, DEAR READER, IS AS FAR AS JACK KIRBY AND I GOT WITH OUR STORY, BEFORE THE UNEXPECTED HAPPENED! BUT, LET US SHOW YOU JUST HOW IT ALL CAME ABOUT...OUR SCENE NOW CHANGES TO THE STUDIO OF KIRBY AND LEE, ON MADISON AVENUE, WHERE WE FIND...
HOW ABOUT SOMEONE LIKE THIS FOR OUR VILLAIN, STAN? WE CAN CALL HIM FALSE-FACE!
NOT BAD, JACK, BUT I THINK HE SOUNDS A LITTLE TOO COMMONPLACE! OUR FANS HAVE GROWN TO EXPECT REAL EXCITING SUPER VILLAINS FROM US!
ANT-MAN
HULK
THOR
TOO BAD THAT DOCTOR DOOM WAS LOST IN SPACE! HE WAS POSSIBLY THE GREATEST VILLAIN OF ALL!
YEAH! WE SURE CAN'T COME UP WITH A MENACE LIKE HIM EVERY DAY!
AND THEN, IT HAPPENED!
DID SOMEONE MENTION MY NAME?
NO! IT CAN'T BE! IT ISN'T POSSIBLE!
BUT IT IS! IT'S DOCTOR DOOM-- HE'S ALIVE!
BUT HOW?? HOW DID YOU SAVE YOURSELF FROM BEING HURLED INTO ENDLESS SPACE??*
IT IS A LONG STORY! WE WILL NOT DISCUSS IT NOW!
FAN MAIL
NOW, I HAVE MORE IMPORTANT MATTERS TO ATTEND TO! NOW IT IS TIME FOR MY REVENGE!
UGH! THAT FACE!
DON'T TAKE OFF YOUR MASK! DON'T!
I DO NOT BLAME YOU FOR SHRINKING FROM THE SIGHT OF ME! I STILL CANNOT BEAR TO GAZE UPON MY FACE MYSELF!
BUT I MUST REMOVE MY MASK AT TIMES-- ELSE I FEEL IT WILL STRANGLE ME!
BUT ENOUGH OF THAT! YOU ARE SEARCHING FOR A STORY-- WELL, I SHALL GIVE YOU ONE! HERE, PHONE MR. FANTASTIC -- SAY WHAT I TELL YOU IF YOU VALUE YOUR LIVES!
5
* SEE FANTASTIC FOUR #6 "THE DIABOLICAL DUO JOIN FORCES!"

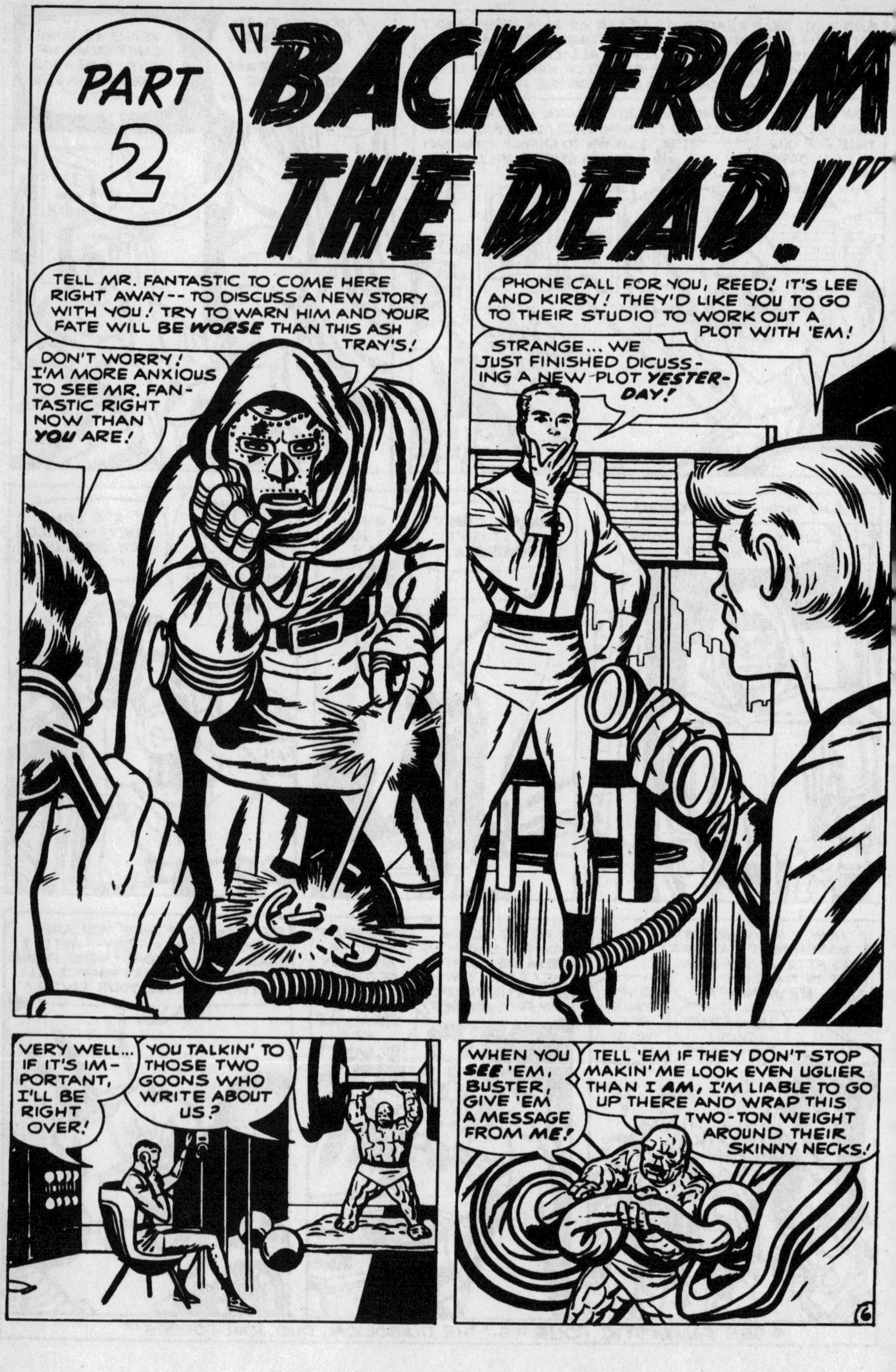
PART 2
"BACK FROM THE DEAD!"
TELL MR. FANTASTIC TO COME HERE RIGHT AWAY-- TO DISCUSS A NEW STORY WITH YOU! TRY TO WARN HIM AND YOUR FATE WILL BE WORSE THAN THIS ASH TRAY'S!
DON'T WORRY! I'M MORE ANXIOUS TO SEE MR. FANTASTIC RIGHT NOW THAN YOU ARE!
PHONE CALL FOR YOU, REED! IT'S LEE AND KIRBY! THEY'D LIKE YOU TO GO TO THEIR STUDIO TO WORK OUT A PLOT WITH 'EM!
STRANGE... WE JUST FINISHED DICUSSING A NEW PLOT YESTERDAY!
VERY WELL... IF IT'S IMPORTANT, I'LL BE RIGHT OVER!
YOU TALKIN' TO THOSE TWO GOONS WHO WRITE ABOUT US?
WHEN YOU SEE 'EM, BUSTER, GIVE 'EM A MESSAGE FROM ME!
TELL 'EM IF THEY DON'T STOP MAKIN' ME LOOK EVEN UGLIER THAN I AM, I'M LIABLE TO GO UP THERE AND WRAP THIS TWO-TON WEIGHT AROUND THEIR SKINNY NECKS!
6

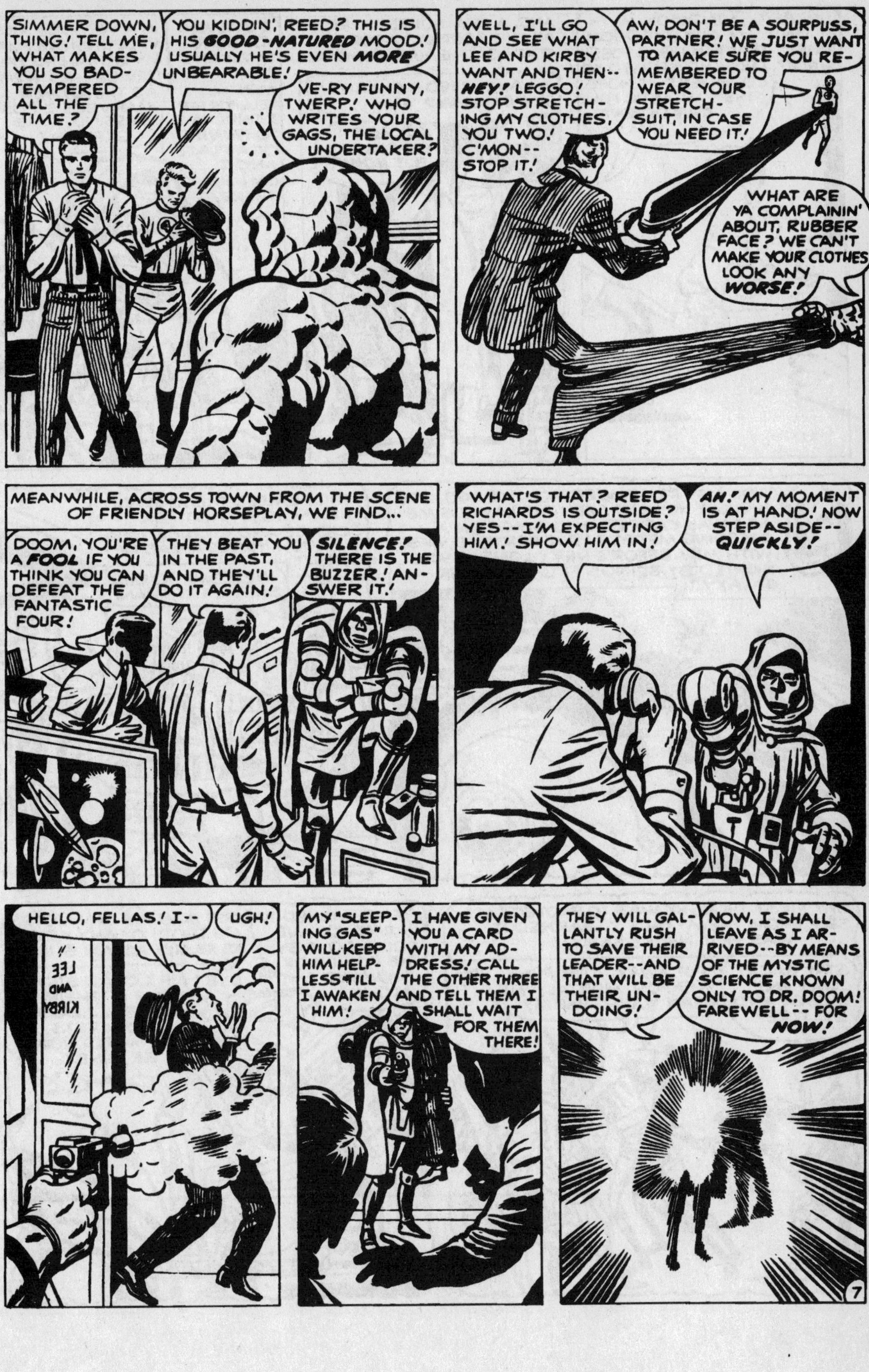
SIMMER DOWN, THING! TELL ME, WHAT MAKES YOU SO BAD-TEMPERED ALL THE TIME?
YOU KIDDIN', REED? THIS IS HIS GOOD-NATURED MOOD! USUALLY HE'S EVEN MORE UNBEARABLE!
VE-RY FUNNY, TWERP! WHO WRITES YOUR GAGS, THE LOCAL UNDERTAKER?
WELL, I'LL GO AND SEE WHAT LEE AND KIRBY WANT AND THEN-- HEY! LEGGO! STOP STRETCHING MY CLOTHES, YOU TWO! C'MON-- STOP IT!
AW, DON'T BE A SOURPUSS, PARTNER! WE JUST WANT TO MAKE SURE YOU REMEMBERED TO WEAR YOUR STRETCH-SUIT, IN CASE YOU NEED IT!
WHAT ARE YA COMPLAININ' ABOUT, RUBBER FACE? WE CAN'T MAKE YOUR CLOTHES LOOK ANY WORSE!
MEANWHILE, ACROSS TOWN FROM THE SCENE OF FRIENDLY HORSEPLAY, WE FIND...
DOOM, YOU'RE A FOOL IF YOU THINK YOU CAN DEFEAT THE FANTASTIC FOUR!
THEY BEAT YOU IN THE PAST, AND THEY'LL DO IT AGAIN!
SILENCE! THERE IS THE BUZZER! ANSWER IT!
WHAT'S THAT? REED RICHARDS IS OUTSIDE? YES-- I'M EXPECTING HIM! SHOW HIM IN!
AH! MY MOMENT IS AT HAND! NOW STEP ASIDE-- QUICKLY!
HELLO, FELLAS! I--
UGH!
MY "SLEEPING GAS" WILL KEEP HIM HELPLESS 'TILL I AWAKEN HIM!
I HAVE GIVEN YOU A CARD WITH MY ADDRESS! CALL THE OTHER THREE AND TELL THEM I SHALL WAIT FOR THEM THERE!
THEY WILL GALLANTLY RUSH TO SAVE THEIR LEADER--AND THAT WILL BE THEIR UNDOING!
NOW, I SHALL LEAVE AS I ARRIVED--BY MEANS OF THE MYSTIC SCIENCE KNOWN ONLY TO DR. DOOM! FAREWELL-- FOR NOW!
7

GULP! IT-- IT ISN'T POSSIBLE!

JACKSON, WITH A GUY LIKE DOOM, ANYTHING IS POSSIBLE! HE SEEMED SO CONFIDENT-- I HOPE THE FANTASTIC FOUR CAN DEFEAT HIM!

AND, A FEW HOURS LATER, AT THE SECRET LABORATORY OF THE MASTER MENACE...

AWAKE, REED RICHARDS! I COMMAND YOU!

DOCTOR DOOM! BUT HOW??

I BROUGHT YOU HERE BY MEANS OF MY MENTAL-TELEPORTER! I ONLY HAVE TO THINK OF A PLACE, AND I CAN BE THERE!

IN A WAY, YOU ARE RESPONSIBLE FOR MY OBTAINING THIS DEVICE--AS WELL AS THE OTHER MARVELS I POSSESS! LET ME EXPLAIN!

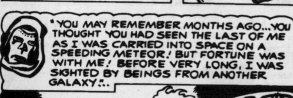

"YOU MAY REMEMBER MONTHS AGO...YOU THOUGHT YOU HAD SEEN THE LAST OF ME AS I WAS CARRIED INTO SPACE ON A SPEEDING METEOR! BUT FORTUNE WAS WITH ME! BEFORE VERY LONG, I WAS SIGHTED BY BEINGS FROM ANOTHER GALAXY..."

"THEY CALLED THEMSELVES THE OVOIDS, AND THEIR SCIENCE AND CULTURE WERE A MILLION YEARS AHEAD OF OURS!"

WELCOME TO OUR SHIP, EARTHMAN!

"MY FIRST THOUGHT WAS TO PROTECT MYSELF FROM THEM--BUT I LEARNED IT WAS NOT NECESSARY!"

STAY BACK! COME ANY CLOSER AND I'LL FIRE!

PUT AWAY YOUR PUNY WEAPON, MORTAL! WE MEAN YOU NO HARM!

IF WE WISHED TO INJURE YOU, WE COULD DO IT BY THE POWER OF THOUGHT ALONE!

SEE HOW WE CAN MOVE OBJECTS OF ANY WEIGHT, AS EASILY AS YOU BLINK YOUR EYE!

IF I COULD STEAL SOME OF THEIR POWERS... LEARN THEIR SECRETS... THE WORLD WOULD BE MINE!

8

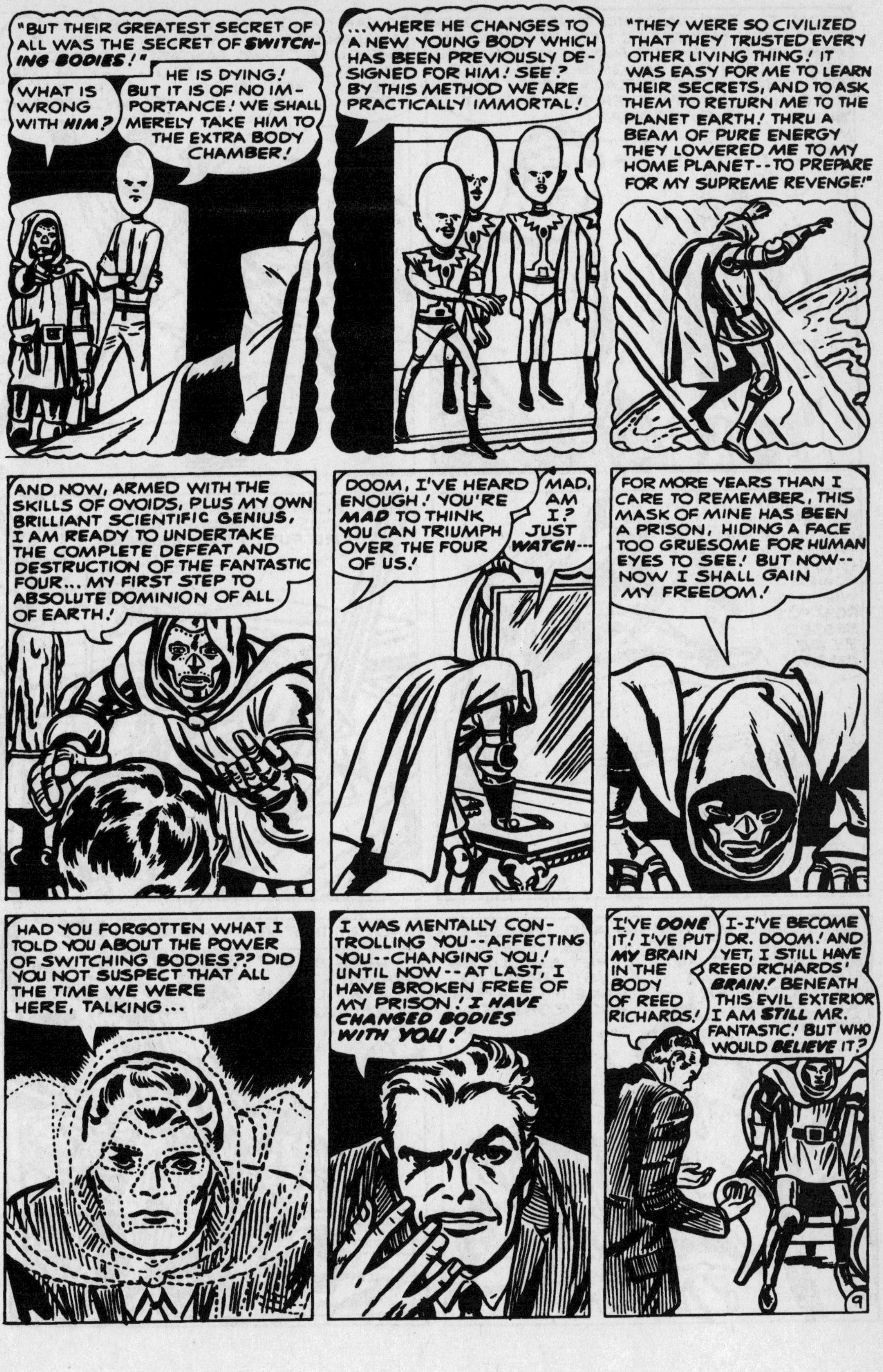
"BUT THEIR GREATEST SECRET OF ALL WAS THE SECRET OF SWITCHING BODIES!"
WHAT IS WRONG WITH HIM?
HE IS DYING! BUT IT IS OF NO IMPORTANCE! WE SHALL MERELY TAKE HIM TO THE EXTRA BODY CHAMBER!
...WHERE HE CHANGES TO A NEW YOUNG BODY WHICH HAS BEEN PREVIOUSLY DESIGNED FOR HIM! SEE? BY THIS METHOD WE ARE PRACTICALLY IMMORTAL!
"THEY WERE SO CIVILIZED THAT THEY TRUSTED EVERY OTHER LIVING THING! IT WAS EASY FOR ME TO LEARN THEIR SECRETS, AND TO ASK THEM TO RETURN ME TO THE PLANET EARTH! THRU A BEAM OF PURE ENERGY THEY LOWERED ME TO MY HOME PLANET--TO PREPARE FOR MY SUPREME REVENGE!"
AND NOW, ARMED WITH THE SKILLS OF OVOIDS, PLUS MY OWN BRILLIANT SCIENTIFIC GENIUS, I AM READY TO UNDERTAKE THE COMPLETE DEFEAT AND DESTRUCTION OF THE FANTASTIC FOUR... MY FIRST STEP TO ABSOLUTE DOMINION OF ALL OF EARTH!
DOOM, I'VE HEARD ENOUGH! YOU'RE MAD TO THINK YOU CAN TRIUMPH OVER THE FOUR OF US!
MAD, AM I? JUST WATCH---
FOR MORE YEARS THAN I CARE TO REMEMBER, THIS MASK OF MINE HAS BEEN A PRISON, HIDING A FACE TOO GRUESOME FOR HUMAN EYES TO SEE! BUT NOW--NOW I SHALL GAIN MY FREEDOM!
HAD YOU FORGOTTEN WHAT I TOLD YOU ABOUT THE POWER OF SWITCHING BODIES?? DID YOU NOT SUSPECT THAT ALL THE TIME WE WERE HERE, TALKING...
I WAS MENTALLY CONTROLLING YOU--AFFECTING YOU--CHANGING YOU! UNTIL NOW--AT LAST, I HAVE BROKEN FREE OF MY PRISON! I HAVE CHANGED BODIES WITH YOU!
I'VE DONE IT! I'VE PUT MY BRAIN IN THE BODY OF REED RICHARDS!
I-I'VE BECOME DR. DOOM! AND YET, I STILL HAVE REED RICHARDS' BRAIN! BENEATH THIS EVIL EXTERIOR I AM STILL MR. FANTASTIC! BUT WHO WOULD BELIEVE IT?
9

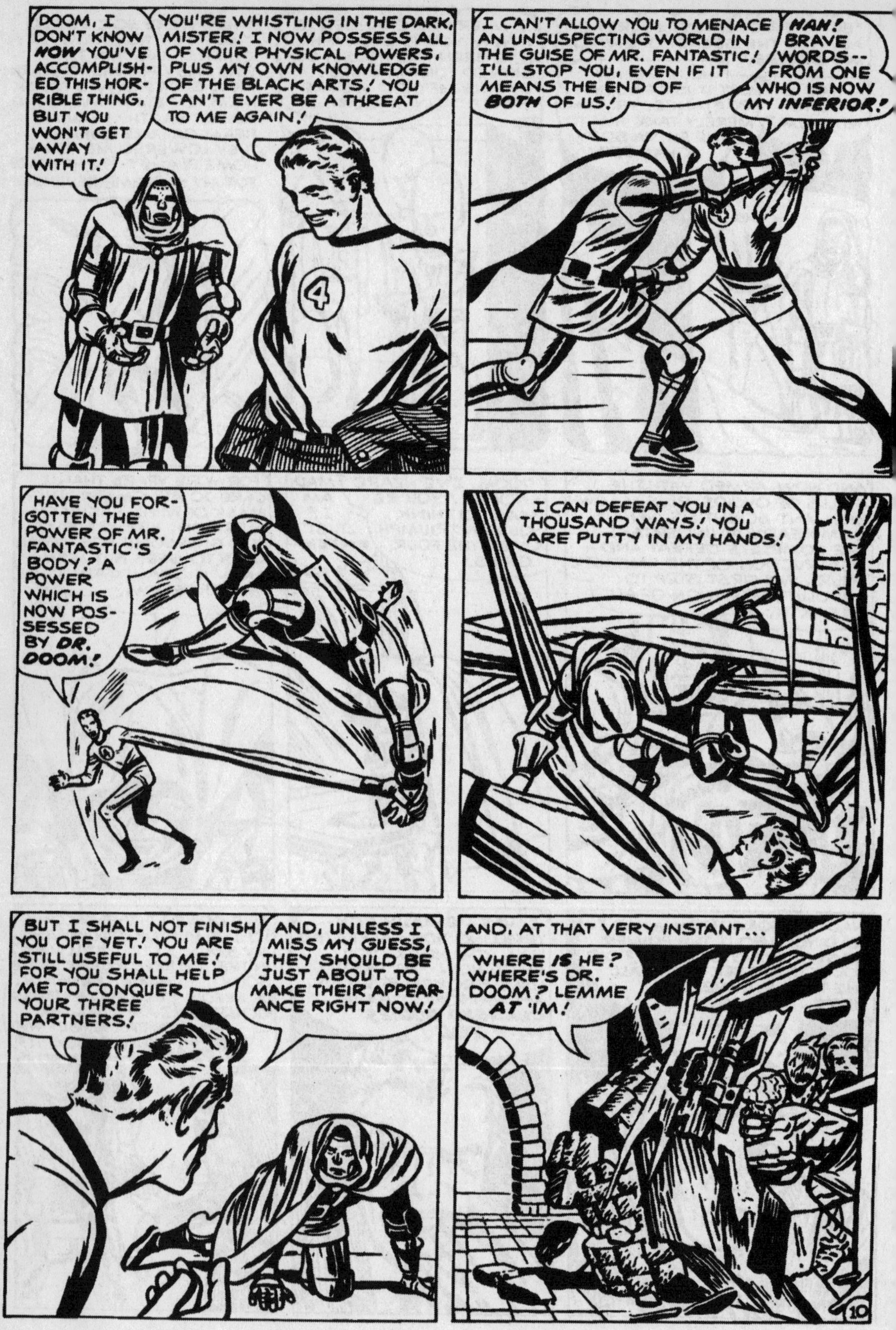
DOOM, I DON'T KNOW **HOW** YOU'VE ACCOMPLISHED THIS HORRIBLE THING, BUT YOU WON'T GET AWAY WITH IT!
YOU'RE WHISTLING IN THE DARK, MISTER! I NOW POSSESS ALL OF YOUR PHYSICAL POWERS, PLUS MY OWN KNOWLEDGE OF THE BLACK ARTS! YOU CAN'T EVER BE A THREAT TO ME AGAIN!
I CAN'T ALLOW YOU TO MENACE AN UNSUSPECTING WORLD IN THE GUISE OF MR. FANTASTIC! I'LL STOP YOU, EVEN IF IT MEANS THE END OF **BOTH** OF US!
HAH! BRAVE WORDS-- FROM ONE WHO IS NOW MY **INFERIOR!**
HAVE YOU FORGOTTEN THE POWER OF MR. FANTASTIC'S BODY? A POWER WHICH IS NOW POSSESSED BY **DR. DOOM!**
I CAN DEFEAT YOU IN A THOUSAND WAYS! YOU ARE PUTTY IN MY HANDS!
BUT I SHALL NOT FINISH YOU OFF YET! YOU ARE STILL USEFUL TO ME! FOR YOU SHALL HELP ME TO CONQUER YOUR THREE PARTNERS!
AND, UNLESS I MISS MY GUESS, THEY SHOULD BE JUST ABOUT TO MAKE THEIR APPEARANCE RIGHT NOW!
AND, AT THAT VERY INSTANT...
WHERE **IS** HE? WHERE'S DR. DOOM? LEMME **AT** 'IM!
10

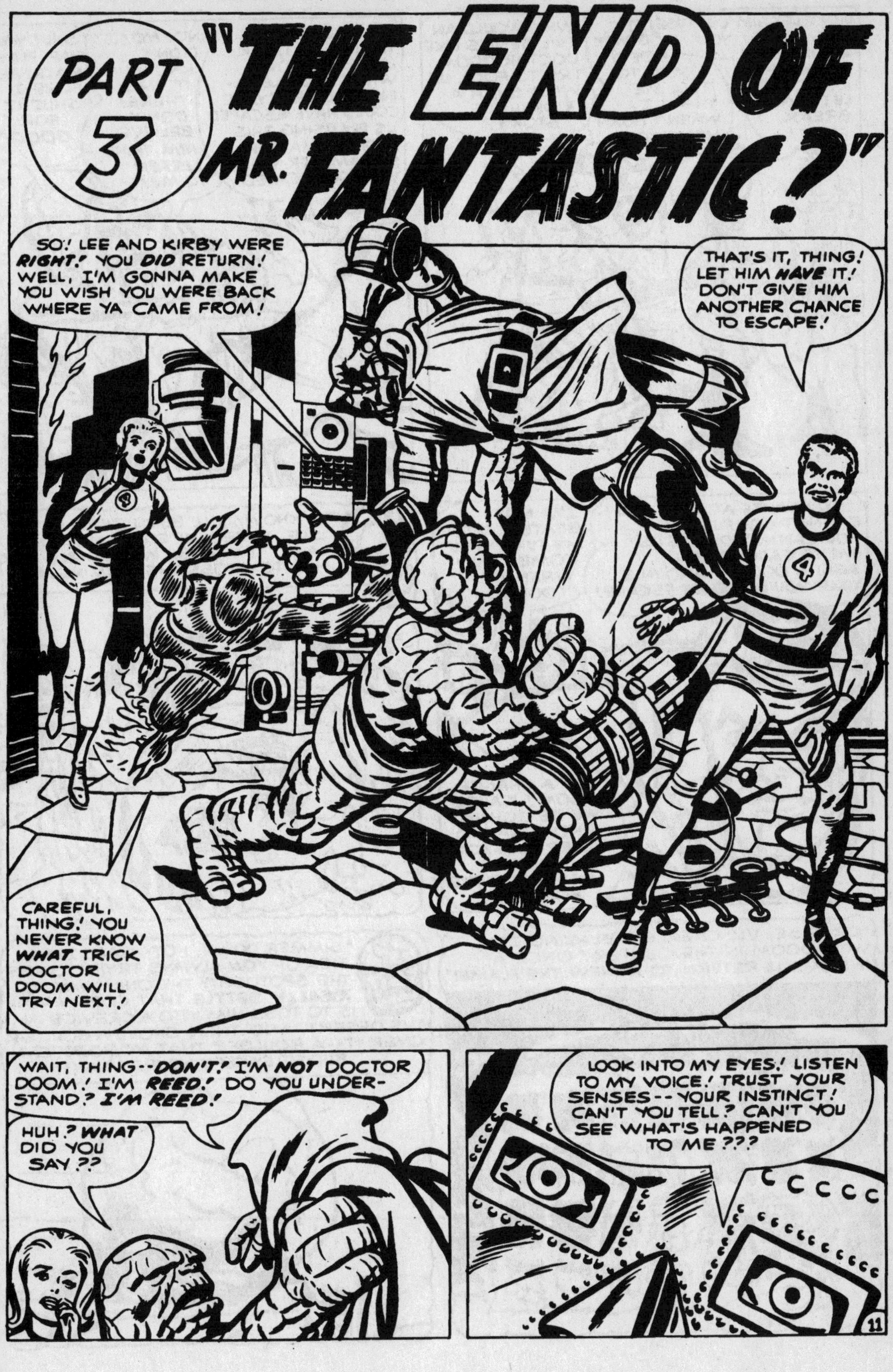
PART 3
"THE END OF MR. FANTASTIC?"
SO! LEE AND KIRBY WERE RIGHT! YOU DID RETURN! WELL, I'M GONNA MAKE YOU WISH YOU WERE BACK WHERE YA CAME FROM!
THAT'S IT, THING! LET HIM HAVE IT! DON'T GIVE HIM ANOTHER CHANCE TO ESCAPE!
CAREFUL, THING! YOU NEVER KNOW WHAT TRICK DOCTOR DOOM WILL TRY NEXT!
WAIT, THING--DON'T! I'M NOT DOCTOR DOOM! I'M REED! DO YOU UNDERSTAND? I'M REED!
HUH? WHAT DID YOU SAY??
LOOK INTO MY EYES! LISTEN TO MY VOICE! TRUST YOUR SENSES--YOUR INSTINCT! CAN'T YOU TELL? CAN'T YOU SEE WHAT'S HAPPENED TO ME???
11

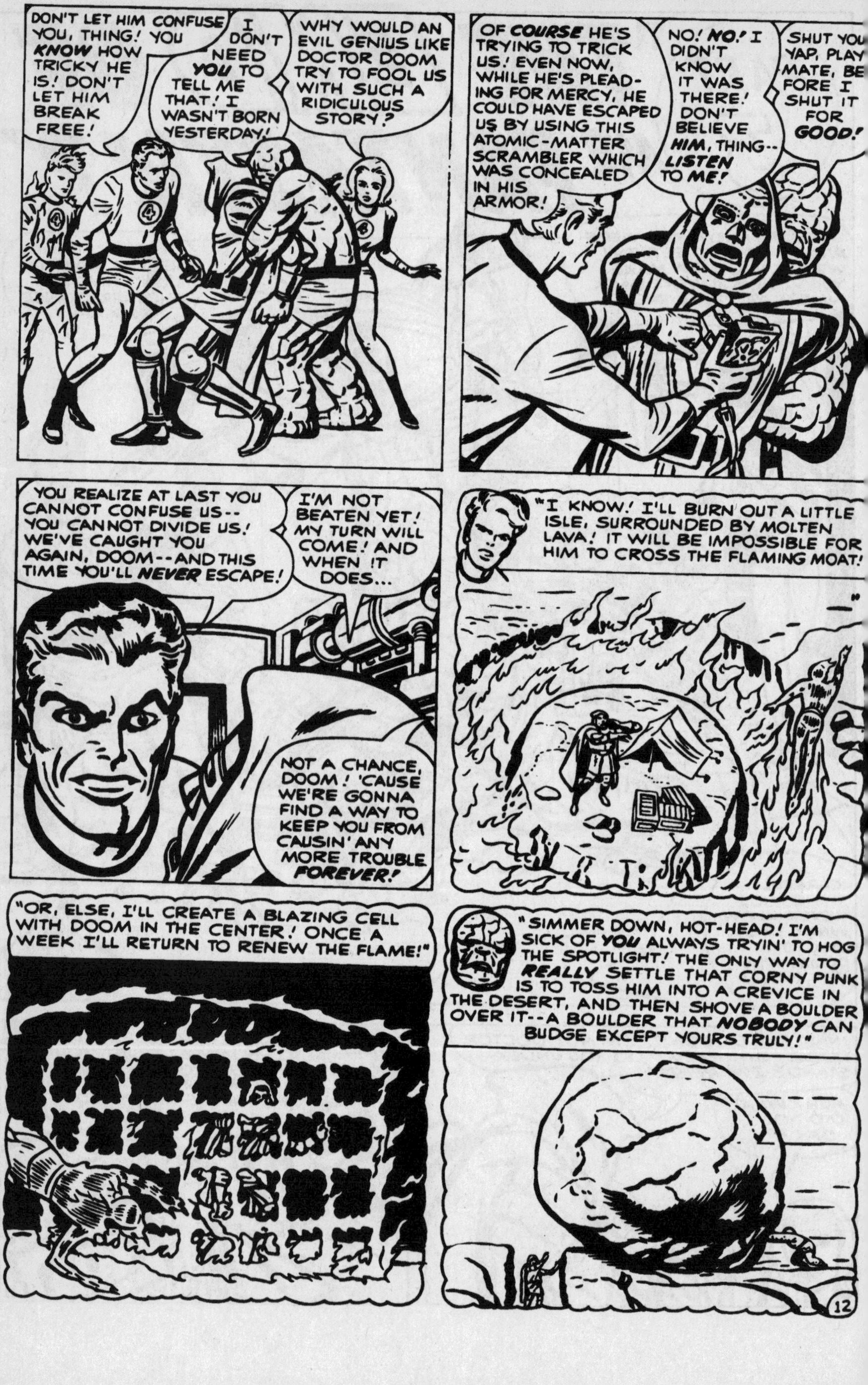
DON'T LET HIM CONFUSE YOU, THING! YOU KNOW HOW TRICKY HE IS! DON'T LET HIM BREAK FREE!
I DON'T NEED YOU TO TELL ME THAT! I WASN'T BORN YESTERDAY!
WHY WOULD AN EVIL GENIUS LIKE DOCTOR DOOM TRY TO FOOL US WITH SUCH A RIDICULOUS STORY?
OF COURSE HE'S TRYING TO TRICK US! EVEN NOW, WHILE HE'S PLEADING FOR MERCY, HE COULD HAVE ESCAPED US BY USING THIS ATOMIC-MATTER SCRAMBLER WHICH WAS CONCEALED IN HIS ARMOR!
NO! NO! I DIDN'T KNOW IT WAS THERE! DON'T BELIEVE HIM, THING-- LISTEN TO ME!
SHUT YOU YAP, PLAY MATE, BE FORE I SHUT IT FOR GOOD!
YOU REALIZE AT LAST YOU CANNOT CONFUSE US-- YOU CANNOT DIVIDE US! WE'VE CAUGHT YOU AGAIN, DOOM--AND THIS TIME YOU'LL NEVER ESCAPE!
I'M NOT BEATEN YET! MY TURN WILL COME! AND WHEN IT DOES...
NOT A CHANCE, DOOM! 'CAUSE WE'RE GONNA FIND A WAY TO KEEP YOU FROM CAUSIN' ANY MORE TROUBLE FOREVER!
"I KNOW! I'LL BURN OUT A LITTLE ISLE, SURROUNDED BY MOLTEN LAVA! IT WILL BE IMPOSSIBLE FOR HIM TO CROSS THE FLAMING MOAT!"
"OR, ELSE, I'LL CREATE A BLAZING CELL WITH DOOM IN THE CENTER! ONCE A WEEK I'LL RETURN TO RENEW THE FLAME!"
"SIMMER DOWN, HOT-HEAD! I'M SICK OF YOU ALWAYS TRYIN' TO HOG THE SPOTLIGHT! THE ONLY WAY TO REALLY SETTLE THAT CORNY PUNK IS TO TOSS HIM INTO A CREVICE IN THE DESERT, AND THEN SHOVE A BOULDER OVER IT--A BOULDER THAT NOBODY CAN BUDGE EXCEPT YOURS TRULY!"
12

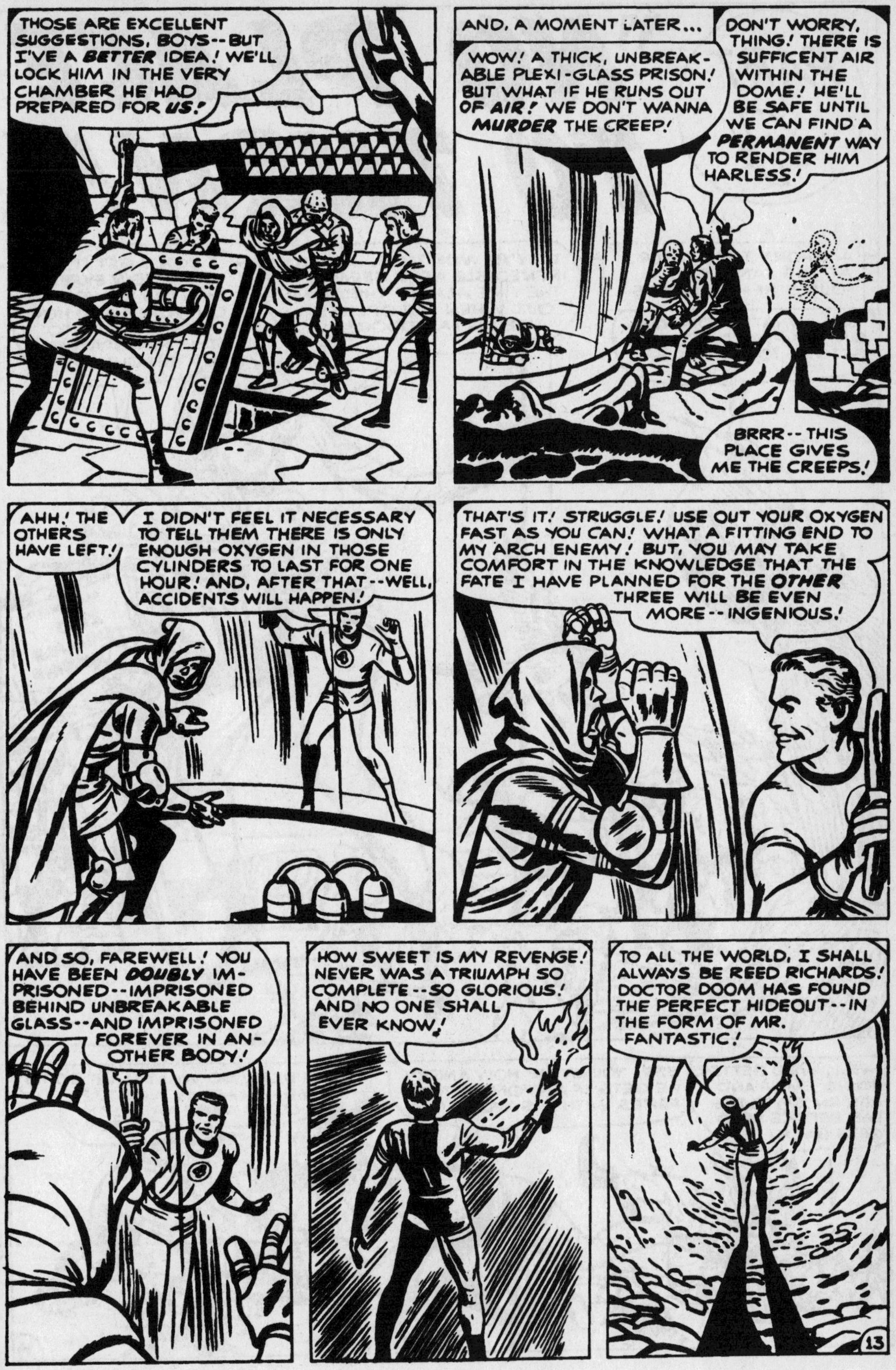
THOSE ARE EXCELLENT SUGGESTIONS, BOYS--BUT I'VE A BETTER IDEA! WE'LL LOCK HIM IN THE VERY CHAMBER HE HAD PREPARED FOR US!
AND, A MOMENT LATER...
WOW! A THICK, UNBREAKABLE PLEXI-GLASS PRISON! BUT WHAT IF HE RUNS OUT OF AIR! WE DON'T WANNA MURDER THE CREEP!
DON'T WORRY, THING! THERE IS SUFFICENT AIR WITHIN THE DOME! HE'LL BE SAFE UNTIL WE CAN FIND A PERMANENT WAY TO RENDER HIM HARLESS!
BRRR--THIS PLACE GIVES ME THE CREEPS!
AHH! THE OTHERS HAVE LEFT!
I DIDN'T FEEL IT NECESSARY TO TELL THEM THERE IS ONLY ENOUGH OXYGEN IN THOSE CYLINDERS TO LAST FOR ONE HOUR! AND, AFTER THAT--WELL, ACCIDENTS WILL HAPPEN!
THAT'S IT! STRUGGLE! USE OUT YOUR OXYGEN FAST AS YOU CAN! WHAT A FITTING END TO MY ARCH ENEMY! BUT, YOU MAY TAKE COMFORT IN THE KNOWLEDGE THAT THE FATE I HAVE PLANNED FOR THE OTHER THREE WILL BE EVEN MORE--INGENIOUS!
AND SO, FAREWELL! YOU HAVE BEEN DOUBLY IMPRISONED--IMPRISONED BEHIND UNBREAKABLE GLASS--AND IMPRISONED FOREVER IN ANOTHER BODY!
HOW SWEET IS MY REVENGE! NEVER WAS A TRIUMPH SO COMPLETE--SO GLORIOUS! AND NO ONE SHALL EVER KNOW!
TO ALL THE WORLD, I SHALL ALWAYS BE REED RICHARDS! DOCTOR DOOM HAS FOUND THE PERFECT HIDEOUT--IN THE FORM OF MR. FANTASTIC!
13

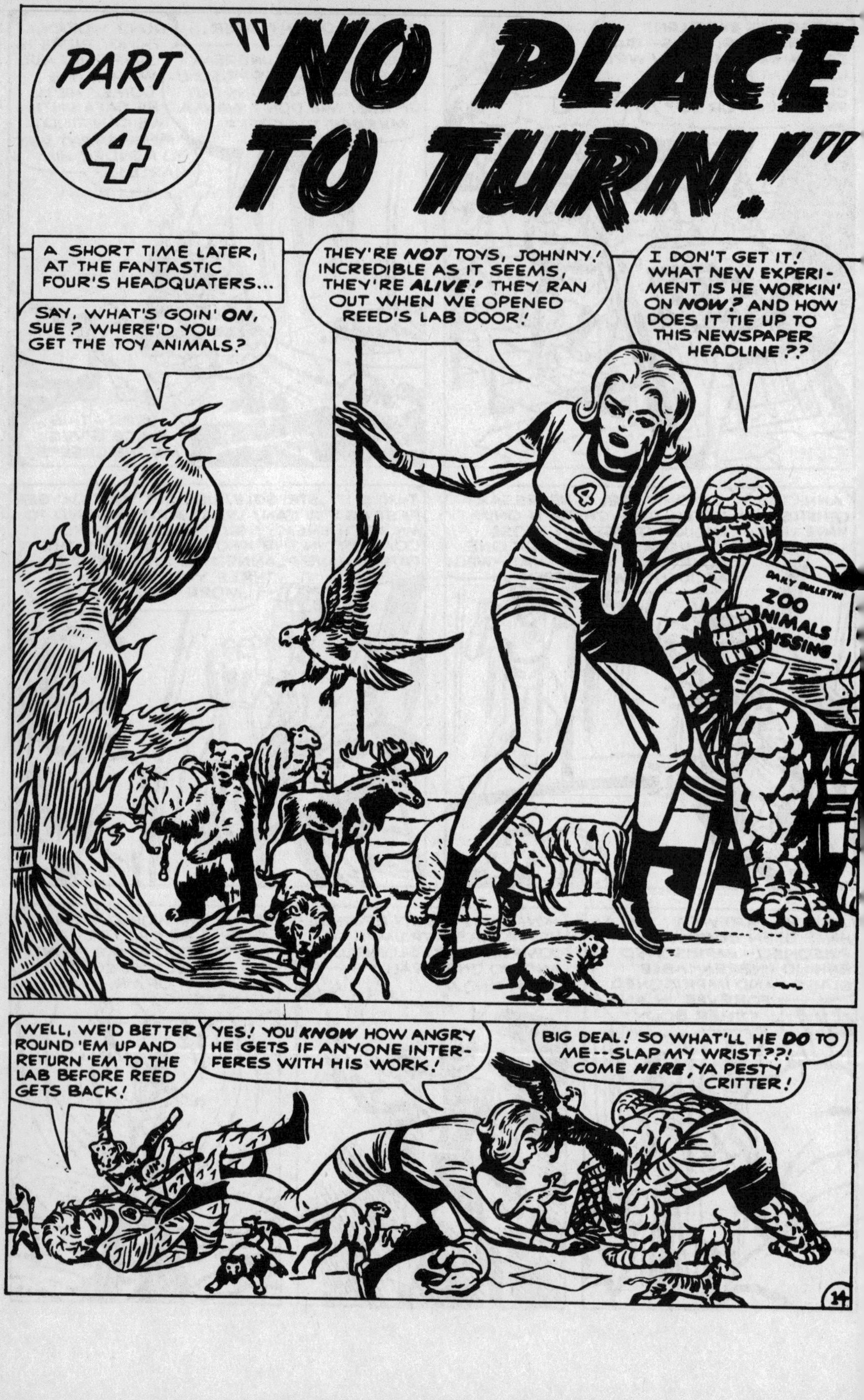
PART 4
"NO PLACE TO TURN!"
A SHORT TIME LATER, AT THE FANTASTIC FOUR'S HEADQUATERS...
SAY, WHAT'S GOIN' ON, SUE? WHERE'D YOU GET THE TOY ANIMALS?
THEY'RE NOT TOYS, JOHNNY! INCREDIBLE AS IT SEEMS, THEY'RE ALIVE! THEY RAN OUT WHEN WE OPENED REED'S LAB DOOR!
I DON'T GET IT! WHAT NEW EXPERIMENT IS HE WORKIN' ON NOW? AND HOW DOES IT TIE UP TO THIS NEWSPAPER HEADLINE??
DAILY BULLETIN
ZOO NIMALS ISSING
WELL, WE'D BETTER ROUND 'EM UP AND RETURN 'EM TO THE LAB BEFORE REED GETS BACK!
YES! YOU KNOW HOW ANGRY HE GETS IF ANYONE INTERFERES WITH HIS WORK!
BIG DEAL! SO WHAT'LL HE DO TO ME--SLAP MY WRIST??! COME HERE, YA PESTY CRITTER!
14

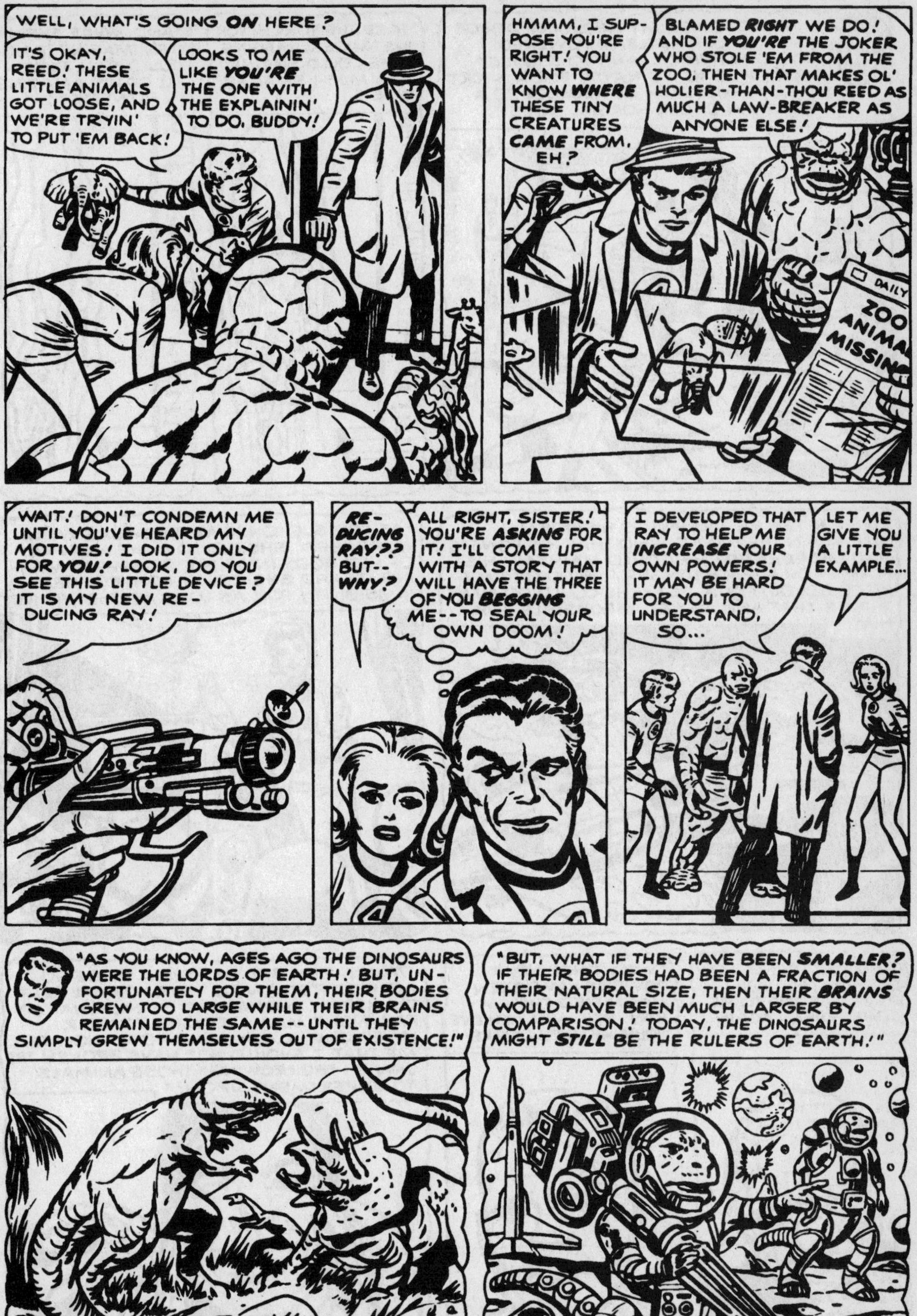

WELL, WHAT'S GOING ON HERE?
IT'S OKAY, REED! THESE LITTLE ANIMALS GOT LOOSE, AND WE'RE TRYIN' TO PUT 'EM BACK!
LOOKS TO ME LIKE YOU'RE THE ONE WITH THE EXPLAININ' TO DO, BUDDY!
HMMM, I SUPPOSE YOU'RE RIGHT! YOU WANT TO KNOW WHERE THESE TINY CREATURES CAME FROM, EH?
BLAMED RIGHT WE DO! AND IF YOU'RE THE JOKER WHO STOLE 'EM FROM THE ZOO, THEN THAT MAKES OL' HOLIER-THAN-THOU REED AS MUCH A LAW-BREAKER AS ANYONE ELSE!
DAILY
ZOO ANIMAL MISSING
WAIT! DON'T CONDEMN ME UNTIL YOU'VE HEARD MY MOTIVES! I DID IT ONLY FOR YOU! LOOK, DO YOU SEE THIS LITTLE DEVICE? IT IS MY NEW REDUCING RAY!
REDUCING RAY?? BUT-- WHY?
ALL RIGHT, SISTER! YOU'RE ASKING FOR IT! I'LL COME UP WITH A STORY THAT WILL HAVE THE THREE OF YOU BEGGING ME--TO SEAL YOUR OWN DOOM!
I DEVELOPED THAT RAY TO HELP ME INCREASE YOUR OWN POWERS! IT MAY BE HARD FOR YOU TO UNDERSTAND, SO...
LET ME GIVE YOU A LITTLE EXAMPLE...
"AS YOU KNOW, AGES AGO THE DINOSAURS WERE THE LORDS OF EARTH! BUT, UNFORTUNATELY FOR THEM, THEIR BODIES GREW TOO LARGE WHILE THEIR BRAINS REMAINED THE SAME--UNTIL THEY SIMPLY GREW THEMSELVES OUT OF EXISTENCE!"
"BUT, WHAT IF THEY HAVE BEEN SMALLER? IF THEIR BODIES HAD BEEN A FRACTION OF THEIR NATURAL SIZE, THEN THEIR BRAINS WOULD HAVE BEEN MUCH LARGER BY COMPARISON! TODAY, THE DINOSAURS MIGHT STILL BE THE RULERS OF EARTH!"
15

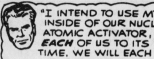 "I INTEND TO USE MY REDUCING DEVICE INSIDE OF OUR NUCLEAR POWERED ATOMIC ACTIVATOR, AND TO SUBJECT *EACH* OF US TO ITS RAYS! FOR A SHORT TIME, WE WILL EACH BE REDUCED TO A FRACTION OF OUR NORMAL SIZES..."

"TAKE THE TORCH, FOR INSTANCE... IMAGINE IF HE COULD SHRINK TO A MUCH SMALLER SIZE.."

"AND, WHILE *SHRINKING*, IMAGINE IF HE COULD STILL RETAIN ALL OF HIS AMAZING POWERS'..."

"THEN AFTER RETURNING TO HIS NORMAL SIZE AGAIN, HE WOULD FIND THAT HIS POWERS HAD *INCREASED*! HE COULD MAINTAIN HIS FLAME FOR A MUCH LONGER PERIOD OF TIME-- HE COULD OUTFLY A JET -- HE COULD DO MANY THINGS THAT ARE AS YET IMPOSSIBLE FOR HIM!"

"AS FOR SUE, ONCE *HER* POWERS WERE INCREASED, SHE COULD MAKE ANY *PART* OF HER BODY INVISIBLE BY SIMPLY WISHING IT! AND SHE COULD CONTROL HER INVISIBILITY FOR AS LONG AS SHE WISHED!"

"AND *YOU*, THING... HOW DESPERATELY YOU HAVE WISHED TO BECOME HUMAN AGAIN!"

"WELL, ONCE YOUR POWERS HAVE BEEN MAGNIFIED THRU MY RAY, YOU WILL ACHIEVE YOUR HEART'S DESIRE!"

"*THINK*, BEN GRIMM! THINK OF BEING ABLE TO RETURN TO YOUR NORMAL SELF BY MERELY *WISHING* IT! THINK WHAT MY RAY MIGHT MEAN TO YOU -- TO YOUR LOVED ONE, ALICIA! AND NOW-- NOW TELL ME THAT I SHOULD NOT HAVE BROKEN THE LAW BY "BORROWING" THOSE ANIMALS TO EXPERIMENT UPON!"

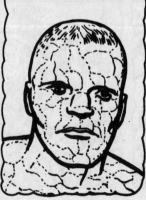

16

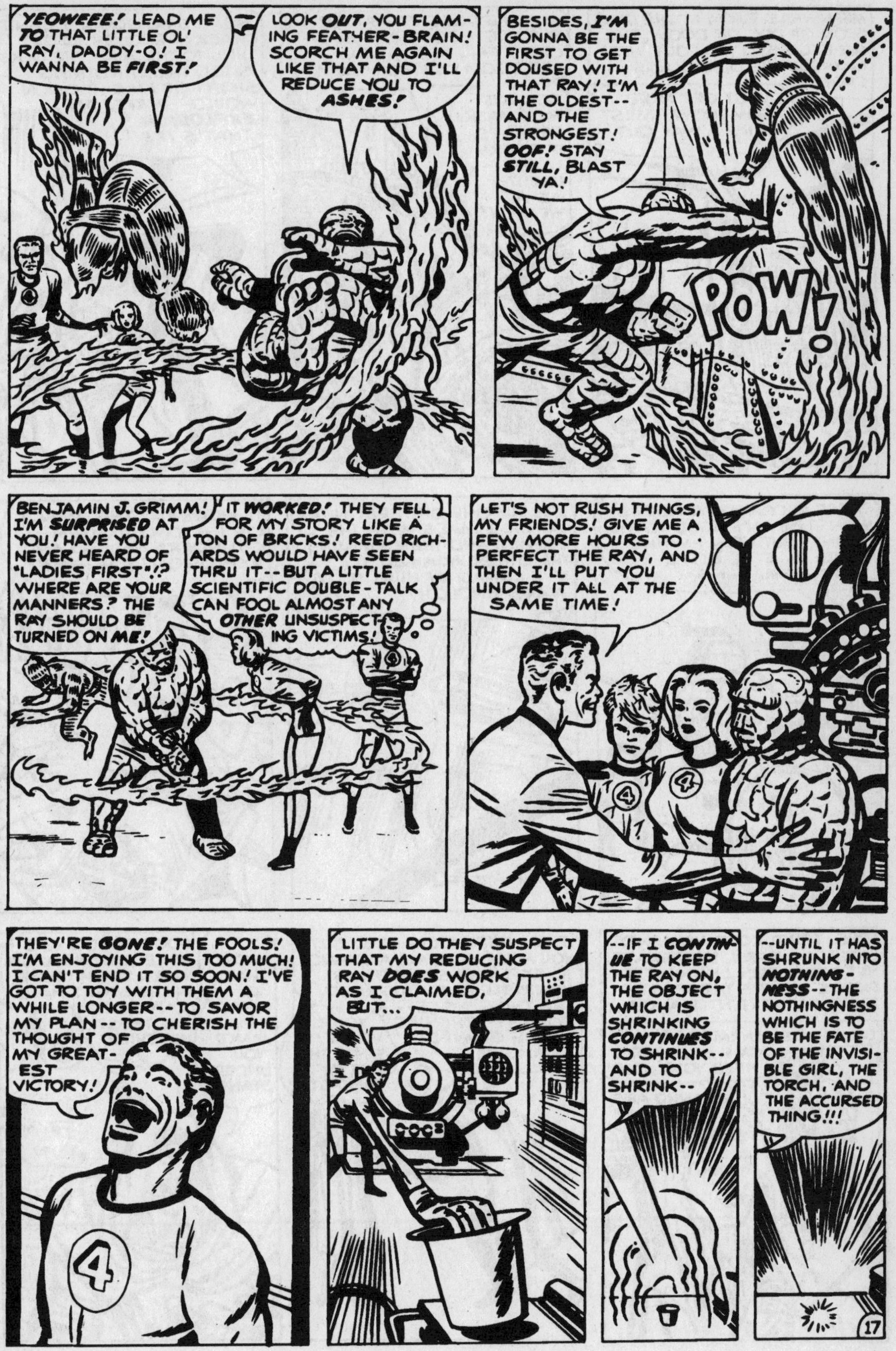
YEOWEEE! LEAD ME TO THAT LITTLE OL' RAY, DADDY-O! I WANNA BE FIRST!
LOOK OUT, YOU FLAMING FEATHER-BRAIN! SCORCH ME AGAIN LIKE THAT AND I'LL REDUCE YOU TO ASHES!
BESIDES, I'M GONNA BE THE FIRST TO GET DOUSED WITH THAT RAY! I'M THE OLDEST--AND THE STRONGEST! OOF! STAY STILL, BLAST YA!
POW!
BENJAMIN J. GRIMM! I'M SURPRISED AT YOU! HAVE YOU NEVER HEARD OF "LADIES FIRST"!? WHERE ARE YOUR MANNERS? THE RAY SHOULD BE TURNED ON ME!
IT WORKED! THEY FELL FOR MY STORY LIKE A TON OF BRICKS! REED RICHARDS WOULD HAVE SEEN THRU IT--BUT A LITTLE SCIENTIFIC DOUBLE-TALK CAN FOOL ALMOST ANY OTHER UNSUSPECTING VICTIMS!
LET'S NOT RUSH THINGS, MY FRIENDS! GIVE ME A FEW MORE HOURS TO PERFECT THE RAY, AND THEN I'LL PUT YOU UNDER IT ALL AT THE SAME TIME!
THEY'RE GONE! THE FOOLS! I'M ENJOYING THIS TOO MUCH! I CAN'T END IT SO SOON! I'VE GOT TO TOY WITH THEM A WHILE LONGER--TO SAVOR MY PLAN--TO CHERISH THE THOUGHT OF MY GREATEST VICTORY!
LITTLE DO THEY SUSPECT THAT MY REDUCING RAY DOES WORK AS I CLAIMED, BUT...
--IF I CONTINUE TO KEEP THE RAY ON, THE OBJECT WHICH IS SHRINKING CONTINUES TO SHRINK--AND TO SHRINK--
--UNTIL IT HAS SHRUNK INTO NOTHINGNESS--THE NOTHINGNESS WHICH IS TO BE THE FATE OF THE INVISIBLE GIRL, THE TORCH, AND THE ACCURSED THING!!!

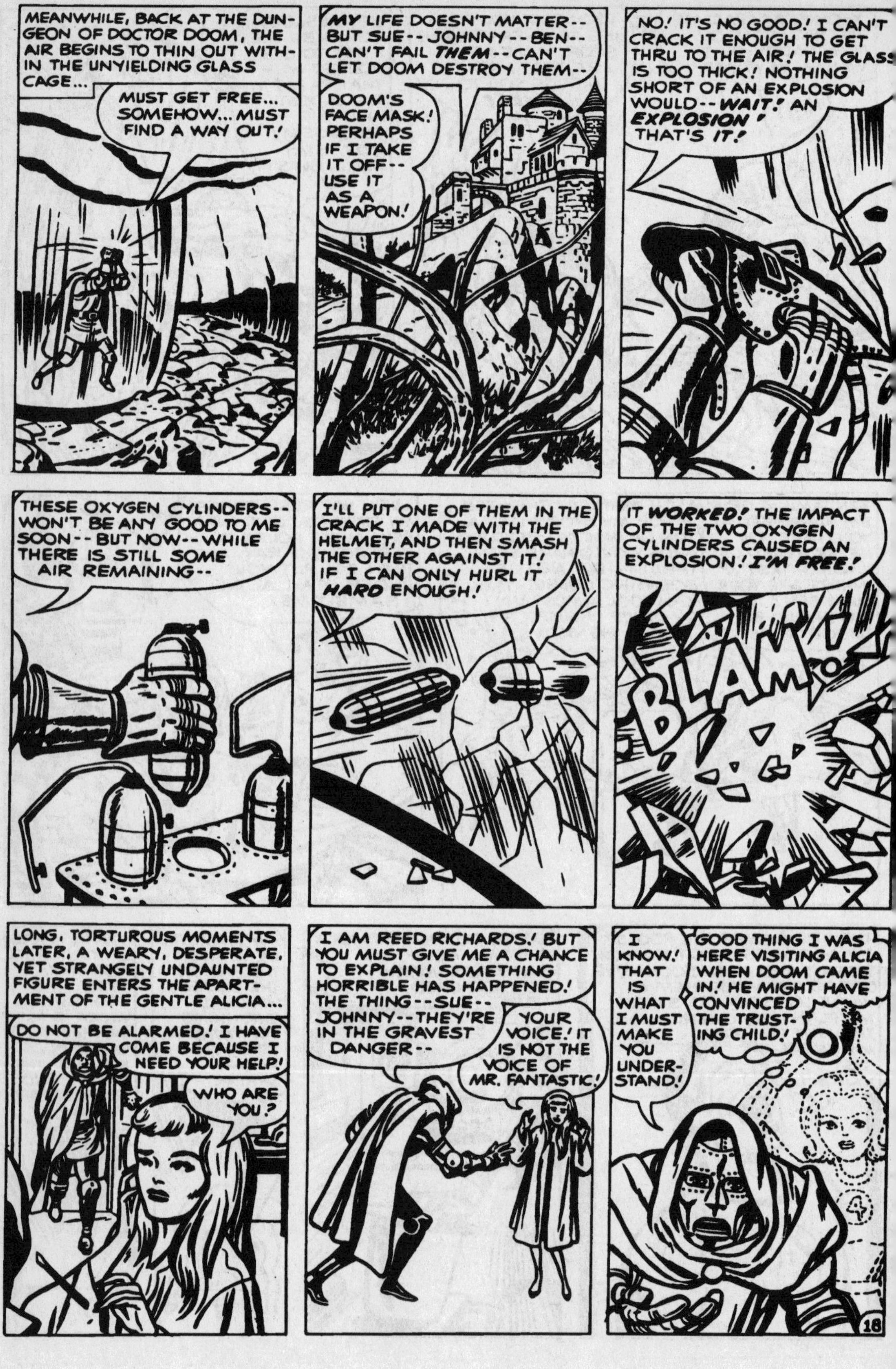
MEANWHILE, BACK AT THE DUNGEON OF DOCTOR DOOM, THE AIR BEGINS TO THIN OUT WITHIN THE UNYIELDING GLASS CAGE...
MUST GET FREE... SOMEHOW... MUST FIND A WAY OUT!
MY LIFE DOESN'T MATTER-- BUT SUE-- JOHNNY-- BEN-- CAN'T FAIL THEM--CAN'T LET DOOM DESTROY THEM--
DOOM'S FACE MASK! PERHAPS IF I TAKE IT OFF-- USE IT AS A WEAPON!
NO! IT'S NO GOOD! I CAN'T CRACK IT ENOUGH TO GET THRU TO THE AIR! THE GLASS IS TOO THICK! NOTHING SHORT OF AN EXPLOSION WOULD--WAIT! AN EXPLOSION! THAT'S IT!
THESE OXYGEN CYLINDERS-- WON'T BE ANY GOOD TO ME SOON--BUT NOW--WHILE THERE IS STILL SOME AIR REMAINING--
I'LL PUT ONE OF THEM IN THE CRACK I MADE WITH THE HELMET, AND THEN SMASH THE OTHER AGAINST IT! IF I CAN ONLY HURL IT HARD ENOUGH!
IT WORKED! THE IMPACT OF THE TWO OXYGEN CYLINDERS CAUSED AN EXPLOSION! I'M FREE!
BLAM!
LONG, TORTUROUS MOMENTS LATER, A WEARY, DESPERATE, YET STRANGELY UNDAUNTED FIGURE ENTERS THE APARTMENT OF THE GENTLE ALICIA...
DO NOT BE ALARMED! I HAVE COME BECAUSE I NEED YOUR HELP!
WHO ARE YOU?
I AM REED RICHARDS! BUT YOU MUST GIVE ME A CHANCE TO EXPLAIN! SOMETHING HORRIBLE HAS HAPPENED! THE THING--SUE-- JOHNNY--THEY'RE IN THE GRAVEST DANGER--
YOUR VOICE! IT IS NOT THE VOICE OF MR. FANTASTIC!
I KNOW! THAT IS WHAT I MUST MAKE YOU UNDERSTAND!
GOOD THING I WAS HERE VISITING ALICIA WHEN DOOM CAME IN! HE MIGHT HAVE CONVINCED THE TRUSTING CHILD!
4
18

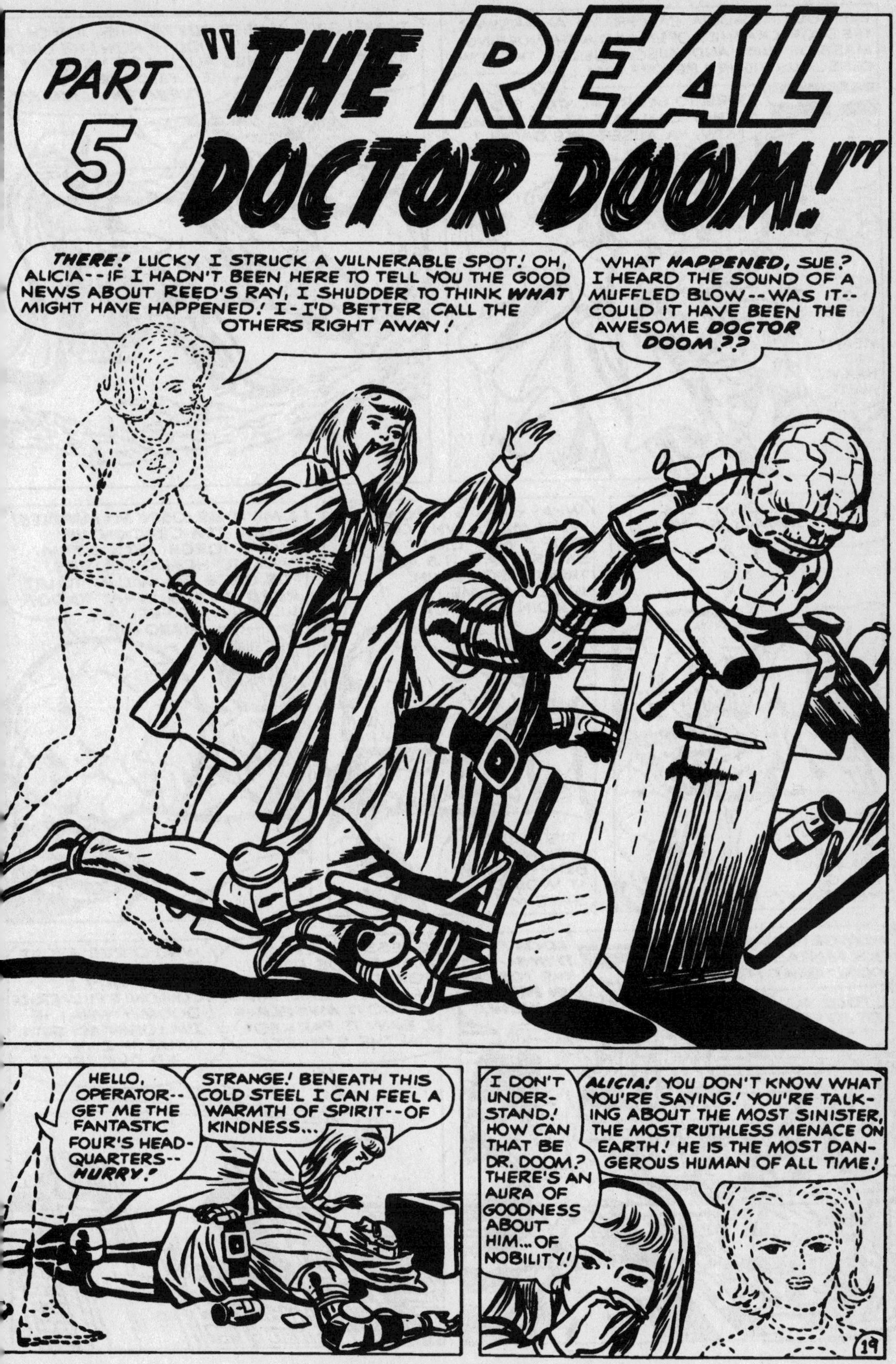
PART 5
"THE REAL DOCTOR DOOM!"
THERE! LUCKY I STRUCK A VULNERABLE SPOT! OH, ALICIA--IF I HADN'T BEEN HERE TO TELL YOU THE GOOD NEWS ABOUT REED'S RAY, I SHUDDER TO THINK WHAT MIGHT HAVE HAPPENED! I-I'D BETTER CALL THE OTHERS RIGHT AWAY!
WHAT HAPPENED, SUE? I HEARD THE SOUND OF A MUFFLED BLOW--WAS IT--COULD IT HAVE BEEN THE AWESOME DOCTOR DOOM??
HELLO, OPERATOR--GET ME THE FANTASTIC FOUR'S HEAD-QUARTERS--HURRY!
STRANGE! BENEATH THIS COLD STEEL I CAN FEEL A WARMTH OF SPIRIT--OF KINDNESS...
I DON'T UNDER-STAND! HOW CAN THAT BE DR. DOOM? THERE'S AN AURA OF GOODNESS ABOUT HIM... OF NOBILITY!
ALICIA! YOU DON'T KNOW WHAT YOU'RE SAYING! YOU'RE TALK-ING ABOUT THE MOST SINISTER, THE MOST RUTHLESS MENACE ON EARTH! HE IS THE MOST DAN-GEROUS HUMAN OF ALL TIME!
19

EVEN BEFORE ALICIA CAN FRAME AN ANSWER, THE DOOR CRASHES OPEN AND A THUNDERING MASS OF FURY AND MUSCLE SEIZES THE NOW-CONSCIOUS FIGURE BEFORE HIM...

SO! YOU TRIED TO SCARE *ALICIA*, DID YA! NOTHIN' CAN SAVE YA FROM ME NOW, YA MISERABLE GHOUL!

NO, THING! I MEANT NO HARM! WAIT--!

THING! GIVE 'IM A CHANCE TO SPEAK! MAYBE...

KEEP *OUTTA* THIS, TORCH! I AIN'T KIDDIN' NOW! HE THREATENED ALICIA! DO YA *HEAR* ME? HE DARED TO *THREATEN ALICIA!!!*

THIS IS *IT*, DOOM! I'M GONNA *DEMOLISH* YA!

NO, THING-- YOU *CAN'T!* YOU MUSTN'T! HEAR ME, THING-- *HEAR ME!*

WHA-WHAT'S *WRONG* WITH ME?? WHY DID I STOP? WHY CAN'T I SMASH YA? IT'S AS THOUGH SOMETHIN' INSIDE OF ME IS HOLDIN' ME BACK!

IT'S YOUR *INSTINCT*, BEN-- I *KNEW* IT WOULD SAVE ME!

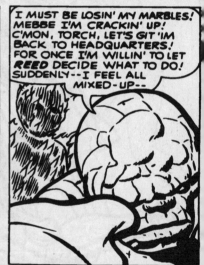

I MUST BE LOSIN' MY MARBLES! MEBBE I'M CRACKIN' UP! C'MON, TORCH, LET'S GIT 'IM BACK TO HEADQUARTERS! FOR ONCE I'M WILLIN' TO LET *REED* DECIDE WHAT TO DO! SUDDENLY-- I FEEL ALL MIXED-UP--

HEY! GET AWAY FROM OUR FANTASTI-CAR, KIDS! *BEAT IT!*

I *TOLD* YA NOT TO PARK IT THERE!

LOOK! THE *THING*--AND THE *TORCH*, IN PERSON! WOW!

GUESS WE CAN'T BLAME KIDS FOR POKIN' AROUND THE FANTASTI-CAR, THING! I'D DO IT *MYSELF* IF I SAW IT PARKED IN THE STREET!

WHO CARES ABOUT *THAT!* I WANNA KNOW WHY I COULDN'T PULVERIZE DOOM!! WHAT IF I'M LOSIN' MY GUTS? WHAT IF I'VE TURNED CHICKEN??

20

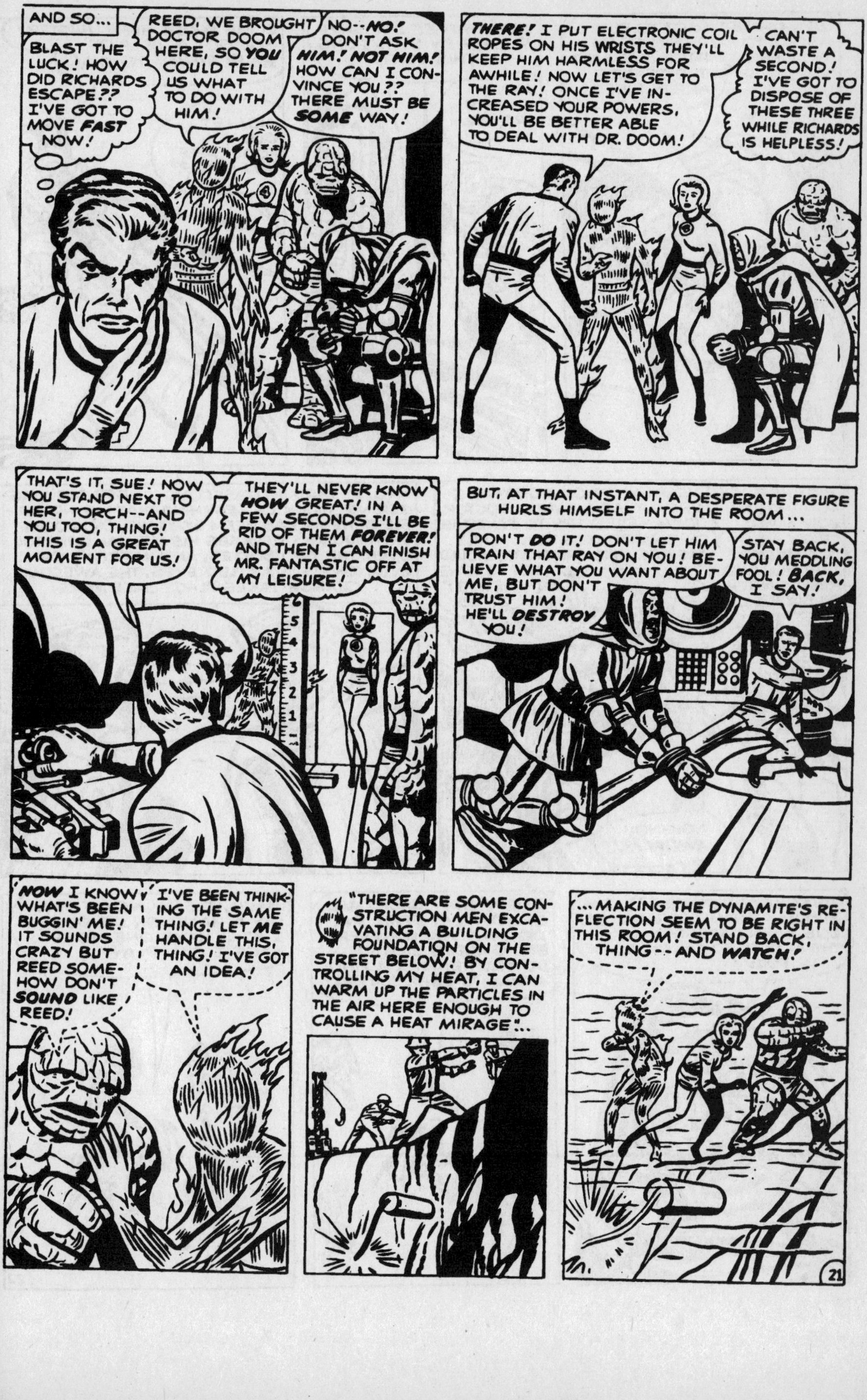
AND SO...
BLAST THE LUCK! HOW DID RICHARDS ESCAPE?? I'VE GOT TO MOVE FAST NOW!
REED, WE BROUGHT DOCTOR DOOM HERE, SO YOU COULD TELL US WHAT TO DO WITH HIM!
NO--NO! DON'T ASK HIM! NOT HIM! HOW CAN I CONVINCE YOU?? THERE MUST BE SOME WAY!
THERE! I PUT ELECTRONIC COIL ROPES ON HIS WRISTS THEY'LL KEEP HIM HARMLESS FOR AWHILE! NOW LET'S GET TO THE RAY! ONCE I'VE INCREASED YOUR POWERS, YOU'LL BE BETTER ABLE TO DEAL WITH DR. DOOM!
CAN'T WASTE A SECOND! I'VE GOT TO DISPOSE OF THESE THREE WHILE RICHARDS IS HELPLESS!
THAT'S IT, SUE! NOW YOU STAND NEXT TO HER, TORCH--AND YOU TOO, THING! THIS IS A GREAT MOMENT FOR US!
THEY'LL NEVER KNOW HOW GREAT! IN A FEW SECONDS I'LL BE RID OF THEM FOREVER! AND THEN I CAN FINISH MR. FANTASTIC OFF AT MY LEISURE!
BUT, AT THAT INSTANT, A DESPERATE FIGURE HURLS HIMSELF INTO THE ROOM...
DON'T DO IT! DON'T LET HIM TRAIN THAT RAY ON YOU! BELIEVE WHAT YOU WANT ABOUT ME, BUT DON'T TRUST HIM! HE'LL DESTROY YOU!
STAY BACK, YOU MEDDLING FOOL! BACK, I SAY!
NOW I KNOW WHAT'S BEEN BUGGIN' ME! IT SOUNDS CRAZY BUT REED SOMEHOW DON'T SOUND LIKE REED!
I'VE BEEN THINKING THE SAME THING! LET ME HANDLE THIS, THING! I'VE GOT AN IDEA!
"THERE ARE SOME CONSTRUCTION MEN EXCAVATING A BUILDING FOUNDATION ON THE STREET BELOW! BY CONTROLLING MY HEAT, I CAN WARM UP THE PARTICLES IN THE AIR HERE ENOUGH TO CAUSE A HEAT MIRAGE"...
...MAKING THE DYNAMITE'S REFLECTION SEEM TO BE RIGHT IN THIS ROOM! STAND BACK, THING--AND WATCH!
21

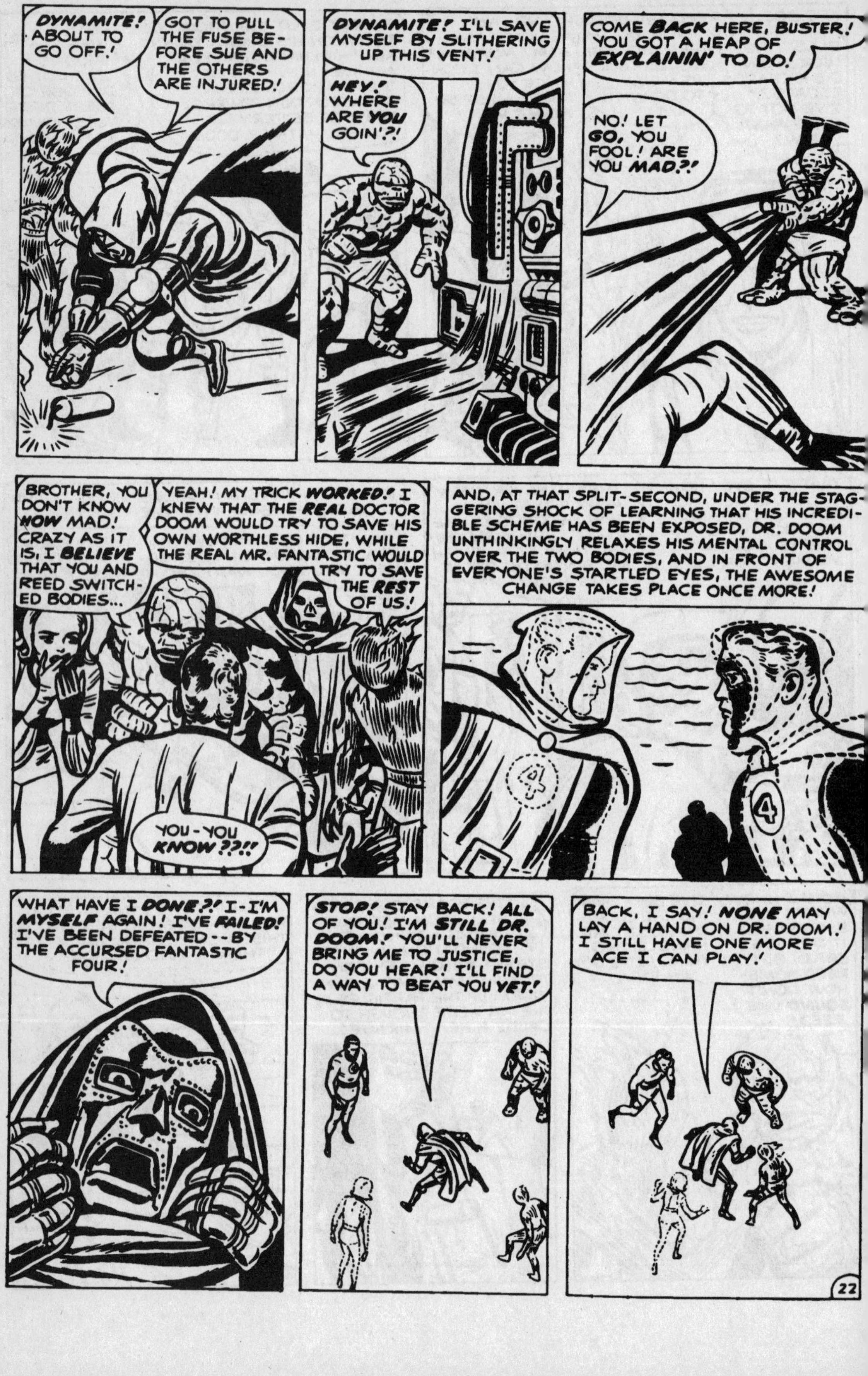
DYNAMITE! ABOUT TO GO OFF!
GOT TO PULL THE FUSE BEFORE SUE AND THE OTHERS ARE INJURED!
DYNAMITE! I'LL SAVE MYSELF BY SLITHERING UP THIS VENT!
HEY! WHERE ARE YOU GOIN'?!
COME BACK HERE, BUSTER! YOU GOT A HEAP OF EXPLAININ' TO DO!
NO! LET GO, YOU FOOL! ARE YOU MAD?!
BROTHER, YOU DON'T KNOW HOW MAD! CRAZY AS IT IS, I BELIEVE THAT YOU AND REED SWITCHED BODIES...
YEAH! MY TRICK WORKED! I KNEW THAT THE REAL DOCTOR DOOM WOULD TRY TO SAVE HIS OWN WORTHLESS HIDE, WHILE THE REAL MR. FANTASTIC WOULD TRY TO SAVE THE REST OF US!
YOU-YOU KNOW??!!
AND, AT THAT SPLIT-SECOND, UNDER THE STAGGERING SHOCK OF LEARNING THAT HIS INCREDIBLE SCHEME HAS BEEN EXPOSED, DR. DOOM UNTHINKINGLY RELAXES HIS MENTAL CONTROL OVER THE TWO BODIES, AND IN FRONT OF EVERYONE'S STARTLED EYES, THE AWESOME CHANGE TAKES PLACE ONCE MORE!
WHAT HAVE I DONE?! I-I'M MYSELF AGAIN! I'VE FAILED! I'VE BEEN DEFEATED--BY THE ACCURSED FANTASTIC FOUR!
STOP! STAY BACK! ALL OF YOU! I'M STILL DR. DOOM! YOU'LL NEVER BRING ME TO JUSTICE, DO YOU HEAR! I'LL FIND A WAY TO BEAT YOU YET!
BACK, I SAY! NONE MAY LAY A HAND ON DR. DOOM! I STILL HAVE ONE MORE ACE I CAN PLAY!
22

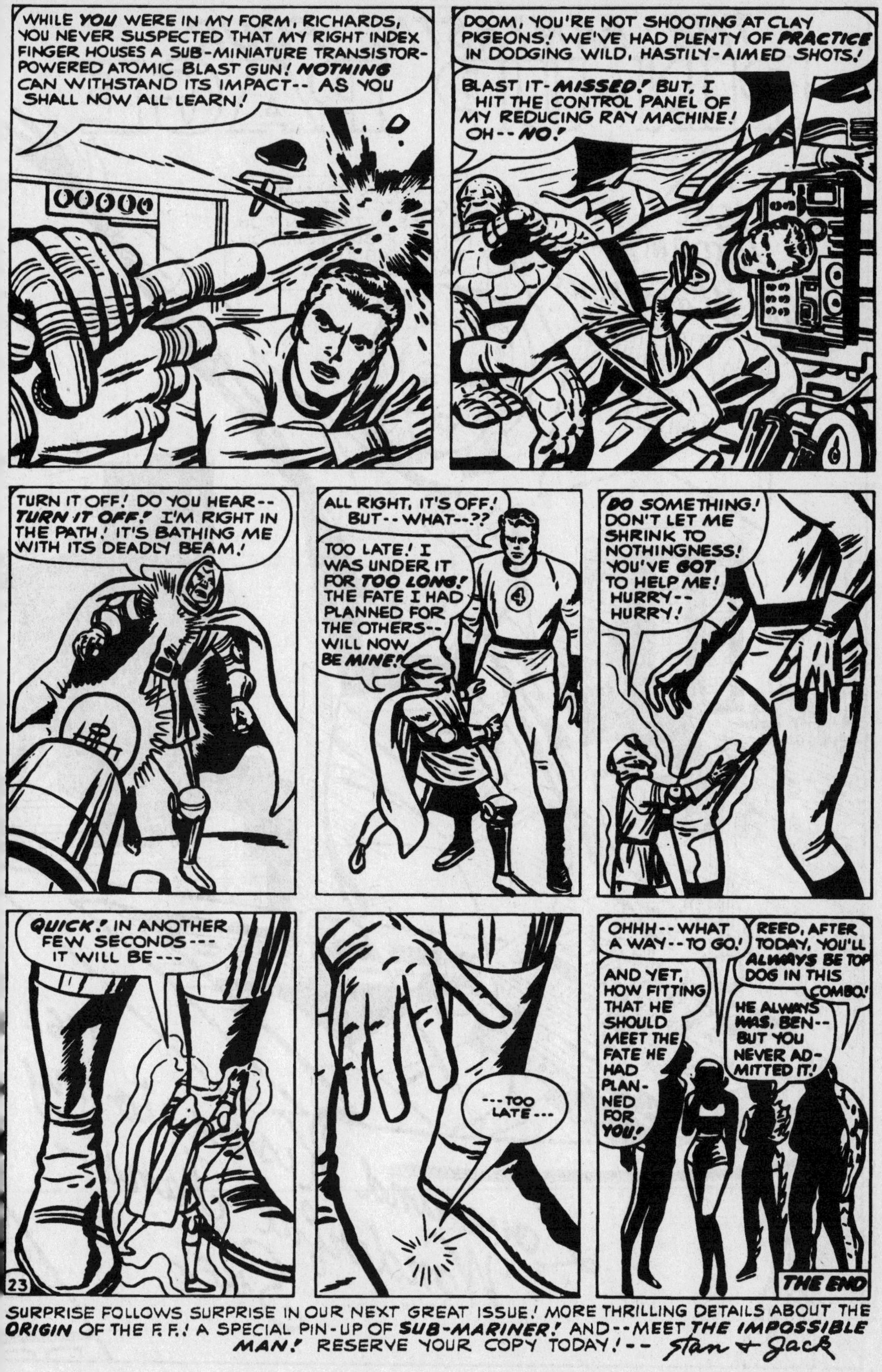
WHILE YOU WERE IN MY FORM, RICHARDS, YOU NEVER SUSPECTED THAT MY RIGHT INDEX FINGER HOUSES A SUB-MINIATURE TRANSISTOR-POWERED ATOMIC BLAST GUN! NOTHING CAN WITHSTAND ITS IMPACT-- AS YOU SHALL NOW ALL LEARN!
DOOM, YOU'RE NOT SHOOTING AT CLAY PIGEONS! WE'VE HAD PLENTY OF PRACTICE IN DODGING WILD, HASTILY-AIMED SHOTS!
BLAST IT-MISSED! BUT, I HIT THE CONTROL PANEL OF MY REDUCING RAY MACHINE! OH--NO!
TURN IT OFF! DO YOU HEAR-- TURN IT OFF! I'M RIGHT IN THE PATH! IT'S BATHING ME WITH ITS DEADLY BEAM!
ALL RIGHT, IT'S OFF! BUT--WHAT--??
TOO LATE! I WAS UNDER IT FOR TOO LONG! THE FATE I HAD PLANNED FOR THE OTHERS-- WILL NOW BE MINE!
DO SOMETHING! DON'T LET ME SHRINK TO NOTHINGNESS! YOU'VE GOT TO HELP ME! HURRY-- HURRY!
QUICK! IN ANOTHER FEW SECONDS--- IT WILL BE---
23
---TOO LATE---
OHHH--WHAT A WAY--TO GO!
AND YET, HOW FITTING THAT HE SHOULD MEET THE FATE HE HAD PLANNED FOR YOU!
REED, AFTER TODAY, YOU'LL ALWAYS BE TOP DOG IN THIS COMBO!
HE ALWAYS WAS, BEN-- BUT YOU NEVER ADMITTED IT!
THE END

SURPRISE FOLLOWS SURPRISE IN OUR NEXT GREAT ISSUE! MORE THRILLING DETAILS ABOUT THE ***ORIGIN*** OF THE F.F.! A SPECIAL PIN-UP OF ***SUB-MARINER!*** AND--MEET ***THE IMPOSSIBLE MAN!*** RESERVE YOUR COPY TODAY!-- Stan + Jack

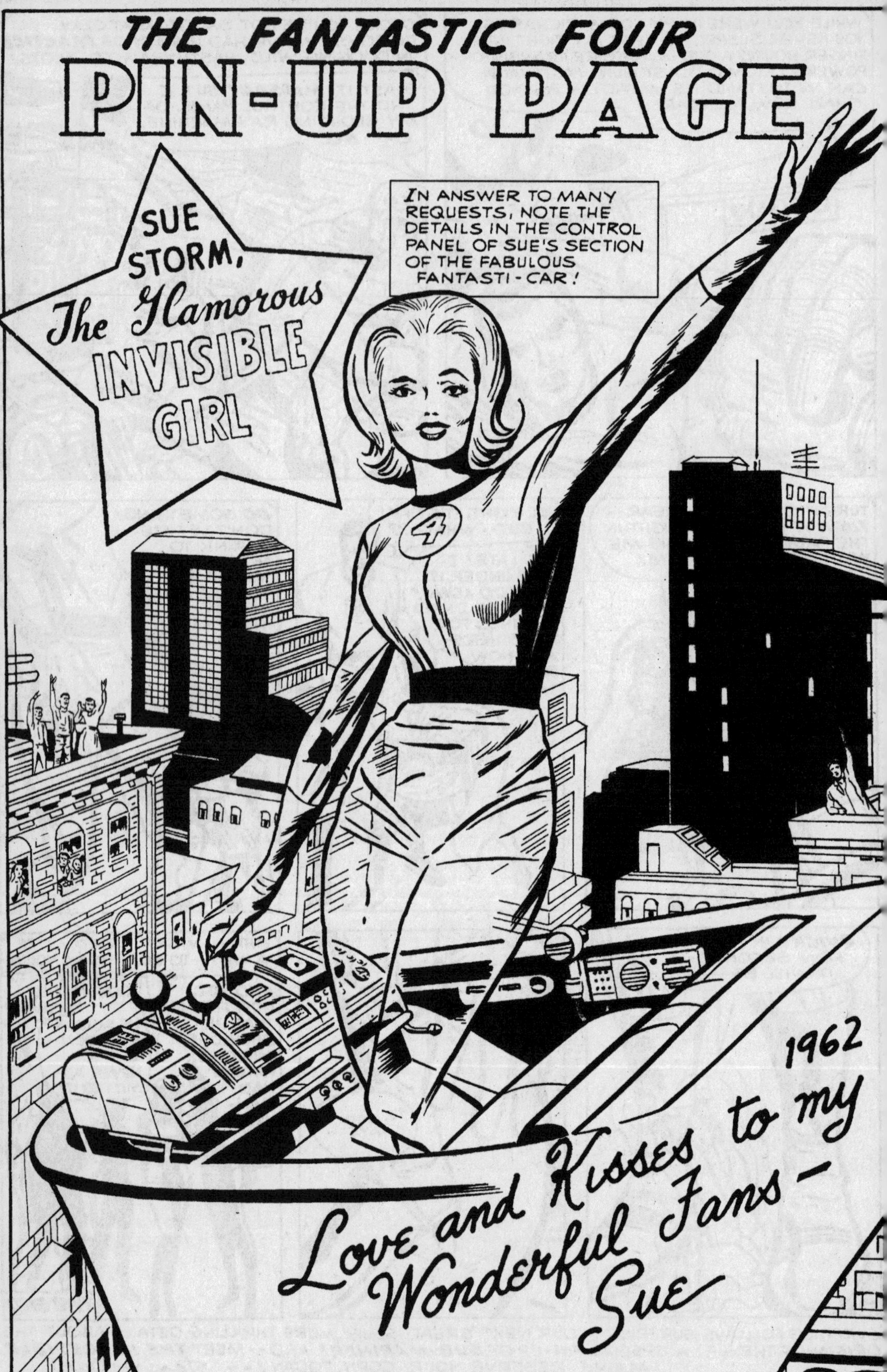
THE FANTASTIC FOUR
PIN-UP PAGE
SUE STORM, The Glamorous INVISIBLE GIRL
IN ANSWER TO MANY REQUESTS, NOTE THE DETAILS IN THE CONTROL PANEL OF SUE'S SECTION OF THE FABULOUS FANTASTI-CAR!
1962
Love and Kisses to my Wonderful Fans- Sue

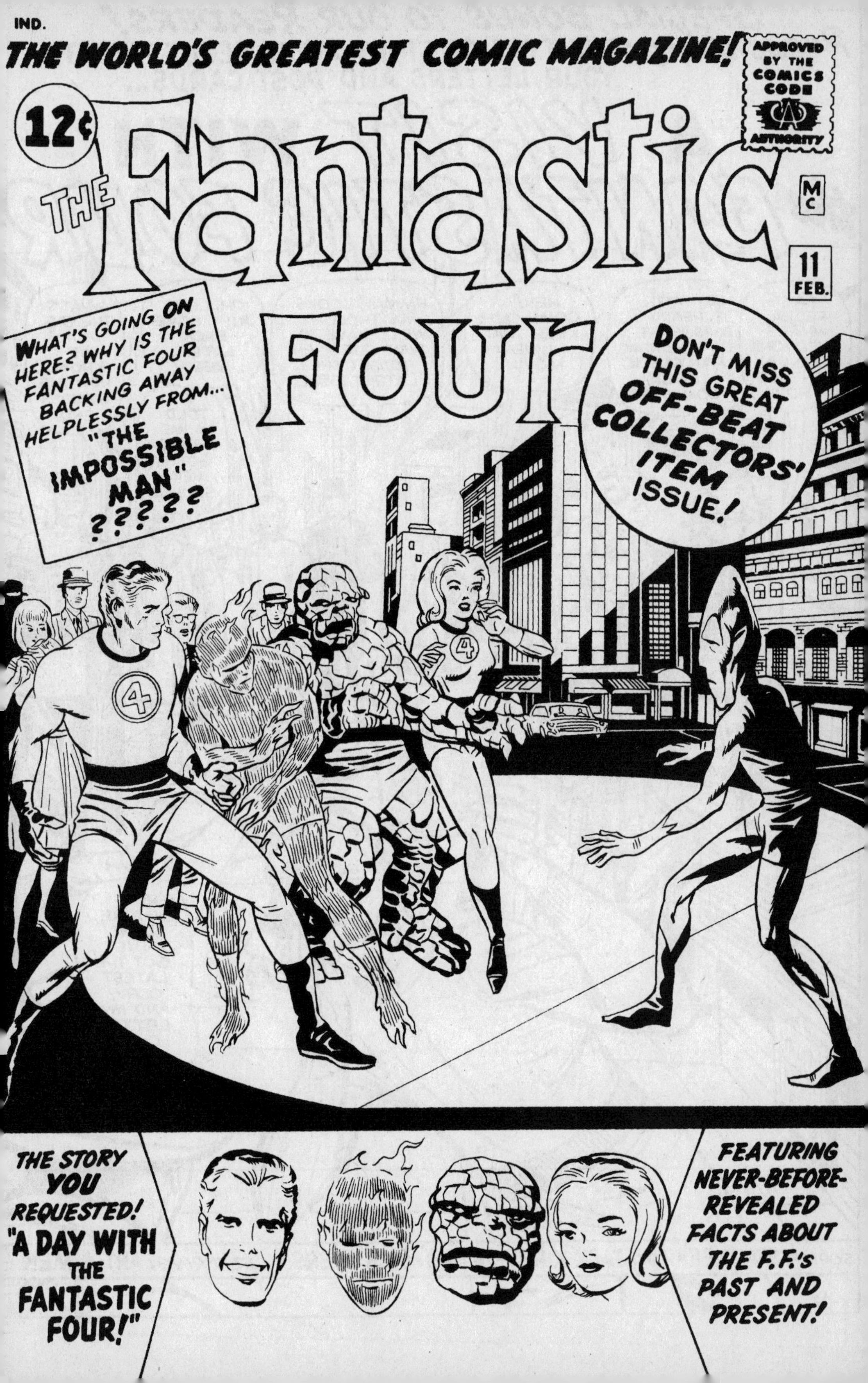

IND.
THE WORLD'S GREATEST COMIC MAGAZINE!
APPROVED BY THE COMICS CODE AUTHORITY
12¢
THE Fantastic Four
MC
11 FEB.
WHAT'S GOING ON HERE? WHY IS THE FANTASTIC FOUR BACKING AWAY HELPLESSLY FROM... "THE IMPOSSIBLE MAN" ?????
DON'T MISS THIS GREAT OFF-BEAT COLLECTORS' ITEM ISSUE!
THE STORY YOU REQUESTED! "A DAY WITH THE FANTASTIC FOUR!"
FEATURING NEVER-BEFORE-REVEALED FACTS ABOUT THE F.F.'s PAST AND PRESENT!

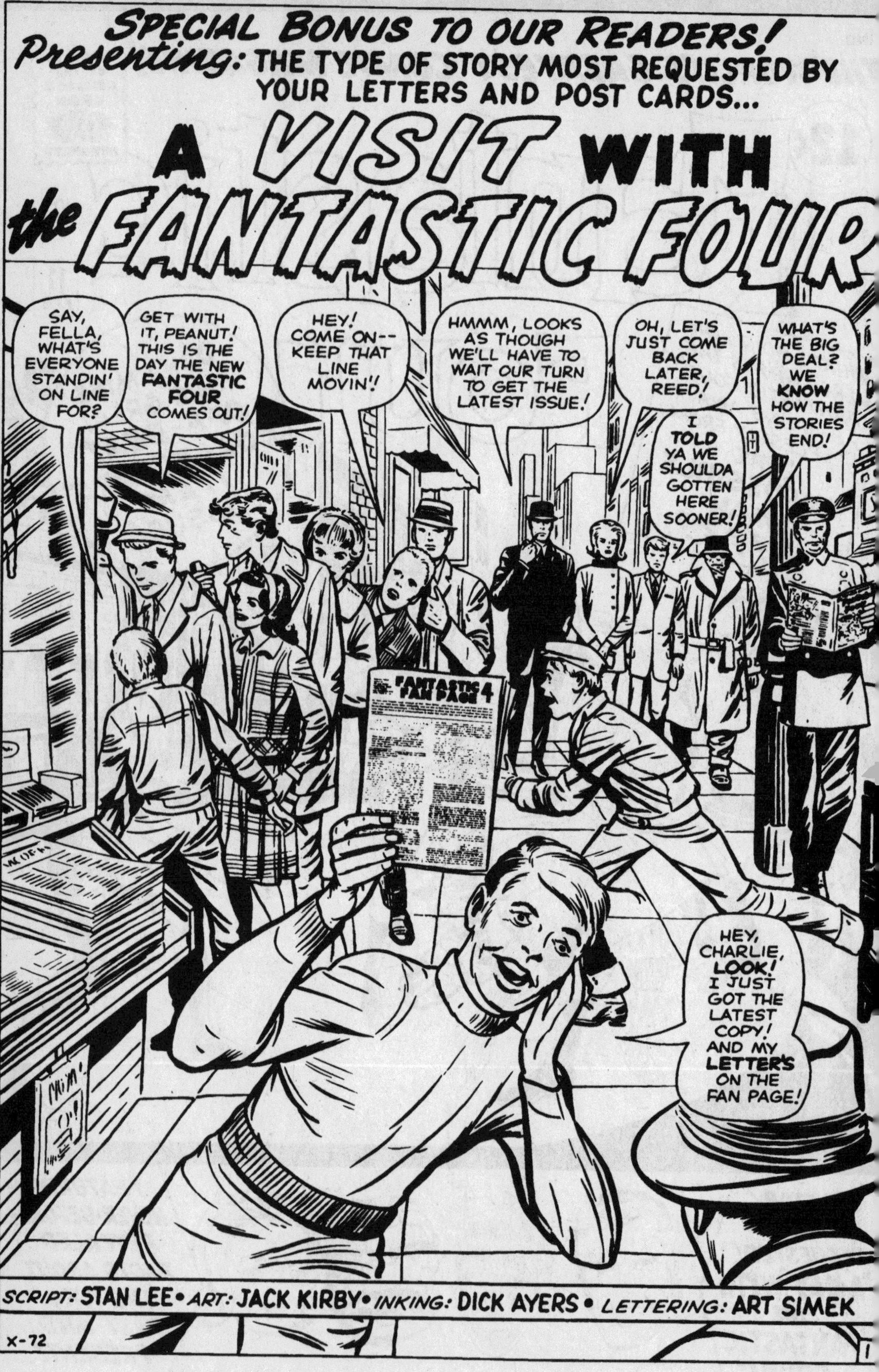

SPECIAL BONUS TO OUR READERS!
Presenting: THE TYPE OF STORY MOST REQUESTED BY YOUR LETTERS AND POST CARDS...
A VISIT WITH the FANTASTIC FOUR
SAY, FELLA, WHAT'S EVERYONE STANDIN' ON LINE FOR?
GET WITH IT, PEANUT! THIS IS THE DAY THE NEW FANTASTIC FOUR COMES OUT!
HEY! COME ON-- KEEP THAT LINE MOVIN'!
HMMM, LOOKS AS THOUGH WE'LL HAVE TO WAIT OUR TURN TO GET THE LATEST ISSUE!
OH, LET'S JUST COME BACK LATER, REED!
I TOLD YA WE SHOULDA GOTTEN HERE SOONER!
WHAT'S THE BIG DEAL? WE KNOW HOW THE STORIES END!
FANTASTIC 4 FAN PAGE
HEY, CHARLIE, LOOK! I JUST GOT THE LATEST COPY! AND MY LETTER'S ON THE FAN PAGE!
SCRIPT: STAN LEE • ART: JACK KIRBY • INKING: DICK AYERS • LETTERING: ART SIMEK
X-72
1

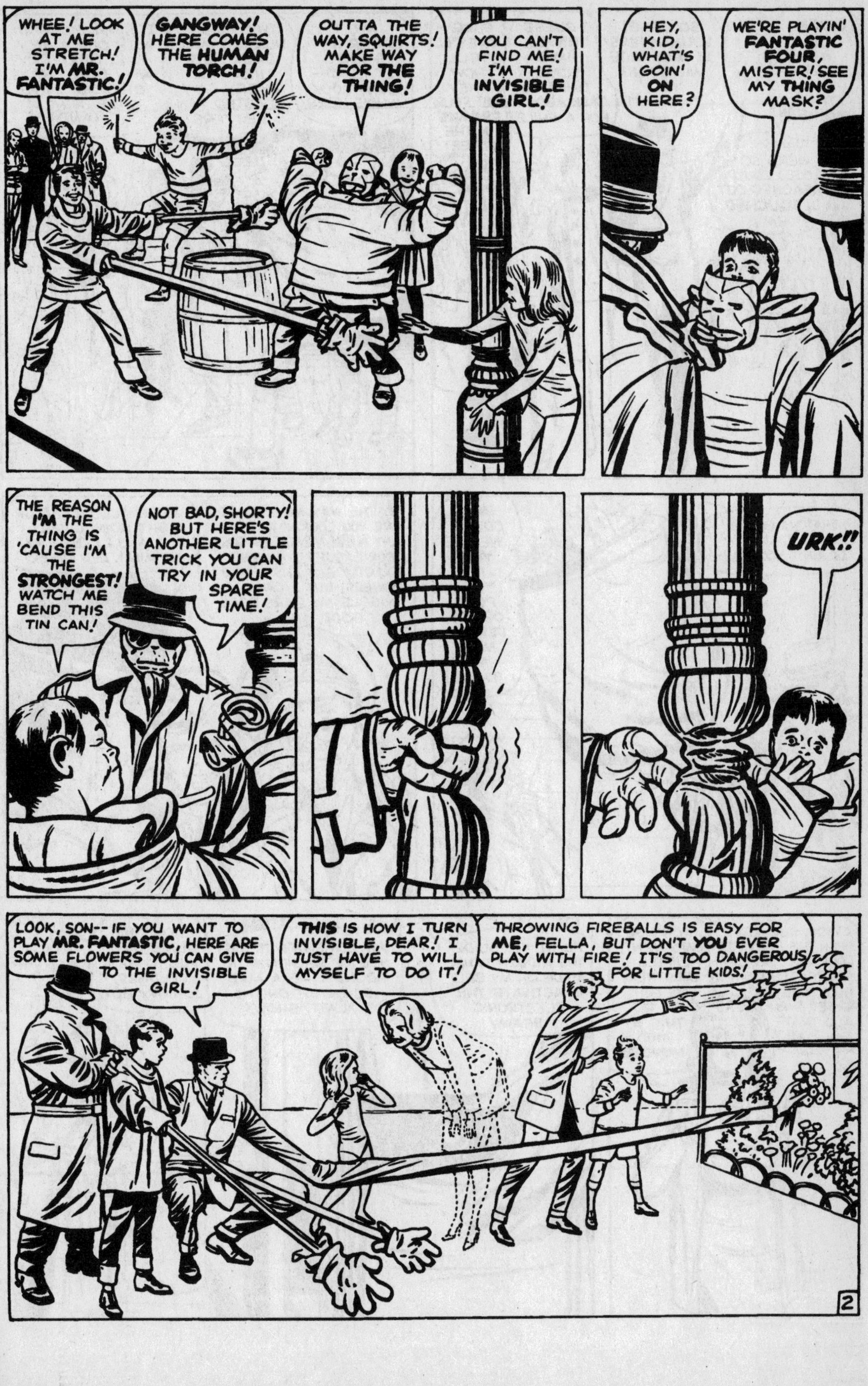

WHEE! LOOK AT ME STRETCH! I'M MR. FANTASTIC!
GANGWAY! HERE COMES THE HUMAN TORCH!
OUTTA THE WAY, SQUIRTS! MAKE WAY FOR THE THING!
YOU CAN'T FIND ME! I'M THE INVISIBLE GIRL!
HEY, KID, WHAT'S GOIN' ON HERE?
WE'RE PLAYIN' FANTASTIC FOUR, MISTER! SEE MY THING MASK?
THE REASON I'M THE THING IS 'CAUSE I'M THE STRONGEST! WATCH ME BEND THIS TIN CAN!
NOT BAD, SHORTY! BUT HERE'S ANOTHER LITTLE TRICK YOU CAN TRY IN YOUR SPARE TIME!
URK!!
LOOK, SON-- IF YOU WANT TO PLAY MR. FANTASTIC, HERE ARE SOME FLOWERS YOU CAN GIVE TO THE INVISIBLE GIRL!
THIS IS HOW I TURN INVISIBLE, DEAR! I JUST HAVE TO WILL MYSELF TO DO IT!
THROWING FIREBALLS IS EASY FOR ME, FELLA, BUT DON'T YOU EVER PLAY WITH FIRE! IT'S TOO DANGEROUS FOR LITTLE KIDS!
2

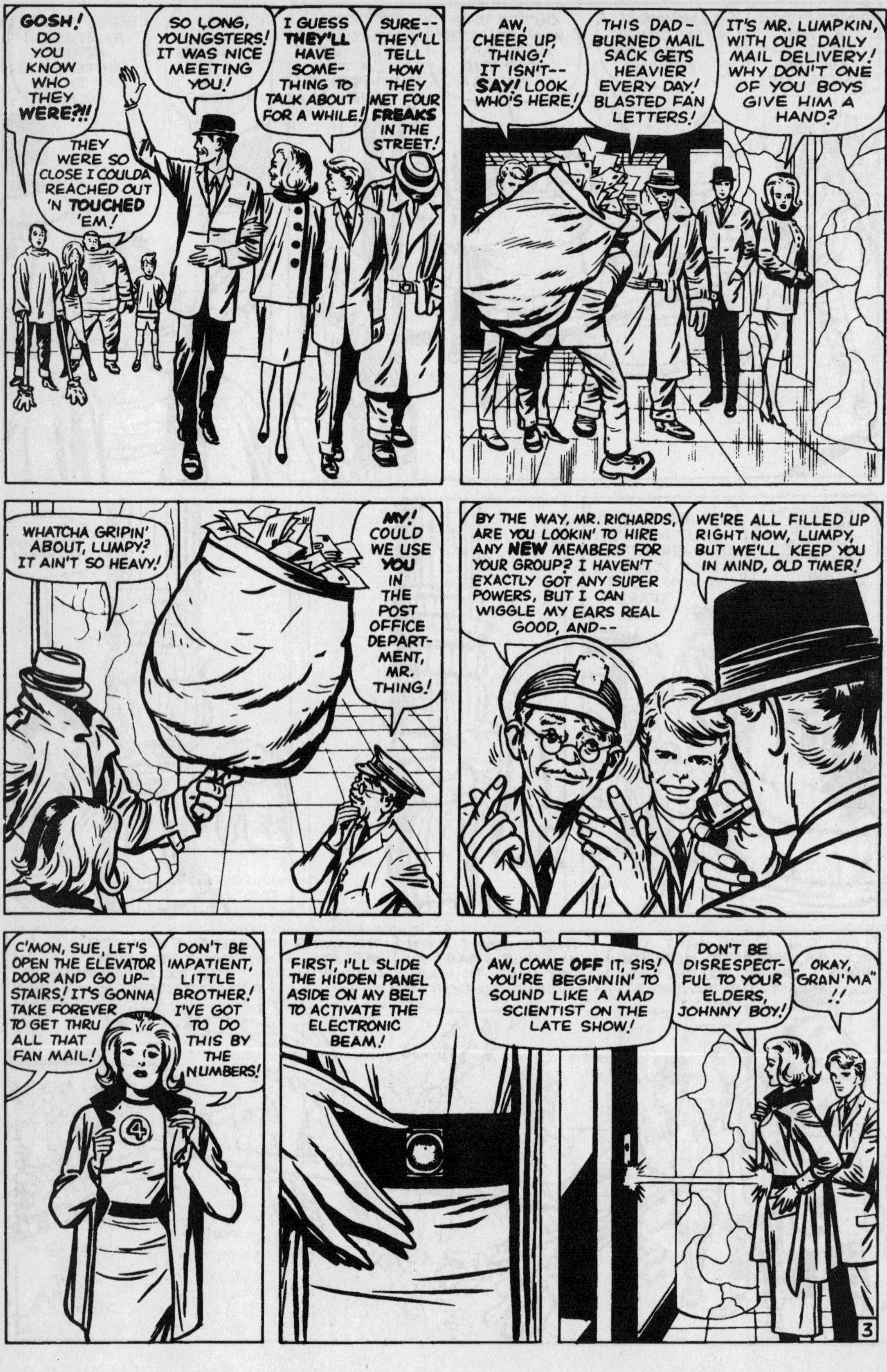
GOSH! DO YOU KNOW WHO THEY WERE?!!
THEY WERE SO CLOSE I COULDA REACHED OUT 'N TOUCHED 'EM!
SO LONG, YOUNGSTERS! IT WAS NICE MEETING YOU!
I GUESS THEY'LL HAVE SOMETHING TO TALK ABOUT FOR A WHILE!
SURE--THEY'LL TELL HOW THEY MET FOUR FREAKS IN THE STREET!
AW, CHEER UP, THING! IT ISN'T--SAY! LOOK WHO'S HERE!
THIS DAD-BURNED MAIL SACK GETS HEAVIER EVERY DAY! BLASTED FAN LETTERS!
IT'S MR. LUMPKIN, WITH OUR DAILY MAIL DELIVERY! WHY DON'T ONE OF YOU BOYS GIVE HIM A HAND?
WHATCHA GRIPIN' ABOUT, LUMPY? IT AIN'T SO HEAVY!
MY! COULD WE USE YOU IN THE POST OFFICE DEPARTMENT, MR. THING!
BY THE WAY, MR. RICHARDS, ARE YOU LOOKIN' TO HIRE ANY NEW MEMBERS FOR YOUR GROUP? I HAVEN'T EXACTLY GOT ANY SUPER POWERS, BUT I CAN WIGGLE MY EARS REAL GOOD, AND--
WE'RE ALL FILLED UP RIGHT NOW, LUMPY, BUT WE'LL KEEP YOU IN MIND, OLD TIMER!
C'MON, SUE, LET'S OPEN THE ELEVATOR DOOR AND GO UPSTAIRS! IT'S GONNA TAKE FOREVER TO GET THRU ALL THAT FAN MAIL!
DON'T BE IMPATIENT, LITTLE BROTHER! I'VE GOT TO DO THIS BY THE NUMBERS!
FIRST, I'LL SLIDE THE HIDDEN PANEL ASIDE ON MY BELT TO ACTIVATE THE ELECTRONIC BEAM!
AW, COME OFF IT, SIS! YOU'RE BEGINNIN' TO SOUND LIKE A MAD SCIENTIST ON THE LATE SHOW!
DON'T BE DISRESPECTFUL TO YOUR ELDERS, JOHNNY BOY!
OKAY, GRAN'MA" !!
3

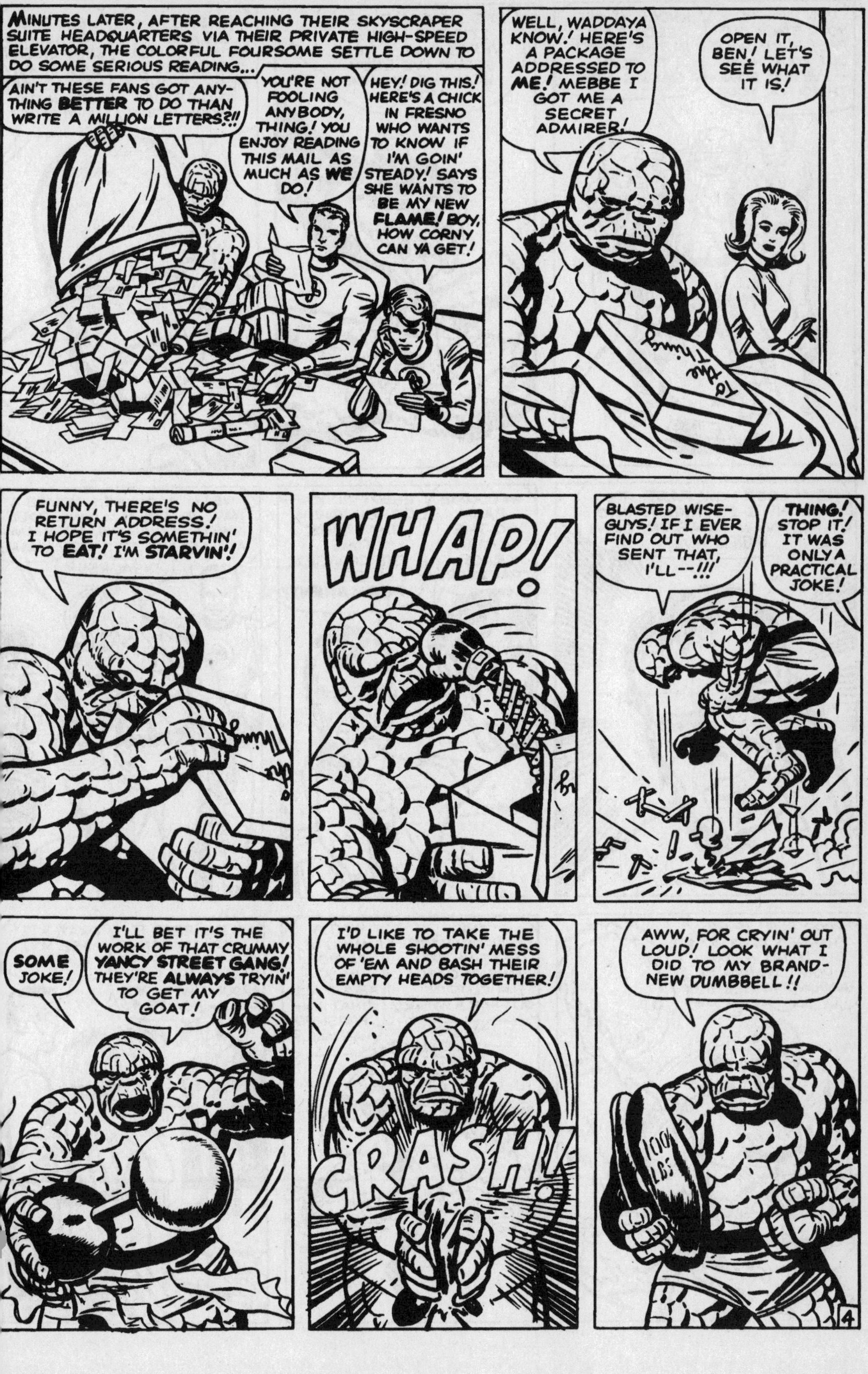
MINUTES LATER, AFTER REACHING THEIR SKYSCRAPER SUITE HEADQUARTERS VIA THEIR PRIVATE HIGH-SPEED ELEVATOR, THE COLORFUL FOURSOME SETTLE DOWN TO DO SOME SERIOUS READING...
AIN'T THESE FANS GOT ANYTHING **BETTER** TO DO THAN WRITE A MILLION LETTERS?!!
YOU'RE NOT FOOLING ANYBODY, THING! YOU ENJOY READING THIS MAIL AS MUCH AS **WE** DO!
HEY! DIG THIS! HERE'S A CHICK IN FRESNO WHO WANTS TO KNOW IF I'M GOIN' STEADY! SAYS SHE WANTS TO BE MY NEW **FLAME!** BOY, HOW CORNY CAN YA GET!
WELL, WADDAYA KNOW! HERE'S A PACKAGE ADDRESSED TO **ME!** MEBBE I GOT ME A SECRET ADMIRER!
OPEN IT, BEN! LET'S SEE WHAT IT IS!
FUNNY, THERE'S NO RETURN ADDRESS! I HOPE IT'S SOMETHIN' TO **EAT!** I'M **STARVIN'!**
WHAP!
BLASTED WISE-GUYS! IF I EVER FIND OUT WHO SENT THAT, I'LL--!!!
THING! STOP IT! IT WAS ONLY A PRACTICAL JOKE!
SOME JOKE!
I'LL BET IT'S THE WORK OF THAT CRUMMY **YANCY STREET GANG!** THEY'RE **ALWAYS** TRYIN' TO GET MY GOAT!
I'D LIKE TO TAKE THE WHOLE SHOOTIN' MESS OF 'EM AND BASH THEIR EMPTY HEADS TOGETHER!
CRASH!
AWW, FOR CRYIN' OUT LOUD! LOOK WHAT I DID TO MY BRAND-NEW DUMBBELL!!

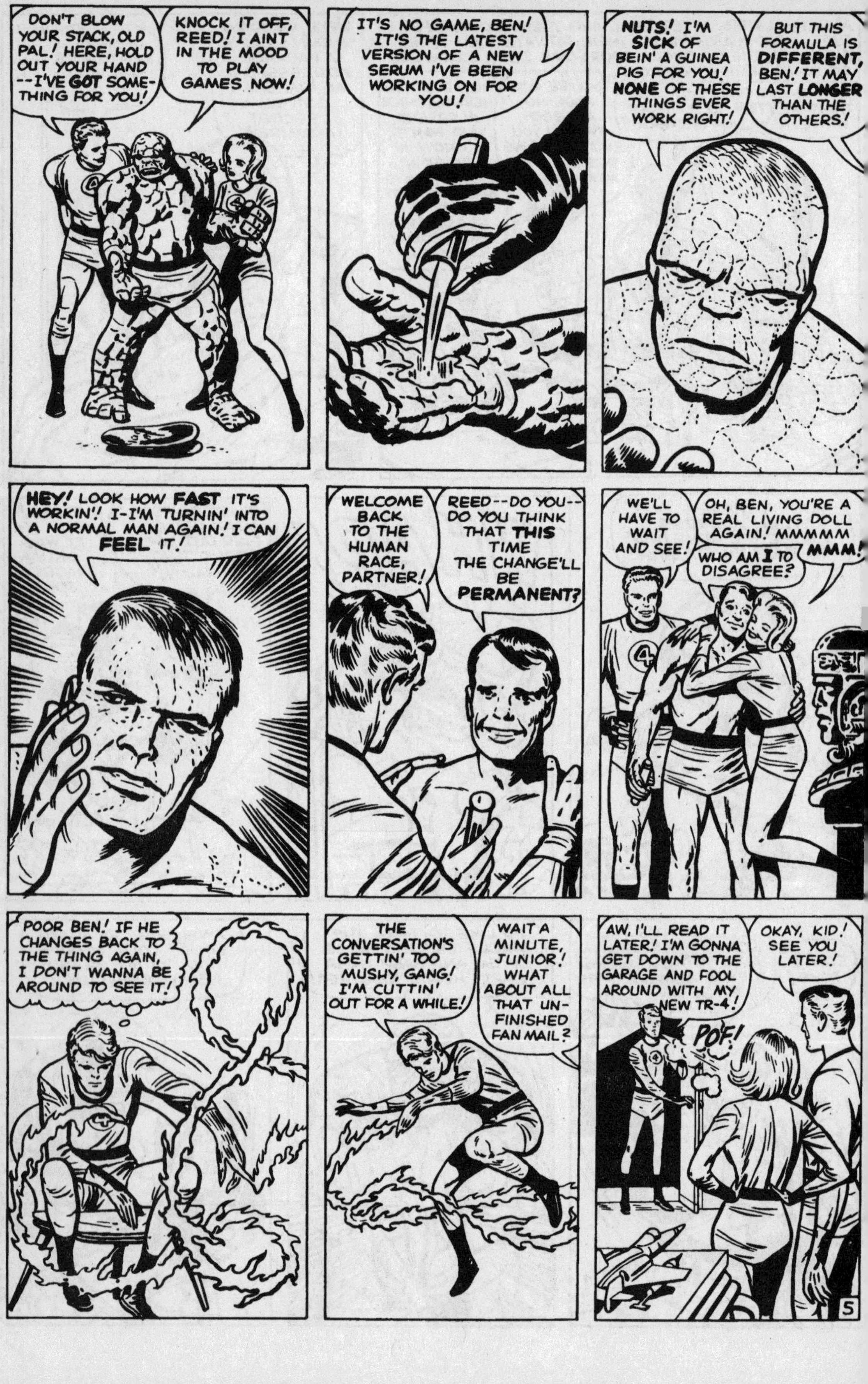
DON'T BLOW YOUR STACK, OLD PAL! HERE, HOLD OUT YOUR HAND --I'VE GOT SOMETHING FOR YOU!
KNOCK IT OFF, REED! I AINT IN THE MOOD TO PLAY GAMES NOW!
IT'S NO GAME, BEN! IT'S THE LATEST VERSION OF A NEW SERUM I'VE BEEN WORKING ON FOR YOU!
NUTS! I'M SICK OF BEIN' A GUINEA PIG FOR YOU! NONE OF THESE THINGS EVER WORK RIGHT!
BUT THIS FORMULA IS DIFFERENT, BEN! IT MAY LAST LONGER THAN THE OTHERS!
HEY! LOOK HOW FAST IT'S WORKIN'! I-I'M TURNIN' INTO A NORMAL MAN AGAIN! I CAN FEEL IT!
WELCOME BACK TO THE HUMAN RACE, PARTNER!
REED--DO YOU--DO YOU THINK THAT THIS TIME THE CHANGE'LL BE PERMANENT?
WE'LL HAVE TO WAIT AND SEE!
OH, BEN, YOU'RE A REAL LIVING DOLL AGAIN! MMMMM MMM!
WHO AM I TO DISAGREE?
POOR BEN! IF HE CHANGES BACK TO THE THING AGAIN, I DON'T WANNA BE AROUND TO SEE IT!
THE CONVERSATION'S GETTIN' TOO MUSHY, GANG! I'M CUTTIN' OUT FOR A WHILE!
WAIT A MINUTE, JUNIOR! WHAT ABOUT ALL THAT UNFINISHED FAN MAIL?
AW, I'LL READ IT LATER! I'M GONNA GET DOWN TO THE GARAGE AND FOOL AROUND WITH MY NEW TR-4!
OKAY, KID! SEE YOU LATER!
POF!
5

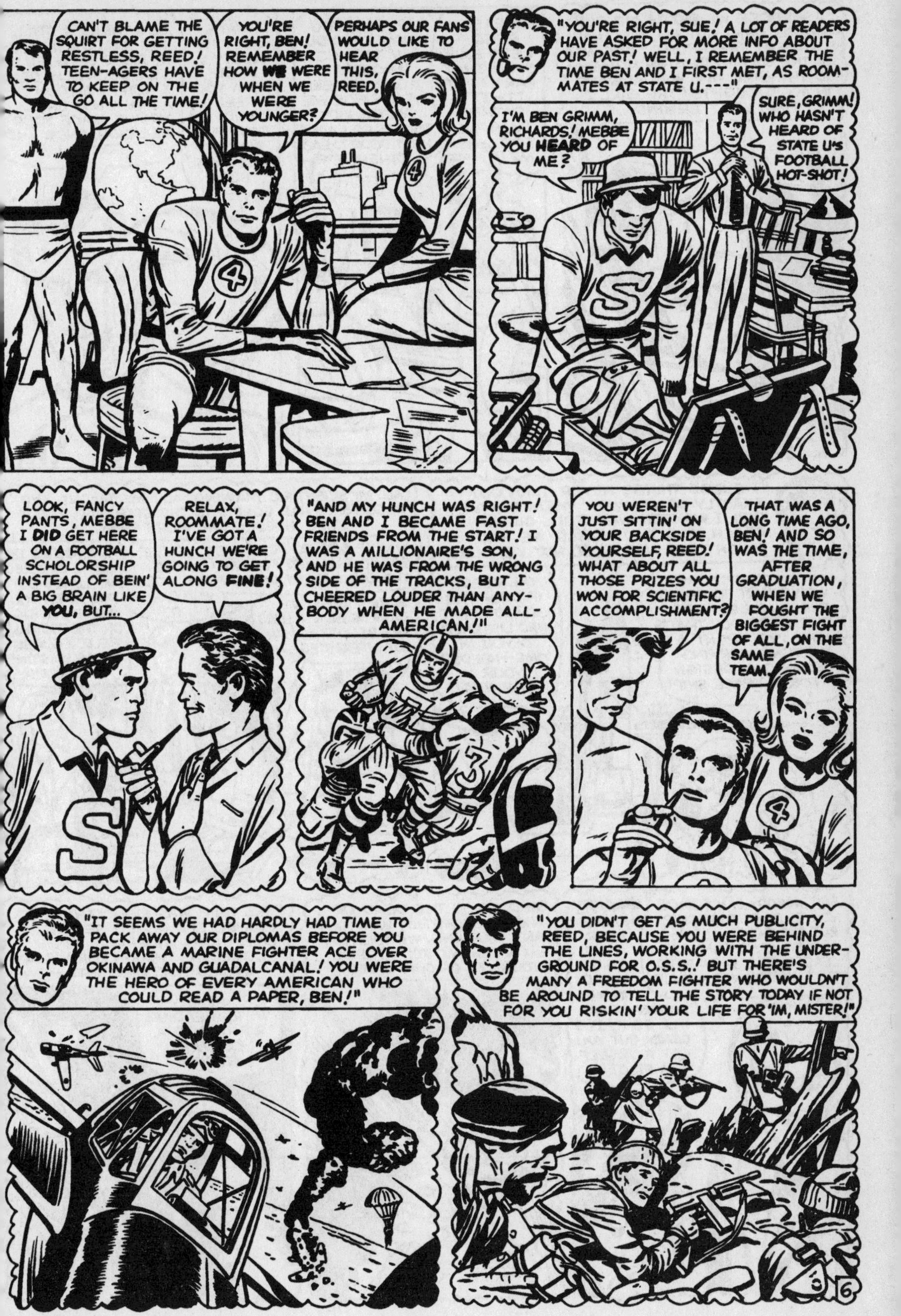
CAN'T BLAME THE SQUIRT FOR GETTING RESTLESS, REED! TEEN-AGERS HAVE TO KEEP ON THE GO ALL THE TIME!
YOU'RE RIGHT, BEN! REMEMBER HOW WE WERE WHEN WE WERE YOUNGER?
PERHAPS OUR FANS WOULD LIKE TO HEAR THIS, REED.
"YOU'RE RIGHT, SUE! A LOT OF READERS HAVE ASKED FOR MORE INFO ABOUT OUR PAST! WELL, I REMEMBER THE TIME BEN AND I FIRST MET, AS ROOM-MATES AT STATE U.---"
I'M BEN GRIMM, RICHARDS! MEBBE YOU HEARD OF ME?
SURE, GRIMM! WHO HASN'T HEARD OF STATE U's FOOTBALL HOT-SHOT!
LOOK, FANCY PANTS, MEBBE I DID GET HERE ON A FOOTBALL SCHOLORSHIP INSTEAD OF BEIN' A BIG BRAIN LIKE YOU, BUT...
RELAX, ROOMMATE! I'VE GOT A HUNCH WE'RE GOING TO GET ALONG FINE!
"AND MY HUNCH WAS RIGHT! BEN AND I BECAME FAST FRIENDS FROM THE START! I WAS A MILLIONAIRE'S SON, AND HE WAS FROM THE WRONG SIDE OF THE TRACKS, BUT I CHEERED LOUDER THAN ANY-BODY WHEN HE MADE ALL-AMERICAN!"
YOU WEREN'T JUST SITTIN' ON YOUR BACKSIDE YOURSELF, REED! WHAT ABOUT ALL THOSE PRIZES YOU WON FOR SCIENTIFIC ACCOMPLISHMENT?
THAT WAS A LONG TIME AGO, BEN! AND SO WAS THE TIME, AFTER GRADUATION, WHEN WE FOUGHT THE BIGGEST FIGHT OF ALL, ON THE SAME TEAM.
"IT SEEMS WE HAD HARDLY HAD TIME TO PACK AWAY OUR DIPLOMAS BEFORE YOU BECAME A MARINE FIGHTER ACE OVER OKINAWA AND GUADALCANAL! YOU WERE THE HERO OF EVERY AMERICAN WHO COULD READ A PAPER, BEN!"
"YOU DIDN'T GET AS MUCH PUBLICITY, REED, BECAUSE YOU WERE BEHIND THE LINES, WORKING WITH THE UNDER-GROUND FOR O.S.S.! BUT THERE'S MANY A FREEDOM FIGHTER WHO WOULDN'T BE AROUND TO TELL THE STORY TODAY IF NOT FOR YOU RISKIN' YOUR LIFE FOR 'IM, MISTER!"
6

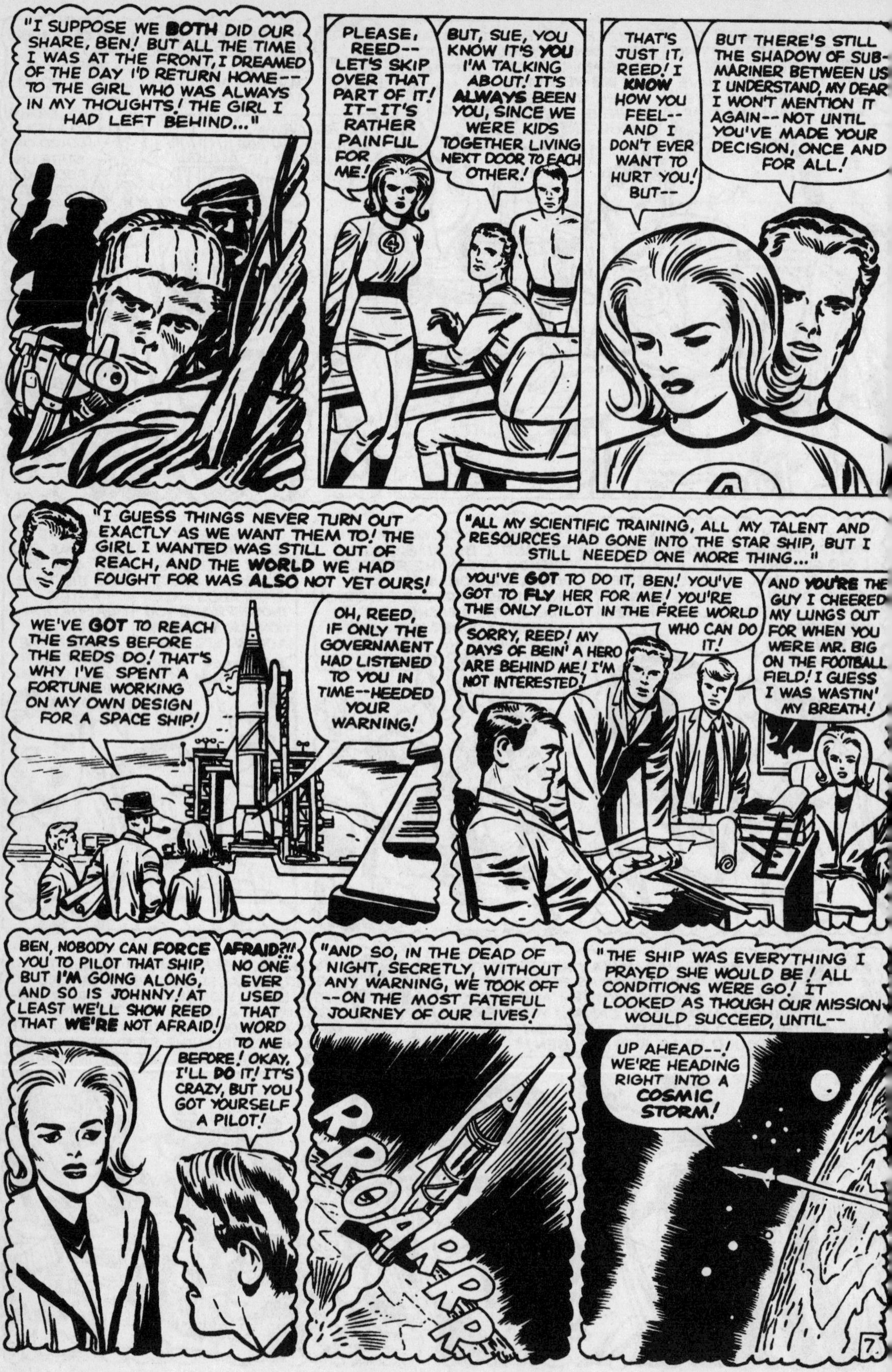
"I SUPPOSE WE BOTH DID OUR SHARE, BEN! BUT ALL THE TIME I WAS AT THE FRONT, I DREAMED OF THE DAY I'D RETURN HOME-- TO THE GIRL WHO WAS ALWAYS IN MY THOUGHTS! THE GIRL I HAD LEFT BEHIND..."
PLEASE, REED-- LET'S SKIP OVER THAT PART OF IT! IT-IT'S RATHER PAINFUL FOR ME!
BUT, SUE, YOU KNOW IT'S YOU I'M TALKING ABOUT! IT'S ALWAYS BEEN YOU, SINCE WE WERE KIDS TOGETHER LIVING NEXT DOOR TO EACH OTHER!
THAT'S JUST IT, REED! I KNOW HOW YOU FEEL-- AND I DON'T EVER WANT TO HURT YOU! BUT--
BUT THERE'S STILL THE SHADOW OF SUB-MARINER BETWEEN US. I UNDERSTAND, MY DEAR. I WON'T MENTION IT AGAIN--NOT UNTIL YOU'VE MADE YOUR DECISION, ONCE AND FOR ALL!
"I GUESS THINGS NEVER TURN OUT EXACTLY AS WE WANT THEM TO! THE GIRL I WANTED WAS STILL OUT OF REACH, AND THE WORLD WE HAD FOUGHT FOR WAS ALSO NOT YET OURS!
WE'VE GOT TO REACH THE STARS BEFORE THE REDS DO! THAT'S WHY I'VE SPENT A FORTUNE WORKING ON MY OWN DESIGN FOR A SPACE SHIP!
OH, REED, IF ONLY THE GOVERNMENT HAD LISTENED TO YOU IN TIME--HEEDED YOUR WARNING!
"ALL MY SCIENTIFIC TRAINING, ALL MY TALENT AND RESOURCES HAD GONE INTO THE STAR SHIP, BUT I STILL NEEDED ONE MORE THING..."
YOU'VE GOT TO DO IT, BEN! YOU'VE GOT TO FLY HER FOR ME! YOU'RE THE ONLY PILOT IN THE FREE WORLD WHO CAN DO IT!
SORRY, REED! MY DAYS OF BEIN' A HERO ARE BEHIND ME! I'M NOT INTERESTED!
AND YOU'RE THE GUY I CHEERED MY LUNGS OUT FOR WHEN YOU WERE MR. BIG ON THE FOOTBALL FIELD! I GUESS I WAS WASTIN' MY BREATH!
BEN, NOBODY CAN FORCE YOU TO PILOT THAT SHIP, BUT I'M GOING ALONG, AND SO IS JOHNNY! AT LEAST WE'LL SHOW REED THAT WE'RE NOT AFRAID!
AFRAID?!! NO ONE EVER USED THAT WORD TO ME BEFORE! OKAY, I'LL DO IT! IT'S CRAZY, BUT YOU GOT YOURSELF A PILOT!
"AND SO, IN THE DEAD OF NIGHT, SECRETLY, WITHOUT ANY WARNING, WE TOOK OFF --ON THE MOST FATEFUL JOURNEY OF OUR LIVES!
RROOARRR
"THE SHIP WAS EVERYTHING I PRAYED SHE WOULD BE! ALL CONDITIONS WERE GO! IT LOOKED AS THOUGH OUR MISSION WOULD SUCCEED, UNTIL--
UP AHEAD--! WE'RE HEADING RIGHT INTO A COSMIC STORM!
7.

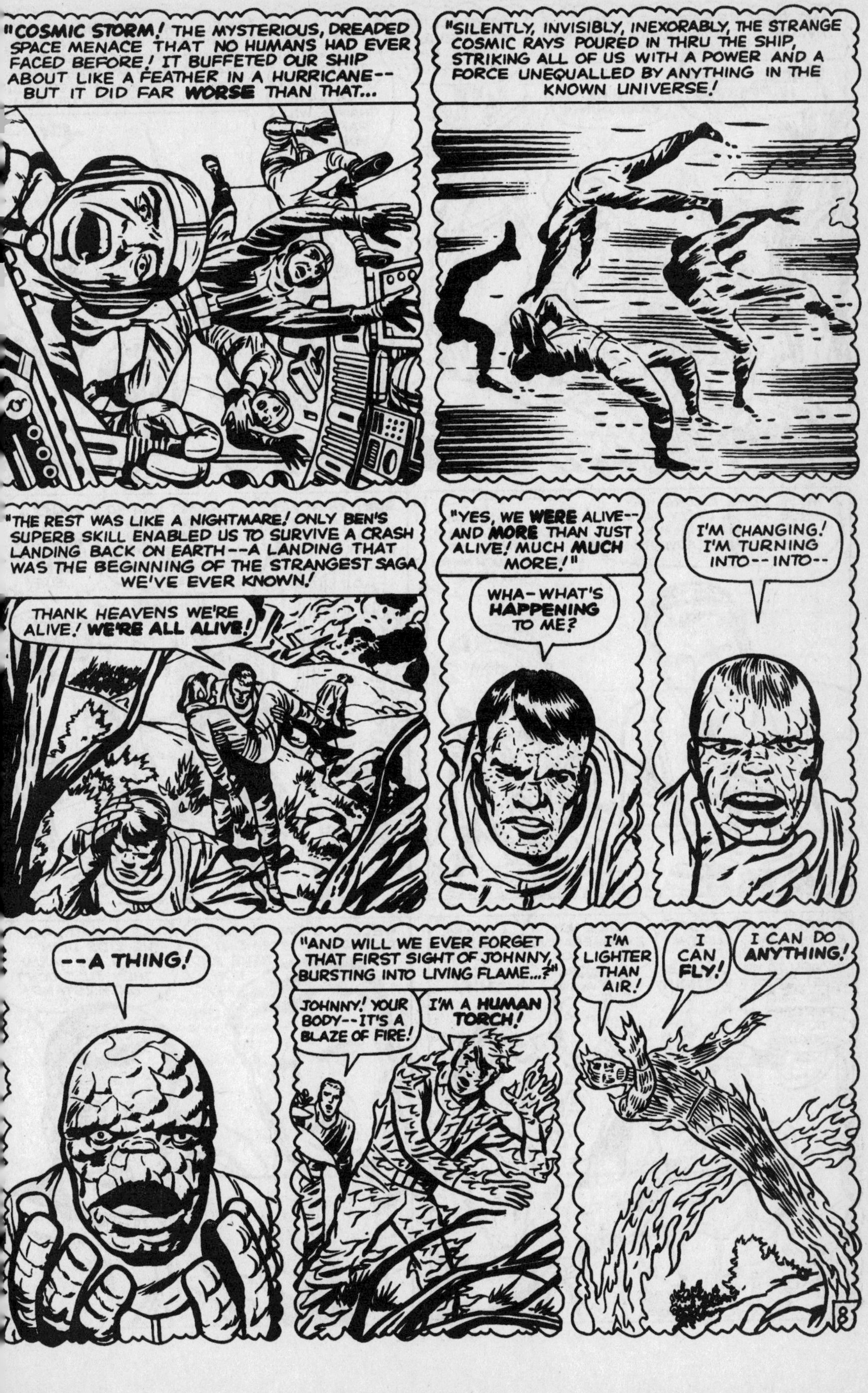

"COSMIC STORM! THE MYSTERIOUS, DREADED SPACE MENACE THAT NO HUMANS HAD EVER FACED BEFORE! IT BUFFETED OUR SHIP ABOUT LIKE A FEATHER IN A HURRICANE-- BUT IT DID FAR WORSE THAN THAT...
"SILENTLY, INVISIBLY, INEXORABLY, THE STRANGE COSMIC RAYS POURED IN THRU THE SHIP, STRIKING ALL OF US WITH A POWER AND A FORCE UNEQUALLED BY ANYTHING IN THE KNOWN UNIVERSE!
"THE REST WAS LIKE A NIGHTMARE! ONLY BEN'S SUPERB SKILL ENABLED US TO SURVIVE A CRASH LANDING BACK ON EARTH--A LANDING THAT WAS THE BEGINNING OF THE STRANGEST SAGA WE'VE EVER KNOWN!
THANK HEAVENS WE'RE ALIVE! WE'RE ALL ALIVE!
"YES, WE WERE ALIVE-- AND MORE THAN JUST ALIVE! MUCH MUCH MORE!"
WHA-WHAT'S HAPPENING TO ME?
I'M CHANGING! I'M TURNING INTO--INTO--
--A THING!
"AND WILL WE EVER FORGET THAT FIRST SIGHT OF JOHNNY, BURSTING INTO LIVING FLAME...?"
JOHNNY! YOUR BODY--IT'S A BLAZE OF FIRE!
I'M A HUMAN TORCH!
I'M LIGHTER THAN AIR!
I CAN FLY!
I CAN DO ANYTHING!
8

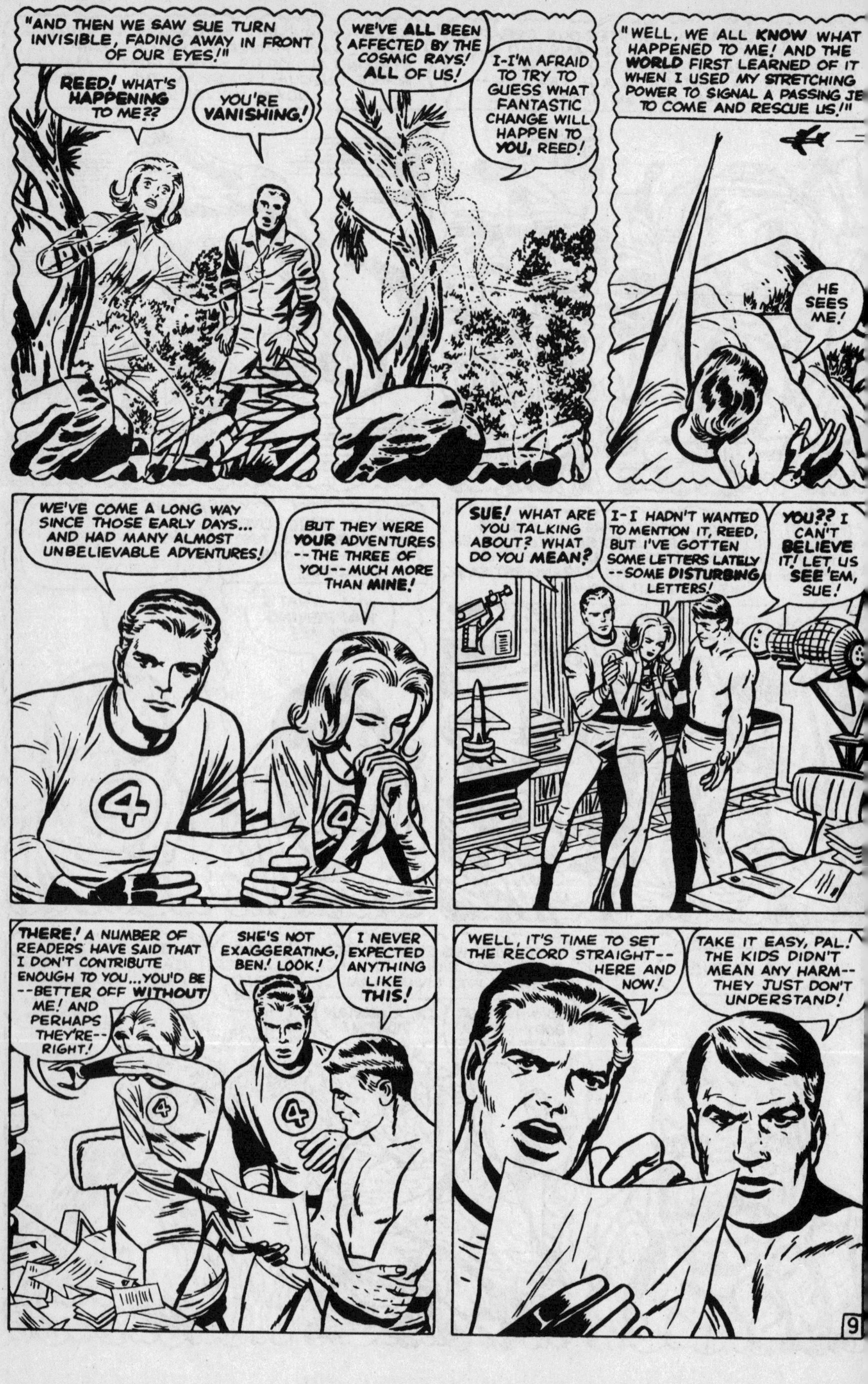
"AND THEN WE SAW SUE TURN INVISIBLE, FADING AWAY IN FRONT OF OUR EYES!"
REED! WHAT'S HAPPENING TO ME??
YOU'RE VANISHING!
WE'VE ALL BEEN AFFECTED BY THE COSMIC RAYS! ALL OF US!
I-I'M AFRAID TO TRY TO GUESS WHAT FANTASTIC CHANGE WILL HAPPEN TO YOU, REED!
"WELL, WE ALL KNOW WHAT HAPPENED TO ME! AND THE WORLD FIRST LEARNED OF IT WHEN I USED MY STRETCHING POWER TO SIGNAL A PASSING JE TO COME AND RESCUE US!"
HE SEES ME!
WE'VE COME A LONG WAY SINCE THOSE EARLY DAYS... AND HAD MANY ALMOST UNBELIEVABLE ADVENTURES!
BUT THEY WERE YOUR ADVENTURES --THE THREE OF YOU--MUCH MORE THAN MINE!
SUE! WHAT ARE YOU TALKING ABOUT? WHAT DO YOU MEAN?
I-I HADN'T WANTED TO MENTION IT, REED, BUT I'VE GOTTEN SOME LETTERS LATELY --SOME DISTURBING LETTERS!
YOU?? I CAN'T BELIEVE IT! LET US SEE 'EM, SUE!
THERE! A NUMBER OF READERS HAVE SAID THAT I DON'T CONTRIBUTE ENOUGH TO YOU...YOU'D BE --BETTER OFF WITHOUT ME! AND PERHAPS THEY'RE--RIGHT!
SHE'S NOT EXAGGERATING, BEN! LOOK!
I NEVER EXPECTED ANYTHING LIKE THIS!
WELL, IT'S TIME TO SET THE RECORD STRAIGHT-- HERE AND NOW!
TAKE IT EASY, PAL! THE KIDS DIDN'T MEAN ANY HARM-- THEY JUST DON'T UNDERSTAND!
9

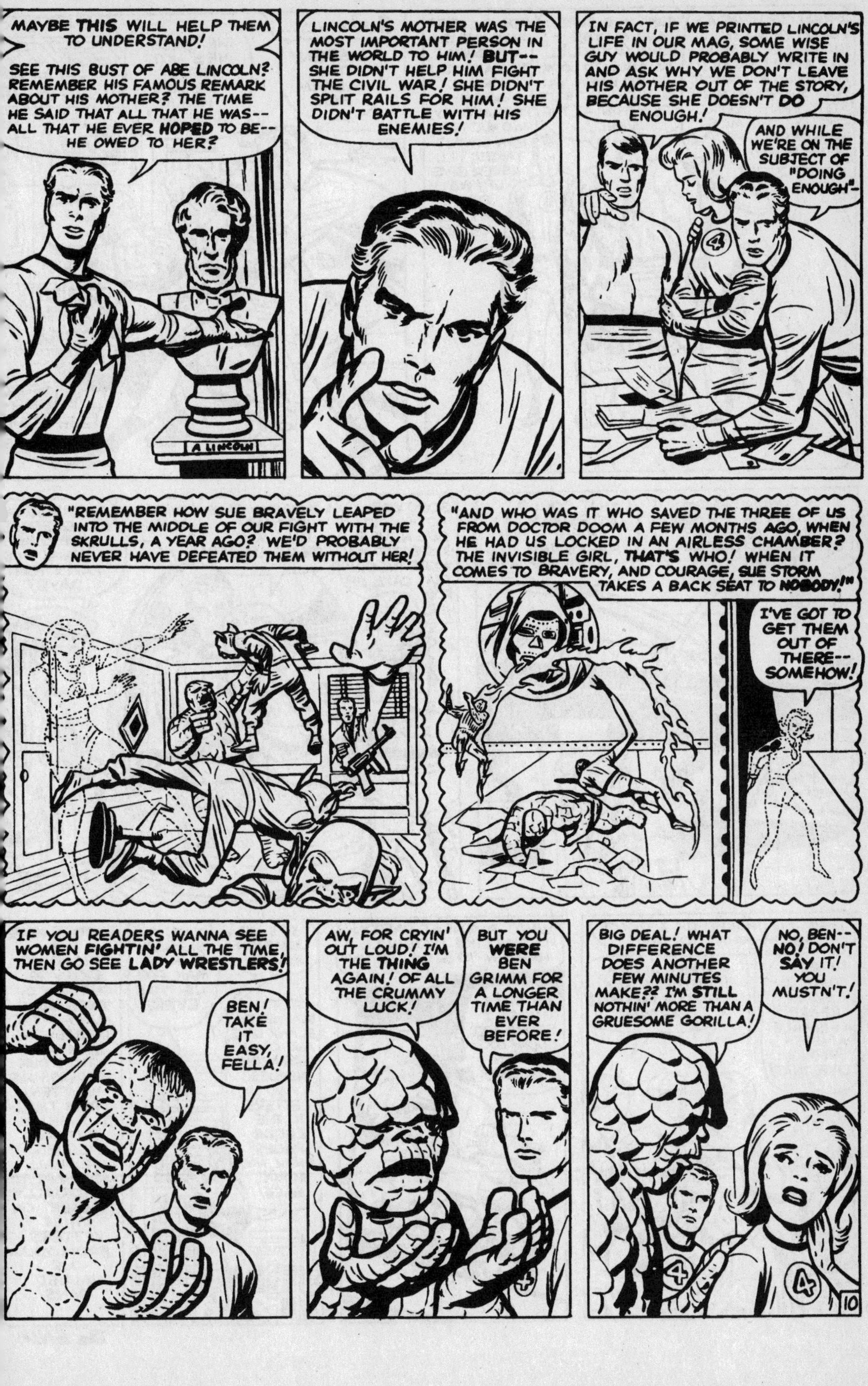
MAYBE THIS WILL HELP THEM TO UNDERSTAND!
SEE THIS BUST OF ABE LINCOLN? REMEMBER HIS FAMOUS REMARK ABOUT HIS MOTHER? THE TIME HE SAID THAT ALL THAT HE WAS-- ALL THAT HE EVER HOPED TO BE-- HE OWED TO HER?
A LINCOLN
LINCOLN'S MOTHER WAS THE MOST IMPORTANT PERSON IN THE WORLD TO HIM! BUT-- SHE DIDN'T HELP HIM FIGHT THE CIVIL WAR! SHE DIDN'T SPLIT RAILS FOR HIM! SHE DIDN'T BATTLE WITH HIS ENEMIES!
IN FACT, IF WE PRINTED LINCOLN'S LIFE IN OUR MAG, SOME WISE GUY WOULD PROBABLY WRITE IN AND ASK WHY WE DON'T LEAVE HIS MOTHER OUT OF THE STORY, BECAUSE SHE DOESN'T DO ENOUGH!
AND WHILE WE'RE ON THE SUBJECT OF "DOING ENOUGH"-
"REMEMBER HOW SUE BRAVELY LEAPED INTO THE MIDDLE OF OUR FIGHT WITH THE SKRULLS, A YEAR AGO? WE'D PROBABLY NEVER HAVE DEFEATED THEM WITHOUT HER!
"AND WHO WAS IT WHO SAVED THE THREE OF US FROM DOCTOR DOOM A FEW MONTHS AGO, WHEN HE HAD US LOCKED IN AN AIRLESS CHAMBER? THE INVISIBLE GIRL, THAT'S WHO! WHEN IT COMES TO BRAVERY, AND COURAGE, SUE STORM TAKES A BACK SEAT TO NOBODY!"
I'VE GOT TO GET THEM OUT OF THERE-- SOMEHOW!
IF YOU READERS WANNA SEE WOMEN FIGHTIN' ALL THE TIME, THEN GO SEE LADY WRESTLERS!
BEN! TAKE IT EASY, FELLA!
AW, FOR CRYIN' OUT LOUD! I'M THE THING AGAIN! OF ALL THE CRUMMY LUCK!
BUT YOU WERE BEN GRIMM FOR A LONGER TIME THAN EVER BEFORE!
BIG DEAL! WHAT DIFFERENCE DOES ANOTHER FEW MINUTES MAKE?? I'M STILL NOTHIN' MORE THAN A GRUESOME GORILLA!
NO, BEN-- NO! DON'T SAY IT! YOU MUSTN'T!
10

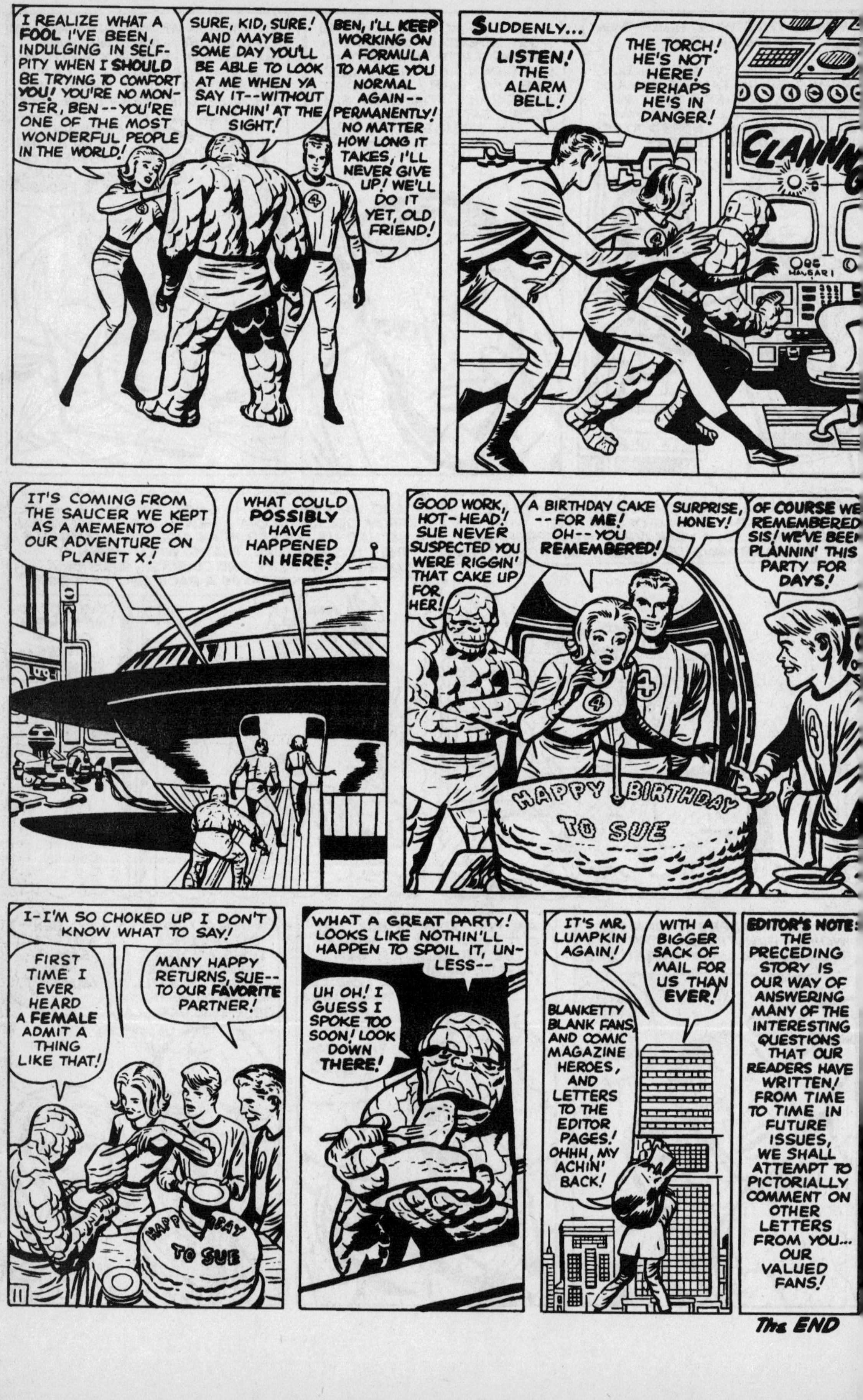
I REALIZE WHAT A **FOOL** I'VE BEEN, INDULGING IN SELF-PITY WHEN I **SHOULD** BE TRYING TO COMFORT **YOU**! YOU'RE NO MONSTER, BEN--YOU'RE ONE OF THE MOST WONDERFUL PEOPLE IN THE WORLD!
SURE, KID, SURE! AND MAYBE SOME DAY YOU'LL BE ABLE TO LOOK AT ME WHEN YA SAY IT--WITHOUT FLINCHIN' AT THE SIGHT!
BEN, I'LL **KEEP** WORKING ON A FORMULA TO MAKE YOU NORMAL AGAIN--PERMANENTLY! NO MATTER HOW LONG IT TAKES, I'LL NEVER GIVE UP! WE'LL DO IT YET, OLD FRIEND!
SUDDENLY...
LISTEN! THE ALARM BELL!
THE TORCH! HE'S NOT HERE! PERHAPS HE'S IN DANGER!
IT'S COMING FROM THE SAUCER WE KEPT AS A MEMENTO OF OUR ADVENTURE ON PLANET X!
WHAT COULD **POSSIBLY** HAVE HAPPENED IN **HERE?**
GOOD WORK, HOT-HEAD! SUE NEVER SUSPECTED YOU WERE RIGGIN' THAT CAKE UP FOR HER!
A BIRTHDAY CAKE --FOR **ME**! OH--YOU **REMEMBERED**!
SURPRISE, HONEY!
OF **COURSE** WE REMEMBERED SIS! WE'VE BEE PLANNIN' THIS PARTY FOR **DAYS**!
HAPPY BIRTHDAY TO SUE
I-I'M SO CHOKED UP I DON'T KNOW WHAT TO SAY!
FIRST TIME I EVER HEARD A **FEMALE** ADMIT A THING LIKE THAT!
MANY HAPPY RETURNS, SUE--TO OUR **FAVORITE** PARTNER!
TO SUE
11
WHAT A GREAT PARTY! LOOKS LIKE NOTHIN'LL HAPPEN TO SPOIL IT, UNLESS--
UH OH! I GUESS I SPOKE TOO SOON! LOOK DOWN **THERE**!
IT'S MR. LUMPKIN AGAIN!
WITH A BIGGER SACK OF MAIL FOR US THAN **EVER**!
BLANKETTY BLANK FANS, AND COMIC MAGAZINE HEROES, AND LETTERS TO THE EDITOR PAGES! OHHH, MY ACHIN' BACK!
EDITOR'S NOTE: THE PRECEDING STORY IS OUR WAY OF ANSWERING MANY OF THE INTERESTING QUESTIONS THAT OUR READERS HAVE WRITTEN! FROM TIME TO TIME IN FUTURE ISSUES, WE SHALL ATTEMPT TO PICTORIALLY COMMENT ON OTHER LETTERS FROM YOU... OUR VALUED FANS!
The END

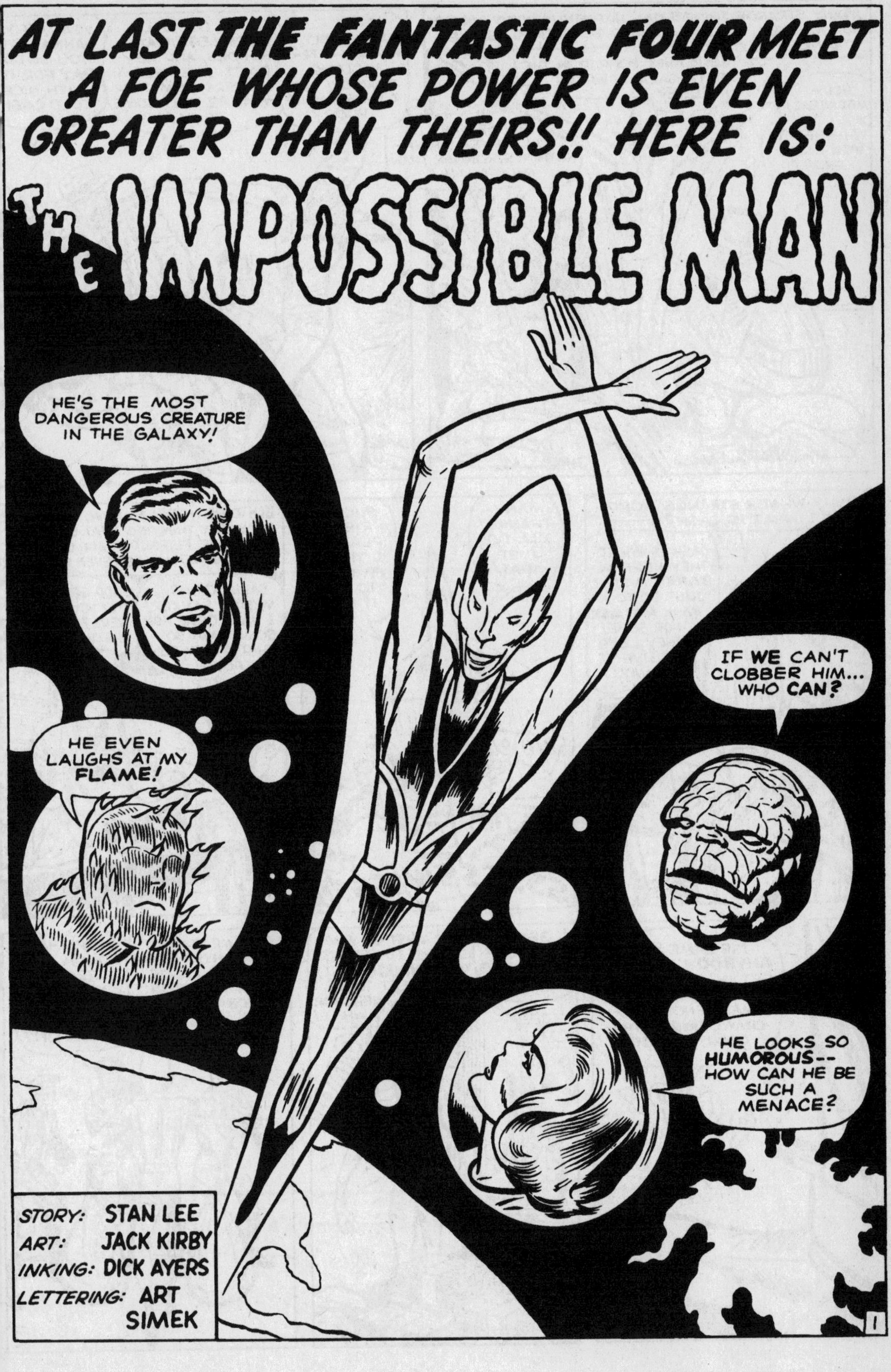

AT LAST THE FANTASTIC FOUR MEET A FOE WHOSE POWER IS EVEN GREATER THAN THEIRS!! HERE IS:
THE IMPOSSIBLE MAN
HE'S THE MOST DANGEROUS CREATURE IN THE GALAXY!
IF WE CAN'T CLOBBER HIM... WHO CAN?
HE EVEN LAUGHS AT MY FLAME!
HE LOOKS SO HUMOROUS-- HOW CAN HE BE SUCH A MENACE?
STORY: STAN LEE
ART: JACK KIRBY
INKING: DICK AYERS
LETTERING: ART SIMEK
1

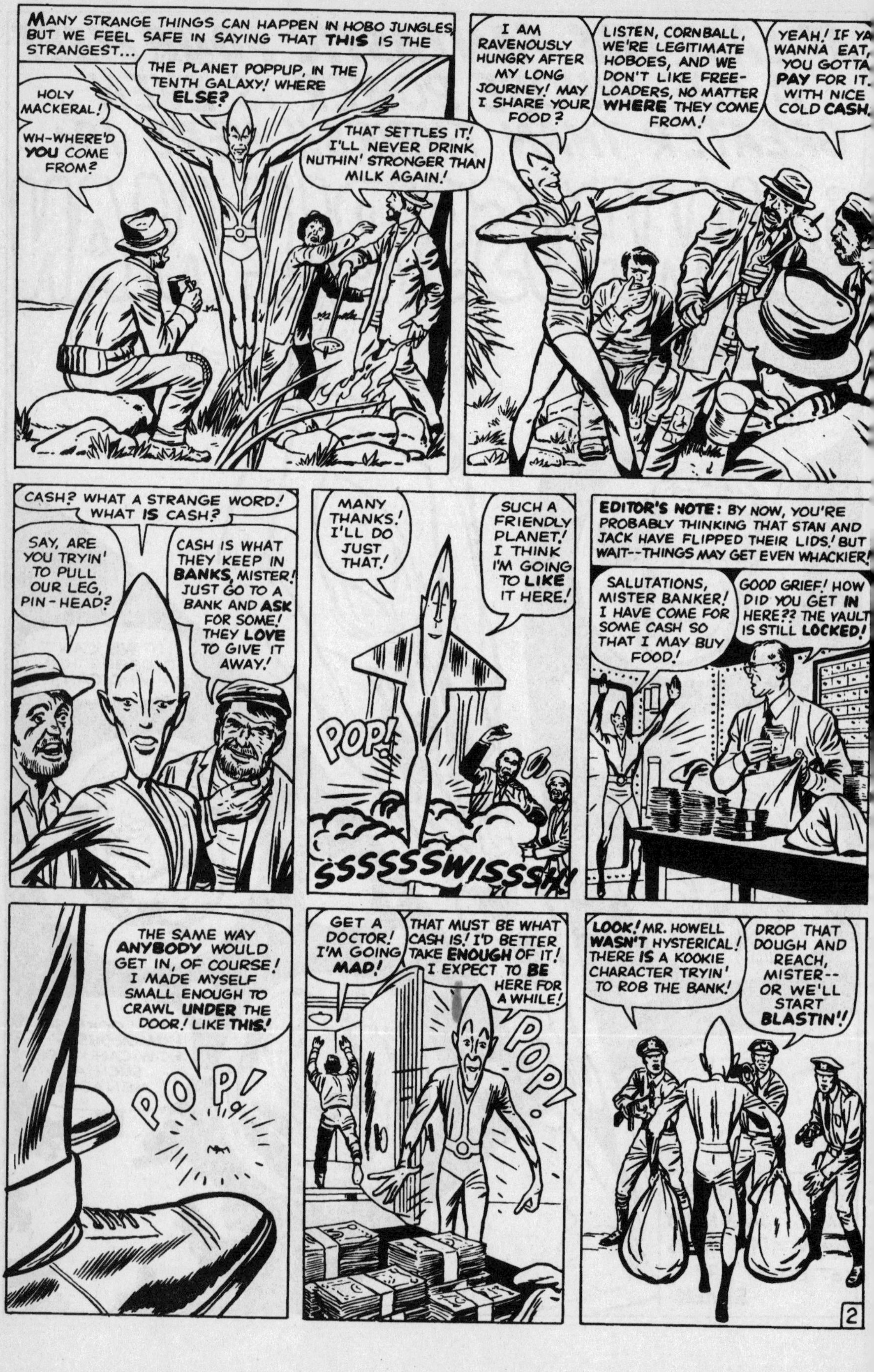

MANY STRANGE THINGS CAN HAPPEN IN HOBO JUNGLES, BUT WE FEEL SAFE IN SAYING THAT THIS IS THE STRANGEST...
HOLY MACKERAL!
WH-WHERE'D YOU COME FROM?
THE PLANET POPPUP, IN THE TENTH GALAXY! WHERE ELSE?
THAT SETTLES IT! I'LL NEVER DRINK NUTHIN' STRONGER THAN MILK AGAIN!
I AM RAVENOUSLY HUNGRY AFTER MY LONG JOURNEY! MAY I SHARE YOUR FOOD?
LISTEN, CORNBALL, WE'RE LEGITIMATE HOBOES, AND WE DON'T LIKE FREE-LOADERS, NO MATTER WHERE THEY COME FROM!
YEAH! IF YA WANNA EAT, YOU GOTTA PAY FOR IT. WITH NICE COLD CASH.
CASH? WHAT A STRANGE WORD! WHAT IS CASH?
SAY, ARE YOU TRYIN' TO PULL OUR LEG, PIN-HEAD?
CASH IS WHAT THEY KEEP IN BANKS, MISTER! JUST GO TO A BANK AND ASK FOR SOME! THEY LOVE TO GIVE IT AWAY!
MANY THANKS! I'LL DO JUST THAT!
SUCH A FRIENDLY PLANET! I THINK I'M GOING TO LIKE IT HERE!
POP!
SSSSSSWISSSSH!
EDITOR'S NOTE: BY NOW, YOU'RE PROBABLY THINKING THAT STAN AND JACK HAVE FLIPPED THEIR LIDS! BUT WAIT--THINGS MAY GET EVEN WHACKIER!
SALUTATIONS, MISTER BANKER! I HAVE COME FOR SOME CASH SO THAT I MAY BUY FOOD!
GOOD GRIEF! HOW DID YOU GET IN HERE?? THE VAULT IS STILL LOCKED!
THE SAME WAY ANYBODY WOULD GET IN, OF COURSE! I MADE MYSELF SMALL ENOUGH TO CRAWL UNDER THE DOOR! LIKE THIS!
POP!
GET A DOCTOR! I'M GOING MAD!
THAT MUST BE WHAT CASH IS! I'D BETTER TAKE ENOUGH OF IT! I EXPECT TO BE HERE FOR A WHILE!
POP!
LOOK! MR. HOWELL WASN'T HYSTERICAL! THERE IS A KOOKIE CHARACTER TRYIN' TO ROB THE BANK!
DROP THAT DOUGH AND REACH, MISTER-- OR WE'LL START BLASTIN'!
2

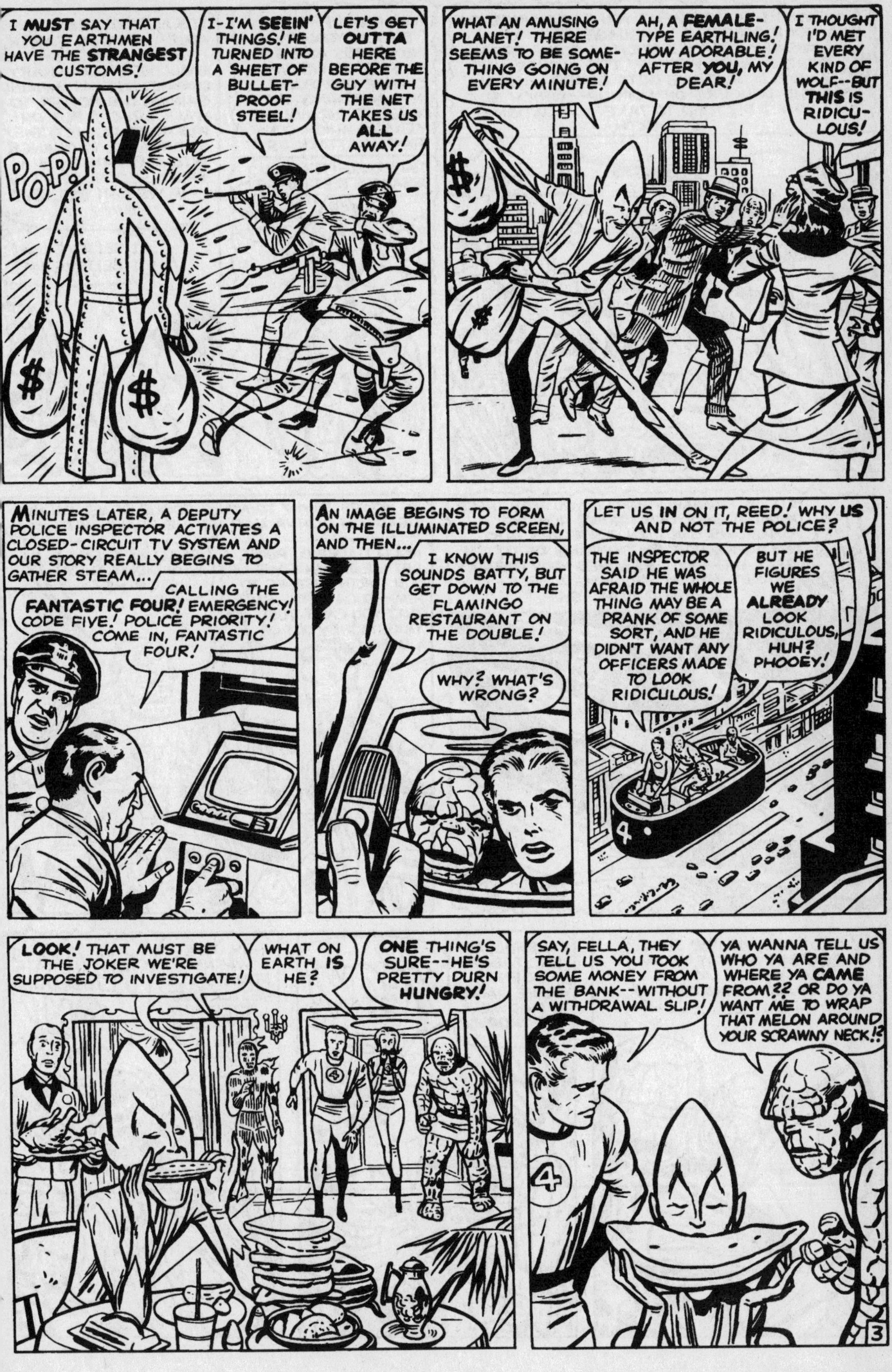
I MUST SAY THAT YOU EARTHMEN HAVE THE STRANGEST CUSTOMS!
I-I'M SEEIN' THINGS! HE TURNED INTO A SHEET OF BULLET-PROOF STEEL!
LET'S GET OUTTA HERE BEFORE THE GUY WITH THE NET TAKES US ALL AWAY!
POP!
WHAT AN AMUSING PLANET! THERE SEEMS TO BE SOMETHING GOING ON EVERY MINUTE!
AH, A FEMALE-TYPE EARTHLING! HOW ADORABLE! AFTER YOU, MY DEAR!
I THOUGHT I'D MET EVERY KIND OF WOLF--BUT THIS IS RIDICULOUS!
MINUTES LATER, A DEPUTY POLICE INSPECTOR ACTIVATES A CLOSED-CIRCUIT TV SYSTEM AND OUR STORY REALLY BEGINS TO GATHER STEAM...
CALLING THE FANTASTIC FOUR! EMERGENCY! CODE FIVE! POLICE PRIORITY! COME IN, FANTASTIC FOUR!
AN IMAGE BEGINS TO FORM ON THE ILLUMINATED SCREEN, AND THEN...
I KNOW THIS SOUNDS BATTY, BUT GET DOWN TO THE FLAMINGO RESTAURANT ON THE DOUBLE!
WHY? WHAT'S WRONG?
LET US IN ON IT, REED! WHY US AND NOT THE POLICE?
THE INSPECTOR SAID HE WAS AFRAID THE WHOLE THING MAY BE A PRANK OF SOME SORT, AND HE DIDN'T WANT ANY OFFICERS MADE TO LOOK RIDICULOUS!
BUT HE FIGURES WE ALREADY LOOK RIDICULOUS, HUH? PHOOEY!
LOOK! THAT MUST BE THE JOKER WE'RE SUPPOSED TO INVESTIGATE!
WHAT ON EARTH IS HE?
ONE THING'S SURE--HE'S PRETTY DURN HUNGRY!
SAY, FELLA, THEY TELL US YOU TOOK SOME MONEY FROM THE BANK--WITHOUT A WITHDRAWAL SLIP!
YA WANNA TELL US WHO YA ARE AND WHERE YA CAME FROM?? OR DO YA WANT ME TO WRAP THAT MELON AROUND YOUR SCRAWNY NECK!?
3

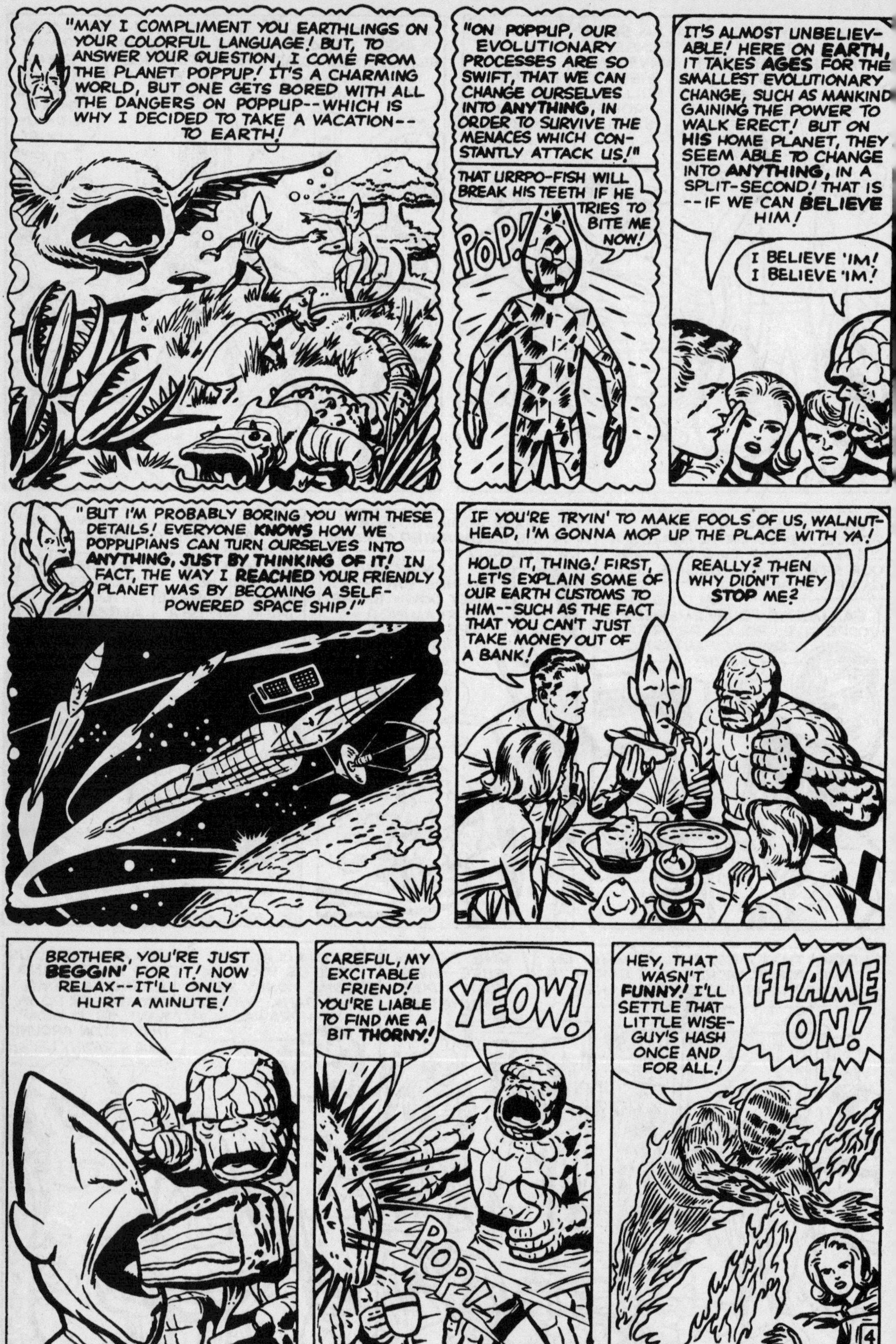
"MAY I COMPLIMENT YOU EARTHLINGS ON YOUR COLORFUL LANGUAGE! BUT, TO ANSWER YOUR QUESTION, I COME FROM THE PLANET POPPUP! IT'S A CHARMING WORLD, BUT ONE GETS BORED WITH ALL THE DANGERS ON POPPUP--WHICH IS WHY I DECIDED TO TAKE A VACATION--TO EARTH!
"ON POPPUP, OUR EVOLUTIONARY PROCESSES ARE SO SWIFT, THAT WE CAN CHANGE OURSELVES INTO ANYTHING, IN ORDER TO SURVIVE THE MENACES WHICH CONSTANTLY ATTACK US!"
THAT URRPO-FISH WILL BREAK HIS TEETH IF HE TRIES TO BITE ME NOW!
POP!
IT'S ALMOST UNBELIEVABLE! HERE ON EARTH, IT TAKES AGES FOR THE SMALLEST EVOLUTIONARY CHANGE, SUCH AS MANKIND GAINING THE POWER TO WALK ERECT! BUT ON HIS HOME PLANET, THEY SEEM ABLE TO CHANGE INTO ANYTHING, IN A SPLIT-SECOND! THAT IS --IF WE CAN BELIEVE HIM!
I BELIEVE 'IM! I BELIEVE 'IM!
"BUT I'M PROBABLY BORING YOU WITH THESE DETAILS! EVERYONE KNOWS HOW WE POPPUPIANS CAN TURN OURSELVES INTO ANYTHING, JUST BY THINKING OF IT! IN FACT, THE WAY I REACHED YOUR FRIENDLY PLANET WAS BY BECOMING A SELF-POWERED SPACE SHIP!"
IF YOU'RE TRYIN' TO MAKE FOOLS OF US, WALNUT-HEAD, I'M GONNA MOP UP THE PLACE WITH YA!
HOLD IT, THING! FIRST, LET'S EXPLAIN SOME OF OUR EARTH CUSTOMS TO HIM--SUCH AS THE FACT THAT YOU CAN'T JUST TAKE MONEY OUT OF A BANK!
REALLY? THEN WHY DIDN'T THEY STOP ME?
BROTHER, YOU'RE JUST BEGGIN' FOR IT! NOW RELAX--IT'LL ONLY HURT A MINUTE!
CAREFUL, MY EXCITABLE FRIEND! YOU'RE LIABLE TO FIND ME A BIT THORNY!
YEOW!
POP!
HEY, THAT WASN'T FUNNY! I'LL SETTLE THAT LITTLE WISE-GUY'S HASH ONCE AND FOR ALL!
FLAME ON!
4

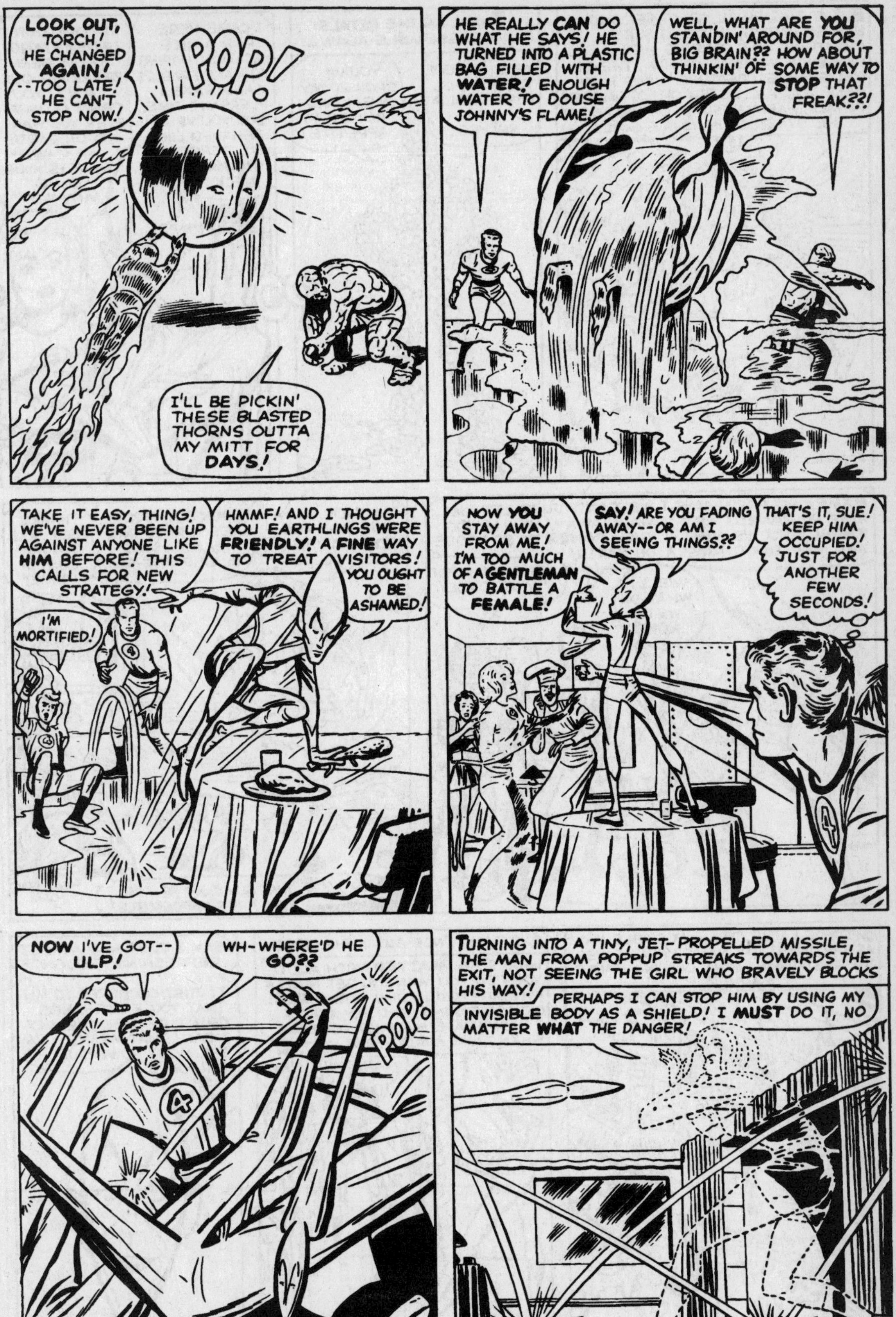

LOOK OUT, TORCH! HE CHANGED AGAIN! --TOO LATE! HE CAN'T STOP NOW!
POP!
I'LL BE PICKIN' THESE BLASTED THORNS OUTTA MY MITT FOR DAYS!
HE REALLY CAN DO WHAT HE SAYS! HE TURNED INTO A PLASTIC BAG FILLED WITH WATER! ENOUGH WATER TO DOUSE JOHNNY'S FLAME!
WELL, WHAT ARE YOU STANDIN' AROUND FOR, BIG BRAIN?? HOW ABOUT THINKIN' OF SOME WAY TO STOP THAT FREAK??!
TAKE IT EASY, THING! WE'VE NEVER BEEN UP AGAINST ANYONE LIKE HIM BEFORE! THIS CALLS FOR NEW STRATEGY!
HMMF! AND I THOUGHT YOU EARTHLINGS WERE FRIENDLY! A FINE WAY TO TREAT VISITORS! YOU OUGHT TO BE ASHAMED!
I'M MORTIFIED!
NOW YOU STAY AWAY FROM ME! I'M TOO MUCH OF A GENTLEMAN TO BATTLE A FEMALE!
SAY! ARE YOU FADING AWAY--OR AM I SEEING THINGS??
THAT'S IT, SUE! KEEP HIM OCCUPIED! JUST FOR ANOTHER FEW SECONDS!
NOW I'VE GOT-- ULP!
WH-WHERE'D HE GO??
POP!
TURNING INTO A TINY, JET-PROPELLED MISSILE, THE MAN FROM POPPUP STREAKS TOWARDS THE EXIT, NOT SEEING THE GIRL WHO BRAVELY BLOCKS HIS WAY!
PERHAPS I CAN STOP HIM BY USING MY INVISIBLE BODY AS A SHIELD! I MUST DO IT, NO MATTER WHAT THE DANGER!
5

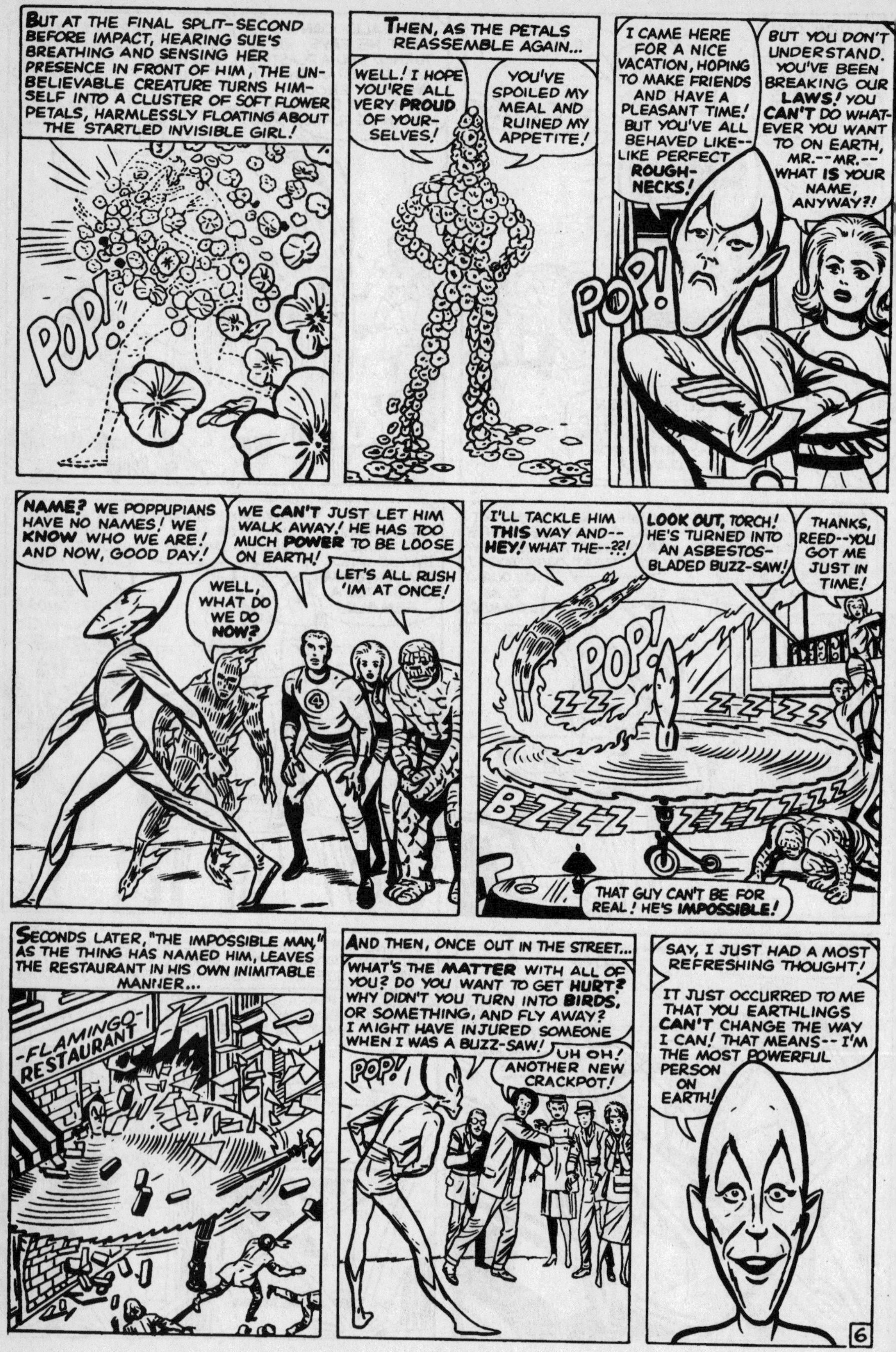
BUT AT THE FINAL SPLIT-SECOND BEFORE IMPACT, HEARING SUE'S BREATHING AND SENSING HER PRESENCE IN FRONT OF HIM, THE UNBELIEVABLE CREATURE TURNS HIMSELF INTO A CLUSTER OF SOFT FLOWER PETALS, HARMLESSLY FLOATING ABOUT THE STARTLED INVISIBLE GIRL!
POP!
THEN, AS THE PETALS REASSEMBLE AGAIN...
WELL! I HOPE YOU'RE ALL VERY PROUD OF YOURSELVES!
YOU'VE SPOILED MY MEAL AND RUINED MY APPETITE!
I CAME HERE FOR A NICE VACATION, HOPING TO MAKE FRIENDS AND HAVE A PLEASANT TIME! BUT YOU'VE ALL BEHAVED LIKE--LIKE PERFECT ROUGHNECKS!
BUT YOU DON'T UNDERSTAND. YOU'VE BEEN BREAKING OUR LAWS! YOU CAN'T DO WHATEVER YOU WANT TO ON EARTH, MR.--MR.--WHAT IS YOUR NAME, ANYWAY?!
POP!
NAME? WE POPPUPIANS HAVE NO NAMES! WE KNOW WHO WE ARE! AND NOW, GOOD DAY!
WE CAN'T JUST LET HIM WALK AWAY! HE HAS TOO MUCH POWER TO BE LOOSE ON EARTH!
LET'S ALL RUSH 'IM AT ONCE!
WELL, WHAT DO WE DO NOW?
I'LL TACKLE HIM THIS WAY AND--HEY! WHAT THE--??!
LOOK OUT, TORCH! HE'S TURNED INTO AN ASBESTOS-BLADED BUZZ-SAW!
THANKS, REED--YOU GOT ME JUST IN TIME!
POP!
ZZ
ZZZZZ
BZZZZ ZZZZZZZZ
THAT GUY CAN'T BE FOR REAL! HE'S IMPOSSIBLE!
SECONDS LATER, "THE IMPOSSIBLE MAN," AS THE THING HAS NAMED HIM, LEAVES THE RESTAURANT IN HIS OWN INIMITABLE MANNER...
-FLAMINGO-RESTAURANT
AND THEN, ONCE OUT IN THE STREET...
WHAT'S THE MATTER WITH ALL OF YOU? DO YOU WANT TO GET HURT? WHY DIDN'T YOU TURN INTO BIRDS, OR SOMETHING, AND FLY AWAY? I MIGHT HAVE INJURED SOMEONE WHEN I WAS A BUZZ-SAW!
POP!
UH OH! ANOTHER NEW CRACKPOT!
SAY, I JUST HAD A MOST REFRESHING THOUGHT!
IT JUST OCCURRED TO ME THAT YOU EARTHLINGS CAN'T CHANGE THE WAY I CAN! THAT MEANS--I'M THE MOST POWERFUL PERSON ON EARTH!
6

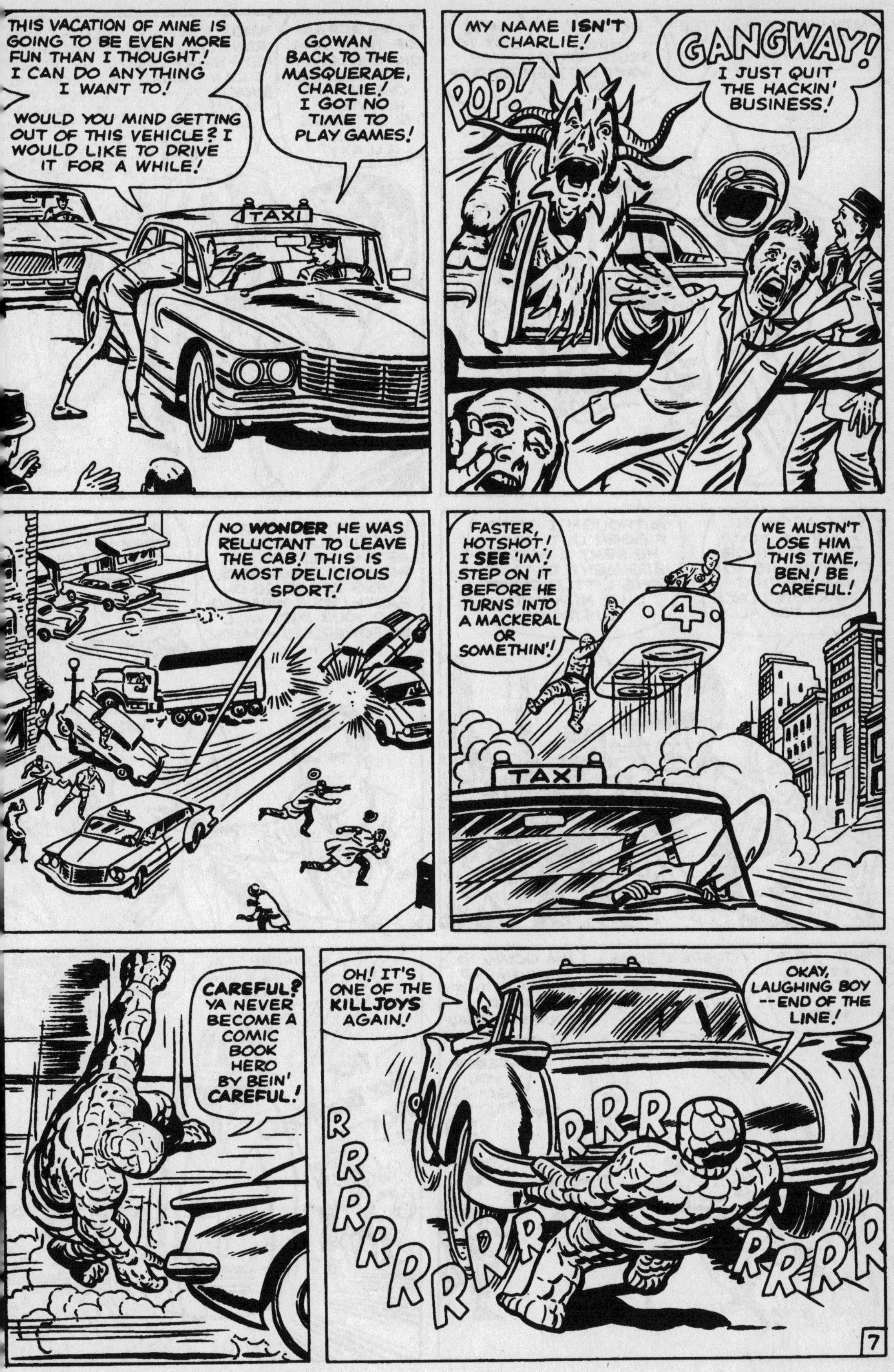
THIS VACATION OF MINE IS GOING TO BE EVEN MORE FUN THAN I THOUGHT! I CAN DO ANYTHING I WANT TO!
WOULD YOU MIND GETTING OUT OF THIS VEHICLE? I WOULD LIKE TO DRIVE IT FOR A WHILE!
GOWAN BACK TO THE MASQUERADE, CHARLIE! I GOT NO TIME TO PLAY GAMES!
TAXI
MY NAME ISN'T CHARLIE!
POP!
GANGWAY! I JUST QUIT THE HACKIN' BUSINESS!
NO WONDER HE WAS RELUCTANT TO LEAVE THE CAB! THIS IS MOST DELICIOUS SPORT!
FASTER, HOTSHOT! I SEE 'IM! STEP ON IT BEFORE HE TURNS INTO A MACKERAL OR SOMETHIN'!
WE MUSTN'T LOSE HIM THIS TIME, BEN! BE CAREFUL!
4
TAXI
CAREFUL? YA NEVER BECOME A COMIC BOOK HERO BY BEIN' CAREFUL!
OH! IT'S ONE OF THE KILLJOYS AGAIN!
OKAY, LAUGHING BOY --END OF THE LINE!
RRRRRRRRR
RRR
RRRR

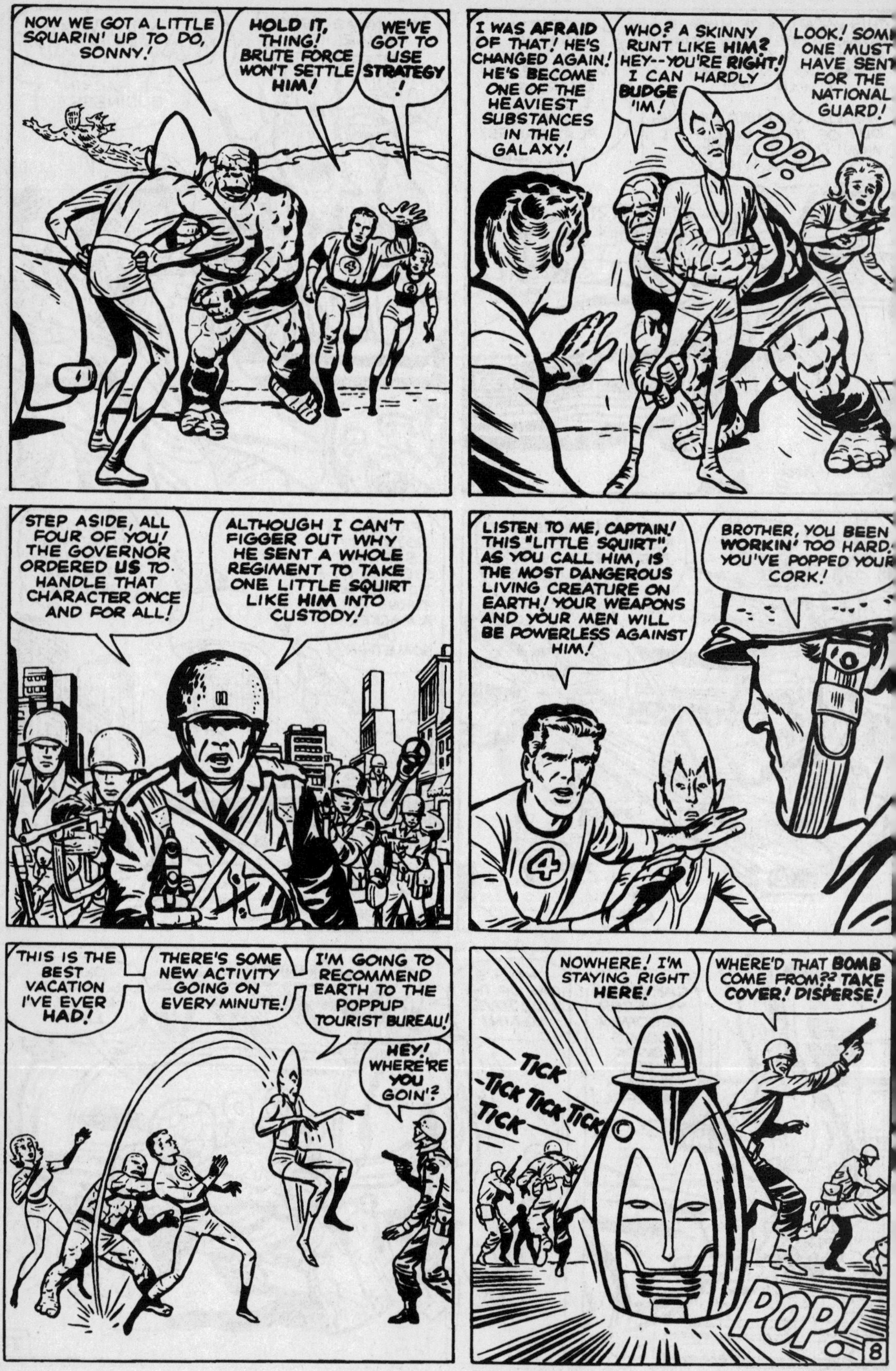
NOW WE GOT A LITTLE SQUARIN' UP TO DO, SONNY!
HOLD IT, THING! BRUTE FORCE WON'T SETTLE HIM!
WE'VE GOT TO USE STRATEGY!
I WAS AFRAID OF THAT! HE'S CHANGED AGAIN! HE'S BECOME ONE OF THE HEAVIEST SUBSTANCES IN THE GALAXY!
WHO? A SKINNY RUNT LIKE HIM? HEY--YOU'RE RIGHT! I CAN HARDLY BUDGE 'IM!
POP!
LOOK! SOME-ONE MUST HAVE SENT FOR THE NATIONAL GUARD!
STEP ASIDE, ALL FOUR OF YOU! THE GOVERNOR ORDERED US TO HANDLE THAT CHARACTER ONCE AND FOR ALL!
ALTHOUGH I CAN'T FIGGER OUT WHY HE SENT A WHOLE REGIMENT TO TAKE ONE LITTLE SQUIRT LIKE HIM INTO CUSTODY!
LISTEN TO ME, CAPTAIN! THIS "LITTLE SQUIRT", AS YOU CALL HIM, IS THE MOST DANGEROUS LIVING CREATURE ON EARTH! YOUR WEAPONS AND YOUR MEN WILL BE POWERLESS AGAINST HIM!
BROTHER, YOU BEEN WORKIN' TOO HARD. YOU'VE POPPED YOUR CORK!
THIS IS THE BEST VACATION I'VE EVER HAD!
THERE'S SOME NEW ACTIVITY GOING ON EVERY MINUTE!
I'M GOING TO RECOMMEND EARTH TO THE POPPUP TOURIST BUREAU!
HEY! WHERE'RE YOU GOIN'?
NOWHERE! I'M STAYING RIGHT HERE!
WHERE'D THAT BOMB COME FROM?? TAKE COVER! DISPERSE!
TICK -TICK TICK TICK TICK
POP!
8

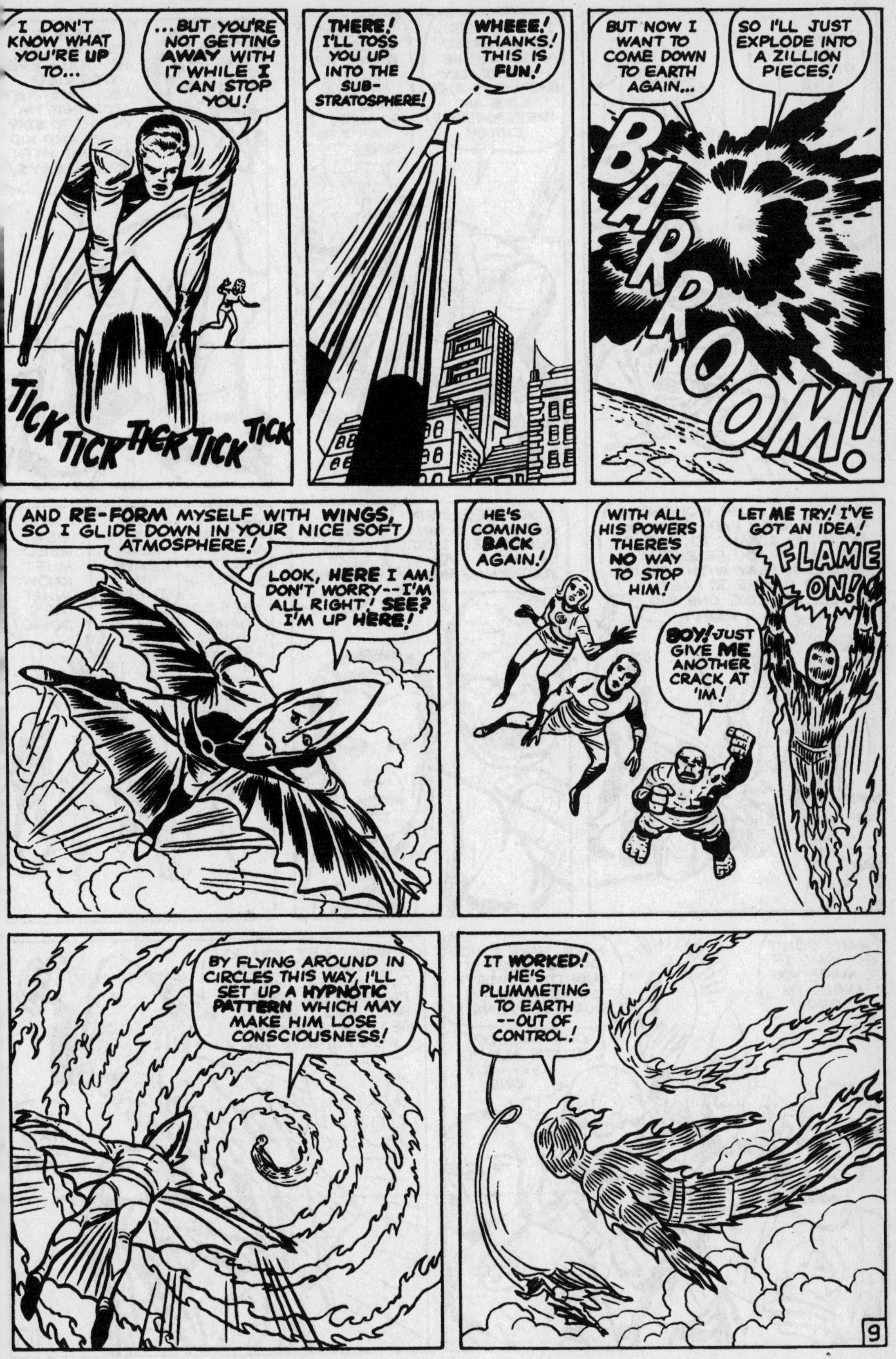
I DON'T KNOW WHAT YOU'RE UP TO...
...BUT YOU'RE NOT GETTING AWAY WITH IT WHILE I CAN STOP YOU!
TICK TICK TICK TICK TICK
THERE! I'LL TOSS YOU UP INTO THE SUB-STRATOSPHERE!
WHEEE! THANKS! THIS IS FUN!
BUT NOW I WANT TO COME DOWN TO EARTH AGAIN...
SO I'LL JUST EXPLODE INTO A ZILLION PIECES!
BARROOM!
AND RE-FORM MYSELF WITH WINGS, SO I GLIDE DOWN IN YOUR NICE SOFT ATMOSPHERE!
LOOK, HERE I AM! DON'T WORRY--I'M ALL RIGHT! SEE? I'M UP HERE!
HE'S COMING BACK AGAIN!
WITH ALL HIS POWERS THERE'S NO WAY TO STOP HIM!
LET ME TRY! I'VE GOT AN IDEA!
FLAME ON!
BOY! JUST GIVE ME ANOTHER CRACK AT 'IM!
BY FLYING AROUND IN CIRCLES THIS WAY, I'LL SET UP A HYPNOTIC PATTERN WHICH MAY MAKE HIM LOSE CONSCIOUSNESS!
IT WORKED! HE'S PLUMMETING TO EARTH --OUT OF CONTROL!
9

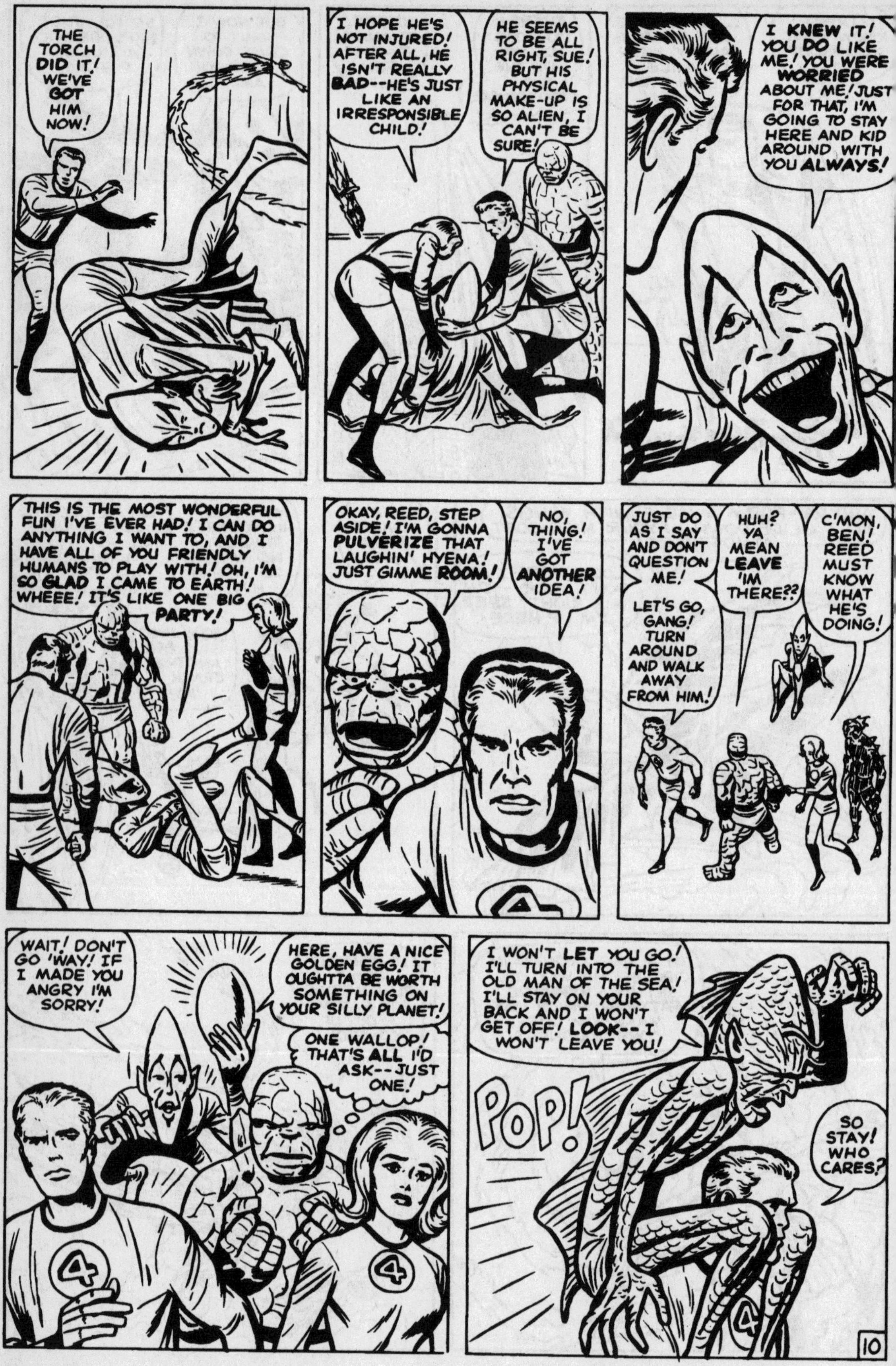
THE TORCH DID IT! WE'VE GOT HIM NOW!
I HOPE HE'S NOT INJURED! AFTER ALL, HE ISN'T REALLY BAD--HE'S JUST LIKE AN IRRESPONSIBLE CHILD!
HE SEEMS TO BE ALL RIGHT, SUE! BUT HIS PHYSICAL MAKE-UP IS SO ALIEN, I CAN'T BE SURE!
I KNEW IT! YOU DO LIKE ME! YOU WERE WORRIED ABOUT ME! JUST FOR THAT, I'M GOING TO STAY HERE AND KID AROUND WITH YOU ALWAYS!
THIS IS THE MOST WONDERFUL FUN I'VE EVER HAD! I CAN DO ANYTHING I WANT TO, AND I HAVE ALL OF YOU FRIENDLY HUMANS TO PLAY WITH! OH, I'M SO GLAD I CAME TO EARTH! WHEEE! IT'S LIKE ONE BIG PARTY!
OKAY, REED, STEP ASIDE! I'M GONNA PULVERIZE THAT LAUGHIN' HYENA! JUST GIMME ROOM!
NO, THING! I'VE GOT ANOTHER IDEA!
JUST DO AS I SAY AND DON'T QUESTION ME!
LET'S GO, GANG! TURN AROUND AND WALK AWAY FROM HIM!
HUH? YA MEAN LEAVE 'IM THERE??
C'MON, BEN! REED MUST KNOW WHAT HE'S DOING!
WAIT! DON'T GO 'WAY! IF I MADE YOU ANGRY I'M SORRY!
HERE, HAVE A NICE GOLDEN EGG! IT OUGHTTA BE WORTH SOMETHING ON YOUR SILLY PLANET!
ONE WALLOP! THAT'S ALL I'D ASK--JUST ONE!
I WON'T LET YOU GO! I'LL TURN INTO THE OLD MAN OF THE SEA! I'LL STAY ON YOUR BACK AND I WON'T GET OFF! LOOK--I WON'T LEAVE YOU!
POP!
SO STAY! WHO CARES?
10

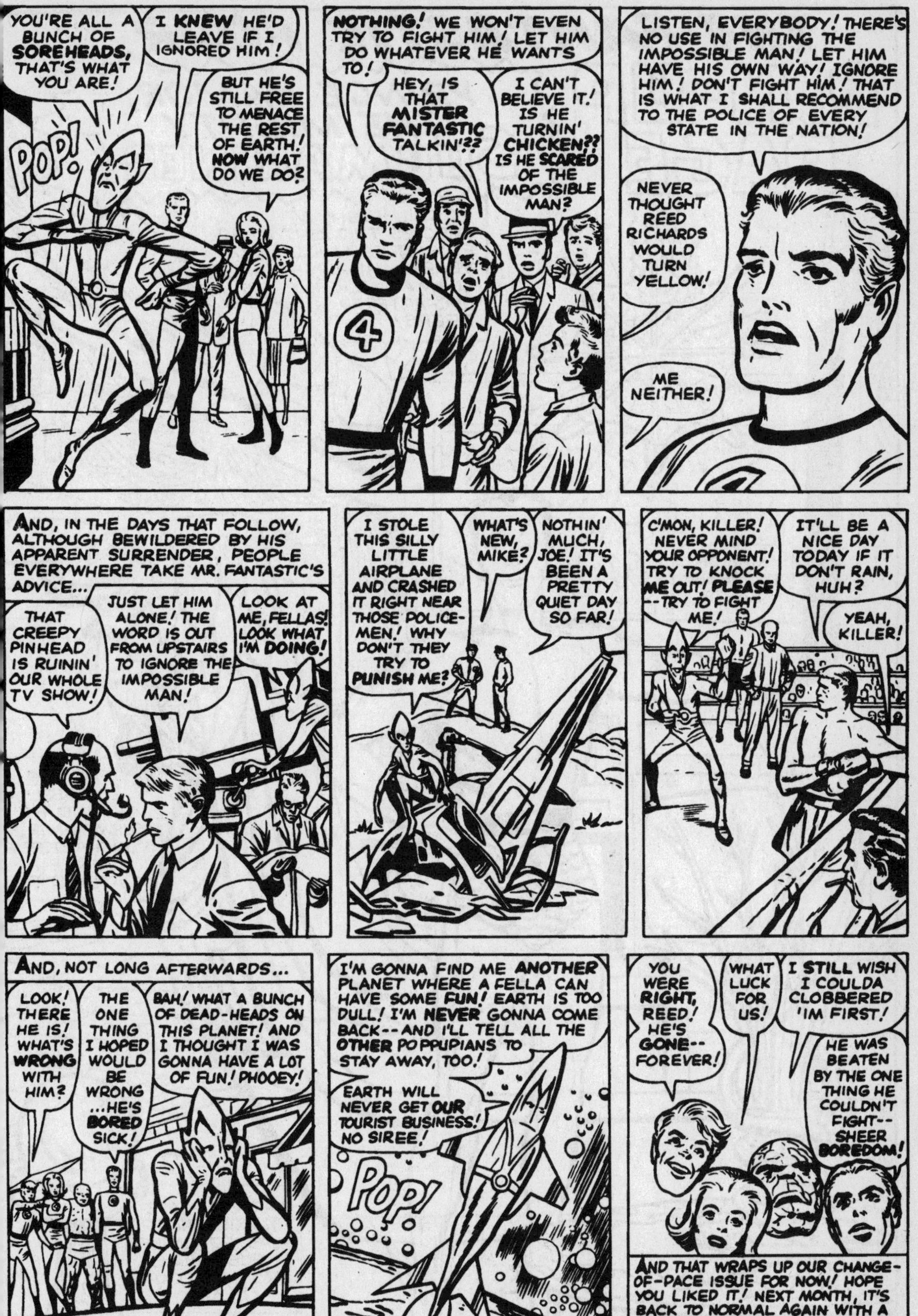
YOU'RE ALL A BUNCH OF SOREHEADS, THAT'S WHAT YOU ARE!
I KNEW HE'D LEAVE IF I IGNORED HIM!
BUT HE'S STILL FREE TO MENACE THE REST OF EARTH! NOW WHAT DO WE DO?
POP!
NOTHING! WE WON'T EVEN TRY TO FIGHT HIM! LET HIM DO WHATEVER HE WANTS TO!
HEY, IS THAT MISTER FANTASTIC TALKIN'??
I CAN'T BELIEVE IT! IS HE TURNIN' CHICKEN?? IS HE SCARED OF THE IMPOSSIBLE MAN?
LISTEN, EVERYBODY! THERE'S NO USE IN FIGHTING THE IMPOSSIBLE MAN! LET HIM HAVE HIS OWN WAY! IGNORE HIM! DON'T FIGHT HIM! THAT IS WHAT I SHALL RECOMMEND TO THE POLICE OF EVERY STATE IN THE NATION!
NEVER THOUGHT REED RICHARDS WOULD TURN YELLOW!
ME NEITHER!
AND, IN THE DAYS THAT FOLLOW, ALTHOUGH BEWILDERED BY HIS APPARENT SURRENDER, PEOPLE EVERYWHERE TAKE MR. FANTASTIC'S ADVICE...
THAT CREEPY PINHEAD IS RUININ' OUR WHOLE TV SHOW!
JUST LET HIM ALONE! THE WORD IS OUT FROM UPSTAIRS TO IGNORE THE IMPOSSIBLE MAN!
LOOK AT ME, FELLAS! LOOK WHAT I'M DOING!
I STOLE THIS SILLY LITTLE AIRPLANE AND CRASHED IT RIGHT NEAR THOSE POLICE-MEN! WHY DON'T THEY TRY TO PUNISH ME?
WHAT'S NEW, MIKE?
NOTHIN' MUCH, JOE! IT'S BEEN A PRETTY QUIET DAY SO FAR!
C'MON, KILLER! NEVER MIND YOUR OPPONENT! TRY TO KNOCK ME OUT! PLEASE --TRY TO FIGHT ME!
IT'LL BE A NICE DAY TODAY IF IT DON'T RAIN, HUH?
YEAH, KILLER!
AND, NOT LONG AFTERWARDS...
LOOK! THERE HE IS! WHAT'S WRONG WITH HIM?
THE ONE THING I HOPED WOULD BE WRONG ...HE'S BORED SICK!
BAH! WHAT A BUNCH OF DEAD-HEADS ON THIS PLANET! AND I THOUGHT I WAS GONNA HAVE A LOT OF FUN! PHOOEY!
11
I'M GONNA FIND ME ANOTHER PLANET WHERE A FELLA CAN HAVE SOME FUN! EARTH IS TOO DULL! I'M NEVER GONNA COME BACK--AND I'LL TELL ALL THE OTHER POPPUPIANS TO STAY AWAY, TOO!
EARTH WILL NEVER GET OUR TOURIST BUSINESS! NO SIREE!
POP!
YOU WERE RIGHT, REED! HE'S GONE-- FOREVER!
WHAT LUCK FOR US!
I STILL WISH I COULDA CLOBBERED 'IM FIRST!
HE WAS BEATEN BY THE ONE THING HE COULDN'T FIGHT-- SHEER BOREDOM!
AND THAT WRAPS UP OUR CHANGE-OF-PACE ISSUE FOR NOW! HOPE YOU LIKED IT! NEXT MONTH, IT'S BACK TO NORMAL AGAIN WITH A SURPRISE-PACKED FULL-LENGTH THRILLER--THE FANTASTIC FOUR MEET--THE HULK! DON'T MISS IT!
THE END

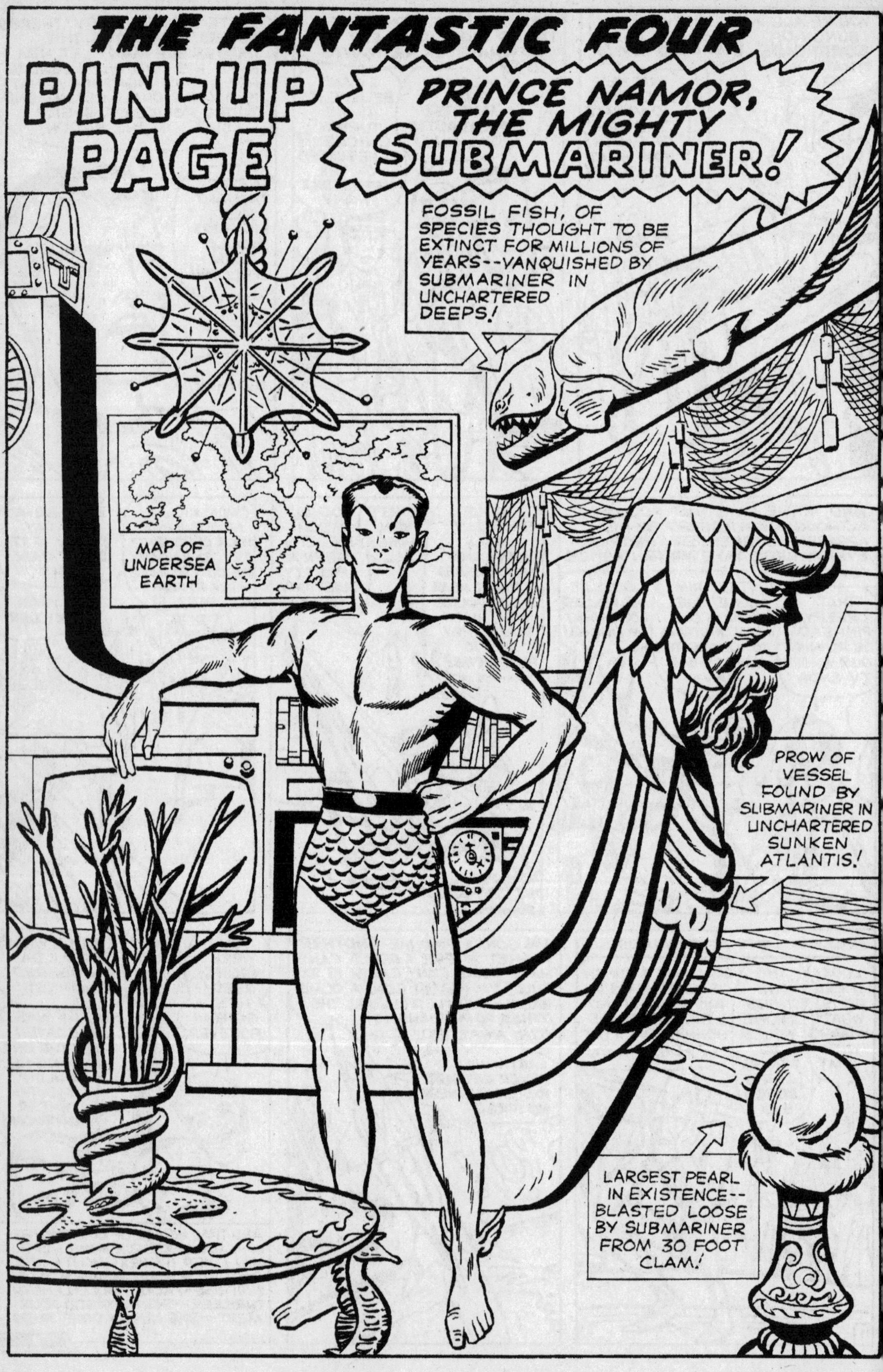
THE FANTASTIC FOUR
PIN-UP PAGE
PRINCE NAMOR, THE MIGHTY SUBMARINER!
FOSSIL FISH, OF SPECIES THOUGHT TO BE EXTINCT FOR MILLIONS OF YEARS--VANQUISHED BY SUBMARINER IN UNCHARTERED DEEPS!
MAP OF UNDERSEA EARTH
PROW OF VESSEL FOUND BY SUBMARINER IN UNCHARTERED SUNKEN ATLANTIS!
LARGEST PEARL IN EXISTENCE--BLASTED LOOSE BY SUBMARINER FROM 30 FOOT CLAM!

IND.
THE WORLD'S GREATEST COMIC MAGAZINE!
APPROVED BY THE COMICS CODE AUTHORITY
12¢
THE Fantastic Four
MC
12 MAR.
AT LAST!!! the FANTASTIC FOUR meet THE HULK!
THE HULK IS NEARBY! I CAN FEEL IT!
ANOTHER SECOND AND I'LL DESTROY THEM ALL!!
A BOOK-LENGTH EPIC!! NEED WE SAY MORE?!!!

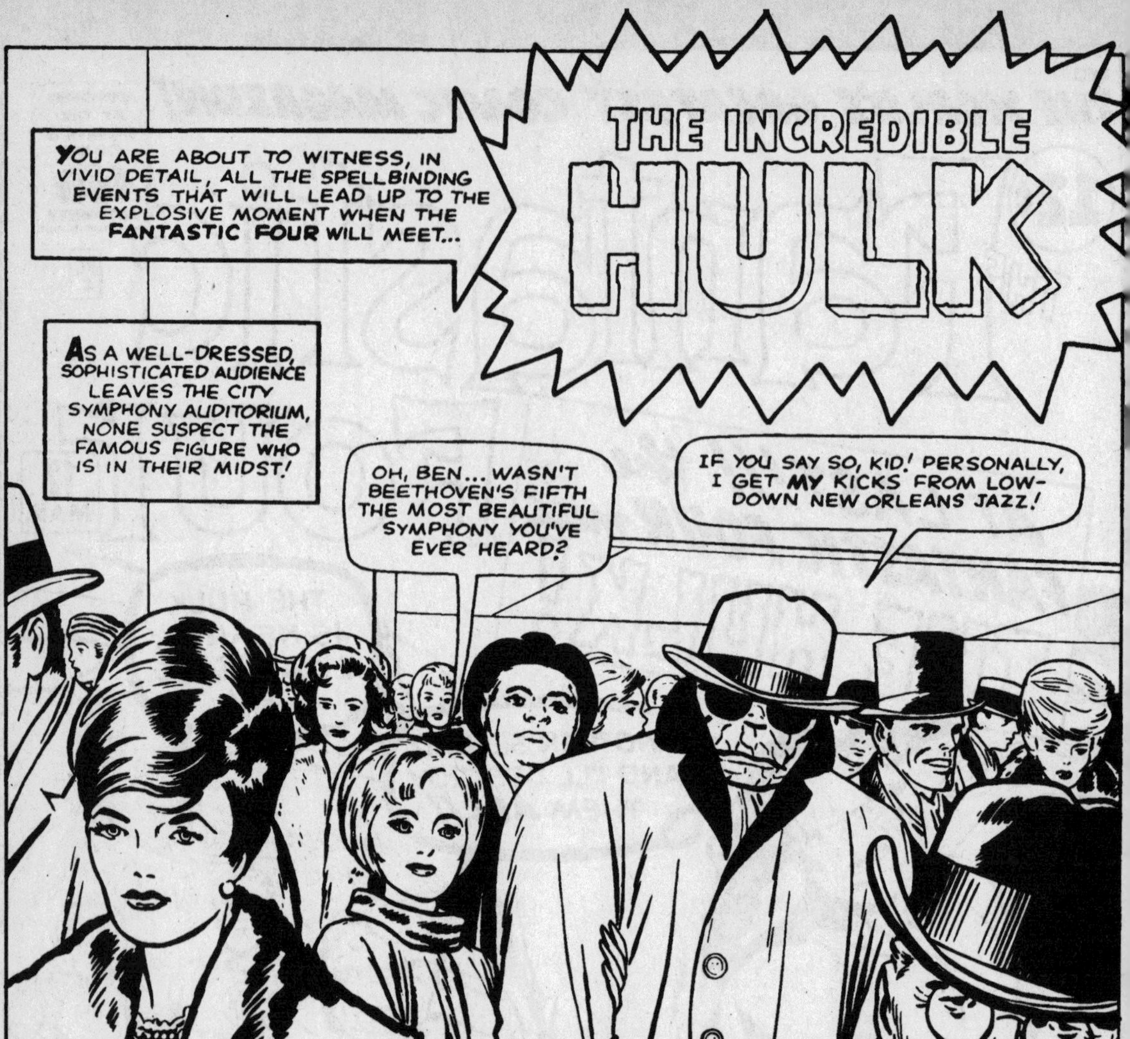
THE INCREDIBLE HULK
YOU ARE ABOUT TO WITNESS, IN VIVID DETAIL, ALL THE SPELLBINDING EVENTS THAT WILL LEAD UP TO THE EXPLOSIVE MOMENT WHEN THE FANTASTIC FOUR WILL MEET...
AS A WELL-DRESSED, SOPHISTICATED AUDIENCE LEAVES THE CITY SYMPHONY AUDITORIUM, NONE SUSPECT THE FAMOUS FIGURE WHO IS IN THEIR MIDST!
OH, BEN... WASN'T BEETHOVEN'S FIFTH THE MOST BEAUTIFUL SYMPHONY YOU'VE EVER HEARD?
IF YOU SAY SO, KID! PERSONALLY, I GET MY KICKS FROM LOW-DOWN NEW ORLEANS JAZZ!
SCRIPT.......... STAN LEE
ART............. JACK KIRBY
INKING........ DICK AYERS
LETTERING... ART SIMEK
X-101
LOOK, MY DEAR! A COMPANY OF INFANTRYMEN! HERE IN NEW YORK!
HEY!
LOOK OUT WHO YOU'RE POKIN'!
1

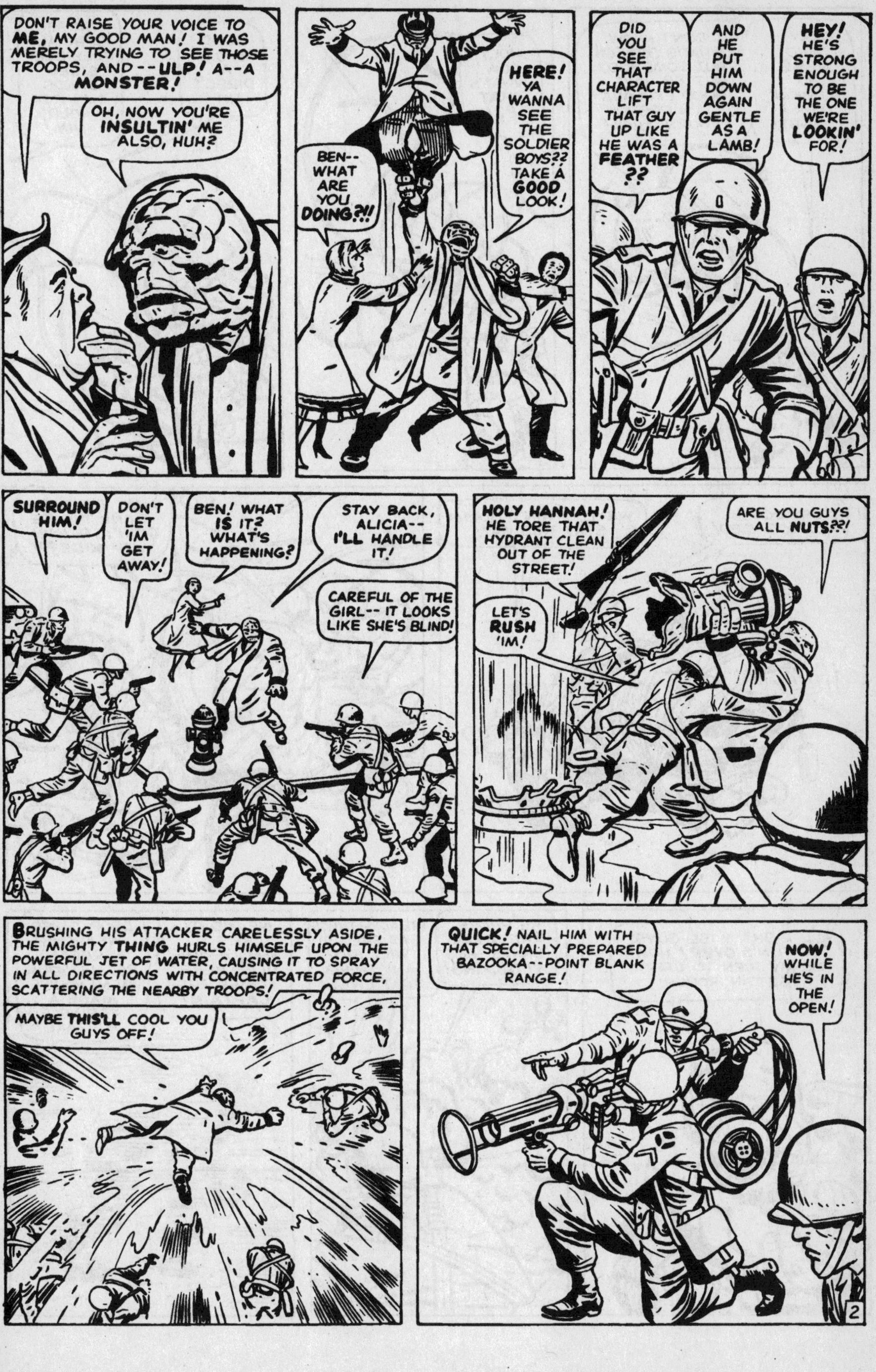
DON'T RAISE YOUR VOICE TO ME, MY GOOD MAN! I WAS MERELY TRYING TO SEE THOSE TROOPS, AND--ULP! A--A MONSTER!
OH, NOW YOU'RE INSULTIN' ME ALSO, HUH?
HERE! YA WANNA SEE THE SOLDIER BOYS?? TAKE A GOOD LOOK!
BEN--WHAT ARE YOU DOING?!!
DID YOU SEE THAT CHARACTER LIFT THAT GUY UP LIKE HE WAS A FEATHER??
AND HE PUT HIM DOWN AGAIN GENTLE AS A LAMB!
HEY! HE'S STRONG ENOUGH TO BE THE ONE WE'RE LOOKIN' FOR!
SURROUND HIM!
DON'T LET 'IM GET AWAY!
BEN! WHAT IS IT? WHAT'S HAPPENING?
STAY BACK, ALICIA--I'LL HANDLE IT!
CAREFUL OF THE GIRL-- IT LOOKS LIKE SHE'S BLIND!
HOLY HANNAH! HE TORE THAT HYDRANT CLEAN OUT OF THE STREET!
ARE YOU GUYS ALL NUTS??!
LET'S RUSH 'IM!
BRUSHING HIS ATTACKER CARELESSLY ASIDE, THE MIGHTY THING HURLS HIMSELF UPON THE POWERFUL JET OF WATER, CAUSING IT TO SPRAY IN ALL DIRECTIONS WITH CONCENTRATED FORCE, SCATTERING THE NEARBY TROOPS!
MAYBE THIS'LL COOL YOU GUYS OFF!
QUICK! NAIL HIM WITH THAT SPECIALLY PREPARED BAZOOKA--POINT BLANK RANGE!
NOW! WHILE HE'S IN THE OPEN!
2

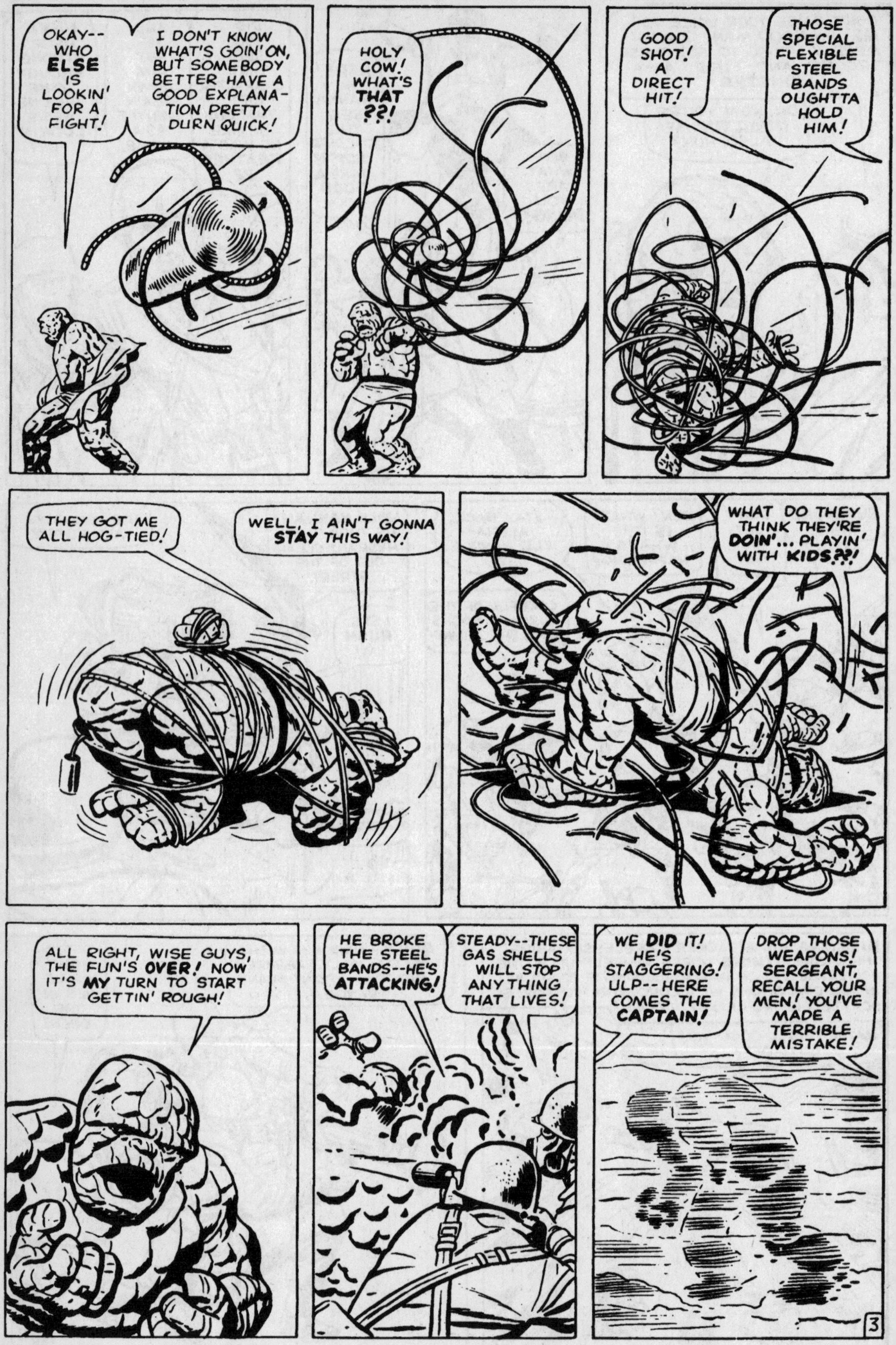
OKAY-- WHO ELSE IS LOOKIN' FOR A FIGHT!
I DON'T KNOW WHAT'S GOIN' ON, BUT SOMEBODY BETTER HAVE A GOOD EXPLANATION PRETTY DURN QUICK!
HOLY COW! WHAT'S THAT ??!
GOOD SHOT! A DIRECT HIT!
THOSE SPECIAL FLEXIBLE STEEL BANDS OUGHTTA HOLD HIM!
THEY GOT ME ALL HOG-TIED!
WELL, I AIN'T GONNA STAY THIS WAY!
WHAT DO THEY THINK THEY'RE DOIN'... PLAYIN' WITH KIDS??!
ALL RIGHT, WISE GUYS, THE FUN'S OVER! NOW IT'S MY TURN TO START GETTIN' ROUGH!
HE BROKE THE STEEL BANDS--HE'S ATTACKING!
STEADY--THESE GAS SHELLS WILL STOP ANYTHING THAT LIVES!
WE DID IT! HE'S STAGGERING! ULP--HERE COMES THE CAPTAIN!
DROP THOSE WEAPONS! SERGEANT, RECALL YOUR MEN! YOU'VE MADE A TERRIBLE MISTAKE!
3

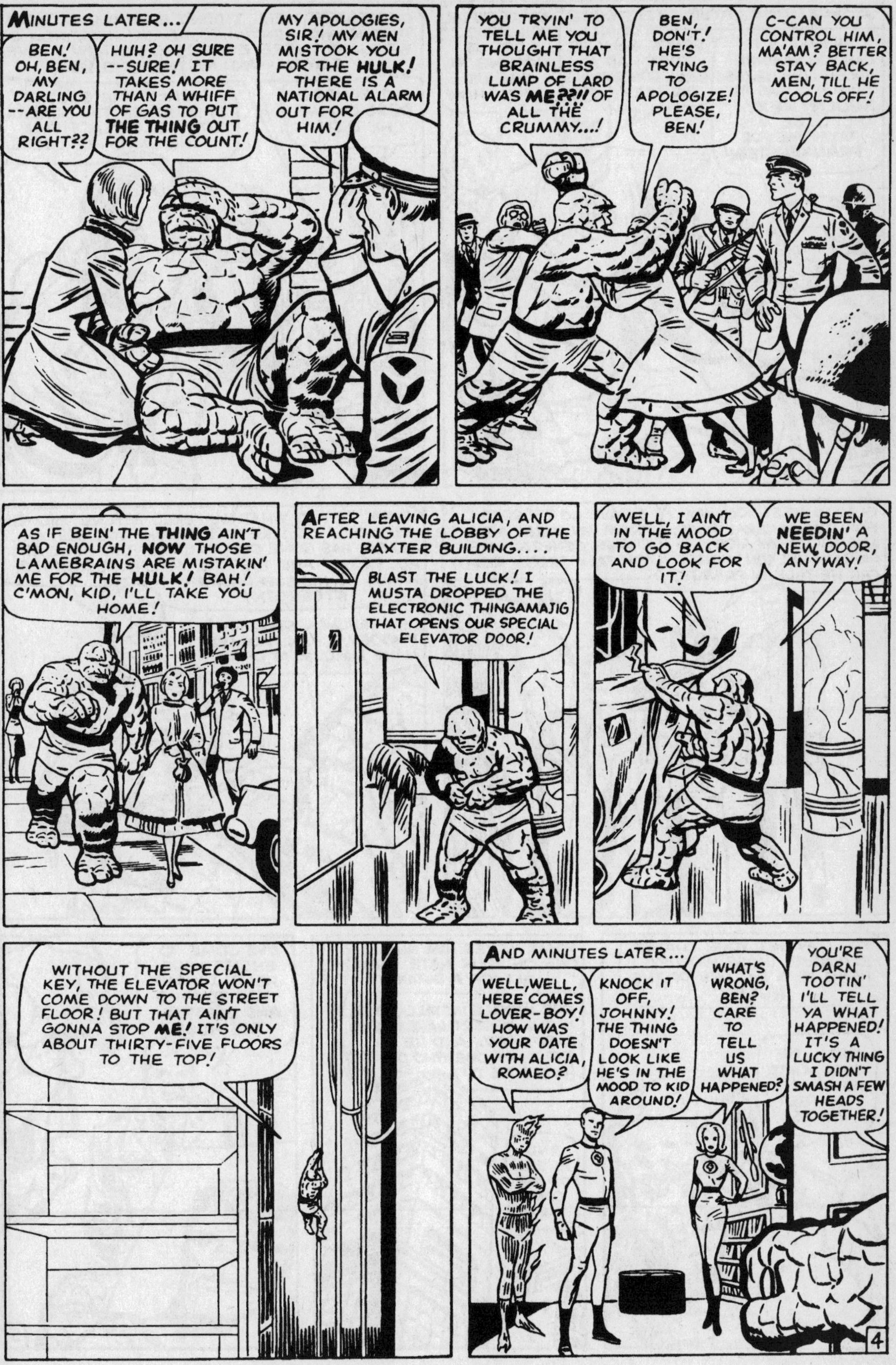
MINUTES LATER...
BEN! OH, BEN, MY DARLING --ARE YOU ALL RIGHT??
HUH? OH SURE --SURE! IT TAKES MORE THAN A WHIFF OF GAS TO PUT THE THING OUT FOR THE COUNT!
MY APOLOGIES, SIR! MY MEN MISTOOK YOU FOR THE HULK! THERE IS A NATIONAL ALARM OUT FOR HIM!
YOU TRYIN' TO TELL ME YOU THOUGHT THAT BRAINLESS LUMP OF LARD WAS ME??!! OF ALL THE CRUMMY...!
BEN, DON'T! HE'S TRYING TO APOLOGIZE! PLEASE, BEN!
C-CAN YOU CONTROL HIM, MA'AM? BETTER STAY BACK, MEN, TILL HE COOLS OFF!
AS IF BEIN' THE THING AIN'T BAD ENOUGH, NOW THOSE LAMEBRAINS ARE MISTAKIN' ME FOR THE HULK! BAH! C'MON, KID, I'LL TAKE YOU HOME!
AFTER LEAVING ALICIA, AND REACHING THE LOBBY OF THE BAXTER BUILDING....
BLAST THE LUCK! I MUSTA DROPPED THE ELECTRONIC THINGAMAJIG THAT OPENS OUR SPECIAL ELEVATOR DOOR!
WELL, I AIN'T IN THE MOOD TO GO BACK AND LOOK FOR IT!
WE BEEN NEEDIN' A NEW DOOR, ANYWAY!
WITHOUT THE SPECIAL KEY, THE ELEVATOR WON'T COME DOWN TO THE STREET FLOOR! BUT THAT AIN'T GONNA STOP ME! IT'S ONLY ABOUT THIRTY-FIVE FLOORS TO THE TOP!
AND MINUTES LATER...
WELL, WELL, HERE COMES LOVER-BOY! HOW WAS YOUR DATE WITH ALICIA, ROMEO?
KNOCK IT OFF, JOHNNY! THE THING DOESN'T LOOK LIKE HE'S IN THE MOOD TO KID AROUND!
WHAT'S WRONG, BEN? CARE TO TELL US WHAT HAPPENED?
YOU'RE DARN TOOTIN' I'LL TELL YA WHAT HAPPENED! IT'S A LUCKY THING I DIDN'T SMASH A FEW HEADS TOGETHER!
4

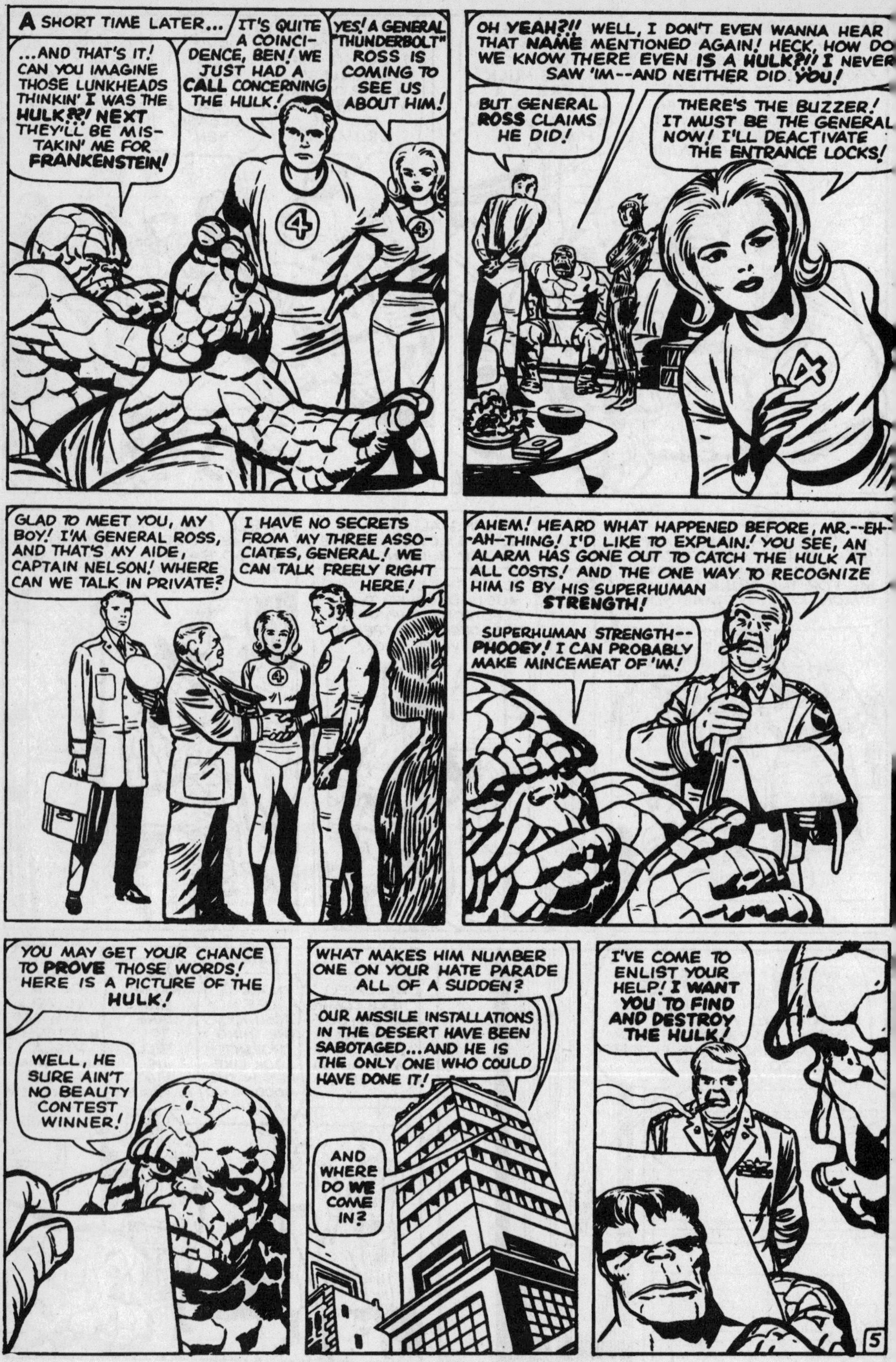
A SHORT TIME LATER...
...AND THAT'S IT! CAN YOU IMAGINE THOSE LUNKHEADS THINKIN' I WAS THE HULK??! NEXT THEY'LL BE MIS-TAKIN' ME FOR FRANKENSTEIN!
IT'S QUITE A COINCI-DENCE, BEN! WE JUST HAD A CALL CONCERNING THE HULK!
YES! A GENERAL "THUNDERBOLT" ROSS IS COMING TO SEE US ABOUT HIM!
OH YEAH?!! WELL, I DON'T EVEN WANNA HEAR THAT NAME MENTIONED AGAIN! HECK, HOW DO WE KNOW THERE EVEN IS A HULK?!! I NEVER SAW 'IM--AND NEITHER DID YOU!
BUT GENERAL ROSS CLAIMS HE DID!
THERE'S THE BUZZER! IT MUST BE THE GENERAL NOW! I'LL DEACTIVATE THE ENTRANCE LOCKS!
GLAD TO MEET YOU, MY BOY! I'M GENERAL ROSS, AND THAT'S MY AIDE, CAPTAIN NELSON! WHERE CAN WE TALK IN PRIVATE?
I HAVE NO SECRETS FROM MY THREE ASSO-CIATES, GENERAL! WE CAN TALK FREELY RIGHT HERE!
AHEM! HEARD WHAT HAPPENED BEFORE, MR.--EH--AH--THING! I'D LIKE TO EXPLAIN! YOU SEE, AN ALARM HAS GONE OUT TO CATCH THE HULK AT ALL COSTS! AND THE ONE WAY TO RECOGNIZE HIM IS BY HIS SUPERHUMAN STRENGTH!
SUPERHUMAN STRENGTH--PHOOEY! I CAN PROBABLY MAKE MINCEMEAT OF 'IM!
YOU MAY GET YOUR CHANCE TO PROVE THOSE WORDS! HERE IS A PICTURE OF THE HULK!
WELL, HE SURE AIN'T NO BEAUTY CONTEST WINNER!
WHAT MAKES HIM NUMBER ONE ON YOUR HATE PARADE ALL OF A SUDDEN?
OUR MISSILE INSTALLATIONS IN THE DESERT HAVE BEEN SABOTAGED...AND HE IS THE ONLY ONE WHO COULD HAVE DONE IT!
AND WHERE DO WE COME IN?
I'VE COME TO ENLIST YOUR HELP! I WANT YOU TO FIND AND DESTROY THE HULK!
5

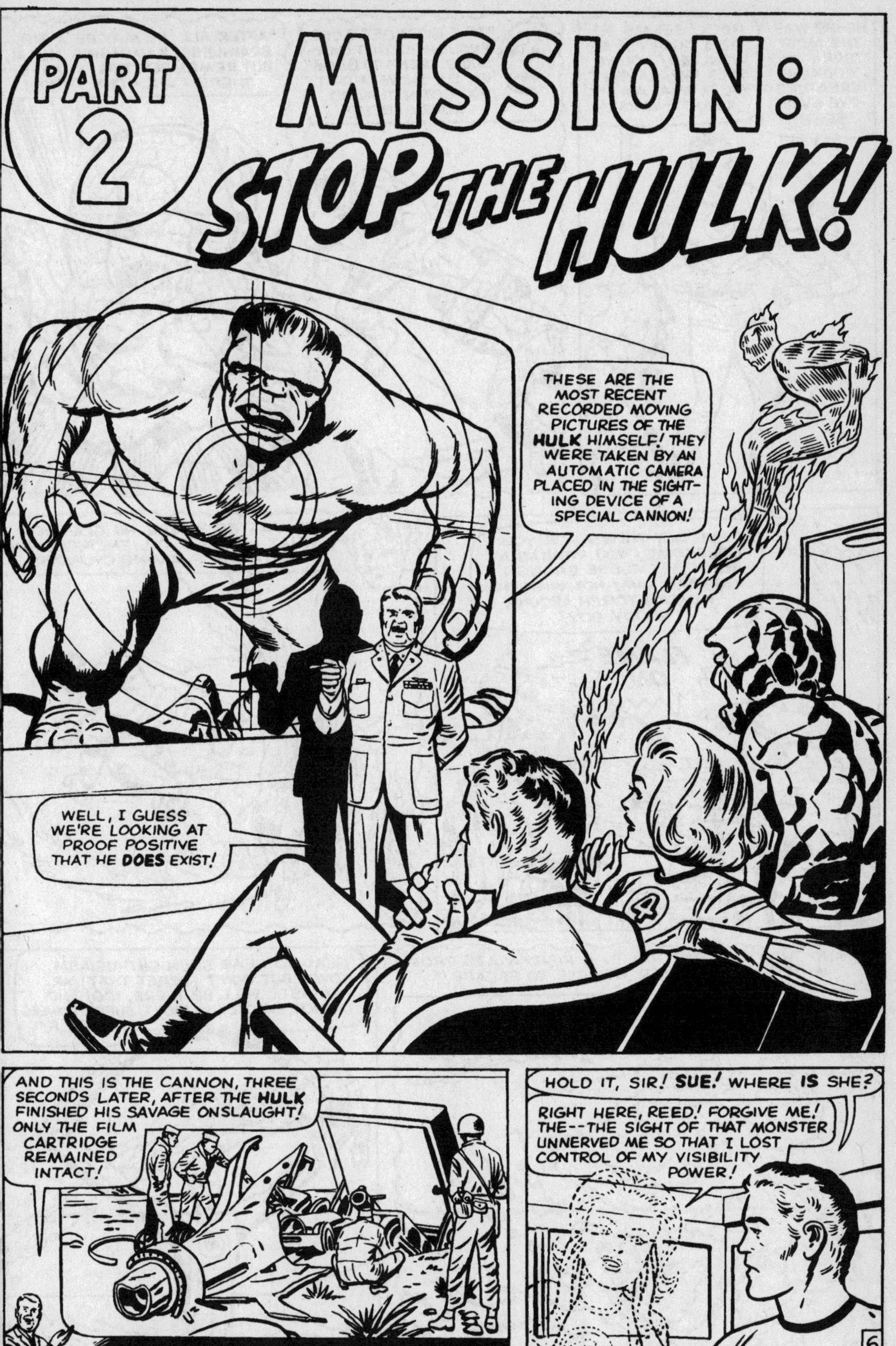
PART 2
MISSION: STOP THE HULK!
THESE ARE THE MOST RECENT RECORDED MOVING PICTURES OF THE HULK HIMSELF! THEY WERE TAKEN BY AN AUTOMATIC CAMERA PLACED IN THE SIGHTING DEVICE OF A SPECIAL CANNON!
WELL, I GUESS WE'RE LOOKING AT PROOF POSITIVE THAT HE DOES EXIST!
AND THIS IS THE CANNON, THREE SECONDS LATER, AFTER THE HULK FINISHED HIS SAVAGE ONSLAUGHT! ONLY THE FILM CARTRIDGE REMAINED INTACT!
HOLD IT, SIR! SUE! WHERE IS SHE?
RIGHT HERE, REED! FORGIVE ME! THE--THE SIGHT OF THAT MONSTER UNNERVED ME SO THAT I LOST CONTROL OF MY VISIBILITY POWER!
6

HE-HE WAS THE MOST TERRIFYING-LOOKING CREATURE I'VE EVER SEEN!

HECK! SEEMS TO ME I OUGHTTA BE INSULTED! YOU'VE SEEN ME, HAVEN'T YOU?? WHAT AM I-- A PANTY-WAIST!?

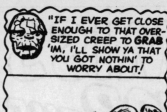

"IF I EVER GET CLOSE ENOUGH TO THAT OVER-SIZED CREEP TO GRAB 'IM, I'LL SHOW YA THAT YOU GOT NOTHIN' TO WORRY ABOUT!"

"AFTER ALL, HE MAY BE A BIG, BRAINLESS, RAMPAGING HULK, BUT REMEMBER THIS, KIDDIES-- THERE'S ONLY ONE THING!"

I'VE GOT NEWS FOR YOU, GRUESOME! YOU PROBABLY WON'T GET CLOSE ENOUGH TO GRAB HIM! NOT WITH THE HUMAN TORCH AROUND, BUDDY BOY!

FLAME ON!

"NO MATTER WHERE HE GOES, OR WHAT HE DOES, I'LL ENCIRCLE HIM WITH MY FLAMING CYLINDER...

"...AND THEN I'LL TRAP HIM IN A FIERY MAZE FROM WHICH HE'LL NEVER BE ABLE TO ESCAPE!"

GLAD TO HEAR SUCH ENTHUSIASM, BOYS! BUT DON'T FORGET THAT MR. FANTASTIC WILL BE THERE, TOO! AND I'M NOT EXACTLY WITHOUT SUPER POWERS MYSELF!

7

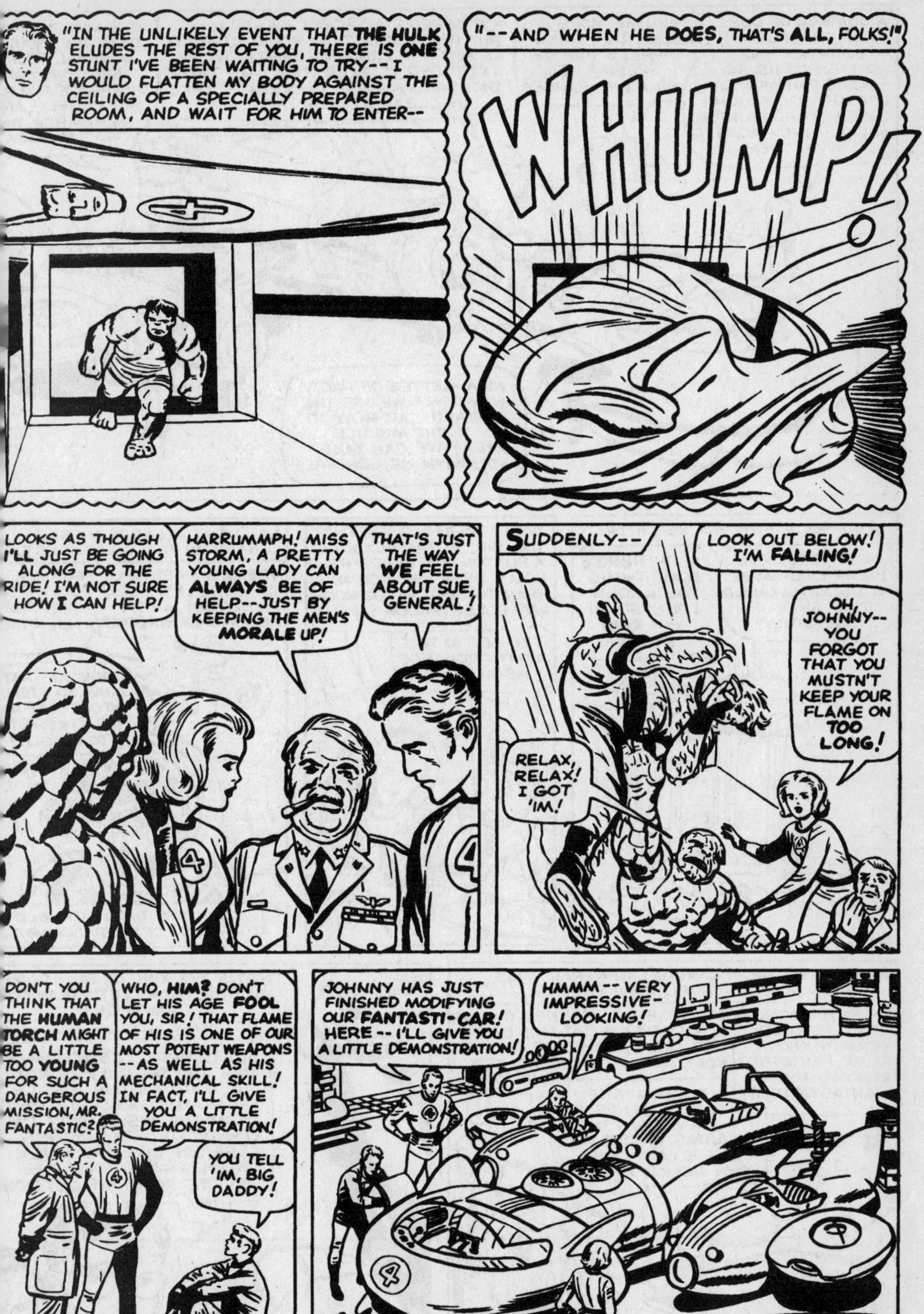
"IN THE UNLIKELY EVENT THAT THE HULK ELUDES THE REST OF YOU, THERE IS ONE STUNT I'VE BEEN WAITING TO TRY-- I WOULD FLATTEN MY BODY AGAINST THE CEILING OF A SPECIALLY PREPARED ROOM, AND WAIT FOR HIM TO ENTER--
"--AND WHEN HE DOES, THAT'S ALL, FOLKS!"
WHUMP!
LOOKS AS THOUGH I'LL JUST BE GOING ALONG FOR THE RIDE! I'M NOT SURE HOW I CAN HELP!
HARRUMMPH! MISS STORM, A PRETTY YOUNG LADY CAN ALWAYS BE OF HELP--JUST BY KEEPING THE MEN'S MORALE UP!
THAT'S JUST THE WAY WE FEEL ABOUT SUE, GENERAL!
SUDDENLY--
LOOK OUT BELOW! I'M FALLING!
OH, JOHNNY-- YOU FORGOT THAT YOU MUSTN'T KEEP YOUR FLAME ON TOO LONG!
RELAX, RELAX! I GOT 'IM!
DON'T YOU THINK THAT THE HUMAN TORCH MIGHT BE A LITTLE TOO YOUNG FOR SUCH A DANGEROUS MISSION, MR. FANTASTIC?
WHO, HIM? DON'T LET HIS AGE FOOL YOU, SIR! THAT FLAME OF HIS IS ONE OF OUR MOST POTENT WEAPONS --AS WELL AS HIS MECHANICAL SKILL! IN FACT, I'LL GIVE YOU A LITTLE DEMONSTRATION!
YOU TELL 'IM, BIG DADDY!
JOHNNY HAS JUST FINISHED MODIFYING OUR FANTASTI-CAR! HERE -- I'LL GIVE YOU A LITTLE DEMONSTRATION!
HMMM -- VERY IMPRESSIVE-LOOKING!
I STILL SAY THEY DON'T BUILD 'EM LIKE THEY USED TO!
8

A NUMBER OF OUR FANS THRUOUT THE COUNTRY HAD WRITTEN TO US SAYING THE FANTASTI-CAR LOOKED TOO MUCH LIKE A FLYING BATHTUB! AND JOHNNNY AGREED WITH THEM!

TELL ME MORE **ABOUT** THIS THING --WHAT'S HER TOP SPEED? HER CRUISING RANGE?

TOP SPEED'S A SECRET, GENERAL-- BUT IT'S FASTER THAN YOU'D SUSPECT! AS FOR HER CRUISING RANGE, WE'VE EXTENDED IT TO BETTER THAN THREE THOUSAND MILES--ENOUGH TO TAKE US CLEAR ACROSS THE U.S.A.!

STOP YAKKIN' AND SHOW THE BRASS HOW ALL FOUR SECTIONS CAN DISENGAGE AND FL SEPARATELY! ANI REMEMBER, THA WAS **MY** IDEA.

AS A MATTER OF FACT, WHY DON'T WE USE THE FANTASTI-CAR **NOW** TO FLY TO THE MISSILE AREA? WE CAN TAKE YOU **WITH** US, GENERAL!

AND SO, A FEW HOURS LATER...

THOSE JET PROPS UNDER EACH SMALL WING REALLY HOLD THIS SHIP UP SMOOTHLY!

UH OH! **HERE'S** SOMETHING YOU HADN'T COUNTED ON -- A **RAIN STORM!**

WE'VE PREPARED FOR **THAT** TOO, SIR! AT THE FLICK OF A BUTTON, THE WINDSHIELD ROLLS OVER AND FORMS A TRANSPARENT WATERPROOF **AND BULLETPROOF** SHIELD!

I'VE GOT TO TELL ARMY ORDNANCE ABOUT THIS!

LATER* AT A LARGE MISSILE BASE IN THE SOUTHWEST...

THERE'S AN EXAMPLE OF THE **HULK'S** WORK! PROJECT 34, ANTI-GRAV MISSILE, **WRECKED!**

BUT HOW CAN YOU BE SURE THE **HULK** DID IT?

LOOK AT THAT TANGLED STEEL NO ONE **ELSE** HA THE STRENGTH TO DO THAT!

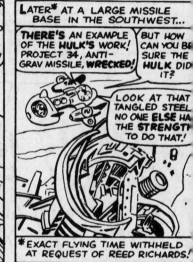

*EXACT FLYING TIME WITHHELD AT REQUEST OF REED RICHARDS!

IMMEDIATELY UPON LANDING, GENERAL ROSS CALLS A HIGH-LEVEL CONFERENCE...

GENTLEMEN, THIS IS REED RICHARDS, KNOWN AS MR. FANTASTIC, REPRESENTING THE **FANTASTIC FOUR!**

I'M DR. BRUCE BANNER, CIVILIAN SCIENTIFIC EXEC AT THIS BASE! THIS IS MY ASSISTANT, DR. KARL KORT, AND MY YOUNG HELPER, RICK JONES!

EVERY MINUTE COUNTS, GENERAL! HOW DOES THE **FANTASTIC FOUR** PROPOSE TO CATCH **THE HULK?**

HI!

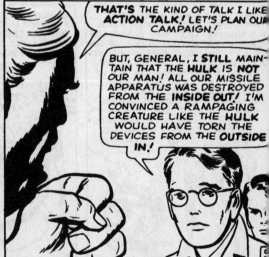

THAT'S THE KIND OF TALK I LIKE **ACTION TALK!** LET'S PLAN OUR CAMPAIGN!

BUT, GENERAL, I **STILL** MAINTAIN THAT THE **HULK** IS **NOT** OUR MAN! ALL OUR MISSILE APPARATUS WAS DESTROYED FROM THE **INSIDE OUT!** I'M CONVINCED A RAMPAGING CREATURE LIKE THE HULK WOULD HAVE TORN THE DEVICES FROM THE **OUTSIDE IN!**

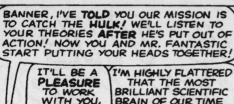

BANNER, I'VE TOLD YOU OUR MISSION IS TO CATCH THE *HULK!* WE'LL LISTEN TO YOUR THEORIES *AFTER* HE'S PUT OUT OF ACTION! NOW YOU AND MR. FANTASTIC START PUTTING YOUR HEADS TOGETHER!

IT'LL BE A *PLEASURE* TO WORK WITH YOU, DR. BANNER! I'VE LONG BEEN AN ADMIRER OF YOUR ATOMIC RESEARCH!

I'M HIGHLY FLATTERED THAT THE MOST BRILLIANT SCIENTIFIC BRAIN OF OUR TIME SHOULD SAY THAT TO ME!

WELL, YOU GENTLEMEN WON'T BE NEEDING ME FOR A WHILE! I'LL GET BACK TO MY WORK!

HEY, SHORTY, HOW MUCH LONGER THEY GONNA KEEP US COOLIN' OUR HEELS OUT HERE?

GASP! WHA-WHAT ARE YOU??!

S'MATTER -- AIN'T YOU NEVER SEEN A *THING* BEFORE??

I'M GETTIN' *FED UP* WITH GUYS DOIN' DOUBLE-TAKES EVERY TIME THEY SEE ME!

LOOK AT 'IM GO! I THINK YOU SCARED THE POOR GUY OUTTA A YEAR'S GROWTH, THING!

AND *HE* CAN'T SPARE IT!

HEY -- HE DROPPED HIS WALLET!

RELAX, BIG FELLA! I'LL GET IT FOR HIM!

I'VE BEEN *WANTING* TO TRY THIS FLAMING LASSO TRICK SINCE I DREAMED IT UP!

NOT BAD, EH? AND I DIDN'T EVEN SINGE THE LEATHER!

I AIN'T IN THE MOOD FOR TRICKS! THEY CAN'T KEEP *ME* WAITIN' OUT HERE ANY LONGER!

OKAY, SOLDIER BOYS! READY OR NOT, HERE I COME!

THING! DON'T! IT'S A PRIVATE MEETING!

EASY WITH THAT CHOPPER, SARGE! WE'RE ON *YOUR* TEAM!

THING! WHAT ARE YOU *DOING??* HAVE YOU LOST YOUR *SENSES?!!*

10

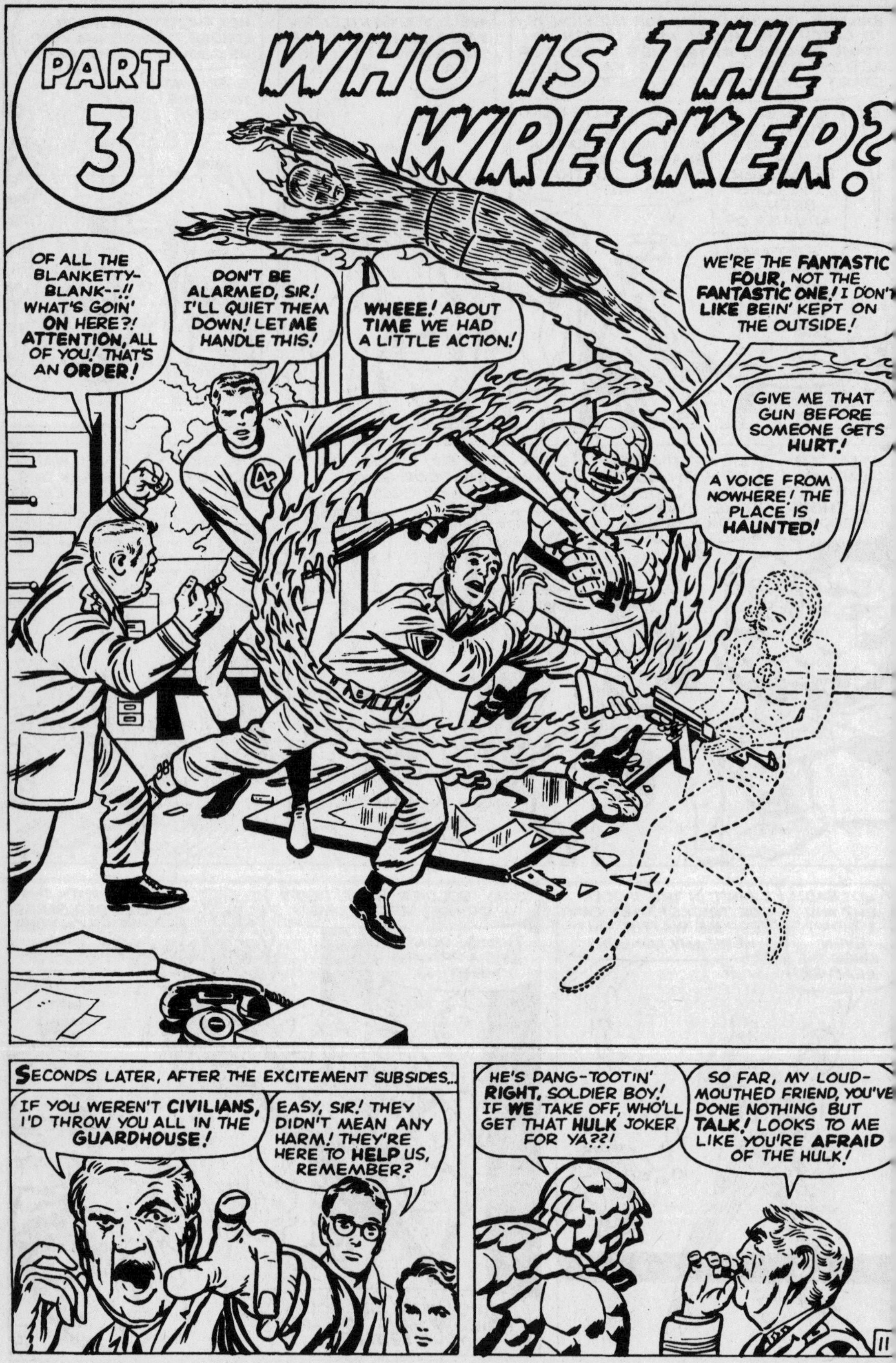
PART 3
WHO IS THE WRECKER?
OF ALL THE BLANKETTY-BLANK--!! WHAT'S GOIN' ON HERE?! ATTENTION, ALL OF YOU! THAT'S AN ORDER!
DON'T BE ALARMED, SIR! I'LL QUIET THEM DOWN! LET ME HANDLE THIS!
WHEEE! ABOUT TIME WE HAD A LITTLE ACTION!
WE'RE THE FANTASTIC FOUR, NOT THE FANTASTIC ONE! I DON'T LIKE BEIN' KEPT ON THE OUTSIDE!
GIVE ME THAT GUN BEFORE SOMEONE GETS HURT!
A VOICE FROM NOWHERE! THE PLACE IS HAUNTED!
SECONDS LATER, AFTER THE EXCITEMENT SUBSIDES...
IF YOU WEREN'T CIVILIANS, I'D THROW YOU ALL IN THE GUARDHOUSE!
EASY, SIR! THEY DIDN'T MEAN ANY HARM! THEY'RE HERE TO HELP US, REMEMBER?
HE'S DANG-TOOTIN' RIGHT, SOLDIER BOY! IF WE TAKE OFF, WHO'LL GET THAT HULK JOKER FOR YA??!
SO FAR, MY LOUD-MOUTHED FRIEND, YOU'VE DONE NOTHING BUT TALK! LOOKS TO ME LIKE YOU'RE AFRAID OF THE HULK!
11

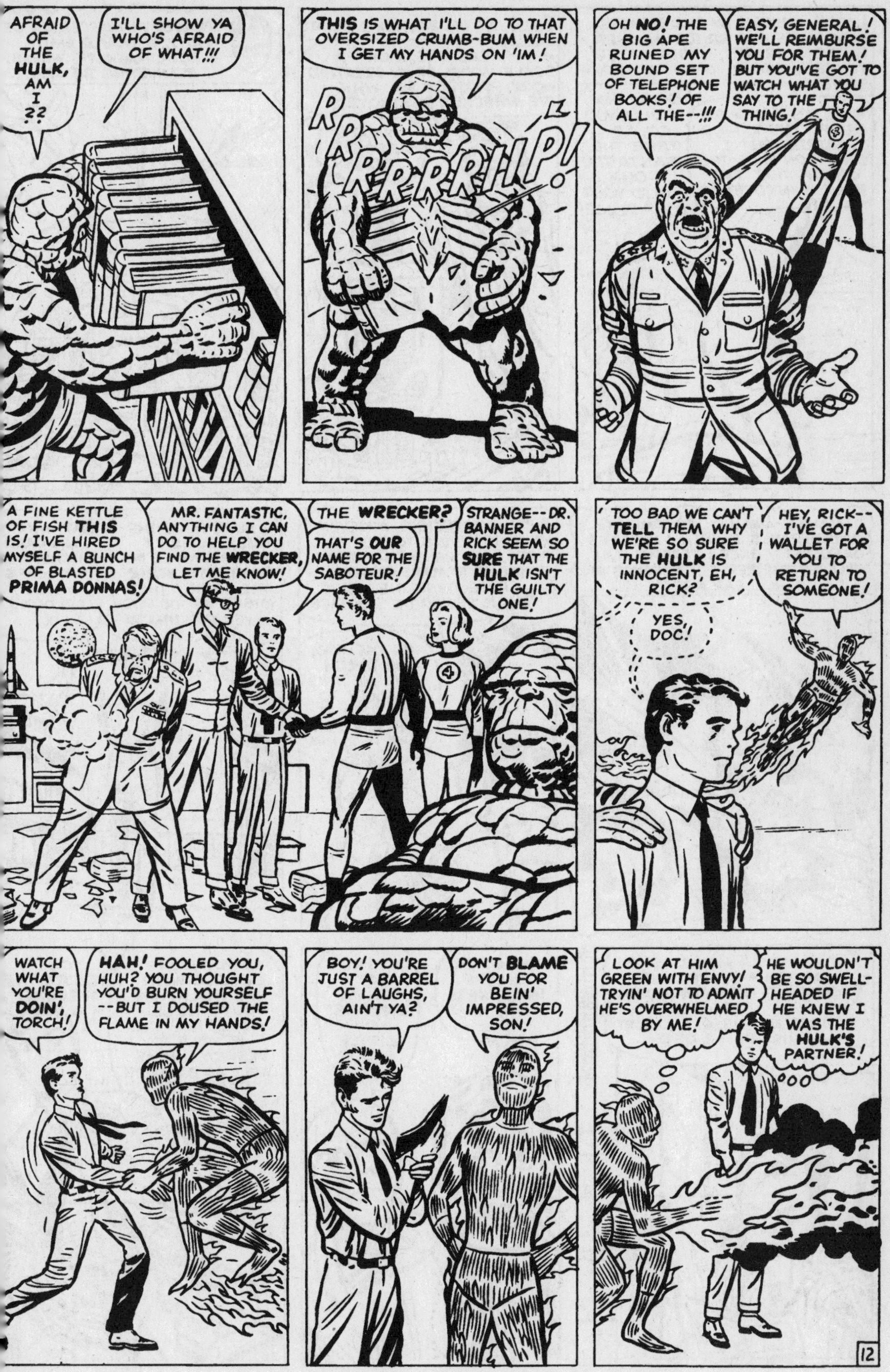

AFRAID OF THE HULK, AM I ??
I'LL SHOW YA WHO'S AFRAID OF WHAT!!!
THIS IS WHAT I'LL DO TO THAT OVERSIZED CRUMB-BUM WHEN I GET MY HANDS ON 'IM!
RRRRRRRIIP!
OH NO! THE BIG APE RUINED MY BOUND SET OF TELEPHONE BOOKS! OF ALL THE--!!!
EASY, GENERAL! WE'LL REIMBURSE YOU FOR THEM! BUT YOU'VE GOT TO WATCH WHAT YOU SAY TO THE THING!
A FINE KETTLE OF FISH THIS IS! I'VE HIRED MYSELF A BUNCH OF BLASTED PRIMA DONNAS!
MR. FANTASTIC, ANYTHING I CAN DO TO HELP YOU FIND THE WRECKER, LET ME KNOW!
THE WRECKER?
THAT'S OUR NAME FOR THE SABOTEUR!
STRANGE--DR. BANNER AND RICK SEEM SO SURE THAT THE HULK ISN'T THE GUILTY ONE!
TOO BAD WE CAN'T TELL THEM WHY WE'RE SO SURE THE HULK IS INNOCENT, EH, RICK?
YES, DOC!
HEY, RICK--I'VE GOT A WALLET FOR YOU TO RETURN TO SOMEONE!
WATCH WHAT YOU'RE DOIN', TORCH!
HAH! FOOLED YOU, HUH? YOU THOUGHT YOU'D BURN YOURSELF --BUT I DOUSED THE FLAME IN MY HANDS!
BOY! YOU'RE JUST A BARREL OF LAUGHS, AIN'T YA?
DON'T BLAME YOU FOR BEIN' IMPRESSED, SON!
LOOK AT HIM GREEN WITH ENVY! TRYIN' NOT TO ADMIT HE'S OVERWHELMED BY ME!
HE WOULDN'T BE SO SWELL-HEADED IF HE KNEW I WAS THE HULK'S PARTNER!
12

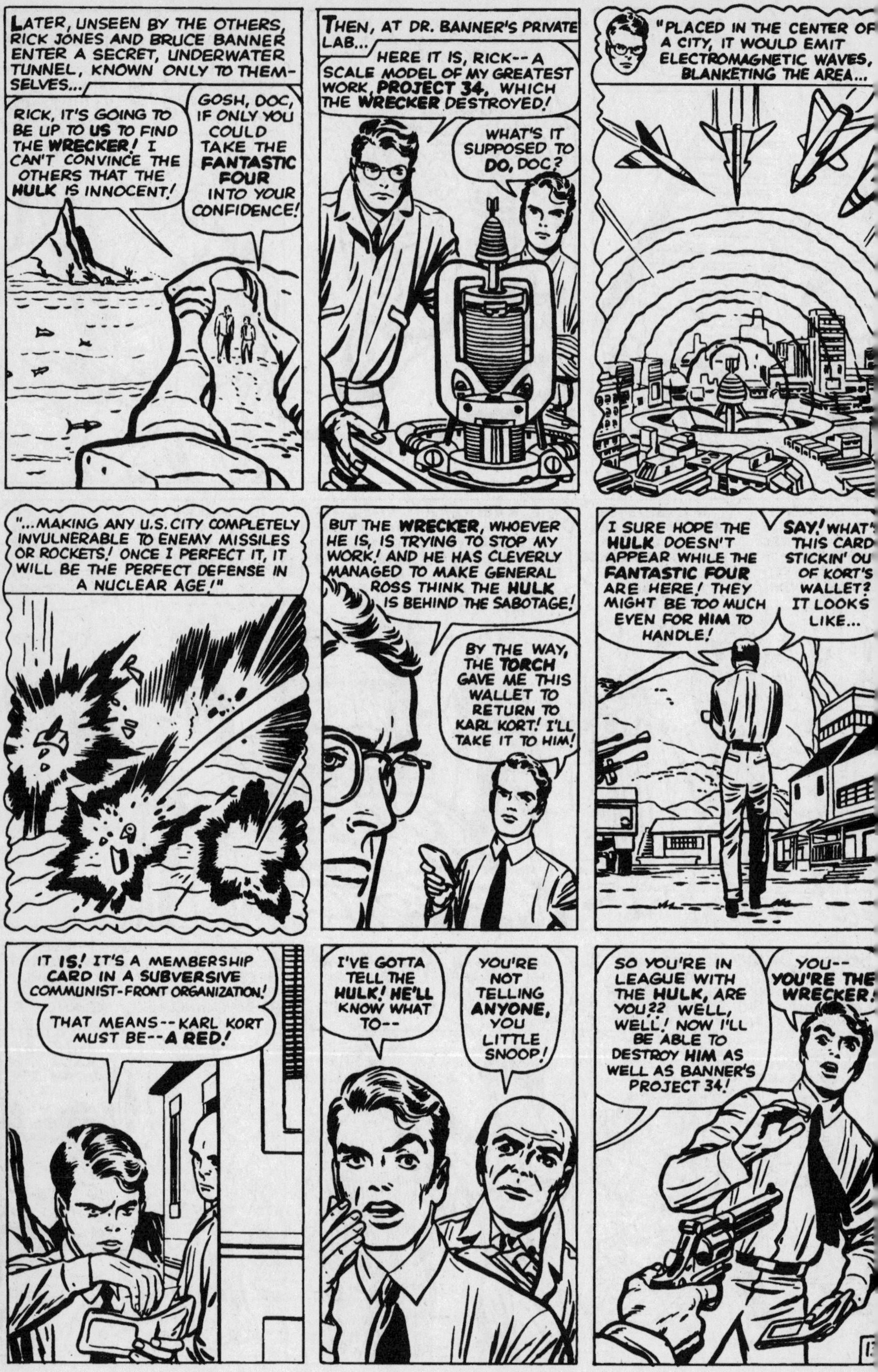
LATER, UNSEEN BY THE OTHERS, RICK JONES AND BRUCE BANNER ENTER A SECRET, UNDERWATER TUNNEL, KNOWN ONLY TO THEMSELVES...
RICK, IT'S GOING TO BE UP TO US TO FIND THE WRECKER! I CAN'T CONVINCE THE OTHERS THAT THE HULK IS INNOCENT!
GOSH, DOC, IF ONLY YOU COULD TAKE THE FANTASTIC FOUR INTO YOUR CONFIDENCE!
THEN, AT DR. BANNER'S PRIVATE LAB...
HERE IT IS, RICK-- A SCALE MODEL OF MY GREATEST WORK, PROJECT 34, WHICH THE WRECKER DESTROYED!
WHAT'S IT SUPPOSED TO DO, DOC?
"PLACED IN THE CENTER OF A CITY, IT WOULD EMIT ELECTROMAGNETIC WAVES, BLANKETING THE AREA...
"...MAKING ANY U.S. CITY COMPLETELY INVULNERABLE TO ENEMY MISSILES OR ROCKETS! ONCE I PERFECT IT, IT WILL BE THE PERFECT DEFENSE IN A NUCLEAR AGE!"
BUT THE WRECKER, WHOEVER HE IS, IS TRYING TO STOP MY WORK! AND HE HAS CLEVERLY MANAGED TO MAKE GENERAL ROSS THINK THE HULK IS BEHIND THE SABOTAGE!
BY THE WAY, THE TORCH GAVE ME THIS WALLET TO RETURN TO KARL KORT! I'LL TAKE IT TO HIM!
I SURE HOPE THE HULK DOESN'T APPEAR WHILE THE FANTASTIC FOUR ARE HERE! THEY MIGHT BE TOO MUCH EVEN FOR HIM TO HANDLE!
SAY! WHAT'S THIS CARD STICKIN' OU OF KORT'S WALLET? IT LOOKS LIKE...
IT IS! IT'S A MEMBERSHIP CARD IN A SUBVERSIVE COMMUNIST-FRONT ORGANIZATION!
THAT MEANS--KARL KORT MUST BE--A RED!
I'VE GOTTA TELL THE HULK! HE'LL KNOW WHAT TO--
YOU'RE NOT TELLING ANYONE, YOU LITTLE SNOOP!
SO YOU'RE IN LEAGUE WITH THE HULK, ARE YOU?? WELL, WELL! NOW I'LL BE ABLE TO DESTROY HIM AS WELL AS BANNER'S PROJECT 34!
YOU-- YOU'RE THE WRECKER!
13

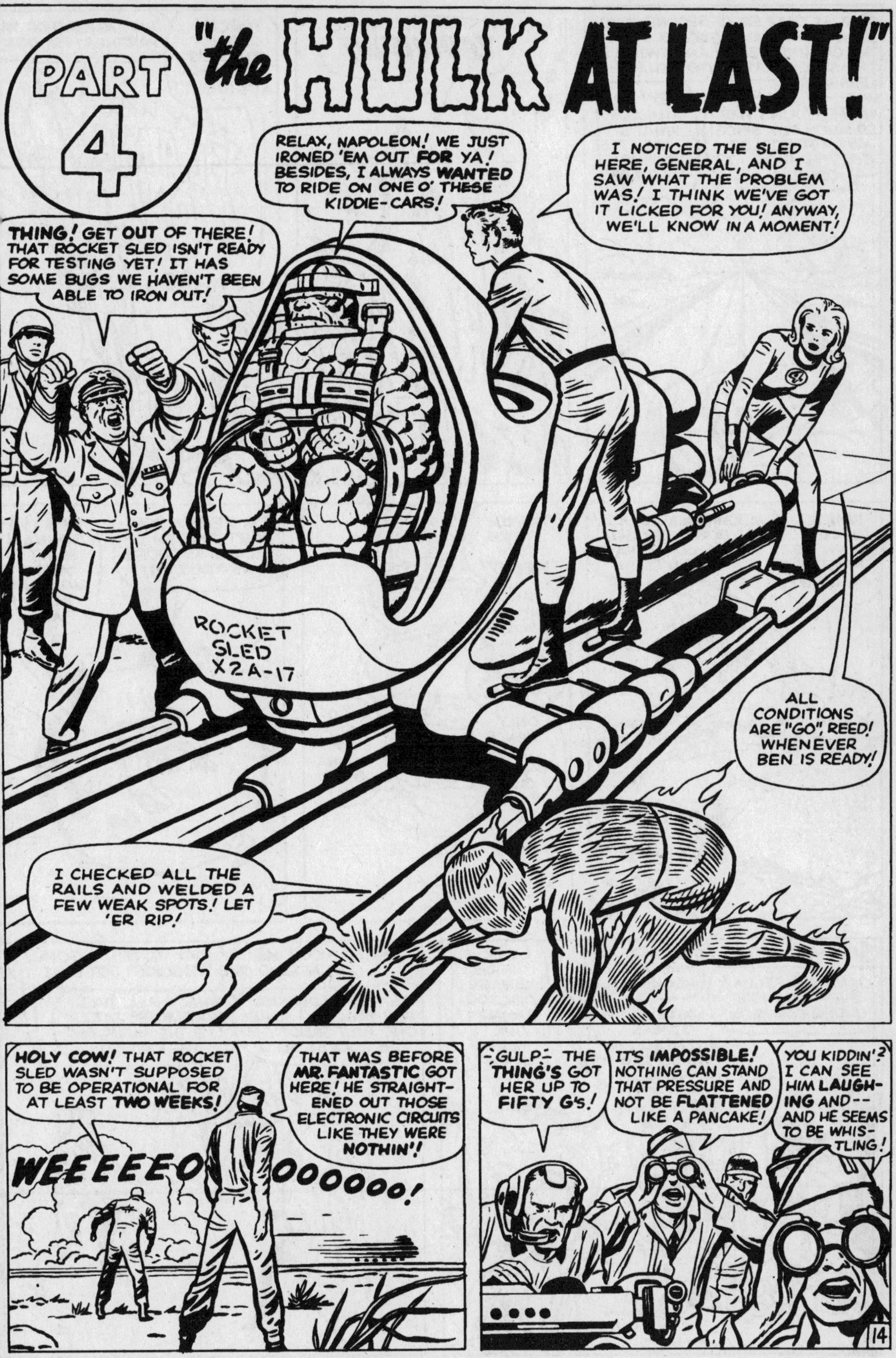

PART 4
"the HULK AT LAST!"
RELAX, NAPOLEON! WE JUST IRONED 'EM OUT FOR YA! BESIDES, I ALWAYS WANTED TO RIDE ON ONE O' THESE KIDDIE-CARS!
I NOTICED THE SLED HERE, GENERAL, AND I SAW WHAT THE PROBLEM WAS! I THINK WE'VE GOT IT LICKED FOR YOU! ANYWAY, WE'LL KNOW IN A MOMENT!
THING! GET OUT OF THERE! THAT ROCKET SLED ISN'T READY FOR TESTING YET! IT HAS SOME BUGS WE HAVEN'T BEEN ABLE TO IRON OUT!
ROCKET SLED X2A-17
ALL CONDITIONS ARE "GO", REED! WHENEVER BEN IS READY!
I CHECKED ALL THE RAILS AND WELDED A FEW WEAK SPOTS! LET 'ER RIP!
HOLY COW! THAT ROCKET SLED WASN'T SUPPOSED TO BE OPERATIONAL FOR AT LEAST TWO WEEKS!
THAT WAS BEFORE MR. FANTASTIC GOT HERE! HE STRAIGHT-ENED OUT THOSE ELECTRONIC CIRCUITS LIKE THEY WERE NOTHIN'!
WEEEEEEOOOOOOOO!
-GULP- THE THING'S GOT HER UP TO FIFTY G'S!
IT'S IMPOSSIBLE! NOTHING CAN STAND THAT PRESSURE AND NOT BE FLATTENED LIKE A PANCAKE!
YOU KIDDIN'? I CAN SEE HIM LAUGH-ING AND-- AND HE SEEMS TO BE WHIS-TLING!
14

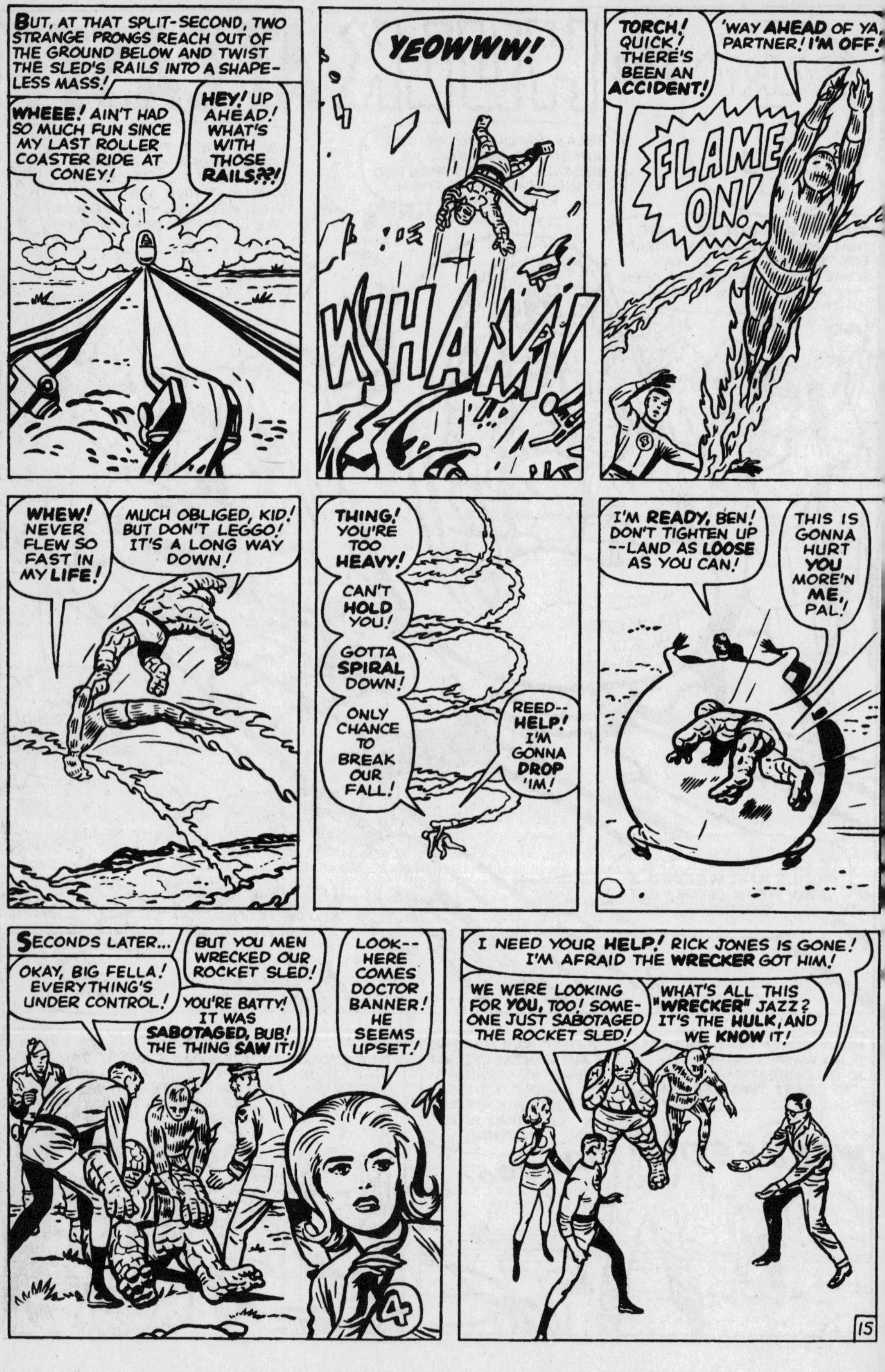

BUT, AT THAT SPLIT-SECOND, TWO STRANGE PRONGS REACH OUT OF THE GROUND BELOW AND TWIST THE SLED'S RAILS INTO A SHAPE-LESS MASS!
WHEEE! AIN'T HAD SO MUCH FUN SINCE MY LAST ROLLER COASTER RIDE AT CONEY!
HEY! UP AHEAD! WHAT'S WITH THOSE RAILS??!
YEOWWW!
WHAM!
TORCH! QUICK! THERE'S BEEN AN ACCIDENT!
'WAY AHEAD OF YA, PARTNER! I'M OFF!
FLAME ON!
WHEW! NEVER FLEW SO FAST IN MY LIFE!
MUCH OBLIGED, KID! BUT DON'T LEGGO! IT'S A LONG WAY DOWN!
THING! YOU'RE TOO HEAVY!
CAN'T HOLD YOU!
GOTTA SPIRAL DOWN!
ONLY CHANCE TO BREAK OUR FALL!
REED-- HELP! I'M GONNA DROP 'IM!
I'M READY, BEN! DON'T TIGHTEN UP --LAND AS LOOSE AS YOU CAN!
THIS IS GONNA HURT YOU MORE'N ME, PAL!
SECONDS LATER...
OKAY, BIG FELLA! EVERYTHING'S UNDER CONTROL!
BUT YOU MEN WRECKED OUR ROCKET SLED!
YOU'RE BATTY! IT WAS SABOTAGED, BUB! THE THING SAW IT!
LOOK-- HERE COMES DOCTOR BANNER! HE SEEMS UPSET!
I NEED YOUR HELP! RICK JONES IS GONE! I'M AFRAID THE WRECKER GOT HIM!
WE WERE LOOKING FOR YOU, TOO! SOME-ONE JUST SABOTAGED THE ROCKET SLED!
WHAT'S ALL THIS "WRECKER" JAZZ? IT'S THE HULK, AND WE KNOW IT!
15

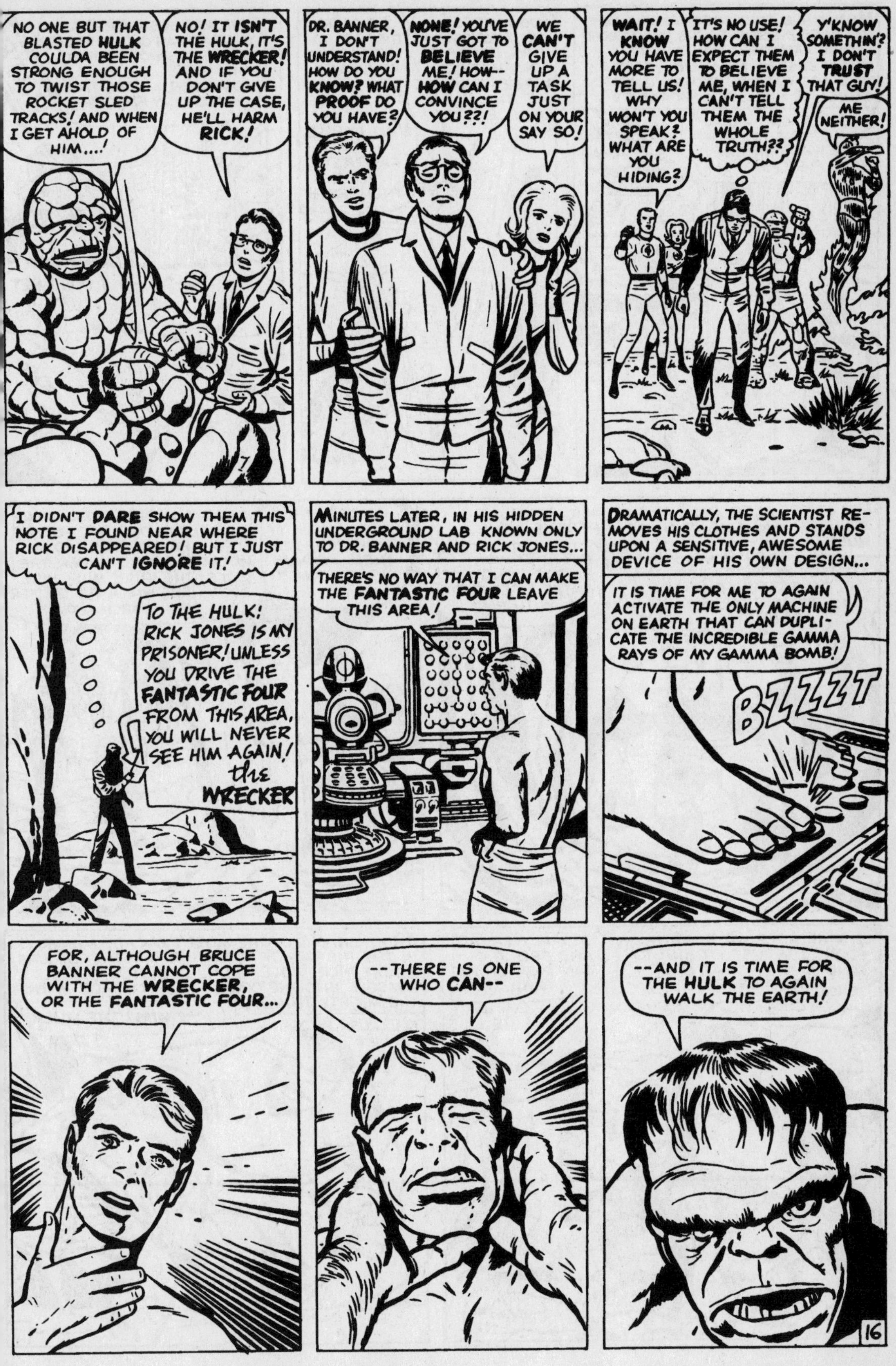

NO ONE BUT THAT BLASTED HULK COULDA BEEN STRONG ENOUGH TO TWIST THOSE ROCKET SLED TRACKS! AND WHEN I GET AHOLD OF HIM....!
NO! IT ISN'T THE HULK, IT'S THE WRECKER! AND IF YOU DON'T GIVE UP THE CASE, HE'LL HARM RICK!
DR. BANNER, I DON'T UNDERSTAND! HOW DO YOU KNOW? WHAT PROOF DO YOU HAVE?
NONE! YOU'VE JUST GOT TO BELIEVE ME! HOW-- HOW CAN I CONVINCE YOU??!
WE CAN'T GIVE UP A TASK JUST ON YOUR SAY SO!
WAIT! I KNOW YOU HAVE MORE TO TELL US! WHY WON'T YOU SPEAK? WHAT ARE YOU HIDING?
IT'S NO USE! HOW CAN I EXPECT THEM TO BELIEVE ME, WHEN I CAN'T TELL THEM THE WHOLE TRUTH??
Y'KNOW SOMETHIN'? I DON'T TRUST THAT GUY!
ME NEITHER!
I DIDN'T DARE SHOW THEM THIS NOTE I FOUND NEAR WHERE RICK DISAPPEARED! BUT I JUST CAN'T IGNORE IT!
TO THE HULK! RICK JONES IS MY PRISONER! UNLESS YOU DRIVE THE FANTASTIC FOUR FROM THIS AREA, YOU WILL NEVER SEE HIM AGAIN! the WRECKER
MINUTES LATER, IN HIS HIDDEN UNDERGROUND LAB KNOWN ONLY TO DR. BANNER AND RICK JONES...
THERE'S NO WAY THAT I CAN MAKE THE FANTASTIC FOUR LEAVE THIS AREA!
DRAMATICALLY, THE SCIENTIST REMOVES HIS CLOTHES AND STANDS UPON A SENSITIVE, AWESOME DEVICE OF HIS OWN DESIGN...
IT IS TIME FOR ME TO AGAIN ACTIVATE THE ONLY MACHINE ON EARTH THAT CAN DUPLICATE THE INCREDIBLE GAMMA RAYS OF MY GAMMA BOMB!
BZZZT
FOR, ALTHOUGH BRUCE BANNER CANNOT COPE WITH THE WRECKER, OR THE FANTASTIC FOUR...
--THERE IS ONE WHO CAN--
--AND IT IS TIME FOR THE HULK TO AGAIN WALK THE EARTH!
16

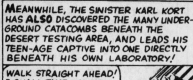

MEANWHILE, THE SINISTER KARL KORT HAS **ALSO** DISCOVERED THE MANY UNDERGROUND CATACOMBS BENEATH THE DESERT TESTING AREA, AND LEADS HIS TEEN-AGE CAPTIVE INTO ONE DIRECTLY BENEATH HIS OWN LABORATORY!

WALK STRAIGHT AHEAD! I SHALL TAKE YOU TO A PLACE WHERE **NO ONE** SHALL EVER FIND YOU!

YOU AIN'T GONNA GET **AWAY** WITH THIS, DADDY-O! NO MATTER **WHERE** YOU TAKE ME, THE HULK WILL FIND ME!

I BEG TO DIFFER, MY ARROGANT FRIEND! I SHALL HANDLE THE **HULK** AS EASILY AS I SHALL DISPOSE OF THE **FANTASTIC FOUR** THEMSELVES!

WE ARE NOW DIRECTLY BENEATH AN OLD, DESERTED WESTERN GHOST TOWN! THIS SHALL BE YOUR HOME FOR A LONG TIME --POSSIBLY **FOREVER**!

DON'T **BET** ON IT, GRAMPS!

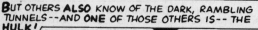

BUT OTHERS **ALSO** KNOW OF THE DARK, RAMBLING TUNNELS --AND **ONE** OF THOSE OTHERS IS -- THE **HULK**!

I OUGHTTA BE UNDER PROJECT 34 PRETTY SOON, AND THE **FANTASTIC FOUR** ARE SURE TO BE SOMEWHERE AROUND!

BUT THEY WON'T BE FOR LONG, NOT AFTER **I** GET THRU WITH 'EM!

VOICES! THIS IS BETTER'N I EXPECTED! IT'S **THEM** --COMIN' RIGHT TOWARD ME!

I HAD A **HUNCH** THERE WERE TUNNELS UNDER THAT ROCKET SLED! THE GROUND HAD A **HOLLOW** SOUND UNDER THE RAILS! THE **HULK** MUST HIDE DOWN HERE WHILE THE SOLDIER BOYS SEARCH ABOVE!

I SURE HOPE WE **FIND** 'IM SOON! I'M JUST **ITCHIN'** TO TANGLE WITH THAT OVER-RATED CREEP!

I'LL FLY AHEAD AND SEE IF I CAN PICK UP HIS TRAIL!

AND THEN, ONE OF THE MOST DRAMATIC MOMENTS IN THE HISTORY OF ADVENTURE-FANTASY OCCURS, AS THE INCREDIBLE **HULK** SUDDENLY HURLS HIMSELF INTO THE OPEN, FACE-TO-FACE WITH THE MIGHTY **THING**!

I'LL CRUSH YOU LIKE A FLEA!

IT'S **HIM**! THE HULK!

17

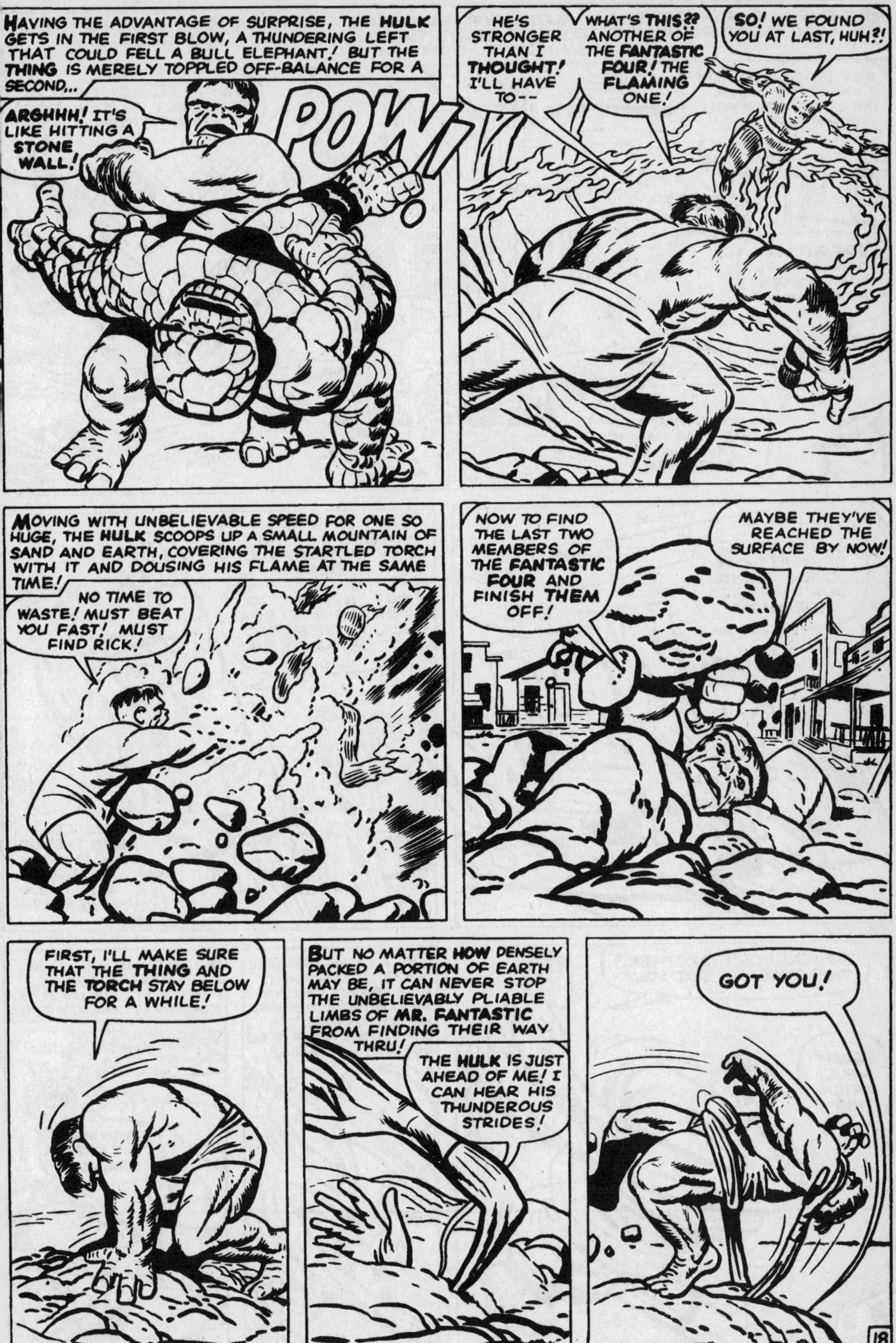
HAVING THE ADVANTAGE OF SURPRISE, THE HULK GETS IN THE FIRST BLOW, A THUNDERING LEFT THAT COULD FELL A BULL ELEPHANT! BUT THE THING IS MERELY TOPPLED OFF-BALANCE FOR A SECOND...
ARGHHH! IT'S LIKE HITTING A STONE WALL!
POW!
HE'S STRONGER THAN I THOUGHT! I'LL HAVE TO--
WHAT'S THIS?? ANOTHER OF THE FANTASTIC FOUR! THE FLAMING ONE!
SO! WE FOUND YOU AT LAST, HUH?!
MOVING WITH UNBELIEVABLE SPEED FOR ONE SO HUGE, THE HULK SCOOPS UP A SMALL MOUNTAIN OF SAND AND EARTH, COVERING THE STARTLED TORCH WITH IT AND DOUSING HIS FLAME AT THE SAME TIME!
NO TIME TO WASTE! MUST BEAT YOU FAST! MUST FIND RICK!
NOW TO FIND THE LAST TWO MEMBERS OF THE FANTASTIC FOUR AND FINISH THEM OFF!
MAYBE THEY'VE REACHED THE SURFACE BY NOW!
FIRST, I'LL MAKE SURE THAT THE THING AND THE TORCH STAY BELOW FOR A WHILE!
BUT NO MATTER HOW DENSELY PACKED A PORTION OF EARTH MAY BE, IT CAN NEVER STOP THE UNBELIEVABLY PLIABLE LIMBS OF MR. FANTASTIC FROM FINDING THEIR WAY THRU!
THE HULK IS JUST AHEAD OF ME! I CAN HEAR HIS THUNDEROUS STRIDES!
GOT YOU!
18

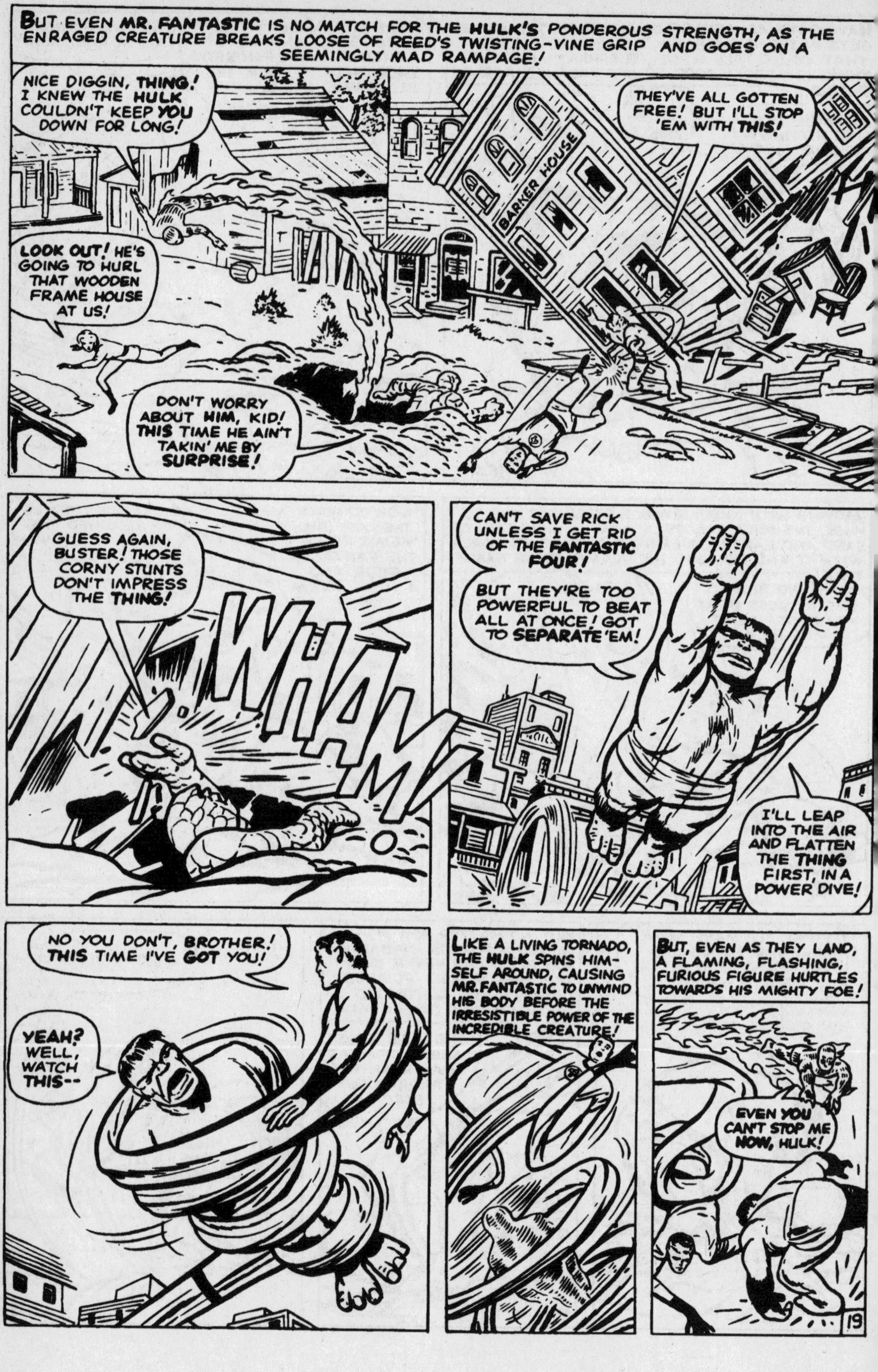

BUT EVEN MR. FANTASTIC IS NO MATCH FOR THE HULK'S PONDEROUS STRENGTH, AS THE ENRAGED CREATURE BREAKS LOOSE OF REED'S TWISTING-VINE GRIP AND GOES ON A SEEMINGLY MAD RAMPAGE!
NICE DIGGIN, THING! I KNEW THE HULK COULDN'T KEEP YOU DOWN FOR LONG!
LOOK OUT! HE'S GOING TO HURL THAT WOODEN FRAME HOUSE AT US!
DON'T WORRY ABOUT HIM, KID! THIS TIME HE AIN'T TAKIN' ME BY SURPRISE!
BARKER HOUSE
THEY'VE ALL GOTTEN FREE! BUT I'LL STOP 'EM WITH THIS!
GUESS AGAIN, BUSTER! THOSE CORNY STUNTS DON'T IMPRESS THE THING!
WHAM!
CAN'T SAVE RICK UNLESS I GET RID OF THE FANTASTIC FOUR!
BUT THEY'RE TOO POWERFUL TO BEAT ALL AT ONCE! GOT TO SEPARATE 'EM!
I'LL LEAP INTO THE AIR AND FLATTEN THE THING FIRST, IN A POWER DIVE!
NO YOU DON'T, BROTHER! THIS TIME I'VE GOT YOU!
YEAH? WELL, WATCH THIS--
LIKE A LIVING TORNADO, THE HULK SPINS HIMSELF AROUND, CAUSING MR. FANTASTIC TO UNWIND HIS BODY BEFORE THE IRRESISTIBLE POWER OF THE INCREDIBLE CREATURE!
BUT, EVEN AS THEY LAND, A FLAMING, FLASHING, FURIOUS FIGURE HURTLES TOWARDS HIS MIGHTY FOE!
EVEN YOU CAN'T STOP ME NOW, HULK!

BUT THE HULK HAS ONE MORE POWER HE CAN USE--ONE THAT NEVER FAILS TO STOP THOSE WHO DO NOT EXPECT IT!

BRACE YOURSELF FOR A LITTLE SURPRISE, YOU FLAMING BRAT!

SO MIGHTY ARE HIS ARMS, THAT WHEN HE CLAPS HIS HANDS TOGETHER WITH FULL FORCE, IT HAS THE EFFECT OF A SUPERSONIC BOOM SHOCK WAVE!

HERE'S A LITTLE LULLABY FROM ME TO YOU!

HA! THAT'LL KEEP 'EM OUTTA ACTION FOR A WHILE!

BUT WHERE'S THE FOURTH ONE? WHERE'S THE THING?

RIGHT HERE, GRUESOME! THERE AIN'T A SOUND YOU CAN LISTEN TO THAT I CAN'T HANDLE ALSO!

WELL, WELL! SO THE BIG BAD HULK IS THROWIN' THINGS, HUH? THAT AIN'T GONNA HELP YOU NOW!

ANYONE CAN FIGHT WITH HIS MOUTH! BUT WHEN I GET MY HANDS ON YOU...

AND SO THE TWO HUMAN BEHEMOTHS MEET HEAD-ON, AS THE VERY EARTH BENEATH THEIR FEET TREMBLES FROM THE IMPACT!

I BEEN LOOKIN' FORWARD TO THIS FOR A LONG, LONG TIME!

NOW I'VE GOT YOU!

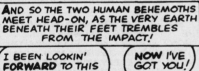

SLOWLY, INEXORABLY, THE LARGER HULK LIFTS THE RAGING THING OFF HIS FEET, AS THE MIND-STAGGERING BATTLE REACHES ITS FINAL CLIMAX! BUT THEN--AT THAT INSTANT--A STRANGE, ATOM-POWERED RAY SHOOTS OUT FROM THE TUNNEL BELOW, AND...

DON'T MOVE, MISTER! MY PILE-DRIVER PUNCH IS COMIN' RIGHT AT YA!

I'LL SMASH YOU TO THE GROUND LIKE A PANCAKE! I'LL-- UGHHHH!

20

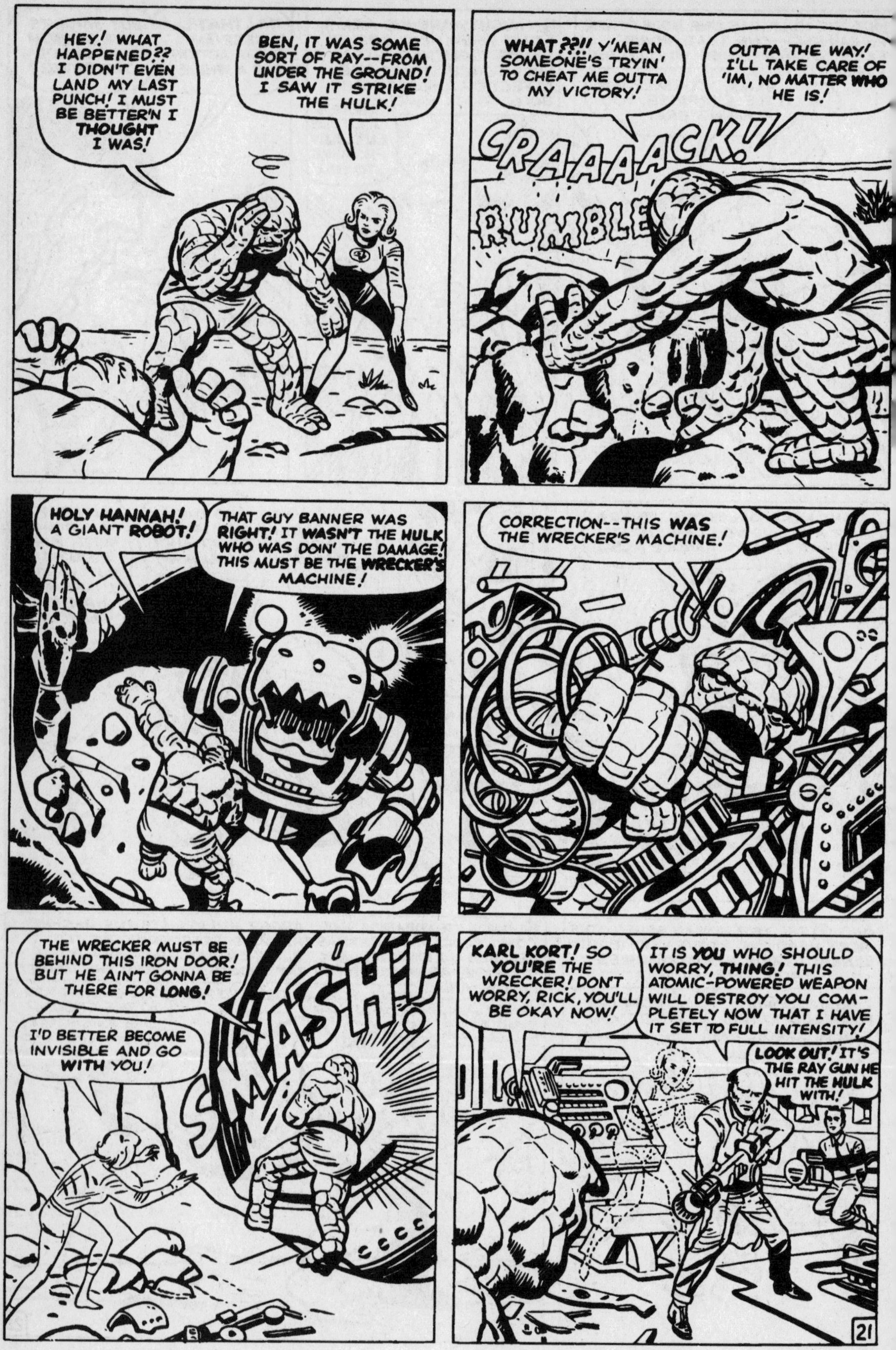
HEY! WHAT HAPPENED?? I DIDN'T EVEN LAND MY LAST PUNCH! I MUST BE BETTER'N I THOUGHT I WAS!
BEN, IT WAS SOME SORT OF RAY--FROM UNDER THE GROUND! I SAW IT STRIKE THE HULK!
WHAT??!! Y'MEAN SOMEONE'S TRYIN' TO CHEAT ME OUTTA MY VICTORY!
OUTTA THE WAY! I'LL TAKE CARE OF 'IM, NO MATTER WHO HE IS!
CRAAAACK!
RUMBLE
HOLY HANNAH! A GIANT ROBOT!
THAT GUY BANNER WAS RIGHT! IT WASN'T THE HULK WHO WAS DOIN' THE DAMAGE! THIS MUST BE THE WRECKER'S MACHINE!
CORRECTION--THIS WAS THE WRECKER'S MACHINE!
THE WRECKER MUST BE BEHIND THIS IRON DOOR! BUT HE AIN'T GONNA BE THERE FOR LONG!
SMASH!
I'D BETTER BECOME INVISIBLE AND GO WITH YOU!
KARL KORT! SO YOU'RE THE WRECKER! DON'T WORRY, RICK, YOU'LL BE OKAY NOW!
IT IS YOU WHO SHOULD WORRY, THING! THIS ATOMIC-POWERED WEAPON WILL DESTROY YOU COMPLETELY NOW THAT I HAVE IT SET TO FULL INTENSITY!
LOOK OUT! IT'S THE RAY GUN HE HIT THE HULK WITH!
21

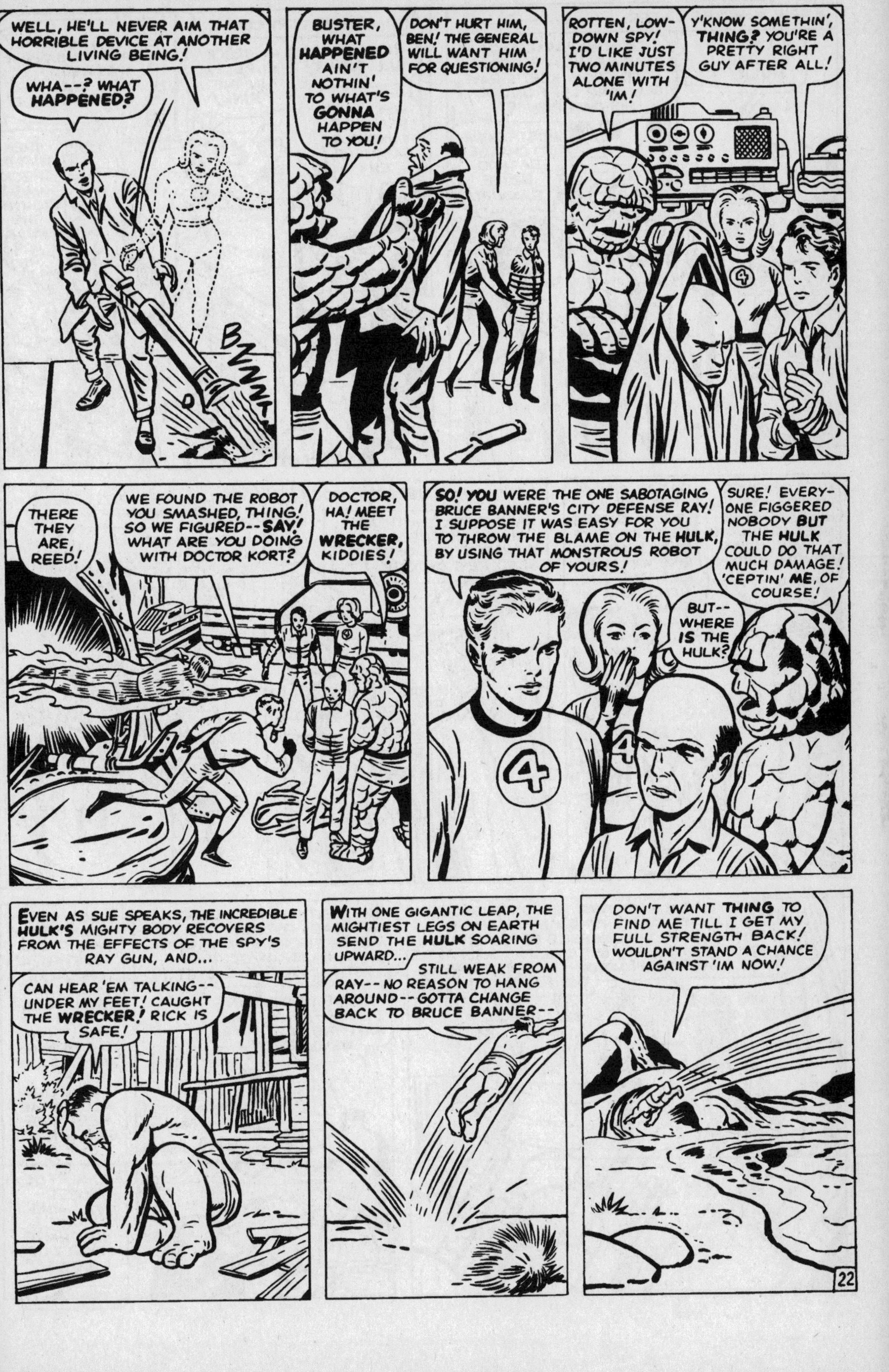

WELL, HE'LL NEVER AIM THAT HORRIBLE DEVICE AT ANOTHER LIVING BEING!
WHA--? WHAT HAPPENED?
BZZZZT
BUSTER, WHAT HAPPENED AIN'T NOTHIN' TO WHAT'S GONNA HAPPEN TO YOU!
DON'T HURT HIM, BEN! THE GENERAL WILL WANT HIM FOR QUESTIONING!
ROTTEN, LOW-DOWN SPY! I'D LIKE JUST TWO MINUTES ALONE WITH 'IM!
Y'KNOW SOMETHIN', THING? YOU'RE A PRETTY RIGHT GUY AFTER ALL!
THERE THEY ARE, REED!
WE FOUND THE ROBOT YOU SMASHED, THING! SO WE FIGURED--SAY! WHAT ARE YOU DOING WITH DOCTOR KORT?
DOCTOR, HA! MEET THE WRECKER, KIDDIES!
SO! YOU WERE THE ONE SABOTAGING BRUCE BANNER'S CITY DEFENSE RAY! I SUPPOSE IT WAS EASY FOR YOU TO THROW THE BLAME ON THE HULK, BY USING THAT MONSTROUS ROBOT OF YOURS!
SURE! EVERY-ONE FIGGERED NOBODY BUT THE HULK COULD DO THAT MUCH DAMAGE! 'CEPTIN' ME, OF COURSE!
BUT--WHERE IS THE HULK?
EVEN AS SUE SPEAKS, THE INCREDIBLE HULK'S MIGHTY BODY RECOVERS FROM THE EFFECTS OF THE SPY'S RAY GUN, AND...
CAN HEAR 'EM TALKING--UNDER MY FEET! CAUGHT THE WRECKER! RICK IS SAFE!
WITH ONE GIGANTIC LEAP, THE MIGHTIEST LEGS ON EARTH SEND THE HULK SOARING UPWARD...
STILL WEAK FROM RAY--NO REASON TO HANG AROUND--GOTTA CHANGE BACK TO BRUCE BANNER--
DON'T WANT THING TO FIND ME TILL I GET MY FULL STRENGTH BACK! WOULDN'T STAND A CHANCE AGAINST 'IM NOW!
22

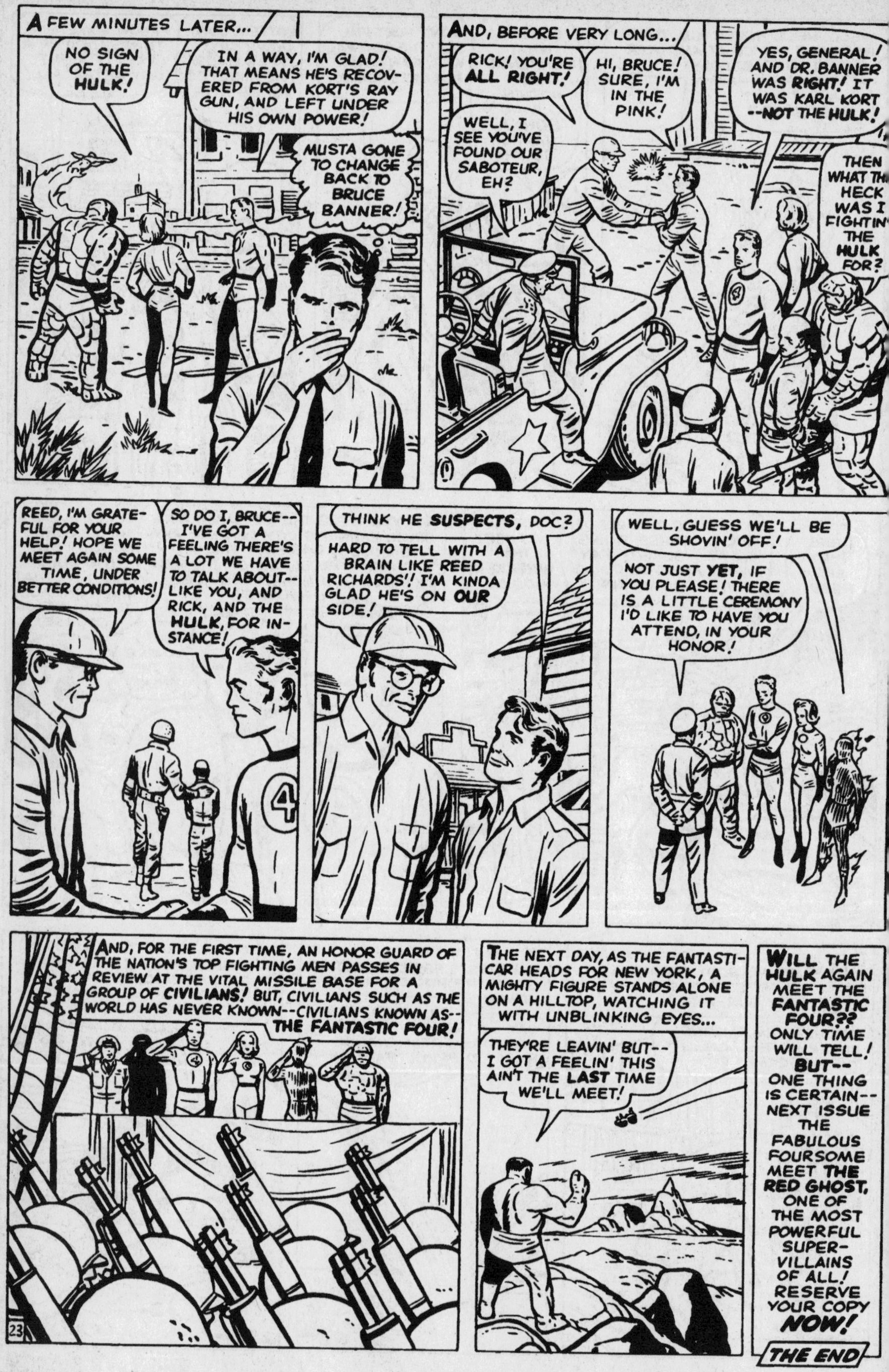
A FEW MINUTES LATER...
NO SIGN OF THE HULK!
IN A WAY, I'M GLAD! THAT MEANS HE'S RECOVERED FROM KORT'S RAY GUN, AND LEFT UNDER HIS OWN POWER!
MUSTA GONE TO CHANGE BACK TO BRUCE BANNER!
AND, BEFORE VERY LONG...
RICK! YOU'RE ALL RIGHT!
HI, BRUCE! SURE, I'M IN THE PINK!
WELL, I SEE YOU'VE FOUND OUR SABOTEUR, EH?
YES, GENERAL! AND DR. BANNER WAS RIGHT! IT WAS KARL KORT --NOT THE HULK!
THEN WHAT TH' HECK WAS I FIGHTIN' THE HULK FOR?
REED, I'M GRATEFUL FOR YOUR HELP! HOPE WE MEET AGAIN SOME TIME, UNDER BETTER CONDITIONS!
SO DO I, BRUCE-- I'VE GOT A FEELING THERE'S A LOT WE HAVE TO TALK ABOUT-- LIKE YOU, AND RICK, AND THE HULK, FOR INSTANCE!
THINK HE SUSPECTS, DOC?
HARD TO TELL WITH A BRAIN LIKE REED RICHARDS'! I'M KINDA GLAD HE'S ON OUR SIDE!
WELL, GUESS WE'LL BE SHOVIN' OFF!
NOT JUST YET, IF YOU PLEASE! THERE IS A LITTLE CEREMONY I'D LIKE TO HAVE YOU ATTEND, IN YOUR HONOR!
AND, FOR THE FIRST TIME, AN HONOR GUARD OF THE NATION'S TOP FIGHTING MEN PASSES IN REVIEW AT THE VITAL MISSILE BASE FOR A GROUP OF CIVILIANS! BUT, CIVILIANS SUCH AS THE WORLD HAS NEVER KNOWN--CIVILIANS KNOWN AS-- THE FANTASTIC FOUR!
23
THE NEXT DAY, AS THE FANTASTI-CAR HEADS FOR NEW YORK, A MIGHTY FIGURE STANDS ALONE ON A HILLTOP, WATCHING IT WITH UNBLINKING EYES...
THEY'RE LEAVIN' BUT-- I GOT A FEELIN' THIS AIN'T THE LAST TIME WE'LL MEET!
WILL THE HULK AGAIN MEET THE FANTASTIC FOUR?? ONLY TIME WILL TELL! BUT-- ONE THING IS CERTAIN-- NEXT ISSUE THE FABULOUS FOURSOME MEET THE RED GHOST, ONE OF THE MOST POWERFUL SUPER-VILLAINS OF ALL! RESERVE YOUR COPY NOW!
THE END

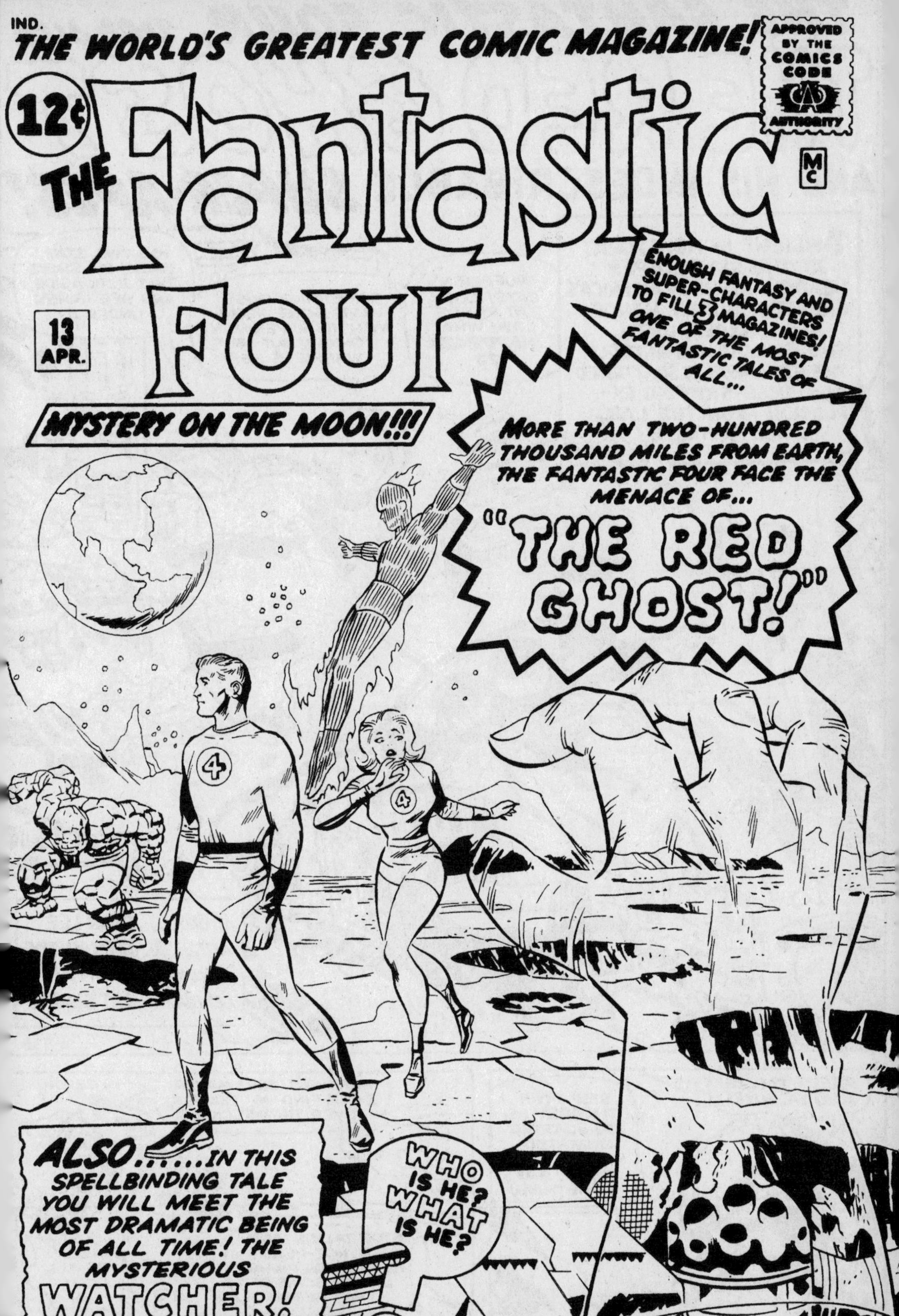
IND.
THE WORLD'S GREATEST COMIC MAGAZINE!
APPROVED BY THE COMICS CODE AUTHORITY
12¢
THE Fantastic Four
MC
13 APR.
ENOUGH FANTASY AND SUPER-CHARACTERS TO FILL 3 MAGAZINES! ONE OF THE MOST FANTASTIC TALES OF ALL...
MYSTERY ON THE MOON!!!
MORE THAN TWO-HUNDRED THOUSAND MILES FROM EARTH, THE FANTASTIC FOUR FACE THE MENACE OF...
"THE RED GHOST!"
ALSO......IN THIS SPELLBINDING TALE YOU WILL MEET THE MOST DRAMATIC BEING OF ALL TIME! THE MYSTERIOUS WATCHER!
WHO IS HE? WHAT IS HE?

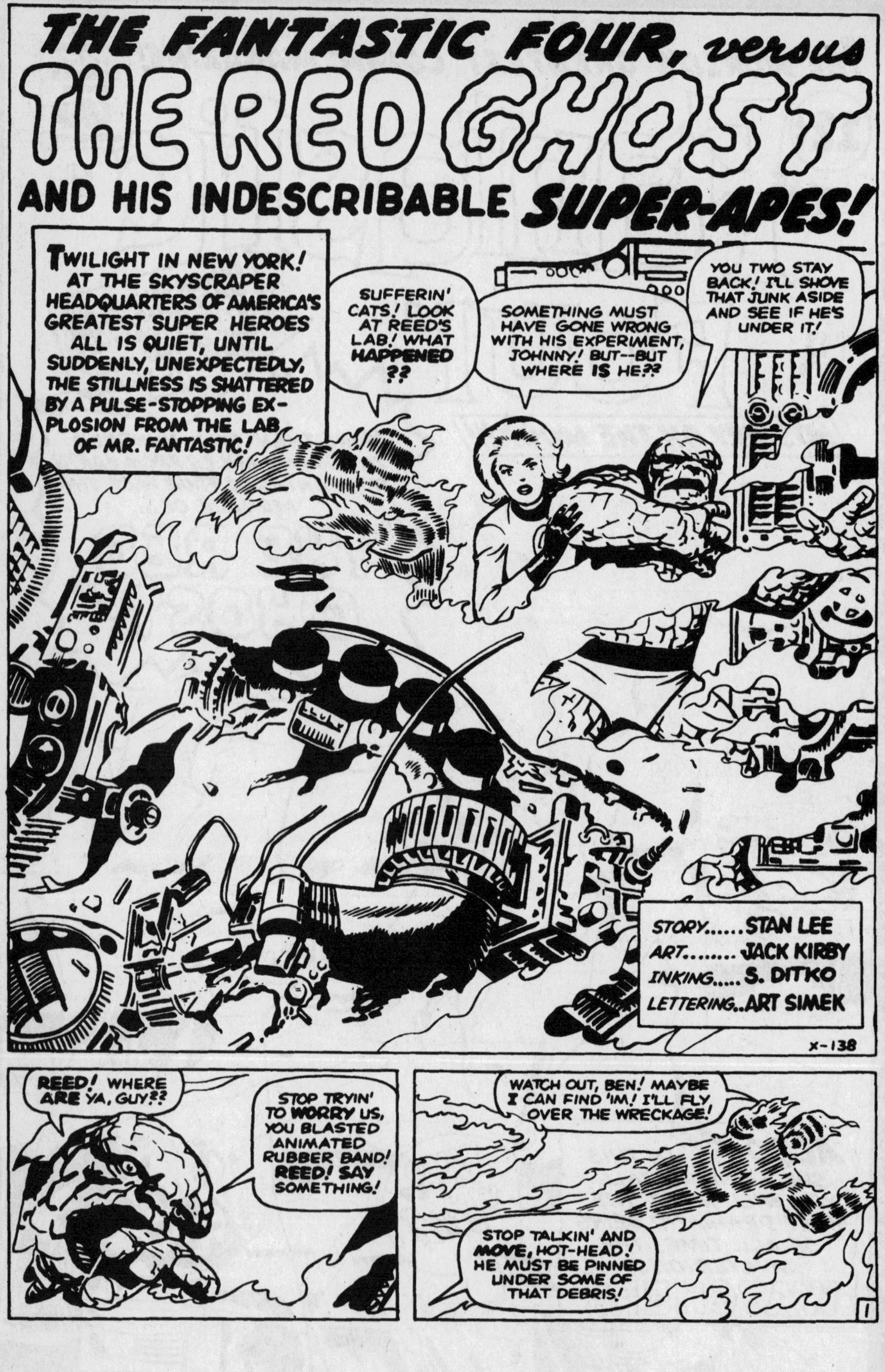
THE FANTASTIC FOUR, versus
THE RED GHOST
AND HIS INDESCRIBABLE SUPER-APES!
TWILIGHT IN NEW YORK! AT THE SKYSCRAPER HEADQUARTERS OF AMERICA'S GREATEST SUPER HEROES ALL IS QUIET, UNTIL SUDDENLY, UNEXPECTEDLY, THE STILLNESS IS SHATTERED BY A PULSE-STOPPING EX-PLOSION FROM THE LAB OF MR. FANTASTIC!
SUFFERIN' CATS! LOOK AT REED'S LAB! WHAT HAPPENED ??
SOMETHING MUST HAVE GONE WRONG WITH HIS EXPERIMENT, JOHNNY! BUT--BUT WHERE IS HE??
YOU TWO STAY BACK! I'LL SHOVE THAT JUNK ASIDE AND SEE IF HE'S UNDER IT!
STORY......STAN LEE
ART........JACK KIRBY
INKING.....S. DITKO
LETTERING..ART SIMEK
X-138
REED! WHERE ARE YA, GUY??
STOP TRYIN' TO WORRY US, YOU BLASTED ANIMATED RUBBER BAND! REED! SAY SOMETHING!
WATCH OUT, BEN! MAYBE I CAN FIND 'IM! I'LL FLY OVER THE WRECKAGE!
STOP TALKIN' AND MOVE, HOT-HEAD! HE MUST BE PINNED UNDER SOME OF THAT DEBRIS!
1

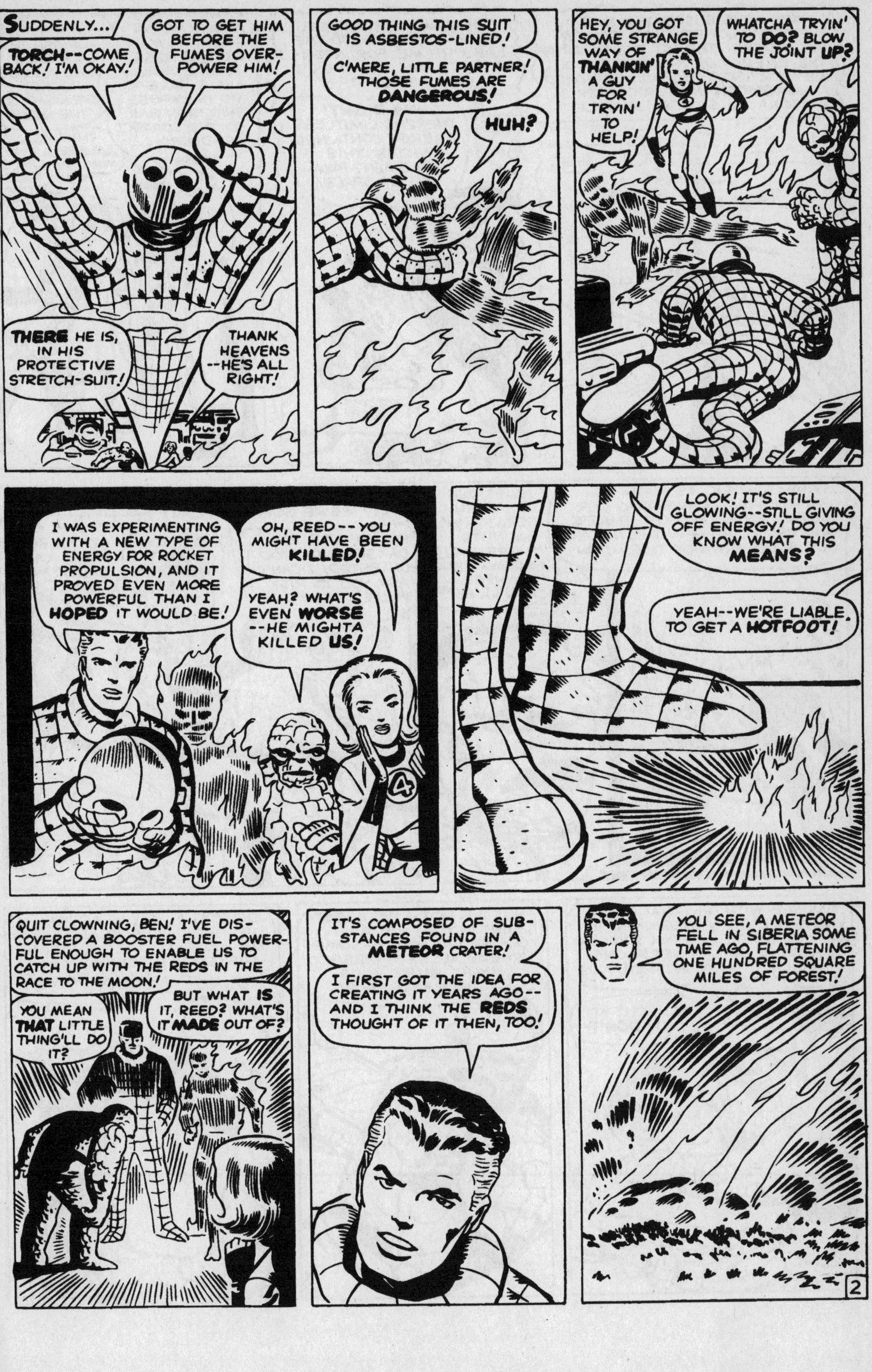
SUDDENLY...
TORCH--COME BACK! I'M OKAY!
GOT TO GET HIM BEFORE THE FUMES OVER-POWER HIM!
THERE HE IS, IN HIS PROTECTIVE STRETCH-SUIT!
THANK HEAVENS --HE'S ALL RIGHT!
GOOD THING THIS SUIT IS ASBESTOS-LINED!
C'MERE, LITTLE PARTNER! THOSE FUMES ARE DANGEROUS!
HUH?
HEY, YOU GOT SOME STRANGE WAY OF THANKIN' A GUY FOR TRYIN' TO HELP!
WHATCHA TRYIN' TO DO? BLOW THE JOINT UP?
I WAS EXPERIMENTING WITH A NEW TYPE OF ENERGY FOR ROCKET PROPULSION, AND IT PROVED EVEN MORE POWERFUL THAN I HOPED IT WOULD BE!
OH, REED--YOU MIGHT HAVE BEEN KILLED!
YEAH? WHAT'S EVEN WORSE --HE MIGHTA KILLED US!
LOOK! IT'S STILL GLOWING--STILL GIVING OFF ENERGY! DO YOU KNOW WHAT THIS MEANS?
YEAH--WE'RE LIABLE TO GET A HOTFOOT!
QUIT CLOWNING, BEN! I'VE DIS-COVERED A BOOSTER FUEL POWER-FUL ENOUGH TO ENABLE US TO CATCH UP WITH THE REDS IN THE RACE TO THE MOON!
YOU MEAN THAT LITTLE THING'LL DO IT?
BUT WHAT IS IT, REED? WHAT'S IT MADE OUT OF?
IT'S COMPOSED OF SUB-STANCES FOUND IN A METEOR CRATER!
I FIRST GOT THE IDEA FOR CREATING IT YEARS AGO-- AND I THINK THE REDS THOUGHT OF IT THEN, TOO!
YOU SEE, A METEOR FELL IN SIBERIA SOME TIME AGO, FLATTENING ONE HUNDRED SQUARE MILES OF FOREST!
2

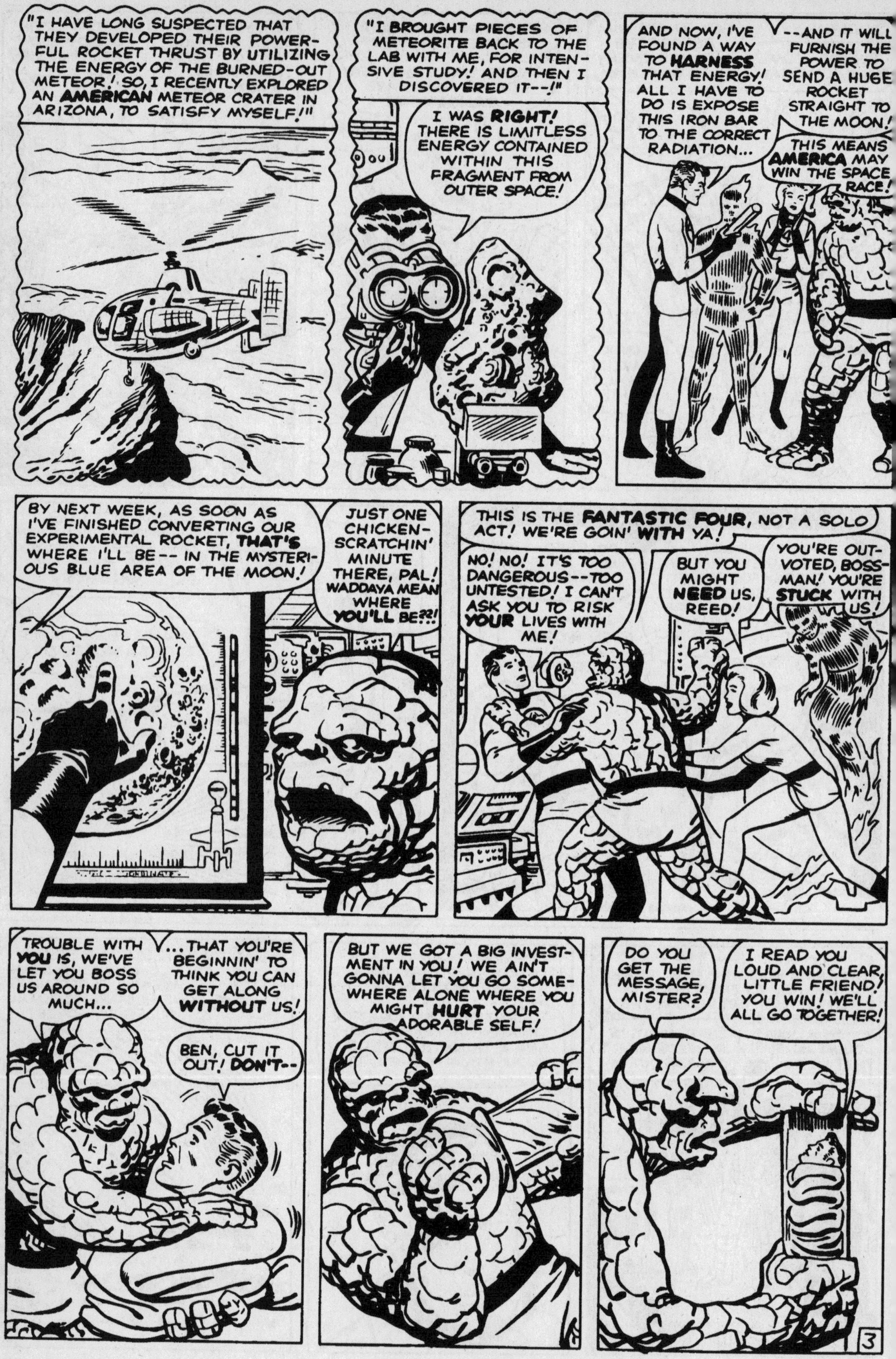
"I HAVE LONG SUSPECTED THAT THEY DEVELOPED THEIR POWERFUL ROCKET THRUST BY UTILIZING THE ENERGY OF THE BURNED-OUT METEOR! SO, I RECENTLY EXPLORED AN AMERICAN METEOR CRATER IN ARIZONA, TO SATISFY MYSELF!"
"I BROUGHT PIECES OF METEORITE BACK TO THE LAB WITH ME, FOR INTENSIVE STUDY! AND THEN I DISCOVERED IT--!"
I WAS RIGHT! THERE IS LIMITLESS ENERGY CONTAINED WITHIN THIS FRAGMENT FROM OUTER SPACE!
AND NOW, I'VE FOUND A WAY TO HARNESS THAT ENERGY! ALL I HAVE TO DO IS EXPOSE THIS IRON BAR TO THE CORRECT RADIATION...
--AND IT WILL FURNISH THE POWER TO SEND A HUGE ROCKET STRAIGHT TO THE MOON!
THIS MEANS AMERICA MAY WIN THE SPACE RACE!
BY NEXT WEEK, AS SOON AS I'VE FINISHED CONVERTING OUR EXPERIMENTAL ROCKET, THAT'S WHERE I'LL BE-- IN THE MYSTERIOUS BLUE AREA OF THE MOON!
JUST ONE CHICKEN-SCRATCHIN' MINUTE THERE, PAL! WADDAYA MEAN WHERE YOU'LL BE??!
THIS IS THE FANTASTIC FOUR, NOT A SOLO ACT! WE'RE GOIN' WITH YA!
NO! NO! IT'S TOO DANGEROUS--TOO UNTESTED! I CAN'T ASK YOU TO RISK YOUR LIVES WITH ME!
BUT YOU MIGHT NEED US, REED!
YOU'RE OUT-VOTED, BOSS-MAN! YOU'RE STUCK WITH US!
TROUBLE WITH YOU IS, WE'VE LET YOU BOSS US AROUND SO MUCH...
...THAT YOU'RE BEGINNIN' TO THINK YOU CAN GET ALONG WITHOUT US!
BEN, CUT IT OUT! DON'T--
BUT WE GOT A BIG INVESTMENT IN YOU! WE AIN'T GONNA LET YOU GO SOMEWHERE ALONE WHERE YOU MIGHT HURT YOUR ADORABLE SELF!
DO YOU GET THE MESSAGE, MISTER?
I READ YOU LOUD AND CLEAR, LITTLE FRIEND! YOU WIN! WE'LL ALL GO TOGETHER!

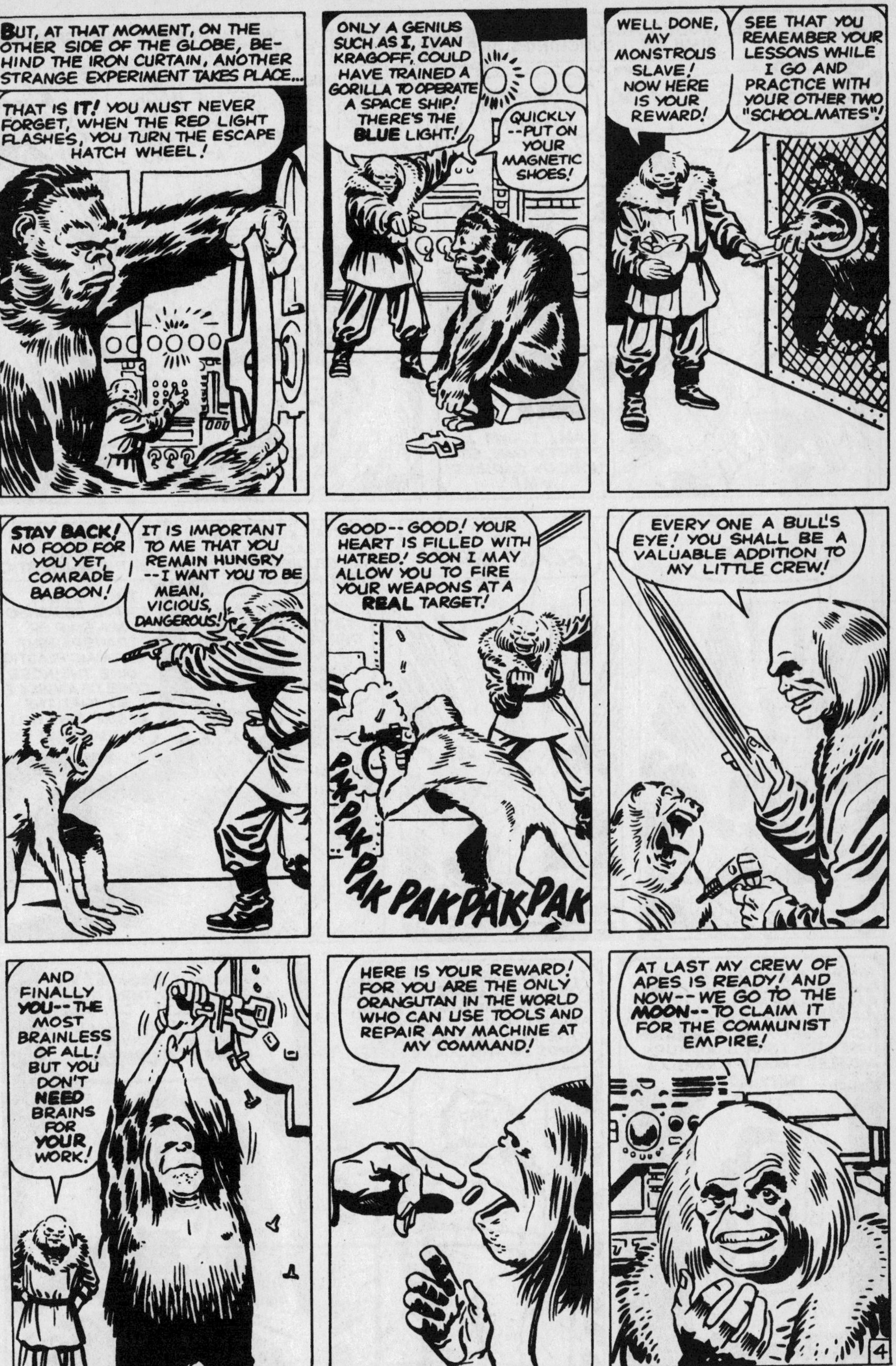

BUT, AT THAT MOMENT, ON THE OTHER SIDE OF THE GLOBE, BEHIND THE IRON CURTAIN, ANOTHER STRANGE EXPERIMENT TAKES PLACE...
THAT IS IT! YOU MUST NEVER FORGET, WHEN THE RED LIGHT FLASHES, YOU TURN THE ESCAPE HATCH WHEEL!
ONLY A GENIUS SUCH AS I, IVAN KRAGOFF, COULD HAVE TRAINED A GORILLA TO OPERATE A SPACE SHIP! THERE'S THE BLUE LIGHT!
QUICKLY --PUT ON YOUR MAGNETIC SHOES!
WELL DONE, MY MONSTROUS SLAVE! NOW HERE IS YOUR REWARD!
SEE THAT YOU REMEMBER YOUR LESSONS WHILE I GO AND PRACTICE WITH YOUR OTHER TWO "SCHOOLMATES"!
STAY BACK! NO FOOD FOR YOU YET, COMRADE BABOON!
IT IS IMPORTANT TO ME THAT YOU REMAIN HUNGRY --I WANT YOU TO BE MEAN, VICIOUS, DANGEROUS!
GOOD-- GOOD! YOUR HEART IS FILLED WITH HATRED! SOON I MAY ALLOW YOU TO FIRE YOUR WEAPONS AT A REAL TARGET!
PAK PAK PAK PAK PAK PAK PAK
EVERY ONE A BULL'S EYE! YOU SHALL BE A VALUABLE ADDITION TO MY LITTLE CREW!
AND FINALLY YOU-- THE MOST BRAINLESS OF ALL! BUT YOU DON'T NEED BRAINS FOR YOUR WORK!
HERE IS YOUR REWARD! FOR YOU ARE THE ONLY ORANGUTAN IN THE WORLD WHO CAN USE TOOLS AND REPAIR ANY MACHINE AT MY COMMAND!
AT LAST MY CREW OF APES IS READY! AND NOW-- WE GO TO THE MOON-- TO CLAIM IT FOR THE COMMUNIST EMPIRE!
4

AND, AS FATE WOULD HAVE IT, AT THE EXACT MOMENT IN TWO DIFFERENT HEMISPHERES, SIMILAR LAUNCHINGS, ARE ABOUT TO TAKE PLACE...

HERE, SUE, LET ME GIVE YOU A HAND UP TO THE ENTRY HATCH!

THIS SURE BEATS USING A GANTRY!

BAH! I AIN'T A PRETTY GAL, SO NOBODY CARRIES ME!

SET THE CONTROLS, COMRADE GORILLA!

YOU OTHERS SETTLE BACK IN YOUR SAFETY SEATS! OUR GREAT MOMENT IS AT HAND!

BLAST OFF!

BLAST OFF!

BUT IVAN KRAGOFF'S MISSION IS **MORE** THAN JUST REACHING THE MOON! FOR KRAGOFF HAS STUDIED THE HISTORY OF THE **FANTASTIC FOUR** FOR MONTHS!

THE MIGHTY **FANTASTIC FOUR** DERIVED THEIR GREAT POWERS BY BEING BOMBARDED WITH **COSMIC RAYS!**

THAT IS WHY I HAVE DESIGNED MY SHIP OF TRANSPARENT CERAMIC PLASTIC, LIKE THE NOSE CONE OF A MISSILE, SO THAT THE COSMIC RAYS WILL BOMBARD ME, TOO!

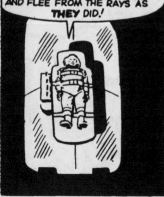

MY SHIP IS COMPLETELY UN-SHIELDED AGAINST THE COSMIC RAYS! WHATEVER DOSE OF RAYS THE **FANTASTIC FOUR** RECEIVED, I SHALL GET AN EVEN **GREATER** DOSE--FOR I SHALL NOT TURN AND FLEE FROM THE RAYS AS **THEY** DID!

I, IVAN KRAGOFF, SHALL BE-COME EVEN **MORE** POWERFUL THAN THE **FANTASTIC FOUR**... AND SO SHALL MY **APES!** TOGETHER, WE SHALL BE LORDS OF THE SOLAR SYSTEM!

AND NOW IT **BEGINS!** WE ARE PASSING THRU THE COSMIC BELT! I CAN **FEEL** THE RAYS! THEY SHALL GIVE ME POWER! **POWER! POWER!**

5

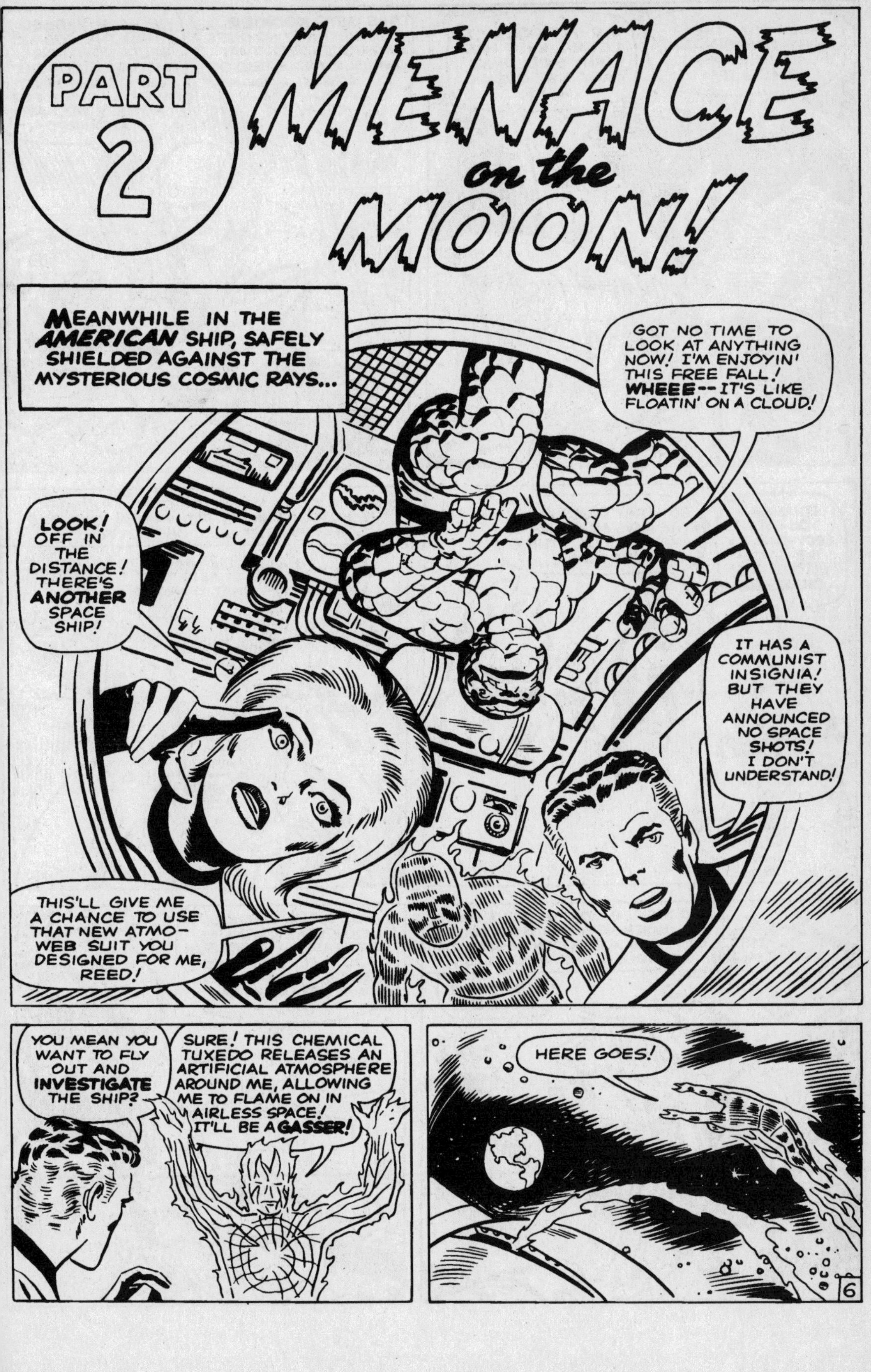

PART 2
MENACE on the MOON!
MEANWHILE IN THE AMERICAN SHIP, SAFELY SHIELDED AGAINST THE MYSTERIOUS COSMIC RAYS...
GOT NO TIME TO LOOK AT ANYTHING NOW! I'M ENJOYIN' THIS FREE FALL! WHEEE-- IT'S LIKE FLOATIN' ON A CLOUD!
LOOK! OFF IN THE DISTANCE! THERE'S ANOTHER SPACE SHIP!
IT HAS A COMMUNIST INSIGNIA! BUT THEY HAVE ANNOUNCED NO SPACE SHOTS! I DON'T UNDERSTAND!
THIS'LL GIVE ME A CHANCE TO USE THAT NEW ATMO-WEB SUIT YOU DESIGNED FOR ME, REED!
YOU MEAN YOU WANT TO FLY OUT AND INVESTIGATE THE SHIP?
SURE! THIS CHEMICAL TUXEDO RELEASES AN ARTIFICIAL ATMOSPHERE AROUND ME, ALLOWING ME TO FLAME ON IN AIRLESS SPACE! IT'LL BE A GASSER!
HERE GOES!
6

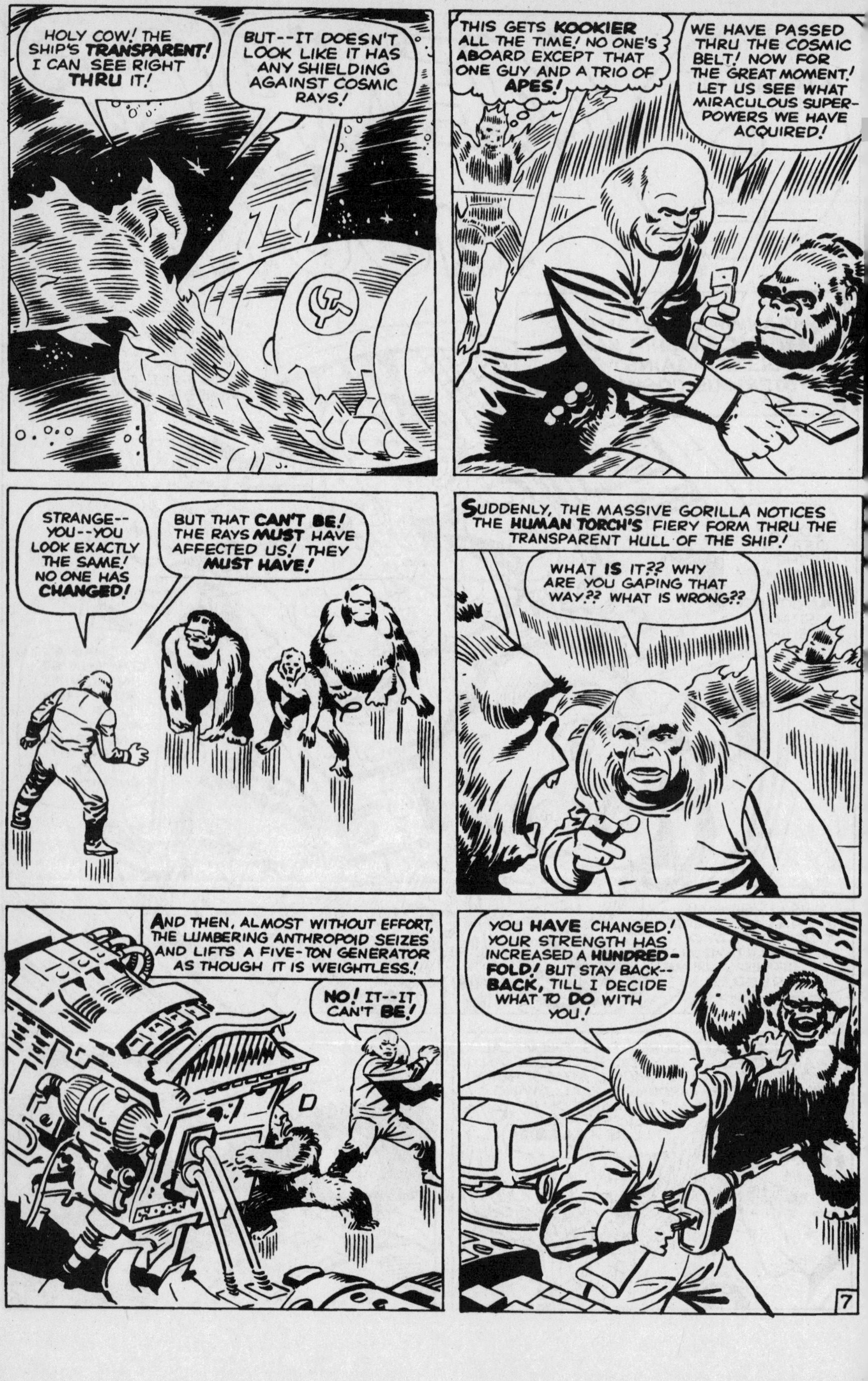
HOLY COW! THE SHIP'S TRANSPARENT! I CAN SEE RIGHT THRU IT!
BUT--IT DOESN'T LOOK LIKE IT HAS ANY SHIELDING AGAINST COSMIC RAYS!
THIS GETS KOOKIER ALL THE TIME! NO ONE'S ABOARD EXCEPT THAT ONE GUY AND A TRIO OF APES!
WE HAVE PASSED THRU THE COSMIC BELT! NOW FOR THE GREAT MOMENT! LET US SEE WHAT MIRACULOUS SUPER-POWERS WE HAVE ACQUIRED!
STRANGE--YOU--YOU LOOK EXACTLY THE SAME! NO ONE HAS CHANGED!
BUT THAT CAN'T BE! THE RAYS MUST HAVE AFFECTED US! THEY MUST HAVE!
SUDDENLY, THE MASSIVE GORILLA NOTICES THE HUMAN TORCH'S FIERY FORM THRU THE TRANSPARENT HULL OF THE SHIP!
WHAT IS IT?? WHY ARE YOU GAPING THAT WAY?? WHAT IS WRONG??
AND THEN, ALMOST WITHOUT EFFORT, THE LUMBERING ANTHROPOID SEIZES AND LIFTS A FIVE-TON GENERATOR AS THOUGH IT IS WEIGHTLESS!
NO! IT--IT CAN'T BE!
YOU HAVE CHANGED! YOUR STRENGTH HAS INCREASED A HUNDRED-FOLD! BUT STAY BACK--BACK, TILL I DECIDE WHAT TO DO WITH YOU!
7

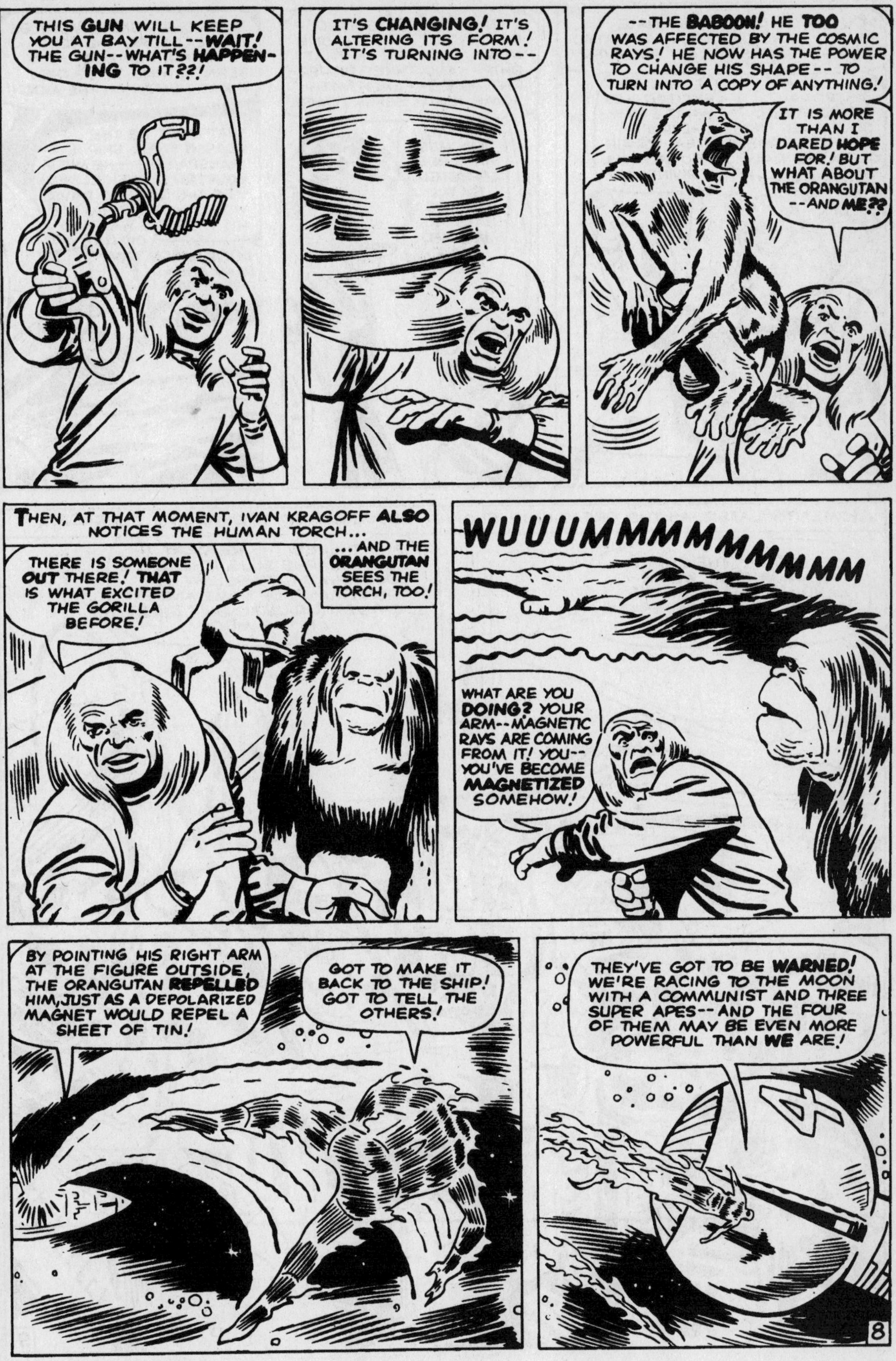

THIS GUN WILL KEEP YOU AT BAY TILL--WAIT! THE GUN--WHAT'S HAPPENING TO IT??!
IT'S CHANGING! IT'S ALTERING ITS FORM! IT'S TURNING INTO--
--THE BABOON! HE TOO WAS AFFECTED BY THE COSMIC RAYS! HE NOW HAS THE POWER TO CHANGE HIS SHAPE-- TO TURN INTO A COPY OF ANYTHING!
IT IS MORE THAN I DARED HOPE FOR! BUT WHAT ABOUT THE ORANGUTAN --AND ME??
THEN, AT THAT MOMENT, IVAN KRAGOFF ALSO NOTICES THE HUMAN TORCH...
THERE IS SOMEONE OUT THERE! THAT IS WHAT EXCITED THE GORILLA BEFORE!
...AND THE ORANGUTAN SEES THE TORCH, TOO!
WUUUMMMMMMMMMM
WHAT ARE YOU DOING? YOUR ARM--MAGNETIC RAYS ARE COMING FROM IT! YOU--YOU'VE BECOME MAGNETIZED SOMEHOW!
BY POINTING HIS RIGHT ARM AT THE FIGURE OUTSIDE, THE ORANGUTAN REPELLED HIM, JUST AS A DEPOLARIZED MAGNET WOULD REPEL A SHEET OF TIN!
GOT TO MAKE IT BACK TO THE SHIP! GOT TO TELL THE OTHERS!
THEY'VE GOT TO BE WARNED! WE'RE RACING TO THE MOON WITH A COMMUNIST AND THREE SUPER APES--AND THE FOUR OF THEM MAY BE EVEN MORE POWERFUL THAN WE ARE!
4
8

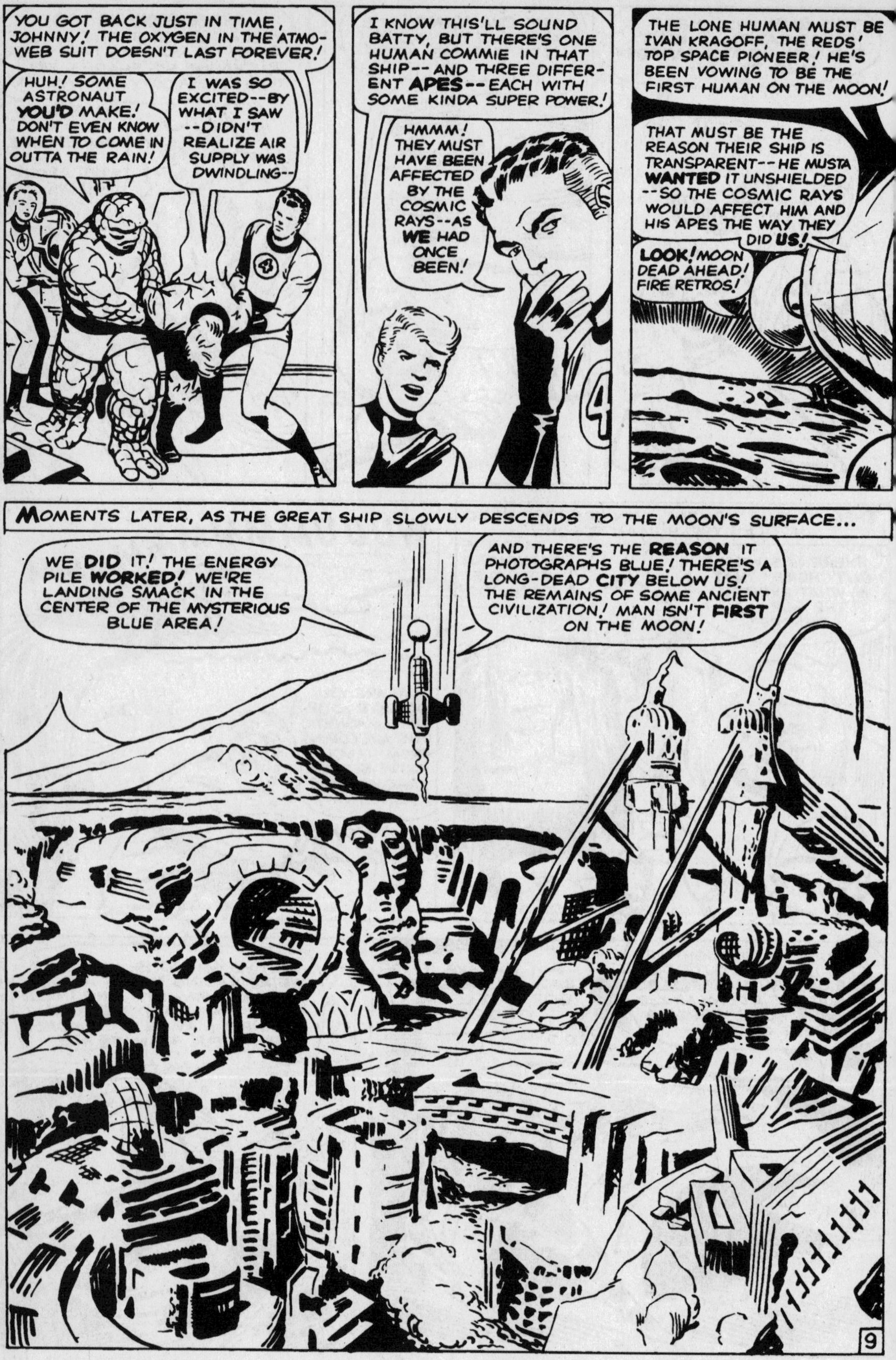
YOU GOT BACK JUST IN TIME, JOHNNY! THE OXYGEN IN THE ATMO-WEB SUIT DOESN'T LAST FOREVER!
HUH! SOME ASTRONAUT YOU'D MAKE! DON'T EVEN KNOW WHEN TO COME IN OUTTA THE RAIN!
I WAS SO EXCITED--BY WHAT I SAW --DIDN'T REALIZE AIR SUPPLY WAS DWINDLING--
I KNOW THIS'LL SOUND BATTY, BUT THERE'S ONE HUMAN COMMIE IN THAT SHIP-- AND THREE DIFFERENT APES-- EACH WITH SOME KINDA SUPER POWER!
HMMM! THEY MUST HAVE BEEN AFFECTED BY THE COSMIC RAYS--AS WE HAD ONCE BEEN!
THE LONE HUMAN MUST BE IVAN KRAGOFF, THE REDS' TOP SPACE PIONEER! HE'S BEEN VOWING TO BE THE FIRST HUMAN ON THE MOON!
THAT MUST BE THE REASON THEIR SHIP IS TRANSPARENT-- HE MUSTA WANTED IT UNSHIELDED --SO THE COSMIC RAYS WOULD AFFECT HIM AND HIS APES THE WAY THEY DID US!
LOOK! MOON DEAD AHEAD! FIRE RETROS!
MOMENTS LATER, AS THE GREAT SHIP SLOWLY DESCENDS TO THE MOON'S SURFACE...
WE DID IT! THE ENERGY PILE WORKED! WE'RE LANDING SMACK IN THE CENTER OF THE MYSTERIOUS BLUE AREA!
AND THERE'S THE REASON IT PHOTOGRAPHS BLUE! THERE'S A LONG-DEAD CITY BELOW US! THE REMAINS OF SOME ANCIENT CIVILIZATION! MAN ISN'T FIRST ON THE MOON!
9

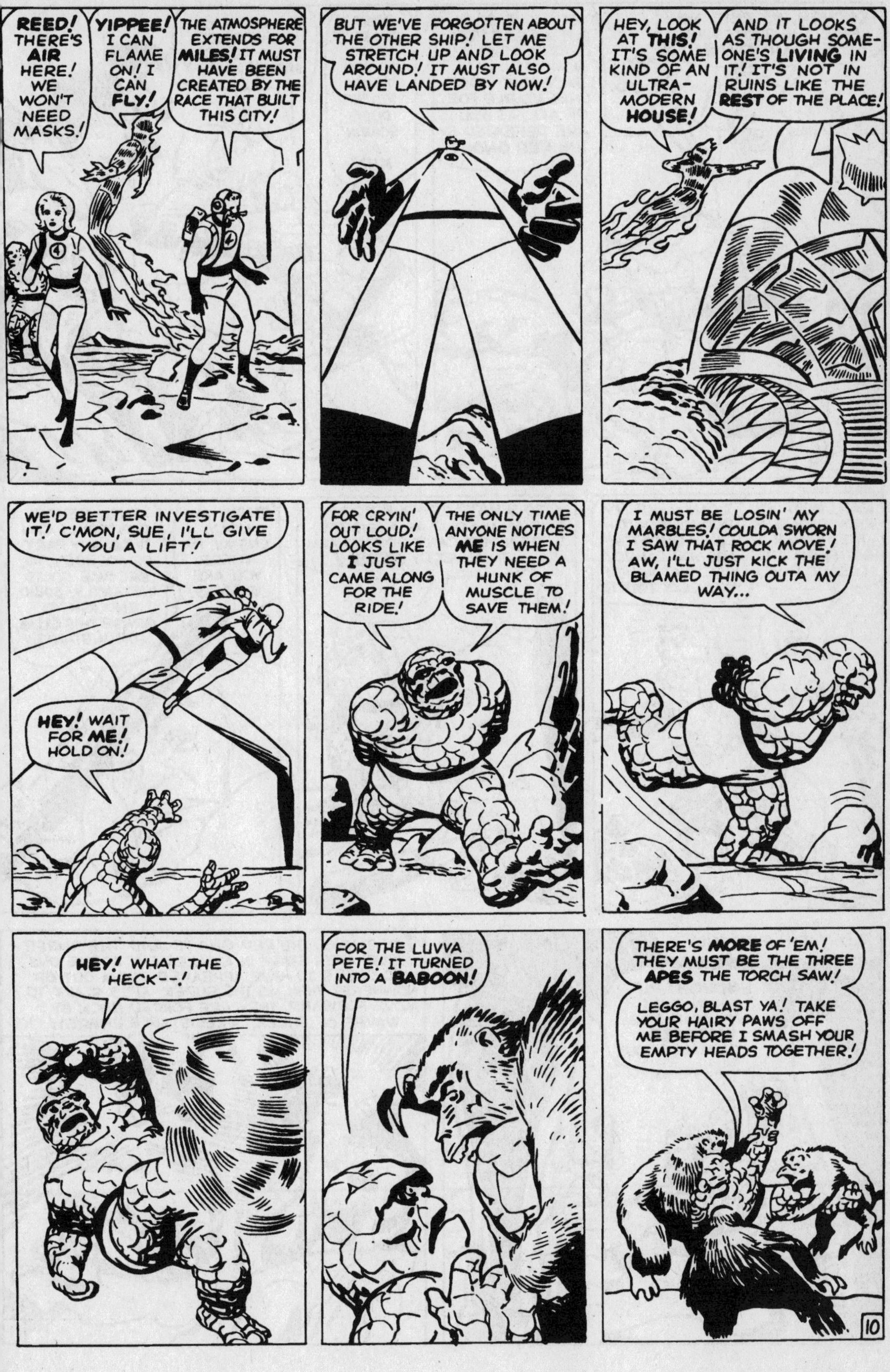
REED! THERE'S AIR HERE! WE WON'T NEED MASKS!
YIPPEE! I CAN FLAME ON! I CAN FLY!
THE ATMOSPHERE EXTENDS FOR MILES! IT MUST HAVE BEEN CREATED BY THE RACE THAT BUILT THIS CITY!
BUT WE'VE FORGOTTEN ABOUT THE OTHER SHIP! LET ME STRETCH UP AND LOOK AROUND! IT MUST ALSO HAVE LANDED BY NOW!
HEY, LOOK AT THIS! IT'S SOME KIND OF AN ULTRA-MODERN HOUSE!
AND IT LOOKS AS THOUGH SOME-ONE'S LIVING IN IT! IT'S NOT IN RUINS LIKE THE REST OF THE PLACE!
WE'D BETTER INVESTIGATE IT! C'MON, SUE, I'LL GIVE YOU A LIFT!
HEY! WAIT FOR ME! HOLD ON!
FOR CRYIN' OUT LOUD! LOOKS LIKE I JUST CAME ALONG FOR THE RIDE!
THE ONLY TIME ANYONE NOTICES ME IS WHEN THEY NEED A HUNK OF MUSCLE TO SAVE THEM!
I MUST BE LOSIN' MY MARBLES! COULDA SWORN I SAW THAT ROCK MOVE! AW, I'LL JUST KICK THE BLAMED THING OUTA MY WAY...
HEY! WHAT THE HECK--!
FOR THE LUVVA PETE! IT TURNED INTO A BABOON!
THERE'S MORE OF 'EM! THEY MUST BE THE THREE APES THE TORCH SAW!
LEGGO, BLAST YA! TAKE YOUR HAIRY PAWS OFF ME BEFORE I SMASH YOUR EMPTY HEADS TOGETHER!
10

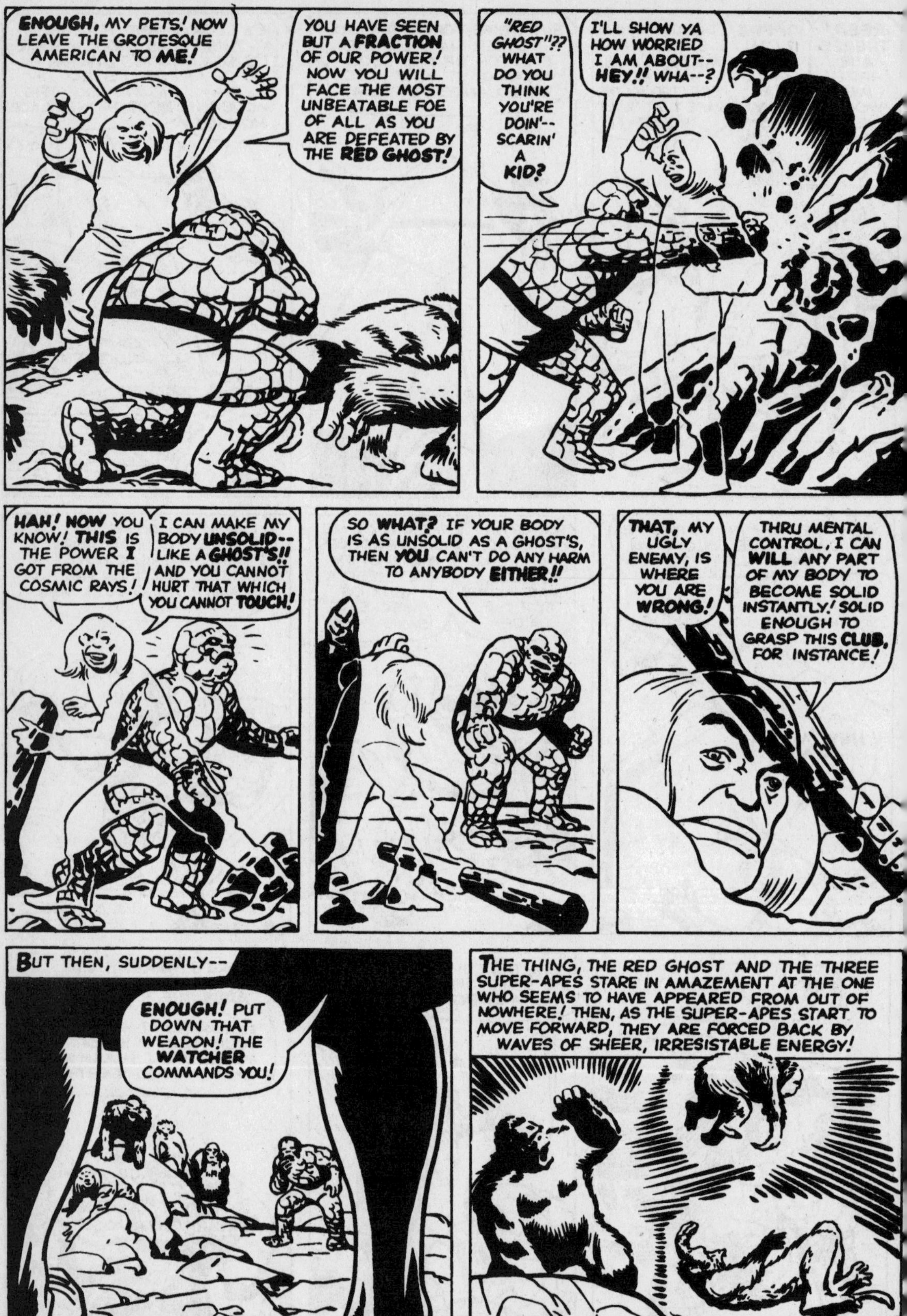
ENOUGH, MY PETS! NOW LEAVE THE GROTESQUE AMERICAN TO ME!
YOU HAVE SEEN BUT A FRACTION OF OUR POWER! NOW YOU WILL FACE THE MOST UNBEATABLE FOE OF ALL AS YOU ARE DEFEATED BY THE RED GHOST!
"RED GHOST"?? WHAT DO YOU THINK YOU'RE DOIN'-- SCARIN' A KID?
I'LL SHOW YA HOW WORRIED I AM ABOUT-- HEY!! WHA--?
HAH! NOW YOU KNOW! THIS IS THE POWER I GOT FROM THE COSMIC RAYS!
I CAN MAKE MY BODY UNSOLID-- LIKE A GHOST'S!! AND YOU CANNOT HURT THAT WHICH YOU CANNOT TOUCH!
SO WHAT? IF YOUR BODY IS AS UNSOLID AS A GHOST'S, THEN YOU CAN'T DO ANY HARM TO ANYBODY EITHER!!
THAT, MY UGLY ENEMY, IS WHERE YOU ARE WRONG!
THRU MENTAL CONTROL, I CAN WILL ANY PART OF MY BODY TO BECOME SOLID INSTANTLY! SOLID ENOUGH TO GRASP THIS CLUB, FOR INSTANCE!
BUT THEN, SUDDENLY--
ENOUGH! PUT DOWN THAT WEAPON! THE WATCHER COMMANDS YOU!
THE THING, THE RED GHOST AND THE THREE SUPER-APES STARE IN AMAZEMENT AT THE ONE WHO SEEMS TO HAVE APPEARED FROM OUT OF NOWHERE! THEN, AS THE SUPER-APES START TO MOVE FORWARD, THEY ARE FORCED BACK BY WAVES OF SHEER, IRRESISTABLE ENERGY!
11

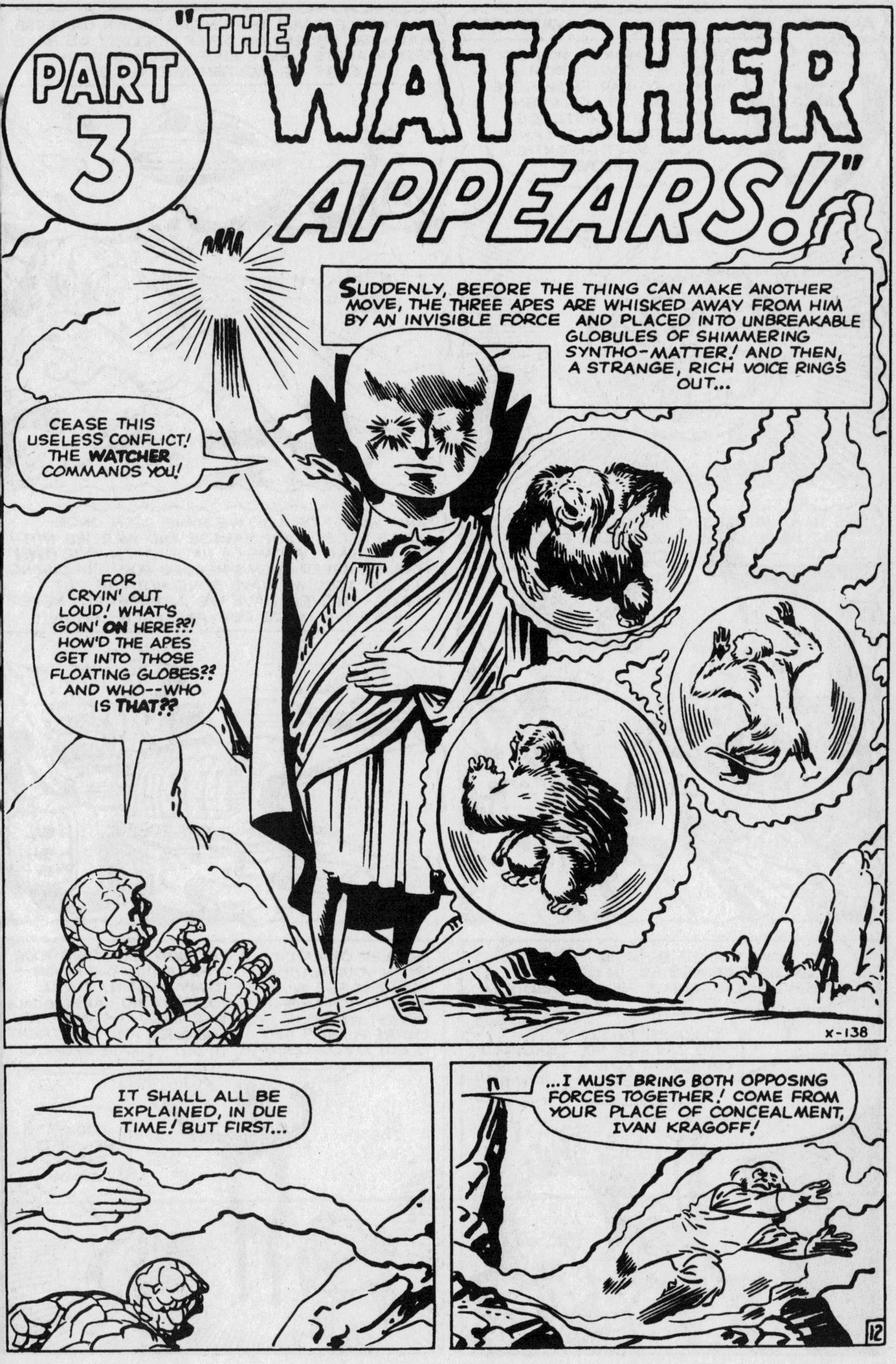
PART 3
"THE WATCHER APPEARS!"
SUDDENLY, BEFORE THE THING CAN MAKE ANOTHER MOVE, THE THREE APES ARE WHISKED AWAY FROM HIM BY AN INVISIBLE FORCE AND PLACED INTO UNBREAKABLE GLOBULES OF SHIMMERING SYNTHO-MATTER! AND THEN, A STRANGE, RICH VOICE RINGS OUT...
CEASE THIS USELESS CONFLICT! THE WATCHER COMMANDS YOU!
FOR CRYIN' OUT LOUD! WHAT'S GOIN' ON HERE??! HOW'D THE APES GET INTO THOSE FLOATING GLOBES?? AND WHO--WHO IS THAT??
X-138
IT SHALL ALL BE EXPLAINED, IN DUE TIME! BUT FIRST...
...I MUST BRING BOTH OPPOSING FORCES TOGETHER! COME FROM YOUR PLACE OF CONCEALMENT, IVAN KRAGOFF!
12

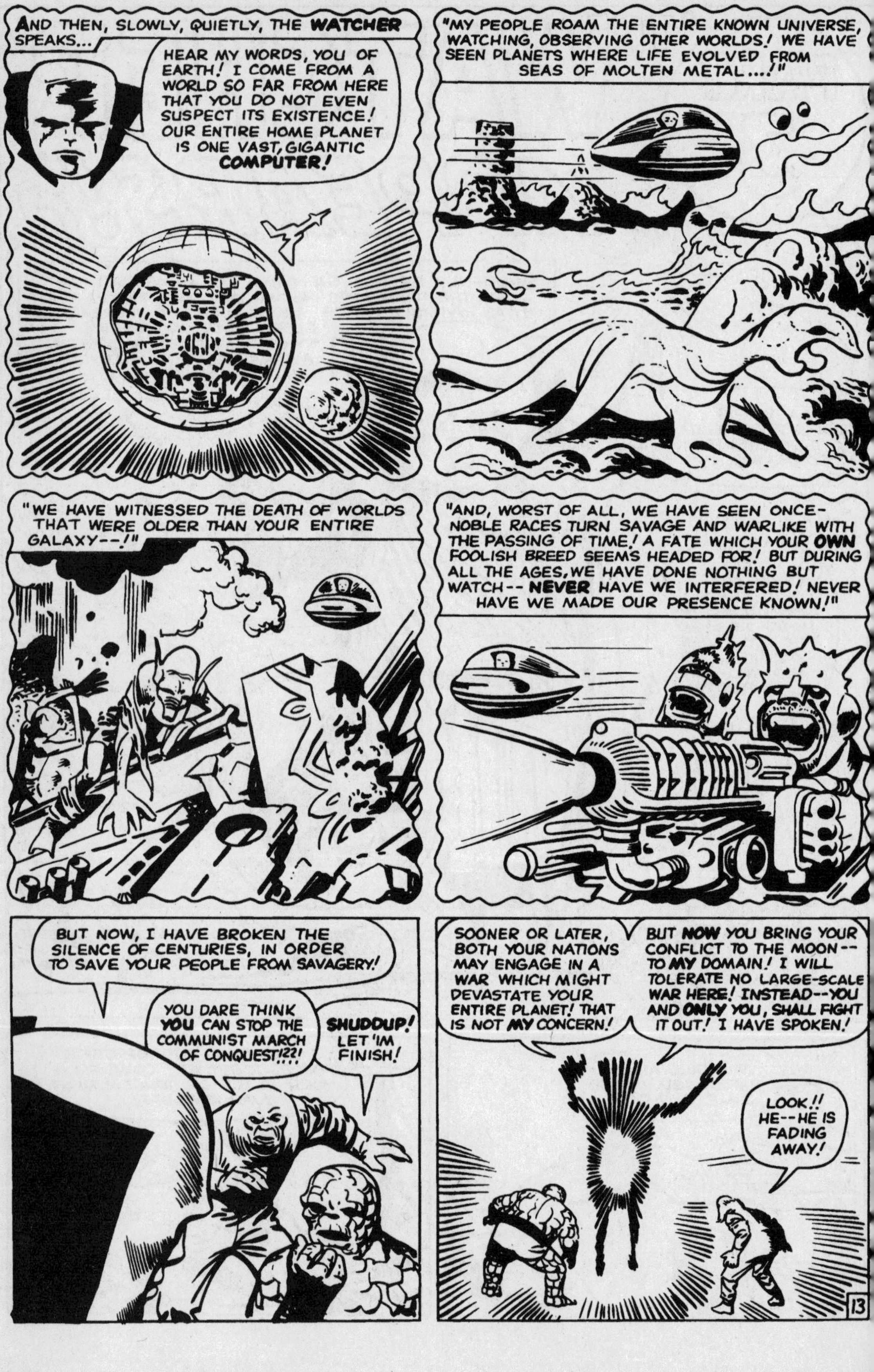
AND THEN, SLOWLY, QUIETLY, THE WATCHER SPEAKS...
HEAR MY WORDS, YOU OF EARTH! I COME FROM A WORLD SO FAR FROM HERE THAT YOU DO NOT EVEN SUSPECT ITS EXISTENCE! OUR ENTIRE HOME PLANET IS ONE VAST, GIGANTIC COMPUTER!
"MY PEOPLE ROAM THE ENTIRE KNOWN UNIVERSE, WATCHING, OBSERVING OTHER WORLDS! WE HAVE SEEN PLANETS WHERE LIFE EVOLVED FROM SEAS OF MOLTEN METAL....!"
"WE HAVE WITNESSED THE DEATH OF WORLDS THAT WERE OLDER THAN YOUR ENTIRE GALAXY--!"
"AND, WORST OF ALL, WE HAVE SEEN ONCE-NOBLE RACES TURN SAVAGE AND WARLIKE WITH THE PASSING OF TIME! A FATE WHICH YOUR OWN FOOLISH BREED SEEMS HEADED FOR! BUT DURING ALL THE AGES, WE HAVE DONE NOTHING BUT WATCH-- NEVER HAVE WE INTERFERED! NEVER HAVE WE MADE OUR PRESENCE KNOWN!"
BUT NOW, I HAVE BROKEN THE SILENCE OF CENTURIES, IN ORDER TO SAVE YOUR PEOPLE FROM SAVAGERY!
YOU DARE THINK YOU CAN STOP THE COMMUNIST MARCH OF CONQUEST!?!
SHUDDUP! LET 'IM FINISH!
SOONER OR LATER, BOTH YOUR NATIONS MAY ENGAGE IN A WAR WHICH MIGHT DEVASTATE YOUR ENTIRE PLANET! THAT IS NOT MY CONCERN!
BUT NOW YOU BRING YOUR CONFLICT TO THE MOON-- TO MY DOMAIN! I WILL TOLERATE NO LARGE-SCALE WAR HERE! INSTEAD--YOU AND ONLY YOU, SHALL FIGHT IT OUT! I HAVE SPOKEN!
LOOK!! HE--HE IS FADING AWAY!
13

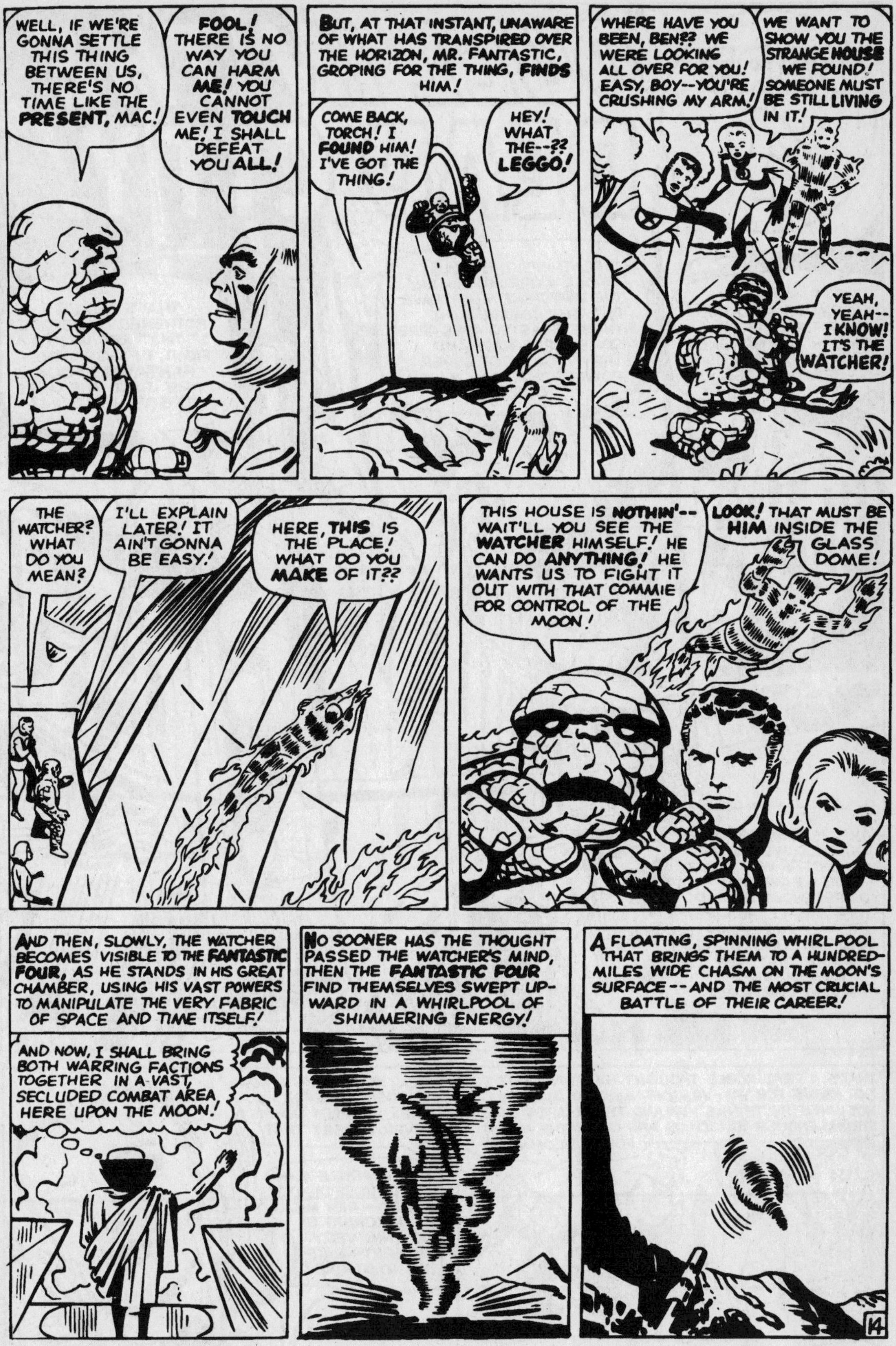
WELL, IF WE'RE GONNA SETTLE THIS THING BETWEEN US, THERE'S NO TIME LIKE THE PRESENT, MAC!
FOOL! THERE IS NO WAY YOU CAN HARM ME! YOU CANNOT EVEN TOUCH ME! I SHALL DEFEAT YOU ALL!
BUT, AT THAT INSTANT, UNAWARE OF WHAT HAS TRANSPIRED OVER THE HORIZON, MR. FANTASTIC, GROPING FOR THE THING, FINDS HIM!
COME BACK, TORCH! I FOUND HIM! I'VE GOT THE THING!
HEY! WHAT THE--?? LEGGO!
WHERE HAVE YOU BEEN, BEN?? WE WERE LOOKING ALL OVER FOR YOU! EASY, BOY--YOU'RE CRUSHING MY ARM!
WE WANT TO SHOW YOU THE STRANGE HOUSE WE FOUND! SOMEONE MUST BE STILL LIVING IN IT!
YEAH, YEAH--I KNOW! IT'S THE WATCHER!
THE WATCHER? WHAT DO YOU MEAN?
I'LL EXPLAIN LATER! IT AIN'T GONNA BE EASY!
HERE, THIS IS THE PLACE! WHAT DO YOU MAKE OF IT??
THIS HOUSE IS NOTHIN'--WAIT'LL YOU SEE THE WATCHER HIMSELF! HE CAN DO ANYTHING! HE WANTS US TO FIGHT IT OUT WITH THAT COMMIE FOR CONTROL OF THE MOON!
LOOK! THAT MUST BE HIM INSIDE THE GLASS DOME!
AND THEN, SLOWLY, THE WATCHER BECOMES VISIBLE TO THE FANTASTIC FOUR, AS HE STANDS IN HIS GREAT CHAMBER, USING HIS VAST POWERS TO MANIPULATE THE VERY FABRIC OF SPACE AND TIME ITSELF!
AND NOW, I SHALL BRING BOTH WARRING FACTIONS TOGETHER IN A VAST, SECLUDED COMBAT AREA HERE UPON THE MOON!
NO SOONER HAS THE THOUGHT PASSED THE WATCHER'S MIND, THEN THE FANTASTIC FOUR FIND THEMSELVES SWEPT UPWARD IN A WHIRLPOOL OF SHIMMERING ENERGY!
A FLOATING, SPINNING WHIRLPOOL THAT BRINGS THEM TO A HUNDRED-MILES WIDE CHASM ON THE MOON'S SURFACE--AND THE MOST CRUCIAL BATTLE OF THEIR CAREER!
14

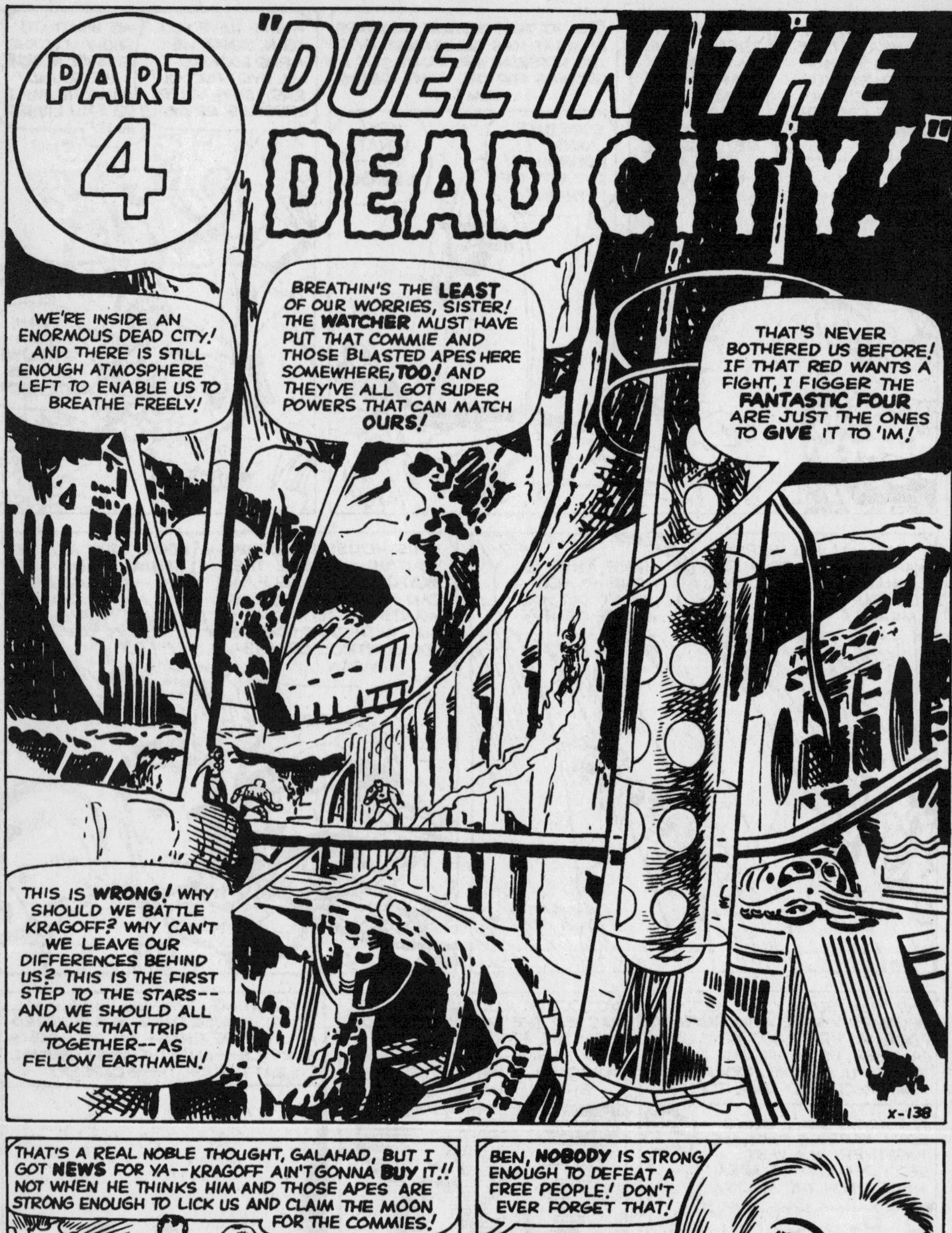
PART 4
"DUEL IN THE DEAD CITY!"
WE'RE INSIDE AN ENORMOUS DEAD CITY! AND THERE IS STILL ENOUGH ATMOSPHERE LEFT TO ENABLE US TO BREATHE FREELY!
BREATHIN'S THE LEAST OF OUR WORRIES, SISTER! THE WATCHER MUST HAVE PUT THAT COMMIE AND THOSE BLASTED APES HERE SOMEWHERE, TOO! AND THEY'VE ALL GOT SUPER POWERS THAT CAN MATCH OURS!
THAT'S NEVER BOTHERED US BEFORE! IF THAT RED WANTS A FIGHT, I FIGGER THE FANTASTIC FOUR ARE JUST THE ONES TO GIVE IT TO 'IM!
THIS IS WRONG! WHY SHOULD WE BATTLE KRAGOFF? WHY CAN'T WE LEAVE OUR DIFFERENCES BEHIND US? THIS IS THE FIRST STEP TO THE STARS--AND WE SHOULD ALL MAKE THAT TRIP TOGETHER--AS FELLOW EARTHMEN!
X-138
THAT'S A REAL NOBLE THOUGHT, GALAHAD, BUT I GOT NEWS FOR YA--KRAGOFF AIN'T GONNA BUY IT!! NOT WHEN HE THINKS HIM AND THOSE APES ARE STRONG ENOUGH TO LICK US AND CLAIM THE MOON FOR THE COMMIES!
BEN, NOBODY IS STRONG ENOUGH TO DEFEAT A FREE PEOPLE! DON'T EVER FORGET THAT!
THAT HORRIBLE MAN--AND THOSE DEADLY BEASTS--THEY MIGHT BE WATCHING US AT THIS VERY MOMENT--WAITING TO STRIKE!
15

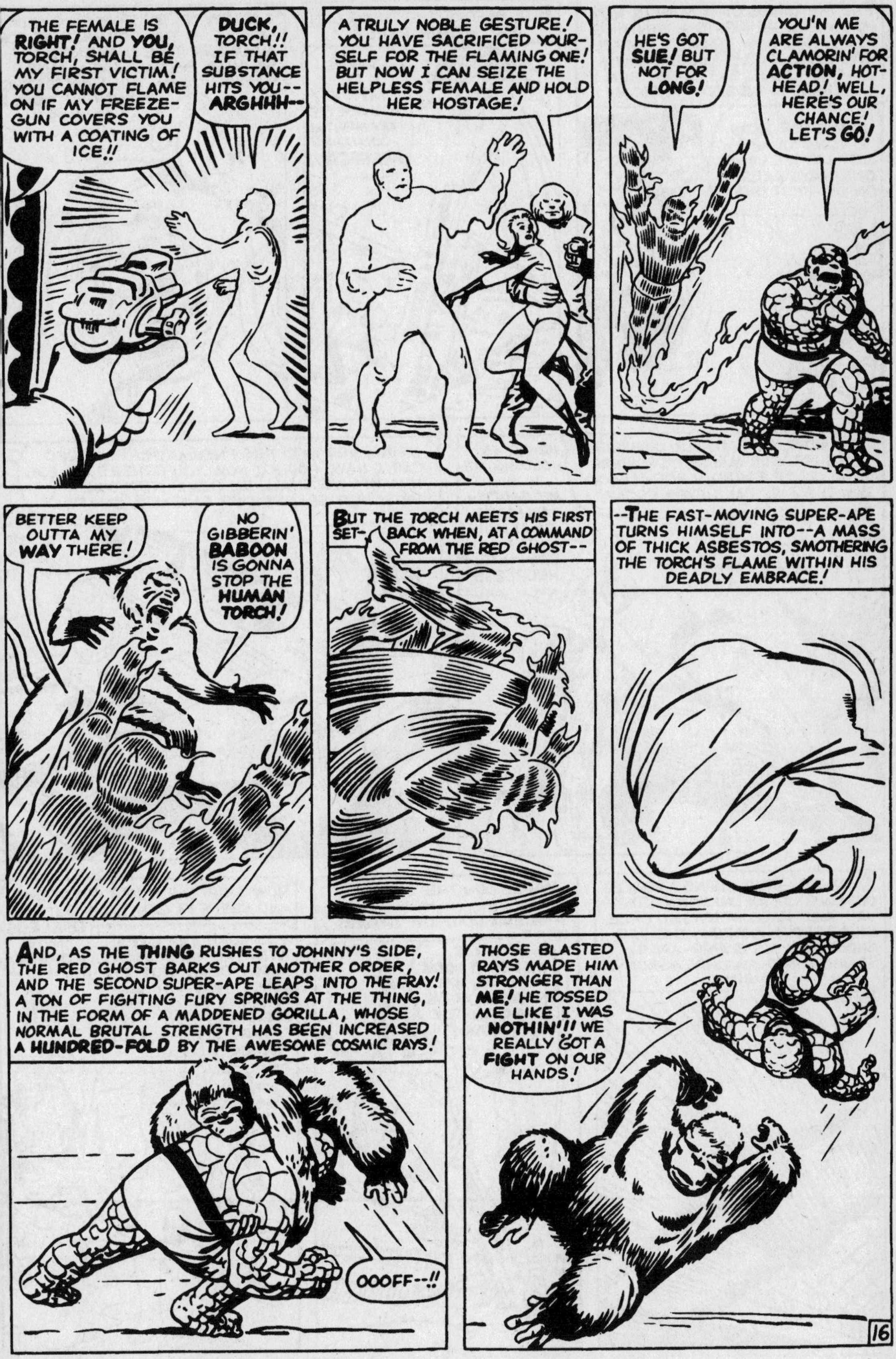

THE FEMALE IS RIGHT! AND YOU, TORCH, SHALL BE MY FIRST VICTIM! YOU CANNOT FLAME ON IF MY FREEZE-GUN COVERS YOU WITH A COATING OF ICE!!
DUCK, TORCH!! IF THAT SUBSTANCE HITS YOU-- ARGHHH--
A TRULY NOBLE GESTURE! YOU HAVE SACRIFICED YOURSELF FOR THE FLAMING ONE! BUT NOW I CAN SEIZE THE HELPLESS FEMALE AND HOLD HER HOSTAGE!
HE'S GOT SUE! BUT NOT FOR LONG!
YOU'N ME ARE ALWAYS CLAMORIN' FOR ACTION, HOT-HEAD! WELL, HERE'S OUR CHANCE! LET'S GO!
BETTER KEEP OUTTA MY WAY THERE!
NO GIBBERIN' BABOON IS GONNA STOP THE HUMAN TORCH!
BUT THE TORCH MEETS HIS FIRST SET-BACK WHEN, AT A COMMAND FROM THE RED GHOST--
--THE FAST-MOVING SUPER-APE TURNS HIMSELF INTO--A MASS OF THICK ASBESTOS, SMOTHERING THE TORCH'S FLAME WITHIN HIS DEADLY EMBRACE!
AND, AS THE THING RUSHES TO JOHNNY'S SIDE, THE RED GHOST BARKS OUT ANOTHER ORDER, AND THE SECOND SUPER-APE LEAPS INTO THE FRAY! A TON OF FIGHTING FURY SPRINGS AT THE THING, IN THE FORM OF A MADDENED GORILLA, WHOSE NORMAL BRUTAL STRENGTH HAS BEEN INCREASED A HUNDRED-FOLD BY THE AWESOME COSMIC RAYS!
OOOFF--!!
THOSE BLASTED RAYS MADE HIM STRONGER THAN ME! HE TOSSED ME LIKE I WAS NOTHIN'!! WE REALLY GOT A FIGHT ON OUR HANDS!
16

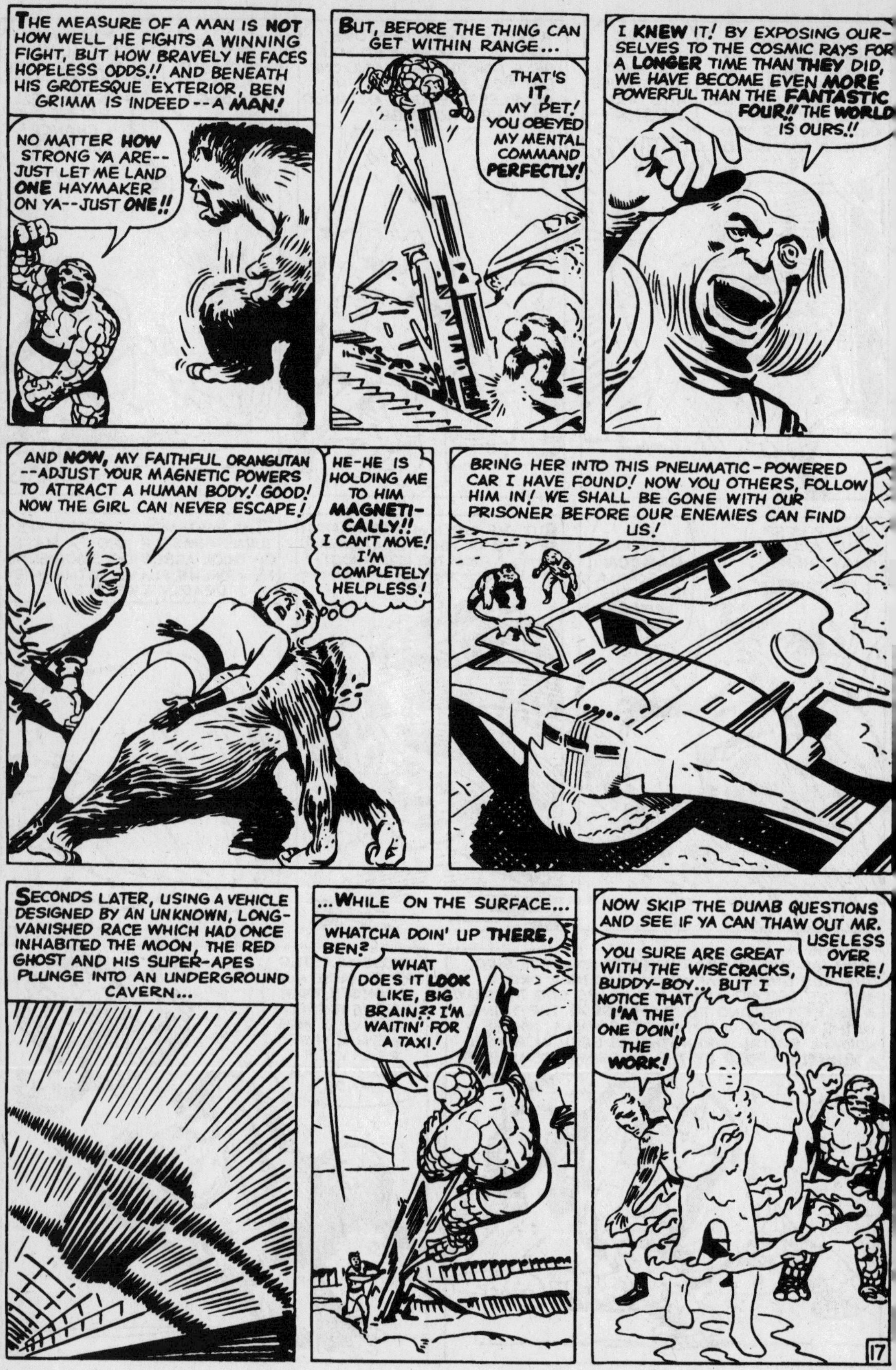
THE MEASURE OF A MAN IS NOT HOW WELL HE FIGHTS A WINNING FIGHT, BUT HOW BRAVELY HE FACES HOPELESS ODDS!! AND BENEATH HIS GROTESQUE EXTERIOR, BEN GRIMM IS INDEED--A MAN!
NO MATTER HOW STRONG YA ARE--JUST LET ME LAND ONE HAYMAKER ON YA--JUST ONE!!
BUT, BEFORE THE THING CAN GET WITHIN RANGE...
THAT'S IT, MY PET! YOU OBEYED MY MENTAL COMMAND PERFECTLY!
I KNEW IT! BY EXPOSING OURSELVES TO THE COSMIC RAYS FOR A LONGER TIME THAN THEY DID, WE HAVE BECOME EVEN MORE POWERFUL THAN THE FANTASTIC FOUR!! THE WORLD IS OURS!!
AND NOW, MY FAITHFUL ORANGUTAN--ADJUST YOUR MAGNETIC POWERS TO ATTRACT A HUMAN BODY! GOOD! NOW THE GIRL CAN NEVER ESCAPE!
HE-HE IS HOLDING ME TO HIM MAGNETICALLY!! I CAN'T MOVE! I'M COMPLETELY HELPLESS!
BRING HER INTO THIS PNEUMATIC-POWERED CAR I HAVE FOUND! NOW YOU OTHERS, FOLLOW HIM IN! WE SHALL BE GONE WITH OUR PRISONER BEFORE OUR ENEMIES CAN FIND US!
SECONDS LATER, USING A VEHICLE DESIGNED BY AN UNKNOWN, LONG-VANISHED RACE WHICH HAD ONCE INHABITED THE MOON, THE RED GHOST AND HIS SUPER-APES PLUNGE INTO AN UNDERGROUND CAVERN...
...WHILE ON THE SURFACE...
WHATCHA DOIN' UP THERE, BEN?
WHAT DOES IT LOOK LIKE, BIG BRAIN?? I'M WAITIN' FOR A TAXI!
NOW SKIP THE DUMB QUESTIONS AND SEE IF YA CAN THAW OUT MR. USELESS OVER THERE!
YOU SURE ARE GREAT WITH THE WISECRACKS, BUDDY-BOY... BUT I NOTICE THAT I'M THE ONE DOIN' THE WORK!
17

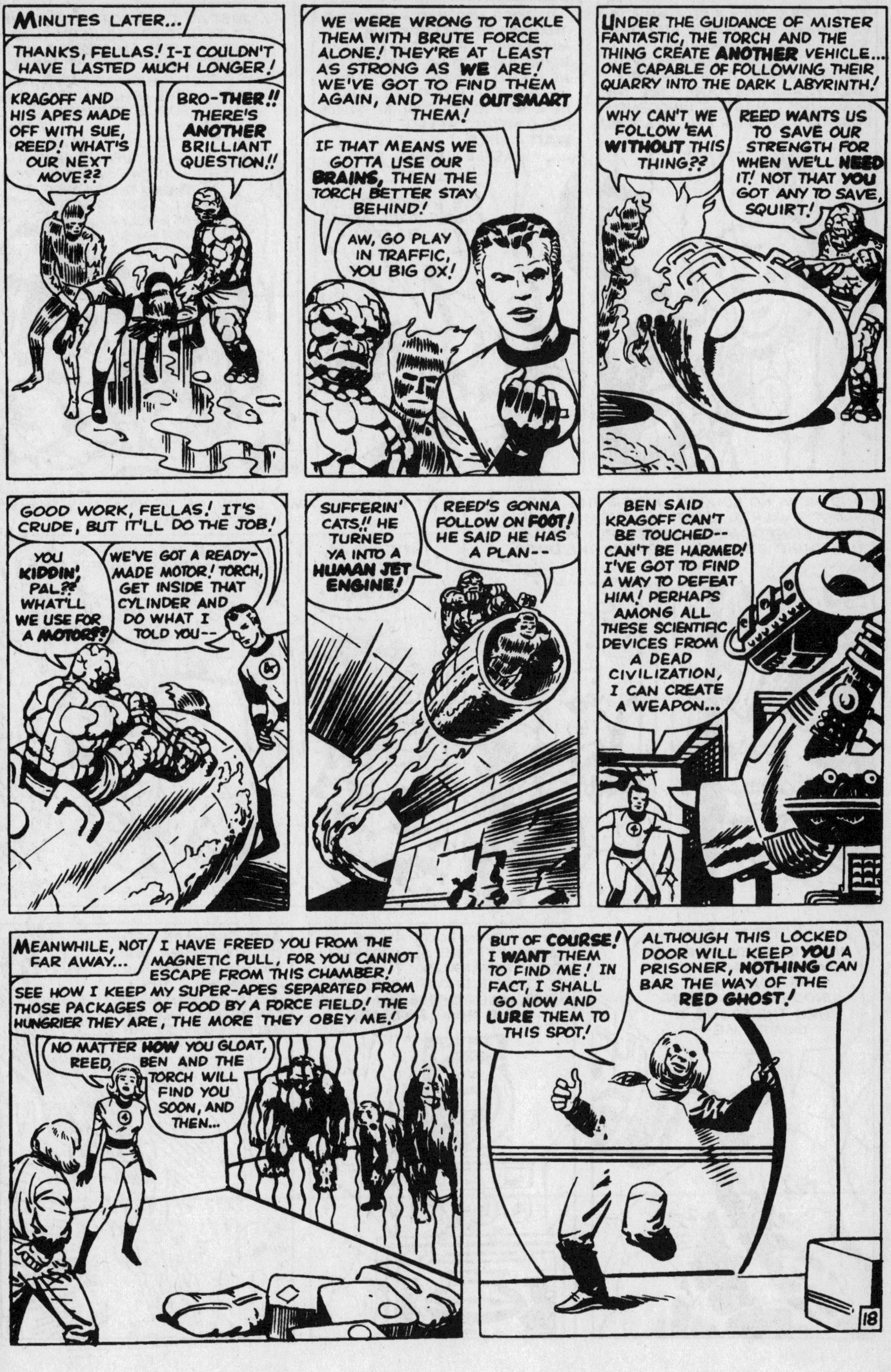
MINUTES LATER...
THANKS, FELLAS! I-I COULDN'T HAVE LASTED MUCH LONGER!
KRAGOFF AND HIS APES MADE OFF WITH SUE, REED! WHAT'S OUR NEXT MOVE??
BRO-THER!! THERE'S ANOTHER BRILLIANT QUESTION!!
WE WERE WRONG TO TACKLE THEM WITH BRUTE FORCE ALONE! THEY'RE AT LEAST AS STRONG AS WE ARE! WE'VE GOT TO FIND THEM AGAIN, AND THEN OUTSMART THEM!
IF THAT MEANS WE GOTTA USE OUR BRAINS, THEN THE TORCH BETTER STAY BEHIND!
AW, GO PLAY IN TRAFFIC, YOU BIG OX!
UNDER THE GUIDANCE OF MISTER FANTASTIC, THE TORCH AND THE THING CREATE ANOTHER VEHICLE... ONE CAPABLE OF FOLLOWING THEIR QUARRY INTO THE DARK LABYRINTH!
WHY CAN'T WE FOLLOW 'EM WITHOUT THIS THING??
REED WANTS US TO SAVE OUR STRENGTH FOR WHEN WE'LL NEED IT! NOT THAT YOU GOT ANY TO SAVE, SQUIRT!
GOOD WORK, FELLAS! IT'S CRUDE, BUT IT'LL DO THE JOB!
YOU KIDDIN', PAL?? WHAT'LL WE USE FOR A MOTOR??
WE'VE GOT A READY-MADE MOTOR! TORCH, GET INSIDE THAT CYLINDER AND DO WHAT I TOLD YOU--
SUFFERIN' CATS!! HE TURNED YA INTO A HUMAN JET ENGINE!
REED'S GONNA FOLLOW ON FOOT! HE SAID HE HAS A PLAN--
BEN SAID KRAGOFF CAN'T BE TOUCHED-- CAN'T BE HARMED! I'VE GOT TO FIND A WAY TO DEFEAT HIM! PERHAPS AMONG ALL THESE SCIENTIFIC DEVICES FROM A DEAD CIVILIZATION, I CAN CREATE A WEAPON...
MEANWHILE, NOT FAR AWAY...
I HAVE FREED YOU FROM THE MAGNETIC PULL, FOR YOU CANNOT ESCAPE FROM THIS CHAMBER!
SEE HOW I KEEP MY SUPER-APES SEPARATED FROM THOSE PACKAGES OF FOOD BY A FORCE FIELD! THE HUNGRIER THEY ARE, THE MORE THEY OBEY ME!
NO MATTER HOW YOU GLOAT, REED, BEN AND THE TORCH WILL FIND YOU SOON, AND THEN...
BUT OF COURSE! I WANT THEM TO FIND ME! IN FACT, I SHALL GO NOW AND LURE THEM TO THIS SPOT!
ALTHOUGH THIS LOCKED DOOR WILL KEEP YOU A PRISONER, NOTHING CAN BAR THE WAY OF THE RED GHOST!
18

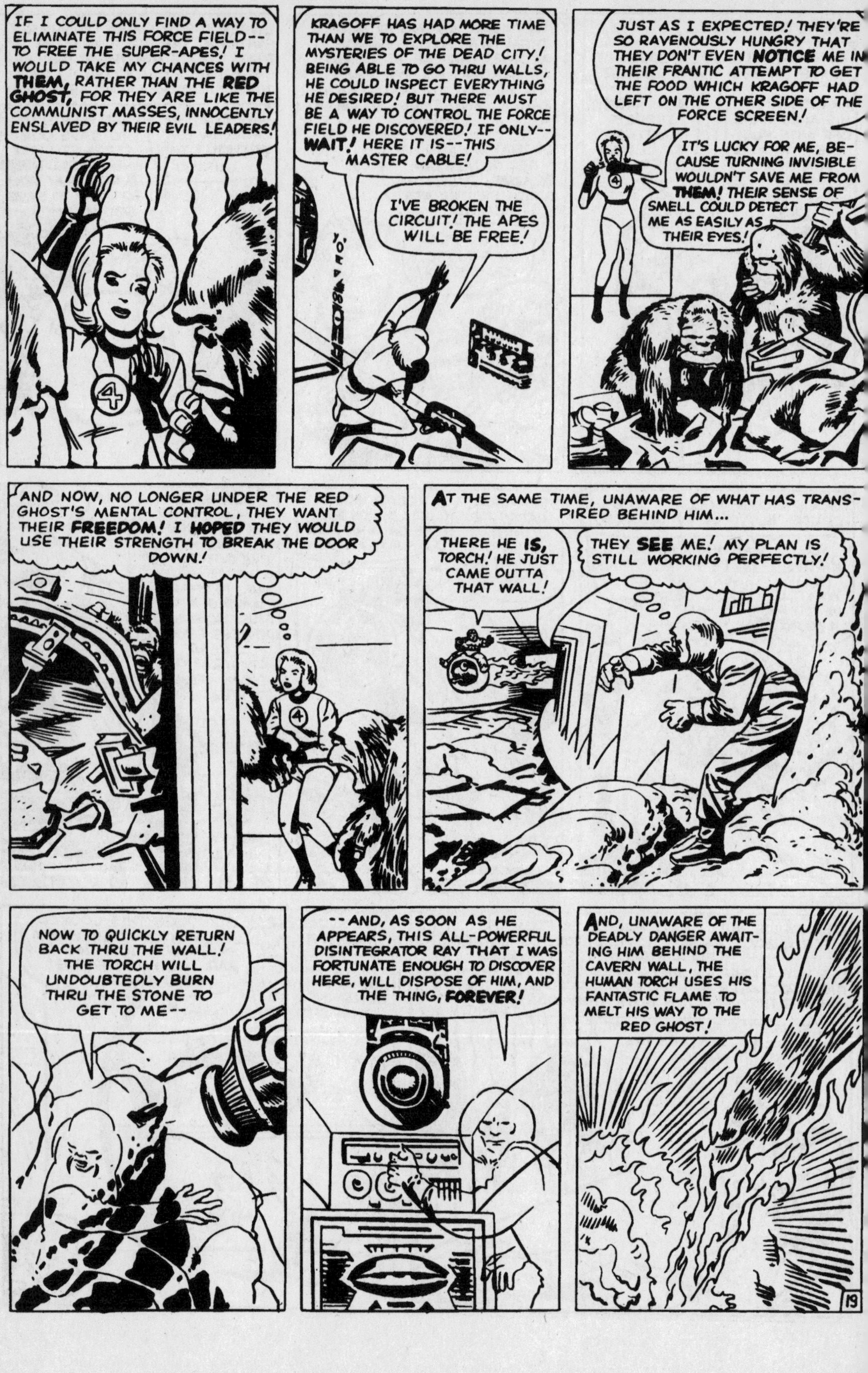

IF I COULD ONLY FIND A WAY TO ELIMINATE THIS FORCE FIELD-- TO FREE THE SUPER-APES! I WOULD TAKE MY CHANCES WITH THEM, RATHER THAN THE RED GHOST, FOR THEY ARE LIKE THE COMMUNIST MASSES, INNOCENTLY ENSLAVED BY THEIR EVIL LEADERS!
KRAGOFF HAS HAD MORE TIME THAN WE TO EXPLORE THE MYSTERIES OF THE DEAD CITY! BEING ABLE TO GO THRU WALLS, HE COULD INSPECT EVERYTHING HE DESIRED! BUT THERE MUST BE A WAY TO CONTROL THE FORCE FIELD HE DISCOVERED! IF ONLY-- WAIT! HERE IT IS--THIS MASTER CABLE!
I'VE BROKEN THE CIRCUIT! THE APES WILL BE FREE!
JUST AS I EXPECTED! THEY'RE SO RAVENOUSLY HUNGRY THAT THEY DON'T EVEN NOTICE ME IN THEIR FRANTIC ATTEMPT TO GET THE FOOD WHICH KRAGOFF HAD LEFT ON THE OTHER SIDE OF THE FORCE SCREEN!
IT'S LUCKY FOR ME, BECAUSE TURNING INVISIBLE WOULDN'T SAVE ME FROM THEM! THEIR SENSE OF SMELL COULD DETECT ME AS EASILY AS THEIR EYES!
AND NOW, NO LONGER UNDER THE RED GHOST'S MENTAL CONTROL, THEY WANT THEIR FREEDOM! I HOPED THEY WOULD USE THEIR STRENGTH TO BREAK THE DOOR DOWN!
AT THE SAME TIME, UNAWARE OF WHAT HAS TRANSPIRED BEHIND HIM...
THERE HE IS, TORCH! HE JUST CAME OUTTA THAT WALL!
THEY SEE ME! MY PLAN IS STILL WORKING PERFECTLY!
NOW TO QUICKLY RETURN BACK THRU THE WALL! THE TORCH WILL UNDOUBTEDLY BURN THRU THE STONE TO GET TO ME--
--AND, AS SOON AS HE APPEARS, THIS ALL-POWERFUL DISINTEGRATOR RAY THAT I WAS FORTUNATE ENOUGH TO DISCOVER HERE, WILL DISPOSE OF HIM, AND THE THING, FOREVER!
AND, UNAWARE OF THE DEADLY DANGER AWAITING HIM BEHIND THE CAVERN WALL, THE HUMAN TORCH USES HIS FANTASTIC FLAME TO MELT HIS WAY TO THE RED GHOST!
19

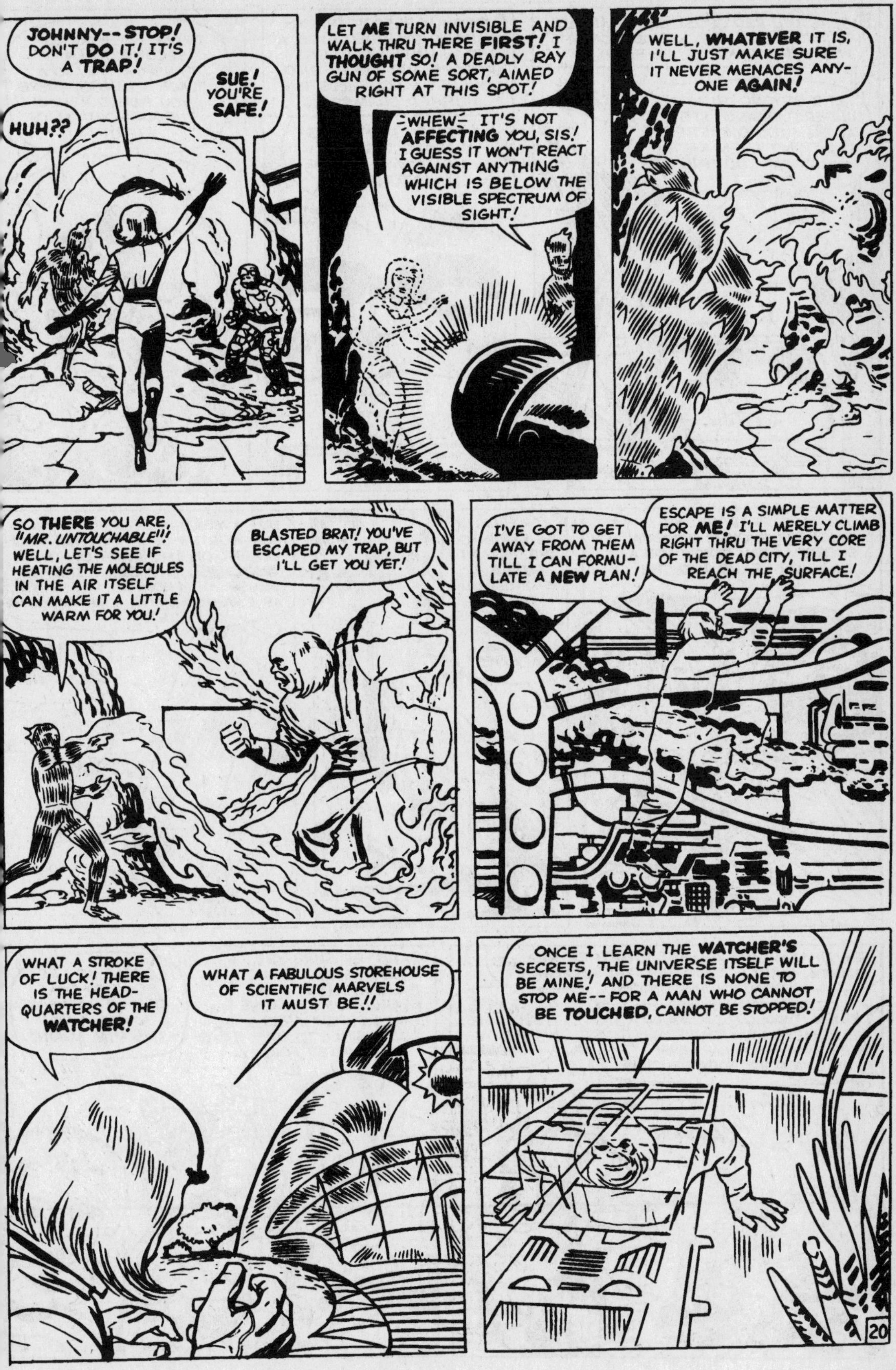
JOHNNY-- STOP! DON'T DO IT! IT'S A TRAP!
HUH??
SUE! YOU'RE SAFE!
LET ME TURN INVISIBLE AND WALK THRU THERE FIRST! I THOUGHT SO! A DEADLY RAY GUN OF SOME SORT, AIMED RIGHT AT THIS SPOT!
WHEW! IT'S NOT AFFECTING YOU, SIS! I GUESS IT WON'T REACT AGAINST ANYTHING WHICH IS BELOW THE VISIBLE SPECTRUM OF SIGHT!
WELL, WHATEVER IT IS, I'LL JUST MAKE SURE IT NEVER MENACES ANY-ONE AGAIN!
SO THERE YOU ARE, "MR. UNTOUCHABLE"! WELL, LET'S SEE IF HEATING THE MOLECULES IN THE AIR ITSELF CAN MAKE IT A LITTLE WARM FOR YOU!
BLASTED BRAT! YOU'VE ESCAPED MY TRAP, BUT I'LL GET YOU YET!
I'VE GOT TO GET AWAY FROM THEM TILL I CAN FORMU-LATE A NEW PLAN!
ESCAPE IS A SIMPLE MATTER FOR ME! I'LL MERELY CLIMB RIGHT THRU THE VERY CORE OF THE DEAD CITY, TILL I REACH THE SURFACE!
WHAT A STROKE OF LUCK! THERE IS THE HEAD-QUARTERS OF THE WATCHER!
WHAT A FABULOUS STOREHOUSE OF SCIENTIFIC MARVELS IT MUST BE!!
ONCE I LEARN THE WATCHER'S SECRETS, THE UNIVERSE ITSELF WILL BE MINE! AND THERE IS NONE TO STOP ME-- FOR A MAN WHO CANNOT BE TOUCHED, CANNOT BE STOPPED!
20

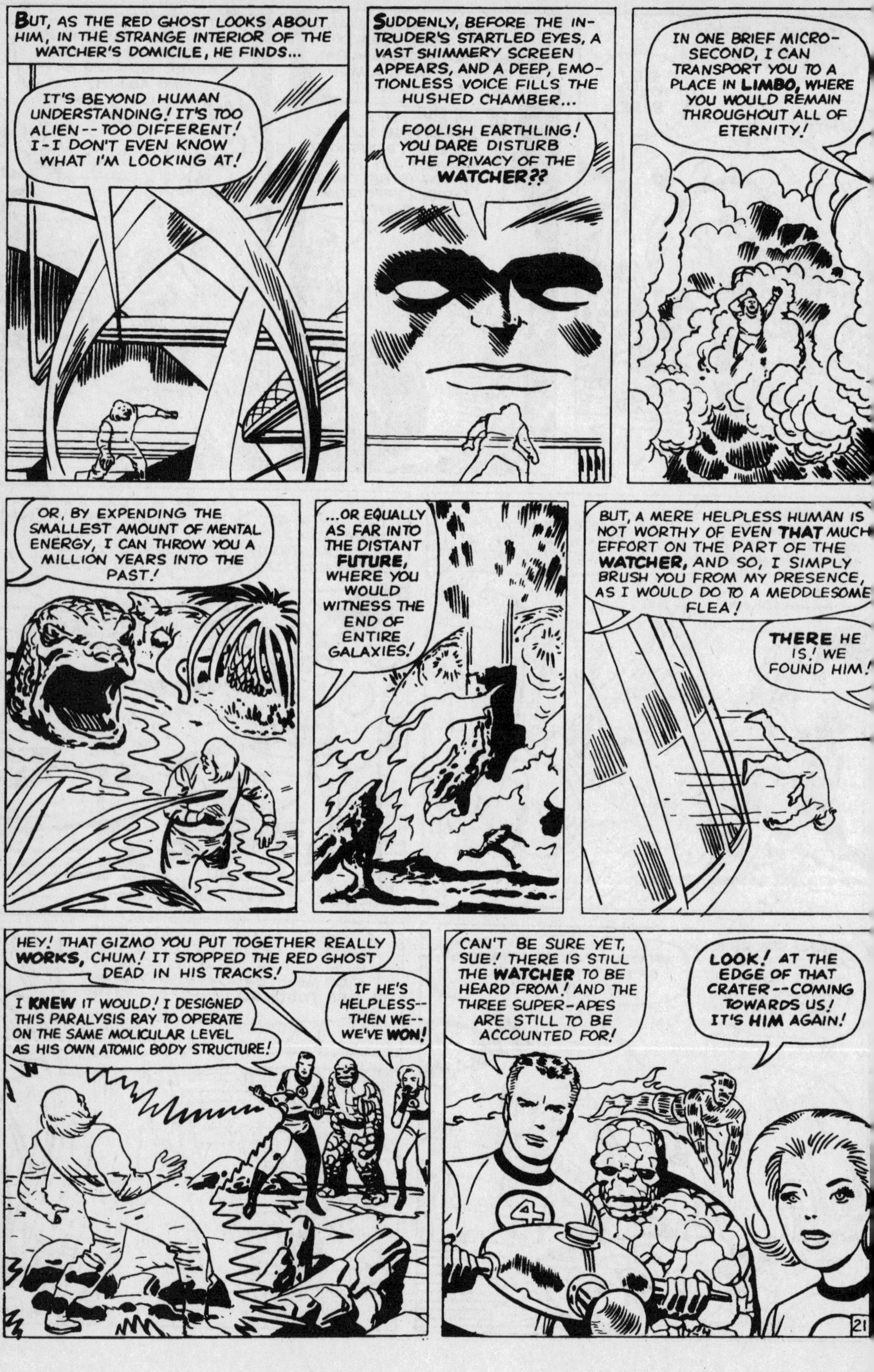
BUT, AS THE RED GHOST LOOKS ABOUT HIM, IN THE STRANGE INTERIOR OF THE WATCHER'S DOMICILE, HE FINDS...
IT'S BEYOND HUMAN UNDERSTANDING! IT'S TOO ALIEN-- TOO DIFFERENT! I-I DON'T EVEN KNOW WHAT I'M LOOKING AT!
SUDDENLY, BEFORE THE INTRUDER'S STARTLED EYES, A VAST SHIMMERY SCREEN APPEARS, AND A DEEP, EMOTIONLESS VOICE FILLS THE HUSHED CHAMBER...
FOOLISH EARTHLING! YOU DARE DISTURB THE PRIVACY OF THE WATCHER??
IN ONE BRIEF MICRO-SECOND, I CAN TRANSPORT YOU TO A PLACE IN LIMBO, WHERE YOU WOULD REMAIN THROUGHOUT ALL OF ETERNITY!
OR, BY EXPENDING THE SMALLEST AMOUNT OF MENTAL ENERGY, I CAN THROW YOU A MILLION YEARS INTO THE PAST!
...OR EQUALLY AS FAR INTO THE DISTANT FUTURE, WHERE YOU WOULD WITNESS THE END OF ENTIRE GALAXIES!
BUT, A MERE HELPLESS HUMAN IS NOT WORTHY OF EVEN THAT MUCH EFFORT ON THE PART OF THE WATCHER, AND SO, I SIMPLY BRUSH YOU FROM MY PRESENCE, AS I WOULD DO TO A MEDDLESOME FLEA!
THERE HE IS! WE FOUND HIM!
HEY! THAT GIZMO YOU PUT TOGETHER REALLY WORKS, CHUM! IT STOPPED THE RED GHOST DEAD IN HIS TRACKS!
I KNEW IT WOULD! I DESIGNED THIS PARALYSIS RAY TO OPERATE ON THE SAME MOLICULAR LEVEL AS HIS OWN ATOMIC BODY STRUCTURE!
IF HE'S HELPLESS-- THEN WE-- WE'VE WON!
CAN'T BE SURE YET, SUE! THERE IS STILL THE WATCHER TO BE HEARD FROM! AND THE THREE SUPER-APES ARE STILL TO BE ACCOUNTED FOR!
LOOK! AT THE EDGE OF THAT CRATER--COMING TOWARDS US! IT'S HIM AGAIN!
21

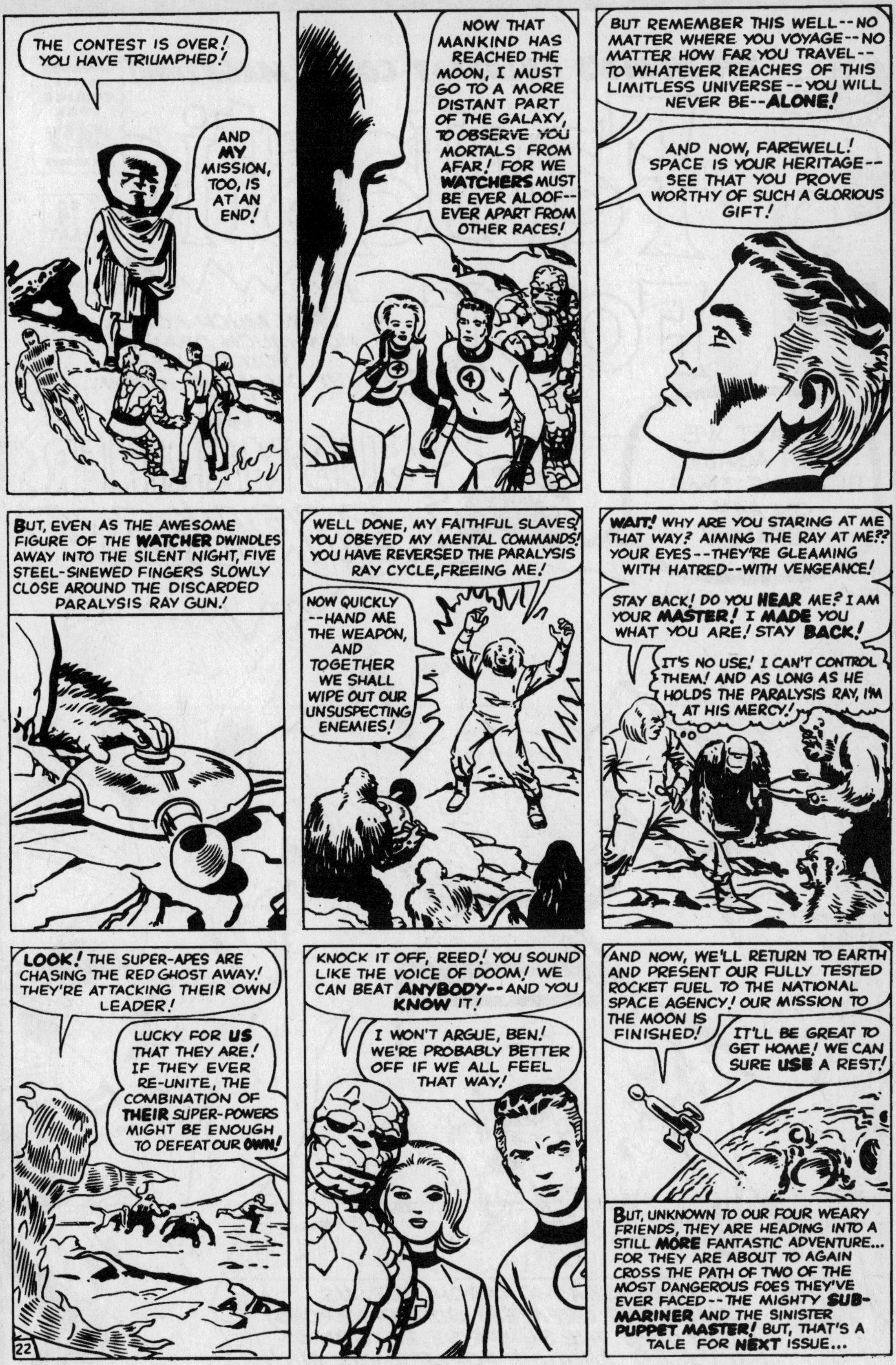
THE CONTEST IS OVER! YOU HAVE TRIUMPHED!
AND MY MISSION, TOO, IS AT AN END!
NOW THAT MANKIND HAS REACHED THE MOON, I MUST GO TO A MORE DISTANT PART OF THE GALAXY, TO OBSERVE YOU MORTALS FROM AFAR! FOR WE WATCHERS MUST BE EVER ALOOF-- EVER APART FROM OTHER RACES!
BUT REMEMBER THIS WELL--NO MATTER WHERE YOU VOYAGE--NO MATTER HOW FAR YOU TRAVEL-- TO WHATEVER REACHES OF THIS LIMITLESS UNIVERSE--YOU WILL NEVER BE--ALONE!
AND NOW, FAREWELL! SPACE IS YOUR HERITAGE-- SEE THAT YOU PROVE WORTHY OF SUCH A GLORIOUS GIFT!
BUT, EVEN AS THE AWESOME FIGURE OF THE WATCHER DWINDLES AWAY INTO THE SILENT NIGHT, FIVE STEEL-SINEWED FINGERS SLOWLY CLOSE AROUND THE DISCARDED PARALYSIS RAY GUN!
WELL DONE, MY FAITHFUL SLAVES! YOU OBEYED MY MENTAL COMMANDS! YOU HAVE REVERSED THE PARALYSIS RAY CYCLE, FREEING ME!
NOW QUICKLY --HAND ME THE WEAPON, AND TOGETHER WE SHALL WIPE OUT OUR UNSUSPECTING ENEMIES!
WAIT! WHY ARE YOU STARING AT ME THAT WAY? AIMING THE RAY AT ME?? YOUR EYES--THEY'RE GLEAMING WITH HATRED--WITH VENGEANCE!
STAY BACK! DO YOU HEAR ME? I AM YOUR MASTER! I MADE YOU WHAT YOU ARE! STAY BACK!
IT'S NO USE! I CAN'T CONTROL THEM! AND AS LONG AS HE HOLDS THE PARALYSIS RAY, I'M AT HIS MERCY!
LOOK! THE SUPER-APES ARE CHASING THE RED GHOST AWAY! THEY'RE ATTACKING THEIR OWN LEADER!
LUCKY FOR US THAT THEY ARE! IF THEY EVER RE-UNITE, THE COMBINATION OF THEIR SUPER-POWERS MIGHT BE ENOUGH TO DEFEAT OUR OWN!
KNOCK IT OFF, REED! YOU SOUND LIKE THE VOICE OF DOOM! WE CAN BEAT ANYBODY--AND YOU KNOW IT!
I WON'T ARGUE, BEN! WE'RE PROBABLY BETTER OFF IF WE ALL FEEL THAT WAY!
AND NOW, WE'LL RETURN TO EARTH AND PRESENT OUR FULLY TESTED ROCKET FUEL TO THE NATIONAL SPACE AGENCY! OUR MISSION TO THE MOON IS FINISHED!
IT'LL BE GREAT TO GET HOME! WE CAN SURE USE A REST!
BUT, UNKNOWN TO OUR FOUR WEARY FRIENDS, THEY ARE HEADING INTO A STILL MORE FANTASTIC ADVENTURE... FOR THEY ARE ABOUT TO AGAIN CROSS THE PATH OF TWO OF THE MOST DANGEROUS FOES THEY'VE EVER FACED--THE MIGHTY SUB-MARINER AND THE SINISTER PUPPET MASTER! BUT, THAT'S A TALE FOR NEXT ISSUE...
22

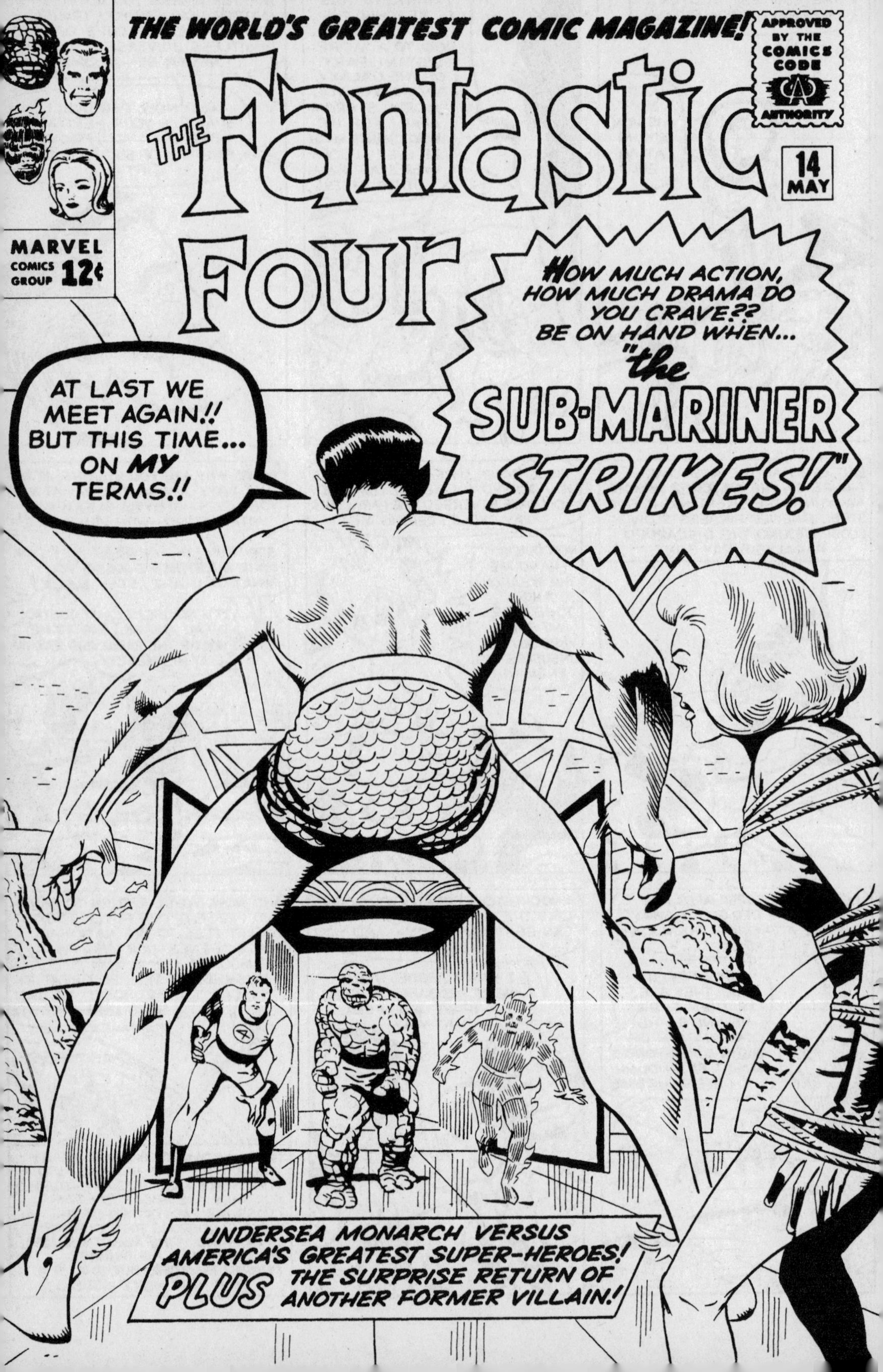

THE WORLD'S GREATEST COMIC MAGAZINE!
APPROVED BY THE COMICS CODE AUTHORITY
THE Fantastic Four
14 MAY
MARVEL COMICS GROUP 12¢
HOW MUCH ACTION, HOW MUCH DRAMA DO YOU CRAVE?? BE ON HAND WHEN... "the SUB-MARINER STRIKES!"
AT LAST WE MEET AGAIN!! BUT THIS TIME... ON MY TERMS!!
UNDERSEA MONARCH VERSUS AMERICA'S GREATEST SUPER-HEROES!
PLUS THE SURPRISE RETURN OF ANOTHER FORMER VILLAIN!

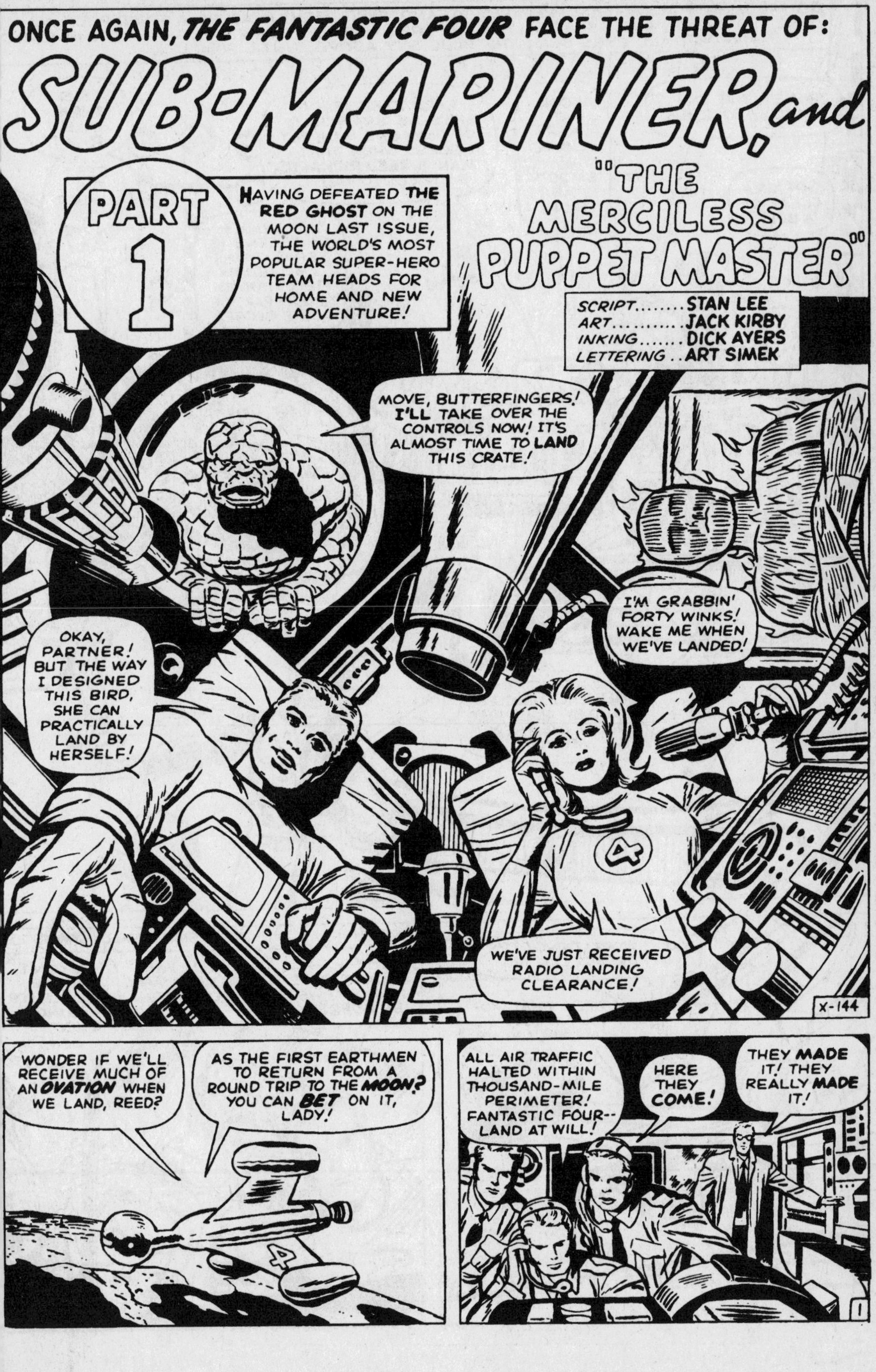
ONCE AGAIN, THE FANTASTIC FOUR FACE THE THREAT OF:
SUB-MARINER, and
"THE MERCILESS PUPPET MASTER"
PART 1
HAVING DEFEATED THE RED GHOST ON THE MOON LAST ISSUE, THE WORLD'S MOST POPULAR SUPER-HERO TEAM HEADS FOR HOME AND NEW ADVENTURE!
SCRIPT........STAN LEE
ART...........JACK KIRBY
INKING.......DICK AYERS
LETTERING..ART SIMEK
MOVE, BUTTERFINGERS! I'LL TAKE OVER THE CONTROLS NOW! IT'S ALMOST TIME TO LAND THIS CRATE!
OKAY, PARTNER! BUT THE WAY I DESIGNED THIS BIRD, SHE CAN PRACTICALLY LAND BY HERSELF!
I'M GRABBIN' FORTY WINKS! WAKE ME WHEN WE'VE LANDED!
WE'VE JUST RECEIVED RADIO LANDING CLEARANCE!
X-144
WONDER IF WE'LL RECEIVE MUCH OF AN OVATION WHEN WE LAND, REED?
AS THE FIRST EARTHMEN TO RETURN FROM A ROUND TRIP TO THE MOON? YOU CAN BET ON IT, LADY!
ALL AIR TRAFFIC HALTED WITHIN THOUSAND-MILE PERIMETER! FANTASTIC FOUR-- LAND AT WILL!
HERE THEY COME!
THEY MADE IT! THEY REALLY MADE IT!
1

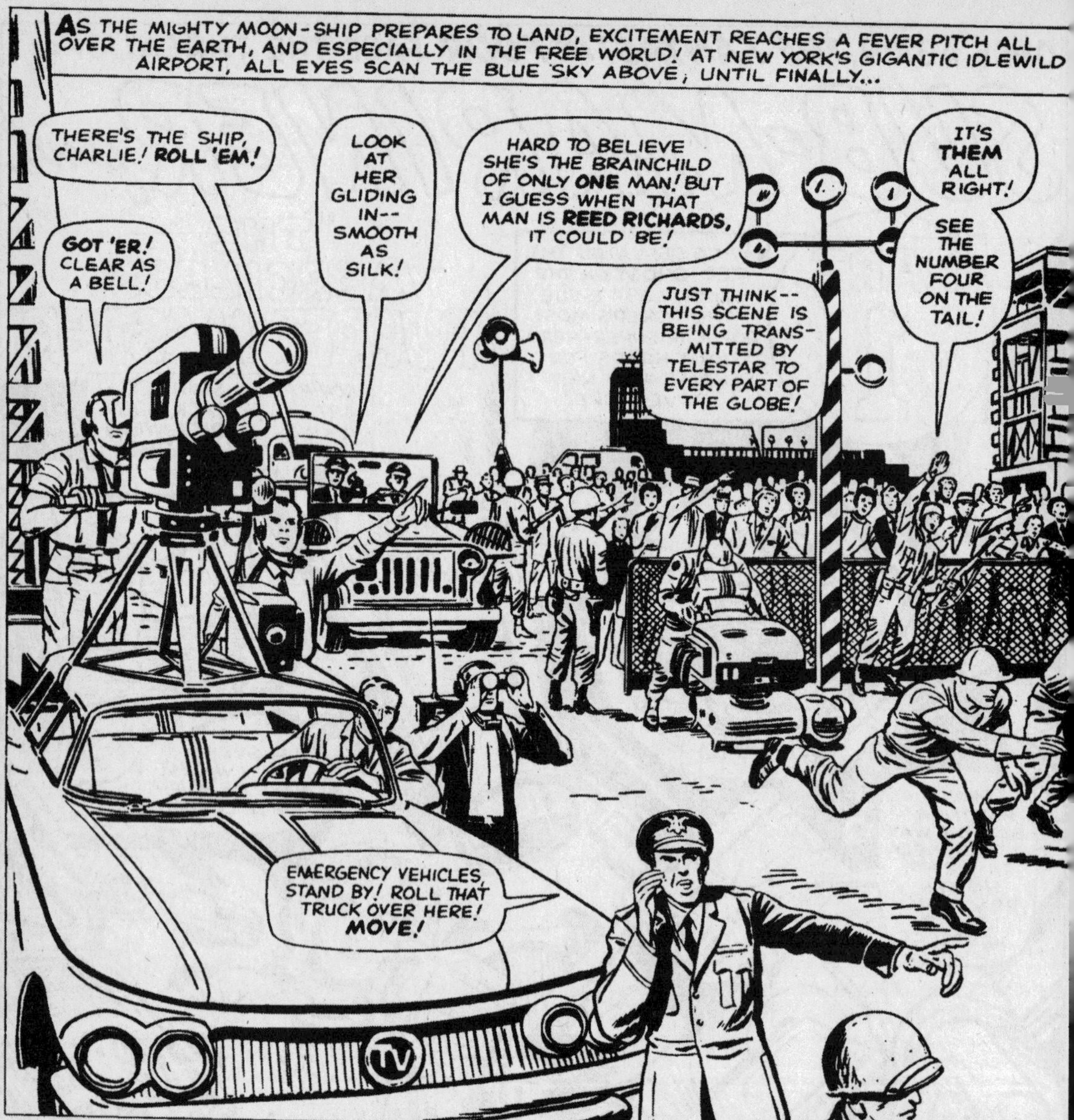
AS THE MIGHTY MOON-SHIP PREPARES TO LAND, EXCITEMENT REACHES A FEVER PITCH ALL OVER THE EARTH, AND ESPECIALLY IN THE FREE WORLD! AT NEW YORK'S GIGANTIC IDLEWILD AIRPORT, ALL EYES SCAN THE BLUE SKY ABOVE, UNTIL FINALLY...
THERE'S THE SHIP, CHARLIE! ROLL 'EM!
GOT 'ER! CLEAR AS A BELL!
LOOK AT HER GLIDING IN-- SMOOTH AS SILK!
HARD TO BELIEVE SHE'S THE BRAINCHILD OF ONLY ONE MAN! BUT I GUESS WHEN THAT MAN IS REED RICHARDS, IT COULD BE!
IT'S THEM ALL RIGHT!
SEE THE NUMBER FOUR ON THE TAIL!
JUST THINK-- THIS SCENE IS BEING TRANS-MITTED BY TELESTAR TO EVERY PART OF THE GLOBE!
EMERGENCY VEHICLES, STAND BY! ROLL THAT TRUCK OVER HERE! MOVE!
TV

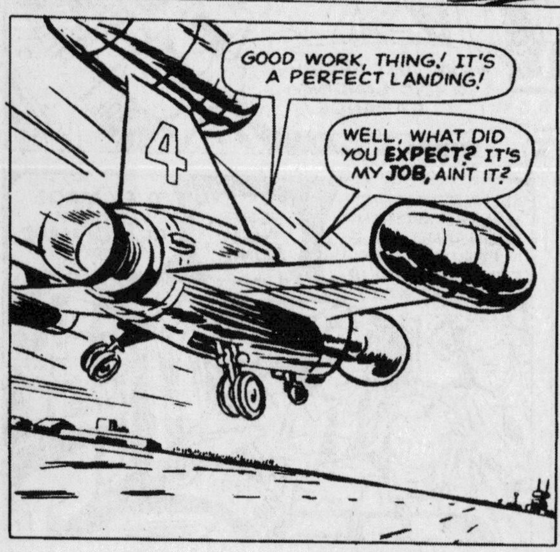
GOOD WORK, THING! IT'S A PERFECT LANDING!
WELL, WHAT DID YOU EXPECT? IT'S MY JOB, AINT IT?
4

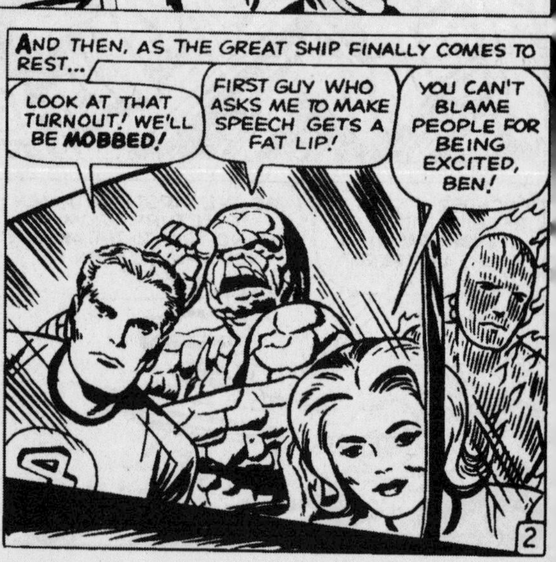
AND THEN, AS THE GREAT SHIP FINALLY COMES TO REST...
LOOK AT THAT TURNOUT! WE'LL BE MOBBED!
FIRST GUY WHO ASKS ME TO MAKE SPEECH GETS A FAT LIP!
YOU CAN'T BLAME PEOPLE FOR BEING EXCITED, BEN!

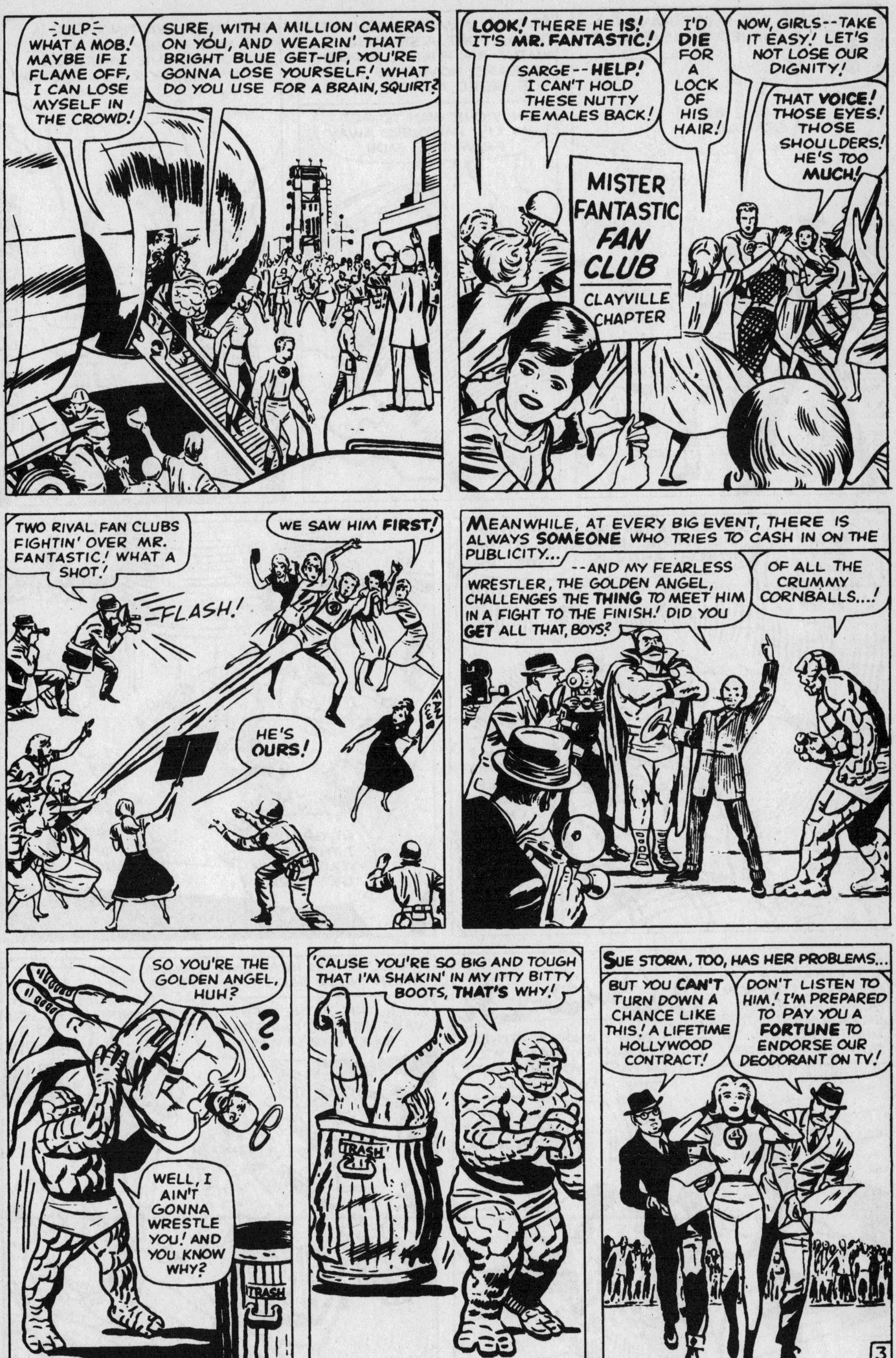

-ULP- WHAT A MOB! MAYBE IF I FLAME OFF, I CAN LOSE MYSELF IN THE CROWD!
SURE, WITH A MILLION CAMERAS ON YOU, AND WEARIN' THAT BRIGHT BLUE GET-UP, YOU'RE GONNA LOSE YOURSELF! WHAT DO YOU USE FOR A BRAIN, SQUIRT?
LOOK! THERE HE IS! IT'S MR. FANTASTIC!
SARGE--HELP! I CAN'T HOLD THESE NUTTY FEMALES BACK!
I'D DIE FOR A LOCK OF HIS HAIR!
NOW, GIRLS--TAKE IT EASY! LET'S NOT LOSE OUR DIGNITY!
THAT VOICE! THOSE EYES! THOSE SHOULDERS! HE'S TOO MUCH!
MISTER FANTASTIC FAN CLUB CLAYVILLE CHAPTER
TWO RIVAL FAN CLUBS FIGHTIN' OVER MR. FANTASTIC! WHAT A SHOT!
WE SAW HIM FIRST!
FLASH!
HE'S OURS!
MEANWHILE, AT EVERY BIG EVENT, THERE IS ALWAYS SOMEONE WHO TRIES TO CASH IN ON THE PUBLICITY...
--AND MY FEARLESS WRESTLER, THE GOLDEN ANGEL, CHALLENGES THE THING TO MEET HIM IN A FIGHT TO THE FINISH! DID YOU GET ALL THAT, BOYS?
OF ALL THE CRUMMY CORNBALLS...!
SO YOU'RE THE GOLDEN ANGEL, HUH?
?
WELL, I AIN'T GONNA WRESTLE YOU! AND YOU KNOW WHY?
TRASH
'CAUSE YOU'RE SO BIG AND TOUGH THAT I'M SHAKIN' IN MY ITTY BITTY BOOTS, THAT'S WHY!
TRASH
SUE STORM, TOO, HAS HER PROBLEMS...
BUT YOU CAN'T TURN DOWN A CHANCE LIKE THIS! A LIFETIME HOLLYWOOD CONTRACT!
DON'T LISTEN TO HIM! I'M PREPARED TO PAY YOU A FORTUNE TO ENDORSE OUR DEODORANT ON TV!
3

WHERE DID SHE GO?

SHE MUST HAVE TURNED INVISIBLE!

SOME PEOPLE JUST HAVE NO GRATITUDE!

AT THAT MOMENT, HIGH OVER THE AIRPORT, A STRANGE, WARM-AIR FUNNEL SUDDENLY APPEARS, HOVERING OVER SUE, REED, AND THE THING...

ONLY ONE WAY TO GET MY LI'L PARTNERS AWAY FROM THAT MOB!

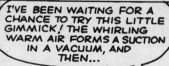

I'VE BEEN WAITING FOR A CHANCE TO TRY THIS LITTLE GIMMICK! THE WHIRLING WARM AIR FORMS A SUCTION IN A VACUUM, AND THEN...

REED! BEN! WHAT'S HAPPENING?

WE'RE BEING DRAWN UP INTO THIS WARM AIR FUNNEL BY THE TORCH! AND JUST IN TIME, TOO!

AWW, I DIDN'T EVEN GET A CHANCE TO CLOBBER ANYBODY BACK THERE IN THE MOB!

HI, GROUP! I THOUGHT YOU'D NEVER GET HERE!

AFTER CATCHING THEIR BREATH, THE COLORFUL FOURSOME HEADS FOR THEIR SKYSCRAPER SUITE VIA THEIR PRIVATE ROOFTOP ELEVATOR!

I DON'T KNOW WHETHER I OUGHTTA THANK YOU, OR PASTE YOU ONE, HOT-HEAD!

WHY DON'T YOU GO GET A JOB AS A FOOD TESTER IN A POISON FACTORY?!

FINALLY, UPON REACHING THEIR INNER SANCTUM...

AHHH, THIS IS THE LIFE! WAKE ME UP AT CHRISTMAS! NEXT CHRISTMAS!

HMMM, I THINK I'D BETTER DO A LITTLE HOUSE-CLEANING!

JUST SO LONG AS YOU DO IT SILENTLY.

4

BUT, A FEW HOURS LATER, THINGS ARE BACK TO NORMAL AGAIN WITH THE **FANTASTIC FOUR...**

THERE! THAT FINISHES MY SCIENTIFIC REPORT TO N.A.S.A. ABOUT OUR NEW ROCKET FUEL!

NOW I'LL FIND SUE AND ASK HER TO TYPE IT UP SO THAT WE CAN DISPATCH IT TO WASHINGTON VIA SPECIAL COURIER!

HMMM, THERE SHE IS, OPERATING MY NEW EXPERIMENTAL "ROVING-EYE" TV APPARATUS! SHE'S GOT IT FOCUSED ON THE BOTTOM OF THE SEA!

SO **THERE** YOU ARE, SUE! I'VE BEEN LOOKING FOR YOU!

OH! REED! YOU--YOU **STARTLED** ME!

SHE BLANKED IT OUT IN ALARM! AND I'M SURE I KNOW WHY!

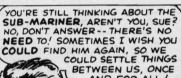

YOU'RE STILL THINKING ABOUT THE **SUB-MARINER,** AREN'T YOU, SUE? NO, DON'T ANSWER -- THERE'S NO **NEED** TO! SOMETIMES I WISH YOU **COULD** FIND HIM AGAIN, SO WE COULD SETTLE THINGS BETWEEN US, ONCE AND FOR ALL!

AND THEN, AFTER GIVING SUE THE REPORT TO TYPE...

STRANGE HOW NOBODY IS EVER REALLY MASTER OF HIS OWN FATE!

I'VE ALWAYS THOUGHT OF MYSELF AS BEING ABLE TO ACCOMPLISH ALMOST ANYTHING! WITH MY SCIENTIFIC TALENT, AND MY SUPER-FLEXIBLE BODY, IT SEEMED THAT NOTHING COULD EVER DEFEAT ME!

"NOTHING COULD OUTSMART ME -- NO PROBLEM COULD LONG REMAIN UNSOLVED WHEN I PUT MY MIND TO IT! NO OBSTACLE COULD STOP ME IF I DIDN'T WISH TO BE STOPPED!"

"PERHAPS I ALLOWED MY-SELF TO GET TOO OVER-CONFIDENT, TOO CONVINCED OF MY OWN ABILITY TO ACCOMPLISH ANYTHING I SET MY MIND TO!"

FOR NOW, THOUGH THE WORLD KNOWS ME AS THE INVINCIBLE **MISTER FANTASTIC,** I AM UNABLE TO WIN MY MOST CHERISHED GOAL! I AM UNABLE TO COMPLETELY CONQUER THE HEART OF THE GIRL I LOVE!

5

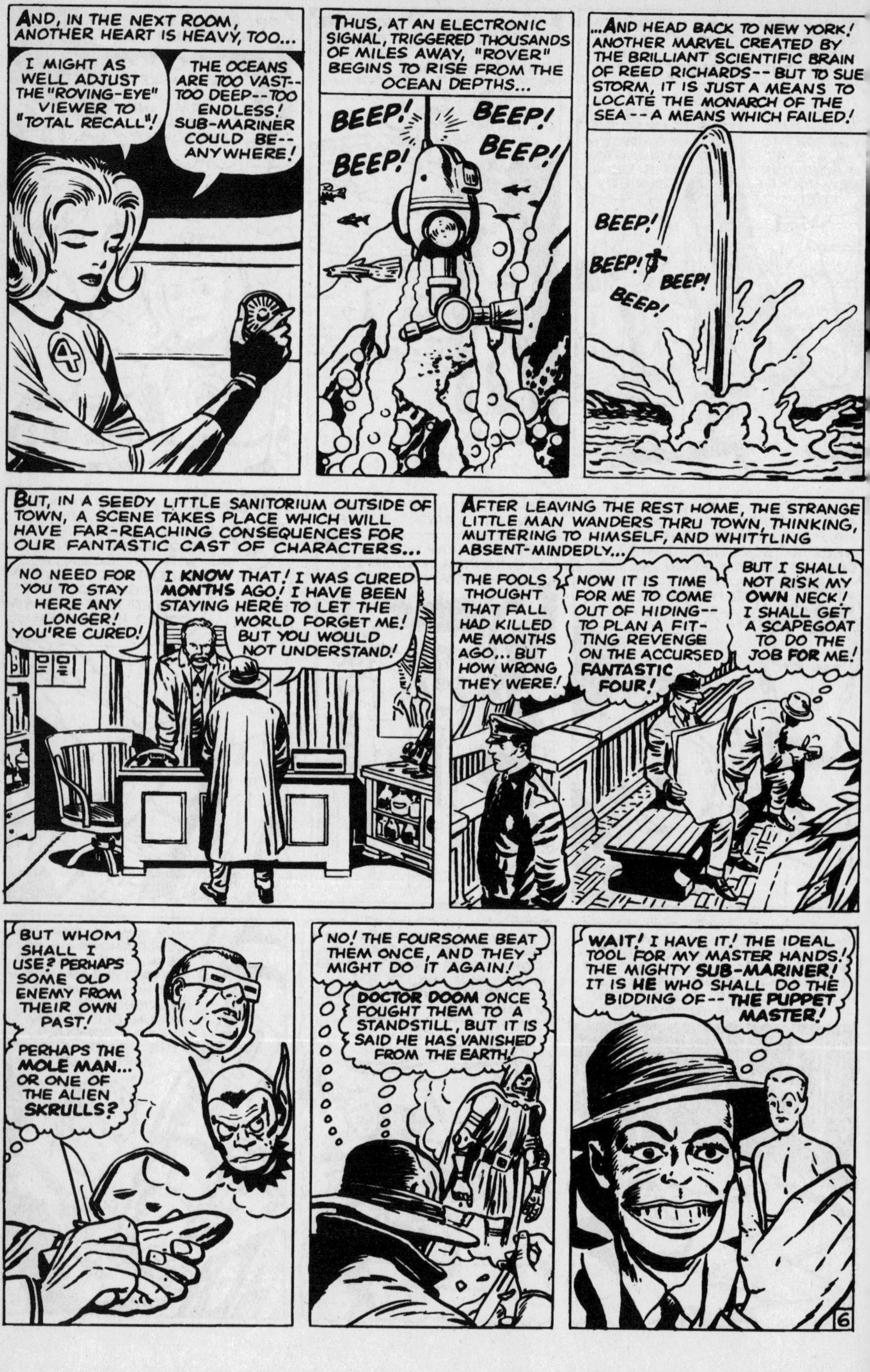
AND, IN THE NEXT ROOM, ANOTHER HEART IS HEAVY, TOO...
I MIGHT AS WELL ADJUST THE "ROVING-EYE" VIEWER TO "TOTAL RECALL"!
THE OCEANS ARE TOO VAST--TOO DEEP--TOO ENDLESS! SUB-MARINER COULD BE--ANYWHERE!
THUS, AT AN ELECTRONIC SIGNAL, TRIGGERED THOUSANDS OF MILES AWAY, "ROVER" BEGINS TO RISE FROM THE OCEAN DEPTHS...
BEEP! BEEP! BEEP! BEEP!
...AND HEAD BACK TO NEW YORK! ANOTHER MARVEL CREATED BY THE BRILLIANT SCIENTIFIC BRAIN OF REED RICHARDS--BUT TO SUE STORM, IT IS JUST A MEANS TO LOCATE THE MONARCH OF THE SEA--A MEANS WHICH FAILED!
BEEP! BEEP! BEEP! BEEP!
BUT, IN A SEEDY LITTLE SANITORIUM OUTSIDE OF TOWN, A SCENE TAKES PLACE WHICH WILL HAVE FAR-REACHING CONSEQUENCES FOR OUR FANTASTIC CAST OF CHARACTERS...
NO NEED FOR YOU TO STAY HERE ANY LONGER! YOU'RE CURED!
I KNOW THAT! I WAS CURED MONTHS AGO! I HAVE BEEN STAYING HERE TO LET THE WORLD FORGET ME! BUT YOU WOULD NOT UNDERSTAND!
AFTER LEAVING THE REST HOME, THE STRANGE LITTLE MAN WANDERS THRU TOWN, THINKING, MUTTERING TO HIMSELF, AND WHITTLING ABSENT-MINDEDLY...
THE FOOLS THOUGHT THAT FALL HAD KILLED ME MONTHS AGO... BUT HOW WRONG THEY WERE!
NOW IT IS TIME FOR ME TO COME OUT OF HIDING--TO PLAN A FITTING REVENGE ON THE ACCURSED FANTASTIC FOUR!
BUT I SHALL NOT RISK MY OWN NECK! I SHALL GET A SCAPEGOAT TO DO THE JOB FOR ME!
BUT WHOM SHALL I USE? PERHAPS SOME OLD ENEMY FROM THEIR OWN PAST!
PERHAPS THE MOLE MAN... OR ONE OF THE ALIEN SKRULLS?
NO! THE FOURSOME BEAT THEM ONCE, AND THEY MIGHT DO IT AGAIN!
DOCTOR DOOM ONCE FOUGHT THEM TO A STANDSTILL, BUT IT IS SAID HE HAS VANISHED FROM THE EARTH!
WAIT! I HAVE IT! THE IDEAL TOOL FOR MY MASTER HANDS! THE MIGHTY SUB-MARINER! IT IS HE WHO SHALL DO THE BIDDING OF--THE PUPPET MASTER!
6

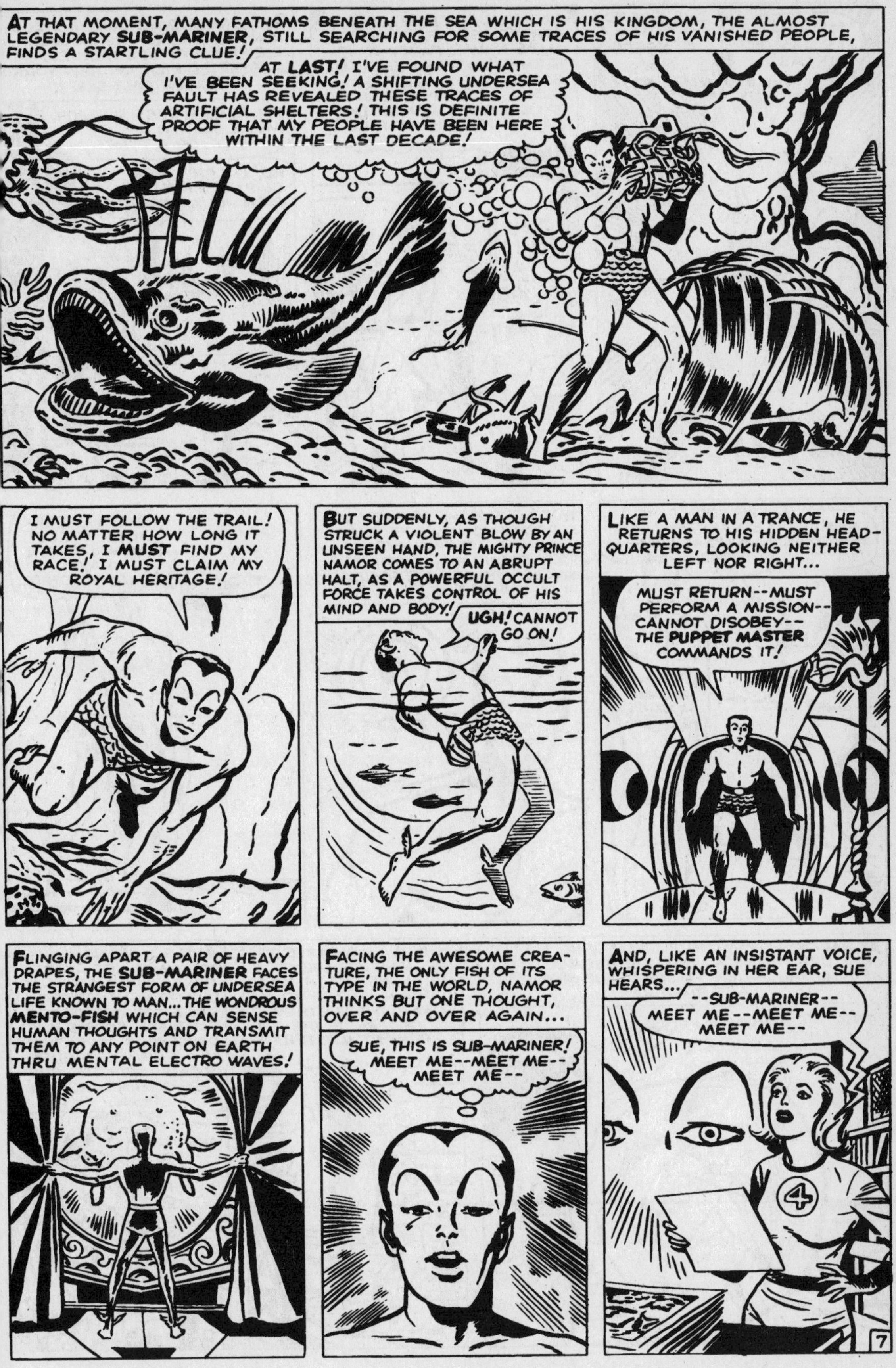

AT THAT MOMENT, MANY FATHOMS BENEATH THE SEA WHICH IS HIS KINGDOM, THE ALMOST LEGENDARY SUB-MARINER, STILL SEARCHING FOR SOME TRACES OF HIS VANISHED PEOPLE, FINDS A STARTLING CLUE!
AT LAST! I'VE FOUND WHAT I'VE BEEN SEEKING! A SHIFTING UNDERSEA FAULT HAS REVEALED THESE TRACES OF ARTIFICIAL SHELTERS! THIS IS DEFINITE PROOF THAT MY PEOPLE HAVE BEEN HERE WITHIN THE LAST DECADE!
I MUST FOLLOW THE TRAIL! NO MATTER HOW LONG IT TAKES, I MUST FIND MY RACE! I MUST CLAIM MY ROYAL HERITAGE!
BUT SUDDENLY, AS THOUGH STRUCK A VIOLENT BLOW BY AN UNSEEN HAND, THE MIGHTY PRINCE NAMOR COMES TO AN ABRUPT HALT, AS A POWERFUL OCCULT FORCE TAKES CONTROL OF HIS MIND AND BODY!
UGH! CANNOT GO ON!
LIKE A MAN IN A TRANCE, HE RETURNS TO HIS HIDDEN HEAD-QUARTERS, LOOKING NEITHER LEFT NOR RIGHT...
MUST RETURN--MUST PERFORM A MISSION--CANNOT DISOBEY--THE PUPPET MASTER COMMANDS IT!
FLINGING APART A PAIR OF HEAVY DRAPES, THE SUB-MARINER FACES THE STRANGEST FORM OF UNDERSEA LIFE KNOWN TO MAN...THE WONDROUS MENTO-FISH WHICH CAN SENSE HUMAN THOUGHTS AND TRANSMIT THEM TO ANY POINT ON EARTH THRU MENTAL ELECTRO WAVES!
FACING THE AWESOME CREATURE, THE ONLY FISH OF ITS TYPE IN THE WORLD, NAMOR THINKS BUT ONE THOUGHT, OVER AND OVER AGAIN...
SUE, THIS IS SUB-MARINER! MEET ME--MEET ME--MEET ME--
AND, LIKE AN INSISTANT VOICE, WHISPERING IN HER EAR, SUE HEARS...
--SUB-MARINER--MEET ME--MEET ME--MEET ME--
4
7

IT'S HIM! IT'S NAMOR! AT LAST!

I'VE GOT TO GO TO HIM! HE **NEEDS** ME!

BUT I MUSTN'T LET THE OTHERS SEE ME! THEY'LL MAKE A WAR PARTY OF IT IF THEY KNOW WHERE I'M GOING! AND I **MUST** GO ALONE--IT'S MY ONE CHANCE TO LEARN IF I REALLY **DO** CARE FOR SUB-MARINER!

FOLLOWING THE SILENT INSTRUCTIONS WHISPERED IN HER BRAIN, SUE FINALLY FINDS HERSELF AT A DESERTED PIER, ON NEW YORK'S LOWER EAST SIDE...

I'LL REMAIN INVISIBLE UNTIL I MAKE CERTAIN IT ISN'T A TRICK, OR A TRAP!

NO! IT CAN'T BE A TRAP! IT'S **HIM**! I'D KNOW HIM **ANYWHERE**!

NAMOR! I'VE COME! I--

WHY DON'T YOU SPEAK? WHY DON'T YOU SAY SOMETHING?

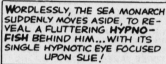

WORDLESSLY, THE SEA MONARCH SUDDENLY MOVES ASIDE, TO REVEAL A FLUTTERING **HYPNO-FISH** BEHIND HIM...WITH ITS SINGLE HYPNOTIC EYE FOCUSED UPON SUE!

SHE IS UNDER YOUR SPELL! NOW DO AS I HAVE INSTRUCTED...

AT NAMOR'S COMMAND, THE AMAZING CREATURE FORMS A HUGE AIR BUBBLE AROUND THE DOCILE FIGURE OF SUE STORM! AND THEN...

INTO THE SEA WITH HER!

SHE WILL BE ABLE TO BREATHE NORMALLY UNTIL WE REACH MY DOMAIN...THERE TO AWAIT THE FURTHER ORDERS OF THE **PUPPET MASTER**!

AND SO, HAVING BLINDLY FOLLOWED HER HEART, THE INVISIBLE GIRL HAS UNWITTINGLY SET THE STAGE FOR ONE OF THE **FANTASTIC FOUR'S** MOST DANGEROUS ADVENTURES, AS A GRINNING FIGURE GLOATS OVER THE SUCCESS OF HIS VENGEFUL PLAN!

AND NOW --IT IS TIME FOR STEP TWO!

8

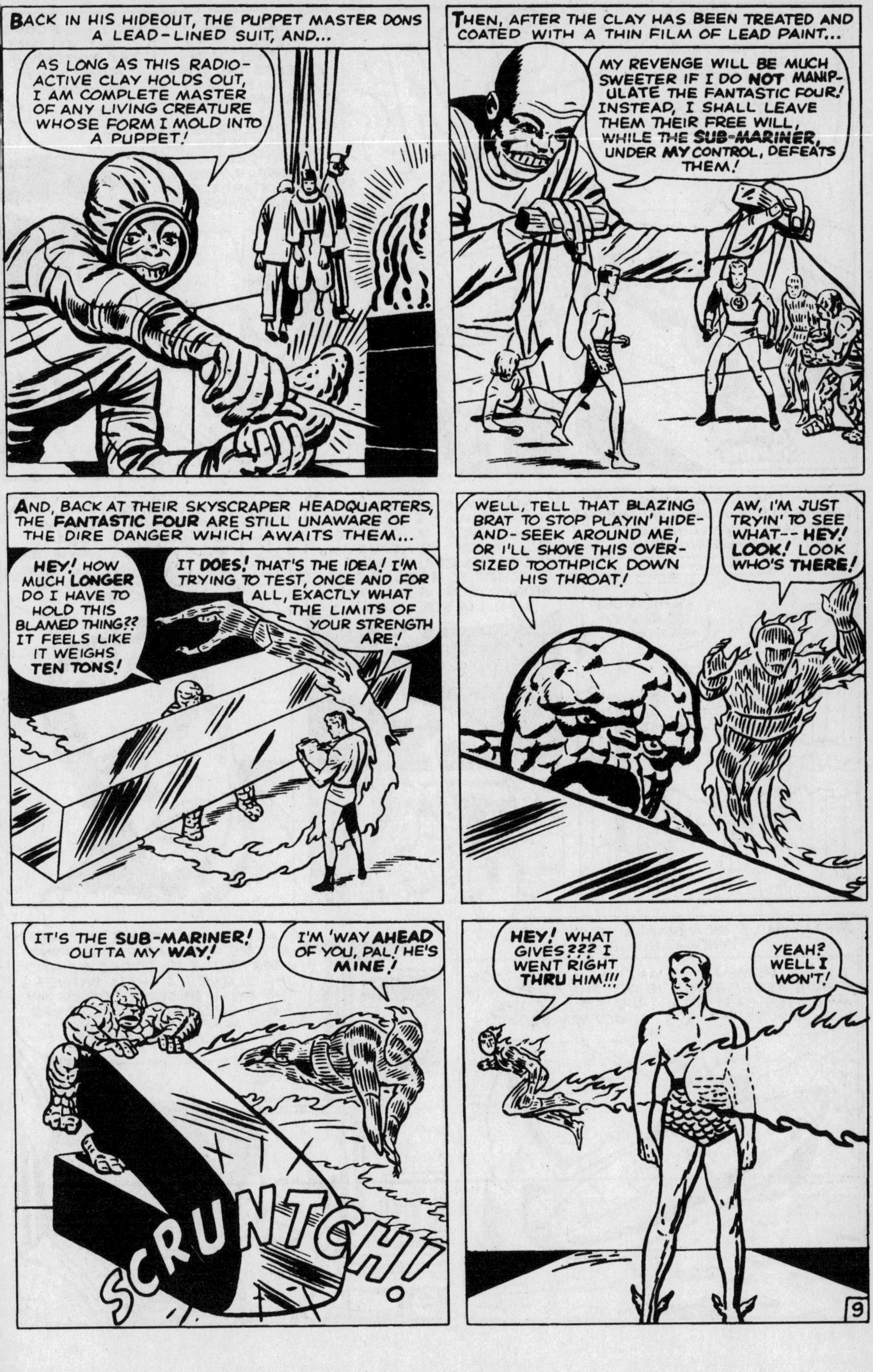
BACK IN HIS HIDEOUT, THE PUPPET MASTER DONS A LEAD-LINED SUIT, AND...
AS LONG AS THIS RADIO-ACTIVE CLAY HOLDS OUT, I AM COMPLETE MASTER OF ANY LIVING CREATURE WHOSE FORM I MOLD INTO A PUPPET!
THEN, AFTER THE CLAY HAS BEEN TREATED AND COATED WITH A THIN FILM OF LEAD PAINT...
MY REVENGE WILL BE MUCH SWEETER IF I DO NOT MANIPULATE THE FANTASTIC FOUR! INSTEAD, I SHALL LEAVE THEM THEIR FREE WILL, WHILE THE SUB-MARINER, UNDER MY CONTROL, DEFEATS THEM!
AND, BACK AT THEIR SKYSCRAPER HEADQUARTERS, THE FANTASTIC FOUR ARE STILL UNAWARE OF THE DIRE DANGER WHICH AWAITS THEM...
HEY! HOW MUCH LONGER DO I HAVE TO HOLD THIS BLAMED THING?? IT FEELS LIKE IT WEIGHS TEN TONS!
IT DOES! THAT'S THE IDEA! I'M TRYING TO TEST, ONCE AND FOR ALL, EXACTLY WHAT THE LIMITS OF YOUR STRENGTH ARE!
WELL, TELL THAT BLAZING BRAT TO STOP PLAYIN' HIDE-AND-SEEK AROUND ME, OR I'LL SHOVE THIS OVER-SIZED TOOTHPICK DOWN HIS THROAT!
AW, I'M JUST TRYIN' TO SEE WHAT-- HEY! LOOK! LOOK WHO'S THERE!
IT'S THE SUB-MARINER! OUTTA MY WAY!
I'M 'WAY AHEAD OF YOU, PAL! HE'S MINE!
SCRUNTCH!
HEY! WHAT GIVES??? I WENT RIGHT THRU HIM!!!
YEAH? WELL I WON'T!
9

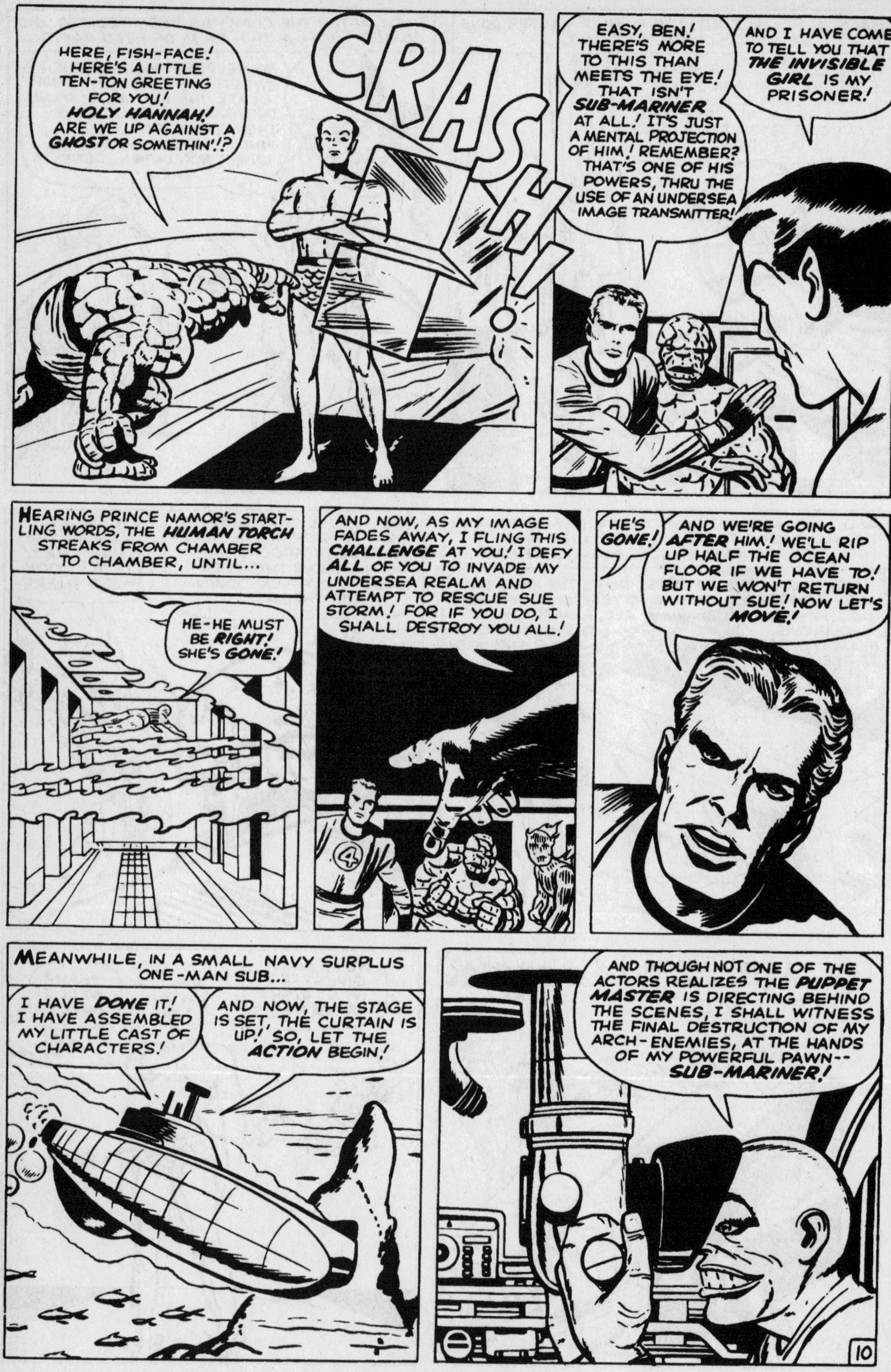
HERE, FISH-FACE! HERE'S A LITTLE TEN-TON GREETING FOR YOU! HOLY HANNAH! ARE WE UP AGAINST A GHOST OR SOMETHIN'!?
CRASH!
EASY, BEN! THERE'S MORE TO THIS THAN MEETS THE EYE! THAT ISN'T SUB-MARINER AT ALL! IT'S JUST A MENTAL PROJECTION OF HIM! REMEMBER? THAT'S ONE OF HIS POWERS, THRU THE USE OF AN UNDERSEA IMAGE TRANSMITTER!
AND I HAVE COME TO TELL YOU THAT THE INVISIBLE GIRL IS MY PRISONER!
HEARING PRINCE NAMOR'S STARTLING WORDS, THE HUMAN TORCH STREAKS FROM CHAMBER TO CHAMBER, UNTIL...
HE-HE MUST BE RIGHT! SHE'S GONE!
AND NOW, AS MY IMAGE FADES AWAY, I FLING THIS CHALLENGE AT YOU! I DEFY ALL OF YOU TO INVADE MY UNDERSEA REALM AND ATTEMPT TO RESCUE SUE STORM! FOR IF YOU DO, I SHALL DESTROY YOU ALL!
HE'S GONE!
AND WE'RE GOING AFTER HIM! WE'LL RIP UP HALF THE OCEAN FLOOR IF WE HAVE TO! BUT WE WON'T RETURN WITHOUT SUE! NOW LET'S MOVE!
MEANWHILE, IN A SMALL NAVY SURPLUS ONE-MAN SUB...
I HAVE DONE IT! I HAVE ASSEMBLED MY LITTLE CAST OF CHARACTERS!
AND NOW, THE STAGE IS SET, THE CURTAIN IS UP! SO, LET THE ACTION BEGIN!
AND THOUGH NOT ONE OF THE ACTORS REALIZES THE PUPPET MASTER IS DIRECTING BEHIND THE SCENES, I SHALL WITNESS THE FINAL DESTRUCTION OF MY ARCH-ENEMIES, AT THE HANDS OF MY POWERFUL PAWN-- SUB-MARINER!
10

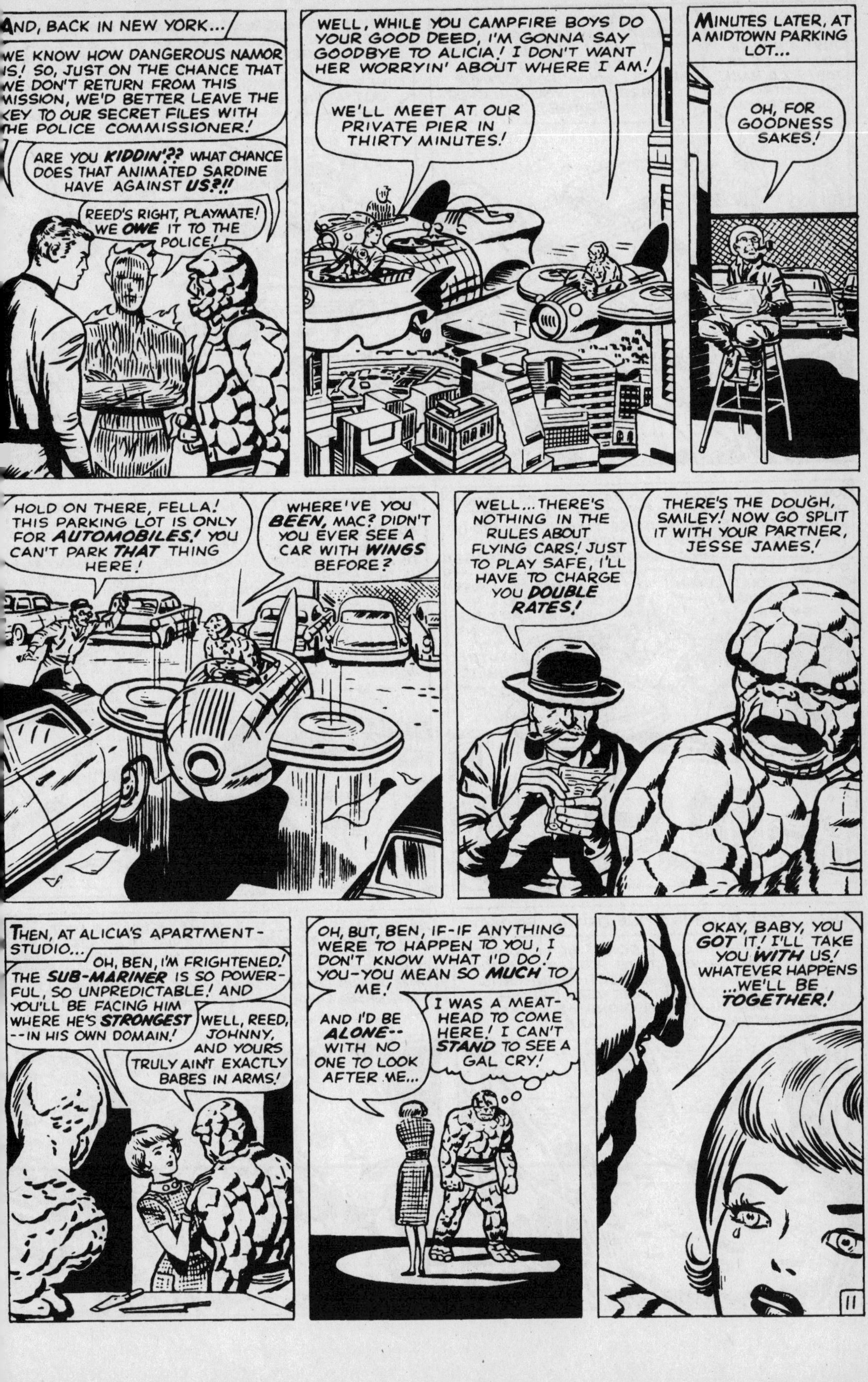

AND, BACK IN NEW YORK...
WE KNOW HOW DANGEROUS NAMOR IS! SO, JUST ON THE CHANCE THAT WE DON'T RETURN FROM THIS MISSION, WE'D BETTER LEAVE THE KEY TO OUR SECRET FILES WITH THE POLICE COMMISSIONER!
ARE YOU KIDDIN'?? WHAT CHANCE DOES THAT ANIMATED SARDINE HAVE AGAINST US?!!
REED'S RIGHT, PLAYMATE! WE OWE IT TO THE POLICE!
WELL, WHILE YOU CAMPFIRE BOYS DO YOUR GOOD DEED, I'M GONNA SAY GOODBYE TO ALICIA! I DON'T WANT HER WORRYIN' ABOUT WHERE I AM!
WE'LL MEET AT OUR PRIVATE PIER IN THIRTY MINUTES!
MINUTES LATER, AT A MIDTOWN PARKING LOT...
OH, FOR GOODNESS SAKES!
HOLD ON THERE, FELLA! THIS PARKING LOT IS ONLY FOR AUTOMOBILES! YOU CAN'T PARK THAT THING HERE!
WHERE'VE YOU BEEN, MAC? DIDN'T YOU EVER SEE A CAR WITH WINGS BEFORE?
WELL... THERE'S NOTHING IN THE RULES ABOUT FLYING CARS! JUST TO PLAY SAFE, I'LL HAVE TO CHARGE YOU DOUBLE RATES!
THERE'S THE DOUGH, SMILEY! NOW GO SPLIT IT WITH YOUR PARTNER, JESSE JAMES!
THEN, AT ALICIA'S APARTMENT-STUDIO...
OH, BEN, I'M FRIGHTENED! THE SUB-MARINER IS SO POWERFUL, SO UNPREDICTABLE! AND YOU'LL BE FACING HIM WHERE HE'S STRONGEST --IN HIS OWN DOMAIN!
WELL, REED, JOHNNY, AND YOURS TRULY AIN'T EXACTLY BABES IN ARMS!
OH, BUT, BEN, IF-IF ANYTHING WERE TO HAPPEN TO YOU, I DON'T KNOW WHAT I'D DO! YOU-YOU MEAN SO MUCH TO ME!
AND I'D BE ALONE-- WITH NO ONE TO LOOK AFTER ME...
I WAS A MEAT-HEAD TO COME HERE! I CAN'T STAND TO SEE A GAL CRY!
OKAY, BABY, YOU GOT IT! I'LL TAKE YOU WITH US! WHATEVER HAPPENS ...WE'LL BE TOGETHER!
11

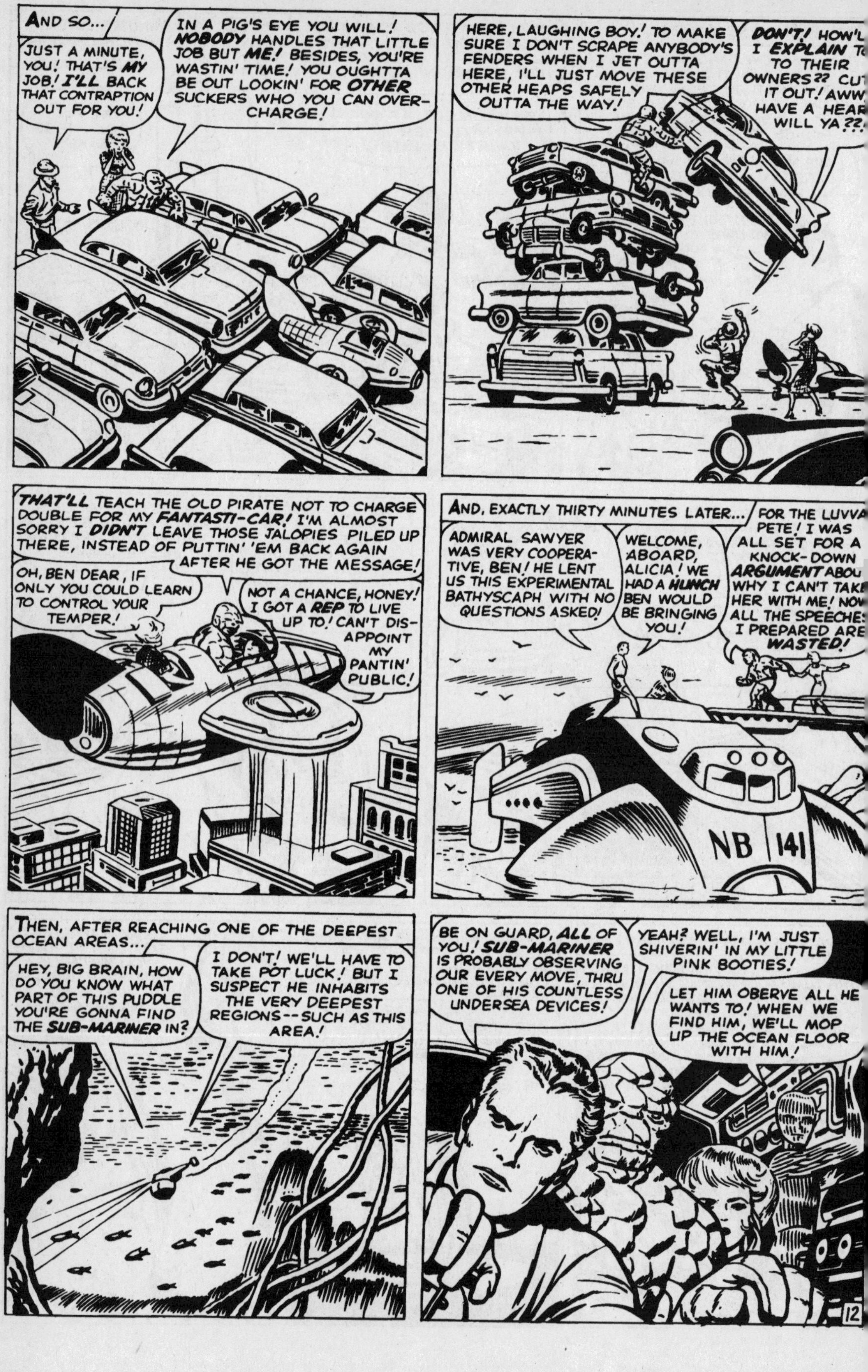
AND SO...
JUST A MINUTE, YOU! THAT'S MY JOB! I'LL BACK THAT CONTRAPTION OUT FOR YOU!
IN A PIG'S EYE YOU WILL! NOBODY HANDLES THAT LITTLE JOB BUT ME! BESIDES, YOU'RE WASTIN' TIME! YOU OUGHTTA BE OUT LOOKIN' FOR OTHER SUCKERS WHO YOU CAN OVER-CHARGE!
HERE, LAUGHING BOY! TO MAKE SURE I DON'T SCRAPE ANYBODY'S FENDERS WHEN I JET OUTTA HERE, I'LL JUST MOVE THESE OTHER HEAPS SAFELY OUTTA THE WAY!
THAT'LL TEACH THE OLD PIRATE NOT TO CHARGE DOUBLE FOR MY FANTASTI-CAR! I'M ALMOST SORRY I DIDN'T LEAVE THOSE JALOPIES PILED UP THERE, INSTEAD OF PUTTIN' 'EM BACK AGAIN AFTER HE GOT THE MESSAGE!
OH, BEN DEAR, IF ONLY YOU COULD LEARN TO CONTROL YOUR TEMPER!
NOT A CHANCE, HONEY! I GOT A REP TO LIVE UP TO! CAN'T DIS-APPOINT MY PANTIN' PUBLIC!
AND, EXACTLY THIRTY MINUTES LATER...
ADMIRAL SAWYER WAS VERY COOPERA-TIVE, BEN! HE LENT US THIS EXPERIMENTAL BATHYSCAPH WITH NO QUESTIONS ASKED!
WELCOME, ALICIA! WE HAD A HUNCH BEN WOULD BE BRINGING YOU!
NB 141
THEN, AFTER REACHING ONE OF THE DEEPEST OCEAN AREAS...
HEY, BIG BRAIN, HOW DO YOU KNOW WHAT PART OF THIS PUDDLE YOU'RE GONNA FIND THE SUB-MARINER IN?
I DON'T! WE'LL HAVE TO TAKE POT LUCK! BUT I SUSPECT HE INHABITS THE VERY DEEPEST REGIONS--SUCH AS THIS AREA!
BE ON GUARD, ALL OF YOU! SUB-MARINER IS PROBABLY OBSERVING OUR EVERY MOVE, THRU ONE OF HIS COUNTLESS UNDERSEA DEVICES!
YEAH? WELL, I'M JUST SHIVERIN' IN MY LITTLE PINK BOOTIES!
LET HIM OBSERVE ALL HE WANTS TO! WHEN WE FIND HIM, WE'LL MOP UP THE OCEAN FLOOR WITH HIM!
12

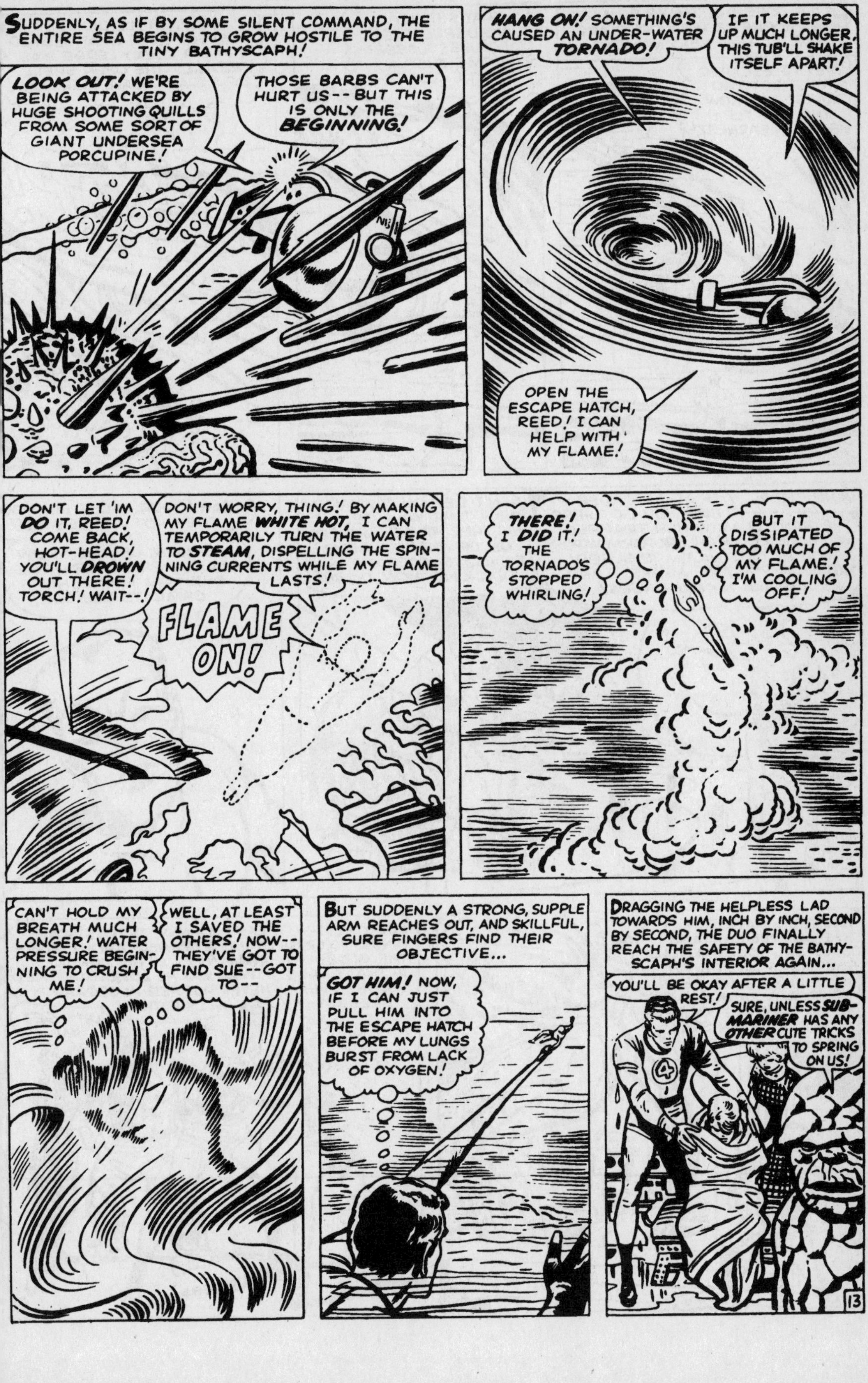
SUDDENLY, AS IF BY SOME SILENT COMMAND, THE ENTIRE SEA BEGINS TO GROW HOSTILE TO THE TINY BATHYSCAPH!
LOOK OUT! WE'RE BEING ATTACKED BY HUGE SHOOTING QUILLS FROM SOME SORT OF GIANT UNDERSEA PORCUPINE!
THOSE BARBS CAN'T HURT US--BUT THIS IS ONLY THE BEGINNING!
HANG ON! SOMETHING'S CAUSED AN UNDER-WATER TORNADO!
IF IT KEEPS UP MUCH LONGER, THIS TUB'LL SHAKE ITSELF APART!
OPEN THE ESCAPE HATCH, REED! I CAN HELP WITH MY FLAME!
DON'T LET 'IM DO IT, REED! COME BACK, HOT-HEAD! YOU'LL DROWN OUT THERE! TORCH! WAIT--!
DON'T WORRY, THING! BY MAKING MY FLAME WHITE HOT, I CAN TEMPORARILY TURN THE WATER TO STEAM, DISPELLING THE SPINNING CURRENTS WHILE MY FLAME LASTS!
FLAME ON!
THERE! I DID IT! THE TORNADO'S STOPPED WHIRLING!
BUT IT DISSIPATED TOO MUCH OF MY FLAME! I'M COOLING OFF!
CAN'T HOLD MY BREATH MUCH LONGER! WATER PRESSURE BEGINNING TO CRUSH ME!
WELL, AT LEAST I SAVED THE OTHERS! NOW--THEY'VE GOT TO FIND SUE--GOT TO--
BUT SUDDENLY A STRONG, SUPPLE ARM REACHES OUT, AND SKILLFUL, SURE FINGERS FIND THEIR OBJECTIVE...
GOT HIM! NOW, IF I CAN JUST PULL HIM INTO THE ESCAPE HATCH BEFORE MY LUNGS BURST FROM LACK OF OXYGEN!
DRAGGING THE HELPLESS LAD TOWARDS HIM, INCH BY INCH, SECOND BY SECOND, THE DUO FINALLY REACH THE SAFETY OF THE BATHYSCAPH'S INTERIOR AGAIN...
YOU'LL BE OKAY AFTER A LITTLE REST!
SURE, UNLESS SUB-MARINER HAS ANY OTHER CUTE TRICKS TO SPRING ON US!
13

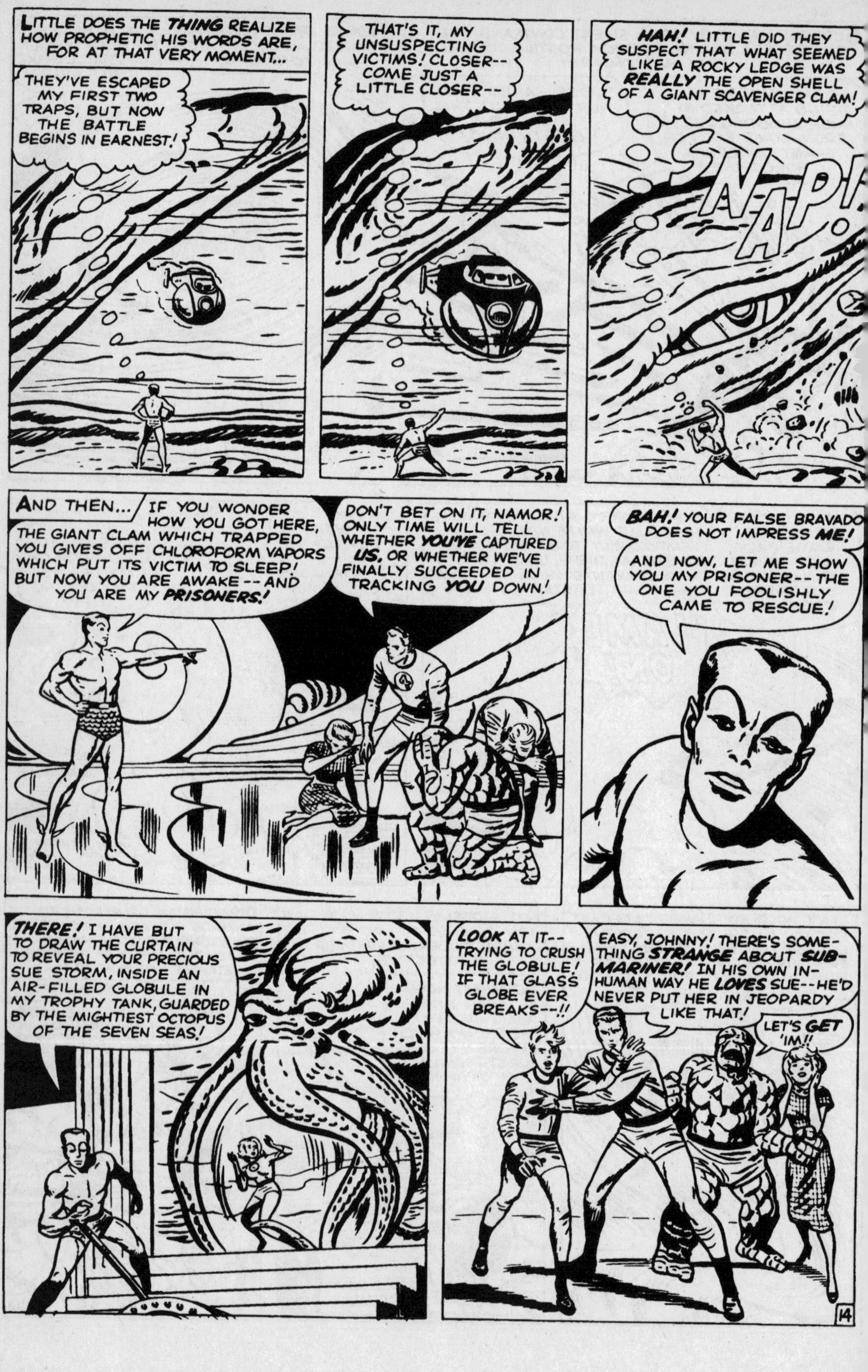
LITTLE DOES THE THING REALIZE HOW PROPHETIC HIS WORDS ARE, FOR AT THAT VERY MOMENT...
THEY'VE ESCAPED MY FIRST TWO TRAPS, BUT NOW THE BATTLE BEGINS IN EARNEST!
THAT'S IT, MY UNSUSPECTING VICTIMS! CLOSER-- COME JUST A LITTLE CLOSER--
HAH! LITTLE DID THEY SUSPECT THAT WHAT SEEMED LIKE A ROCKY LEDGE WAS REALLY THE OPEN SHELL OF A GIANT SCAVENGER CLAM!
SNAP!
AND THEN...
IF YOU WONDER HOW YOU GOT HERE, THE GIANT CLAM WHICH TRAPPED YOU GIVES OFF CHLOROFORM VAPORS WHICH PUT ITS VICTIM TO SLEEP! BUT NOW YOU ARE AWAKE--AND YOU ARE MY PRISONERS!
DON'T BET ON IT, NAMOR! ONLY TIME WILL TELL WHETHER YOU'VE CAPTURED US, OR WHETHER WE'VE FINALLY SUCCEEDED IN TRACKING YOU DOWN!
BAH! YOUR FALSE BRAVADO DOES NOT IMPRESS ME!
AND NOW, LET ME SHOW YOU MY PRISONER--THE ONE YOU FOOLISHLY CAME TO RESCUE!
THERE! I HAVE BUT TO DRAW THE CURTAIN TO REVEAL YOUR PRECIOUS SUE STORM, INSIDE AN AIR-FILLED GLOBULE IN MY TROPHY TANK, GUARDED BY THE MIGHTIEST OCTOPUS OF THE SEVEN SEAS!
LOOK AT IT-- TRYING TO CRUSH THE GLOBULE! IF THAT GLASS GLOBE EVER BREAKS--!!
EASY, JOHNNY! THERE'S SOMETHING STRANGE ABOUT SUB-MARINER! IN HIS OWN INHUMAN WAY HE LOVES SUE--HE'D NEVER PUT HER IN JEOPARDY LIKE THAT!
LET'S GET 'IM!!
14

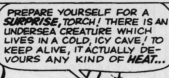

I'LL BATTLE YOU ONE BY ONE, AS IS THE CUSTOM OF MY PEOPLE! WHO SHALL BE THE FIRST?

ME, YOU FLAT-HEADED CREEP! THAT'S MY SISTER IN THERE!

FLAME ON!

PREPARE YOURSELF FOR A SURPRISE, TORCH! THERE IS AN UNDERSEA CREATURE WHICH LIVES IN A COLD, ICY CAVE! TO KEEP ALIVE, IT ACTUALLY DEVOURS ANY KIND OF HEAT...

AND THIS IS IT! THE LIVING WEAPON WITH WHICH I SHALL DEFEAT YOUR FLAMING POWER ONCE AND FOR ALL! A RAVENOUS UNTHINKING FLAME-EATER!

IT'S WORKING! HE IS ABSORBING THE HEAT FROM YOUR BODY AS A SPONGE ABSORBS WATER!

GETTING WEAK --ALL THE FLAME--ALL THE STRENGTH --DRAINING AWAY FROM ME--CAN'T --CAN'T STAY ALOFT--

LOOK AT YOURSELF, TORCH! BEHOLD THE FABULOUS, FABLED HERO OF MILLIONS!

BUT MY FLAME-EATER HAS HAD ENOUGH! HE CAN ABSORB NO MORE! HE HAS DONE HIS TASK WELL!

ALL THAT REMAINS IS FOR ME TO FINISH THE JOB, WITH MY BARE HANDS!

WELL, WHAT ARE YOU WAITIN' FOR? I NEVER LEARNED HOW TO SAY "UNCLE"!!

OH NO YOU DON'T, FISH-FACE! THAT BRAVE LITTLE KID IS WORTH A DOZEN DOUBLE-CROSSERS LIKE YOU!

THIS WAS SUPPOSED TO BE A HAND-TO-HAND FIGHT! IF YOU CAN BRING IN THOSE CREEPY SEA-CREATURES OF YOURS, THEN THE TORCH CAN USE A LITTLE HELP, TOO! AND, BROTHER, HE'S GONNA GET IT!

15

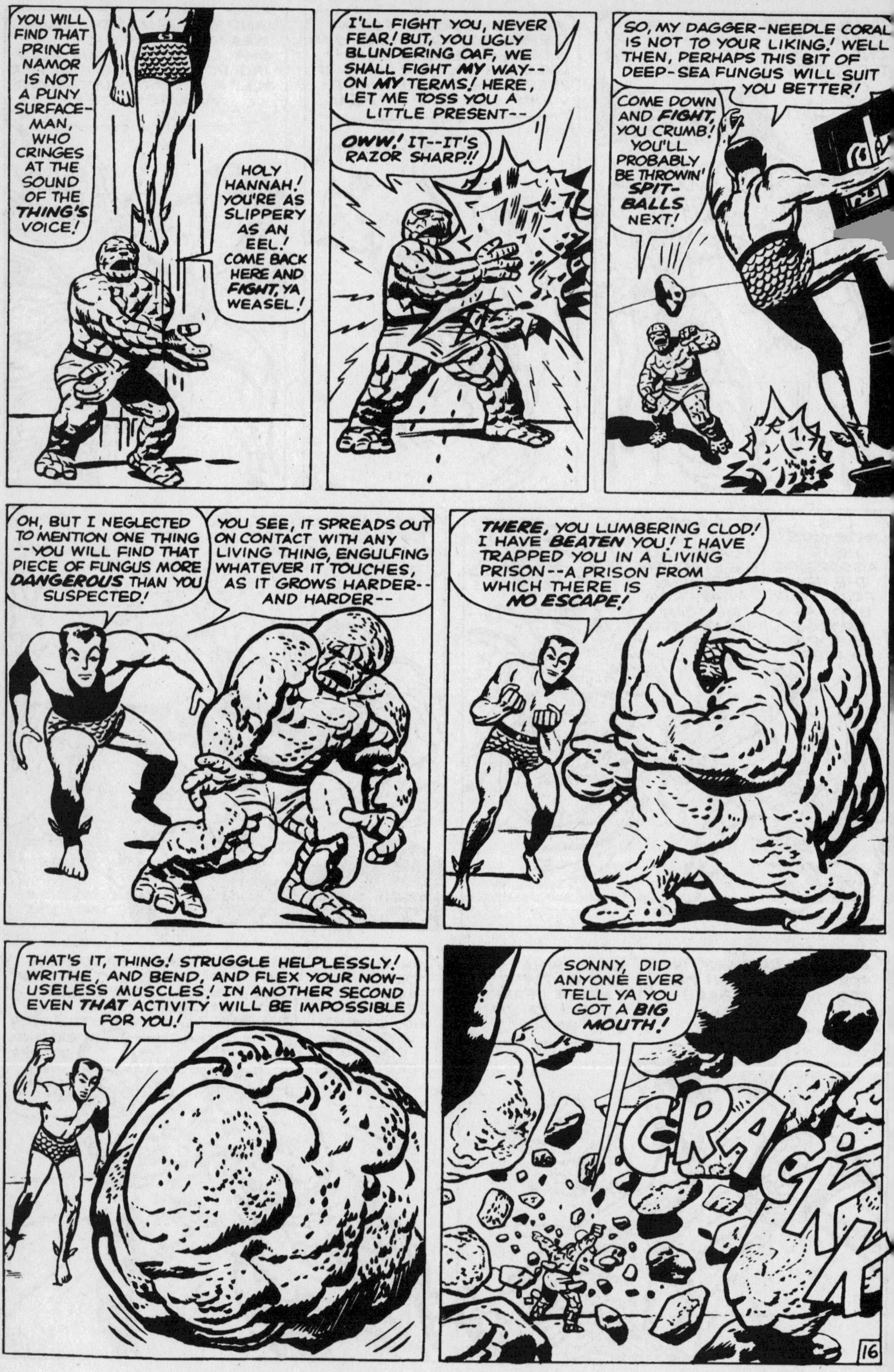
YOU WILL FIND THAT PRINCE NAMOR IS NOT A PUNY SURFACE-MAN, WHO CRINGES AT THE SOUND OF THE THING'S VOICE!
HOLY HANNAH! YOU'RE AS SLIPPERY AS AN EEL! COME BACK HERE AND FIGHT, YA WEASEL!
I'LL FIGHT YOU, NEVER FEAR! BUT, YOU UGLY BLUNDERING OAF, WE SHALL FIGHT MY WAY-- ON MY TERMS! HERE, LET ME TOSS YOU A LITTLE PRESENT--
OWW! IT--IT'S RAZOR SHARP!!
SO, MY DAGGER-NEEDLE CORAL IS NOT TO YOUR LIKING! WELL THEN, PERHAPS THIS BIT OF DEEP-SEA FUNGUS WILL SUIT YOU BETTER!
COME DOWN AND FIGHT, YOU CRUMB! YOU'LL PROBABLY BE THROWIN' SPIT-BALLS NEXT!
OH, BUT I NEGLECTED TO MENTION ONE THING --YOU WILL FIND THAT PIECE OF FUNGUS MORE DANGEROUS THAN YOU SUSPECTED!
YOU SEE, IT SPREADS OUT ON CONTACT WITH ANY LIVING THING, ENGULFING WHATEVER IT TOUCHES, AS IT GROWS HARDER-- AND HARDER--
THERE, YOU LUMBERING CLOD! I HAVE BEATEN YOU! I HAVE TRAPPED YOU IN A LIVING PRISON--A PRISON FROM WHICH THERE IS NO ESCAPE!
THAT'S IT, THING! STRUGGLE HELPLESSLY! WRITHE, AND BEND, AND FLEX YOUR NOW-USELESS MUSCLES! IN ANOTHER SECOND EVEN THAT ACTIVITY WILL BE IMPOSSIBLE FOR YOU!
SONNY, DID ANYONE EVER TELL YA YOU GOT A BIG MOUTH!
CRACK

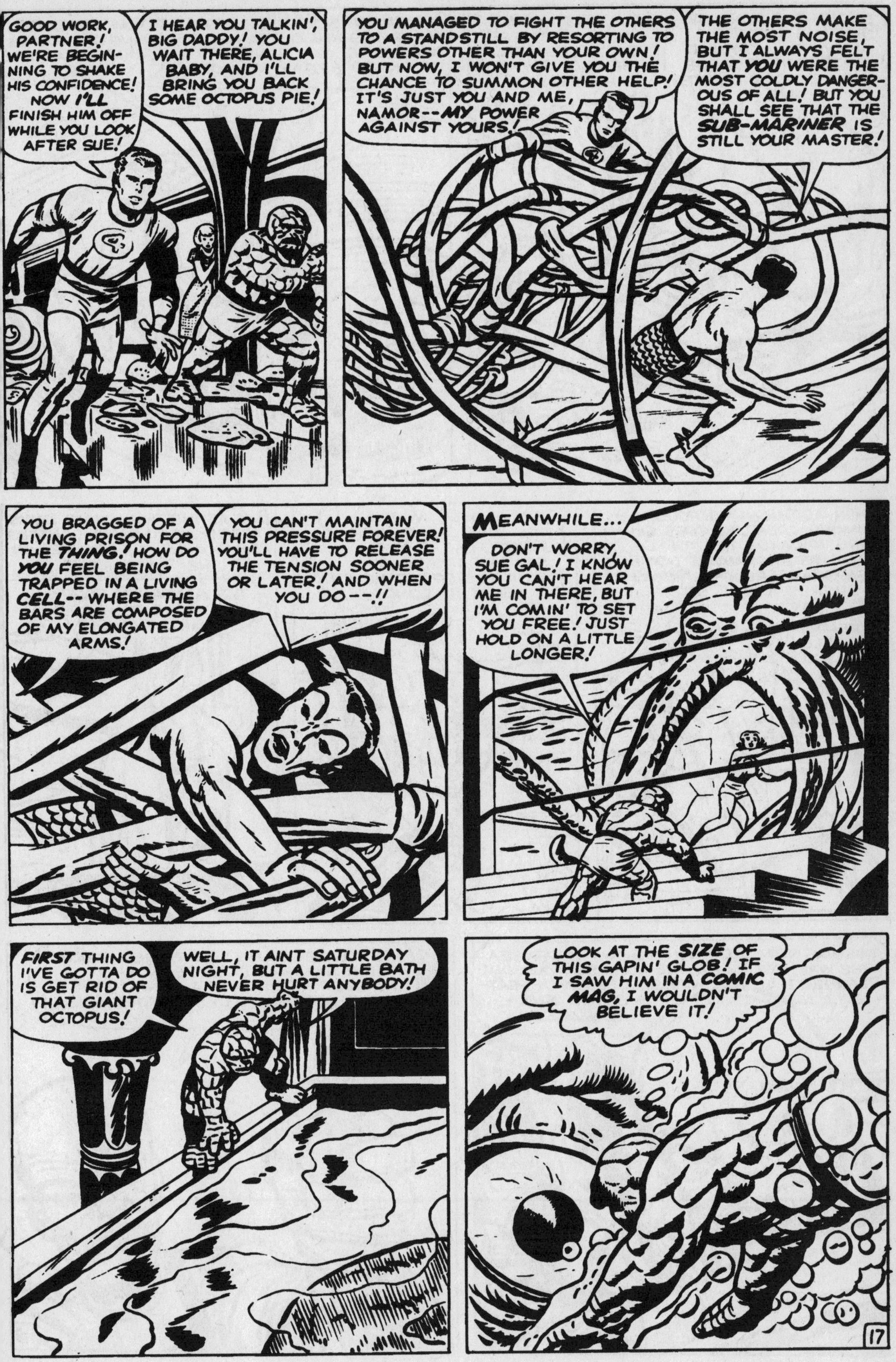
GOOD WORK, PARTNER! WE'RE BEGINNING TO SHAKE HIS CONFIDENCE! NOW I'LL FINISH HIM OFF WHILE YOU LOOK AFTER SUE!
I HEAR YOU TALKIN', BIG DADDY! YOU WAIT THERE, ALICIA BABY, AND I'LL BRING YOU BACK SOME OCTOPUS PIE!
YOU MANAGED TO FIGHT THE OTHERS TO A STANDSTILL BY RESORTING TO POWERS OTHER THAN YOUR OWN! BUT NOW, I WON'T GIVE YOU THE CHANCE TO SUMMON OTHER HELP! IT'S JUST YOU AND ME, NAMOR--MY POWER AGAINST YOURS!
THE OTHERS MAKE THE MOST NOISE, BUT I ALWAYS FELT THAT YOU WERE THE MOST COLDLY DANGEROUS OF ALL! BUT YOU SHALL SEE THAT THE SUB-MARINER IS STILL YOUR MASTER!
YOU BRAGGED OF A LIVING PRISON FOR THE THING! HOW DO YOU FEEL BEING TRAPPED IN A LIVING CELL-- WHERE THE BARS ARE COMPOSED OF MY ELONGATED ARMS!
YOU CAN'T MAINTAIN THIS PRESSURE FOREVER! YOU'LL HAVE TO RELEASE THE TENSION SOONER OR LATER! AND WHEN YOU DO--!!
MEANWHILE...
DON'T WORRY, SUE GAL! I KNOW YOU CAN'T HEAR ME IN THERE, BUT I'M COMIN' TO SET YOU FREE! JUST HOLD ON A LITTLE LONGER!
FIRST THING I'VE GOTTA DO IS GET RID OF THAT GIANT OCTOPUS!
WELL, IT AINT SATURDAY NIGHT, BUT A LITTLE BATH NEVER HURT ANYBODY!
LOOK AT THE SIZE OF THIS GAPIN' GLOB! IF I SAW HIM IN A COMIC MAG, I WOULDN'T BELIEVE IT!
17

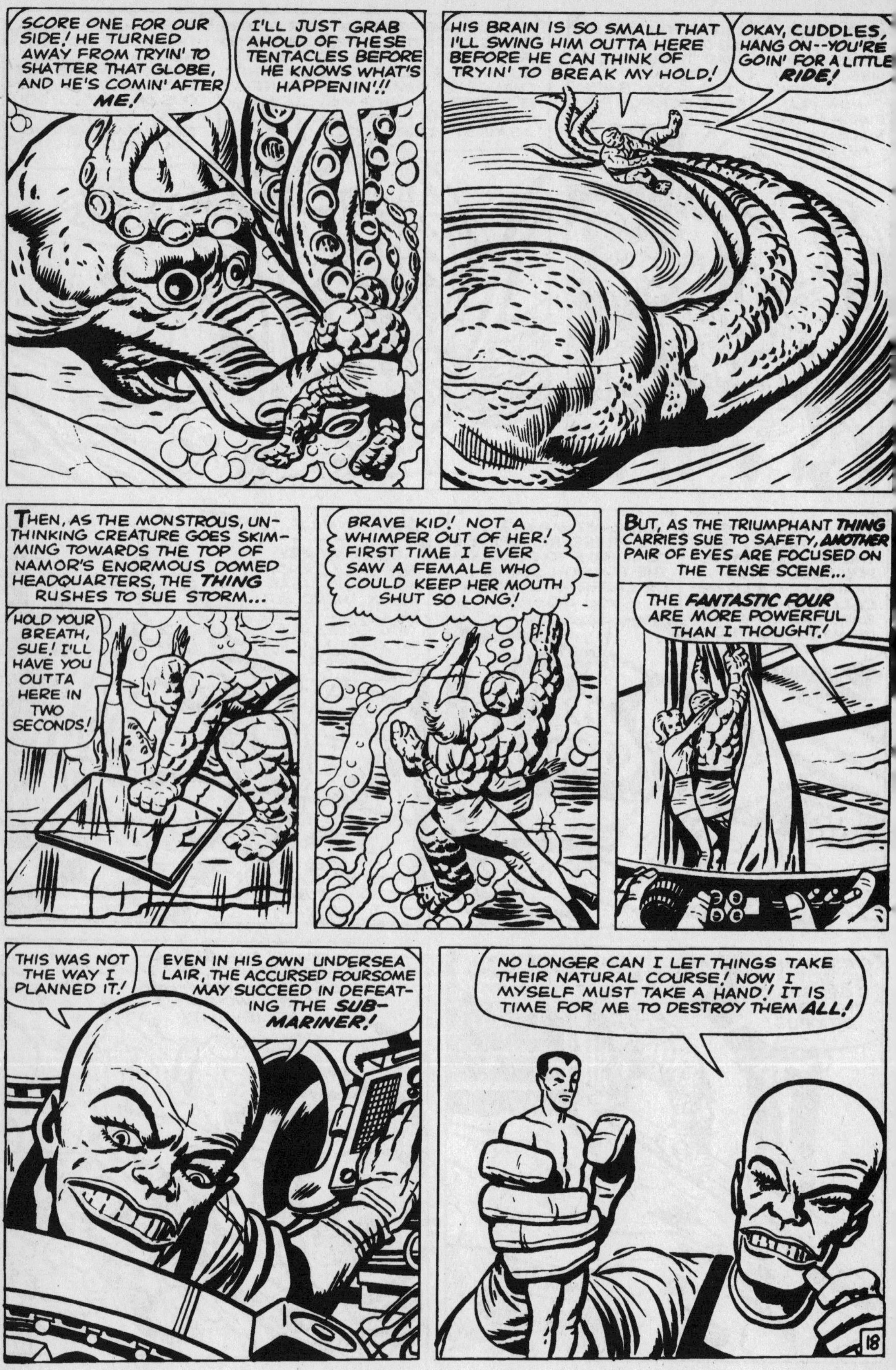

SCORE ONE FOR OUR SIDE! HE TURNED AWAY FROM TRYIN' TO SHATTER THAT GLOBE, AND HE'S COMIN' AFTER ME!
I'LL JUST GRAB AHOLD OF THESE TENTACLES BEFORE HE KNOWS WHAT'S HAPPENIN'!!
HIS BRAIN IS SO SMALL THAT I'LL SWING HIM OUTTA HERE BEFORE HE CAN THINK OF TRYIN' TO BREAK MY HOLD!
OKAY, CUDDLES, HANG ON--YOU'RE GOIN' FOR A LITTLE RIDE!
THEN, AS THE MONSTROUS, UNTHINKING CREATURE GOES SKIMMING TOWARDS THE TOP OF NAMOR'S ENORMOUS DOMED HEADQUARTERS, THE THING RUSHES TO SUE STORM...
HOLD YOUR BREATH, SUE! I'LL HAVE YOU OUTTA HERE IN TWO SECONDS!
BRAVE KID! NOT A WHIMPER OUT OF HER! FIRST TIME I EVER SAW A FEMALE WHO COULD KEEP HER MOUTH SHUT SO LONG!
BUT, AS THE TRIUMPHANT THING CARRIES SUE TO SAFETY, ANOTHER PAIR OF EYES ARE FOCUSED ON THE TENSE SCENE...
THE FANTASTIC FOUR ARE MORE POWERFUL THAN I THOUGHT!
THIS WAS NOT THE WAY I PLANNED IT!
EVEN IN HIS OWN UNDERSEA LAIR, THE ACCURSED FOURSOME MAY SUCCEED IN DEFEATING THE SUB-MARINER!
NO LONGER CAN I LET THINGS TAKE THEIR NATURAL COURSE! NOW I MYSELF MUST TAKE A HAND! IT IS TIME FOR ME TO DESTROY THEM ALL!
18

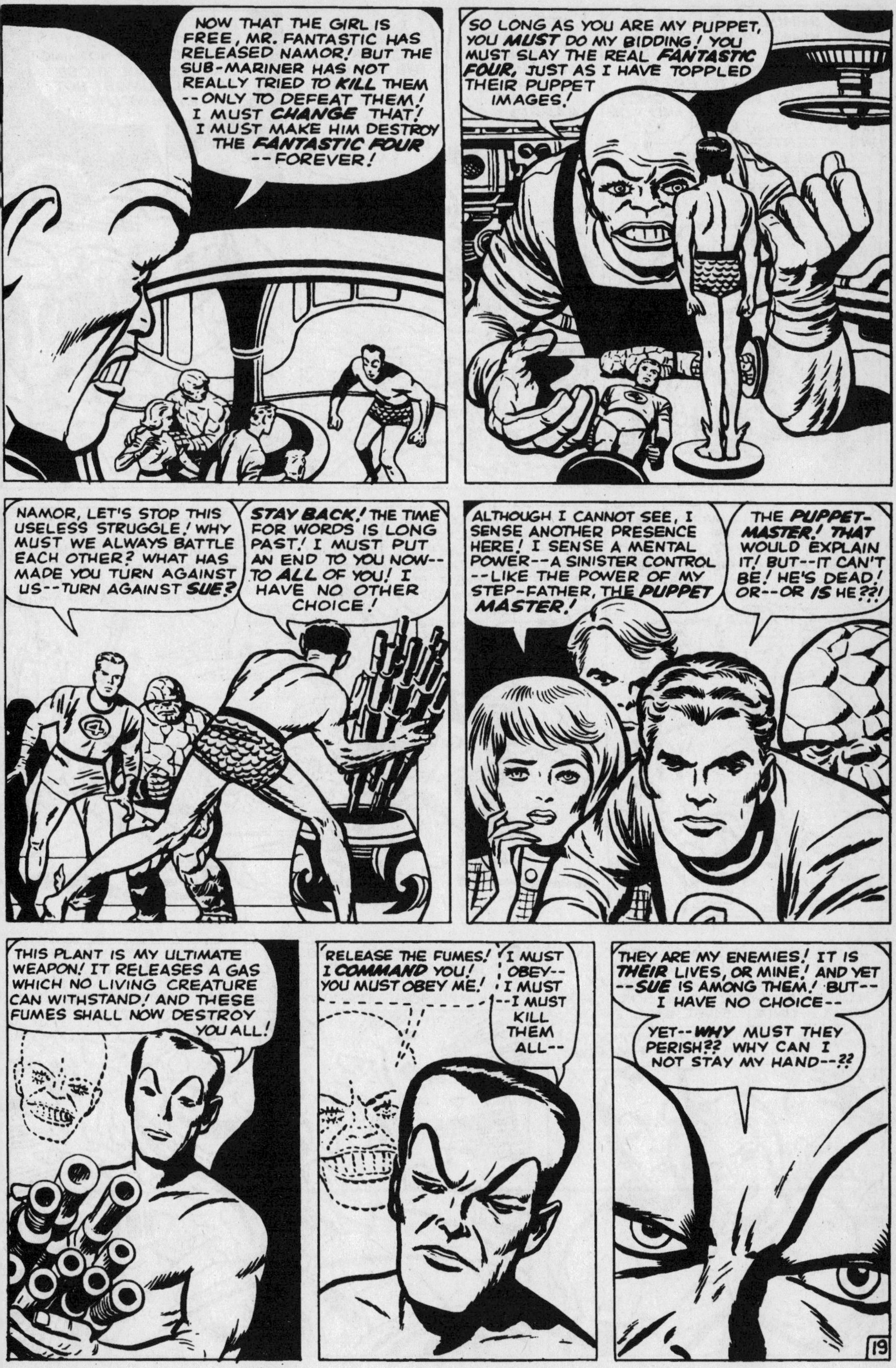
NOW THAT THE GIRL IS FREE, MR. FANTASTIC HAS RELEASED NAMOR! BUT THE SUB-MARINER HAS NOT REALLY TRIED TO KILL THEM --ONLY TO DEFEAT THEM! I MUST CHANGE THAT! I MUST MAKE HIM DESTROY THE FANTASTIC FOUR --FOREVER!
SO LONG AS YOU ARE MY PUPPET, YOU MUST DO MY BIDDING! YOU MUST SLAY THE REAL FANTASTIC FOUR, JUST AS I HAVE TOPPLED THEIR PUPPET IMAGES!
NAMOR, LET'S STOP THIS USELESS STRUGGLE! WHY MUST WE ALWAYS BATTLE EACH OTHER? WHAT HAS MADE YOU TURN AGAINST US--TURN AGAINST SUE?
STAY BACK! THE TIME FOR WORDS IS LONG PAST! I MUST PUT AN END TO YOU NOW--TO ALL OF YOU! I HAVE NO OTHER CHOICE!
ALTHOUGH I CANNOT SEE, I SENSE ANOTHER PRESENCE HERE! I SENSE A MENTAL POWER--A SINISTER CONTROL --LIKE THE POWER OF MY STEP-FATHER, THE PUPPET MASTER!
THE PUPPET-MASTER! THAT WOULD EXPLAIN IT! BUT--IT CAN'T BE! HE'S DEAD! OR--OR IS HE??!
THIS PLANT IS MY ULTIMATE WEAPON! IT RELEASES A GAS WHICH NO LIVING CREATURE CAN WITHSTAND! AND THESE FUMES SHALL NOW DESTROY YOU ALL!
RELEASE THE FUMES! I COMMAND YOU! YOU MUST OBEY ME!
I MUST OBEY--I MUST--I MUST KILL THEM ALL--
THEY ARE MY ENEMIES! IT IS THEIR LIVES, OR MINE! AND YET --SUE IS AMONG THEM! BUT--I HAVE NO CHOICE--
YET--WHY MUST THEY PERISH?? WHY CAN I NOT STAY MY HAND--??
19

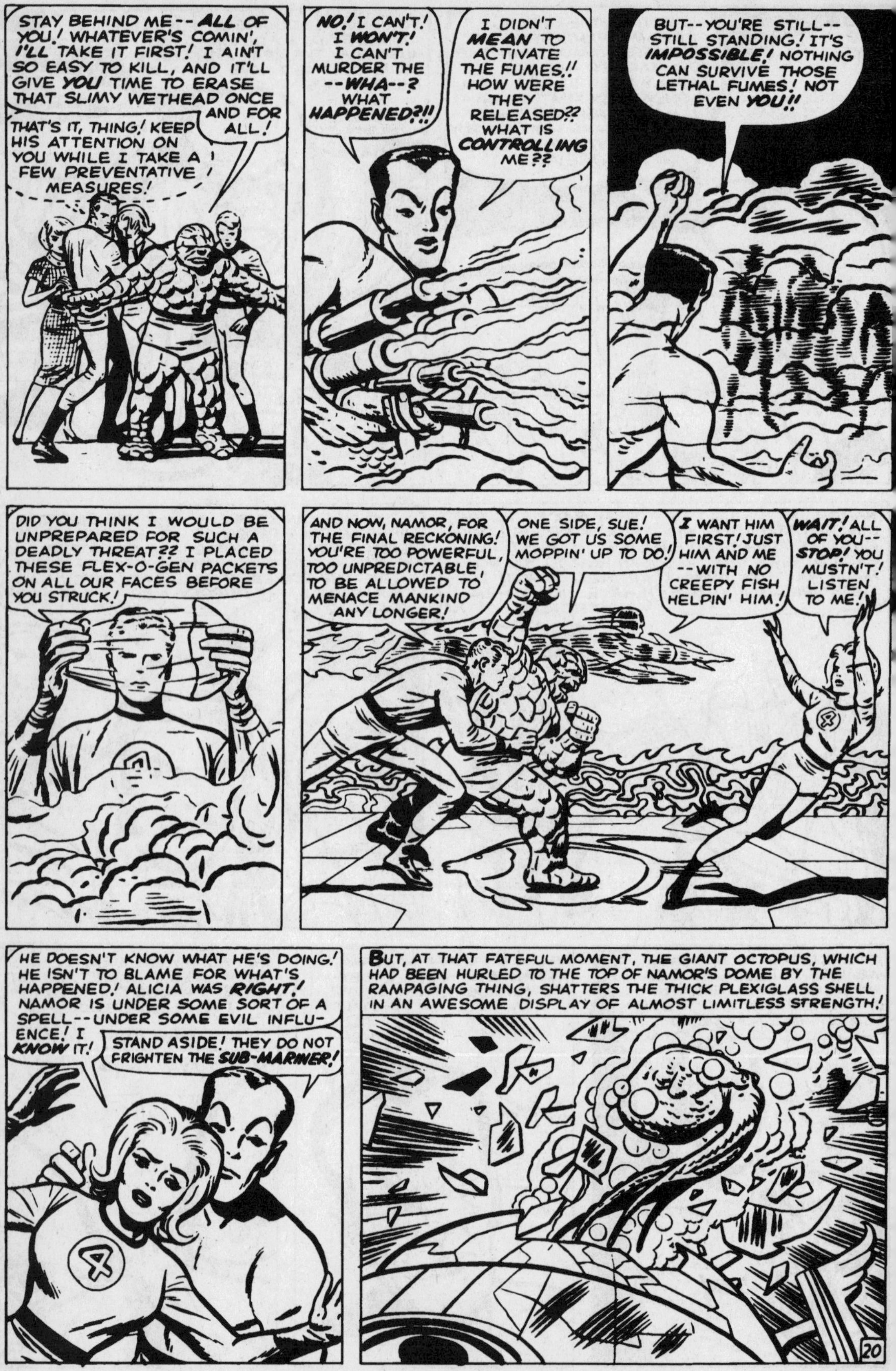
STAY BEHIND ME-- ALL OF YOU! WHATEVER'S COMIN', I'LL TAKE IT FIRST! I AIN'T SO EASY TO KILL, AND IT'LL GIVE YOU TIME TO ERASE THAT SLIMY WETHEAD ONCE AND FOR ALL!
THAT'S IT, THING! KEEP HIS ATTENTION ON YOU WHILE I TAKE A FEW PREVENTATIVE MEASURES!
NO! I CAN'T! I WON'T! I CAN'T MURDER THE --WHA--? WHAT HAPPENED?!!
I DIDN'T MEAN TO ACTIVATE THE FUMES!! HOW WERE THEY RELEASED?? WHAT IS CONTROLLING ME??
BUT--YOU'RE STILL-- STILL STANDING! IT'S IMPOSSIBLE! NOTHING CAN SURVIVE THOSE LETHAL FUMES! NOT EVEN YOU!!
DID YOU THINK I WOULD BE UNPREPARED FOR SUCH A DEADLY THREAT?? I PLACED THESE FLEX-O-GEN PACKETS ON ALL OUR FACES BEFORE YOU STRUCK!
AND NOW, NAMOR, FOR THE FINAL RECKONING! YOU'RE TOO POWERFUL, TOO UNPREDICTABLE, TO BE ALLOWED TO MENACE MANKIND ANY LONGER!
ONE SIDE, SUE! WE GOT US SOME MOPPIN' UP TO DO!
I WANT HIM FIRST! JUST HIM AND ME --WITH NO CREEPY FISH HELPIN' HIM!
WAIT! ALL OF YOU-- STOP! YOU MUSTN'T! LISTEN TO ME!
HE DOESN'T KNOW WHAT HE'S DOING! HE ISN'T TO BLAME FOR WHAT'S HAPPENED! ALICIA WAS RIGHT! NAMOR IS UNDER SOME SORT OF A SPELL--UNDER SOME EVIL INFLUENCE! I KNOW IT!
STAND ASIDE! THEY DO NOT FRIGHTEN THE SUB-MARINER!
BUT, AT THAT FATEFUL MOMENT, THE GIANT OCTOPUS, WHICH HAD BEEN HURLED TO THE TOP OF NAMOR'S DOME BY THE RAMPAGING THING, SHATTERS THE THICK PLEXIGLASS SHELL IN AN AWESOME DISPLAY OF ALMOST LIMITLESS STRENGTH!
20

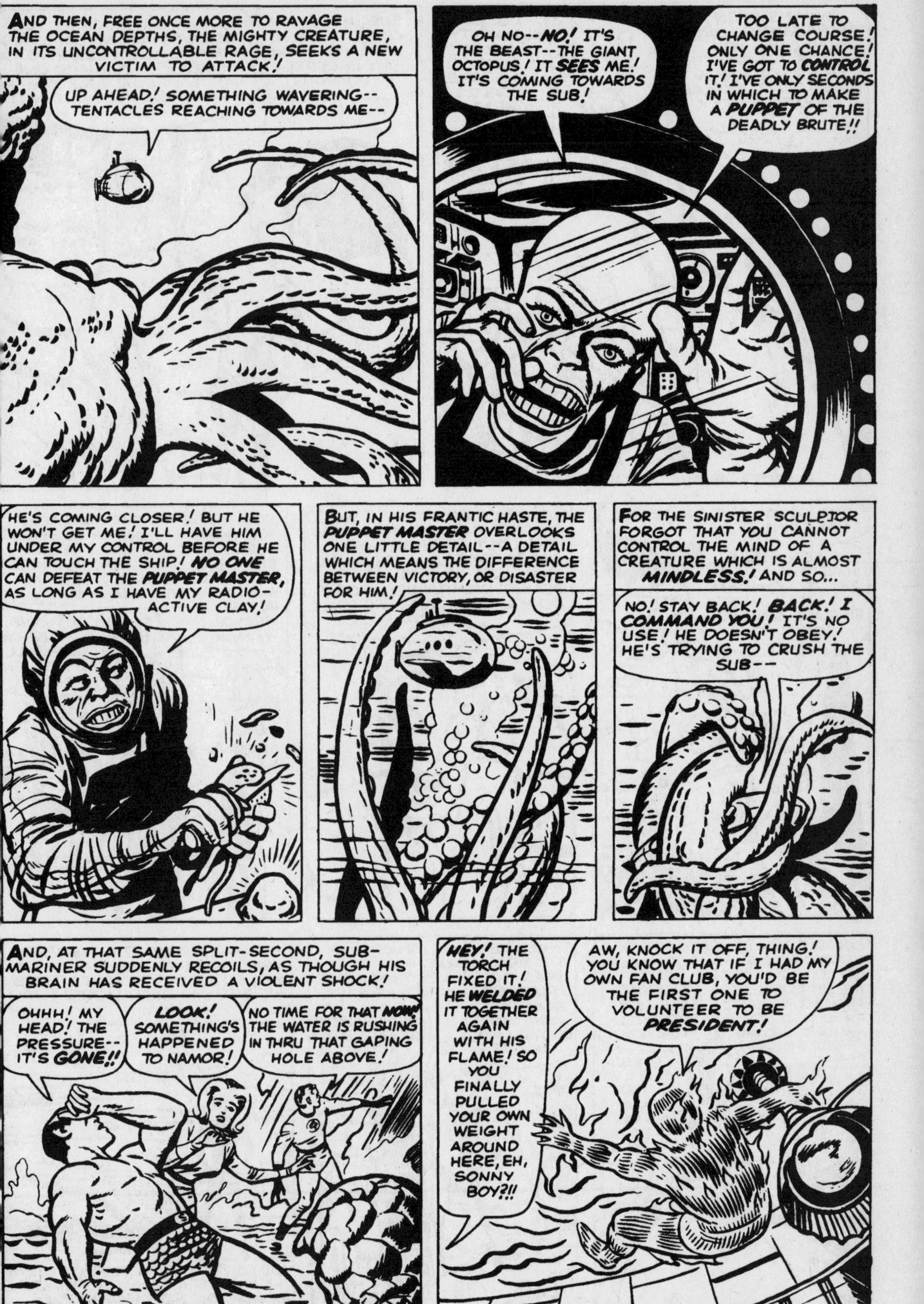

AND THEN, FREE ONCE MORE TO RAVAGE THE OCEAN DEPTHS, THE MIGHTY CREATURE, IN ITS UNCONTROLLABLE RAGE, SEEKS A NEW VICTIM TO ATTACK!
UP AHEAD! SOMETHING WAVERING-- TENTACLES REACHING TOWARDS ME--
OH NO--NO! IT'S THE BEAST--THE GIANT OCTOPUS! IT SEES ME! IT'S COMING TOWARDS THE SUB!
TOO LATE TO CHANGE COURSE! ONLY ONE CHANCE! I'VE GOT TO CONTROL IT! I'VE ONLY SECONDS IN WHICH TO MAKE A PUPPET OF THE DEADLY BRUTE!!
HE'S COMING CLOSER! BUT HE WON'T GET ME! I'LL HAVE HIM UNDER MY CONTROL BEFORE HE CAN TOUCH THE SHIP! NO ONE CAN DEFEAT THE PUPPET MASTER, AS LONG AS I HAVE MY RADIO-ACTIVE CLAY!
BUT, IN HIS FRANTIC HASTE, THE PUPPET MASTER OVERLOOKS ONE LITTLE DETAIL--A DETAIL WHICH MEANS THE DIFFERENCE BETWEEN VICTORY, OR DISASTER FOR HIM!
FOR THE SINISTER SCULPTOR FORGOT THAT YOU CANNOT CONTROL THE MIND OF A CREATURE WHICH IS ALMOST MINDLESS! AND SO...
NO! STAY BACK! BACK! I COMMAND YOU! IT'S NO USE! HE DOESN'T OBEY! HE'S TRYING TO CRUSH THE SUB--
AND, AT THAT SAME SPLIT-SECOND, SUB-MARINER SUDDENLY RECOILS, AS THOUGH HIS BRAIN HAS RECEIVED A VIOLENT SHOCK!
OHHH! MY HEAD! THE PRESSURE-- IT'S GONE!!
LOOK! SOMETHING'S HAPPENED TO NAMOR!
NO TIME FOR THAT NOW! THE WATER IS RUSHING IN THRU THAT GAPING HOLE ABOVE!
HEY! THE TORCH FIXED IT! HE WELDED IT TOGETHER AGAIN WITH HIS FLAME! SO YOU FINALLY PULLED YOUR OWN WEIGHT AROUND HERE, EH, SONNY BOY?!!
AW, KNOCK IT OFF, THING! YOU KNOW THAT IF I HAD MY OWN FAN CLUB, YOU'D BE THE FIRST ONE TO VOLUNTEER TO BE PRESIDENT!
21

Namor: WHAT'S BEEN *HAPPENING* HERE? HOW DARE YOU INVADE THE SANCTUM OF PRINCE NAMOR..?! *EXPLAIN YOURSELVES!*

Thing: I'LL BE *BLANKETTY-BLANKED!* HE'S EITHER THE WORLD'S BEST *ACTOR,* OR ELSE HE REALLY *WAS* UNDER SOME KINDA SPELL!!

Namor: SUE, HAVE YOU *COME* TO ME AT LAST-- TO SHARE MY UNDERSEA DOMAIN?

Sue: NO, NAMOR! MUCH AS YOU FASCINATE ME, MY LOYALTIES ARE STILL WITH *REED!* AS FOR MY *HEART*--PERHAPS ONE DAY IT WILL BE ABLE TO MAKE A FINAL CHOICE--BUT NOT YET!

Namor: ENOUGH OF THIS! A *PRINCE* DOES NOT BEG! AS FOR *ME,* I HAVE A MISSION YET TO COMPLETE --I STILL MUST FIND MY VANISHED PEOPLE!

Map of UNDER SEA EARTH

Namor: SOONER OR LATER, I SHALL LOCATE THEM! I SHALL FIND THE LOST RACE OF *SUB-MARINERS!* AND THEN WE SHALL *SEE* TO WHOM THIS PLANET RIGHTLY BELONGS!! DO YOU HEAR ME-- WE SHALL *SEE!!!*

Namor: NOW, RETURN TO THE SURFACE! YOU HAVE NO FURTHER BUSINESS HERE! TAKE THE GIRL, REED RICHARDS--TAKE HER, AND HOLD HER IF YOU CAN! BUT HEED MY WORDS--NEVER SHALL SHE FORGET PRINCE NAMOR!

Thing: I'LL GO GET OUR BATHYSCAPH BEFORE THAT CORNBALL STARTS RECITIN' HAMLET!

Reed: GOODBYE, NAMOR! I PRAY THAT SOME-DAY YOU WILL LOSE THE BITTERNESS FROM YOUR HEART, AND THAT YOU MIGHT BECOME --OUR FRIEND!

Thing: FRIEND? THAT IS TOO MILD A WORD FOR THE *SUB-MARINER!* FAREWELL-- FOR NOW! YEECH! ALL WE NEED NOW IS A BRASS BAND!

Sue: I WONDER IF IT REALLY *WAS* THE *PUPPET MASTER* WHO WAS CONTROLLING NAMOR?

Reed: LET US HOPE NOT! FOR IF HE STILL LIVES, THEN *NONE* OF US ARE SAFE!

Johnny: YOU'LL *ALWAYS* BE SAFE, BABY --AS LONG AS I'M AROUND!

Namor: STRANGE, I CANNOT REMEMBER WHAT BROUGHT THEM HERE--AND YET, I FEEL AS THOUGH A TERRIBLE WEIGHT HAS BEEN LIFTED FROM ME!

AND SO, THE *FANTASTIC FOUR* LEAVE THE UNDERSEA REALM OF *PRINCE NAMOR,* THE *SUB-MARINER,* AS THEY HEAD FOR ONE OF THE MOST BIZARRE ADVENTURES OF ALL TIME! BUT THAT'S A TALE FOR *NEXT* ISSUE!

22

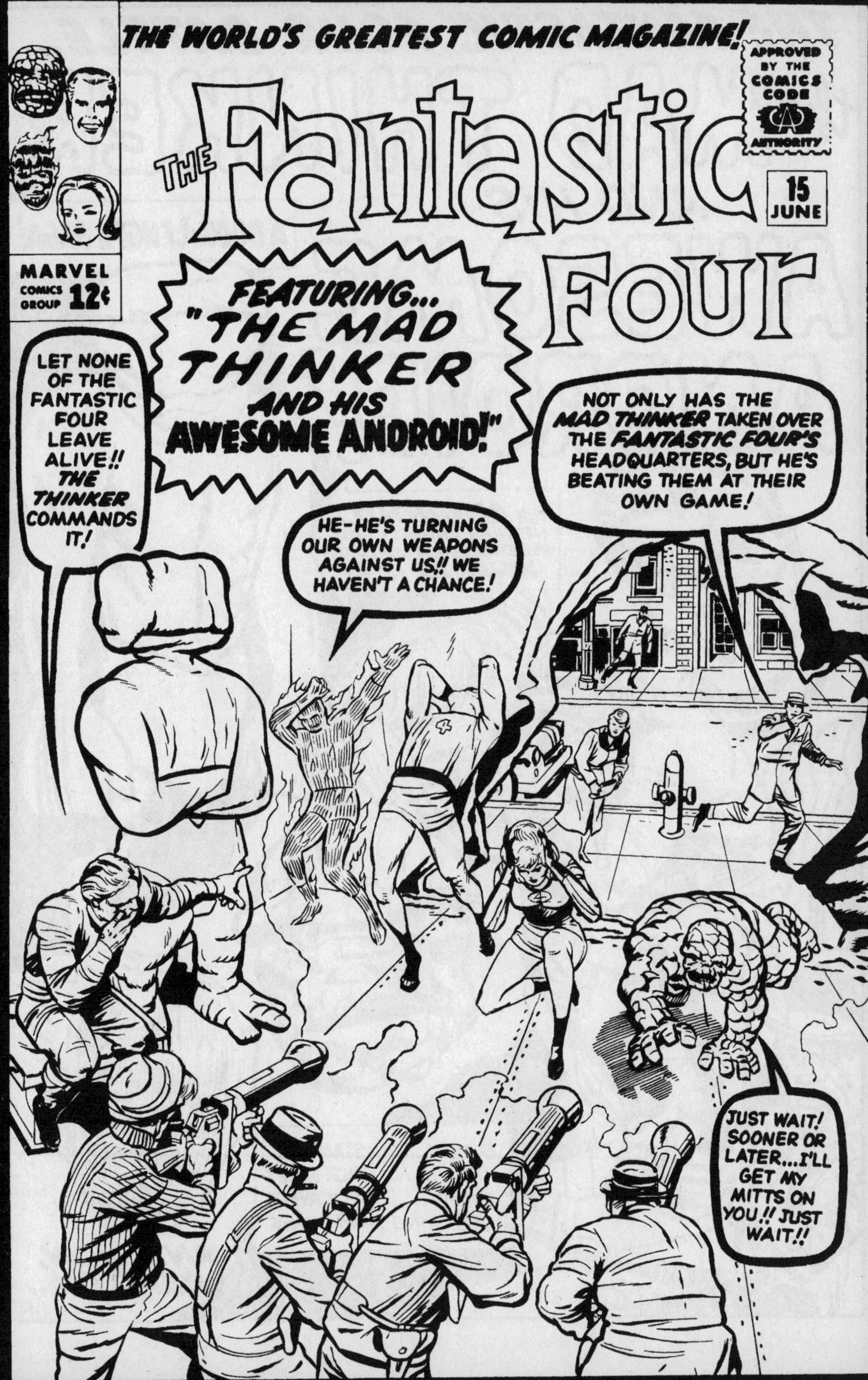
THE WORLD'S GREATEST COMIC MAGAZINE!
APPROVED BY THE COMICS CODE AUTHORITY
THE Fantastic Four
15 JUNE
MARVEL COMICS GROUP 12¢
FEATURING... "THE MAD THINKER AND HIS AWESOME ANDROID!"
LET NONE OF THE FANTASTIC FOUR LEAVE ALIVE!! THE THINKER COMMANDS IT!
HE-HE'S TURNING OUR OWN WEAPONS AGAINST US!! WE HAVEN'T A CHANCE!
NOT ONLY HAS THE MAD THINKER TAKEN OVER THE FANTASTIC FOUR'S HEADQUARTERS, BUT HE'S BEATING THEM AT THEIR OWN GAME!
JUST WAIT! SOONER OR LATER...I'LL GET MY MITTS ON YOU!! JUST WAIT!!

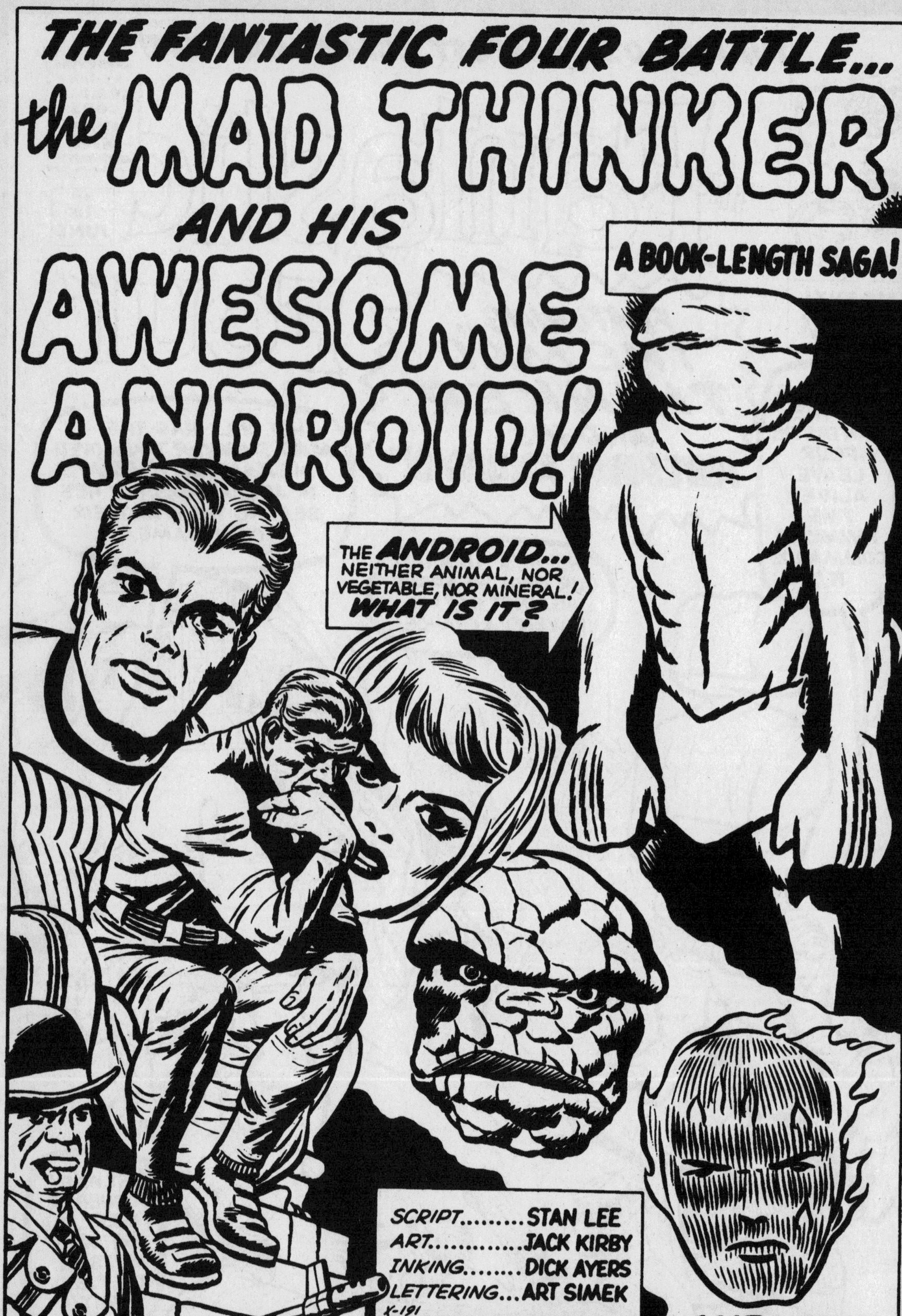
THE FANTASTIC FOUR BATTLE...
the MAD THINKER
AND HIS
AWESOME
ANDROID!
A BOOK-LENGTH SAGA!
THE ANDROID... NEITHER ANIMAL, NOR VEGETABLE, NOR MINERAL! WHAT IS IT?
SCRIPT.........STAN LEE
ART.............JACK KIRBY
INKING........DICK AYERS
LETTERING...ART SIMEK
X-191
AND NOW, READ ON...
1

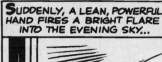

YOU ARE NOW EXPERIENCING ONE OF THE MOST EXCITING MOMENTS IN MAGAZINE READING: THE START OF AN ALL-NEW *FANTASTIC FOUR* ADVENTURE! THIS IS NEW YORK, HOME OF THE FAMOUS *BAXTER BUILDING*, WHICH HOUSES THE *FANTASTIC FOUR'S* SKYSCRAPER HEADQUARTERS!

SUDDENLY, A LEAN, POWERFUL HAND FIRES A BRIGHT FLARE INTO THE EVENING SKY...

...AND OUR ADVENTURE INTO FANTASY BEGINS!

LOOK! THE RED ALERT SIGNAL OF THE *FANTASTIC FOUR*!

NOT FAR AWAY, IN A QUIET LANE IN CENTRAL PARK, WE FIND A TEEN-AGER AND HIS DATE...

OF *COURSE* I'M ANGRY, JOHNNY! DO YOU KNOW HOW MANY DATES YOU'VE BROKEN WITH ME??

AW, PEGGY, YOU *KNOW* I COULDN'T HELP IT! BUT I'M HERE *NOW*, AND THERE'S A MOON ABOVE, AND YOU SURE LOOK GORGEOUS...

OH, JOHNNY, HOW I'VE *LONGED* FOR THIS WONDERFUL MOMENT!

GREAT BALLS OF FIRE!! AT A TIME LIKE *THIS!*

SORRY, PEG, I'LL HAVE TO LEAVE YOU FOR A WHILE! HOPE YOU CAN DRIVE!

FLAME ON!

OH *NO!* NOT *AGAIN!!*

AND, IN A CHI-CHI BEAUTY PARLOR ON FIFTH AVENUE...

I JUST *KNOW* I'VE SEEN THAT GIRL SOMEWHERE!

AH, MISS STORM, NOW FOR THE SUPREME MOMENT! I, PERSONALLY, SHALL CREATE YOUR NEW HAIR-DO!

I HAVE CANCELLED ALL OTHER APPOINTMENTS SO THAT I COULD DEVOTE MYSELF ENTIRELY TO *YOU* TODAY!

REED'S SIGNAL! IT MEANS COME A'RUNNING, NO MATTER WHAT!

2

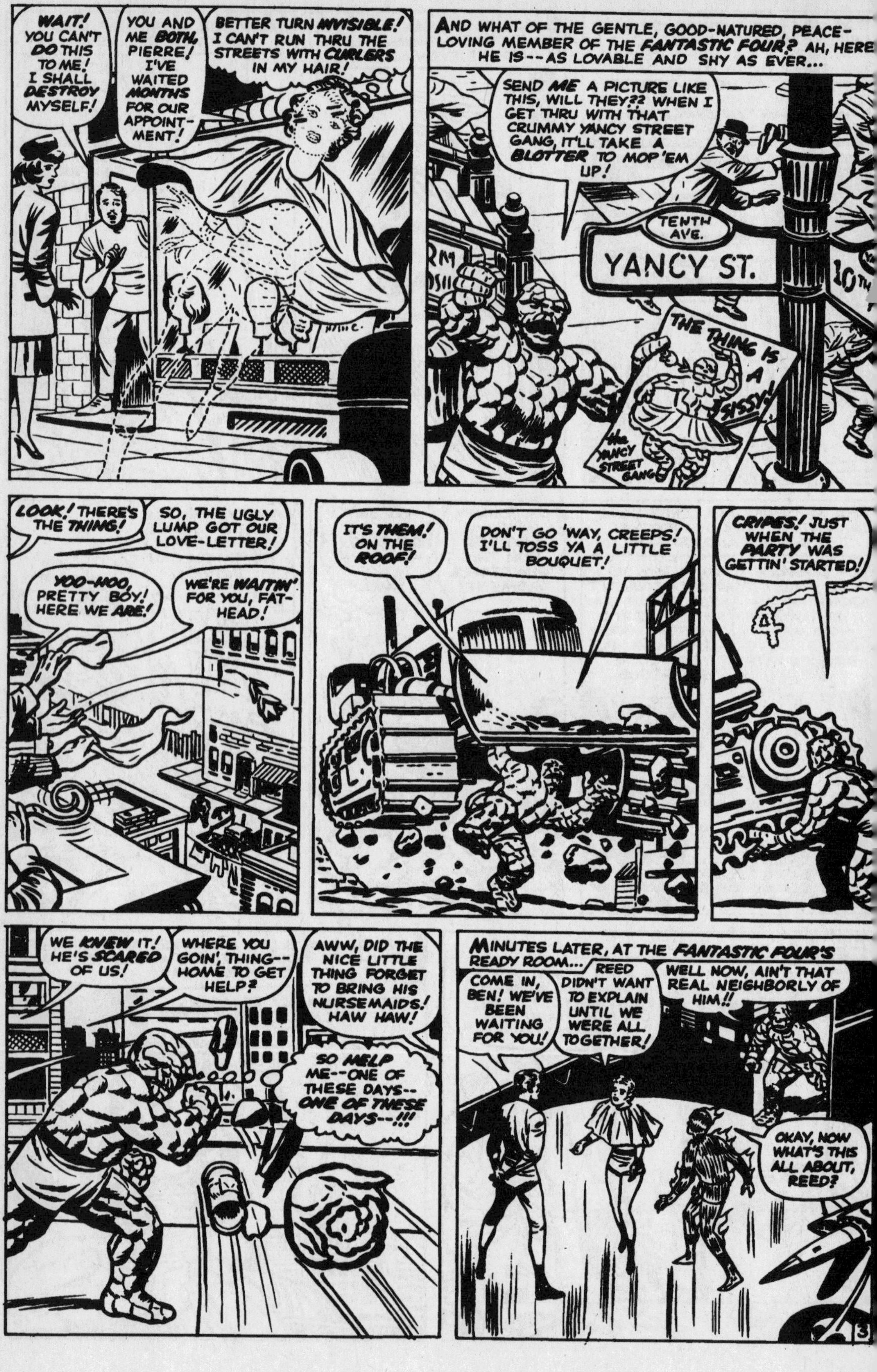
WAIT! YOU CAN'T DO THIS TO ME! I SHALL DESTROY MYSELF!
YOU AND ME BOTH, PIERRE! I'VE WAITED MONTHS FOR OUR APPOINT-MENT!
BETTER TURN INVISIBLE! I CAN'T RUN THRU THE STREETS WITH CURLERS IN MY HAIR!
AND WHAT OF THE GENTLE, GOOD-NATURED, PEACE-LOVING MEMBER OF THE FANTASTIC FOUR? AH, HERE HE IS--AS LOVABLE AND SHY AS EVER...
SEND ME A PICTURE LIKE THIS, WILL THEY?? WHEN I GET THRU WITH THAT CRUMMY YANCY STREET GANG, IT'LL TAKE A BLOTTER TO MOP 'EM UP!
TENTH AVE.
YANCY ST.
THE THING IS A SISSY!
the YANCY STREET GANG
LOOK! THERE'S THE THING!
SO, THE UGLY LUMP GOT OUR LOVE-LETTER!
YOO-HOO, PRETTY BOY! HERE WE ARE!
WE'RE WAITIN' FOR YOU, FAT-HEAD!
IT'S THEM! ON THE ROOF!
DON'T GO 'WAY, CREEPS! I'LL TOSS YA A LITTLE BOUQUET!
CRIPES! JUST WHEN THE PARTY WAS GETTIN' STARTED!
WE KNEW IT! HE'S SCARED OF US!
WHERE YOU GOIN', THING--HOME TO GET HELP?
AWW, DID THE NICE LITTLE THING FORGET TO BRING HIS NURSEMAIDS! HAW HAW!
SO HELP ME--ONE OF THESE DAYS--ONE OF THESE DAYS--!!!
MINUTES LATER, AT THE FANTASTIC FOUR'S READY ROOM...
COME IN, BEN! WE'VE BEEN WAITING FOR YOU!
REED DIDN'T WANT TO EXPLAIN UNTIL WE WERE ALL TOGETHER!
WELL NOW, AIN'T THAT REAL NEIGHBORLY OF HIM!!
OKAY, NOW WHAT'S THIS ALL ABOUT, REED?
3

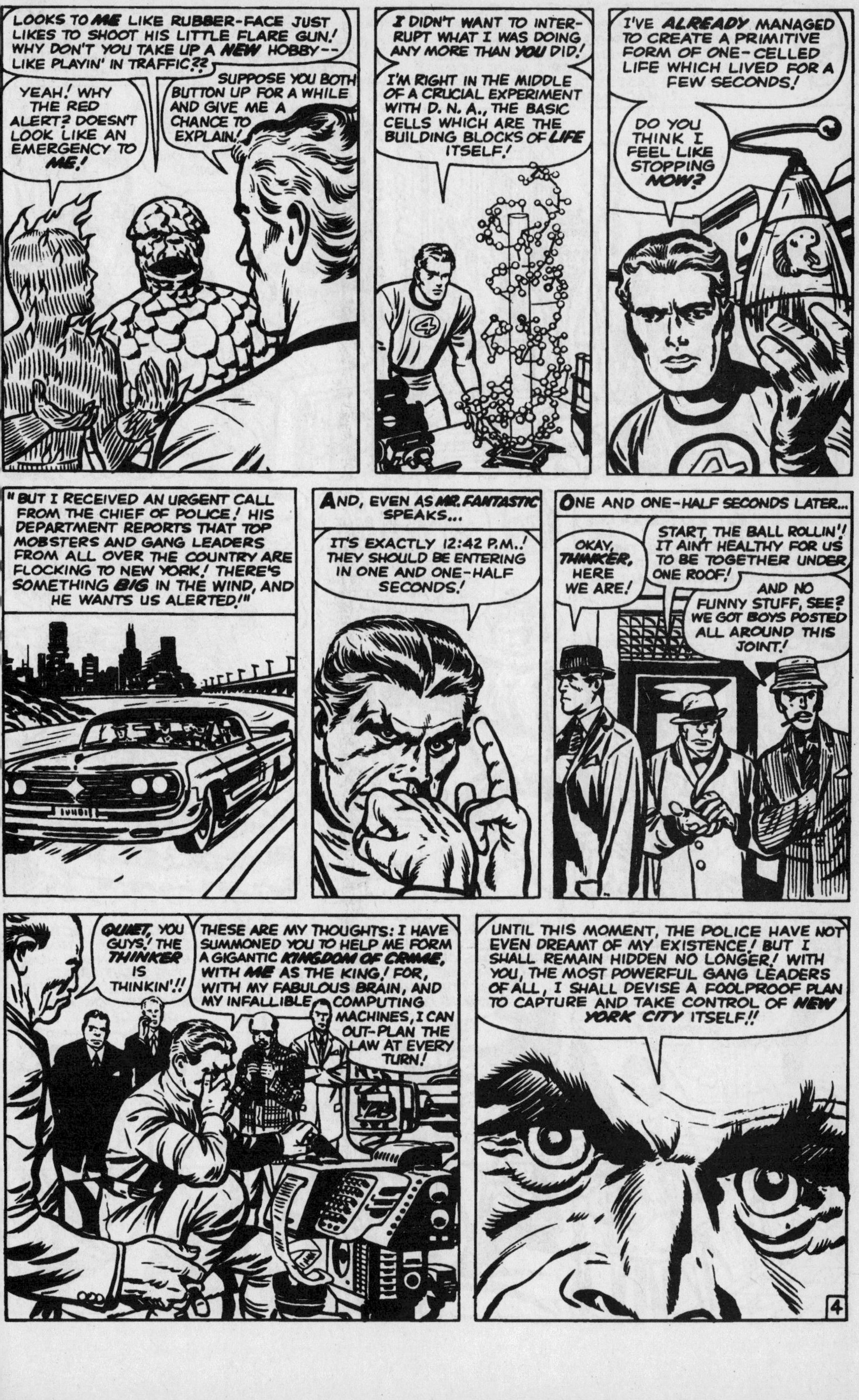

LOOKS TO ME LIKE RUBBER-FACE JUST LIKES TO SHOOT HIS LITTLE FLARE GUN! WHY DON'T YOU TAKE UP A NEW HOBBY--LIKE PLAYIN' IN TRAFFIC??
YEAH! WHY THE RED ALERT? DOESN'T LOOK LIKE AN EMERGENCY TO ME!
SUPPOSE YOU BOTH BUTTON UP FOR A WHILE AND GIVE ME A CHANCE TO EXPLAIN!
I DIDN'T WANT TO INTERRUPT WHAT I WAS DOING ANY MORE THAN YOU DID!
I'M RIGHT IN THE MIDDLE OF A CRUCIAL EXPERIMENT WITH D. N. A., THE BASIC CELLS WHICH ARE THE BUILDING BLOCKS OF LIFE ITSELF!
I'VE ALREADY MANAGED TO CREATE A PRIMITIVE FORM OF ONE-CELLED LIFE WHICH LIVED FOR A FEW SECONDS!
DO YOU THINK I FEEL LIKE STOPPING NOW?
"BUT I RECEIVED AN URGENT CALL FROM THE CHIEF OF POLICE! HIS DEPARTMENT REPORTS THAT TOP MOBSTERS AND GANG LEADERS FROM ALL OVER THE COUNTRY ARE FLOCKING TO NEW YORK! THERE'S SOMETHING BIG IN THE WIND, AND HE WANTS US ALERTED!"
AND, EVEN AS MR. FANTASTIC SPEAKS...
IT'S EXACTLY 12:42 P.M.! THEY SHOULD BE ENTERING IN ONE AND ONE-HALF SECONDS!
ONE AND ONE-HALF SECONDS LATER...
OKAY, THINKER, HERE WE ARE!
START THE BALL ROLLIN'! IT AIN'T HEALTHY FOR US TO BE TOGETHER UNDER ONE ROOF!
AND NO FUNNY STUFF, SEE? WE GOT BOYS POSTED ALL AROUND THIS JOINT!
QUIET, YOU GUYS! THE THINKER IS THINKIN'!!
THESE ARE MY THOUGHTS: I HAVE SUMMONED YOU TO HELP ME FORM A GIGANTIC KINGDOM OF CRIME, WITH ME AS THE KING! FOR, WITH MY FABULOUS BRAIN, AND MY INFALLIBLE COMPUTING MACHINES, I CAN OUT-PLAN THE LAW AT EVERY TURN!
UNTIL THIS MOMENT, THE POLICE HAVE NOT EVEN DREAMT OF MY EXISTENCE! BUT I SHALL REMAIN HIDDEN NO LONGER! WITH YOU, THE MOST POWERFUL GANG LEADERS OF ALL, I SHALL DEVISE A FOOLPROOF PLAN TO CAPTURE AND TAKE CONTROL OF NEW YORK CITY ITSELF!!
4

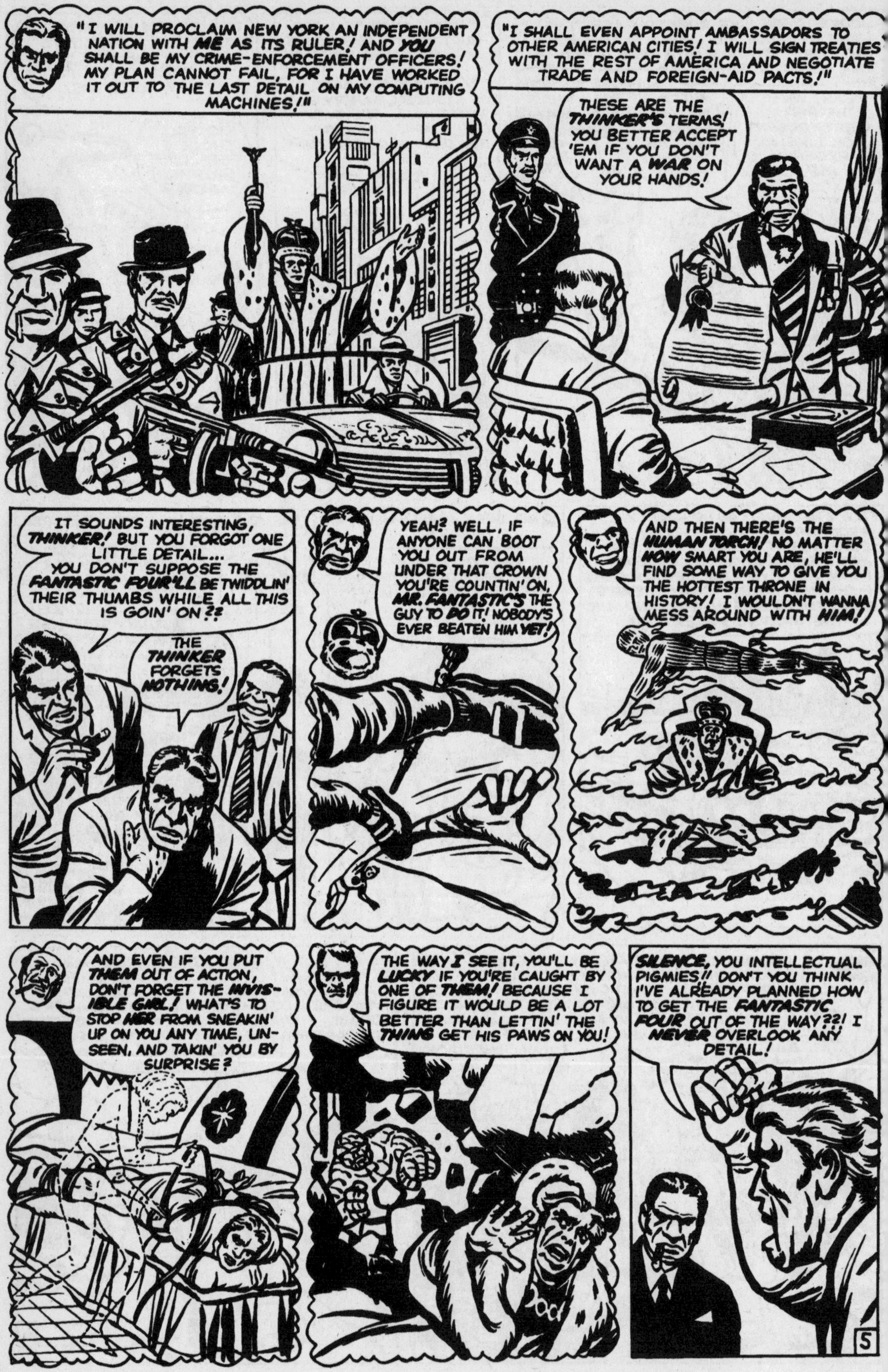
"I WILL PROCLAIM NEW YORK AN INDEPENDENT NATION WITH ME AS ITS RULER! AND YOU SHALL BE MY CRIME-ENFORCEMENT OFFICERS! MY PLAN CANNOT FAIL, FOR I HAVE WORKED IT OUT TO THE LAST DETAIL ON MY COMPUTING MACHINES!"
"I SHALL EVEN APPOINT AMBASSADORS TO OTHER AMERICAN CITIES! I WILL SIGN TREATIES WITH THE REST OF AMERICA AND NEGOTIATE TRADE AND FOREIGN-AID PACTS!"
THESE ARE THE THINKER'S TERMS! YOU BETTER ACCEPT 'EM IF YOU DON'T WANT A WAR ON YOUR HANDS!
IT SOUNDS INTERESTING, THINKER! BUT YOU FORGOT ONE LITTLE DETAIL... YOU DON'T SUPPOSE THE FANTASTIC FOUR'LL BE TWIDDLIN' THEIR THUMBS WHILE ALL THIS IS GOIN' ON??
THE THINKER FORGETS NOTHING!
YEAH? WELL, IF ANYONE CAN BOOT YOU OUT FROM UNDER THAT CROWN YOU'RE COUNTIN' ON, MR. FANTASTIC'S THE GUY TO DO IT! NOBODY'S EVER BEATEN HIM YET!
AND THEN THERE'S THE HUMAN TORCH! NO MATTER HOW SMART YOU ARE, HE'LL FIND SOME WAY TO GIVE YOU THE HOTTEST THRONE IN HISTORY! I WOULDN'T WANNA MESS AROUND WITH HIM!
AND EVEN IF YOU PUT THEM OUT OF ACTION, DON'T FORGET THE INVISIBLE GIRL! WHAT'S TO STOP HER FROM SNEAKIN' UP ON YOU ANY TIME, UNSEEN, AND TAKIN' YOU BY SURPRISE?
THE WAY I SEE IT, YOU'LL BE LUCKY IF YOU'RE CAUGHT BY ONE OF THEM! BECAUSE I FIGURE IT WOULD BE A LOT BETTER THAN LETTIN' THE THING GET HIS PAWS ON YOU!
SILENCE, YOU INTELLECTUAL PIGMIES!! DON'T YOU THINK I'VE ALREADY PLANNED HOW TO GET THE FANTASTIC FOUR OUT OF THE WAY??! I NEVER OVERLOOK ANY DETAIL!
5

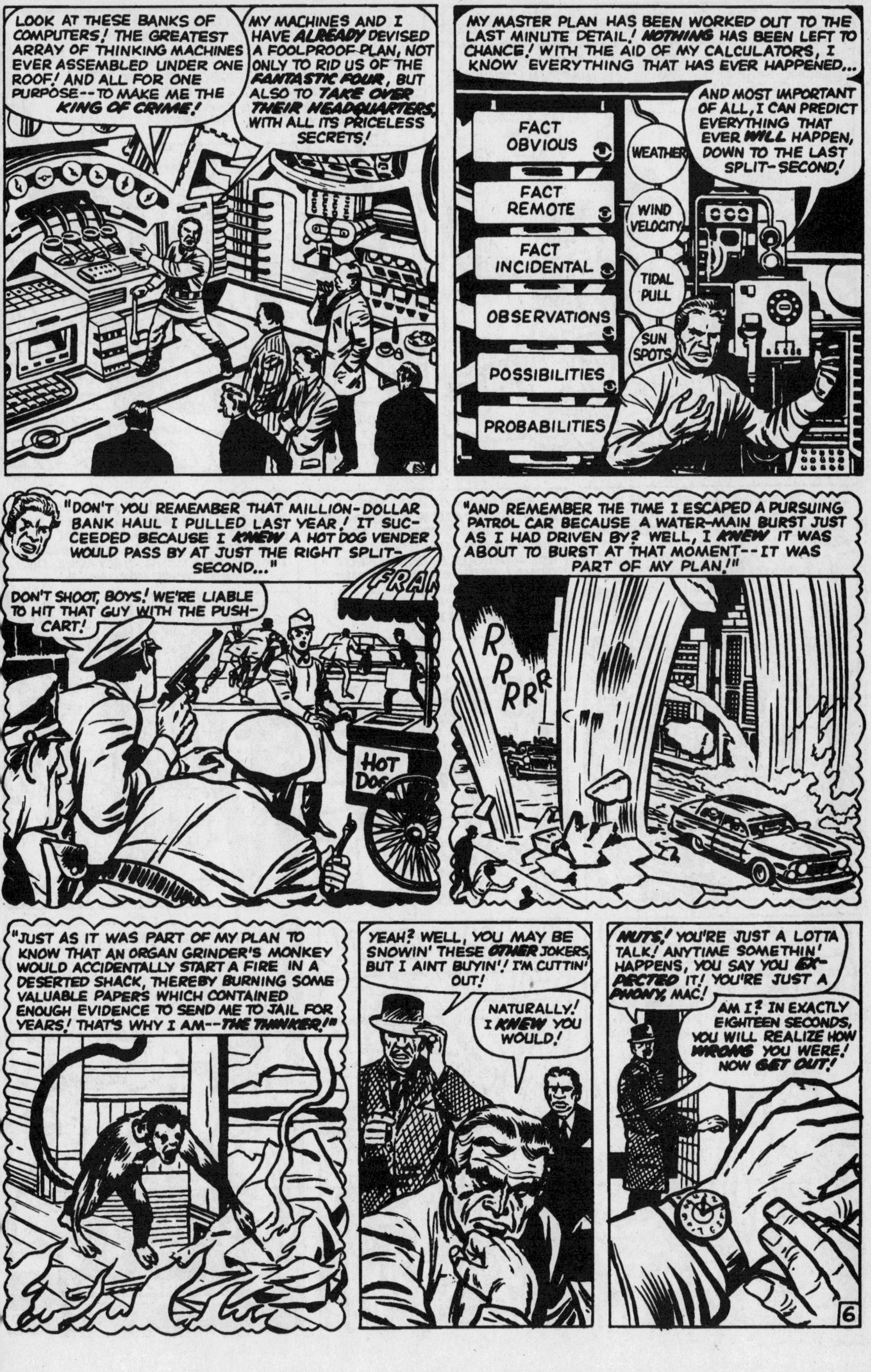
LOOK AT THESE BANKS OF COMPUTERS! THE GREATEST ARRAY OF THINKING MACHINES EVER ASSEMBLED UNDER ONE ROOF! AND ALL FOR ONE PURPOSE--TO MAKE ME THE KING OF CRIME!
MY MACHINES AND I HAVE ALREADY DEVISED A FOOLPROOF PLAN, NOT ONLY TO RID US OF THE FANTASTIC FOUR, BUT ALSO TO TAKE OVER THEIR HEADQUARTERS, WITH ALL ITS PRICELESS SECRETS!
MY MASTER PLAN HAS BEEN WORKED OUT TO THE LAST MINUTE DETAIL! NOTHING HAS BEEN LEFT TO CHANCE! WITH THE AID OF MY CALCULATORS, I KNOW EVERYTHING THAT HAS EVER HAPPENED...
AND MOST IMPORTANT OF ALL, I CAN PREDICT EVERYTHING THAT EVER WILL HAPPEN, DOWN TO THE LAST SPLIT-SECOND!
FACT OBVIOUS
FACT REMOTE
FACT INCIDENTAL
OBSERVATIONS
POSSIBILITIES
PROBABILITIES
WEATHER
WIND VELOCITY
TIDAL PULL
SUN SPOTS
"DON'T YOU REMEMBER THAT MILLION-DOLLAR BANK HAUL I PULLED LAST YEAR! IT SUCCEEDED BECAUSE I KNEW A HOT DOG VENDER WOULD PASS BY AT JUST THE RIGHT SPLIT-SECOND..."
DON'T SHOOT, BOYS! WE'RE LIABLE TO HIT THAT GUY WITH THE PUSH-CART!
HOT DOG
"AND REMEMBER THE TIME I ESCAPED A PURSUING PATROL CAR BECAUSE A WATER-MAIN BURST JUST AS I HAD DRIVEN BY? WELL, I KNEW IT WAS ABOUT TO BURST AT THAT MOMENT--IT WAS PART OF MY PLAN!"
RRRRR
"JUST AS IT WAS PART OF MY PLAN TO KNOW THAT AN ORGAN GRINDER'S MONKEY WOULD ACCIDENTALLY START A FIRE IN A DESERTED SHACK, THEREBY BURNING SOME VALUABLE PAPERS WHICH CONTAINED ENOUGH EVIDENCE TO SEND ME TO JAIL FOR YEARS! THAT'S WHY I AM--THE THINKER!"
YEAH? WELL, YOU MAY BE SNOWIN' THESE OTHER JOKERS, BUT I AINT BUYIN'! I'M CUTTIN' OUT!
NATURALLY! I KNEW YOU WOULD!
NUTS! YOU'RE JUST A LOTTA TALK! ANYTIME SOMETHIN' HAPPENS, YOU SAY YOU EXPECTED IT! YOU'RE JUST A PHONY, MAC!
AM I? IN EXACTLY EIGHTEEN SECONDS, YOU WILL REALIZE HOW WRONG YOU WERE! NOW GET OUT!
6

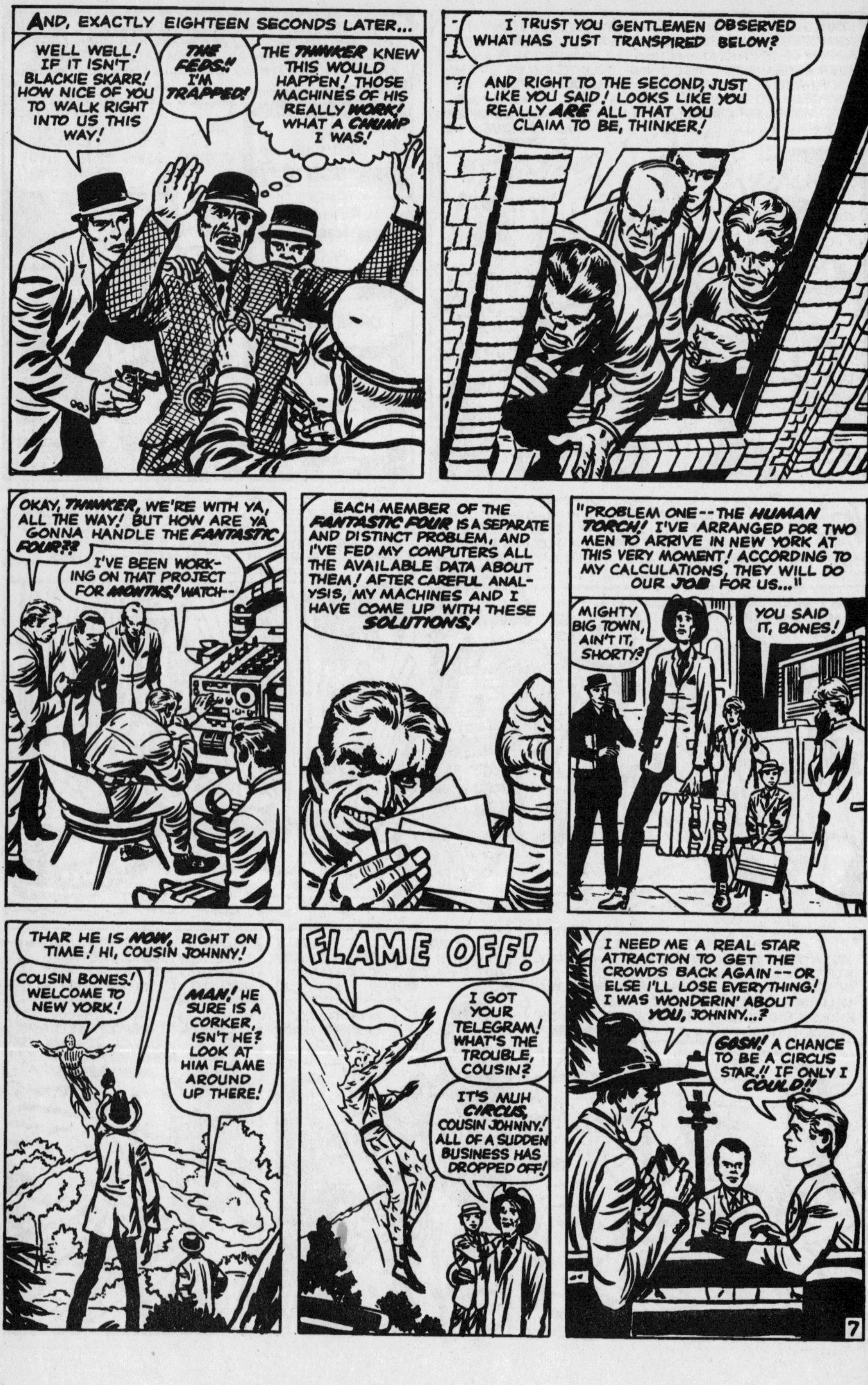

AND, EXACTLY EIGHTEEN SECONDS LATER...
WELL WELL! IF IT ISN'T BLACKIE SKARR! HOW NICE OF YOU TO WALK RIGHT INTO US THIS WAY!
THE FEDS!! I'M TRAPPED!
THE THINKER KNEW THIS WOULD HAPPEN! THOSE MACHINES OF HIS REALLY WORK! WHAT A CHUMP I WAS!
I TRUST YOU GENTLEMEN OBSERVED WHAT HAS JUST TRANSPIRED BELOW?
AND RIGHT TO THE SECOND, JUST LIKE YOU SAID! LOOKS LIKE YOU REALLY ARE ALL THAT YOU CLAIM TO BE, THINKER!
OKAY, THINKER, WE'RE WITH YA, ALL THE WAY! BUT HOW ARE YA GONNA HANDLE THE FANTASTIC FOUR??
I'VE BEEN WORKING ON THAT PROJECT FOR MONTHS! WATCH--
EACH MEMBER OF THE FANTASTIC FOUR IS A SEPARATE AND DISTINCT PROBLEM, AND I'VE FED MY COMPUTERS ALL THE AVAILABLE DATA ABOUT THEM! AFTER CAREFUL ANALYSIS, MY MACHINES AND I HAVE COME UP WITH THESE SOLUTIONS!
"PROBLEM ONE--THE HUMAN TORCH! I'VE ARRANGED FOR TWO MEN TO ARRIVE IN NEW YORK AT THIS VERY MOMENT! ACCORDING TO MY CALCULATIONS, THEY WILL DO OUR JOB FOR US..."
MIGHTY BIG TOWN, AIN'T IT, SHORTY?
YOU SAID IT, BONES!
THAR HE IS NOW, RIGHT ON TIME! HI, COUSIN JOHNNY!
COUSIN BONES! WELCOME TO NEW YORK!
MAN! HE SURE IS A CORKER, ISN'T HE? LOOK AT HIM FLAME AROUND UP THERE!
FLAME OFF!
I GOT YOUR TELEGRAM! WHAT'S THE TROUBLE, COUSIN?
IT'S MUH CIRCUS, COUSIN JOHNNY! ALL OF A SUDDEN BUSINESS HAS DROPPED OFF!
I NEED ME A REAL STAR ATTRACTION TO GET THE CROWDS BACK AGAIN--OR ELSE I'LL LOSE EVERYTHING! I WAS WONDERIN' ABOUT YOU, JOHNNY...?
GOSH! A CHANCE TO BE A CIRCUS STAR!! IF ONLY I COULD!!

PROBLEM TWO--*MISTER FANTASTIC!* AT THE EXECUTIVE OFFICES OF GENERAL ELECTRONICS, LTD...

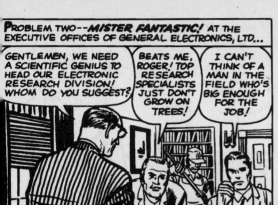

GENTLEMEN, WE NEED A SCIENTIFIC GENIUS TO HEAD OUR ELECTRONIC RESEARCH DIVISION! WHOM DO YOU SUGGEST?

BEATS ME, ROGER! TOP RESEARCH SPECIALISTS JUST DON'T GROW ON TREES!

I CAN'T THINK OF A MAN IN THE FIELD WHO'S BIG ENOUGH FOR THE JOB!

AT THAT MOMENT, AS THOUGH PREARRANGED BY FATE, A JANITOR CARELESSLY LAYS A COPY OF A MAGAZINE HE HAD BEEN READING ON A MASSIVE OAK DESK...

WELL, KEEP WORKING ON IT, GENTLEMEN! WE *MUST* FIND THE RIGHT MAN FOR THE JOB, AND *SOON!*

I'LL JUST LEAVE THIS HERE FOR A FEW MINUTES WHILE I MOP UP THE HALL!

THEN, JUST AS THE *THINKER* KNEW IT WOULD, THE BRIGHTLY-COLORED COVER CATCHES THE INDUSTRIALIST'S EYE, AND...

CARTWRIGHT! VAN DORN! COME HERE! I'VE *FOUND* THE MAN WE'RE LOOKING FOR!

IN THE *FANTASTIC FOUR* COMIC MAGAZINE?? WHAT DO YOU *MEAN,* ROGER?

OF *COURSE!* WE SHOULD HAVE THOUGHT OF IT BEFORE! *REED RICHARDS!* THE MOST GIFTED INVENTIVE GENIUS OF OUR TIME! WE'LL SEND FOR HIM *IMMEDIATELY!*

PROBLEM THREE-- THE *THING!* IN A LOCAL GYM, A SHIFTY-EYED WRESTLING MANAGER MAKES BEN GRIMM A TEMPTING OFFER...

I TELL YA, *THING,* IF YA SIGN UP WITH *ME* WE CAN MAKE A *FORTUNE!* YOU'D BE THE BIGGEST WRESTLIN' ATTRACTION SINCE STRANGLER LEWIS!

YEAH YEAH, I KNOW! IT SOUNDS GOOD, BUT I GOT *OTHER* THINGS TO DO!

THAT SO? COULD BE YOU'RE *AFRAID* TO MEET *FATAL FINNEGAN,* THE IDOL OF THE *YANCY STREET GANG?!!*

ME, *AFRAID??!*

I DON'T *LIKE* THAT KINDA TALK, SQUIRT!

NOW JUST YOU WAIT THERE TILL I GET BACK! I GOTTA TALK THIS OVER WITH MY PARTNERS!

S-SURE, *THING,* I-I'LL -ULP- HANG AROUND!

8

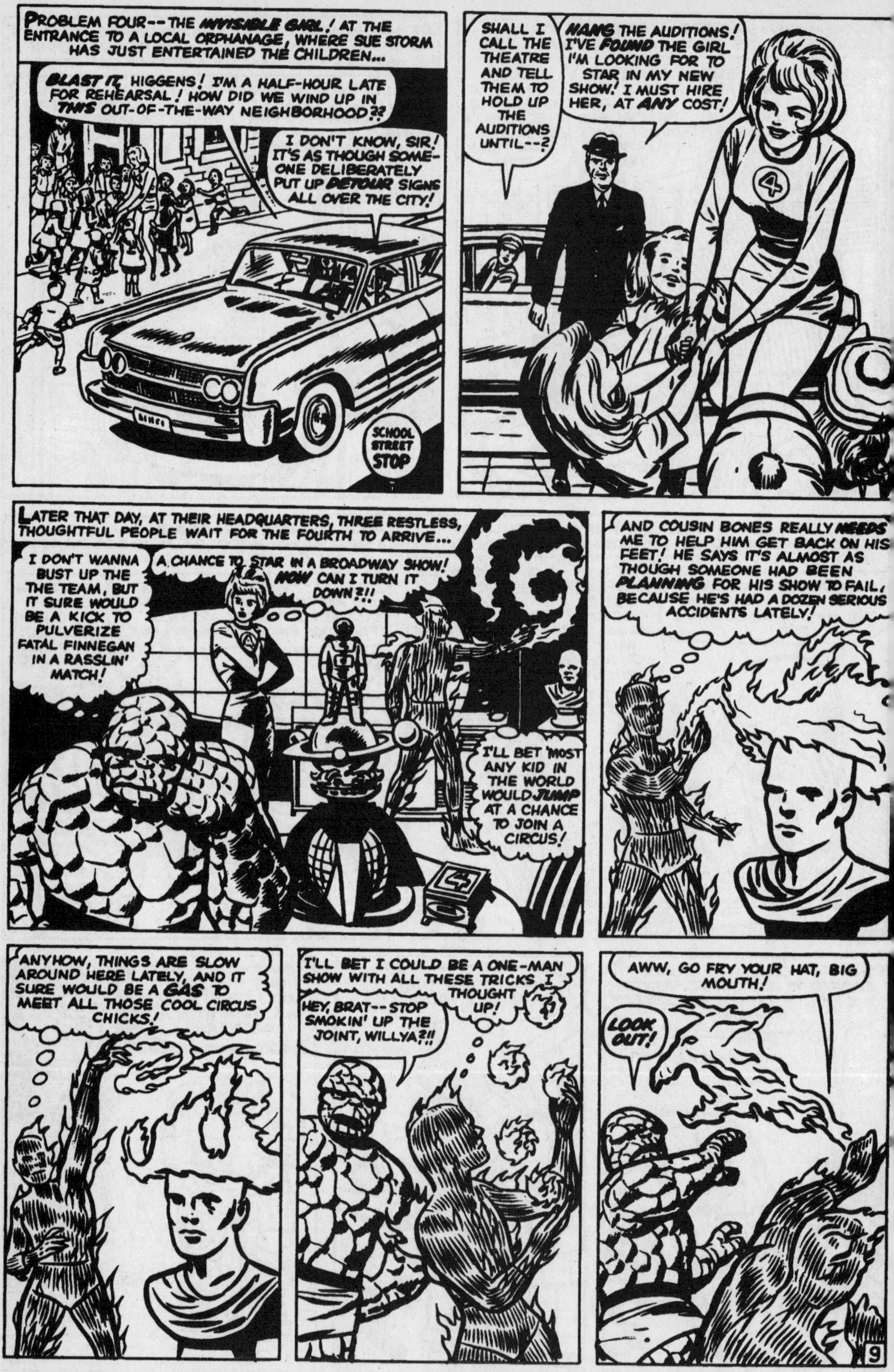
PROBLEM FOUR--THE INVISIBLE GIRL! AT THE ENTRANCE TO A LOCAL ORPHANAGE, WHERE SUE STORM HAS JUST ENTERTAINED THE CHILDREN...
BLAST IT, HIGGENS! I'M A HALF-HOUR LATE FOR REHEARSAL! HOW DID WE WIND UP IN THIS OUT-OF-THE-WAY NEIGHBORHOOD??
I DON'T KNOW, SIR! IT'S AS THOUGH SOME-ONE DELIBERATELY PUT UP DETOUR SIGNS ALL OVER THE CITY!
SCHOOL STREET STOP
SHALL I CALL THE THEATRE AND TELL THEM TO HOLD UP THE AUDITIONS UNTIL--?
HANG THE AUDITIONS! I'VE FOUND THE GIRL I'M LOOKING FOR TO STAR IN MY NEW SHOW! I MUST HIRE HER, AT ANY COST!
LATER THAT DAY, AT THEIR HEADQUARTERS, THREE RESTLESS, THOUGHTFUL PEOPLE WAIT FOR THE FOURTH TO ARRIVE...
I DON'T WANNA BUST UP THE THE TEAM, BUT IT SURE WOULD BE A KICK TO PULVERIZE FATAL FINNEGAN IN A RASSLIN' MATCH!
A CHANCE TO STAR IN A BROADWAY SHOW! HOW CAN I TURN IT DOWN?!!
I'LL BET 'MOST ANY KID IN THE WORLD WOULD JUMP AT A CHANCE TO JOIN A CIRCUS!
AND COUSIN BONES REALLY NEEDS ME TO HELP HIM GET BACK ON HIS FEET! HE SAYS IT'S ALMOST AS THOUGH SOMEONE HAD BEEN PLANNING FOR HIS SHOW TO FAIL, BECAUSE HE'S HAD A DOZEN SERIOUS ACCIDENTS LATELY!
ANYHOW, THINGS ARE SLOW AROUND HERE LATELY, AND IT SURE WOULD BE A GAS TO MEET ALL THOSE COOL CIRCUS CHICKS!
I'LL BET I COULD BE A ONE-MAN SHOW WITH ALL THESE TRICKS I THOUGHT UP!
HEY, BRAT--STOP SMOKIN' UP THE JOINT, WILLYA?!!
AWW, GO FRY YOUR HAT, BIG MOUTH!
LOOK OUT!
9

THAT *DOES* IT! I'M GONNA DOUSE THAT FLAME OF YOURS, AND THEN--

THING! TORCH! KNOCK IT OFF!

HECK, REED! THIS IS THE MOST FUN ANYONE'S HAD AROUND HERE FOR DAYS!

LET'S FACE IT, PAL, JOHNNY'S *RIGHT!* WE AINT CUT OUT FOR TWIDDLIN' OUR THUMBS! WE'RE ALL GETTIN' RESTLESS!

YES! PERHAPS WE ALL NEED A VACATION!

I WAS ABOUT TO SUGGEST THE SAME THING! MAYBE A TEMPORARY SEPARATION WOULD DO US ALL SOME GOOD!

THAT'S THE *COOLEST!* BUT WHAT ABOUT THOSE MOBSTERS HITTIN' NEW YORK, AND THE TROUBLE WE'RE SUPPOSED TO BE WATCHIN' FOR??

WE CAN ALWAYS RETURN TO HOME BASE IN A HURRY! *I* CAN BE REACHED AT GENERAL ELECTRONICS, IN NEW ENGLAND!

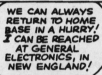

ME, I'LL BE TRAVELLIN' THRU THE SOUTH WITH THE BONES 'N BAILEY CIRCUS!

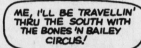

YOU'LL READ ABOUT *ME* IN THE PAPERS! I'M GONNA BE THE NEXT SENSATION OF THE GRUNT 'N GROAN CIRCUIT IN THE MIDWEST!

AND I'LL BE IN HOLLYWOOD, REHEARSING FOR MY VERY FIRST STARRING ROLE! ≥SIGH≤

*A*ND SO, UNSUSPECTED BY THE *FANTASTIC FOUR*, ALL THE TINY DETAILS OF THE *THINKER'S* MASTER PLAN FALL NEATLY INTO PLACE! HE HAS WON THE FIRST ROUND OF A FIGHT WHICH THE COLORFUL QUARTET DOESN'T EVEN KNOW IT IS FIGHTING!

Y'KNOW SOMETHIN'? THIS IS THE FIRST TIME WE EVER BUSTED UP! IT'S A SPOOKY FEELIN'!

YOU'RE *RIGHT*, BEN!

AW, WE'LL GET TOGETHER AGAIN AFTER A WHILE!

AT *LAST* I CAN DRESS THE WAY I'VE ALWAYS *WANTED* TO!

NEVER THOUGHT I'D SAY THIS, SMALL FRY, BUT I'M GONNA *MISS* YOU!

SURE, YA BIG LUG! NOBODY ELSE WOULD PUT UP WITH YA! TAKE CARE OF YOURSELF, BIG FELLA!

FOR TWO CENTS I'D TRY TO GET 'EM TO CALL THE WHOLE THING OFF! *NUTS!* WHAT'S THE MATTER WITH ME! IT AIN'T THE END OF THE WORLD! *EVERYBODY* NEEDS A VACATION SOME TIME!

10

AND NOW, BACK TO THE MAN WHOSE METICULOUS PLANNING HAS BROUGHT ABOUT THE EVENTS YOU HAVE JUST WITNESSED! BACK TO --THE *THINKER!*

IT IS NOW EXACTLY THREE MINUTES AFTER FOUR! THEY SHOULD JUST BE LEAVING THEIR HEADQUARTERS AT THIS MOMENT!

OKAY, *THINKER,* LET'S SAY THEY *ARE!* SO WHAT GOOD DOES THAT DO *US?*

YEAH! WHAT'S OUR *NEXT* MOVE? HOW DO WE TAKE OVER THE CITY?

THE VERY FORCES OF NATURE HERSELF WILL HELP US! MY MACHINES HAVE CALCULATED THE COURSE OF AN APPROACHING METEOR, WHICH WILL STRIKE NEW YORK HARBOR IN EXACTLY FIFTEEN SECONDS!

I KNEW OF THIS IMPENDING EVENT *WEEKS* AGO, AND INCLUDED IT IN MY PLANS! IT WILL BE OUR SIGNAL TO *STRIKE!*

AT THE PRECISE SPLIT-SECOND PREDICTED BY THE *THINKER,* A HURTLING METEOR DOES INDEED PLUMMET INTO THE WATERS OUTSIDE OF NEW YORK'S LOWER BAY...

ALTHOUGH NO ONE IS INJURED, THE SHOCK OF IMPACT CAUSES A TEMPORARY PANIC AMONG THE POPULACE...

WHAT *HAPPENED??* WHAT WAS *THAT??!*

MAYBE WE'RE BEING *ATTACKED!!* IT MUST BE *WAR!*

MINUTES LATER, AS THE SHOCK WEARS OFF, THE TRUTH IS LEARNED AND THE PANIC ENDS! BUT A *NEW* DANGER APPEARS! THE VIOLENT EARTH TREMOR HAS KNOCKED OUT ALL ELECTRIC POWER IN THE SPRAWLING CITY, AND CAUSED NUMEROUS SMALL FIRES AND EXPLOSIONS!

WOW! DID ONE LITTLE METEORITE DO ALL *THAT??*

LOOK! ALL THE STREET LIGHTS HAVE GONE OUT--AND THERE ARE FLAMES IN CENTRAL PARK!

IT'LL TAKE *HOURS* TO GET THINGS BACK TO NORMAL IN MIDTOWN NEW YORK!

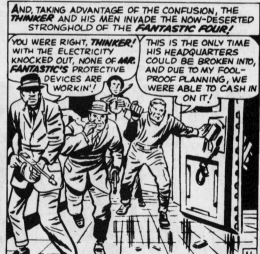

AND, TAKING ADVANTAGE OF THE CONFUSION, THE *THINKER* AND HIS MEN INVADE THE NOW-DESERTED STRONGHOLD OF THE *FANTASTIC FOUR!*

YOU WERE RIGHT, *THINKER!* WITH THE ELECTRICITY KNOCKED OUT, NONE OF *MR. FANTASTIC'S* PROTECTIVE DEVICES ARE WORKIN'!

THIS IS THE ONLY TIME HIS HEADQUARTERS COULD BE BROKEN INTO, AND DUE TO MY FOOLPROOF PLANNING, WE WERE ABLE TO CASH IN ON IT!

11

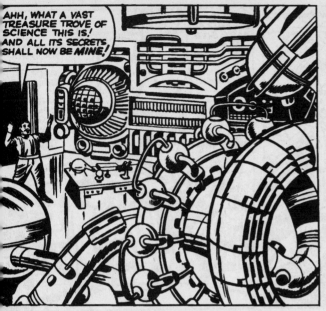

AHH, WHAT A VAST TREASURE TROVE OF SCIENCE THIS IS! AND ALL ITS SECRETS SHALL NOW BE *MINE!*

THIS IS EVEN BETTER THAN I EXPECTED!! HERE ARE *MR. FANTASTIC'S* NOTES CONCERNING HIS WORK WITH D.N.A., THE BUILDING BLOCKS OF *LIFE ITSELF!*

USING THIS INFORMATION, I SHOULD BE ABLE TO CREATE A NEW FORM OF *LIFE*-- ONE WHICH WILL SERVE ONLY-- THE *THINKER!!*

BUT LET US TAKE OUR LEAVE OF THE *THINKER* FOR A WHILE, AND VIEW A SCENE WHICH TAKES PLACE DAYS LATER, IN THE NORTHERN PART OF FLORIDA...

IT'S *AMAZING!* EVER SINCE THE *TORCH* HAS BEEN THE STAR OF OUR CIRCUS, WE'VE PLAYED TO CAPACITY CROWDS AT EVERY SHOW!

'YAY!!

LOOK AT *THAT!*

AND NOW, FOR HIS FINAL ACT, THE FANTASTIC *HUMAN TORCH* WILL PERFORM EVERY KNOWN CIRCUS STUNT AT THE SAME TIME!!

THE TORCH CAN DO *ANYTHING!*

MORE! *MORE!*

BUT, WHEN THE FINAL PERFORMANCE OF THE DAY HAS ENDED, IN THE SOLITUDE OF HIS ROOM, JOHNNY STORM BEGINS TO BROOD...

I NEVER REALIZED HOW *EMPTY* THE SOUND OF APPLAUSE CAN BE!

SAME OLD ACT, DAY AFTER DAY! I CAN'T TAKE MUCH MORE OF IT!

I WONDER HOW THE *OTHERS* ARE DOIN' NOW?

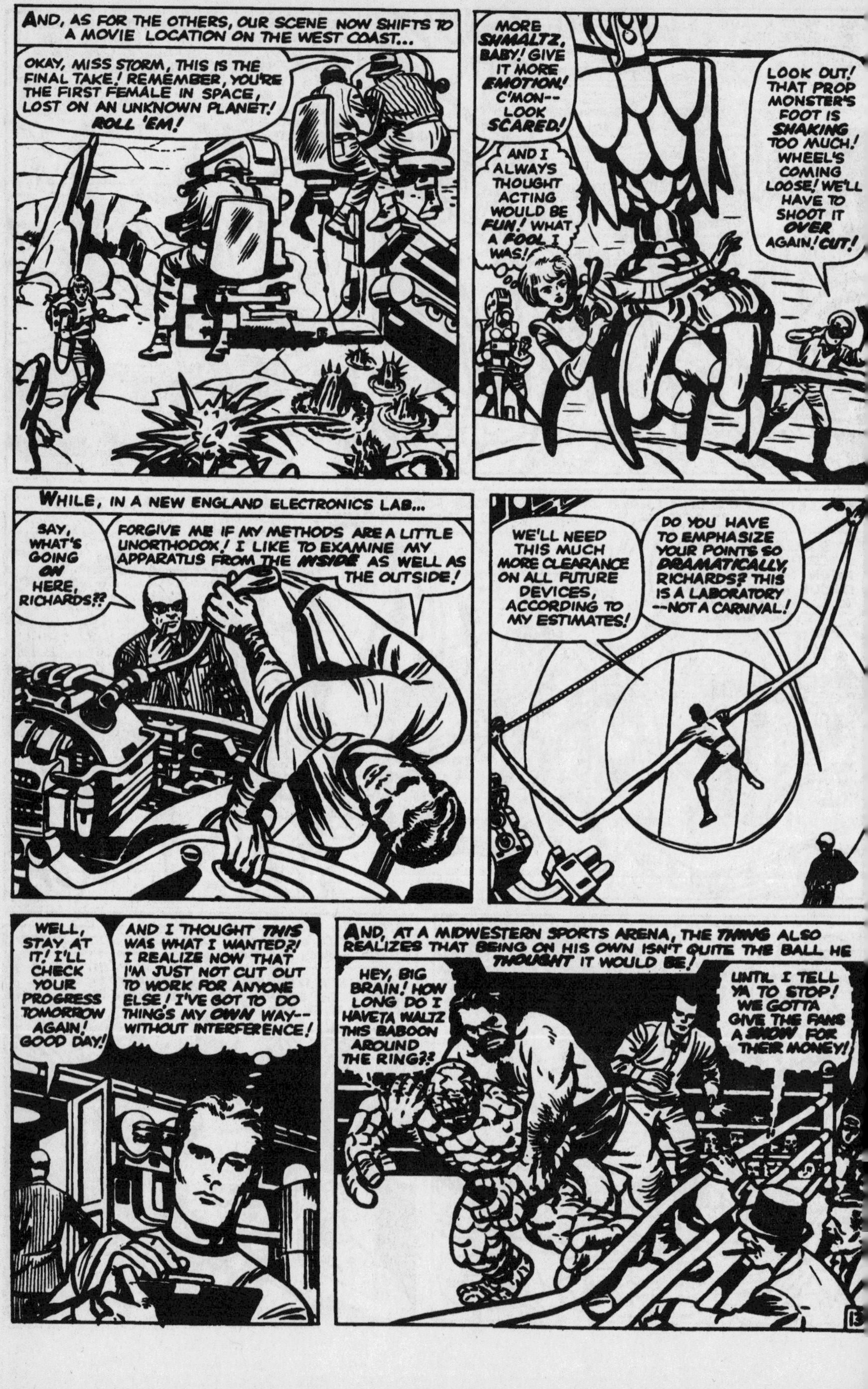

AND, AS FOR THE OTHERS, OUR SCENE NOW SHIFTS TO A MOVIE LOCATION ON THE WEST COAST...
OKAY, MISS STORM, THIS IS THE FINAL TAKE! REMEMBER, YOU'RE THE FIRST FEMALE IN SPACE, LOST ON AN UNKNOWN PLANET! ROLL 'EM!
MORE SHMALTZ, BABY! GIVE IT MORE EMOTION! C'MON-- LOOK SCARED!
AND I ALWAYS THOUGHT ACTING WOULD BE FUN! WHAT A FOOL I WAS!
LOOK OUT! THAT PROP MONSTER'S FOOT IS SHAKING TOO MUCH! WHEEL'S COMING LOOSE! WE'LL HAVE TO SHOOT IT OVER AGAIN! CUT!
WHILE, IN A NEW ENGLAND ELECTRONICS LAB...
SAY, WHAT'S GOING ON HERE, RICHARDS??
FORGIVE ME IF MY METHODS ARE A LITTLE UNORTHODOX! I LIKE TO EXAMINE MY APPARATUS FROM THE INSIDE AS WELL AS THE OUTSIDE!
WE'LL NEED THIS MUCH MORE CLEARANCE ON ALL FUTURE DEVICES, ACCORDING TO MY ESTIMATES!
DO YOU HAVE TO EMPHASIZE YOUR POINTS SO DRAMATICALLY, RICHARDS? THIS IS A LABORATORY --NOT A CARNIVAL!
WELL, STAY AT IT! I'LL CHECK YOUR PROGRESS TOMORROW AGAIN! GOOD DAY!
AND I THOUGHT THIS WAS WHAT I WANTED?! I REALIZE NOW THAT I'M JUST NOT CUT OUT TO WORK FOR ANYONE ELSE! I'VE GOT TO DO THINGS MY OWN WAY-- WITHOUT INTERFERENCE!
AND, AT A MIDWESTERN SPORTS ARENA, THE THING ALSO REALIZES THAT BEING ON HIS OWN ISN'T QUITE THE BALL HE THOUGHT IT WOULD BE!
HEY, BIG BRAIN! HOW LONG DO I HAVETA WALTZ THIS BABOON AROUND THE RING??
UNTIL I TELL YA TO STOP! WE GOTTA GIVE THE FANS A SHOW FOR THEIR MONEY!
13

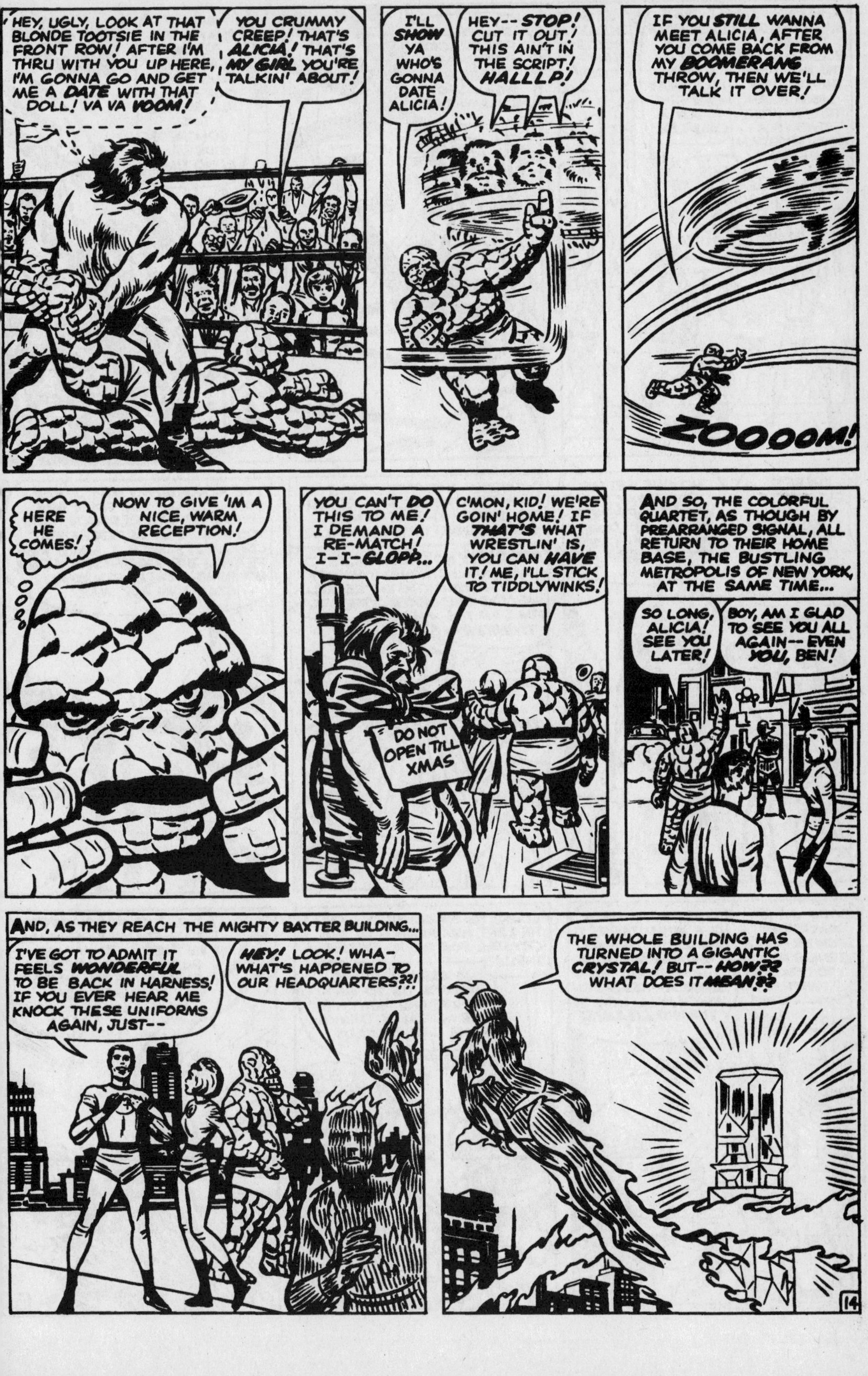
HEY, UGLY, LOOK AT THAT BLONDE TOOTSIE IN THE FRONT ROW! AFTER I'M THRU WITH YOU UP HERE, I'M GONNA GO AND GET ME A DATE WITH THAT DOLL! VA VA VOOM!
YOU CRUMMY CREEP! THAT'S ALICIA! THAT'S MY GIRL YOU'RE TALKIN' ABOUT!
I'LL SHOW YA WHO'S GONNA DATE ALICIA!
HEY-- STOP! CUT IT OUT! THIS AIN'T IN THE SCRIPT! HALLLP!
IF YOU STILL WANNA MEET ALICIA, AFTER YOU COME BACK FROM MY BOOMERANG THROW, THEN WE'LL TALK IT OVER!
ZOOOOOM!
HERE HE COMES!
NOW TO GIVE 'IM A NICE, WARM RECEPTION!
YOU CAN'T DO THIS TO ME! I DEMAND A RE-MATCH! I-I-GLOPP...
C'MON, KID! WE'RE GOIN' HOME! IF THAT'S WHAT WRESTLIN' IS, YOU CAN HAVE IT! ME, I'LL STICK TO TIDDLYWINKS!
DO NOT OPEN TILL XMAS
AND SO, THE COLORFUL QUARTET, AS THOUGH BY PREARRANGED SIGNAL, ALL RETURN TO THEIR HOME BASE, THE BUSTLING METROPOLIS OF NEW YORK, AT THE SAME TIME...
SO LONG, ALICIA! SEE YOU LATER!
BOY, AM I GLAD TO SEE YOU ALL AGAIN-- EVEN YOU, BEN!
AND, AS THEY REACH THE MIGHTY BAXTER BUILDING...
I'VE GOT TO ADMIT IT FEELS WONDERFUL TO BE BACK IN HARNESS! IF YOU EVER HEAR ME KNOCK THESE UNIFORMS AGAIN, JUST--
HEY! LOOK! WHA- WHAT'S HAPPENED TO OUR HEADQUARTERS??!
THE WHOLE BUILDING HAS TURNED INTO A GIGANTIC CRYSTAL! BUT-- HOW?? WHAT DOES IT MEAN??
14

IT'S *INCREDIBLE!* THE VERY ELEMENTS OF THE BUILDING THEMSELVES HAVE BEEN *TRANSMUTED!* THIS IS A NEW, UNKNOWN SUBSTANCE!

I CAN'T EVEN POKE A HOLE THRU IT! A THING LIKE THAT CAN GIVE A GUY A *COMPLEX!*

IT'S HEAT RESIS-TANT, TOO!

THIS MEANS WE'RE LOCKED OUT OF OUR OWN HEAD-QUARTERS!

I'LL PROBE FOR CRACKS --PERHAPS THERE'S A WEAK SPOT SOMEWHERE!

PHOOY! THAT'S TOO *SLOW!* MEBBE I CAN JUST *DIG* OUR WAY IN! I'LL BE THRU THIS CONCRETE SIDEWALK IN NO TIME!

THERE'S EVEN MORE TO THIS THAN MEETS THE EYE! LOOK AT ALL THE PASSERS-BY!

NO ONE SEEMS TO *NOTICE* WHAT'S HAPPENED TO THE BUILDING! THEY DON'T EVEN SEEM TO *SEE* IT!

SUDDENLY, THE FACE OF THE THINKER APPEARS, PROJECTED RIGHT THRU THE STRANGE, SHIMMERING CRYSTAL WALL!

NATURALLY NO ONE NOTICES! I HAVE AN ELECTRONIC HYPNO-RAY FIELD AROUND THIS ENTIRE BUILD-ING! I'VE BEEN *EXPECTING* YOU-- FOR I AM THE *THINKER!*

THE *THINKER?*

I'VE MODIFIED MY HYPNO-RAY SO THAT ONLY YOU FOUR ARE AWARE OF MY PRESENCE! FOR YOU ARE TO BE MY GREATEST CONQUEST! ONCE I HAVE DE-FEATED THE *FANTASTIC FOUR,* NO POWER ON EARTH CAN STAND IN MY WAY!

GOOD GRIEF! *ANOTHER* POWER-MAD GENIUS FOR US TO CONTEND WITH!

TRUE! BUT I HAVE ONE ADVANTAGE! I HAVE THE USE OF *MR. FANTASTIC'S* SCIENTIFIC RE-SEARCH--RESEARCH WHICH WILL NOW BE TURNED *AGAINST YOU!*

LOOK! HE FADED AWAY! AND HE LEFT AN OPENING IN THE CRYSTAL FOR US TO ENTER THRU!

HE *MEANS* IT! HE *WANTS* US TO GET INSIDE AND FIGHT HIM! HE ACTUALLY THINKS HE CAN BEAT US!

WELL-- WHAT ARE WE *WAITIN'* FOR??

I'LL JUST TOSS A SPEEDY BLUE-FLAME FIRE-BALL IN THERE, TO MAKE SURE THERE AREN'T ANY LITTLE TRAPS WAIT-ING FOR US!

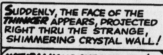

15

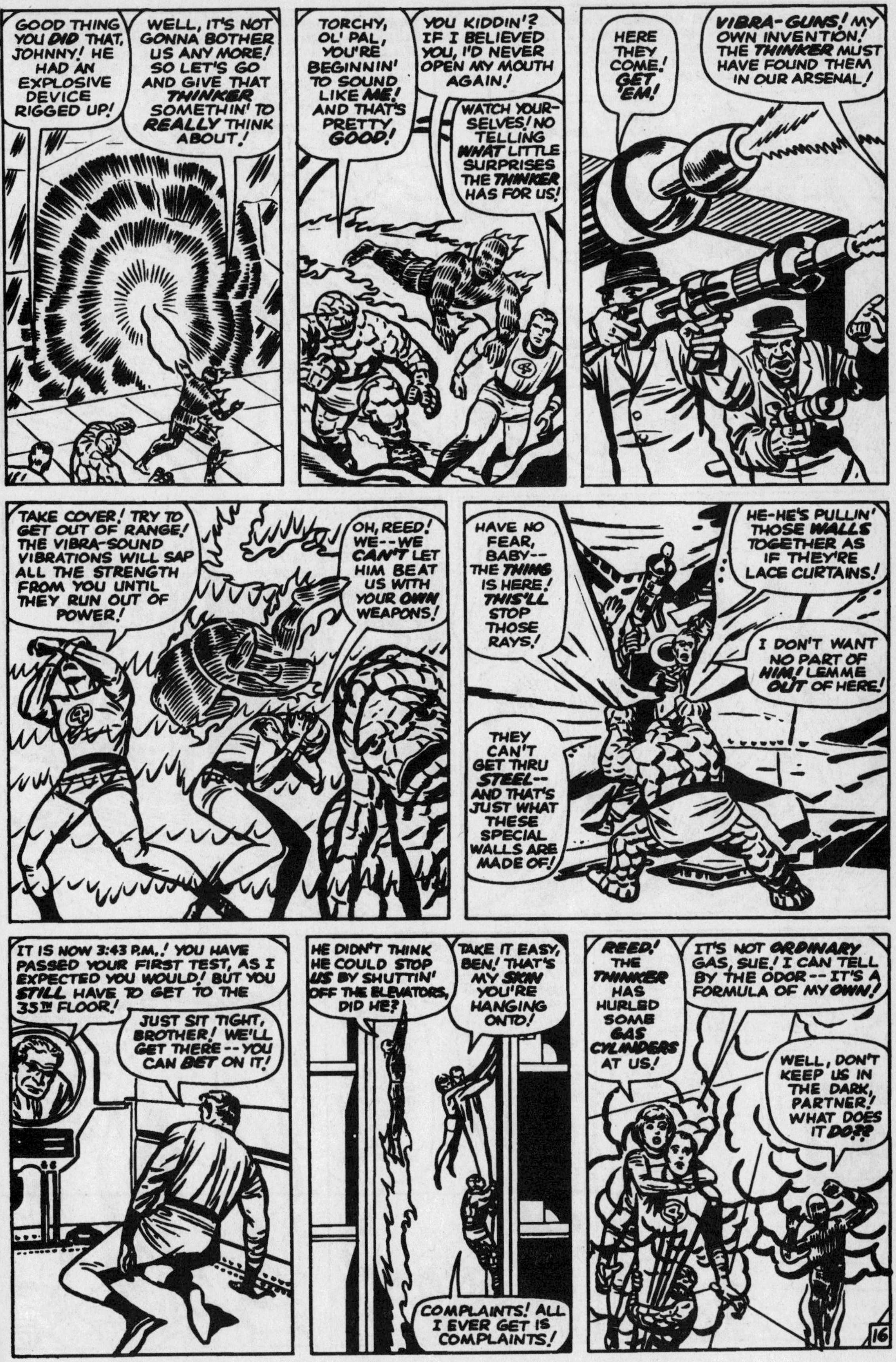
GOOD THING YOU DID THAT, JOHNNY! HE HAD AN EXPLOSIVE DEVICE RIGGED UP!
WELL, IT'S NOT GONNA BOTHER US ANY MORE! SO LET'S GO AND GIVE THAT THINKER SOMETHIN' TO REALLY THINK ABOUT!
TORCHY, OL' PAL, YOU'RE BEGINNIN' TO SOUND LIKE ME! AND THAT'S PRETTY GOOD!
YOU KIDDIN'? IF I BELIEVED YOU, I'D NEVER OPEN MY MOUTH AGAIN!
WATCH YOURSELVES! NO TELLING WHAT LITTLE SURPRISES THE THINKER HAS FOR US!
HERE THEY COME! GET 'EM!
VIBRA-GUNS! MY OWN INVENTION! THE THINKER MUST HAVE FOUND THEM IN OUR ARSENAL!
TAKE COVER! TRY TO GET OUT OF RANGE! THE VIBRA-SOUND VIBRATIONS WILL SAP ALL THE STRENGTH FROM YOU UNTIL THEY RUN OUT OF POWER!
OH, REED! WE--WE CAN'T LET HIM BEAT US WITH YOUR OWN WEAPONS!
HAVE NO FEAR, BABY-- THE THING IS HERE! THIS'LL STOP THOSE RAYS!
HE-HE'S PULLIN' THOSE WALLS TOGETHER AS IF THEY'RE LACE CURTAINS!
I DON'T WANT NO PART OF HIM! LEMME OUT OF HERE!
THEY CAN'T GET THRU STEEL-- AND THAT'S JUST WHAT THESE SPECIAL WALLS ARE MADE OF!
IT IS NOW 3:43 P.M.! YOU HAVE PASSED YOUR FIRST TEST, AS I EXPECTED YOU WOULD! BUT YOU STILL HAVE TO GET TO THE 35TH FLOOR!
JUST SIT TIGHT, BROTHER! WE'LL GET THERE--YOU CAN BET ON IT!
HE DIDN'T THINK HE COULD STOP US BY SHUTTIN' OFF THE ELEVATORS, DID HE?
TAKE IT EASY, BEN! THAT'S MY SKIN YOU'RE HANGING ONTO!
COMPLAINTS! ALL I EVER GET IS COMPLAINTS!
REED! THE THINKER HAS HURLED SOME GAS CYLINDERS AT US!
IT'S NOT ORDINARY GAS, SUE! I CAN TELL BY THE ODOR--IT'S A FORMULA OF MY OWN!
WELL, DON'T KEEP US IN THE DARK, PARTNER! WHAT DOES IT DO??
16

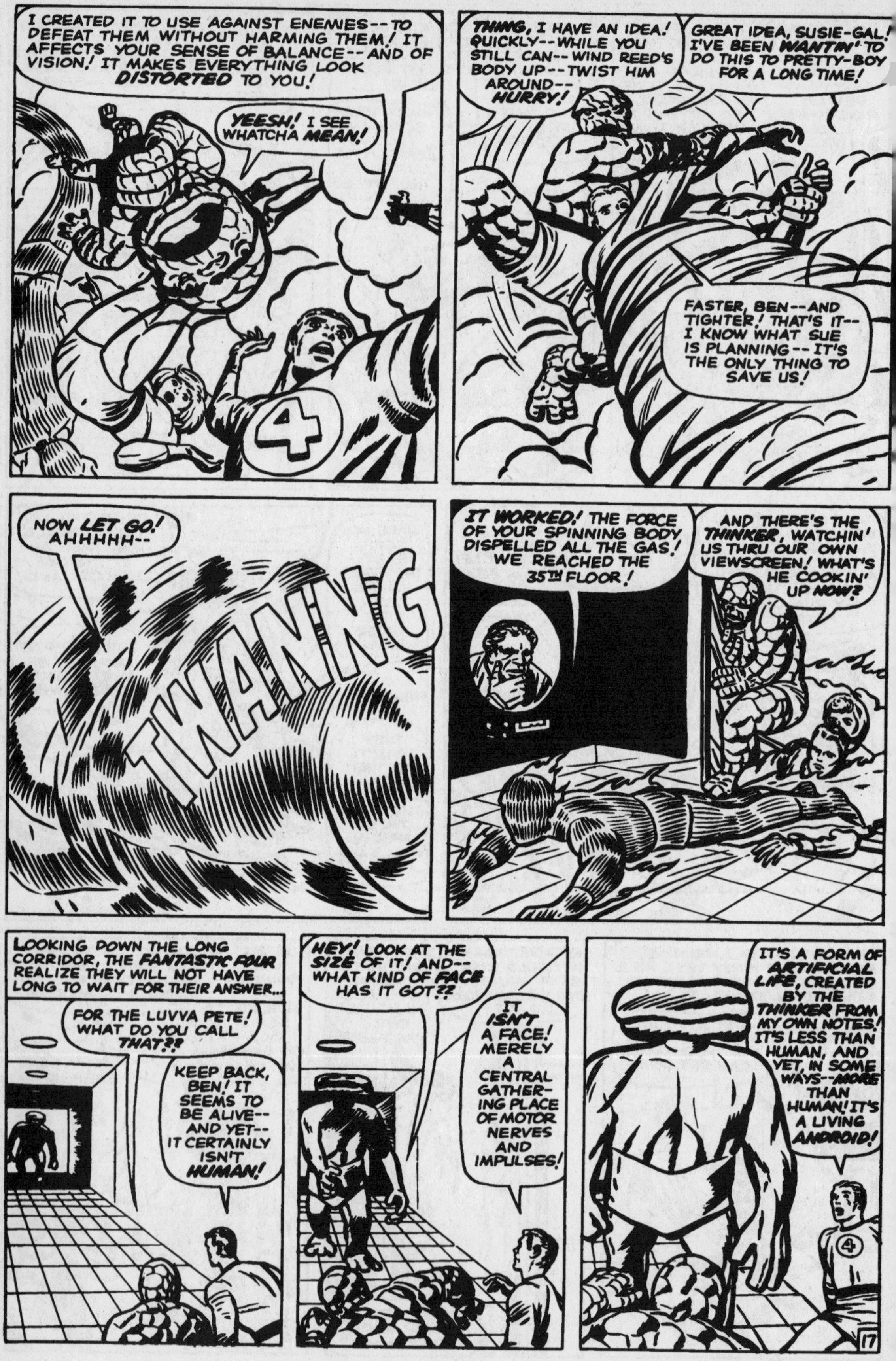
I CREATED IT TO USE AGAINST ENEMIES--TO DEFEAT THEM WITHOUT HARMING THEM! IT AFFECTS YOUR SENSE OF BALANCE--AND OF VISION! IT MAKES EVERYTHING LOOK DISTORTED TO YOU!
YEESH! I SEE WHATCHA MEAN!
THING, I HAVE AN IDEA! QUICKLY--WHILE YOU STILL CAN--WIND REED'S BODY UP--TWIST HIM AROUND--HURRY!
GREAT IDEA, SUSIE-GAL! I'VE BEEN WANTIN' TO DO THIS TO PRETTY-BOY FOR A LONG TIME!
FASTER, BEN--AND TIGHTER! THAT'S IT--I KNOW WHAT SUE IS PLANNING--IT'S THE ONLY THING TO SAVE US!
NOW LET GO! AHHHHH--
TWANNG
IT WORKED! THE FORCE OF YOUR SPINNING BODY DISPELLED ALL THE GAS! WE REACHED THE 35TH FLOOR!
AND THERE'S THE THINKER, WATCHIN' US THRU OUR OWN VIEWSCREEN! WHAT'S HE COOKIN' UP NOW?
LOOKING DOWN THE LONG CORRIDOR, THE FANTASTIC FOUR REALIZE THEY WILL NOT HAVE LONG TO WAIT FOR THEIR ANSWER...
FOR THE LUVVA PETE! WHAT DO YOU CALL THAT??
KEEP BACK, BEN! IT SEEMS TO BE ALIVE--AND YET--IT CERTAINLY ISN'T HUMAN!
HEY! LOOK AT THE SIZE OF IT! AND--WHAT KIND OF FACE HAS IT GOT??
IT ISN'T A FACE! MERELY A CENTRAL GATHERING PLACE OF MOTOR NERVES AND IMPULSES!
IT'S A FORM OF ARTIFICIAL LIFE, CREATED BY THE THINKER FROM MY OWN NOTES! IT'S LESS THAN HUMAN, AND YET, IN SOME WAYS--MORE THAN HUMAN! IT'S A LIVING ANDROID!
17

WAIT, JOHNNY! DON'T ATTACK IT YET! NOT TILL WE KNOW MORE **ABOUT** IT!

AWW, WHAT DO I HAVE TO WORRY ABOUT FROM A BIG HUNK LIKE THAT??

SUDDENLY, AS THE BLAZING **TORCH** FLAMES TOWARDS IT, THE **ANDROID** SPEWS FORTH A HURRICANE-INTENSITY BLAST OF WIND--

WHOOSH

YEOWW! IT'S LIKE FLYING INTO THE MOUTH OF A **TORNADO!** IT-IT'S BLOWING OUT MY FLAME!

WHOOOOOSH

STEP ASIDE, PLAYMATES! AS USUAL, I CAN SEE IT'S UP TO LITTLE OLD **ME** TO TAKE CARE OF THIS OVER-SIZED RAG DOLL!

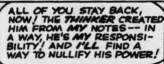

HEY! NOW WHAT'S HAPPENIN'??

I WAS **AFRAID** OF THAT, BEN! THE **ANDROID** HAS THE POWER OF **MIMICRY** BUILT INTO IT-- IT'S TURNING INTO--**YOU!**

BUT IT'S A STILL BIGGER, STRONGER VERSION OF THE **THING!** DUCK, BEN-- GET AWAY FROM IT!

WHAT DO YA THINK I'M **TRYIN'** TO DO, MISTER??

THANKS, SUE, FOR HELPING ME PULL HIM OUT OF THE WAY! LUCKILY THE **ANDROID** IS SLOW-MOVING! WE'VE GOT A FEW SECONDS TO THINK OF SOME WAY TO DEFEAT IT!

ALL OF YOU STAY BACK, NOW! THE **THINKER** CREATED HIM FROM **MY** NOTES-- IN A WAY, HE'S **MY** RESPONSIBILITY! AND **I'LL** FIND A WAY TO NULLIFY HIS POWER!

REED! I CAN'T LET YOU FACE THAT **CREATURE** ALONE! IF-IF ANYTHING SHOULD HAPPEN TO YOU--

IF I CAN'T STOP YOU, SUE, THEN AT LEAST TURN **INVISIBLE**-- IT MAY SAVE YOUR LIFE!

18

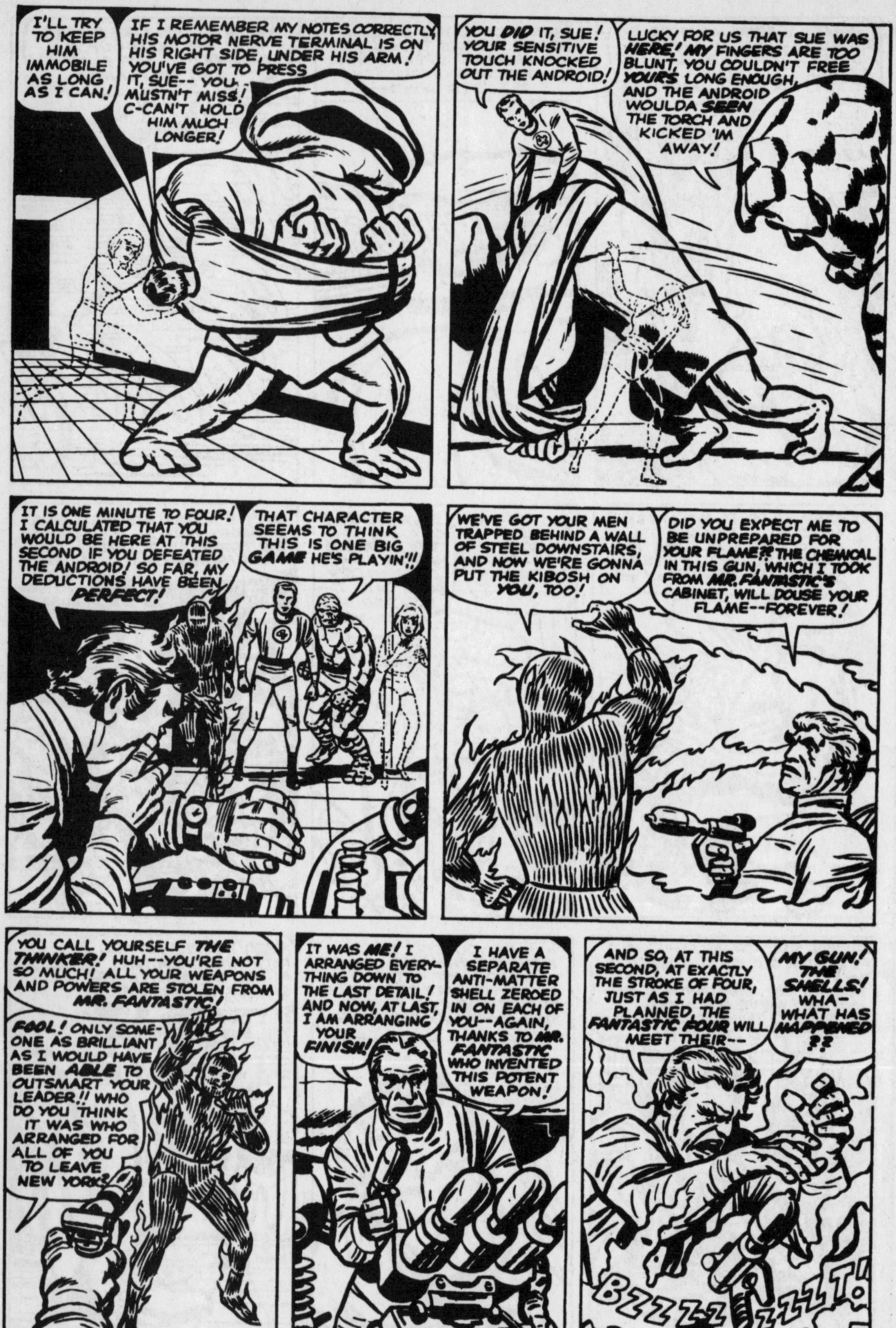
I'LL TRY TO KEEP HIM IMMOBILE AS LONG AS I CAN!
IF I REMEMBER MY NOTES CORRECTLY, HIS MOTOR NERVE TERMINAL IS ON HIS RIGHT SIDE, UNDER HIS ARM! YOU'VE GOT TO PRESS IT, SUE-- YOU MUSTN'T MISS! C-CAN'T HOLD HIM MUCH LONGER!
YOU DID IT, SUE! YOUR SENSITIVE TOUCH KNOCKED OUT THE ANDROID!
LUCKY FOR US THAT SUE WAS HERE! MY FINGERS ARE TOO BLUNT, YOU COULDN'T FREE YOURS LONG ENOUGH, AND THE ANDROID WOULDA SEEN THE TORCH AND KICKED 'IM AWAY!
IT IS ONE MINUTE TO FOUR! I CALCULATED THAT YOU WOULD BE HERE AT THIS SECOND IF YOU DEFEATED THE ANDROID! SO FAR, MY DEDUCTIONS HAVE BEEN PERFECT!
THAT CHARACTER SEEMS TO THINK THIS IS ONE BIG GAME HE'S PLAYIN'!!
WE'VE GOT YOUR MEN TRAPPED BEHIND A WALL OF STEEL DOWNSTAIRS, AND NOW WE'RE GONNA PUT THE KIBOSH ON YOU, TOO!
DID YOU EXPECT ME TO BE UNPREPARED FOR YOUR FLAME?? THE CHEMICAL IN THIS GUN, WHICH I TOOK FROM MR. FANTASTIC'S CABINET, WILL DOUSE YOUR FLAME--FOREVER!
YOU CALL YOURSELF THE THINKER! HUH--YOU'RE NOT SO MUCH! ALL YOUR WEAPONS AND POWERS ARE STOLEN FROM MR. FANTASTIC!
FOOL! ONLY SOMEONE AS BRILLIANT AS I WOULD HAVE BEEN ABLE TO OUTSMART YOUR LEADER!! WHO DO YOU THINK IT WAS WHO ARRANGED FOR ALL OF YOU TO LEAVE NEW YORK?
IT WAS ME! I ARRANGED EVERYTHING DOWN TO THE LAST DETAIL! AND NOW, AT LAST, I AM ARRANGING YOUR FINISH!
I HAVE A SEPARATE ANTI-MATTER SHELL ZEROED IN ON EACH OF YOU--AGAIN, THANKS TO MR. FANTASTIC WHO INVENTED THIS POTENT WEAPON!
AND SO, AT THIS SECOND, AT EXACTLY THE STROKE OF FOUR, JUST AS I HAD PLANNED, THE FANTASTIC FOUR WILL MEET THEIR--
MY GUN! THE SHELLS! WHA-WHAT HAS HAPPENED??
BZZZZZZZZZT!
19

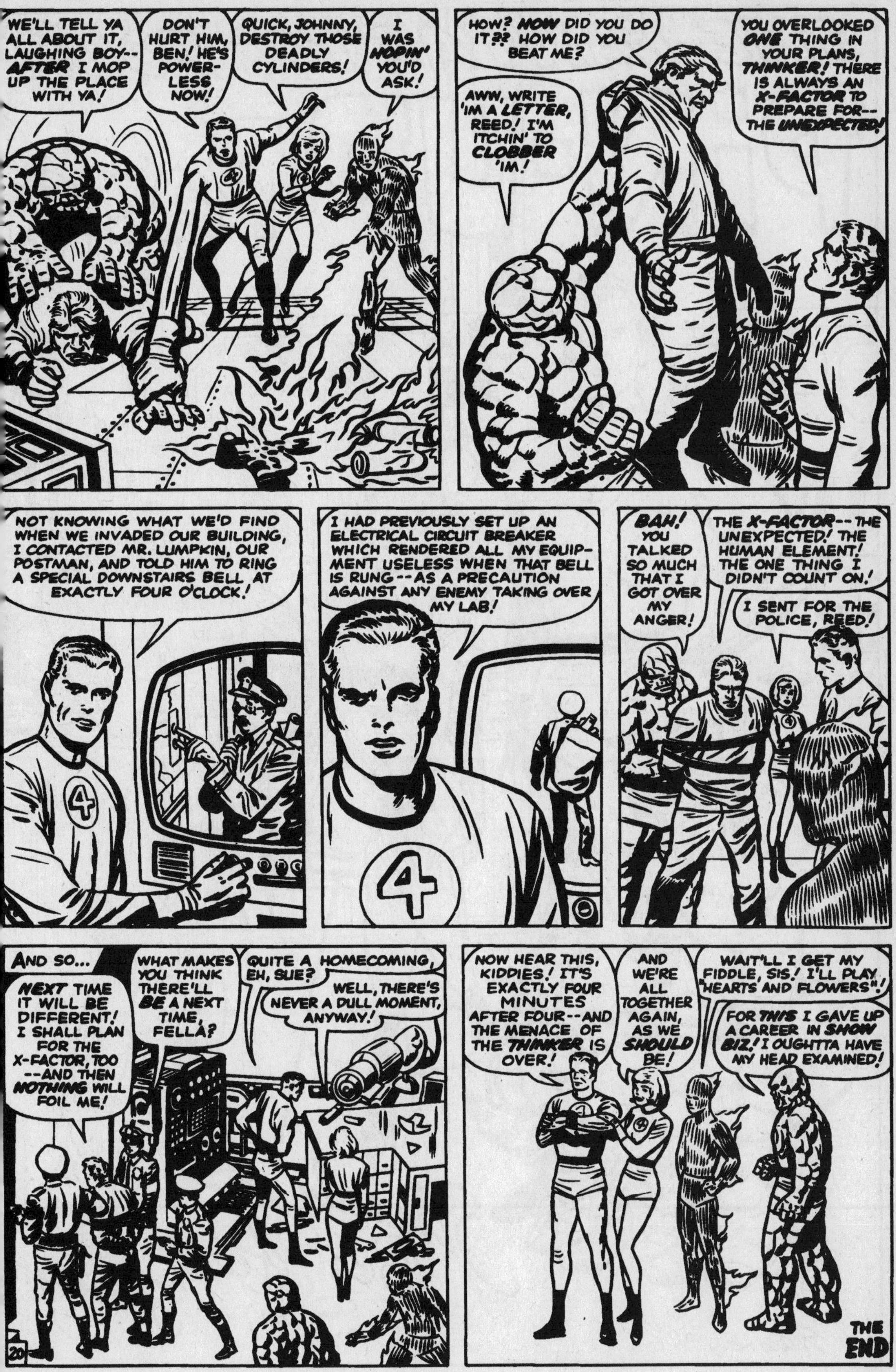
WE'LL TELL YA ALL ABOUT IT, LAUGHING BOY-- AFTER I MOP UP THE PLACE WITH YA!
DON'T HURT HIM, BEN! HE'S POWER-LESS NOW!
QUICK, JOHNNY, DESTROY THOSE DEADLY CYLINDERS!
I WAS HOPIN' YOU'D ASK!
HOW? HOW DID YOU DO IT?? HOW DID YOU BEAT ME?
YOU OVERLOOKED ONE THING IN YOUR PLANS, THINKER! THERE IS ALWAYS AN X-FACTOR TO PREPARE FOR-- THE UNEXPECTED!
AWW, WRITE 'IM A LETTER, REED! I'M ITCHIN' TO CLOBBER 'IM!
NOT KNOWING WHAT WE'D FIND WHEN WE INVADED OUR BUILDING, I CONTACTED MR. LUMPKIN, OUR POSTMAN, AND TOLD HIM TO RING A SPECIAL DOWNSTAIRS BELL AT EXACTLY FOUR O'CLOCK!
I HAD PREVIOUSLY SET UP AN ELECTRICAL CIRCUIT BREAKER WHICH RENDERED ALL MY EQUIP-MENT USELESS WHEN THAT BELL IS RUNG--AS A PRECAUTION AGAINST ANY ENEMY TAKING OVER MY LAB!
BAH! YOU TALKED SO MUCH THAT I GOT OVER MY ANGER!
THE X-FACTOR--THE UNEXPECTED! THE HUMAN ELEMENT! THE ONE THING I DIDN'T COUNT ON!
I SENT FOR THE POLICE, REED!
AND SO...
NEXT TIME IT WILL BE DIFFERENT! I SHALL PLAN FOR THE X-FACTOR, TOO --AND THEN NOTHING WILL FOIL ME!
WHAT MAKES YOU THINK THERE'LL BE A NEXT TIME, FELLA?
QUITE A HOMECOMING, EH, SUE?
WELL, THERE'S NEVER A DULL MOMENT, ANYWAY!
NOW HEAR THIS, KIDDIES! IT'S EXACTLY FOUR MINUTES AFTER FOUR--AND THE MENACE OF THE THINKER IS OVER!
AND WE'RE ALL TOGETHER AGAIN, AS WE SHOULD BE!
WAIT'LL I GET MY FIDDLE, SIS! I'LL PLAY "HEARTS AND FLOWERS"!
FOR THIS I GAVE UP A CAREER IN SHOW BIZ! I OUGHTTA HAVE MY HEAD EXAMINED!
THE END

THE FANTASTIC FOUR
PiN-UP Page

Sincerely,
Ben, Reed,
Sue, & Johnny—

—& Stan & JACK

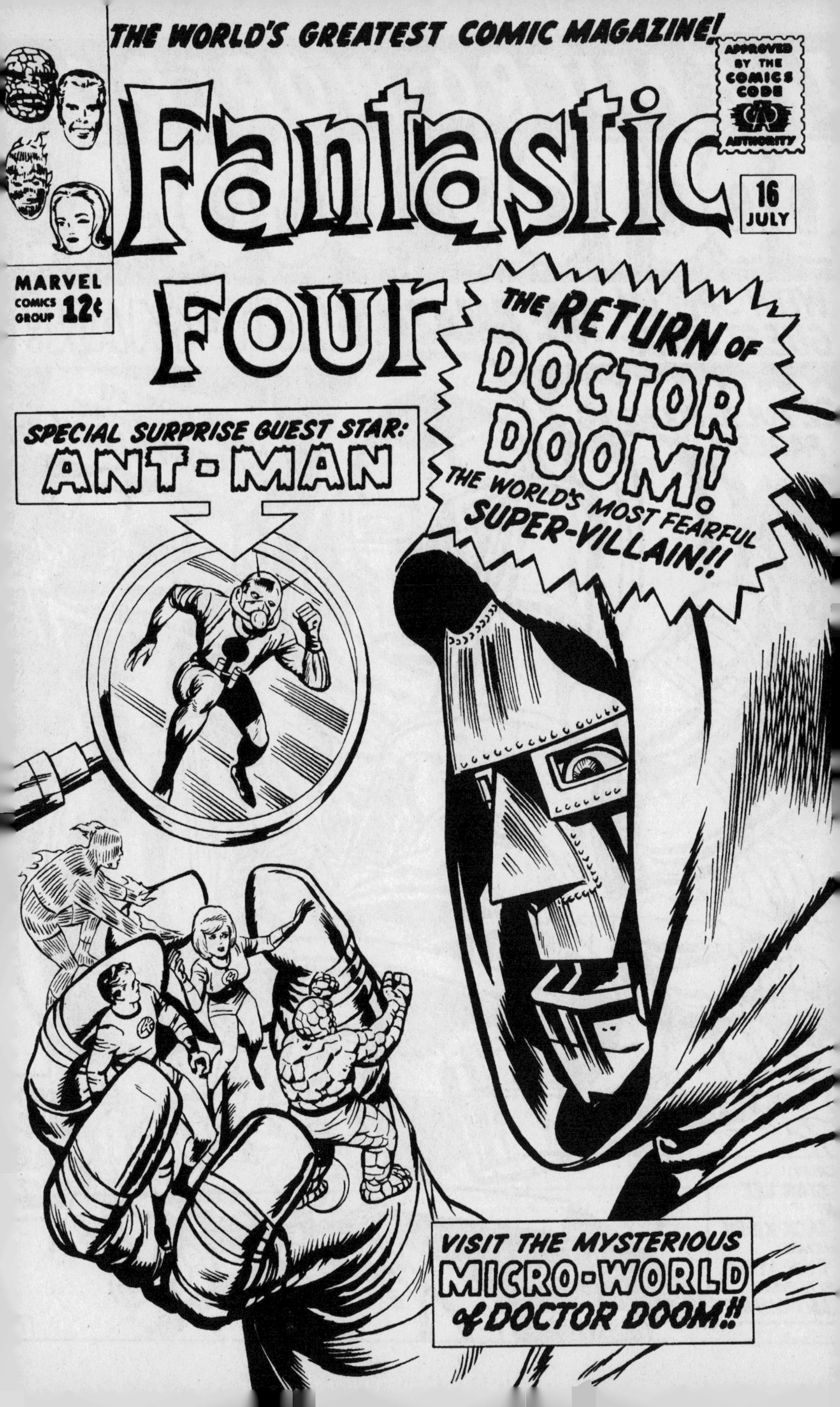

THE WORLD'S GREATEST COMIC MAGAZINE!
APPROVED BY THE COMICS CODE AUTHORITY
Fantastic Four
16 JULY
MARVEL COMICS GROUP 12¢
THE RETURN OF DOCTOR DOOM! THE WORLD'S MOST FEARFUL SUPER-VILLAIN!!
SPECIAL SURPRISE GUEST STAR: ANT-MAN
VISIT THE MYSTERIOUS MICRO-WORLD of DOCTOR DOOM!!

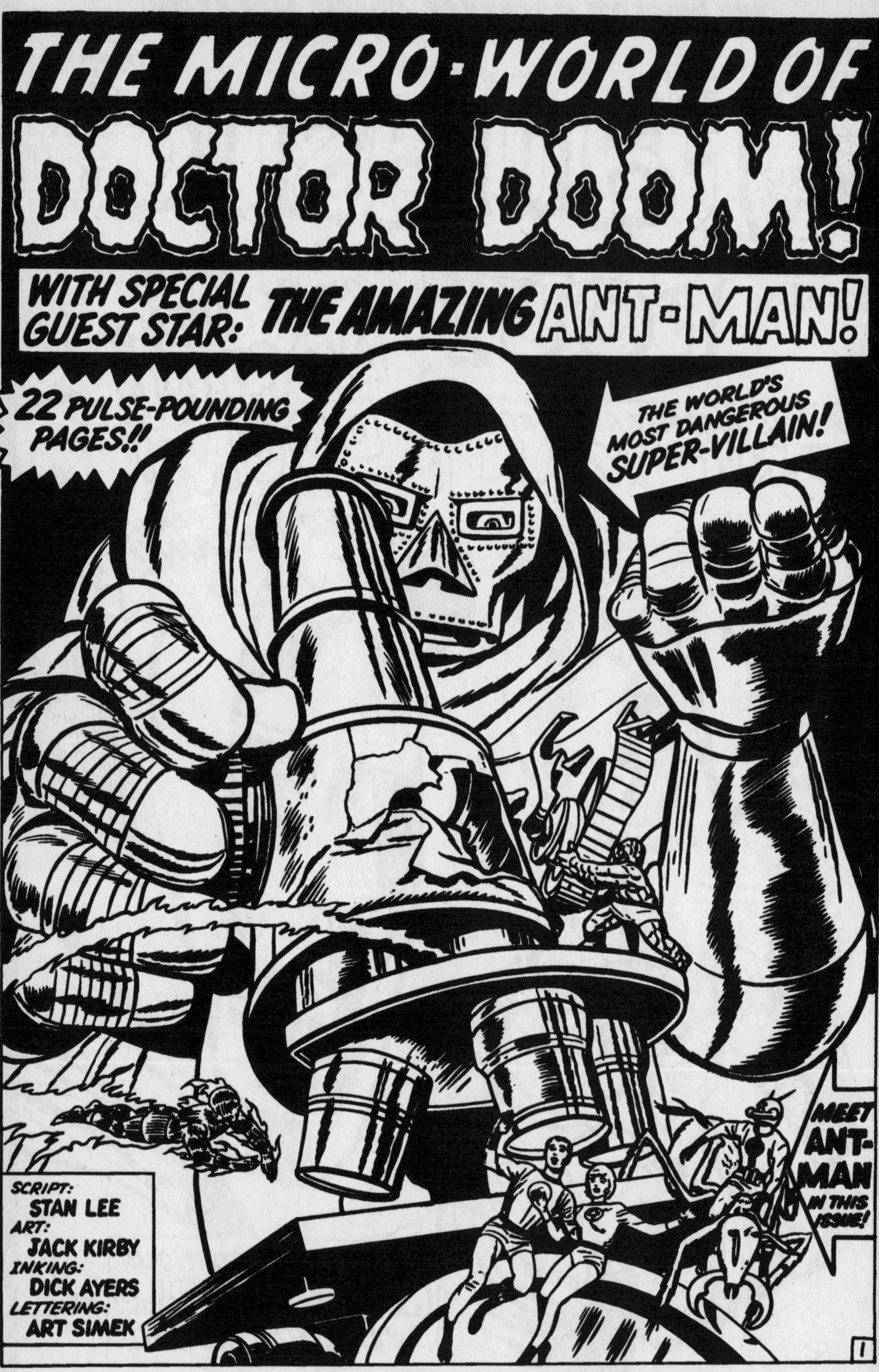
THE MICRO-WORLD OF
DOCTOR DOOM!
WITH SPECIAL GUEST STAR: THE AMAZING ANT-MAN!
22 PULSE-POUNDING PAGES!!
THE WORLD'S MOST DANGEROUS SUPER-VILLAIN!
MEET ANT-MAN IN THIS ISSUE!
SCRIPT: STAN LEE
ART: JACK KIRBY
INKING: DICK AYERS
LETTERING: ART SIMEK
1

ATOP A NEIGHBORHOOD BUILDING IN NEW YORK CITY, AN AMATEUR ASTRONOMER EXCITEDLY SHOUTS...

I'LL BE *FAMOUS!!* I'VE DISCOVERED A NEW, BLAZING *COMET!*

NOT FAR AWAY, IN THE OPERATING ROOM OF A LARGE HOSPITAL...

WHAT A LUCKY COINCIDENCE! THAT BLAZING STREAK IN THE SKY GAVE US ENOUGH LIGHT TO COMPLETE OUR SURGERY WHEN THE POWER FAILED!

BUT WHAT ON EARTH CAN IT *BE?*

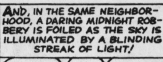

AND, IN THE SAME NEIGHBORHOOD, A DARING MIDNIGHT ROBBERY IS FOILED AS THE SKY IS ILLUMINATED BY A BLINDING STREAK OF LIGHT!

WHAT HAPPENED?? WHERE'D THAT *LIGHT* COME FROM??

THEY GOT THE GOODS ON US!

DON'T MAKE A MOVE. WE'VE GOT YOU DEAD TO RIGHTS!

LIKE A FIERY METEOR, THE CAUSE OF WHAT WE HAVE JUST SEEN BLAZES THRU THE SKY AT ALMOST UNIMAGINABLE SPEED! ONCE AGAIN THE *HUMAN TORCH* IS FLAMING OVERHEAD!

SOMETHING'S WRONG AT HEADQUARTERS! NOBODY ANSWERED MY SIGNAL! GOT TO GET THERE *PRONTO!*

BUT WHAT COULD HAVE *HAPPENED??* THERE'S NOT A POWER ON EARTH THAT CAN PUT THE *FANTASTIC FOUR* OUT OF ACTION!!

OR-- GULP *IS* THERE??

REED! BEN! SUE! WHERE ARE YA??

FLAMING FIREBALLS!!! THERE'S NOT A SIGN OF LIFE!!!

IS ANYBODY *HERE??* SPEAK UP!! WHAT'S GOIN' ON??

AND THEN, SUDDENLY, THE *TORCH* HEARS A THIN, FAINT VOICE... AND, AS HE LOOKS DOWN...

HERE, JOHNNY! DOWN *HERE!!*

NO! *NO!* IT CAN'T *BE!!*

YOU-YOU'VE ALL BEEN REDUCED TO THE SIZE OF *TOYS!!!*

DON'T JUST *STAND* THERE, HOT-HEAD! *GRAB* US, BEFORE WE'RE PULLED INTO THAT AIR-DUCT!

HURRY, JOHNNY!! CAN'T HOLD ON MUCH LONGER!

2

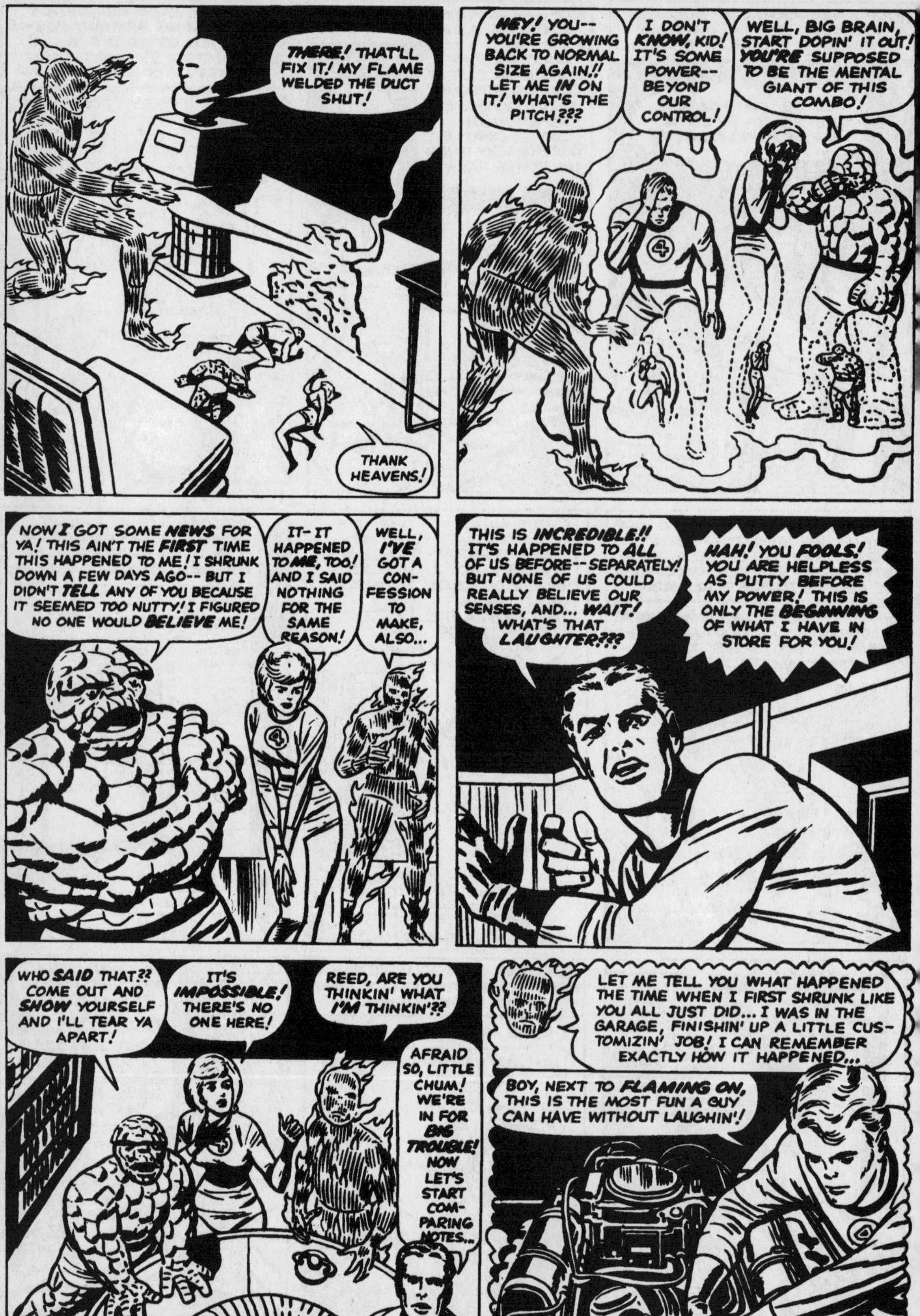
THERE! THAT'LL FIX IT! MY FLAME WELDED THE DUCT SHUT!
THANK HEAVENS!
HEY! YOU-- YOU'RE GROWING BACK TO NORMAL SIZE AGAIN!! LET ME IN ON IT! WHAT'S THE PITCH???
I DON'T KNOW, KID! IT'S SOME POWER-- BEYOND OUR CONTROL!
WELL, BIG BRAIN, START DOPIN' IT OUT! YOU'RE SUPPOSED TO BE THE MENTAL GIANT OF THIS COMBO!
NOW I GOT SOME NEWS FOR YA! THIS AIN'T THE FIRST TIME THIS HAPPENED TO ME! I SHRUNK DOWN A FEW DAYS AGO-- BUT I DIDN'T TELL ANY OF YOU BECAUSE IT SEEMED TOO NUTTY! I FIGURED NO ONE WOULD BELIEVE ME!
IT- IT HAPPENED TO ME, TOO! AND I SAID NOTHING FOR THE SAME REASON!
WELL, I'VE GOT A CON- FESSION TO MAKE, ALSO...
THIS IS INCREDIBLE!! IT'S HAPPENED TO ALL OF US BEFORE--SEPARATELY! BUT NONE OF US COULD REALLY BELIEVE OUR SENSES, AND... WAIT! WHAT'S THAT LAUGHTER???
HAH! YOU FOOLS! YOU ARE HELPLESS AS PUTTY BEFORE MY POWER! THIS IS ONLY THE BEGINNING OF WHAT I HAVE IN STORE FOR YOU!
WHO SAID THAT?? COME OUT AND SHOW YOURSELF AND I'LL TEAR YA APART!
IT'S IMPOSSIBLE! THERE'S NO ONE HERE!
REED, ARE YOU THINKIN' WHAT I'M THINKIN'??
AFRAID SO, LITTLE CHUM! WE'RE IN FOR BIG TROUBLE! NOW LET'S START COM- PARING NOTES...
LET ME TELL YOU WHAT HAPPENED THE TIME WHEN I FIRST SHRUNK LIKE YOU ALL JUST DID... I WAS IN THE GARAGE, FINISHIN' UP A LITTLE CUS- TOMIZIN' JOB! I CAN REMEMBER EXACTLY HOW IT HAPPENED...
BOY, NEXT TO FLAMING ON, THIS IS THE MOST FUN A GUY CAN HAVE WITHOUT LAUGHIN'!
3

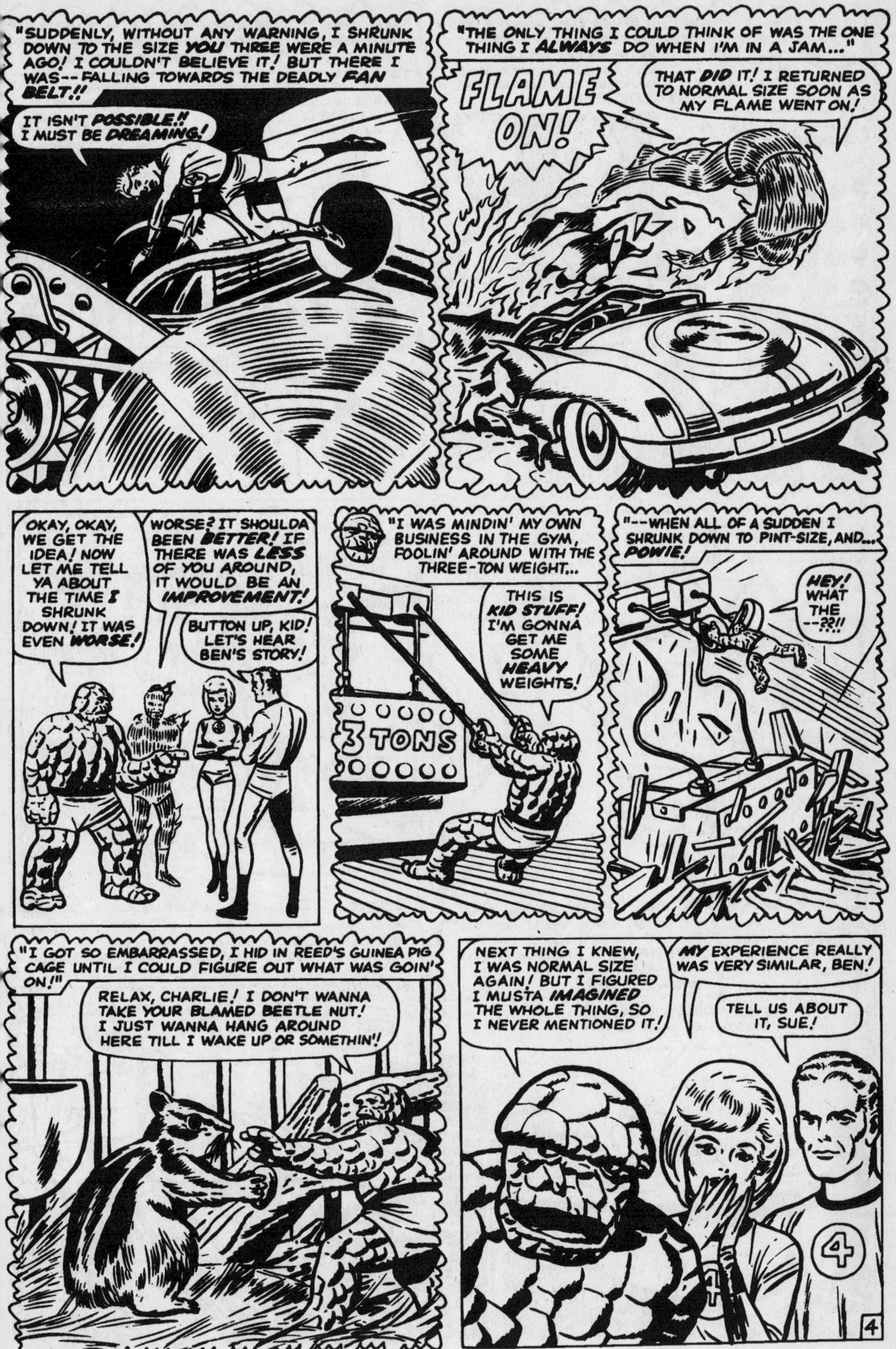
"SUDDENLY, WITHOUT ANY WARNING, I SHRUNK DOWN TO THE SIZE YOU THREE WERE A MINUTE AGO! I COULDN'T BELIEVE IT! BUT THERE I WAS-- FALLING TOWARDS THE DEADLY FAN BELT!!
IT ISN'T POSSIBLE!! I MUST BE DREAMING!
"THE ONLY THING I COULD THINK OF WAS THE ONE THING I ALWAYS DO WHEN I'M IN A JAM..."
FLAME ON!
THAT DID IT! I RETURNED TO NORMAL SIZE SOON AS MY FLAME WENT ON!
OKAY, OKAY, WE GET THE IDEA! NOW LET ME TELL YA ABOUT THE TIME I SHRUNK DOWN! IT WAS EVEN WORSE!
WORSE? IT SHOULDA BEEN BETTER! IF THERE WAS LESS OF YOU AROUND, IT WOULD BE AN IMPROVEMENT!
BUTTON UP, KID! LET'S HEAR BEN'S STORY!
"I WAS MINDIN' MY OWN BUSINESS IN THE GYM, FOOLIN' AROUND WITH THE THREE-TON WEIGHT...
THIS IS KID STUFF! I'M GONNA GET ME SOME HEAVY WEIGHTS!
3 TONS
"--WHEN ALL OF A SUDDEN I SHRUNK DOWN TO PINT-SIZE, AND... POWIE!
HEY! WHAT THE --??!!
"I GOT SO EMBARRASSED, I HID IN REED'S GUINEA PIG CAGE UNTIL I COULD FIGURE OUT WHAT WAS GOIN' ON!"
RELAX, CHARLIE! I DON'T WANNA TAKE YOUR BLAMED BEETLE NUT! I JUST WANNA HANG AROUND HERE TILL I WAKE UP OR SOMETHIN'!
NEXT THING I KNEW, I WAS NORMAL SIZE AGAIN! BUT I FIGURED I MUSTA IMAGINED THE WHOLE THING, SO I NEVER MENTIONED IT!
MY EXPERIENCE REALLY WAS VERY SIMILAR, BEN!
TELL US ABOUT IT, SUE!
4

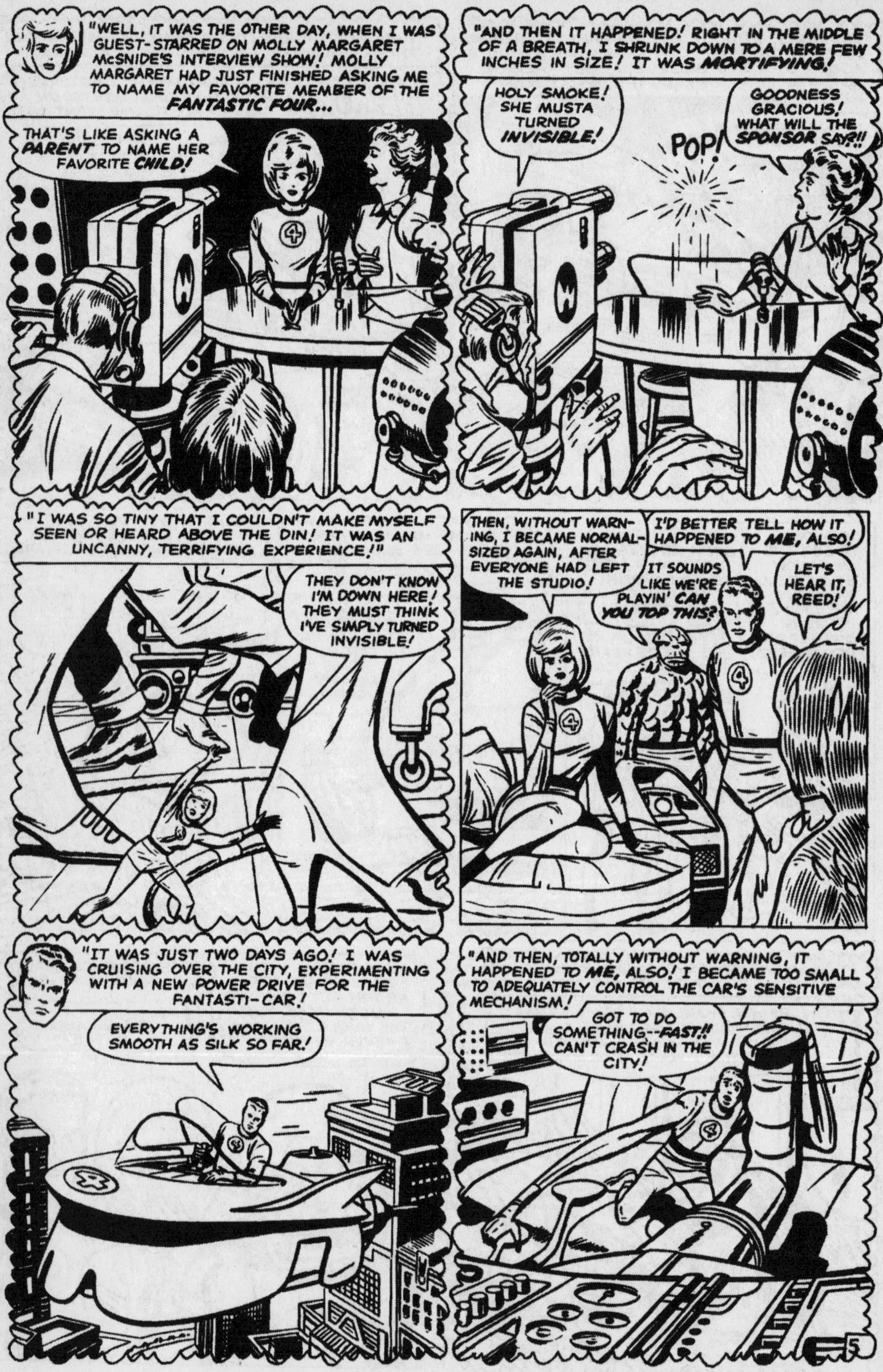
"WELL, IT WAS THE OTHER DAY, WHEN I WAS GUEST-STARRED ON MOLLY MARGARET McSNIDE'S INTERVIEW SHOW! MOLLY MARGARET HAD JUST FINISHED ASKING ME TO NAME MY FAVORITE MEMBER OF THE FANTASTIC FOUR...
THAT'S LIKE ASKING A PARENT TO NAME HER FAVORITE CHILD!
"AND THEN IT HAPPENED! RIGHT IN THE MIDDLE OF A BREATH, I SHRUNK DOWN TO A MERE FEW INCHES IN SIZE! IT WAS MORTIFYING!
HOLY SMOKE! SHE MUSTA TURNED INVISIBLE!
GOODNESS GRACIOUS! WHAT WILL THE SPONSOR SAY?!!
POP!
"I WAS SO TINY THAT I COULDN'T MAKE MYSELF SEEN OR HEARD ABOVE THE DIN! IT WAS AN UNCANNY, TERRIFYING EXPERIENCE!"
THEY DON'T KNOW I'M DOWN HERE! THEY MUST THINK I'VE SIMPLY TURNED INVISIBLE!
THEN, WITHOUT WARNING, I BECAME NORMAL-SIZED AGAIN, AFTER EVERYONE HAD LEFT THE STUDIO!
I'D BETTER TELL HOW IT HAPPENED TO ME, ALSO!
IT SOUNDS LIKE WE'RE PLAYIN' CAN YOU TOP THIS?
LET'S HEAR IT, REED!
"IT WAS JUST TWO DAYS AGO! I WAS CRUISING OVER THE CITY, EXPERIMENTING WITH A NEW POWER DRIVE FOR THE FANTASTI-CAR!
EVERYTHING'S WORKING SMOOTH AS SILK SO FAR!
"AND THEN, TOTALLY WITHOUT WARNING, IT HAPPENED TO ME, ALSO! I BECAME TOO SMALL TO ADEQUATELY CONTROL THE CAR'S SENSITIVE MECHANISM!
GOT TO DO SOMETHING--FAST!! CAN'T CRASH IN THE CITY!
5

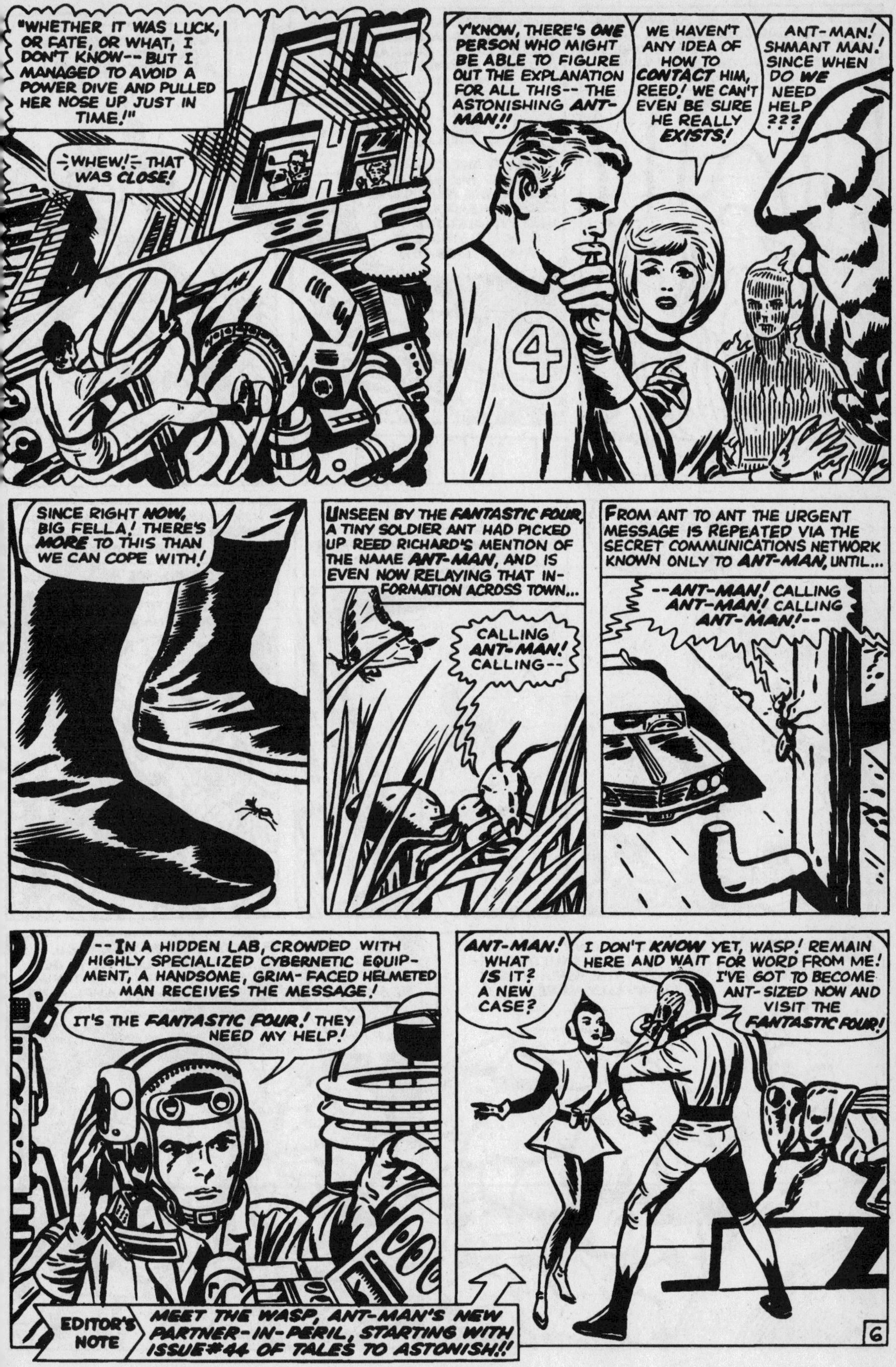
"WHETHER IT WAS LUCK, OR FATE, OR WHAT, I DON'T KNOW-- BUT I MANAGED TO AVOID A POWER DIVE AND PULLED HER NOSE UP JUST IN TIME!"
WHEW! THAT WAS CLOSE!
Y'KNOW, THERE'S ONE PERSON WHO MIGHT BE ABLE TO FIGURE OUT THE EXPLANATION FOR ALL THIS-- THE ASTONISHING ANT-MAN!!
WE HAVEN'T ANY IDEA OF HOW TO CONTACT HIM, REED! WE CAN'T EVEN BE SURE HE REALLY EXISTS!
ANT-MAN! SHMANT MAN! SINCE WHEN DO WE NEED HELP ???
SINCE RIGHT NOW, BIG FELLA! THERE'S MORE TO THIS THAN WE CAN COPE WITH!
UNSEEN BY THE FANTASTIC FOUR, A TINY SOLDIER ANT HAD PICKED UP REED RICHARD'S MENTION OF THE NAME ANT-MAN, AND IS EVEN NOW RELAYING THAT INFORMATION ACROSS TOWN...
CALLING ANT-MAN! CALLING--
FROM ANT TO ANT THE URGENT MESSAGE IS REPEATED VIA THE SECRET COMMUNICATIONS NETWORK KNOWN ONLY TO ANT-MAN, UNTIL...
--ANT-MAN! CALLING ANT-MAN! CALLING ANT-MAN!--
--IN A HIDDEN LAB, CROWDED WITH HIGHLY SPECIALIZED CYBERNETIC EQUIPMENT, A HANDSOME, GRIM-FACED HELMETED MAN RECEIVES THE MESSAGE!
IT'S THE FANTASTIC FOUR! THEY NEED MY HELP!
ANT-MAN! WHAT IS IT? A NEW CASE?
I DON'T KNOW YET, WASP! REMAIN HERE AND WAIT FOR WORD FROM ME! I'VE GOT TO BECOME ANT-SIZED NOW AND VISIT THE FANTASTIC FOUR!
EDITOR'S NOTE
MEET THE WASP, ANT-MAN'S NEW PARTNER-IN-PERIL, STARTING WITH ISSUE #44 OF TALES TO ASTONISH!!
6

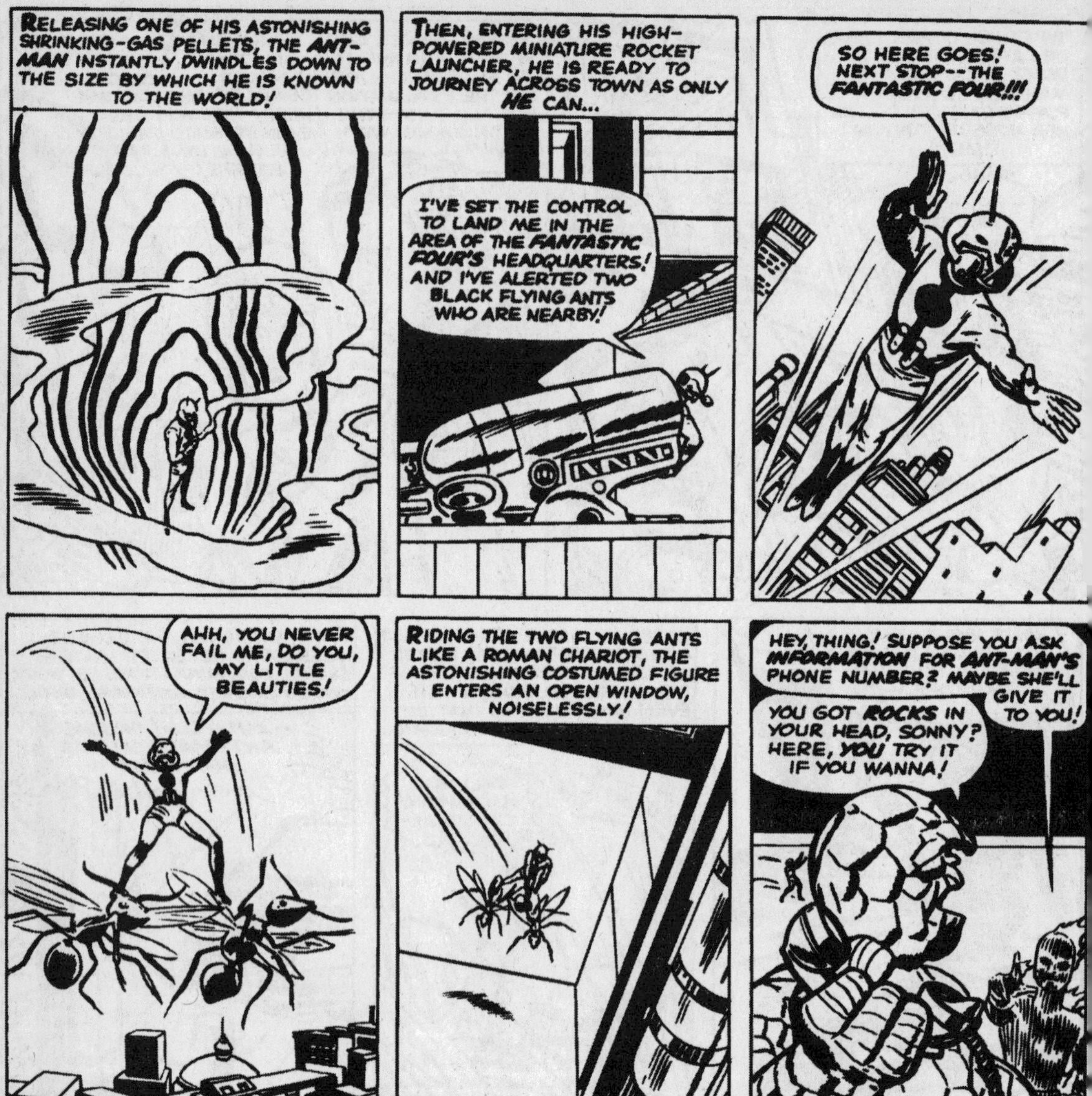
RELEASING ONE OF HIS ASTONISHING SHRINKING-GAS PELLETS, THE ANT-MAN INSTANTLY DWINDLES DOWN TO THE SIZE BY WHICH HE IS KNOWN TO THE WORLD!
THEN, ENTERING HIS HIGH-POWERED MINIATURE ROCKET LAUNCHER, HE IS READY TO JOURNEY ACROSS TOWN AS ONLY HE CAN...
I'VE SET THE CONTROL TO LAND ME IN THE AREA OF THE FANTASTIC FOUR'S HEADQUARTERS! AND I'VE ALERTED TWO BLACK FLYING ANTS WHO ARE NEARBY!
SO HERE GOES! NEXT STOP--THE FANTASTIC FOUR!!!
AHH, YOU NEVER FAIL ME, DO YOU, MY LITTLE BEAUTIES!
RIDING THE TWO FLYING ANTS LIKE A ROMAN CHARIOT, THE ASTONISHING COSTUMED FIGURE ENTERS AN OPEN WINDOW, NOISELESSLY!
HEY, THING! SUPPOSE YOU ASK INFORMATION FOR ANT-MAN'S PHONE NUMBER? MAYBE SHE'LL GIVE IT TO YOU!
YOU GOT ROCKS IN YOUR HEAD, SONNY? HERE, YOU TRY IT IF YOU WANNA!
NO NEED TO PHONE, THING! I'M HERE!
WELL, BRUSH MY TEETH AND CALL ME SMILEY!! IT'S HIM! THE SONUVAGUN IS REALLY HERE!
BUT--HOW--?!?
BOY! EVEN ELEVATOR SHOES WOULDN'T HELP HIM!
IT'S HARD TO HEAR YOU, ANT-MAN! LET ME PLACE THIS CRYSTAL MAGNIFYING AMPLIFIER OVER YOU...
7

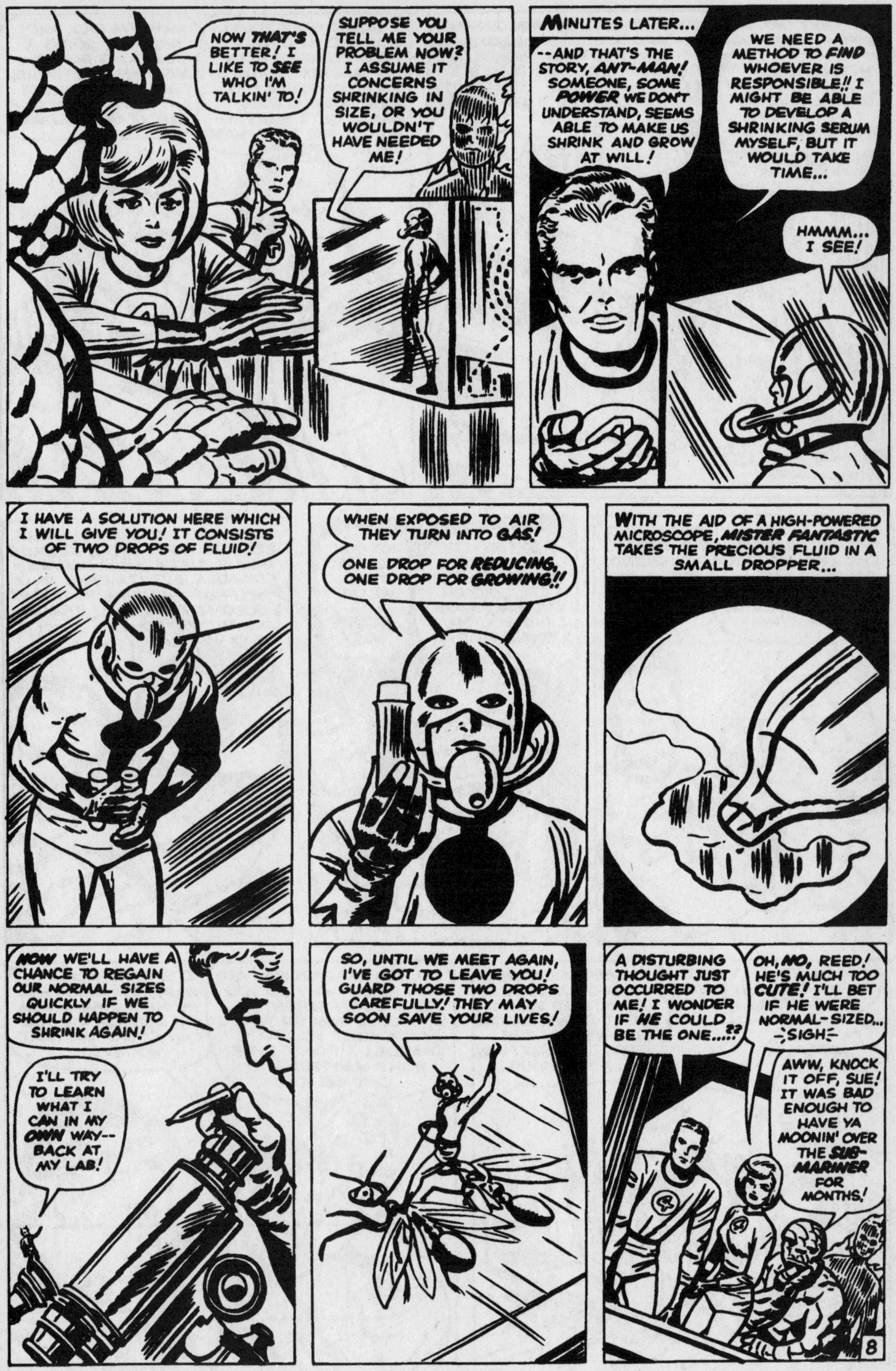
NOW THAT'S BETTER! I LIKE TO SEE WHO I'M TALKIN' TO!
SUPPOSE YOU TELL ME YOUR PROBLEM NOW? I ASSUME IT CONCERNS SHRINKING IN SIZE, OR YOU WOULDN'T HAVE NEEDED ME!
MINUTES LATER...
--AND THAT'S THE STORY, ANT-MAN! SOMEONE, SOME POWER WE DON'T UNDERSTAND, SEEMS ABLE TO MAKE US SHRINK AND GROW AT WILL!
WE NEED A METHOD TO FIND WHOEVER IS RESPONSIBLE!! I MIGHT BE ABLE TO DEVELOP A SHRINKING SERUM MYSELF, BUT IT WOULD TAKE TIME...
HMMM... I SEE!
I HAVE A SOLUTION HERE WHICH I WILL GIVE YOU! IT CONSISTS OF TWO DROPS OF FLUID!
WHEN EXPOSED TO AIR THEY TURN INTO GAS!
ONE DROP FOR REDUCING, ONE DROP FOR GROWING!!
WITH THE AID OF A HIGH-POWERED MICROSCOPE, MISTER FANTASTIC TAKES THE PRECIOUS FLUID IN A SMALL DROPPER...
NOW WE'LL HAVE A CHANCE TO REGAIN OUR NORMAL SIZES QUICKLY IF WE SHOULD HAPPEN TO SHRINK AGAIN!
I'LL TRY TO LEARN WHAT I CAN IN MY OWN WAY-- BACK AT MY LAB!
SO, UNTIL WE MEET AGAIN, I'VE GOT TO LEAVE YOU! GUARD THOSE TWO DROPS CAREFULLY! THEY MAY SOON SAVE YOUR LIVES!
A DISTURBING THOUGHT JUST OCCURRED TO ME! I WONDER IF HE COULD BE THE ONE....??
OH, NO, REED! HE'S MUCH TOO CUTE! I'LL BET IF HE WERE NORMAL-SIZED... -SIGH-
AWW, KNOCK IT OFF, SUE! IT WAS BAD ENOUGH TO HAVE YA MOONIN' OVER THE SUB-MARINER FOR MONTHS!
8

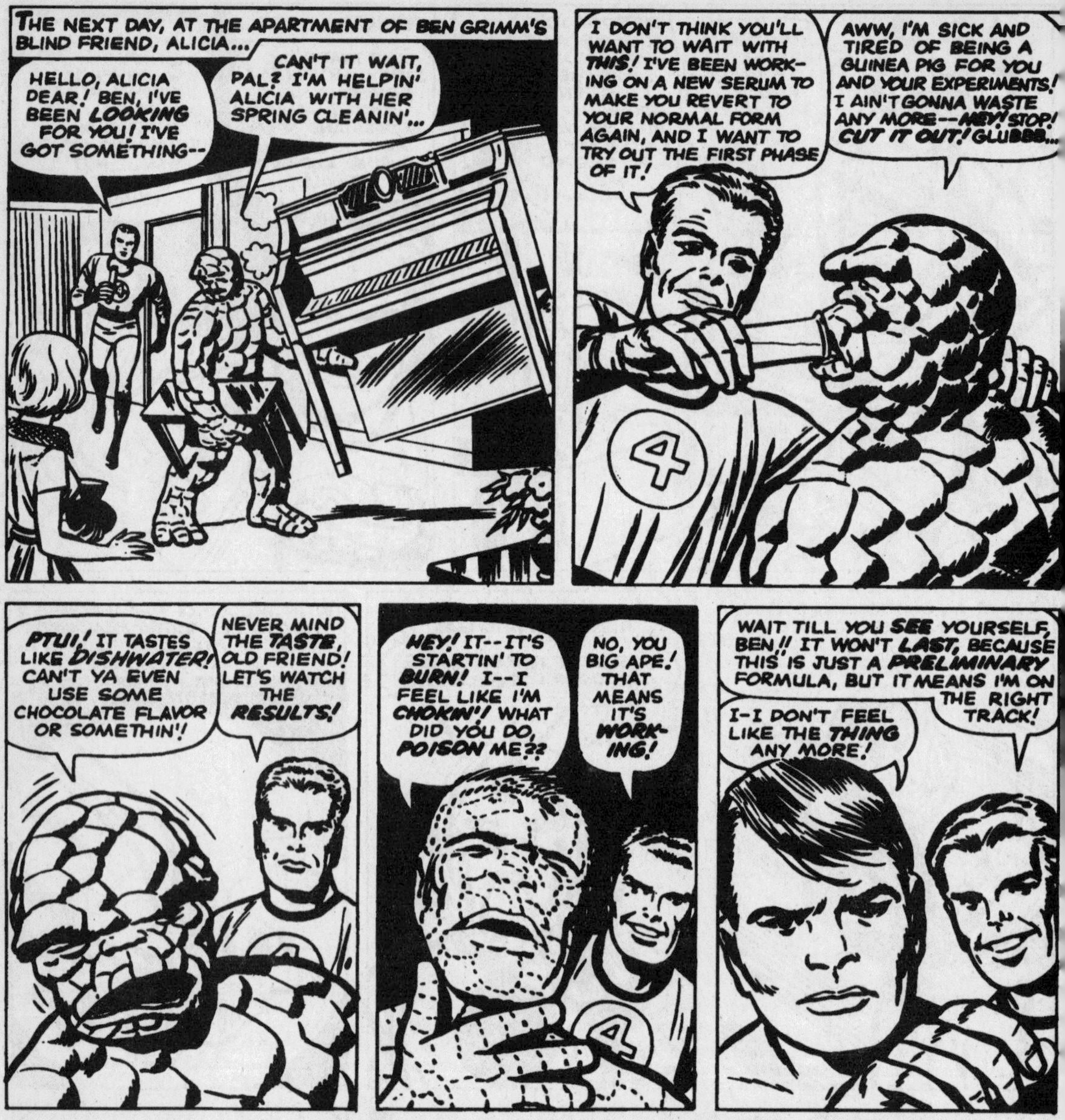
THE NEXT DAY, AT THE APARTMENT OF BEN GRIMM'S BLIND FRIEND, ALICIA...
HELLO, ALICIA DEAR! BEN, I'VE BEEN LOOKING FOR YOU! I'VE GOT SOMETHING--
CAN'T IT WAIT, PAL? I'M HELPIN' ALICIA WITH HER SPRING CLEANIN'...
I DON'T THINK YOU'LL WANT TO WAIT WITH THIS! I'VE BEEN WORKING ON A NEW SERUM TO MAKE YOU REVERT TO YOUR NORMAL FORM AGAIN, AND I WANT TO TRY OUT THE FIRST PHASE OF IT!
AWW, I'M SICK AND TIRED OF BEING A GUINEA PIG FOR YOU AND YOUR EXPERIMENTS! I AIN'T GONNA WASTE ANY MORE--HEY! STOP! CUT IT OUT! GLUBBB...
PTUI! IT TASTES LIKE DISHWATER! CAN'T YA EVEN USE SOME CHOCOLATE FLAVOR OR SOMETHIN'!
NEVER MIND THE TASTE, OLD FRIEND! LET'S WATCH THE RESULTS!
HEY! IT--IT'S STARTIN' TO BURN! I--I FEEL LIKE I'M CHOKIN'! WHAT DID YOU DO, POISON ME??
NO, YOU BIG APE! THAT MEANS IT'S WORKING!
WAIT TILL YOU SEE YOURSELF, BEN!! IT WON'T LAST, BECAUSE THIS IS JUST A PRELIMINARY FORMULA, BUT IT MEANS I'M ON THE RIGHT TRACK!
I-I DON'T FEEL LIKE THE THING ANY MORE!
LOOK OUT! CAN'T HOLD THE PIANO UP ANY MORE!! GANGWAY!
IT'S MY FAULT, BEN! I SHOULD HAVE REMINDED YOU TO PUT IT DOWN BEFORE I GAVE YOU THE FORMULA! BUT I WAS SO ANXIOUS...
BONNNG
OH, BEN! MY DARLING! ARE YOU HURT? WHY DO YOU FEEL SO DIFFERENT?? I--I LOVE YOU SO THAT I DON'T WANT YOU TO CHANGE! I DON'T EVER WANT ANYTHING TO CHANGE YOU!
IT'S OKAY, ALICIA BABY! I'M OKAY! AND NOTHIN'S EVER GONNA CHANGE FOR US! YOU CAN COUNT ON THAT, HONEY!
9

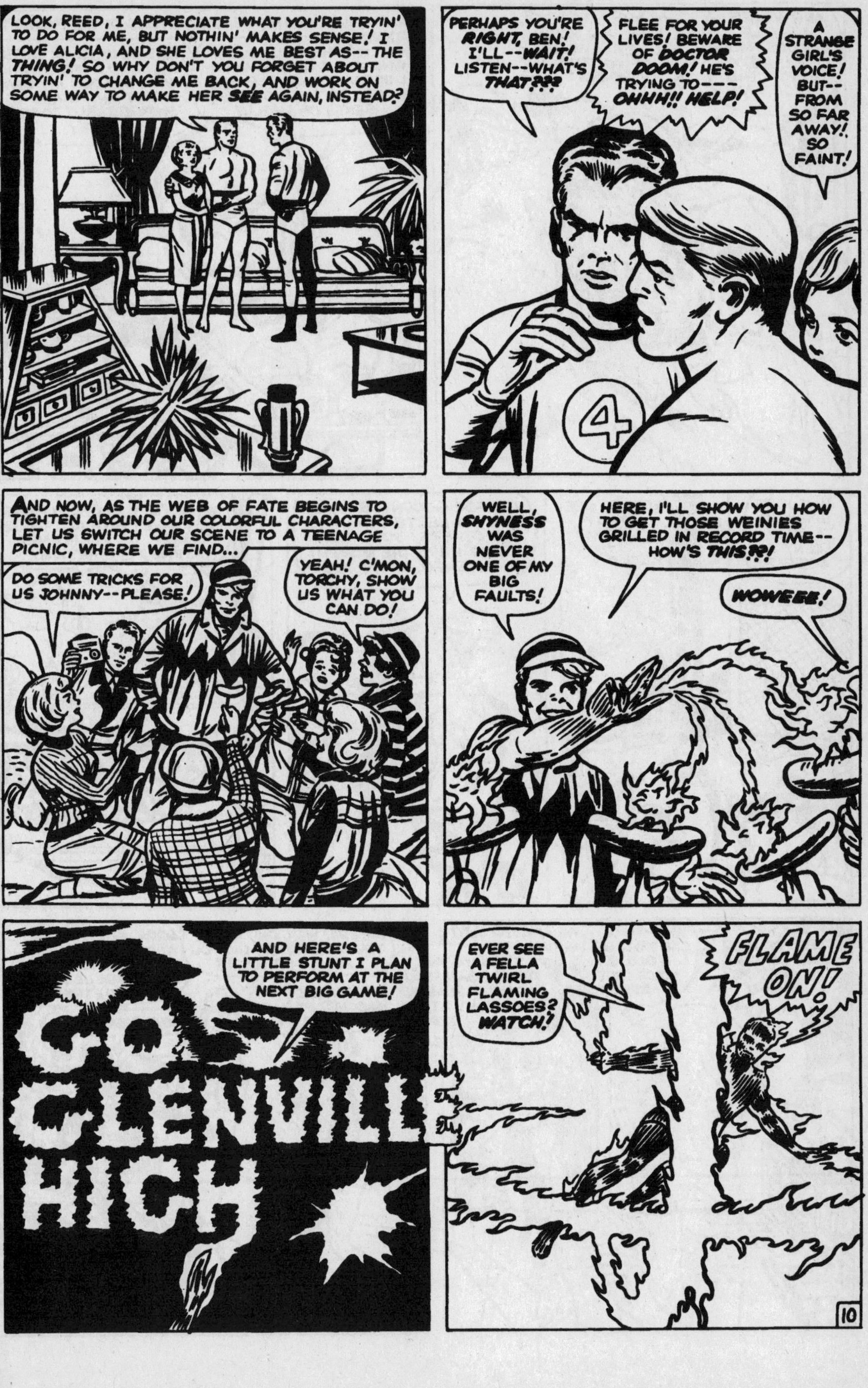

LOOK, REED, I APPRECIATE WHAT YOU'RE TRYIN' TO DO FOR ME, BUT NOTHIN' MAKES SENSE! I LOVE ALICIA, AND SHE LOVES ME BEST AS-- THE THING! SO WHY DON'T YOU FORGET ABOUT TRYIN' TO CHANGE ME BACK, AND WORK ON SOME WAY TO MAKE HER SEE AGAIN, INSTEAD?
PERHAPS YOU'RE RIGHT, BEN! I'LL--WAIT! LISTEN--WHAT'S THAT???
FLEE FOR YOUR LIVES! BEWARE OF DOCTOR DOOM! HE'S TRYING TO--- OHHH!! HELP!
A STRANGE GIRL'S VOICE! BUT-- FROM SO FAR AWAY!, SO FAINT!
AND NOW, AS THE WEB OF FATE BEGINS TO TIGHTEN AROUND OUR COLORFUL CHARACTERS, LET US SWITCH OUR SCENE TO A TEENAGE PICNIC, WHERE WE FIND...
DO SOME TRICKS FOR US JOHNNY--PLEASE!
YEAH! C'MON, TORCHY, SHOW US WHAT YOU CAN DO!
WELL, SHYNESS WAS NEVER ONE OF MY BIG FAULTS!
HERE, I'LL SHOW YOU HOW TO GET THOSE WEINIES GRILLED IN RECORD TIME-- HOW'S THIS??!
WOWEEE!
AND HERE'S A LITTLE STUNT I PLAN TO PERFORM AT THE NEXT BIG GAME!
GO GLENVILLE HIGH
EVER SEE A FELLA TWIRL FLAMING LASSOES? WATCH!
FLAME ON!
10

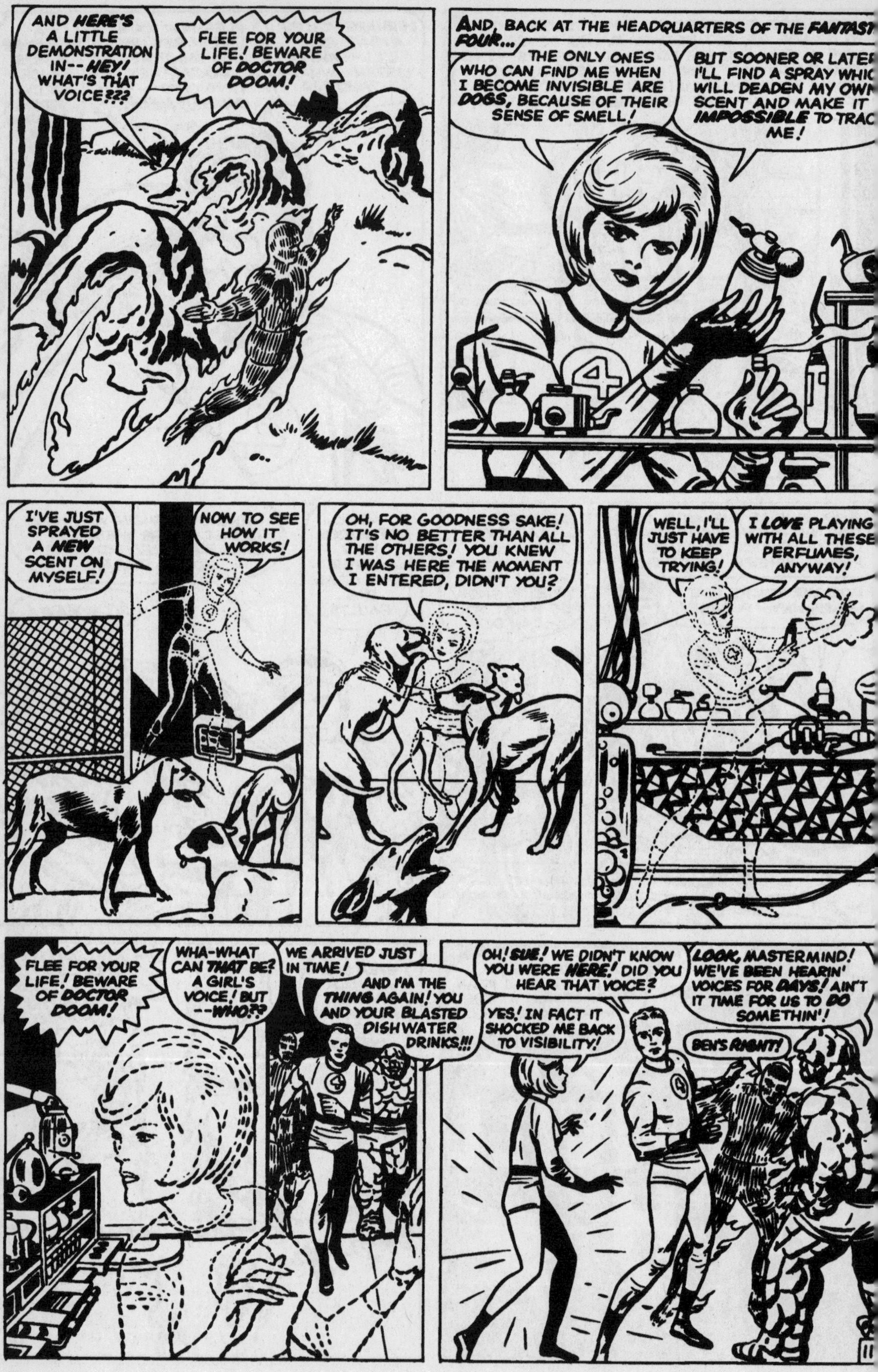
AND HERE'S A LITTLE DEMONSTRATION IN--HEY! WHAT'S THAT VOICE???
FLEE FOR YOUR LIFE! BEWARE OF DOCTOR DOOM!
AND, BACK AT THE HEADQUARTERS OF THE FANTASTI FOUR...
THE ONLY ONES WHO CAN FIND ME WHEN I BECOME INVISIBLE ARE DOGS, BECAUSE OF THEIR SENSE OF SMELL!
BUT SOONER OR LATER I'LL FIND A SPRAY WHIC WILL DEADEN MY OWN SCENT AND MAKE IT IMPOSSIBLE TO TRAC ME!
I'VE JUST SPRAYED A NEW SCENT ON MYSELF!
NOW TO SEE HOW IT WORKS!
OH, FOR GOODNESS SAKE! IT'S NO BETTER THAN ALL THE OTHERS! YOU KNEW I WAS HERE THE MOMENT I ENTERED, DIDN'T YOU?
WELL, I'LL JUST HAVE TO KEEP TRYING!
I LOVE PLAYING WITH ALL THESE PERFUMES, ANYWAY!
FLEE FOR YOUR LIFE! BEWARE OF DOCTOR DOOM!
WHA-WHAT CAN THAT BE? A GIRL'S VOICE! BUT --WHO??
WE ARRIVED JUST IN TIME!
AND I'M THE THING AGAIN! YOU AND YOUR BLASTED DISHWATER DRINKS!!!
OH! SUE! WE DIDN'T KNOW YOU WERE HERE! DID YOU HEAR THAT VOICE?
YES! IN FACT IT SHOCKED ME BACK TO VISIBILITY!
LOOK, MASTERMIND! WE'VE BEEN HEARIN' VOICES FOR DAYS! AIN'T IT TIME FOR US TO DO SOMETHIN'!
BEN'S RIGHT!
11

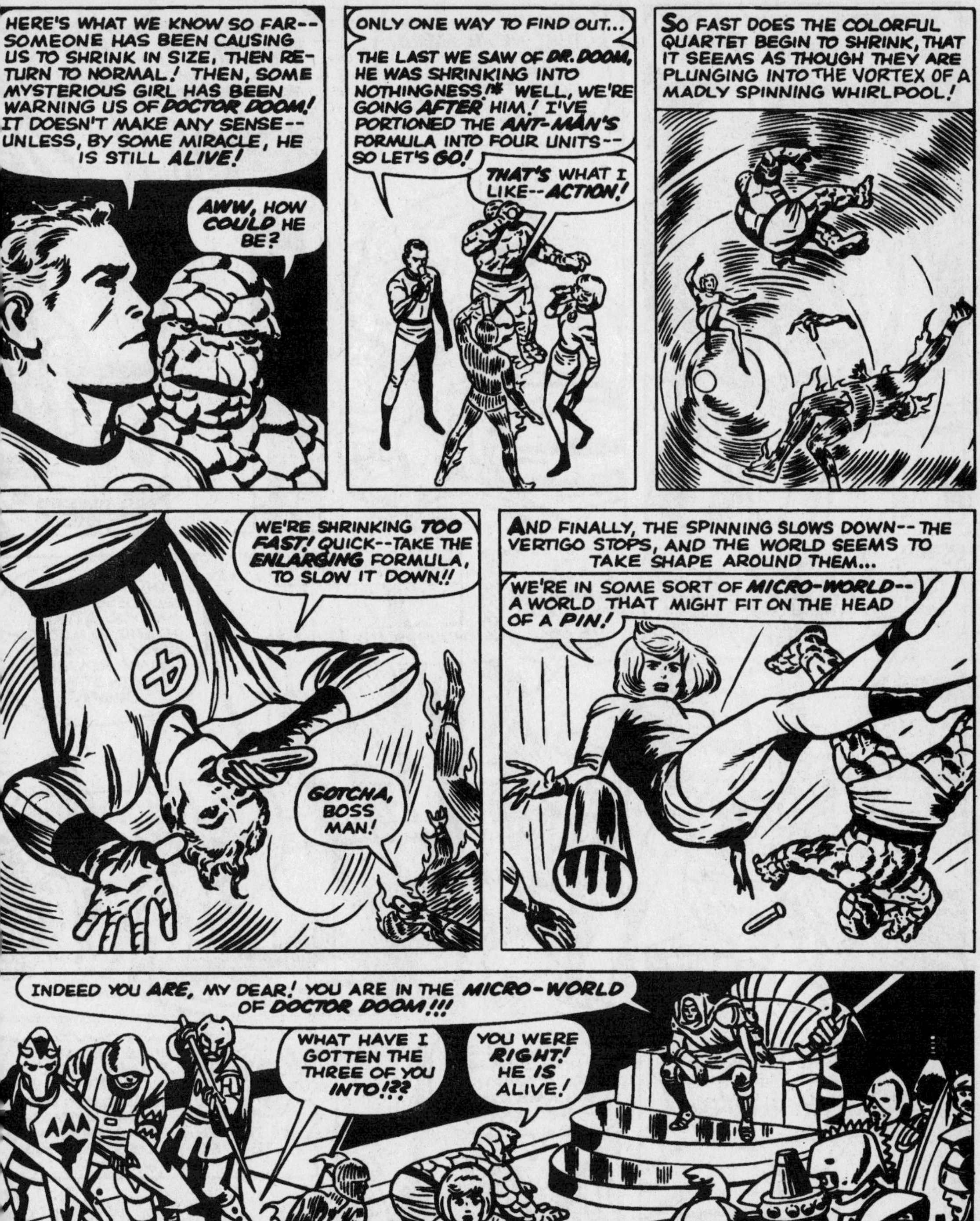
HERE'S WHAT WE KNOW SO FAR-- SOMEONE HAS BEEN CAUSING US TO SHRINK IN SIZE, THEN RETURN TO NORMAL! THEN, SOME MYSTERIOUS GIRL HAS BEEN WARNING US OF DOCTOR DOOM! IT DOESN'T MAKE ANY SENSE-- UNLESS, BY SOME MIRACLE, HE IS STILL ALIVE!
AWW, HOW COULD HE BE?
ONLY ONE WAY TO FIND OUT...
THE LAST WE SAW OF DR. DOOM, HE WAS SHRINKING INTO NOTHINGNESS!* WELL, WE'RE GOING AFTER HIM! I'VE PORTIONED THE ANT-MAN'S FORMULA INTO FOUR UNITS-- SO LET'S GO!
THAT'S WHAT I LIKE--ACTION!
SO FAST DOES THE COLORFUL QUARTET BEGIN TO SHRINK, THAT IT SEEMS AS THOUGH THEY ARE PLUNGING INTO THE VORTEX OF A MADLY SPINNING WHIRLPOOL!
WE'RE SHRINKING TOO FAST! QUICK--TAKE THE ENLARGING FORMULA, TO SLOW IT DOWN!!
GOTCHA, BOSS MAN!
AND FINALLY, THE SPINNING SLOWS DOWN-- THE VERTIGO STOPS, AND THE WORLD SEEMS TO TAKE SHAPE AROUND THEM...
WE'RE IN SOME SORT OF MICRO-WORLD-- A WORLD THAT MIGHT FIT ON THE HEAD OF A PIN!
INDEED YOU ARE, MY DEAR! YOU ARE IN THE MICRO-WORLD OF DOCTOR DOOM!!!
WHAT HAVE I GOTTEN THE THREE OF YOU INTO!??
YOU WERE RIGHT! HE IS ALIVE!
*NOTE: THE COMPLETE STORY OF THE FANTASTIC FOUR'S LAST ENCOUNTER WITH DR. DOOM WAS TOLD IN FANTASTIC FOUR #10, SEPT.
12

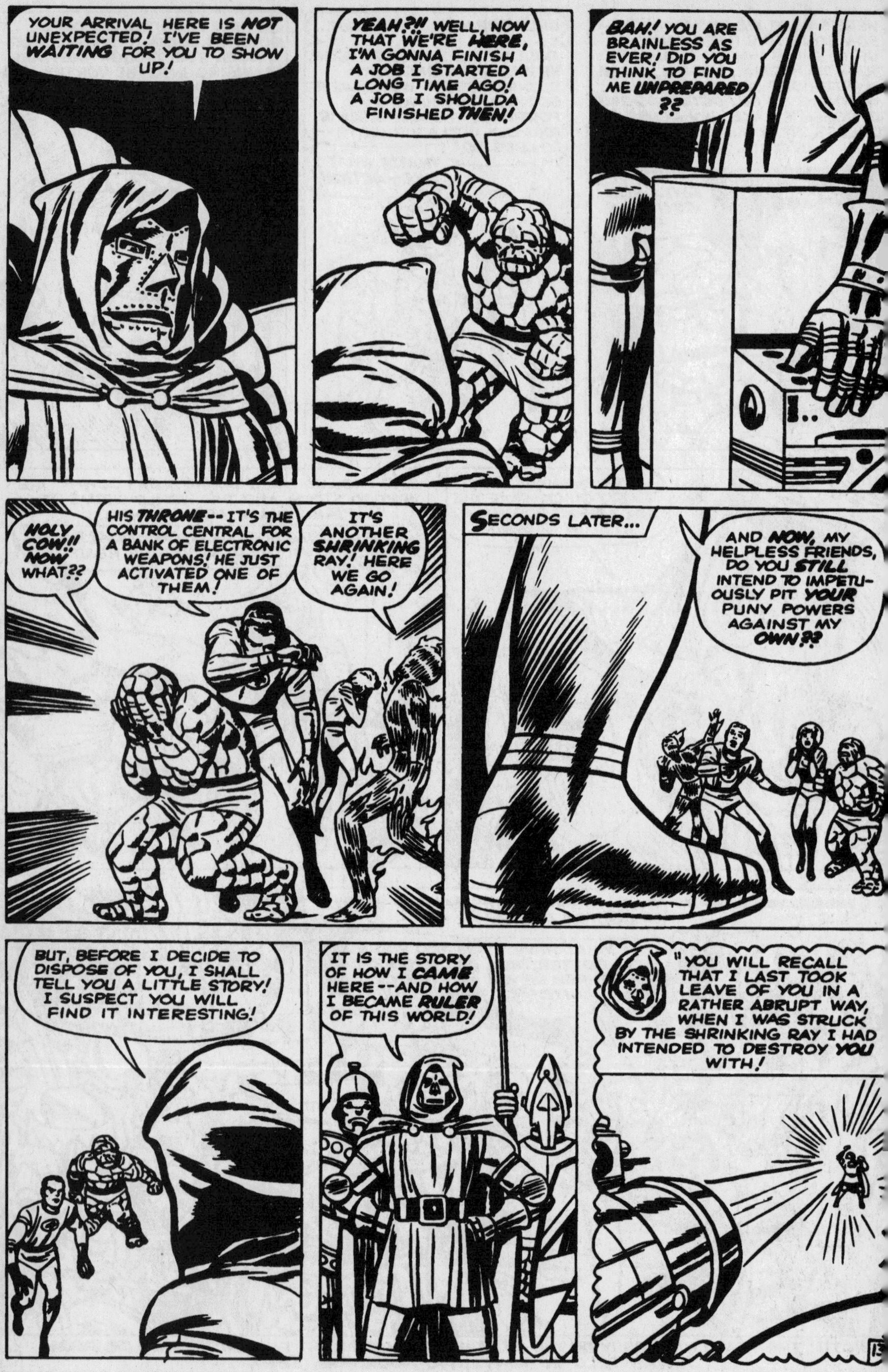
YOUR ARRIVAL HERE IS NOT UNEXPECTED! I'VE BEEN WAITING FOR YOU TO SHOW UP!
YEAH?!! WELL, NOW THAT WE'RE HERE, I'M GONNA FINISH A JOB I STARTED A LONG TIME AGO! A JOB I SHOULDA FINISHED THEN!
BAH! YOU ARE BRAINLESS AS EVER! DID YOU THINK TO FIND ME UNPREPARED ??
HOLY COW!! NOW WHAT??
HIS THRONE-- IT'S THE CONTROL CENTRAL FOR A BANK OF ELECTRONIC WEAPONS! HE JUST ACTIVATED ONE OF THEM!
IT'S ANOTHER SHRINKING RAY! HERE WE GO AGAIN!
SECONDS LATER...
AND NOW, MY HELPLESS FRIENDS, DO YOU STILL INTEND TO IMPETUOUSLY PIT YOUR PUNY POWERS AGAINST MY OWN??
BUT, BEFORE I DECIDE TO DISPOSE OF YOU, I SHALL TELL YOU A LITTLE STORY! I SUSPECT YOU WILL FIND IT INTERESTING!
IT IS THE STORY OF HOW I CAME HERE--AND HOW I BECAME RULER OF THIS WORLD!
"YOU WILL RECALL THAT I LAST TOOK LEAVE OF YOU IN A RATHER ABRUPT WAY, WHEN I WAS STRUCK BY THE SHRINKING RAY I HAD INTENDED TO DESTROY YOU WITH!
13

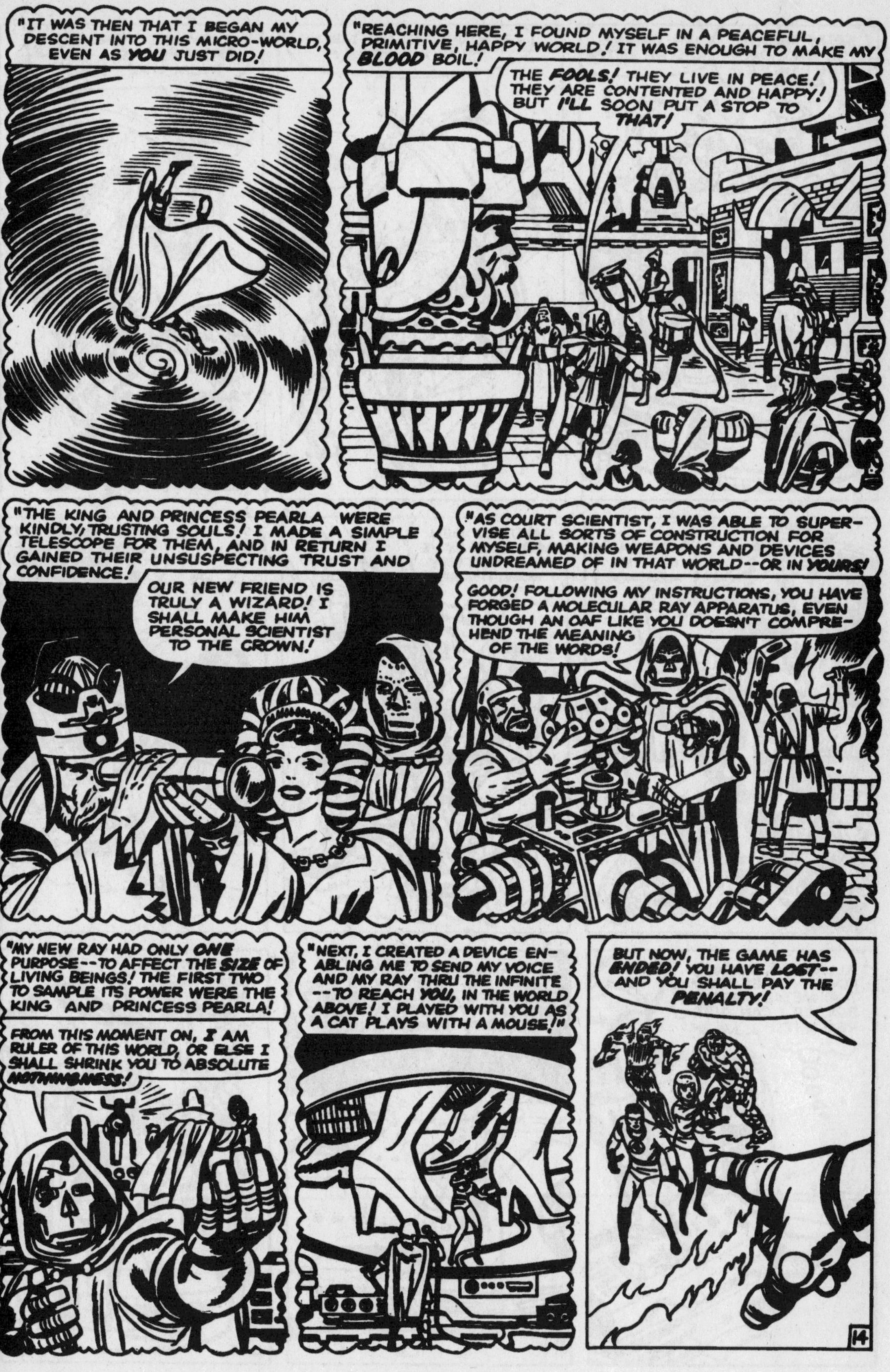
"IT WAS THEN THAT I BEGAN MY DESCENT INTO THIS MICRO-WORLD, EVEN AS YOU JUST DID!
"REACHING HERE, I FOUND MYSELF IN A PEACEFUL, PRIMITIVE, HAPPY WORLD! IT WAS ENOUGH TO MAKE MY BLOOD BOIL!
THE FOOLS! THEY LIVE IN PEACE! THEY ARE CONTENTED AND HAPPY! BUT I'LL SOON PUT A STOP TO THAT!
"THE KING AND PRINCESS PEARLA WERE KINDLY, TRUSTING SOULS! I MADE A SIMPLE TELESCOPE FOR THEM, AND IN RETURN I GAINED THEIR UNSUSPECTING TRUST AND CONFIDENCE!
OUR NEW FRIEND IS TRULY A WIZARD! I SHALL MAKE HIM PERSONAL SCIENTIST TO THE CROWN!
"AS COURT SCIENTIST, I WAS ABLE TO SUPERVISE ALL SORTS OF CONSTRUCTION FOR MYSELF, MAKING WEAPONS AND DEVICES UNDREAMED OF IN THAT WORLD--OR IN YOURS!
GOOD! FOLLOWING MY INSTRUCTIONS, YOU HAVE FORGED A MOLECULAR RAY APPARATUS, EVEN THOUGH AN OAF LIKE YOU DOESN'T COMPREHEND THE MEANING OF THE WORDS!
"MY NEW RAY HAD ONLY ONE PURPOSE--TO AFFECT THE SIZE OF LIVING BEINGS! THE FIRST TWO TO SAMPLE ITS POWER WERE THE KING AND PRINCESS PEARLA!
FROM THIS MOMENT ON, I AM RULER OF THIS WORLD, OR ELSE I SHALL SHRINK YOU TO ABSOLUTE NOTHINGNESS!
"NEXT, I CREATED A DEVICE ENABLING ME TO SEND MY VOICE AND MY RAY THRU THE INFINITE --TO REACH YOU, IN THE WORLD ABOVE! I PLAYED WITH YOU AS A CAT PLAYS WITH A MOUSE!"
BUT NOW, THE GAME HAS ENDED! YOU HAVE LOST-- AND YOU SHALL PAY THE PENALTY!
14

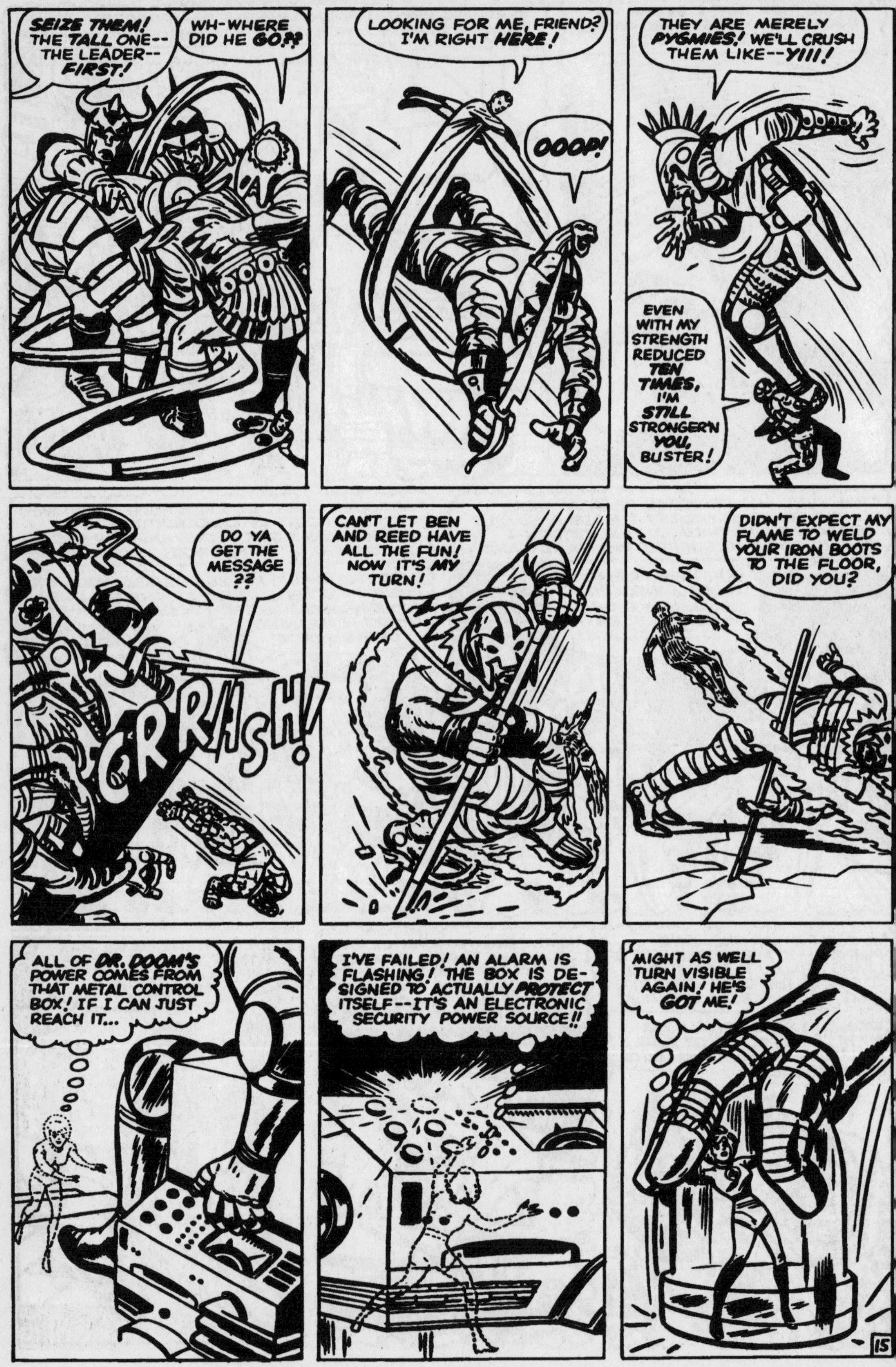
SEIZE THEM! THE TALL ONE-- THE LEADER-- FIRST!
WH-WHERE DID HE GO??
LOOKING FOR ME, FRIEND? I'M RIGHT HERE!
OOOP!
THEY ARE MERELY PYGMIES! WE'LL CRUSH THEM LIKE--YIII!
EVEN WITH MY STRENGTH REDUCED TEN TIMES, I'M STILL STRONGER'N YOU, BUSTER!
DO YA GET THE MESSAGE ??
CRRASH!
CAN'T LET BEN AND REED HAVE ALL THE FUN! NOW IT'S MY TURN!
DIDN'T EXPECT MY FLAME TO WELD YOUR IRON BOOTS TO THE FLOOR, DID YOU?
ALL OF DR. DOOM'S POWER COMES FROM THAT METAL CONTROL BOX! IF I CAN JUST REACH IT...
I'VE FAILED! AN ALARM IS FLASHING! THE BOX IS DESIGNED TO ACTUALLY PROTECT ITSELF--IT'S AN ELECTRONIC SECURITY POWER SOURCE!!
MIGHT AS WELL TURN VISIBLE AGAIN! HE'S GOT ME!
15

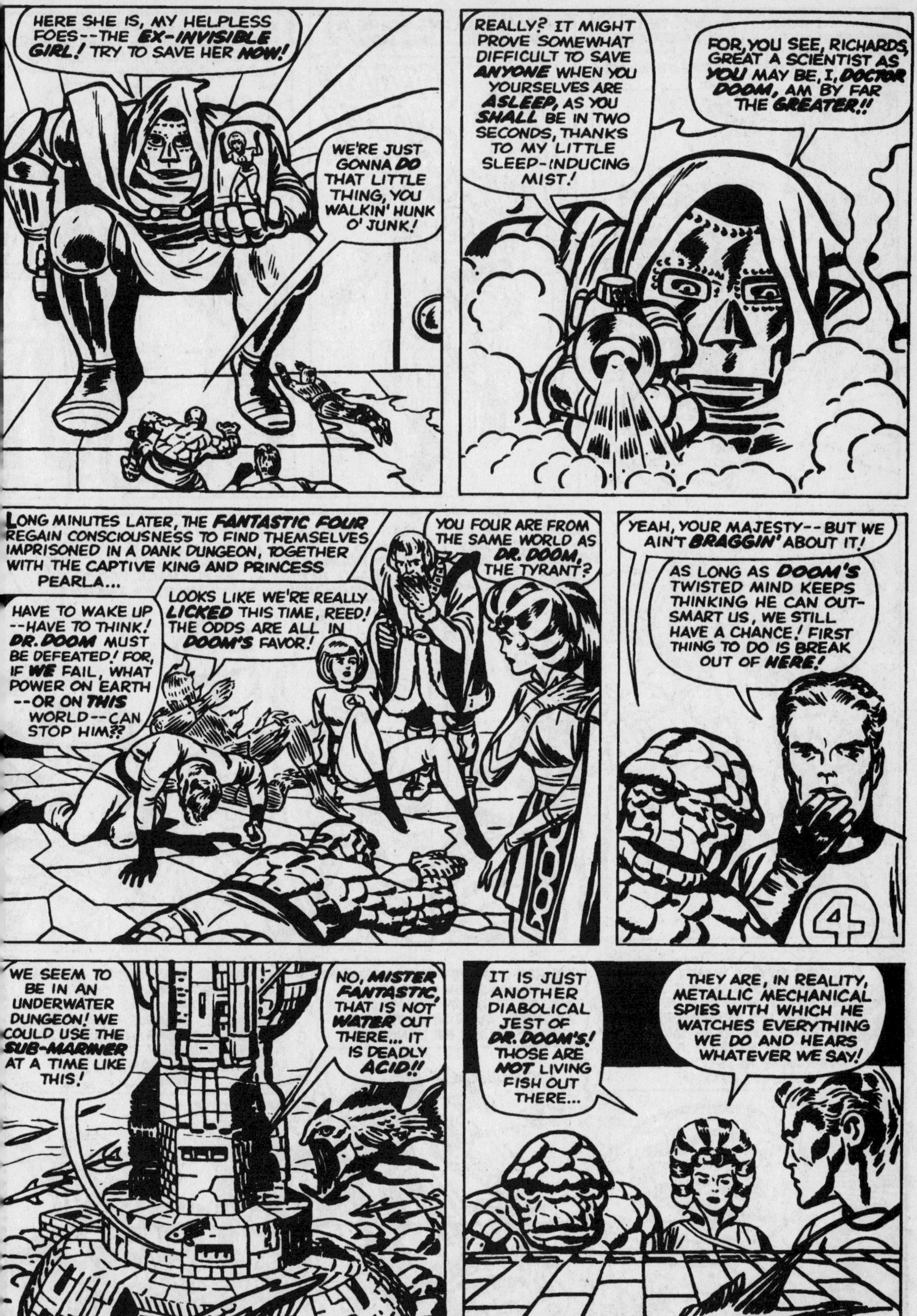
HERE SHE IS, MY HELPLESS FOES--THE EX-INVISIBLE GIRL! TRY TO SAVE HER NOW!
WE'RE JUST GONNA DO THAT LITTLE THING, YOU WALKIN' HUNK O' JUNK!
REALLY? IT MIGHT PROVE SOMEWHAT DIFFICULT TO SAVE ANYONE WHEN YOU YOURSELVES ARE ASLEEP, AS YOU SHALL BE IN TWO SECONDS, THANKS TO MY LITTLE SLEEP-INDUCING MIST!
FOR, YOU SEE, RICHARDS, GREAT A SCIENTIST AS YOU MAY BE, I, DOCTOR DOOM, AM BY FAR THE GREATER!!
LONG MINUTES LATER, THE FANTASTIC FOUR REGAIN CONSCIOUSNESS TO FIND THEMSELVES IMPRISONED IN A DANK DUNGEON, TOGETHER WITH THE CAPTIVE KING AND PRINCESS PEARLA...
HAVE TO WAKE UP --HAVE TO THINK! DR. DOOM MUST BE DEFEATED! FOR, IF WE FAIL, WHAT POWER ON EARTH --OR ON THIS WORLD--CAN STOP HIM??
LOOKS LIKE WE'RE REALLY LICKED THIS TIME, REED! THE ODDS ARE ALL IN DOOM'S FAVOR!
YOU FOUR ARE FROM THE SAME WORLD AS DR. DOOM, THE TYRANT?
YEAH, YOUR MAJESTY--BUT WE AIN'T BRAGGIN' ABOUT IT!
AS LONG AS DOOM'S TWISTED MIND KEEPS THINKING HE CAN OUT-SMART US, WE STILL HAVE A CHANCE! FIRST THING TO DO IS BREAK OUT OF HERE!
WE SEEM TO BE IN AN UNDERWATER DUNGEON! WE COULD USE THE SUB-MARINER AT A TIME LIKE THIS!
NO, MISTER FANTASTIC, THAT IS NOT WATER OUT THERE... IT IS DEADLY ACID!!
IT IS JUST ANOTHER DIABOLICAL JEST OF DR. DOOM'S! THOSE ARE NOT LIVING FISH OUT THERE...
THEY ARE, IN REALITY, METALLIC MECHANICAL SPIES WITH WHICH HE WATCHES EVERYTHING WE DO AND HEARS WHATEVER WE SAY!

DON'T YOU WORRY PRINCESS! WE'LL STILL MANAGE TO COME OUTTA THIS OKAY!
OH! THAT FLAME! IT'S SO-- FRIGHTENING!
HECK! I WOULDN'T SCARE A LIVING DOLL LIKE YOU!
FLAME OFF!
WHEN THINGS LOOK THE MOST HOPELESS FOR US, THAT'S WHEN OUR ENEMIES BETTER RUN FOR THE HILLS, CHICK!
AS FOR ME, THE HUMAN TORCH IS GONNA SEE TO IT THAT NOBODY HURTS ONE LITTLE FINGER-NAIL OF THAT DAINTY LITTLE HAND!
OHH...
C'MON, SQUIRT! LEAVE THE SPEECHES FOR TONY CURTIS! WE GOT WORK TO DO!
LEGGO, YA BIG OX! HAVEN'T YOU ANY ROMANCE IN YOUR SOUL??
WAIT A MINUTE! IT MUST HAVE BEEN YOUR VOICE WE HEARD, TRYING TO WARN US!
IT WAS! I KNEW HE WAS TRYING TO LURE YOU HERE-- SO I USED HIS RAY MACHINE A FEW TIMES WHEN HE WASN'T THERE!
"DR. DOOM WANTS ME TO MARRY HIM! BUT I DESPISE HIM! THAT IS WHY I AM HIS PRISONER, TOO! HE PLANS TO BETRAY THIS ENTIRE WORLD IF I REFUSE HIM! EVEN NOW HE IS CONTACTING THE PLANET TOK!
"HE HAS OFFERED TOK A REWARD FOR JOINING HIM! YOU FOUR ARE TO BE THEIR REWARD--AS SLAVES! EVEN NOW, THE TOK SHIP MUST BE LANDING...
"THE TERRIBLE WARRIORS OF TOK ARE FEARED THRUOUT OUR UNIVERSE! THEY ARE HUGE AND POWERFUL, COMING FROM A HEAVY PLANET WITH GRAVITY A DOZEN TIMES STRONGER THAN OURS! AND THEY ARE COMING FOR-- YOU!
17

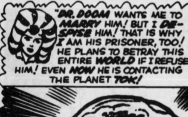

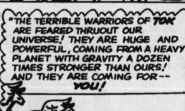

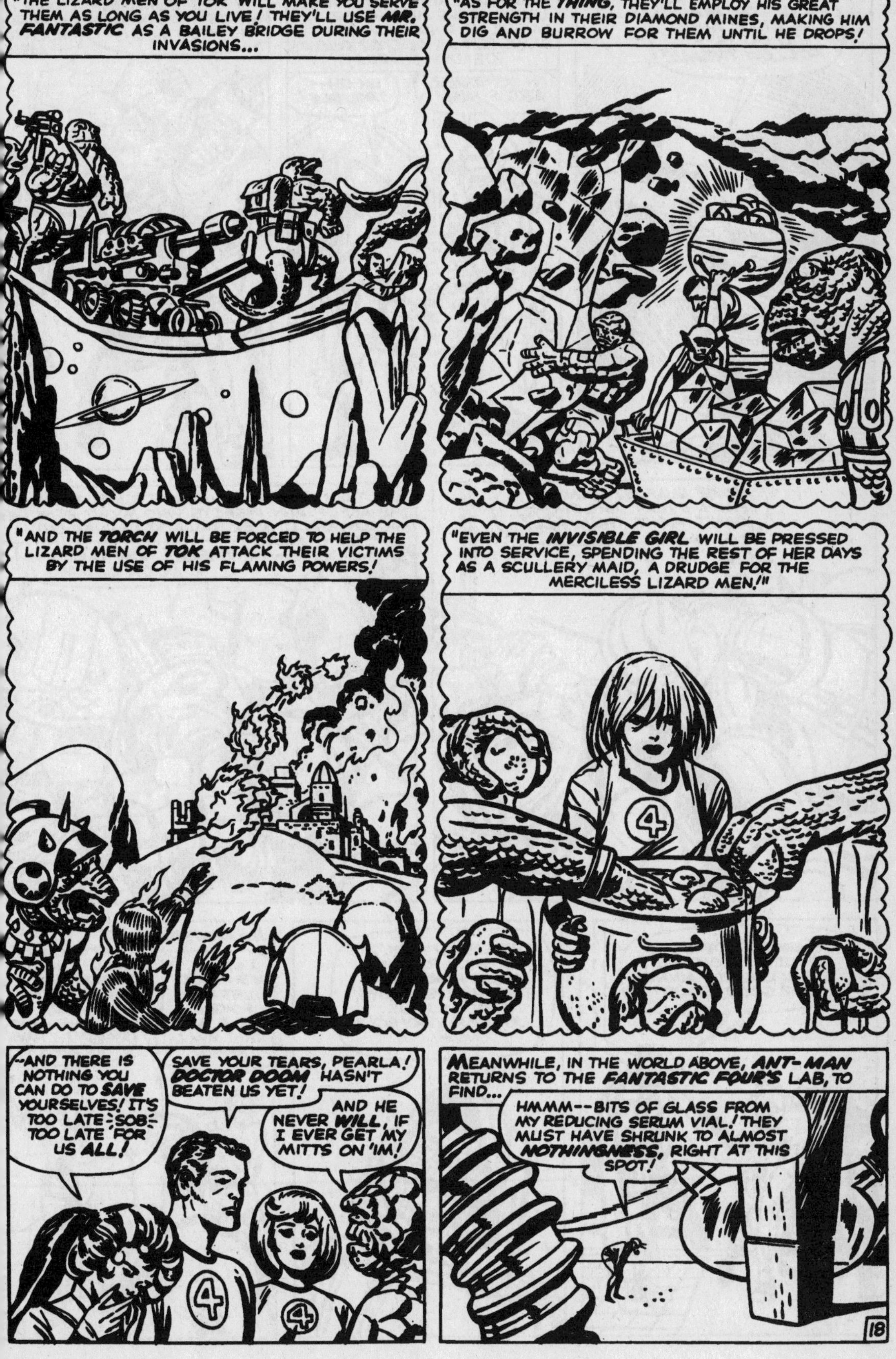

"THE LIZARD MEN OF TOK WILL MAKE YOU SERVE THEM AS LONG AS YOU LIVE! THEY'LL USE MR. FANTASTIC AS A BAILEY BRIDGE DURING THEIR INVASIONS...
"AS FOR THE THING, THEY'LL EMPLOY HIS GREAT STRENGTH IN THEIR DIAMOND MINES, MAKING HIM DIG AND BURROW FOR THEM UNTIL HE DROPS!
"AND THE TORCH WILL BE FORCED TO HELP THE LIZARD MEN OF TOK ATTACK THEIR VICTIMS BY THE USE OF HIS FLAMING POWERS!
"EVEN THE INVISIBLE GIRL WILL BE PRESSED INTO SERVICE, SPENDING THE REST OF HER DAYS AS A SCULLERY MAID, A DRUDGE FOR THE MERCILESS LIZARD MEN!"
--AND THERE IS NOTHING YOU CAN DO TO SAVE YOURSELVES! IT'S TOO LATE--SOB--TOO LATE FOR US ALL!
SAVE YOUR TEARS, PEARLA! DOCTOR DOOM HASN'T BEATEN US YET!
AND HE NEVER WILL, IF I EVER GET MY MITTS ON 'IM!
MEANWHILE, IN THE WORLD ABOVE, ANT-MAN RETURNS TO THE FANTASTIC FOUR'S LAB, TO FIND...
HMMM--BITS OF GLASS FROM MY REDUCING SERUM VIAL! THEY MUST HAVE SHRUNK TO ALMOST NOTHINGNESS, RIGHT AT THIS SPOT!
18

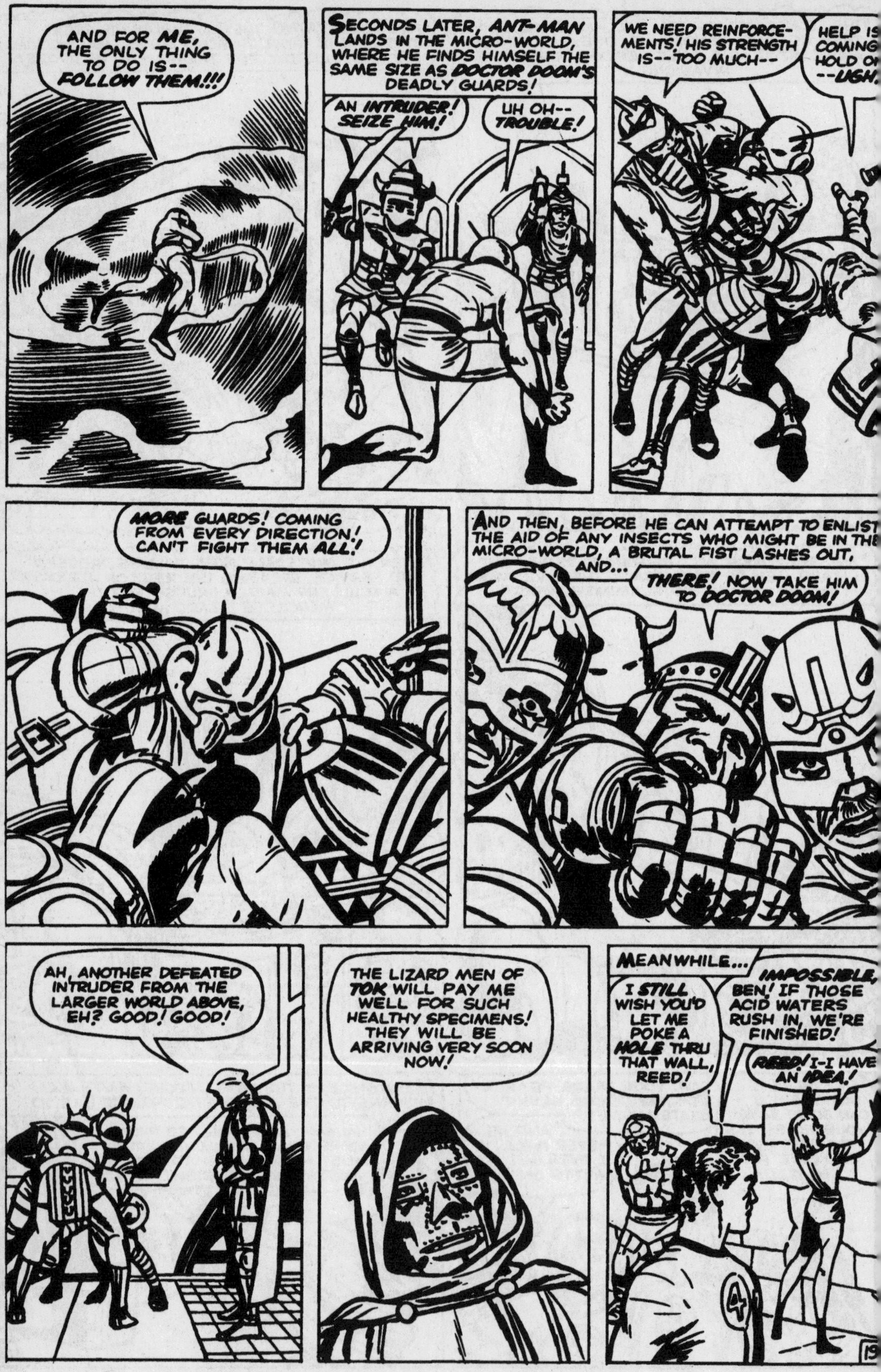
AND FOR ME, THE ONLY THING TO DO IS-- FOLLOW THEM!!!
SECONDS LATER, ANT-MAN LANDS IN THE MICRO-WORLD, WHERE HE FINDS HIMSELF THE SAME SIZE AS DOCTOR DOOM'S DEADLY GUARDS!
AN INTRUDER! SEIZE HIM!
UH OH-- TROUBLE!
WE NEED REINFORCE-MENTS! HIS STRENGTH IS--TOO MUCH--
HELP IS COMING HOLD OI --UGH
MORE GUARDS! COMING FROM EVERY DIRECTION! CAN'T FIGHT THEM ALL!
AND THEN, BEFORE HE CAN ATTEMPT TO ENLIST THE AID OF ANY INSECTS WHO MIGHT BE IN THE MICRO-WORLD, A BRUTAL FIST LASHES OUT, AND...
THERE! NOW TAKE HIM TO DOCTOR DOOM!
AH, ANOTHER DEFEATED INTRUDER FROM THE LARGER WORLD ABOVE, EH? GOOD! GOOD!
THE LIZARD MEN OF TOK WILL PAY ME WELL FOR SUCH HEALTHY SPECIMENS! THEY WILL BE ARRIVING VERY SOON NOW!
MEANWHILE...
I STILL WISH YOU'D LET ME POKE A HOLE THRU THAT WALL, REED!
IMPOSSIBLE, BEN! IF THOSE ACID WATERS RUSH IN, WE'RE FINISHED!
REED! I-I HAVE AN IDEA!
19

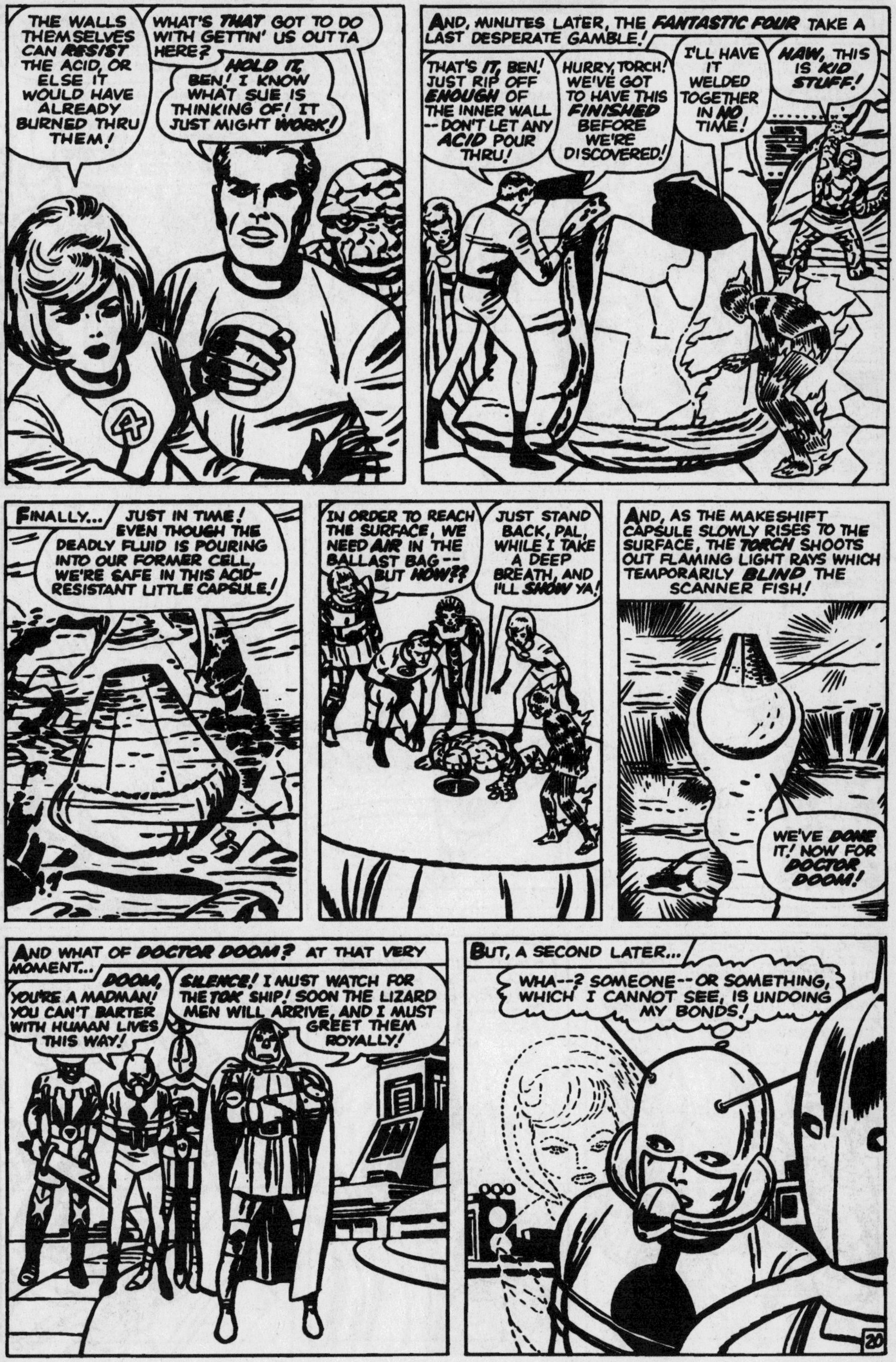
THE WALLS THEMSELVES CAN RESIST THE ACID, OR ELSE IT WOULD HAVE ALREADY BURNED THRU THEM!
WHAT'S THAT GOT TO DO WITH GETTIN' US OUTTA HERE?
HOLD IT, BEN! I KNOW WHAT SUE IS THINKING OF! IT JUST MIGHT WORK!
AND, MINUTES LATER, THE FANTASTIC FOUR TAKE A LAST DESPERATE GAMBLE!
THAT'S IT, BEN! JUST RIP OFF ENOUGH OF THE INNER WALL -- DON'T LET ANY ACID POUR THRU!
HURRY, TORCH! WE'VE GOT TO HAVE THIS FINISHED BEFORE WE'RE DISCOVERED!
I'LL HAVE IT WELDED TOGETHER IN NO TIME!
HAW, THIS IS KID STUFF!
FINALLY...
JUST IN TIME! EVEN THOUGH THE DEADLY FLUID IS POURING INTO OUR FORMER CELL, WE'RE SAFE IN THIS ACID-RESISTANT LITTLE CAPSULE!
IN ORDER TO REACH THE SURFACE, WE NEED AIR IN THE BALLAST BAG -- BUT HOW??
JUST STAND BACK, PAL, WHILE I TAKE A DEEP BREATH, AND I'LL SHOW YA!
AND, AS THE MAKESHIFT CAPSULE SLOWLY RISES TO THE SURFACE, THE TORCH SHOOTS OUT FLAMING LIGHT RAYS WHICH TEMPORARILY BLIND THE SCANNER FISH!
WE'VE DONE IT! NOW FOR DOCTOR DOOM!
AND WHAT OF DOCTOR DOOM? AT THAT VERY MOMENT...
DOOM, YOU'RE A MADMAN! YOU CAN'T BARTER WITH HUMAN LIVES THIS WAY!
SILENCE! I MUST WATCH FOR THE TOK SHIP! SOON THE LIZARD MEN WILL ARRIVE, AND I MUST GREET THEM ROYALLY!
BUT, A SECOND LATER...
WHA--? SOMEONE--OR SOMETHING, WHICH I CANNOT SEE, IS UNDOING MY BONDS!
20

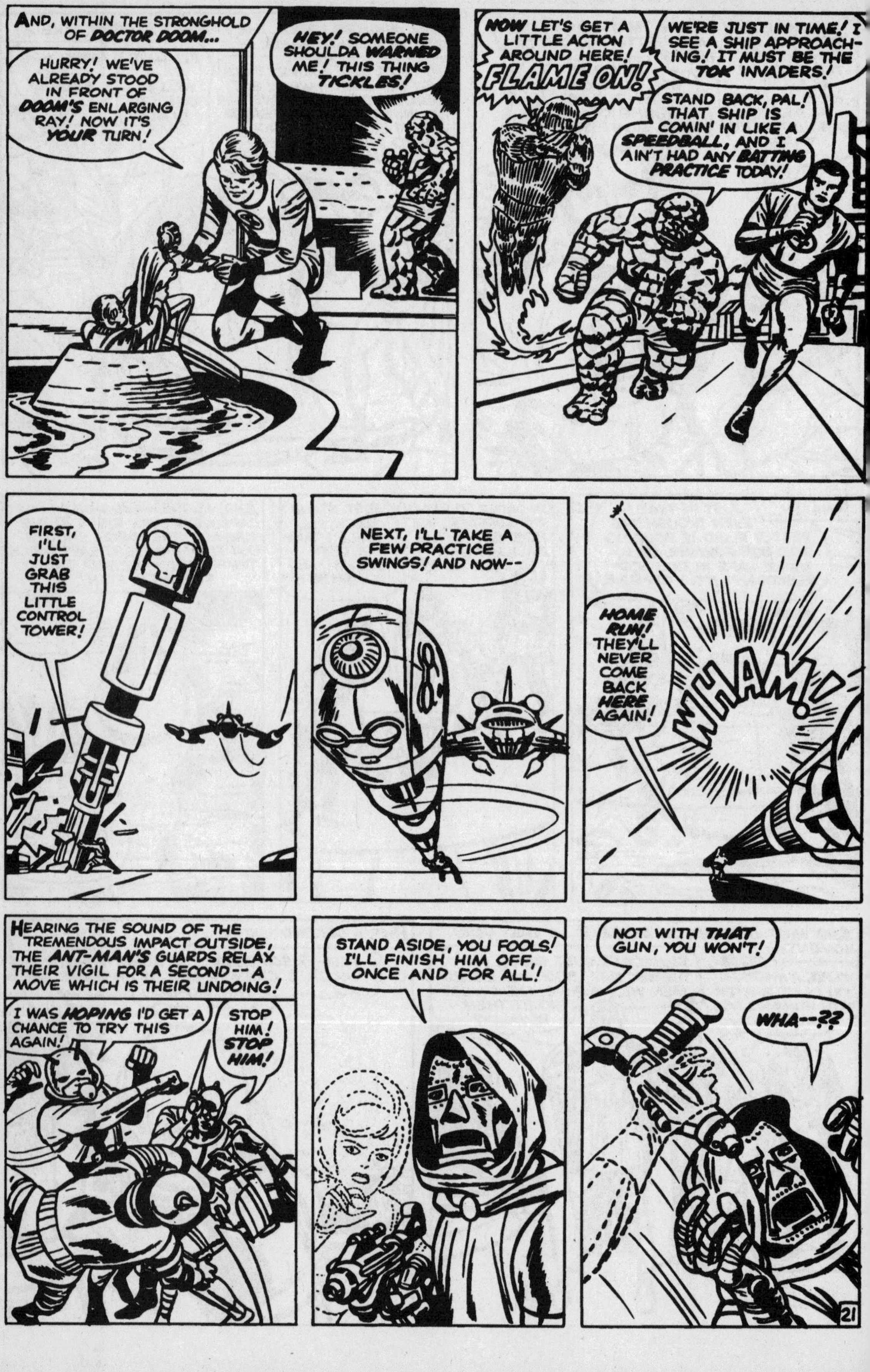
AND, WITHIN THE STRONGHOLD OF DOCTOR DOOM...
HURRY! WE'VE ALREADY STOOD IN FRONT OF DOOM'S ENLARGING RAY! NOW IT'S YOUR TURN!
HEY! SOMEONE SHOULDA WARNED ME! THIS THING TICKLES!
NOW LET'S GET A LITTLE ACTION AROUND HERE! FLAME ON!
WE'RE JUST IN TIME! I SEE A SHIP APPROACHING! IT MUST BE THE TOK INVADERS!
STAND BACK, PAL! THAT SHIP IS COMIN' IN LIKE A SPEEDBALL, AND I AIN'T HAD ANY BATTING PRACTICE TODAY!
FIRST, I'LL JUST GRAB THIS LITTLE CONTROL TOWER!
NEXT, I'LL TAKE A FEW PRACTICE SWINGS! AND NOW--
HOME RUN! THEY'LL NEVER COME BACK HERE AGAIN!
WHAM!
HEARING THE SOUND OF THE TREMENDOUS IMPACT OUTSIDE, THE ANT-MAN'S GUARDS RELAX THEIR VIGIL FOR A SECOND -- A MOVE WHICH IS THEIR UNDOING!
I WAS HOPING I'D GET A CHANCE TO TRY THIS AGAIN!
STOP HIM! STOP HIM!
STAND ASIDE, YOU FOOLS! I'LL FINISH HIM OFF, ONCE AND FOR ALL!
NOT WITH THAT GUN, YOU WON'T!
WHA--??
21

A DISEMBODIED VOICE! IT CAN ONLY MEAN ONE THING-- THE *INVISIBLE GIRL* IS FREE!

I'VE GOT TO FLEE TO SAFETY-- THRU THIS TRAP DOOR!

IF THE *INVISIBLE GIRL* IS FREE, THEN *ALL* OF THE *FANTASTIC FOUR* MUST BE FREE, TOO!

BUT BY THE TIME THEY FIGURE OUT WHERE TO FIND ME, I'LL BE *GONE!*

I'LL BE WAITING FOR THEM--BACK ON THE SURFACE OF OUR *OWN* WORLD! I'LL GIVE THEM A RECEPTION THEY'LL *NEVER* FORGET!

WITH *DOCTOR DOOM* GONE, ALL THE FIGHT GOES OUT OF HIS GUARDS, AND SO...

I'LL RELEASE MY FLAMING FENCE FROM AROUND YOU GUYS! I FIGURE YOU'VE HAD *ENOUGH!*

I'LL KEEP THIS LAST BATCH TIED UP TILL YOU GET THEM TO HIS MAJESTY! AND STOP CLOWNING-- USE *BOTH* HANDS!

RELAX, RUBBER-HEAD! IF I DROP YOU, YOU'LL ONLY *BOUNCE!*

YOU HAVE SAVED MY KINGDOM! YOU HAVE DRIVEN *DOCTOR DOOM* BACK TO HIS OWN WORLD! HOW CAN I EVER REPAY YOU?

NO NEED FOR THAT, YOUR MAJESTY! SIMPLY PERMIT US TO USE YOUR EN-LARGING RAY, SO THAT WE CAN GO AFTER *DOCTOR DOOM!*

WISH GRANTED!

YOU--YOU ARE THE MOST FAS-CINATING MAN I HAVE EVER MET! MUST *YOU* GO, TOO??? PERHAPS IF YOU REMAINED HERE...??

I CAN'T LEAVE MY PARDS, PEARLA--BUT MAYBE SOME DAY I'LL BE BACK--!!

KNOCK OFF THE MUSH STUFF, HOT HEAD! WE *STILL* HAVEN'T CAUGHT *DOCTOR DOOM,* REMEMBER?!!

22

AND SO, STEPPING IN FRONT OF THE ENLARGER RAYS AS THEY PREPARE TO RETURN TO THEIR OWN WORLD, THE *FANTASTIC FOUR* AND *ANT-MAN* BID FAREWELL TO THE DWELLERS OF THE MICRO-WORLD...

...AS THEY AGAIN TAKE UP THE HUNT FOR *DOCTOR DOOM,* THE MOST DANGEROUS MAN ON EARTH! BUT, THAT'S A TALE FOR *NEXT* ISSUE...

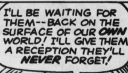

THE END

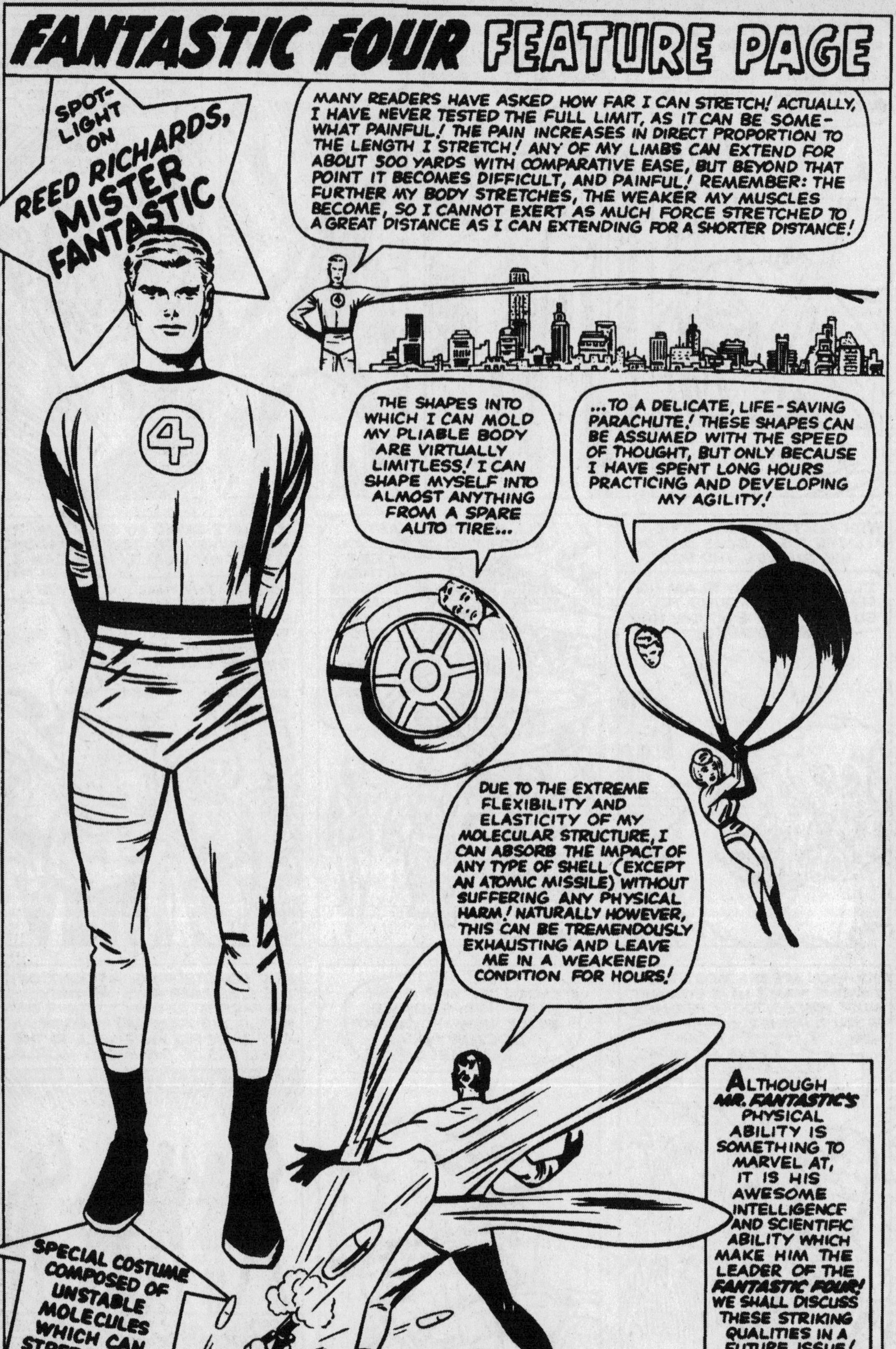
FANTASTIC FOUR FEATURE PAGE
SPOT-LIGHT ON REED RICHARDS, MISTER FANTASTIC
MANY READERS HAVE ASKED HOW FAR I CAN STRETCH! ACTUALLY, I HAVE NEVER TESTED THE FULL LIMIT, AS IT CAN BE SOME-WHAT PAINFUL! THE PAIN INCREASES IN DIRECT PROPORTION TO THE LENGTH I STRETCH! ANY OF MY LIMBS CAN EXTEND FOR ABOUT 500 YARDS WITH COMPARATIVE EASE, BUT BEYOND THAT POINT IT BECOMES DIFFICULT, AND PAINFUL! REMEMBER: THE FURTHER MY BODY STRETCHES, THE WEAKER MY MUSCLES BECOME, SO I CANNOT EXERT AS MUCH FORCE STRETCHED TO A GREAT DISTANCE AS I CAN EXTENDING FOR A SHORTER DISTANCE!
THE SHAPES INTO WHICH I CAN MOLD MY PLIABLE BODY ARE VIRTUALLY LIMITLESS! I CAN SHAPE MYSELF INTO ALMOST ANYTHING FROM A SPARE AUTO TIRE...
...TO A DELICATE, LIFE-SAVING PARACHUTE! THESE SHAPES CAN BE ASSUMED WITH THE SPEED OF THOUGHT, BUT ONLY BECAUSE I HAVE SPENT LONG HOURS PRACTICING AND DEVELOPING MY AGILITY!
DUE TO THE EXTREME FLEXIBILITY AND ELASTICITY OF MY MOLECULAR STRUCTURE, I CAN ABSORB THE IMPACT OF ANY TYPE OF SHELL (EXCEPT AN ATOMIC MISSILE) WITHOUT SUFFERING ANY PHYSICAL HARM! NATURALLY HOWEVER, THIS CAN BE TREMENDOUSLY EXHAUSTING AND LEAVE ME IN A WEAKENED CONDITION FOR HOURS!
SPECIAL COSTUME COMPOSED OF UNSTABLE MOLECULES WHICH CAN STRETCH AND CONTRACT AS BODY DOES!
ALTHOUGH MR. FANTASTIC'S PHYSICAL ABILITY IS SOMETHING TO MARVEL AT, IT IS HIS AWESOME INTELLIGENCE AND SCIENTIFIC ABILITY WHICH MAKE HIM THE LEADER OF THE FANTASTIC FOUR! WE SHALL DISCUSS THESE STRIKING QUALITIES IN A FUTURE ISSUE!

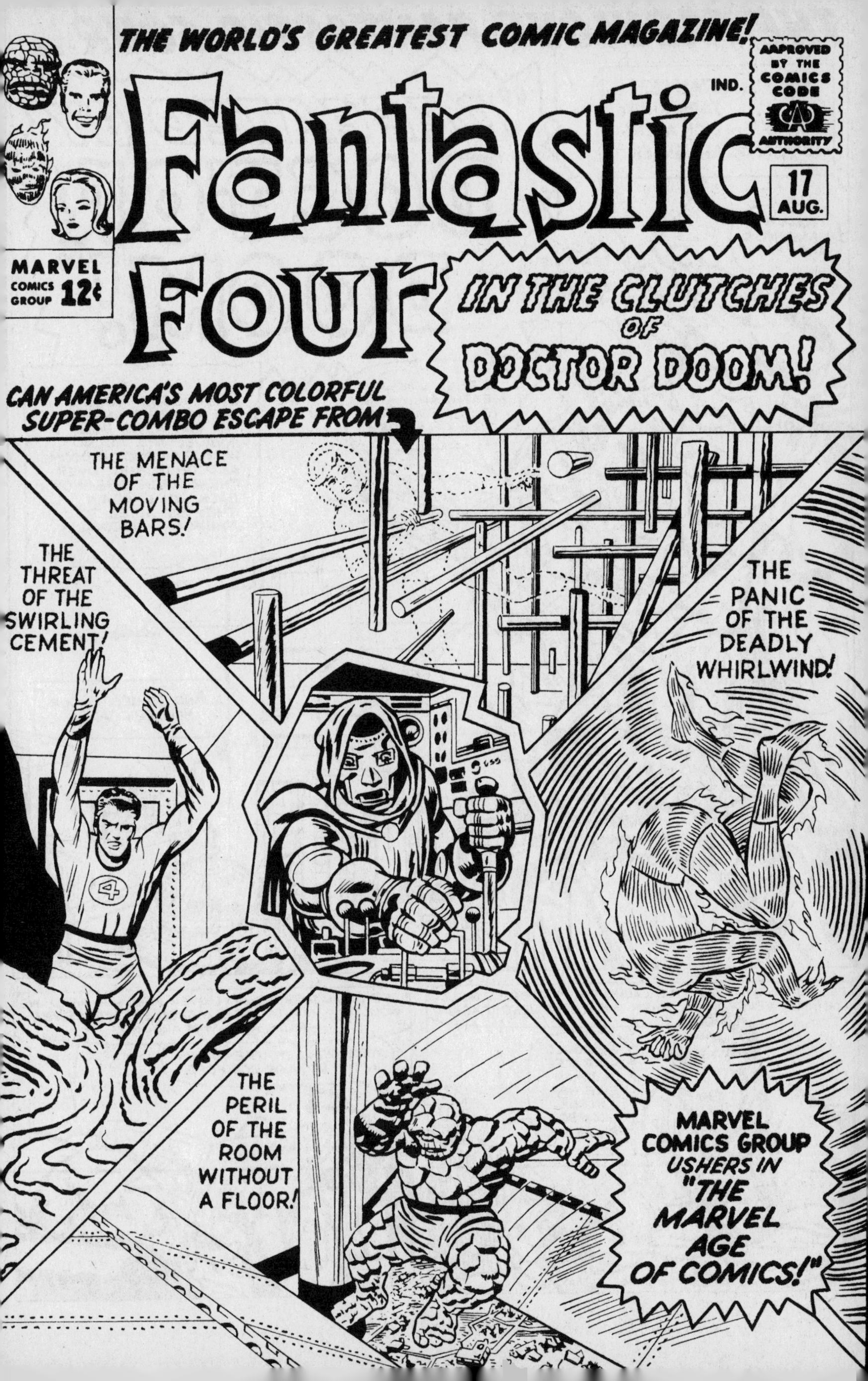
THE WORLD'S GREATEST COMIC MAGAZINE!
APPROVED BY THE COMICS CODE AUTHORITY
IND.
Fantastic Four
17 AUG.
MARVEL COMICS GROUP 12¢
IN THE CLUTCHES OF DOCTOR DOOM!
CAN AMERICA'S MOST COLORFUL SUPER-COMBO ESCAPE FROM
THE MENACE OF THE MOVING BARS!
THE THREAT OF THE SWIRLING CEMENT!
THE PANIC OF THE DEADLY WHIRLWIND!
THE PERIL OF THE ROOM WITHOUT A FLOOR!
MARVEL COMICS GROUP USHERS IN "THE MARVEL AGE OF COMICS!"

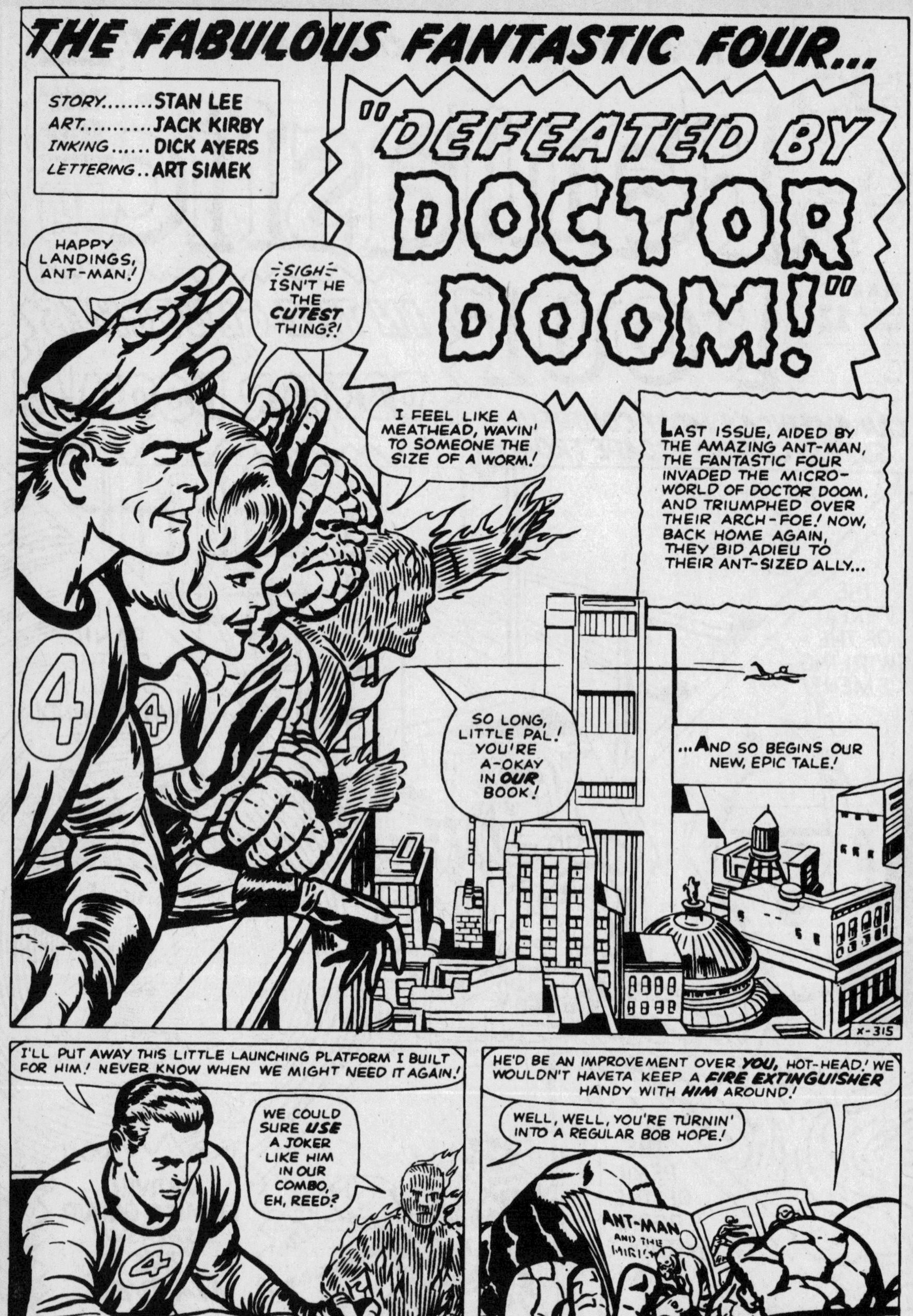
THE FABULOUS FANTASTIC FOUR...
STORY........STAN LEE
ART...........JACK KIRBY
INKING......DICK AYERS
LETTERING..ART SIMEK
"DEFEATED BY DOCTOR DOOM!"
HAPPY LANDINGS, ANT-MAN!
-SIGH- ISN'T HE THE CUTEST THING?!
I FEEL LIKE A MEATHEAD, WAVIN' TO SOMEONE THE SIZE OF A WORM!
LAST ISSUE, AIDED BY THE AMAZING ANT-MAN, THE FANTASTIC FOUR INVADED THE MICRO-WORLD OF DOCTOR DOOM, AND TRIUMPHED OVER THEIR ARCH-FOE! NOW, BACK HOME AGAIN, THEY BID ADIEU TO THEIR ANT-SIZED ALLY...
SO LONG, LITTLE PAL! YOU'RE A-OKAY IN OUR BOOK!
...AND SO BEGINS OUR NEW, EPIC TALE!
X-315
I'LL PUT AWAY THIS LITTLE LAUNCHING PLATFORM I BUILT FOR HIM! NEVER KNOW WHEN WE MIGHT NEED IT AGAIN!
WE COULD SURE USE A JOKER LIKE HIM IN OUR COMBO, EH, REED?
HE'D BE AN IMPROVEMENT OVER YOU, HOT-HEAD! WE WOULDN'T HAVETA KEEP A FIRE EXTINGUISHER HANDY WITH HIM AROUND!
WELL, WELL, YOU'RE TURNIN' INTO A REGULAR BOB HOPE!
ANT-MAN AND THE
1

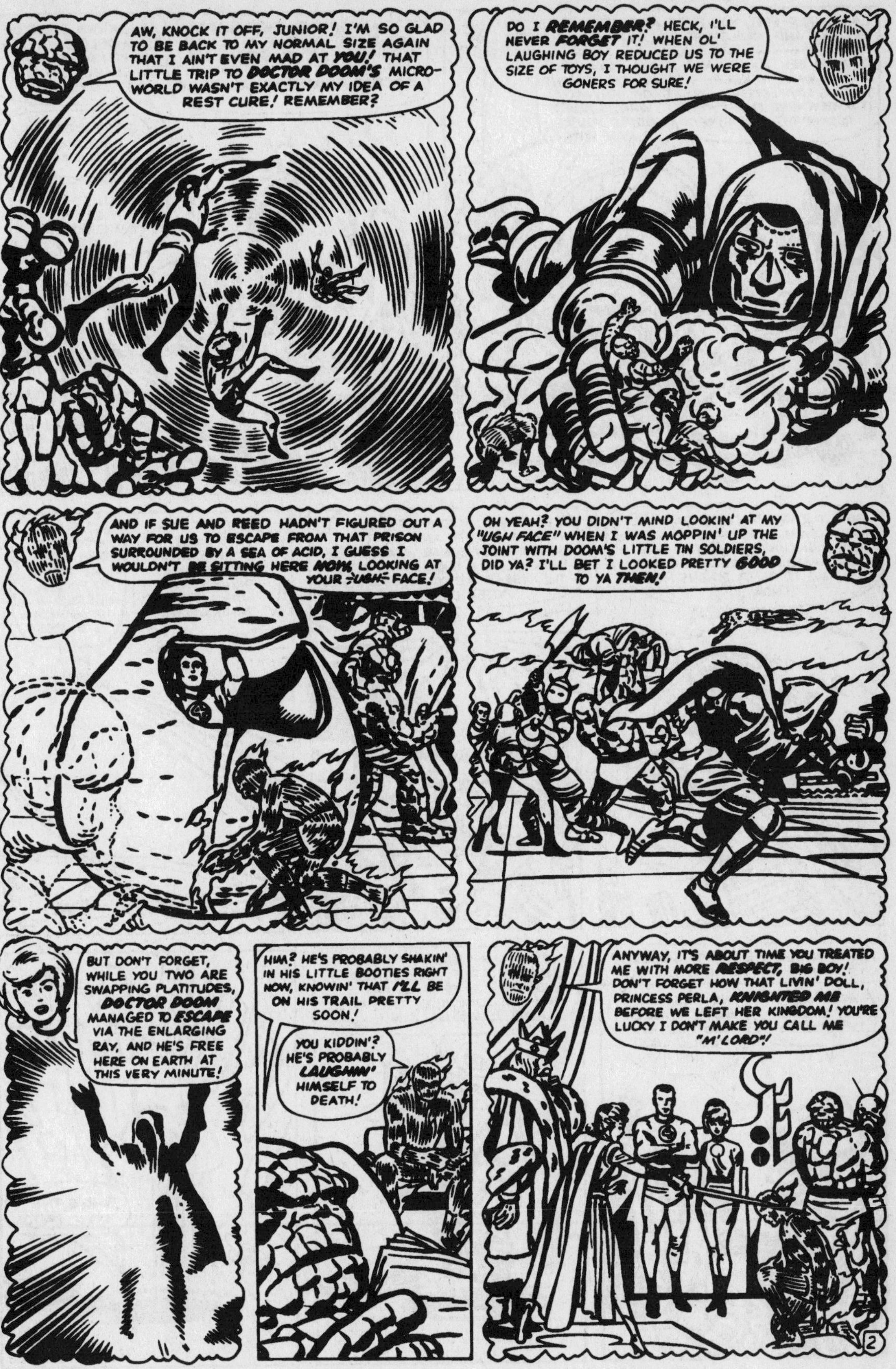
AW, KNOCK IT OFF, JUNIOR! I'M SO GLAD TO BE BACK TO MY NORMAL SIZE AGAIN THAT I AIN'T EVEN MAD AT YOU! THAT LITTLE TRIP TO DOCTOR DOOM'S MICRO-WORLD WASN'T EXACTLY MY IDEA OF A REST CURE! REMEMBER?
DO I REMEMBER? HECK, I'LL NEVER FORGET IT! WHEN OL' LAUGHING BOY REDUCED US TO THE SIZE OF TOYS, I THOUGHT WE WERE GONERS FOR SURE!
AND IF SUE AND REED HADN'T FIGURED OUT A WAY FOR US TO ESCAPE FROM THAT PRISON SURROUNDED BY A SEA OF ACID, I GUESS I WOULDN'T BE SITTING HERE NOW, LOOKING AT YOUR "UGH" FACE!
OH YEAH? YOU DIDN'T MIND LOOKIN' AT MY "UGH FACE" WHEN I WAS MOPPIN' UP THE JOINT WITH DOOM'S LITTLE TIN SOLDIERS, DID YA? I'LL BET I LOOKED PRETTY GOOD TO YA THEN!
BUT DON'T FORGET, WHILE YOU TWO ARE SWAPPING PLATITUDES, DOCTOR DOOM MANAGED TO ESCAPE VIA THE ENLARGING RAY, AND HE'S FREE HERE ON EARTH AT THIS VERY MINUTE!
HIM? HE'S PROBABLY SHAKIN' IN HIS LITTLE BOOTIES RIGHT NOW, KNOWIN' THAT I'LL BE ON HIS TRAIL PRETTY SOON!
YOU KIDDIN'? HE'S PROBABLY LAUGHIN' HIMSELF TO DEATH!
ANYWAY, IT'S ABOUT TIME YOU TREATED ME WITH MORE RESPECT, BIG BOY! DON'T FORGET HOW THAT LIVIN' DOLL, PRINCESS PERLA, KNIGHTED ME BEFORE WE LEFT HER KINGDOM! YOU'RE LUCKY I DON'T MAKE YOU CALL ME "M'LORD"!
2

LOOK, HALF-PINT, YOU EVER ASK ME TO CALL YOU "M'LORD," AND YOU'LL END UP CHEWIN' ON A FISTFUL OF KNUCKLES!!!

CLAM UP, BEN! IF YOU AND JOHNNY WANT TO KEEP TRADING LOVE LETTERS, DO IT SOMEWHERE ELSE! YOU'RE ROCKIN' THE BOAT HERE!

OKAY, OKAY! I'M ALL TALKED OUT NOW, ANYWAY! WHAT'S THAT GIZMO YOU'RE PLAYIN' WITH?

IT'S A HIGHLY REFINED RADAR SET, EXTRA SENSITIVE TO HUMAN FLESH COVERED BY STEEL! I'M HOPING TO GET A CLUE TO DOCTOR DOOM'S WHEREABOUTS!

I THINK THE THREE OF US SHOULD BE HELPING YOU RIGHT NOW, BY SEARCHING THE CITY OURSELVES!

GOOD IDEA, SIS! I COULD USE A LITTLE ACTION!

YEAH, JUST LIKE THEY SAY IN COMIC BOOKS, HUH?

BOY, IF I DIDN'T LOVE THAT BIG APE SO MUCH, I'D GIVE 'IM A HOT-FOOT RIGHT IN THE SEAT OF HIS BAGGY PANTS! OH WELL, I GUESS IT'S TIME TO TEND TO BUSINESS NOW...

I'LL CLIMB UP TO A COUPLE THOUSAND FEET AND START SENDING OUT SONAR HEAT WAVES! WITH A LITTLE LUCK, I MAY DETECT THE VIBRATIONS OF DOOM'S STEEL OUTER COVERING!

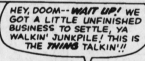

YES SIREE, IT SURE WAS A GREAT IDEA! THERE'S ONLY ONE LITTLE THING WRONG--

--IT'S NOT WORKIN'!! TOO MUCH LIKE TRYIN' TO FIND A NEEDLE IN A HAYSTACK, I GUESS!

MEANWHILE, THE THING SEEMS TO HAVE BETTER LUCK...

HOLY COW! IT'S HIM!! I FOUND 'IM!!

HE MUST BE NUTS TO WALK AROUND IN PUBLIC LIKE THAT!

HEY, DOOM-- WAIT UP! WE GOT A LITTLE UNFINISHED BUSINESS TO SETTLE, YA WALKIN' JUNKPILE! THIS IS THE THING TALKIN'!!

WHUMP!

WHO'S THE WISE GUY??!

3

HOW THE #?#!!#?# DO I GET OUTTA HERE??!
LADY! LOOK OUT!
MY BRAKES ARE JAMMED!!
I AIN'T GOT TIME TO FIND THE RIGHT EXIT, SO I'LL JUST--
HEY! A GUY COULD GET A CHARLEY HORSE THIS WAY!!
OH! YOU-- YOU SAVED MY LIFE!
SURE, SURE! I'M JUST A BIG, FAT, HANDSOME HERO! NOW GET OUTTA THE WAY--I GOT THINGS TO DO!
WOW! IT'S THE THING! LOOK AT THAT BIG FELLA MOVE!
HE--HE'S SO GROTESQUE THAT HE'S ALMOST BEAUTIFUL!
HAH! I KNEW I'D CATCH UP TO 'IM! BOY, AM I GONNA ENJOY THIS!
HEY, BUSTER! TURN AROUND! I WANNA GAZE INTO YOUR BABY BLUES WHILE I MOP UP THE STREET WITH YA!
WHAT GIVES, MISTER?? YOU SOME KINDA FANATIC, OR SOMETHIN'??
I'LL BE A MONKEY'S UNCLE!! I BEEN ROBBED!!
TODAY AT THE BIJOU THEATER "WHEN KNIGHTS WERE BOLD!" SEE IT NOW!
AND, IN ANOTHER PART OF TOWN...
IF DOCTOR DOOM IS IN THE CITY, HE'LL BE SURE TO CONTACT SOME HARDENED CRIMINALS TO HELP HIM! SO, IF I INVISIBLY FOLLOW SOME UNDERWORLD TYPES, PERHAPS...
-GASP!- I WOULDN'T HAVE EXPECTED ANYTHING AS BLATANT AS THIS TO TAKE PLACE RIGHT OUT IN THE OPEN!
I THINK THIS IS WHAT YOU'VE BEEN WAITING FOR, MR. SPADE!
YEAH! LET ME HAVE IT, PROFESSOR, AND I'LL SEE IF IT'S THE ONE I WANT!
THIS SPECIAL ADAPTER IS WHAT WILL MAKE THE DIFFERENCE! NOTICE HOW SMOOTHLY IT FITS ON THE BARREL OF THE GUN! IT'S EASY TO HANDLE AND NEVER MISSES!
4

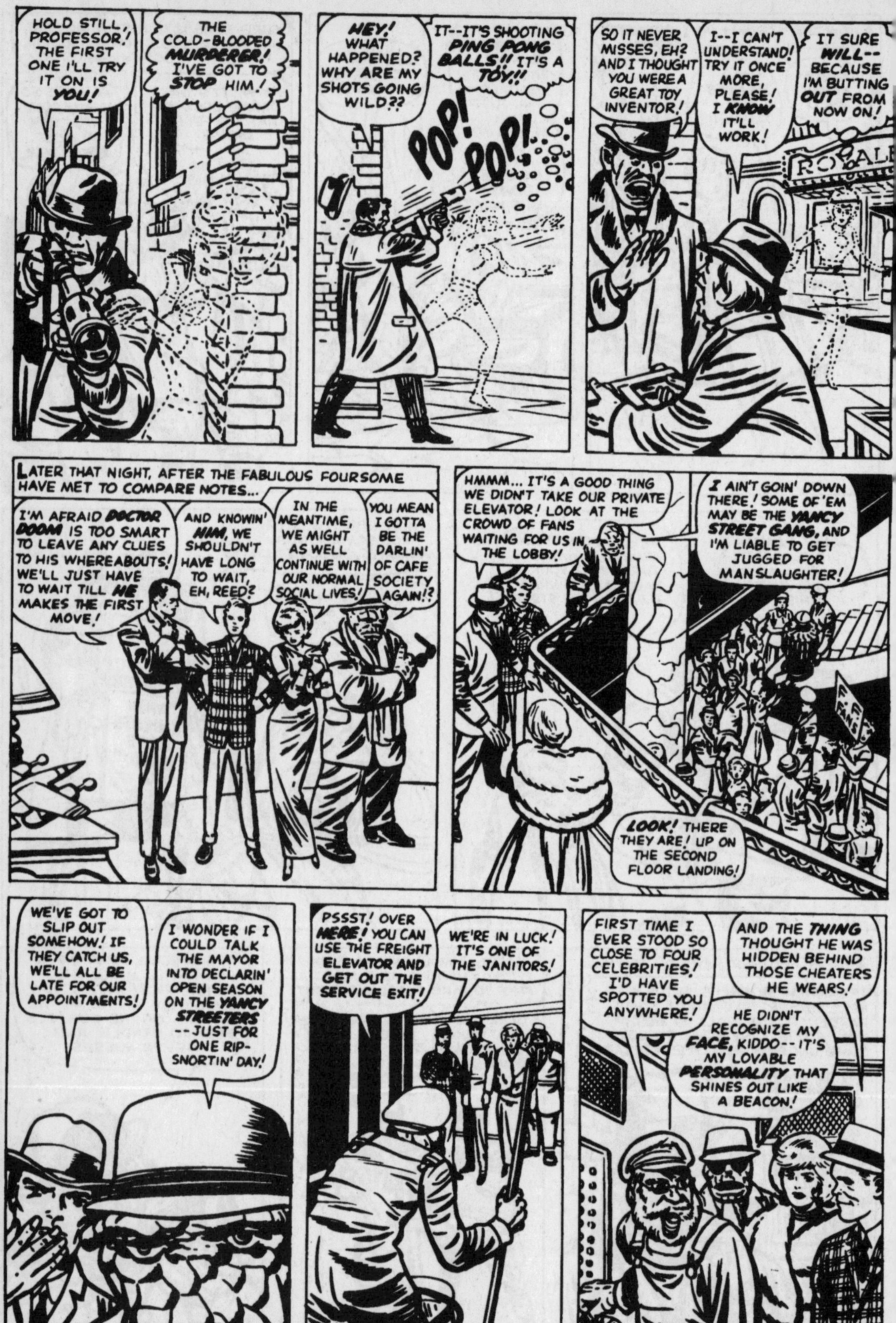
HOLD STILL, PROFESSOR! THE FIRST ONE I'LL TRY IT ON IS YOU!
THE COLD-BLOODED MURDERER! I'VE GOT TO STOP HIM!
HEY! WHAT HAPPENED? WHY ARE MY SHOTS GOING WILD??
IT--IT'S SHOOTING PING PONG BALLS!! IT'S A TOY!!
POP! POP!
SO IT NEVER MISSES, EH? AND I THOUGHT YOU WERE A GREAT TOY INVENTOR!
I--I CAN'T UNDERSTAND! TRY IT ONCE MORE, PLEASE! I KNOW IT'LL WORK!
IT SURE WILL-- BECAUSE I'M BUTTING OUT FROM NOW ON!
LATER THAT NIGHT, AFTER THE FABULOUS FOURSOME HAVE MET TO COMPARE NOTES...
I'M AFRAID DOCTOR DOOM IS TOO SMART TO LEAVE ANY CLUES TO HIS WHEREABOUTS! WE'LL JUST HAVE TO WAIT TILL HE MAKES THE FIRST MOVE!
AND KNOWIN' HIM, WE SHOULDN'T HAVE LONG TO WAIT, EH, REED?
IN THE MEANTIME, WE MIGHT AS WELL CONTINUE WITH OUR NORMAL SOCIAL LIVES!
YOU MEAN I GOTTA BE THE DARLIN' OF CAFE SOCIETY AGAIN!?
HMMM... IT'S A GOOD THING WE DIDN'T TAKE OUR PRIVATE ELEVATOR! LOOK AT THE CROWD OF FANS WAITING FOR US IN THE LOBBY!
I AIN'T GOIN' DOWN THERE! SOME OF 'EM MAY BE THE YANCY STREET GANG, AND I'M LIABLE TO GET JUGGED FOR MANSLAUGHTER!
F.F. FANS
LOOK! THERE THEY ARE! UP ON THE SECOND FLOOR LANDING!
WE'VE GOT TO SLIP OUT SOMEHOW! IF THEY CATCH US, WE'LL ALL BE LATE FOR OUR APPOINTMENTS!
I WONDER IF I COULD TALK THE MAYOR INTO DECLARIN' OPEN SEASON ON THE YANCY STREETERS --JUST FOR ONE RIP-SNORTIN' DAY!
PSSST! OVER HERE! YOU CAN USE THE FREIGHT ELEVATOR AND GET OUT THE SERVICE EXIT!
WE'RE IN LUCK! IT'S ONE OF THE JANITORS!
FIRST TIME I EVER STOOD SO CLOSE TO FOUR CELEBRITIES! I'D HAVE SPOTTED YOU ANYWHERE!
AND THE THING THOUGHT HE WAS HIDDEN BEHIND THOSE CHEATERS HE WEARS!
HE DIDN'T RECOGNIZE MY FACE, KIDDO--IT'S MY LOVABLE PERSONALITY THAT SHINES OUT LIKE A BEACON!
5

Panel 1: "I'D SURE APPRECIATE IT IF I COULD SHAKE HANDS WITH YOU ALL BEFORE YOU GO!"

"SURE, OLD FELLA! BUT DON'T SQUEEZE ME TOO HARD! HEH HEH!"

"IT'S A PLEASURE, SIR! AND THANK YOU FOR HELPING US!"

Panel 2: AS THEY LEAVE, NONE OF THE COLORFUL QUARTET NOTICE THAT THE "JANITOR" HAS SECRETLY AFFIXED A TINY, TISSUE-THIN PLASTIC DISC TO EACH OF THEIR HANDS!

"IT WORKED LIKE A CHARM--AS *ALL* MY PLANS DO!"

Panel 3: THEN, DASHING INTO A NEARBY BROOM CLOSET, HE REMOVES HIS OVERALLS, CAP, FALSE BEARD, AND FACE MASK...

"WITH THOSE SPECIALLY TREATED IDENTO-DISCS ON THEIR HANDS, MY LITTLE *'FOLLOWERS'* WILL BE ABLE TO TRACK THE *FANTASTIC FOUR* WHEREVER THEY GO!"

Panel 4: "AND NOW, I'LL RETURN TO MY HIDDEN LAB TO PUT *PHASE ONE* OF MY MASTER PLAN INTO OPERATION! *THIS* TIME NOTHING SHALL STOP ME FROM DEFEATING THE *FANTASTIC FOUR*-- AS ONLY *DOCTOR DOOM* CAN!"

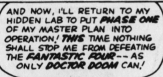

Panel 5: A SHORT TIME LATER...

"*GO*, MY FOLLOWERS! I RELEASE YOU TO DO THE JOB FOR WHICH I CREATED YOU!"

"EACH OF YOU LIGHTER-THAN-AIR ROBOTS ARE ATTUNED TO ONE SPECIAL DISC--NOW FIND YOUR OBJECTIVES!"

Panel 6: AND SO...

"GOSH, HELEN, I THOUGHT YOU'D *NEVER* SAY YES TO A DATE WITH ME!"

"WELL, I'LL ADMIT I WAS A LITTLE NERVOUS ABOUT GOING OUT WITH THE FAMOUS *HUMAN TORCH*, JOHNNY! BUT NOW I'M *GLAD* WE'RE TOGETHER!"

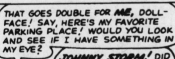

Panel 7: "THAT GOES DOUBLE FOR *ME*, DOLL-FACE! SAY, HERE'S MY FAVORITE PARKING PLACE! WOULD YOU LOOK AND SEE IF I HAVE SOMETHING IN MY EYE?"

"JOHNNY STORM! DID ANYONE EVER TELL YOU WHAT A FAST WORKER YOU--?? JOHNNY!! WHAT'S THAT??!!..."

Panel 8: "HUH? WHAT'S WHA--???"

"*BLAZIN' BEARCATS!!* I DON'T KNOW WHAT THAT THING *IS*, BUT DON'T WORRY, HONEY, I'LL GET *RID* OF IT!"

Panel 9: *FLAME ON!*

"*HEY!* WHAT THE--?? I FLEW RIGHT *THRU* IT!"

"IF THIS IS *YOUR* IDEA OF A *FUN* EVENING, JOHNNY STORM, IT ISN'T *MINE!* I'M *WALKING HOME!* GOODBYE FOREVER!"

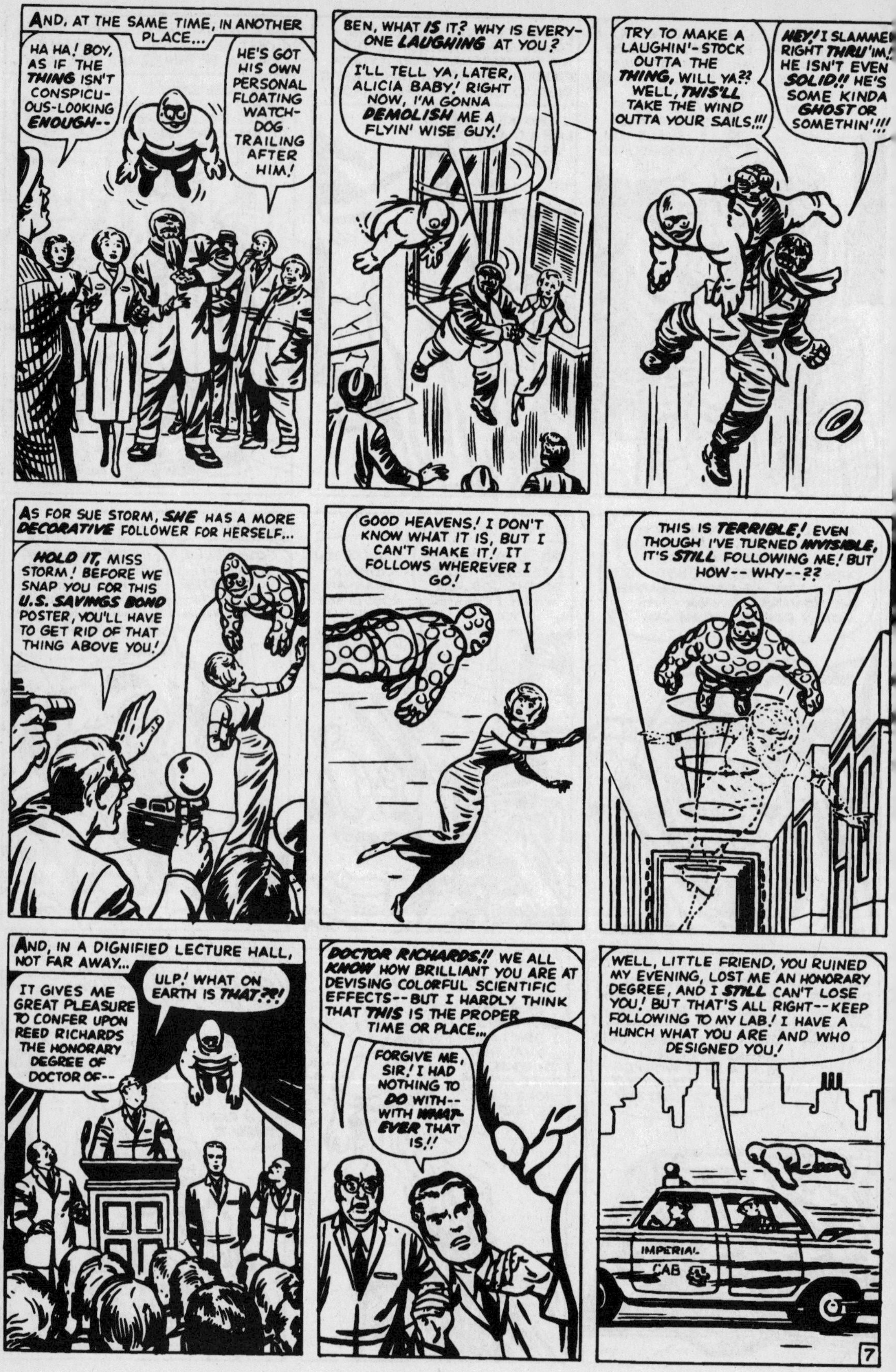

AND, AT THE SAME TIME, IN ANOTHER PLACE...
HA HA! BOY, AS IF THE THING ISN'T CONSPICU-OUS-LOOKING ENOUGH--
HE'S GOT HIS OWN PERSONAL FLOATING WATCH-DOG TRAILING AFTER HIM!
BEN, WHAT IS IT? WHY IS EVERY-ONE LAUGHING AT YOU?
I'LL TELL YA, LATER, ALICIA BABY! RIGHT NOW, I'M GONNA DEMOLISH ME A FLYIN' WISE GUY!
TRY TO MAKE A LAUGHIN'-STOCK OUTTA THE THING, WILL YA?? WELL, THIS'LL TAKE THE WIND OUTTA YOUR SAILS!!!
HEY! I SLAMMED RIGHT THRU 'IM! HE ISN'T EVEN SOLID!! HE'S SOME KINDA GHOST OR SOMETHIN'!!!
AS FOR SUE STORM, SHE HAS A MORE DECORATIVE FOLLOWER FOR HERSELF...
HOLD IT, MISS STORM! BEFORE WE SNAP YOU FOR THIS U.S. SAVINGS BOND POSTER, YOU'LL HAVE TO GET RID OF THAT THING ABOVE YOU!
GOOD HEAVENS! I DON'T KNOW WHAT IT IS, BUT I CAN'T SHAKE IT! IT FOLLOWS WHEREVER I GO!
THIS IS TERRIBLE! EVEN THOUGH I'VE TURNED INVISIBLE, IT'S STILL FOLLOWING ME! BUT HOW-- WHY--??
AND, IN A DIGNIFIED LECTURE HALL, NOT FAR AWAY...
IT GIVES ME GREAT PLEASURE TO CONFER UPON REED RICHARDS THE HONORARY DEGREE OF DOCTOR OF--
ULP! WHAT ON EARTH IS THAT??!
DOCTOR RICHARDS!! WE ALL KNOW HOW BRILLIANT YOU ARE AT DEVISING COLORFUL SCIENTIFIC EFFECTS--BUT I HARDLY THINK THAT THIS IS THE PROPER TIME OR PLACE...
FORGIVE ME, SIR! I HAD NOTHING TO DO WITH-- WITH WHAT-EVER THAT IS!!
WELL, LITTLE FRIEND, YOU RUINED MY EVENING, LOST ME AN HONORARY DEGREE, AND I STILL CAN'T LOSE YOU! BUT THAT'S ALL RIGHT--KEEP FOLLOWING TO MY LAB! I HAVE A HUNCH WHAT YOU ARE AND WHO DESIGNED YOU!
IMPERIAL CAB
7

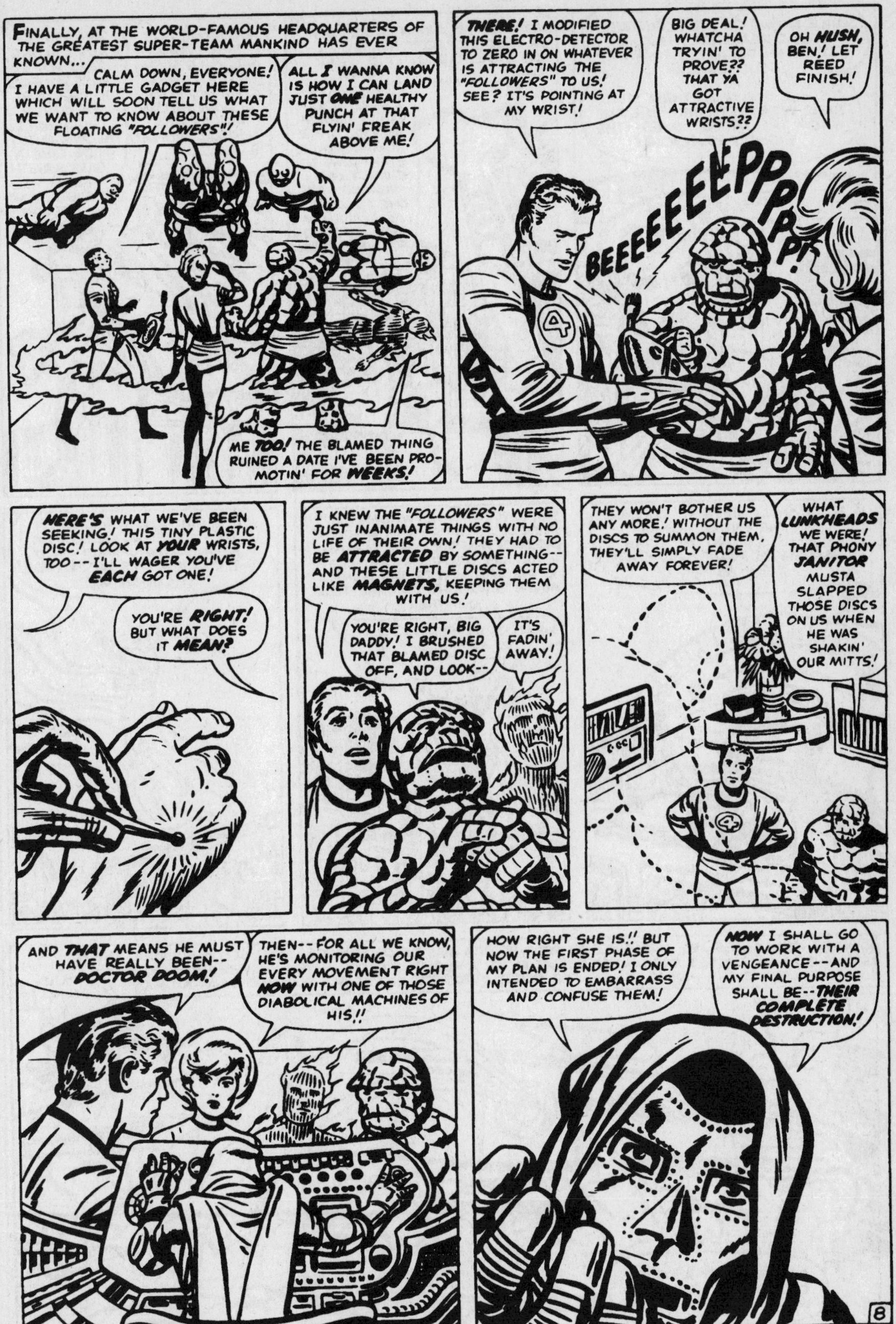

FINALLY, AT THE WORLD-FAMOUS HEADQUARTERS OF THE GREATEST SUPER-TEAM MANKIND HAS EVER KNOWN...
CALM DOWN, EVERYONE! I HAVE A LITTLE GADGET HERE WHICH WILL SOON TELL US WHAT WE WANT TO KNOW ABOUT THESE FLOATING "FOLLOWERS"!
ALL I WANNA KNOW IS HOW I CAN LAND JUST ONE HEALTHY PUNCH AT THAT FLYIN' FREAK ABOVE ME!
ME TOO! THE BLAMED THING RUINED A DATE I'VE BEEN PROMOTIN' FOR WEEKS!
THERE! I MODIFIED THIS ELECTRO-DETECTOR TO ZERO IN ON WHATEVER IS ATTRACTING THE "FOLLOWERS" TO US! SEE? IT'S POINTING AT MY WRIST!
BIG DEAL! WHATCHA TRYIN' TO PROVE?? THAT YA GOT ATTRACTIVE WRISTS??
OH HUSH, BEN! LET REED FINISH!
BEEEEEEELPPPP!
HERE'S WHAT WE'VE BEEN SEEKING! THIS TINY PLASTIC DISC! LOOK AT YOUR WRISTS, TOO--I'LL WAGER YOU'VE EACH GOT ONE!
YOU'RE RIGHT! BUT WHAT DOES IT MEAN?
I KNEW THE "FOLLOWERS" WERE JUST INANIMATE THINGS WITH NO LIFE OF THEIR OWN! THEY HAD TO BE ATTRACTED BY SOMETHING--AND THESE LITTLE DISCS ACTED LIKE MAGNETS, KEEPING THEM WITH US!
YOU'RE RIGHT, BIG DADDY! I BRUSHED THAT BLAMED DISC OFF, AND LOOK--
IT'S FADIN' AWAY!
THEY WON'T BOTHER US ANY MORE! WITHOUT THE DISCS TO SUMMON THEM, THEY'LL SIMPLY FADE AWAY FOREVER!
WHAT LUNKHEADS WE WERE! THAT PHONY JANITOR MUSTA SLAPPED THOSE DISCS ON US WHEN HE WAS SHAKIN' OUR MITTS!
AND THAT MEANS HE MUST HAVE REALLY BEEN--DOCTOR DOOM!
THEN--FOR ALL WE KNOW, HE'S MONITORING OUR EVERY MOVEMENT RIGHT NOW WITH ONE OF THOSE DIABOLICAL MACHINES OF HIS!!
HOW RIGHT SHE IS!! BUT NOW THE FIRST PHASE OF MY PLAN IS ENDED! I ONLY INTENDED TO EMBARRASS AND CONFUSE THEM!
NOW I SHALL GO TO WORK WITH A VENGEANCE--AND MY FINAL PURPOSE SHALL BE--THEIR COMPLETE DESTRUCTION!
8

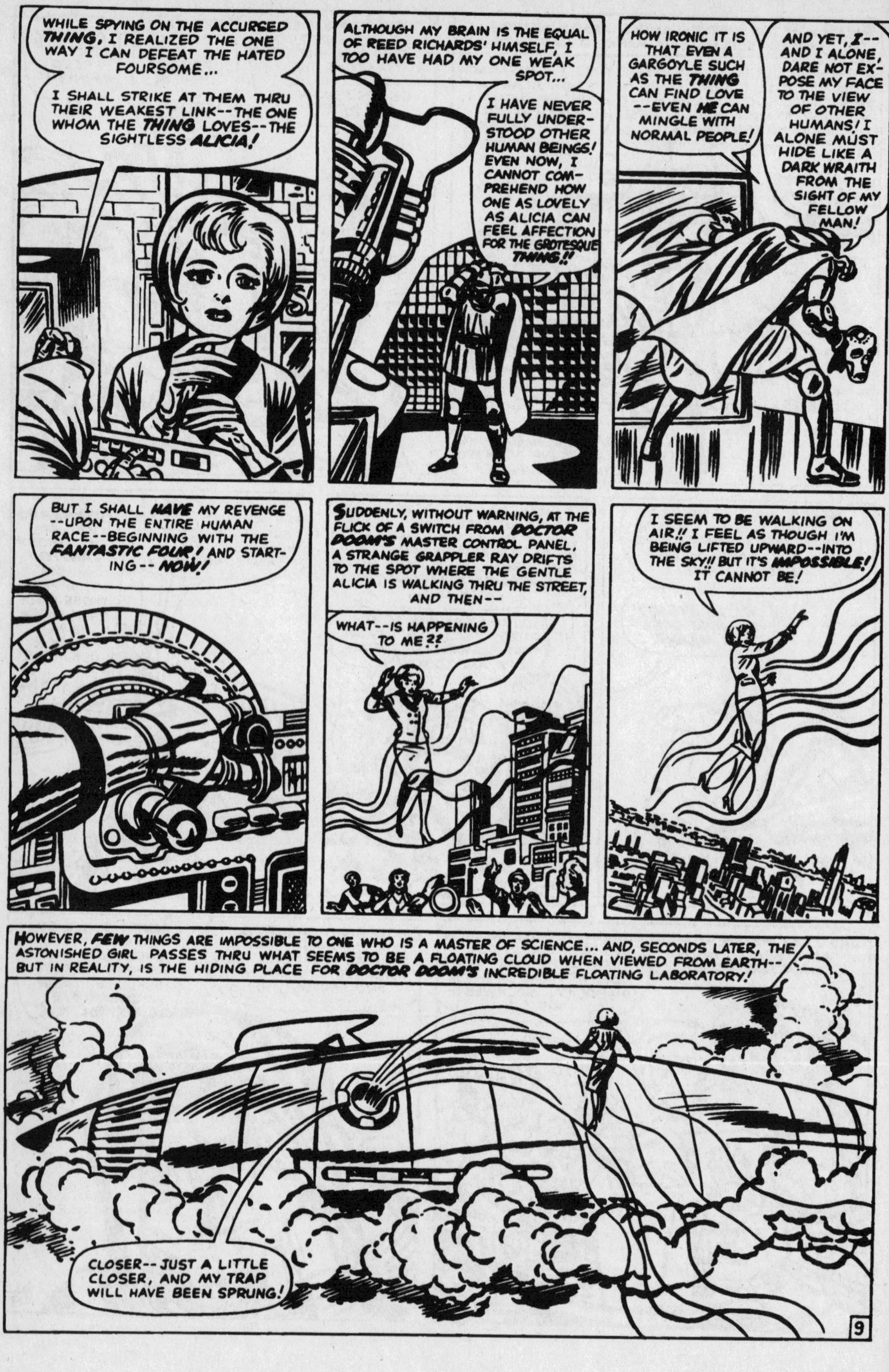
WHILE SPYING ON THE ACCURSED THING, I REALIZED THE ONE WAY I CAN DEFEAT THE HATED FOURSOME...
I SHALL STRIKE AT THEM THRU THEIR WEAKEST LINK--THE ONE WHOM THE THING LOVES--THE SIGHTLESS ALICIA!
ALTHOUGH MY BRAIN IS THE EQUAL OF REED RICHARDS' HIMSELF, I TOO HAVE HAD MY ONE WEAK SPOT...
I HAVE NEVER FULLY UNDERSTOOD OTHER HUMAN BEINGS! EVEN NOW, I CANNOT COMPREHEND HOW ONE AS LOVELY AS ALICIA CAN FEEL AFFECTION FOR THE GROTESQUE THING!!
HOW IRONIC IT IS THAT EVEN A GARGOYLE SUCH AS THE THING CAN FIND LOVE --EVEN HE CAN MINGLE WITH NORMAL PEOPLE!
AND YET, I-- AND I ALONE, DARE NOT EXPOSE MY FACE TO THE VIEW OF OTHER HUMANS! I ALONE MUST HIDE LIKE A DARK WRAITH FROM THE SIGHT OF MY FELLOW MAN!
BUT I SHALL HAVE MY REVENGE --UPON THE ENTIRE HUMAN RACE--BEGINNING WITH THE FANTASTIC FOUR! AND STARTING--NOW!
SUDDENLY, WITHOUT WARNING, AT THE FLICK OF A SWITCH FROM DOCTOR DOOM'S MASTER CONTROL PANEL, A STRANGE GRAPPLER RAY DRIFTS TO THE SPOT WHERE THE GENTLE ALICIA IS WALKING THRU THE STREET, AND THEN--
WHAT--IS HAPPENING TO ME??
I SEEM TO BE WALKING ON AIR!! I FEEL AS THOUGH I'M BEING LIFTED UPWARD--INTO THE SKY!! BUT IT'S IMPOSSIBLE! IT CANNOT BE!
HOWEVER, FEW THINGS ARE IMPOSSIBLE TO ONE WHO IS A MASTER OF SCIENCE... AND, SECONDS LATER, THE ASTONISHED GIRL PASSES THRU WHAT SEEMS TO BE A FLOATING CLOUD WHEN VIEWED FROM EARTH-- BUT IN REALITY, IS THE HIDING PLACE FOR DOCTOR DOOM'S INCREDIBLE FLOATING LABORATORY!
CLOSER-- JUST A LITTLE CLOSER, AND MY TRAP WILL HAVE BEEN SPRUNG!
9

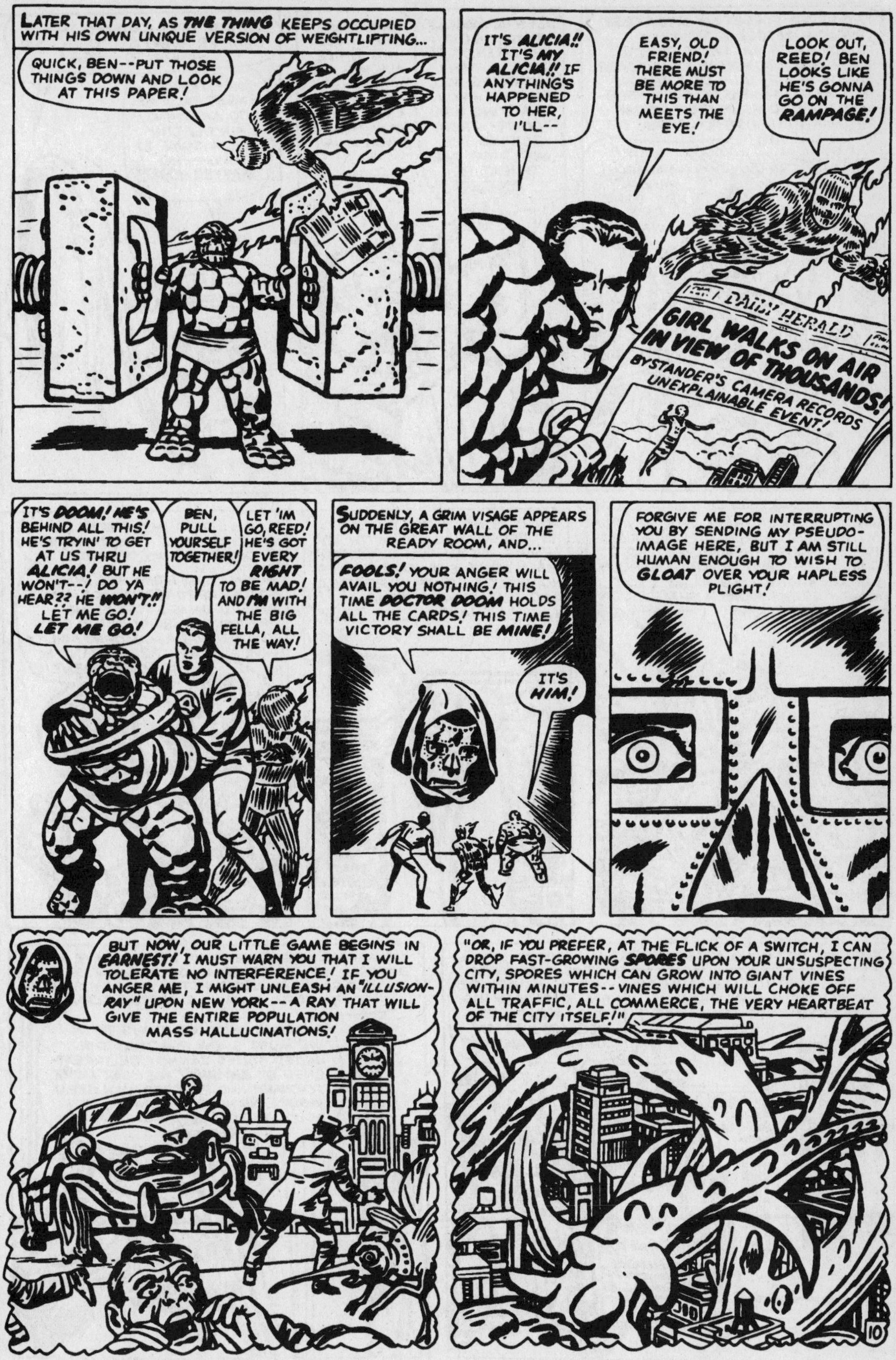
LATER THAT DAY, AS THE THING KEEPS OCCUPIED WITH HIS OWN UNIQUE VERSION OF WEIGHTLIFTING...
QUICK, BEN--PUT THOSE THINGS DOWN AND LOOK AT THIS PAPER!
IT'S ALICIA!! IT'S MY ALICIA!! IF ANYTHING'S HAPPENED TO HER, I'LL--
EASY, OLD FRIEND! THERE MUST BE MORE TO THIS THAN MEETS THE EYE!
LOOK OUT, REED! BEN LOOKS LIKE HE'S GONNA GO ON THE RAMPAGE!
DAILY HERALD
GIRL WALKS ON AIR IN VIEW OF THOUSANDS!
BYSTANDER'S CAMERA RECORDS UNEXPLAINABLE EVENT!
IT'S DOOM! HE'S BEHIND ALL THIS! HE'S TRYIN' TO GET AT US THRU ALICIA! BUT HE WON'T--! DO YA HEAR?? HE WON'T!! LET ME GO! LET ME GO!
BEN, PULL YOURSELF TOGETHER!
LET 'IM GO, REED! HE'S GOT EVERY RIGHT TO BE MAD! AND I'M WITH THE BIG FELLA, ALL THE WAY!
SUDDENLY, A GRIM VISAGE APPEARS ON THE GREAT WALL OF THE READY ROOM, AND...
FOOLS! YOUR ANGER WILL AVAIL YOU NOTHING! THIS TIME DOCTOR DOOM HOLDS ALL THE CARDS! THIS TIME VICTORY SHALL BE MINE!
IT'S HIM!
FORGIVE ME FOR INTERRUPTING YOU BY SENDING MY PSEUDO-IMAGE HERE, BUT I AM STILL HUMAN ENOUGH TO WISH TO GLOAT OVER YOUR HAPLESS PLIGHT!
BUT NOW, OUR LITTLE GAME BEGINS IN EARNEST! I MUST WARN YOU THAT I WILL TOLERATE NO INTERFERENCE! IF YOU ANGER ME, I MIGHT UNLEASH AN "ILLUSION-RAY" UPON NEW YORK--A RAY THAT WILL GIVE THE ENTIRE POPULATION MASS HALLUCINATIONS!
"OR, IF YOU PREFER, AT THE FLICK OF A SWITCH, I CAN DROP FAST-GROWING SPORES UPON YOUR UNSUSPECTING CITY, SPORES WHICH CAN GROW INTO GIANT VINES WITHIN MINUTES--VINES WHICH WILL CHOKE OFF ALL TRAFFIC, ALL COMMERCE, THE VERY HEARTBEAT OF THE CITY ITSELF!"
10

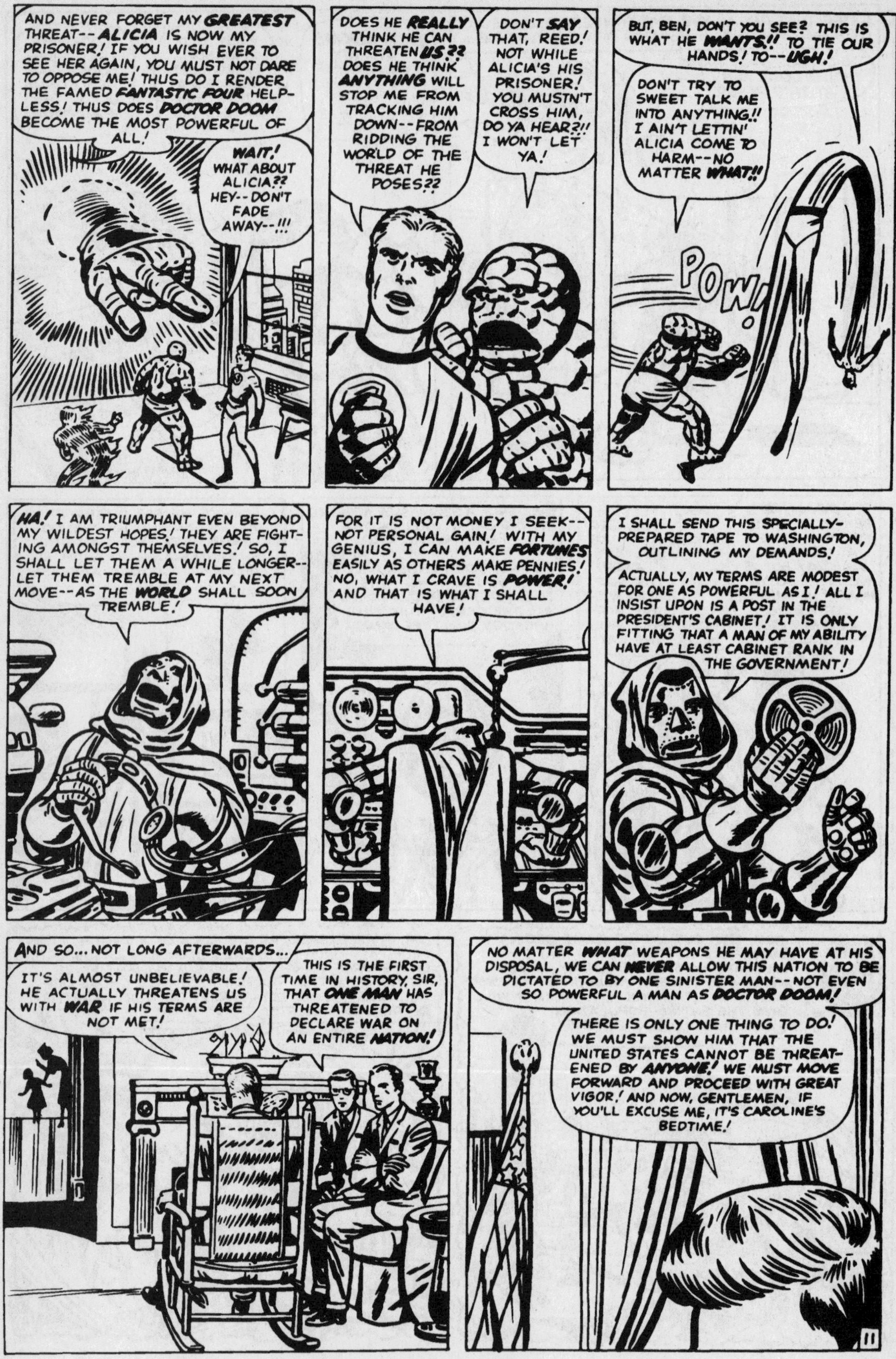
AND NEVER FORGET MY GREATEST THREAT--ALICIA IS NOW MY PRISONER! IF YOU WISH EVER TO SEE HER AGAIN, YOU MUST NOT DARE TO OPPOSE ME! THUS DO I RENDER THE FAMED FANTASTIC FOUR HELPLESS! THUS DOES DOCTOR DOOM BECOME THE MOST POWERFUL OF ALL!
WAIT! WHAT ABOUT ALICIA?? HEY--DON'T FADE AWAY--!!!
DOES HE REALLY THINK HE CAN THREATEN US?? DOES HE THINK ANYTHING WILL STOP ME FROM TRACKING HIM DOWN--FROM RIDDING THE WORLD OF THE THREAT HE POSES??
DON'T SAY THAT, REED! NOT WHILE ALICIA'S HIS PRISONER! YOU MUSTN'T CROSS HIM, DO YA HEAR?!! I WON'T LET YA!
BUT, BEN, DON'T YOU SEE? THIS IS WHAT HE WANTS!! TO TIE OUR HANDS! TO--UGH!
DON'T TRY TO SWEET TALK ME INTO ANYTHING!! I AIN'T LETTIN' ALICIA COME TO HARM--NO MATTER WHAT!!
POW!
HA! I AM TRIUMPHANT EVEN BEYOND MY WILDEST HOPES! THEY ARE FIGHTING AMONGST THEMSELVES! SO, I SHALL LET THEM A WHILE LONGER--LET THEM TREMBLE AT MY NEXT MOVE--AS THE WORLD SHALL SOON TREMBLE!
FOR IT IS NOT MONEY I SEEK--NOT PERSONAL GAIN! WITH MY GENIUS, I CAN MAKE FORTUNES EASILY AS OTHERS MAKE PENNIES! NO, WHAT I CRAVE IS POWER! AND THAT IS WHAT I SHALL HAVE!
I SHALL SEND THIS SPECIALLY-PREPARED TAPE TO WASHINGTON, OUTLINING MY DEMANDS!
ACTUALLY, MY TERMS ARE MODEST FOR ONE AS POWERFUL AS I! ALL I INSIST UPON IS A POST IN THE PRESIDENT'S CABINET! IT IS ONLY FITTING THAT A MAN OF MY ABILITY HAVE AT LEAST CABINET RANK IN THE GOVERNMENT!
AND SO... NOT LONG AFTERWARDS...
IT'S ALMOST UNBELIEVABLE! HE ACTUALLY THREATENS US WITH WAR IF HIS TERMS ARE NOT MET!
THIS IS THE FIRST TIME IN HISTORY, SIR, THAT ONE MAN HAS THREATENED TO DECLARE WAR ON AN ENTIRE NATION!
NO MATTER WHAT WEAPONS HE MAY HAVE AT HIS DISPOSAL, WE CAN NEVER ALLOW THIS NATION TO BE DICTATED TO BY ONE SINISTER MAN--NOT EVEN SO POWERFUL A MAN AS DOCTOR DOOM!
THERE IS ONLY ONE THING TO DO! WE MUST SHOW HIM THAT THE UNITED STATES CANNOT BE THREATENED BY ANYONE! WE MUST MOVE FORWARD AND PROCEED WITH GREAT VIGOR! AND NOW, GENTLEMEN, IF YOU'LL EXCUSE ME, IT'S CAROLINE'S BEDTIME!
11

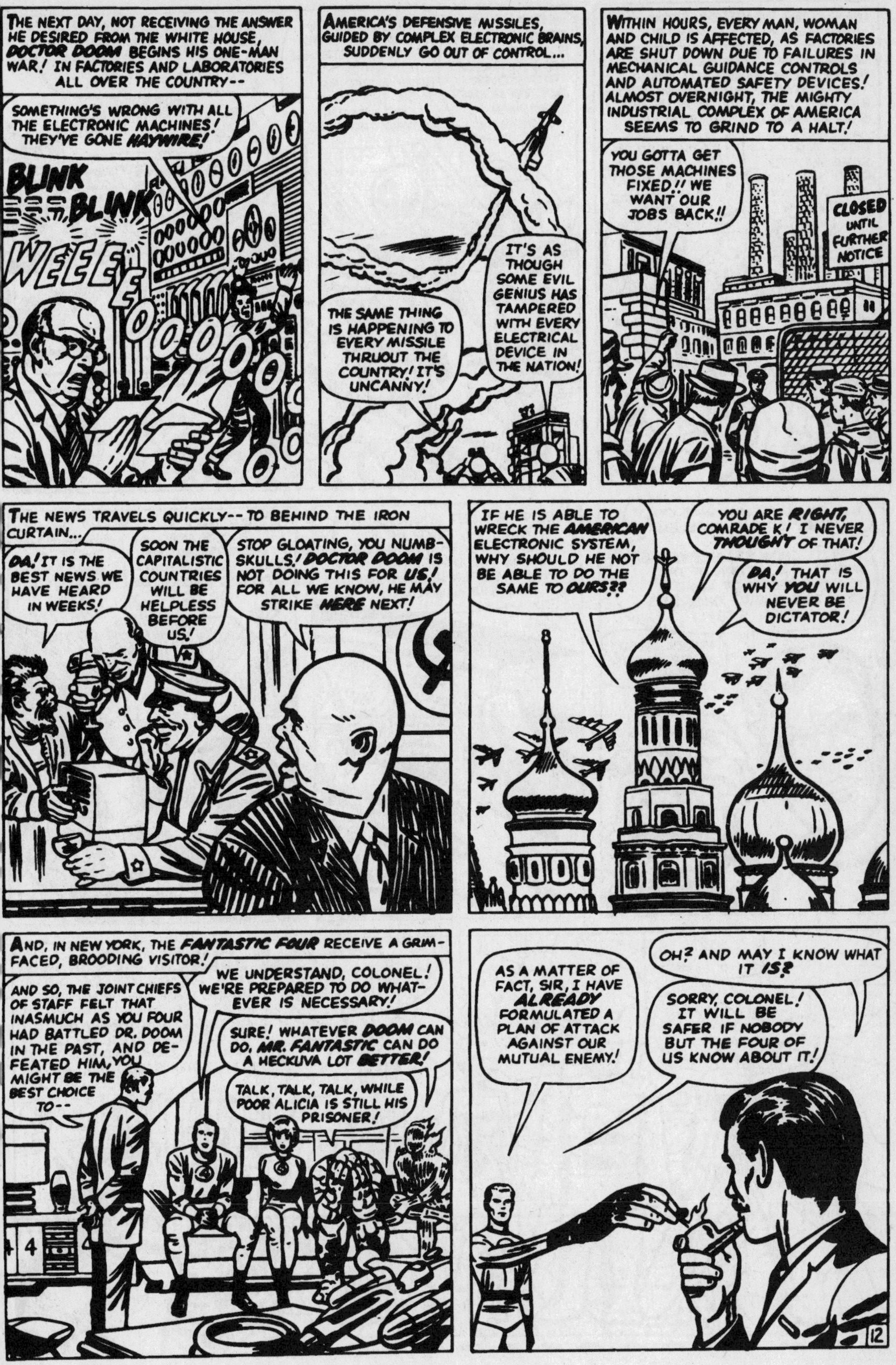
THE NEXT DAY, NOT RECEIVING THE ANSWER HE DESIRED FROM THE WHITE HOUSE, DOCTOR DOOM BEGINS HIS ONE-MAN WAR! IN FACTORIES AND LABORATORIES ALL OVER THE COUNTRY--
SOMETHING'S WRONG WITH ALL THE ELECTRONIC MACHINES! THEY'VE GONE HAYWIRE!
BLINK
BLINK
WEEEEOOOOOOO
AMERICA'S DEFENSIVE MISSILES, GUIDED BY COMPLEX ELECTRONIC BRAINS, SUDDENLY GO OUT OF CONTROL...
THE SAME THING IS HAPPENING TO EVERY MISSILE THRUOUT THE COUNTRY! IT'S UNCANNY!
IT'S AS THOUGH SOME EVIL GENIUS HAS TAMPERED WITH EVERY ELECTRICAL DEVICE IN THE NATION!
WITHIN HOURS, EVERY MAN, WOMAN AND CHILD IS AFFECTED, AS FACTORIES ARE SHUT DOWN DUE TO FAILURES IN MECHANICAL GUIDANCE CONTROLS AND AUTOMATED SAFETY DEVICES! ALMOST OVERNIGHT, THE MIGHTY INDUSTRIAL COMPLEX OF AMERICA SEEMS TO GRIND TO A HALT!
YOU GOTTA GET THOSE MACHINES FIXED!! WE WANT OUR JOBS BACK!!
CLOSED UNTIL FURTHER NOTICE
THE NEWS TRAVELS QUICKLY-- TO BEHIND THE IRON CURTAIN...
DA! IT IS THE BEST NEWS WE HAVE HEARD IN WEEKS!
SOON THE CAPITALISTIC COUNTRIES WILL BE HELPLESS BEFORE US!
STOP GLOATING, YOU NUMBSKULLS! DOCTOR DOOM IS NOT DOING THIS FOR US! FOR ALL WE KNOW, HE MAY STRIKE HERE NEXT!
IF HE IS ABLE TO WRECK THE AMERICAN ELECTRONIC SYSTEM, WHY SHOULD HE NOT BE ABLE TO DO THE SAME TO OURS??
YOU ARE RIGHT, COMRADE K! I NEVER THOUGHT OF THAT!
DA! THAT IS WHY YOU WILL NEVER BE DICTATOR!
AND, IN NEW YORK, THE FANTASTIC FOUR RECEIVE A GRIM-FACED, BROODING VISITOR!
AND SO, THE JOINT CHIEFS OF STAFF FELT THAT INASMUCH AS YOU FOUR HAD BATTLED DR. DOOM IN THE PAST, AND DEFEATED HIM, YOU MIGHT BE THE BEST CHOICE TO--
WE UNDERSTAND, COLONEL! WE'RE PREPARED TO DO WHATEVER IS NECESSARY!
SURE! WHATEVER DOOM CAN DO, MR. FANTASTIC CAN DO A HECKUVA LOT BETTER!
TALK, TALK, TALK, WHILE POOR ALICIA IS STILL HIS PRISONER!
AS A MATTER OF FACT, SIR, I HAVE ALREADY FORMULATED A PLAN OF ATTACK AGAINST OUR MUTUAL ENEMY!
OH? AND MAY I KNOW WHAT IT IS?
SORRY, COLONEL! IT WILL BE SAFER IF NOBODY BUT THE FOUR OF US KNOW ABOUT IT!
12

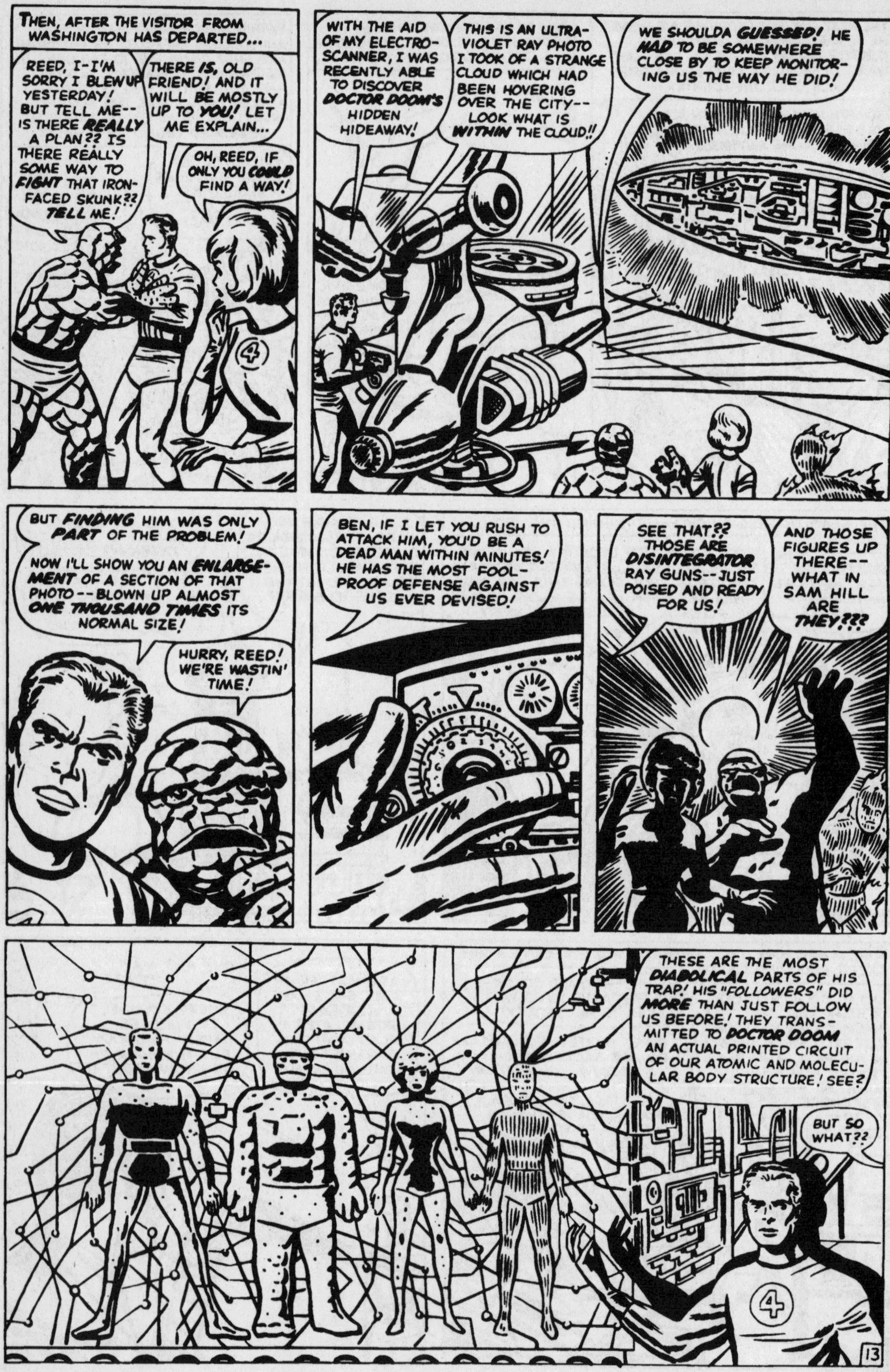

THEN, AFTER THE VISITOR FROM WASHINGTON HAS DEPARTED...
REED, I-I'M SORRY I BLEW UP YESTERDAY! BUT TELL ME-- IS THERE REALLY A PLAN?? IS THERE REALLY SOME WAY TO FIGHT THAT IRON-FACED SKUNK?? TELL ME!
THERE IS, OLD FRIEND! AND IT WILL BE MOSTLY UP TO YOU! LET ME EXPLAIN...
OH, REED, IF ONLY YOU COULD FIND A WAY!
WITH THE AID OF MY ELECTRO-SCANNER, I WAS RECENTLY ABLE TO DISCOVER DOCTOR DOOM'S HIDDEN HIDEAWAY!
THIS IS AN ULTRA-VIOLET RAY PHOTO I TOOK OF A STRANGE CLOUD WHICH HAD BEEN HOVERING OVER THE CITY-- LOOK WHAT IS WITHIN THE CLOUD!!
WE SHOULDA GUESSED! HE HAD TO BE SOMEWHERE CLOSE BY TO KEEP MONITORING US THE WAY HE DID!
BUT FINDING HIM WAS ONLY PART OF THE PROBLEM!
NOW I'LL SHOW YOU AN ENLARGEMENT OF A SECTION OF THAT PHOTO--BLOWN UP ALMOST ONE THOUSAND TIMES ITS NORMAL SIZE!
HURRY, REED! WE'RE WASTIN' TIME!
BEN, IF I LET YOU RUSH TO ATTACK HIM, YOU'D BE A DEAD MAN WITHIN MINUTES! HE HAS THE MOST FOOL-PROOF DEFENSE AGAINST US EVER DEVISED!
SEE THAT?? THOSE ARE DISINTEGRATOR RAY GUNS--JUST POISED AND READY FOR US!
AND THOSE FIGURES UP THERE-- WHAT IN SAM HILL ARE THEY???
THESE ARE THE MOST DIABOLICAL PARTS OF HIS TRAP! HIS "FOLLOWERS" DID MORE THAN JUST FOLLOW US BEFORE! THEY TRANSMITTED TO DOCTOR DOOM AN ACTUAL PRINTED CIRCUIT OF OUR ATOMIC AND MOLECULAR BODY STRUCTURE! SEE?
BUT SO WHAT??
13

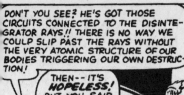

DON'T YOU SEE? HE'S GOT THOSE CIRCUITS CONNECTED TO THE DISINTEGRATOR RAYS!! THERE IS NO WAY WE COULD SLIP PAST THE RAYS WITHOUT THE VERY ATOMIC STRUCTURE OF OUR BODIES TRIGGERING OUR OWN DESTRUCTION!

THEN-- IT'S HOPELESS! BUT, YOU SAID YOU HAD A WAY--??

I DO! AND THE WHOLE THING DEPENDS ON YOU!

HOW? FOR THE LOVE OF PETE, SPILL IT, WILLYA??!

THERE IS ONLY ONE OF US WHO CAN CHANGE HIS ATOMIC STRUCTURE! WHEN YOU BECOME BEN GRIMM, YOUR ATOMS AND MOLECULES ARE COMPLETELY RE-ARRANGED! THAT'S THE ONE THING DOOM DIDN'T PROVIDE FOR IN HIS TRAP!

I'VE GOT TO PREPARE A SOLUTION THAT WILL TURN YOU BACK TO BEN GRIMM LONG ENOUGH TO SLIP BY DOOM'S DEFENSES!

THE MINUTES TURN TO LONG HOURS AS MR. FANTASTIC WORKS AS NO SCIENTIST HAS EVER WORKED BEFORE...

I CAN'T AFFORD A MISTAKE! IF HE CHANGES BACK TO THE THING TOO SOON, THE RAYS WILL STRIKE HIM!!

WHAT HAPPENED TO THE HEATING UNIT?? I MUST HAVE MORE CONCENTRATED HEAT!!

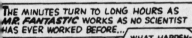

QUICKLY, TORCH, WHILE THE SERUM IS STILL VOLATILE!

I HEAR YOU TALKIN', BOSS! THIS OUGHTTA DO THE TRICK!

FINALLY, AS REED'S TALL FRAME SLUMPS INTO A CHAIR, ON THE VERGE OF EXHAUSTION...

BEN, BEN... I CAN'T GUARANTEE IT WILL MAINTAIN ITS POTENCY LONG ENOUGH! IF YOU CHANGE TO THE THING TOO SOON--YOU KNOW WHAT IT WILL MEAN??

GIMME THAT STUFF, MISTER! ALICIA'S LIFE MAY BE AT STAKE UP THERE!

NO MATTER WHAT HAPPENS, REED, I KNOW YOU TRIED YOUR BEST! AND IF MY LIFE'S GOTTA DEPEND ON SOMEONE, I'D RATHER IT BE YOU THAN ANYONE I KNOW, YA OLD HOUND DOG!

WELL, BOTTOMS UP, KIDDIES!

IT'S WORKING! I CAN FEEL IT! IT'S WORKING!

I KNEW IT WOULD, BEN GRIMM! THE ONLY QUESTION NOW IS-- FOR HOW LONG???

14

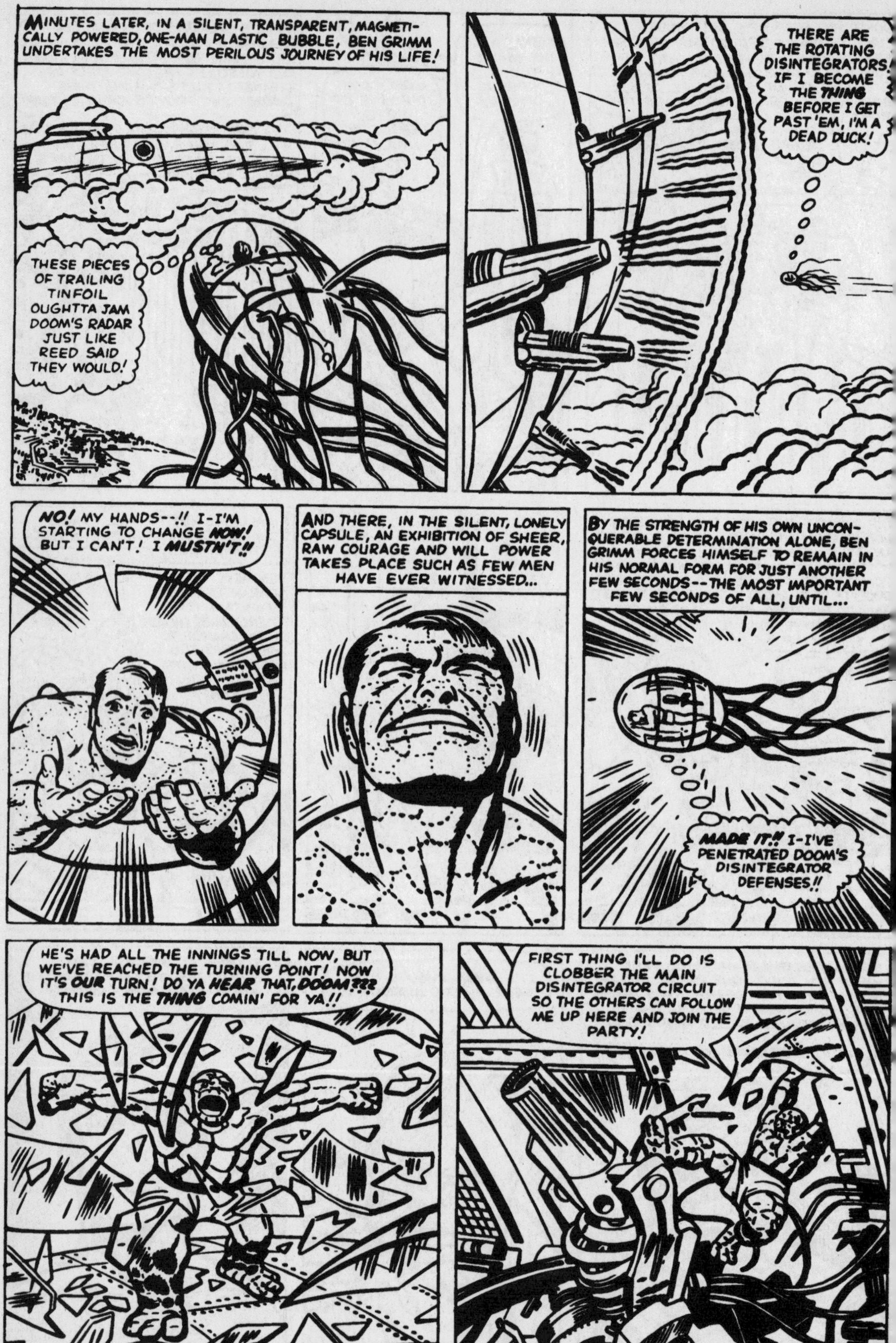
MINUTES LATER, IN A SILENT, TRANSPARENT, MAGNETICALLY POWERED, ONE-MAN PLASTIC BUBBLE, BEN GRIMM UNDERTAKES THE MOST PERILOUS JOURNEY OF HIS LIFE!
THESE PIECES OF TRAILING TINFOIL OUGHTTA JAM DOOM'S RADAR JUST LIKE REED SAID THEY WOULD!
THERE ARE THE ROTATING DISINTEGRATORS. IF I BECOME THE THING BEFORE I GET PAST 'EM, I'M A DEAD DUCK!
NO! MY HANDS--!! I-I'M STARTING TO CHANGE NOW! BUT I CAN'T! I MUSTN'T!!
AND THERE, IN THE SILENT, LONELY CAPSULE, AN EXHIBITION OF SHEER, RAW COURAGE AND WILL POWER TAKES PLACE SUCH AS FEW MEN HAVE EVER WITNESSED...
BY THE STRENGTH OF HIS OWN UNCONQUERABLE DETERMINATION ALONE, BEN GRIMM FORCES HIMSELF TO REMAIN IN HIS NORMAL FORM FOR JUST ANOTHER FEW SECONDS--THE MOST IMPORTANT FEW SECONDS OF ALL, UNTIL...
MADE IT!! I-I'VE PENETRATED DOOM'S DISINTEGRATOR DEFENSES!!
HE'S HAD ALL THE INNINGS TILL NOW, BUT WE'VE REACHED THE TURNING POINT! NOW IT'S OUR TURN! DO YA HEAR THAT, DOOM??? THIS IS THE THING COMIN' FOR YA!!
FIRST THING I'LL DO IS CLOBBER THE MAIN DISINTEGRATOR CIRCUIT SO THE OTHERS CAN FOLLOW ME UP HERE AND JOIN THE PARTY!
15

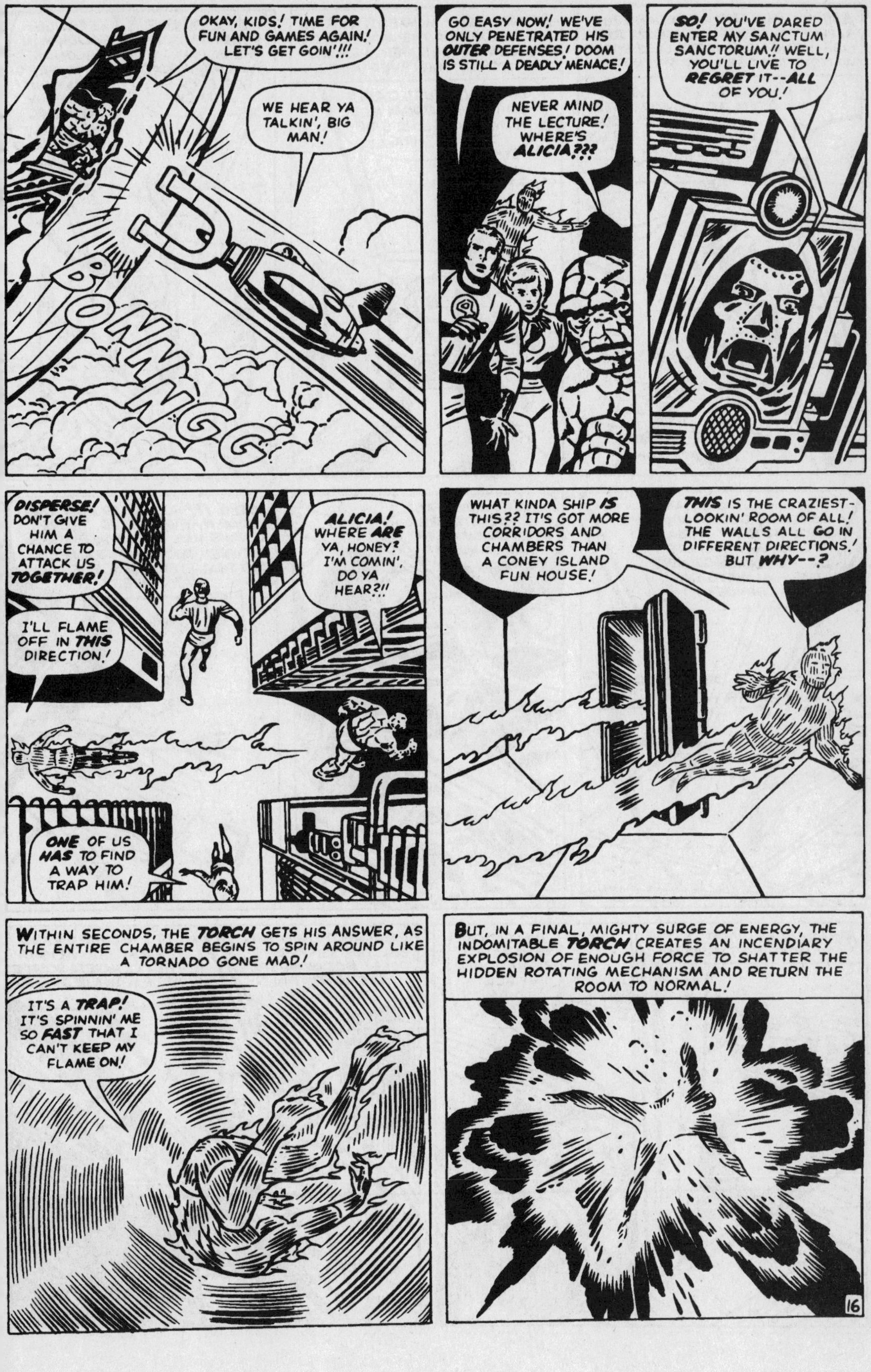
OKAY, KIDS! TIME FOR FUN AND GAMES AGAIN! LET'S GET GOIN'!!!
WE HEAR YA TALKIN', BIG MAN!
BONNNGG
GO EASY NOW! WE'VE ONLY PENETRATED HIS OUTER DEFENSES! DOOM IS STILL A DEADLY MENACE!
NEVER MIND THE LECTURE! WHERE'S ALICIA???
SO! YOU'VE DARED ENTER MY SANCTUM SANCTORUM!! WELL, YOU'LL LIVE TO REGRET IT--ALL OF YOU!
DISPERSE! DON'T GIVE HIM A CHANCE TO ATTACK US TOGETHER!
I'LL FLAME OFF IN THIS DIRECTION!
ALICIA! WHERE ARE YA, HONEY? I'M COMIN', DO YA HEAR?!!
ONE OF US HAS TO FIND A WAY TO TRAP HIM!
WHAT KINDA SHIP IS THIS?? IT'S GOT MORE CORRIDORS AND CHAMBERS THAN A CONEY ISLAND FUN HOUSE!
THIS IS THE CRAZIEST-LOOKIN' ROOM OF ALL! THE WALLS ALL GO IN DIFFERENT DIRECTIONS! BUT WHY--?
WITHIN SECONDS, THE TORCH GETS HIS ANSWER, AS THE ENTIRE CHAMBER BEGINS TO SPIN AROUND LIKE A TORNADO GONE MAD!
IT'S A TRAP! IT'S SPINNIN' ME SO FAST THAT I CAN'T KEEP MY FLAME ON!
BUT, IN A FINAL, MIGHTY SURGE OF ENERGY, THE INDOMITABLE TORCH CREATES AN INCENDIARY EXPLOSION OF ENOUGH FORCE TO SHATTER THE HIDDEN ROTATING MECHANISM AND RETURN THE ROOM TO NORMAL!
16

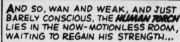

Panel 1:

AND SO, WAN AND WEAK, AND JUST BARELY CONSCIOUS, THE *HUMAN TORCH* LIES IN THE NOW-MOTIONLESS ROOM, WAITING TO REGAIN HIS STRENGTH...

GUESS THIS PUTS *ME* OUTTA ACTION FOR A FEW MINUTES, BUT *DOC DOOM* IS STILL GONNA HAVE HIS HANDS FULL WITH MY THREE PARDS!

Panel 2:

AT THAT VERY MOMENT, WE FIND THE LEADER OF THE MOST COLORFUL COMBO OF SUPER HEROES THE WORLD HAS EVER KNOWN...

THAT DOOR JUST CLOSED BEHIND ME! *DOOM* MUST BE WATCHING! HE'S UP TO SOMETHING!

Panel 3:

WET CEMENT POURING INTO THE ROOM! HE WAS *PREPARED* FOR SUCH AN ATTACK!

IT WILL SOLIDIFY IN SECONDS, AND THERE'S NO WAY OUT! --FOR ANY *NORMAL* HUMAN, THAT IS!

Panel 4:

BUT A MAN WHO CAN MAKE HIS BODY THIN ENOUGH TO FIT THRU THE OXYGEN POCKETS OF THE POROUS CEMENT ITSELF *ALWAYS* HAS A CHANCE!

Panel 5:

HAVE TO MOVE FAST! THE POCKETS ARE GROWING SMALLER AND SMALLER!

Panel 6:

MADE IT! NO MATTER *HOW* TIGHT A DOOR MAY BE FITTED, THERE ALWAYS HAS TO BE *SOME* SPACE BETWEEN DOOR AND FRAME-- AND THAT LITTLE SPACE IS ALL THAT I NEED!

Panel 7:

MEANWHILE, WHAT OF THE RAMPAGING *THING*???

THE FLOOR SEPARATED RIGHT UNDER MY FEET!! I-I'M FALLIN'!!

Panel 8:

CAN'T HOLD ONTO THIS BLASTED SLIPPERY POLE! *DOOM* MUSTA *GREASED* IT IN ADVANCE!

IF I HIT THE GROUND FROM THIS HEIGHT, THEY'LL HAVETA SCRAPE ME UP WITH A *BLOTTER!*

17

BUT I CAN'T FALL!! ALICIA'S DEPENDIN' ON ME! I CAN'T FAIL HER!
I GOTTA HANG ON! I GOTTA!!
I DID IT-- -GASP-! NOW-- IF I CAN JUST GET BACK UP--
THAT'S IT! JUST A LITTLE FURTHER! AND THEN--IT'LL BE DOCTOR DOOM AN' ME!
BUT, AT THAT VERY MOMENT, IN HIS HIDDEN VIEWING CHAMBER...
BAH! THAT ACCURSED FOURSOME HAS MORE LIVES THAN A PACK OF CATS!!
BUT EVEN THE FANTASTIC FOUR WILL NOT BE ABLE TO SURVIVE THE DREAD FURY OF MY HURTLING POWER SPHERES!
THERE THEY ARE NOW, TOGETHER AGAIN! I DO NOT SEE THE GIRL, BUT SHE IS UNIMPORTANT! ONCE MY POWER SPHERES HAVE DESTROYED THEM, I CAN DISPOSE OF THE INVISIBLE GIRL AT MY LEISURE!
AH, MY GREATEST WEAPONS ARE WORKING PERFECTLY! ATTRACTED BY THEIR BODY HEAT, THE SPHERES ARE COMPLETELY ENCASING THE TRAPPED TRIO!
18

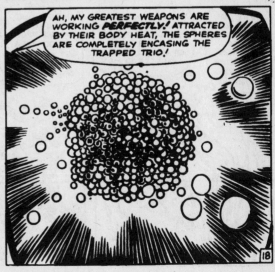

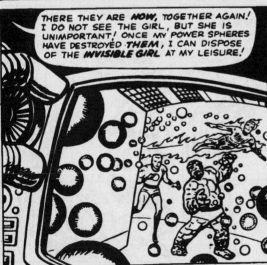

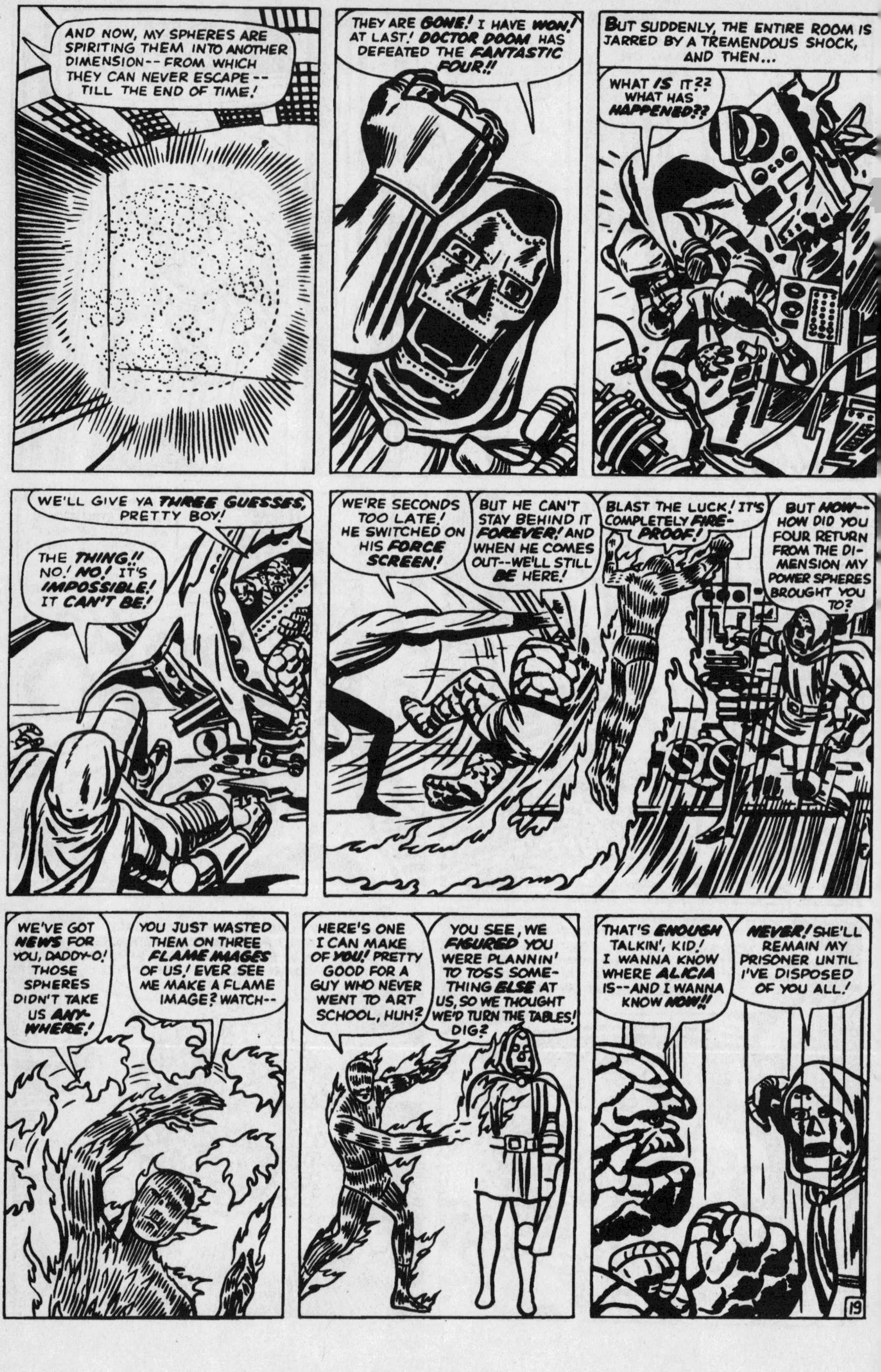
AND NOW, MY SPHERES ARE SPIRITING THEM INTO ANOTHER DIMENSION-- FROM WHICH THEY CAN NEVER ESCAPE-- TILL THE END OF TIME!
THEY ARE GONE! I HAVE WON! AT LAST! DOCTOR DOOM HAS DEFEATED THE FANTASTIC FOUR!!
BUT SUDDENLY, THE ENTIRE ROOM IS JARRED BY A TREMENDOUS SHOCK, AND THEN...
WHAT IS IT?? WHAT HAS HAPPENED??
WE'LL GIVE YA THREE GUESSES, PRETTY BOY!
THE THING!! NO! NO! IT'S IMPOSSIBLE! IT CAN'T BE!
WE'RE SECONDS TOO LATE! HE SWITCHED ON HIS FORCE SCREEN!
BUT HE CAN'T STAY BEHIND IT FOREVER! AND WHEN HE COMES OUT--WE'LL STILL BE HERE!
BLAST THE LUCK! IT'S COMPLETELY FIRE-PROOF!
BUT HOW--HOW DID YOU FOUR RETURN FROM THE DIMENSION MY POWER SPHERES BROUGHT YOU TO?
WE'VE GOT NEWS FOR YOU, DADDY-O! THOSE SPHERES DIDN'T TAKE US ANYWHERE!
YOU JUST WASTED THEM ON THREE FLAME IMAGES OF US! EVER SEE ME MAKE A FLAME IMAGE? WATCH--
HERE'S ONE I CAN MAKE OF YOU! PRETTY GOOD FOR A GUY WHO NEVER WENT TO ART SCHOOL, HUH?
YOU SEE, WE FIGURED YOU WERE PLANNIN' TO TOSS SOMETHING ELSE AT US, SO WE THOUGHT WE'D TURN THE TABLES! DIG?
THAT'S ENOUGH TALKIN', KID! I WANNA KNOW WHERE ALICIA IS--AND I WANNA KNOW NOW!!
NEVER! SHE'LL REMAIN MY PRISONER UNTIL I'VE DISPOSED OF YOU ALL!
19

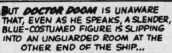

BUT DOCTOR DOOM IS UNAWARE THAT, EVEN AS HE SPEAKS, A SLENDER, BLUE-COSTUMED FIGURE IS SLIPPING INTO AN UNGUARDED ROOM AT THE OTHER END OF THE SHIP...

AT LAST! I'VE FOUND HER...

FOOTSTEPS!! WHO--?

ALICIA DEAR, IT'S ME, SUE STORM! DON'T SAY A WORD! JUST DO AS I SAY! DOCTOR DOOM WILL RETURN AT ANY MOMENT!

AND SO, A HURRIED EXCHANGE TAKES PLACE...

BUT, SUE-- WHEN HE FINDS YOU HERE IN MY PLACE, YOUR LIFE WON'T BE WORTH--

HUSH! JUST HIDE IN THAT CORRIDOR, AS I TOLD YOU!

AND, SECONDS LATER, DOCTOR DOOM ENTERS FROM THE OTHER DOOR...

NOW TO SEIZE HER AND USE HER AS A HOSTAGE! THEY WON'T DARE ATTACK ME SO LONG AS I HAVE THE GIRL!

IT'S HIM! THIS IS THE SHOW-DOWN!

WHA--?? SHE--SHE VANISHED!! BUT THAT ISN'T POSSIBLE-- UNLESS--

OF COURSE! I SHOULD HAVE GUESSED! IT'S THE INVISIBLE GIRL! SHE MUST HAVE CHANGED PLACES WITH ALICIA!

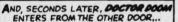

YOU FOOL! ONE HOSTAGE IS AS GOOD AS ANOTHER TO ME! YOU SHALL SERVE AS MY PRISONER JUST AS WELL AS THE BLIND GIRL!

YOU'RE MAKING ONE SMALL MISTAKE, MY FRIEND! IT IS YOU WHO ARE MY PRISONER!

SLAM!

YOU DARE SPEAK SO TO DOCTOR DOOM??! YOU SHALL LIVE TO REGRET IT, WOMAN!

WE'LL SEE WHO'S GOING TO REGRET WHAT! I'VE BEEN WAITING FOR A CHANCE TO PROVE WHAT I CAN DO WITHOUT THE OTHER THREE... AND NOW I'VE GOT IT!

OOOF!

20

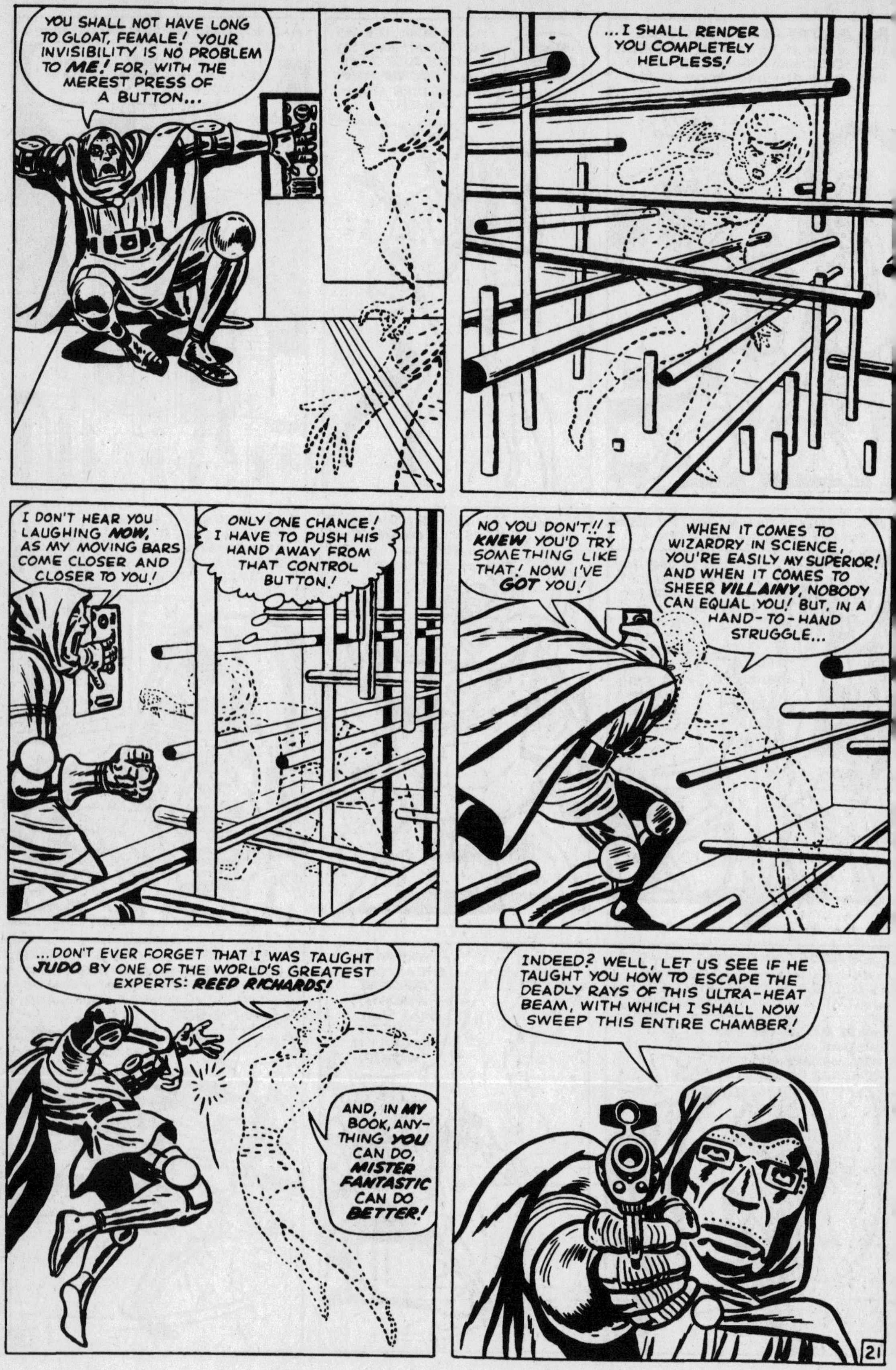
YOU SHALL NOT HAVE LONG TO GLOAT, FEMALE! YOUR INVISIBILITY IS NO PROBLEM TO ME! FOR, WITH THE MEREST PRESS OF A BUTTON...
...I SHALL RENDER YOU COMPLETELY HELPLESS!
I DON'T HEAR YOU LAUGHING NOW, AS MY MOVING BARS COME CLOSER AND CLOSER TO YOU!
ONLY ONE CHANCE! I HAVE TO PUSH HIS HAND AWAY FROM THAT CONTROL BUTTON!
NO YOU DON'T!! I KNEW YOU'D TRY SOMETHING LIKE THAT! NOW I'VE GOT YOU!
WHEN IT COMES TO WIZARDRY IN SCIENCE, YOU'RE EASILY MY SUPERIOR! AND WHEN IT COMES TO SHEER VILLAINY, NOBODY CAN EQUAL YOU! BUT, IN A HAND-TO-HAND STRUGGLE...
...DON'T EVER FORGET THAT I WAS TAUGHT JUDO BY ONE OF THE WORLD'S GREATEST EXPERTS: REED RICHARDS!
AND, IN MY BOOK, ANYTHING YOU CAN DO, MISTER FANTASTIC CAN DO BETTER!
INDEED? WELL, LET US SEE IF HE TAUGHT YOU HOW TO ESCAPE THE DEADLY RAYS OF THIS ULTRA-HEAT BEAM, WITH WHICH I SHALL NOW SWEEP THIS ENTIRE CHAMBER!
21

BUT, SUDDENLY...

BROTHER, YOUR CHAMBER-SWEEPIN' DAYS ARE *OVER!*

YOU--YOU *FOUND ME*-- SO *SOON??!*

BUT I SHALL *NEVER* SUFFER THE HUMILIATION OF BEING CAPTURED BY THE LIKES OF *YOU!!*

COME BACK! YA CAN'T CHEAT ME OUTTA MY REVENGE THIS WAY!!

BEN! GET OUT OF THE WAY! I CAN STILL REACH OUT AND GRAB HIM-- BEN--NO! IT'S *TOO LATE* NOW!

SWIFTLY, SILENTLY, THE AWESOME FORM OF THE GREATEST MENACE OF OUR AGE PLUMMETS EARTHWARD... DOWN-- DOWN-- DOWN-- UNTIL IT IS LOST FROM SIGHT IN THE BILLOWING CLOUDS BELOW!

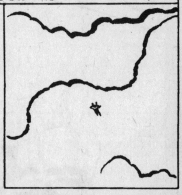

A FEW SECONDS LATER...

BEN? MY DARLING-- IT'S *YOU!* I *KNOW* IT IS!

ALICIA! I'M *HERE*, BABY! EVERY-THING'S OKAY NOW!

JOHNNY! *SUE* IS GONE! WE'VE GOT TO *FIND* HER!

DON'T WORRY, REED DEAR-- YOU NEVER *LOST* ME!

SUE! YOU'RE ALL RIGHT! THAT MEANS OUR TRIUMPH IS COMPLETE!

SUE, DARLING --IF ANYTHING HAD HAPPENED TO YOU--

BENJAMIN GRIMM-- *STOP!* YOU'RE MAKING MY *HEAD* SPIN!

THAT'S WHAT *YOU* DO TO *ME*, DOLL-- EVERY TIME I *LOOK* AT YA!

YEESH! WHAT A LOT OF *MUSH!* I DON'T *BLAME* DOCTOR DOOM FOR *JUMPIN'!!*

BUT THE TORCH HASN'T MUCH TIME TO WORRY ABOUT THAT "MUSH" FOR NEXT ISSUE THE *F.F.* BATTLE A FOE WHO HAS ALL THE POWERS *THEY* HAVE-- AND *MORE!* SEE YOU THEN!

22

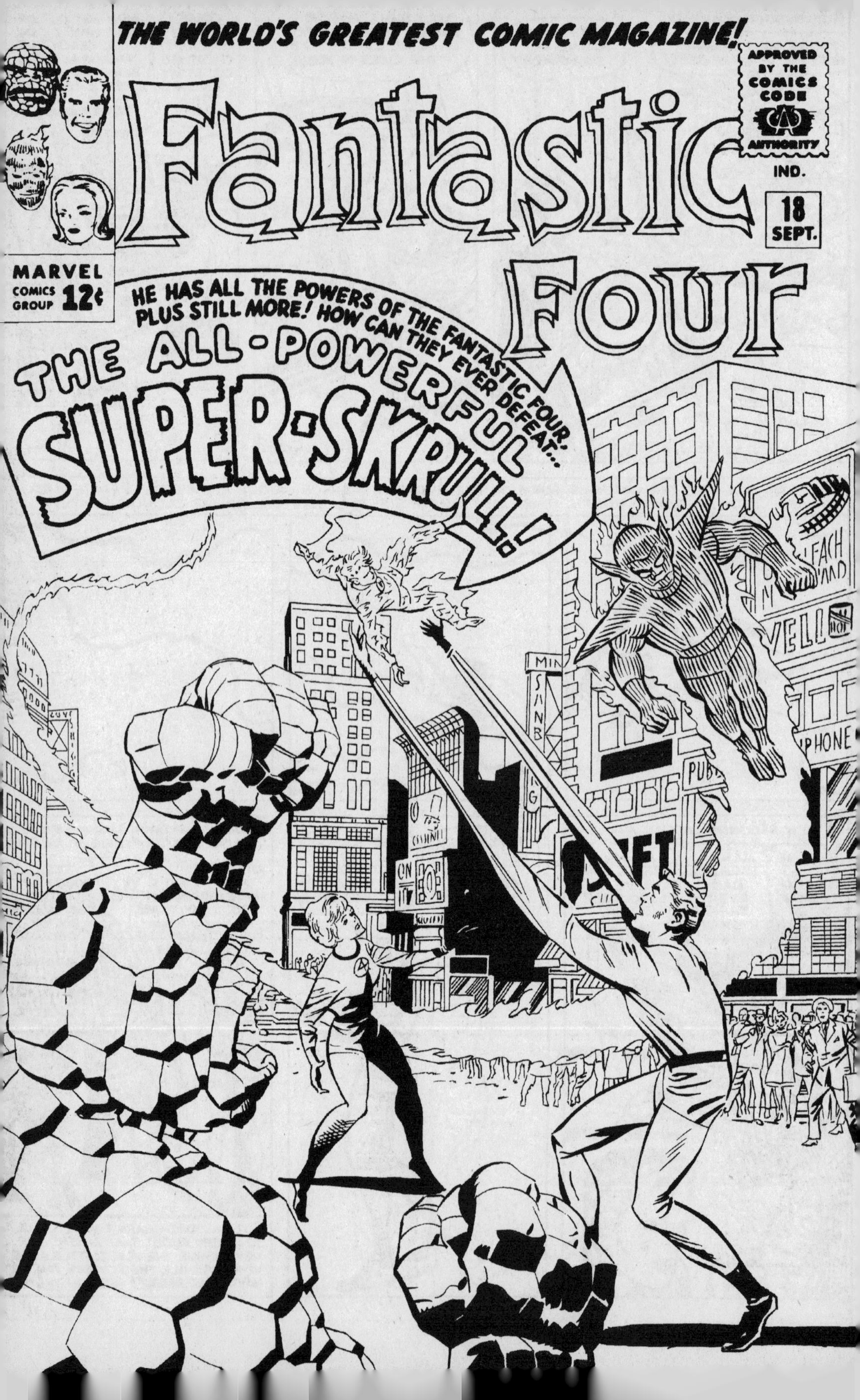
THE WORLD'S GREATEST COMIC MAGAZINE!
APPROVED BY THE COMICS CODE AUTHORITY
Fantastic Four
IND.
18 SEPT.
MARVEL COMICS GROUP 12¢
HE HAS ALL THE POWERS OF THE FANTASTIC FOUR, PLUS STILL MORE! HOW CAN THEY EVER DEFEAT...
THE ALL-POWERFUL SUPER-SKRULL!

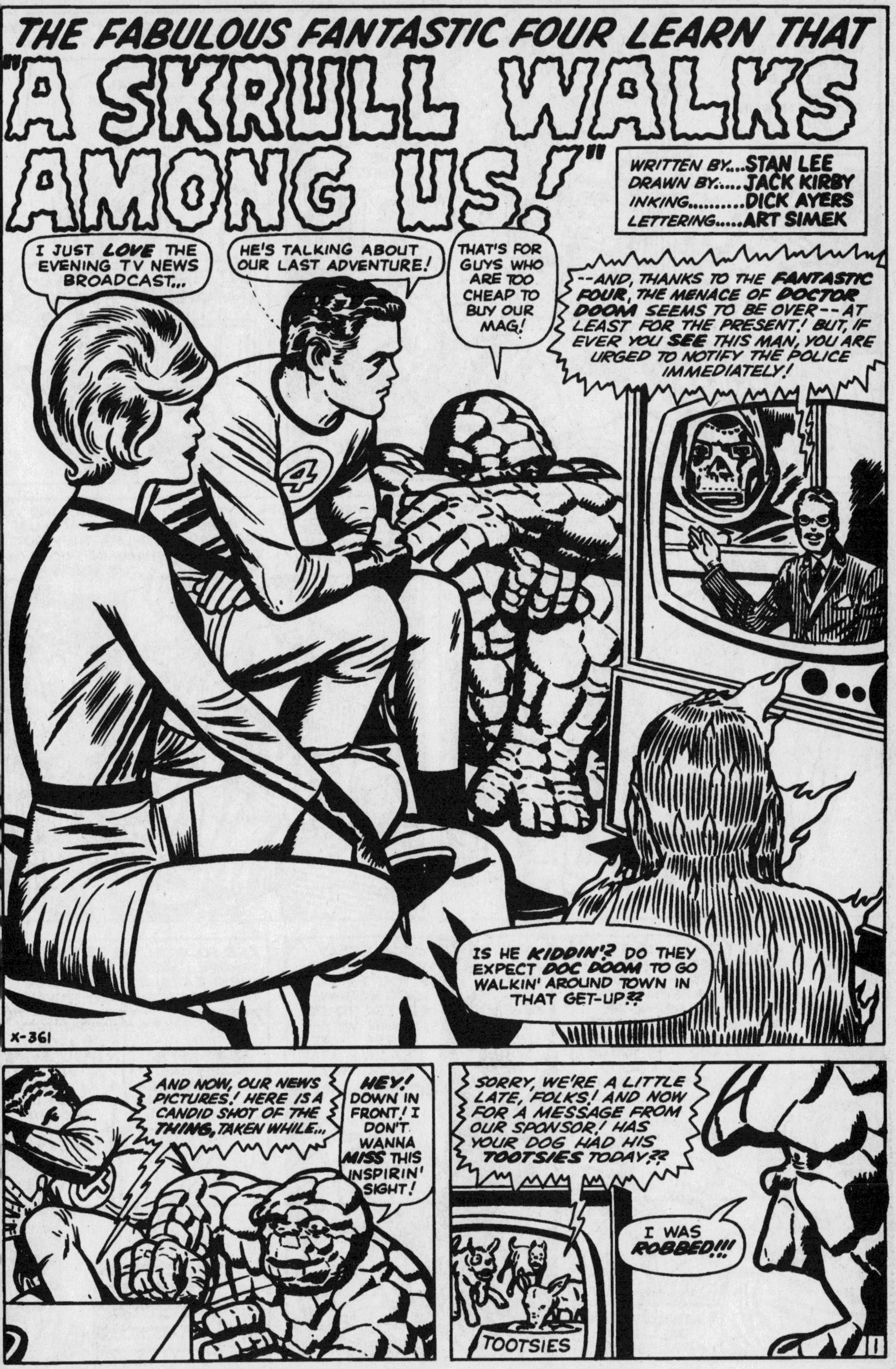
THE FABULOUS FANTASTIC FOUR LEARN THAT
"A SKRULL WALKS AMONG US!"
WRITTEN BY....STAN LEE
DRAWN BY.....JACK KIRBY
INKING..........DICK AYERS
LETTERING.....ART SIMEK
I JUST LOVE THE EVENING TV NEWS BROADCAST...
HE'S TALKING ABOUT OUR LAST ADVENTURE!
THAT'S FOR GUYS WHO ARE TOO CHEAP TO BUY OUR MAG!
--AND, THANKS TO THE FANTASTIC FOUR, THE MENACE OF DOCTOR DOOM SEEMS TO BE OVER-- AT LEAST FOR THE PRESENT! BUT, IF EVER YOU SEE THIS MAN, YOU ARE URGED TO NOTIFY THE POLICE IMMEDIATELY!
IS HE KIDDIN'? DO THEY EXPECT DOC DOOM TO GO WALKIN' AROUND TOWN IN THAT GET-UP??
X-361
AND NOW, OUR NEWS PICTURES! HERE IS A CANDID SHOT OF THE THING, TAKEN WHILE...
HEY! DOWN IN FRONT! I DON'T WANNA MISS THIS INSPIRIN' SIGHT!
SORRY, WE'RE A LITTLE LATE, FOLKS! AND NOW FOR A MESSAGE FROM OUR SPONSOR! HAS YOUR DOG HAD HIS TOOTSIES TODAY??
I WAS ROBBED!!!
TOOTSIES
1

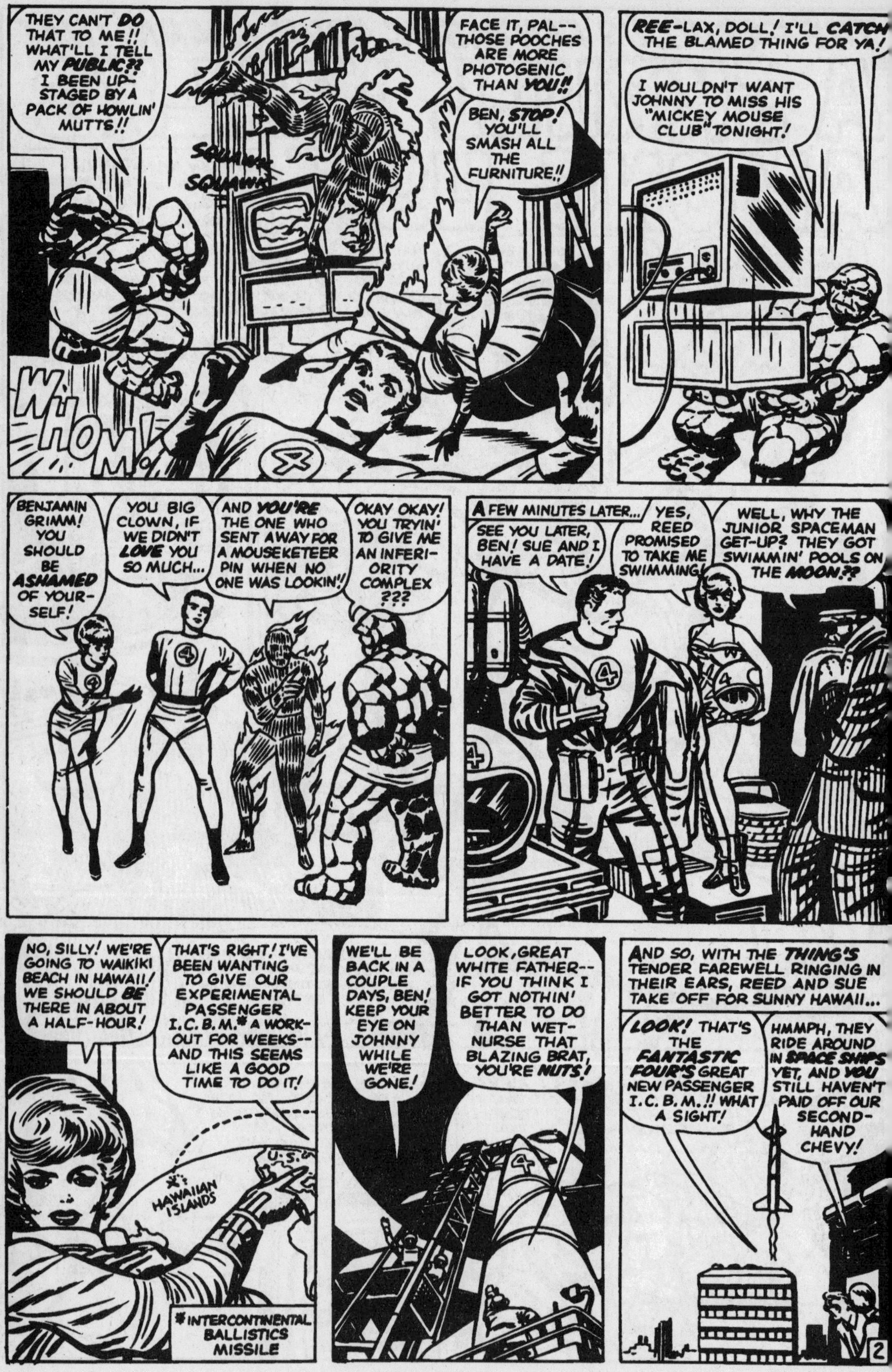
THEY CAN'T DO THAT TO ME!! WHAT'LL I TELL MY PUBLIC?? I BEEN UP-STAGED BY A PACK OF HOWLIN' MUTTS!!
FACE IT, PAL-- THOSE POOCHES ARE MORE PHOTOGENIC THAN YOU!!
BEN, STOP! YOU'LL SMASH ALL THE FURNITURE!!
WHOM!
REE-LAX, DOLL! I'LL CATCH THE BLAMED THING FOR YA!
I WOULDN'T WANT JOHNNY TO MISS HIS "MICKEY MOUSE CLUB" TONIGHT!
BENJAMIN GRIMM! YOU SHOULD BE ASHAMED OF YOURSELF!
YOU BIG CLOWN, IF WE DIDN'T LOVE YOU SO MUCH...
AND YOU'RE THE ONE WHO SENT AWAY FOR A MOUSEKETEER PIN WHEN NO ONE WAS LOOKIN'!
OKAY OKAY! YOU TRYIN' TO GIVE ME AN INFERIORITY COMPLEX ???
A FEW MINUTES LATER...
SEE YOU LATER, BEN! SUE AND I HAVE A DATE!
YES, REED PROMISED TO TAKE ME SWIMMING!
WELL, WHY THE JUNIOR SPACEMAN GET-UP? THEY GOT SWIMMIN' POOLS ON THE MOON??
NO, SILLY! WE'RE GOING TO WAIKIKI BEACH IN HAWAII! WE SHOULD BE THERE IN ABOUT A HALF-HOUR!
THAT'S RIGHT! I'VE BEEN WANTING TO GIVE OUR EXPERIMENTAL PASSENGER I.C.B.M.* A WORK-OUT FOR WEEKS-- AND THIS SEEMS LIKE A GOOD TIME TO DO IT!
U.S.
HAWAIIAN ISLANDS
*INTERCONTINENTAL BALLISTICS MISSILE
WE'LL BE BACK IN A COUPLE DAYS, BEN! KEEP YOUR EYE ON JOHNNY WHILE WE'RE GONE!
LOOK, GREAT WHITE FATHER-- IF YOU THINK I GOT NOTHIN' BETTER TO DO THAN WET-NURSE THAT BLAZING BRAT, YOU'RE NUTS!
AND SO, WITH THE THING'S TENDER FAREWELL RINGING IN THEIR EARS, REED AND SUE TAKE OFF FOR SUNNY HAWAII...
LOOK! THAT'S THE FANTASTIC FOUR'S GREAT NEW PASSENGER I.C.B.M.!! WHAT A SIGHT!
HMMPH, THEY RIDE AROUND IN SPACE SHIPS YET, AND YOU STILL HAVEN'T PAID OFF OUR SECOND-HAND CHEVY!
2

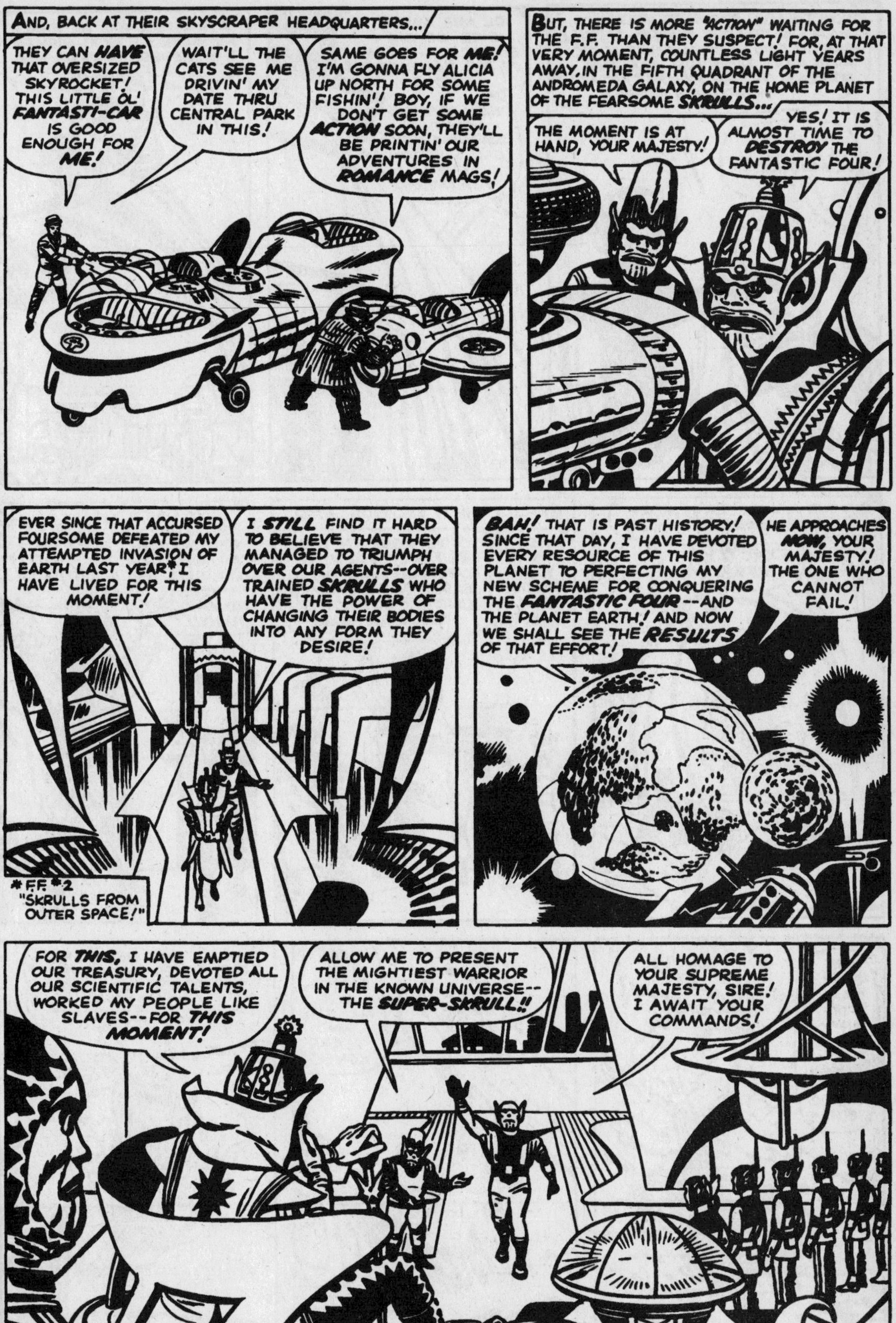

AND, BACK AT THEIR SKYSCRAPER HEADQUARTERS...
THEY CAN HAVE THAT OVERSIZED SKYROCKET! THIS LITTLE OL' FANTASTI-CAR IS GOOD ENOUGH FOR ME!
WAIT'LL THE CATS SEE ME DRIVIN' MY DATE THRU CENTRAL PARK IN THIS!
SAME GOES FOR ME! I'M GONNA FLY ALICIA UP NORTH FOR SOME FISHIN'! BOY, IF WE DON'T GET SOME ACTION SOON, THEY'LL BE PRINTIN' OUR ADVENTURES IN ROMANCE MAGS!
BUT, THERE IS MORE "ACTION" WAITING FOR THE F.F. THAN THEY SUSPECT! FOR, AT THAT VERY MOMENT, COUNTLESS LIGHT YEARS AWAY, IN THE FIFTH QUADRANT OF THE ANDROMEDA GALAXY, ON THE HOME PLANET OF THE FEARSOME SKRULLS...
THE MOMENT IS AT HAND, YOUR MAJESTY!
YES! IT IS ALMOST TIME TO DESTROY THE FANTASTIC FOUR!
EVER SINCE THAT ACCURSED FOURSOME DEFEATED MY ATTEMPTED INVASION OF EARTH LAST YEAR,* I HAVE LIVED FOR THIS MOMENT!
I STILL FIND IT HARD TO BELIEVE THAT THEY MANAGED TO TRIUMPH OVER OUR AGENTS--OVER TRAINED SKRULLS WHO HAVE THE POWER OF CHANGING THEIR BODIES INTO ANY FORM THEY DESIRE!
*F.F. #2 "SKRULLS FROM OUTER SPACE!"
BAH! THAT IS PAST HISTORY! SINCE THAT DAY, I HAVE DEVOTED EVERY RESOURCE OF THIS PLANET TO PERFECTING MY NEW SCHEME FOR CONQUERING THE FANTASTIC FOUR--AND THE PLANET EARTH! AND NOW WE SHALL SEE THE RESULTS OF THAT EFFORT!
HE APPROACHES NOW, YOUR MAJESTY! THE ONE WHO CANNOT FAIL!
FOR THIS, I HAVE EMPTIED OUR TREASURY, DEVOTED ALL OUR SCIENTIFIC TALENTS, WORKED MY PEOPLE LIKE SLAVES--FOR THIS MOMENT!
ALLOW ME TO PRESENT THE MIGHTIEST WARRIOR IN THE KNOWN UNIVERSE--THE SUPER-SKRULL!!
ALL HOMAGE TO YOUR SUPREME MAJESTY, SIRE! I AWAIT YOUR COMMANDS!

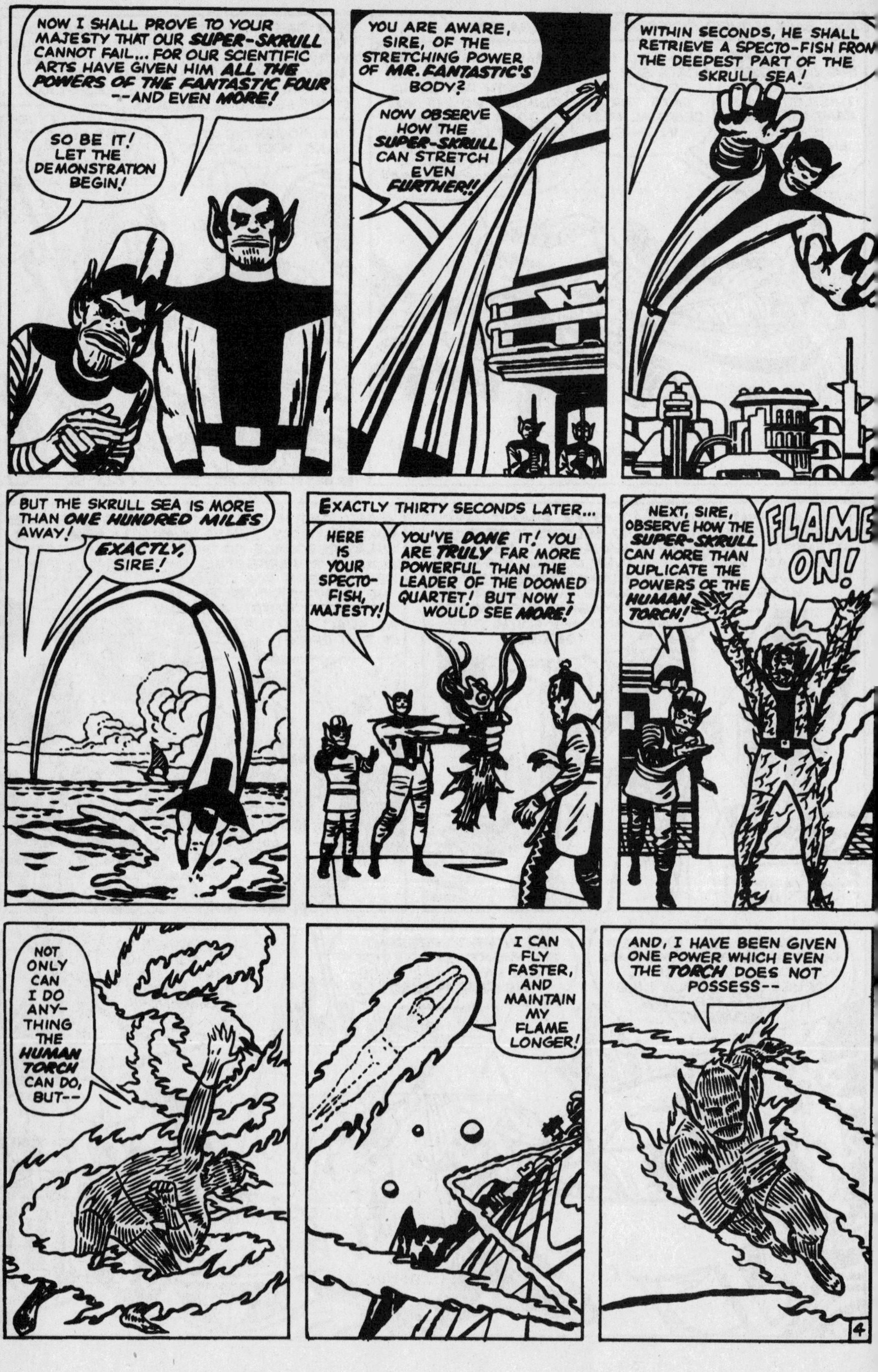
NOW I SHALL PROVE TO YOUR MAJESTY THAT OUR SUPER-SKRULL CANNOT FAIL... FOR OUR SCIENTIFIC ARTS HAVE GIVEN HIM ALL THE POWERS OF THE FANTASTIC FOUR --AND EVEN MORE!
SO BE IT! LET THE DEMONSTRATION BEGIN!
YOU ARE AWARE, SIRE, OF THE STRETCHING POWER OF MR. FANTASTIC'S BODY?
NOW OBSERVE HOW THE SUPER-SKRULL CAN STRETCH EVEN FURTHER!!
WITHIN SECONDS, HE SHALL RETRIEVE A SPECTO-FISH FROM THE DEEPEST PART OF THE SKRULL SEA!
BUT THE SKRULL SEA IS MORE THAN ONE HUNDRED MILES AWAY!
EXACTLY, SIRE!
EXACTLY THIRTY SECONDS LATER...
HERE IS YOUR SPECTO-FISH, MAJESTY!
YOU'VE DONE IT! YOU ARE TRULY FAR MORE POWERFUL THAN THE LEADER OF THE DOOMED QUARTET! BUT NOW I WOULD SEE MORE!
NEXT, SIRE, OBSERVE HOW THE SUPER-SKRULL CAN MORE THAN DUPLICATE THE POWERS OF THE HUMAN TORCH!
FLAME ON!
NOT ONLY CAN I DO ANY-THING THE HUMAN TORCH CAN DO, BUT--
I CAN FLY FASTER, AND MAINTAIN MY FLAME LONGER!
AND, I HAVE BEEN GIVEN ONE POWER WHICH EVEN THE TORCH DOES NOT POSSESS--
4

MY *ANTI-MATTER* FIRE-BALL CAN DESTROY *ANYTHING* --EVEN THE PEAK OF A SMALL MOUNTAIN!!

ENOUGH! I AM ROYALLY IMPRESSED! NOW SHOW ME HIS *OTHER* POWERS! FOR *THIS* TIME WE DARE NOT FAIL!

BEHOLD, MY LORD, HOW THE *SUPER-SKRULL* SHALL NOW EXHIBIT A *STRENGTH* THAT SURPASSES THAT OF THE MIGHTY *THING!*

STANDING ATOP A SPECIALLY CON-STRUCTED PLATFORM, HE SHALL LIFT THE *COSMIC GENERATOR* THAT SUPPLIES ALL THE POWER OF OUR PLANET!

IMPOSSIBLE!

NO, MY LORD--IT IS POSSIBLE--BUT ONLY FOR THE *SUPER-SKRULL!!* THERE IS NO *MACHINE* THAT COULD PERFORM SUCH A FEAT, AND YET--

HE IS *DOING* IT! THIS EXCEEDS MY WILDEST HOPES!

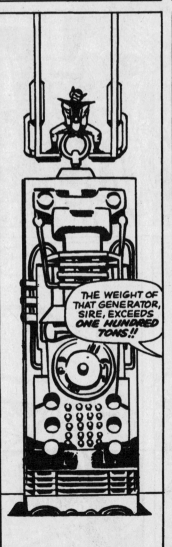

THE WEIGHT OF THAT GENERATOR, SIRE, EXCEEDS *ONE HUNDRED TONS!!*

AND, AS FAR AS WE CAN DETERMINE, THE ABSOLUTE LIMIT WHICH THE *THING* CAN LIFT IS *FIVE TONS!*

5

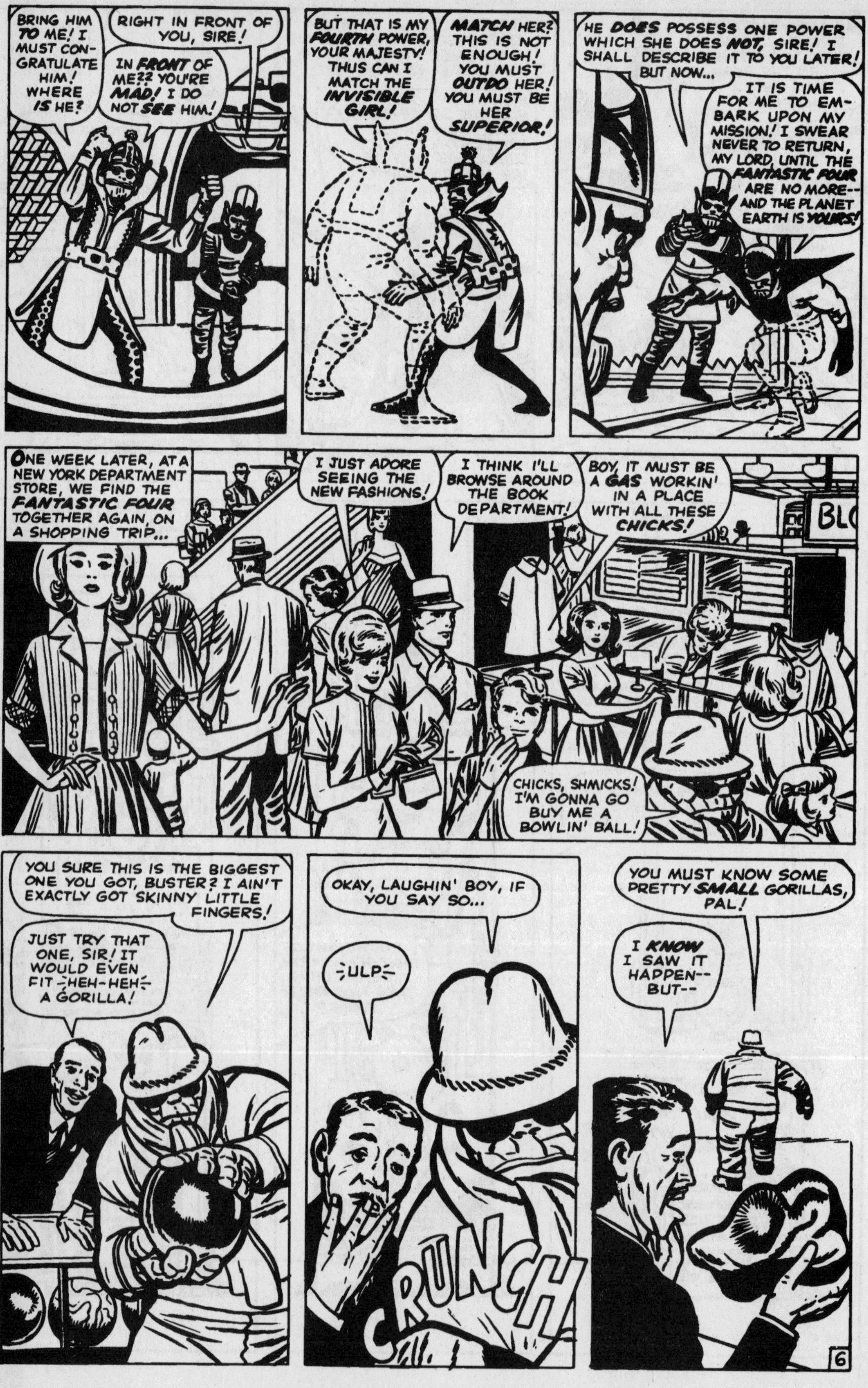

BRING HIM TO ME! I MUST CONGRATULATE HIM! WHERE IS HE?
RIGHT IN FRONT OF YOU, SIRE!
IN FRONT OF ME?? YOU'RE MAD! I DO NOT SEE HIM!
BUT THAT IS MY FOURTH POWER, YOUR MAJESTY! THUS CAN I MATCH THE INVISIBLE GIRL!
MATCH HER? THIS IS NOT ENOUGH! YOU MUST OUTDO HER! YOU MUST BE HER SUPERIOR!
HE DOES POSSESS ONE POWER WHICH SHE DOES NOT, SIRE! I SHALL DESCRIBE IT TO YOU LATER! BUT NOW...
IT IS TIME FOR ME TO EMBARK UPON MY MISSION! I SWEAR NEVER TO RETURN, MY LORD, UNTIL THE FANTASTIC FOUR ARE NO MORE-- AND THE PLANET EARTH IS YOURS!
ONE WEEK LATER, AT A NEW YORK DEPARTMENT STORE, WE FIND THE FANTASTIC FOUR TOGETHER AGAIN, ON A SHOPPING TRIP...
I JUST ADORE SEEING THE NEW FASHIONS!
I THINK I'LL BROWSE AROUND THE BOOK DEPARTMENT!
BOY, IT MUST BE A GAS WORKIN' IN A PLACE WITH ALL THESE CHICKS!
CHICKS, SHMICKS! I'M GONNA GO BUY ME A BOWLIN' BALL!
YOU SURE THIS IS THE BIGGEST ONE YOU GOT, BUSTER? I AIN'T EXACTLY GOT SKINNY LITTLE FINGERS!
JUST TRY THAT ONE, SIR! IT WOULD EVEN FIT -HEH-HEH- A GORILLA!
OKAY, LAUGHIN' BOY, IF YOU SAY SO...
ULP
CRUNCH
YOU MUST KNOW SOME PRETTY SMALL GORILLAS, PAL!
I KNOW I SAW IT HAPPEN-- BUT--
6

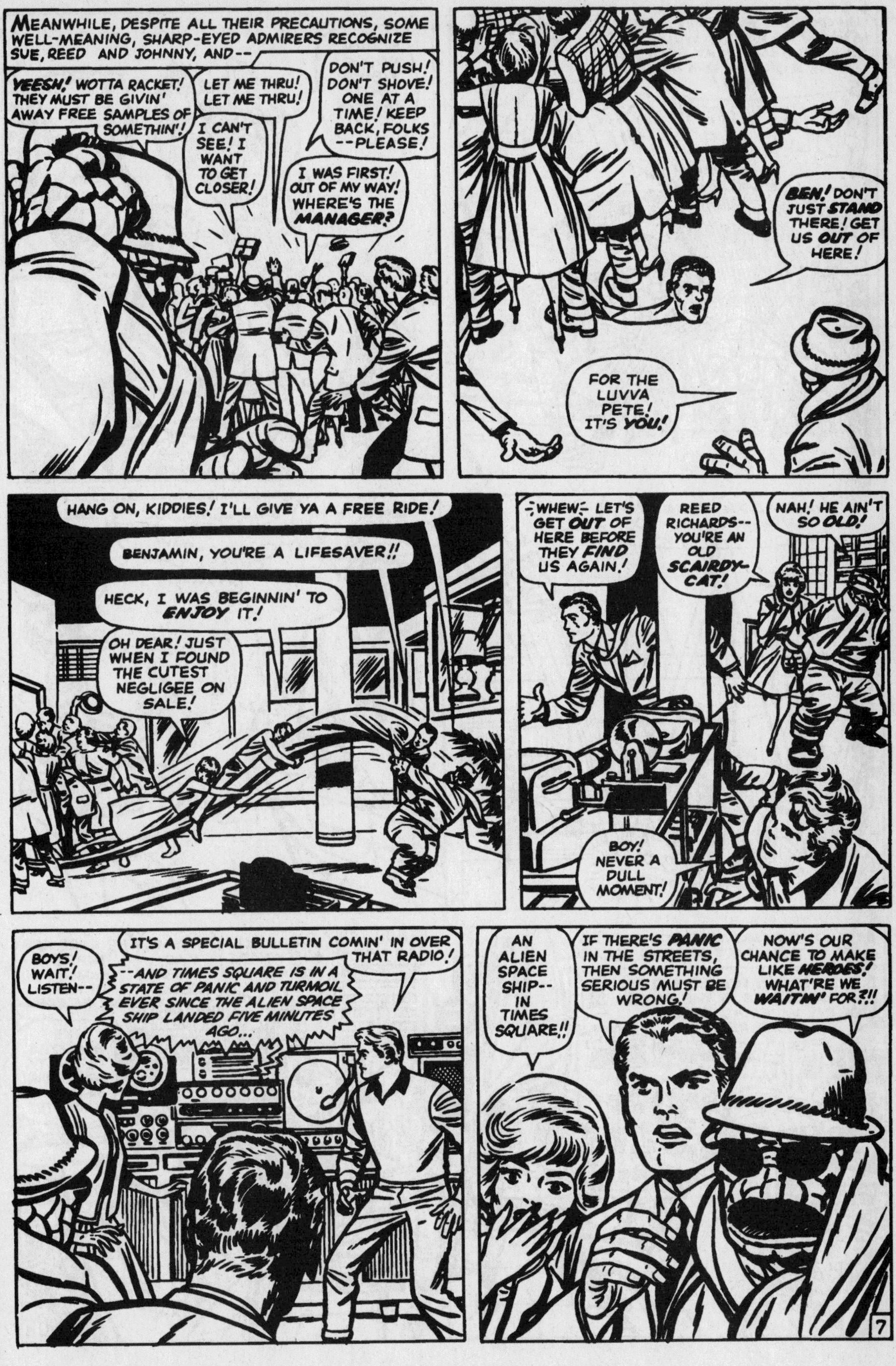
MEANWHILE, DESPITE ALL THEIR PRECAUTIONS, SOME WELL-MEANING, SHARP-EYED ADMIRERS RECOGNIZE SUE, REED AND JOHNNY, AND--
YEESH! WOTTA RACKET! THEY MUST BE GIVIN' AWAY FREE SAMPLES OF SOMETHIN'!
LET ME THRU! LET ME THRU!
I CAN'T SEE! I WANT TO GET CLOSER!
DON'T PUSH! DON'T SHOVE! ONE AT A TIME! KEEP BACK, FOLKS --PLEASE!
I WAS FIRST! OUT OF MY WAY! WHERE'S THE MANAGER?
BEN! DON'T JUST STAND THERE! GET US OUT OF HERE!
FOR THE LUVVA PETE! IT'S YOU!
HANG ON, KIDDIES! I'LL GIVE YA A FREE RIDE!
BENJAMIN, YOU'RE A LIFESAVER!!
HECK, I WAS BEGINNIN' TO ENJOY IT!
OH DEAR! JUST WHEN I FOUND THE CUTEST NEGLIGEE ON SALE!
WHEW - LET'S GET OUT OF HERE BEFORE THEY FIND US AGAIN!
REED RICHARDS-- YOU'RE AN OLD SCAIRDY-CAT!
NAH! HE AIN'T SO OLD!
BOY! NEVER A DULL MOMENT!
BOYS! WAIT! LISTEN--
IT'S A SPECIAL BULLETIN COMIN' IN OVER THAT RADIO!
--AND TIMES SQUARE IS IN A STATE OF PANIC AND TURMOIL EVER SINCE THE ALIEN SPACE SHIP LANDED FIVE MINUTES AGO...
AN ALIEN SPACE SHIP-- IN TIMES SQUARE!!
IF THERE'S PANIC IN THE STREETS, THEN SOMETHING SERIOUS MUST BE WRONG!
NOW'S OUR CHANCE TO MAKE LIKE HEROES! WHAT'RE WE WAITIN' FOR?!!
7

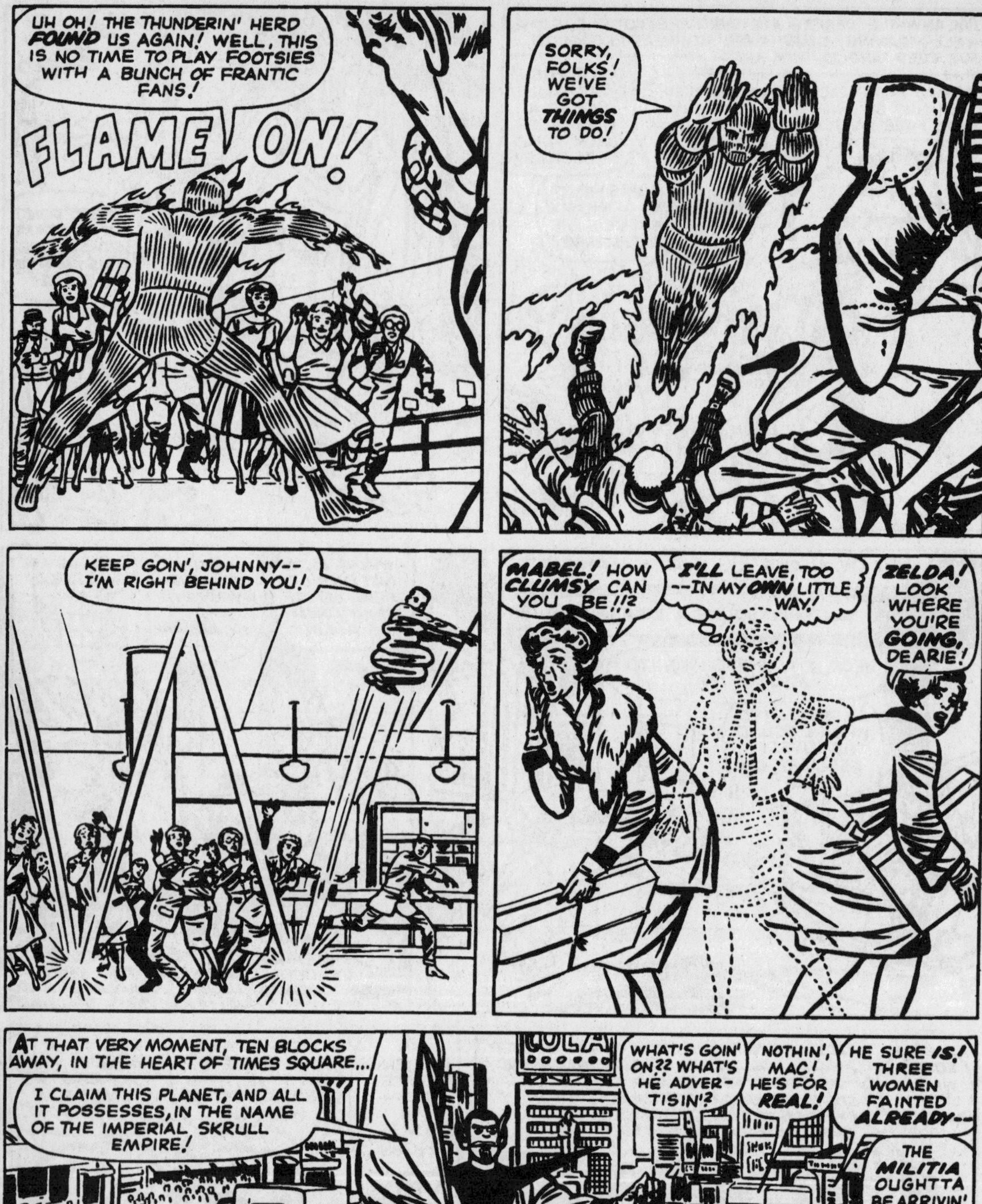
UH OH! THE THUNDERIN' HERD FOUND US AGAIN! WELL, THIS IS NO TIME TO PLAY FOOTSIES WITH A BUNCH OF FRANTIC FANS!
FLAME ON!
SORRY, FOLKS! WE'VE GOT THINGS TO DO!
KEEP GOIN', JOHNNY-- I'M RIGHT BEHIND YOU!
MABEL! HOW CLUMSY CAN YOU BE!!?
I'LL LEAVE, TOO --IN MY OWN LITTLE WAY!
ZELDA! LOOK WHERE YOU'RE GOING, DEARIE!
AT THAT VERY MOMENT, TEN BLOCKS AWAY, IN THE HEART OF TIMES SQUARE...
I CLAIM THIS PLANET, AND ALL IT POSSESSES, IN THE NAME OF THE IMPERIAL SKRULL EMPIRE!
WHAT'S GOIN' ON?? WHAT'S HE ADVER-TISIN'?
NOTHIN', MAC! HE'S FOR REAL!
HE SURE IS! THREE WOMEN FAINTED ALREADY--
THE MILITIA OUGHTTA BE ARRIVIN' HERE ANY MINUTE!
8

I'LL PLANT MY BANNER TO MARK THE SPOT WHERE I LANDED, AND...

THE GROUND IS TOO HARD! IT WILL NOT PENETRATE!

BUT THAT IS NO PROBLEM TO THE SUPER-SKRULL!

L-LOOK! HE'S LIKE AN ALIEN HUMAN TORCH!

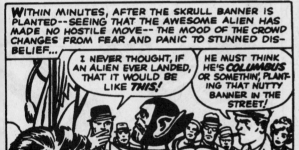

WITHIN MINUTES, AFTER THE SKRULL BANNER IS PLANTED--SEEING THAT THE AWESOME ALIEN HAS MADE NO HOSTILE MOVE-- THE MOOD OF THE CROWD CHANGES FROM FEAR AND PANIC TO STUNNED DISBELIEF...

I NEVER THOUGHT, IF AN ALIEN EVER LANDED, THAT IT WOULD BE LIKE THIS!

HE MUST THINK HE'S COLUMBUS OR SOMETHIN', PLANTING THAT NUTTY BANNER IN THE STREET!

YOU MAY ALL DISPERSE NOW, AND RETURN TO YOUR EVERY-DAY TASKS!

BEFORE LONG, I SHALL ISSUE THE FIRST IMPERIAL ORDERS FROM YOUR NEW PROVISIONAL SKRULL GOVERNMENT!

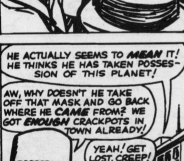

HE ACTUALLY SEEMS TO MEAN IT! HE THINKS HE HAS TAKEN POSSESSION OF THIS PLANET!

AW, WHY DOESN'T HE TAKE OFF THAT MASK AND GO BACK WHERE HE CAME FROM? WE GOT ENOUGH CRACKPOTS IN TOWN ALREADY!

YEAH! GET LOST, CREEP!

YOU DARE SPEAK THUS TO YOUR NEW MASTER??? BEGONE, BEFORE I FORGET HOW WEAK AND DEFENSELESS YOU ARE!

9

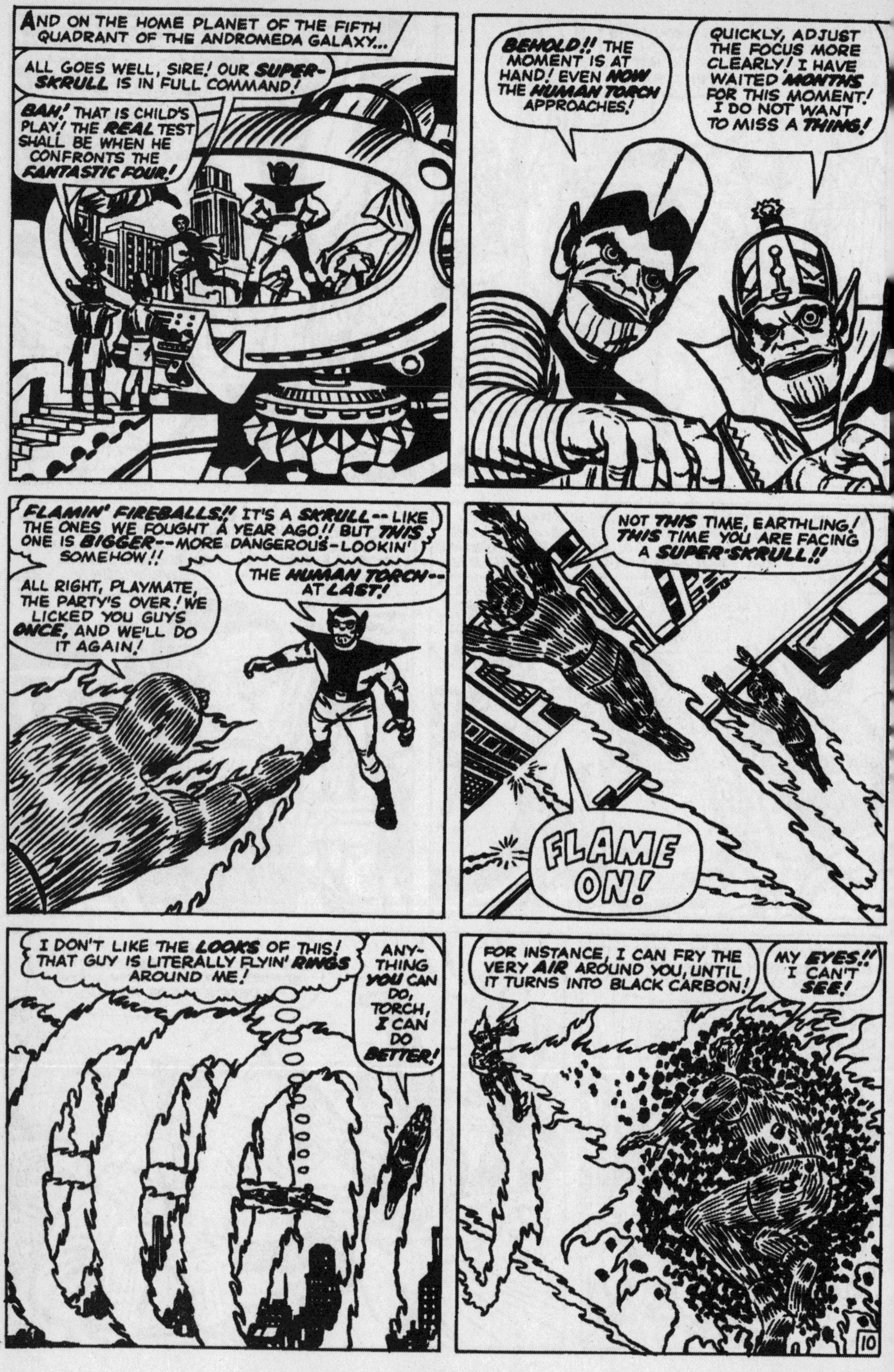
AND ON THE HOME PLANET OF THE FIFTH QUADRANT OF THE ANDROMEDA GALAXY...
ALL GOES WELL, SIRE! OUR SUPER-SKRULL IS IN FULL COMMAND!
BAH! THAT IS CHILD'S PLAY! THE REAL TEST SHALL BE WHEN HE CONFRONTS THE FANTASTIC FOUR!
BEHOLD!! THE MOMENT IS AT HAND! EVEN NOW THE HUMAN TORCH APPROACHES!
QUICKLY, ADJUST THE FOCUS MORE CLEARLY! I HAVE WAITED MONTHS FOR THIS MOMENT! I DO NOT WANT TO MISS A THING!
FLAMIN' FIREBALLS!! IT'S A SKRULL--LIKE THE ONES WE FOUGHT A YEAR AGO!! BUT THIS ONE IS BIGGER--MORE DANGEROUS-LOOKIN' SOMEHOW!!
ALL RIGHT, PLAYMATE, THE PARTY'S OVER! WE LICKED YOU GUYS ONCE, AND WE'LL DO IT AGAIN!
THE HUMAN TORCH--AT LAST!
NOT THIS TIME, EARTHLING! THIS TIME YOU ARE FACING A SUPER-SKRULL!!
FLAME ON!
I DON'T LIKE THE LOOKS OF THIS! THAT GUY IS LITERALLY FLYIN' RINGS AROUND ME!
ANY-THING YOU CAN DO, TORCH, I CAN DO BETTER!
FOR INSTANCE, I CAN FRY THE VERY AIR AROUND YOU, UNTIL IT TURNS INTO BLACK CARBON!
MY EYES!! I CAN'T SEE!
10

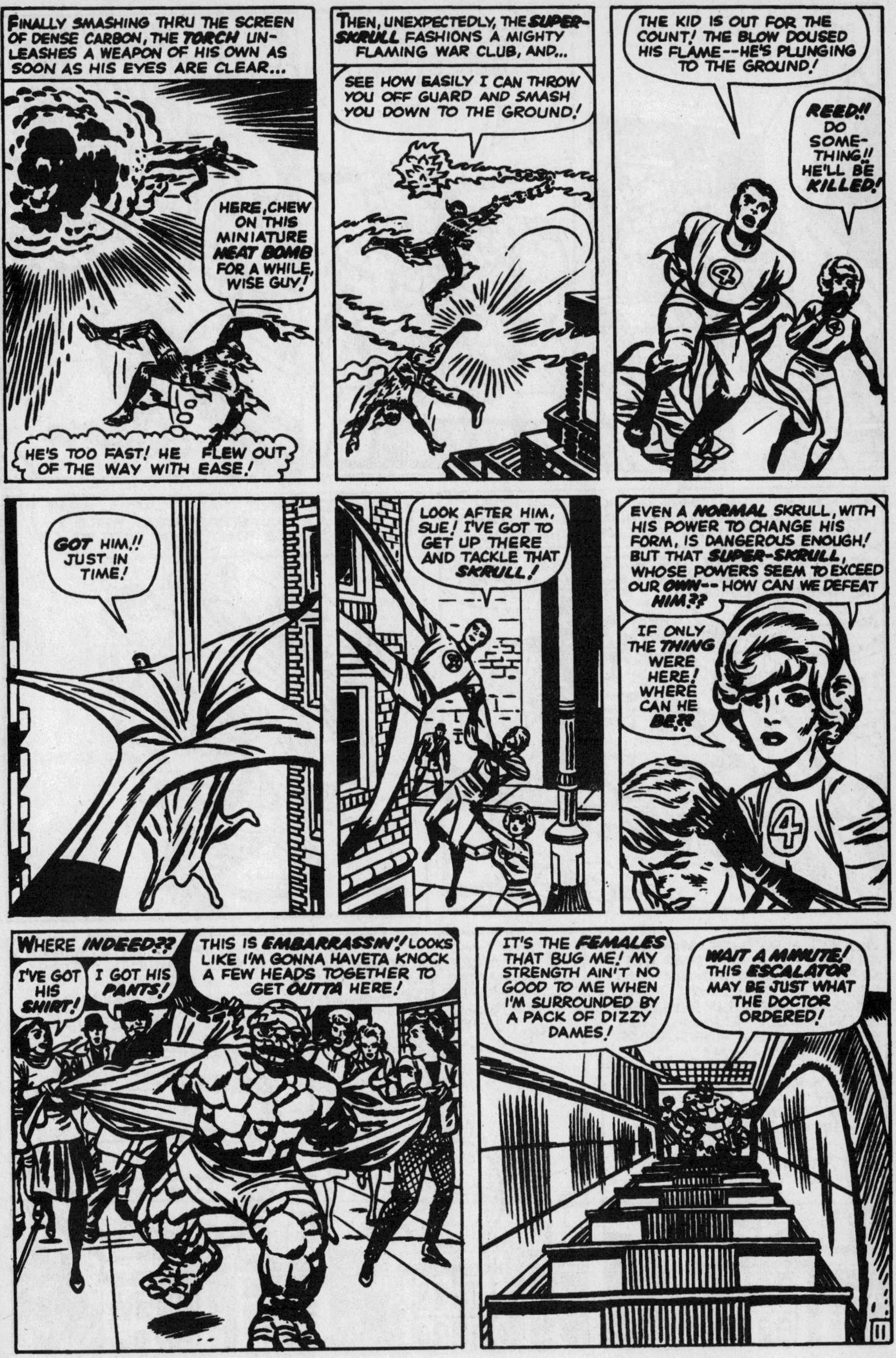

FINALLY SMASHING THRU THE SCREEN OF DENSE CARBON, THE TORCH UNLEASHES A WEAPON OF HIS OWN AS SOON AS HIS EYES ARE CLEAR...
HERE, CHEW ON THIS MINIATURE HEAT BOMB FOR A WHILE, WISE GUY!
HE'S TOO FAST! HE FLEW OUT OF THE WAY WITH EASE!
THEN, UNEXPECTEDLY, THE SUPER-SKRULL FASHIONS A MIGHTY FLAMING WAR CLUB, AND...
SEE HOW EASILY I CAN THROW YOU OFF GUARD AND SMASH YOU DOWN TO THE GROUND!
THE KID IS OUT FOR THE COUNT! THE BLOW DOUSED HIS FLAME--HE'S PLUNGING TO THE GROUND!
REED!! DO SOMETHING!! HE'LL BE KILLED!
GOT HIM!! JUST IN TIME!
LOOK AFTER HIM, SUE! I'VE GOT TO GET UP THERE AND TACKLE THAT SKRULL!
EVEN A NORMAL SKRULL, WITH HIS POWER TO CHANGE HIS FORM, IS DANGEROUS ENOUGH! BUT THAT SUPER-SKRULL, WHOSE POWERS SEEM TO EXCEED OUR OWN-- HOW CAN WE DEFEAT HIM??
IF ONLY THE THING WERE HERE! WHERE CAN HE BE??
WHERE INDEED??
I'VE GOT HIS SHIRT!
I GOT HIS PANTS!
THIS IS EMBARRASSIN'! LOOKS LIKE I'M GONNA HAVETA KNOCK A FEW HEADS TOGETHER TO GET OUTTA HERE!
IT'S THE FEMALES THAT BUG ME! MY STRENGTH AIN'T NO GOOD TO ME WHEN I'M SURROUNDED BY A PACK OF DIZZY DAMES!
WAIT A MINUTE! THIS ESCALATOR MAY BE JUST WHAT THE DOCTOR ORDERED!
11

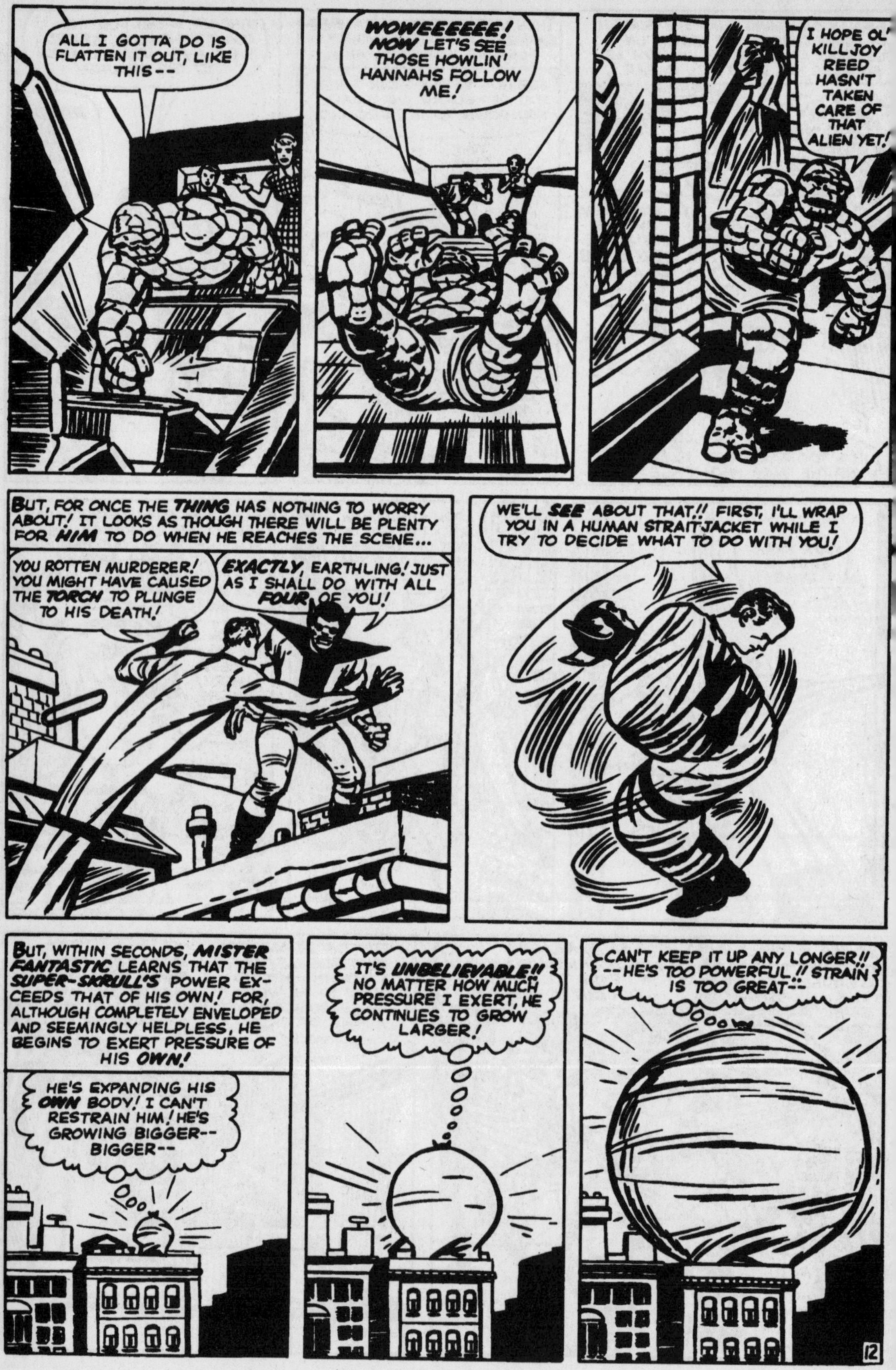
ALL I GOTTA DO IS FLATTEN IT OUT, LIKE THIS--
WOWEEEEEE! NOW LET'S SEE THOSE HOWLIN' HANNAHS FOLLOW ME!
I HOPE OL' KILLJOY REED HASN'T TAKEN CARE OF THAT ALIEN YET!
BUT, FOR ONCE THE THING HAS NOTHING TO WORRY ABOUT! IT LOOKS AS THOUGH THERE WILL BE PLENTY FOR HIM TO DO WHEN HE REACHES THE SCENE...
YOU ROTTEN MURDERER! YOU MIGHT HAVE CAUSED THE TORCH TO PLUNGE TO HIS DEATH!
EXACTLY, EARTHLING! JUST AS I SHALL DO WITH ALL FOUR OF YOU!
WE'LL SEE ABOUT THAT!! FIRST, I'LL WRAP YOU IN A HUMAN STRAIT-JACKET WHILE I TRY TO DECIDE WHAT TO DO WITH YOU!
BUT, WITHIN SECONDS, MISTER FANTASTIC LEARNS THAT THE SUPER-SKRULL'S POWER EXCEEDS THAT OF HIS OWN! FOR, ALTHOUGH COMPLETELY ENVELOPED AND SEEMINGLY HELPLESS, HE BEGINS TO EXERT PRESSURE OF HIS OWN!
HE'S EXPANDING HIS OWN BODY! I CAN'T RESTRAIN HIM! HE'S GROWING BIGGER-- BIGGER--
IT'S UNBELIEVABLE!! NO MATTER HOW MUCH PRESSURE I EXERT, HE CONTINUES TO GROW LARGER!
CAN'T KEEP IT UP ANY LONGER!! --HE'S TOO POWERFUL!! STRAIN IS TOO GREAT--
12

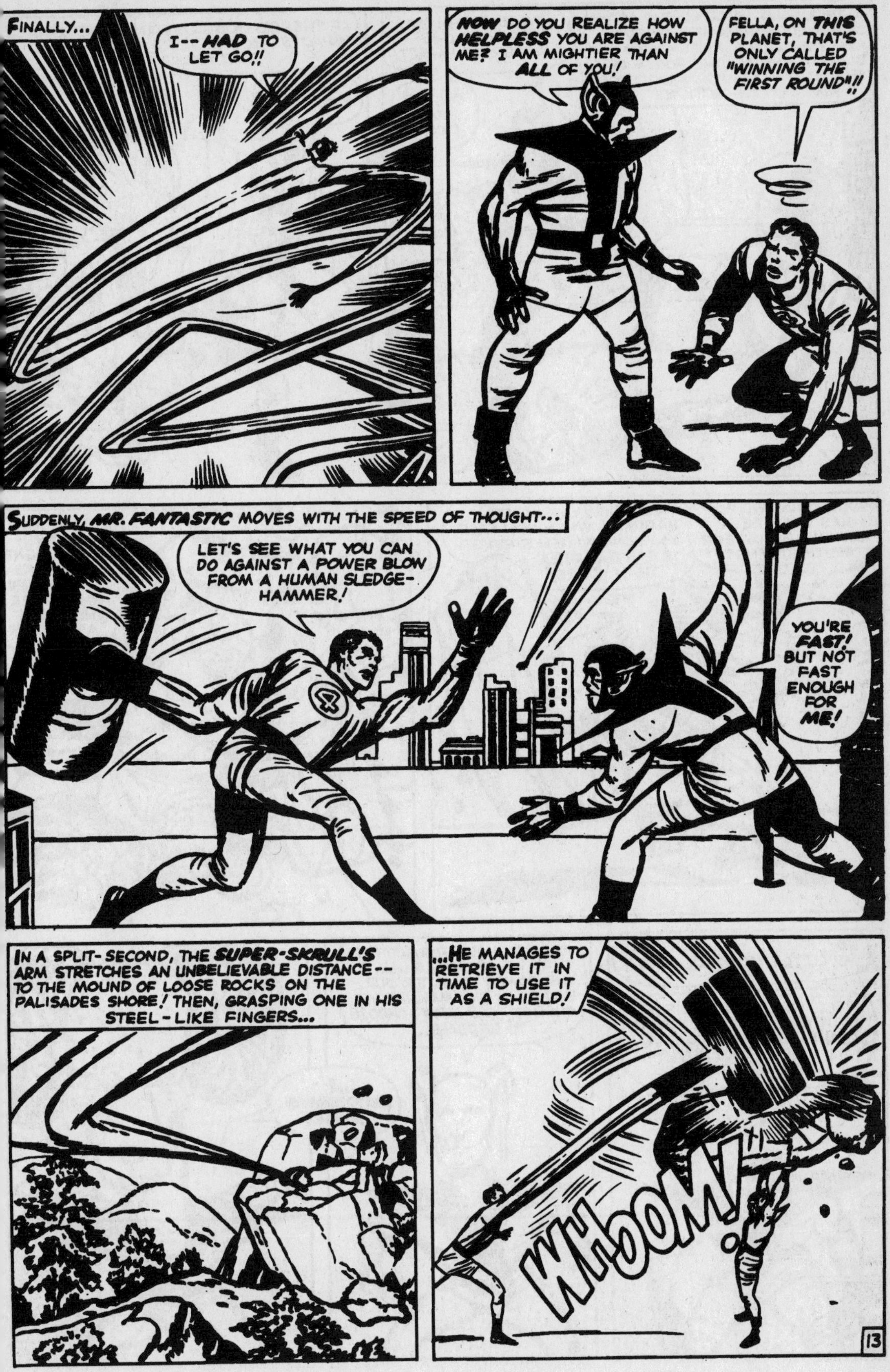
FINALLY...
I--HAD TO LET GO!!
NOW DO YOU REALIZE HOW HELPLESS YOU ARE AGAINST ME? I AM MIGHTIER THAN ALL OF YOU!
FELLA, ON THIS PLANET, THAT'S ONLY CALLED "WINNING THE FIRST ROUND"!!
SUDDENLY, MR. FANTASTIC MOVES WITH THE SPEED OF THOUGHT...
LET'S SEE WHAT YOU CAN DO AGAINST A POWER BLOW FROM A HUMAN SLEDGE-HAMMER!
YOU'RE FAST! BUT NOT FAST ENOUGH FOR ME!
IN A SPLIT-SECOND, THE SUPER-SKRULL'S ARM STRETCHES AN UNBELIEVABLE DISTANCE--TO THE MOUND OF LOOSE ROCKS ON THE PALISADES SHORE! THEN, GRASPING ONE IN HIS STEEL-LIKE FINGERS...
...HE MANAGES TO RETRIEVE IT IN TIME TO USE IT AS A SHIELD!
WHOOM!
13

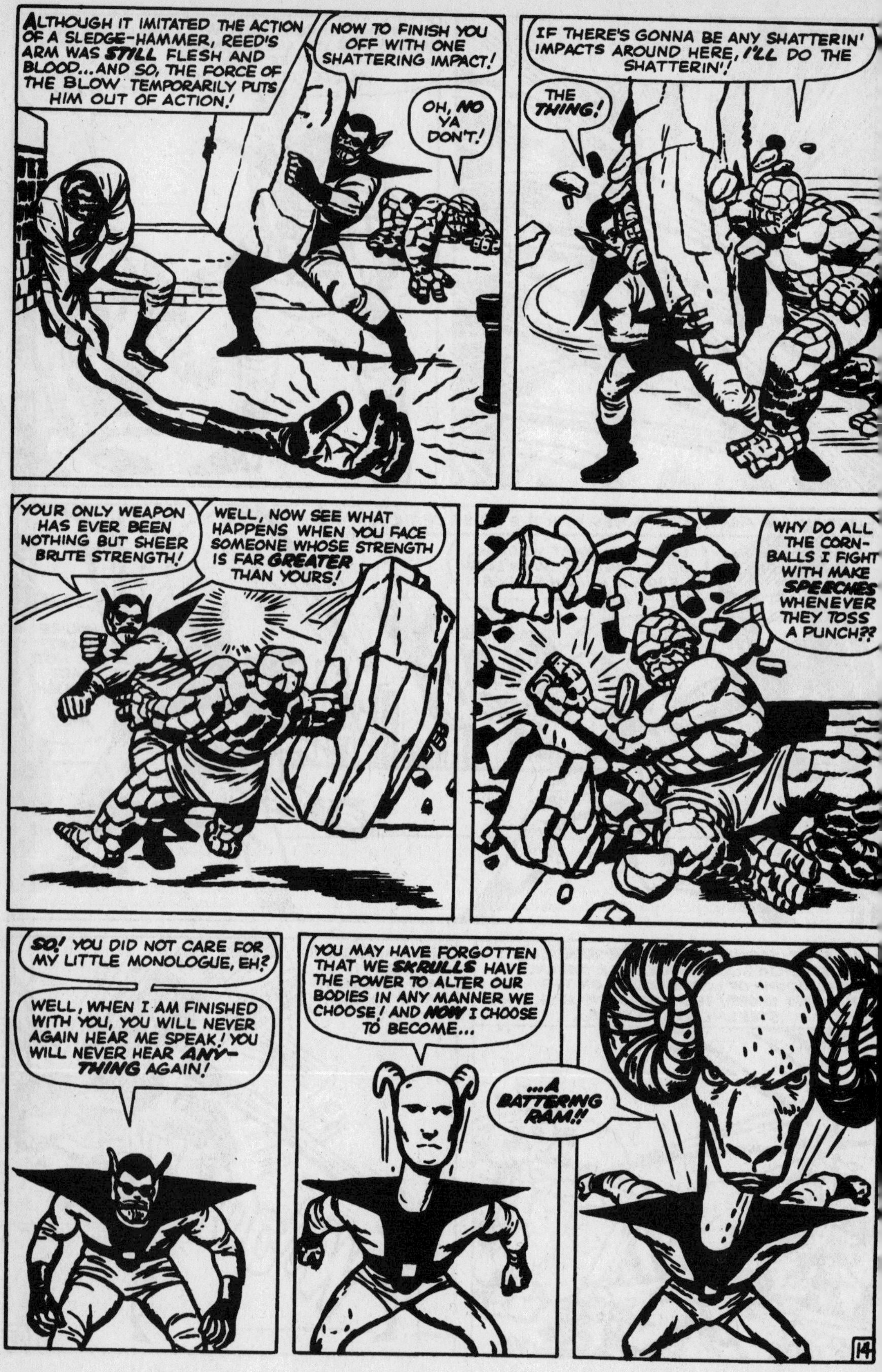

ALTHOUGH IT IMITATED THE ACTION OF A SLEDGE-HAMMER, REED'S ARM WAS STILL FLESH AND BLOOD...AND SO, THE FORCE OF THE BLOW TEMPORARILY PUTS HIM OUT OF ACTION!
NOW TO FINISH YOU OFF WITH ONE SHATTERING IMPACT!
OH, NO YA DON'T!
IF THERE'S GONNA BE ANY SHATTERIN' IMPACTS AROUND HERE, I'LL DO THE SHATTERIN'!
THE THING!
YOUR ONLY WEAPON HAS EVER BEEN NOTHING BUT SHEER BRUTE STRENGTH!
WELL, NOW SEE WHAT HAPPENS WHEN YOU FACE SOMEONE WHOSE STRENGTH IS FAR GREATER THAN YOURS!
WHY DO ALL THE CORN-BALLS I FIGHT WITH MAKE SPEECHES WHENEVER THEY TOSS A PUNCH??
SO! YOU DID NOT CARE FOR MY LITTLE MONOLOGUE, EH?
WELL, WHEN I AM FINISHED WITH YOU, YOU WILL NEVER AGAIN HEAR ME SPEAK! YOU WILL NEVER HEAR ANY-THING AGAIN!
YOU MAY HAVE FORGOTTEN THAT WE SKRULLS HAVE THE POWER TO ALTER OUR BODIES IN ANY MANNER WE CHOOSE! AND NOW I CHOOSE TO BECOME...
...A BATTERING RAM!!
14

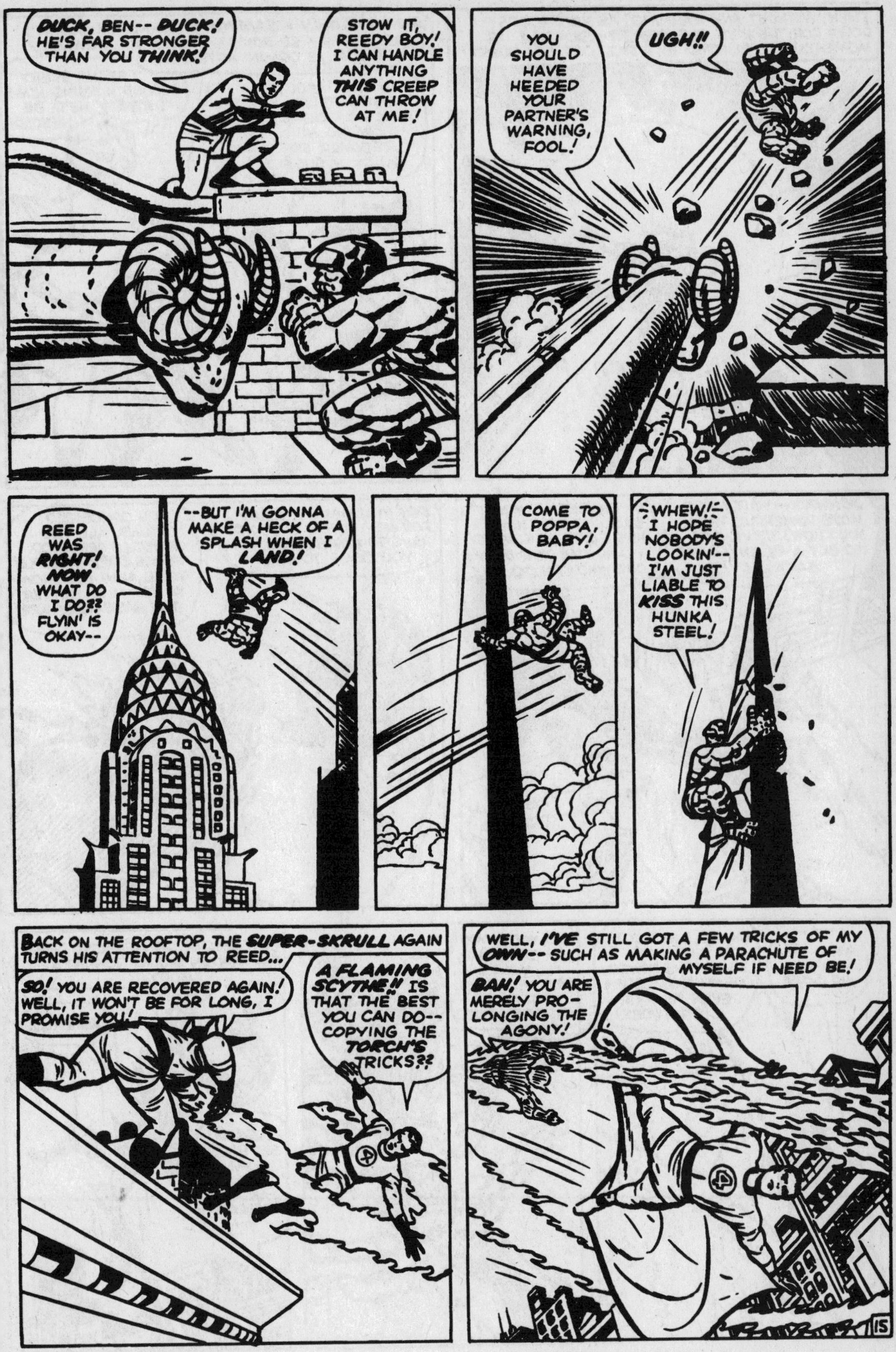
DUCK, BEN-- DUCK! HE'S FAR STRONGER THAN YOU THINK!
STOW IT, REEDY BOY! I CAN HANDLE ANYTHING THIS CREEP CAN THROW AT ME!
YOU SHOULD HAVE HEEDED YOUR PARTNER'S WARNING, FOOL!
UGH!!
REED WAS RIGHT! NOW WHAT DO I DO?? FLYIN' IS OKAY--
--BUT I'M GONNA MAKE A HECK OF A SPLASH WHEN I LAND!
COME TO POPPA, BABY!
WHEW! I HOPE NOBODY'S LOOKIN'-- I'M JUST LIABLE TO KISS THIS HUNKA STEEL!
BACK ON THE ROOFTOP, THE SUPER-SKRULL AGAIN TURNS HIS ATTENTION TO REED...
SO! YOU ARE RECOVERED AGAIN! WELL, IT WON'T BE FOR LONG, I PROMISE YOU!
A FLAMING SCYTHE!! IS THAT THE BEST YOU CAN DO-- COPYING THE TORCH'S TRICKS??
WELL, I'VE STILL GOT A FEW TRICKS OF MY OWN-- SUCH AS MAKING A PARACHUTE OF MYSELF IF NEED BE!
BAH! YOU ARE MERELY PRO-LONGING THE AGONY!
15

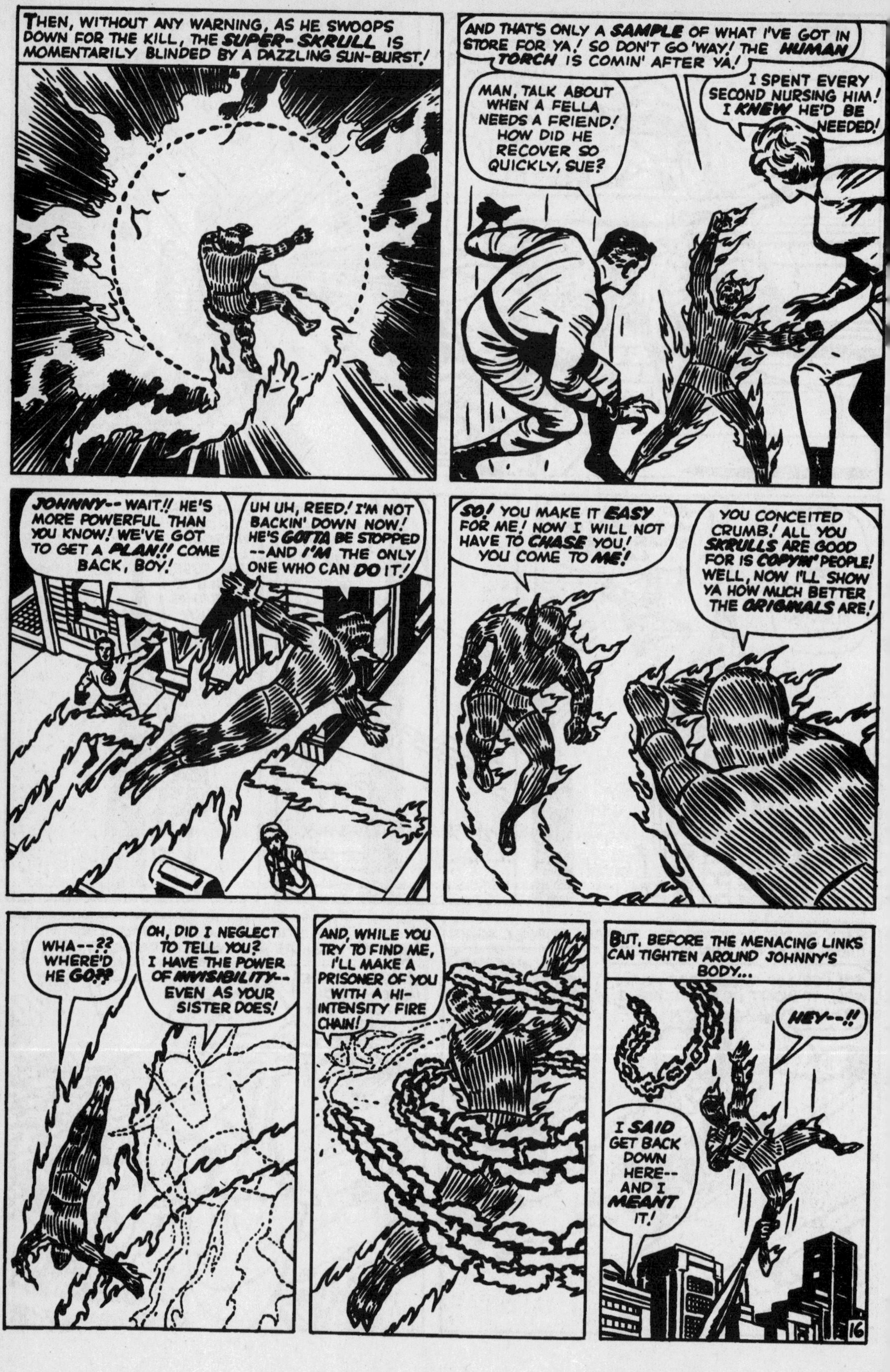
THEN, WITHOUT ANY WARNING, AS HE SWOOPS DOWN FOR THE KILL, THE SUPER-SKRULL IS MOMENTARILY BLINDED BY A DAZZLING SUN-BURST!
AND THAT'S ONLY A SAMPLE OF WHAT I'VE GOT IN STORE FOR YA! SO DON'T GO 'WAY! THE HUMAN TORCH IS COMIN' AFTER YA!
MAN, TALK ABOUT WHEN A FELLA NEEDS A FRIEND! HOW DID HE RECOVER SO QUICKLY, SUE?
I SPENT EVERY SECOND NURSING HIM! I KNEW HE'D BE NEEDED!
JOHNNY-- WAIT!! HE'S MORE POWERFUL THAN YOU KNOW! WE'VE GOT TO GET A PLAN!! COME BACK, BOY!
UH UH, REED! I'M NOT BACKIN' DOWN NOW! HE'S GOTTA BE STOPPED --AND I'M THE ONLY ONE WHO CAN DO IT!
SO! YOU MAKE IT EASY FOR ME! NOW I WILL NOT HAVE TO CHASE YOU! YOU COME TO ME!
YOU CONCEITED CRUMB! ALL YOU SKRULLS ARE GOOD FOR IS COPYIN' PEOPLE! WELL, NOW I'LL SHOW YA HOW MUCH BETTER THE ORIGINALS ARE!
WHA--?? WHERE'D HE GO??
OH, DID I NEGLECT TO TELL YOU? I HAVE THE POWER OF INVISIBILITY-- EVEN AS YOUR SISTER DOES!
AND, WHILE YOU TRY TO FIND ME, I'LL MAKE A PRISONER OF YOU WITH A HI-INTENSITY FIRE CHAIN!
BUT, BEFORE THE MENACING LINKS CAN TIGHTEN AROUND JOHNNY'S BODY...
HEY--!!
I SAID GET BACK DOWN HERE-- AND I MEANT IT!
16

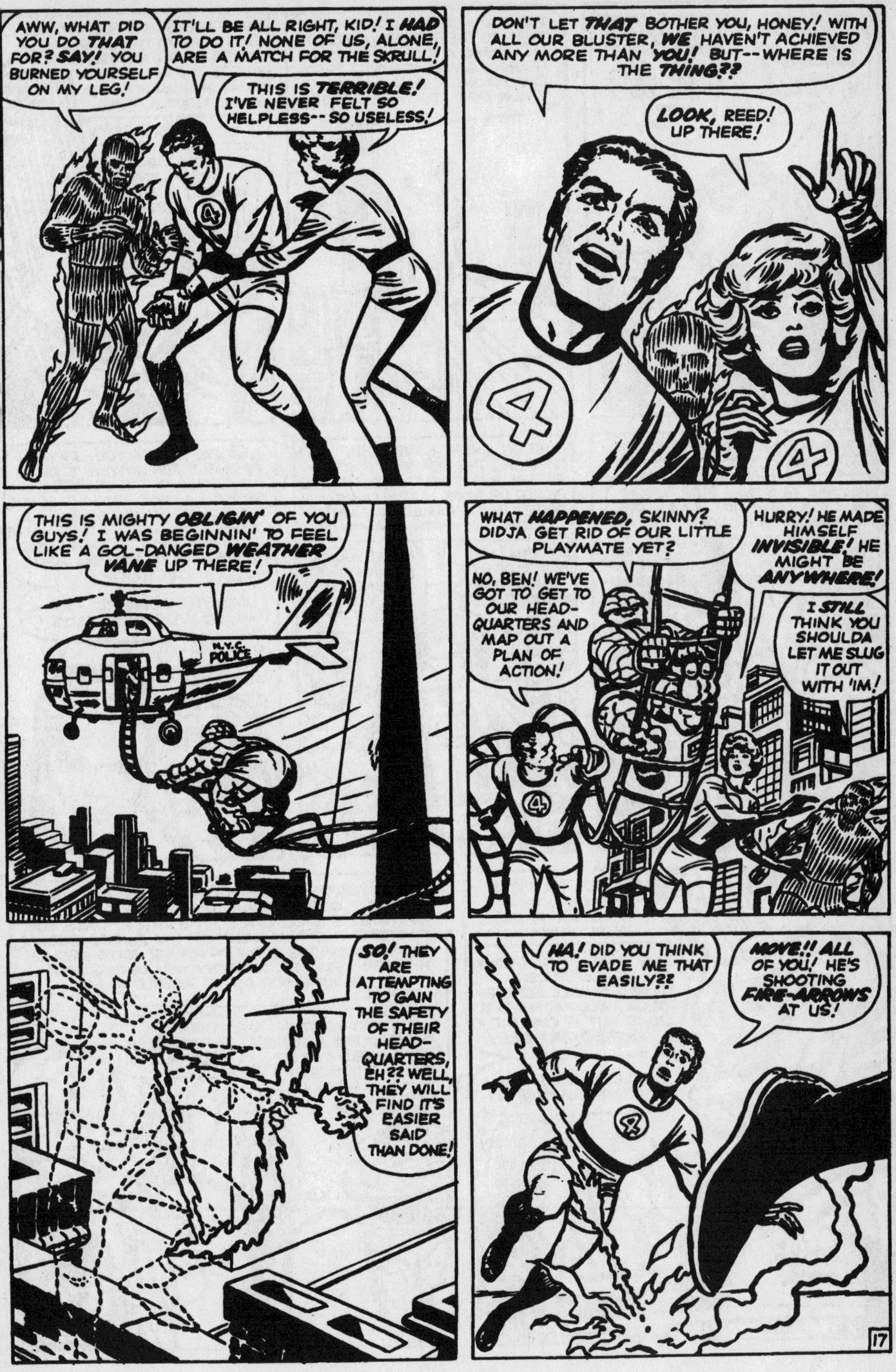

AWW, WHAT DID YOU DO THAT FOR? SAY! YOU BURNED YOURSELF ON MY LEG!
IT'LL BE ALL RIGHT, KID! I HAD TO DO IT! NONE OF US, ALONE, ARE A MATCH FOR THE SKRULL!
THIS IS TERRIBLE! I'VE NEVER FELT SO HELPLESS--SO USELESS!
DON'T LET THAT BOTHER YOU, HONEY! WITH ALL OUR BLUSTER, WE HAVEN'T ACHIEVED ANY MORE THAN YOU! BUT--WHERE IS THE THING??
LOOK, REED! UP THERE!
THIS IS MIGHTY OBLIGIN' OF YOU GUYS! I WAS BEGINNIN' TO FEEL LIKE A GOL-DANGED WEATHER VANE UP THERE!
N.Y.C. POLICE
WHAT HAPPENED, SKINNY? DIDJA GET RID OF OUR LITTLE PLAYMATE YET?
NO, BEN! WE'VE GOT TO GET TO OUR HEAD-QUARTERS AND MAP OUT A PLAN OF ACTION!
HURRY! HE MADE HIMSELF INVISIBLE! HE MIGHT BE ANYWHERE!
I STILL THINK YOU SHOULDA LET ME SLUG IT OUT WITH 'IM!
SO! THEY ARE ATTEMPTING TO GAIN THE SAFETY OF THEIR HEAD-QUARTERS, EH?? WELL, THEY WILL FIND IT'S EASIER SAID THAN DONE!
HA! DID YOU THINK TO EVADE ME THAT EASILY??
MOVE!! ALL OF YOU! HE'S SHOOTING FIRE-ARROWS AT US!

HA! LET THEM RUN! I SHALL NOT DESCEND TO THEIR LEVEL BY PURSUING THEM!

NOW I KNOW I AM MORE POWERFUL THAN ALL OF THEM-- AND THEY KNOW IT, TOO!

I SHALL ALLOW THEM TO RETURN TO THEIR HEADQUARTERS AND SPEND A SLEEPLESS NIGHT FEARING MY NEXT MOVE! THEN, TOMORROW, I SHALL FINISH THEM OFF AT MY LEISURE!

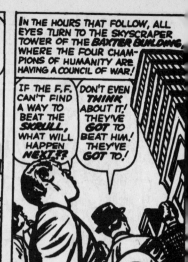

IN THE HOURS THAT FOLLOW, ALL EYES TURN TO THE SKYSCRAPER TOWER OF THE BAXTER BUILDING, WHERE THE FOUR CHAMPIONS OF HUMANITY ARE HAVING A COUNCIL OF WAR!

IF THE F.F. CAN'T FIND A WAY TO BEAT THE SKRULL, WHAT WILL HAPPEN NEXT??

DON'T EVEN THINK ABOUT IT! THEY'VE GOT TO BEAT HIM! THEY'VE GOT TO!

AND, IN MR. FANTASTIC'S EXPERIMENTAL LAB...

HEY, STRINGBEAN, WHEN ARE YA GONNA STOP MAKIN' LIKE A MAD SCIENTIST IN A B-MOVIE AND COME UP WITH SOMETHIN'??

HUSH, BEN! REED'S TRYING HIS BEST!

I THINK I'VE GOT SOMETHING AT LAST!

JUST ON A HUNCH, I'VE BEEN CHECKING THE HEAVENS FOR ANY UNUSUAL MANIFESTATIONS, AND I'VE PICKED UP SOME ULTRA-SONIC POWER RAYS BEAMED TO EARTH FROM THE FIFTH QUADRANT!

BUT WHAT HAS THAT TO DO WITH THE SUPER-SKRULL, REED?

NUTS! YOU'RE BEGINNIN' TO SOUND LIKE THE POOR MAN'S VINCENT PRICE!

LISTEN, ALL OF YOU! IT ISN'T POSSIBLE FOR ANYONE TO BE AS POWERFUL AS THE SUPER-SKRULL-- NOT WITHOUT SOME ADDITIONAL POWER SOURCE! I SUSPECT HIS HOME PLANET, IN THE FIFTH QUADRANT, IS BEAMING POWER RAYS TO HIM HERE ON EARTH!

AND I'M GOING TO FIND A WAY TO STOP THOSE RAYS!!!

OH, REED-- IF ONLY YOU COULD!

SLOWLY, SILENTLY, THE LONG, TENSE MINUTES PASS, UNTIL FINALLY...

I'VE GOT IT! THIS TINY SUB-MINIATURIZED "JAMMER" WILL DO THE TRICK! ALL WE HAVE TO DO IS PUT IT ON THE SUPER-SKRULL!

WILL DO, BOSS MAN! LEMME HAVE IT!

SORRY, TORCH, YOU WOULDN'T HAVE A CHANCE TO GET CLOSE ENOUGH TO HIM! ONLY THE INVISIBLE GIRL CAN DO THE TRICK! ONCE SUE FASTENS THIS "JAMMER" ON THE SUPER-SKRULL, IT WILL STOP THE FLOW OF POWER-RAYS FROM HIS HOME PLANET, THEREBY WEAKENING HIM ENOUGH FOR US TO HANDLE HIM!

BUT WHAT IF YOU'RE WRONG, REED?? WHAT IF IT DOESN'T WORK?

THEN HE'LL APOLOGIZE, LOUD-MOUTH!

18

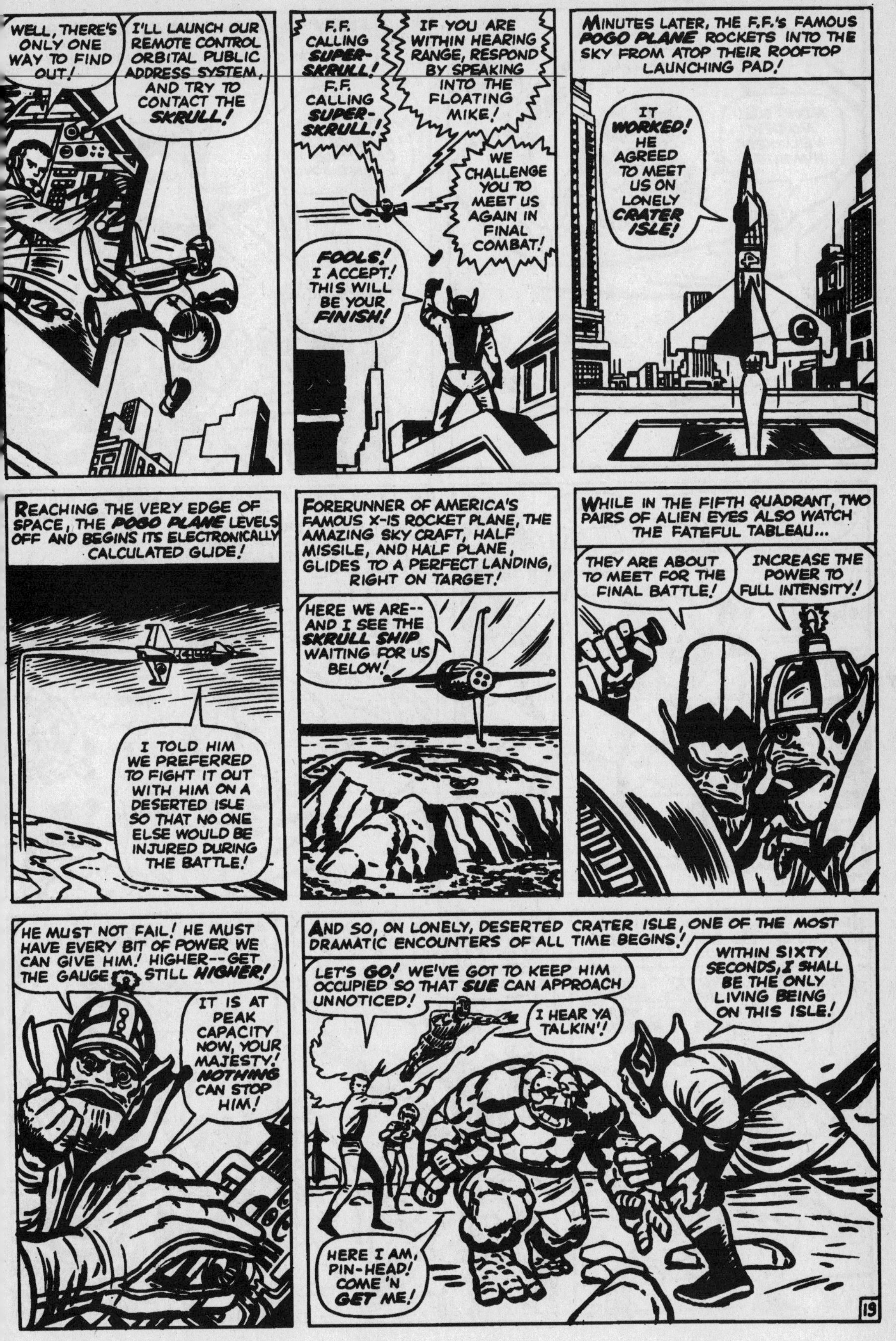
WELL, THERE'S ONLY ONE WAY TO FIND OUT!
I'LL LAUNCH OUR REMOTE CONTROL ORBITAL PUBLIC ADDRESS SYSTEM, AND TRY TO CONTACT THE SKRULL!
F.F. CALLING SUPER-SKRULL! F.F. CALLING SUPER-SKRULL!
IF YOU ARE WITHIN HEARING RANGE, RESPOND BY SPEAKING INTO THE FLOATING MIKE!
WE CHALLENGE YOU TO MEET US AGAIN IN FINAL COMBAT!
FOOLS! I ACCEPT! THIS WILL BE YOUR FINISH!
MINUTES LATER, THE F.F.'s FAMOUS POGO PLANE ROCKETS INTO THE SKY FROM ATOP THEIR ROOFTOP LAUNCHING PAD!
IT WORKED! HE AGREED TO MEET US ON LONELY CRATER ISLE!
REACHING THE VERY EDGE OF SPACE, THE POGO PLANE LEVELS OFF AND BEGINS ITS ELECTRONICALLY CALCULATED GLIDE!
I TOLD HIM WE PREFERRED TO FIGHT IT OUT WITH HIM ON A DESERTED ISLE SO THAT NO ONE ELSE WOULD BE INJURED DURING THE BATTLE!
FORERUNNER OF AMERICA'S FAMOUS X-15 ROCKET PLANE, THE AMAZING SKY CRAFT, HALF MISSILE, AND HALF PLANE, GLIDES TO A PERFECT LANDING, RIGHT ON TARGET!
HERE WE ARE-- AND I SEE THE SKRULL SHIP WAITING FOR US BELOW!
WHILE IN THE FIFTH QUADRANT, TWO PAIRS OF ALIEN EYES ALSO WATCH THE FATEFUL TABLEAU...
THEY ARE ABOUT TO MEET FOR THE FINAL BATTLE!
INCREASE THE POWER TO FULL INTENSITY!
HE MUST NOT FAIL! HE MUST HAVE EVERY BIT OF POWER WE CAN GIVE HIM! HIGHER--GET THE GAUGE STILL HIGHER!
IT IS AT PEAK CAPACITY NOW, YOUR MAJESTY! NOTHING CAN STOP HIM!
AND SO, ON LONELY, DESERTED CRATER ISLE, ONE OF THE MOST DRAMATIC ENCOUNTERS OF ALL TIME BEGINS!
LET'S GO! WE'VE GOT TO KEEP HIM OCCUPIED SO THAT SUE CAN APPROACH UNNOTICED!
I HEAR YA TALKIN'!
WITHIN SIXTY SECONDS, I SHALL BE THE ONLY LIVING BEING ON THIS ISLE!
HERE I AM, PIN-HEAD! COME 'N GET ME!

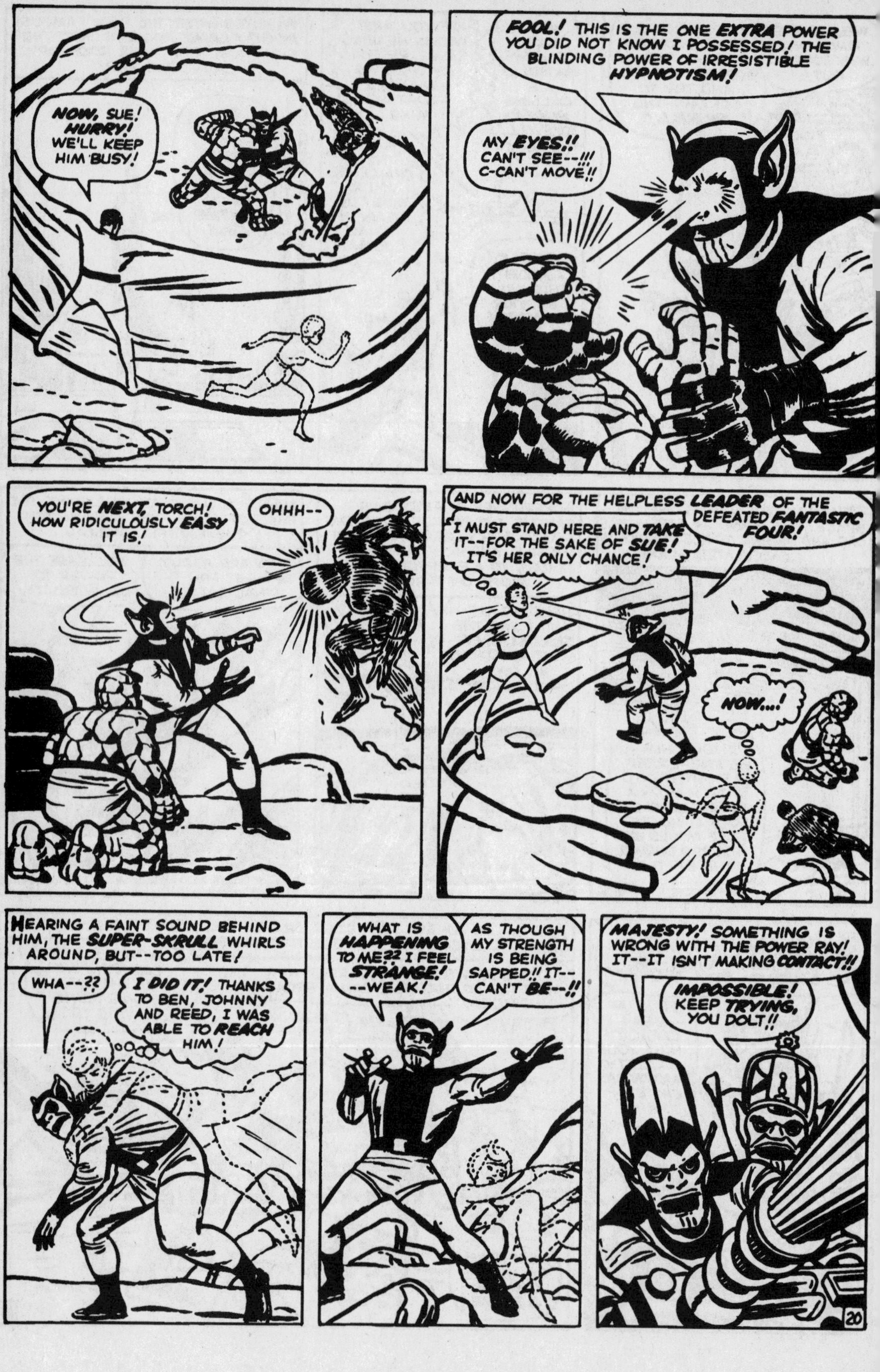
NOW, SUE! HURRY! WE'LL KEEP HIM BUSY!
FOOL! THIS IS THE ONE EXTRA POWER YOU DID NOT KNOW I POSSESSED! THE BLINDING POWER OF IRRESISTIBLE HYPNOTISM!
MY EYES!! CAN'T SEE--!!! C-CAN'T MOVE!!
YOU'RE NEXT, TORCH! HOW RIDICULOUSLY EASY IT IS!
OHHH--
AND NOW FOR THE HELPLESS LEADER OF THE DEFEATED FANTASTIC FOUR!
I MUST STAND HERE AND TAKE IT--FOR THE SAKE OF SUE! IT'S HER ONLY CHANCE!
NOW...!
HEARING A FAINT SOUND BEHIND HIM, THE SUPER-SKRULL WHIRLS AROUND, BUT--TOO LATE!
WHA--??
I DID IT! THANKS TO BEN, JOHNNY AND REED, I WAS ABLE TO REACH HIM!
WHAT IS HAPPENING TO ME?? I FEEL STRANGE! --WEAK!
AS THOUGH MY STRENGTH IS BEING SAPPED!! IT--CAN'T BE--!!
MAJESTY! SOMETHING IS WRONG WITH THE POWER RAY! IT--IT ISN'T MAKING CONTACT!!
IMPOSSIBLE! KEEP TRYING, YOU DOLT!!
20

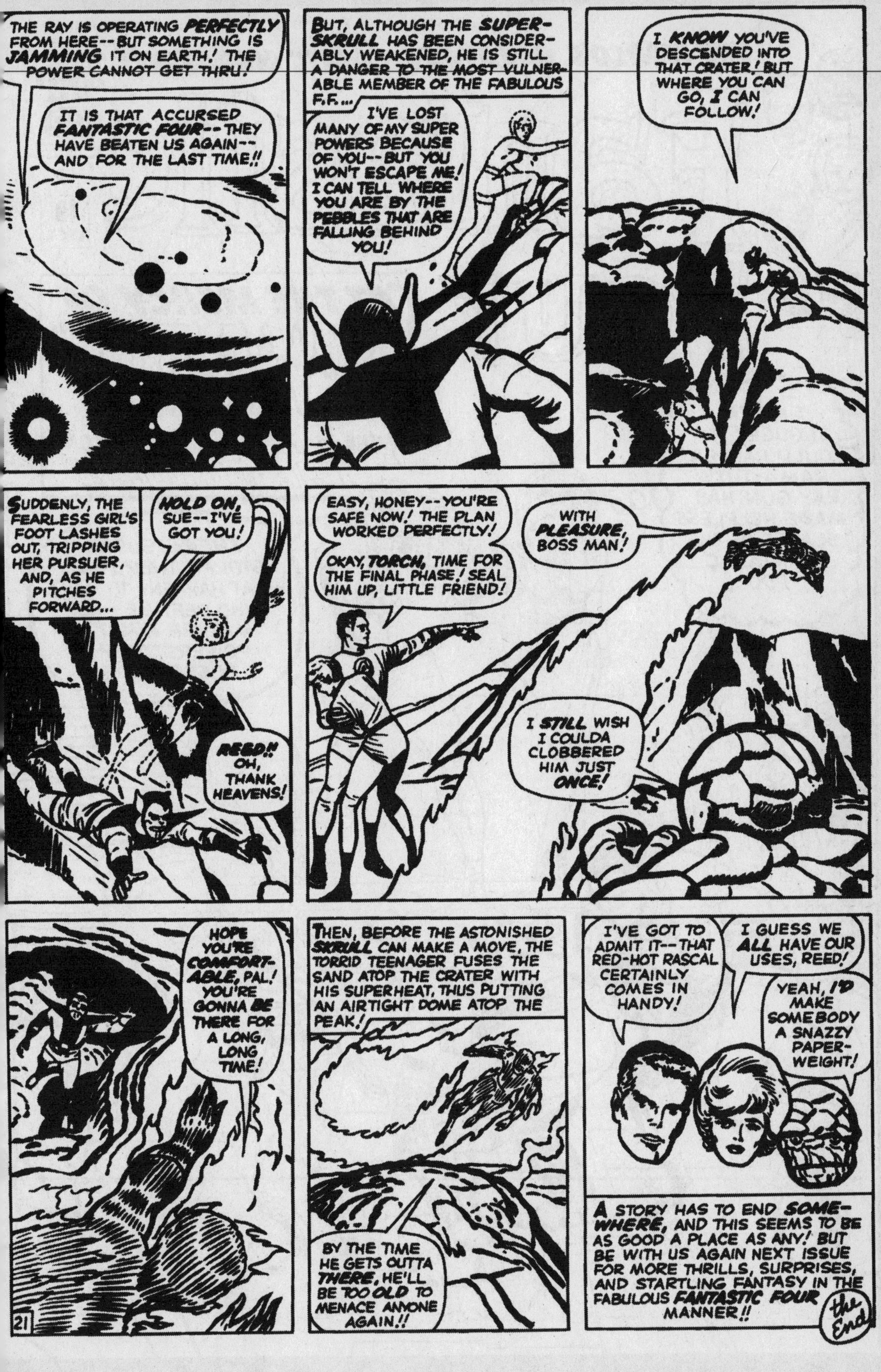
THE RAY IS OPERATING PERFECTLY FROM HERE--BUT SOMETHING IS JAMMING IT ON EARTH! THE POWER CANNOT GET THRU!
IT IS THAT ACCURSED FANTASTIC FOUR--THEY HAVE BEATEN US AGAIN--AND FOR THE LAST TIME!!
BUT, ALTHOUGH THE SUPER-SKRULL HAS BEEN CONSIDERABLY WEAKENED, HE IS STILL A DANGER TO THE MOST VULNERABLE MEMBER OF THE FABULOUS F.F....
I'VE LOST MANY OF MY SUPER POWERS BECAUSE OF YOU--BUT YOU WON'T ESCAPE ME! I CAN TELL WHERE YOU ARE BY THE PEBBLES THAT ARE FALLING BEHIND YOU!
I KNOW YOU'VE DESCENDED INTO THAT CRATER! BUT WHERE YOU CAN GO, I CAN FOLLOW!
SUDDENLY, THE FEARLESS GIRL'S FOOT LASHES OUT, TRIPPING HER PURSUER, AND, AS HE PITCHES FORWARD...
HOLD ON, SUE--I'VE GOT YOU!
REED!! OH, THANK HEAVENS!
EASY, HONEY--YOU'RE SAFE NOW! THE PLAN WORKED PERFECTLY!
OKAY, TORCH, TIME FOR THE FINAL PHASE! SEAL HIM UP, LITTLE FRIEND!
WITH PLEASURE, BOSS MAN!
I STILL WISH I COULDA CLOBBERED HIM JUST ONCE!
HOPE YOU'RE COMFORTABLE, PAL! YOU'RE GONNA BE THERE FOR A LONG, LONG TIME!
21
THEN, BEFORE THE ASTONISHED SKRULL CAN MAKE A MOVE, THE TORRID TEENAGER FUSES THE SAND ATOP THE CRATER WITH HIS SUPERHEAT, THUS PUTTING AN AIRTIGHT DOME ATOP THE PEAK!
BY THE TIME HE GETS OUTTA THERE, HE'LL BE TOO OLD TO MENACE ANYONE AGAIN!!
I'VE GOT TO ADMIT IT--THAT RED-HOT RASCAL CERTAINLY COMES IN HANDY!
I GUESS WE ALL HAVE OUR USES, REED!
YEAH, I'D MAKE SOMEBODY A SNAZZY PAPER-WEIGHT!
A STORY HAS TO END SOMEWHERE, AND THIS SEEMS TO BE AS GOOD A PLACE AS ANY! BUT BE WITH US AGAIN NEXT ISSUE FOR MORE THRILLS, SURPRISES, AND STARTLING FANTASY IN THE FABULOUS FANTASTIC FOUR MANNER!!
the End

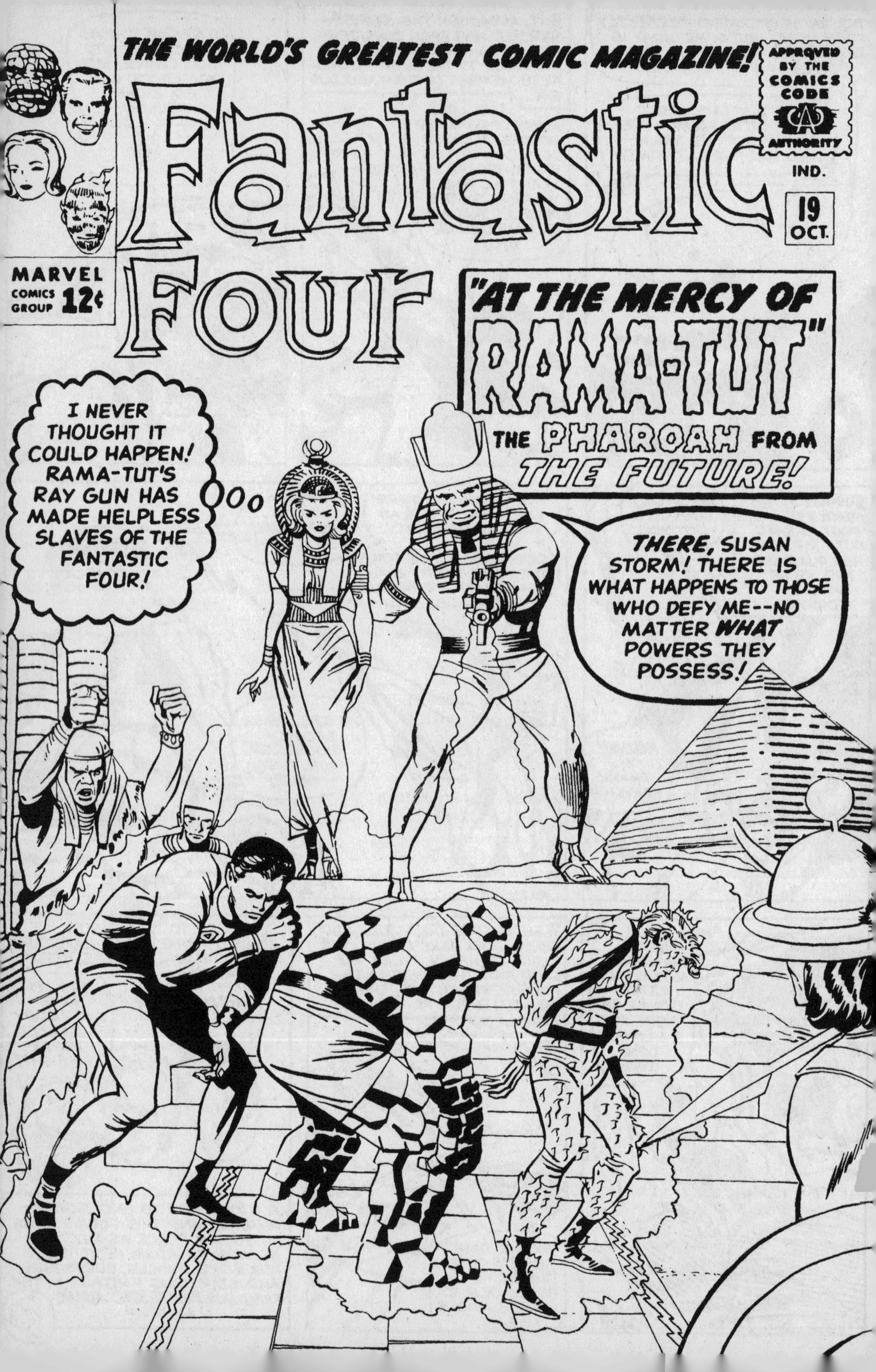
THE WORLD'S GREATEST COMIC MAGAZINE!
APPROVED BY THE COMICS CODE AUTHORITY
IND.
Fantastic Four
19 OCT.
MARVEL COMICS GROUP 12¢
"AT THE MERCY OF RAMA-TUT"
THE PHAROAH FROM THE FUTURE!
I NEVER THOUGHT IT COULD HAPPEN! RAMA-TUT'S RAY GUN HAS MADE HELPLESS SLAVES OF THE FANTASTIC FOUR!
THERE, SUSAN STORM! THERE IS WHAT HAPPENS TO THOSE WHO DEFY ME--NO MATTER WHAT POWERS THEY POSSESS!

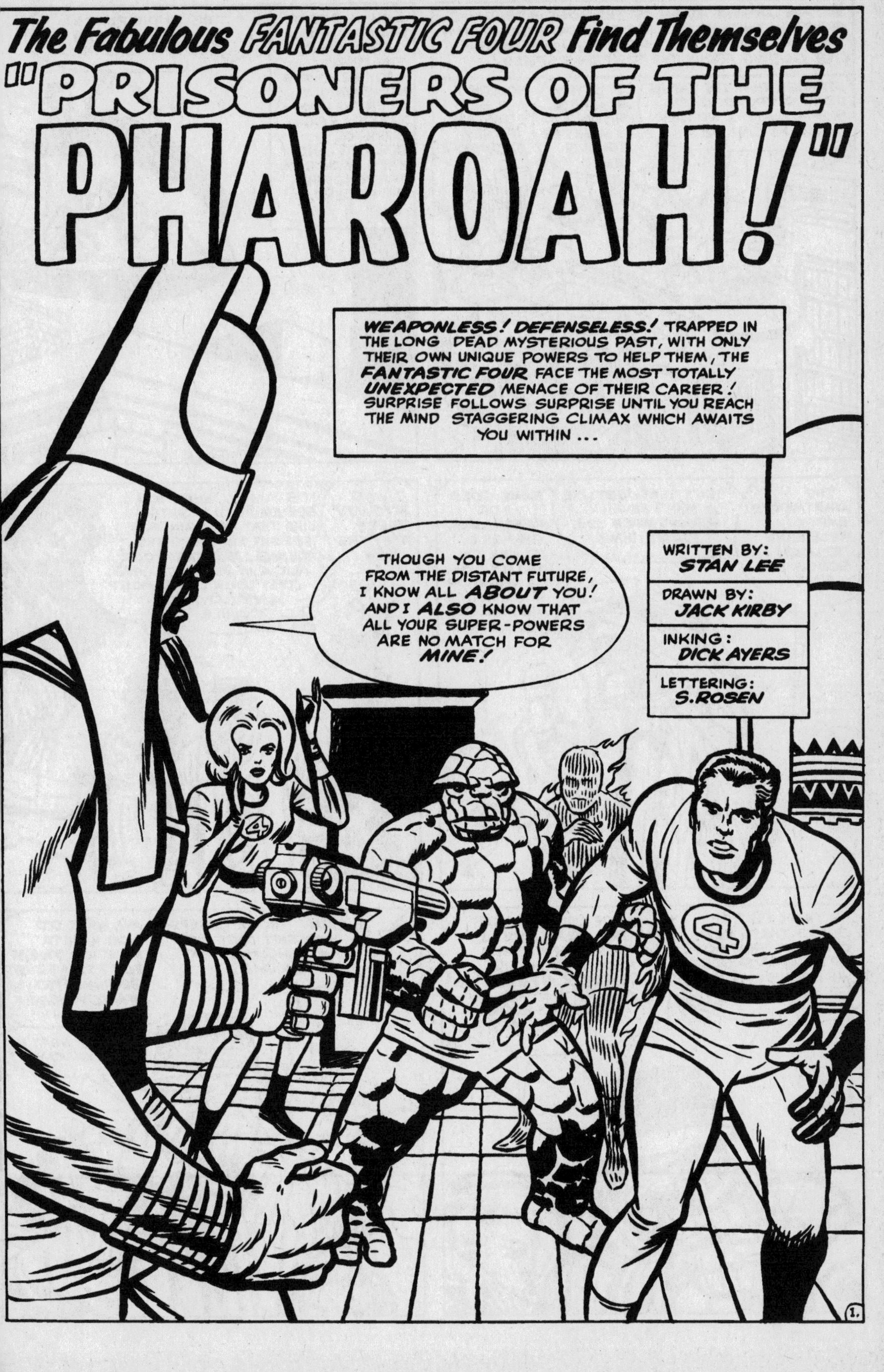
The Fabulous FANTASTIC FOUR Find Themselves
"PRISONERS OF THE PHAROAH!"
WEAPONLESS! DEFENSELESS! TRAPPED IN THE LONG DEAD MYSTERIOUS PAST, WITH ONLY THEIR OWN UNIQUE POWERS TO HELP THEM, THE FANTASTIC FOUR FACE THE MOST TOTALLY UNEXPECTED MENACE OF THEIR CAREER! SURPRISE FOLLOWS SURPRISE UNTIL YOU REACH THE MIND STAGGERING CLIMAX WHICH AWAITS YOU WITHIN ...
THOUGH YOU COME FROM THE DISTANT FUTURE, I KNOW ALL ABOUT YOU! AND I ALSO KNOW THAT ALL YOUR SUPER-POWERS ARE NO MATCH FOR MINE!
WRITTEN BY: STAN LEE
DRAWN BY: JACK KIRBY
INKING: DICK AYERS
LETTERING: S.ROSEN
1.

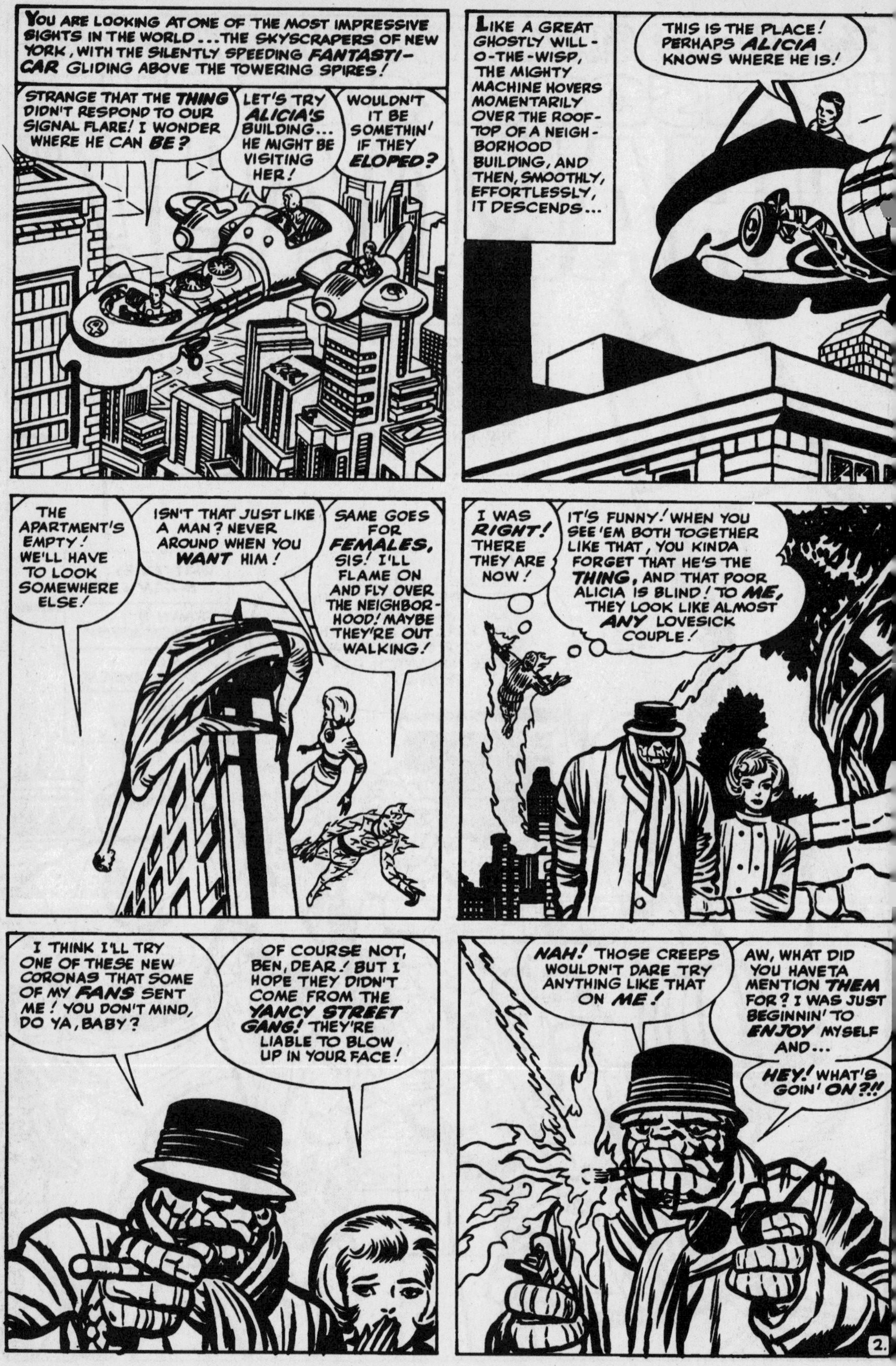
YOU ARE LOOKING AT ONE OF THE MOST IMPRESSIVE SIGHTS IN THE WORLD... THE SKYSCRAPERS OF NEW YORK, WITH THE SILENTLY SPEEDING FANTASTI-CAR GLIDING ABOVE THE TOWERING SPIRES!
STRANGE THAT THE THING DIDN'T RESPOND TO OUR SIGNAL FLARE! I WONDER WHERE HE CAN BE?
LET'S TRY ALICIA'S BUILDING... HE MIGHT BE VISITING HER!
WOULDN'T IT BE SOMETHIN' IF THEY ELOPED?
LIKE A GREAT GHOSTLY WILL-O-THE-WISP, THE MIGHTY MACHINE HOVERS MOMENTARILY OVER THE ROOF-TOP OF A NEIGHBORHOOD BUILDING, AND THEN, SMOOTHLY, EFFORTLESSLY, IT DESCENDS...
THIS IS THE PLACE! PERHAPS ALICIA KNOWS WHERE HE IS!
THE APARTMENT'S EMPTY! WE'LL HAVE TO LOOK SOMEWHERE ELSE!
ISN'T THAT JUST LIKE A MAN? NEVER AROUND WHEN YOU WANT HIM!
SAME GOES FOR FEMALES, SIS! I'LL FLAME ON AND FLY OVER THE NEIGHBORHOOD! MAYBE THEY'RE OUT WALKING!
I WAS RIGHT! THERE THEY ARE NOW!
IT'S FUNNY! WHEN YOU SEE 'EM BOTH TOGETHER LIKE THAT, YOU KINDA FORGET THAT HE'S THE THING, AND THAT POOR ALICIA IS BLIND! TO ME, THEY LOOK LIKE ALMOST ANY LOVESICK COUPLE!
I THINK I'LL TRY ONE OF THESE NEW CORONAS THAT SOME OF MY FANS SENT ME! YOU DON'T MIND, DO YA, BABY?
OF COURSE NOT, BEN, DEAR! BUT I HOPE THEY DIDN'T COME FROM THE YANCY STREET GANG! THEY'RE LIABLE TO BLOW UP IN YOUR FACE!
NAH! THOSE CREEPS WOULDN'T DARE TRY ANYTHING LIKE THAT ON ME!
AW, WHAT DID YOU HAVETA MENTION THEM FOR? I WAS JUST BEGINNIN' TO ENJOY MYSELF AND...
HEY! WHAT'S GOIN' ON?!!

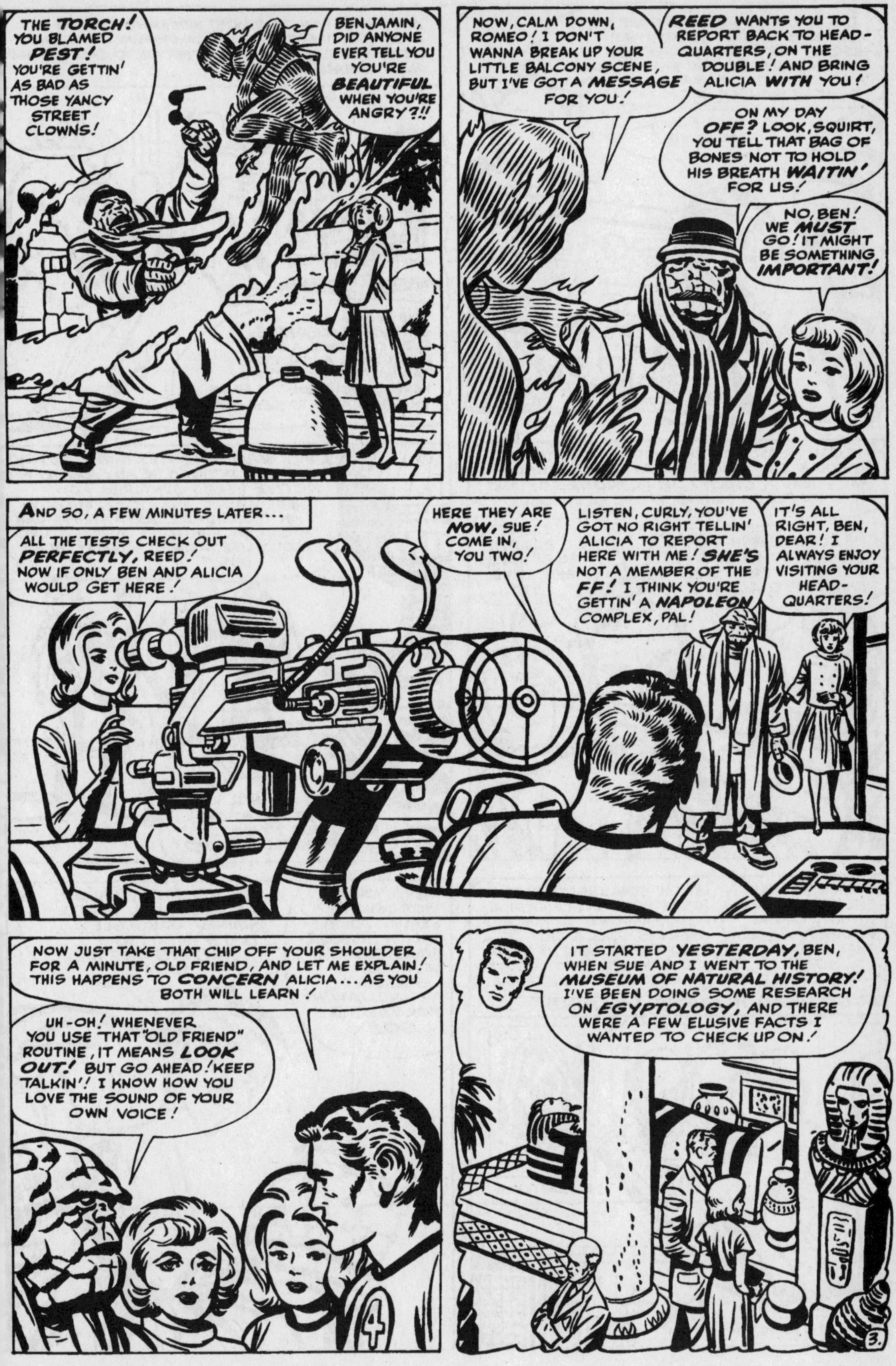
THE TORCH! YOU BLAMED PEST! YOU'RE GETTIN' AS BAD AS THOSE YANCY STREET CLOWNS!
BENJAMIN, DID ANYONE EVER TELL YOU YOU'RE BEAUTIFUL WHEN YOU'RE ANGRY?!!
NOW, CALM DOWN, ROMEO! I DON'T WANNA BREAK UP YOUR LITTLE BALCONY SCENE, BUT I'VE GOT A MESSAGE FOR YOU!
REED WANTS YOU TO REPORT BACK TO HEAD-QUARTERS, ON THE DOUBLE! AND BRING ALICIA WITH YOU!
ON MY DAY OFF? LOOK, SQUIRT, YOU TELL THAT BAG OF BONES NOT TO HOLD HIS BREATH WAITIN' FOR US!
NO, BEN! WE MUST GO! IT MIGHT BE SOMETHING IMPORTANT!
AND SO, A FEW MINUTES LATER...
ALL THE TESTS CHECK OUT PERFECTLY, REED! NOW IF ONLY BEN AND ALICIA WOULD GET HERE!
HERE THEY ARE NOW, SUE! COME IN, YOU TWO!
LISTEN, CURLY, YOU'VE GOT NO RIGHT TELLIN' ALICIA TO REPORT HERE WITH ME! SHE'S NOT A MEMBER OF THE FF! I THINK YOU'RE GETTIN' A NAPOLEON COMPLEX, PAL!
IT'S ALL RIGHT, BEN, DEAR! I ALWAYS ENJOY VISITING YOUR HEAD-QUARTERS!
NOW JUST TAKE THAT CHIP OFF YOUR SHOULDER FOR A MINUTE, OLD FRIEND, AND LET ME EXPLAIN! THIS HAPPENS TO CONCERN ALICIA... AS YOU BOTH WILL LEARN!
UH-OH! WHENEVER YOU USE THAT "OLD FRIEND" ROUTINE, IT MEANS LOOK OUT! BUT GO AHEAD! KEEP TALKIN'! I KNOW HOW YOU LOVE THE SOUND OF YOUR OWN VOICE!
IT STARTED YESTERDAY, BEN, WHEN SUE AND I WENT TO THE MUSEUM OF NATURAL HISTORY! I'VE BEEN DOING SOME RESEARCH ON EGYPTOLOGY, AND THERE WERE A FEW ELUSIVE FACTS I WANTED TO CHECK UP ON!
3.

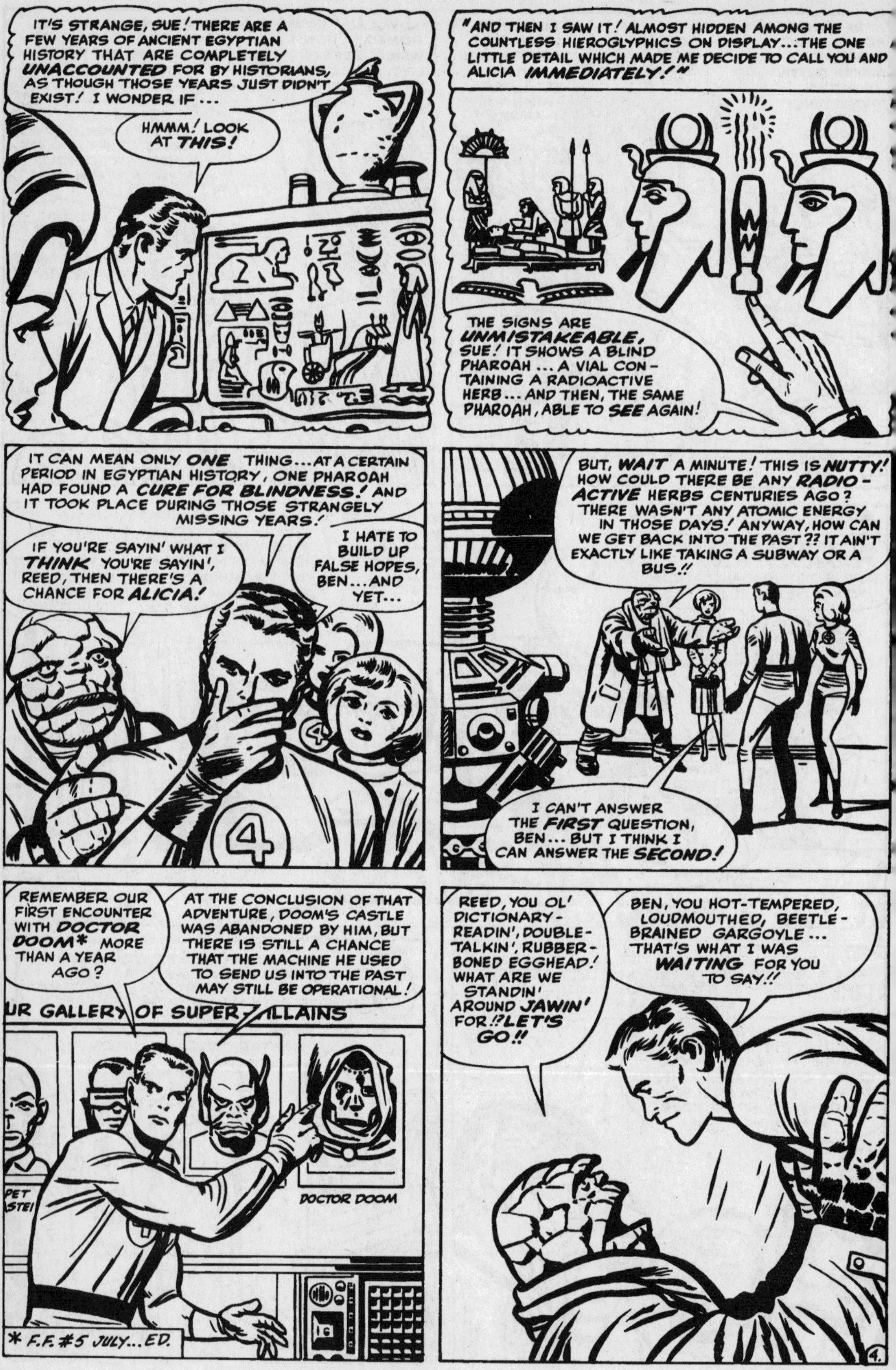
IT'S STRANGE, SUE! THERE ARE A FEW YEARS OF ANCIENT EGYPTIAN HISTORY THAT ARE COMPLETELY UNACCOUNTED FOR BY HISTORIANS, AS THOUGH THOSE YEARS JUST DIDN'T EXIST! I WONDER IF ...
HMMM! LOOK AT THIS!
"AND THEN I SAW IT! ALMOST HIDDEN AMONG THE COUNTLESS HIEROGLYPHICS ON DISPLAY...THE ONE LITTLE DETAIL WHICH MADE ME DECIDE TO CALL YOU AND ALICIA IMMEDIATELY!"
THE SIGNS ARE UNMISTAKEABLE, SUE! IT SHOWS A BLIND PHAROAH ... A VIAL CONTAINING A RADIOACTIVE HERB ... AND THEN, THE SAME PHAROAH, ABLE TO SEE AGAIN!
IT CAN MEAN ONLY ONE THING...AT A CERTAIN PERIOD IN EGYPTIAN HISTORY, ONE PHAROAH HAD FOUND A CURE FOR BLINDNESS! AND IT TOOK PLACE DURING THOSE STRANGELY MISSING YEARS!
IF YOU'RE SAYIN' WHAT I THINK YOU'RE SAYIN', REED, THEN THERE'S A CHANCE FOR ALICIA!
I HATE TO BUILD UP FALSE HOPES, BEN...AND YET...
BUT, WAIT A MINUTE! THIS IS NUTTY! HOW COULD THERE BE ANY RADIO-ACTIVE HERBS CENTURIES AGO? THERE WASN'T ANY ATOMIC ENERGY IN THOSE DAYS! ANYWAY, HOW CAN WE GET BACK INTO THE PAST?? IT AIN'T EXACTLY LIKE TAKING A SUBWAY OR A BUS!!
I CAN'T ANSWER THE FIRST QUESTION, BEN... BUT I THINK I CAN ANSWER THE SECOND!
REMEMBER OUR FIRST ENCOUNTER WITH DOCTOR DOOM* MORE THAN A YEAR AGO?
AT THE CONCLUSION OF THAT ADVENTURE, DOOM'S CASTLE WAS ABANDONED BY HIM, BUT THERE IS STILL A CHANCE THAT THE MACHINE HE USED TO SEND US INTO THE PAST MAY STILL BE OPERATIONAL!
UR GALLERY OF SUPER-VILLAINS
DOCTOR DOOM
* F.F. #5 JULY... ED.
REED, YOU OL' DICTIONARY-READIN', DOUBLE-TALKIN', RUBBER-BONED EGGHEAD! WHAT ARE WE STANDIN' AROUND JAWIN' FOR!? LET'S GO!!
BEN, YOU HOT-TEMPERED, LOUDMOUTHED, BEETLE-BRAINED GARGOYLE... THAT'S WHAT I WAS WAITING FOR YOU TO SAY!!
4.

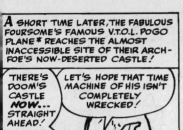

A SHORT TIME LATER, THE FABULOUS FOURSOME'S FAMOUS V.T.O.L.* POGO PLANE* REACHES THE ALMOST INACCESSIBLE SITE OF THEIR ARCH-FOE'S NOW-DESERTED CASTLE!

THERE'S DOOM'S CASTLE **NOW**... STRAIGHT AHEAD!

LET'S HOPE THAT TIME MACHINE OF HIS ISN'T COMPLETELY WRECKED!

*V.T.O.L.-VERTICAL TAKE-OFF AND LANDING.

I'LL FLY OVER THE WALL AND LOWER THE DRAWBRIDGE FOR YOU THREE LANDLUBBERS!

EVERYTHING SEEMS TO BE ALMOST AS DOOM LEFT IT!

YEAH, EXCEPT THAT OL' IRON-HEAD AIN'T AROUND!

THEN, AS THE MIGHTY DRAWBRIDGE CREAKS DOWN...

HI, KIDS! IF I KNEW YOU WERE COMING, I'D HAVE BAKED A CAKE!

HEY, WE'RE IN LUCK! HERE'S THE PANEL WE STOOD ON WHEN WE TOOK OUR LITTLE TRIP! LOOKS AS GOOD AS NEW!

LUCKY FOR US THAT DOCTOR DOOM MADE ALMOST EVERYTHING **FIREPROOF** TO PROTECT HIM-SELF AGAINST **YOU**, JOHNNY!

THE CONTROLS WHICH HE WORKED WHILE SITTING IN HIS SPECIALLY-BUILT CHAIR ALL SEEM TO BE INTACT!

ALICIA, BABY, YOU'LL HAVE TO STAY BEHIND AND OPERATE THIS GIZMO TO GET US THERE AND BACK! THINK YOU CAN HANDLE IT?

I'VE **GOT** TO, BEN! IF YOU EXPLAIN IT CAREFULLY, I'LL TRY TO DO IT BY **TOUCH!**

BUT, BEN...MY DARLING...IF THERE WILL BE ANY DANGER TO YOU... TO **ANY** OF YOU...THEN IT ISN'T **WORTH** IT IF... I COULDN'T **BEAR** IT IF...

FORGET IT, KID! DANGER IS OUR BUSINESS, LIKE THEY SAY IN THE MOVIES!

AND THEN, AFTER HOURS OF PRACTICE...

GOOD LUCK, YOU DEAR, WONDER-FUL FRIENDS...

REMEMBER, ALICIA...WORK THOSE BUTTONS IN EXACTLY THE PATTERN WE SHOWED YOU! IF ALL GOES WELL, WE'LL RETURN IN TWENTY-FOUR HOURS!

FAREWELL, YOU BRAVE, NOBLE, UNSELFISH ADVENTURERS! FARE-WELL, BEN...MY OWN DARLING LOVE...

5.

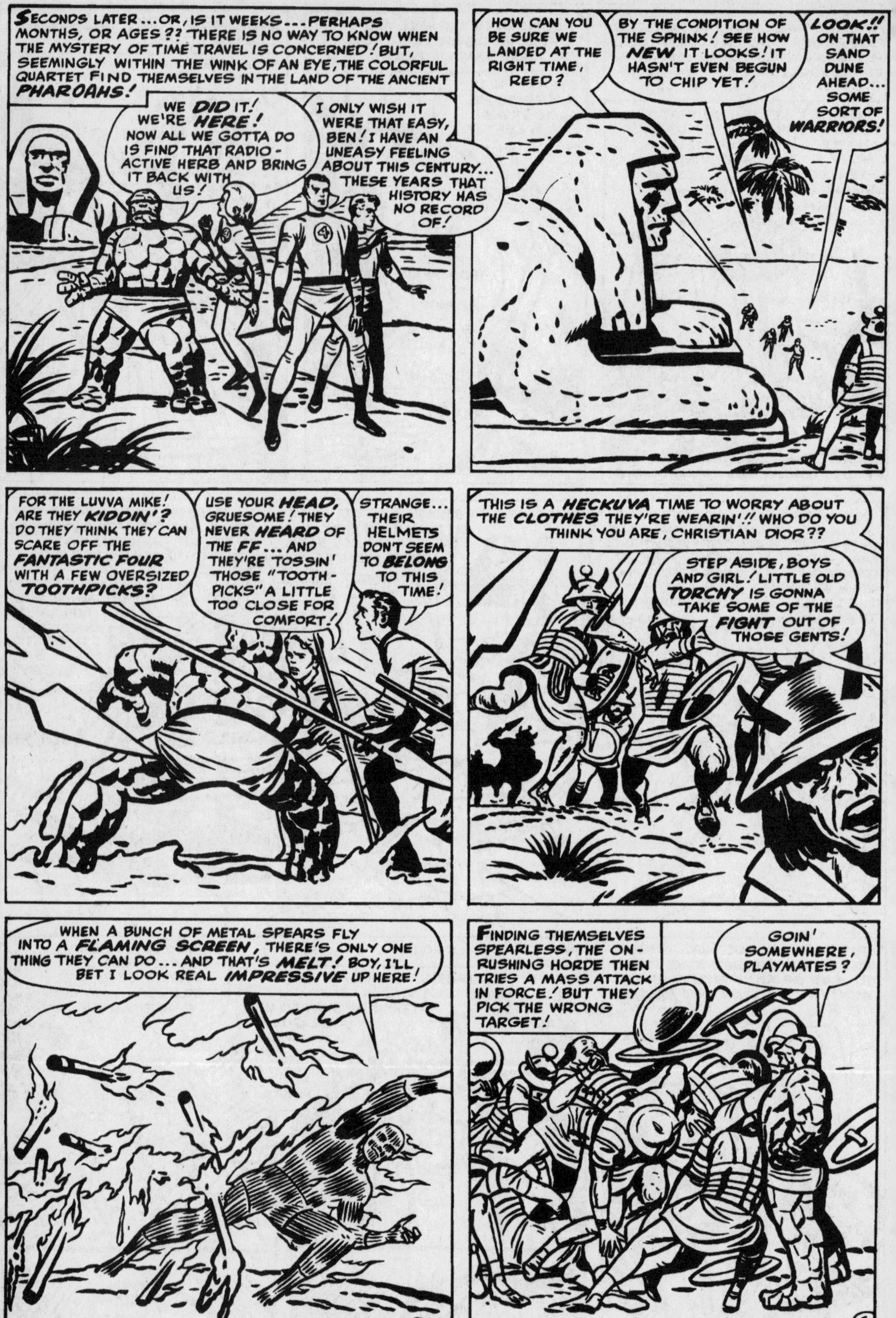
SECONDS LATER ... OR, IS IT WEEKS ... PERHAPS MONTHS, OR AGES?? THERE IS NO WAY TO KNOW WHEN THE MYSTERY OF TIME TRAVEL IS CONCERNED! BUT, SEEMINGLY WITHIN THE WINK OF AN EYE, THE COLORFUL QUARTET FIND THEMSELVES IN THE LAND OF THE ANCIENT PHAROAHS!
WE DID IT! WE'RE HERE! NOW ALL WE GOTTA DO IS FIND THAT RADIO-ACTIVE HERB AND BRING IT BACK WITH US!
I ONLY WISH IT WERE THAT EASY, BEN! I HAVE AN UNEASY FEELING ABOUT THIS CENTURY... THESE YEARS THAT HISTORY HAS NO RECORD OF!
HOW CAN YOU BE SURE WE LANDED AT THE RIGHT TIME, REED?
BY THE CONDITION OF THE SPHINX! SEE HOW NEW IT LOOKS! IT HASN'T EVEN BEGUN TO CHIP YET!
LOOK!! ON THAT SAND DUNE AHEAD... SOME SORT OF WARRIORS!
FOR THE LUVVA MIKE! ARE THEY KIDDIN'? DO THEY THINK THEY CAN SCARE OFF THE FANTASTIC FOUR WITH A FEW OVERSIZED TOOTHPICKS?
USE YOUR HEAD, GRUESOME! THEY NEVER HEARD OF THE FF... AND THEY'RE TOSSIN' THOSE "TOOTH-PICKS" A LITTLE TOO CLOSE FOR COMFORT!
STRANGE... THEIR HELMETS DON'T SEEM TO BELONG TO THIS TIME!
THIS IS A HECKUVA TIME TO WORRY ABOUT THE CLOTHES THEY'RE WEARIN'!! WHO DO YOU THINK YOU ARE, CHRISTIAN DIOR??
STEP ASIDE, BOYS AND GIRL! LITTLE OLD TORCHY IS GONNA TAKE SOME OF THE FIGHT OUT OF THOSE GENTS!
WHEN A BUNCH OF METAL SPEARS FLY INTO A FLAMING SCREEN, THERE'S ONLY ONE THING THEY CAN DO... AND THAT'S MELT! BOY, I'LL BET I LOOK REAL IMPRESSIVE UP HERE!
FINDING THEMSELVES SPEARLESS, THE ON-RUSHING HORDE THEN TRIES A MASS ATTACK IN FORCE! BUT THEY PICK THE WRONG TARGET!
GOIN' SOMEWHERE, PLAYMATES?
6.

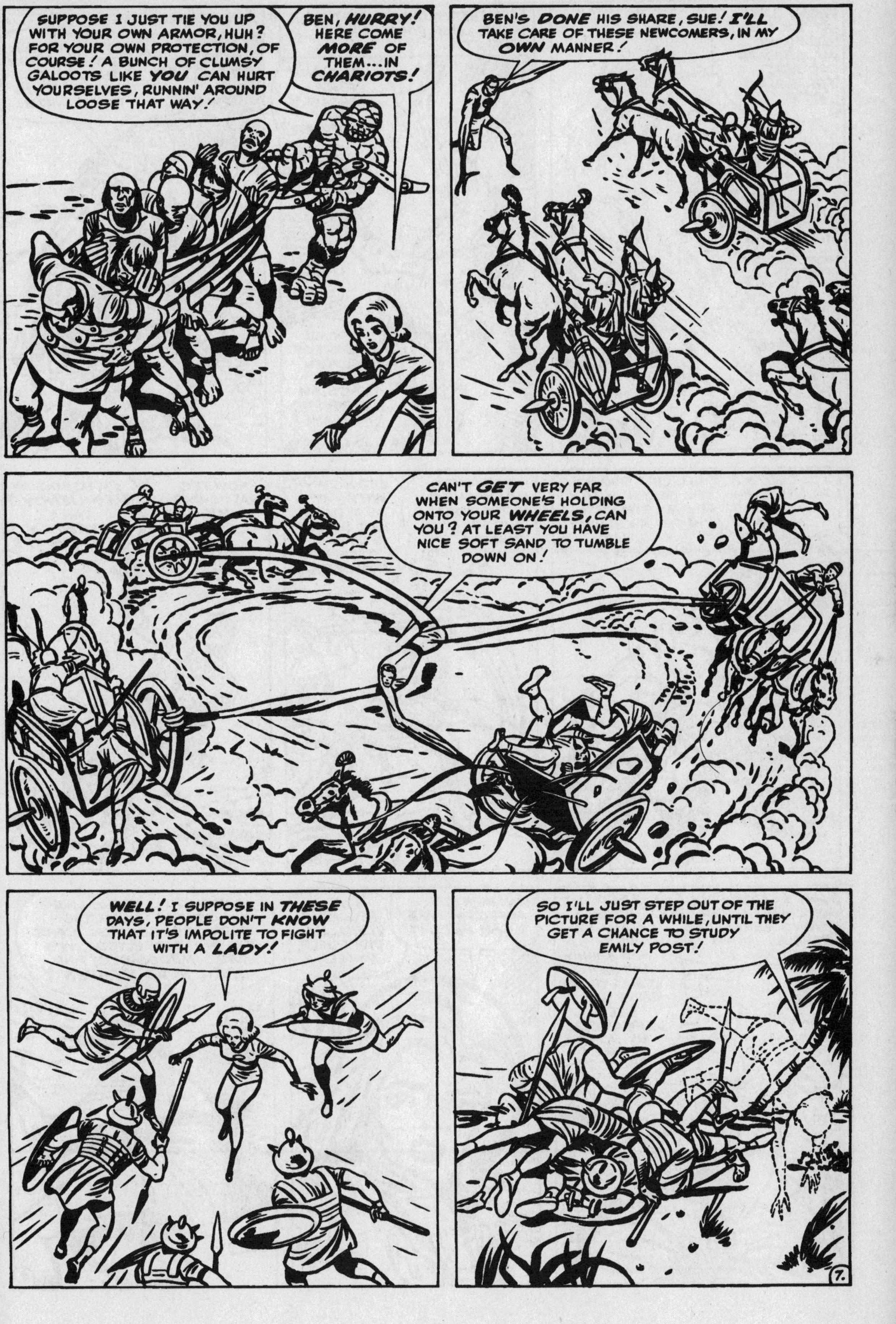
SUPPOSE I JUST TIE YOU UP WITH YOUR OWN ARMOR, HUH? FOR YOUR OWN PROTECTION, OF COURSE! A BUNCH OF CLUMSY GALOOTS LIKE YOU CAN HURT YOURSELVES, RUNNIN' AROUND LOOSE THAT WAY!
BEN, HURRY! HERE COME MORE OF THEM...IN CHARIOTS!
BEN'S DONE HIS SHARE, SUE! I'LL TAKE CARE OF THESE NEWCOMERS, IN MY OWN MANNER!
CAN'T GET VERY FAR WHEN SOMEONE'S HOLDING ONTO YOUR WHEELS, CAN YOU? AT LEAST YOU HAVE NICE SOFT SAND TO TUMBLE DOWN ON!
WELL! I SUPPOSE IN THESE DAYS, PEOPLE DON'T KNOW THAT IT'S IMPOLITE TO FIGHT WITH A LADY!
SO I'LL JUST STEP OUT OF THE PICTURE FOR A WHILE, UNTIL THEY GET A CHANCE TO STUDY EMILY POST!
7.

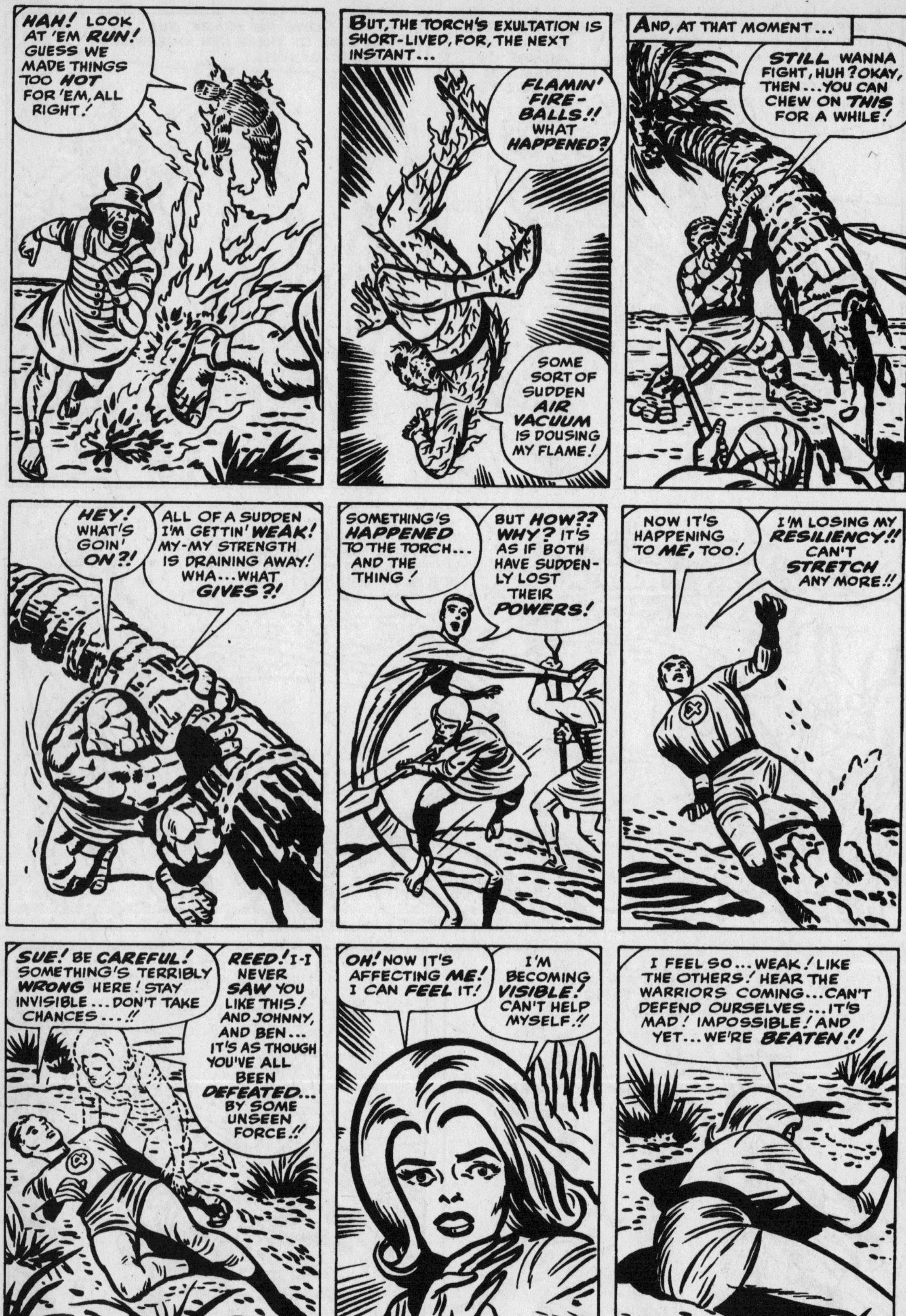
HAH! LOOK AT 'EM RUN! GUESS WE MADE THINGS TOO HOT FOR 'EM, ALL RIGHT!
BUT, THE TORCH'S EXULTATION IS SHORT-LIVED, FOR, THE NEXT INSTANT...
FLAMIN' FIRE-BALLS!! WHAT HAPPENED?
SOME SORT OF SUDDEN AIR VACUUM IS DOUSING MY FLAME!
AND, AT THAT MOMENT...
STILL WANNA FIGHT, HUH? OKAY, THEN... YOU CAN CHEW ON THIS FOR A WHILE!
HEY! WHAT'S GOIN' ON?!
ALL OF A SUDDEN I'M GETTIN' WEAK! MY-MY STRENGTH IS DRAINING AWAY! WHA... WHAT GIVES?!
SOMETHING'S HAPPENED TO THE TORCH... AND THE THING!
BUT HOW?? WHY? IT'S AS IF BOTH HAVE SUDDENLY LOST THEIR POWERS!
NOW IT'S HAPPENING TO ME, TOO!
I'M LOSING MY RESILIENCY!! CAN'T STRETCH ANY MORE!!
SUE! BE CAREFUL! SOMETHING'S TERRIBLY WRONG HERE! STAY INVISIBLE... DON'T TAKE CHANCES...!!
REED! I-I NEVER SAW YOU LIKE THIS! AND JOHNNY, AND BEN... IT'S AS THOUGH YOU'VE ALL BEEN DEFEATED... BY SOME UNSEEN FORCE!!
OH! NOW IT'S AFFECTING ME! I CAN FEEL IT!
I'M BECOMING VISIBLE! CAN'T HELP MYSELF!!
I FEEL SO... WEAK! LIKE THE OTHERS! HEAR THE WARRIORS COMING... CAN'T DEFEND OURSELVES... IT'S MAD! IMPOSSIBLE! AND YET... WE'RE BEATEN!!
8.

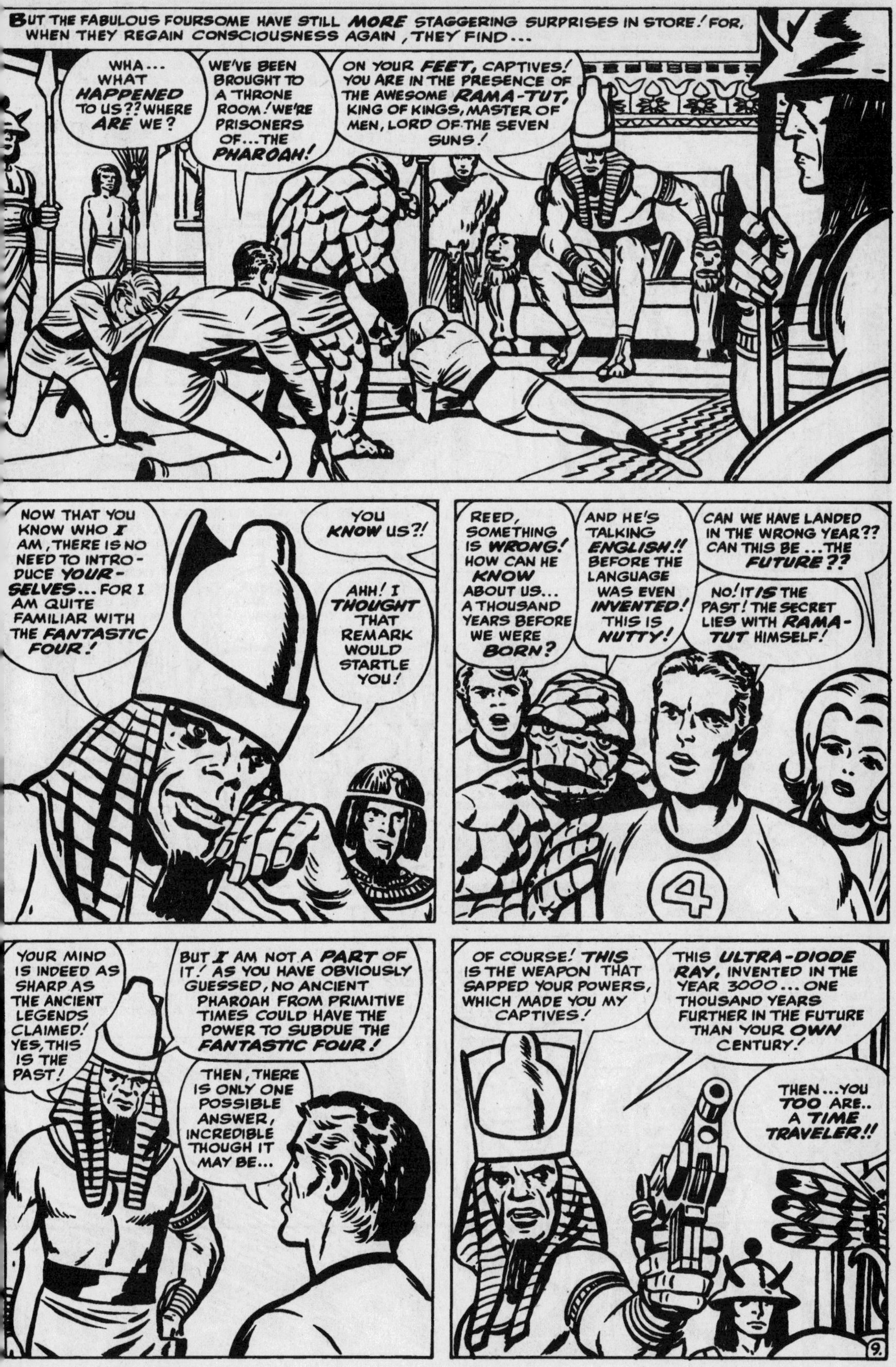

BUT THE FABULOUS FOURSOME HAVE STILL MORE STAGGERING SURPRISES IN STORE! FOR, WHEN THEY REGAIN CONSCIOUSNESS AGAIN, THEY FIND...
WHA... WHAT HAPPENED TO US?? WHERE ARE WE?
WE'VE BEEN BROUGHT TO A THRONE ROOM! WE'RE PRISONERS OF... THE PHAROAH!
ON YOUR FEET, CAPTIVES! YOU ARE IN THE PRESENCE OF THE AWESOME RAMA-TUT, KING OF KINGS, MASTER OF MEN, LORD OF THE SEVEN SUNS!
NOW THAT YOU KNOW WHO I AM, THERE IS NO NEED TO INTRODUCE YOURSELVES... FOR I AM QUITE FAMILIAR WITH THE FANTASTIC FOUR!
YOU KNOW US?!
AHH! I THOUGHT THAT REMARK WOULD STARTLE YOU!
REED, SOMETHING IS WRONG! HOW CAN HE KNOW ABOUT US... A THOUSAND YEARS BEFORE WE WERE BORN?
AND HE'S TALKING ENGLISH!! BEFORE THE LANGUAGE WAS EVEN INVENTED! THIS IS NUTTY!
CAN WE HAVE LANDED IN THE WRONG YEAR?? CAN THIS BE ... THE FUTURE??
NO! IT IS THE PAST! THE SECRET LIES WITH RAMA-TUT HIMSELF!
YOUR MIND IS INDEED AS SHARP AS THE ANCIENT LEGENDS CLAIMED! YES, THIS IS THE PAST!
BUT I AM NOT A PART OF IT! AS YOU HAVE OBVIOUSLY GUESSED, NO ANCIENT PHAROAH FROM PRIMITIVE TIMES COULD HAVE THE POWER TO SUBDUE THE FANTASTIC FOUR!
THEN, THERE IS ONLY ONE POSSIBLE ANSWER, INCREDIBLE THOUGH IT MAY BE...
OF COURSE! THIS IS THE WEAPON THAT SAPPED YOUR POWERS, WHICH MADE YOU MY CAPTIVES!
THIS ULTRA-DIODE RAY, INVENTED IN THE YEAR 3000... ONE THOUSAND YEARS FURTHER IN THE FUTURE THAN YOUR OWN CENTURY!
THEN... YOU TOO ARE.. A TIME TRAVELER!!
9.

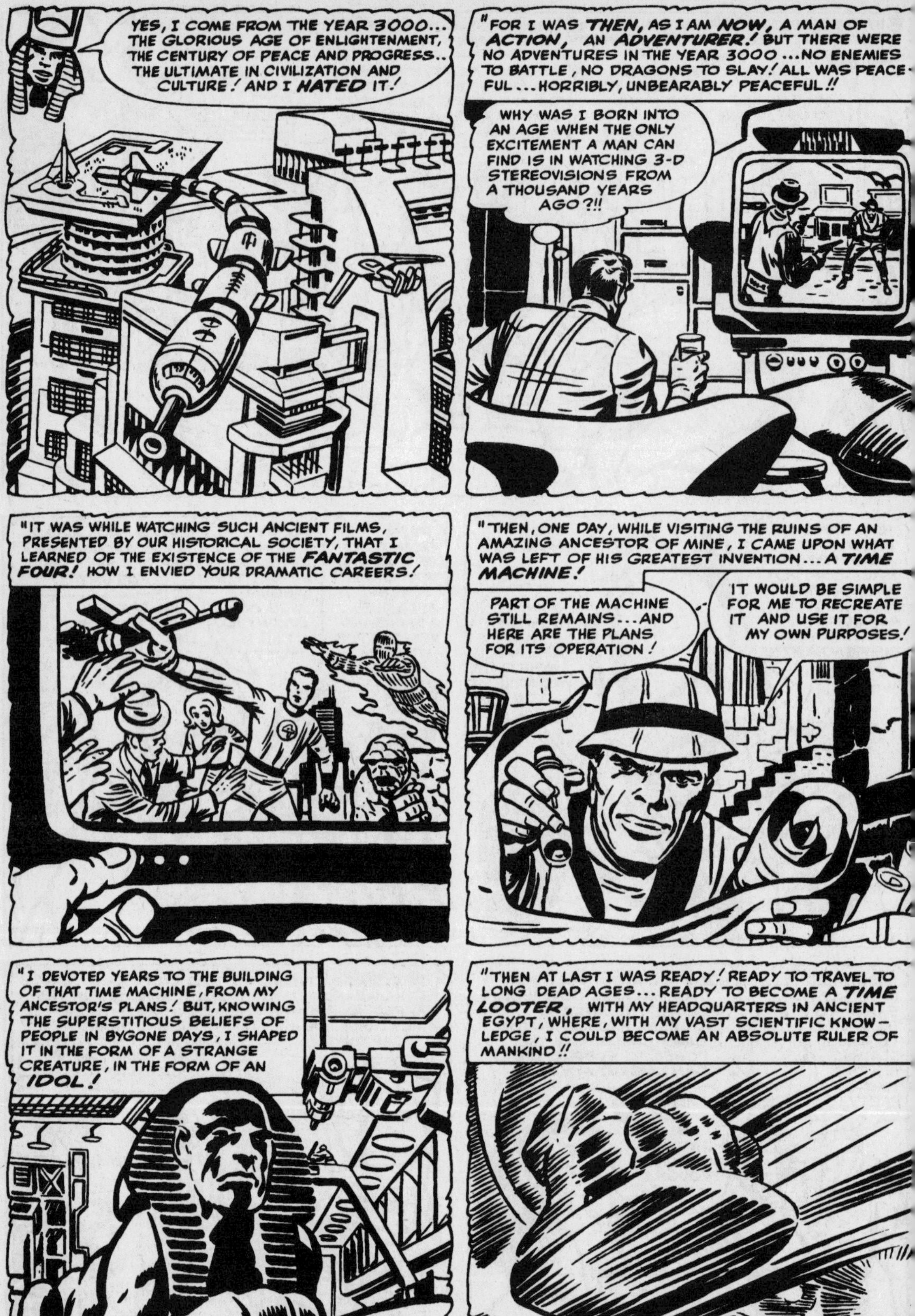
YES, I COME FROM THE YEAR 3000... THE GLORIOUS AGE OF ENLIGHTENMENT, THE CENTURY OF PEACE AND PROGRESS.. THE ULTIMATE IN CIVILIZATION AND CULTURE! AND I HATED IT!
"FOR I WAS THEN, AS I AM NOW, A MAN OF ACTION, AN ADVENTURER! BUT THERE WERE NO ADVENTURES IN THE YEAR 3000 ...NO ENEMIES TO BATTLE, NO DRAGONS TO SLAY! ALL WAS PEACEFUL ... HORRIBLY, UNBEARABLY PEACEFUL!!
WHY WAS I BORN INTO AN AGE WHEN THE ONLY EXCITEMENT A MAN CAN FIND IS IN WATCHING 3-D STEREOVISIONS FROM A THOUSAND YEARS AGO?!!
"IT WAS WHILE WATCHING SUCH ANCIENT FILMS, PRESENTED BY OUR HISTORICAL SOCIETY, THAT I LEARNED OF THE EXISTENCE OF THE FANTASTIC FOUR! HOW I ENVIED YOUR DRAMATIC CAREERS!
"THEN, ONE DAY, WHILE VISITING THE RUINS OF AN AMAZING ANCESTOR OF MINE, I CAME UPON WHAT WAS LEFT OF HIS GREATEST INVENTION ... A TIME MACHINE!
PART OF THE MACHINE STILL REMAINS... AND HERE ARE THE PLANS FOR ITS OPERATION!
IT WOULD BE SIMPLE FOR ME TO RECREATE IT AND USE IT FOR MY OWN PURPOSES!
"I DEVOTED YEARS TO THE BUILDING OF THAT TIME MACHINE, FROM MY ANCESTOR'S PLANS! BUT, KNOWING THE SUPERSTITIOUS BELIEFS OF PEOPLE IN BYGONE DAYS, I SHAPED IT IN THE FORM OF A STRANGE CREATURE, IN THE FORM OF AN IDOL!
"THEN AT LAST I WAS READY! READY TO TRAVEL TO LONG DEAD AGES... READY TO BECOME A TIME LOOTER, WITH MY HEADQUARTERS IN ANCIENT EGYPT, WHERE, WITH MY VAST SCIENTIFIC KNOW-LEDGE, I COULD BECOME AN ABSOLUTE RULER OF MANKIND!!
10

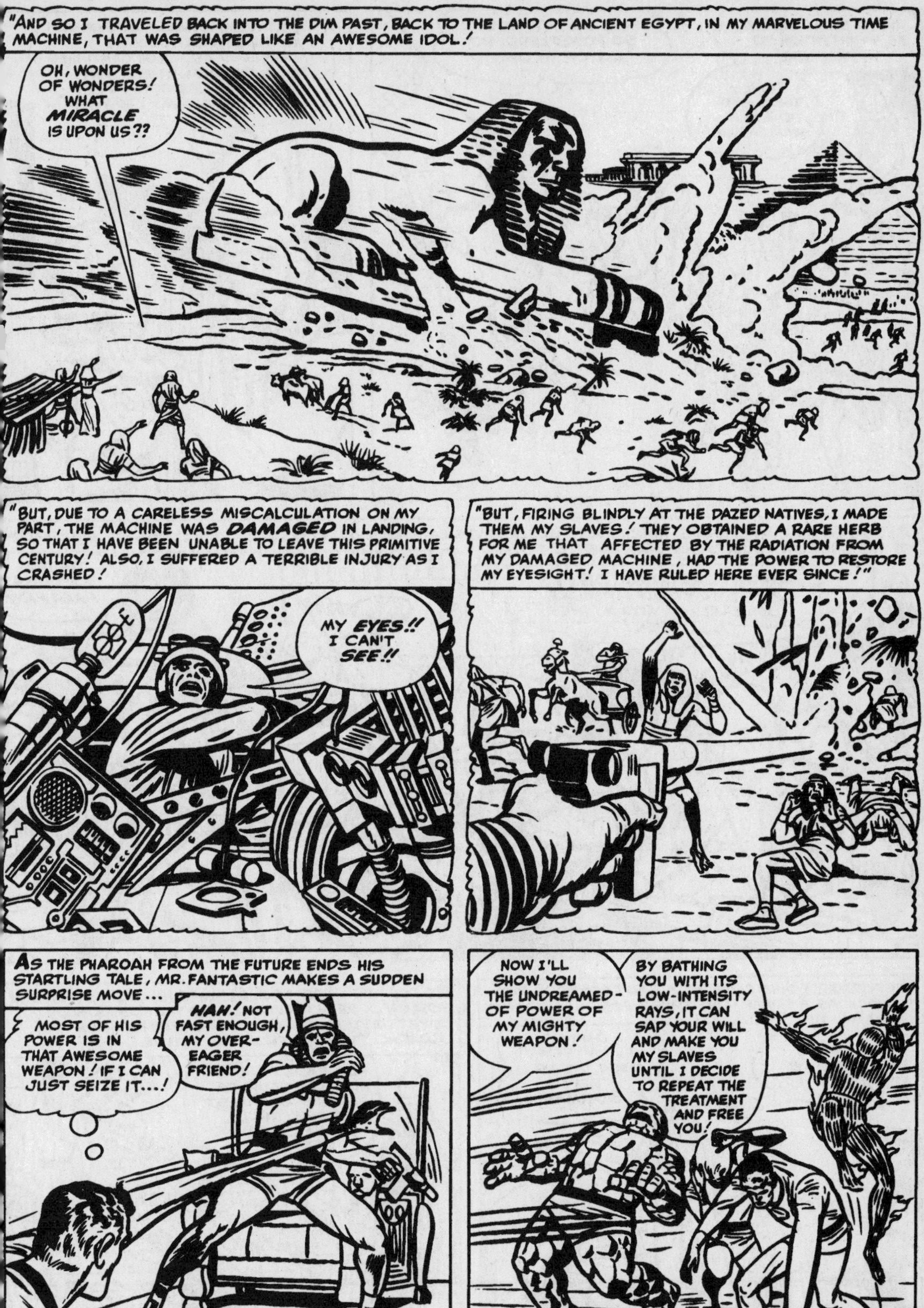

"AND SO I TRAVELED BACK INTO THE DIM PAST, BACK TO THE LAND OF ANCIENT EGYPT, IN MY MARVELOUS TIME MACHINE, THAT WAS SHAPED LIKE AN AWESOME IDOL!
OH, WONDER OF WONDERS! WHAT MIRACLE IS UPON US??
"BUT, DUE TO A CARELESS MISCALCULATION ON MY PART, THE MACHINE WAS DAMAGED IN LANDING, SO THAT I HAVE BEEN UNABLE TO LEAVE THIS PRIMITIVE CENTURY! ALSO, I SUFFERED A TERRIBLE INJURY AS I CRASHED!
MY EYES!! I CAN'T SEE!!
"BUT, FIRING BLINDLY AT THE DAZED NATIVES, I MADE THEM MY SLAVES! THEY OBTAINED A RARE HERB FOR ME THAT AFFECTED BY THE RADIATION FROM MY DAMAGED MACHINE, HAD THE POWER TO RESTORE MY EYESIGHT! I HAVE RULED HERE EVER SINCE!"
AS THE PHAROAH FROM THE FUTURE ENDS HIS STARTLING TALE, MR. FANTASTIC MAKES A SUDDEN SURPRISE MOVE...
MOST OF HIS POWER IS IN THAT AWESOME WEAPON! IF I CAN JUST SEIZE IT...!
HAH! NOT FAST ENOUGH, MY OVER-EAGER FRIEND!
NOW I'LL SHOW YOU THE UNDREAMED-OF POWER OF MY MIGHTY WEAPON!
BY BATHING YOU WITH ITS LOW-INTENSITY RAYS, IT CAN SAP YOUR WILL AND MAKE YOU MY SLAVES UNTIL I DECIDE TO REPEAT THE TREATMENT AND FREE YOU!
11

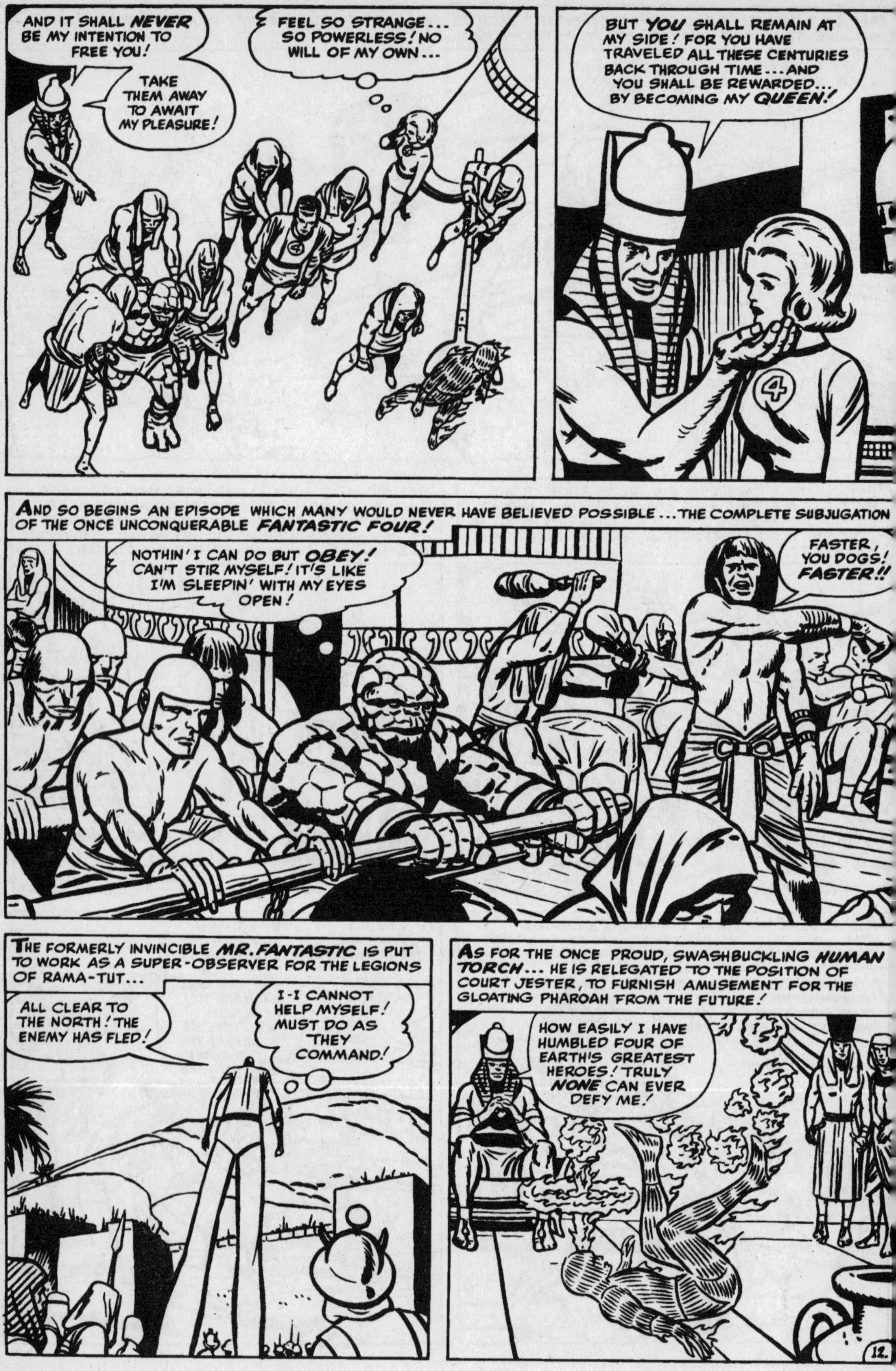
AND IT SHALL NEVER BE MY INTENTION TO FREE YOU!
TAKE THEM AWAY TO AWAIT MY PLEASURE!
FEEL SO STRANGE... SO POWERLESS! NO WILL OF MY OWN...
BUT YOU SHALL REMAIN AT MY SIDE! FOR YOU HAVE TRAVELED ALL THESE CENTURIES BACK THROUGH TIME... AND YOU SHALL BE REWARDED... BY BECOMING MY QUEEN!
AND SO BEGINS AN EPISODE WHICH MANY WOULD NEVER HAVE BELIEVED POSSIBLE... THE COMPLETE SUBJUGATION OF THE ONCE UNCONQUERABLE FANTASTIC FOUR!
NOTHIN' I CAN DO BUT OBEY! CAN'T STIR MYSELF! IT'S LIKE I'M SLEEPIN' WITH MY EYES OPEN!
FASTER, YOU DOGS! FASTER!!
THE FORMERLY INVINCIBLE MR. FANTASTIC IS PUT TO WORK AS A SUPER-OBSERVER FOR THE LEGIONS OF RAMA-TUT...
ALL CLEAR TO THE NORTH! THE ENEMY HAS FLED!
I-I CANNOT HELP MYSELF! MUST DO AS THEY COMMAND!
AS FOR THE ONCE PROUD, SWASHBUCKLING HUMAN TORCH... HE IS RELEGATED TO THE POSITION OF COURT JESTER, TO FURNISH AMUSEMENT FOR THE GLOATING PHAROAH FROM THE FUTURE!
HOW EASILY I HAVE HUMBLED FOUR OF EARTH'S GREATEST HEROES! TRULY NONE CAN EVER DEFY ME!
12.

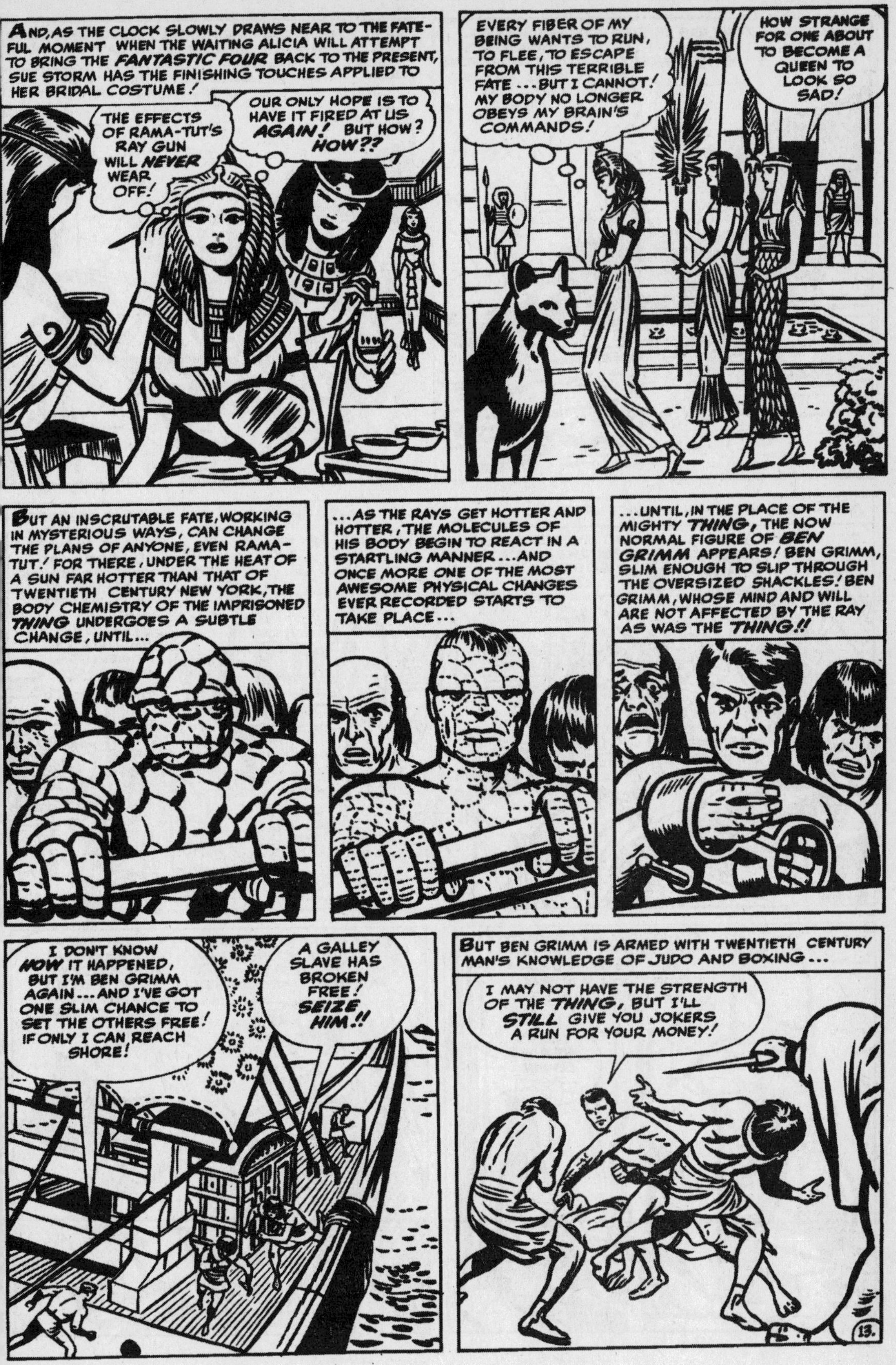
AND, AS THE CLOCK SLOWLY DRAWS NEAR TO THE FATEFUL MOMENT WHEN THE WAITING ALICIA WILL ATTEMPT TO BRING THE FANTASTIC FOUR BACK TO THE PRESENT, SUE STORM HAS THE FINISHING TOUCHES APPLIED TO HER BRIDAL COSTUME!
THE EFFECTS OF RAMA-TUT'S RAY GUN WILL NEVER WEAR OFF!
OUR ONLY HOPE IS TO HAVE IT FIRED AT US AGAIN! BUT HOW? HOW??
EVERY FIBER OF MY BEING WANTS TO RUN, TO FLEE, TO ESCAPE FROM THIS TERRIBLE FATE ... BUT I CANNOT! MY BODY NO LONGER OBEYS MY BRAIN'S COMMANDS!
HOW STRANGE FOR ONE ABOUT TO BECOME A QUEEN TO LOOK SO SAD!
BUT AN INSCRUTABLE FATE, WORKING IN MYSTERIOUS WAYS, CAN CHANGE THE PLANS OF ANYONE, EVEN RAMA-TUT! FOR THERE, UNDER THE HEAT OF A SUN FAR HOTTER THAN THAT OF TWENTIETH CENTURY NEW YORK, THE BODY CHEMISTRY OF THE IMPRISONED THING UNDERGOES A SUBTLE CHANGE, UNTIL...
...AS THE RAYS GET HOTTER AND HOTTER, THE MOLECULES OF HIS BODY BEGIN TO REACT IN A STARTLING MANNER ... AND ONCE MORE ONE OF THE MOST AWESOME PHYSICAL CHANGES EVER RECORDED STARTS TO TAKE PLACE...
...UNTIL, IN THE PLACE OF THE MIGHTY THING, THE NOW NORMAL FIGURE OF BEN GRIMM APPEARS! BEN GRIMM, SLIM ENOUGH TO SLIP THROUGH THE OVERSIZED SHACKLES! BEN GRIMM, WHOSE MIND AND WILL ARE NOT AFFECTED BY THE RAY AS WAS THE THING!!
I DON'T KNOW HOW IT HAPPENED, BUT I'M BEN GRIMM AGAIN ... AND I'VE GOT ONE SLIM CHANCE TO SET THE OTHERS FREE! IF ONLY I CAN REACH SHORE!
A GALLEY SLAVE HAS BROKEN FREE! SEIZE HIM!!
BUT BEN GRIMM IS ARMED WITH TWENTIETH CENTURY MAN'S KNOWLEDGE OF JUDO AND BOXING ...
I MAY NOT HAVE THE STRENGTH OF THE THING, BUT I'LL STILL GIVE YOU JOKERS A RUN FOR YOUR MONEY!
13.

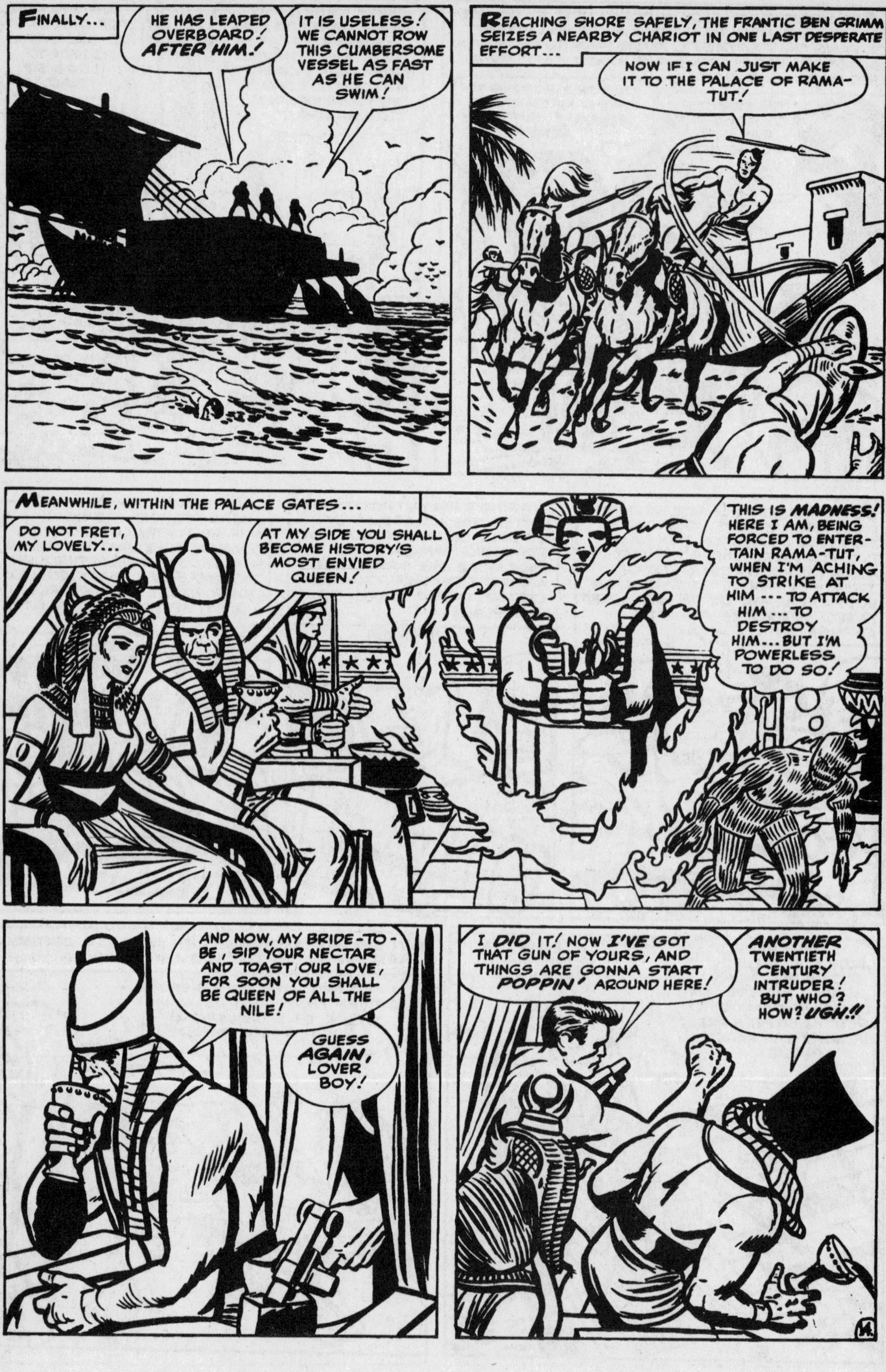

FINALLY...
HE HAS LEAPED OVERBOARD! AFTER HIM!
IT IS USELESS! WE CANNOT ROW THIS CUMBERSOME VESSEL AS FAST AS HE CAN SWIM!
REACHING SHORE SAFELY, THE FRANTIC BEN GRIMM SEIZES A NEARBY CHARIOT IN ONE LAST DESPERATE EFFORT...
NOW IF I CAN JUST MAKE IT TO THE PALACE OF RAMA-TUT!
MEANWHILE, WITHIN THE PALACE GATES...
DO NOT FRET, MY LOVELY...
AT MY SIDE YOU SHALL BECOME HISTORY'S MOST ENVIED QUEEN!
THIS IS MADNESS! HERE I AM, BEING FORCED TO ENTERTAIN RAMA-TUT, WHEN I'M ACHING TO STRIKE AT HIM --- TO ATTACK HIM ... TO DESTROY HIM ... BUT I'M POWERLESS TO DO SO!
AND NOW, MY BRIDE-TO-BE, SIP YOUR NECTAR AND TOAST OUR LOVE, FOR SOON YOU SHALL BE QUEEN OF ALL THE NILE!
GUESS AGAIN, LOVER BOY!
I DID IT! NOW I'VE GOT THAT GUN OF YOURS, AND THINGS ARE GONNA START POPPIN' AROUND HERE!
ANOTHER TWENTIETH CENTURY INTRUDER! BUT WHO? HOW? UGH!!
14.

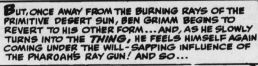

BUT, ONCE AWAY FROM THE BURNING RAYS OF THE PRIMITIVE DESERT SUN, BEN GRIMM BEGINS TO REVERT TO HIS OTHER FORM... AND, AS HE SLOWLY TURNS INTO THE *THING*, HE FEELS HIMSELF AGAIN COMING UNDER THE WILL-SAPPING INFLUENCE OF THE PHAROAH'S RAY GUN! AND SO...

MUST FREE *SUE* BEFORE I GO UNDER... CAN'T LET MY ESCAPE HAVE BEEN IN VAIN! MUSTN'T MISS... JUST ONE BLAST... JUST *ONE*...

THE RAYS STRUCK HER A SECOND TIME! SHE'S *NORMAL* AGAIN! MUST GET THE GUN FROM HER!

YOU *SAVED* ME, BEN! NOW *I* HAVE THE GUN! IT'S UP TO *ME*... AND I WON'T LET YOU DOWN! I WON'T FAIL THE FANTASTIC FOUR!

GIVE ME THAT RAY GUN, WOMAN! IT WON'T HELP YOU! I'LL SEIZE IT BEFORE YOU CAN LEARN HOW TO OPERATE IT!

I'VE GOT TO STALL FOR TIME! EVEN A FEW SECONDS!

YOU ARE ELUSIVE, MY QUEEN-TO-BE! BUT TURNING INVISIBLE WILL DO NO GOOD! I CAN STILL SEE YOUR GARMENTS!

I FORGOT! I'M NOT WEARING MY UNSTABLE-MOLECULE COSTUME! ONLY ONE CHANCE LEFT.. I'LL FIRE AT THE *TORCH*!

I DID IT! IT WORKED! THE RAY IS BATHING HIM!

YIPPEE! I'M *MYSELF* AGAIN! I CAN DO WHAT I *WANT* TO! STAND BACK NOW, SIS, AND WATCH MY STEAM!

NO! STAY BACK! STOP! I COMMAND YOU!!

MISTER, YOUR COMMANDIN' DAYS ARE *OVER*! THIS IS JUST A *SAMPLE* OF WHAT YOU'LL GET WHEN I SNAP THE *THING* AND *MR. FANTASTIC* OUT OF *THEIR* SPELLS, TOO!

15.

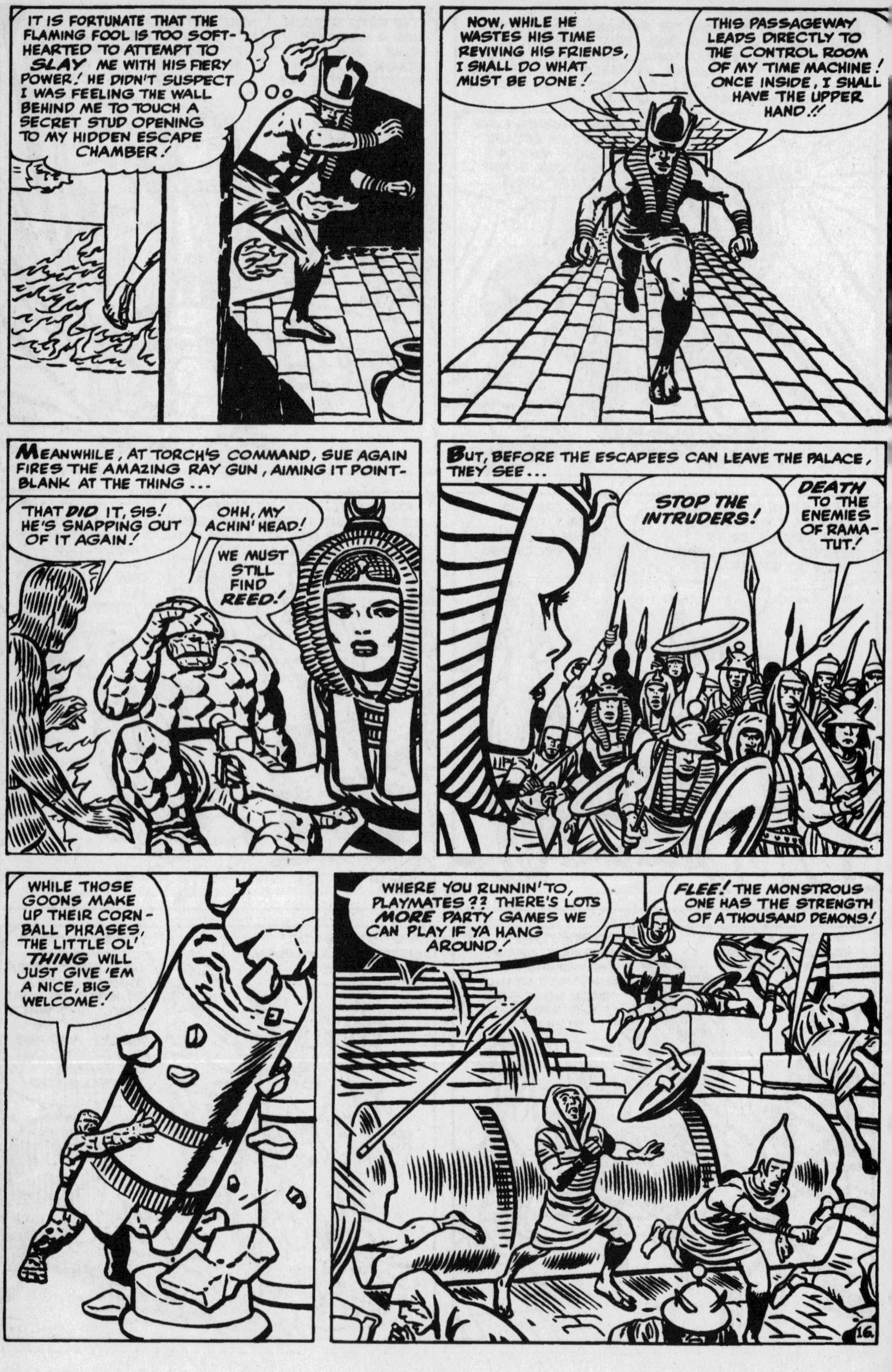
IT IS FORTUNATE THAT THE FLAMING FOOL IS TOO SOFT-HEARTED TO ATTEMPT TO SLAY ME WITH HIS FIERY POWER! HE DIDN'T SUSPECT I WAS FEELING THE WALL BEHIND ME TO TOUCH A SECRET STUD OPENING TO MY HIDDEN ESCAPE CHAMBER!
NOW, WHILE HE WASTES HIS TIME REVIVING HIS FRIENDS, I SHALL DO WHAT MUST BE DONE!
THIS PASSAGEWAY LEADS DIRECTLY TO THE CONTROL ROOM OF MY TIME MACHINE! ONCE INSIDE, I SHALL HAVE THE UPPER HAND!!
MEANWHILE, AT TORCH'S COMMAND, SUE AGAIN FIRES THE AMAZING RAY GUN, AIMING IT POINT-BLANK AT THE THING...
THAT DID IT, SIS! HE'S SNAPPING OUT OF IT AGAIN!
OHH, MY ACHIN' HEAD!
WE MUST STILL FIND REED!
BUT, BEFORE THE ESCAPEES CAN LEAVE THE PALACE, THEY SEE...
STOP THE INTRUDERS!
DEATH TO THE ENEMIES OF RAMA-TUT!
WHILE THOSE GOONS MAKE UP THEIR CORN-BALL PHRASES, THE LITTLE OL' THING WILL JUST GIVE 'EM A NICE, BIG WELCOME!
WHERE YOU RUNNIN' TO, PLAYMATES?? THERE'S LOTS MORE PARTY GAMES WE CAN PLAY IF YA HANG AROUND!
FLEE! THE MONSTROUS ONE HAS THE STRENGTH OF A THOUSAND DEMONS!
16.

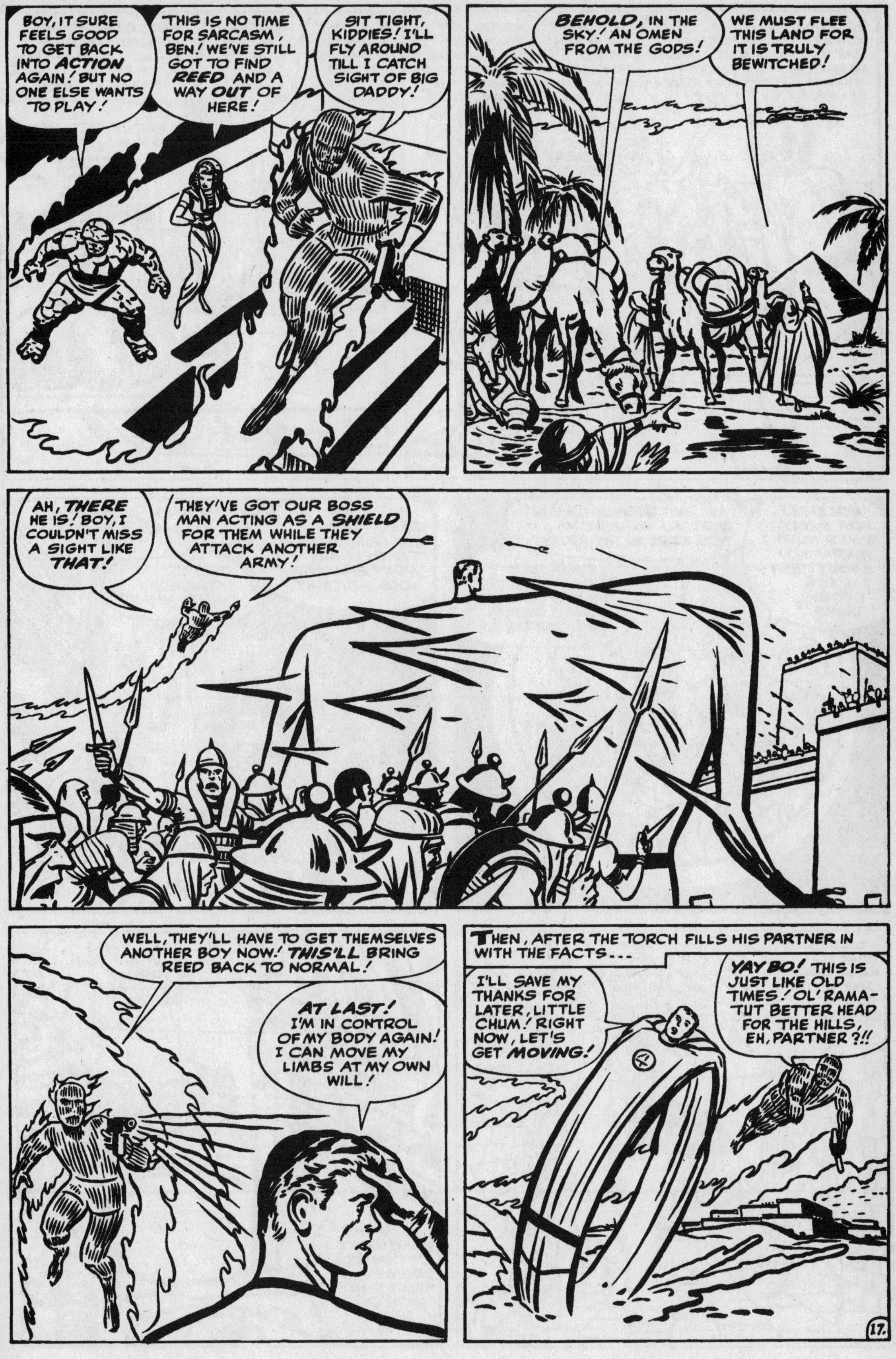
BOY, IT SURE FEELS GOOD TO GET BACK INTO ACTION AGAIN! BUT NO ONE ELSE WANTS TO PLAY!
THIS IS NO TIME FOR SARCASM, BEN! WE'VE STILL GOT TO FIND REED AND A WAY OUT OF HERE!
SIT TIGHT, KIDDIES! I'LL FLY AROUND TILL I CATCH SIGHT OF BIG DADDY!
BEHOLD, IN THE SKY! AN OMEN FROM THE GODS!
WE MUST FLEE THIS LAND FOR IT IS TRULY BEWITCHED!
AH, THERE HE IS! BOY, I COULDN'T MISS A SIGHT LIKE THAT!
THEY'VE GOT OUR BOSS MAN ACTING AS A SHIELD FOR THEM WHILE THEY ATTACK ANOTHER ARMY!
WELL, THEY'LL HAVE TO GET THEMSELVES ANOTHER BOY NOW! THIS'LL BRING REED BACK TO NORMAL!
AT LAST! I'M IN CONTROL OF MY BODY AGAIN! I CAN MOVE MY LIMBS AT MY OWN WILL!
THEN, AFTER THE TORCH FILLS HIS PARTNER IN WITH THE FACTS...
I'LL SAVE MY THANKS FOR LATER, LITTLE CHUM! RIGHT NOW, LET'S GET MOVING!
YAY BO! THIS IS JUST LIKE OLD TIMES! OL' RAMA-TUT BETTER HEAD FOR THE HILLS, EH, PARTNER?!!
17.

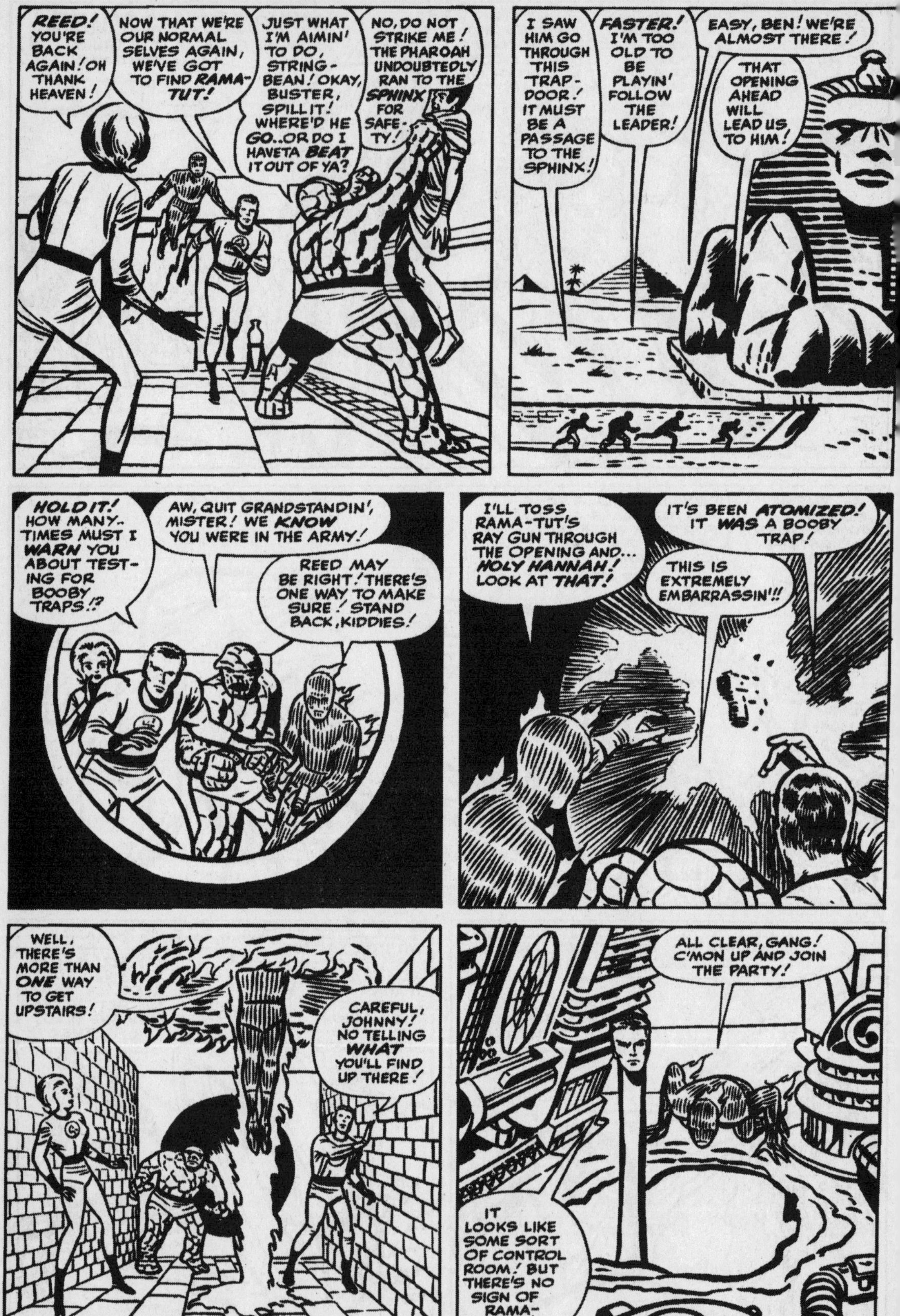
REED! YOU'RE BACK AGAIN! OH THANK HEAVEN!
NOW THAT WE'RE OUR NORMAL SELVES AGAIN, WE'VE GOT TO FIND RAMA-TUT!
JUST WHAT I'M AIMIN' TO DO, STRING-BEAN! OKAY, BUSTER, SPILL IT! WHERE'D HE GO..OR DO I HAVETA BEAT IT OUT OF YA?
NO, DO NOT STRIKE ME! THE PHAROAH UNDOUBTEDLY RAN TO THE SPHINX FOR SAFE-TY!
I SAW HIM GO THROUGH THIS TRAP-DOOR! IT MUST BE A PASSAGE TO THE SPHINX!
FASTER! I'M TOO OLD TO BE PLAYIN' FOLLOW THE LEADER!
EASY, BEN! WE'RE ALMOST THERE!
THAT OPENING AHEAD WILL LEAD US TO HIM!
HOLD IT! HOW MANY.. TIMES MUST I WARN YOU ABOUT TESTING FOR BOOBY TRAPS!?
AW, QUIT GRANDSTANDIN', MISTER! WE KNOW YOU WERE IN THE ARMY!
REED MAY BE RIGHT! THERE'S ONE WAY TO MAKE SURE! STAND BACK, KIDDIES!
I'LL TOSS RAMA-TUT'S RAY GUN THROUGH THE OPENING AND... HOLY HANNAH! LOOK AT THAT!
IT'S BEEN ATOMIZED! IT WAS A BOOBY TRAP!
THIS IS EXTREMELY EMBARRASSIN'!!!
WELL, THERE'S MORE THAN ONE WAY TO GET UPSTAIRS!
CAREFUL, JOHNNY! NO TELLING WHAT YOU'LL FIND UP THERE!
ALL CLEAR, GANG! C'MON UP AND JOIN THE PARTY!
IT LOOKS LIKE SOME SORT OF CONTROL ROOM! BUT THERE'S NO SIGN OF RAMA-TUT!

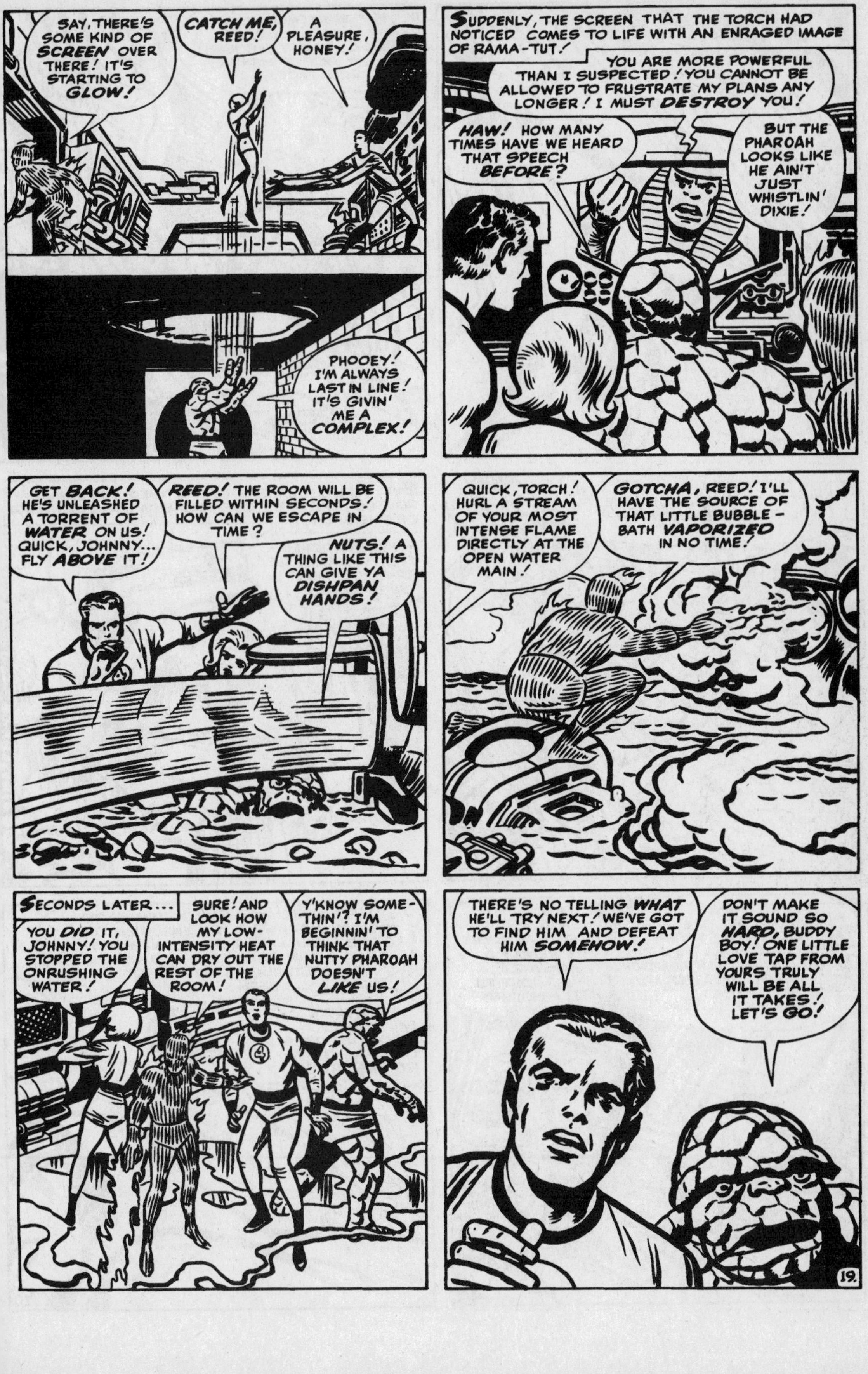
SAY, THERE'S SOME KIND OF SCREEN OVER THERE! IT'S STARTING TO GLOW!
CATCH ME, REED!
A PLEASURE, HONEY!
PHOOEY! I'M ALWAYS LAST IN LINE! IT'S GIVIN' ME A COMPLEX!
SUDDENLY, THE SCREEN THAT THE TORCH HAD NOTICED COMES TO LIFE WITH AN ENRAGED IMAGE OF RAMA-TUT!
YOU ARE MORE POWERFUL THAN I SUSPECTED! YOU CANNOT BE ALLOWED TO FRUSTRATE MY PLANS ANY LONGER! I MUST DESTROY YOU!
HAW! HOW MANY TIMES HAVE WE HEARD THAT SPEECH BEFORE?
BUT THE PHAROAH LOOKS LIKE HE AIN'T JUST WHISTLIN' DIXIE!
GET BACK! HE'S UNLEASHED A TORRENT OF WATER ON US! QUICK, JOHNNY... FLY ABOVE IT!
REED! THE ROOM WILL BE FILLED WITHIN SECONDS! HOW CAN WE ESCAPE IN TIME?
NUTS! A THING LIKE THIS CAN GIVE YA DISHPAN HANDS!
QUICK, TORCH! HURL A STREAM OF YOUR MOST INTENSE FLAME DIRECTLY AT THE OPEN WATER MAIN!
GOTCHA, REED! I'LL HAVE THE SOURCE OF THAT LITTLE BUBBLE-BATH VAPORIZED IN NO TIME!
SECONDS LATER...
YOU DID IT, JOHNNY! YOU STOPPED THE ONRUSHING WATER!
SURE! AND LOOK HOW MY LOW-INTENSITY HEAT CAN DRY OUT THE REST OF THE ROOM!
Y'KNOW SOME-THIN'? I'M BEGINNIN' TO THINK THAT NUTTY PHAROAH DOESN'T LIKE US!
THERE'S NO TELLING WHAT HE'LL TRY NEXT! WE'VE GOT TO FIND HIM AND DEFEAT HIM SOMEHOW!
DON'T MAKE IT SOUND SO HARD, BUDDY BOY! ONE LITTLE LOVE TAP FROM YOURS TRULY WILL BE ALL IT TAKES! LET'S GO!

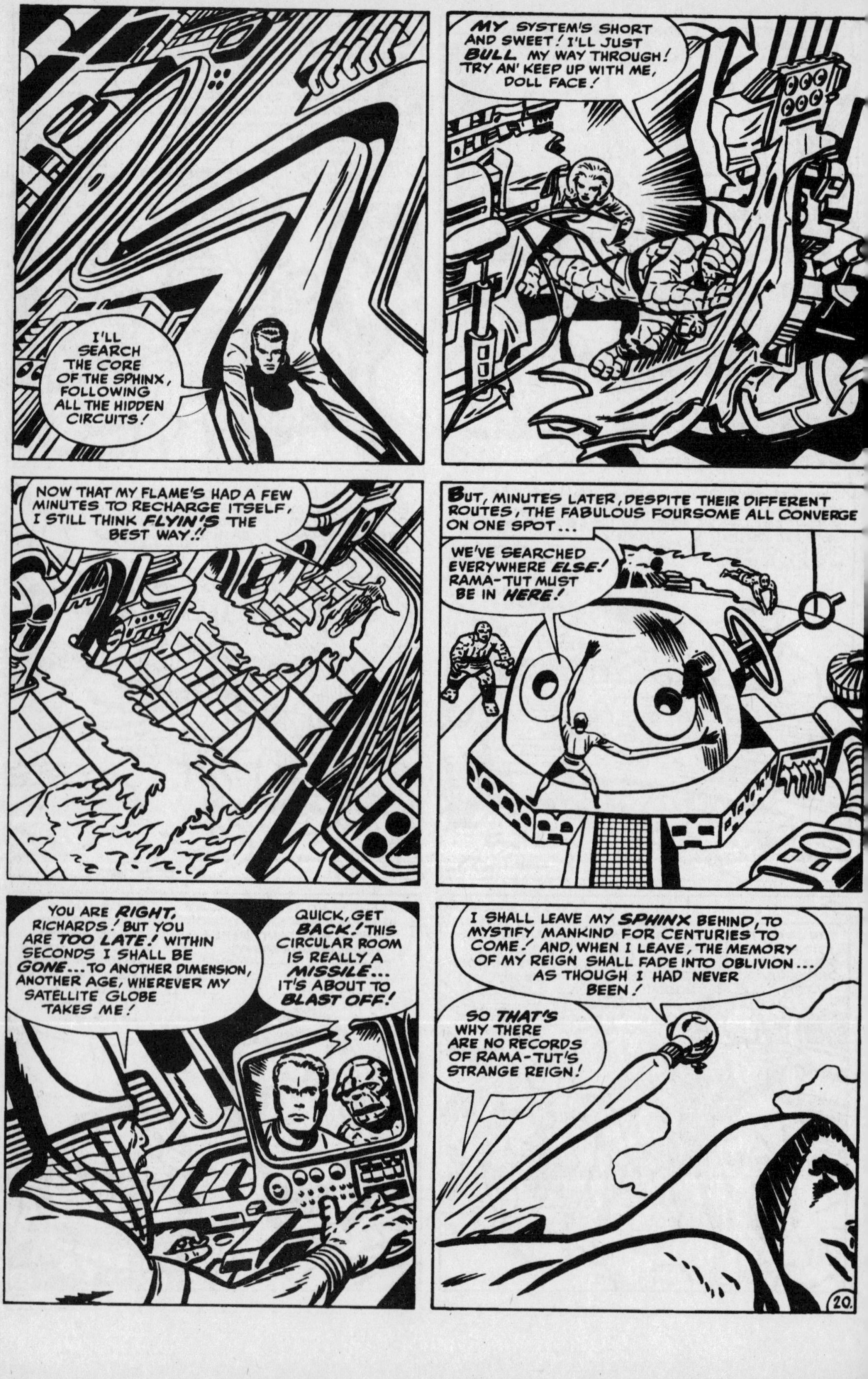

I'LL SEARCH THE CORE OF THE SPHINX, FOLLOWING ALL THE HIDDEN CIRCUITS!
MY SYSTEM'S SHORT AND SWEET! I'LL JUST BULL MY WAY THROUGH! TRY AN' KEEP UP WITH ME, DOLL FACE!
NOW THAT MY FLAME'S HAD A FEW MINUTES TO RECHARGE ITSELF, I STILL THINK FLYIN'S THE BEST WAY!!
BUT, MINUTES LATER, DESPITE THEIR DIFFERENT ROUTES, THE FABULOUS FOURSOME ALL CONVERGE ON ONE SPOT...
WE'VE SEARCHED EVERYWHERE ELSE! RAMA-TUT MUST BE IN HERE!
YOU ARE RIGHT, RICHARDS! BUT YOU ARE TOO LATE! WITHIN SECONDS I SHALL BE GONE... TO ANOTHER DIMENSION, ANOTHER AGE, WHEREVER MY SATELLITE GLOBE TAKES ME!
QUICK, GET BACK! THIS CIRCULAR ROOM IS REALLY A MISSILE... IT'S ABOUT TO BLAST OFF!
I SHALL LEAVE MY SPHINX BEHIND, TO MYSTIFY MANKIND FOR CENTURIES TO COME! AND, WHEN I LEAVE, THE MEMORY OF MY REIGN SHALL FADE INTO OBLIVION... AS THOUGH I HAD NEVER BEEN!
SO THAT'S WHY THERE ARE NO RECORDS OF RAMA-TUT'S STRANGE REIGN!
20.

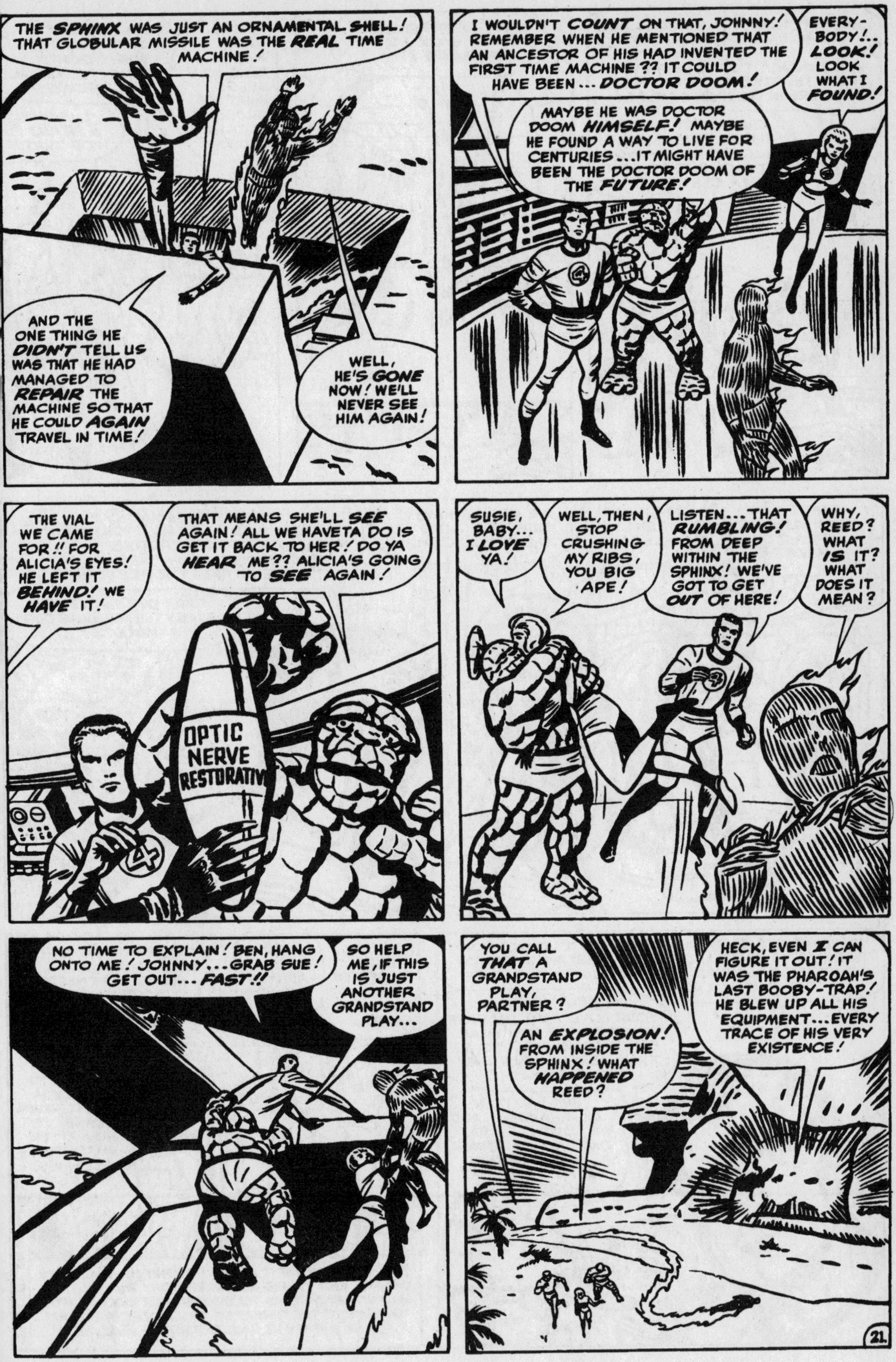
THE SPHINX WAS JUST AN ORNAMENTAL SHELL! THAT GLOBULAR MISSILE WAS THE REAL TIME MACHINE!
AND THE ONE THING HE DIDN'T TELL US WAS THAT HE HAD MANAGED TO REPAIR THE MACHINE SO THAT HE COULD AGAIN TRAVEL IN TIME!
WELL, HE'S GONE NOW! WE'LL NEVER SEE HIM AGAIN!
I WOULDN'T COUNT ON THAT, JOHNNY! REMEMBER WHEN HE MENTIONED THAT AN ANCESTOR OF HIS HAD INVENTED THE FIRST TIME MACHINE?? IT COULD HAVE BEEN... DOCTOR DOOM!
EVERY-BODY!.. LOOK! LOOK WHAT I FOUND!
MAYBE HE WAS DOCTOR DOOM HIMSELF! MAYBE HE FOUND A WAY TO LIVE FOR CENTURIES... IT MIGHT HAVE BEEN THE DOCTOR DOOM OF THE FUTURE!
THE VIAL WE CAME FOR!! FOR ALICIA'S EYES! HE LEFT IT BEHIND! WE HAVE IT!
THAT MEANS SHE'LL SEE AGAIN! ALL WE HAVETA DO IS GET IT BACK TO HER! DO YA HEAR ME?? ALICIA'S GOING TO SEE AGAIN!
OPTIC NERVE RESTORATIVE
SUSIE, BABY... I LOVE YA!
WELL, THEN, STOP CRUSHING MY RIBS, YOU BIG APE!
LISTEN... THAT RUMBLING! FROM DEEP WITHIN THE SPHINX! WE'VE GOT TO GET OUT OF HERE!
WHY, REED? WHAT IS IT? WHAT DOES IT MEAN?
NO TIME TO EXPLAIN! BEN, HANG ONTO ME! JOHNNY... GRAB SUE! GET OUT... FAST!!
SO HELP ME, IF THIS IS JUST ANOTHER GRANDSTAND PLAY...
YOU CALL THAT A GRANDSTAND PLAY, PARTNER?
AN EXPLOSION! FROM INSIDE THE SPHINX! WHAT HAPPENED REED?
HECK, EVEN I CAN FIGURE IT OUT! IT WAS THE PHAROAH'S LAST BOOBY-TRAP! HE BLEW UP ALL HIS EQUIPMENT... EVERY TRACE OF HIS VERY EXISTENCE!
21

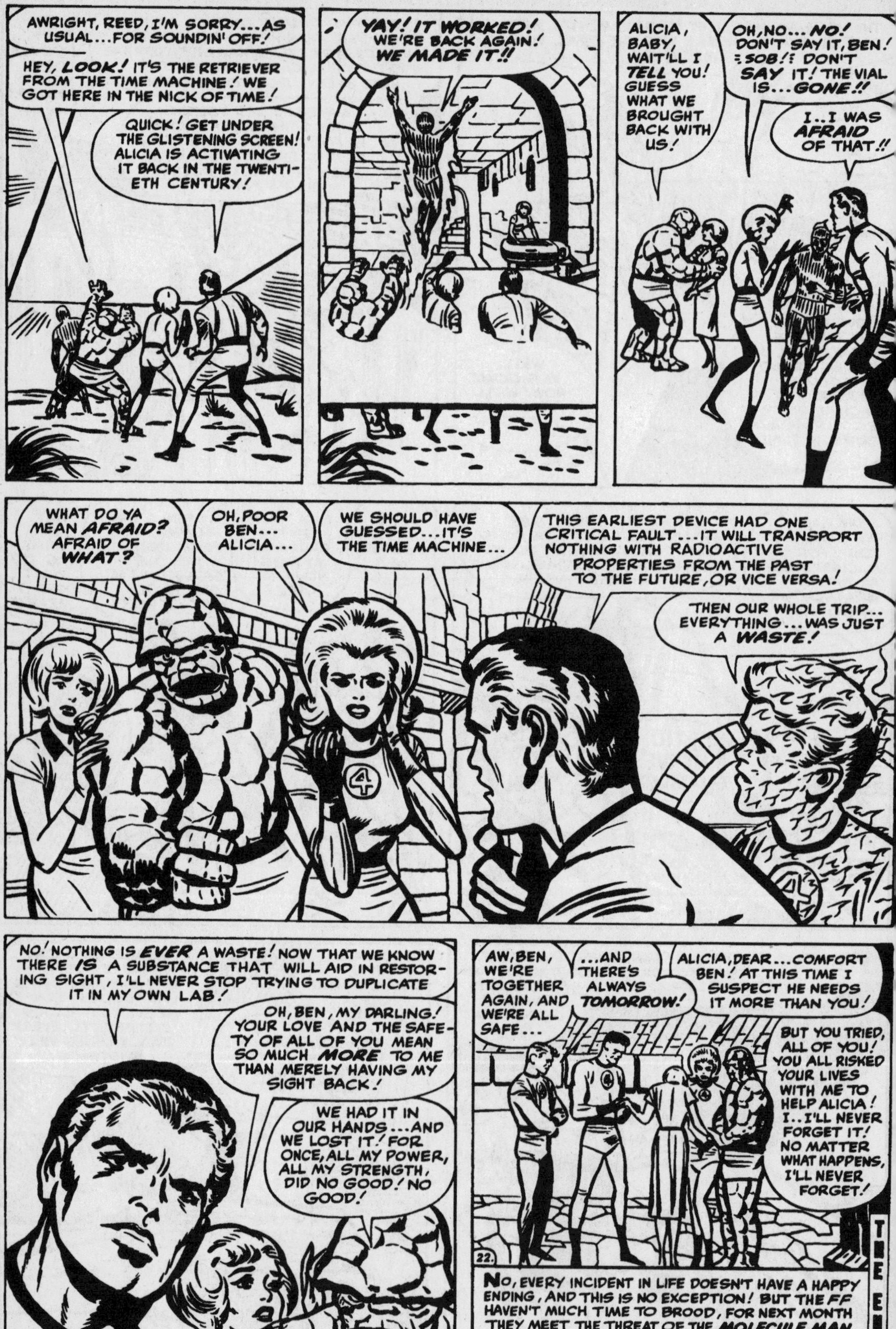

AWRIGHT, REED, I'M SORRY... AS USUAL... FOR SOUNDIN' OFF!
HEY, LOOK! IT'S THE RETRIEVER FROM THE TIME MACHINE! WE GOT HERE IN THE NICK OF TIME!
QUICK! GET UNDER THE GLISTENING SCREEN! ALICIA IS ACTIVATING IT BACK IN THE TWENTIETH CENTURY!
YAY! IT WORKED! WE'RE BACK AGAIN! WE MADE IT!!
ALICIA, BABY, WAIT'LL I TELL YOU! GUESS WHAT WE BROUGHT BACK WITH US!
OH, NO... NO! DON'T SAY IT, BEN! :SOB!: DON'T SAY IT! THE VIAL IS... GONE!!
I.. I WAS AFRAID OF THAT!!
WHAT DO YA MEAN AFRAID? AFRAID OF WHAT?
OH, POOR BEN... ALICIA...
WE SHOULD HAVE GUESSED... IT'S THE TIME MACHINE...
THIS EARLIEST DEVICE HAD ONE CRITICAL FAULT... IT WILL TRANSPORT NOTHING WITH RADIOACTIVE PROPERTIES FROM THE PAST TO THE FUTURE, OR VICE VERSA!
THEN OUR WHOLE TRIP... EVERYTHING... WAS JUST A WASTE!
NO! NOTHING IS EVER A WASTE! NOW THAT WE KNOW THERE IS A SUBSTANCE THAT WILL AID IN RESTORING SIGHT, I'LL NEVER STOP TRYING TO DUPLICATE IT IN MY OWN LAB!
OH, BEN, MY DARLING! YOUR LOVE AND THE SAFETY OF ALL OF YOU MEAN SO MUCH MORE TO ME THAN MERELY HAVING MY SIGHT BACK!
WE HAD IT IN OUR HANDS... AND WE LOST IT! FOR ONCE, ALL MY POWER, ALL MY STRENGTH, DID NO GOOD! NO GOOD!
AW, BEN, WE'RE TOGETHER AGAIN, AND WE'RE ALL SAFE...
...AND THERE'S ALWAYS TOMORROW!
ALICIA, DEAR... COMFORT BEN! AT THIS TIME I SUSPECT HE NEEDS IT MORE THAN YOU!
BUT YOU TRIED, ALL OF YOU! YOU ALL RISKED YOUR LIVES WITH ME TO HELP ALICIA! I.. I'LL NEVER FORGET IT! NO MATTER WHAT HAPPENS, I'LL NEVER FORGET!
22.
NO, EVERY INCIDENT IN LIFE DOESN'T HAVE A HAPPY ENDING, AND THIS IS NO EXCEPTION! BUT THE FF HAVEN'T MUCH TIME TO BROOD, FOR NEXT MONTH THEY MEET THE THREAT OF THE MOLECULE MAN.. A FOE SO MIGHTY HE CAN DESTROY A GALAXY!
THE END

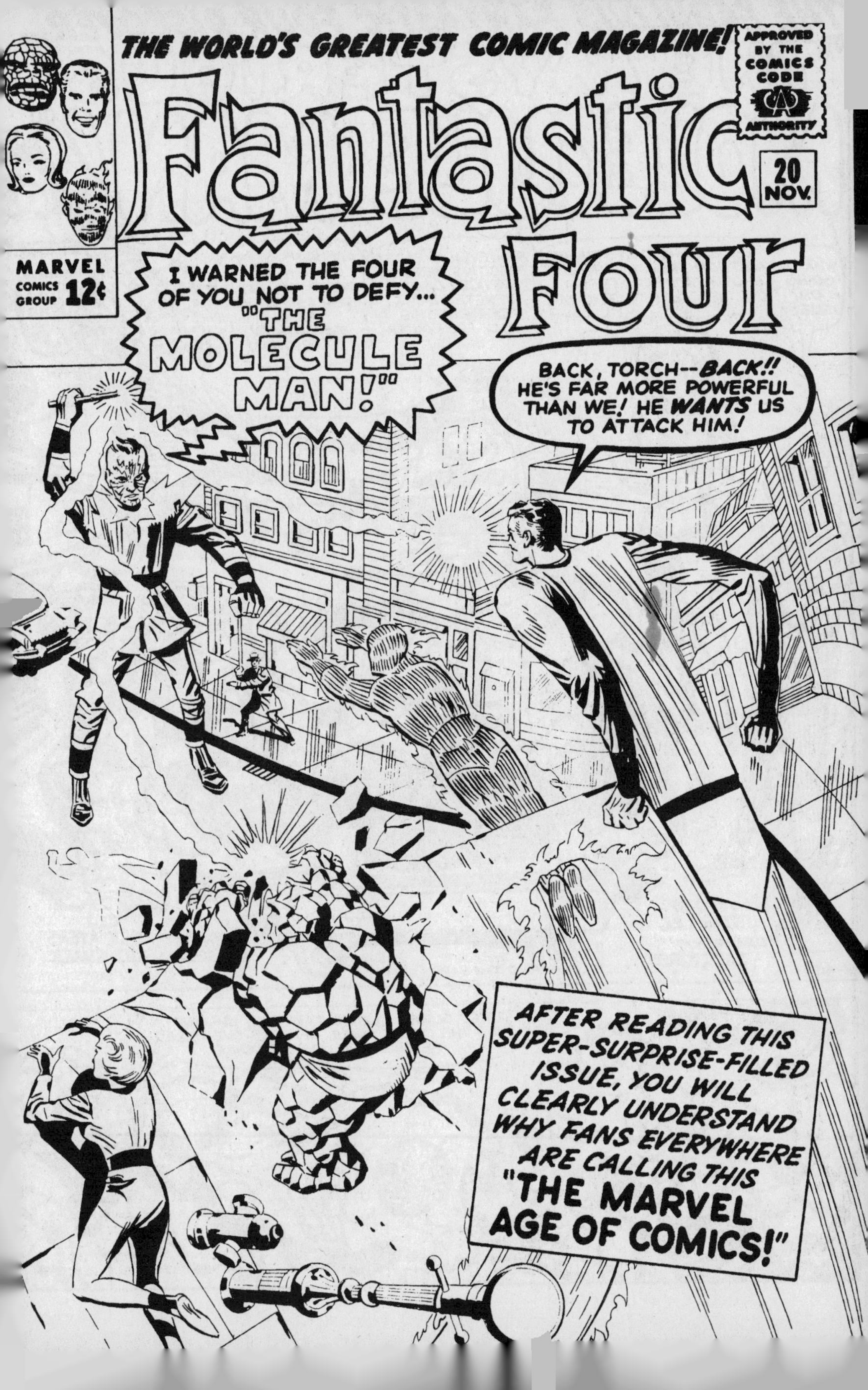
THE WORLD'S GREATEST COMIC MAGAZINE!
APPROVED BY THE COMICS CODE AUTHORITY
Fantastic Four
MARVEL COMICS GROUP 12¢
20 NOV.
I WARNED THE FOUR OF YOU NOT TO DEFY... "THE MOLECULE MAN!"
BACK, TORCH--BACK!! HE'S FAR MORE POWERFUL THAN WE! HE WANTS US TO ATTACK HIM!
AFTER READING THIS SUPER-SURPRISE-FILLED ISSUE, YOU WILL CLEARLY UNDERSTAND WHY FANS EVERYWHERE ARE CALLING THIS "THE MARVEL AGE OF COMICS!"

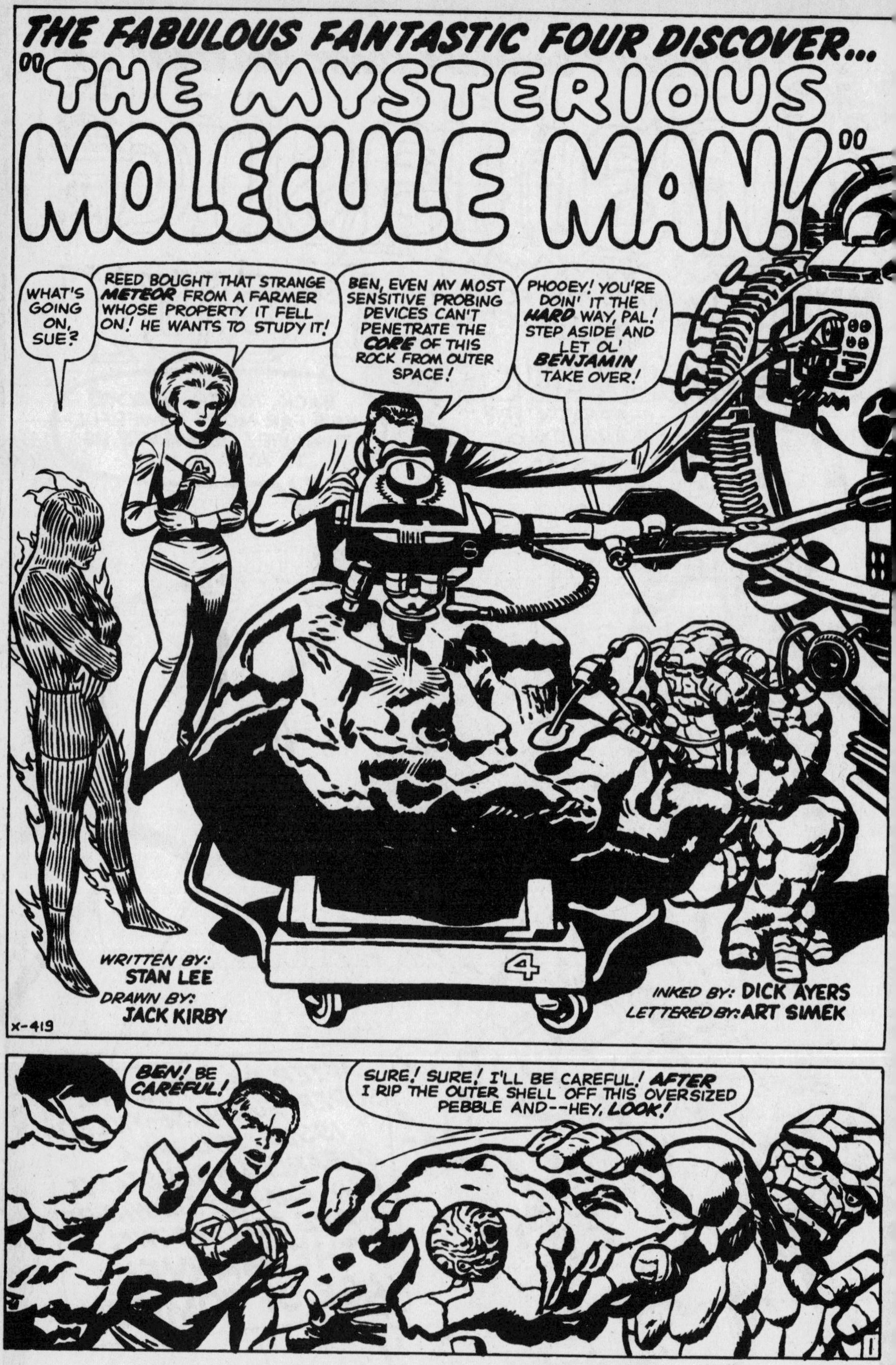
THE FABULOUS FANTASTIC FOUR DISCOVER...
"THE MYSTERIOUS MOLECULE MAN!"
WHAT'S GOING ON, SUE?
REED BOUGHT THAT STRANGE METEOR FROM A FARMER WHOSE PROPERTY IT FELL ON! HE WANTS TO STUDY IT!
BEN, EVEN MY MOST SENSITIVE PROBING DEVICES CAN'T PENETRATE THE CORE OF THIS ROCK FROM OUTER SPACE!
PHOOEY! YOU'RE DOIN' IT THE HARD WAY, PAL! STEP ASIDE AND LET OL' BENJAMIN TAKE OVER!
WRITTEN BY: STAN LEE
DRAWN BY: JACK KIRBY
INKED BY: DICK AYERS
LETTERED BY: ART SIMEK
X-419
BEN! BE CAREFUL!
SURE! SURE! I'LL BE CAREFUL! AFTER I RIP THE OUTER SHELL OFF THIS OVERSIZED PEBBLE AND--HEY, LOOK!
1

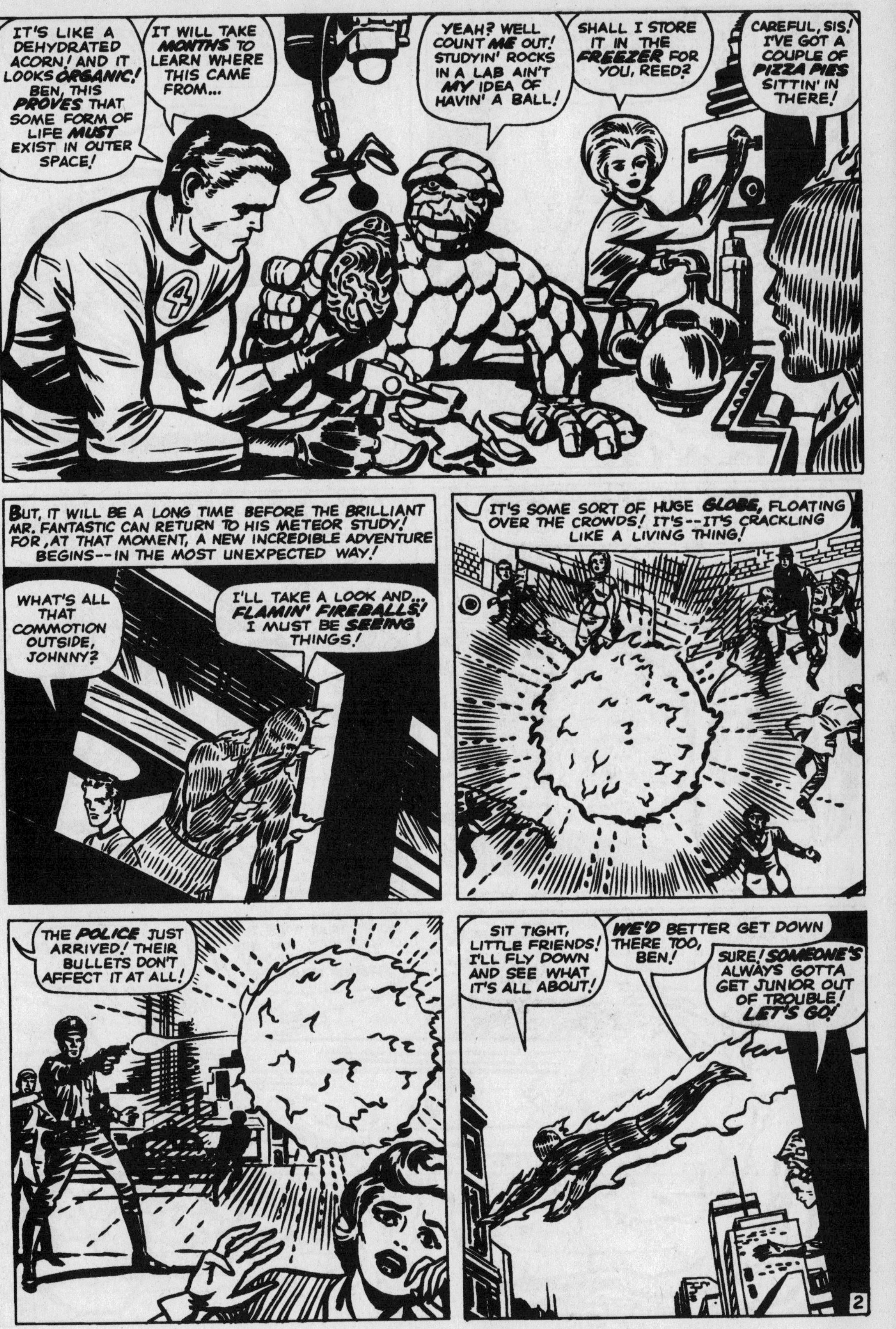
IT'S LIKE A DEHYDRATED ACORN! AND IT LOOKS ORGANIC! BEN, THIS PROVES THAT SOME FORM OF LIFE MUST EXIST IN OUTER SPACE!
IT WILL TAKE MONTHS TO LEARN WHERE THIS CAME FROM...
YEAH? WELL COUNT ME OUT! STUDYIN' ROCKS IN A LAB AIN'T MY IDEA OF HAVIN' A BALL!
SHALL I STORE IT IN THE FREEZER FOR YOU, REED?
CAREFUL, SIS! I'VE GOT A COUPLE OF PIZZA PIES SITTIN' IN THERE!
BUT, IT WILL BE A LONG TIME BEFORE THE BRILLIANT MR. FANTASTIC CAN RETURN TO HIS METEOR STUDY! FOR, AT THAT MOMENT, A NEW INCREDIBLE ADVENTURE BEGINS--IN THE MOST UNEXPECTED WAY!
WHAT'S ALL THAT COMMOTION OUTSIDE, JOHNNY?
I'LL TAKE A LOOK AND... FLAMIN' FIREBALLS! I MUST BE SEEING THINGS!
IT'S SOME SORT OF HUGE GLOBE, FLOATING OVER THE CROWDS! IT'S--IT'S CRACKLING LIKE A LIVING THING!
THE POLICE JUST ARRIVED! THEIR BULLETS DON'T AFFECT IT AT ALL!
SIT TIGHT, LITTLE FRIENDS! I'LL FLY DOWN AND SEE WHAT IT'S ALL ABOUT!
WE'D BETTER GET DOWN THERE TOO, BEN!
SURE! SOMEONE'S ALWAYS GOTTA GET JUNIOR OUT OF TROUBLE! LET'S GO!
2

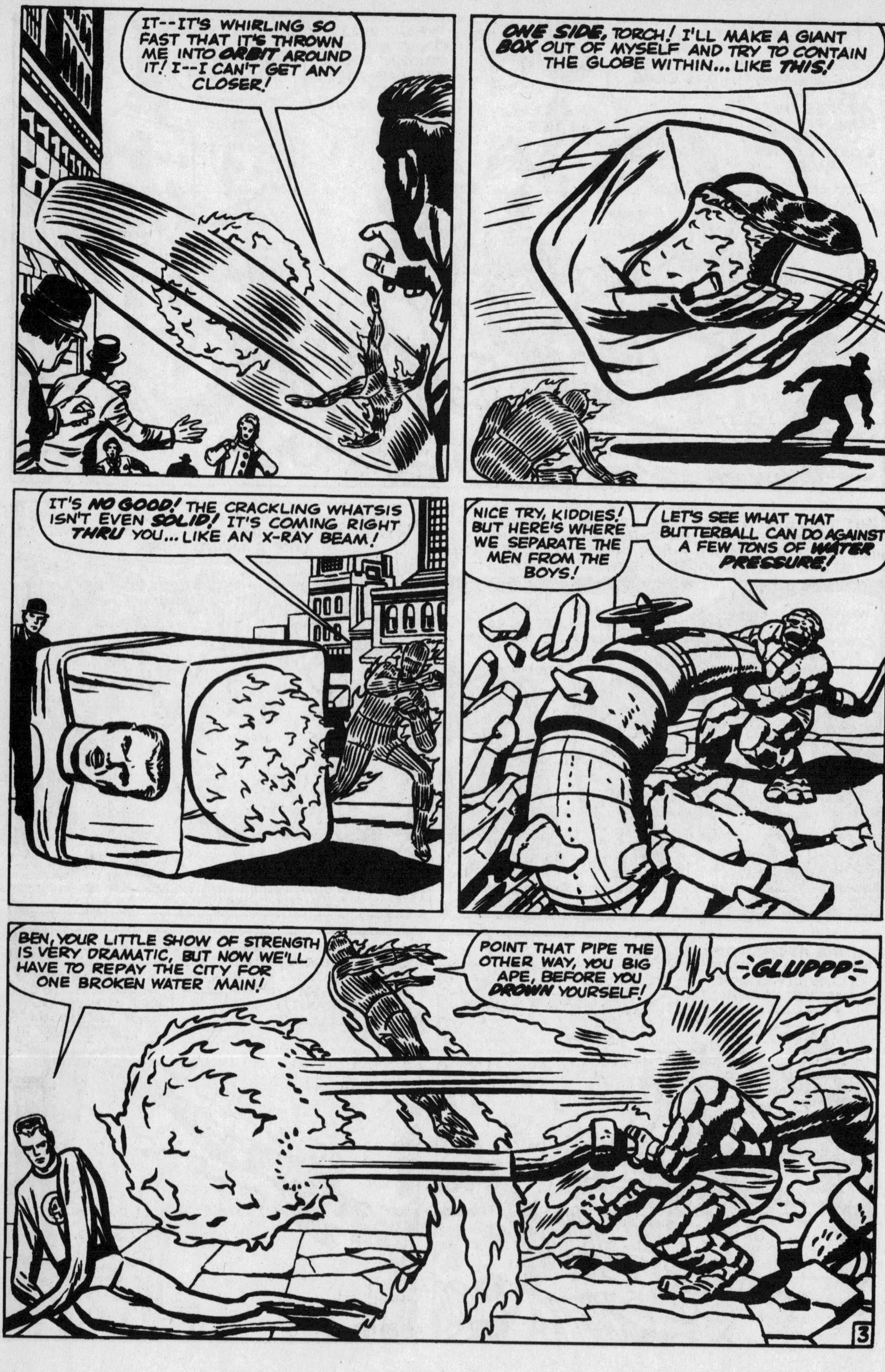
IT--IT'S WHIRLING SO FAST THAT IT'S THROWN ME INTO ORBIT AROUND IT! I--I CAN'T GET ANY CLOSER!
ONE SIDE, TORCH! I'LL MAKE A GIANT BOX OUT OF MYSELF AND TRY TO CONTAIN THE GLOBE WITHIN... LIKE THIS!
IT'S NO GOOD! THE CRACKLING WHATSIS ISN'T EVEN SOLID! IT'S COMING RIGHT THRU YOU... LIKE AN X-RAY BEAM!
NICE TRY, KIDDIES! BUT HERE'S WHERE WE SEPARATE THE MEN FROM THE BOYS!
LET'S SEE WHAT THAT BUTTERBALL CAN DO AGAINST A FEW TONS OF WATER PRESSURE!
BEN, YOUR LITTLE SHOW OF STRENGTH IS VERY DRAMATIC, BUT NOW WE'LL HAVE TO REPAY THE CITY FOR ONE BROKEN WATER MAIN!
POINT THAT PIPE THE OTHER WAY, YOU BIG APE, BEFORE YOU DROWN YOURSELF!
GLUPPP
3

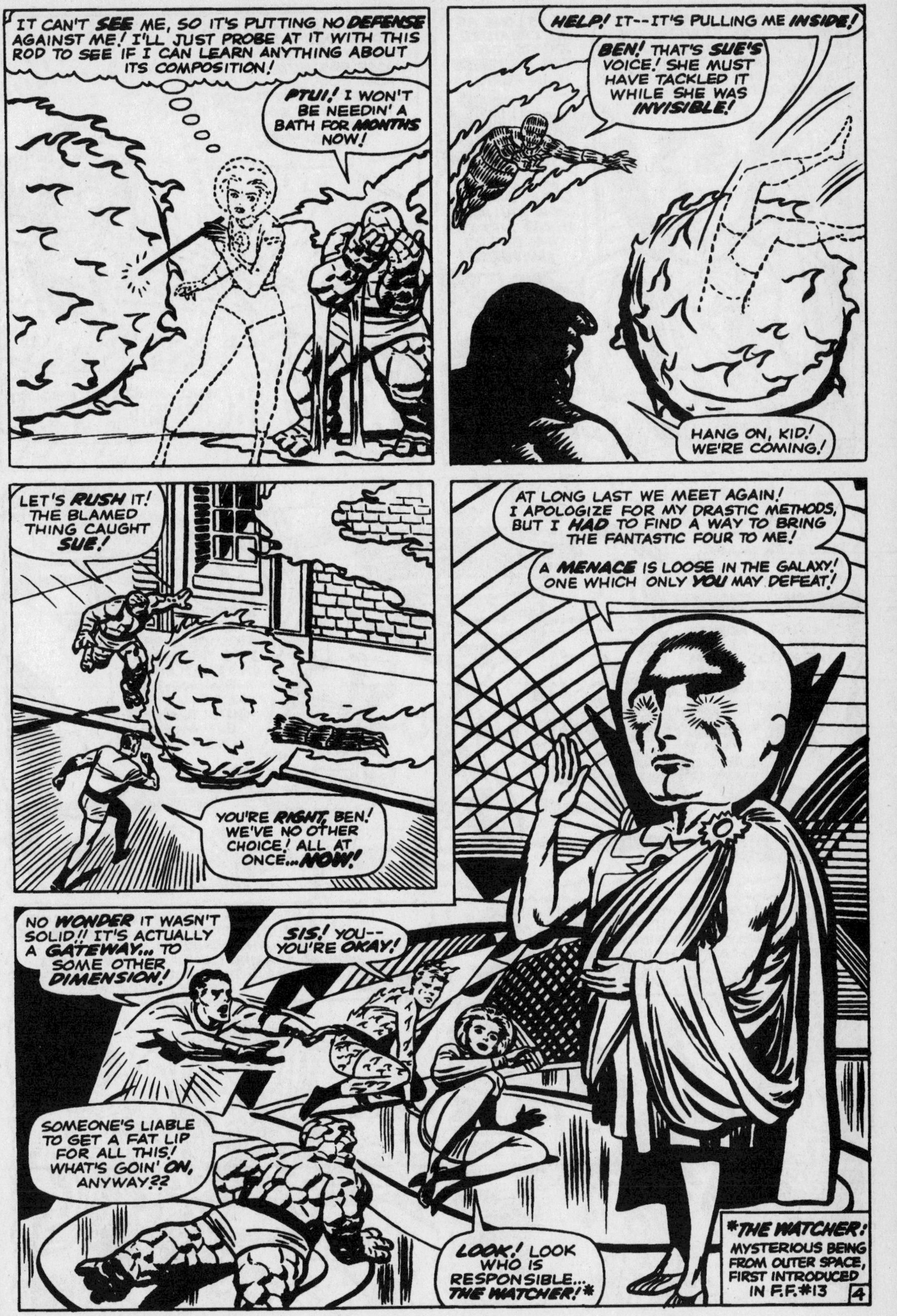
IT CAN'T SEE ME, SO IT'S PUTTING NO DEFENSE AGAINST ME! I'LL JUST PROBE AT IT WITH THIS ROD TO SEE IF I CAN LEARN ANYTHING ABOUT ITS COMPOSITION!
PTUI! I WON'T BE NEEDIN' A BATH FOR MONTHS NOW!
HELP! IT--IT'S PULLING ME INSIDE!
BEN! THAT'S SUE'S VOICE! SHE MUST HAVE TACKLED IT WHILE SHE WAS INVISIBLE!
HANG ON, KID! WE'RE COMING!
LET'S RUSH IT! THE BLAMED THING CAUGHT SUE!
YOU'RE RIGHT, BEN! WE'VE NO OTHER CHOICE! ALL AT ONCE...NOW!
AT LONG LAST WE MEET AGAIN! I APOLOGIZE FOR MY DRASTIC METHODS, BUT I HAD TO FIND A WAY TO BRING THE FANTASTIC FOUR TO ME!
A MENACE IS LOOSE IN THE GALAXY! ONE WHICH ONLY YOU MAY DEFEAT!
NO WONDER IT WASN'T SOLID!! IT'S ACTUALLY A GATEWAY... TO SOME OTHER DIMENSION!
SIS! YOU-- YOU'RE OKAY!
SOMEONE'S LIABLE TO GET A FAT LIP FOR ALL THIS! WHAT'S GOIN' ON, ANYWAY??
LOOK! LOOK WHO IS RESPONSIBLE... THE WATCHER!*
*THE WATCHER: MYSTERIOUS BEING FROM OUTER SPACE, FIRST INTRODUCED IN F.F.#13

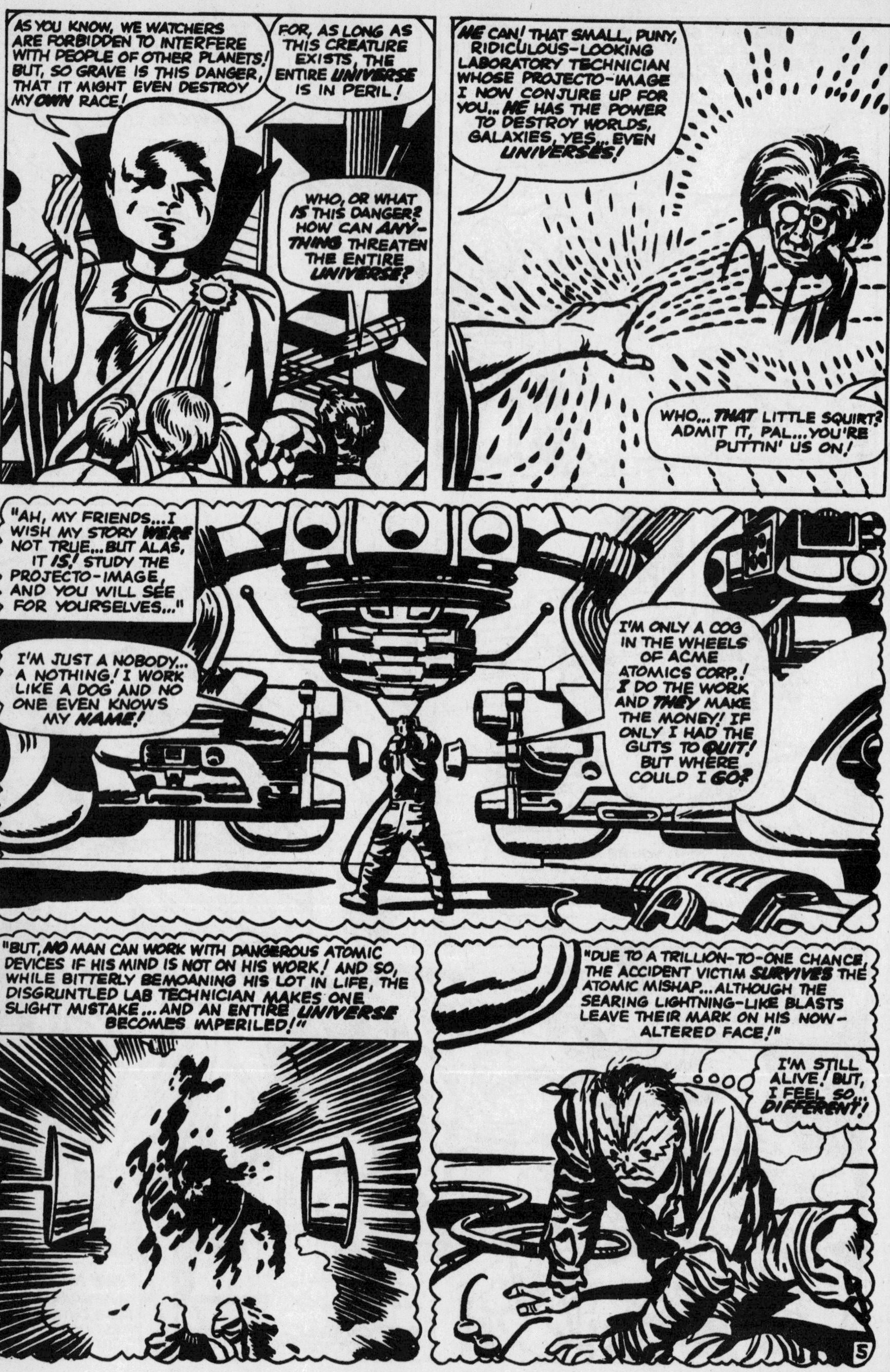
AS YOU KNOW, WE WATCHERS ARE FORBIDDEN TO INTERFERE WITH PEOPLE OF OTHER PLANETS! BUT, SO GRAVE IS THIS DANGER, THAT IT MIGHT EVEN DESTROY MY OWN RACE!
FOR, AS LONG AS THIS CREATURE EXISTS, THE ENTIRE UNIVERSE IS IN PERIL!
WHO, OR WHAT IS THIS DANGER? HOW CAN ANYTHING THREATEN THE ENTIRE UNIVERSE?
HE CAN! THAT SMALL, PUNY, RIDICULOUS-LOOKING LABORATORY TECHNICIAN WHOSE PROJECTO-IMAGE I NOW CONJURE UP FOR YOU... HE HAS THE POWER TO DESTROY WORLDS, GALAXIES, YES... EVEN UNIVERSES!
WHO... THAT LITTLE SQUIRT? ADMIT IT, PAL... YOU'RE PUTTIN' US ON!
"AH, MY FRIENDS... I WISH MY STORY WERE NOT TRUE... BUT ALAS, IT IS! STUDY THE PROJECTO-IMAGE, AND YOU WILL SEE FOR YOURSELVES..."
I'M JUST A NOBODY... A NOTHING! I WORK LIKE A DOG AND NO ONE EVEN KNOWS MY NAME!
I'M ONLY A COG IN THE WHEELS OF ACME ATOMICS CORP.! I DO THE WORK AND THEY MAKE THE MONEY! IF ONLY I HAD THE GUTS TO QUIT! BUT WHERE COULD I GO?
"BUT, NO MAN CAN WORK WITH DANGEROUS ATOMIC DEVICES IF HIS MIND IS NOT ON HIS WORK! AND SO, WHILE BITTERLY BEMOANING HIS LOT IN LIFE, THE DISGRUNTLED LAB TECHNICIAN MAKES ONE SLIGHT MISTAKE... AND AN ENTIRE UNIVERSE BECOMES IMPERILED!"
"DUE TO A TRILLION-TO-ONE CHANCE, THE ACCIDENT VICTIM SURVIVES THE ATOMIC MISHAP... ALTHOUGH THE SEARING LIGHTNING-LIKE BLASTS LEAVE THEIR MARK ON HIS NOW-ALTERED FACE!"
I'M STILL ALIVE! BUT, I FEEL SO... DIFFERENT!
5

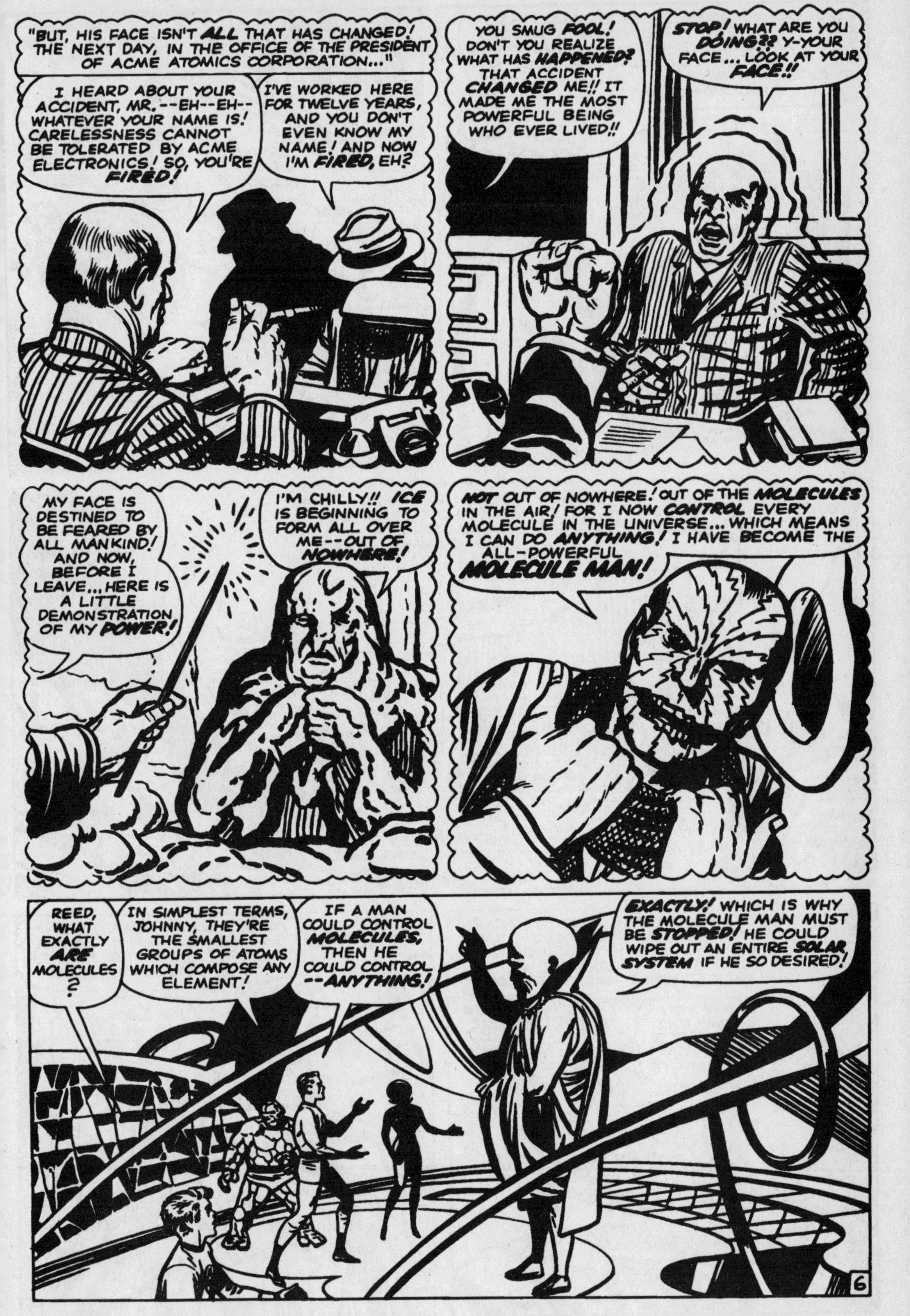
"BUT, HIS FACE ISN'T ALL THAT HAS CHANGED! THE NEXT DAY, IN THE OFFICE OF THE PRESIDENT OF ACME ATOMICS CORPORATION..."
I HEARD ABOUT YOUR ACCIDENT, MR.--EH--EH-- WHATEVER YOUR NAME IS! CARELESSNESS CANNOT BE TOLERATED BY ACME ELECTRONICS! SO, YOU'RE FIRED!
I'VE WORKED HERE FOR TWELVE YEARS, AND YOU DON'T EVEN KNOW MY NAME! AND NOW I'M FIRED, EH?
YOU SMUG FOOL! DON'T YOU REALIZE WHAT HAS HAPPENED? THAT ACCIDENT CHANGED ME!! IT MADE ME THE MOST POWERFUL BEING WHO EVER LIVED!!
STOP! WHAT ARE YOU DOING?? Y-YOUR FACE... LOOK AT YOUR FACE!!
MY FACE IS DESTINED TO BE FEARED BY ALL MANKIND! AND NOW, BEFORE I LEAVE... HERE IS A LITTLE DEMONSTRATION OF MY POWER!
I'M CHILLY!! ICE IS BEGINNING TO FORM ALL OVER ME--OUT OF NOWHERE!
NOT OUT OF NOWHERE! OUT OF THE MOLECULES IN THE AIR! FOR I NOW CONTROL EVERY MOLECULE IN THE UNIVERSE... WHICH MEANS I CAN DO ANYTHING! I HAVE BECOME THE ALL-POWERFUL MOLECULE MAN!
REED, WHAT EXACTLY ARE MOLECULES?
IN SIMPLEST TERMS, JOHNNY, THEY'RE THE SMALLEST GROUPS OF ATOMS WHICH COMPOSE ANY ELEMENT!
IF A MAN COULD CONTROL MOLECULES, THEN HE COULD CONTROL --ANYTHING!
EXACTLY! WHICH IS WHY THE MOLECULE MAN MUST BE STOPPED! HE COULD WIPE OUT AN ENTIRE SOLAR SYSTEM IF HE SO DESIRED!
6

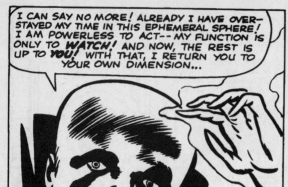

I CAN SAY NO MORE! ALREADY I HAVE OVER-STAYED MY TIME IN THIS EPHEMERAL SPHERE! I AM POWERLESS TO ACT-- MY FUNCTION IS ONLY TO *WATCH!* AND NOW, THE REST IS UP TO *YOU!* WITH THAT, I RETURN YOU TO YOUR OWN DIMENSION...

THE BLUE SPHERE FADED AWAY!

LOOK! WE'RE *BACK!*

SUE! JOHNNY! BEN! LOOK!! OVER *THERE--!*

OUR HEADQUARTERS BUILDING--*IT'S GONE!!*

LOOKS LIKE IT WAS SCOOPED OUT OF ITS FOUNDATION BY A GIANT CRANE!

IT ISN'T *POSSIBLE!* WE MUST BE *DREAMING!*

EVEN THE *YANCY STREETERS* COULDN'T HAVE DONE *THIS!*

FIRST THE *WATCHER* APPEARS...THEN WE LEARN OF AN ALL-POWERFUL *MOLECULE MAN--* AND NOW, AN ENTIRE SKYSCRAPER BUILDING COMPLETELY VANISHES! IT-- IT'S ALMOST AS THOUGH THE WHOLE WORLD HAS GONE *MAD!*

AND HOW COME THE *STREET'S* SO EMPTY?

YEAH! WHERE *IS* EVERYBODY?

HERE'S YOUR ANSWER! EVERY-ONE HAS FLOCKED TO *TIMES SQUARE!* HERE'S THE ANSWER TO *EVERYTHING!* LOOK!

I'M LOOKIN'... I'M SEEIN'... BUT I *STILL* DON'T BELIEVE IT!

7

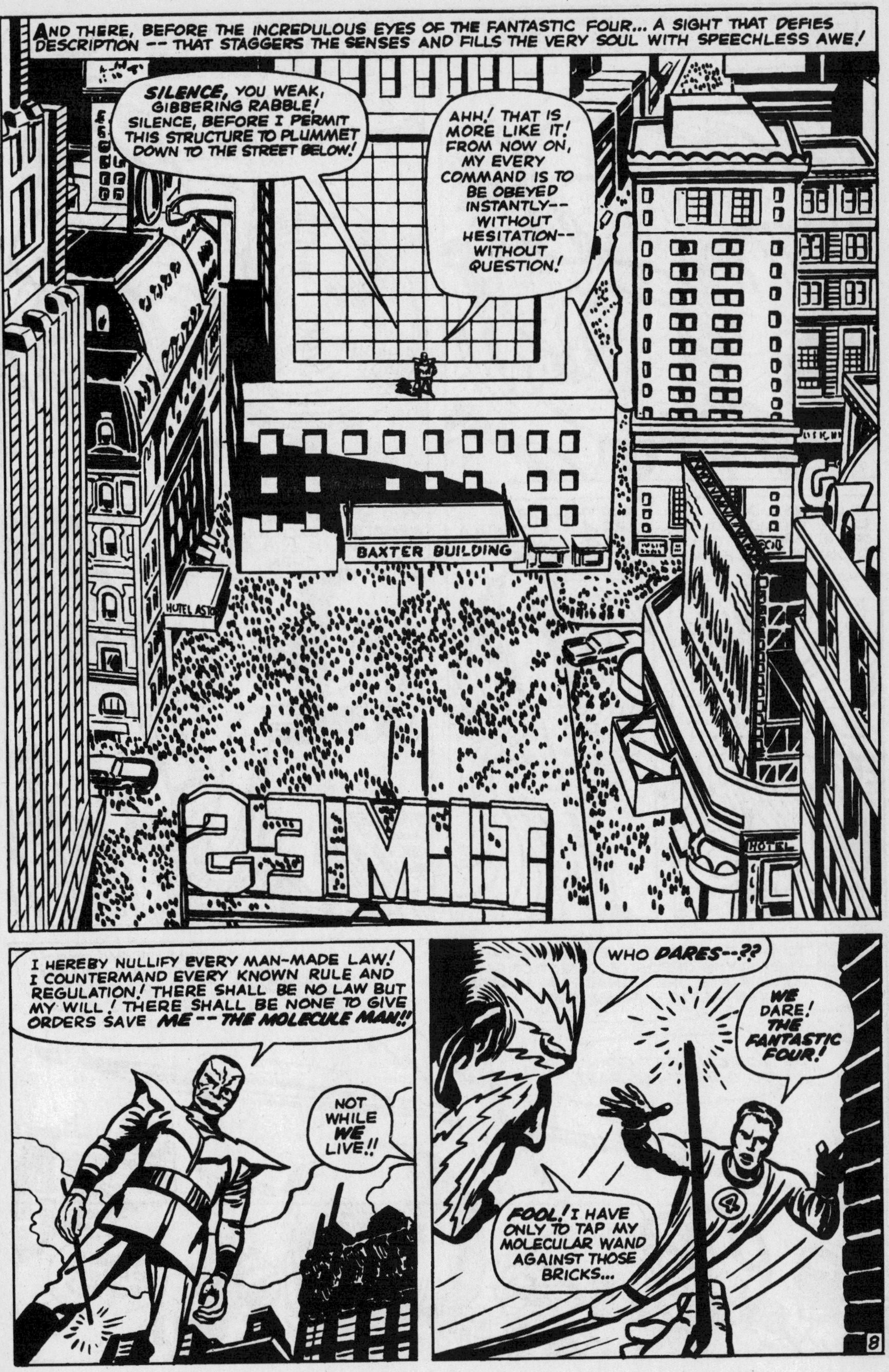
AND THERE, BEFORE THE INCREDULOUS EYES OF THE FANTASTIC FOUR... A SIGHT THAT DEFIES DESCRIPTION -- THAT STAGGERS THE SENSES AND FILLS THE VERY SOUL WITH SPEECHLESS AWE!
SILENCE, YOU WEAK, GIBBERING RABBLE! SILENCE, BEFORE I PERMIT THIS STRUCTURE TO PLUMMET DOWN TO THE STREET BELOW!
AHH! THAT IS MORE LIKE IT! FROM NOW ON, MY EVERY COMMAND IS TO BE OBEYED INSTANTLY-- WITHOUT HESITATION-- WITHOUT QUESTION!
BAXTER BUILDING
HOTEL ASTO
TIMES
HOTEL
I HEREBY NULLIFY EVERY MAN-MADE LAW! I COUNTERMAND EVERY KNOWN RULE AND REGULATION! THERE SHALL BE NO LAW BUT MY WILL! THERE SHALL BE NONE TO GIVE ORDERS SAVE ME -- THE MOLECULE MAN!!
NOT WHILE WE LIVE!!
WHO DARES--??
WE DARE! THE FANTASTIC FOUR!
FOOL! I HAVE ONLY TO TAP MY MOLECULAR WAND AGAINST THOSE BRICKS...
8

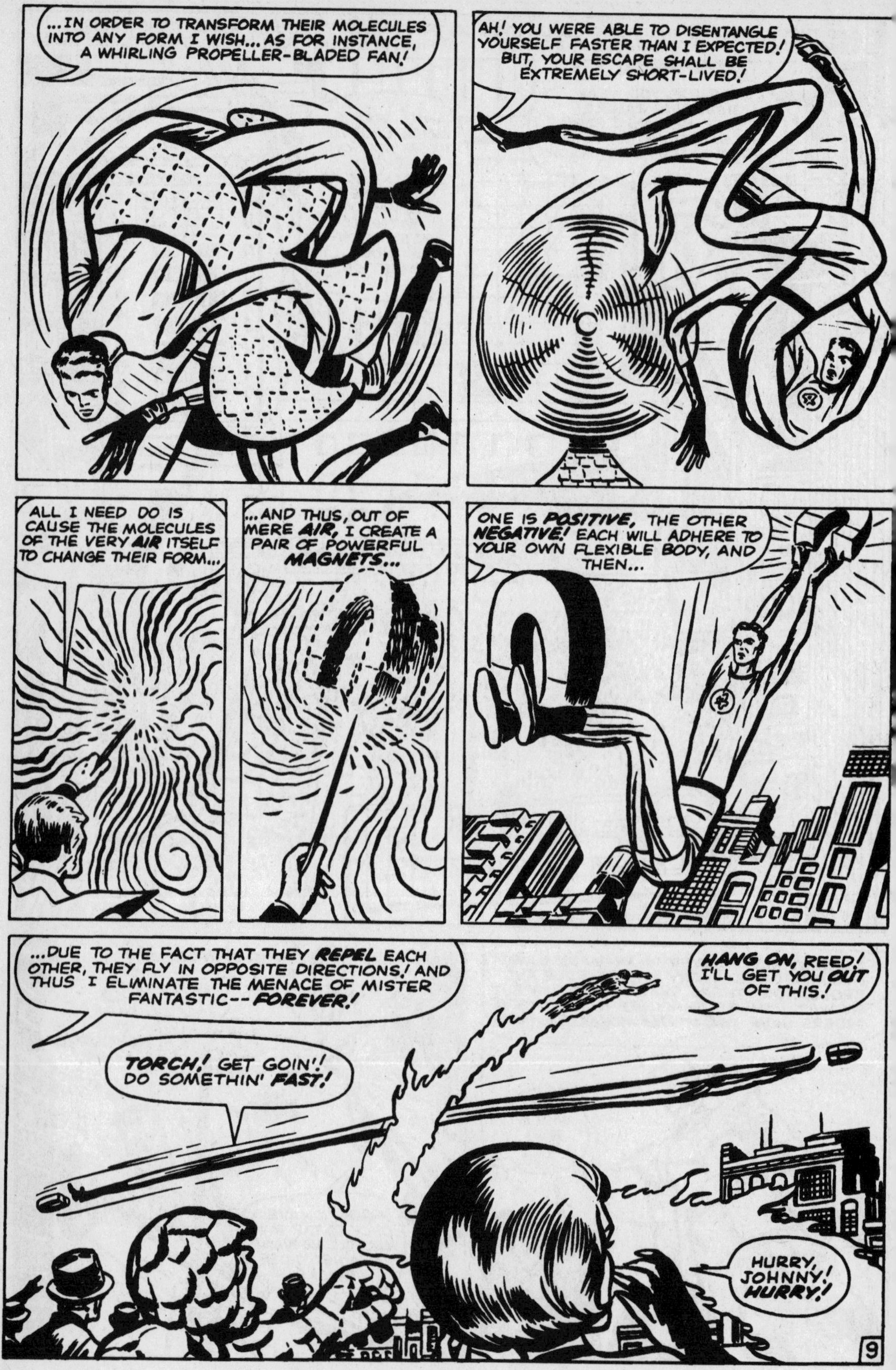
...IN ORDER TO TRANSFORM THEIR MOLECULES INTO ANY FORM I WISH... AS FOR INSTANCE, A WHIRLING PROPELLER-BLADED FAN!
AH! YOU WERE ABLE TO DISENTANGLE YOURSELF FASTER THAN I EXPECTED! BUT, YOUR ESCAPE SHALL BE EXTREMELY SHORT-LIVED!
ALL I NEED DO IS CAUSE THE MOLECULES OF THE VERY AIR ITSELF TO CHANGE THEIR FORM...
...AND THUS, OUT OF MERE AIR, I CREATE A PAIR OF POWERFUL MAGNETS...
ONE IS POSITIVE, THE OTHER NEGATIVE! EACH WILL ADHERE TO YOUR OWN FLEXIBLE BODY, AND THEN...
...DUE TO THE FACT THAT THEY REPEL EACH OTHER, THEY FLY IN OPPOSITE DIRECTIONS! AND THUS I ELIMINATE THE MENACE OF MISTER FANTASTIC--FOREVER!
HANG ON, REED! I'LL GET YOU OUT OF THIS!
TORCH! GET GOIN'! DO SOMETHIN' FAST!
HURRY, JOHNNY! HURRY!
9

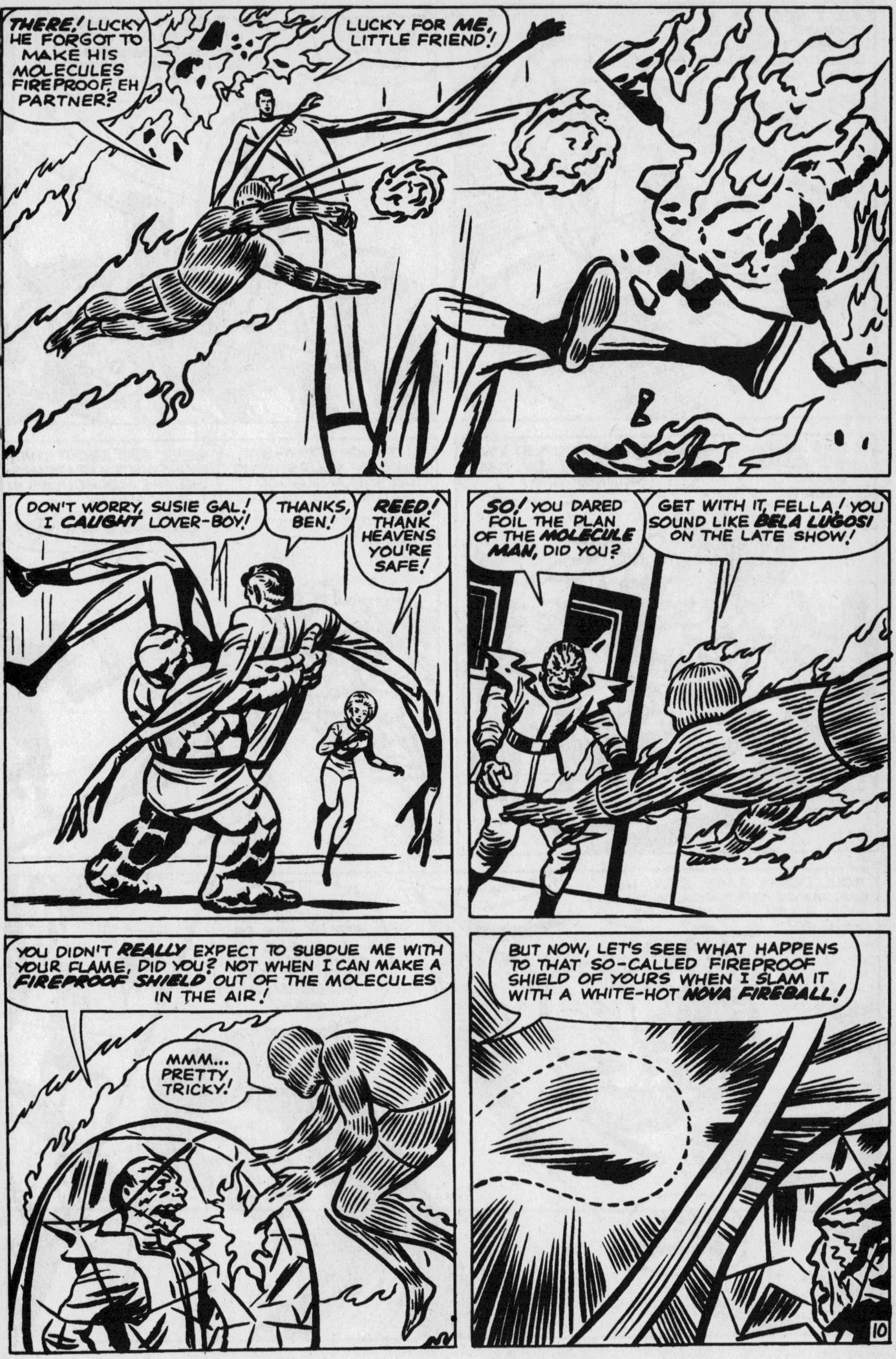
THERE! LUCKY HE FORGOT TO MAKE HIS MOLECULES FIREPROOF, EH PARTNER?
LUCKY FOR ME, LITTLE FRIEND!
DON'T WORRY, SUSIE GAL! I CAUGHT LOVER-BOY!
THANKS, BEN!
REED! THANK HEAVENS YOU'RE SAFE!
SO! YOU DARED FOIL THE PLAN OF THE MOLECULE MAN, DID YOU?
GET WITH IT, FELLA! YOU SOUND LIKE BELA LUGOSI ON THE LATE SHOW!
YOU DIDN'T REALLY EXPECT TO SUBDUE ME WITH YOUR FLAME, DID YOU? NOT WHEN I CAN MAKE A FIREPROOF SHIELD OUT OF THE MOLECULES IN THE AIR!
MMM... PRETTY TRICKY!
BUT NOW, LET'S SEE WHAT HAPPENS TO THAT SO-CALLED FIREPROOF SHIELD OF YOURS WHEN I SLAM IT WITH A WHITE-HOT NOVA FIREBALL!
10

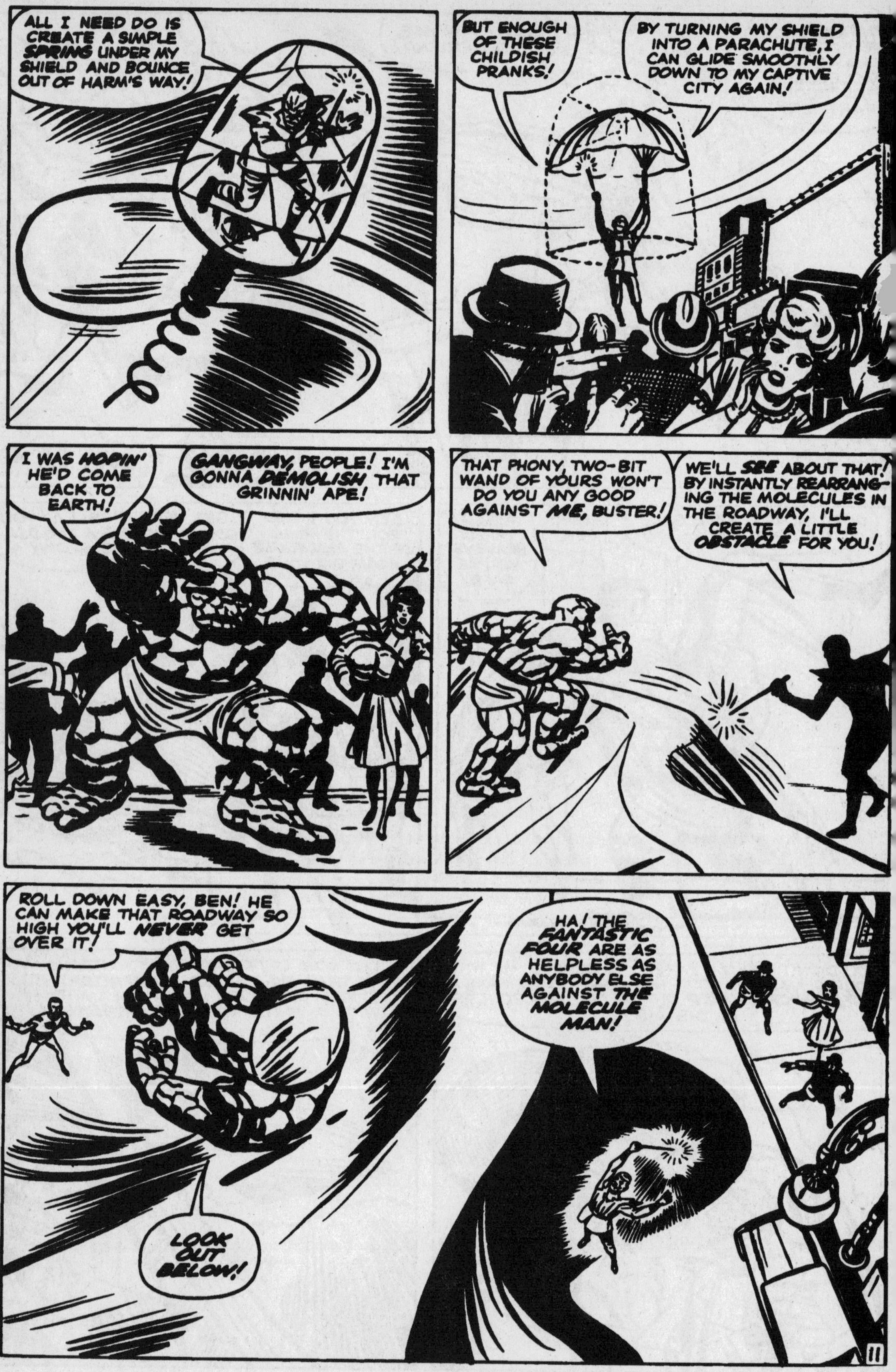

ALL I NEED DO IS CREATE A SIMPLE SPRING UNDER MY SHIELD AND BOUNCE OUT OF HARM'S WAY!
BUT ENOUGH OF THESE CHILDISH PRANKS!
BY TURNING MY SHIELD INTO A PARACHUTE, I CAN GLIDE SMOOTHLY DOWN TO MY CAPTIVE CITY AGAIN!
I WAS HOPIN' HE'D COME BACK TO EARTH!
GANGWAY, PEOPLE! I'M GONNA DEMOLISH THAT GRINNIN' APE!
THAT PHONY, TWO-BIT WAND OF YOURS WON'T DO YOU ANY GOOD AGAINST ME, BUSTER!
WE'LL SEE ABOUT THAT! BY INSTANTLY REARRANGING THE MOLECULES IN THE ROADWAY, I'LL CREATE A LITTLE OBSTACLE FOR YOU!
ROLL DOWN EASY, BEN! HE CAN MAKE THAT ROADWAY SO HIGH YOU'LL NEVER GET OVER IT!
LOOK OUT BELOW!
HA! THE FANTASTIC FOUR ARE AS HELPLESS AS ANYBODY ELSE AGAINST THE MOLECULE MAN!
11

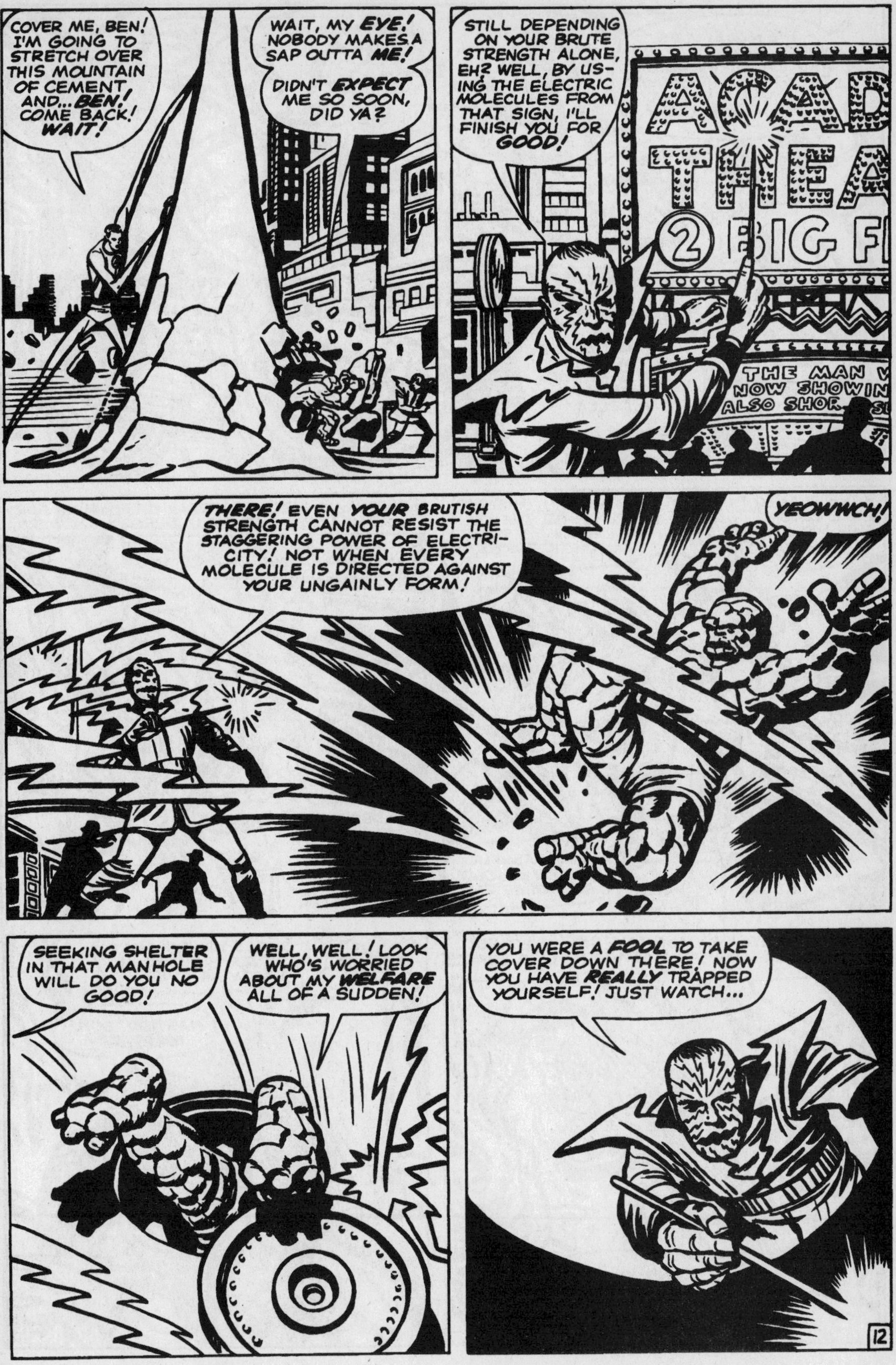
COVER ME, BEN! I'M GOING TO STRETCH OVER THIS MOUNTAIN OF CEMENT, AND... BEN! COME BACK! WAIT!
WAIT, MY EYE! NOBODY MAKES A SAP OUTTA ME!
DIDN'T EXPECT ME SO SOON, DID YA?
STILL DEPENDING ON YOUR BRUTE STRENGTH ALONE, EH? WELL, BY USING THE ELECTRIC MOLECULES FROM THAT SIGN, I'LL FINISH YOU FOR GOOD!
2 BIG F
THE MAN W
NOW SHOWIN
ALSO SHOR
THERE! EVEN YOUR BRUTISH STRENGTH CANNOT RESIST THE STAGGERING POWER OF ELECTRICITY! NOT WHEN EVERY MOLECULE IS DIRECTED AGAINST YOUR UNGAINLY FORM!
YEOWWCH!
SEEKING SHELTER IN THAT MANHOLE WILL DO YOU NO GOOD!
WELL, WELL! LOOK WHO'S WORRIED ABOUT MY WELFARE ALL OF A SUDDEN!
YOU WERE A FOOL TO TAKE COVER DOWN THERE! NOW YOU HAVE REALLY TRAPPED YOURSELF! JUST WATCH...
12

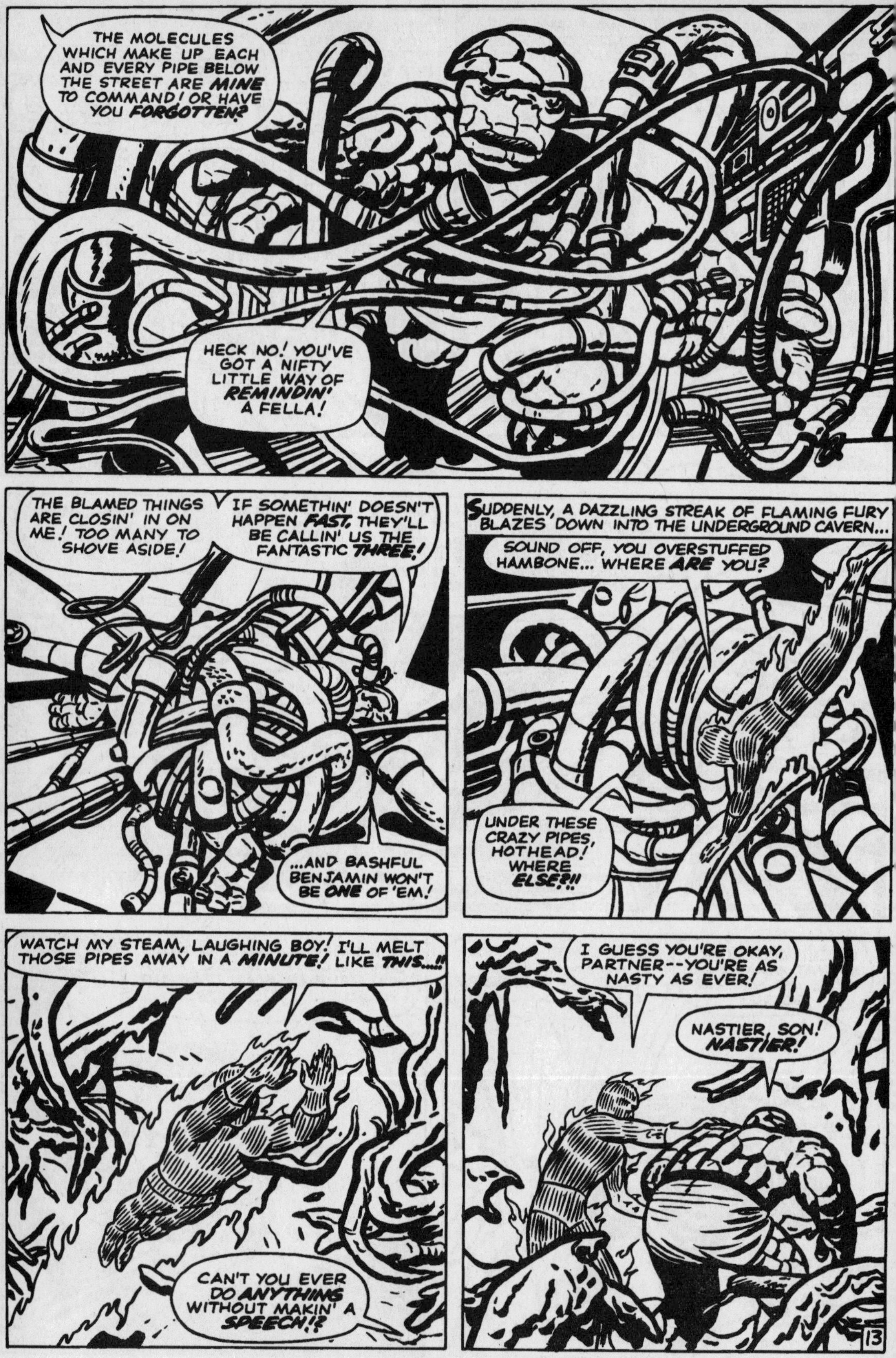
THE MOLECULES WHICH MAKE UP EACH AND EVERY PIPE BELOW THE STREET ARE MINE TO COMMAND! OR HAVE YOU FORGOTTEN?
HECK NO! YOU'VE GOT A NIFTY LITTLE WAY OF REMINDIN' A FELLA!
THE BLAMED THINGS ARE CLOSIN' IN ON ME! TOO MANY TO SHOVE ASIDE!
IF SOMETHIN' DOESN'T HAPPEN FAST, THEY'LL BE CALLIN' US THE FANTASTIC THREE!
...AND BASHFUL BENJAMIN WON'T BE ONE OF 'EM!
SUDDENLY, A DAZZLING STREAK OF FLAMING FURY BLAZES DOWN INTO THE UNDERGROUND CAVERN...
SOUND OFF, YOU OVERSTUFFED HAMBONE... WHERE ARE YOU?
UNDER THESE CRAZY PIPES, HOTHEAD! WHERE ELSE?!!
WATCH MY STEAM, LAUGHING BOY! I'LL MELT THOSE PIPES AWAY IN A MINUTE! LIKE THIS...!!
CAN'T YOU EVER DO ANYTHING WITHOUT MAKIN' A SPEECH!?
I GUESS YOU'RE OKAY, PARTNER--YOU'RE AS NASTY AS EVER!
NASTIER, SON! NASTIER!

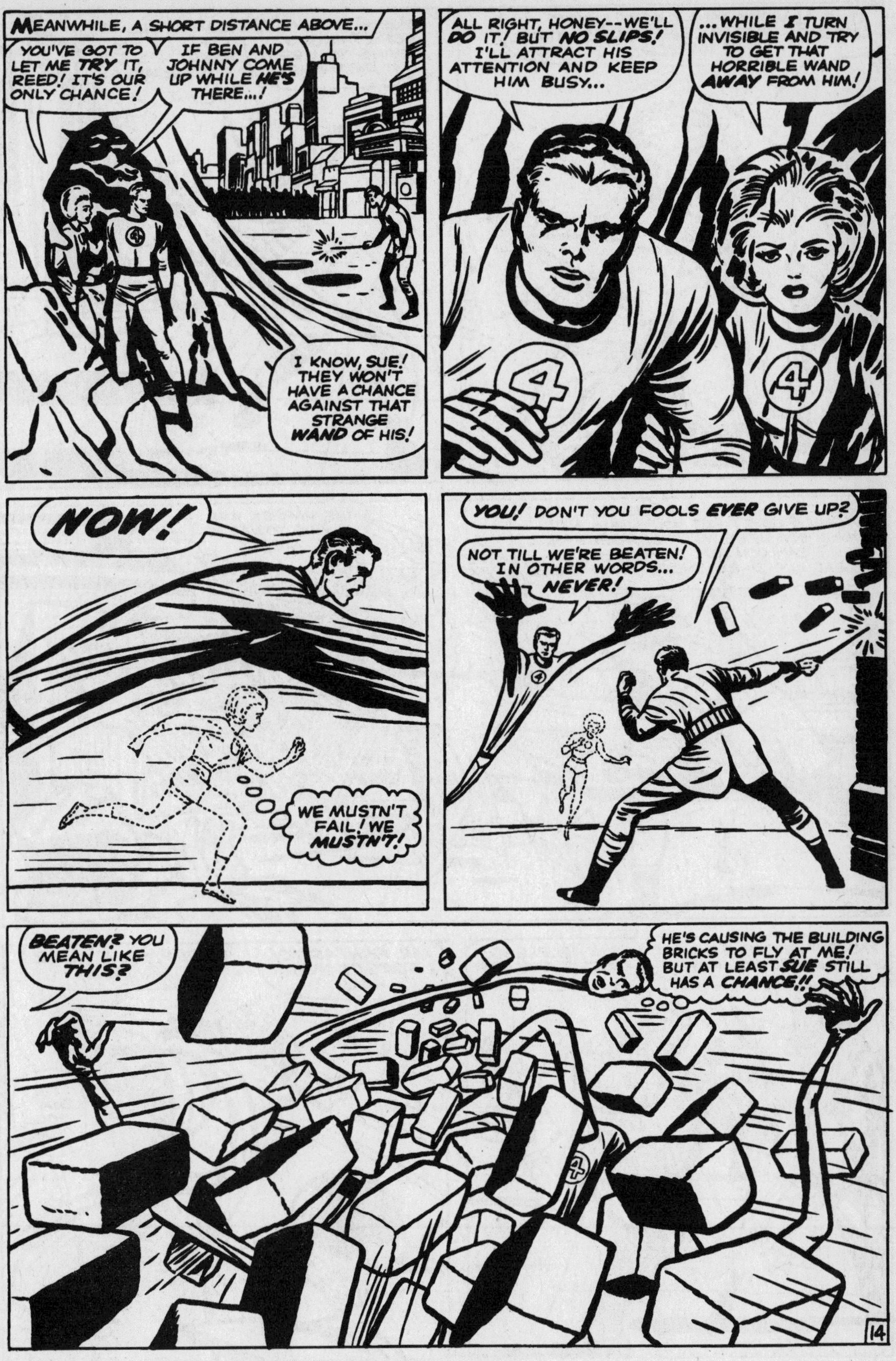
MEANWHILE, A SHORT DISTANCE ABOVE...
YOU'VE GOT TO LET ME TRY IT, REED! IT'S OUR ONLY CHANCE!
IF BEN AND JOHNNY COME UP WHILE HE'S THERE...!
I KNOW, SUE! THEY WON'T HAVE A CHANCE AGAINST THAT STRANGE WAND OF HIS!
ALL RIGHT, HONEY--WE'LL DO IT! BUT NO SLIPS! I'LL ATTRACT HIS ATTENTION AND KEEP HIM BUSY...
...WHILE I TURN INVISIBLE AND TRY TO GET THAT HORRIBLE WAND AWAY FROM HIM!
NOW!
WE MUSTN'T FAIL! WE MUSTN'T!
YOU! DON'T YOU FOOLS EVER GIVE UP?
NOT TILL WE'RE BEATEN! IN OTHER WORDS... NEVER!
BEATEN? YOU MEAN LIKE THIS?
HE'S CAUSING THE BUILDING BRICKS TO FLY AT ME! BUT AT LEAST SUE STILL HAS A CHANCE!!
14

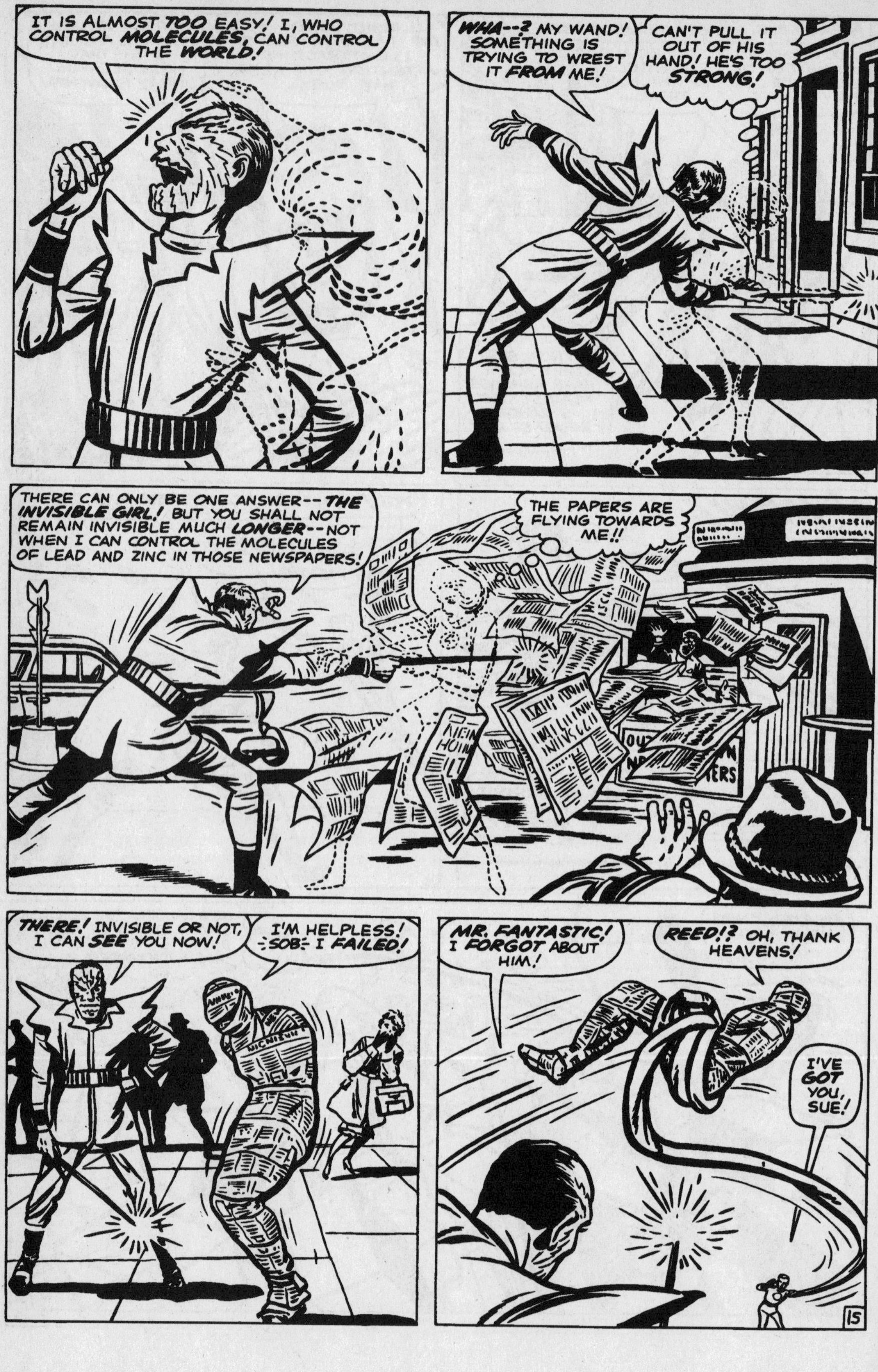
IT IS ALMOST TOO EASY! I, WHO CONTROL MOLECULES, CAN CONTROL THE WORLD!
WHA--? MY WAND! SOMETHING IS TRYING TO WREST IT FROM ME!
CAN'T PULL IT OUT OF HIS HAND! HE'S TOO STRONG!
THERE CAN ONLY BE ONE ANSWER--THE INVISIBLE GIRL! BUT YOU SHALL NOT REMAIN INVISIBLE MUCH LONGER--NOT WHEN I CAN CONTROL THE MOLECULES OF LEAD AND ZINC IN THOSE NEWSPAPERS!
THE PAPERS ARE FLYING TOWARDS ME!!
THERE! INVISIBLE OR NOT, I CAN SEE YOU NOW!
I'M HELPLESS! -SOB- I FAILED!
MR. FANTASTIC! I FORGOT ABOUT HIM!
REED!? OH, THANK HEAVENS!
I'VE GOT YOU, SUE!
15

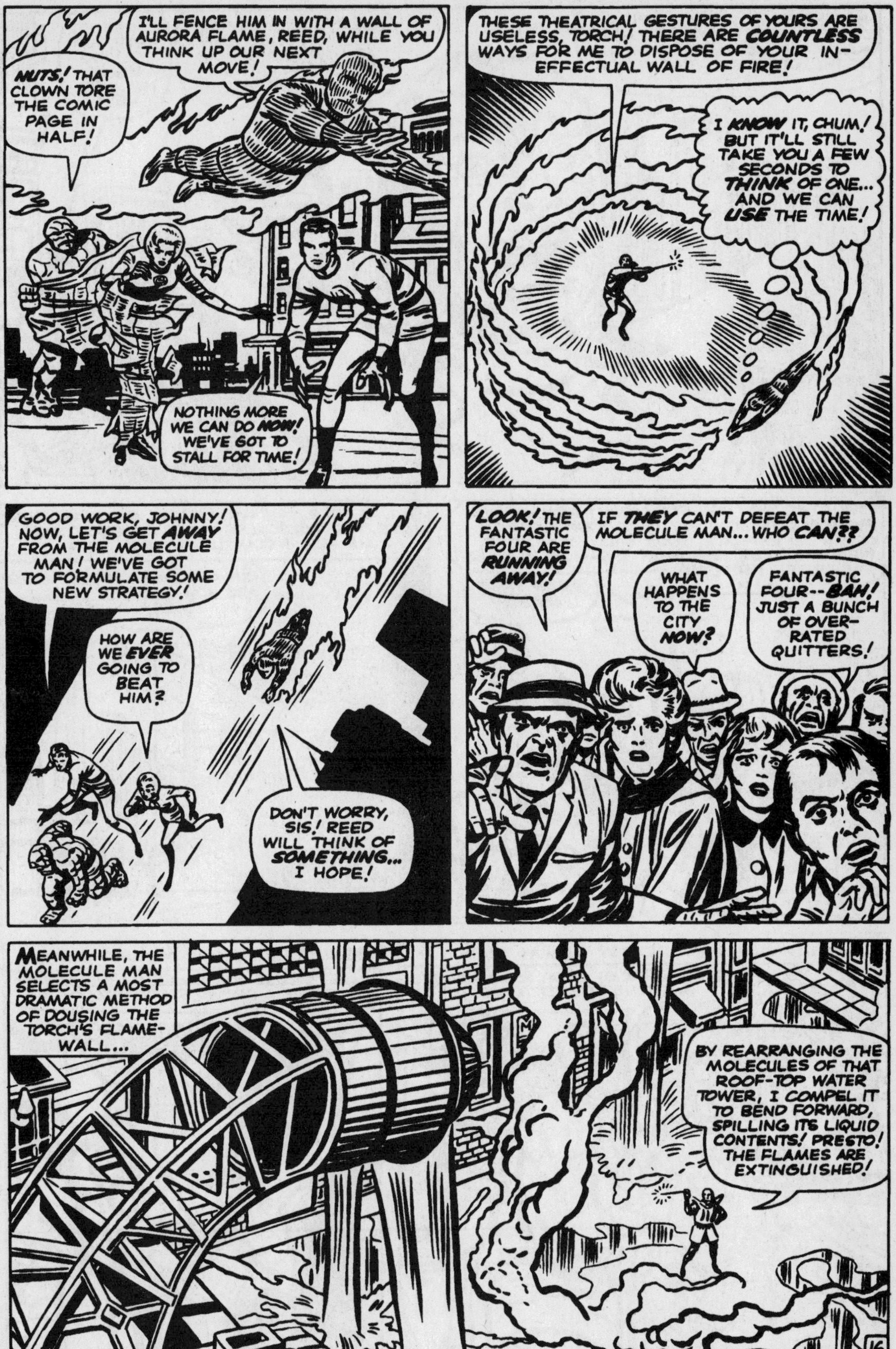
I'LL FENCE HIM IN WITH A WALL OF AURORA FLAME, REED, WHILE YOU THINK UP OUR NEXT MOVE!
NUTS! THAT CLOWN TORE THE COMIC PAGE IN HALF!
NOTHING MORE WE CAN DO NOW! WE'VE GOT TO STALL FOR TIME!
THESE THEATRICAL GESTURES OF YOURS ARE USELESS, TORCH! THERE ARE COUNTLESS WAYS FOR ME TO DISPOSE OF YOUR IN-EFFECTUAL WALL OF FIRE!
I KNOW IT, CHUM! BUT IT'LL STILL TAKE YOU A FEW SECONDS TO THINK OF ONE... AND WE CAN USE THE TIME!
GOOD WORK, JOHNNY! NOW, LET'S GET AWAY FROM THE MOLECULE MAN! WE'VE GOT TO FORMULATE SOME NEW STRATEGY!
HOW ARE WE EVER GOING TO BEAT HIM?
DON'T WORRY, SIS! REED WILL THINK OF SOMETHING... I HOPE!
LOOK! THE FANTASTIC FOUR ARE RUNNING AWAY!
IF THEY CAN'T DEFEAT THE MOLECULE MAN... WHO CAN??
WHAT HAPPENS TO THE CITY NOW?
FANTASTIC FOUR--BAH! JUST A BUNCH OF OVER-RATED QUITTERS!
MEANWHILE, THE MOLECULE MAN SELECTS A MOST DRAMATIC METHOD OF DOUSING THE TORCH'S FLAME-WALL...
BY REARRANGING THE MOLECULES OF THAT ROOF-TOP WATER TOWER, I COMPEL IT TO BEND FORWARD, SPILLING ITS LIQUID CONTENTS! PRESTO! THE FLAMES ARE EXTINGUISHED!

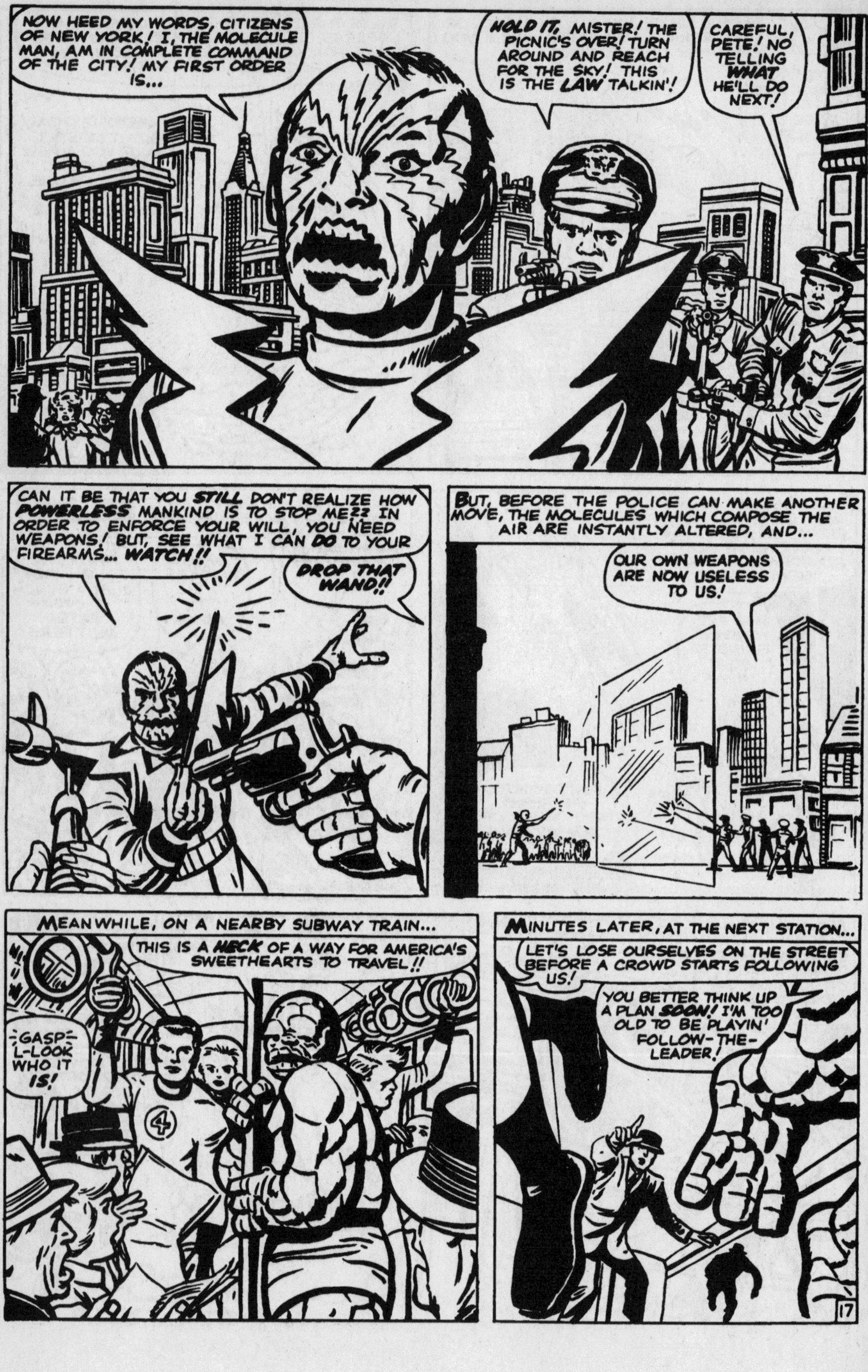
NOW HEED MY WORDS, CITIZENS OF NEW YORK! I, THE MOLECULE MAN, AM IN COMPLETE COMMAND OF THE CITY! MY FIRST ORDER IS...
HOLD IT, MISTER! THE PICNIC'S OVER! TURN AROUND AND REACH FOR THE SKY! THIS IS THE LAW TALKIN'!
CAREFUL, PETE! NO TELLING WHAT HE'LL DO NEXT!
CAN IT BE THAT YOU STILL DON'T REALIZE HOW POWERLESS MANKIND IS TO STOP ME?? IN ORDER TO ENFORCE YOUR WILL, YOU NEED WEAPONS! BUT, SEE WHAT I CAN DO TO YOUR FIREARMS... WATCH!!
DROP THAT WAND!!
BUT, BEFORE THE POLICE CAN MAKE ANOTHER MOVE, THE MOLECULES WHICH COMPOSE THE AIR ARE INSTANTLY ALTERED, AND...
OUR OWN WEAPONS ARE NOW USELESS TO US!
MEANWHILE, ON A NEARBY SUBWAY TRAIN...
THIS IS A HECK OF A WAY FOR AMERICA'S SWEETHEARTS TO TRAVEL!!
-GASP- L-LOOK WHO IT IS!
MINUTES LATER, AT THE NEXT STATION...
LET'S LOSE OURSELVES ON THE STREET BEFORE A CROWD STARTS FOLLOWING US!
YOU BETTER THINK UP A PLAN SOON! I'M TOO OLD TO BE PLAYIN' FOLLOW-THE-LEADER!
17

AND, BACK AT TIMES SQUARE... I INTEND TO HOLD THE ENTIRE CITY OF NEW YORK *HOSTAGE* UNTIL THE FANTASTIC FOUR ARE MY PRISONERS! YOU ARE ORDERED TO *FIND* THEM-- AND BRING THEM TO ME!

ALL I NEED DO IS REARRANGE THE MOLECULES IN THE AIR ONCE MORE... THE MOLECULES OVER WHICH I HAVE ABSOLUTE CONTROL...

UNTIL THEY ARE MY CAPTIVES, NO ONE CAN ENTER OR LEAVE THE CITY!

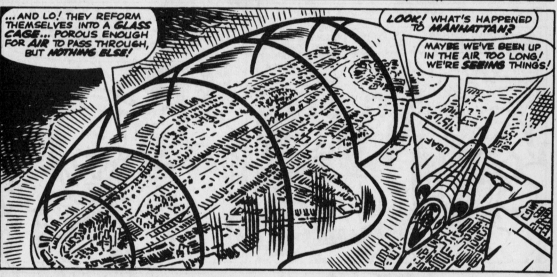

...AND LO! THEY REFORM THEMSELVES INTO A *GLASS CAGE*... POROUS ENOUGH FOR *AIR* TO PASS THROUGH, BUT *NOTHING ELSE!*

LOOK! WHAT'S HAPPENED TO *MANHATTAN?*

MAYBE WE'VE BEEN UP IN THE AIR TOO LONG! WE'RE *SEEING* THINGS!

IN THE HOURS THAT FOLLOW, AMERICA'S MOST FAMOUS QUARTET FINDS ITSELF THE OBJECT OF NEW YORK'S BIGGEST MANHUNT...

IF WE FIND THE F.F., WHAT DO WE *DO,* CHARLIE?

BOY! EVERYONE'S SO SCARED OF THE MOLECULE MAN, THEY'D TURN IN THEIR BEST FRIEND IF HE TOLD 'EM TO!

NOTIFY THE MOLECULE MAN IMMEDI-ATELY! WE'VE NO OTHER CHOICE!

THEN, SUDDENLY...

PSST! HEY, GRUESOME! C'MERE!

SOMEONE *SPOTTED* US!

18

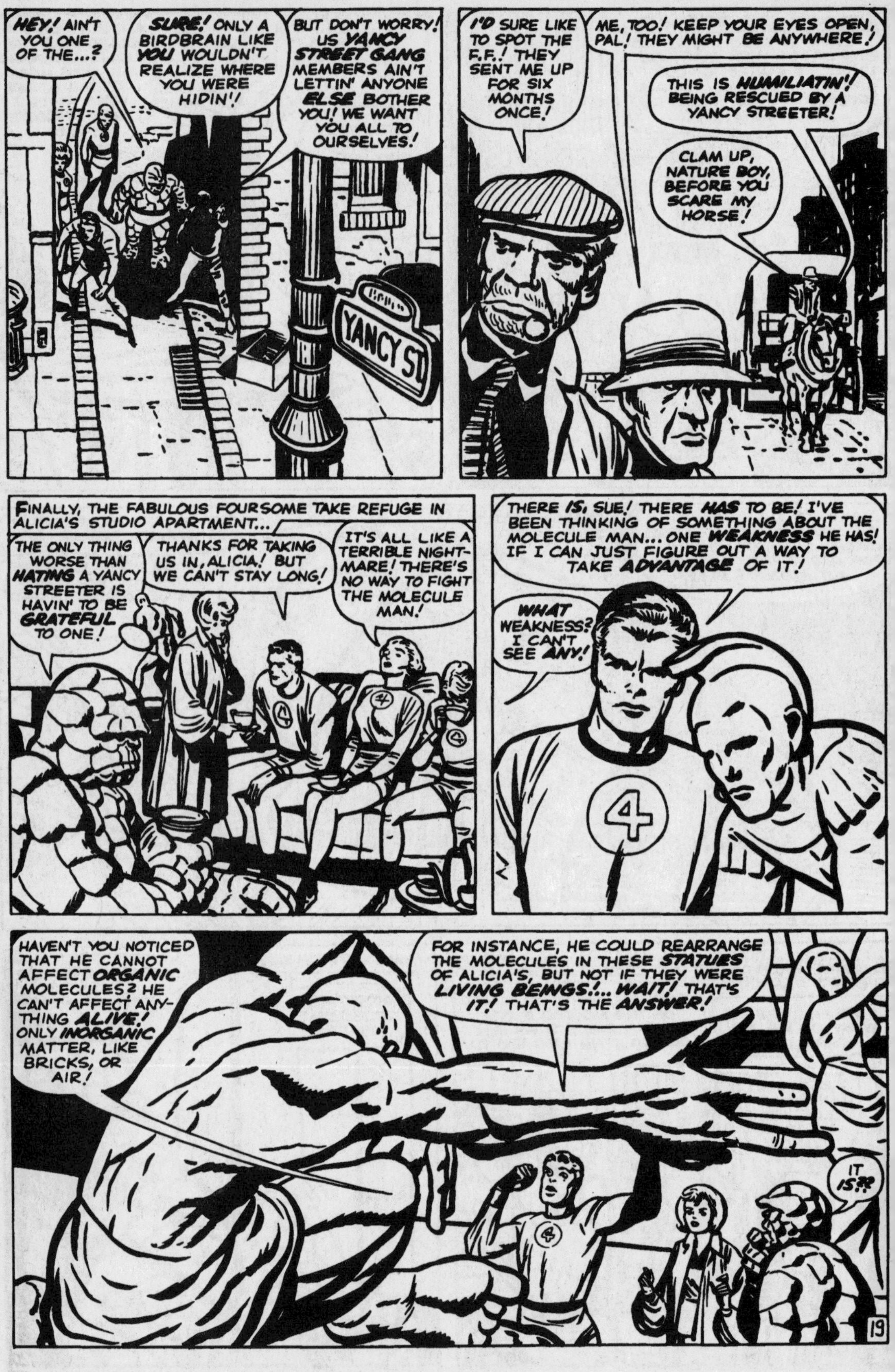

HEY! AIN'T YOU ONE OF THE...?
SURE! ONLY A BIRDBRAIN LIKE YOU WOULDN'T REALIZE WHERE YOU WERE HIDIN'!
BUT DON'T WORRY! US YANCY STREET GANG MEMBERS AIN'T LETTIN' ANYONE ELSE BOTHER YOU! WE WANT YOU ALL TO OURSELVES!
YANCY ST
I'D SURE LIKE TO SPOT THE F.F.! THEY SENT ME UP FOR SIX MONTHS ONCE!
ME, TOO! KEEP YOUR EYES OPEN, PAL! THEY MIGHT BE ANYWHERE!
THIS IS HUMILIATIN'! BEING RESCUED BY A YANCY STREETER!
CLAM UP, NATURE BOY, BEFORE YOU SCARE MY HORSE!
FINALLY, THE FABULOUS FOURSOME TAKE REFUGE IN ALICIA'S STUDIO APARTMENT...
THE ONLY THING WORSE THAN HATING A YANCY STREETER IS HAVIN' TO BE GRATEFUL TO ONE!
THANKS FOR TAKING US IN, ALICIA! BUT WE CAN'T STAY LONG!
IT'S ALL LIKE A TERRIBLE NIGHT-MARE! THERE'S NO WAY TO FIGHT THE MOLECULE MAN!
THERE IS, SUE! THERE HAS TO BE! I'VE BEEN THINKING OF SOMETHING ABOUT THE MOLECULE MAN... ONE WEAKNESS HE HAS! IF I CAN JUST FIGURE OUT A WAY TO TAKE ADVANTAGE OF IT!
WHAT WEAKNESS? I CAN'T SEE ANY!
HAVEN'T YOU NOTICED THAT HE CANNOT AFFECT ORGANIC MOLECULES? HE CAN'T AFFECT ANY-THING ALIVE! ONLY INORGANIC MATTER, LIKE BRICKS, OR AIR!
FOR INSTANCE, HE COULD REARRANGE THE MOLECULES IN THESE STATUES OF ALICIA'S, BUT NOT IF THEY WERE LIVING BEINGS!... WAIT! THAT'S IT! THAT'S THE ANSWER!
IT IS?!
19

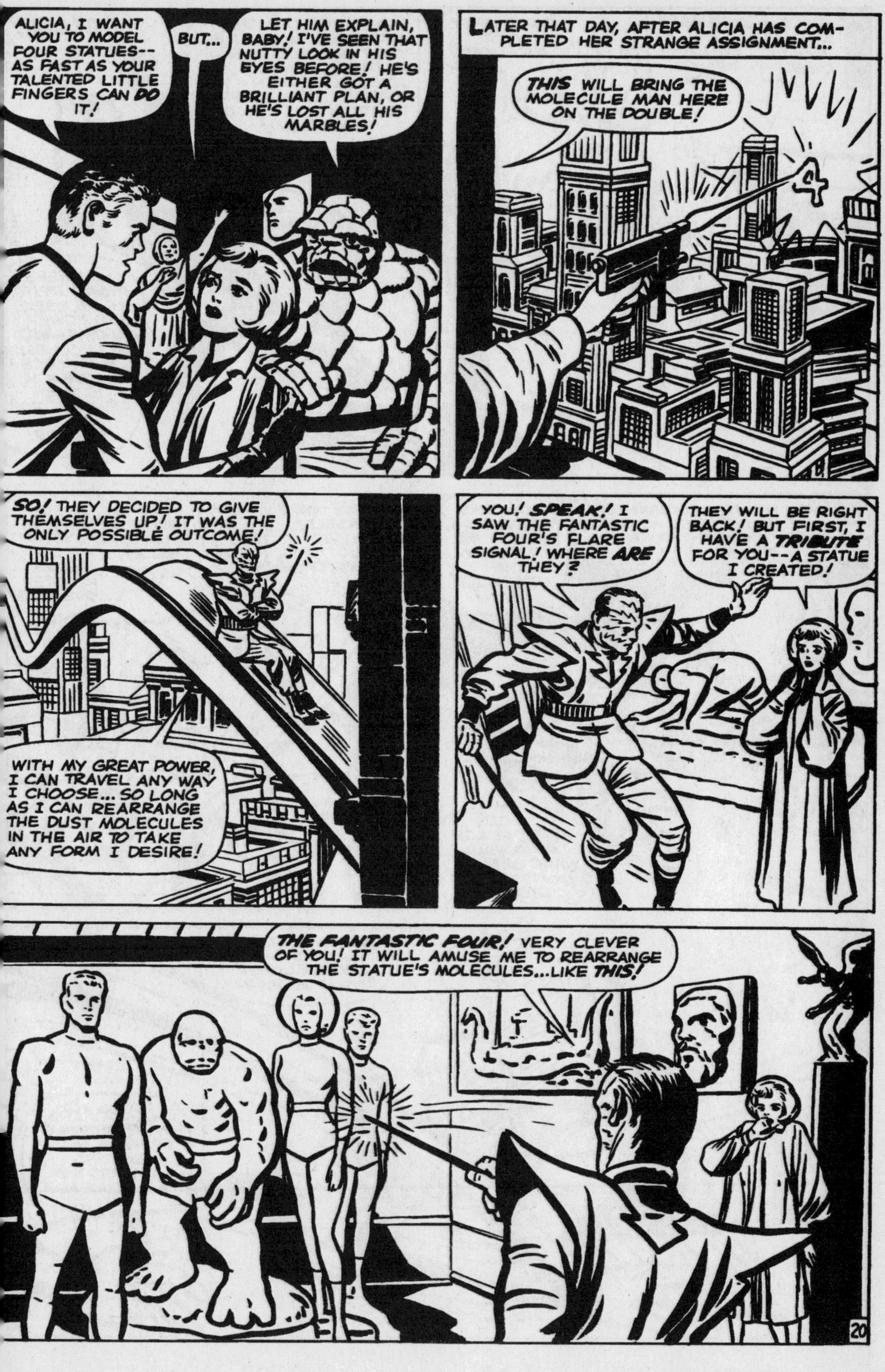
ALICIA, I WANT YOU TO MODEL FOUR STATUES-- AS FAST AS YOUR TALENTED LITTLE FINGERS CAN DO IT!
BUT...
LET HIM EXPLAIN, BABY! I'VE SEEN THAT NUTTY LOOK IN HIS EYES BEFORE! HE'S EITHER GOT A BRILLIANT PLAN, OR HE'S LOST ALL HIS MARBLES!
LATER THAT DAY, AFTER ALICIA HAS COMPLETED HER STRANGE ASSIGNMENT...
THIS WILL BRING THE MOLECULE MAN HERE ON THE DOUBLE!
SO! THEY DECIDED TO GIVE THEMSELVES UP! IT WAS THE ONLY POSSIBLE OUTCOME!
WITH MY GREAT POWER, I CAN TRAVEL ANY WAY I CHOOSE... SO LONG AS I CAN REARRANGE THE DUST MOLECULES IN THE AIR TO TAKE ANY FORM I DESIRE!
YOU! SPEAK! I SAW THE FANTASTIC FOUR'S FLARE SIGNAL! WHERE ARE THEY?
THEY WILL BE RIGHT BACK! BUT FIRST, I HAVE A TRIBUTE FOR YOU--A STATUE I CREATED!
THE FANTASTIC FOUR! VERY CLEVER OF YOU! IT WILL AMUSE ME TO REARRANGE THE STATUE'S MOLECULES...LIKE THIS!
20

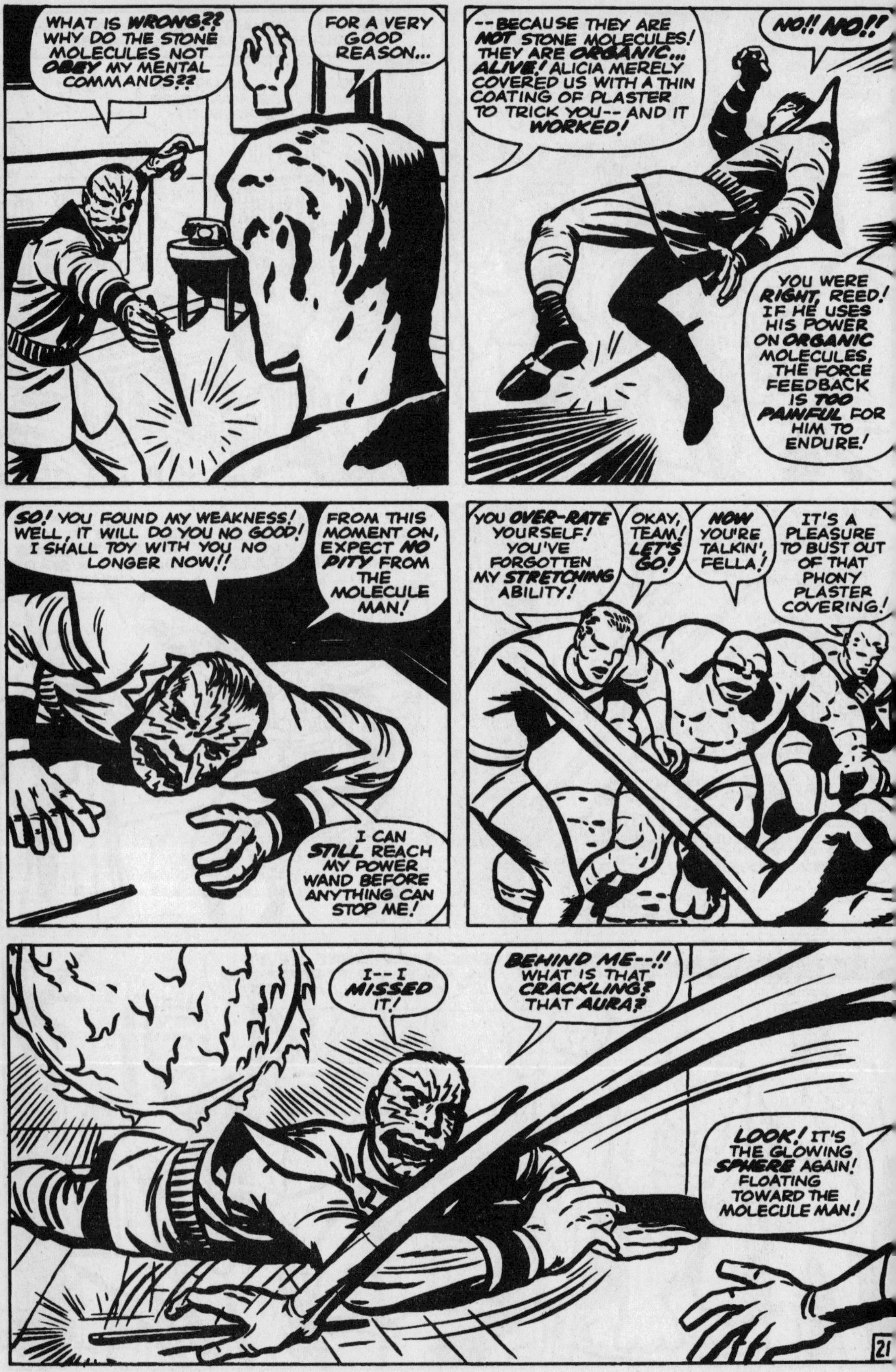
WHAT IS WRONG?? WHY DO THE STONE MOLECULES NOT OBEY MY MENTAL COMMANDS??
FOR A VERY GOOD REASON...
--BECAUSE THEY ARE NOT STONE MOLECULES! THEY ARE ORGANIC... ALIVE! ALICIA MERELY COVERED US WITH A THIN COATING OF PLASTER TO TRICK YOU-- AND IT WORKED!
NO!! NO!!
YOU WERE RIGHT, REED! IF HE USES HIS POWER ON ORGANIC MOLECULES, THE FORCE FEEDBACK IS TOO PAINFUL FOR HIM TO ENDURE!
SO! YOU FOUND MY WEAKNESS! WELL, IT WILL DO YOU NO GOOD! I SHALL TOY WITH YOU NO LONGER NOW!!
FROM THIS MOMENT ON, EXPECT NO PITY FROM THE MOLECULE MAN!
I CAN STILL REACH MY POWER WAND BEFORE ANYTHING CAN STOP ME!
YOU OVER-RATE YOURSELF! YOU'VE FORGOTTEN MY STRETCHING ABILITY!
OKAY, TEAM! LET'S GO!
NOW YOU'RE TALKIN', FELLA!
IT'S A PLEASURE TO BUST OUT OF THAT PHONY PLASTER COVERING!
I-- I MISSED IT!
BEHIND ME--!! WHAT IS THAT CRACKLING? THAT AURA?
LOOK! IT'S THE GLOWING SPHERE AGAIN! FLOATING TOWARD THE MOLECULE MAN!
21

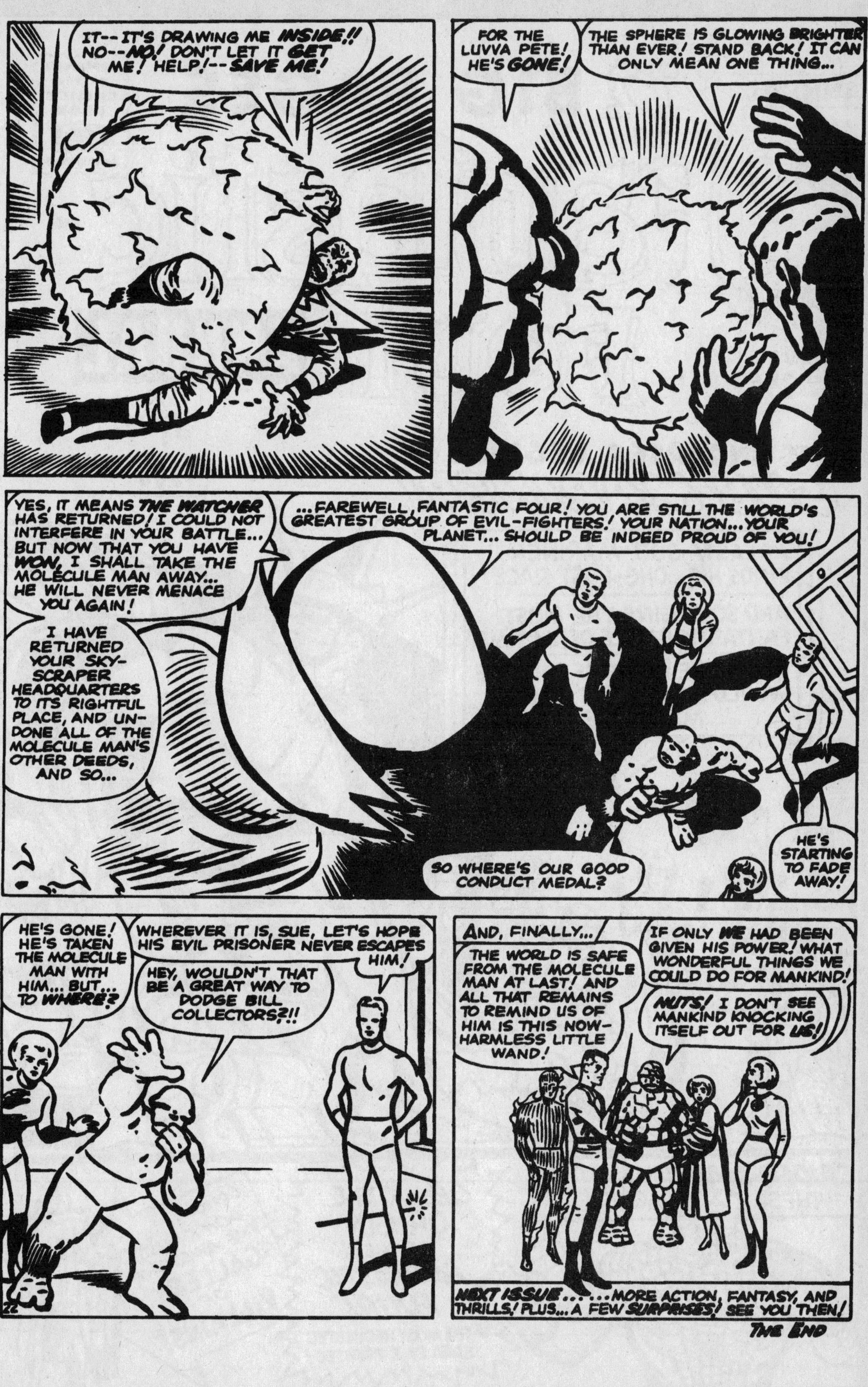
IT-- IT'S DRAWING ME INSIDE!! NO--NO! DON'T LET IT GET ME! HELP!--SAVE ME!
FOR THE LUVVA PETE! HE'S GONE!
THE SPHERE IS GLOWING BRIGHTER THAN EVER! STAND BACK! IT CAN ONLY MEAN ONE THING...
YES, IT MEANS THE WATCHER HAS RETURNED! I COULD NOT INTERFERE IN YOUR BATTLE... BUT NOW THAT YOU HAVE WON, I SHALL TAKE THE MOLECULE MAN AWAY... HE WILL NEVER MENACE YOU AGAIN!
I HAVE RETURNED YOUR SKY-SCRAPER HEADQUARTERS TO ITS RIGHTFUL PLACE, AND UNDONE ALL OF THE MOLECULE MAN'S OTHER DEEDS, AND SO...
...FAREWELL, FANTASTIC FOUR! YOU ARE STILL THE WORLD'S GREATEST GROUP OF EVIL-FIGHTERS! YOUR NATION... YOUR PLANET... SHOULD BE INDEED PROUD OF YOU!
SO WHERE'S OUR GOOD CONDUCT MEDAL?
HE'S STARTING TO FADE AWAY!
HE'S GONE! HE'S TAKEN THE MOLECULE MAN WITH HIM... BUT... TO WHERE?
WHEREVER IT IS, SUE, LET'S HOPE HIS EVIL PRISONER NEVER ESCAPES HIM!
HEY, WOULDN'T THAT BE A GREAT WAY TO DODGE BILL COLLECTORS?!!
22
AND, FINALLY...
THE WORLD IS SAFE FROM THE MOLECULE MAN AT LAST! AND ALL THAT REMAINS TO REMIND US OF HIM IS THIS NOW-HARMLESS LITTLE WAND!
IF ONLY WE HAD BEEN GIVEN HIS POWER! WHAT WONDERFUL THINGS WE COULD DO FOR MANKIND!
NUTS! I DON'T SEE MANKIND KNOCKING ITSELF OUT FOR US!
NEXT ISSUE.......MORE ACTION, FANTASY, AND THRILLS! PLUS... A FEW SURPRISES! SEE YOU THEN!
THE END

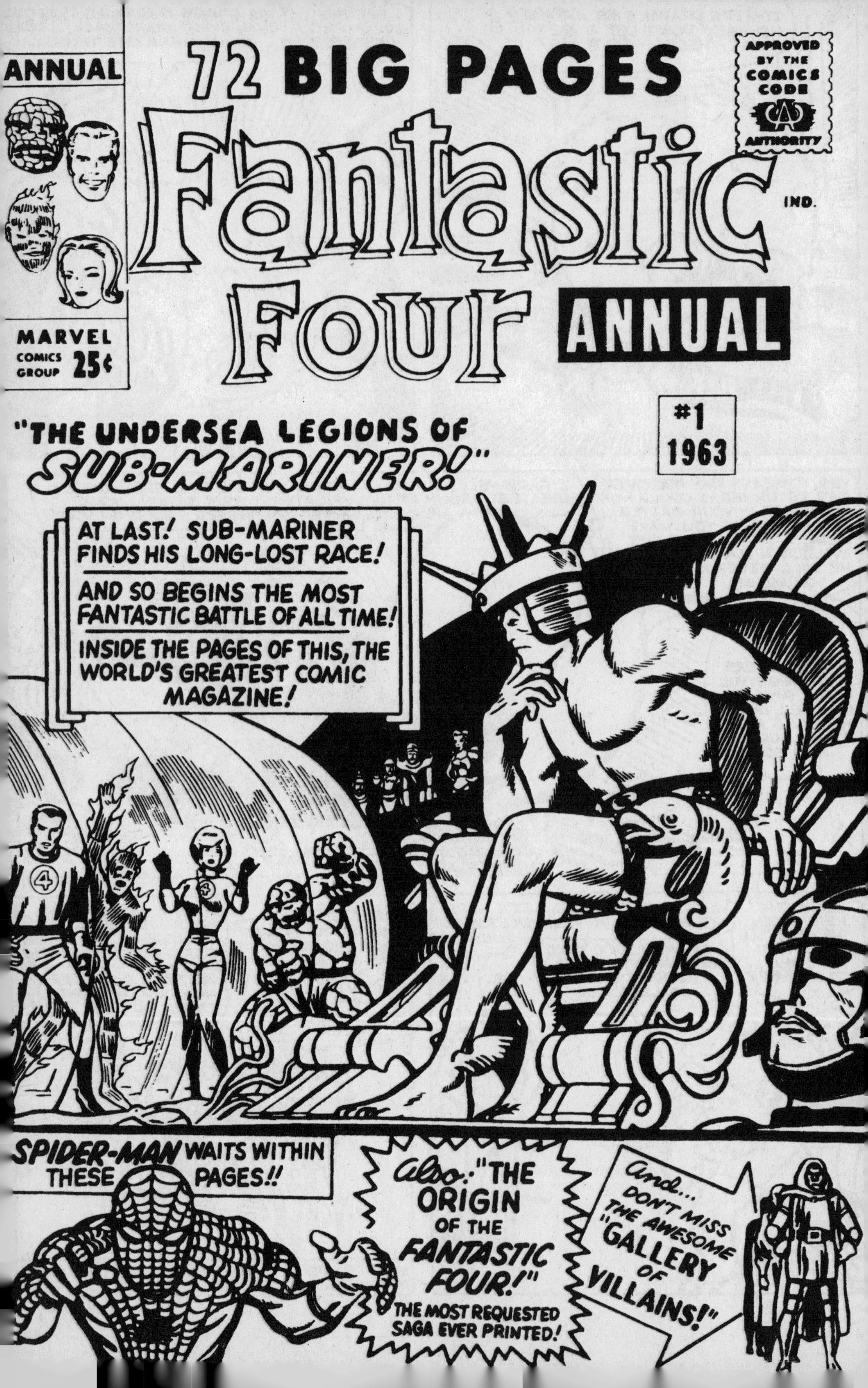

ANNUAL
72 BIG PAGES
APPROVED BY THE COMICS CODE AUTHORITY
Fantastic Four
IND.
ANNUAL
MARVEL COMICS GROUP 25¢
#1 1963
"THE UNDERSEA LEGIONS OF SUB-MARINER!"
AT LAST! SUB-MARINER FINDS HIS LONG-LOST RACE!
AND SO BEGINS THE MOST FANTASTIC BATTLE OF ALL TIME!
INSIDE THE PAGES OF THIS, THE WORLD'S GREATEST COMIC MAGAZINE!
SPIDER-MAN WAITS WITHIN THESE PAGES!!
Also: "THE ORIGIN OF THE FANTASTIC FOUR!"
THE MOST REQUESTED SAGA EVER PRINTED!
And... DON'T MISS THE AWESOME "GALLERY OF VILLAINS!"

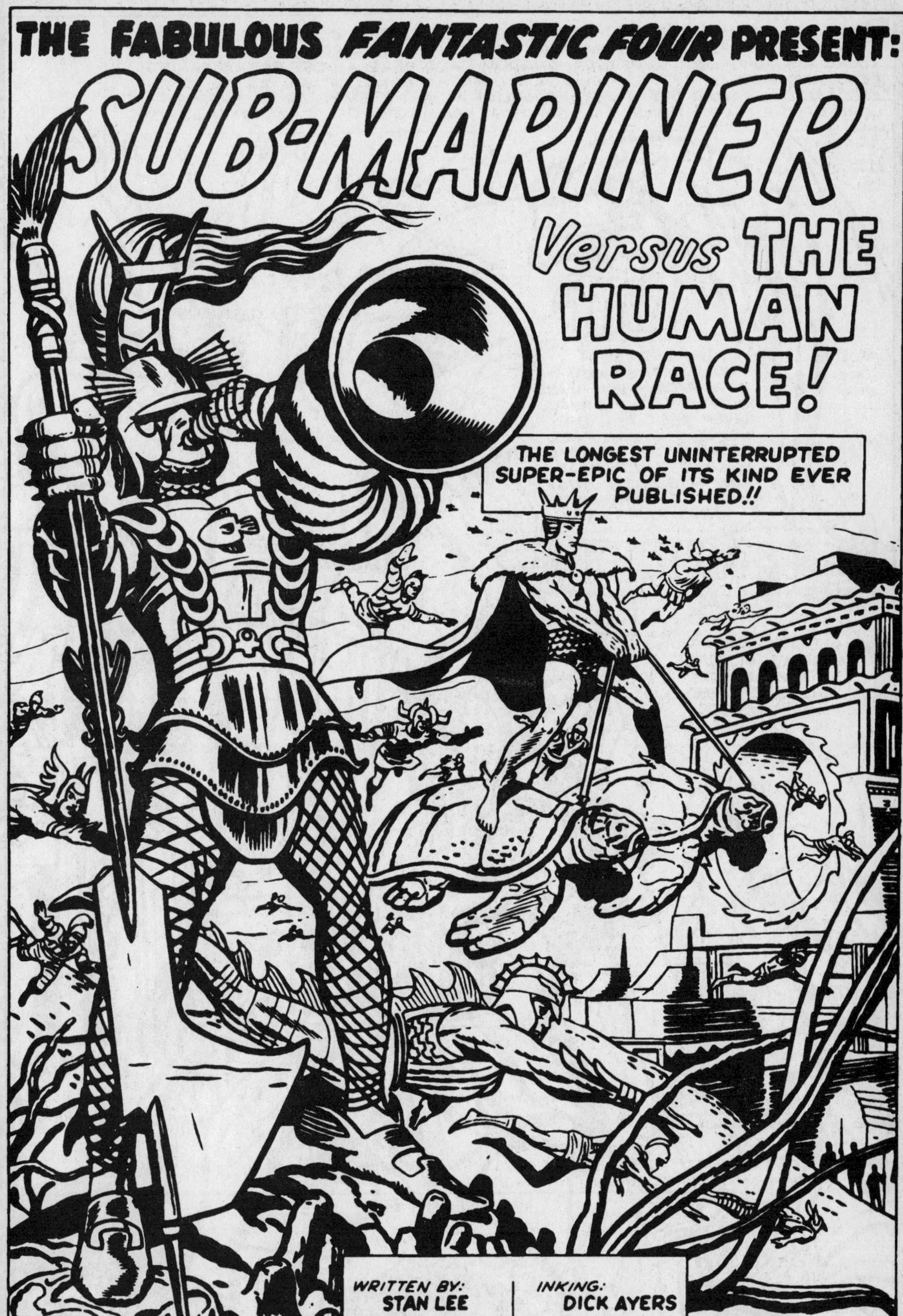
THE FABULOUS FANTASTIC FOUR PRESENT:
SUB-MARINER
Versus THE HUMAN RACE!
THE LONGEST UNINTERRUPTED SUPER-EPIC OF ITS KIND EVER PUBLISHED!!
WRITTEN BY: STAN LEE
DRAWN BY: JACK KIRBY
INKING: DICK AYERS
LETTERING: ART SIMEK
1

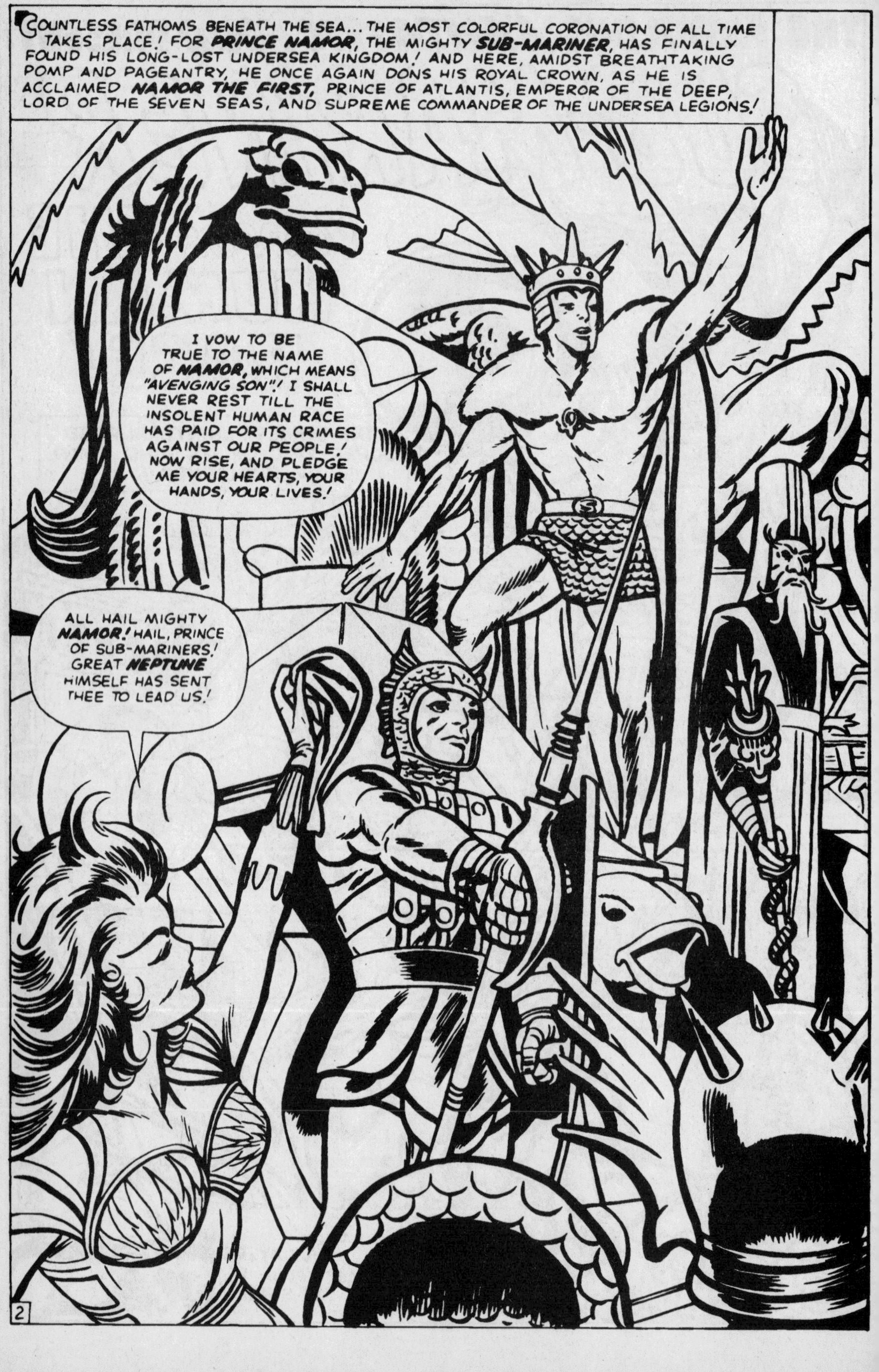
COUNTLESS FATHOMS BENEATH THE SEA... THE MOST COLORFUL CORONATION OF ALL TIME TAKES PLACE! FOR PRINCE NAMOR, THE MIGHTY SUB-MARINER, HAS FINALLY FOUND HIS LONG-LOST UNDERSEA KINGDOM! AND HERE, AMIDST BREATHTAKING POMP AND PAGEANTRY, HE ONCE AGAIN DONS HIS ROYAL CROWN, AS HE IS ACCLAIMED NAMOR THE FIRST, PRINCE OF ATLANTIS, EMPEROR OF THE DEEP, LORD OF THE SEVEN SEAS, AND SUPREME COMMANDER OF THE UNDERSEA LEGIONS!
I VOW TO BE TRUE TO THE NAME OF NAMOR, WHICH MEANS "AVENGING SON"! I SHALL NEVER REST TILL THE INSOLENT HUMAN RACE HAS PAID FOR ITS CRIMES AGAINST OUR PEOPLE! NOW RISE, AND PLEDGE ME YOUR HEARTS, YOUR HANDS, YOUR LIVES!
ALL HAIL MIGHTY NAMOR! HAIL, PRINCE OF SUB-MARINERS! GREAT NEPTUNE HIMSELF HAS SENT THEE TO LEAD US!
2

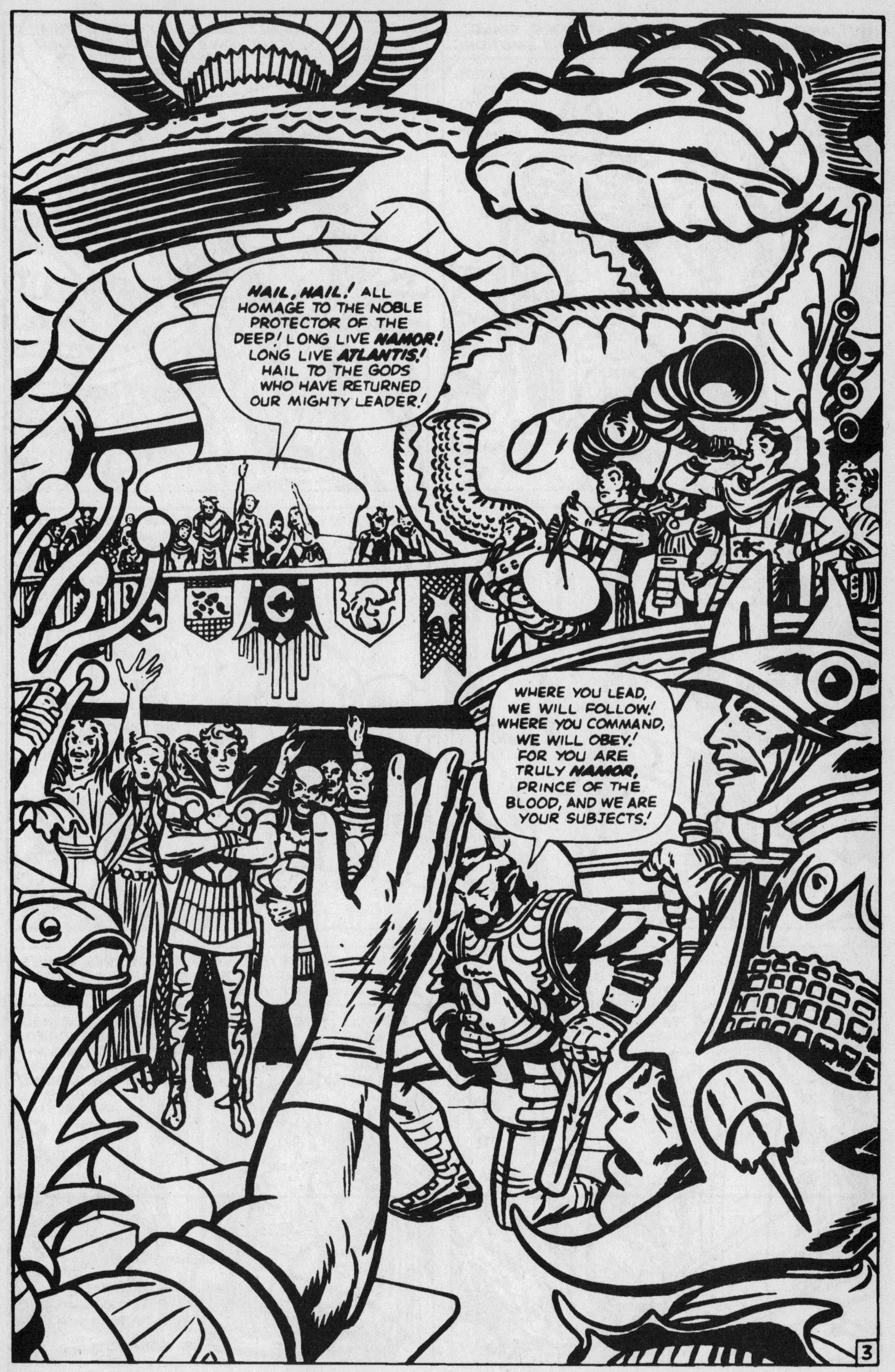
HAIL, HAIL! ALL HOMAGE TO THE NOBLE PROTECTOR OF THE DEEP! LONG LIVE NAMOR! LONG LIVE ATLANTIS! HAIL TO THE GODS WHO HAVE RETURNED OUR MIGHTY LEADER!
WHERE YOU LEAD, WE WILL FOLLOW! WHERE YOU COMMAND, WE WILL OBEY! FOR YOU ARE TRULY NAMOR, PRINCE OF THE BLOOD, AND WE ARE YOUR SUBJECTS!

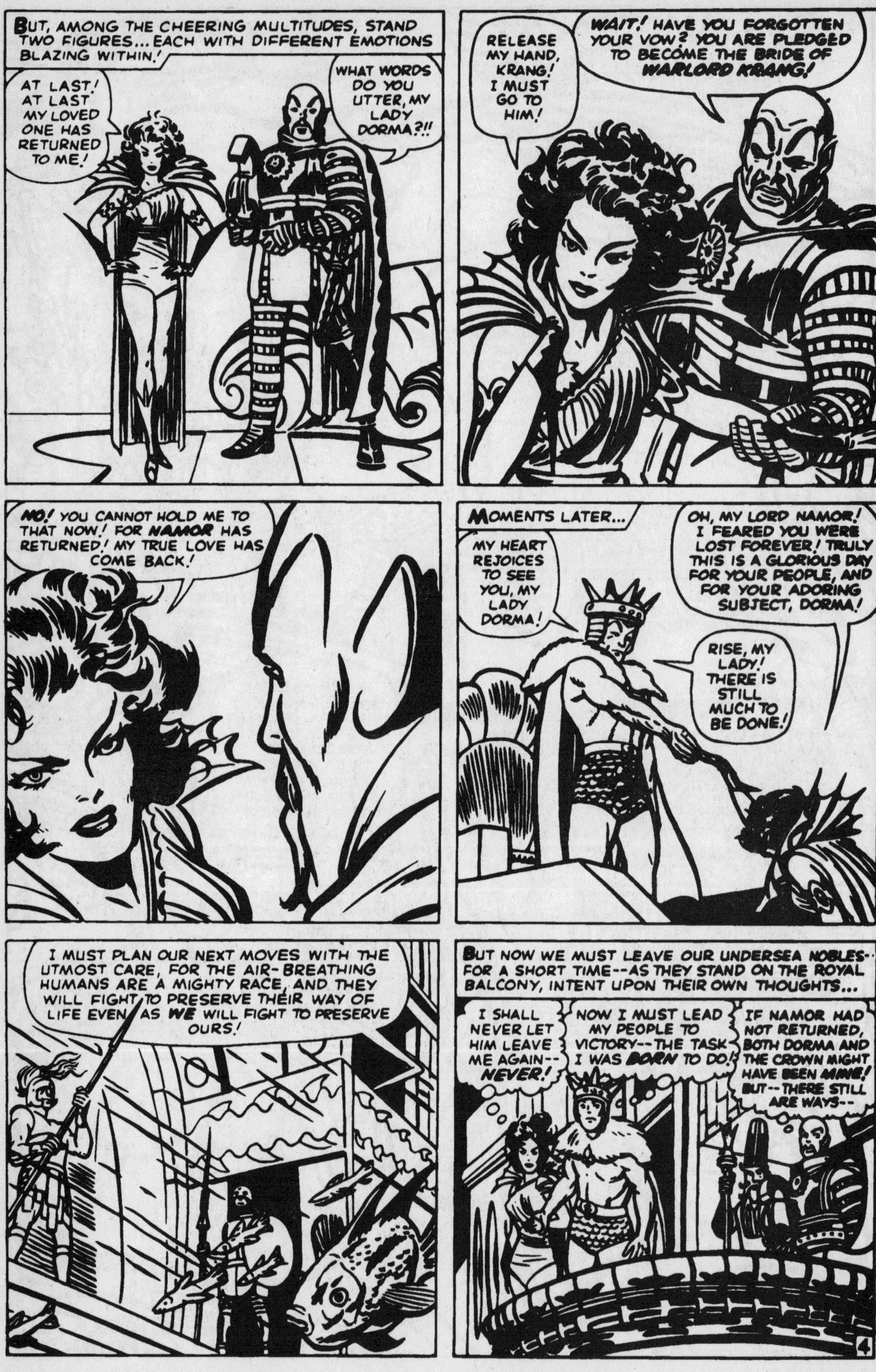
BUT, AMONG THE CHEERING MULTITUDES, STAND TWO FIGURES... EACH WITH DIFFERENT EMOTIONS BLAZING WITHIN!
AT LAST! AT LAST MY LOVED ONE HAS RETURNED TO ME!
WHAT WORDS DO YOU UTTER, MY LADY DORMA?!!
RELEASE MY HAND, KRANG! I MUST GO TO HIM!
WAIT! HAVE YOU FORGOTTEN YOUR VOW? YOU ARE PLEDGED TO BECOME THE BRIDE OF WARLORD KRANG!
NO! YOU CANNOT HOLD ME TO THAT NOW! FOR NAMOR HAS RETURNED! MY TRUE LOVE HAS COME BACK!
MOMENTS LATER...
OH, MY LORD NAMOR! I FEARED YOU WERE LOST FOREVER! TRULY THIS IS A GLORIOUS DAY FOR YOUR PEOPLE, AND FOR YOUR ADORING SUBJECT, DORMA!
MY HEART REJOICES TO SEE YOU, MY LADY DORMA!
RISE, MY LADY! THERE IS STILL MUCH TO BE DONE!
I MUST PLAN OUR NEXT MOVES WITH THE UTMOST CARE, FOR THE AIR-BREATHING HUMANS ARE A MIGHTY RACE, AND THEY WILL FIGHT TO PRESERVE THEIR WAY OF LIFE EVEN AS WE WILL FIGHT TO PRESERVE OURS!
BUT NOW WE MUST LEAVE OUR UNDERSEA NOBLES-- FOR A SHORT TIME--AS THEY STAND ON THE ROYAL BALCONY, INTENT UPON THEIR OWN THOUGHTS...
I SHALL NEVER LET HIM LEAVE ME AGAIN-- NEVER!
NOW I MUST LEAD MY PEOPLE TO VICTORY--THE TASK I WAS BORN TO DO!
IF NAMOR HAD NOT RETURNED, BOTH DORMA AND THE CROWN MIGHT HAVE BEEN MINE! BUT--THERE STILL ARE WAYS--
4

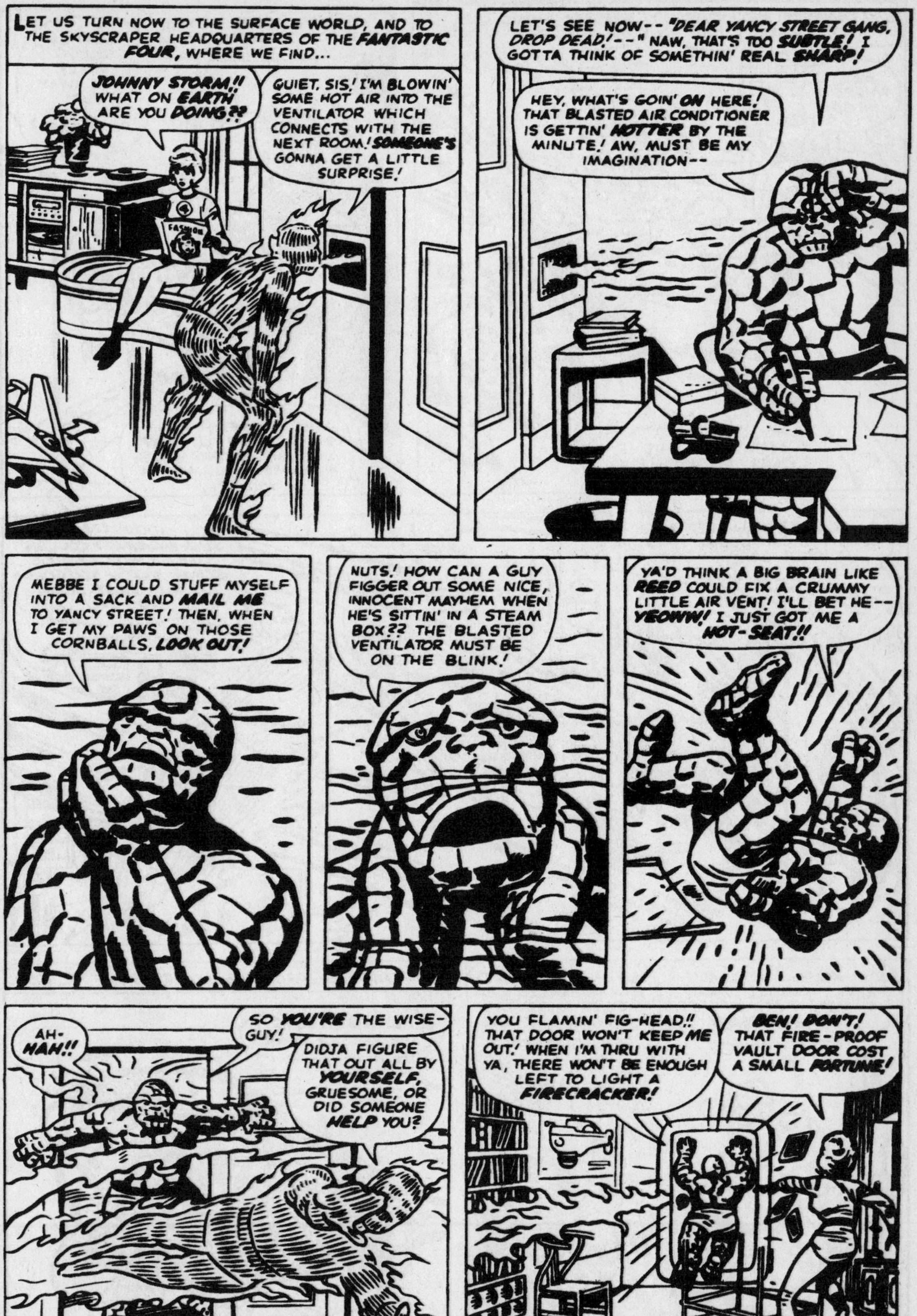
LET US TURN NOW TO THE SURFACE WORLD, AND TO THE SKYSCRAPER HEADQUARTERS OF THE FANTASTIC FOUR, WHERE WE FIND...
JOHNNY STORM!! WHAT ON EARTH ARE YOU DOING??
QUIET, SIS! I'M BLOWIN' SOME HOT AIR INTO THE VENTILATOR WHICH CONNECTS WITH THE NEXT ROOM! SOMEONE'S GONNA GET A LITTLE SURPRISE!
LET'S SEE NOW-- "DEAR YANCY STREET GANG, DROP DEAD!--" NAW, THAT'S TOO SUBTLE! I GOTTA THINK OF SOMETHIN' REAL SHARP!
HEY, WHAT'S GOIN' ON HERE! THAT BLASTED AIR CONDITIONER IS GETTIN' HOTTER BY THE MINUTE! AW, MUST BE MY IMAGINATION--
MEBBE I COULD STUFF MYSELF INTO A SACK AND MAIL ME TO YANCY STREET! THEN, WHEN I GET MY PAWS ON THOSE CORNBALLS, LOOK OUT!
NUTS! HOW CAN A GUY FIGGER OUT SOME NICE, INNOCENT MAYHEM WHEN HE'S SITTIN' IN A STEAM BOX?? THE BLASTED VENTILATOR MUST BE ON THE BLINK!
YA'D THINK A BIG BRAIN LIKE REED COULD FIX A CRUMMY LITTLE AIR VENT! I'LL BET HE-- YEOWW! I JUST GOT ME A HOT-SEAT!!
AH-HAH!!
SO YOU'RE THE WISE-GUY!
DIDJA FIGURE THAT OUT ALL BY YOURSELF, GRUESOME, OR DID SOMEONE HELP YOU?
YOU FLAMIN' FIG-HEAD!! THAT DOOR WON'T KEEP ME OUT! WHEN I'M THRU WITH YA, THERE WON'T BE ENOUGH LEFT TO LIGHT A FIRECRACKER!
BEN! DON'T! THAT FIRE-PROOF VAULT DOOR COST A SMALL FORTUNE!
5

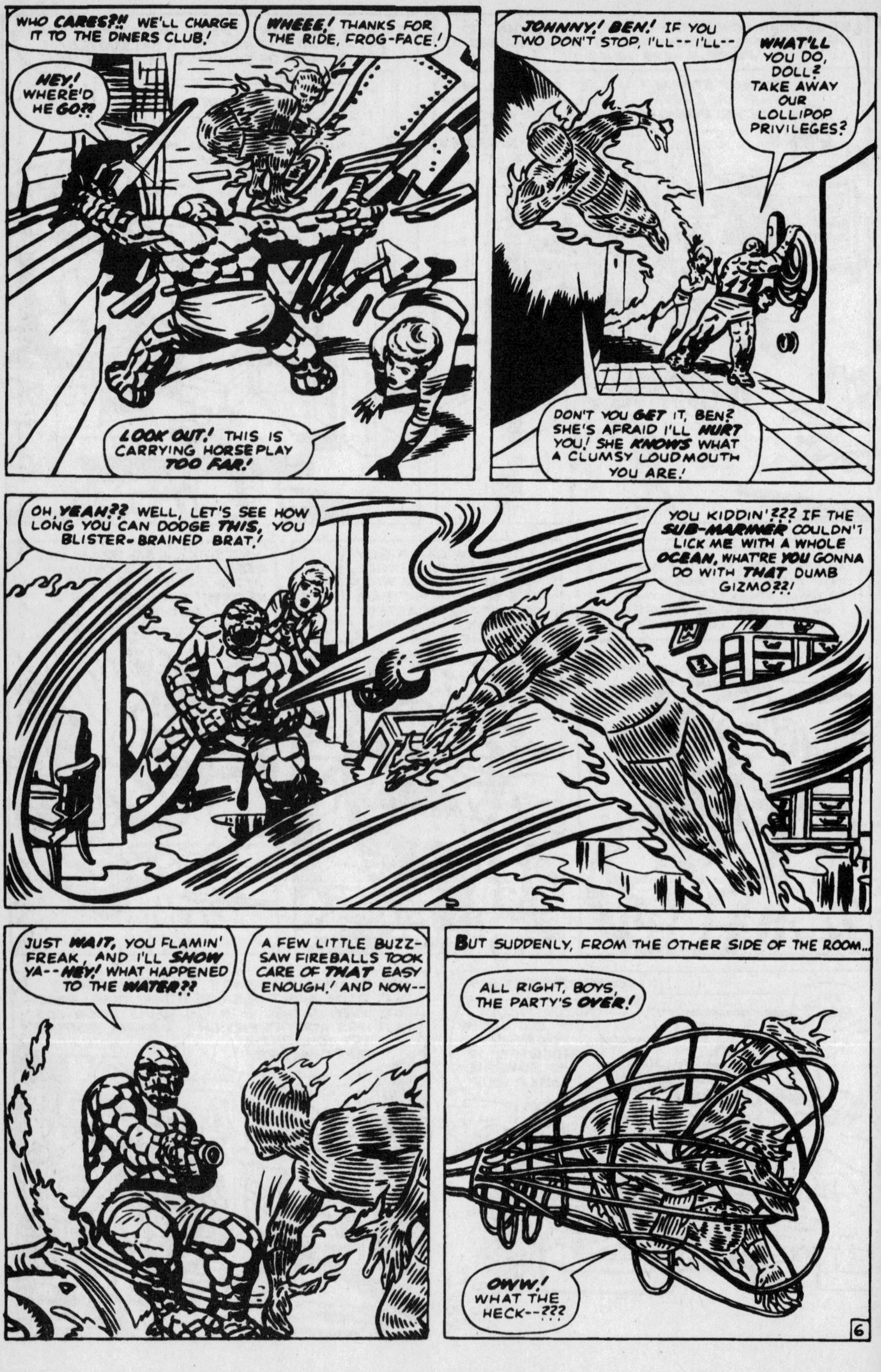

WHO CARES?!! WE'LL CHARGE IT TO THE DINERS CLUB!
WHEEE! THANKS FOR THE RIDE, FROG-FACE!
HEY! WHERE'D HE GO??
LOOK OUT! THIS IS CARRYING HORSEPLAY TOO FAR!
JOHNNY! BEN! IF YOU TWO DON'T STOP, I'LL-- I'LL--
WHAT'LL YOU DO, DOLL? TAKE AWAY OUR LOLLIPOP PRIVILEGES?
DON'T YOU GET IT, BEN? SHE'S AFRAID I'LL HURT YOU! SHE KNOWS WHAT A CLUMSY LOUDMOUTH YOU ARE!
OH, YEAH?? WELL, LET'S SEE HOW LONG YOU CAN DODGE THIS, YOU BLISTER-BRAINED BRAT!
YOU KIDDIN'??? IF THE SUB-MARINER COULDN'T LICK ME WITH A WHOLE OCEAN, WHAT'RE YOU GONNA DO WITH THAT DUMB GIZMO??!
JUST WAIT, YOU FLAMIN' FREAK, AND I'LL SHOW YA--HEY! WHAT HAPPENED TO THE WATER??
A FEW LITTLE BUZZ-SAW FIREBALLS TOOK CARE OF THAT EASY ENOUGH! AND NOW--
BUT SUDDENLY, FROM THE OTHER SIDE OF THE ROOM...
ALL RIGHT, BOYS, THE PARTY'S OVER!
OWW! WHAT THE HECK--???
6

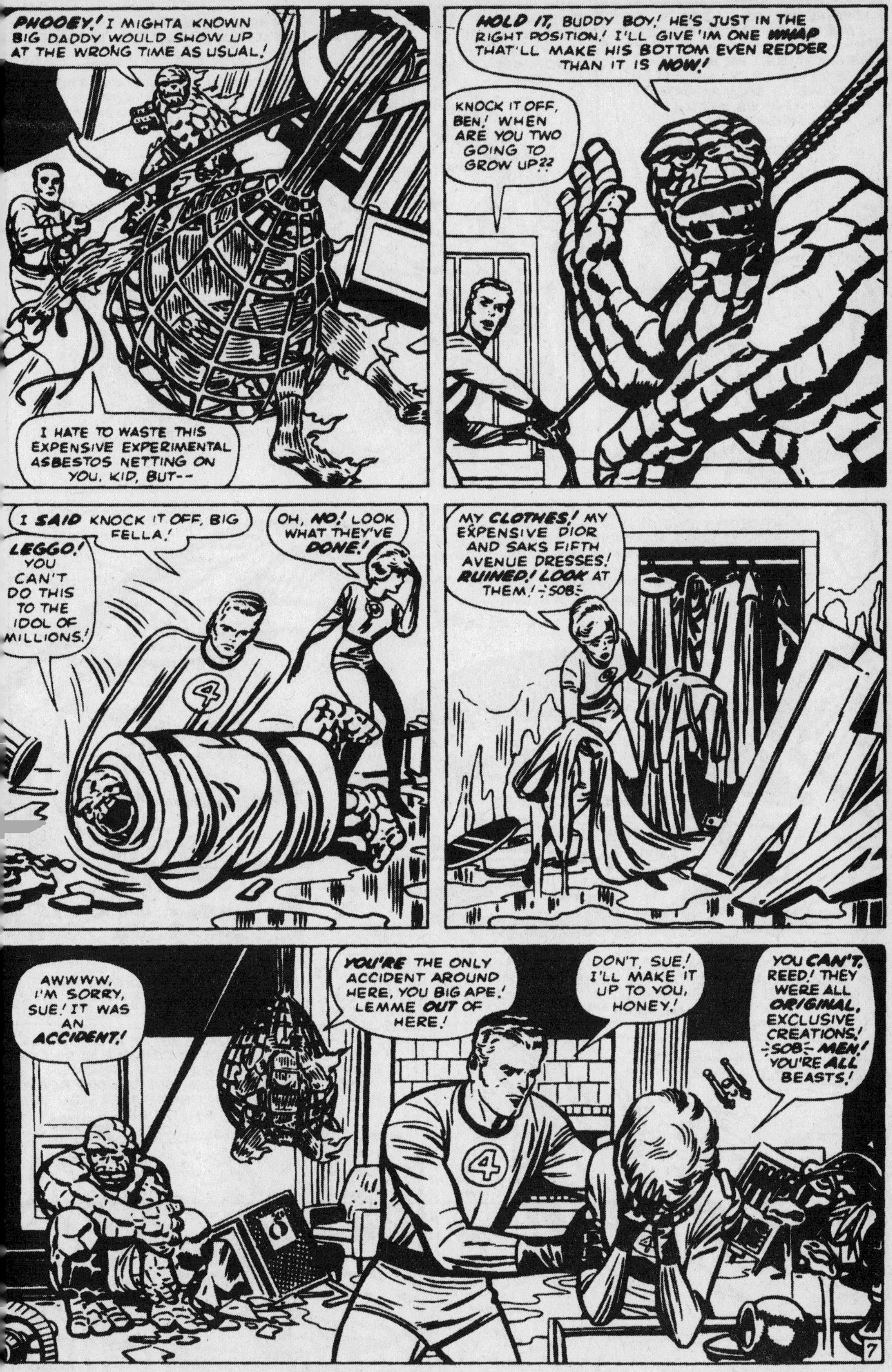
PHOOEY! I MIGHTA KNOWN BIG DADDY WOULD SHOW UP AT THE WRONG TIME AS USUAL!
I HATE TO WASTE THIS EXPENSIVE EXPERIMENTAL ASBESTOS NETTING ON YOU, KID, BUT--
HOLD IT, BUDDY BOY! HE'S JUST IN THE RIGHT POSITION! I'LL GIVE 'IM ONE WHAP THAT'LL MAKE HIS BOTTOM EVEN REDDER THAN IT IS NOW!
KNOCK IT OFF, BEN! WHEN ARE YOU TWO GOING TO GROW UP??
I SAID KNOCK IT OFF, BIG FELLA!
LEGGO! YOU CAN'T DO THIS TO THE IDOL OF MILLIONS!
OH, NO! LOOK WHAT THEY'VE DONE!
MY CLOTHES! MY EXPENSIVE DIOR AND SAKS FIFTH AVENUE DRESSES! RUINED! LOOK AT THEM! -SOB-
AWWWW, I'M SORRY, SUE! IT WAS AN ACCIDENT!
YOU'RE THE ONLY ACCIDENT AROUND HERE, YOU BIG APE! LEMME OUT OF HERE!
DON'T, SUE! I'LL MAKE IT UP TO YOU, HONEY!
YOU CAN'T, REED! THEY WERE ALL ORIGINAL, EXCLUSIVE CREATIONS! -SOB- MEN! YOU'RE ALL BEASTS!
7

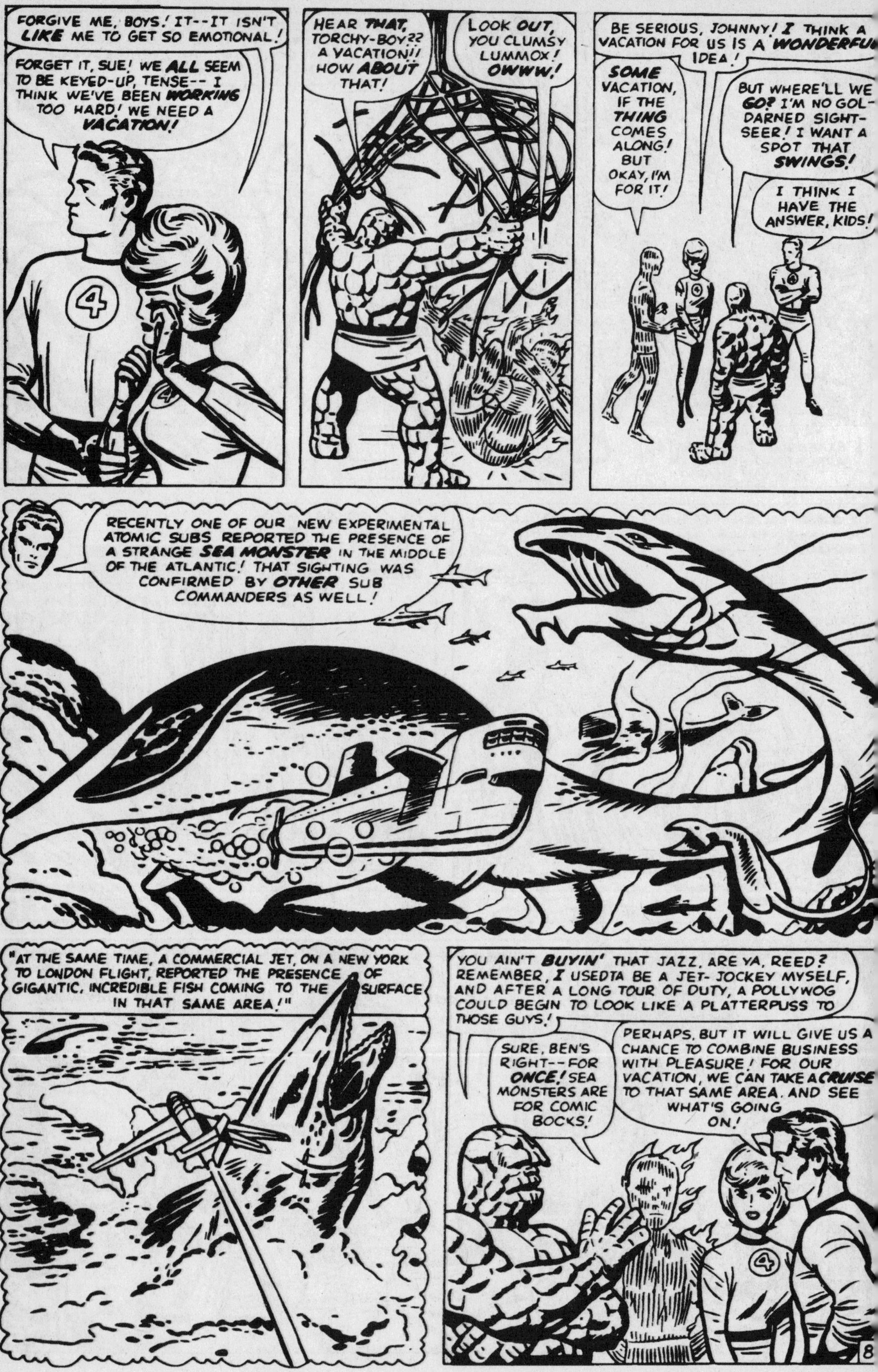
FORGIVE ME, BOYS! IT--IT ISN'T LIKE ME TO GET SO EMOTIONAL!
FORGET IT, SUE! WE ALL SEEM TO BE KEYED-UP, TENSE-- I THINK WE'VE BEEN WORKING TOO HARD! WE NEED A VACATION!
HEAR THAT, TORCHY-BOY?? A VACATION!! HOW ABOUT THAT!
LOOK OUT, YOU CLUMSY LUMMOX! OWWW!
BE SERIOUS, JOHNNY! I THINK A VACATION FOR US IS A WONDERFU IDEA!
SOME VACATION, IF THE THING COMES ALONG! BUT OKAY, I'M FOR IT!
BUT WHERE'LL WE GO? I'M NO GOL-DARNED SIGHT-SEER! I WANT A SPOT THAT SWINGS!
I THINK I HAVE THE ANSWER, KIDS!
RECENTLY ONE OF OUR NEW EXPERIMENTAL ATOMIC SUBS REPORTED THE PRESENCE OF A STRANGE SEA MONSTER IN THE MIDDLE OF THE ATLANTIC! THAT SIGHTING WAS CONFIRMED BY OTHER SUB COMMANDERS AS WELL!
"AT THE SAME TIME, A COMMERCIAL JET, ON A NEW YORK TO LONDON FLIGHT, REPORTED THE PRESENCE OF GIGANTIC, INCREDIBLE FISH COMING TO THE SURFACE IN THAT SAME AREA!"
YOU AIN'T BUYIN' THAT JAZZ, ARE YA, REED? REMEMBER, I USEDTA BE A JET-JOCKEY MYSELF, AND AFTER A LONG TOUR OF DUTY, A POLLYWOG COULD BEGIN TO LOOK LIKE A PLATTERPUSS TO THOSE GUYS!
SURE, BEN'S RIGHT--FOR ONCE! SEA MONSTERS ARE FOR COMIC BOOKS!
PERHAPS, BUT IT WILL GIVE US A CHANCE TO COMBINE BUSINESS WITH PLEASURE! FOR OUR VACATION, WE CAN TAKE A CRUISE TO THAT SAME AREA, AND SEE WHAT'S GOING ON!

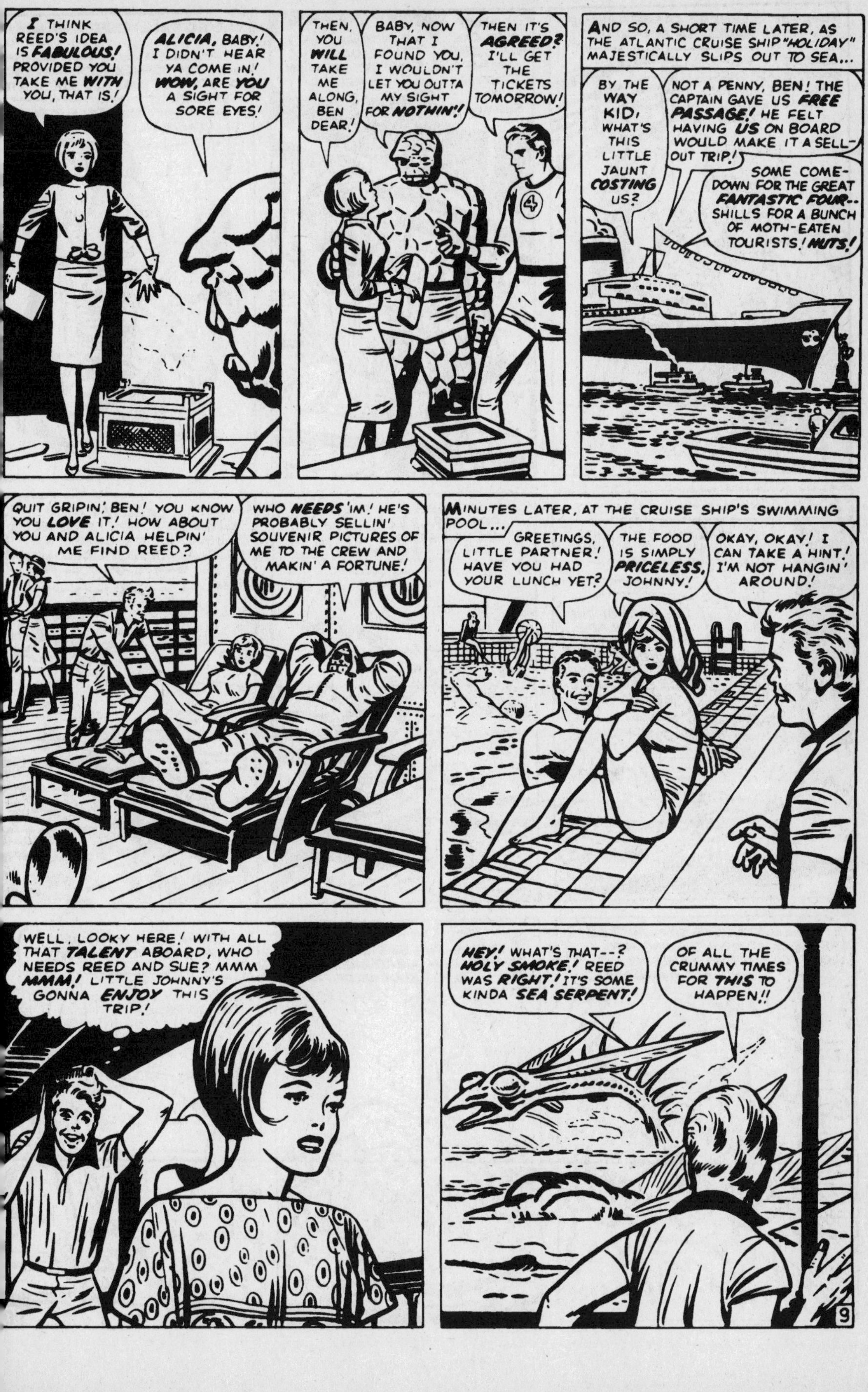

I THINK REED'S IDEA IS FABULOUS! PROVIDED YOU TAKE ME WITH YOU, THAT IS!
ALICIA, BABY! I DIDN'T HEAR YA COME IN! WOW, ARE YOU A SIGHT FOR SORE EYES!
THEN, YOU WILL TAKE ME ALONG, BEN DEAR!
BABY, NOW THAT I FOUND YOU, I WOULDN'T LET YOU OUTTA MY SIGHT FOR NOTHIN'!
THEN IT'S AGREED? I'LL GET THE TICKETS TOMORROW!
AND SO, A SHORT TIME LATER, AS THE ATLANTIC CRUISE SHIP "HOLIDAY" MAJESTICALLY SLIPS OUT TO SEA...
BY THE WAY KID, WHAT'S THIS LITTLE JAUNT COSTING US?
NOT A PENNY, BEN! THE CAPTAIN GAVE US FREE PASSAGE! HE FELT HAVING US ON BOARD WOULD MAKE IT A SELL-OUT TRIP!
SOME COME-DOWN FOR THE GREAT FANTASTIC FOUR-- SHILLS FOR A BUNCH OF MOTH-EATEN TOURISTS! NUTS!
QUIT GRIPIN', BEN! YOU KNOW YOU LOVE IT! HOW ABOUT YOU AND ALICIA HELPIN' ME FIND REED?
WHO NEEDS 'IM! HE'S PROBABLY SELLIN' SOUVENIR PICTURES OF ME TO THE CREW AND MAKIN' A FORTUNE!
MINUTES LATER, AT THE CRUISE SHIP'S SWIMMING POOL...
GREETINGS, LITTLE PARTNER! HAVE YOU HAD YOUR LUNCH YET?
THE FOOD IS SIMPLY PRICELESS, JOHNNY!
OKAY, OKAY! I CAN TAKE A HINT! I'M NOT HANGIN' AROUND!
WELL, LOOKY HERE! WITH ALL THAT TALENT ABOARD, WHO NEEDS REED AND SUE? MMM MMM! LITTLE JOHNNY'S GONNA ENJOY THIS TRIP!
HEY! WHAT'S THAT--? HOLY SMOKE! REED WAS RIGHT! IT'S SOME KINDA SEA SERPENT!
OF ALL THE CRUMMY TIMES FOR THIS TO HAPPEN!!
9

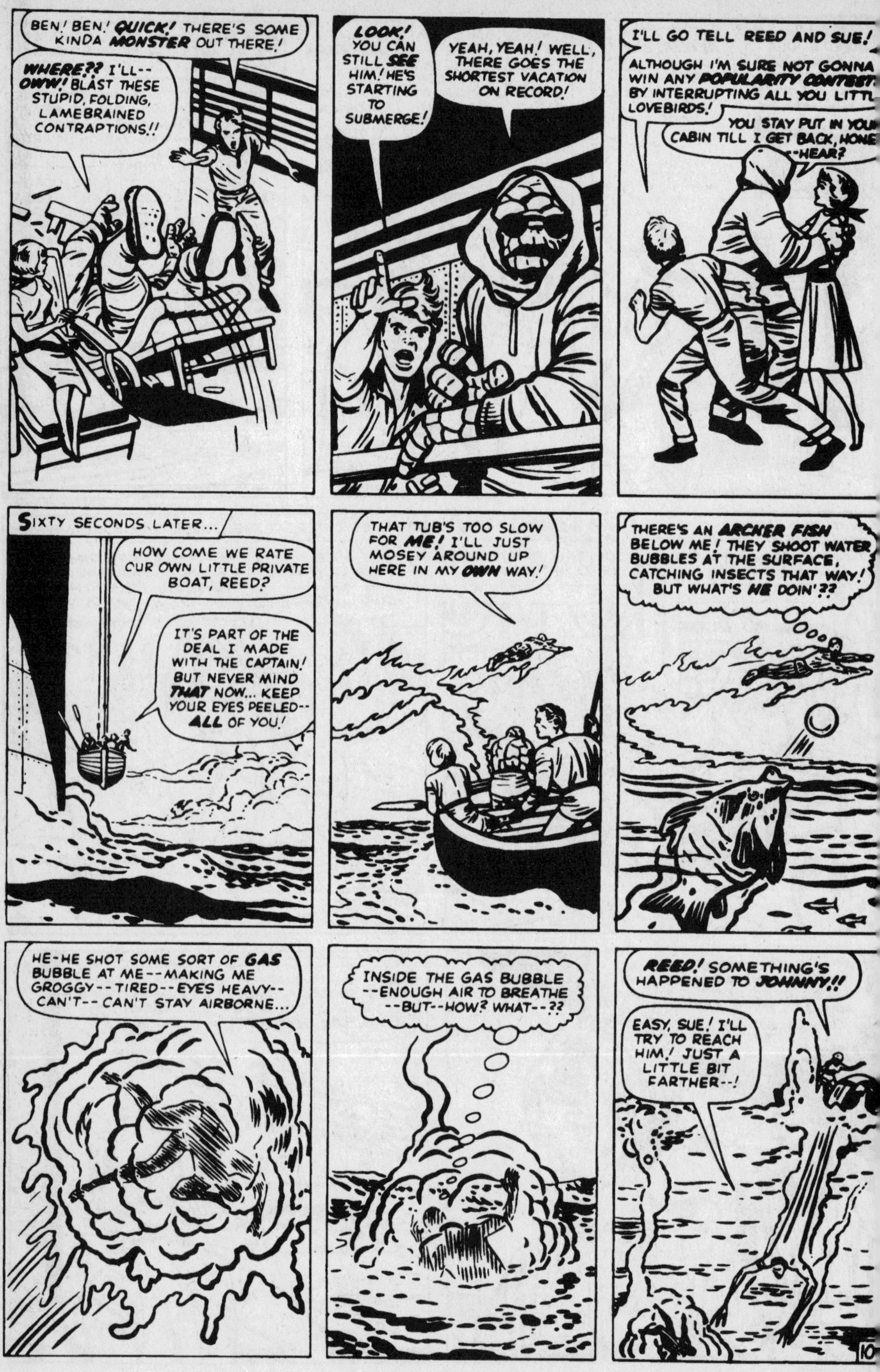
BEN! BEN! QUICK! THERE'S SOME KINDA MONSTER OUT THERE!
WHERE?? I'LL-- OWW! BLAST THESE STUPID, FOLDING, LAMEBRAINED CONTRAPTIONS!!
LOOK! YOU CAN STILL SEE HIM! HE'S STARTING TO SUBMERGE!
YEAH, YEAH! WELL, THERE GOES THE SHORTEST VACATION ON RECORD!
I'LL GO TELL REED AND SUE!
ALTHOUGH I'M SURE NOT GONNA WIN ANY POPULARITY CONTEST BY INTERRUPTING ALL YOU LITTLE LOVEBIRDS!
YOU STAY PUT IN YOUR CABIN TILL I GET BACK, HONE --HEAR?
SIXTY SECONDS LATER...
HOW COME WE RATE OUR OWN LITTLE PRIVATE BOAT, REED?
IT'S PART OF THE DEAL I MADE WITH THE CAPTAIN! BUT NEVER MIND THAT NOW... KEEP YOUR EYES PEELED-- ALL OF YOU!
THAT TUB'S TOO SLOW FOR ME! I'LL JUST MOSEY AROUND UP HERE IN MY OWN WAY!
THERE'S AN ARCHER FISH BELOW ME! THEY SHOOT WATER BUBBLES AT THE SURFACE, CATCHING INSECTS THAT WAY! BUT WHAT'S HE DOIN'??
HE-HE SHOT SOME SORT OF GAS BUBBLE AT ME--MAKING ME GROGGY--TIRED--EYES HEAVY-- CAN'T--CAN'T STAY AIRBORNE...
INSIDE THE GAS BUBBLE --ENOUGH AIR TO BREATHE --BUT--HOW? WHAT--??
REED! SOMETHING'S HAPPENED TO JOHNNY!!
EASY, SUE! I'LL TRY TO REACH HIM! JUST A LITTLE BIT FARTHER--!
10

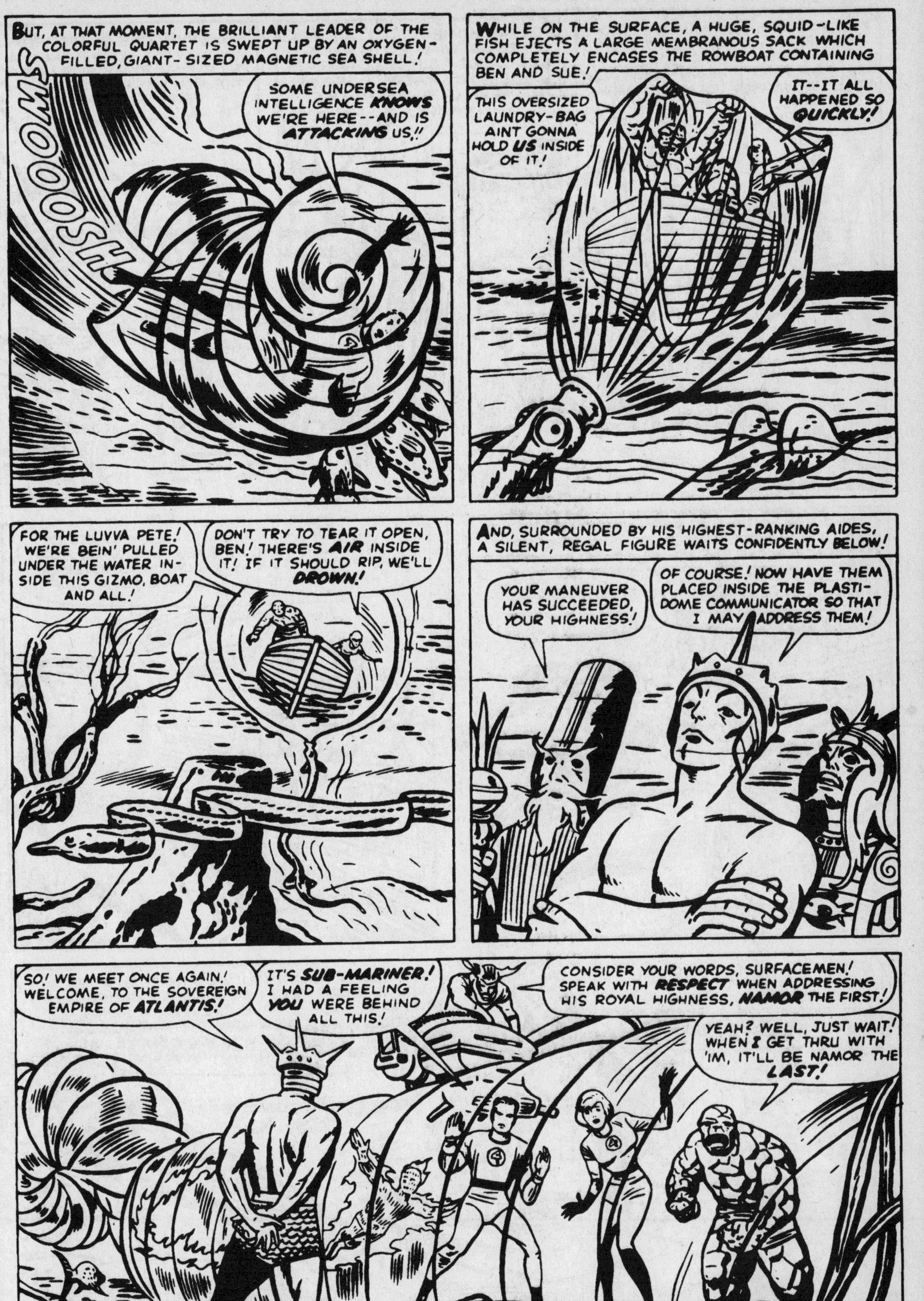
BUT, AT THAT MOMENT, THE BRILLIANT LEADER OF THE COLORFUL QUARTET IS SWEPT UP BY AN OXYGEN-FILLED, GIANT-SIZED MAGNETIC SEA SHELL!
SWOOOOSH
SOME UNDERSEA INTELLIGENCE KNOWS WE'RE HERE--AND IS ATTACKING US!!
WHILE ON THE SURFACE, A HUGE, SQUID-LIKE FISH EJECTS A LARGE MEMBRANOUS SACK WHICH COMPLETELY ENCASES THE ROWBOAT CONTAINING BEN AND SUE!
THIS OVERSIZED LAUNDRY-BAG AINT GONNA HOLD US INSIDE OF IT!
IT--IT ALL HAPPENED SO QUICKLY!
FOR THE LUVVA PETE! WE'RE BEIN' PULLED UNDER THE WATER IN-SIDE THIS GIZMO, BOAT AND ALL!
DON'T TRY TO TEAR IT OPEN, BEN! THERE'S AIR INSIDE IT! IF IT SHOULD RIP, WE'LL DROWN!
AND, SURROUNDED BY HIS HIGHEST-RANKING AIDES, A SILENT, REGAL FIGURE WAITS CONFIDENTLY BELOW!
YOUR MANEUVER HAS SUCCEEDED, YOUR HIGHNESS!
OF COURSE! NOW HAVE THEM PLACED INSIDE THE PLASTI-DOME COMMUNICATOR SO THAT I MAY ADDRESS THEM!
SO! WE MEET ONCE AGAIN! WELCOME, TO THE SOVEREIGN EMPIRE OF ATLANTIS!
IT'S SUB-MARINER! I HAD A FEELING YOU WERE BEHIND ALL THIS!
CONSIDER YOUR WORDS, SURFACEMEN! SPEAK WITH RESPECT WHEN ADDRESSING HIS ROYAL HIGHNESS, NAMOR THE FIRST!
YEAH? WELL, JUST WAIT! WHEN I GET THRU WITH 'IM, IT'LL BE NAMOR THE LAST!
11

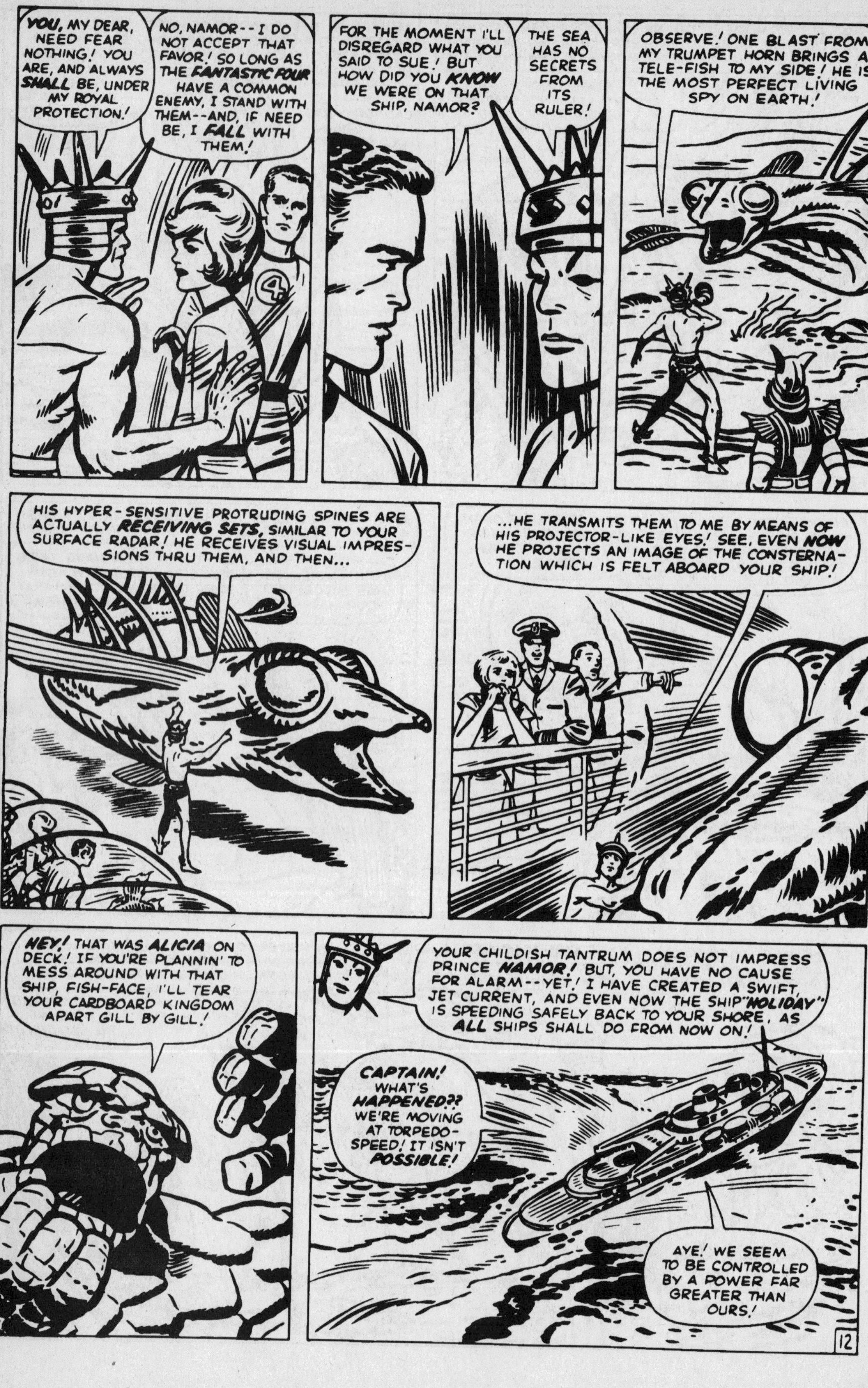
YOU, MY DEAR, NEED FEAR NOTHING! YOU ARE, AND ALWAYS SHALL BE, UNDER MY ROYAL PROTECTION!
NO, NAMOR--I DO NOT ACCEPT THAT FAVOR! SO LONG AS THE FANTASTIC FOUR HAVE A COMMON ENEMY, I STAND WITH THEM--AND, IF NEED BE, I FALL WITH THEM!
FOR THE MOMENT I'LL DISREGARD WHAT YOU SAID TO SUE! BUT HOW DID YOU KNOW WE WERE ON THAT SHIP, NAMOR?
THE SEA HAS NO SECRETS FROM ITS RULER!
OBSERVE! ONE BLAST FROM MY TRUMPET HORN BRINGS A TELE-FISH TO MY SIDE! HE IS THE MOST PERFECT LIVING SPY ON EARTH!
HIS HYPER-SENSITIVE PROTRUDING SPINES ARE ACTUALLY RECEIVING SETS, SIMILAR TO YOUR SURFACE RADAR! HE RECEIVES VISUAL IMPRESSIONS THRU THEM, AND THEN...
...HE TRANSMITS THEM TO ME BY MEANS OF HIS PROJECTOR-LIKE EYES! SEE, EVEN NOW HE PROJECTS AN IMAGE OF THE CONSTERNATION WHICH IS FELT ABOARD YOUR SHIP!
HEY! THAT WAS ALICIA ON DECK! IF YOU'RE PLANNIN' TO MESS AROUND WITH THAT SHIP, FISH-FACE, I'LL TEAR YOUR CARDBOARD KINGDOM APART GILL BY GILL!
YOUR CHILDISH TANTRUM DOES NOT IMPRESS PRINCE NAMOR! BUT, YOU HAVE NO CAUSE FOR ALARM--YET! I HAVE CREATED A SWIFT JET CURRENT, AND EVEN NOW THE SHIP "HOLIDAY" IS SPEEDING SAFELY BACK TO YOUR SHORE, AS ALL SHIPS SHALL DO FROM NOW ON!
CAPTAIN! WHAT'S HAPPENED?? WE'RE MOVING AT TORPEDO-SPEED! IT ISN'T POSSIBLE!
AYE! WE SEEM TO BE CONTROLLED BY A POWER FAR GREATER THAN OURS!
12

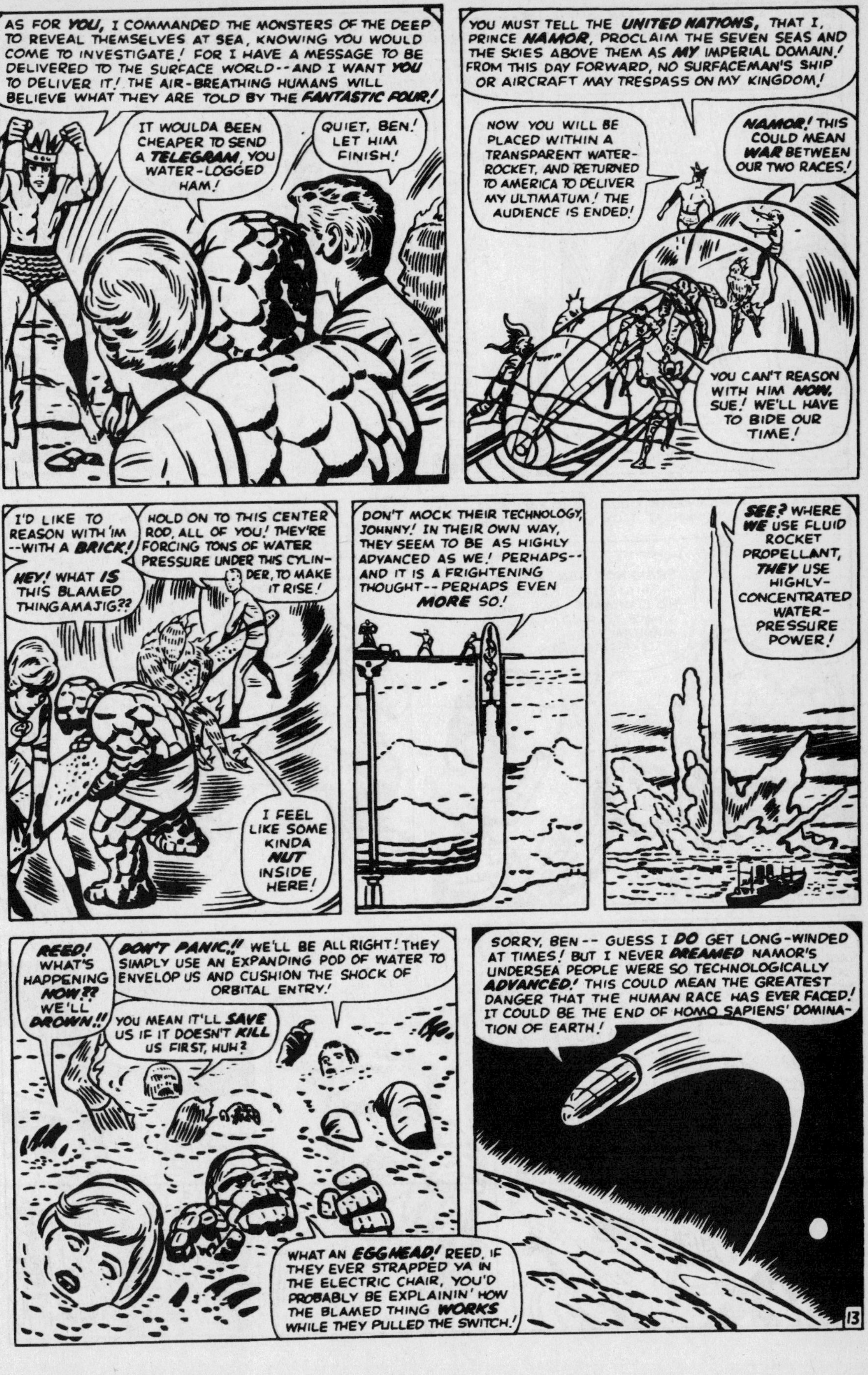
AS FOR YOU, I COMMANDED THE MONSTERS OF THE DEEP TO REVEAL THEMSELVES AT SEA, KNOWING YOU WOULD COME TO INVESTIGATE! FOR I HAVE A MESSAGE TO BE DELIVERED TO THE SURFACE WORLD--AND I WANT YOU TO DELIVER IT! THE AIR-BREATHING HUMANS WILL BELIEVE WHAT THEY ARE TOLD BY THE FANTASTIC FOUR!
IT WOULDA BEEN CHEAPER TO SEND A TELEGRAM, YOU WATER-LOGGED HAM!
QUIET, BEN! LET HIM FINISH!
YOU MUST TELL THE UNITED NATIONS, THAT I, PRINCE NAMOR, PROCLAIM THE SEVEN SEAS AND THE SKIES ABOVE THEM AS MY IMPERIAL DOMAIN! FROM THIS DAY FORWARD, NO SURFACEMAN'S SHIP OR AIRCRAFT MAY TRESPASS ON MY KINGDOM!
NOW YOU WILL BE PLACED WITHIN A TRANSPARENT WATER-ROCKET, AND RETURNED TO AMERICA TO DELIVER MY ULTIMATUM! THE AUDIENCE IS ENDED!
NAMOR! THIS COULD MEAN WAR BETWEEN OUR TWO RACES!
YOU CAN'T REASON WITH HIM NOW, SUE! WE'LL HAVE TO BIDE OUR TIME!
I'D LIKE TO REASON WITH 'IM --WITH A BRICK!
HOLD ON TO THIS CENTER ROD, ALL OF YOU! THEY'RE FORCING TONS OF WATER PRESSURE UNDER THIS CYLINDER, TO MAKE IT RISE!
HEY! WHAT IS THIS BLAMED THINGAMAJIG??
I FEEL LIKE SOME KINDA NUT INSIDE HERE!
DON'T MOCK THEIR TECHNOLOGY, JOHNNY! IN THEIR OWN WAY, THEY SEEM TO BE AS HIGHLY ADVANCED AS WE! PERHAPS--AND IT IS A FRIGHTENING THOUGHT--PERHAPS EVEN MORE SO!
SEE? WHERE WE USE FLUID ROCKET PROPELLANT, THEY USE HIGHLY-CONCENTRATED WATER-PRESSURE POWER!
REED! WHAT'S HAPPENING NOW?? WE'LL DROWN!!
DON'T PANIC!! WE'LL BE ALL RIGHT! THEY SIMPLY USE AN EXPANDING POD OF WATER TO ENVELOP US AND CUSHION THE SHOCK OF ORBITAL ENTRY!
YOU MEAN IT'LL SAVE US IF IT DOESN'T KILL US FIRST, HUH?
WHAT AN EGGHEAD! REED, IF THEY EVER STRAPPED YA IN THE ELECTRIC CHAIR, YOU'D PROBABLY BE EXPLAININ' HOW THE BLAMED THING WORKS WHILE THEY PULLED THE SWITCH!
SORRY, BEN -- GUESS I DO GET LONG-WINDED AT TIMES! BUT I NEVER DREAMED NAMOR'S UNDERSEA PEOPLE WERE SO TECHNOLOGICALLY ADVANCED! THIS COULD MEAN THE GREATEST DANGER THAT THE HUMAN RACE HAS EVER FACED! IT COULD BE THE END OF HOMO SAPIENS' DOMINATION OF EARTH!
13

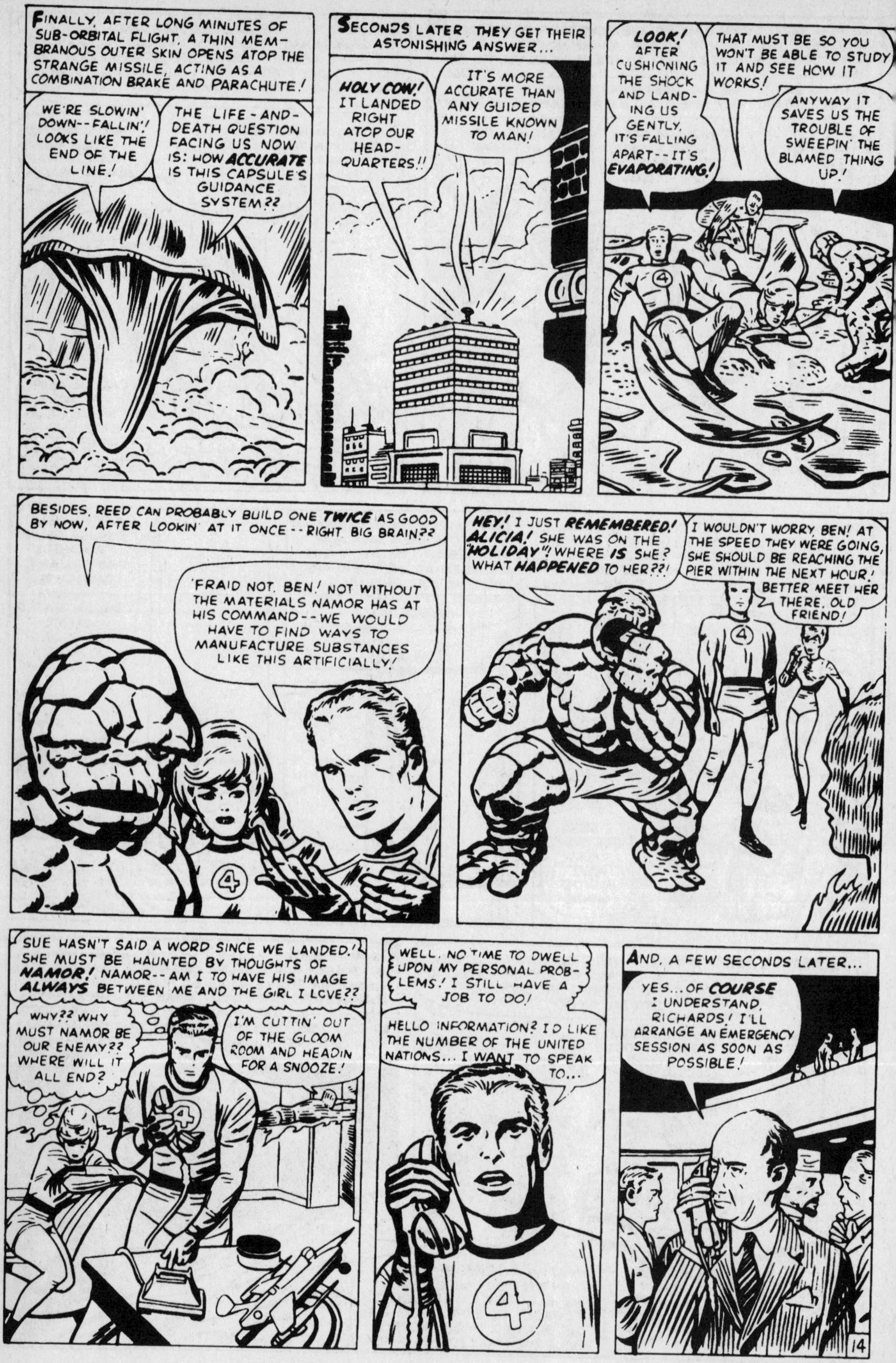
FINALLY, AFTER LONG MINUTES OF SUB-ORBITAL FLIGHT, A THIN MEMBRANOUS OUTER SKIN OPENS ATOP THE STRANGE MISSILE, ACTING AS A COMBINATION BRAKE AND PARACHUTE!
WE'RE SLOWIN' DOWN--FALLIN'! LOOKS LIKE THE END OF THE LINE!
THE LIFE-AND-DEATH QUESTION FACING US NOW IS: HOW ACCURATE IS THIS CAPSULE'S GUIDANCE SYSTEM??
SECONDS LATER THEY GET THEIR ASTONISHING ANSWER...
HOLY COW! IT LANDED RIGHT ATOP OUR HEAD-QUARTERS!!
IT'S MORE ACCURATE THAN ANY GUIDED MISSILE KNOWN TO MAN!
LOOK! AFTER CUSHIONING THE SHOCK AND LANDING US GENTLY, IT'S FALLING APART--IT'S EVAPORATING!
THAT MUST BE SO YOU WON'T BE ABLE TO STUDY IT AND SEE HOW IT WORKS!
ANYWAY IT SAVES US THE TROUBLE OF SWEEPIN' THE BLAMED THING UP!
BESIDES, REED CAN PROBABLY BUILD ONE TWICE AS GOOD BY NOW, AFTER LOOKIN' AT IT ONCE--RIGHT, BIG BRAIN??
'FRAID NOT, BEN! NOT WITHOUT THE MATERIALS NAMOR HAS AT HIS COMMAND--WE WOULD HAVE TO FIND WAYS TO MANUFACTURE SUBSTANCES LIKE THIS ARTIFICIALLY!
HEY! I JUST REMEMBERED! ALICIA! SHE WAS ON THE "HOLIDAY"! WHERE IS SHE? WHAT HAPPENED TO HER??!
I WOULDN'T WORRY, BEN! AT THE SPEED THEY WERE GOING, SHE SHOULD BE REACHING THE PIER WITHIN THE NEXT HOUR!
BETTER MEET HER THERE, OLD FRIEND!
SUE HASN'T SAID A WORD SINCE WE LANDED! SHE MUST BE HAUNTED BY THOUGHTS OF NAMOR! NAMOR--AM I TO HAVE HIS IMAGE ALWAYS BETWEEN ME AND THE GIRL I LOVE??
WHY?? WHY MUST NAMOR BE OUR ENEMY?? WHERE WILL IT ALL END?
I'M CUTTIN' OUT OF THE GLOOM ROOM AND HEADIN FOR A SNOOZE!
WELL, NO TIME TO DWELL UPON MY PERSONAL PROBLEMS! I STILL HAVE A JOB TO DO!
HELLO INFORMATION? I'D LIKE THE NUMBER OF THE UNITED NATIONS... I WANT TO SPEAK TO...
AND, A FEW SECONDS LATER...
YES... OF COURSE I UNDERSTAND, RICHARDS! I'LL ARRANGE AN EMERGENCY SESSION AS SOON AS POSSIBLE!
14

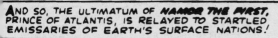

AND SO, THE ULTIMATUM OF *NAMOR THE FIRST*, PRINCE OF ATLANTIS, IS RELAYED TO STARTLED EMISSARIES OF EARTH'S SURFACE NATIONS!

...AND I CANNOT EMPHASIZE TOO STRONGLY THE GRAVITY OF THE THREAT! THIS IS NO BLUSTERING TYRANT TRYING TO BLUFF THE U.N.! THIS IS THE SUPREME RULER OF A POWERFUL UNDERSEA EMPIRE, WHO FEELS HE IS FIGHTING FOR WHAT IS *DUE* HIM! AND THERE IS EVERY POSSIBILITY THAT HE HAS THE ARMED *MIGHT* TO ACHIEVE HIS OBJECTIVES!

BAH! IT IS ALL A PACK OF CAPITALISTIC LIES!

NO MATTER WHAT THE DEMOCRACIES SAY, I VOTE *NYET! NYET! NYET!*

BAM BAM BAM

WE ANTICIPATED THE FACT THAT SOME MEMBER NATIONS MIGHT DOUBT THE EXISTENCE OF THE *SUB-MARINER*, AND SO I PRESENT DR. G. W. FALTON, AN EMINENT AUTHORITY ON UNDERSEA LIFE, WHO HAS VOLUNTEERED TO EXPLAIN THE ORIGIN OF *NAMOR* AND HIS ALMOST LEGENDARY RACE!

IF THE DELEGATE WILL KINDLY STOP POUNDING HIS SHOE, I WILL TRY TO ALLAY HIS UNFOUNDED SUSPICIONS!

I CALL YOUR ATTENTION TO THIS RARE SKULL FOSSIL EVIDENCE OF THE EXISTENCE OF A RACE KNOWN AS *HOMO MERMANUS* OR 'MAN OF THE SEA!'

AT THE DAWN OF TIME, MANY FORMS OF LIFE EVOLVED FROM THE SEA ...AND SOME OF THEM LATER *RETURNED* TO THE SEA, SUCH AS THE MAMMAL WE CALL *WHALE!*

"BUT THERE WAS *ANOTHER* FORM OF MAMMAL WHICH LATER RETURNED TO THE SEA-- THE MAMMAL WHICH WOULD COME TO BE KNOWN AS *HOMO MERMANUS!* WE SHALL NEVER KNOW WHAT AWESOME MENACE DROVE HIM BACK TO THE DEEP, BUT OF ONE THING WE CAN BE CERTAIN..."

"...*HOMO MERMANUS* EVOLVED INTO AN INTELLIGENT, WATER-BREATHING RACE...RIVALING THE DEVELOPMENT OF OUR OWN EARLY CAVE MEN!"

ARTIST'S INTERPRETATION OF ANCIENT SEA PEOPLE BATTLING THE ACTUAL ANCESTOR OF OUR PRESENT DAY SHARK.

15

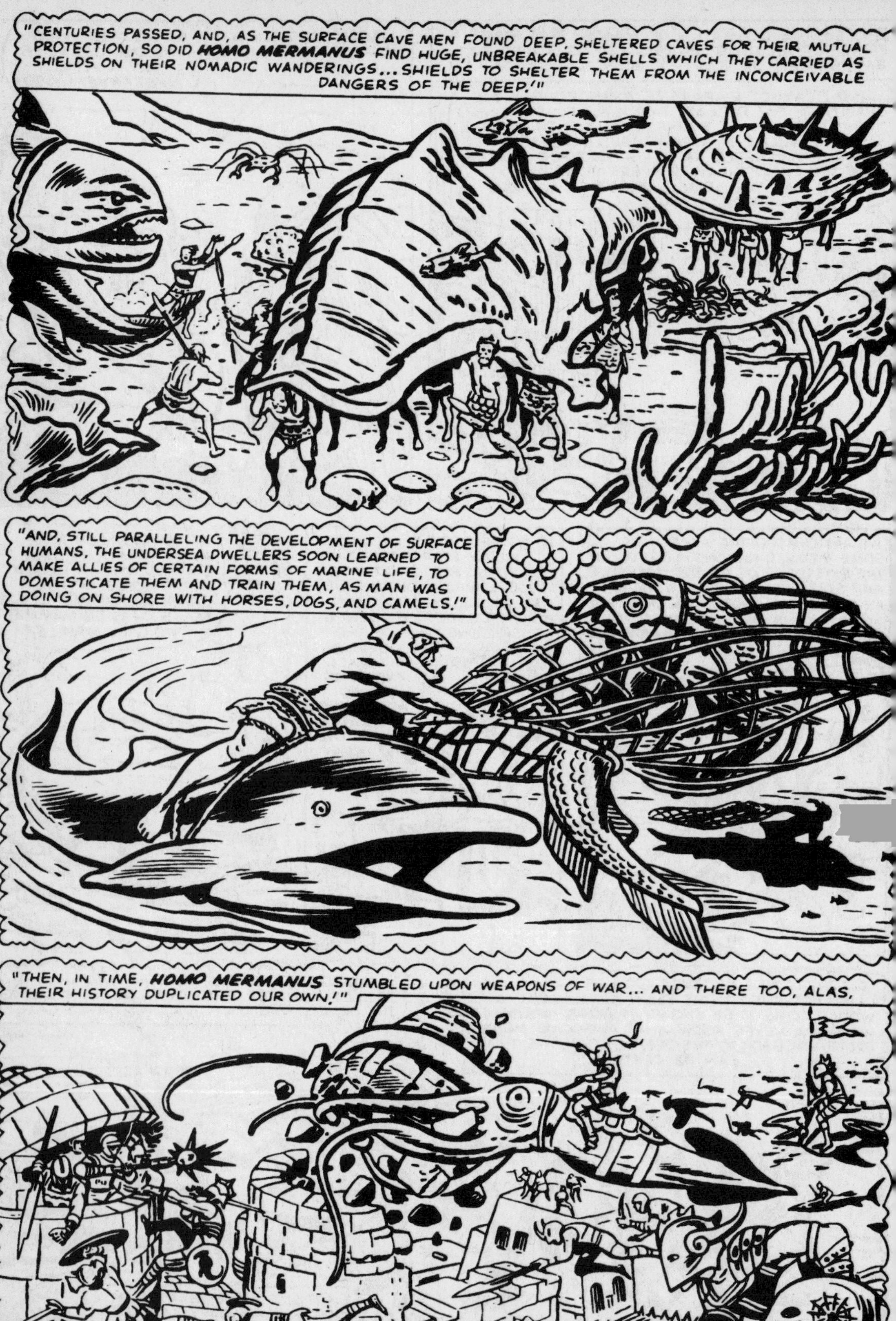
"CENTURIES PASSED, AND, AS THE SURFACE CAVE MEN FOUND DEEP, SHELTERED CAVES FOR THEIR MUTUAL PROTECTION, SO DID HOMO MERMANUS FIND HUGE, UNBREAKABLE SHELLS WHICH THEY CARRIED AS SHIELDS ON THEIR NOMADIC WANDERINGS... SHIELDS TO SHELTER THEM FROM THE INCONCEIVABLE DANGERS OF THE DEEP.'"
"AND, STILL PARALLELING THE DEVELOPMENT OF SURFACE HUMANS, THE UNDERSEA DWELLERS SOON LEARNED TO MAKE ALLIES OF CERTAIN FORMS OF MARINE LIFE, TO DOMESTICATE THEM AND TRAIN THEM, AS MAN WAS DOING ON SHORE WITH HORSES, DOGS, AND CAMELS!"
"THEN, IN TIME, HOMO MERMANUS STUMBLED UPON WEAPONS OF WAR... AND THERE TOO, ALAS, THEIR HISTORY DUPLICATED OUR OWN!'"
16

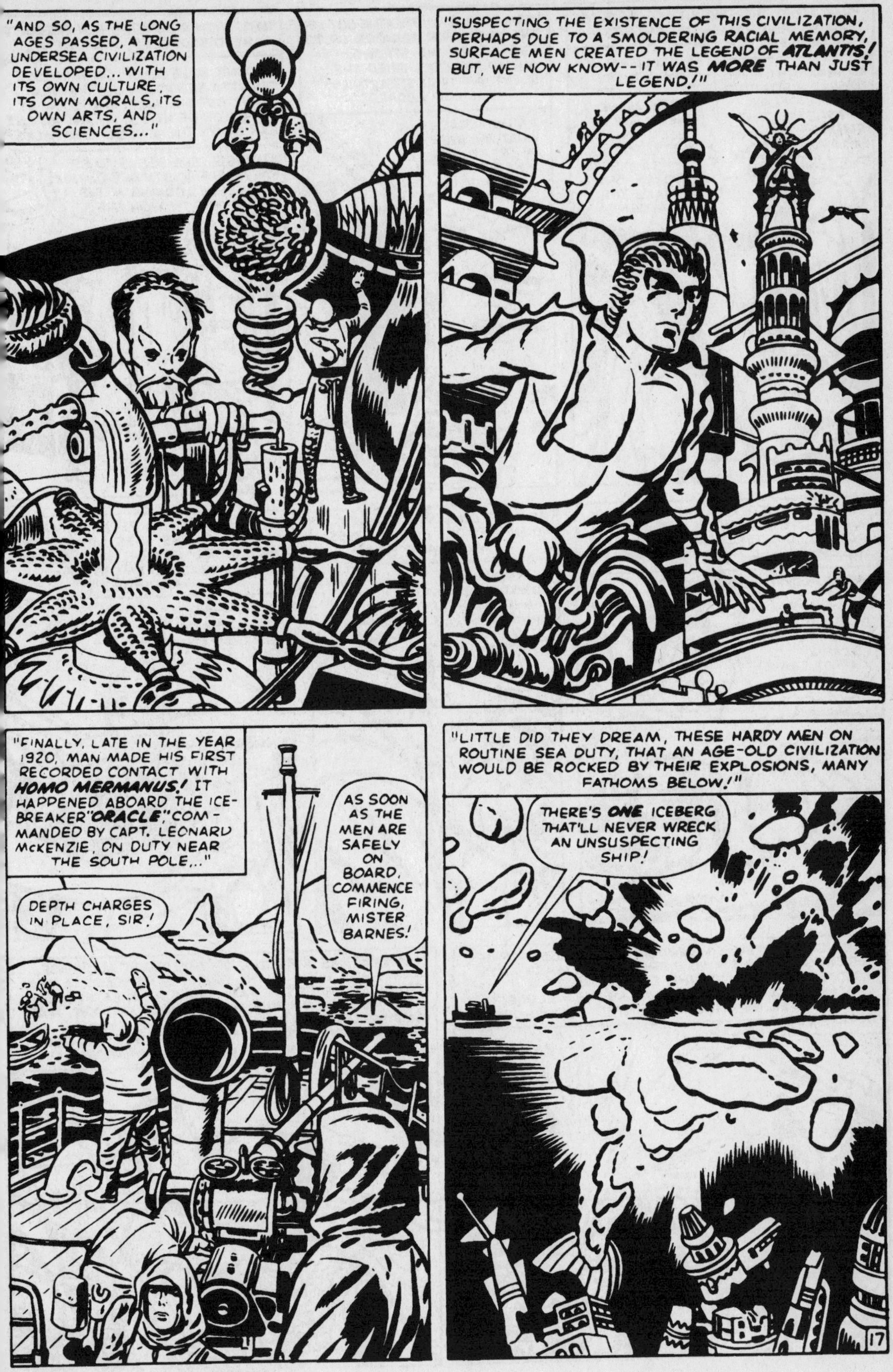
"AND SO, AS THE LONG AGES PASSED, A TRUE UNDERSEA CIVILIZATION DEVELOPED... WITH ITS OWN CULTURE, ITS OWN MORALS, ITS OWN ARTS, AND SCIENCES..."
"SUSPECTING THE EXISTENCE OF THIS CIVILIZATION, PERHAPS DUE TO A SMOLDERING RACIAL MEMORY, SURFACE MEN CREATED THE LEGEND OF ATLANTIS! BUT, WE NOW KNOW-- IT WAS MORE THAN JUST LEGEND!"
"FINALLY, LATE IN THE YEAR 1920, MAN MADE HIS FIRST RECORDED CONTACT WITH HOMO MERMANUS! IT HAPPENED ABOARD THE ICE-BREAKER "ORACLE," COMMANDED BY CAPT. LEONARD McKENZIE, ON DUTY NEAR THE SOUTH POLE..."
DEPTH CHARGES IN PLACE, SIR!
AS SOON AS THE MEN ARE SAFELY ON BOARD, COMMENCE FIRING, MISTER BARNES!
"LITTLE DID THEY DREAM, THESE HARDY MEN ON ROUTINE SEA DUTY, THAT AN AGE-OLD CIVILIZATION WOULD BE ROCKED BY THEIR EXPLOSIONS, MANY FATHOMS BELOW!"
THERE'S ONE ICEBERG THAT'LL NEVER WRECK AN UNSUSPECTING SHIP!
17

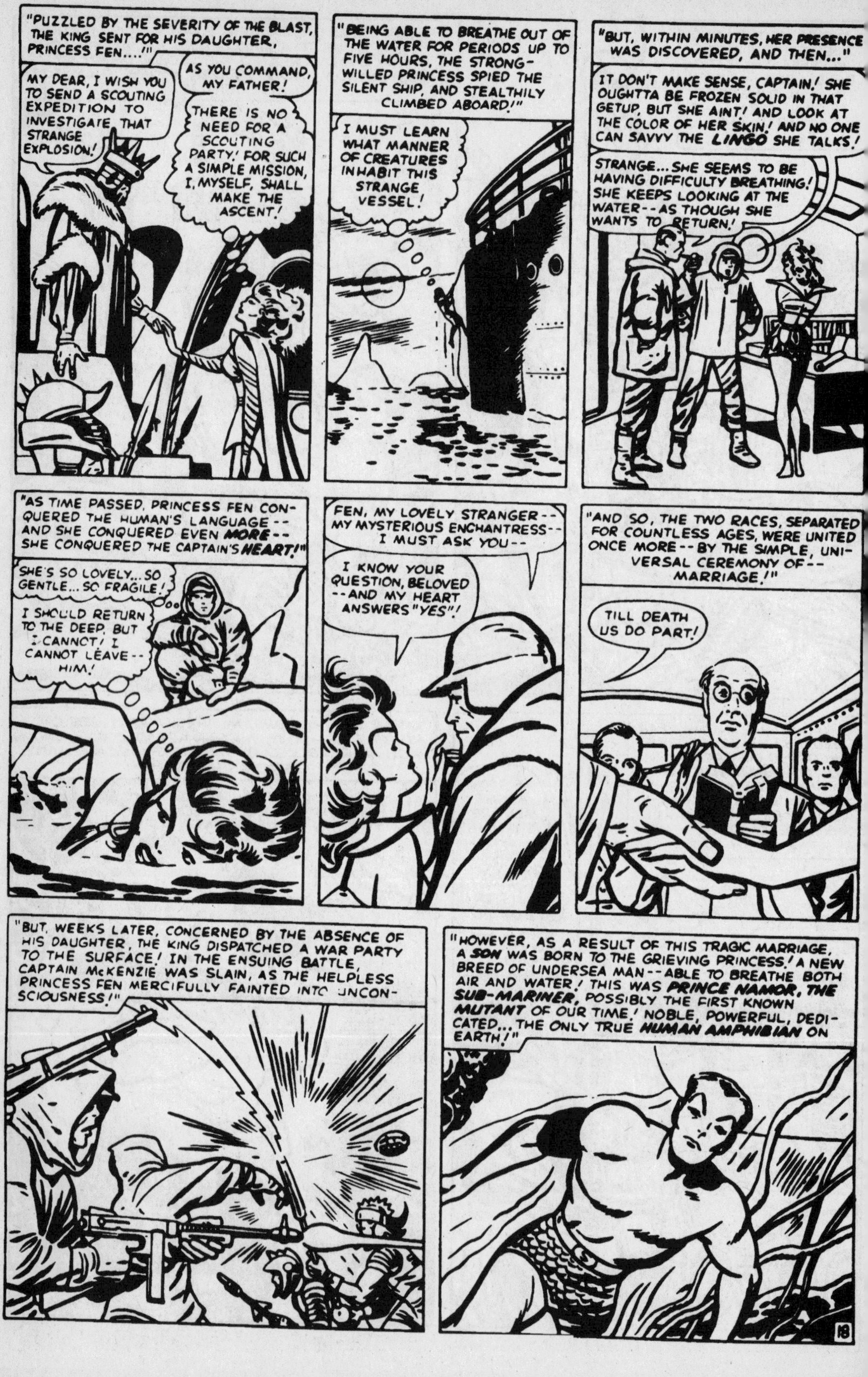
"PUZZLED BY THE SEVERITY OF THE BLAST, THE KING SENT FOR HIS DAUGHTER, PRINCESS FEN....!"
MY DEAR, I WISH YOU TO SEND A SCOUTING EXPEDITION TO INVESTIGATE THAT STRANGE EXPLOSION!
AS YOU COMMAND, MY FATHER!
THERE IS NO NEED FOR A SCOUTING PARTY! FOR SUCH A SIMPLE MISSION, I, MYSELF, SHALL MAKE THE ASCENT!
"BEING ABLE TO BREATHE OUT OF THE WATER FOR PERIODS UP TO FIVE HOURS, THE STRONG-WILLED PRINCESS SPIED THE SILENT SHIP, AND STEALTHILY CLIMBED ABOARD!"
I MUST LEARN WHAT MANNER OF CREATURES INHABIT THIS STRANGE VESSEL!
"BUT, WITHIN MINUTES, HER PRESENCE WAS DISCOVERED, AND THEN..."
IT DON'T MAKE SENSE, CAPTAIN! SHE OUGHTTA BE FROZEN SOLID IN THAT GETUP, BUT SHE AINT! AND LOOK AT THE COLOR OF HER SKIN! AND NO ONE CAN SAVVY THE LINGO SHE TALKS!
STRANGE... SHE SEEMS TO BE HAVING DIFFICULTY BREATHING! SHE KEEPS LOOKING AT THE WATER--AS THOUGH SHE WANTS TO RETURN!
"AS TIME PASSED, PRINCESS FEN CONQUERED THE HUMAN'S LANGUAGE--AND SHE CONQUERED EVEN MORE--SHE CONQUERED THE CAPTAIN'S HEART!"
SHE'S SO LOVELY... SO GENTLE... SO FRAGILE!
I SHOULD RETURN TO THE DEEP, BUT I CANNOT! I CANNOT LEAVE--HIM!
FEN, MY LOVELY STRANGER--MY MYSTERIOUS ENCHANTRESS--I MUST ASK YOU--
I KNOW YOUR QUESTION, BELOVED--AND MY HEART ANSWERS "YES"!
"AND SO, THE TWO RACES, SEPARATED FOR COUNTLESS AGES, WERE UNITED ONCE MORE--BY THE SIMPLE, UNIVERSAL CEREMONY OF--MARRIAGE!"
TILL DEATH US DO PART!
"BUT, WEEKS LATER, CONCERNED BY THE ABSENCE OF HIS DAUGHTER, THE KING DISPATCHED A WAR PARTY TO THE SURFACE! IN THE ENSUING BATTLE, CAPTAIN McKENZIE WAS SLAIN, AS THE HELPLESS PRINCESS FEN MERCIFULLY FAINTED INTO UNCONSCIOUSNESS!"
"HOWEVER, AS A RESULT OF THIS TRAGIC MARRIAGE, A SON WAS BORN TO THE GRIEVING PRINCESS! A NEW BREED OF UNDERSEA MAN--ABLE TO BREATHE BOTH AIR AND WATER! THIS WAS PRINCE NAMOR, THE SUB-MARINER, POSSIBLY THE FIRST KNOWN MUTANT OF OUR TIME! NOBLE, POWERFUL, DEDICATED... THE ONLY TRUE HUMAN AMPHIBIAN ON EARTH!"
18

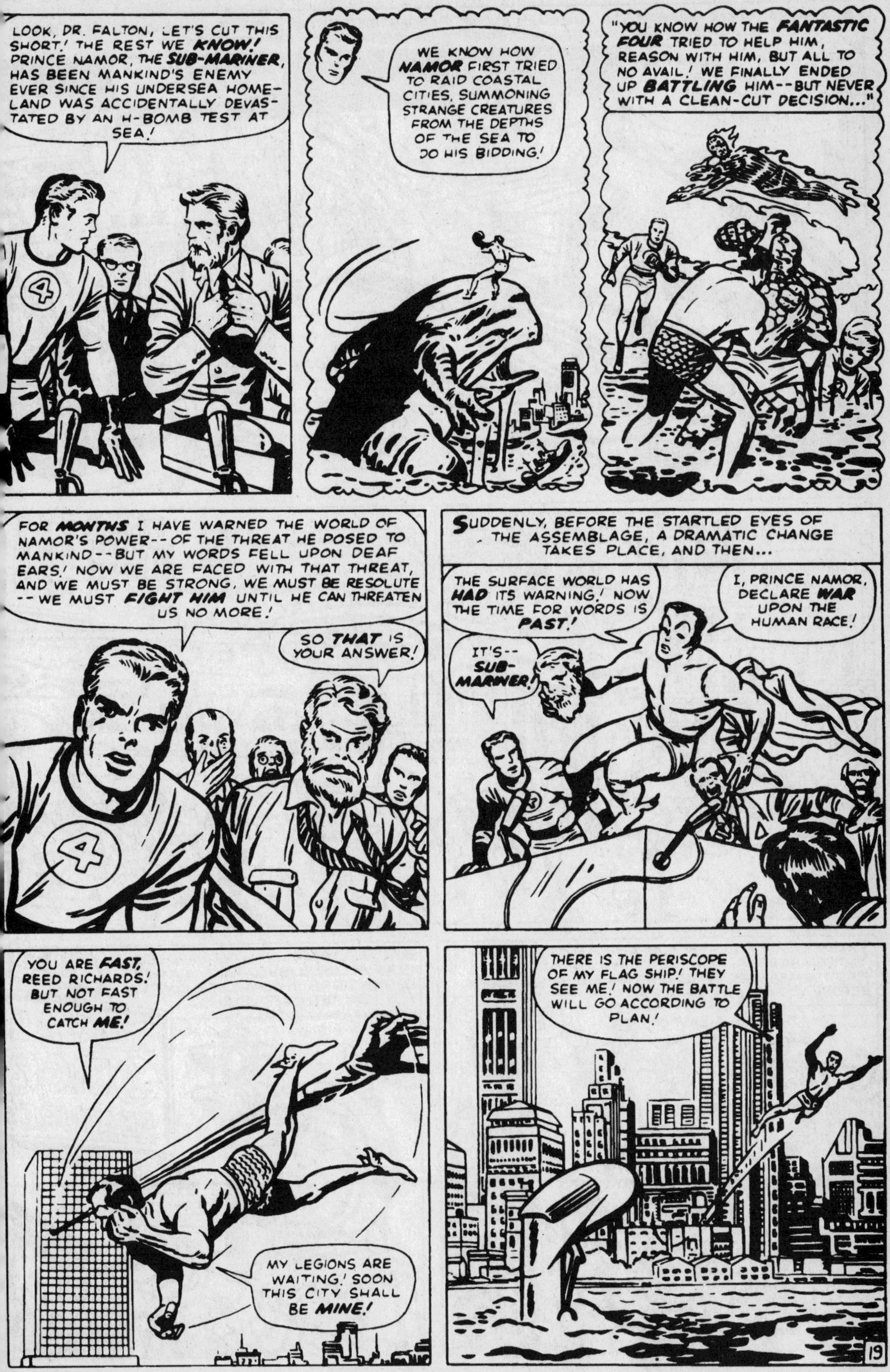

LOOK, DR. FALTON, LET'S CUT THIS SHORT! THE REST WE KNOW! PRINCE NAMOR, THE SUB-MARINER, HAS BEEN MANKIND'S ENEMY EVER SINCE HIS UNDERSEA HOMELAND WAS ACCIDENTALLY DEVASTATED BY AN H-BOMB TEST AT SEA!
WE KNOW HOW NAMOR FIRST TRIED TO RAID COASTAL CITIES, SUMMONING STRANGE CREATURES FROM THE DEPTHS OF THE SEA TO DO HIS BIDDING!
"YOU KNOW HOW THE FANTASTIC FOUR TRIED TO HELP HIM, REASON WITH HIM, BUT ALL TO NO AVAIL! WE FINALLY ENDED UP BATTLING HIM--BUT NEVER WITH A CLEAN-CUT DECISION..."
FOR MONTHS I HAVE WARNED THE WORLD OF NAMOR'S POWER--OF THE THREAT HE POSED TO MANKIND--BUT MY WORDS FELL UPON DEAF EARS! NOW WE ARE FACED WITH THAT THREAT, AND WE MUST BE STRONG, WE MUST BE RESOLUTE--WE MUST FIGHT HIM UNTIL HE CAN THREATEN US NO MORE!
SO THAT IS YOUR ANSWER!
SUDDENLY, BEFORE THE STARTLED EYES OF THE ASSEMBLAGE, A DRAMATIC CHANGE TAKES PLACE, AND THEN...
THE SURFACE WORLD HAS HAD ITS WARNING! NOW THE TIME FOR WORDS IS PAST!
I, PRINCE NAMOR, DECLARE WAR UPON THE HUMAN RACE!
IT'S--SUB-MARINER!
YOU ARE FAST, REED RICHARDS! BUT NOT FAST ENOUGH TO CATCH ME!
MY LEGIONS ARE WAITING! SOON THIS CITY SHALL BE MINE!
THERE IS THE PERISCOPE OF MY FLAG SHIP! THEY SEE ME! NOW THE BATTLE WILL GO ACCORDING TO PLAN!

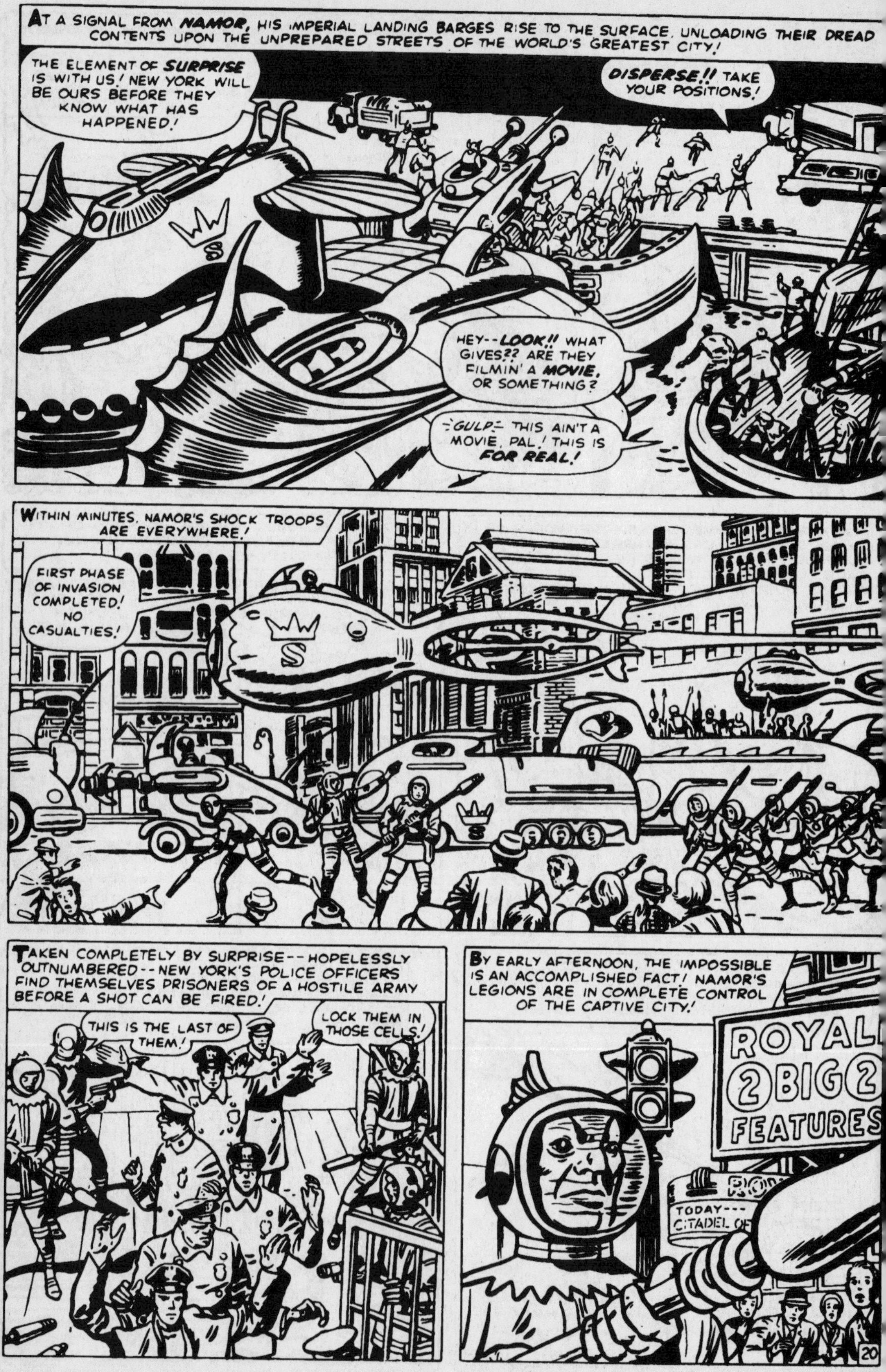

AT A SIGNAL FROM NAMOR, HIS IMPERIAL LANDING BARGES RISE TO THE SURFACE, UNLOADING THEIR DREAD CONTENTS UPON THE UNPREPARED STREETS OF THE WORLD'S GREATEST CITY!
THE ELEMENT OF SURPRISE IS WITH US! NEW YORK WILL BE OURS BEFORE THEY KNOW WHAT HAS HAPPENED!
DISPERSE!! TAKE YOUR POSITIONS!
HEY--LOOK!! WHAT GIVES?? ARE THEY FILMIN' A MOVIE, OR SOMETHING?
-GULP- THIS AIN'T A MOVIE, PAL! THIS IS FOR REAL!
WITHIN MINUTES, NAMOR'S SHOCK TROOPS ARE EVERYWHERE!
FIRST PHASE OF INVASION COMPLETED! NO CASUALTIES!
TAKEN COMPLETELY BY SURPRISE--HOPELESSLY OUTNUMBERED--NEW YORK'S POLICE OFFICERS FIND THEMSELVES PRISONERS OF A HOSTILE ARMY BEFORE A SHOT CAN BE FIRED!
THIS IS THE LAST OF THEM!
LOCK THEM IN THOSE CELLS!
BY EARLY AFTERNOON, THE IMPOSSIBLE IS AN ACCOMPLISHED FACT! NAMOR'S LEGIONS ARE IN COMPLETE CONTROL OF THE CAPTIVE CITY!
ROYAL
2 BIG 2
FEATURES
TODAY---
CITADEL OF
20

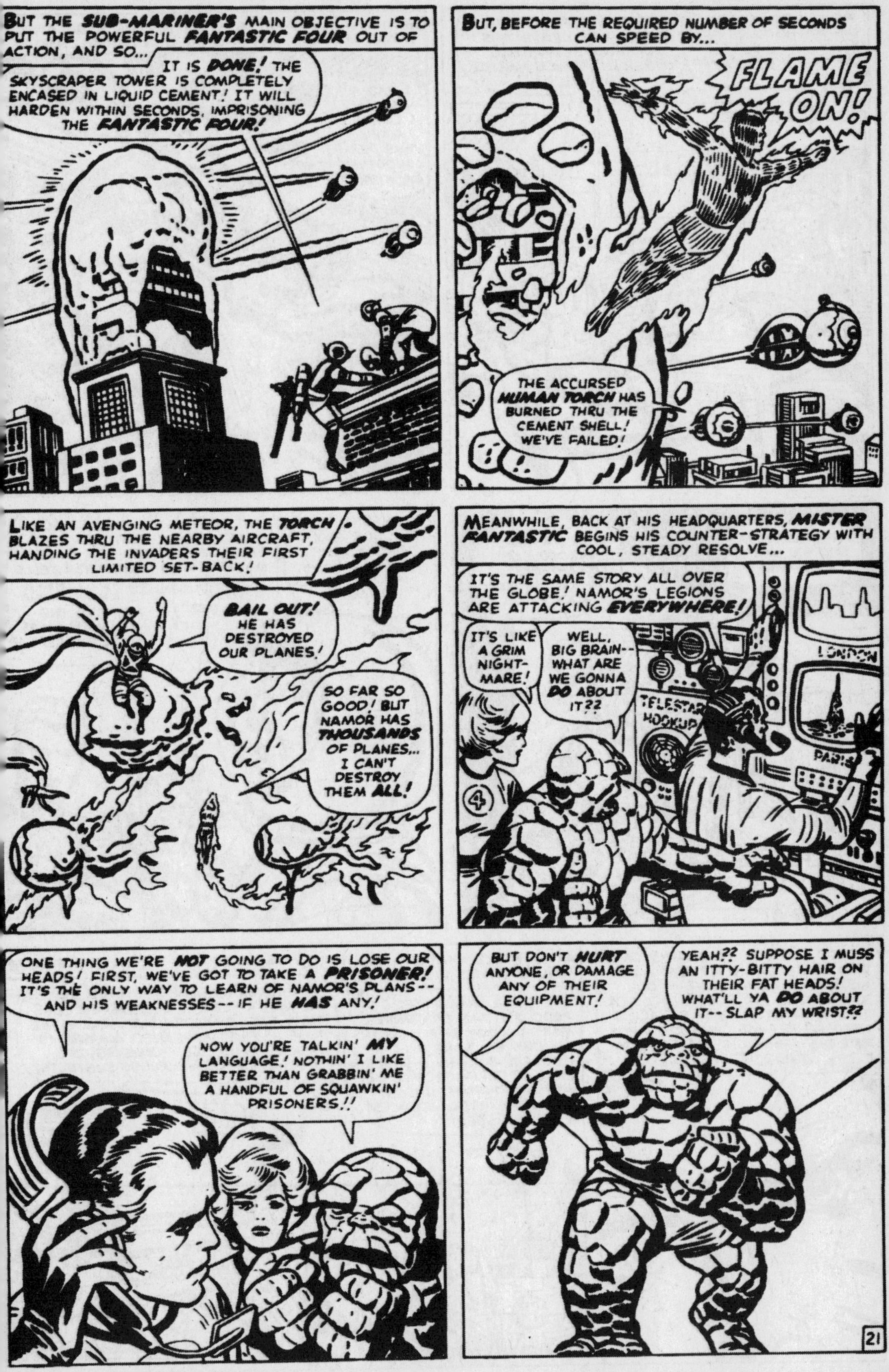
BUT THE SUB-MARINER'S MAIN OBJECTIVE IS TO PUT THE POWERFUL FANTASTIC FOUR OUT OF ACTION, AND SO...
IT IS DONE! THE SKYSCRAPER TOWER IS COMPLETELY ENCASED IN LIQUID CEMENT! IT WILL HARDEN WITHIN SECONDS, IMPRISONING THE FANTASTIC FOUR!
BUT, BEFORE THE REQUIRED NUMBER OF SECONDS CAN SPEED BY...
FLAME ON!
THE ACCURSED HUMAN TORCH HAS BURNED THRU THE CEMENT SHELL! WE'VE FAILED!
LIKE AN AVENGING METEOR, THE TORCH BLAZES THRU THE NEARBY AIRCRAFT, HANDING THE INVADERS THEIR FIRST LIMITED SET-BACK!
BAIL OUT! HE HAS DESTROYED OUR PLANES!
SO FAR SO GOOD! BUT NAMOR HAS THOUSANDS OF PLANES... I CAN'T DESTROY THEM ALL!
MEANWHILE, BACK AT HIS HEADQUARTERS, MISTER FANTASTIC BEGINS HIS COUNTER-STRATEGY WITH COOL, STEADY RESOLVE...
IT'S THE SAME STORY ALL OVER THE GLOBE! NAMOR'S LEGIONS ARE ATTACKING EVERYWHERE!
IT'S LIKE A GRIM NIGHT-MARE!
WELL, BIG BRAIN-- WHAT ARE WE GONNA DO ABOUT IT??
LONDON
TELESTAR HOOKUP
PARIS
ONE THING WE'RE NOT GOING TO DO IS LOSE OUR HEADS! FIRST, WE'VE GOT TO TAKE A PRISONER! IT'S THE ONLY WAY TO LEARN OF NAMOR'S PLANS-- AND HIS WEAKNESSES-- IF HE HAS ANY!
NOW YOU'RE TALKIN' MY LANGUAGE! NOTHIN' I LIKE BETTER THAN GRABBIN' ME A HANDFUL OF SQUAWKIN' PRISONERS!!
BUT DON'T HURT ANYONE, OR DAMAGE ANY OF THEIR EQUIPMENT!
YEAH?? SUPPOSE I MUSS AN ITTY-BITTY HAIR ON THEIR FAT HEADS! WHAT'LL YA DO ABOUT IT-- SLAP MY WRIST??
21

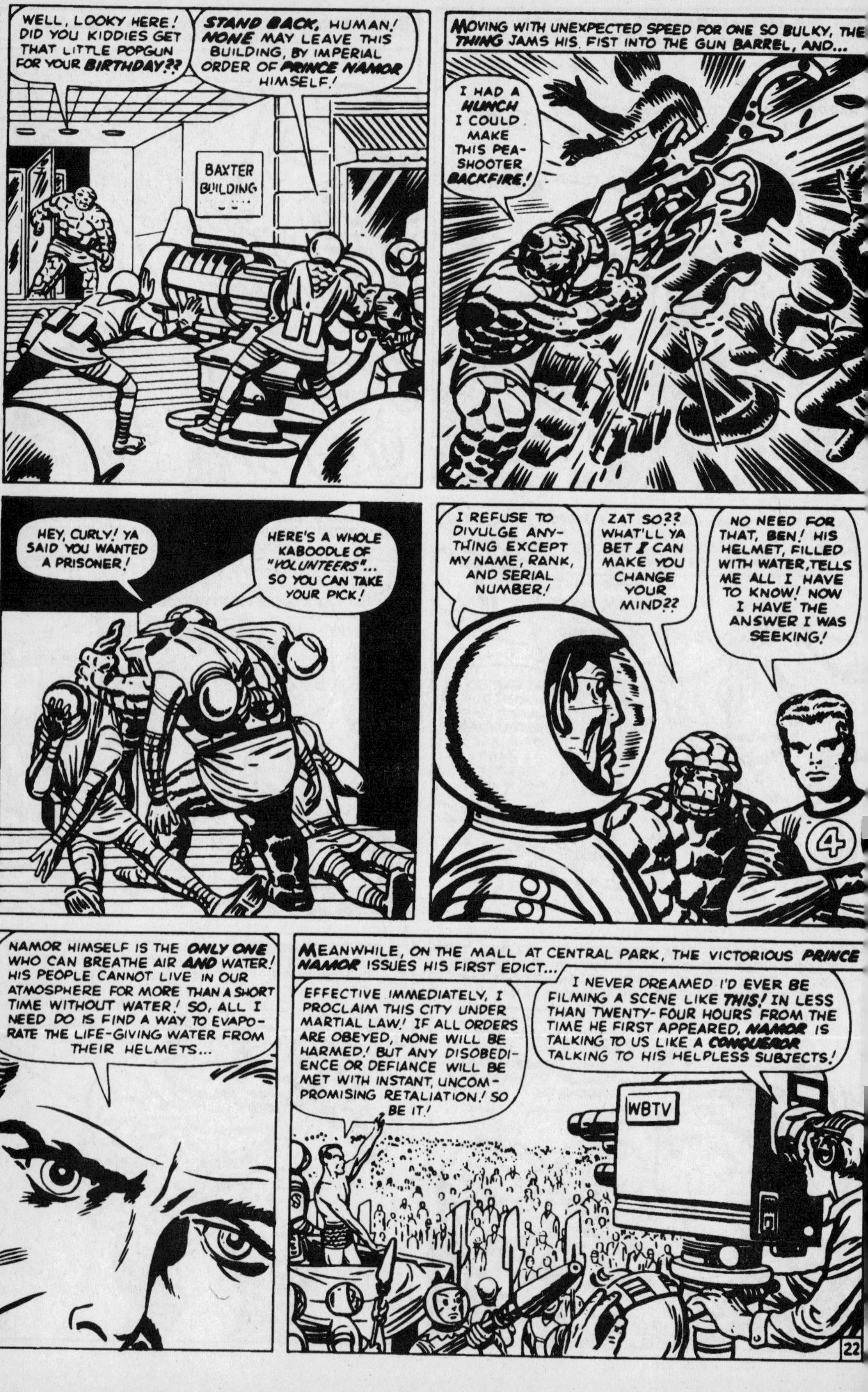
WELL, LOOKY HERE! DID YOU KIDDIES GET THAT LITTLE POPGUN FOR YOUR BIRTHDAY??
STAND BACK, HUMAN! NONE MAY LEAVE THIS BUILDING, BY IMPERIAL ORDER OF PRINCE NAMOR HIMSELF!
BAXTER BUILDING
MOVING WITH UNEXPECTED SPEED FOR ONE SO BULKY, THE THING JAMS HIS FIST INTO THE GUN BARREL, AND...
I HAD A HUNCH I COULD MAKE THIS PEA-SHOOTER BACKFIRE!
HEY, CURLY! YA SAID YOU WANTED A PRISONER!
HERE'S A WHOLE KABOODLE OF "VOLUNTEERS"... SO YOU CAN TAKE YOUR PICK!
I REFUSE TO DIVULGE ANYTHING EXCEPT MY NAME, RANK, AND SERIAL NUMBER!
ZAT SO?? WHAT'LL YA BET I CAN MAKE YOU CHANGE YOUR MIND??
NO NEED FOR THAT, BEN! HIS HELMET, FILLED WITH WATER, TELLS ME ALL I HAVE TO KNOW! NOW I HAVE THE ANSWER I WAS SEEKING!
NAMOR HIMSELF IS THE ONLY ONE WHO CAN BREATHE AIR AND WATER! HIS PEOPLE CANNOT LIVE IN OUR ATMOSPHERE FOR MORE THAN A SHORT TIME WITHOUT WATER! SO, ALL I NEED DO IS FIND A WAY TO EVAPORATE THE LIFE-GIVING WATER FROM THEIR HELMETS...
MEANWHILE, ON THE MALL AT CENTRAL PARK, THE VICTORIOUS PRINCE NAMOR ISSUES HIS FIRST EDICT...
EFFECTIVE IMMEDIATELY, I PROCLAIM THIS CITY UNDER MARTIAL LAW! IF ALL ORDERS ARE OBEYED, NONE WILL BE HARMED! BUT ANY DISOBEDIENCE OR DEFIANCE WILL BE MET WITH INSTANT, UNCOMPROMISING RETALIATION! SO BE IT!
I NEVER DREAMED I'D EVER BE FILMING A SCENE LIKE THIS! IN LESS THAN TWENTY-FOUR HOURS FROM THE TIME HE FIRST APPEARED, NAMOR IS TALKING TO US LIKE A CONQUEROR TALKING TO HIS HELPLESS SUBJECTS!
WBTV

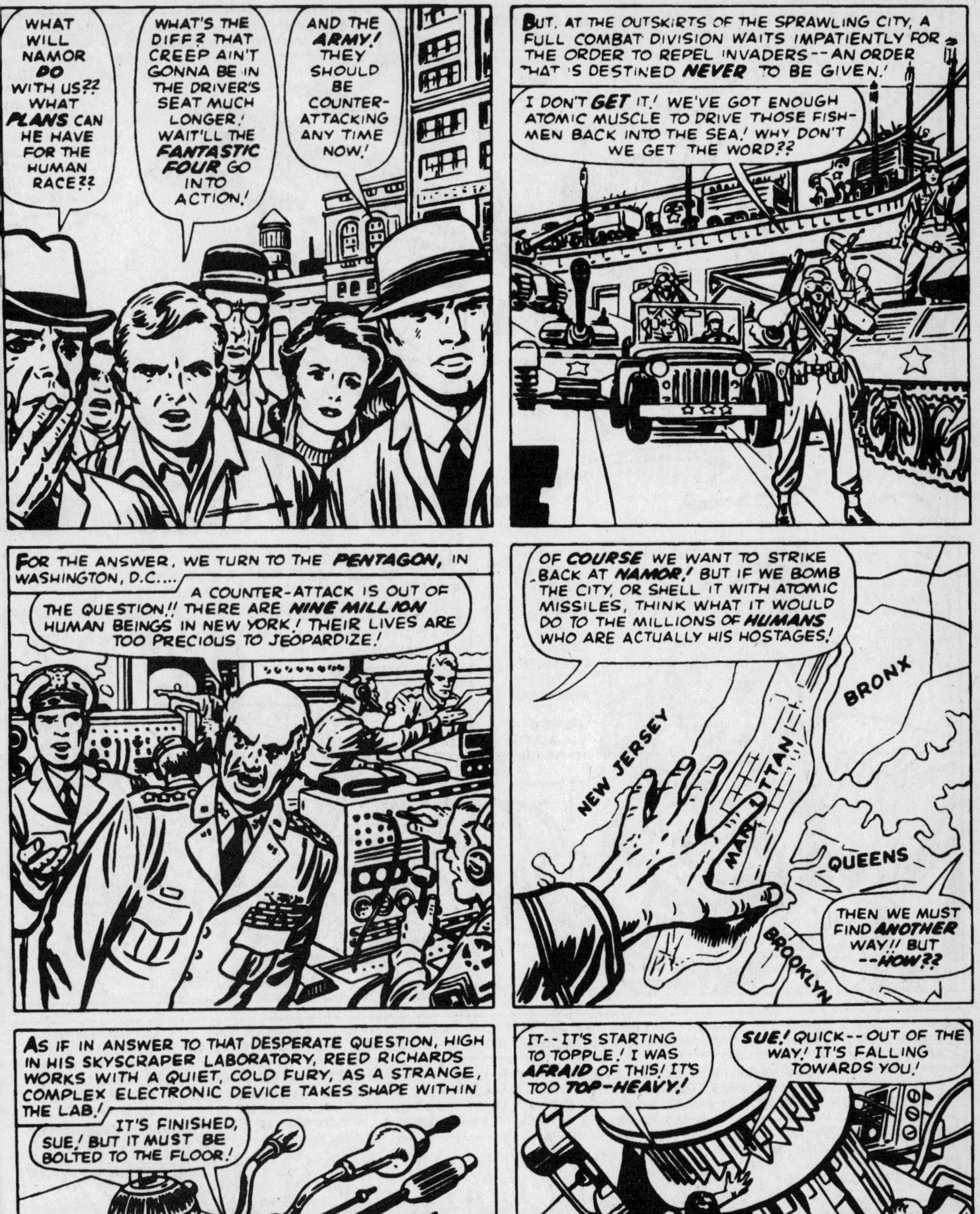

WHAT WILL NAMOR DO WITH US?? WHAT PLANS CAN HE HAVE FOR THE HUMAN RACE??
WHAT'S THE DIFF? THAT CREEP AIN'T GONNA BE IN THE DRIVER'S SEAT MUCH LONGER! WAIT'LL THE FANTASTIC FOUR GO INTO ACTION!
AND THE ARMY! THEY SHOULD BE COUNTER-ATTACKING ANY TIME NOW!
BUT, AT THE OUTSKIRTS OF THE SPRAWLING CITY, A FULL COMBAT DIVISION WAITS IMPATIENTLY FOR THE ORDER TO REPEL INVADERS--AN ORDER THAT IS DESTINED NEVER TO BE GIVEN!
I DON'T GET IT! WE'VE GOT ENOUGH ATOMIC MUSCLE TO DRIVE THOSE FISH-MEN BACK INTO THE SEA! WHY DON'T WE GET THE WORD??
FOR THE ANSWER, WE TURN TO THE PENTAGON, IN WASHINGTON, D.C....
A COUNTER-ATTACK IS OUT OF THE QUESTION!! THERE ARE NINE MILLION HUMAN BEINGS IN NEW YORK! THEIR LIVES ARE TOO PRECIOUS TO JEOPARDIZE!
OF COURSE WE WANT TO STRIKE BACK AT NAMOR! BUT IF WE BOMB THE CITY, OR SHELL IT WITH ATOMIC MISSILES, THINK WHAT IT WOULD DO TO THE MILLIONS OF HUMANS WHO ARE ACTUALLY HIS HOSTAGES!
NEW JERSEY
MANHATTAN
BRONX
QUEENS
BROOKLYN
THEN WE MUST FIND ANOTHER WAY!! BUT --HOW??
AS IF IN ANSWER TO THAT DESPERATE QUESTION, HIGH IN HIS SKYSCRAPER LABORATORY, REED RICHARDS WORKS WITH A QUIET, COLD FURY, AS A STRANGE, COMPLEX ELECTRONIC DEVICE TAKES SHAPE WITHIN THE LAB!
IT'S FINISHED, SUE! BUT IT MUST BE BOLTED TO THE FLOOR!
IT--IT'S STARTING TO TOPPLE! I WAS AFRAID OF THIS! IT'S TOO TOP-HEAVY!
SUE! QUICK--OUT OF THE WAY! IT'S FALLING TOWARDS YOU!

PUSHING THE STARTLED GIRL TO SAFETY, *MR. FANTASTIC* ABSORBS THE FULL FORCE OF THE IMPACT HIMSELF!

BEN! COME QUICK! REED IS *HURT!*

UHHHH...

HURRY, GET 'IM ON THE COUCH! IF-- IF ANYTHING *HAPPENS* TO THAT LONG DRINK O' WATER, IT'LL BE MY OWN STUPID FAULT FOR NOT *BEIN'* HERE IN TIME!

OH, REED--MY DARLING! YOU COULD HAVE MOVED ASIDE IN TIME-- BUT YOU REMAINED --TO SAVE *ME!*

BEN-- HE'S *ALL RIGHT!* HE'S COMING TO!

SURE! HE'S TOO *ORNERY* TO CONK OUT ON US!

LISTEN, BOTH OF YOU! IT'S UP TO *YOU* TO OPERATE THE MACHINE -- TO DEFEAT NAMOR'S INVASION...

AND SO, FOLLOWING THE INSTRUCTIONS OF THE WEAKENED *MR. FANTASTIC*, THE *THING* AND SUE WORK FEVERISHLY TO MAKE THE COMPLEX ELECTRONIC DEVICE OPERATIONAL!

THAT'S IT! NOW SET IT TO MAXIMUM INTENSITY...

THIS IS LIKE A CORNY SCENE FROM SOME OLD *FRANKENSTEIN* MOVIE!

IT'S ALL SET NOW, REED! LET'S JUST PRAY THAT IT *WORKS!*

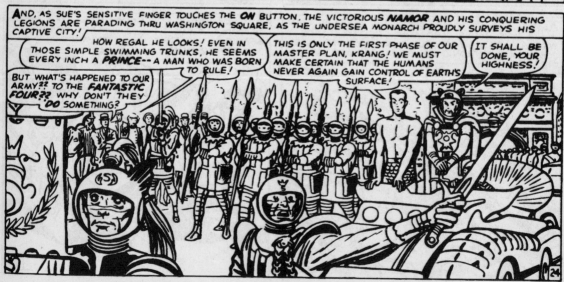

AND, AS SUE'S SENSITIVE FINGER TOUCHES THE *ON* BUTTON, THE VICTORIOUS *NAMOR* AND HIS CONQUERING LEGIONS ARE PARADING THRU WASHINGTON SQUARE, AS THE UNDERSEA MONARCH PROUDLY SURVEYS HIS CAPTIVE CITY!

HOW REGAL HE LOOKS! EVEN IN THOSE SIMPLE SWIMMING TRUNKS, HE SEEMS EVERY INCH A *PRINCE*-- A MAN WHO WAS BORN TO RULE!

THIS IS ONLY THE FIRST PHASE OF OUR MASTER PLAN, KRANG! WE MUST MAKE CERTAIN THAT THE HUMANS NEVER AGAIN GAIN CONTROL OF EARTH'S SURFACE!

IT SHALL BE DONE, YOUR HIGHNESS!

BUT WHAT'S HAPPENED TO OUR ARMY?? TO THE *FANTASTIC FOUR??* WHY DON'T THEY *DO* SOMETHING?

24

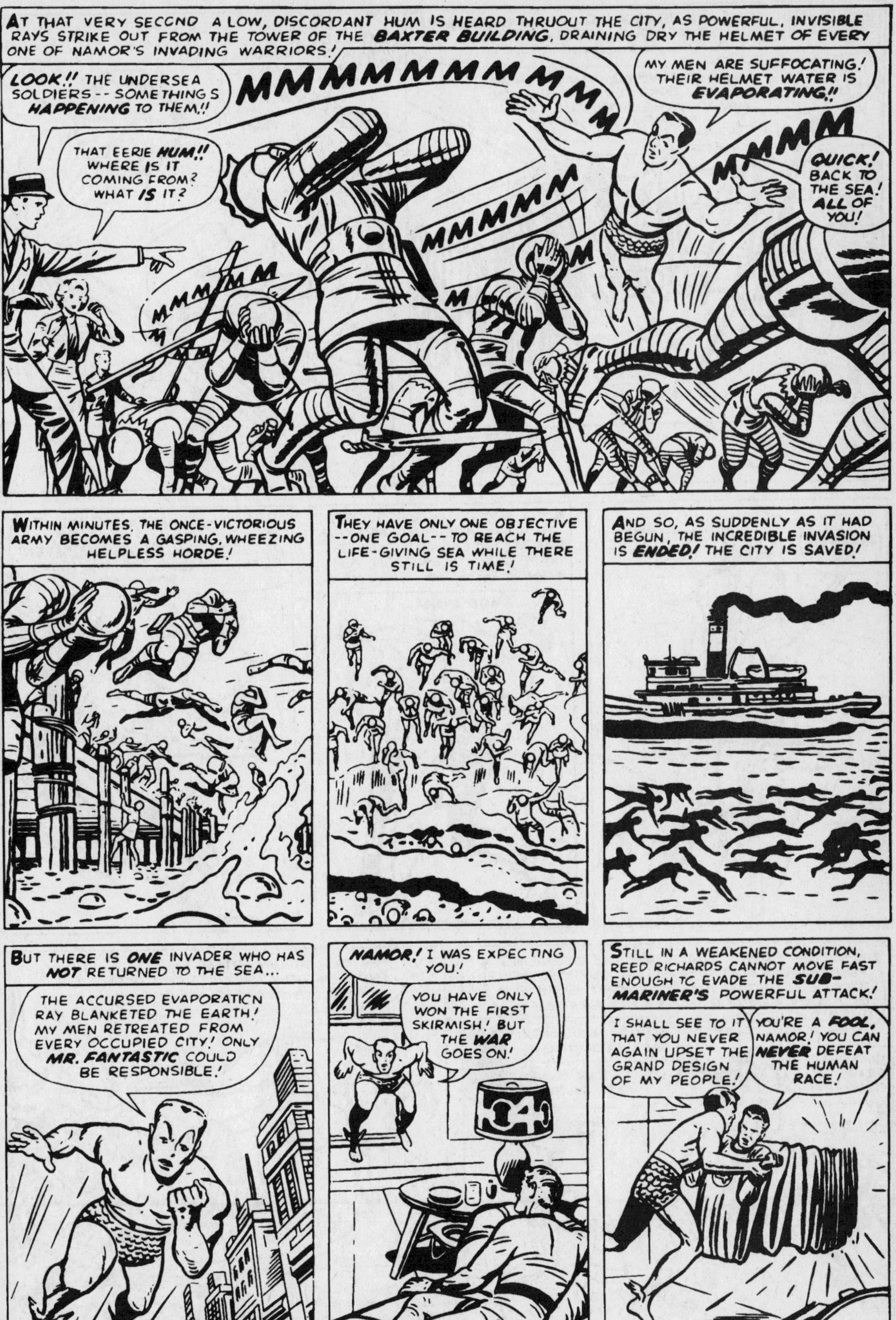

AT THAT VERY SECOND A LOW, DISCORDANT HUM IS HEARD THRUOUT THE CITY, AS POWERFUL, INVISIBLE RAYS STRIKE OUT FROM THE TOWER OF THE BAXTER BUILDING, DRAINING DRY THE HELMET OF EVERY ONE OF NAMOR'S INVADING WARRIORS!
LOOK!! THE UNDERSEA SOLDIERS -- SOMETHING'S HAPPENING TO THEM!!
MMMMMMMMMMMMMMM
MY MEN ARE SUFFOCATING! THEIR HELMET WATER IS EVAPORATING!!
THAT EERIE HUM!! WHERE IS IT COMING FROM? WHAT IS IT?
MMMMMMM
MMMMMM
QUICK! BACK TO THE SEA! ALL OF YOU!
MMMMM
WITHIN MINUTES, THE ONCE-VICTORIOUS ARMY BECOMES A GASPING, WHEEZING HELPLESS HORDE!
THEY HAVE ONLY ONE OBJECTIVE --ONE GOAL-- TO REACH THE LIFE-GIVING SEA WHILE THERE STILL IS TIME!
AND SO, AS SUDDENLY AS IT HAD BEGUN, THE INCREDIBLE INVASION IS ENDED! THE CITY IS SAVED!
BUT THERE IS ONE INVADER WHO HAS NOT RETURNED TO THE SEA...
THE ACCURSED EVAPORATION RAY BLANKETED THE EARTH! MY MEN RETREATED FROM EVERY OCCUPIED CITY! ONLY MR. FANTASTIC COULD BE RESPONSIBLE!
NAMOR! I WAS EXPECTING YOU!
YOU HAVE ONLY WON THE FIRST SKIRMISH! BUT THE WAR GOES ON!
STILL IN A WEAKENED CONDITION, REED RICHARDS CANNOT MOVE FAST ENOUGH TO EVADE THE SUB-MARINER'S POWERFUL ATTACK!
I SHALL SEE TO IT THAT YOU NEVER AGAIN UPSET THE GRAND DESIGN OF MY PEOPLE!
YOU'RE A FOOL, NAMOR! YOU CAN NEVER DEFEAT THE HUMAN RACE!

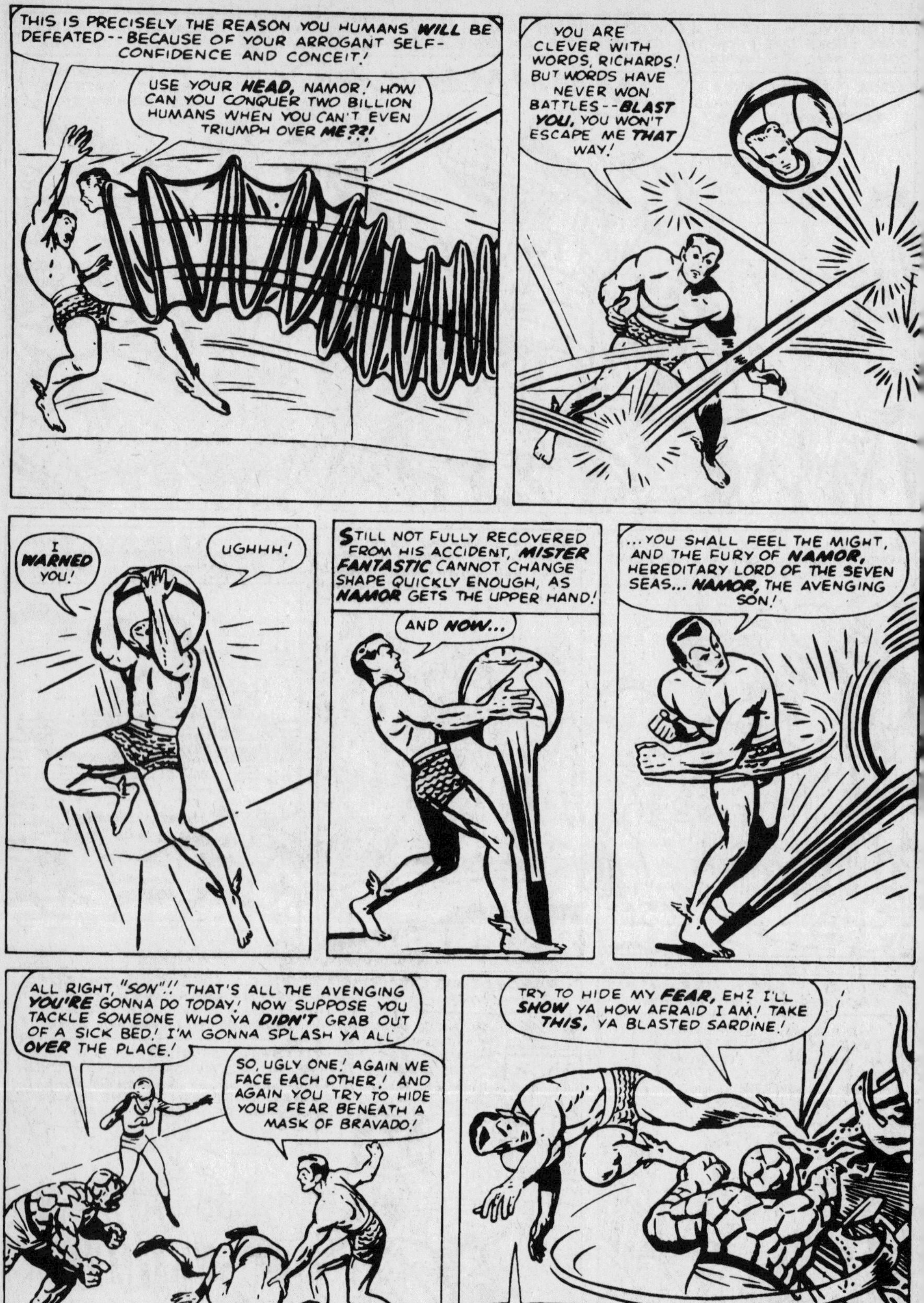

THIS IS PRECISELY THE REASON YOU HUMANS WILL BE DEFEATED--BECAUSE OF YOUR ARROGANT SELF-CONFIDENCE AND CONCEIT!
USE YOUR HEAD, NAMOR! HOW CAN YOU CONQUER TWO BILLION HUMANS WHEN YOU CAN'T EVEN TRIUMPH OVER ME??!
YOU ARE CLEVER WITH WORDS, RICHARDS! BUT WORDS HAVE NEVER WON BATTLES--BLAST YOU, YOU WON'T ESCAPE ME THAT WAY!
I WARNED YOU!
UGHHH!
STILL NOT FULLY RECOVERED FROM HIS ACCIDENT, MISTER FANTASTIC CANNOT CHANGE SHAPE QUICKLY ENOUGH, AS NAMOR GETS THE UPPER HAND!
AND NOW...
...YOU SHALL FEEL THE MIGHT, AND THE FURY OF NAMOR, HEREDITARY LORD OF THE SEVEN SEAS... NAMOR, THE AVENGING SON!
ALL RIGHT, "SON"!! THAT'S ALL THE AVENGING YOU'RE GONNA DO TODAY! NOW SUPPOSE YOU TACKLE SOMEONE WHO YA DIDN'T GRAB OUT OF A SICK BED! I'M GONNA SPLASH YA ALL OVER THE PLACE!
SO, UGLY ONE! AGAIN WE FACE EACH OTHER! AND AGAIN YOU TRY TO HIDE YOUR FEAR BENEATH A MASK OF BRAVADO!
TRY TO HIDE MY FEAR, EH? I'LL SHOW YA HOW AFRAID I AM! TAKE THIS, YA BLASTED SARDINE!
YOU THICK-SKINNED CLOD! NONE MAY LAY HANDS ON THE ROYAL PERSON OF NAMOR!
26

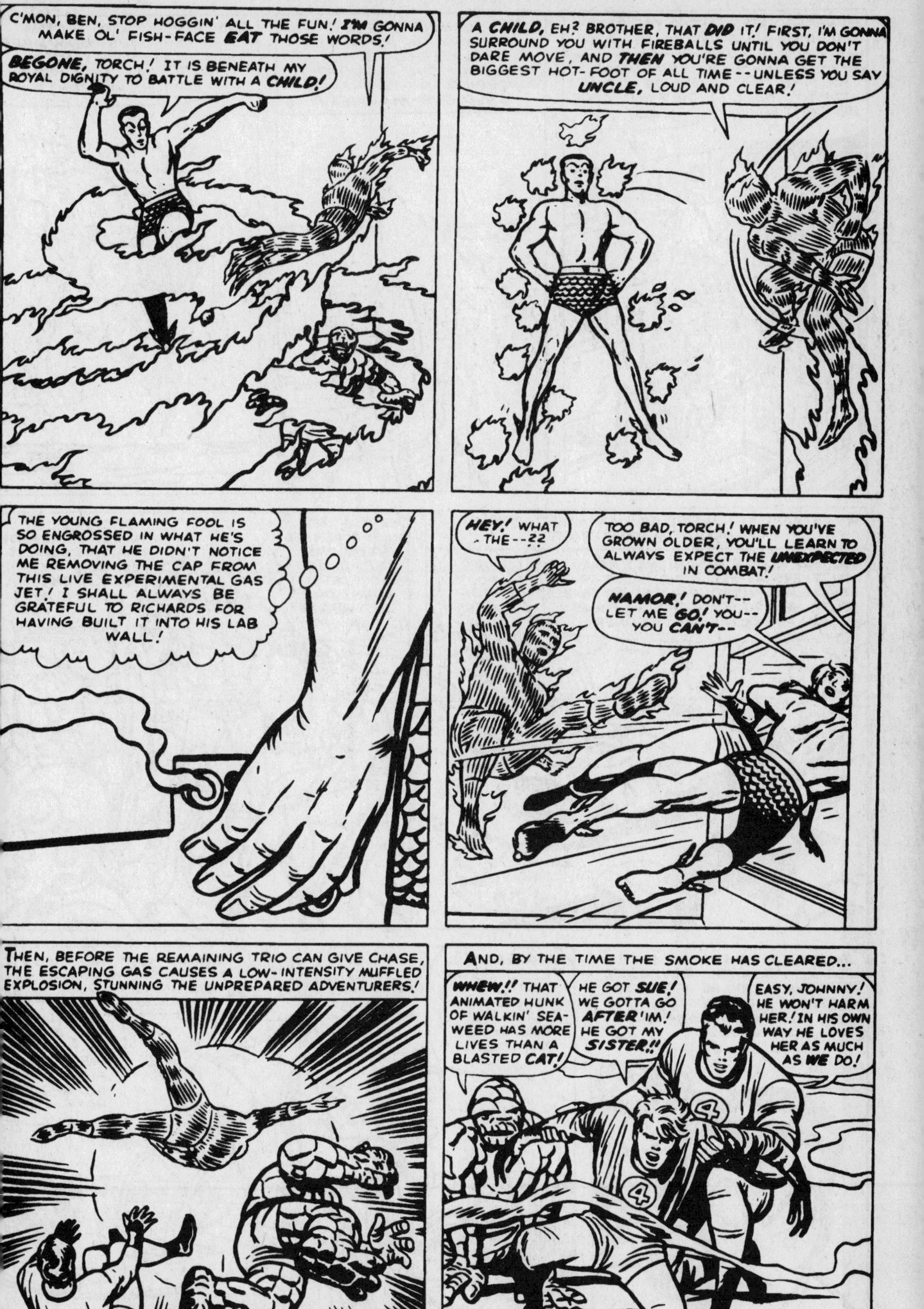
C'MON, BEN, STOP HOGGIN' ALL THE FUN! I'M GONNA MAKE OL' FISH-FACE EAT THOSE WORDS!
BEGONE, TORCH! IT IS BENEATH MY ROYAL DIGNITY TO BATTLE WITH A CHILD!
A CHILD, EH? BROTHER, THAT DID IT! FIRST, I'M GONNA SURROUND YOU WITH FIREBALLS UNTIL YOU DON'T DARE MOVE, AND THEN YOU'RE GONNA GET THE BIGGEST HOT-FOOT OF ALL TIME--UNLESS YOU SAY UNCLE, LOUD AND CLEAR!
THE YOUNG FLAMING FOOL IS SO ENGROSSED IN WHAT HE'S DOING, THAT HE DIDN'T NOTICE ME REMOVING THE CAP FROM THIS LIVE EXPERIMENTAL GAS JET! I SHALL ALWAYS BE GRATEFUL TO RICHARDS FOR HAVING BUILT IT INTO HIS LAB WALL!
HEY! WHAT THE--??
TOO BAD, TORCH! WHEN YOU'VE GROWN OLDER, YOU'LL LEARN TO ALWAYS EXPECT THE UNEXPECTED IN COMBAT!
NAMOR! DON'T-- LET ME GO! YOU-- YOU CAN'T--
THEN, BEFORE THE REMAINING TRIO CAN GIVE CHASE, THE ESCAPING GAS CAUSES A LOW-INTENSITY MUFFLED EXPLOSION, STUNNING THE UNPREPARED ADVENTURERS!
AND, BY THE TIME THE SMOKE HAS CLEARED...
WHEW!! THAT ANIMATED HUNK OF WALKIN' SEA-WEED HAS MORE LIVES THAN A BLASTED CAT!
HE GOT SUE! WE GOTTA GO AFTER 'IM! HE GOT MY SISTER!!
EASY, JOHNNY! HE WON'T HARM HER! IN HIS OWN WAY HE LOVES HER AS MUCH AS WE DO!
27

MINUTES LATER, AFTER THE FABULOUS FOURSOME HAS DRAWN UP A HASTY BATTLE PLAN..

YOU **FIND** THEM, JOHNNY! WE'LL BE RIGHT BEHIND YOU!

REMEMBER, JUNIOR--LEAVE THE FIGHTIN' FOR **US!**

FLAME ON!

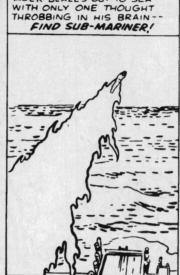

LIKE A FLAMING STREAK OF LIVING FURY, THE FIERY TEEN-AGER BLAZES OUT TO SEA WITH ONLY ONE THOUGHT THROBBING IN HIS BRAIN-- **FIND SUB-MARINER!**

AND THEN...

NOW F I CAN JUST REMEMBER HOW REED TOLD ME TO WHIP UP A FLAMING PROBING DEVICE... HEY, **THAT'S** IT!

WHILE MANY FATHOMS BELOW, IN NAMOR'S IMPERIAL AMPHIBIOUS COMMAND CRAFT...

YOU MAY REMOVE YOUR HELMET, KRANG! AND YOU OTHERS, AS WELL! THE WALLS OF THIS VEHICLE ARE MOISTURE-LINED, TO ENABLE YOU TO BREATHE, EVEN THOUGH THERE IS AIR FOR OUR HUMAN PRISONER!

YES, YOUR HIGHNESS!

WE MUST NOT ALLOW OURSELVES TO BECOME DISCOURAGED BY ONE DEFEAT! I HAVE ONLY JUST **BEGUN** TO FIGHT!

OF COURSE, MY PRINCE! AND NO MATTE WHAT FATE BEFALLS US, KNOW YOU THAT LADY **DORMA** SHALL ALWAYS BE AT YOUR SIDE!

ENOUGH! I HAVE NO PATIENCE FOR SUCH TALK! THE **FANTASTIC FOUR** WILL SOON BE AFTER US TO RESCUE THEIR ABDUCTED MEMBER! WE MUST PREPARE OUR DEFENSES!

MAJESTY! I DETECT SONAR HEAT BLIPS FROM THE SURFACE, FOLLOWING OUR COURSE!

IT CAN ONLY MEAN ONE THING-- THE **HUMAN TORCH** HAS FOUND US!

NAMOR--WAIT! HE--HE'S ONLY A **BOY!** WHAT ARE YOU GOING TO DO??

I SHALL DO WHAT I **MUST!** OUR PEOPLES ARE AT **WAR!** ... AND I MUST NOT SHIRK MY ROYAL DUTY!

28

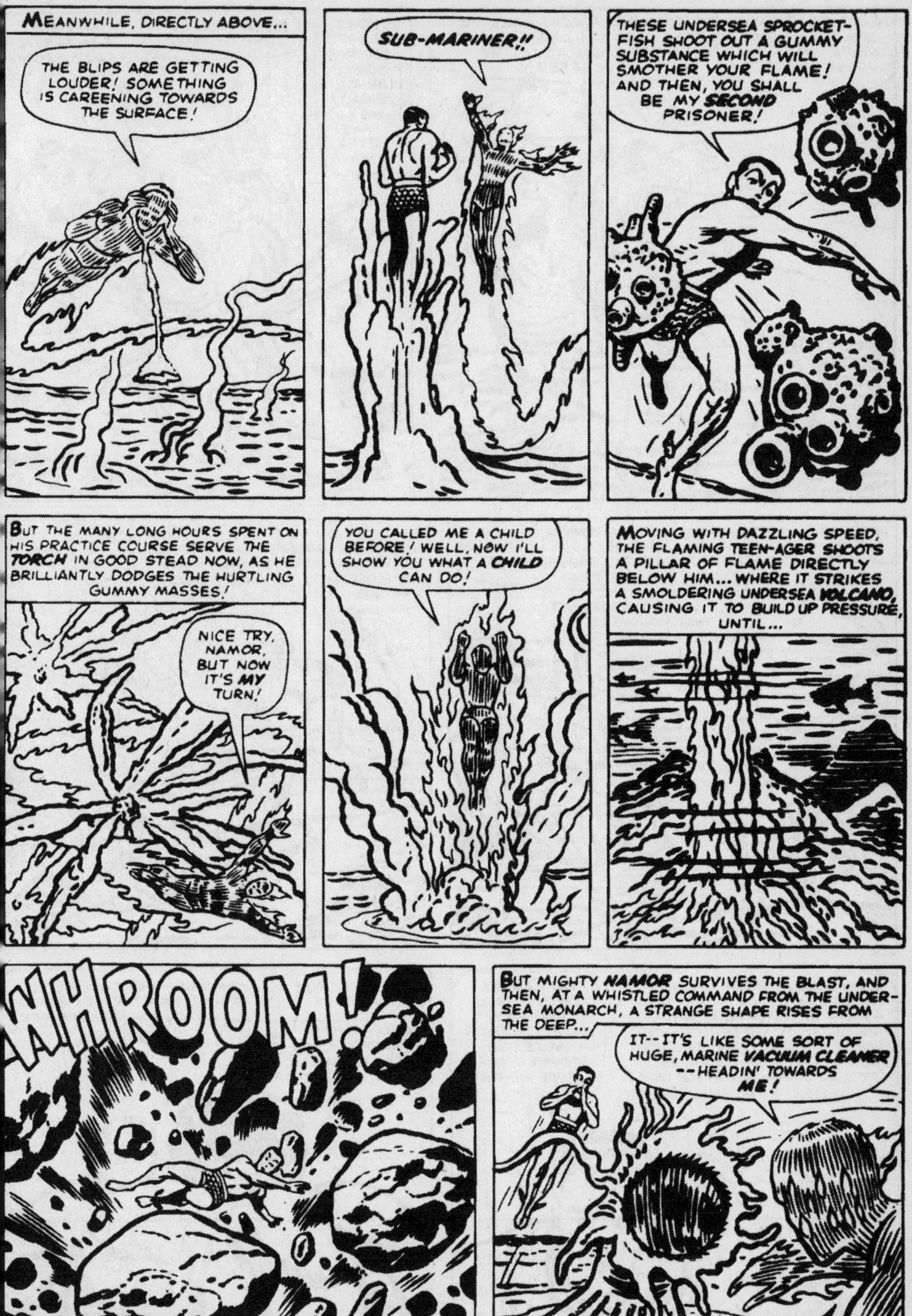
MEANWHILE, DIRECTLY ABOVE...
THE BLIPS ARE GETTING LOUDER! SOMETHING IS CAREENING TOWARDS THE SURFACE!
SUB-MARINER!!
THESE UNDERSEA SPROCKET-FISH SHOOT OUT A GUMMY SUBSTANCE WHICH WILL SMOTHER YOUR FLAME! AND THEN, YOU SHALL BE MY SECOND PRISONER!
BUT THE MANY LONG HOURS SPENT ON HIS PRACTICE COURSE SERVE THE TORCH IN GOOD STEAD NOW, AS HE BRILLIANTLY DODGES THE HURTLING GUMMY MASSES!
NICE TRY, NAMOR, BUT NOW IT'S MY TURN!
YOU CALLED ME A CHILD BEFORE! WELL, NOW I'LL SHOW YOU WHAT A CHILD CAN DO!
MOVING WITH DAZZLING SPEED, THE FLAMING TEEN-AGER SHOOTS A PILLAR OF FLAME DIRECTLY BELOW HIM... WHERE IT STRIKES A SMOLDERING UNDERSEA VOLCANO, CAUSING IT TO BUILD UP PRESSURE, UNTIL...
WHROOM!
BUT MIGHTY NAMOR SURVIVES THE BLAST, AND THEN, AT A WHISTLED COMMAND FROM THE UNDER-SEA MONARCH, A STRANGE SHAPE RISES FROM THE DEEP...
IT--IT'S LIKE SOME SORT OF HUGE, MARINE VACUUM CLEANER --HEADIN' TOWARDS ME!
29

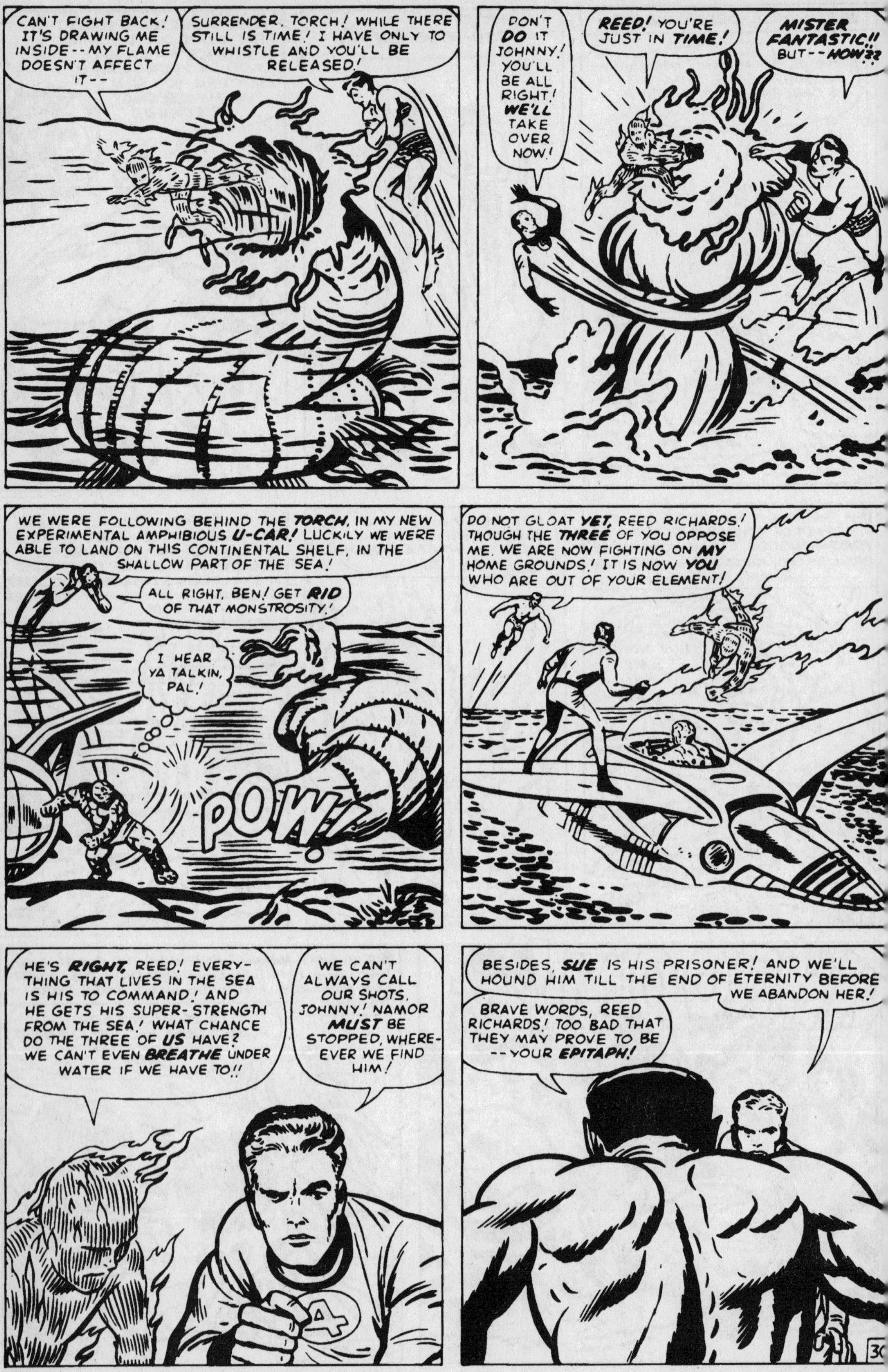
CAN'T FIGHT BACK! IT'S DRAWING ME INSIDE--MY FLAME DOESN'T AFFECT IT--
SURRENDER, TORCH! WHILE THERE STILL IS TIME! I HAVE ONLY TO WHISTLE AND YOU'LL BE RELEASED!
DON'T DO IT JOHNNY! YOU'LL BE ALL RIGHT! WE'LL TAKE OVER NOW!
REED! YOU'RE JUST IN TIME!
MISTER FANTASTIC!! BUT--HOW??
WE WERE FOLLOWING BEHIND THE TORCH, IN MY NEW EXPERIMENTAL AMPHIBIOUS U-CAR! LUCKILY WE WERE ABLE TO LAND ON THIS CONTINENTAL SHELF, IN THE SHALLOW PART OF THE SEA!
ALL RIGHT, BEN! GET RID OF THAT MONSTROSITY!
I HEAR YA TALKIN, PAL!
POW!
DO NOT GLOAT YET, REED RICHARDS! THOUGH THE THREE OF YOU OPPOSE ME, WE ARE NOW FIGHTING ON MY HOME GROUNDS! IT IS NOW YOU WHO ARE OUT OF YOUR ELEMENT!
HE'S RIGHT, REED! EVERYTHING THAT LIVES IN THE SEA IS HIS TO COMMAND! AND HE GETS HIS SUPER-STRENGTH FROM THE SEA! WHAT CHANCE DO THE THREE OF US HAVE? WE CAN'T EVEN BREATHE UNDER WATER IF WE HAVE TO!!
WE CAN'T ALWAYS CALL OUR SHOTS, JOHNNY! NAMOR MUST BE STOPPED, WHEREEVER WE FIND HIM!
BESIDES, SUE IS HIS PRISONER! AND WE'LL HOUND HIM TILL THE END OF ETERNITY BEFORE WE ABANDON HER!
BRAVE WORDS, REED RICHARDS! TOO BAD THAT THEY MAY PROVE TO BE --YOUR EPITAPH!
30

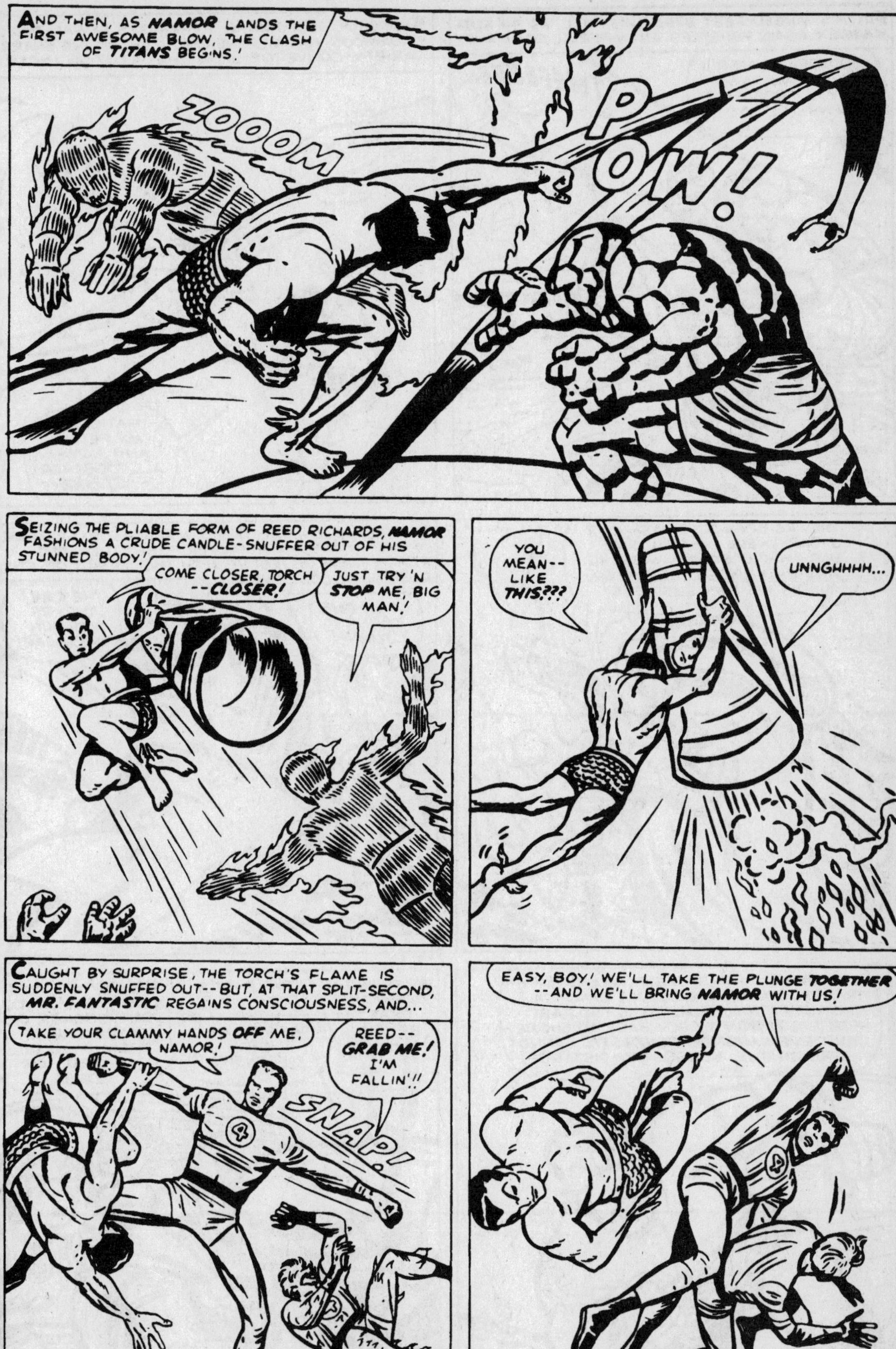
AND THEN, AS NAMOR LANDS THE FIRST AWESOME BLOW, THE CLASH OF TITANS BEGINS!
ZOOOM
POW!
SEIZING THE PLIABLE FORM OF REED RICHARDS, NAMOR FASHIONS A CRUDE CANDLE-SNUFFER OUT OF HIS STUNNED BODY!
COME CLOSER, TORCH --CLOSER!
JUST TRY 'N STOP ME, BIG MAN!
YOU MEAN-- LIKE THIS???
UNNGHHHH...
CAUGHT BY SURPRISE, THE TORCH'S FLAME IS SUDDENLY SNUFFED OUT--BUT, AT THAT SPLIT-SECOND, MR. FANTASTIC REGAINS CONSCIOUSNESS, AND...
TAKE YOUR CLAMMY HANDS OFF ME, NAMOR!
REED-- GRAB ME! I'M FALLIN'!!
SNAP!
EASY, BOY! WE'LL TAKE THE PLUNGE TOGETHER --AND WE'LL BRING NAMOR WITH US!
31

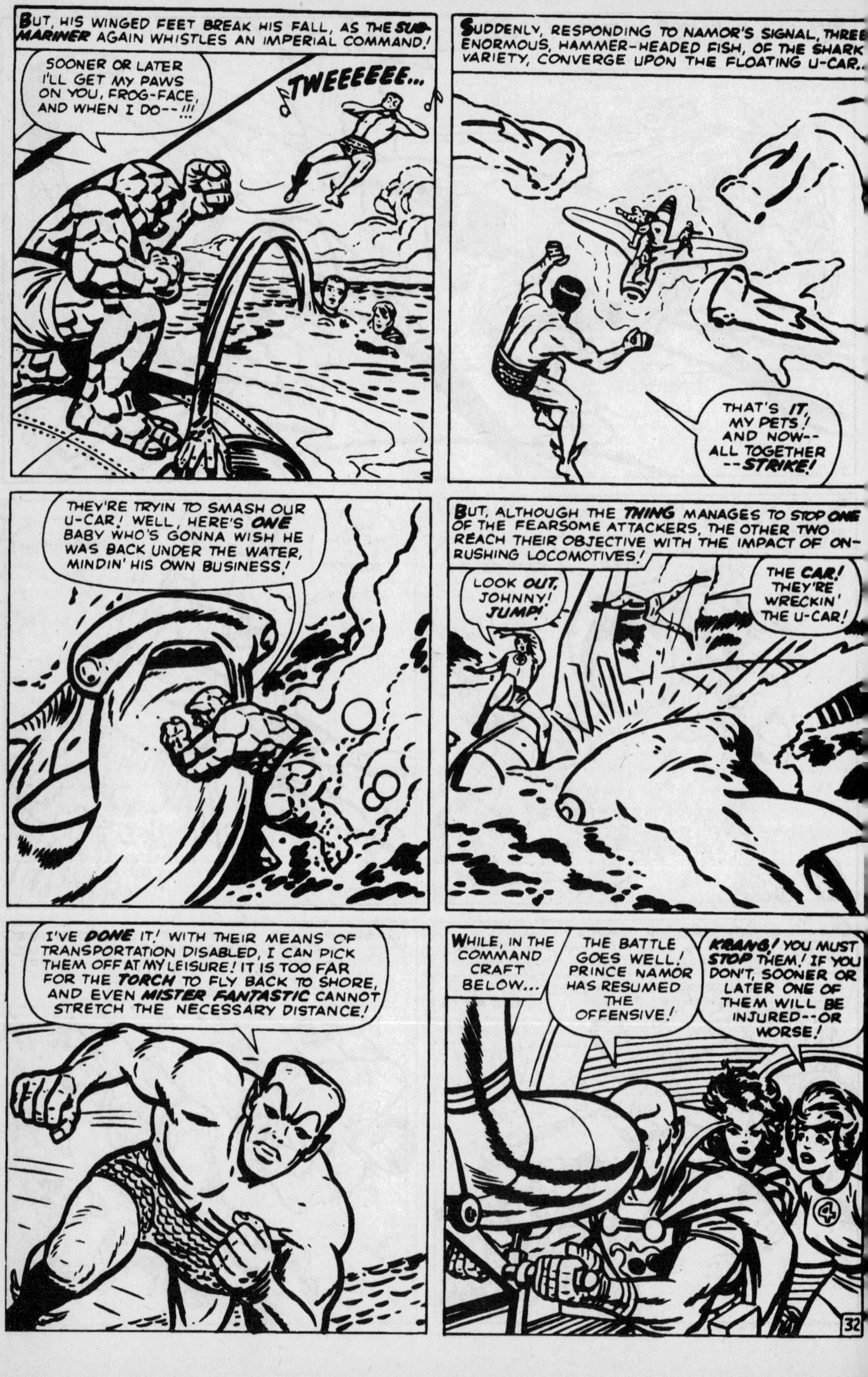
BUT, HIS WINGED FEET BREAK HIS FALL, AS THE SUB-MARINER AGAIN WHISTLES AN IMPERIAL COMMAND!
SOONER OR LATER I'LL GET MY PAWS ON YOU, FROG-FACE, AND WHEN I DO--!!!
TWEEEEEE...
SUDDENLY, RESPONDING TO NAMOR'S SIGNAL, THREE ENORMOUS, HAMMER-HEADED FISH, OF THE SHARK VARIETY, CONVERGE UPON THE FLOATING U-CAR...
THAT'S IT, MY PETS! AND NOW-- ALL TOGETHER --STRIKE!
THEY'RE TRYIN TO SMASH OUR U-CAR! WELL, HERE'S ONE BABY WHO'S GONNA WISH HE WAS BACK UNDER THE WATER, MINDIN' HIS OWN BUSINESS!
BUT, ALTHOUGH THE THING MANAGES TO STOP ONE OF THE FEARSOME ATTACKERS, THE OTHER TWO REACH THEIR OBJECTIVE WITH THE IMPACT OF ON-RUSHING LOCOMOTIVES!
LOOK OUT, JOHNNY! JUMP!
THE CAR! THEY'RE WRECKIN' THE U-CAR!
I'VE DONE IT! WITH THEIR MEANS OF TRANSPORTATION DISABLED, I CAN PICK THEM OFF AT MY LEISURE! IT IS TOO FAR FOR THE TORCH TO FLY BACK TO SHORE, AND EVEN MISTER FANTASTIC CANNOT STRETCH THE NECESSARY DISTANCE!
WHILE, IN THE COMMAND CRAFT BELOW...
THE BATTLE GOES WELL! PRINCE NAMOR HAS RESUMED THE OFFENSIVE!
KRANG! YOU MUST STOP THEM! IF YOU DON'T, SOONER OR LATER ONE OF THEM WILL BE INJURED--OR WORSE!
32

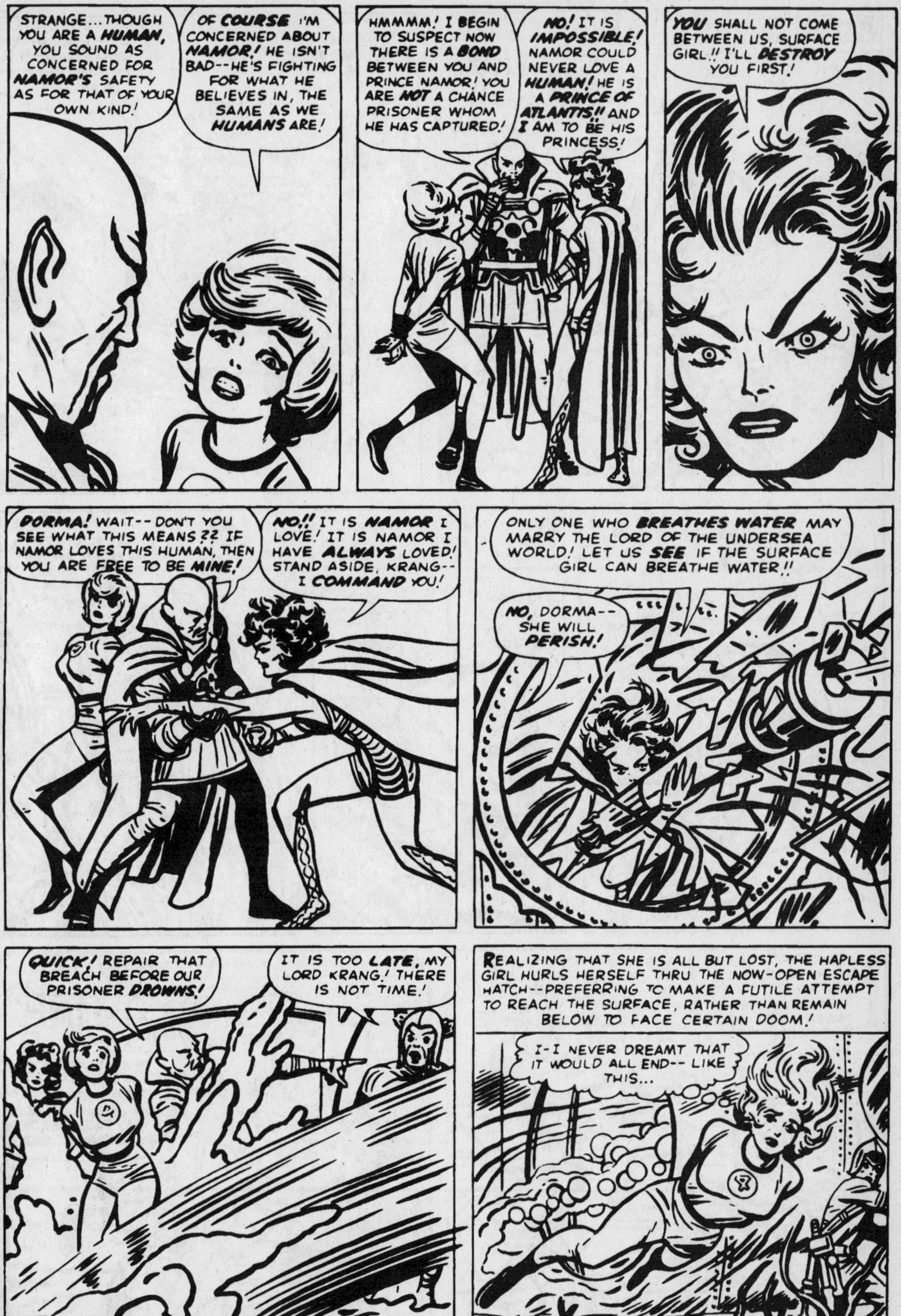
STRANGE...THOUGH YOU ARE A HUMAN, YOU SOUND AS CONCERNED FOR NAMOR'S SAFETY AS FOR THAT OF YOUR OWN KIND!
OF COURSE I'M CONCERNED ABOUT NAMOR! HE ISN'T BAD--HE'S FIGHTING FOR WHAT HE BELIEVES IN, THE SAME AS WE HUMANS ARE!
HMMMM! I BEGIN TO SUSPECT NOW THERE IS A BOND BETWEEN YOU AND PRINCE NAMOR! YOU ARE NOT A CHANCE PRISONER WHOM HE HAS CAPTURED!
NO! IT IS IMPOSSIBLE! NAMOR COULD NEVER LOVE A HUMAN! HE IS A PRINCE OF ATLANTIS!! AND I AM TO BE HIS PRINCESS!
YOU SHALL NOT COME BETWEEN US, SURFACE GIRL!! I'LL DESTROY YOU FIRST!
DORMA! WAIT-- DON'T YOU SEE WHAT THIS MEANS?? IF NAMOR LOVES THIS HUMAN, THEN YOU ARE FREE TO BE MINE!
NO!! IT IS NAMOR I LOVE! IT IS NAMOR I HAVE ALWAYS LOVED! STAND ASIDE, KRANG-- I COMMAND YOU!
ONLY ONE WHO BREATHES WATER MAY MARRY THE LORD OF THE UNDERSEA WORLD! LET US SEE IF THE SURFACE GIRL CAN BREATHE WATER!!
NO, DORMA-- SHE WILL PERISH!
QUICK! REPAIR THAT BREACH BEFORE OUR PRISONER DROWNS!
IT IS TOO LATE, MY LORD KRANG! THERE IS NOT TIME!
REALIZING THAT SHE IS ALL BUT LOST, THE HAPLESS GIRL HURLS HERSELF THRU THE NOW-OPEN ESCAPE HATCH--PREFERRING TO MAKE A FUTILE ATTEMPT TO REACH THE SURFACE, RATHER THAN REMAIN BELOW TO FACE CERTAIN DOOM!
I-I NEVER DREAMT THAT IT WOULD ALL END-- LIKE THIS...
33

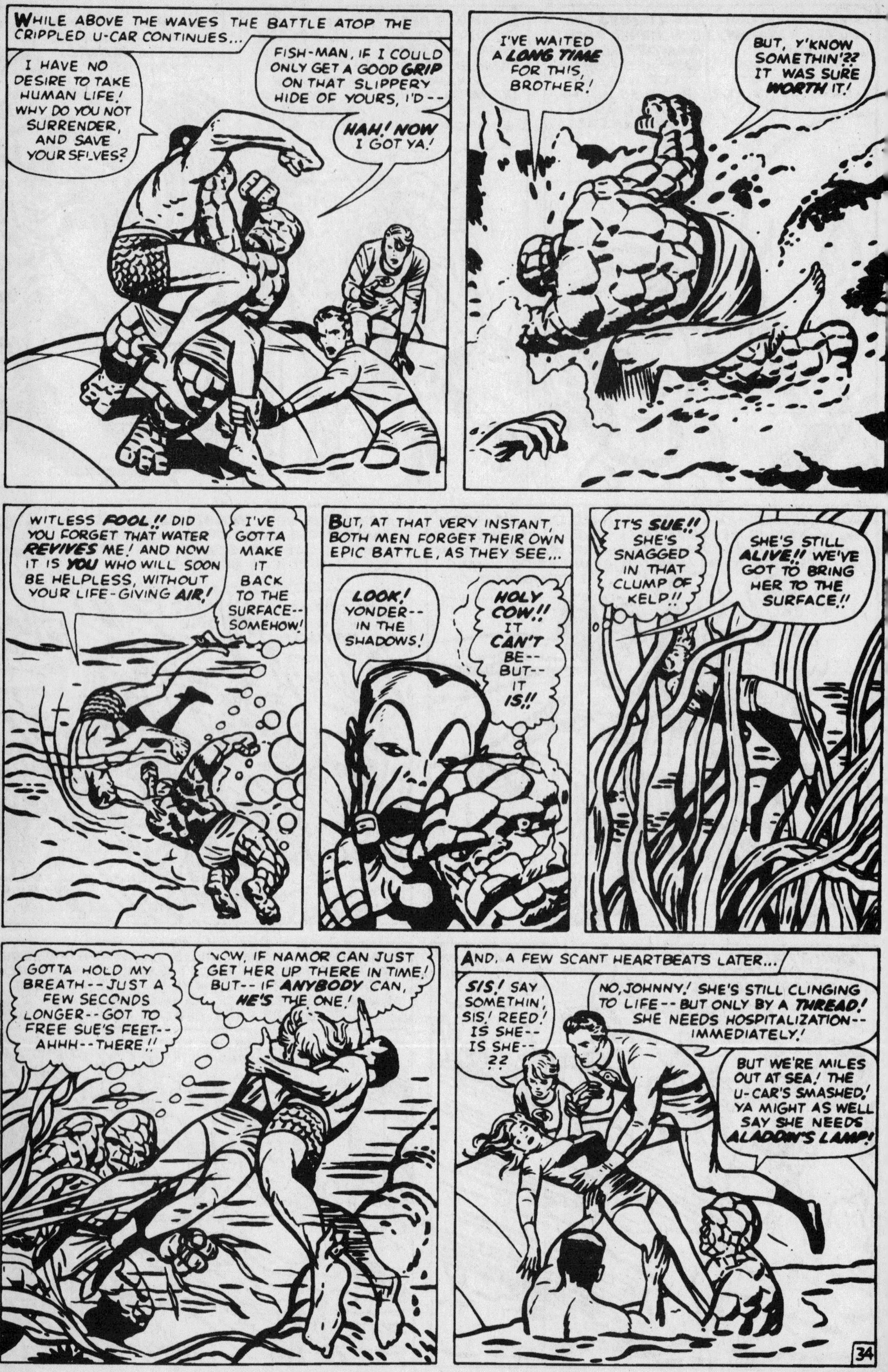
WHILE ABOVE THE WAVES THE BATTLE ATOP THE CRIPPLED U-CAR CONTINUES...
I HAVE NO DESIRE TO TAKE HUMAN LIFE! WHY DO YOU NOT SURRENDER, AND SAVE YOURSELVES?
FISH-MAN, IF I COULD ONLY GET A GOOD GRIP ON THAT SLIPPERY HIDE OF YOURS, I'D--
HAH! NOW I GOT YA!
I'VE WAITED A LONG TIME FOR THIS, BROTHER!
BUT, Y'KNOW SOMETHIN'?? IT WAS SURE WORTH IT!
WITLESS FOOL!! DID YOU FORGET THAT WATER REVIVES ME! AND NOW IT IS YOU WHO WILL SOON BE HELPLESS, WITHOUT YOUR LIFE-GIVING AIR!
I'VE GOTTA MAKE IT BACK TO THE SURFACE-- SOMEHOW!
BUT, AT THAT VERY INSTANT, BOTH MEN FORGET THEIR OWN EPIC BATTLE, AS THEY SEE...
LOOK! YONDER-- IN THE SHADOWS!
HOLY COW!! IT CAN'T BE-- BUT-- IT IS!!
IT'S SUE!! SHE'S SNAGGED IN THAT CLUMP OF KELP!!
SHE'S STILL ALIVE!! WE'VE GOT TO BRING HER TO THE SURFACE!!
GOTTA HOLD MY BREATH-- JUST A FEW SECONDS LONGER-- GOT TO FREE SUE'S FEET-- AHHH-- THERE!!
NOW, IF NAMOR CAN JUST GET HER UP THERE IN TIME! BUT-- IF ANYBODY CAN, HE'S THE ONE!
AND, A FEW SCANT HEARTBEATS LATER...
SIS! SAY SOMETHIN', SIS! REED! IS SHE-- IS SHE-- ??
NO, JOHNNY! SHE'S STILL CLINGING TO LIFE-- BUT ONLY BY A THREAD! SHE NEEDS HOSPITALIZATION-- IMMEDIATELY!
BUT WE'RE MILES OUT AT SEA! THE U-CAR'S SMASHED! YA MIGHT AS WELL SAY SHE NEEDS ALADDIN'S LAMP!
34

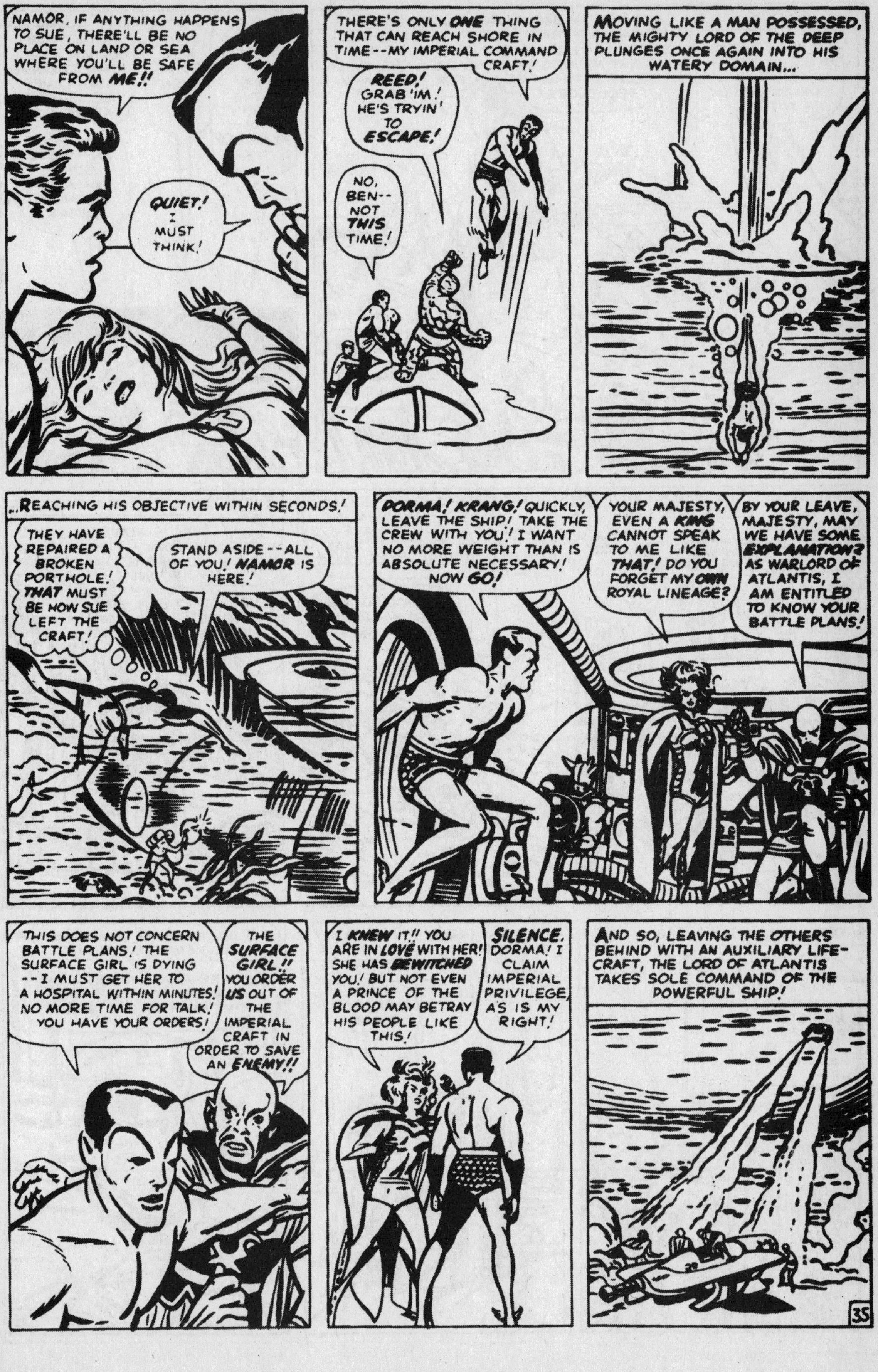

NAMOR, IF ANYTHING HAPPENS TO SUE, THERE'LL BE NO PLACE ON LAND OR SEA WHERE YOU'LL BE SAFE FROM ME!!
QUIET! I MUST THINK!
THERE'S ONLY ONE THING THAT CAN REACH SHORE IN TIME--MY IMPERIAL COMMAND CRAFT!
REED! GRAB 'IM! HE'S TRYIN' TO ESCAPE!
NO, BEN--NOT THIS TIME!
MOVING LIKE A MAN POSSESSED, THE MIGHTY LORD OF THE DEEP PLUNGES ONCE AGAIN INTO HIS WATERY DOMAIN...
...REACHING HIS OBJECTIVE WITHIN SECONDS!
THEY HAVE REPAIRED A BROKEN PORTHOLE! THAT MUST BE HOW SUE LEFT THE CRAFT!
STAND ASIDE--ALL OF YOU! NAMOR IS HERE!
DORMA! KRANG! QUICKLY, LEAVE THE SHIP! TAKE THE CREW WITH YOU! I WANT NO MORE WEIGHT THAN IS ABSOLUTE NECESSARY! NOW GO!
YOUR MAJESTY, EVEN A KING CANNOT SPEAK TO ME LIKE THAT! DO YOU FORGET MY OWN ROYAL LINEAGE?
BY YOUR LEAVE, MAJESTY, MAY WE HAVE SOME EXPLANATION? AS WARLORD OF ATLANTIS, I AM ENTITLED TO KNOW YOUR BATTLE PLANS!
THIS DOES NOT CONCERN BATTLE PLANS! THE SURFACE GIRL IS DYING --I MUST GET HER TO A HOSPITAL WITHIN MINUTES! NO MORE TIME FOR TALK! YOU HAVE YOUR ORDERS!
THE SURFACE GIRL!! YOU ORDER US OUT OF THE IMPERIAL CRAFT IN ORDER TO SAVE AN ENEMY!!
I KNEW IT!! YOU ARE IN LOVE WITH HER! SHE HAS BEWITCHED YOU! BUT NOT EVEN A PRINCE OF THE BLOOD MAY BETRAY HIS PEOPLE LIKE THIS!
SILENCE, DORMA! I CLAIM IMPERIAL PRIVILEGE, AS IS MY RIGHT!
AND SO, LEAVING THE OTHERS BEHIND WITH AN AUXILIARY LIFE-CRAFT, THE LORD OF ATLANTIS TAKES SOLE COMMAND OF THE POWERFUL SHIP!
35

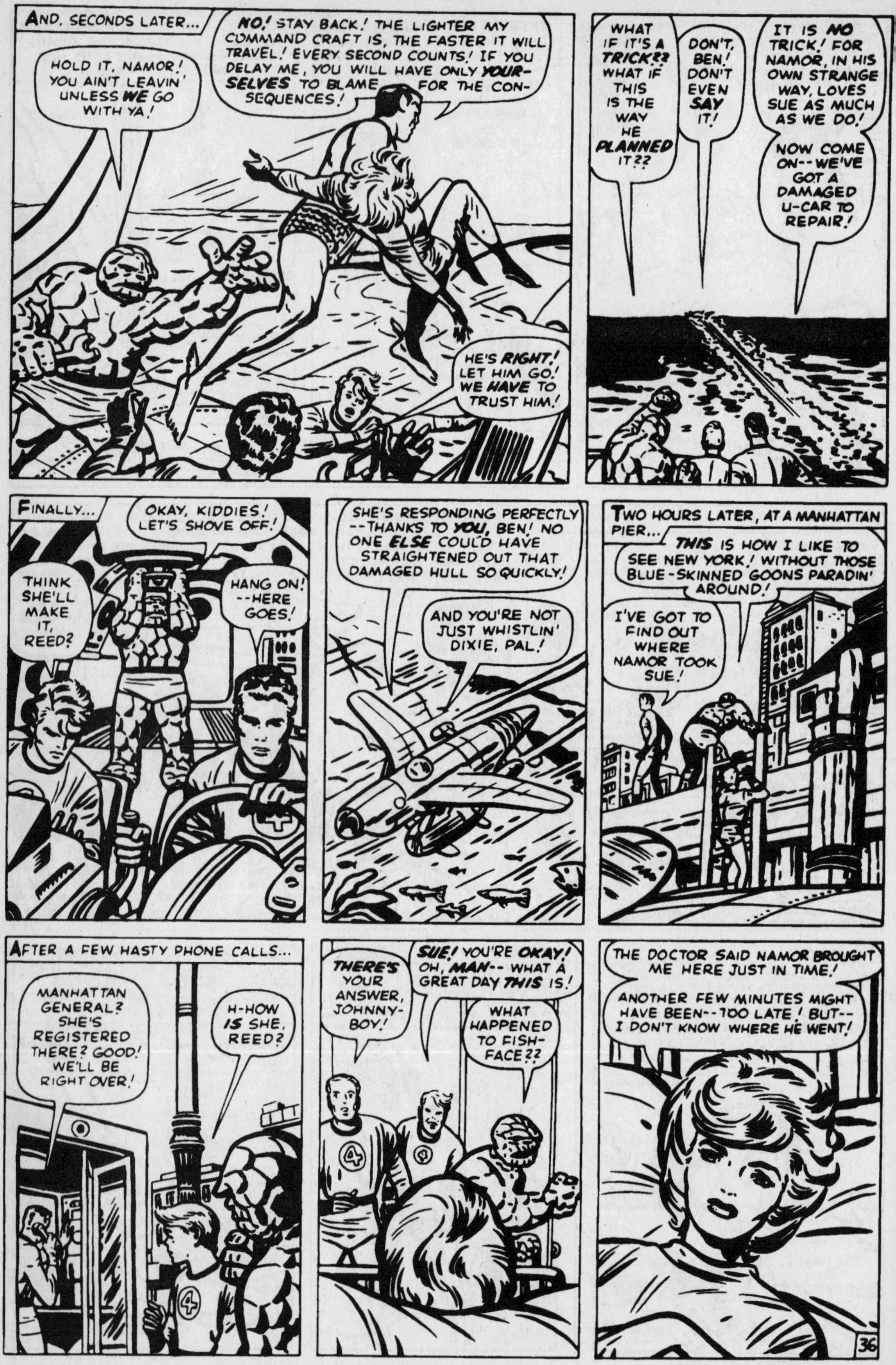
AND, SECONDS LATER...
HOLD IT, NAMOR! YOU AIN'T LEAVIN' UNLESS WE GO WITH YA!
NO! STAY BACK! THE LIGHTER MY COMMAND CRAFT IS, THE FASTER IT WILL TRAVEL! EVERY SECOND COUNTS! IF YOU DELAY ME, YOU WILL HAVE ONLY YOURSELVES TO BLAME FOR THE CONSEQUENCES!
HE'S RIGHT! LET HIM GO! WE HAVE TO TRUST HIM!
WHAT IF IT'S A TRICK?? WHAT IF THIS IS THE WAY HE PLANNED IT??
DON'T, BEN! DON'T EVEN SAY IT!
IT IS NO TRICK! FOR NAMOR, IN HIS OWN STRANGE WAY, LOVES SUE AS MUCH AS WE DO!
NOW COME ON--WE'VE GOT A DAMAGED U-CAR TO REPAIR!
FINALLY...
OKAY, KIDDIES! LET'S SHOVE OFF!
THINK SHE'LL MAKE IT, REED?
HANG ON! --HERE GOES!
SHE'S RESPONDING PERFECTLY --THANKS TO YOU, BEN! NO ONE ELSE COULD HAVE STRAIGHTENED OUT THAT DAMAGED HULL SO QUICKLY!
AND YOU'RE NOT JUST WHISTLIN' DIXIE, PAL!
TWO HOURS LATER, AT A MANHATTAN PIER...
THIS IS HOW I LIKE TO SEE NEW YORK! WITHOUT THOSE BLUE-SKINNED GOONS PARADIN' AROUND!
I'VE GOT TO FIND OUT WHERE NAMOR TOOK SUE!
AFTER A FEW HASTY PHONE CALLS...
MANHATTAN GENERAL? SHE'S REGISTERED THERE? GOOD! WE'LL BE RIGHT OVER!
H-HOW IS SHE, REED?
THERE'S YOUR ANSWER, JOHNNY-BOY!
SUE! YOU'RE OKAY! OH, MAN-- WHAT A GREAT DAY THIS IS!
WHAT HAPPENED TO FISH-FACE??
THE DOCTOR SAID NAMOR BROUGHT ME HERE JUST IN TIME!
ANOTHER FEW MINUTES MIGHT HAVE BEEN--TOO LATE! BUT-- I DON'T KNOW WHERE HE WENT!

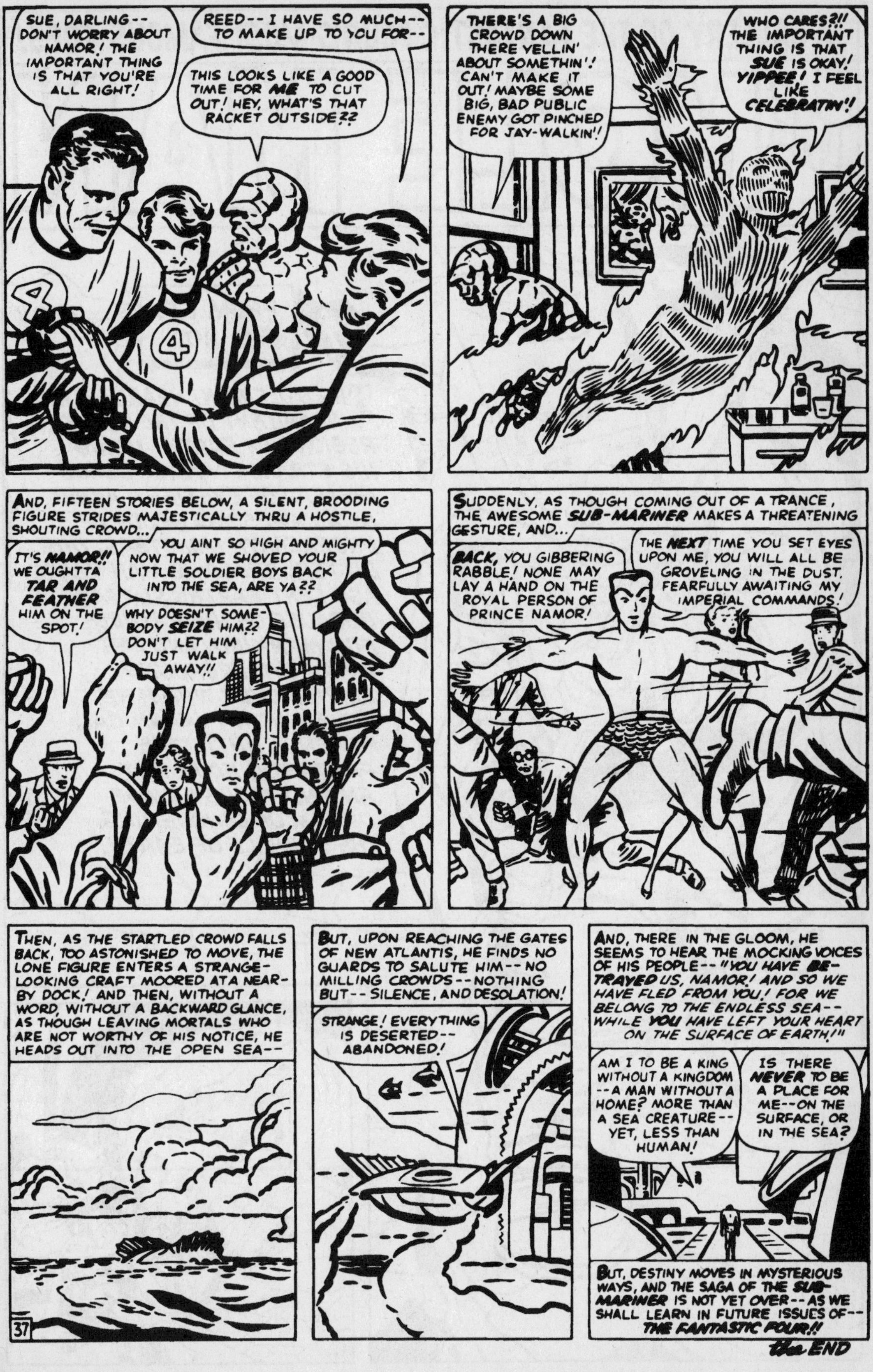
SUE, DARLING-- DON'T WORRY ABOUT NAMOR! THE IMPORTANT THING IS THAT YOU'RE ALL RIGHT!
REED-- I HAVE SO MUCH-- TO MAKE UP TO YOU FOR--
THIS LOOKS LIKE A GOOD TIME FOR ME TO CUT OUT! HEY, WHAT'S THAT RACKET OUTSIDE??
THERE'S A BIG CROWD DOWN THERE YELLIN' ABOUT SOMETHIN'! CAN'T MAKE IT OUT! MAYBE SOME BIG, BAD PUBLIC ENEMY GOT PINCHED FOR JAY-WALKIN'!
WHO CARES?!! THE IMPORTANT THING IS THAT SUE IS OKAY! YIPPEE! I FEEL LIKE CELEBRATIN'!
AND, FIFTEEN STORIES BELOW, A SILENT, BROODING FIGURE STRIDES MAJESTICALLY THRU A HOSTILE, SHOUTING CROWD...
IT'S NAMOR!! WE OUGHTTA TAR AND FEATHER HIM ON THE SPOT!
YOU AINT SO HIGH AND MIGHTY NOW THAT WE SHOVED YOUR LITTLE SOLDIER BOYS BACK INTO THE SEA, ARE YA??
WHY DOESN'T SOMEBODY SEIZE HIM?? DON'T LET HIM JUST WALK AWAY!!
SUDDENLY, AS THOUGH COMING OUT OF A TRANCE, THE AWESOME SUB-MARINER MAKES A THREATENING GESTURE, AND...
BACK, YOU GIBBERING RABBLE! NONE MAY LAY A HAND ON THE ROYAL PERSON OF PRINCE NAMOR!
THE NEXT TIME YOU SET EYES UPON ME, YOU WILL ALL BE GROVELING IN THE DUST, FEARFULLY AWAITING MY IMPERIAL COMMANDS!
THEN, AS THE STARTLED CROWD FALLS BACK, TOO ASTONISHED TO MOVE, THE LONE FIGURE ENTERS A STRANGE-LOOKING CRAFT MOORED AT A NEAR-BY DOCK! AND THEN, WITHOUT A WORD, WITHOUT A BACKWARD GLANCE, AS THOUGH LEAVING MORTALS WHO ARE NOT WORTHY OF HIS NOTICE, HE HEADS OUT INTO THE OPEN SEA--
BUT, UPON REACHING THE GATES OF NEW ATLANTIS, HE FINDS NO GUARDS TO SALUTE HIM-- NO MILLING CROWDS-- NOTHING BUT-- SILENCE, AND DESOLATION!
STRANGE! EVERYTHING IS DESERTED-- ABANDONED!
AND, THERE IN THE GLOOM, HE SEEMS TO HEAR THE MOCKING VOICES OF HIS PEOPLE-- "YOU HAVE BETRAYED US, NAMOR! AND SO WE HAVE FLED FROM YOU! FOR WE BELONG TO THE ENDLESS SEA-- WHILE YOU HAVE LEFT YOUR HEART ON THE SURFACE OF EARTH!"
AM I TO BE A KING WITHOUT A KINGDOM --A MAN WITHOUT A HOME? MORE THAN A SEA CREATURE-- YET, LESS THAN HUMAN!
IS THERE NEVER TO BE A PLACE FOR ME--ON THE SURFACE, OR IN THE SEA?
BUT, DESTINY MOVES IN MYSTERIOUS WAYS, AND THE SAGA OF THE SUB-MARINER IS NOT YET OVER-- AS WE SHALL LEARN IN FUTURE ISSUES OF-- THE FANTASTIC FOUR!!
37
the END

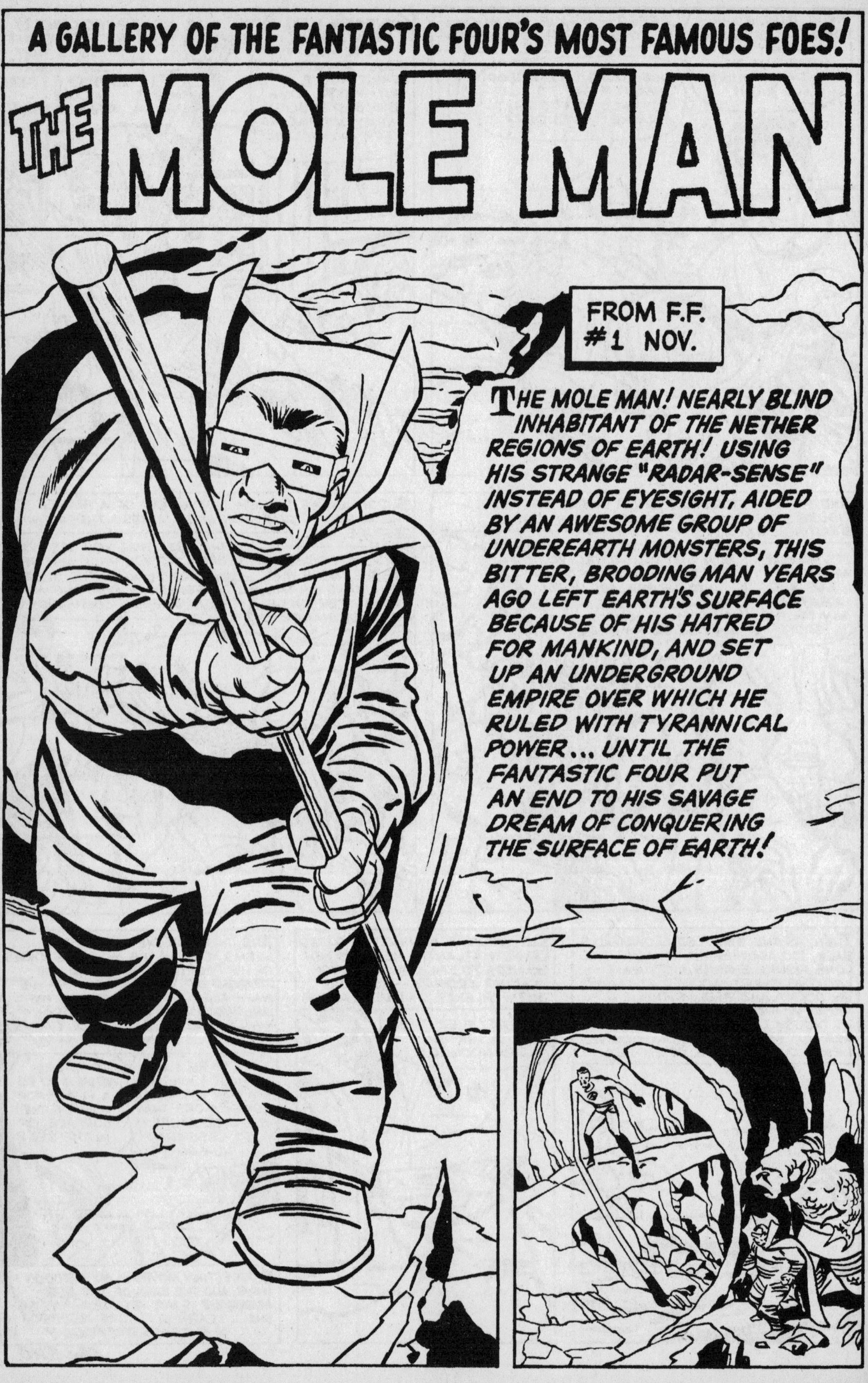
A GALLERY OF THE FANTASTIC FOUR'S MOST FAMOUS FOES!
THE MOLE MAN
FROM F.F. #1 NOV.
THE MOLE MAN! NEARLY BLIND INHABITANT OF THE NETHER REGIONS OF EARTH! USING HIS STRANGE "RADAR-SENSE" INSTEAD OF EYESIGHT, AIDED BY AN AWESOME GROUP OF UNDEREARTH MONSTERS, THIS BITTER, BROODING MAN YEARS AGO LEFT EARTH'S SURFACE BECAUSE OF HIS HATRED FOR MANKIND, AND SET UP AN UNDERGROUND EMPIRE OVER WHICH HE RULED WITH TYRANNICAL POWER... UNTIL THE FANTASTIC FOUR PUT AN END TO HIS SAVAGE DREAM OF CONQUERING THE SURFACE OF EARTH!

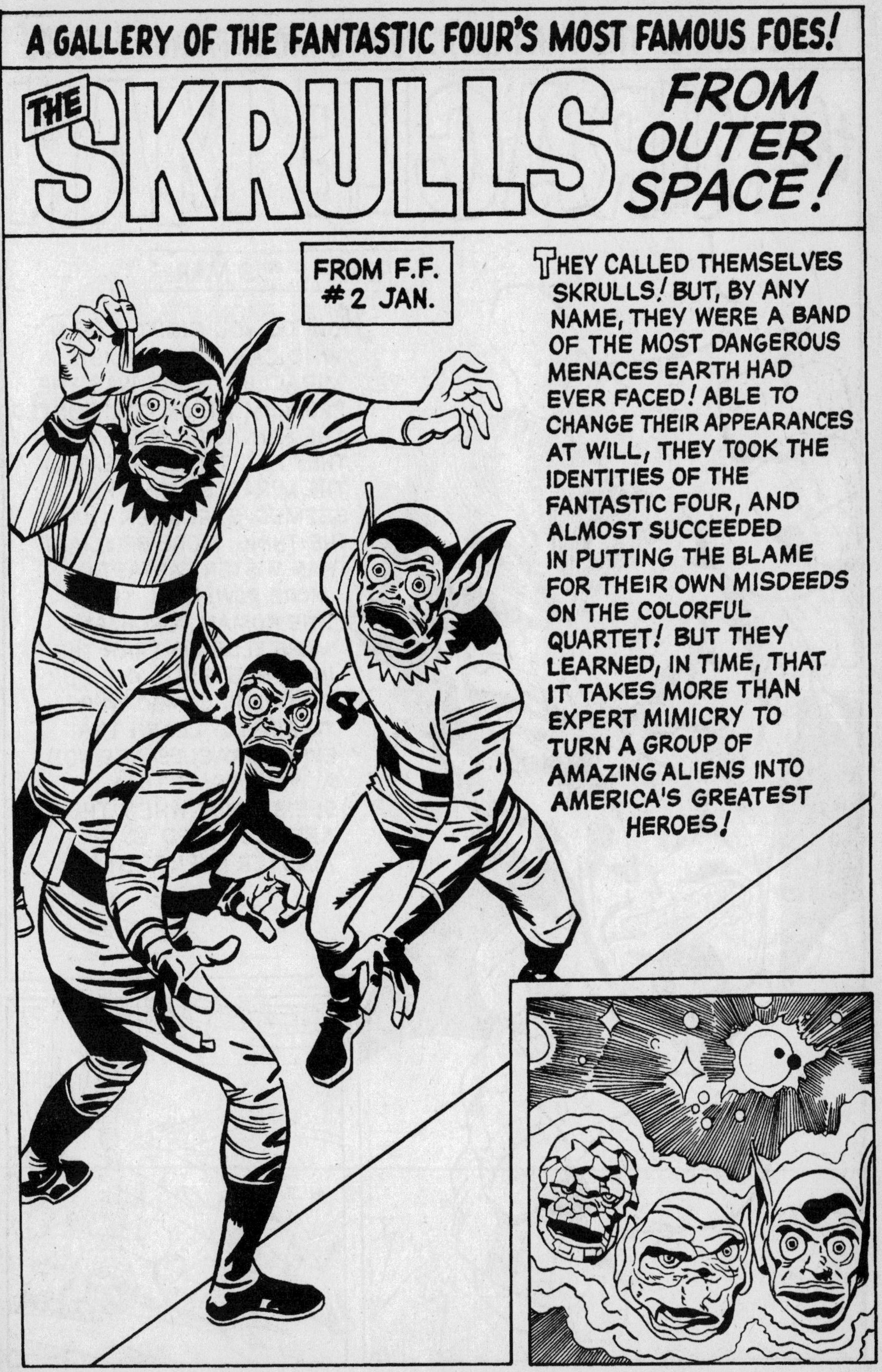
A GALLERY OF THE FANTASTIC FOUR'S MOST FAMOUS FOES!
THE SKRULLS FROM OUTER SPACE!
FROM F.F. #2 JAN.
THEY CALLED THEMSELVES SKRULLS! BUT, BY ANY NAME, THEY WERE A BAND OF THE MOST DANGEROUS MENACES EARTH HAD EVER FACED! ABLE TO CHANGE THEIR APPEARANCES AT WILL, THEY TOOK THE IDENTITIES OF THE FANTASTIC FOUR, AND ALMOST SUCCEEDED IN PUTTING THE BLAME FOR THEIR OWN MISDEEDS ON THE COLORFUL QUARTET! BUT THEY LEARNED, IN TIME, THAT IT TAKES MORE THAN EXPERT MIMICRY TO TURN A GROUP OF AMAZING ALIENS INTO AMERICA'S GREATEST HEROES!

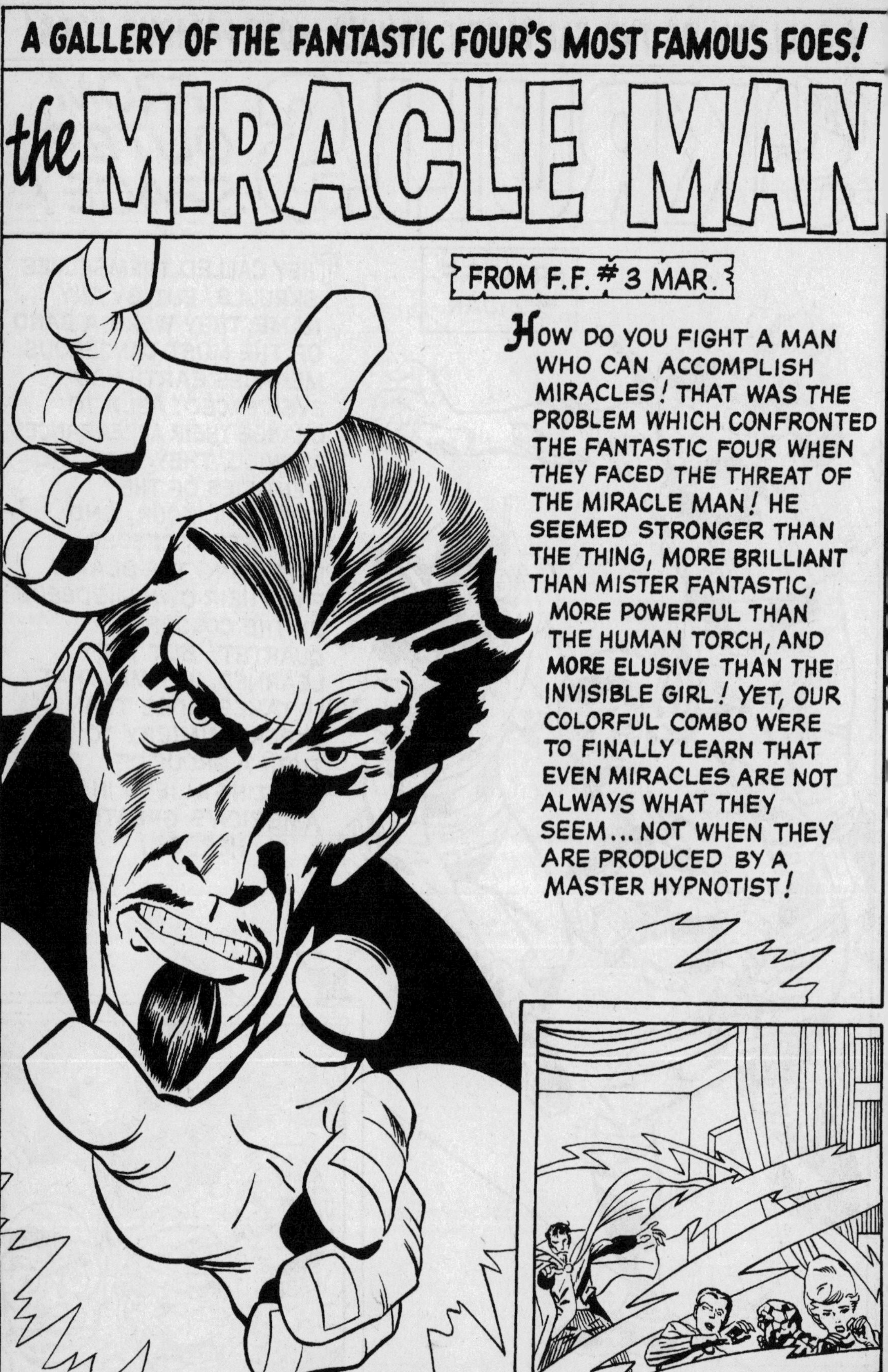
A GALLERY OF THE FANTASTIC FOUR'S MOST FAMOUS FOES!
the MIRACLE MAN
FROM F.F. # 3 MAR.
HOW DO YOU FIGHT A MAN WHO CAN ACCOMPLISH MIRACLES! THAT WAS THE PROBLEM WHICH CONFRONTED THE FANTASTIC FOUR WHEN THEY FACED THE THREAT OF THE MIRACLE MAN! HE SEEMED STRONGER THAN THE THING, MORE BRILLIANT THAN MISTER FANTASTIC, MORE POWERFUL THAN THE HUMAN TORCH, AND MORE ELUSIVE THAN THE INVISIBLE GIRL! YET, OUR COLORFUL COMBO WERE TO FINALLY LEARN THAT EVEN MIRACLES ARE NOT ALWAYS WHAT THEY SEEM... NOT WHEN THEY ARE PRODUCED BY A MASTER HYPNOTIST!

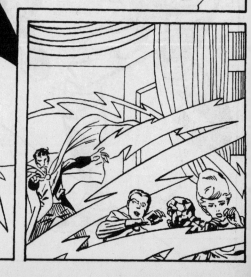

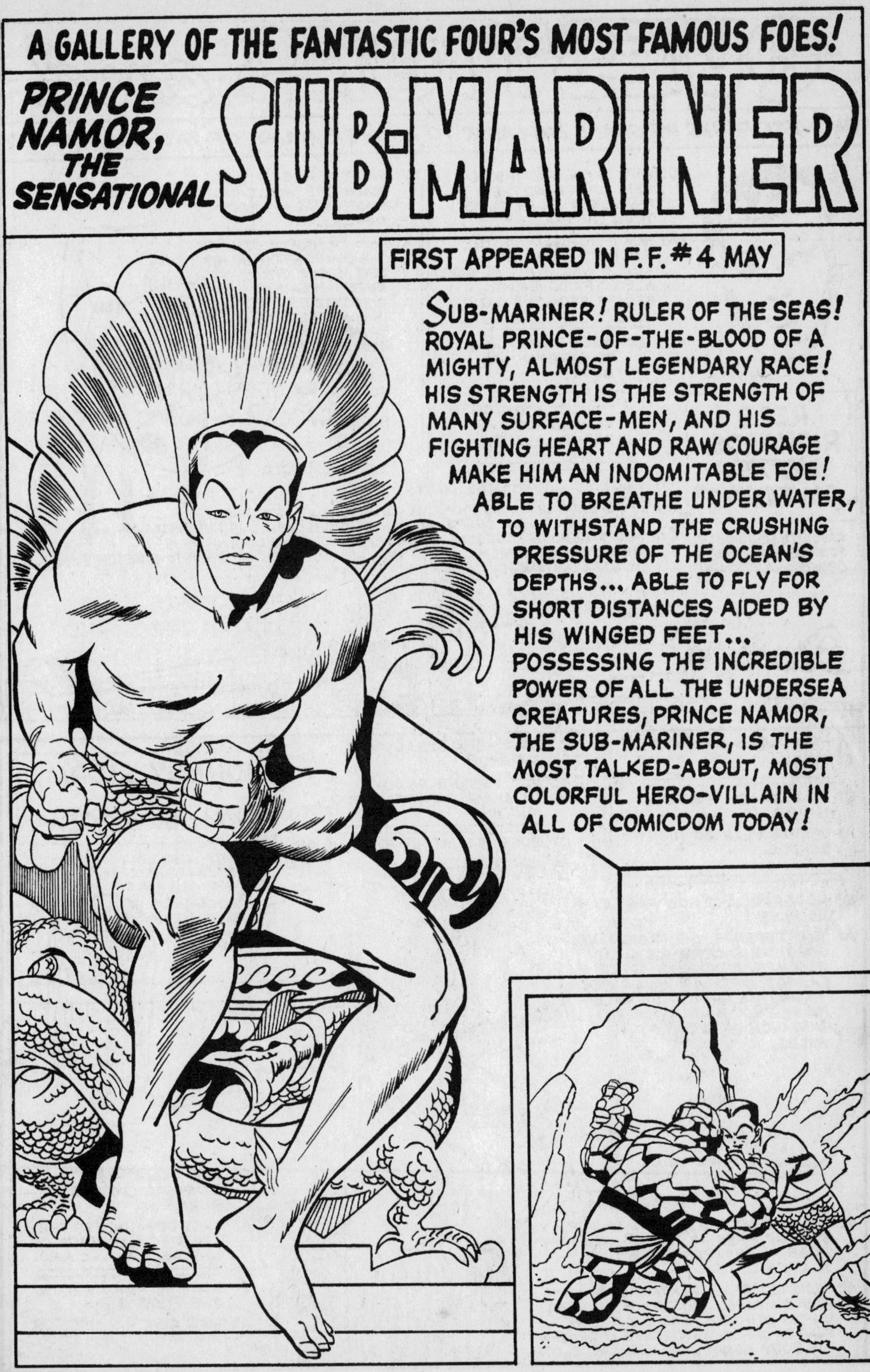
A GALLERY OF THE FANTASTIC FOUR'S MOST FAMOUS FOES!
PRINCE NAMOR, THE SENSATIONAL
SUB-MARINER
FIRST APPEARED IN F.F. #4 MAY
SUB-MARINER! RULER OF THE SEAS! ROYAL PRINCE-OF-THE-BLOOD OF A MIGHTY, ALMOST LEGENDARY RACE! HIS STRENGTH IS THE STRENGTH OF MANY SURFACE-MEN, AND HIS FIGHTING HEART AND RAW COURAGE MAKE HIM AN INDOMITABLE FOE! ABLE TO BREATHE UNDER WATER, TO WITHSTAND THE CRUSHING PRESSURE OF THE OCEAN'S DEPTHS... ABLE TO FLY FOR SHORT DISTANCES AIDED BY HIS WINGED FEET... POSSESSING THE INCREDIBLE POWER OF ALL THE UNDERSEA CREATURES, PRINCE NAMOR, THE SUB-MARINER, IS THE MOST TALKED-ABOUT, MOST COLORFUL HERO-VILLAIN IN ALL OF COMICDOM TODAY!

QUESTIONS and

ON THESE PAGES WE SHALL ENDEAVOR TO ANSWER MANY OF THE MOST-ASKED

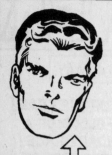

REED RICHARDS, *"MISTER FANTASTIC"*

FAVORITE HOBBIES: *SCIENCE, INVENTING, CRIME DEDUCTION.*

Q: WHY IS MR. FANTASTIC'S HAIR WHITE AT THE TEMPLES? IS HE OLDER THAN HE LOOKS?

A: NO! IT TURNED WHITE DURING THE SECOND WORLD WAR WHEN HE AIDED ALLIED PRISONERS TO ESCAPE FROM THE NAZIS.

Q: DOES IT HURT HIM TO STRETCH HIS BODY?

A: NO! ONLY IF HE TRIES TO STRETCH BEYOND HIS NORMAL LIMITS.

Q: WHAT IS REED'S SUIT MADE OF? HOW CAN IT STRETCH AS HIS BODY DOES?

A: THE PRINCIPLE BEHIND THE COMPOSITION OF HIS SUIT IS ONE OF REED'S GREATEST DISCOVERIES. IT IS COMPOSED OF ***UNSTABLE MOLECULES*** WHICH EXACTLY FOLLOW THE POSITION OF HIS BODY!

Q: WHAT *IS* HIS NORMAL LIMIT?

A: IT DEPENDS UPON HIS PHYSICAL CONDITION AT ANY GIVEN TIME! WHEN IN TOP SHAPE, HE CAN STRETCH OVER ONE HUNDRED YARDS BEFORE IT BEGINS TO GROW PAINFUL! HOWEVER, IF HE IS TIRED, OR NOT FEELING UP TO PAR, HE WILL ONLY BE ABLE TO STRETCH FOR SHORTER DISTANCES.

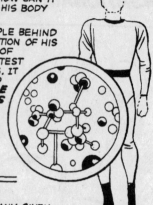

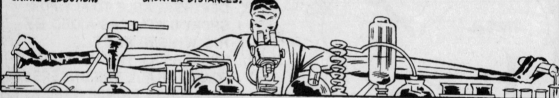

Q: HOW OLD IS JOHNNY?

A: SIXTEEN.

Q: WHAT GRADE IN SCHOOL IS HE?

A: SENIOR YEAR OF HIGH SCHOOL.

Q: HOW FAR, AND HOW FAST CAN HE FLY?

A: THAT DEPENDS. THE FASTER HE GOES, THE SHORTER HIS LIMIT BECOMES. AT NORMAL SPEED (*ABOUT FIFTY AIR MILES PER HOUR*) HE SHOULD BE ABLE TO FLY FOR A HALF-HOUR, A DISTANCE OF TWENTY-FIVE MILES.

Q: HAS HE A STEADY GIRL FRIEND?

A: NOT YET. HE ENJOYS *"PLAYING THE FIELD"* TOO MUCH.

Q: DOES IT HURT HIM TO FLAME ON?

A: NOT AT ALL.

JOHNNY STORM, *"THE HUMAN TORCH"*

FAVORITE HOBBIES: *SPORTS CARS, JAZZ RECORDS, AND GIRLS.* (THOUGH NOT NECESSARILY IN THAT ORDER.)

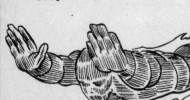

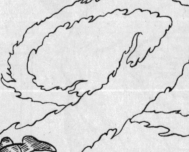

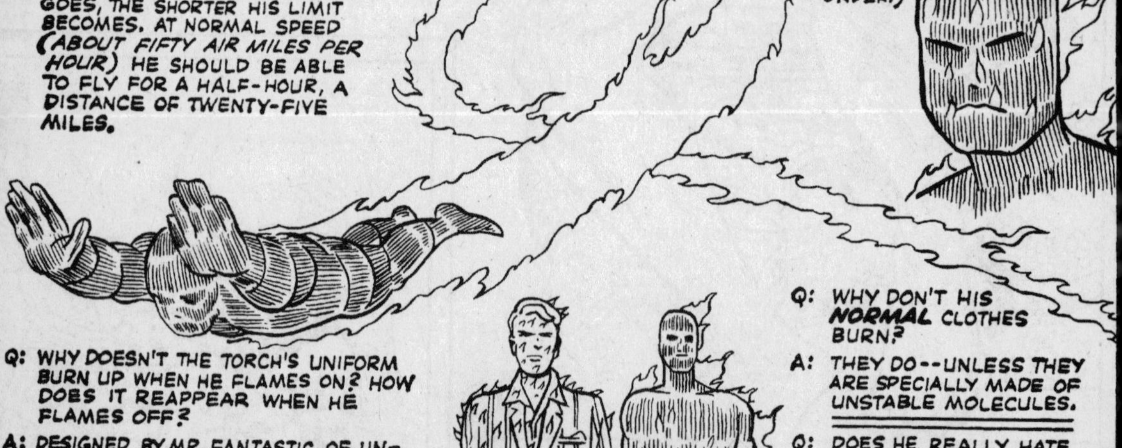

Q: WHY DOESN'T THE TORCH'S UNIFORM BURN UP WHEN HE FLAMES ON? HOW DOES IT REAPPEAR WHEN HE FLAMES OFF?

A: DESIGNED BY MR. FANTASTIC, OF UNSTABLE MOLECULES, TORCH'S UNIFORM UNITES WITH THE FLAME UNTIL HE FLAMES OFF, AT WHICH TIME IT DRAPES HIS BODY AGAIN LIKE NORMAL CLOTH.

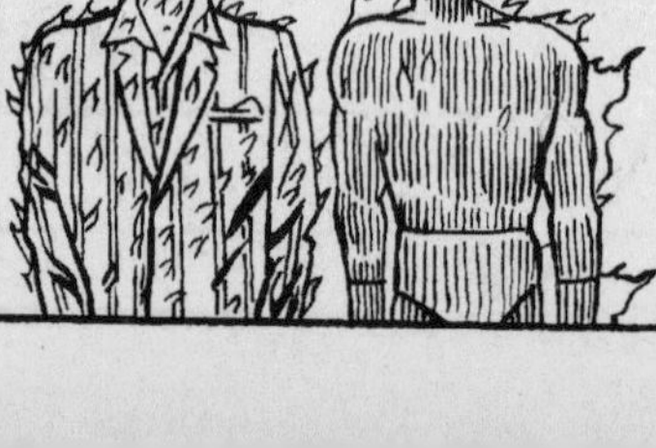

Q: WHY DON'T HIS ***NORMAL*** CLOTHES BURN?

A: THEY DO--UNLESS THEY ARE SPECIALLY MADE OF UNSTABLE MOLECULES.

Q: DOES HE REALLY HATE THE ***THING?***

A: HE'D RISK HIS LIFE FOR HIM WITHOUT QUESTION!

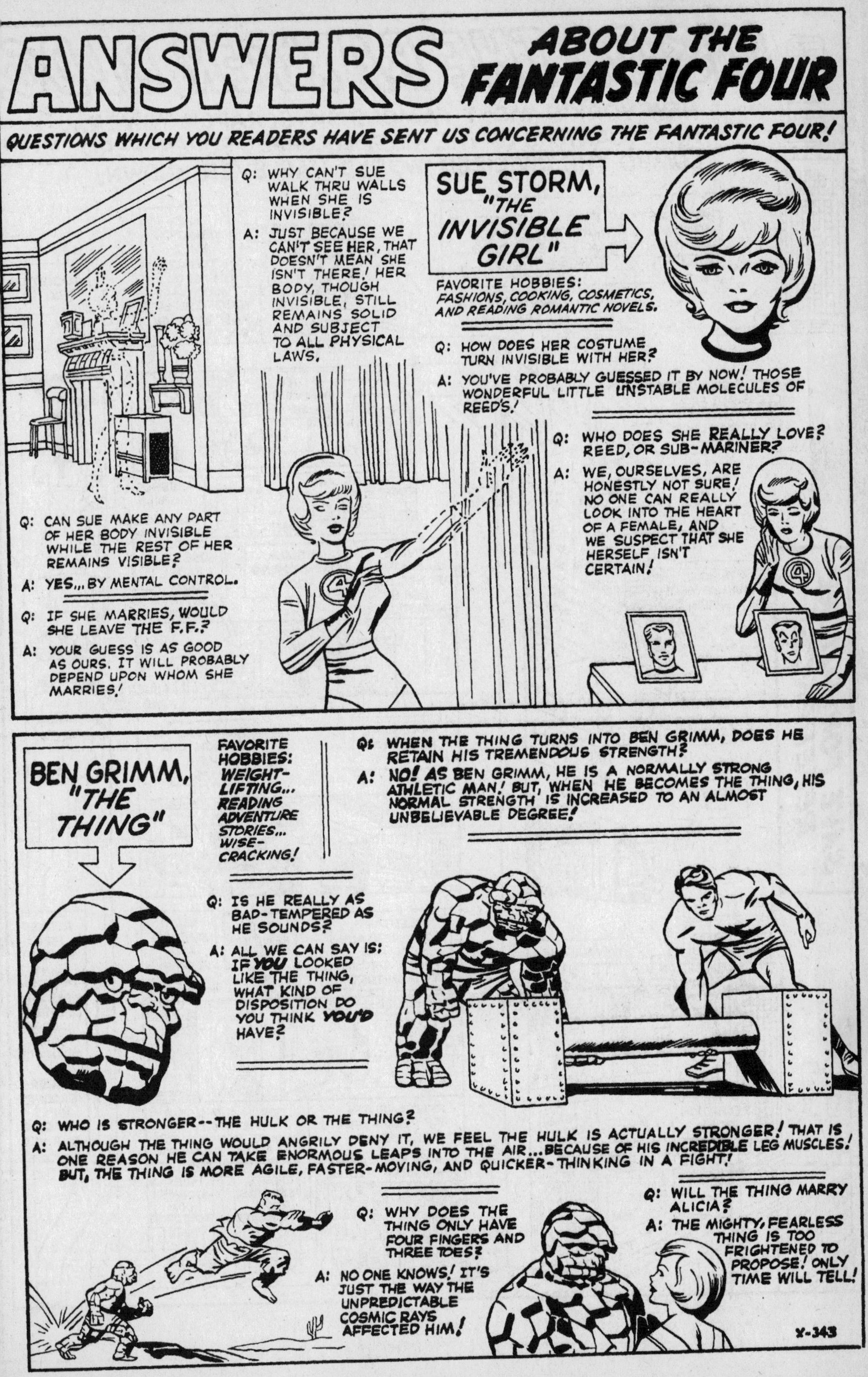
ANSWERS ABOUT THE FANTASTIC FOUR
QUESTIONS WHICH YOU READERS HAVE SENT US CONCERNING THE FANTASTIC FOUR!
Q: WHY CAN'T SUE WALK THRU WALLS WHEN SHE IS INVISIBLE?
A: JUST BECAUSE WE CAN'T SEE HER, THAT DOESN'T MEAN SHE ISN'T THERE! HER BODY, THOUGH INVISIBLE, STILL REMAINS SOLID AND SUBJECT TO ALL PHYSICAL LAWS.
SUE STORM, "THE INVISIBLE GIRL"
FAVORITE HOBBIES: FASHIONS, COOKING, COSMETICS, AND READING ROMANTIC NOVELS.
Q: HOW DOES HER COSTUME TURN INVISIBLE WITH HER?
A: YOU'VE PROBABLY GUESSED IT BY NOW! THOSE WONDERFUL LITTLE UNSTABLE MOLECULES OF REED'S!
Q: WHO DOES SHE REALLY LOVE? REED, OR SUB-MARINER?
A: WE, OURSELVES, ARE HONESTLY NOT SURE! NO ONE CAN REALLY LOOK INTO THE HEART OF A FEMALE, AND WE SUSPECT THAT SHE HERSELF ISN'T CERTAIN!
Q: CAN SUE MAKE ANY PART OF HER BODY INVISIBLE WHILE THE REST OF HER REMAINS VISIBLE?
A: YES... BY MENTAL CONTROL.
Q: IF SHE MARRIES, WOULD SHE LEAVE THE F.F.?
A: YOUR GUESS IS AS GOOD AS OURS. IT WILL PROBABLY DEPEND UPON WHOM SHE MARRIES!
BEN GRIMM, "THE THING"
FAVORITE HOBBIES: WEIGHT-LIFTING... READING ADVENTURE STORIES... WISE-CRACKING!
Q: WHEN THE THING TURNS INTO BEN GRIMM, DOES HE RETAIN HIS TREMENDOUS STRENGTH?
A: NO! AS BEN GRIMM, HE IS A NORMALLY STRONG ATHLETIC MAN! BUT, WHEN HE BECOMES THE THING, HIS NORMAL STRENGTH IS INCREASED TO AN ALMOST UNBELIEVABLE DEGREE!
Q: IS HE REALLY AS BAD-TEMPERED AS HE SOUNDS?
A: ALL WE CAN SAY IS: IF YOU LOOKED LIKE THE THING, WHAT KIND OF DISPOSITION DO YOU THINK YOU'D HAVE?
Q: WHO IS STRONGER--THE HULK OR THE THING?
A: ALTHOUGH THE THING WOULD ANGRILY DENY IT, WE FEEL THE HULK IS ACTUALLY STRONGER! THAT IS ONE REASON HE CAN TAKE ENORMOUS LEAPS INTO THE AIR... BECAUSE OF HIS INCREDIBLE LEG MUSCLES! BUT, THE THING IS MORE AGILE, FASTER-MOVING, AND QUICKER-THINKING IN A FIGHT!
Q: WHY DOES THE THING ONLY HAVE FOUR FINGERS AND THREE TOES?
A: NO ONE KNOWS! IT'S JUST THE WAY THE UNPREDICTABLE COSMIC RAYS AFFECTED HIM!
Q: WILL THE THING MARRY ALICIA?
A: THE MIGHTY, FEARLESS THING IS TOO FRIGHTENED TO PROPOSE! ONLY TIME WILL TELL!
X-343

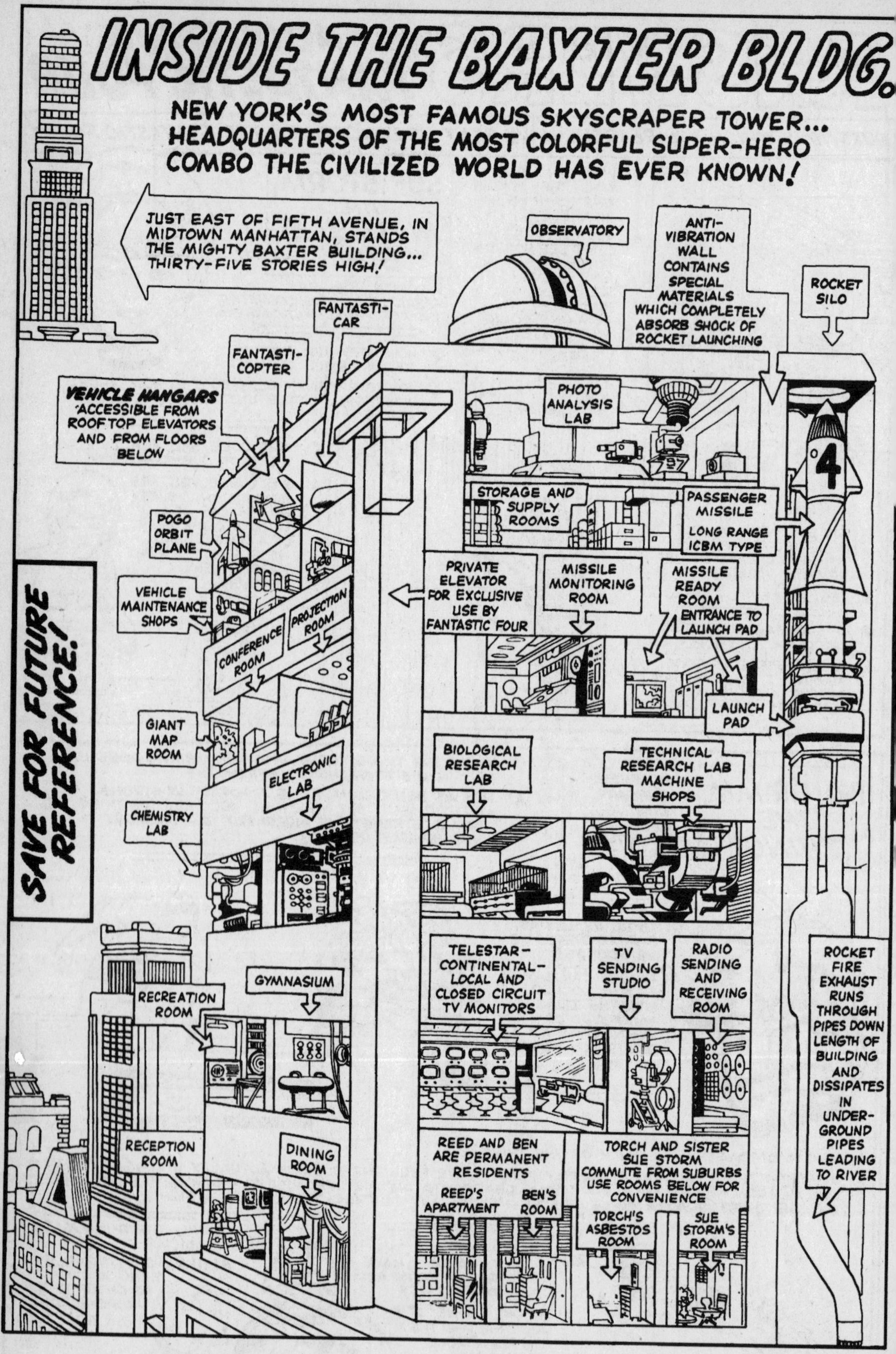
INSIDE THE BAXTER BLDG.
NEW YORK'S MOST FAMOUS SKYSCRAPER TOWER... HEADQUARTERS OF THE MOST COLORFUL SUPER-HERO COMBO THE CIVILIZED WORLD HAS EVER KNOWN!
JUST EAST OF FIFTH AVENUE, IN MIDTOWN MANHATTAN, STANDS THE MIGHTY BAXTER BUILDING... THIRTY-FIVE STORIES HIGH!
OBSERVATORY
ANTI-VIBRATION WALL CONTAINS SPECIAL MATERIALS WHICH COMPLETELY ABSORB SHOCK OF ROCKET LAUNCHING
ROCKET SILO
FANTASTI-CAR
FANTASTI-COPTER
VEHICLE HANGARS ACCESSIBLE FROM ROOF TOP ELEVATORS AND FROM FLOORS BELOW
PHOTO ANALYSIS LAB
4
STORAGE AND SUPPLY ROOMS
PASSENGER MISSILE
LONG RANGE ICBM TYPE
POGO ORBIT PLANE
VEHICLE MAINTENANCE SHOPS
SAVE FOR FUTURE REFERENCE!
PRIVATE ELEVATOR FOR EXCLUSIVE USE BY FANTASTIC FOUR
MISSILE MONITORING ROOM
MISSILE READY ROOM ENTRANCE TO LAUNCH PAD
CONFERENCE ROOM
PROJECTION ROOM
LAUNCH PAD
GIANT MAP ROOM
ELECTRONIC LAB
BIOLOGICAL RESEARCH LAB
TECHNICAL RESEARCH LAB MACHINE SHOPS
CHEMISTRY LAB
GYMNASIUM
RECREATION ROOM
TELESTAR-CONTINENTAL-LOCAL AND CLOSED CIRCUIT TV MONITORS
TV SENDING STUDIO
RADIO SENDING AND RECEIVING ROOM
ROCKET FIRE EXHAUST RUNS THROUGH PIPES DOWN LENGTH OF BUILDING AND DISSIPATES IN UNDER-GROUND PIPES LEADING TO RIVER
RECEPTION ROOM
DINING ROOM
REED AND BEN ARE PERMANENT RESIDENTS
REED'S APARTMENT
BEN'S ROOM
TORCH AND SISTER SUE STORM COMMUTE FROM SUBURBS USE ROOMS BELOW FOR CONVENIENCE
TORCH'S ASBESTOS ROOM
SUE STORM'S ROOM

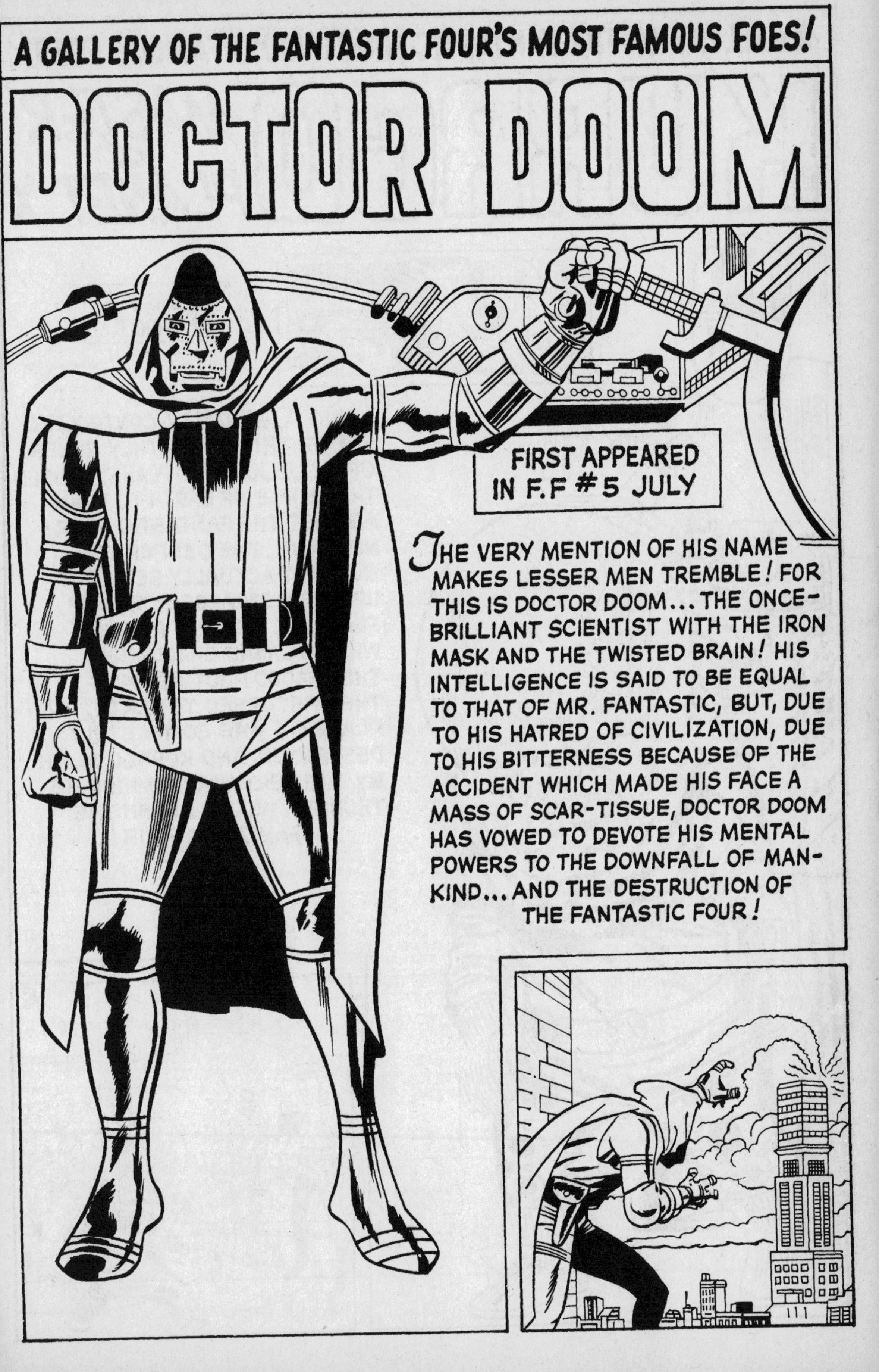
A GALLERY OF THE FANTASTIC FOUR'S MOST FAMOUS FOES!
DOCTOR DOOM
FIRST APPEARED IN F.F #5 JULY
THE VERY MENTION OF HIS NAME MAKES LESSER MEN TREMBLE! FOR THIS IS DOCTOR DOOM... THE ONCE-BRILLIANT SCIENTIST WITH THE IRON MASK AND THE TWISTED BRAIN! HIS INTELLIGENCE IS SAID TO BE EQUAL TO THAT OF MR. FANTASTIC, BUT, DUE TO HIS HATRED OF CIVILIZATION, DUE TO HIS BITTERNESS BECAUSE OF THE ACCIDENT WHICH MADE HIS FACE A MASS OF SCAR-TISSUE, DOCTOR DOOM HAS VOWED TO DEVOTE HIS MENTAL POWERS TO THE DOWNFALL OF MANKIND... AND THE DESTRUCTION OF THE FANTASTIC FOUR!

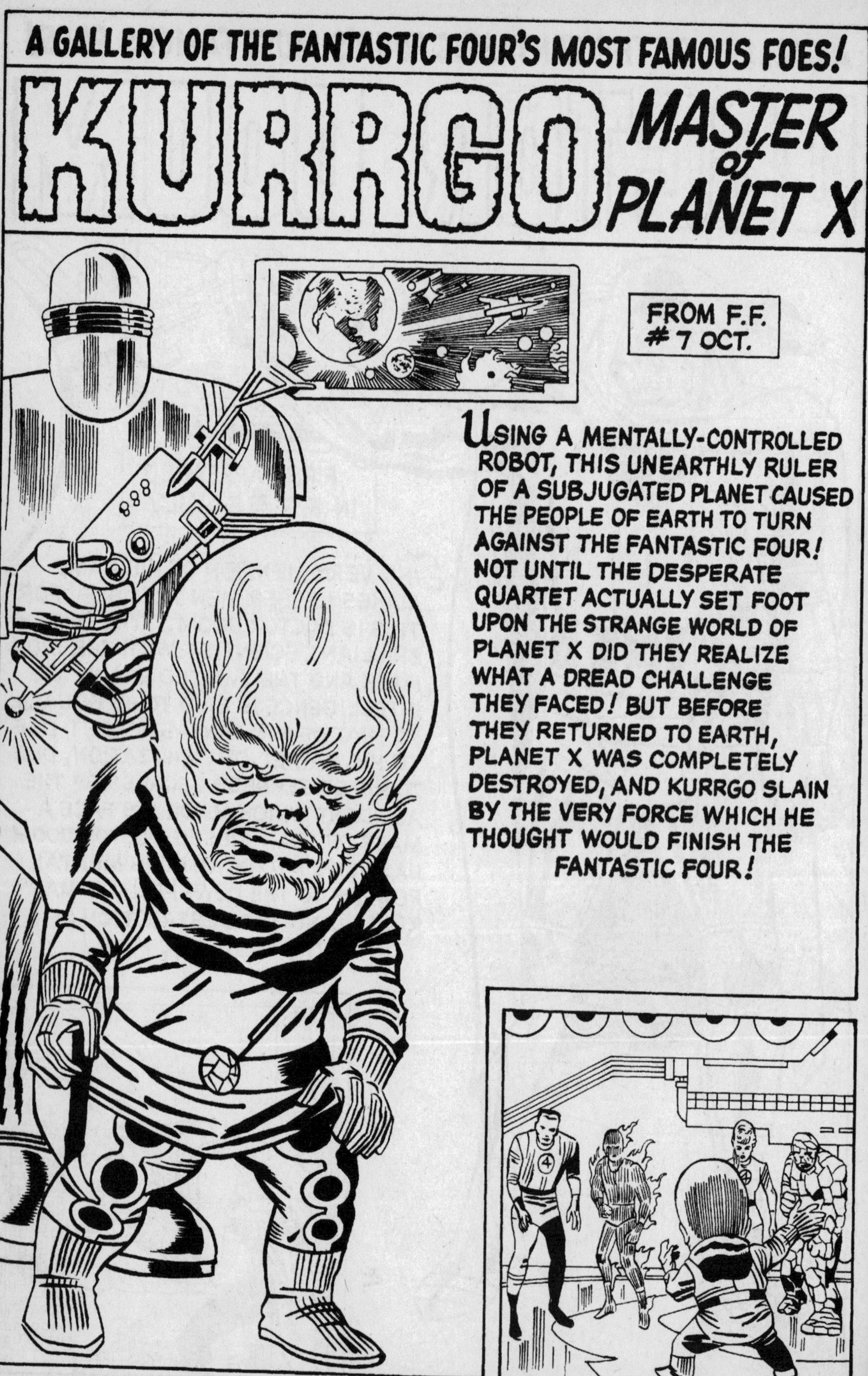
A GALLERY OF THE FANTASTIC FOUR'S MOST FAMOUS FOES!
KURRGO MASTER of PLANET X
FROM F.F. # 7 OCT.
USING A MENTALLY-CONTROLLED ROBOT, THIS UNEARTHLY RULER OF A SUBJUGATED PLANET CAUSED THE PEOPLE OF EARTH TO TURN AGAINST THE FANTASTIC FOUR! NOT UNTIL THE DESPERATE QUARTET ACTUALLY SET FOOT UPON THE STRANGE WORLD OF PLANET X DID THEY REALIZE WHAT A DREAD CHALLENGE THEY FACED! BUT BEFORE THEY RETURNED TO EARTH, PLANET X WAS COMPLETELY DESTROYED, AND KURRGO SLAIN BY THE VERY FORCE WHICH HE THOUGHT WOULD FINISH THE FANTASTIC FOUR!

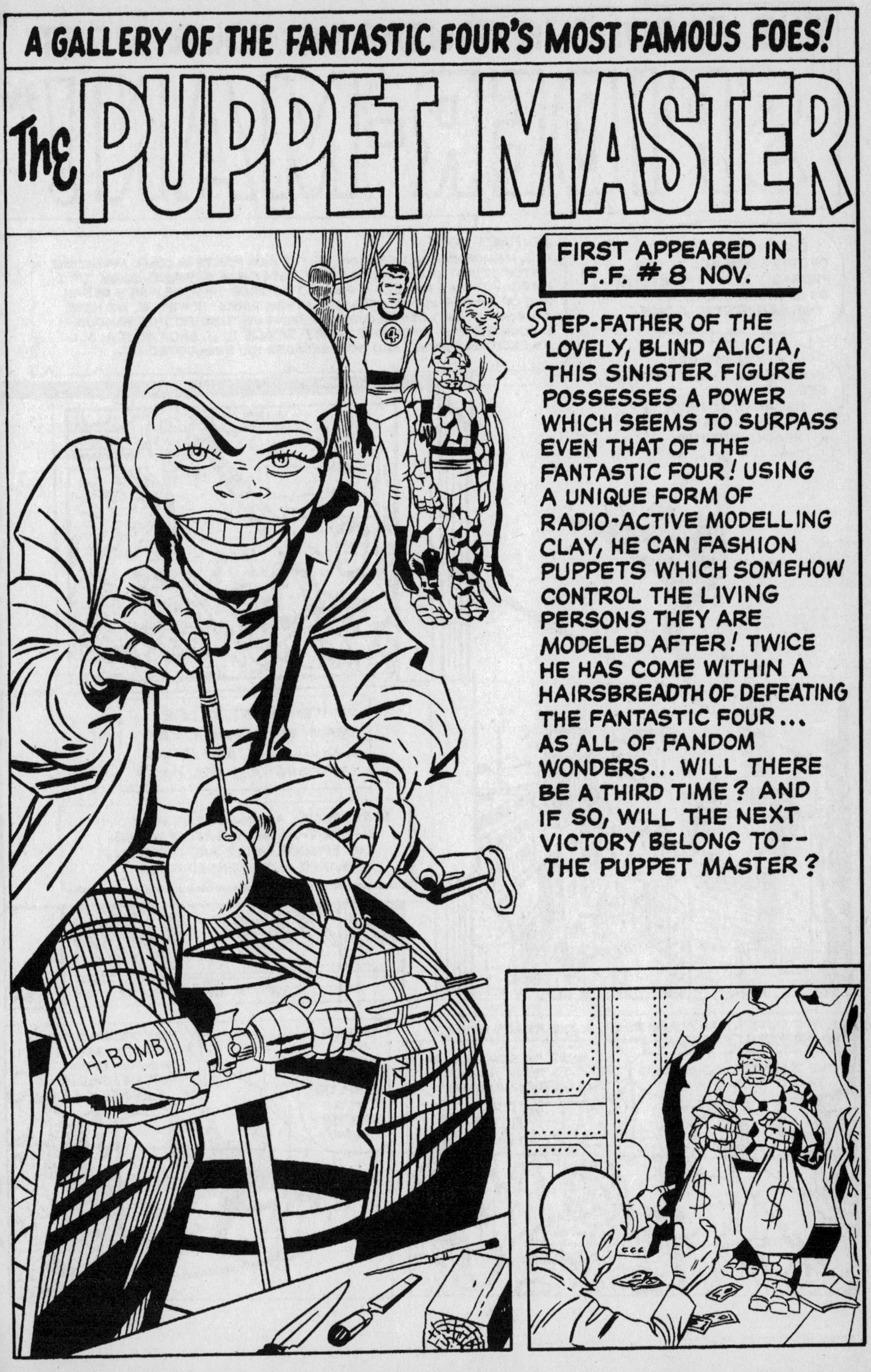
A GALLERY OF THE FANTASTIC FOUR'S MOST FAMOUS FOES!
THE PUPPET MASTER
FIRST APPEARED IN F.F. # 8 NOV.
STEP-FATHER OF THE LOVELY, BLIND ALICIA, THIS SINISTER FIGURE POSSESSES A POWER WHICH SEEMS TO SURPASS EVEN THAT OF THE FANTASTIC FOUR! USING A UNIQUE FORM OF RADIO-ACTIVE MODELLING CLAY, HE CAN FASHION PUPPETS WHICH SOMEHOW CONTROL THE LIVING PERSONS THEY ARE MODELED AFTER! TWICE HE HAS COME WITHIN A HAIRSBREADTH OF DEFEATING THE FANTASTIC FOUR... AS ALL OF FANDOM WONDERS... WILL THERE BE A THIRD TIME? AND IF SO, WILL THE NEXT VICTORY BELONG TO-- THE PUPPET MASTER?
H-BOMB

THE FABULOUS FANTASTIC FOUR MEET SPIDER-MAN!*

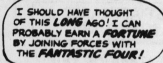

I SHOULD HAVE THOUGHT OF THIS *LONG* AGO! I CAN PROBABLY EARN A *FORTUNE* BY JOINING FORCES WITH THE *FANTASTIC FOUR!*

THEY'LL BE REAL IMPRESSED WHEN THEY SEE HOW EASILY I CAN BREAK INTO THEIR SKYSCRAPER HEADQUARTERS!

EDITOR'S NOTE:
THIS MEMORABLE INCIDENT, ONE OF THE HIGH POINTS IN COMIC MAGAZINE HISTORY, FIRST OCCURRED IN "*THE AMAZING SPIDER-MAN*" # 1, MARCH! IT WAS MERELY A SMALL, TWO-PAGE EPISODE WHICH BEGAN ONE OF SPIDER-MAN'S GREATEST ADVENTURES! HOWEVER, WE HAVE RECEIVED COUNTLESS REQUESTS ASKING US TO RE-DO THIS FAMOUS ENCOUNTER, BUT TO DEVOTE *MORE SPACE* TO IT, SHOWING IT IN ALL ITS EXCITING DETAIL! AND SO-- BECAUSE YOU REQUESTED IT...

WRITTEN BY: *STAN LEE*
DRAWN BY: *JACK KIRBY*
INKING: *STEVE DITKO*
LETTERING: *RAY HOLLOWAY*

* BY SPECIAL ARRANGEMENT WITH *SPIDER-MAN* MAGAZINE WHERE THIS EPISODE, BY LEE AND DITKO, FIRST APPEARED IN CONDENSED FORM!

X-344

AT THAT MOMENT, AN ALARM RINGS IN THE READY-ROOM OF THE *FANTASTIC FOUR!*

THE *ALARM!* SOMEONE IS TRYING TO SNEAK IN!

HE MUST BE SOME KINDA *NUT* TO THINK HE CAN TAKE US BY SURPRISE!

BRIN-NG

THERE'S HIS PICTURE ON OUR VIEWPLATE! IT'S *SPIDER-MAN!*

HOW OBLIGING OF THEM TO LEAVE A WINDOW OPEN FOR ME! THIS IS A *BREEZE!*

1

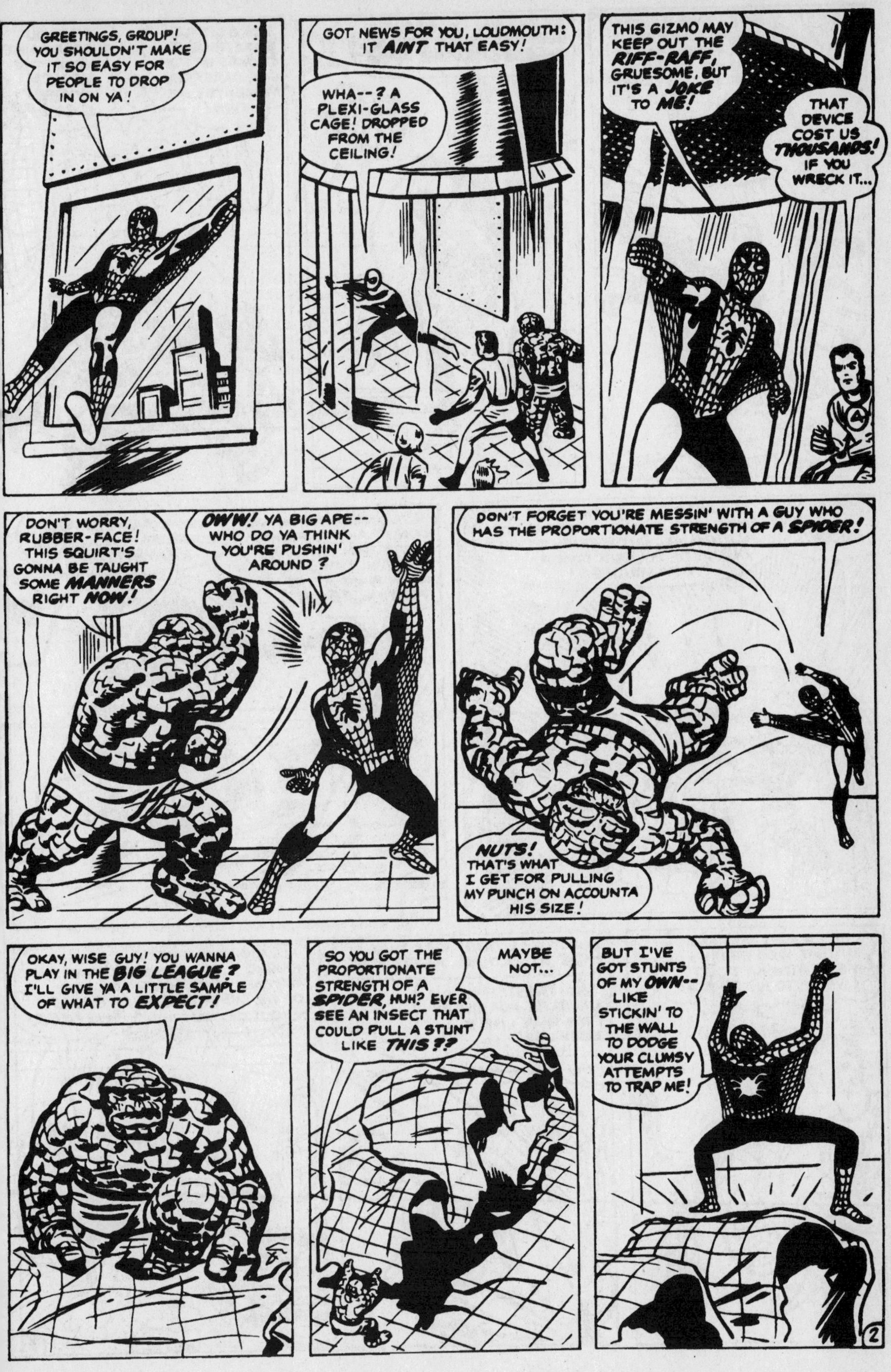
GREETINGS, GROUP! YOU SHOULDN'T MAKE IT SO EASY FOR PEOPLE TO DROP IN ON YA!
GOT NEWS FOR YOU, LOUDMOUTH: IT AINT THAT EASY!
WHA--? A PLEXI-GLASS CAGE! DROPPED FROM THE CEILING!
THIS GIZMO MAY KEEP OUT THE RIFF-RAFF, GRUESOME, BUT IT'S A JOKE TO ME!
THAT DEVICE COST US THOUSANDS! IF YOU WRECK IT...
DON'T WORRY, RUBBER-FACE! THIS SQUIRT'S GONNA BE TAUGHT SOME MANNERS RIGHT NOW!
OWW! YA BIG APE-- WHO DO YA THINK YOU'RE PUSHIN' AROUND?
DON'T FORGET YOU'RE MESSIN' WITH A GUY WHO HAS THE PROPORTIONATE STRENGTH OF A SPIDER!
NUTS! THAT'S WHAT I GET FOR PULLING MY PUNCH ON ACCOUNTA HIS SIZE!
OKAY, WISE GUY! YOU WANNA PLAY IN THE BIG LEAGUE? I'LL GIVE YA A LITTLE SAMPLE OF WHAT TO EXPECT!
SO YOU GOT THE PROPORTIONATE STRENGTH OF A SPIDER, HUH? EVER SEE AN INSECT THAT COULD PULL A STUNT LIKE THIS??
MAYBE NOT...
BUT I'VE GOT STUNTS OF MY OWN-- LIKE STICKIN' TO THE WALL TO DODGE YOUR CLUMSY ATTEMPTS TO TRAP ME!
2

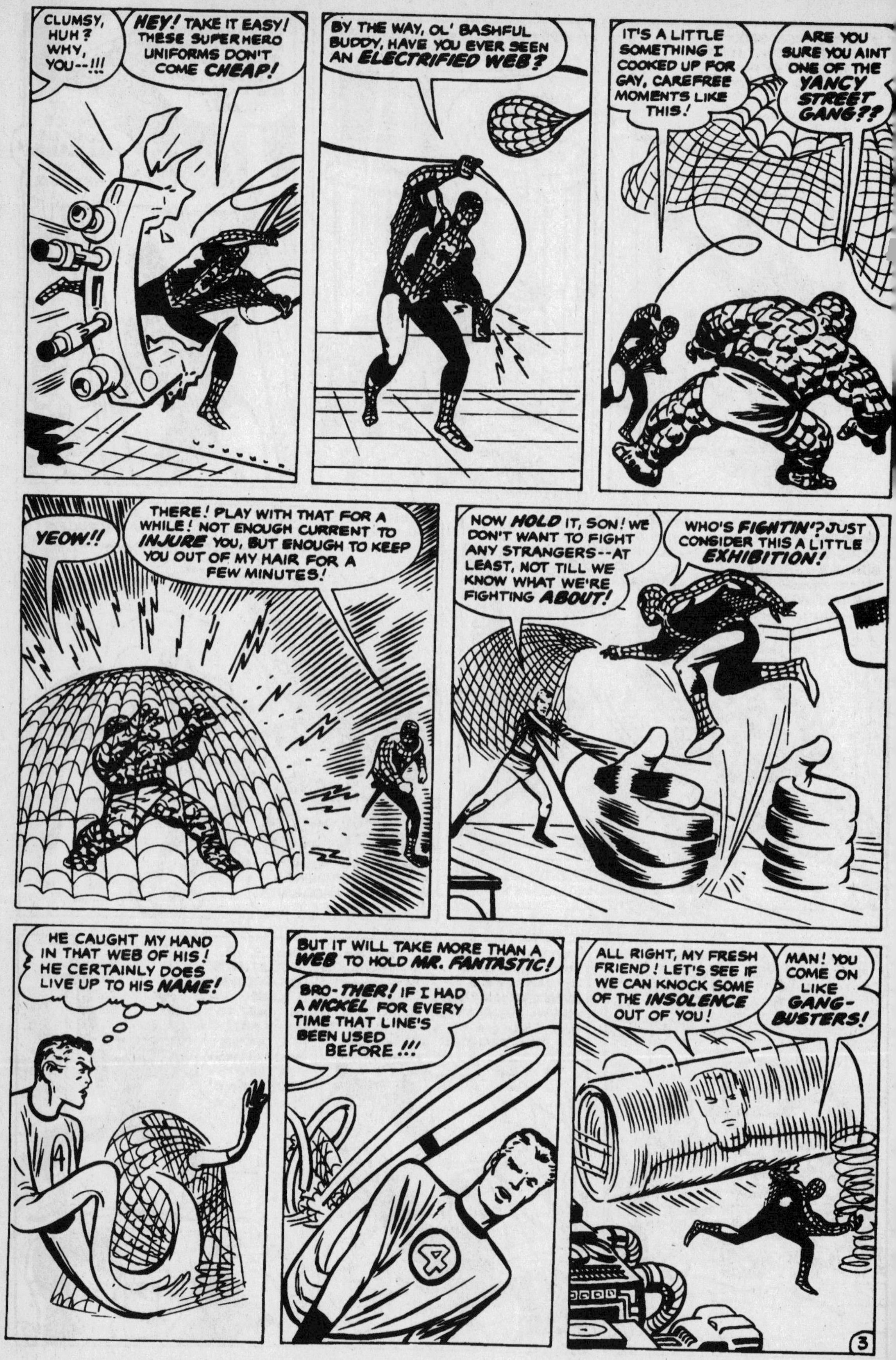
CLUMSY, HUH? WHY, YOU--!!!
HEY! TAKE IT EASY! THESE SUPERHERO UNIFORMS DON'T COME CHEAP!
BY THE WAY, OL' BASHFUL BUDDY, HAVE YOU EVER SEEN AN ELECTRIFIED WEB?
IT'S A LITTLE SOMETHING I COOKED UP FOR GAY, CAREFREE MOMENTS LIKE THIS!
ARE YOU SURE YOU AINT ONE OF THE YANCY STREET GANG??
YEOW!!
THERE! PLAY WITH THAT FOR A WHILE! NOT ENOUGH CURRENT TO INJURE YOU, BUT ENOUGH TO KEEP YOU OUT OF MY HAIR FOR A FEW MINUTES!
NOW HOLD IT, SON! WE DON'T WANT TO FIGHT ANY STRANGERS--AT LEAST, NOT TILL WE KNOW WHAT WE'RE FIGHTING ABOUT!
WHO'S FIGHTIN'? JUST CONSIDER THIS A LITTLE EXHIBITION!
HE CAUGHT MY HAND IN THAT WEB OF HIS! HE CERTAINLY DOES LIVE UP TO HIS NAME!
BUT IT WILL TAKE MORE THAN A WEB TO HOLD MR. FANTASTIC!
BRO-THER! IF I HAD A NICKEL FOR EVERY TIME THAT LINE'S BEEN USED BEFORE!!!
ALL RIGHT, MY FRESH FRIEND! LET'S SEE IF WE CAN KNOCK SOME OF THE INSOLENCE OUT OF YOU!
MAN! YOU COME ON LIKE GANG-BUSTERS!
3

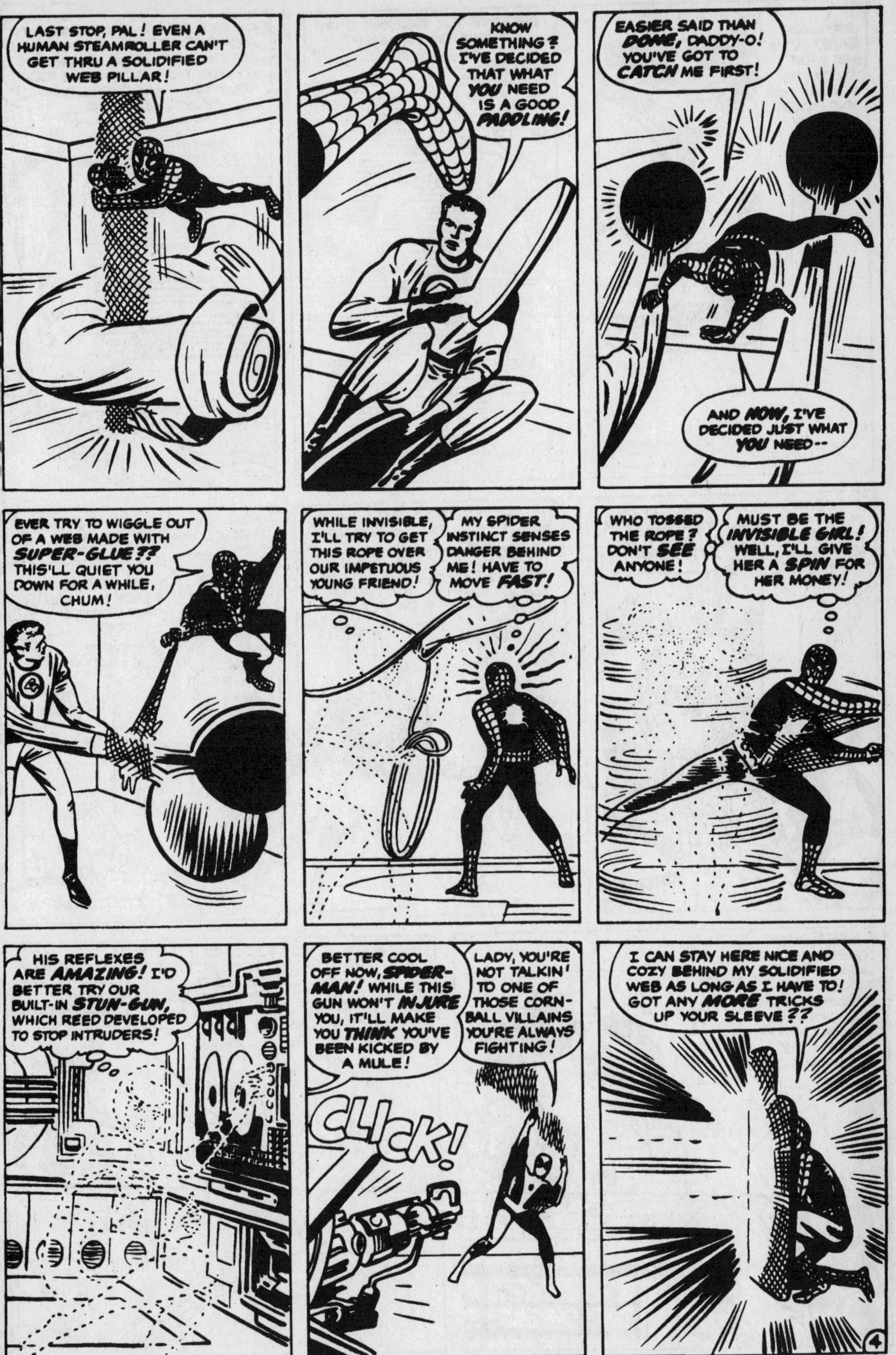
LAST STOP, PAL! EVEN A HUMAN STEAMROLLER CAN'T GET THRU A SOLIDIFIED WEB PILLAR!
KNOW SOMETHING? I'VE DECIDED THAT WHAT YOU NEED IS A GOOD PADDLING!
EASIER SAID THAN DONE, DADDY-O! YOU'VE GOT TO CATCH ME FIRST!
AND NOW, I'VE DECIDED JUST WHAT YOU NEED--
EVER TRY TO WIGGLE OUT OF A WEB MADE WITH SUPER-GLUE?? THIS'LL QUIET YOU DOWN FOR A WHILE, CHUM!
WHILE INVISIBLE, I'LL TRY TO GET THIS ROPE OVER OUR IMPETUOUS YOUNG FRIEND!
MY SPIDER INSTINCT SENSES DANGER BEHIND ME! HAVE TO MOVE FAST!
WHO TOSSED THE ROPE? DON'T SEE ANYONE!
MUST BE THE INVISIBLE GIRL! WELL, I'LL GIVE HER A SPIN FOR HER MONEY!
HIS REFLEXES ARE AMAZING! I'D BETTER TRY OUR BUILT-IN STUN-GUN, WHICH REED DEVELOPED TO STOP INTRUDERS!
BETTER COOL OFF NOW, SPIDER-MAN! WHILE THIS GUN WON'T INJURE YOU, IT'LL MAKE YOU THINK YOU'VE BEEN KICKED BY A MULE!
LADY, YOU'RE NOT TALKIN' TO ONE OF THOSE CORN-BALL VILLAINS YOU'RE ALWAYS FIGHTING!
CLICK!
I CAN STAY HERE NICE AND COZY BEHIND MY SOLIDIFIED WEB AS LONG AS I HAVE TO! GOT ANY MORE TRICKS UP YOUR SLEEVE??
4

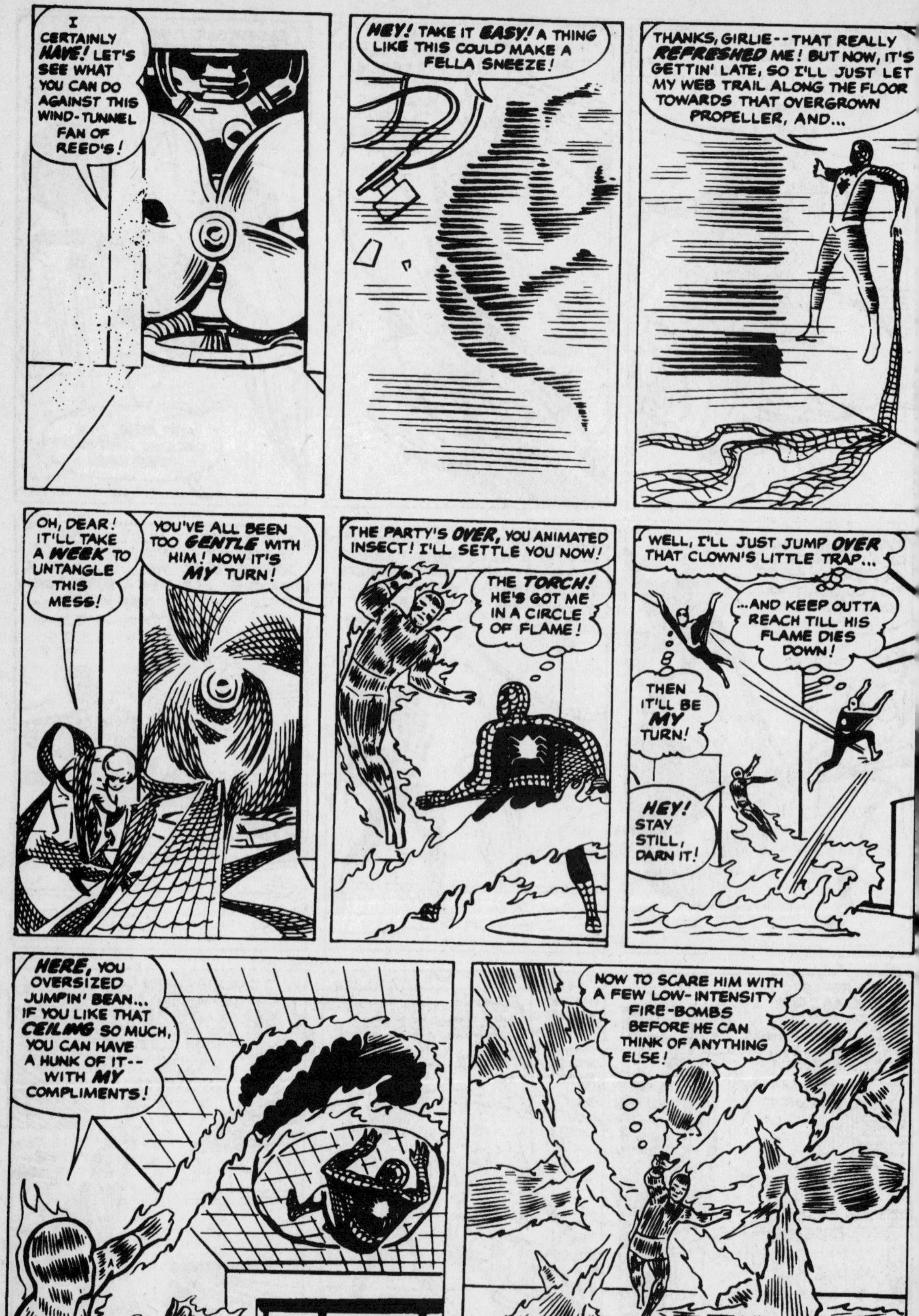
I CERTAINLY HAVE! LET'S SEE WHAT YOU CAN DO AGAINST THIS WIND-TUNNEL FAN OF REED'S!
HEY! TAKE IT EASY! A THING LIKE THIS COULD MAKE A FELLA SNEEZE!
THANKS, GIRLIE--THAT REALLY REFRESHED ME! BUT NOW, IT'S GETTIN' LATE, SO I'LL JUST LET MY WEB TRAIL ALONG THE FLOOR TOWARDS THAT OVERGROWN PROPELLER, AND...
OH, DEAR! IT'LL TAKE A WEEK TO UNTANGLE THIS MESS!
YOU'VE ALL BEEN TOO GENTLE WITH HIM! NOW IT'S MY TURN!
THE PARTY'S OVER, YOU ANIMATED INSECT! I'LL SETTLE YOU NOW!
THE TORCH! HE'S GOT ME IN A CIRCLE OF FLAME!
WELL, I'LL JUST JUMP OVER THAT CLOWN'S LITTLE TRAP...
...AND KEEP OUTTA REACH TILL HIS FLAME DIES DOWN!
THEN IT'LL BE MY TURN!
HEY! STAY STILL, DARN IT!
HERE, YOU OVERSIZED JUMPIN' BEAN... IF YOU LIKE THAT CEILING SO MUCH, YOU CAN HAVE A HUNK OF IT-- WITH MY COMPLIMENTS!
NOW TO SCARE HIM WITH A FEW LOW-INTENSITY FIRE-BOMBS BEFORE HE CAN THINK OF ANYTHING ELSE!
5

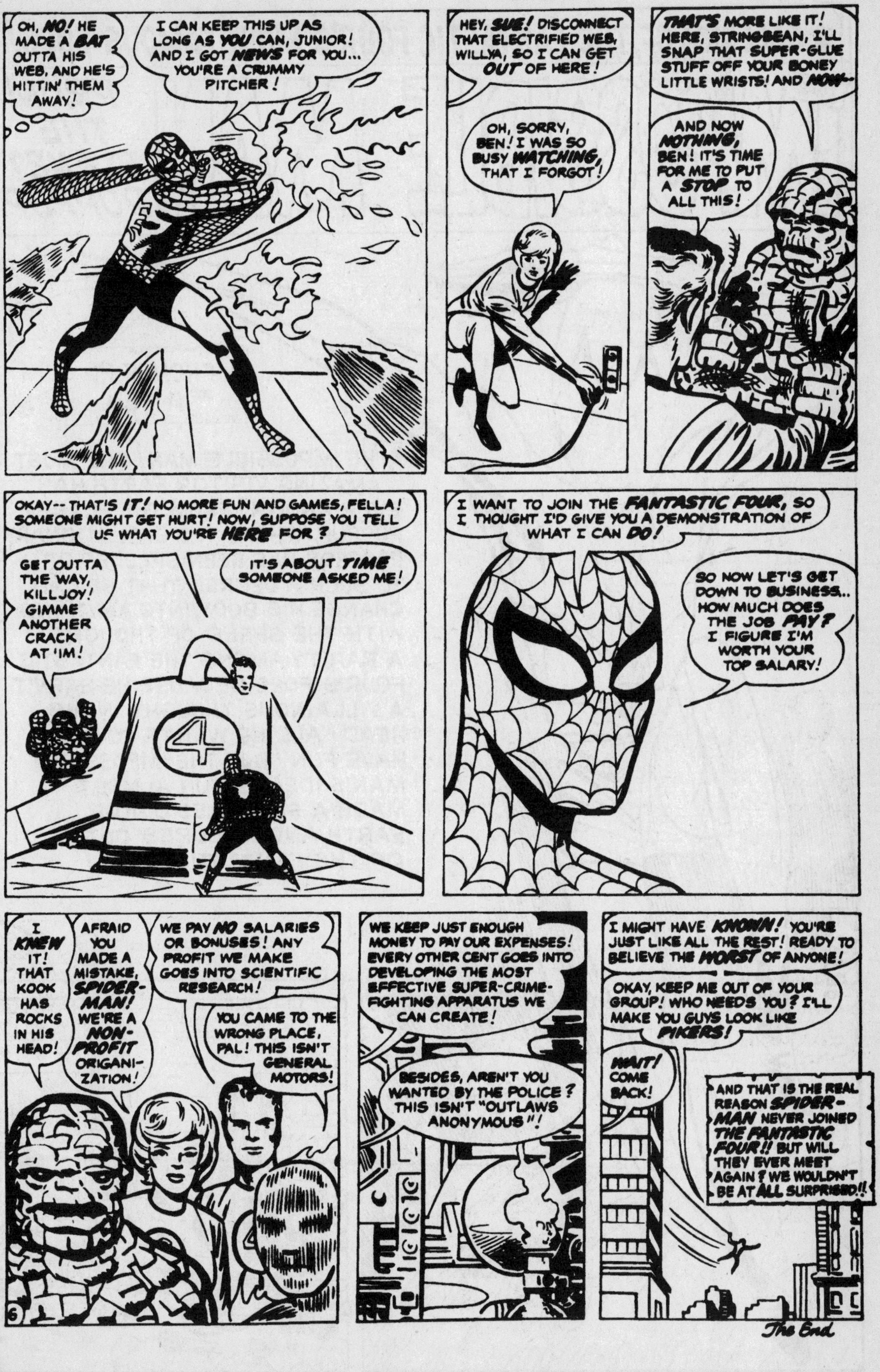

OH, NO! HE MADE A BAT OUTTA HIS WEB, AND HE'S HITTIN' THEM AWAY!
I CAN KEEP THIS UP AS LONG AS YOU CAN, JUNIOR! AND I GOT NEWS FOR YOU... YOU'RE A CRUMMY PITCHER!
HEY, SUE! DISCONNECT THAT ELECTRIFIED WEB, WILLYA, SO I CAN GET OUT OF HERE!
OH, SORRY, BEN! I WAS SO BUSY WATCHING, THAT I FORGOT!
THAT'S MORE LIKE IT! HERE, STRINGBEAN, I'LL SNAP THAT SUPER-GLUE STUFF OFF YOUR BONEY LITTLE WRISTS! AND NOW--
AND NOW NOTHING, BEN! IT'S TIME FOR ME TO PUT A STOP TO ALL THIS!
OKAY-- THAT'S IT! NO MORE FUN AND GAMES, FELLA! SOMEONE MIGHT GET HURT! NOW, SUPPOSE YOU TELL US WHAT YOU'RE HERE FOR?
GET OUTTA THE WAY, KILLJOY! GIMME ANOTHER CRACK AT 'IM!
IT'S ABOUT TIME SOMEONE ASKED ME!
I WANT TO JOIN THE FANTASTIC FOUR, SO I THOUGHT I'D GIVE YOU A DEMONSTRATION OF WHAT I CAN DO!
SO NOW LET'S GET DOWN TO BUSINESS... HOW MUCH DOES THE JOB PAY? I FIGURE I'M WORTH YOUR TOP SALARY!
I KNEW IT! THAT KOOK HAS ROCKS IN HIS HEAD!
AFRAID YOU MADE A MISTAKE, SPIDER-MAN! WE'RE A NON-PROFIT ORGANI-ZATION!
WE PAY NO SALARIES OR BONUSES! ANY PROFIT WE MAKE GOES INTO SCIENTIFIC RESEARCH!
YOU CAME TO THE WRONG PLACE, PAL! THIS ISN'T GENERAL MOTORS!
6
WE KEEP JUST ENOUGH MONEY TO PAY OUR EXPENSES! EVERY OTHER CENT GOES INTO DEVELOPING THE MOST EFFECTIVE SUPER-CRIME-FIGHTING APPARATUS WE CAN CREATE!
BESIDES, AREN'T YOU WANTED BY THE POLICE? THIS ISN'T "OUTLAWS ANONYMOUS"!
I MIGHT HAVE KNOWN! YOU'RE JUST LIKE ALL THE REST! READY TO BELIEVE THE WORST OF ANYONE!
OKAY, KEEP ME OUT OF YOUR GROUP! WHO NEEDS YOU? I'LL MAKE YOU GUYS LOOK LIKE PIKERS!
WAIT! COME BACK!
AND THAT IS THE REAL REASON SPIDER-MAN NEVER JOINED THE FANTASTIC FOUR!! BUT WILL THEY EVER MEET AGAIN? WE WOULDN'T BE AT ALL SURPRISED!!

The End

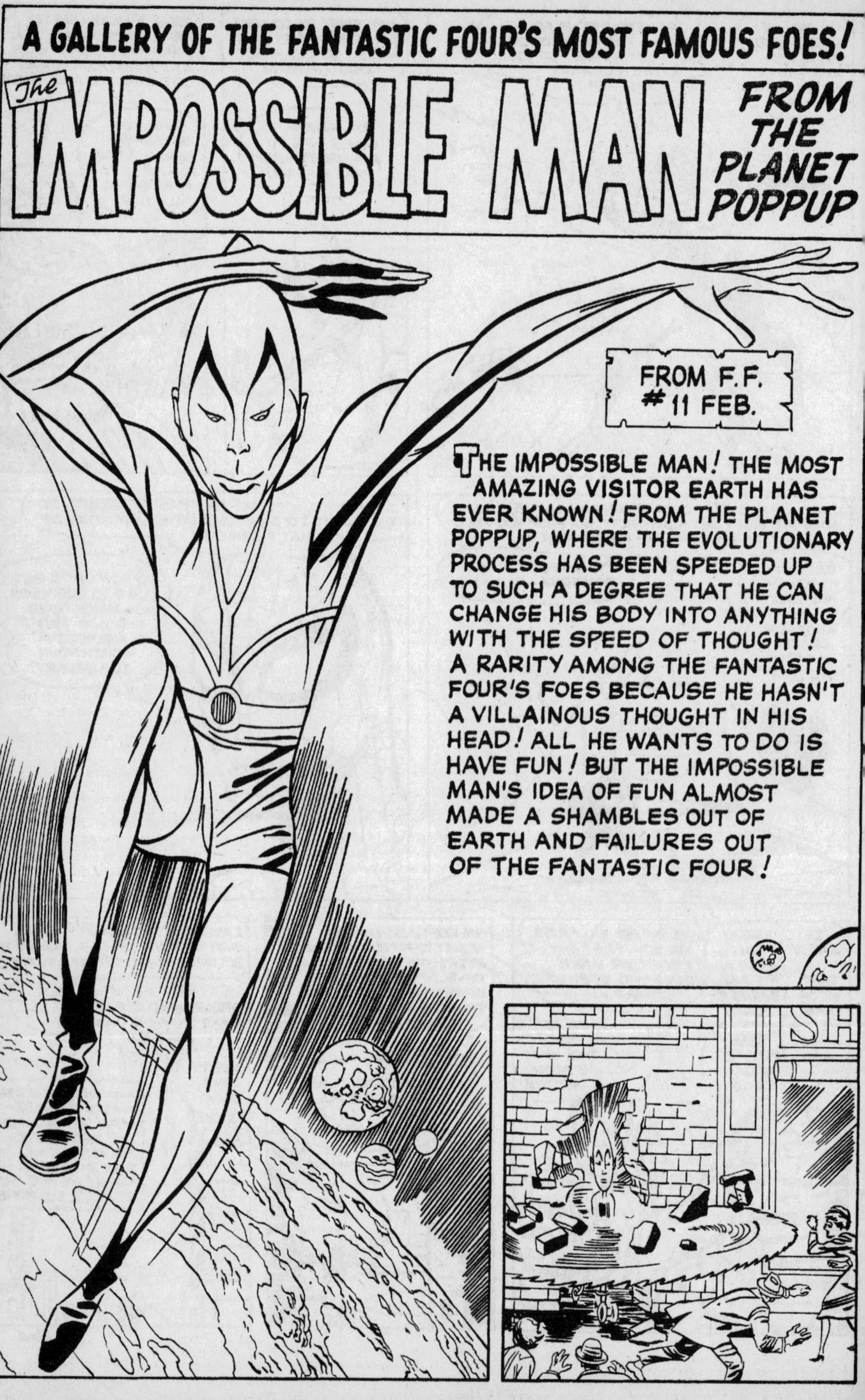
A GALLERY OF THE FANTASTIC FOUR'S MOST FAMOUS FOES!
The IMPOSSIBLE MAN FROM THE PLANET POPPUP
FROM F.F. #11 FEB.
THE IMPOSSIBLE MAN! THE MOST AMAZING VISITOR EARTH HAS EVER KNOWN! FROM THE PLANET POPPUP, WHERE THE EVOLUTIONARY PROCESS HAS BEEN SPEEDED UP TO SUCH A DEGREE THAT HE CAN CHANGE HIS BODY INTO ANYTHING WITH THE SPEED OF THOUGHT! A RARITY AMONG THE FANTASTIC FOUR'S FOES BECAUSE HE HASN'T A VILLAINOUS THOUGHT IN HIS HEAD! ALL HE WANTS TO DO IS HAVE FUN! BUT THE IMPOSSIBLE MAN'S IDEA OF FUN ALMOST MADE A SHAMBLES OUT OF EARTH AND FAILURES OUT OF THE FANTASTIC FOUR!

A GALLERY OF THE FANTASTIC FOUR'S MOST FAMOUS FOES!

THE INCREDIBLE HULK

FROM F.F. # 12 MAR.

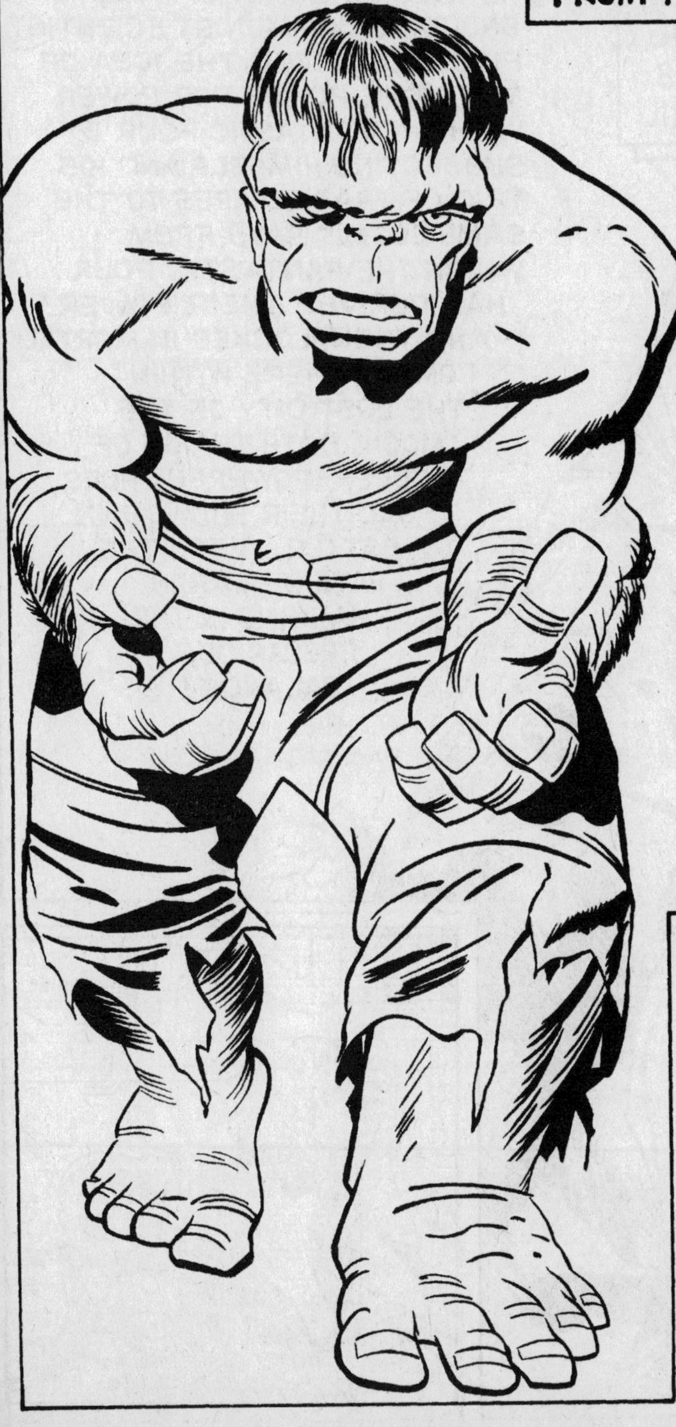

POSSIBILY THE MOST POWERFUL LIVING CREATURE TO WALK THE EARTH... THIS IS THE HULK! ONLY ONE OTHER PERSON KNOWS HIS WELL-GUARDED SECRET... THE FACT THAT HE IS ACTUALLY DR. BRUCE BANNER, A SCIENTIST ALMOST AS FAMOUS AS REED RICHARDS HIMSELF! BUT, WHEN HE STEPS IN FRONT OF HIS UNIQUE GAMMA-RAY MACHINE, THE RESPECTED DR. BANNER BECOMES THE RAGING, UNCONTROLLABLE, RAMPAGING MOUNTAIN OF MUSCLE... THE INCREDIBLE HULK! FANS STILL TALK OF THE EPIC BATTLE BETWEEN THE HULK AND THE THING... AND WONDER IF THEY'LL EVER MEET AGAIN!

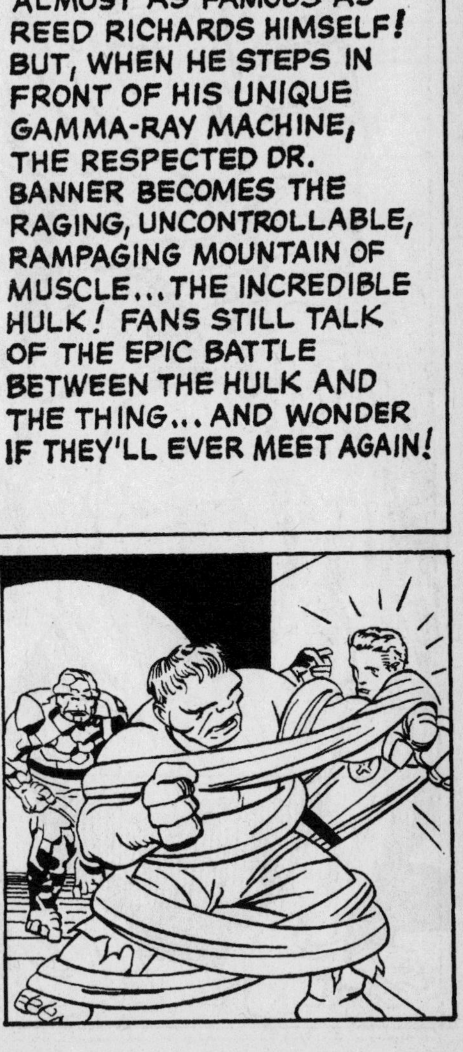

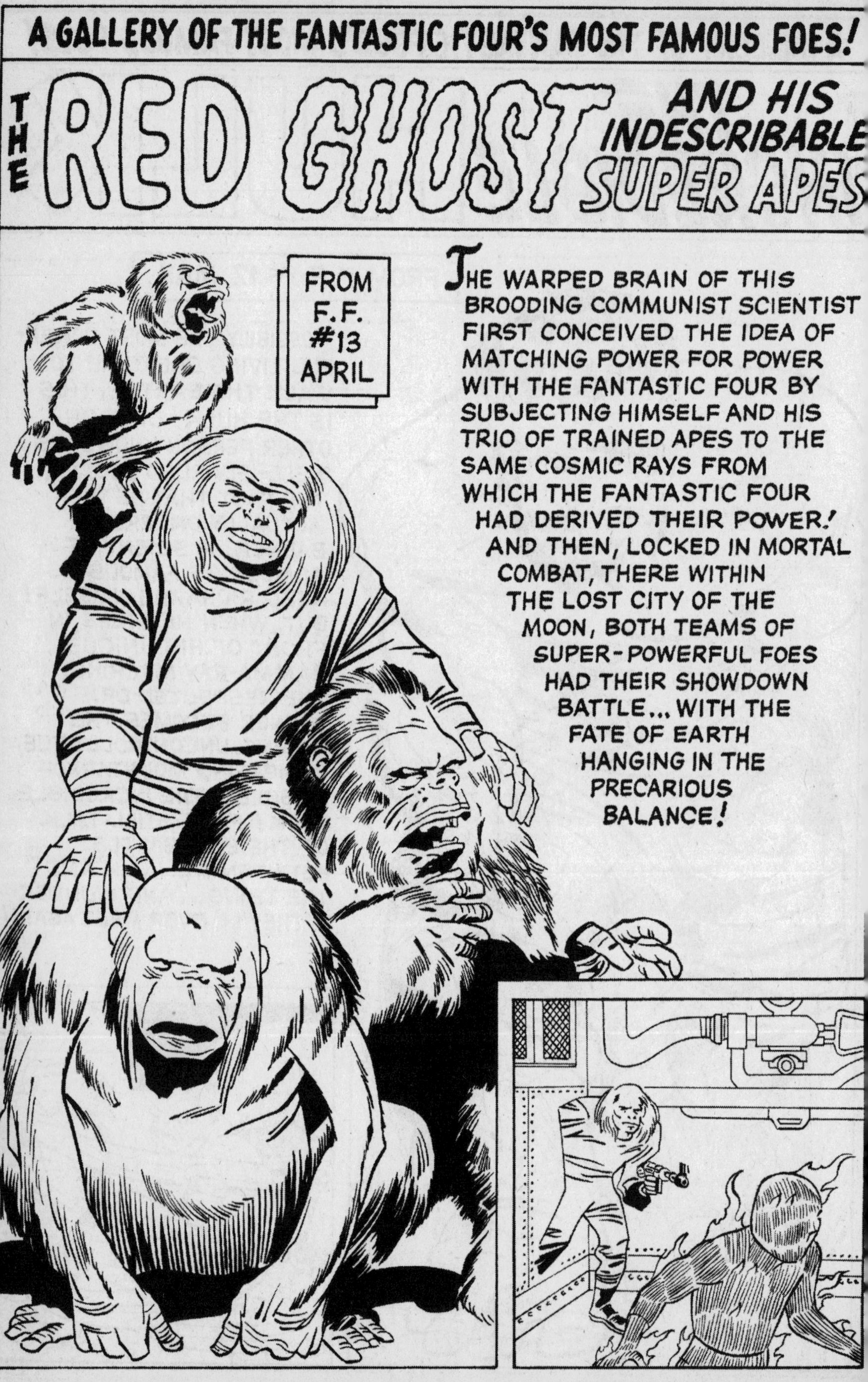
A GALLERY OF THE FANTASTIC FOUR'S MOST FAMOUS FOES!
THE RED GHOST AND HIS INDESCRIBABLE SUPER APES
FROM F.F. #13 APRIL
THE WARPED BRAIN OF THIS BROODING COMMUNIST SCIENTIST FIRST CONCEIVED THE IDEA OF MATCHING POWER FOR POWER WITH THE FANTASTIC FOUR BY SUBJECTING HIMSELF AND HIS TRIO OF TRAINED APES TO THE SAME COSMIC RAYS FROM WHICH THE FANTASTIC FOUR HAD DERIVED THEIR POWER! AND THEN, LOCKED IN MORTAL COMBAT, THERE WITHIN THE LOST CITY OF THE MOON, BOTH TEAMS OF SUPER-POWERFUL FOES HAD THEIR SHOWDOWN BATTLE... WITH THE FATE OF EARTH HANGING IN THE PRECARIOUS BALANCE!

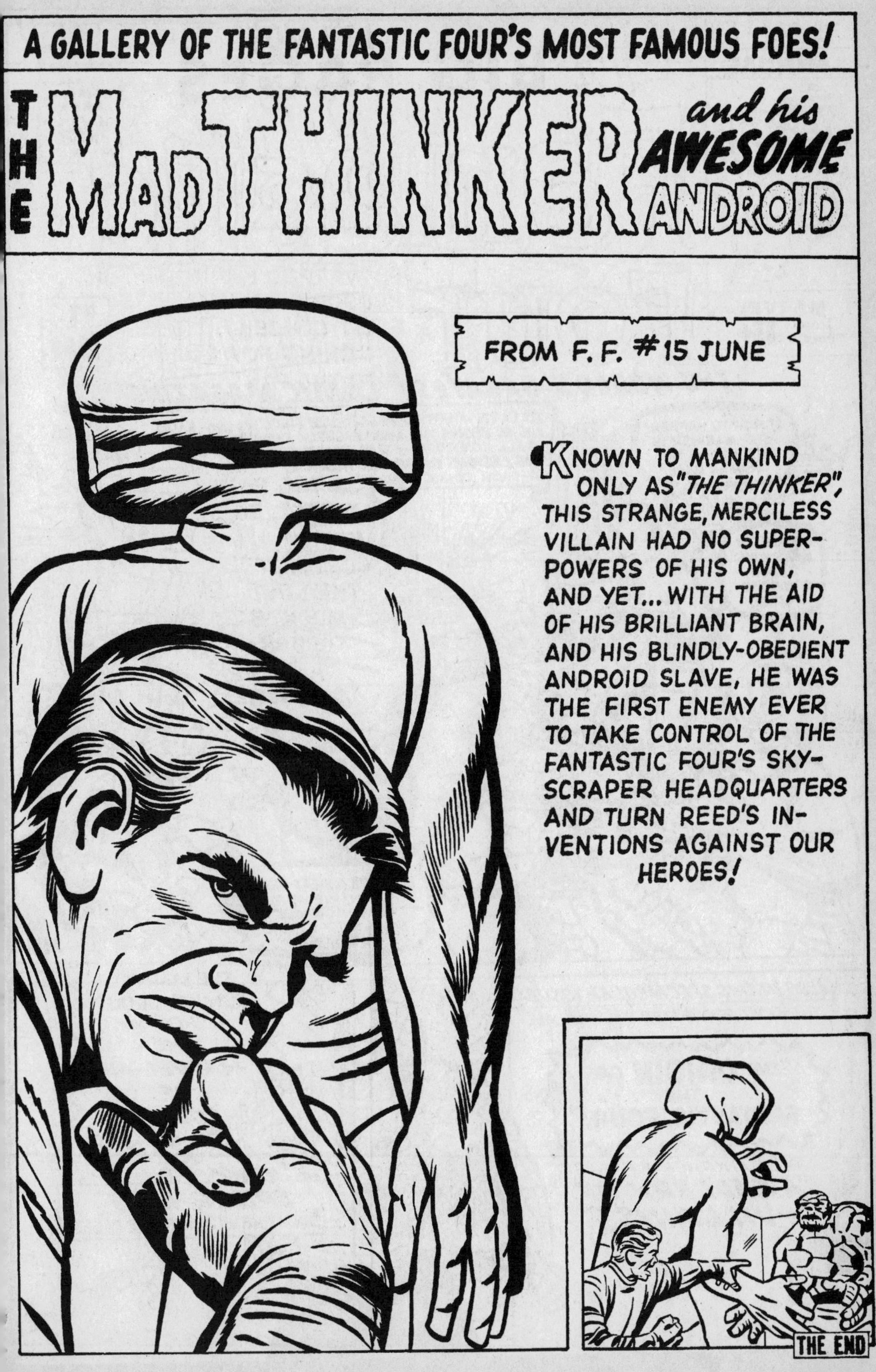
A GALLERY OF THE FANTASTIC FOUR'S MOST FAMOUS FOES!
THE MAD THINKER and his AWESOME ANDROID
FROM F. F. #15 JUNE
KNOWN TO MANKIND ONLY AS "THE THINKER", THIS STRANGE, MERCILESS VILLAIN HAD NO SUPER-POWERS OF HIS OWN, AND YET... WITH THE AID OF HIS BRILLIANT BRAIN, AND HIS BLINDLY-OBEDIENT ANDROID SLAVE, HE WAS THE FIRST ENEMY EVER TO TAKE CONTROL OF THE FANTASTIC FOUR'S SKY-SCRAPER HEADQUARTERS AND TURN REED'S IN-VENTIONS AGAINST OUR HEROES!
THE END

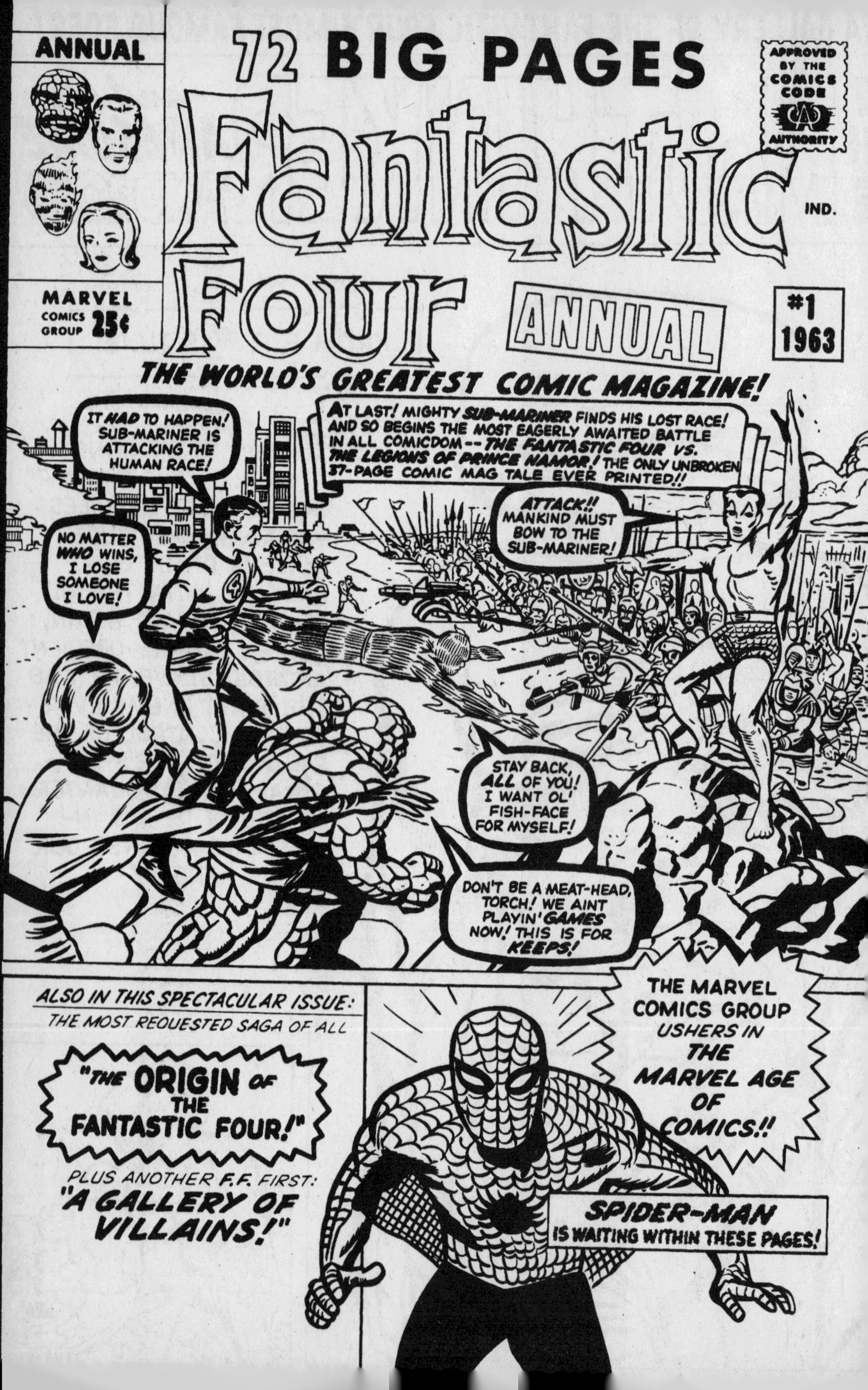
ANNUAL
72 BIG PAGES
APPROVED BY THE COMICS CODE AUTHORITY
Fantastic Four
IND.
MARVEL COMICS GROUP 25¢
ANNUAL
#1 1963
THE WORLD'S GREATEST COMIC MAGAZINE!
IT HAD TO HAPPEN! SUB-MARINER IS ATTACKING THE HUMAN RACE!
AT LAST! MIGHTY SUB-MARINER FINDS HIS LOST RACE! AND SO BEGINS THE MOST EAGERLY AWAITED BATTLE IN ALL COMICDOM -- THE FANTASTIC FOUR VS. THE LEGIONS OF PRINCE NAMOR! THE ONLY UNBROKEN 37-PAGE COMIC MAG TALE EVER PRINTED!!
ATTACK!! MANKIND MUST BOW TO THE SUB-MARINER!
NO MATTER WHO WINS, I LOSE SOMEONE I LOVE!
STAY BACK, ALL OF YOU! I WANT OL' FISH-FACE FOR MYSELF!
DON'T BE A MEAT-HEAD, TORCH! WE AINT PLAYIN' GAMES NOW! THIS IS FOR KEEPS!
ALSO IN THIS SPECTACULAR ISSUE: THE MOST REQUESTED SAGA OF ALL
"THE ORIGIN OF THE FANTASTIC FOUR!"
PLUS ANOTHER F.F. FIRST: "A GALLERY OF VILLAINS!"
THE MARVEL COMICS GROUP USHERS IN THE MARVEL AGE OF COMICS!!
SPIDER-MAN IS WAITING WITHIN THESE PAGES!